# Lecture Notes in Computer Science 6187

*Commenced Publication in 1973*
Founding and Former Series Editors:
Gerhard Goos, Juris Hartmanis, and Jan van Leeuwen

Michael Gertz   Bertram Ludäscher (Eds.)

# Scientific and Statistical Database Management

22nd International Conference, SSDBM 2010
Heidelberg, Germany, June 30–July 2, 2010
Proceedings

Springer

Volume Editors

Michael Gertz
University of Heidelberg
Institute of Computer Science
69120 Heidelberg, Germany
E-mail: gertz@informatik.uni-heidelberg.de

Bertram Ludäscher
University of California
Dept. of Computer Science and Genome Center
One Shields Avenue, Davis, CA 95616, USA
E-mail: ludaesch@ucdavis.edu

Library of Congress Control Number: 2010929609

CR Subject Classification (1998): H.3, I.2, H.4, C.2, H.2.8, H.5

LNCS Sublibrary: SL 3 – Information Systems and Application, incl. Internet/Web and HCI

ISSN 0302-9743
ISBN-10 3-642-13817-9 Springer Berlin Heidelberg New York
ISBN-13 978-3-642-13817-1 Springer Berlin Heidelberg New York



springer.com


Printed in Germany

Typesetting: Camera-ready by author, data conversion by Scientific Publishing Services, Chennai, India
Printed on acid-free paper 06/3180

# Preface

The International Conference on Scientific and Statistical Database Management (SSDBM) is an established forum for the exchange of the latest research results on concepts, tools, and techniques for scientific database applications. The 2010 meeting marked the 22$^{nd}$ time that scientific domain experts, databases researchers, practitioners, and developers came together to share their insights and to discuss future research directions in a stimulating environment. The conference was held from June 30 to July 2 at Villa Bosch, near the Carl Bosch Museum and Heidelberg Castle, overlooking the picturesque Neckar Valley. The conference was organized at and co-sponsored by Heidelberg University and HITS, the Heidelberg Institute for Theoretical Studies, established in January 2010 by Dr. Klaus Tschira, co-founder of SAP AG, as a successor to the EML Research Institute. HITS focuses on new approaches and foundations towards interpreting the rapidly increasing amounts of experimental data. Heidelberg University, the oldest university in Germany, was founded in 1386, is a German Excellence University, and a top-ranking university in Europe and worldwide, known among other things for its excellence in the natural sciences and medicine. The university also hosts a unique Interdisciplinary Center for Scientific Computing (IWR) where grand challenges in the computational sciences are tackled, e.g., climate and ocean modeling, turbulent flows, combustion, bio-molecules, and drug design.

In 2010, SSDBM received a near-record number of 94 submissions from 27 countries. Each submission was reviewed by at least three of the 38 PC members or external reviewers. After careful consideration, 41 papers (≈44%) overall where accepted, 30 as long papers (≈32%) and 11 short papers and demonstrations. The reviewing process was managed by the EasyChair Conference System (www.easychair.org), an excellent free conference management system, developed by Andrei Voronkov. SSDBM 2010 featured two keynotes: Daniel Abadi from Yale University discussed "Trade-offs Between Parallel Database Systems, Hadoop, and HadoopDB as Platforms for Petabyte-Scale Analysis" and described experiences using existing parallel databases and MapReduce systems, and HadoopDB, a hybrid system under development at Yale. In his keynote, Roger Barga from Microsoft Research presented "Emerging Trends and Converging Technologies in Data-Intensive Scalable Computing."

The program and activities of SSDBM 2010 were the result of a large effort by the authors, reviewers, presenters, and organizers. We thank them all for helping to make this conference a success! In particular, we thank the General Chair, Andreas Reuter for offering to host SSDBM at Villa Bosch, for supporting SSDBM in general, and for organizing the SSDBM sponsors. We also thank Wolfgang Müller from HITS for the local organization and Conny Franke for compiling the proceedings. Last not least, we would like to thank the "father of SSDBM" and Chair of the Steering Committee, Arie Shoshani, for guidance throughout the process of organzing SSDBM. We hope you enjoy the proceedings!

April 2010

Michael Gertz
Bertram Ludäscher

# Conference Organization

## General and Program Chairs

Andreas Reuter (General Chair)
Michael Gertz (PC Chair)
Tony Hey (PC Co-chair)
Bertram Ludäscher (PC Co-chair)

## Local Organization

Wolfgang Müller

## Proceedings Chair

Conny Franke

## Program Committee

Ilkay Altintas
Walid G. Aref
Elisa Bertino
Shawn Bowers
Isabel F. Cruz
Conny Franke
Juliana Freire
Johann Gamper
Floris Geerts
Amarnath Gupta
Ralf Hartmut Güting
Bill Howe
Theo Härder
Christian S. Jensen
Martin Kersten
Peer Kröger
Zoé Lacroix
Ulf Leser
David Maier
Paolo Missier
Mohamed F. Mokbel
Suman Nath
Silvia Nittel

Dimitris Papadias
Panagiotis Papapetrou
Norman W. Paton
Tore Risch
Carlos Rueda
Nagiza F. Samatova
Thomas Seidl
Rishi Rakesh Sinha
Kurt Stockinger
Alex S. Szalay
Yufei Tao
Nesime Tatbul
Can Türker
Jianwu Wang
Daniel Zinn

## External Reviewers

Ira Assent
Sebastian Bächle
Jie Bao
Roger Barga
Christian Beecks
Thomas Behr
Khalid Belhajjame
Thomas Bernecker
Roger Castillo
Vasa Curcin
Biplob Debnath
Robin Dhamankar
Tobias Emrich
Ines Färber
Alvaro A.A. Fernandes
Sergej Fries
Ixent Galpin
Gabriel Ghinita
Rigel Gjomemo
Keith Grochow
Alasdair J.G. Gray
Todd Green
Stephan Günnemann
Cornelia Hedeler
Abdeltawab Hendawi
Volker Hudlet
Hoyoung Jeung
Mouna Kacimi
Murat Kantarcioglu
Mohamed Khalefa
Kraig King
Andre Koschmieder
Hardy Kremer
YongChul Kwon
Xiang Lian
Qinghan Liang
Jefrey Lijffijt
Hyo-Sang Lim
Hua Lu
Angela Maduko
Soumyadeb Mitra
Emmanuel Müller
Mohamed Nabeel
Kjell Orsborn
Stavros Papadopoulos
Astrid Rheinländer
Dimitris Sacharidis
Satya Sahoo
Mahmoud Sakr
Daniel Schall
Karsten Schmidt
Christian Sengstock
Silvia Stefanova
Arash Termehchy

George Trimponias
Silke Trissl
Lixing Wang
Andreas Weiner
Marc Wichterich
Dingming Wu
Yin Yang
Ying Yang
Jun Zhao
Erik Zeitler
Andreas Züfle

# Table of Contents

## Invited Talks



## Query Processing



## Scientific Data Management and Analysis

## Data Mining

## Indexes and Data Representation



## Scientific Workflow and Provenance

## Similarity



## Data Stream Processing

# Tradeoffs between Parallel Database Systems, Hadoop, and HadoopDB as Platforms for Petabyte-Scale Analysis

Daniel J. Abadi

Yale University
dna@cs.yale.edu

**Abstract.** As the market demand for analyzing data sets of increasing variety and scale continues to explode, the software options for performing this analysis are beginning to proliferate. No fewer than a dozen companies have launched in the past few years that sell parallel database products to meet this market demand. At the same time, MapReduce-based options, such as the open source Hadoop framework are becoming increasingly popular, and there have been a plethora of research publications in the past two years that demonstrate how MapReduce can be used to accelerate and scale various data analysis tasks.

Both parallel databases and MapReduce-based options have strengths and weaknesses that a practitioner must be aware of before selecting an analytical data management platform. In this talk, I describe some experiences in using these systems, and the advantages and disadvantages of the popular implementations of these systems. I then discuss a hybrid system that we are building at Yale University, called HadoopDB, that attempts to combine the advantages of both types of platforms. Finally, I discuss our experience in using HadoopDB for both traditional decision support workloads (i.e., TPC-H) and also scientific data management (analyzing the Uniprot protein sequence, function, and annotation data).

**Keywords:** MapReduce, parallel databases, scalable dystems, fault tolerant systems, analytical data management.

## 1 Introduction

The amount of data that needs to be stored and processed by analytical applications is exploding. This is partly due to the increased automation with which data can be produced (more processes are becoming digitized), the proliferation of sensors and tracking devices, the increased computational power and data output of scientific machinery, and an increasing desire for more historical data to be kept online (in its raw, granular format) for analysis. It is no longer uncommon to hear of applications producing more than a terabyte of structured data per day (e.g., clickstreams, network event logs, scientific experimental data, telecom CDR records, and high-throughput genomic sequencing).

Given the exploding data problem, there is an increased demand for computer systems that can store, process, manage, and analyze data at this tremendous

M. Gertz and B. Ludäscher (Eds.): SSDBM 2010, LNCS 6187, pp. 1–3, 2010.

scale. Some applications attempt to use relational database (RDBMS) technology such as Oracle, Teradata, or IBM DB2 for storing and analyzing their data. Unfortunately, this technology is often unsuitable for the types of applications mentioned above, for two reasons. First, RDBMSs require data to be carefully modeled and loaded into two-dimensional tables before it can be used, and this requirement is too constraining for some of the applications mentioned above, which require more flexibility.

Second, while these relational databases have been proven to scale really well into the tens of servers involved in parallel data processing (arranged in a shared-nothing MPP architecture), there are very few known parallel RDBMS deployments consisting of more than one hundred servers, and to the best of our knowledge, there exists no published deployment of a parallel RDBMS with servers numbering into the thousands. There are two primary reasons why parallel database systems generally do not scale well into the hundreds of servers. First, failures become increasingly common as one adds more servers to a system, yet RDBMS technology tends to be designed with the assumption that failures are a rare event. Second, RDBMSs generally assume a homogeneous array of machines, yet it is nearly impossible to achieve pure homogeneity at scale (especially on shared infracture such as public or private cloud environments). As the data that needs to be analyzed continues to grow, the number of applications that require more than one hundred servers is starting to multiply.

Some people argue that MapReduce-based systems are well suited for large scale data analysis. Even though MapReduce was originally designed for unstructured text data processing (to help Google build its Web index) [2], it was architected from the beginning to scale to thousands of servers, and has had proven scalability success in Googles internal operations and on the TeraSort benchmark [3]. Unfortunately, MapReduce yields an order of magnitude slower performance than RDBMS technology on structured data analysis workloads (largely due to the fact that MapReduce was not originally designed to perform structured data analysis) [3]. This yields commensurate increases in the number of machines and energy consumption needed to perform a particular task (which is becoming an increasingly important concern).

At Yale, we are building a system, called HadoopDB that combines the flexibility and scalability advantages of MapReduce with the performance and efficiency advantages of RDBMSs to achieve a hybrid system that is well suited for analytical data management applications and can handle the future demands of data intensive applications. In a recent paper [1], we described our architectural vision of HadoopDB. The basic idea is to use Hadoop (an open source implementation of MapReduce) as the communication and job scheduling layer above multiple nodes running DBMS instances. Queries are expressed in SQL, translated into MapReduce, and as much work as possible is pushed into the higher performing single node databases. However, data that does not fit into a relational data model need not be stored in the database systems; rather it can be kept in Hadoop's distributed file system (HDFS) and combined with data stored in the database systems on the fly.

This talk focuses on both the generic problems with using parallel database systems and Hadoop for large scale data analysis and also the specific details of the architecture of the HadoopDB hybrid system. I will discuss some interesting architectural tradeoffs between common analytical platform implementations, including:

1. Fault Tolerance
2. Loading Time
3. Schema Flexibility
4. Join Performance
5. Straggler Node Handling

HadoopDB makes some interesting design decisions with respect to these tradeoffs, often finding a flexible mechanism for a user to adjust the desired middle ground between tradeoff extremes depending on a particular workload.

Finally I will discuss the status of the HadoopDB project, including the open source initiative around the codebase, recent benchmark studies (including some promising numbers on TPC-H), and some interesting applications we have found for HadoopDB (such as analyzing the Uniprot protein sequence, function, and annotation data).

## 2 Bio

Daniel Abadi is an Assistant Professor at Yale University. His research interests are in database system architecture and implementation, scalable data management, and cloud computing. He received his Ph.D. from the Massachusetts Institute of Technology where his work on query execution in column-oriented database systems resulted in the SIGMOD Jim Gray Doctoral Dissertation Award. Abadi has also been a recipient of a Churchill Scholarship, an NSF CAREER Award, and the 2007 VLDB best paper award.

## References

1. Abouzeid, A., Bajda-Pawlikowski, K., Abadi, D.J., Silberschatz, A., Rasin, A.: HadoopDB: An Architectural Hybrid of MapReduce and DBMS Technologies for Analytical Workloads. In: VLDB (2009)
2. Dean, J., Ghemawat, S.: MapReduce: Simplified Data Processing on Large Clusters. In: OSDI (2004)
3. Pavlo, A., Rasin, A., Madden, S., Stonebraker, M., DeWitt, D., Paulson, E., Shrinivas, L., Abadi, D.J.: A Comparison of Approaches to Large Scale Data Analysis. In: Proc. of SIGMOD (2009)

# Emerging Trends and Converging Technologies in Data Intensive Scalable Computing

Roger S. Barga

Microsoft Research, Microsoft Corporation
One Microsoft Way, Redmond, WA, USA, 98073
barga@microsft.com

There is today wide agreement that data-intensive scalable computing methods are essential to advancing research in many disciplines. Such methods are expected to play an increasing important role in providing support for well-informed technical decisions and policies. They are therefore of great scientific and social importance.

The growing wealth of data is manifest as increasing numbers of data collections, varying from curated databases to assemblies of files. The former provide reference resources, preservation and computational access whilst the latter are often structured as spreadsheets or CSV files and stored on individual researchers' computers. Many of these collections are growing both in size and complexity. As computer technology and laboratory automation increases in speed and reduces in cost, more and more primary sources of data are deployed and the flow of data from each one is increased.

At the same time, a growing number of researchers and decision makers are both contributing to the data and expecting to exploit this abundance of data for their own work. They require new combinations of data, new and ever more sophisticated data analysis methods and substantial improvements in the ways in which results are presented. And it is not just the volume of information but also its scope. It's becoming more important for different fields of science to work collaboratively to drive new discoveries. While cross-disciplinary collaboration is helping drive new understanding, it also imposes even greater levels of complexity.

This pervasive change is part of a research revolution that introduces a wave of data-driven approaches termed "The Fourth Paradigm" by Jim Gray, as it is so transformative. Current strategies for supporting it demonstrate the power and potential of these new methods. However, they are not a sustainable strategy as they demand far too much expertise and help to address each new task. In order to carry out these tasks effectively and repeatedly, we must tease out the principles that underpinned their success, and through clarification, articulation, and tools, make it possible to replicate that success widely with fewer demands for exceptional talents. And this will allow researchers to spend more of their time on research.

M. Gertz and B. Ludäscher (Eds.): SSDBM 2010, LNCS 6187, pp. 4–5, 2010.

This talk will take an opinionated look at the past, present, and future of data intensive scalable computing. I will outline trends that have recently emerged in the computer industry to cope with data intensive scalable computing, show why existing software systems are ill-equipped to handle this new reality, and point towards some bright spots on the horizon and share predictions of technology convergence.

# Deriving Spatio-temporal Query Results in Sensor Networks

Markus Bestehorn, Klemens Böhm, Patrick Bradley, and Erik Buchmann

Karlsruhe Institute of Technology, 76131 Karlsruhe, Germany
{bestehorn,klemens.boehm,bradley,erik.buchmann}@kit.edu
http://www.kit.edu

**Abstract.** Tracking moving objects in relation to regions of interest, e.g., for pollution control or habitat monitoring, is an important application of Sensor Networks (SN). Research on Moving Object Databases has resulted in sophisticated mechanisms for querying moving objects and regions declaratively. Applying these results to SN in a straightforward way is not possible: First, sensor nodes typically can only determine that an object is in their vicinity, but not the exact position. Second, nodes may fail, or areas may be unobservable. All this is problematic because the evaluation of spatio-temporal queries requires precise knowledge about object positions. In this paper we specify meaningful results of spatio-temporal queries, given those SN-specific phenomena, and say how to derive them from object detections by sensor nodes. We distinguish between objects which definitely fulfill the query and those that could possibly do so, but where those inaccuracies are in the way of a definite answer. We study both spatio-temporal predicates as well as spatio-temporal developments, i.e., sequences of predicates describing complex movement patterns of objects.

## 1 Introduction

Spatio-temporal semantics are an inherent property of many applications of Sensor Networks (SN). Examples of such applications range from scientists tracking animals [1, 2, 3] to governmental authorities observing if unauthorized persons or vehicles enter sensitive regions [4, 5, 6].

Researchers studying SN have noted the advantages of declarative query processing (e.g., [7, 8]), but have focused on relational queries so far. However, relational query languages are not well-suited to express spatio-temporal semantics [9]. This is because they do not offer spatio-temporal data types to model the movement of objects. Even simple spatio-temporal queries are difficult to formulate. To solve this problem, researchers on *Moving Object Databases (MOD)* have proposed languages to query moving objects and regions.

Applying these advances from MOD to SN in a straightforward way is not possible due to the well-known limitations of SN: MOD tend to assume precise and complete information on objects queried. This is typically not the case for data acquired on moving objects by SN: First, the area monitored by a sensor

M. Gertz and B. Ludäscher (Eds.): SSDBM 2010, LNCS 6187, pp. 6–23, 2010.

node is bounded, and there exist temporarily or permanently unobserved areas. This may be due to failed nodes, non-uniform deployment of nodes or external influences such as objects physically blocking the detection hardware. Another problem is the accuracy of most sensing devices commonly used in SN: They typically only detect the presence of objects in their vicinity, but cannot determine their position. Thus, they might be unable to determine if some object is "inside", "on the border" or "outside" of a region. It is the combination of these problems that is challenging, given the assumptions commonly used in MOD.

In this paper, we show how to obtain meaningful results for spatio-temporal queries based on incomplete, imprecise object detections in SN. As a first step, we provide a formal framework for the description of object movements that is applicable to any detection mechanism. We show how to deduce results for spatio-temporal queries from information acquired through object detection, together with information on the accuracy of query results. We distinguish between three kinds of results: For some objects, the SN can determine that their movement conforms to the query despite the inaccuracy of object detection for sure. In the second case, object detection is not sufficiently accurate to yield a definite answer. The third case is that the SN can rule out that a movement conforms to the query. Note that we abstract from the implementation of communication protocols or data types that may be used to compute the results.

More importantly, we show for all results that they are optimal considering the limitations of object detection by the SN: First, we say how to derive a set of objects definitely fulfilling the query of the user. We show for this set that it is maximal, i.e., contains all objects for which SN can guarantee that they fulfill the query, under non-restrictive assumptions. Second, we say how to derive the set of objects that possibly fulfill the query. Similar to the first set, we show for this set that it does not contain objects from the first category or objects that definitely do not fulfill the query. We show how to compute such result sets for both spatio-temporal predicates as well as spatio-temporal developments. The latter are sequences of predicates that describe complex object movements [10].

Our results are not trivial: The number of possible sequences of object detections is infinite, and the difficulty is finding few good abstractions from individual detection sequences, which give way to meaningful conclusions. Further, this abstraction must keep our approach applicable to a wide range of SN and detection mechanisms.

Paper outline: Section 2 introduces our running example. In Section 3 we briefly review query processing in MOD. Section 4 introduces an abstract node and network model which we use to study the processing of predicates and developments in SN in Sections 5 and 6 respectively. We conclude in Section 7.

## 2 Application Scenario

In the following, we use an application from research on vehicle-target detection and classification called "A Line in the Sand" [6] as a running example. We introduce this application and describe several properties of the SN our approach aims at. The objective of this application is detecting vehicles or humans along a perimeter or within a region defined by geo-coordinates using a sensor network, as illustrated in Figure 1.

Sensor nodes like MicaZ [11] or Sun SPOT [12] are deployed, e.g., by dropping them out of an airplane or by manually installing them. We take different deployment methods into account by distinguishing between three *coverage assumptions (CA)*:

$\mathtt{CA}^{\varnothing}$: Nodes are deployed randomly, and it is not fixed a priori which parts of the space are observed.

$\mathtt{CA}^{\mathtt{B}}$: By deploying nodes in a controlled manner, it is guaranteed that the border of the region is completely observed, i.e., objects cannot move over the border without being detected.

$\mathtt{CA}^{\mathtt{BI}}$: The deployment guarantees that objects inside the region as well as objects moving over the border are detected at any time.

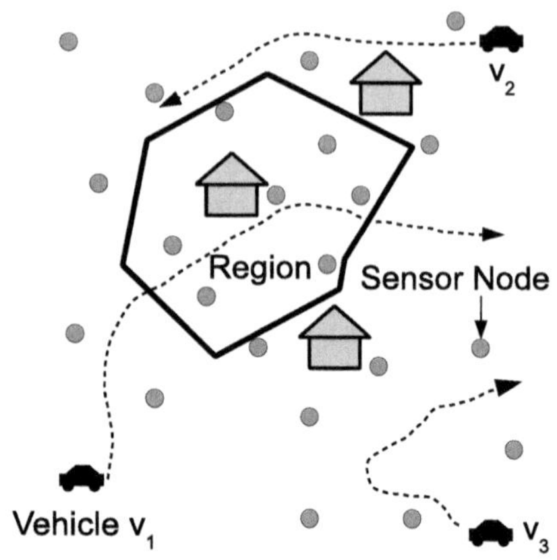


**Fig. 1.** Illustration of the application scenario

Each node is equipped with a GPS receiver to determine its position and sensing hardware to detect moving objects and classify them as, say, vehicles or humans. There exist several approaches for this: For example, acoustic sensors like condenser microphones detect vehicles based on noise emitted by the engine or propulsion gear [13]. Other examples are passive infrared (PIR) motion detectors or magnetics sensors [5].

A simple spatio-temporal query in our scenario is which vehicles have moved from outside of a user-defined region **R** into the region. We use this query as our running example. The application scenario just described also fixes the scope of this paper: To ease presentation, we limit the discussion to queries regarding the spatio-temporal relationship between moving objects and one static region. Next, we assume that sensor nodes do not move, and that the detection mechanism can distinguish between query-relevant objects and irrelevant ones. Further, it is able to identify objects. For instance, if Sensor `Si` detects a certain object, and `Sj` detects the object later on, the SN knows that it is the same object. Such an identification is usually available, e.g., for pedestrians carrying a cellular phone or vehicles emitting a certain noise-pattern.

Another important aspect is the *temporal resolution* of detection mechanisms: From an abstract point of view, such a mechanism checks for objects in range. It does so with a certain temporal resolution, e.g., measurements are taken every $t$ seconds. This temporal resolution determines the speed of the objects the mechanism can detect. If objects travel faster than implicitly assumed, they may remain undetected. We assume in the following that this is not the case.

Finally, the temporal resolution never is infinitely high, but bounded by the physical limits of the hardware used.

## 3 Spatio-temporal Query Processing and Related Work

In this section we briefly review related work and introduce some fundamentals of spatio-temporal query processing. See [10] for further details.

### 3.1 Spatial Relationships

Spatio-temporal query processing is based on the point-set topology [14]. It defines the spatial entities *points*, *lines* and *regions* for the Euclidean space $\mathbf{E^d}$. To ease presentation, we focus on the 2-dimensional space $\mathbf{E^2}$. Every element of the space is a point $p \in \mathbf{E^2}$ with $p := < latitude, longitude >$. An entity is a set of points which divides the space into three pair-wise disjoint subsets: the *interior*, the *border* and the *exterior*. For a region $\mathbf{R}$, the border $\mathbf{R}^B$ contains all points of the line that delimits the region. The interior $\mathbf{R}^I$ covers all points within the region. The points that are neither in $\mathbf{R}^I$ nor in $\mathbf{R}^B$ are the exterior $\mathbf{R}^O$ (See [15] for formal definitions.). In contrast to regions, points do not have a border and only an interior.

$$\begin{pmatrix} A^B \cap B^B \neq \emptyset & A^B \cap B^I \neq \emptyset & A^B \cap B^O \neq \emptyset \\ A^I \cap B^B \neq \emptyset & A^I \cap B^I \neq \emptyset & A^I \cap B^O \neq \emptyset \\ A^O \cap B^B \neq \emptyset & A^O \cap B^I \neq \emptyset & A^O \cap B^O \neq \emptyset \end{pmatrix}$$

**Fig. 2.** 9-Intersection Model for two spatial entities A and B

$$\begin{pmatrix} F & F & F \\ F & T & F \\ T & T & T \end{pmatrix} \quad \begin{pmatrix} F & F & F \\ T & F & F \\ T & T & T \end{pmatrix} \quad \begin{pmatrix} F & F & F \\ F & F & T \\ T & T & T \end{pmatrix}$$

*inside* $(p_3, \mathbf{R})$ *meet* $(p_2, \mathbf{R})$ *disjoint* $(p_1, \mathbf{R})$

**Fig. 3.** 9-Intersection representation of spatial predicates ($A = p_i$ and $B = \mathbf{R}$)

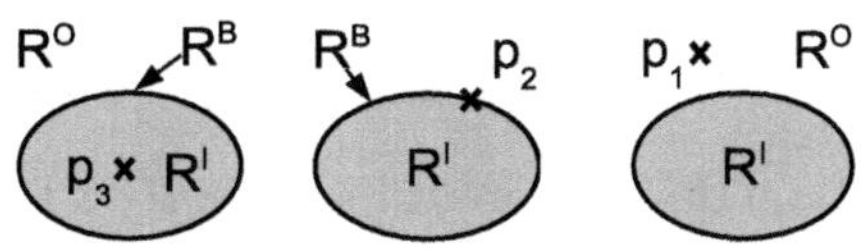


*inside* $(p_3, \mathbf{R})$ *meet* $(p_2, \mathbf{R})$ *disjoint* $(p_1, \mathbf{R})$

**Fig. 4.** Spatial Predicates for Point/Region relations

There exist three predicates to describe the relationship between a point and a region: *disjoint* $(p_1, \mathbf{R})$, *meet* $(p_2, \mathbf{R})$ and *inside* $(p_3, \mathbf{R})$, see Figure 4. The 9-intersection model [15, 16] describes the topological relationship between two spatial entities $A$ and $B$. It is based on the nine possible intersections of interior, border and exterior of $A$ with the interior, border and exterior of $B$, as shown in Figure 2. Each intersection is either empty or not. The intersection matrix consisting of the nine resulting boolean values describes the topological relationship between $A$ and $B$.

**Example 1:** *inside* $(p_3, \mathbf{R})$ is true if the interior of $\mathbf{R}$ contains the point $p_3$. The intersection matrix in Figure 3 represents the intersections of the partitions corresponding to $p_3$ and of the ones corresponding to $\mathbf{R}$: For $p_3$ to be in $\mathbf{R}$, $p_3^I \cap \mathbf{R}^I \neq \varnothing$. This corresponds to the middle value of the second row. Since $p_3$ is a point, the border ${p_3}^B$ is an empty set and thus does not intersect with any part of $\mathbf{R}$. ${p_3}^O$ contains all remaining points of the space and intersects with all parts of $\mathbf{R}$. The last row illustrates this. □

Note that only a subset of all $2^9 = 512$ possible intersection configurations makes sense. For example, if both interior and exterior of two entities intersect, the borders of these two entities must intersect as well.

### 3.2 Spatio-temporal Relationships

When objects or regions move, their topological relation may change over time. To express such changes, one needs to consider time. *Temporal lifting* [9] represents time as real numbers ($time \subset \mathbb{R}$). It models a spatial value $\alpha$ that changes over time as a *temporal function* $\theta(\alpha) : time \rightarrow \alpha$.

Temporal lifting can be leveraged to model *moving objects* and *evolving regions.* In this paper, an object is fully represented by its position, i.e., modeled as a point $p \in \mathbf{E^2}$. A *moving object* is one whose position changes over time:

**Definition 1 (Moving Object):** A *moving object* is a lifted object, i.e., a function $\theta\left(\mathbf{E^2}\right) : time \rightarrow \mathbf{E^2} \cup \{\bot\}$. If an object does not exist at some point in time $t \in time$, the function returns $\bot$. □

The set $\mathfrak{P}$ contains all possible point sets and a region $\mathbf{r}$ is represented by an element of $\mathfrak{P}$.

**Definition 2 (Evolving Region):** An *evolving region* $\mathbf{R}$ is a function $\theta(\mathbf{r})$ : $time \rightarrow \mathfrak{P} \cup \{\bot\}$, i.e., points are added/removed over time. □

A spatio-temporal predicate $P(\mathbf{x}, \mathbf{R})$ is a function that returns $T$, $F$ or $\bot$, depending on the topological relation of $\mathbf{x}$ to $\mathbf{R}$ over time. Spatio-temporal predicates are lifted spatial predicates.

**Example 2:** The spatial predicate *inside* $(\mathbf{x}, \mathbf{R})$ returns $T$ if $\mathbf{x}$ is in $\mathbf{R}^I$. To reflect that $\mathbf{R}$ and $\mathbf{x}$ might change over time, *Inside* $(\mathbf{x}, \mathbf{R})$ is a function $\theta\,(inside\,(\mathbf{x}, \mathbf{R})) : time \rightarrow \{T, F, \bot\}$ that returns $T$ whenever $\mathbf{x}$ is in $\mathbf{R}^I$. □

Example 2 illustrates the lifting of a spatial predicate. We use lower-case letters for spatial predicates like *inside* $(\mathbf{x}, \mathbf{R})$ and upper-case letters for lifted, spatio-temporal predicates, e.g., *Inside* $(\mathbf{x}, \mathbf{R})$. In general, to describe the changing topological relation between $\mathbf{x}$ and $\mathbf{R}$, the predicate $p(\mathbf{x}, \mathbf{R})$ is lifted:

$$\theta\,(p\,(\mathbf{x}, \mathbf{R})) : time \rightarrow \{T, F, \bot\} \tag{1}$$

Next, [10] defines the concatenation operator $\triangleright$ to express more complex changes of relationships between spatio-temporal entities.

**Definition 3 (Concatenation):** The concatenation of two predicates, $P(\mathbf{x}, \mathbf{R}) \rhd Q(\mathbf{x}, \mathbf{R})$, is true if $P(\mathbf{x}, \mathbf{R})$ is true for some time interval $[t_0; t_1[$, and $Q(\mathbf{x}, \mathbf{R})$ is true at $t_1$. □

Using this concatenation operator, one can construct *sequences* of spatio-temporal predicates $P_1(\mathbf{x}, \mathbf{R}) \rhd P_2(\mathbf{x}, \mathbf{R}) \rhd \ldots \rhd P_p(\mathbf{x}, \mathbf{R})$. A *spatio-temporal development* is a sequence of spatio-temporal predicates.

**Example 3:** The user in Section 2 wants to know which vehicles have moved into region $\mathbf{R}$. To fulfill the query, a vehicle must be outside of $\mathbf{R}$, then move over the border $\mathbf{R}^B$ into the interior $\mathbf{R}^I$. This query is expressed as follows:

$$Disjoint(\mathbf{x}, \mathbf{R}) \rhd Meet(\mathbf{x}, \mathbf{R}) \rhd Inside(\mathbf{x}, \mathbf{R}) \tag{2}$$

This spatio-temporal development usually is referred to as $Enter(\mathbf{x}, \mathbf{R})$. Another commonly used spatio-temporal development is $Touch(\mathbf{x}, \mathbf{R})$:

$$Disjoint(\mathbf{x}, \mathbf{R}) \rhd Meet(\mathbf{x}, \mathbf{R}) \rhd Disjoint(\mathbf{x}, \mathbf{R}) \tag{3}$$

□

Any sequence that describes the changing relationship between an object and a region consists of the three predicates $Disjoint(\mathbf{x}, \mathbf{R})$, $Meet(\mathbf{x}, \mathbf{R})$ and $Inside(\mathbf{x}, \mathbf{R})$. While infinite sequences of spatio-temporal predicates are possible, [10] has shown that it is sufficient to explicitly consider a canonical collection of 28 developments. From these 28 developments, more complex ones can be constructed by means of concatenation. In line with [10], we use this canonical collection in Section 6 to limit the number of predicate sequences we must consider explicitly.

## 4 Network and Node Model

The main notion introduced next is abstract detection mechanism. We also say, how objects are localized in a SN based on object detection.

**Notation (SN):** A *sensor network* is a set $\mathsf{N} = \{\mathtt{S1}, \mathtt{S2}, \ldots, \mathtt{Sn}\}$ of $n$ sensor nodes. $p_i$ is the position of $\mathtt{Si}$ after the deployment.

To process spatial or spatio-temporal predicates, sensor nodes must be able to detect objects moving in the area where the sensor network is deployed. There exist numerous approaches for the detection and localization of objects such as humans or vehicles, most of them with different characteristics.

**Example 4:** Acoustic vehicle detection or PIR sensors detect if a vehicle is in the vicinity of the node hosting the sensing device. Laser scanners or range finders yield better results. They can detect the distance of an object to the sensor node. Even more sophisticated mechanisms, e.g., radar, precisely locate objects in the area observed by the node, i.e., the result are coordinates. □

To keep our approach independent of the detection mechanism used, we abstract from it as follows: To detect an object, the object must be 'in range', i.e., in the area observed by the detection mechanism.

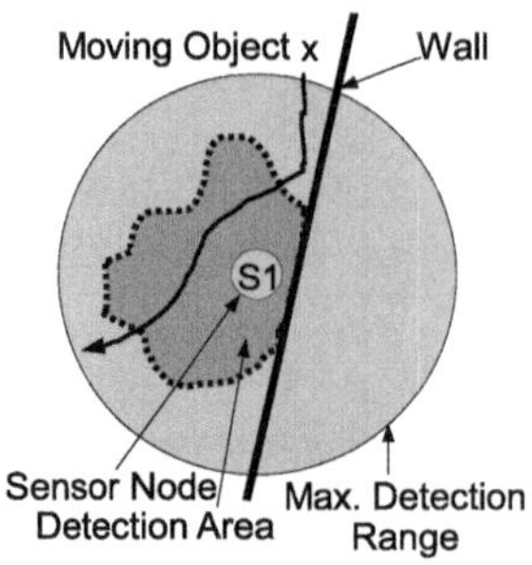


**Fig. 5.** Illustration of the node model

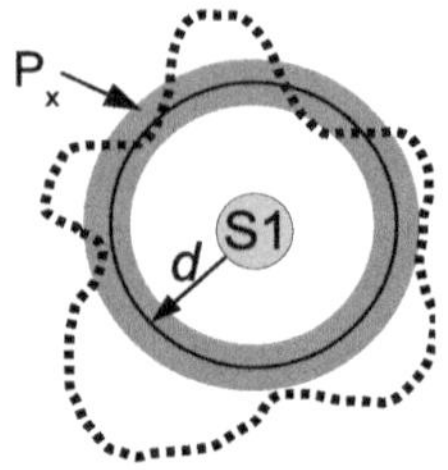


**Fig. 6.** Object detection with distance estimation

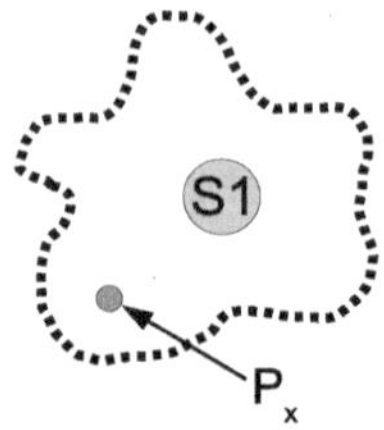


**Fig. 7.** Position-Precise Object Detection

**Definition 4 (Detection Area):** The *detection area* of node Si is the set of points $\mathbf{D}_i \subseteq \mathbf{E}^2$ where Si can detect an object. □

As illustrated in Figure 5, the detection area can have any shape or size and may change over time. Another important aspect is that most detection mechanisms cannot determine their actual detection area.

**Notation (Maximum Detection Range):** We refer to the maximum distance between the node hosting the detection mechanism and an object detected as *maximum detection range* $\mathcal{D}_{max}$.

The maximum detection range is usually provided externally, e.g., by the manufacturer of the sensing hardware, or determined through calibration prior to deployment. Figure 5 and Example 5 illustrate the difference between the detection area and the maximum detection range.

**Example 5:** For PIR-based motion detectors, $\mathcal{D}_{max} \approx 30$ meters. The sensor node in Figure 5 has been deployed close to a wall and cannot detect any object behind it. Thus, the area observed is much smaller than $\mathcal{D}_{max}$. Next, if there is an object in front of the lens of such a sensor, the area observed may be only a few centimeters. Nodes cannot detect this. □

It is the aim of any detection mechanism to narrow down the actual position of a detected object as precisely as possible. Thus, independently of the mechanism used, the result of object detection is modelled as a point set.

**Definition 5 (Possible Object Positions):** The *possible positions of an object* **x** *detected by* Si is a set $\mathbf{POP^i_x}$ containing all points $p \in \mathbf{E}^2$ where **x** could be while being detected by Si. Detection areas may overlap, resulting in *simultaneous detection* of an object by several nodes. In this case, the possible object positions $\mathbf{POP_x}$ are the intersection of all $\mathbf{POP^i_x}$. □

It depends on the detection mechanism how this point set is determined. Example 6 illustrates this, using the detection mechanisms from Example 4.

**Example 6:** Simple mechanisms like acoustic vehicle detection or PIR-based motion detectors cannot observe their detection area and only detect objects in the vicinity of the detecting node `Si`. In these cases, $\mathbf{POP^i_x}$ equals the circle with center $p_i$ and radius $\mathcal{D}_{max}$, see Figure 5. More sophisticated mechanisms determine the distance $d$ from the node to the detected object. Taking into account a certain deviation $\epsilon$, $\mathbf{POP^i_x}$ is ring-shaped, see Figure 6. Figure 7 illustrates $\mathbf{POP^i_x}$ for mechanisms which precisely determine the position of $\mathbf{x}$. □

For certain SN deployments, it is viable to make assumptions on the coverage of the area the SN is deployed in. In Section 2 we introduced three cases which are important for the discussion in the following.

**$\mathtt{CA}^{\varnothing}$:** No assumptions about the coverage are made.
**$\mathtt{CA}^{\mathtt{B}}$:** All points $p \in \mathbf{R}^B$ are in the detection area $\mathbf{D}_i$ of at least one node `Si`:

$$\mathbf{R}^B \subseteq \bigcup_{1 \le i \le n} \mathbf{D}_i \tag{4}$$

**$\mathtt{CA}^{\mathtt{BI}}$:** All points $p \in \mathbf{R}^B \cup \mathbf{R}^I$ are in $\mathbf{D}_i$ for at least one node `Si`:

$$\mathbf{R}^B \cup \mathbf{R}^I \subseteq \bigcup_{1 \le i \le n} \mathbf{D}_i \tag{5}$$

## 5 Deriving Predicate Results from Object Detection

In this section, we show how predicate results can be derived from information acquired through object detection. As a first step, we formalize the information obtained by object detection using so called *detection scenarios*. The detection scenarios also take the accuracy of object detection into account, i.e., nodes typically cannot determine the exact position of objects detected. To solve this problem, we propose to have a three-valued predicate result, to distinguish between objects that are guaranteed to fulfill, those that could possibly fulfill and those that definitely do not fulfill the predicate. The core contribution of this section is a mapping of detection scenarios and predicates to result values. We prove that the results obtained are optimal.

### 5.1 Semantics of Object Detection

When one or more nodes detect an object $\mathbf{x}$, its actual position must be in $\mathbf{POP_x}$. We deduce the result of spatio-temporal predicates from the overlap of $\mathbf{POP_x}$ with the different partitions of $\mathbf{R}$ by defining *detection scenarios*:

**Notation (Detection Scenarios):** A detection scenario describes the overlap of $\mathbf{POP_x}$, which is determined by the detection mechanism, with the different partitions of a region $\mathbf{R}$. In SN, there are the following scenarios:

**$\mathtt{DS}^{\mathtt{N}}$:** There does not exist a node that detects $\mathbf{x}$. In other words, the object is currently unobserved or does not exist: $\mathbf{POP_x} = \varnothing$

$\mathtt{DS^O}$: The set of possible object positions $\mathbf{POP_x}$ only contains points in $\mathbf{R}^O$. Then $\mathbf{x}$ is outside of $\mathbf{R}$: $\mathbf{POP_x} \subseteq \mathbf{R}^O$

$\mathtt{DS^I}$: $\mathbf{POP_x}$ only contains points in $\mathbf{R}^I$. The object $\mathbf{x}$ is inside of $\mathbf{R}$: $\mathbf{POP_x} \subseteq \mathbf{R}^I$

$\mathtt{DS^B}$: $\mathbf{POP_x}$ overlaps with $\mathbf{R}^B$: $\mathbf{R}^B \cap \mathbf{POP_x} \neq \varnothing$.
If $\mathbf{POP_x}$ also contains points of other partitions, it is unclear on which side of the border the object is.

**Lemma 1.** *For any point of time, exactly one detection scenario holds.*

*Proof.* The set of scenarios mentioned is exhaustive because it covers all points in $\mathbf{E^2}$. A point $p \in \mathbf{E^2}$ is either included in at least one detection area or unobserved. $\mathtt{DS^N}$covers all points $\mathbf{E^2} \setminus \bigcup_{\mathtt{Si} \in \mathsf{N}} \mathbf{D}_i$. The observed points $\bigcup_{\mathtt{Si} \in \mathsf{N}} \mathbf{D}_i$ are covered by one of the remaining scenarios: It depends on the detection mechanism which points are covered by $\mathtt{DS^B}$. If the mechanism precisely determines the object positions, $\mathtt{DS^B}$ only covers $\mathbf{R}^B$, while $\mathtt{DS^O}$ and $\mathtt{DS^I}$ cover $\mathbf{R}^O$ and $\mathbf{R}^I$ respectively. For any mechanism that is less accurate, $\mathtt{DS^B}$ also covers points around $\mathbf{R}^B$ from $\mathbf{R}^I$ and $\mathbf{R}^O$. Each of these point sets is pair-wise disjoint with the others, thus at every $t \in time$ exactly one detection scenario holds. □

The detection scenarios are completely independent from the detection mechanism used, the deployment and other external influences. They also take into account simultaneous detection of an object by more than one node:

**Example 7:** Let $\mathsf{N} = \{\mathtt{S1}, \mathtt{S2}, \mathtt{S3}, \mathtt{S4}\}$, and the SN is deployed as shown in Figure 8. Suppose each node only detects objects in its vicinity, e.g., using a PIR-based mechanism. Thus, if Si detects an object $\mathbf{x}$, $\mathbf{POP_x^i}$ contains all points in the circle with radius $\mathcal{D}_{max}$ and center $p_i$. If each Si detects a vehicle $v_i$, $1 \leq i \leq 4$, the following scenarios occur:

$v_1$ : $\mathbf{POP_{v_1}}$ contains only points from $\mathbf{R}^O$, and thus $\mathtt{DS^O}$ occurs.

$v_2$ : $\mathbf{POP_{v_2}}$ contains only points from $\mathbf{R}^I$, and thus $\mathtt{DS^I}$ occurs.

$v_3$ : $\mathbf{POP_{v_3}}$ contains points from all three partitions of the Euclidean space. This means that the detection mechanism is not sufficiently accurate to determine on which side of the border of $\mathbf{R}$ the vehicle $v_3$ is. Thus, $\mathtt{DS^B}$ occurs.

$v_4$ : Analogous to $v_3$.

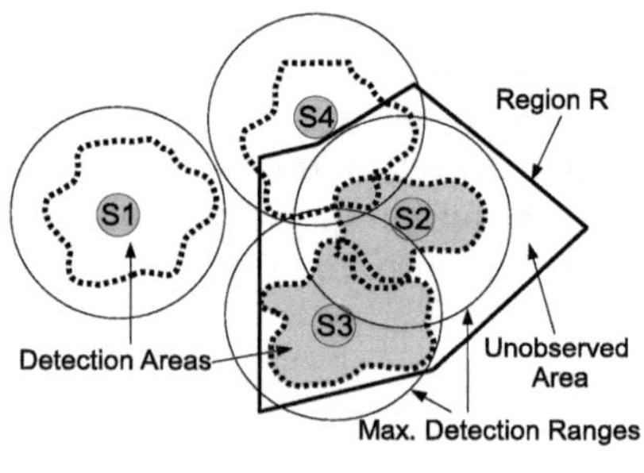


**Fig. 8.** Example of SN, detection areas, detection ranges and a region

In case of simultaneous detection of $v_4$ by S4 and S2, $\mathbf{POP_{v_4}}$ is the intersection of $\mathbf{POP^{S4}_{v_4}}$ and $\mathbf{POP^{S2}_{v_4}}$. It is a subset of $\mathbf{R}^I$ and results in $\mathtt{DS^I}$.

The detection scenarios for these vehicles obviously change if more sophisticated detection mechanisms are used. If S3 could determine its detection area

$D_3$, $\mathbf{POP_{v_3}}$ does not overlap with $\mathbf{R}^B$ anymore, as illustrated in Figure 8. This increased accuracy changes the detection scenario for $v_3$ from $\mathtt{DS^B}$ to $\mathtt{DS^I}$. □

Based on these scenarios, we will show how meaningful predicate results can be obtained. Unless otherwise noted, we assume that nodes cannot precisely locate an object. Thus, in case of $\mathtt{DS^B}$, $\mathbf{POP_x}$ always contains points not in $\mathbf{R}^B$.

### 5.2 Predicate Results

While $\mathtt{DS^O}$ and $\mathtt{DS^I}$ guarantee that the object is in a certain partition of the space, this is not true for $\mathtt{DS^B}$. Thus, objects detected with $\mathtt{DS^O}$ or $\mathtt{DS^I}$ conform to the predicate $p(\mathbf{x}, \mathbf{R})$ in question or not. Contrary to that, objects detected with $\mathtt{DS^B}$ could fulfill $p(\mathbf{x}, \mathbf{R})$, but this is not certain. We take this disparity regarding the certainty of object positions into account by adding a third value $M$(aybe) to the possible results of $p(\mathbf{x}, \mathbf{R})$:

$T$: $p(\mathbf{x}, \mathbf{R})$ returns $T$ if the SN can guarantee that $\mathbf{x}$ fulfills $p(\mathbf{x}, \mathbf{R})$.
$F$: $p(\mathbf{x}, \mathbf{R})$ returns $F$ if the SN can guarantee that $\mathbf{x}$ does not fulfill $p(\mathbf{x}, \mathbf{R})$.
$M$: $p(\mathbf{x}, \mathbf{R})$ returns $M$ otherwise.

**Example 8:** Continuing Example 7, think of a user interested in all vehicles inside the region, i.e., *inside* $(\mathbf{x}, \mathbf{R})$. Recall that a SN can only narrow down the actual position of a detected vehicle $v$: $\mathbf{POP_v^i}$ is the circle with radius $\mathcal{D}_{max}$ around the position $p_i$ of the detecting node `Si`. If node `Si` in Figure 8 detects $v_i$, $1 \leq i \leq 4$, the results are as follows:

$v_1$: The distance between `S1` and $\mathbf{R}$ is greater than $\mathcal{D}_{max}$. Thus, it is certain that $v_1$ is outside of $\mathbf{R}$. This yields *inside* $(v_1, \mathbf{R}) = F$.
$v_2$: $\mathbf{POP_{v_2}^{S2}}$ for $v_2$ is completely inside $\mathbf{R}$. Thus, *inside* $(v_2, \mathbf{R}) = T$.
$v_3$: Since the distance between `S3` and the border of $\mathbf{R}$ is less than $\mathcal{D}_{max}$, the detection area could overlap the border. If a vehicle is detected only by `S3`, the SN cannot determine on which side of the border it is. Thus, *inside* $(v_3, \mathbf{R}) = M$.
$v_4$: Analogously to $v_3$. □

### 5.3 Deriving Predicate Results

To process spatio-temporal queries in SN, we specify the mapping of each detection scenario of Notation 5.1 to a result for any predicate. This mapping is the foundation for meaningful results for spatio-temporal developments in Section 6. To ease the presentation, we do not make any assumptions regarding coverage for the time being, i.e., we use $\mathtt{CA}^{\varnothing}$.

***inside* $(\mathbf{x}, \mathbf{R})$ in SN.** There are three detection scenarios where an object can possibly be in $\mathbf{R}$:

**$\mathtt{DS^I}$: $\mathbf{POP_x}$** only overlaps with $\mathbf{R}^I$. Hence, *inside* $(\mathbf{x}, \mathbf{R})$ is true.

**$\mathtt{DS^B}$: $\mathbf{POP_x}$** partly overlaps with **R**. Thus, it is possible that **x** fulfills *inside* $(\mathbf{x}, \mathbf{R})$, but this is not guaranteed.

**$\mathtt{DS^N}$:** Objects may be within the region without being detected. Thus, **x** might fulfill *inside* $(\mathbf{x}, \mathbf{R})$ while being undetected.

Equation 6 serves as a summary:

$$inside\,(\mathbf{x}, \mathbf{R}) = \begin{cases} T \text{ iff } \mathtt{DS^I} \\ F \text{ iff } \mathtt{DS^O} \\ M \text{ iff } \mathtt{DS^B},\ \mathtt{DS^N} \end{cases} \tag{6}$$

**Lemma 2.** *Let $\Omega_{inside}$ be the set of objects in* **R**. *The set of objects where inside* $(\mathbf{x}, \mathbf{R})$ *yields $T$ or $M$ is the smallest superset of $\Omega_{inside}$ that the SN can derive from the detection scenarios.*

*Rationale.* The remaining detection scenario $\mathtt{DS^O}$ only corresponds to objects that are guaranteed to be outside of **R**. □

**Lemma 3.** *The set of objects where inside* $(\mathbf{x}, \mathbf{R}) = T$ *is the largest subset of $\Omega_{inside}$ that the SN can derive from the detection scenarios.*

*Rationale.* Only $\mathtt{DS^I}$ corresponds to objects that fulfill *inside* $(\mathbf{x}, \mathbf{R})$ for sure. □

We conclude for *inside* $(\mathbf{x}, \mathbf{R})$, that the result in Equation 6 is as accurate as possible, considering the limited view of reality offered by SN.

***meet*** **$(\mathbf{x}, \mathbf{R})$ in SN.** The predicate *meet* $(\mathbf{x}, \mathbf{R})$ is true if **x** is in $\mathbf{R}^B$.

**Lemma 4.** *SN cannot guarantee meet* $(\mathbf{x}, \mathbf{R}) = T$ *for any object detected.*

*Proof.* $\mathtt{DS^B}$ occurs if $\mathbf{POP_x}$ and $\mathbf{R}^B$ overlap. All other detection scenarios either guarantee that **x** is not in $\mathbf{R}^B$ or is undetected. Therefore, only $\mathtt{DS^B}$ needs to be considered here. Even if **x** is on the border $\mathbf{R}^B$, $\mathbf{POP_x}$ also contains points $p \notin \mathbf{R}^B$ (cf. Section 5.1). Thus, the detection mechanism cannot distinguish between objects on the border and objects close to it. □

Even if sophisticated detection mechanisms were used that precisely determine the position of an object, *meet* $(\mathbf{x}, \mathbf{R})$ would be problematic: $\mathbf{R}^B$ is a line, and lines do not have any 'width'. The time it takes for an object to move over a line is infinitely short. Capturing this moment would require sensing hardware with infinitely high temporal resolution. Thus, even those sophisticated mechanisms cannot detect objects on the border reliably.

$\mathtt{DS^B}$ occurs if objects are 'close' to the border, i.e., $\mathtt{DS^B}$ corresponds to objects that possibly are on the border. Without any coverage assumptions, undetected objects might be on the border as well. For the other detection scenarios, the SN guarantees that **x** is not on the border of **R**. See Equation 7:

$$meet\,(\mathbf{x}, \mathbf{R}) = \begin{cases} F \text{ iff } \mathtt{DS^I} \text{ or } \mathtt{DS^O} \\ M \text{ iff } \mathtt{DS^B} \text{ or } \mathtt{DS^N} \end{cases} \tag{7}$$

**Lemma 5.** *The set of objects where meet* $(\mathbf{x}, \mathbf{R}) = M$ *is the smallest superset of objects identifiable by the SN that might conform to meet* $(\mathbf{x}, \mathbf{R})$.

*Proof (Sketch).* Unless detected according to $\mathtt{DS^B}$ or $\mathtt{DS^N}$, objects are not in $\mathbf{R}^B$, because $\mathbf{POP_x}$ does not overlap with it. □

One might now consider removing *meet* $(\mathbf{x}, \mathbf{R})$ from the set of predicates because there does not exist a detection scenario for which *meet* $(\mathbf{x}, \mathbf{R}) = T$. However this is problematic: For example, the development $Touch\,(\mathbf{x}, \mathbf{R})$ would not be expressible without *meet* $(\mathbf{x}, \mathbf{R})$. We will show in Section 6 that there exist spatio-temporal developments containing *meet* $(\mathbf{x}, \mathbf{R})$ whose meaning can be guaranteed despite Lemma 4. Summing up, the result in Equation 7 is as accurate as the detection mechanisms in SN allow.

***disjoint* (x, R) in SN.** To conform to *disjoint* $(\mathbf{x}, \mathbf{R})$, object $\mathbf{x}$ must be in $\mathbf{R}^O$. The mapping to detection scenarios is analogous to *inside* $(\mathbf{x}, \mathbf{R})$:

$$disjoint\,(\mathbf{x}, \mathbf{R}) = \begin{cases} T \text{ iff } \mathtt{DS^O} \\ F \text{ iff } \mathtt{DS^I} \\ M \text{ iff } \mathtt{DS^B} \text{ or } \mathtt{DS^N} \end{cases} \tag{8}$$

Obviously, there are lemmas analogous to Lemmas 2 and 3 for *disjoint* $(\mathbf{x}, \mathbf{R})$.

**Summary.** Table 1 summarizes the mapping of detection scenarios and predicates to result values. Each row in the table corresponds to a predicate and each column to a detection scenario.

**Table 1.** Correspondence of detection scenarios and spatial predicates

| $p\,(\mathbf{x}, \mathbf{R})$ | $\mathtt{DS^N}$ | $\mathtt{DS^O}$ | $\mathtt{DS^I}$ | $\mathtt{DS^B}$ |
|---|---|---|---|---|
| *inside* $(\mathbf{x}, \mathbf{R})$ | $M$ | $F$ | $T$ | $M$ |
| *meet* $(\mathbf{x}, \mathbf{R})$ | $M$ | $F$ | $F$ | $M$ |
| *disjoint* $(\mathbf{x}, \mathbf{R})$ | $M$ | $T$ | $F$ | $M$ |

### 5.4 Impact of Coverage Assumptions on Predicate Results

Table 1 shows the results for predicates in SN without any assumptions regarding coverage. In controlled deployments, assumptions regarding coverage are feasible. Such assumptions influence the results of predicates, as we now show.

$\mathtt{CA^B}$ assumes that any point of the border is observed by at least one sensor node. Thus, undetected objects are guaranteed to be either outside or inside of $\mathbf{R}$, but not on the border. Additionally, if $\mathbf{R}^I$ is observed completely as well (cf. $\mathtt{CA^{BI}}$), undetected objects are guaranteed to be outside of $\mathbf{R}$. Tables 2 and 3 summarize the mapping of detection scenarios and predicates to result values for assumptions $\mathtt{CA^B}$ and $\mathtt{CA^{BI}}$ respectively.

**Table 2.** Predicate results assuming $\mathtt{CA}^{\mathtt{B}}$

| $p(\mathbf{x},\mathbf{R})$ | $\mathtt{DS}^{\mathtt{N}}$ | $\mathtt{DS}^{\mathtt{O}}$ | $\mathtt{DS}^{\mathtt{I}}$ | $\mathtt{DS}^{\mathtt{B}}$ |
|---|---|---|---|---|
| $inside(\mathbf{x},\mathbf{R})$ | $M$ | $F$ | $T$ | $M$ |
| $meet(\mathbf{x},\mathbf{R})$ | $F$ | $F$ | $F$ | $M$ |
| $disjoint(\mathbf{x},\mathbf{R})$ | $M$ | $T$ | $F$ | $M$ |

**Table 3.** Predicate results assuming $\mathtt{CA}^{\mathtt{BI}}$

| $p(\mathbf{x},\mathbf{R})$ | $\mathtt{DS}^{\mathtt{N}}$ | $\mathtt{DS}^{\mathtt{O}}$ | $\mathtt{DS}^{\mathtt{I}}$ | $\mathtt{DS}^{\mathtt{B}}$ |
|---|---|---|---|---|
| $inside(\mathbf{x},\mathbf{R})$ | $F$ | $F$ | $T$ | $M$ |
| $meet(\mathbf{x},\mathbf{R})$ | $F$ | $F$ | $F$ | $M$ |
| $disjoint(\mathbf{x},\mathbf{R})$ | $T$ | $T$ | $F$ | $M$ |

# 6 Spatio-temporal Developments in SN

As a core contribution of this paper, we study in this section how sequences of object detections relate to spatio-temporal developments, i.e., how to compute the result of such developments. As with predicates, the result of spatio-temporal developments is three-valued. We now present our approach in the following three steps; the numbers are in line with the ones of the respective sections:

6.1 We define a framework that allows us to describe object trajectories formally based on sequences of detection scenarios.
6.2 Using the framework and the canonical collection of spatio-temporal developments from [10], we come up with all trajectories that definitely fulfill a predicate sequence.
6.3 We show how the SN can determine which objects definitely do not fulfill the development queried.

All objects not identified in step 6.2 or 6.3 could fulfill the development in question, i.e., the result equals $M$.

## 6.1 Formal Description of Object Detection Sequences

A spatio-temporal development $\mathbb{P}(\mathbf{x},\mathbf{R}) = P_1(\mathbf{x},\mathbf{R}) \rhd P_2(\mathbf{x},\mathbf{R}) \rhd \ldots \rhd P_{\mathtt{q}}(\mathbf{x},\mathbf{R})$ is a sequence of predicates which describes the movement of an object $\mathbf{x}$ in relation to a region $\mathbf{R}$. The trajectory of an object matches such a development if it conforms to the predicates in the given order (cf. Definition 3).

**Definition 6 (Detection Sequence):** The *detection sequence* $\mathbb{D}_{\mathbf{x}}^{\mathbf{R}} = \mathtt{DS}^1 \succ \mathtt{DS}^2 \succ \ldots \succ \mathtt{DS}^{\mathtt{k}}$ describes the trajectory of an object $\mathbf{x}$ in relation to region $\mathbf{R}$. $\mathbb{D}_{\mathbf{x}}^{\mathbf{R}}$ means that for some time interval $[t_1; t_2[$ the detection scenario is $\mathtt{DS}^1$, $\mathtt{DS}^2$ for time interval $[t_2; t_3[$ etc.[1] □

**Lemma 6.** *For every object* $\mathbf{x}$*, there exists exactly one detection sequence* $\mathbb{D}_{\mathbf{x}}^{\mathbf{R}}$ *that represents the information on the movement of* $\mathbf{x}$ *acquired by the SN.*

*Proof (Sketch).* According to Lemma 1, at each $t \in time$ one detection scenario holds. The detection sequence $\mathbb{D}_{\mathbf{x}}^{\mathbf{R}}$ is the concatenation of these scenarios. □

[1] We have chosen right-open intervals here to be in line with the definition of predicate sequences (cf. Definition 3 and [10]). This does not cause any problems, since the temporal resolution of any detection mechanism is limited in any case.

To abstract from detection sequences, we introduce the notion of detection term. The notion is slightly more complex than what is presented next, but we omit some details to keep the presentation concise. More specifically, we only introduce some detection terms. A detection term stands for a (possibly infinite) set of detection sequences.

**Notation (Alternative Detection):** If $\mathtt{DS}^1, \ldots, \mathtt{DS}^k$ are detection scenarios, then $\mathtt{DS}^1 | \ldots | \mathtt{DS}^k$ is a detection term. It represents all detection sequences $\mathbb{D}_{\mathbf{x}}^{\mathbf{R}}$ that contain at least one of $\mathtt{DS}^1, \ldots, \mathtt{DS}^k$. A detection sequence is a detection term as well.

**Notation (Repeated Detection):** If $d$ is a detection term, then $\{d\}$ is a detection term as well. The meaning is that $d$ occurs at least once.

**Example 9:** Consider the development *Enter* $(\mathbf{x}, \mathbf{R})$. The detection sequences $\mathtt{DS}^{\mathtt{O}} \succ \mathtt{DS}^{\mathtt{B}} \succ \mathtt{DS}^{\mathtt{I}}$ as well as $\mathtt{DS}^{\mathtt{O}} \succ \mathtt{DS}^{\mathtt{N}} \succ \mathtt{DS}^{\mathtt{I}}$ describe object trajectories that conform to *Enter* $(\mathbf{x}, \mathbf{R})$. The latter does so because we can infer from the fact that object $\mathbf{x}$ has been detected outside of $\mathbf{R}$ and inside of it afterwards that $\mathbf{x}$ has crossed the border at some point. Additionally, there exists an infinite number of detection scenarios like $\mathtt{DS}^{\mathtt{O}} \succ \mathtt{DS}^{\mathtt{B}} \succ \mathtt{DS}^{\mathtt{N}} \succ \mathtt{DS}^{\mathtt{I}}$ that conform to *Enter* $(\mathbf{x}, \mathbf{R})$ as well. The following detection term reflects this:

$$\mathtt{DS}^{\mathtt{O}} \succ \left\{\mathtt{DS}^{\mathtt{B}} | \mathtt{DS}^{\mathtt{N}}\right\} \succ \mathtt{DS}^{\mathtt{I}} \tag{9}$$

All detection sequences that contain $\mathtt{DS}^{\mathtt{O}}$ once, directly followed by an infinite number of repetitions of either $\mathtt{DS}^{\mathtt{N}}$ or $\mathtt{DS}^{\mathtt{B}}$ and a concluding $\mathtt{DS}^{\mathtt{I}}$ conform to this detection term and at the same time to *Enter* $(\mathbf{x}, \mathbf{R})$. □

**Definition 7 (Detection-Term Conformance):** A detection sequence $\mathbb{D}_{\mathbf{x}}^{\mathbf{R}}$ conforms to a detection term $d$ if $\mathbb{D}_{\mathbf{x}}^{\mathbf{R}}$ contains a substring of detection scenarios that is represented by $d$. □

To conform to a development, it is sufficient that a substring of a detection sequence conforms to the detection term. This is because objects may move in arbitrary patters before or after conforming to the term.

**Example 10:** Continuing Example 9, suppose that a vehicle $\mathbf{x}$ crosses $\mathbf{R}$. This results in $\mathbb{D}_{\mathbf{x}}^{\mathbf{R}} = \mathtt{DS}^{\mathtt{O}} \succ \mathtt{DS}^{\mathtt{B}} \succ \mathtt{DS}^{\mathtt{I}} \succ \mathtt{DS}^{\mathtt{B}} \succ \mathtt{DS}^{\mathtt{O}}$. The substring $\mathtt{DS}^{\mathtt{O}} \succ \mathtt{DS}^{\mathtt{B}} \succ \mathtt{DS}^{\mathtt{I}}$, and thus $\mathbf{x}$, conforms to the detection term in (9) for *Enter* $(\mathbf{x}, \mathbf{R})$. □

There exist various algorithms, e.g., [17], to find a substring conforming to a pattern in a string. In our case, finding a substring in a detection sequence that conforms to a detection term. We now provide *detection terms* for every possible detection sequence that conforms to a given spatio-temporal development.

## 6.2 Determining whether $\mathbb{P}(\mathbf{x}, \mathbf{R}) = T$ from Detection Sequences

As mentioned in Section 3, [10] constructs a canonical collection of possible developments describing the topological relation of an object and a region over time. In this section, we provide a detection term for each development $\mathbb{P}(\mathbf{x}, \mathbf{R})$

in this collection that describes a trajectory that conforms to $\mathbb{P}(\mathbf{x}, \mathbf{R})$ for sure, i.e., results in $\mathbb{P}(\mathbf{x}, \mathbf{R}) = T$.

[10] distinguishes between $meet(\mathbf{x}, \mathbf{R})$ and $Meet(\mathbf{x}, \mathbf{R})$: Using their semantics, $meet(\mathbf{x}, \mathbf{R})$ is true if $\mathbf{x}$ is on the border of $\mathbf{R}$ for exactly one instant of time. Contrary to that, $Meet(\mathbf{x}, \mathbf{R})$ is true if $\mathbf{x}$ stays on the border for a time interval. We omit developments with $meet(\mathbf{x}, \mathbf{R})$ here since this would require object detection with infinite temporal resolution, cf. Lemma 4. This reduces the number of detection sequences that must be considered to 10, which are contained in the left column of Table 4. The right column contains the corresponding detection term. We discuss each entry in the following and show its correctness.

**Table 4.** Detection terms for $\mathbb{P}(\mathbf{x}, \mathbf{R}) = T$

| $\mathbb{P}(\mathbf{x}, \mathbf{R})$ | $\mathbb{P}(\mathbf{x}, \mathbf{R}) = T$ |
|---|---|
| $Disjoint(\mathbf{x}, \mathbf{R}) \triangleright Meet(\mathbf{x}, \mathbf{R})$ | $\mathtt{DS}^{\mathtt{O}} \succ \{\mathtt{DS}^{\mathtt{B}} \mid \mathtt{DS}^{\mathtt{N}}\} \succ \mathtt{DS}^{\mathtt{I}}$ |
| $Meet(\mathbf{x}, \mathbf{R}) \triangleright Inside(\mathbf{x}, \mathbf{R})$ | $\mathtt{DS}^{\mathtt{O}} \succ \{\mathtt{DS}^{\mathtt{B}} \mid \mathtt{DS}^{\mathtt{N}}\} \succ \mathtt{DS}^{\mathtt{I}}$ |
| $Inside(\mathbf{x}, \mathbf{R}) \triangleright Meet(\mathbf{x}, \mathbf{R})$ | $\mathtt{DS}^{\mathtt{I}} \succ \{\mathtt{DS}^{\mathtt{B}} \mid \mathtt{DS}^{\mathtt{N}}\} \succ \mathtt{DS}^{\mathtt{O}}$ |
| $Meet(\mathbf{x}, \mathbf{R}) \triangleright Disjoint(\mathbf{x}, \mathbf{R})$ | $\mathtt{DS}^{\mathtt{I}} \succ \{\mathtt{DS}^{\mathtt{B}} \mid \mathtt{DS}^{\mathtt{N}}\} \succ \mathtt{DS}^{\mathtt{O}}$ |
| $Disjoint(\mathbf{x}, \mathbf{R}) \triangleright Meet(\mathbf{x}, \mathbf{R}) \triangleright Inside(\mathbf{x}, \mathbf{R})$ | $\mathtt{DS}^{\mathtt{O}} \succ \{\mathtt{DS}^{\mathtt{B}} \mid \mathtt{DS}^{\mathtt{N}}\} \succ \mathtt{DS}^{\mathtt{I}}$ |
| $Disjoint(\mathbf{x}, \mathbf{R}) \triangleright Meet(\mathbf{x}, \mathbf{R}) \triangleright Disjoint(\mathbf{x}, \mathbf{R})$ | - |
| $Inside(\mathbf{x}, \mathbf{R}) \triangleright Meet(\mathbf{x}, \mathbf{R}) \triangleright Disjoint(\mathbf{x}, \mathbf{R})$ | $\mathtt{DS}^{\mathtt{I}} \succ \{\mathtt{DS}^{\mathtt{B}} \mid \mathtt{DS}^{\mathtt{N}}\} \succ \mathtt{DS}^{\mathtt{O}}$ |
| $Inside(\mathbf{x}, \mathbf{R}) \triangleright Meet(\mathbf{x}, \mathbf{R}) \triangleright Inside(\mathbf{x}, \mathbf{R})$ | - |
| $Meet(\mathbf{x}, \mathbf{R}) \triangleright Disjoint(\mathbf{x}, \mathbf{R}) \triangleright Meet(\mathbf{x}, \mathbf{R})$ | $\mathtt{DS}^{\mathtt{I}} \succ \{\mathtt{DS}^{\mathtt{B}} \mid \mathtt{DS}^{\mathtt{N}}\} \succ \mathtt{DS}^{\mathtt{O}} \succ \{\mathtt{DS}^{\mathtt{B}} \mid \mathtt{DS}^{\mathtt{N}} \mid \mathtt{DS}^{\mathtt{O}}\} \succ \mathtt{DS}^{\mathtt{I}}$ |
| $Meet(\mathbf{x}, \mathbf{R}) \triangleright Inside(\mathbf{x}, \mathbf{R}) \triangleright Meet(\mathbf{x}, \mathbf{R})$ | $\mathtt{DS}^{\mathtt{O}} \succ \{\mathtt{DS}^{\mathtt{B}} \mid \mathtt{DS}^{\mathtt{N}}\} \succ \mathtt{DS}^{\mathtt{I}} \succ \{\mathtt{DS}^{\mathtt{B}} \mid \mathtt{DS}^{\mathtt{N}} \mid \mathtt{DS}^{\mathtt{I}}\} \succ \mathtt{DS}^{\mathtt{O}}$ |

**Lemma 7.** *Detection sequences conforming to* $\mathtt{DS}^{\mathtt{O}} \succ \{\mathtt{DS}^{\mathtt{B}} | \mathtt{DS}^{\mathtt{N}}\} \succ \mathtt{DS}^{\mathtt{I}}$ *or to* $\mathtt{DS}^{\mathtt{I}} \succ \{\mathtt{DS}^{\mathtt{B}} | \mathtt{DS}^{\mathtt{N}}\} \succ \mathtt{DS}^{\mathtt{O}}$ *imply that* $Meet(\mathbf{x}, \mathbf{R}) = T$. *For any other sequence, this is not the case.*

*Proof (Sketch).* According to Lemma 4, $Meet(\mathbf{x}, \mathbf{R}) = T$ if the object has been detected on both sides of the border for sure. □

Due to Lemma 7, developments consisting of two predicates require detection of the object $\mathbf{x}$ in question on both sides of the border $\mathbf{R}^B$. This also affects developments like $Touch(\mathbf{x}, \mathbf{R})$ or $Inside(\mathbf{x}, \mathbf{R}) \triangleright Meet(\mathbf{x}, \mathbf{R}) \triangleright Inside(\mathbf{x}, \mathbf{R})$:

**Lemma 8.** *Let* $P(\mathbf{x}, \mathbf{R})$ *be an arbitrary predicate. There does not exist a detection sequence which guarantees* $\mathbb{P}(\mathbf{x}, \mathbf{R}) = T$ *for developments* $P(\mathbf{x}, \mathbf{R}) \triangleright Meet(\mathbf{x}, \mathbf{R}) \triangleright P(\mathbf{x}, \mathbf{R})$.

*Proof.* There are two cases: 1. $P(\mathbf{x}, \mathbf{R}) = Disjoint(\mathbf{x}, \mathbf{R})$. 2. $P(\mathbf{x}, \mathbf{R}) = Inside(\mathbf{x}, \mathbf{R})$. We omit $P(\mathbf{x}, \mathbf{R}) = Meet(\mathbf{x}, \mathbf{R})$ here for the following reason:

$$Meet(\mathbf{x}, \mathbf{R}) \triangleright Meet(\mathbf{x}, \mathbf{R}) \triangleright Meet(\mathbf{x}, \mathbf{R}) = Meet(\mathbf{x}, \mathbf{R}) \tag{10}$$

We only discuss Case 1 here, since Case 2 is analogous. According to Lemma 7, $Meet(\mathbf{x}, \mathbf{R}) = T$ is only possible if $\mathbf{x}$ is detected on both sides of $\mathbf{R}^B$ for sure. Thus, to guarantee a movement fulfilling the first part $\mathit{Disjoint}(\mathbf{x},\mathbf{R}) \triangleright \mathit{Meet}(\mathbf{x},\mathbf{R})$, the sequence must conform to $\mathtt{DS}^{\mathtt{O}} \succ \{\mathtt{DS}^{\mathtt{B}}|\mathtt{DS}^{\mathtt{N}}\} \succ \mathtt{DS}^{\mathtt{I}}$. While this movement guarantees $\mathit{Disjoint}(\mathbf{x},\mathbf{R}) \triangleright \mathit{Meet}(\mathbf{x},\mathbf{R})$, it also guarantees $\mathit{Disjoint}(\mathbf{x},\mathbf{R}) \triangleright \mathit{Meet}(\mathbf{x},\mathbf{R}) \triangleright \mathit{Inside}(\mathbf{x},\mathbf{R})$. Thus, the part $\mathit{Meet}(\mathbf{x},\mathbf{R}) \triangleright \mathit{Disjoint}(\mathbf{x},\mathbf{R})$ might not be true. □

Summing up, SN cannot guarantee for any object movement that it conforms to developments like $\mathit{Touch}(\mathbf{x},\mathbf{R})$, as reflected by the '-' entries in Table 4.

**Lemma 9.** *If* $\mathbb{D}_{\mathbf{x}}^{\mathbf{R}}$ *conforms to* $\mathtt{DS}^{\mathtt{I}} \succ \{\mathtt{DS}^{\mathtt{B}}|\mathtt{DS}^{\mathtt{N}}\} \succ \mathtt{DS}^{\mathtt{O}} \succ \{\mathtt{DS}^{\mathtt{B}}|\mathtt{DS}^{\mathtt{N}}|\mathtt{DS}^{\mathtt{O}}\} \succ \mathtt{DS}^{\mathtt{I}}$, *the SN guarantees that* $\mathit{Meet}(\mathbf{x},\mathbf{R}) \triangleright \mathit{Disjoint}(\mathbf{x},\mathbf{R}) \triangleright \mathit{Meet}(\mathbf{x},\mathbf{R}) = T$.

*Proof.* Looking at the first part of the detection sequence, $\mathtt{DS}^{\mathtt{I}} \succ \{\mathtt{DS}^{\mathtt{B}}|\mathtt{DS}^{\mathtt{N}}\} \succ \mathtt{DS}^{\mathtt{O}}$ already guarantees that $\mathit{Meet}(\mathbf{x},\mathbf{R}) \triangleright \mathit{Disjoint}(\mathbf{x},\mathbf{R})$ is true at some time. Afterwards, the object may move outside of $\mathbf{R}$ in any way, as reflected by $\{\mathtt{DS}^{\mathtt{B}}|\mathtt{DS}^{\mathtt{N}}|\mathtt{DS}^{\mathtt{O}}\}$. But this movement does not guarantee that $\mathbf{x}$ crosses $\mathbf{R}^{B}$ another time. This is achieved by adding $\succ \mathtt{DS}^{\mathtt{I}}$, i.e., $\mathtt{DS}^{\mathtt{O}} \succ \{\mathtt{DS}^{\mathtt{B}}|\mathtt{DS}^{\mathtt{N}}|\mathtt{DS}^{\mathtt{O}}\} \succ \mathtt{DS}^{\mathtt{I}}$ guarantees the second part $\mathit{Disjoint}(\mathbf{x},\mathbf{R}) \triangleright \mathit{Meet}(\mathbf{x},\mathbf{R})$. □

We omit a lemma that the entry for $\mathit{Meet}(\mathbf{x},\mathbf{R}) \triangleright \mathit{Inside}(\mathbf{x},\mathbf{R}) \triangleright \mathit{Meet}(\mathbf{x},\mathbf{R})$ in Table 4 is correct because it would be similar to Lemma 9.

### 6.3 Determining whether $\mathbb{P}(\mathbf{x},\mathbf{R}) = F$ from Detection Sequences

In this section we say how to determine systematically that an object movement definitely does not conform to a development.

**Lemma 10.** *Any object which is detected according to* $\mathtt{DS}^{\mathtt{B}}$ *could possibly conform to any spatio-temporal development.*

*Proof (Sketch).* $\mathtt{DS}^{\mathtt{B}}$ occurs if an object is detected 'close' to the border, and the inaccuracy of the detection mechanism prevents a definite answer on which side of the border it is. Thus, while the SN detects $\mathtt{DS}^{\mathtt{B}}$, the object could move around and over the border in any way, repeatedly. □

Recall that we only consider developments that describe topological relations between an object and one region. Lemma 10 implies that detection sequences of objects that definitely do not conform to a development queried may only consist of $\mathtt{DS}^{\mathtt{O}}$, $\mathtt{DS}^{\mathtt{N}}$ and $\mathtt{DS}^{\mathtt{I}}$. Recall that detection areas may have any shape or size, and temporarily undetected objects could cross the border of a region in arbitrary ways unless assumptions regarding the coverage are made. Thus, in case of $\mathtt{CA}^{\varnothing}$, objects that have been temporarily undetected could possibly conform to any spatio-temporal development. This is reflected by Lemma 11.

**Lemma 11.** *An object that is temporarily undetected, i.e.,* $\mathtt{DS}^{\mathtt{N}}$ *occurs, could conform to any development unless assumptions about the coverage are made.*

In SN deployed in a way such that $\mathtt{CA}^{\mathtt{B}}$ or $\mathtt{CA}^{\mathtt{BI}}$ can be assumed, objects cannot cross the border without being detected. In these cases, objects that did not cross the border, i.e., $\mathtt{DS}^{\mathtt{B}}$ never occurred, do not conform to development queried. Summing up, depending on the coverage assumption, the following objects definitely do not conform to any development queried:

$\mathtt{CA}^{\varnothing}$: Taking into account Lemmas 10 and 11, only objects that have been observed during all times according to $\mathtt{DS}^{\mathtt{I}}$ or $\mathtt{DS}^{\mathtt{O}}$ definitely do not conform to any development queried.

$\mathtt{CA}^{\mathtt{B}}$: This assumption implies that objects cannot cross the border without being detected. Thus, only Lemma 10 has to be taken into account to determine which objects do not conform to the development queried.

$\mathtt{CA}^{\mathtt{BI}}$: Since all points of the region are observed, undetected objects cannot exist in the region. Thus, the objects that definitely do not conform to a development are determined similarly to $\mathtt{CA}^{\mathtt{B}}$.

### 6.4 Summary

Equations 11-13 list the result of a development $\mathbb{P}(\mathbf{x}, \mathbf{R})$ for assumptions $\mathtt{CA}^{\varnothing}$, $\mathtt{CA}^{\mathtt{B}}$ and $\mathtt{CA}^{\mathtt{BI}}$ respectively.

$$\mathbb{P}(\mathbf{x}, \mathbf{R}) = \begin{cases} T \text{ iff } \mathbb{D}_{\mathbf{x}}^{\mathbf{R}} \text{ conforms to the corresponding entry in Table 4} \\ F \text{ iff } (\mathbb{D}_{\mathbf{x}}^{\mathbf{R}} = \mathtt{DS}^{\mathtt{I}}) \vee (\mathbb{D}_{\mathbf{x}}^{\mathbf{R}} = \mathtt{DS}^{\mathtt{O}}) \\ M \text{ otherwise} \end{cases} \tag{11}$$

$$\mathbb{P}(\mathbf{x}, \mathbf{R}) = \begin{cases} T \text{ iff } \mathbb{D}_{\mathbf{x}}^{\mathbf{R}} \text{ conforms to the corresponding entry in Table 4} \\ F \text{ iff } (\mathbb{D}_{\mathbf{x}}^{\mathbf{R}} = \{\mathtt{DS}^{\mathtt{N}} | \mathtt{DS}^{\mathtt{O}}\}) \vee (\mathbb{D}_{\mathbf{x}}^{\mathbf{R}} = \{\mathtt{DS}^{\mathtt{N}} | \mathtt{DS}^{\mathtt{I}}\}) \\ M \text{ otherwise} \end{cases} \tag{12}$$

$$\mathbb{P}(\mathbf{x}, \mathbf{R}) = \begin{cases} T \text{ iff } \mathbb{D}_{\mathbf{x}}^{\mathbf{R}} \text{ conforms to the corresponding entry in Table 4} \\ F \text{ iff } (\mathbb{D}_{\mathbf{x}}^{\mathbf{R}} = \{\mathtt{DS}^{\mathtt{N}} | \mathtt{DS}^{\mathtt{O}}\}) \vee (\mathbb{D}_{\mathbf{x}}^{\mathbf{R}} = \mathtt{DS}^{\mathtt{I}}) \\ M \text{ otherwise} \end{cases} \tag{13}$$

**Theorem 1.** *The results for spatio-temporal developments derived in this section are optimal, considering the limitations of detection mechanisms in SN.*

*Proof.* Let $\Omega_{\mathbb{P}(\mathbf{x},\mathbf{R})}$ be the set of objects that conform to $\mathbb{P}(\mathbf{x}, \mathbf{R})$. The set of objects where $\mathbb{P}(\mathbf{x}, \mathbf{R}) = T$ according to lemmas in Section 6.2 is the largest subset of $\mathbb{P}(\mathbf{x}, \mathbf{R})$ the SN can derive. Similarly, the set of objects where $\mathbb{P}(\mathbf{x}, \mathbf{R}) = F$ is the largest set of objects the SN can derive. Therefore, the set of objects where $\mathbb{P}(\mathbf{x}, \mathbf{R}) = M$ is the smallest subset of $\Omega_{\mathbb{P}(\mathbf{x},\mathbf{R})}$ the SN can derive based on the limited accuracy of object detection. □

## 7 Conclusions

In this paper, we have studied the evaluation of spatio-temporal queries with the help of SN. This is important, since SN are widely used to track moving objects. It also is challenging, because MOD typically expect complete knowledge about movements, while SN have limited sensing capabilities. We find classes of detection scenarios that correspond/do not correspond/might correspond to a given spatio-temporal development, for each element of the canonical set of developments. For each of these results, we have shown that it is optimal taking into account the accuracy of object detection of the SN in question.

## References


[1] Mainwaring, A., et al.: Wireless sensor networks for habitat monitoring. In: WSNA 2009, pp. 88–97. ACM, New York (2002)

[2] Cerpa, A., et al.: Habitat monitoring: Application driver for wireless communications technology. SIGCOMM CCR 31(suppl. 2), 20–41 (2001)

[3] Liu, N., et al.: Long-term animal observation by wireless sensor networks with sound recognition. In: Liu, B., Bestavros, A., Du, D.-Z., Wang, J. (eds.) WASA 2009. LNCS, vol. 5682, pp. 1–11. Springer, Heidelberg (2009)

[4] Langendorfer, P., et al.: A Wireless Sensor Network Reliable Architecture for Intrusion Detection. In: NGI, pp. 189–194 (2008)

[5] Ding, J., Cheung, S.Y., Tan, C.W., Varaiya, P.: Signal Processing of Sensor Node Data for Vehicle Detection. In: IEEE ITSC, pp. 70–75 (2004)

[6] Arora, A., et al.: A line in the sand: A wireless sensor network for target detection, classification, and tracking. Computer Networks 46(5), 605–634 (2004)

[7] Yao, Y., Gehrke, J.: The Cougar Approach to In-Network Query Processing in Sensor Networks. SIGMOD Rec. 31(3), 9–18 (2002)

[8] Madden, S., et al.: TinyDB: An Acquisitional Query Processing System for Sensor Networks. ACM TODS 30(1), 122–173 (2005)

[9] Güting, R.H., et al.: A Foundation for Representing and Querying Moving Objects. ACM TODS 25(1), 1–42 (2000)

[10] Erwig, M., Schneider, M.: Spatio-temporal predicates. IEEE TKDE 14(4), 881–901 (2002)

[11] XBow Technology Inc.: Wireless Sensor Network Platforms (2010), `http://www.xbow.com`

[12] SUN Microsystems Inc.: Small Programmable Object Technology (2010), `http://www.sunspotworld.com`

[13] Braunling, R., Jensen, R.M., Gallo, M.A.: Acoustic Target Detection, Tracking, Classification, and Location in a Multiple-Target Environment. In: SPIE, vol. 3081, pp. 57–66 (1997)

[14] Gaal, S.: Point set topology. Academic Press, London (1964)

[15] Egenhofer, M.J., Franzosa, R.D.: Point set topological relations. IJGIS 5, 161–174 (1991)

[16] Clementini, E., et al.: A Small Set of Formal Topological Relationships Suitable for End-User Interaction. In: SSD, London, UK, pp. 277–295. Springer, Heidelberg (1993)

[17] Knuth Jr., D.E., Pratt, V.R.: Fast Pattern Matching in Strings. SIAM Journal on Computing 6(2), 323–350 (1977)

# Efficient and Adaptive Distributed Skyline Computation

George Valkanas[1] and Apostolos N. Papadopoulos[2]

[1] Dept. of Informatics and Telecommunications, University of Athens, Athens, Greece
gvalk@di.uoa.gr

[2] Dept. of Informatics, Aristotle University of Thessaloniki, Thessaloniki, Greece
papadopo@csd.auth.gr

**Abstract.** Skyline queries have attracted considerable attention over the last few years, mainly due to their ability to return interesting objects without the need for user-defined scoring functions. In this work, we study the problem of distributed skyline computation and propose an adaptive algorithm towards controlling the degree of parallelism and the required network traffic. In contrast to state-of-the-art methods, our algorithm handles efficiently diverse preferences imposed on attributes. The key idea is to partition the data using a grid scheme and for each query to build on-the-fly a dependency graph among partitions which can help in effective pruning. Our algorithm operates in two modes: (i) *full-parallel mode*, where processors are activated simultaneously or (ii) *cascading mode*, where processors are activated in a cascading manner using propagation of intermediate results, thus reducing network traffic and potentially increasing throughput. Performance evaluation results, based on real-life and synthetic data sets, demonstrate the scalability with respect to the number of processors and database size.

## 1 Introduction

Skyline queries, in the context of databases, were initially proposed in [1] and since then, they have attracted considerable attention from the database community, primarily due to their applicability in multi-criteria decision making, without the requirement of user-defined scoring functions. The skyline of a data set composed of $d$-dimensional points returns those points that are not dominated by any other, with respect to some specific preference (e.g., min, max) on each dimension. We say that point $p$ dominates point $q$ if $p$ it is at least as good as $q$ in all dimensions and it is strictly better in at least one. A classic example in the bibliography is that of hotels, for which we know their price ($y$-axis) and distance to the beach ($x$-axis), as shown in Fig. 1(a). We are interested in those hotels for which there is none cheaper and closer to the beach at the same time, i.e., hotels $\{a, g, e, n\}$.

There is also a current tendency towards addressing problems in a distributed manner, to enable decentralization and faster computation. P2P and Grid computing are two prominent examples and substantial research has focused on answering skyline queries in these environments [2,3,4,5,6,7,8]. Efficiency involves

M. Gertz and B. Ludäscher (Eds.): SSDBM 2010, LNCS 6187, pp. 24–41, 2010.

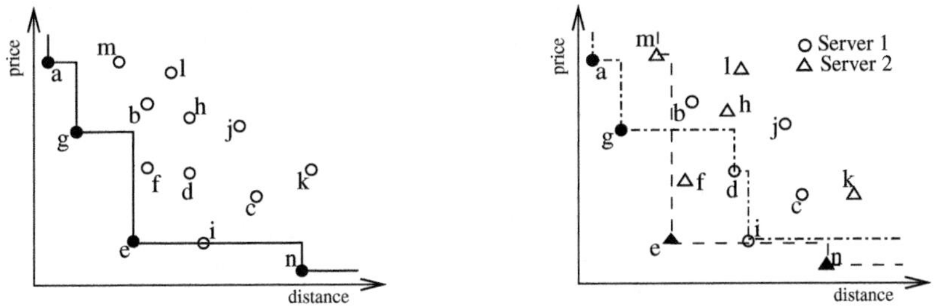


(a) centralized case (b) distributed case

**Fig. 1.** Skyline example of hotels

query processing and propagation, high parallelism, progressiveness and low network traffic. Achieving all these goals is far from trivial.

We focus on answering skyline queries in a *decentralized* setting. The data is distributed to a set of servers, one of which coordinates query execution. Therefore, our technique can be also applied in hierarchical P2P environments, where a superpeer acts as a coordinator which is responsible for a set of peers [9]. An example is given in Fig. 1(b), where points are distributed over two servers. The local skyline in each server is depicted by using different line styles.

Our first contribution is to examine the limitations of existing techniques that address skyline queries in such environments [3,8,10]. These methods mainly focus on ways of data partitioning instead of developing efficient algorithms.

After justifying our choice of one of the partitioning schemes, we make our second contribution: we devise a new algorithm, *ADISC* (Adaptive DIstributed Skyline Computation), that runs in either *full-parallel* or *cascading* mode, without modification, as it uses the same internal structure in both cases. The algorithm incorporates a set of highly tuned optimizations. Following similar research [11], we use specific points from the partitions, to prune areas that will not contribute to the final answer. We exploit these points further, in a novel way, to: i) improve parallelism while maintaining progressiveness, ii) negate relations between partitions which, as a side effect, iii) reduces network traffic and iv) minimizes coordinator workload. Irrelevant points are discarded and *eager* checking [12] is employed to improve performance. Parallel mode is more suitable for light-weighted systems, where response time reduction is desired, while cascading execution is directed towards enhancing progressiveness, reducing network traffic and increasing throughput.

Thirdly, aiming specifically to minimize traffic, we propose the use of *marginal points* as representatives, which is more efficient in the general case than similar techniques [4,8]. Furthermore, for the special case of 2D data we prove optimality of the approach in that each queried processor i) performs minimum I/Os, ii) returns only global skyline points and with a slight modification iii) we minimize network traffic to the greatest extent.

Fourthly, we devise a data propagation algorithm based on skyline properties to determine the way processors must inform each other. Such a method is crucial as it implicitly defines the order of execution, the degree of parallelism and the bandwidth consumption. It is interesting to note that for this reason we use the exact same structure as to determine how partitions must be checked with each other, thus minimizing additional overhead at the coordinator.

A basic property of our algorithm is that it handles different query preferences out of the box. Techniques such as [10] assume that skyline queries will always have fixed semantics regarding the criteria on data attributes and apply a specific partitioning method. However, we argue that this is a serious limitation, since different users may pose different preferences on specific attributes. We give two examples to illustrate the idea. As a first example, consider a multimedia database where images are 3-dimensional points, with each coordinate being the average value of red, green and blue in it. User $U_1$ requires images that are more red, but less green and blue, whereas user $U_2$ is interested in images that are less red but more green and blue. Evidently, $U_1$ issues a skyline query $Q_1$ with preferences <max,min,min>, whereas $U_2$ asks for <min,max,max> in his query $Q_2$. As a second example, consider a decision making application storing 2-dimensional data with bookstore profits, where each bookstore is represented as a $(x, y) = (time, profit)$ point. A query about bookstores with recent low profit is equally valid to one about bookstores with high profit achieved lately. The first is, of course, a <min,max> skyline query whereas the second is a <max,max> skyline query. According to these observations, handling different preferences is considered important towards supporting a broad range of applications.

The rest of the paper is organized as follows. Section 2 presents an overview of related work. Section 3 gives the definition of the problem in the distributed / parallel setting and explains in detail the partitioning schemes and gives some background information on the topic. Our proposal is studied in detail in Section 4 and evaluated experimentally in Section 5. Finally, Section 6 concludes the work and briefly discusses future research in the area.

## 2 Related Work

Primarily known as the maximal vector problem, proposed by Kung et al [13], skyline, or Pareto optimal, queries are a well studied problem in the area of Computational Geometry. It was not until much later that skyline queries were transferred to the context of databases, when Börzsönyi et al introduced the *skyline operator* [1] and proposed two algorithms: a Block-Nested-Loop (BNL) and a divide-and-conquer (D&C) approach. BNL was later improved by presorting the points according to a monotone scoring function, resulting in *Sort-Filter-Skyline* (SFS) [14]. Kossman et al [15] proposed an algorithm based on nearest-neighbor search. Papadias et al. proposed *Branch-and-Bound Skyline* (BBS) [16], which uses a multidimensional index and it is proven to be I/O optimal.

All of these approaches assume a centralized setting. The first work for distributed skyline queries was by Wu et al [3], where a CAN overlay was used to create grid partitions, each assigned to a processor. The main disadvantages of this approach is its low parallelism and that processors exchange the entire skyline which floods the network. Our technique is also different in that it uses a coordinator and processors are unaware of their neighbors' coordinates.

Additional distributed approaches have been developed, with applicability in the Web [2,5], Peer-To-Peer [6,7] and MANETs [4]. Web techniques partition the data vertically, assigning a single dimension to each server instead of a portion of the data, as we do. Peer-To-Peer systems lack any notion of a coordinator and keep distributed indexes. MANETs have limited resources and ad-hoc connectivity, contrary to our wired connection and more resourceful setting.

Parallel approaches include multiprocessor [17] and multi-disk environments [18]. Our setting differs in that we assume a share-nothing architecture in contrast with the shared-memory and shared-disk architecture respectively.

The works mostly related to ours are [8] and [10]. Vlachou et al [10] proposed a partitioning scheme based on hyper-spherical coordinates. Local skylines are computed using BBS, while the global result with SFS. Despite its increased parallelism, the approach has several limitations. First, as it has been noted previously, it assumes that the preference criteria (min or max) are known in advance. Secondly, due to SFS, the technique lacks progressiveness and all processors must report their skyline before any output is returned. This also burdens the coordinator with excessive points that must be kept in main or secondary memory. Finally, all processors must be activated for a skyline query, which may have a negative impact on throughput.

In [8], parallelism of distributed partitions is examined, where processors exchange representative points. Despite the similarities, a major difference is that partitions overlap, unlike our setting. Any parallelism achieved stems only from the initial bounds, whereas we increase parallelism in an innovative way. Partitions that cannot be computed in parallel are assigned a coordinator, hence multiple coordinators exist. Each coordinator creates a linearized execution plan for its partitions, though the details were not given. Finally, our representative points performs better in the general case.

## 3 Background

Given a data set $D$ of $d$-dimensional points, $p = \{p_1, p_2, .., p_d\}$, the skyline contains those points that are not dominated by any other. For simplicity, we assume *min* criteria on all dimensions and w.l.o.g. coordinates are normalized in $[0, 1]^d$. For the remainder of the paper we use the notation shown in Table 1.

**Definition 1.** *Let $D$ be a set of $d$-dimensional points. The skyline of $D$, denoted $SKY(D)$, contains those points that are not dominated by any other. We say that $p$ dominates $p'$, $p \prec p'$, if $p_i \leq p'_i$ $\forall i = 1, 2, .., d$ and $\exists j \in \{1, 2, .., d\}$ such that $p_j < p'_j$. The points in $SKY(D)$ are also referred to as skyline points.*

In the distributed/parallel environment, there are $N$ available processors $P = \{P_1, P_2, .., P_N\}$ and, potentially, a distinct node, termed the *coordinator*, which is responsible for the query execution strategy. The data set $D$ is partitioned offline in $k$ subsets $D_i$, $D = \bigcup_{1 \leq i \leq k} D_i$ and $D_i \cap D_j = \emptyset, \forall i, j$ where $i \neq j$. Each $D_i$

**Table 1.** Frequently used symbols

| Symbol | Interpretation |
|---|---|
| $D$, $n$ | data set and cardinality ($n = \|D\|$) |
| $d$ | data set dimensionality |
| $p$ | a $d$-dimensional point |
| $p_i$ | the $i$-th coordinate of $p$ |
| $D_i$ | the $i$-th partition of $D$ |
| $k$ | number of partitions |
| $P_i$ | the $i$-th processor |
| $N$ | number of processors |
| $SKY(S)$ | the skyline of set $S$ |

is randomly[1] assigned to a processor $P_j$, which is responsible for computing its skyline. The $P_i$s are deployed in a share-nothing architecture and may communicate with each other. We assume one partition per processor, although multiple partitions may be assigned to each processor. The coordinator propagates the query to the $P_i$s, which report their local skyline, and computes the global skyline without indexing the received data, though such an approach could improve performance. The property $SKY(D) = SKY(\bigcup_{1 \leq i \leq k} SKY(D_i))$ [1,17] ensures that the coordinator correctly reports the global skyline by performing a skyline algorithm on the local results.

There are several factors affecting the overall performance: (i) local and global skyline computation, (ii) degree of parallelism, (iii) network traffic, (iv) throughput. Although communicating the entire skyline minimizes I/O, it also floods the network, results in more collisions during data transfer and hinders efficiency. Given that the coordinator also accounts for other tasks, e.g. load balancing, we are interested in minimizing its workload and resource consumption. It is evident that many of these issues are contradictory. For example, high parallelism offers low response times, but in a heavy-loaded system with many concurrent queries, it will impact system throughput, due to increased network traffic. Therefore, answering skyline queries efficiently involves issues such as:

- *Response time*: the time needed to return the full skyline to the user,
- *Parallelism*: the number of parallel executing processors,
- *Network traffic*: the number of points that travel across the network must be minimized,
- *Progressiveness*: results should be returned as they are found and not after all partitions have been checked. However, we also view progressiveness in terms of iterativeness. Skyline queries may return a large number of points on occasions, therefore it would be of interest for the algorithm to produce results upon request, each time returning new skyline points.
- *Diversity*: diverse criteria on the data attributes must be supported and no assumptions should be made on the type of queries that will be invoked.

[1] We note that other assignment techniques (even dynamic ones) could also be applied, since the proposed techniques are orthogonal to the assignment strategy employed.

**Grid-based partitioning.** Grid partitioning was used in [3] by applying a CAN overlay with recursive splits on the coordinates in a round robin fashion. Even workload is ensured by creating partitions with fairly the same amount of points, each one assigned to a processor. An example of grid partitioning is shown in Fig. 2(a). The scheme has several advantages, with the most basic being that partitions preserve skyline properties. Therefore, we can safely exclude those that will certainly not contribute to the result, thus triggering fewer processors. A convenient execution order can be established from partition coordinates which also ensures progressiveness, while parallelism can be achieved for partitions that are certain not to dominate points from each other. Finally, the scheme makes no assumptions regarding the query criteria. This is a very interesting property, since we simply need to develop efficient algorithms to support skyline queries. Despite its advantages, the scheme has some inherent shortcomings. The most prominent is its low parallelism, which is not tackled by existing techniques. Secondly, activating all processors simultaneously returns a lot of unnecessary points from partitions that are certain not to contribute to the final skyline.

**Angle-based partitioning.** This scheme was proposed in [10] to simultaneously execute skyline queries on all processors. To do so, it relies on hyper-spherical coordinates and creates partitions of correlated-like distribution. An example is given in Fig. 2(b). Despite its advantage of parallelism, the scheme has several limitations. Firstly, because of its nature, the coordinator cannot exploit skyline properties on partitions. This leaves SFS as the only option for the global phase, when the received data is not indexed. This may be viable for independent distributions, but it is inefficient for high dimensionality or anti-correlated data, since its complexity is $O(m^2)$ on the number of received data. Secondly, it assumes that the criteria of the queries are known in advance. As shown in Fig. 2(b), the beginning of the axis for the polar coordinates is the same as the beginning of the criteria on the dimensions. Therefore, if *min* preferences are assumed, the scheme cannot answer efficiently a query with a *max* preference, because the underlying partitions were not designed for such a case. This results in a static partitioning and contradicts our goal of diversity. Finally, the scheme is designed to answer skyline queries only. It is unclear how to efficiently answer

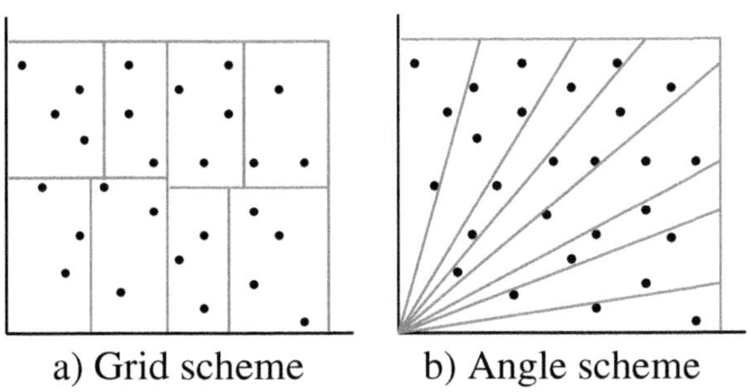


**Fig. 2.** Grid-based and angle-based partitioning schemes

other query types such as top-$k$, range, $k$-nearest neighbor queries, or even skyline variants [19], since the partitions do not maintain Cartesian properties and pruning properties in general, which are required by the aforementioned queries.

# 4 Proposed Approach

Based on the previous discussion, we choose the grid-based partitioning scheme and optimize it, so that its disadvantages are smoothed enough to the point that its advantages are elevated.

## 4.1 Skyline Dependencies

**Definition 2.** *Let $A = [ll^A, ur^A]$ and $B = [ll^B, ur^B]$ be two hyper-rectangles. We say that $B$ depends on $A$, $A \prec B$, if there may be a point from $A$ that dominates any point from $B$.*

**Lemma 1.** *If $A$ and $B$ are two hyper-rectangles, then $A \prec B$ iff $ll^A \leq ur^B$, where for two d-dimensional points $p$ and $p'$, we say $p \leq p' \Leftrightarrow p_i \leq p'_i \ \forall i = 1, 2, .., d$.*

*Proof.* First we will prove sufficiency. If $ll^A \not\leq ur^B \Rightarrow \exists j \in \{1, 2, .., d\}$ such that $ll^A_j > ur^B_j \Rightarrow \forall a \in A, \forall b \in B, a_j > b_j$. Therefore, there is at least one dimension for which $B$ is better, hence no points in $B$ can be dominated by any point in $A \Rightarrow A \nprec B$. For necessity, the proof is that $ll^A$ has the highest dominating region among points from $A$ that dominate $ur^B$. Any points in $B$ that fall in that area are dominated by $ll^A$, assuming it is an actual point. For the same reason, points in $A$ above $ll^A$, below $ur^B$, may also dominate points from $B$. □

In Fig. 3(a), $E \prec A$ whereas $D \nprec B$. Note that relation $\prec$ does not state that such a point exists; only that there might be one. For instance, although $A \prec B$, none of the points in $A$ dominate any of the points in $B$. An immediate result of Lemma 1 is that for any $A$ and $B$, $A \nprec B$ and $B \nprec A$, their points are definitely

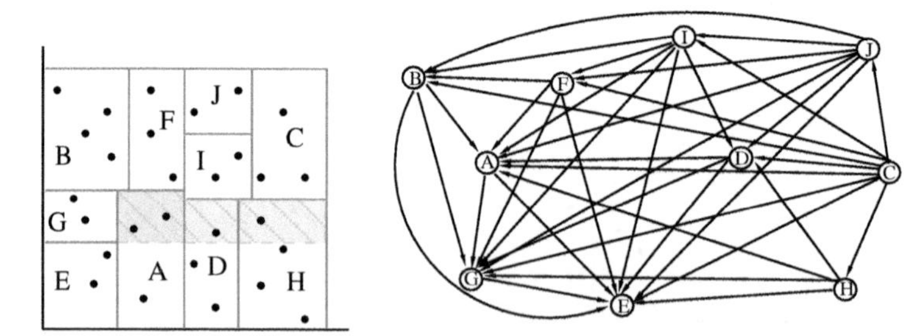

a) Dependencies Example b) Dependency graph

**Fig. 3.** Dependencies and dominating region

skyline with respect to each other. This is of great advantage as such partitions can be computed in parallel. We exploit this observation further so that such partitions are not checked against each other during the global merging phase.

Dependencies can be organized in a graph, where partitions are nodes and there is a directed edge from $B$ to $A$ iff $A \prec B$. This creates a *directed acyclic graph* of dependencies, or a *dependency graph*, as the one in Fig. 3(b) for the partitioning of Fig. 3(a). Such a graph can also be used during data propagation, because if an edge exists from $B$ to $A$, then $A$ may contain data that $B$ can use for pruning, thus $A$ should send its data to $B$. This also illustrates that dependencies define the workflow of query execution.

### 4.2 Cutting-Off Partitions

As in [16], where an R-tree node is not expanded if it is dominated, we can also exclude partitions from being queried if they are dominated by known points. This technique is also used in [11] and it is based on the following lemma.

**Lemma 2.** *Let $p$ be a point and $A = [l^A, u^A]$ an MBR in the $d$-dimensional space. If $p \prec l^A$ (also written as $p \prec A$) then none of the points $a \in A$ will be in the final skyline.*

*Proof.* Since $\forall a \in A$, $a_i \geq l_i^A$ they are all dominated by $p$ and therefore, there is no need to query this partition. □

### 4.3 Increasing Parallelism

Up to this point any achieved parallelism is derived from the partitioning scheme. For example, partitions $B$ and $D$ in Fig. 3(a) will be computed in parallel, because no edges between them exist in the graph. As already mentioned, this does not result in great parallelism.

**Definition 3.** *Let $A = [l^A, u^A]$ and $B = [l^B, u^B]$ be two non intersecting MBRs and $A \prec B$. We define the dominated region of $B$ from $A$, $dr \equiv dr_B(A)$, as the part of $B$ that is dominated by $l^A$.*

The *dominated region* $dr$ is the part of $B$ that is potentially dominated by a point in $A$ and is, in fact, the only reason why the relation $A \prec B$ exists between the two. Points in $B$ outside of $dr$ are skyline with regards to points in $A$, because $\exists j \in \{1, 2, .., d\}$ such that $b_j < l_j^A, b \in B$. Therefore, $dr$ is the sole reason why parallelism is not achieved between them. As an example in Fig. 3(a), the gray region of $A$, $D$, $H$ is the dominating area of $G$ on those partitions.

**Lemma 3.** *Let $A = [l^A, u^A]$ and $B = [l^B, u^B]$ be two non intersecting MBRs and $A \prec B$. Then $A$ and $B$ can be computed in parallel if $\exists$ point $p$, $p \notin A$ such that $p \prec dr$.*

*Proof.* By definition, $A \prec B \Rightarrow l^A \leq u^B \Rightarrow dr$ exists. If $\exists p$, $p \notin A$, $p \prec dr$ then all of the points in $dr$ are dominated according to Lemma 2. Therefore, the points from $B$ that are the reason for $A \prec B$ are no longer present, which negates the dependency of $A$, $B$ and allows them to be computed in parallel. □

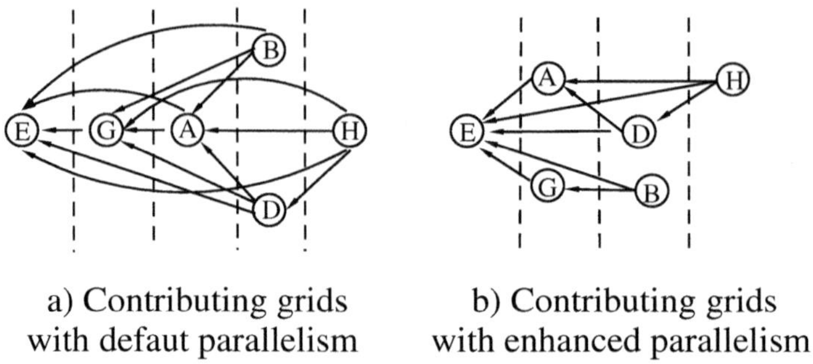


**Fig. 4.** Example of enhanced parallelism

Several observations derive from Lemma 3. First, for the two MBRs $A$ and $B$, it cannot be that $l^A \leq l^B$ because then $dr \equiv B$, in which case $B$ is dominated and will not contribute according to Lemma 2. Second, $p \notin A$ in any case, as that is the reason for the dependency in the first place. Third, assume $p \in C \Rightarrow l^C \leq p$. Since $p$ dominates $dr \Rightarrow p \leq l^{dr} \leq u^B \Rightarrow l^C \leq u^B \Rightarrow C \prec B$. No particular relation exists between $A$ and $C$. This gives us an indication of where to look for such points. Fourth, data will not be exchanged, as the initial dependency has been removed, which reduces traffic. Finally, because $p$ negates the dependency, parallelism is increased and response time is minimized as $B$ no longer has to wait data from $A$. Moreover, points from $A$ and $B$ will not be checked against each other during the global merging phase, thus reducing coordinator workload.

Fig. 4(a) shows the dependency graph of the example in Fig. 3(a), after removing non contributing partitions. The new graph is much simpler, mostly because the removed partitions had a lot of dependencies. Dashed lines indicate when a partition is computed. $B$ and $D$ are by construction independent of each other, hence their parallelism. Figure 4(b) shows the dependency graph after applying our technique. The graph is obviously simpler, even compared to the one in Fig. 4(a). The lower left point of $E$ negates the dependencies of $A$, $D$ and $H$ on $G$ and also removes the dependency of $B$ on $A$. This results in parallelism between $G$ and $A$, which is also more intuitive by looking at the partitioned space. Finally, there is one less dashed line because computations will end earlier than before.

### 4.4 Marginal Points

When processors exchange points, sending the entire skyline may become too cumbersome, not because of the skyline size alone, but because each processor may send it to many others. To alleviate this problem, we use representative points. However, instead of selecting the $k$ points with the highest domination probability [8], also known as entropy points [14], we select targeted points with respect to the partitions they will be sent to. We term these points *marginal*.

**Definition 4.** *The marginal points of a partition are the ones closer to the* $d-1$ *coordinates of the partition's lower left corner based on the L1 distance.*

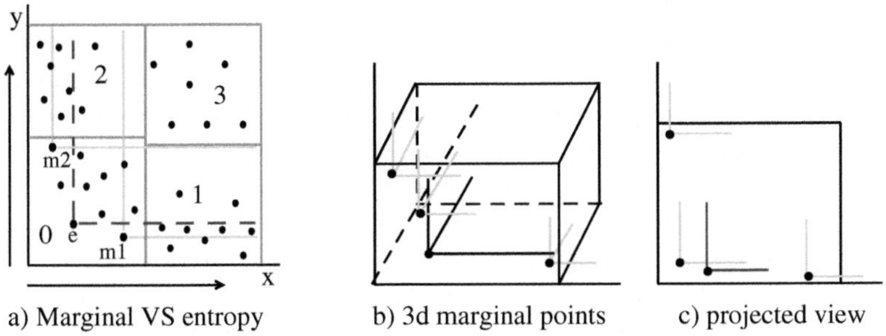


**Fig. 5.** Marginal versus entropy points

For example, in Fig. 5(a) query execution starts at partition 0 and propagated to 1 and 2 (3 is pruned). Although $e$ has the highest probability, it dominates very few points from 1 and 2, whereas $m_1$ and $m_2$ dominate many more (each one separately). Since the receiving partition has at least one greater coordinate, all of its points have greater values in that coordinate. The only way for them to be in the skyline is to have a smaller value on another coordinate. For example, since partition 1 has greater $x$ values, points will be in the skyline only if their $y$ coordinate is better than the current best. Therefore, $m_1$ and $m_2$ are the points closest to $x$ and $y$ axis respectively.

We denote by $m_i$ the marginal point for which the $i$-th coordinate is ignored. There are $d$ such points in a $d$-dimensional space. Explaining the technique for the 3D case gives some additional insight. Assume the marginal points $m_1$, $m_2$, $m_3$ of Fig. 5(b), with gray lines, and the entropy point $e$, with black lines defining their dominating area. Disregarding the $z$ coordinate to find $m_3$ (bottom left in the back), is like projecting on the $xy$ plane, as in Fig. 5(c). On the projected space $m_3$ has a higher domination area than $e$, hence the technique works as if we are selecting the $d$ points with the highest dominating region on the $d-1$ projected subspace. From another perspective, the corner that $m_3$ is closer to can be viewed as the beginning of the axis for partitions of greater $z$. In that sense, we choose points closer to the origin of the partitions that will use them and not of the one that sends them.

### 4.5 Data Propagation

Our algorithm is also able to operate in cascading mode, where processors propagate intermediate results, after computing the local skyline. If a partition sends data to all others that depend on it, the network may be flooded and, most importantly, ignores the fact that representatives are refined thus rendering previous ones unnecessary. Taking into account the fact that skylines propagate mainly along the axis, because inner partitions will be cut-off, we devise a data dissemination algorithm to minimize traffic. The coordinator determines how data will propagate using the dependency graph and skyline properties and informs processors appropriately. If an edge $B \rightarrow A$ exists, the coordinator informs

$A$ it must send data to $B$ and also informs $B$ it must wait data from $A$. Each processor begins computations only after receiving data from all its predecessors.

Multiple dependencies exist between partitions and reducing them minimizes traffic. However, reducing them in a greedy way could have the opposite effect, because less punning will occur and many non skyline points will be returned. Therefore, a natural question is what dependencies can be ignored. A partition should be processed after all of its priors have, thus only edges between nodes that also have an indirect path may be removed, e.g., if $A \prec B$, $A \prec C$ and $C \prec B$, then $A \prec B$ can be neglected. This is as if performing a topological sort among the partitions, visiting nodes once all of its dependencies have been visited. Note that this action does not negate dependencies as when increasing parallelism; it only does not take them into account when finding how points must be exchanged. However, not all such relations can be ignored. Finally, the coordinator only knows partition MBRs and not the actual coordinates of propagated points, so the heuristics should depend on that information alone.

We ignore dependencies $A \prec B$ with an intermediate node $C$, if $A$, $B$ and $C$ share at least one propagation axis i.e. $u_i^A < l_i^C < u_i^C < l_i^B$ as with $E$, $A$ and $D$ in Fig. 3(a). The reason is that by projecting on the remaining $d-1$ dimensions $C$ would send to $B$ the $m_i$ point from $A$ or a refined point from itself.

Another heuristic is to check if $l^A < l^C$, regardless of $B$'s coordinates. This is based on the same assumption as above, but the partitions need not share a propagation axis. This applies in the case of 3 or more dimensions. If neither heuristic applies, the dependency remains and $A$ must send to $B$.

An important issue about marginal points is their optimal behavior in the case of 2D data. We prove that each queried processor: (i) performs the minimum number of I/O operations and (ii) returns only global skyline points. We also prove that by combining the two points, no fewer information can be exchanged without invalidating the above behavior. To prove these, a basic lemma is needed.

**Lemma 4.** *Let $M$ be a 2D MBR. Its marginal points $m_1$ and $m_2$, $m_1 \neq m_2$, dominate the same regions outside $M$ as its entire skyline.*

*Proof.* Let $p \in SKY(M)$, $p \neq m_1$. Then, the dominating area of $p$ outside $M$ for greater $x$, begins at $(u_x^M, p_y)$. Then $m_1 \prec (u_x^M, p_y)$, otherwise $m_1$ would not be marginal. We will prove by contradiction. Since $m_1 \in M \Rightarrow x_{m_1} \leq u_x^M$, so if $m_1 \not\prec (u_x^M, p_y) \Rightarrow y_{m_1} > p_y$. That sets $p$ closer to the $x$ axis, therefore $p$ is the marginal point and not $m_1$, hence the contradiction. The proof is analogous for greater $y$'s and $m_2$. By composition, $p$ dominates a subset of the area dominated by $m_1, m_2$ and therefore, $m_1, m_2$ jointly dominate the same regions as the entire skyline of $M$. □

**Theorem 1.** *(a) Let $D$ be a 2-dimensional data set, partitioned in disjoint MBRs. If processors communicate only the marginal points of a partition, each activated processor: (1) will perform the minimum number of I/Os, (2) will report to the coordinator only global skyline points. (b) Let each partition send a single point to subsequent ones, with coordinates the minimum of its marginal and any other points received. No fewer points can be sent so that (a) still holds.*

*Proof.* (a) Having the entire skyline available, BBS discards all non-contributing areas, which is the reason for its I/O optimality. For the same reason, only global skyline points are retrieved. Since marginal points dominate the same external area as the entire partition skyline (Lemma 4), the number of I/Os of subsequent partitions will be identical in the two cases, hence minimal (1) and only global skyline points will be retrieved and reported to the coordinator (2). (b) Being in the 2D case, points from partitions of at least one greater dimension have only one coordinate to best to be in the skyline, i.e. points of greater $x$ ($y$) will be in the skyline iff their $y$ ($x$) is less than the minimum of received points. Thus, the $x$ ($y$) value of received points is irrelevant and can be safely substituted by any $x \leq u_x^A$ ($y \leq u_y^A$). So we can send ($x_{m_2}$, $y_{m_1}$) and simultaneously define the maximum allowed coordinate for both cases. Combined with the property $SKY_{A \cup B} = SKY(SKY_A \cup SKY_B)$, we derive that the point to send is in fact (min($x$), min($y$)) of local marginal and received points. This incorporates the skyline of previous partitions, which is the global so far (according to $a$). This property and Lemma 4 prove the validity of the technique. Therefore, each partition sends a single point to each subsequent. Due to our first heuristic, each partition receives data from at most two partitions, one for each propagation axis. Since each partition sends a single representative, (b) holds as fewer points means that no points will be sent. As a result no pruning is performed, with unnecessary I/Os and non global skyline points returned. □

Similarly, we can prove that for the 2D case, all non-contributing partitions are pruned, by constructing the marginal points from the partition MBR (which we do), even though we do not explicitly know them. This means that the global minimum of I/Os and traffic is achieved in that setting. Processors, of course, return only global skyline points. We omit the proof due to space restrictions.

### 4.6 Additional Optimizations

Additional optimizations are studied so that the overall efficiency is improved, both at the coordinator and processor side. A first one is *point exclusion.* Assume a point $p$ and a partition $A = [l^A, u^A]$. If $p \not\leq u^A \Rightarrow \exists i$ such that. $p_i > u_i^A$. Such a point will not prune any areas of $A$, hence a processor that receives it can safely discard it. Likewise, if $p \not\geq l^A \Rightarrow \exists j$ such that $p_j < l_j^A$, which means that the coordinator can save time by not checking $p$ against the points from $A$.

Another optimization is *eager checking*, proposed for continuous skyline [12]. Points are checked for domination upon arrival, thus storing only skyline points. The alternative of storing everything until all partitions have reported accumulates data and more time is spent afterwards to discard already stored points.

### 4.7 The ADISC Algorithm

The previous ideas are integrated into the ADISC algorithm. The outline of ADISC is given in Fig. 6. In the sequel, we describe briefly its most important aspects. At first, the coordinator $C$ partitions the data offline and assigns them to processors $P_i$, each of which indexes its local copy with an R-tree and reports back arbitrary representatives. For each grid cell, $C$ stores the MBR and points received. Given a query, $C$ determines all affected partitions (Line 1), by executing a BBS-like pass over the MBRs, since no assumptions are made regarding how such information is organized. Partitions dominated by representatives of $P_i$ are excluded. We also find additional points for pruning, by substituting the $i$-th coordinate of the upper right MBR corner with that of the lower left corner.

For the non-dominated partitions, we create the dependency graph, $dg$, based on the criteria imposed on the attributes (Line 2). At this phase, representative points are used to negate dependencies (Lines 3-4). If in *cascading* mode, the propagation algorithm is executed (Line 5). Each $P_i$ is then informed of the query (Lines 7-8), including its priors and subsequent $P_j$s. In *parallel* mode that information is empty. Then, $C$ waits for results from queried $P_i$s.

---

**Algorithm.** ADISC ($qry$, $P$, $rp$, $mode$)
$qry$: the skyline query, $P$: partitions
$rp$: the representative points from each cell, $mode$: the mode in which to operate

---

1. $F \leftarrow \bigcup p \in P$, s.t. $\forall r \in rp \bigcup$ (other points from F), $r \not\prec p$;
2. $dg \leftarrow$ create dependency graph($F$, $qry.criteria$);
3. $\forall f, g \in F,\ f \prec g$
4.     try negating it with $r \in rp \bigcup$ (other points from F)
5. **if** ( $mode$ = "cascading") **then**
6.     find propagation order( $dg$, $qry.criteria$);
7. $\forall f \in F$
8.     inform( processor($f$), $qry$, $wait(f)$, $send(f)$ )
9. $RPTD \leftarrow \{\}$ ; // no partitions have reported
10. **while** ( not all $f \in F$ reported)
11.     wait(); //until a partition reports
12.     $nprt \leftarrow$ get next reporting partition();
13.     $\forall prt \in RPTD$
14.         checkGrids($dg$, $nprt$, $prt$); //check $nprt$ with previous
15.         **if** ($mode$ = "full-parallel") **then** checkGrids($dg$, $prt$, $nprt$);
16.     $RPTD \leftarrow RPTD \bigcup nprt$;
17.     **if** ($\exists prtn \in RPTD$ s.t. $dg$.depends($prtn$) = 0) **then**
18.         report points from $prtn$;
19. 
20. **function** checkGrids($dg$,$A$,$B$)
21.     **if** $dg$.depends($A$, $B$) **then**
22.         $dg$.removeDepends($A$, $B$);
23.         $\forall a \in A$, **if** ( $a$ isAbove $B$.lowerleft) **then**
24.             $isDomd \leftarrow$ check if $\exists b \in B$, s.t. $b \prec a$;
25.             **if** ($isDomd$ = true) **then** discard $a$;

---

**Fig. 6.** Outline of ADISC algorithm

Each $P_i$ stores the information of prior partitions and subsequent $P_j$s. Whenever data is received from $P_j$, $P_i$ removes $P_j$ from its priors, until the list becomes empty and begins computations. The received data are used for pruning during BBS. The local skyline is reported back to $C$. If subsequent $P_j$s must be informed, representatives are selected and propagated as instructed.

When $C$ receives data, it checks if they are dominated by previously received points. Using $dg$, it finds reported partitions that the new one depends on (Line 14) and checks the points between them. If in *parallel* mode, the symmetric action must also be performed (line 15), since partitions report in unspecified order. Once checked, the dependency is removed, as they do not need to be checked again. A partition without dependencies (Line 17) has been checked against all partitions that could dominate any of its points, thus it contains only global skyline points. Consequently, its data are reported to the user.

## 5 Performance Evaluation Study

The experiments have been conducted on both real and synthetic data, on an Intel Core Duo @1.86GHz, Ubuntu Linux machine with 1GB RAM. R-tree page size has been set to 4KBytes and each processor has 20% of its blocks in buffers. We assume 8ms per page fault and a 100Mbps, collision-free, wired network. Timings show execution time in seconds, averaged over multiple data sets, including network time, whereas traffic graphs refer to the number of points communicated among processors. Synthetic data are generated with independent (IND) and anticorrelated (ANT) distributions. Cardinality varies from 1M to 10M and dimensionality from 2 to 7, with default values $n$=5M and $d$=4. The number of processors varies between 25 and 200, with a default value of 100. For the real data set, we used *forest cover* (FC) (http://kdd.ics.uci.edu).

We compare ANGLE (angle partitioning with $min$ criteria and SFS), ADISC-PRL (parallel ADISC), ADISC-L1 (cascading ADISC, entropy representatives) and ADISC-MRG (marginal representatives). For fairness between ADISC-L1 and ADISC-MRG, processors may exchange at most the same number of points, equal to the data set dimensionality. The darker portion of ADISC-L1/MRG traffic bars show the points exchanged between processors alone.

**The effect of cardinality.** The impact of cardinality on response time is given in Fig. 7(a), (b). ANGLE performs slightly better for IND and $min$ criteria (Fig. 7(b)), since it is especially designed for this case, whereas ADISC-PRL requires more time for some processors to compute their local skyline. High response times of ADISC-L1/MRG are due to the almost sequential execution of some partitions, a result of the data distribution. ADISC-MRG constantly performs slightly better than ADISC-L1, and exchanges fewer points (Fig. 8), due to better pruning of marginal points, which reduces I/O and processing time. However, ANGLE does not behave well in all other cases, to the point that even ADISC-L1 and ADISC-MRG outperform it in the all-$min$, ANT case (Fig. 7(a)). SFS is the reason for this, as more than 90% of the time is spent on merging local

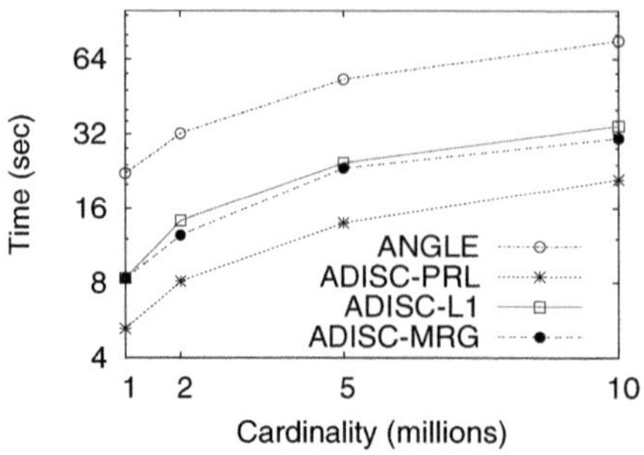


(a) ANT, min preferences

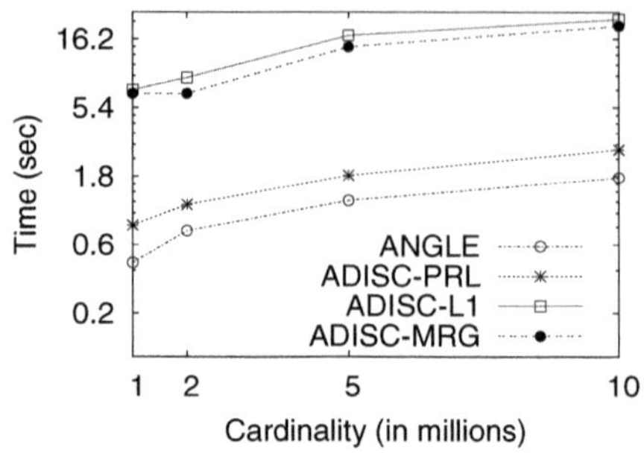


(b) IND, min preferences

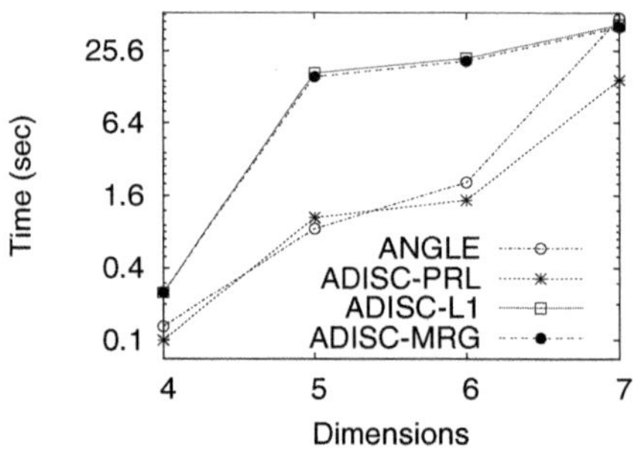


(c) FC, min preferences

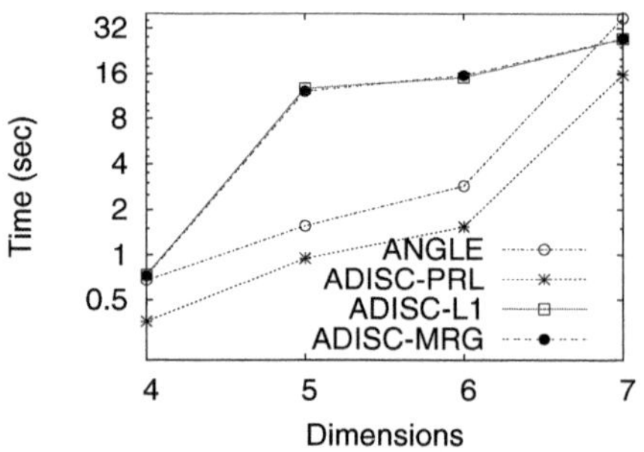


(d) FC, mixed preferences

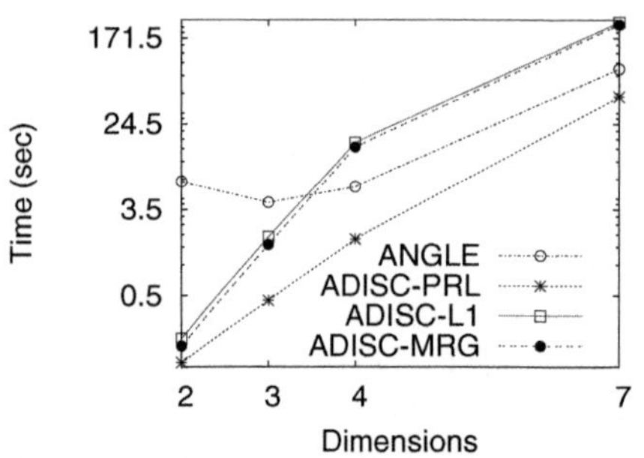


(e) IND, mixed preferences

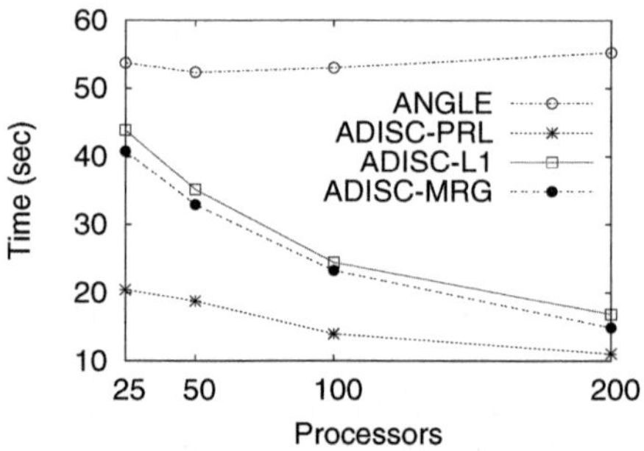


(f) ANT, min preferences

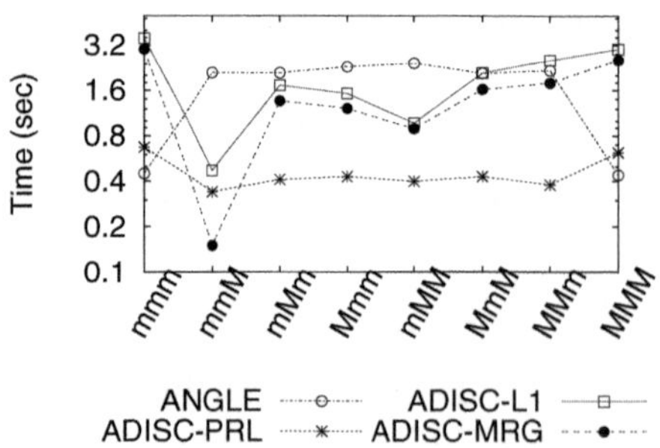


(g) ANT, diverse query criteria

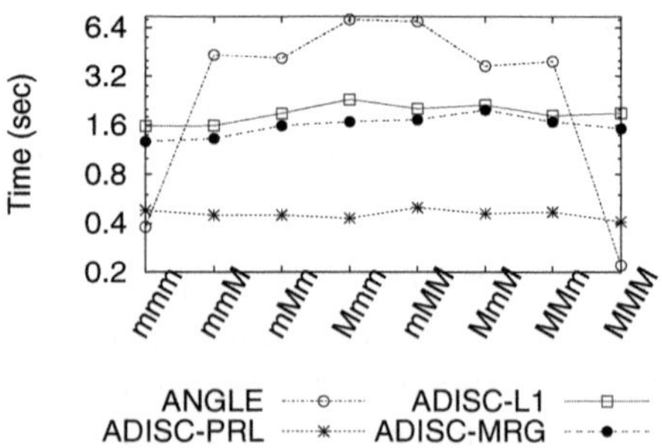


(h) IND, diverse query criteria

**Fig. 7.** Response time results

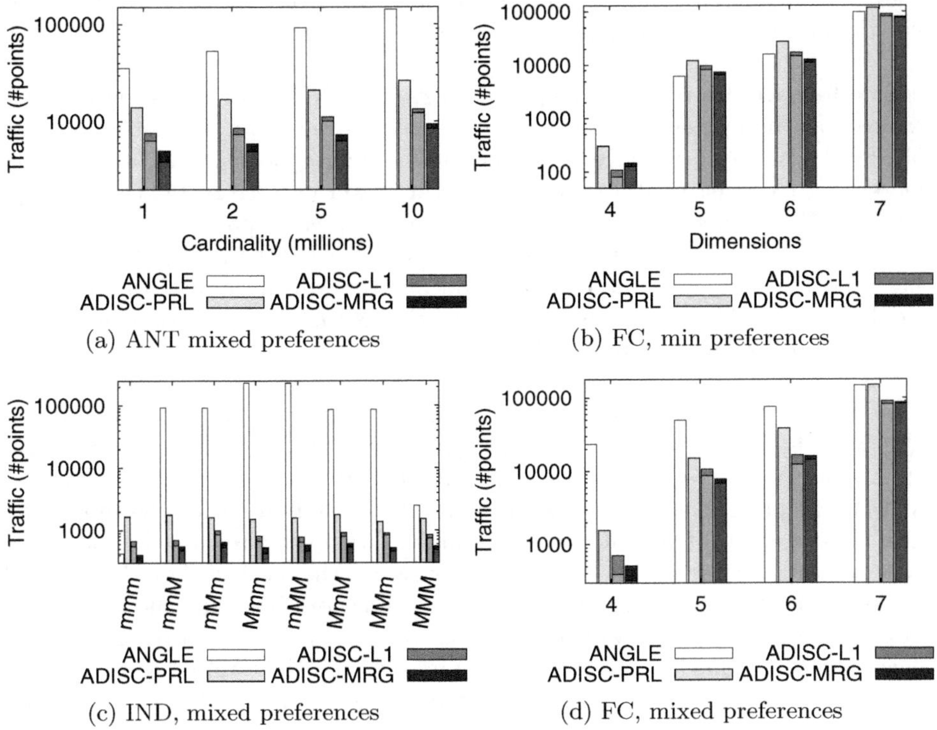


(a) ANT mixed preferences

(b) FC, min preferences

(c) IND, mixed preferences

(d) FC, mixed preferences

**Fig. 8.** Network traffic results

skylines. On the other hand, ADISC's dependency graph and optimizations save valuable time. ANGLE also performs worse than ADISC for mixed criteria.

**The effect of dimensionality.** The impact of dimensionality on response time is shown in Fig. 7(c), (d) and (e). ANGLE performs again slightly better than ADISC-PRL, for few dimensions, all-*min* (Fig. 7(g), (h)). However, for more dimensions (Fig. 7(c), (d)), or even average dimensionality and ANT (Fig. 7(a)), its performance deteriorates. This is due to the fact that skyline computation becomes CPU-bound for high dimensionality and the problems imposed by SFS. Regarding the 2D IND case with diverse criteria, ADISC-PRL is better than ANGLE up to 2 orders of magnitude (Fi.g 7(e)). Processors in ANGLE execute an anticorrelated like skyline, and visit almost all RTree nodes. This also results in exceedingly high traffic (Fig. 8(c)). For more dimensions, the difference is reduced (Fig. 7(c)), as the effect of a single diverse criterion is normalized by the large number of other default criteria. ADISC-PRL also performs better than ANGLE in FC, for almost all cases, with diverse or all-*min* criteria. The problems of SFS are easily seen for 6 dimensions and more, for the all-*min* case, for a data set of low cardinality (~600K) (Fig. 7(c)). With a single *max* criterion, the difference is even greater, for as few as 4 dimensions (Fig. 7(d)). Regarding traffic, ANGLE sends many more points in most, if not all of these occasions. For the all-$min$ case, the number of points is comparable in the two occasions.

**The effect of the number of processors.** For IND and FC, response time is reduced as the number of processors increases. However, an interesting result is observed from Fig. 7(f): ANGLE response time slightly decreases at first but then increases to a point greater than when having fewer processors. On the contrary, all ADISC variants decrease their response time. More processors mean more partitions which do not dominate points from each other. Therefore, time is saved both at the processors and the coordinator, which significantly decreases total response. This could also lead us to the assumption that skyline of ANT data may be easier to compute than IND data.

**The effect of diverse criteria.** The most interesting results are those of Fig. 7(g),(h), where all 8 combinations of criteria on a 3D data set are examined. Apart from $mmm$, ANGLE performs slightly better than ADISC-PRL for $MMM$, as partitions retain the correlated-like distribution for the most part. The sudden drop of ADISC-L1/MRG in Fig. 7(g), $mmM$ case, is due to the generators. By construction, the last dimension is the most likely to have a high value, w.r.t. the other two, to achieve anticorrelation. Inverting the criterion to $max$ is like ignoring the dimension. This results in less anticorrelation, more partitions are pruned, returning less points to $C$ and the total response is lower. However, ANGLE activates all processors, although many do not contribute, hence many points are returned (Fig. 8(a), (c)). Another interesting observation, is that ADISC-PRL shows a particularly steady behavior, almost invariant to the criteria imposed on the attributes, with minor fluctuations due to the different skyline sizes. A similar observation arise for traffic. ANGLE varies greatly, depending not only on the number, but even on the position of a criterion (Fig 8(c)). Such a high number of points floods the network and degrades coordinator performance, since these need to be locally stored, until all points are received.

## 6 Conclusions

In this work, we presented ADISC, an algorithm for efficient and adaptive distributed skyline computation. ADISC may operate in either full-parallel or cascading mode, balancing between the degree of parallelism and network traffic according to system load. The algorithm runs on top of a grid partitioning scheme and integrates several optimizations for efficient computation. It efficiently handles different criteria on the attributes, since the dependency graph is constructed dynamically. We also proved optimality of our approach for the case of 2D data. We finally demonstrated the efficiency of our scheme with experimental results on real-life and synthetic data sets. Future research may include: (i) the study of an *hybrid* mode, where some partitions execute in parallel and others sequentially, for the same query, according to estimated cost and (ii) the design of randomized algorithms trading accuracy for speed.

## References


1. Börzsönyi, S., Kossmann, D., Stocker, K.: The skyline operator. In: Proc. of the 17th ICDE, pp. 421–430 (2001)
2. Balke, W.T., Güntzer, U., Zheng, J.X.: Efficient distributed skylining for web information systems. In: Bertino, E., Christodoulakis, S., Plexousakis, D., Christophides, V., Koubarakis, M., Böhm, K., Ferrari, E. (eds.) EDBT 2004. LNCS, vol. 2992, pp. 256–273. Springer, Heidelberg (2004)
3. Wu, P., Zhang, C., Feng, Y., Zhao, B.Y., Agrawal, D., Abbadi, A.E.: Parallelizing skyline queries for scalable distribution. In: Ioannidis, Y., Scholl, M.H., Schmidt, J.W., Matthes, F., Hatzopoulos, M., Böhm, K., Kemper, A., Grust, T., Böhm, C. (eds.) EDBT 2006. LNCS, vol. 3896, pp. 112–130. Springer, Heidelberg (2006)
4. Huang, Z., Jensen, C.S., Lu, H., Ooi, B.C.: Skyline queries against mobile lightweight devices in manets. In: Proc. of the 22nd ICDE (2006)
5. Lo, E., Yip, K.Y., Lin, K.I., Cheung, D.W.: Progressive skylining over web-accessible databases. Data Knowl. Eng. 57(2), 122–147 (2006)
6. Li, H., Tan, Q., Lee, W.C.: Efficient progressive processing of skyline queries in peer-to-peer systems. In: Proc. of the 1st Int. Conf. on Scalable Inf. Sys. (2006)
7. Wang, S., Ooi, B.C., Tung, A.K.H., Xu, L.: Efficient skyline query processing on peer-to-peer networks. In: Proc. of the 23rd ICDE, pp. 1126–1135 (2007)
8. Cui, B., Lu, H., Xu, Q., Chen, L., Dai, Y., Zhou, Y.: Parallel distributed processing of constrained skyline queries by filtering. In: Proc. of the 24th ICDE (2008)
9. Vlachou, A., Doulkeridis, C., Kotidis, Y.: Skypeer: Efficient subspace skyline computation over distributed data. In: Proc. of the 23rd ICDE, pp. 416–425 (2007)
10. Vlachou, A., Doulkeridis, C., Kotidis, Y.: Angle-based space partitioning for efficient parallel skyline computation. In: Proc. of the 2008 Int. Conf. ACM SIGMOD, pp. 227–238 (2008)
11. Wang, S., Vu, Q.H., Ooi, B.C., Tung, A.K., Xu, L.: Skyframe: a framework for skyline query processing in peer-to-peer systems. The VLDB Journal 18(1), 345–362 (2009)
12. Tao, Y., Papadias, D.: Maintaining sliding window skylines on data streams. IEEE Trans. on Knowl. and Data Eng. 18(3), 377–391 (2006)
13. Kung, H.T., Luccio, F., Preparata, F.P.: On finding the maxima of a set of vectors. Journal of the ACM 22, 469–476 (1975)
14. Chomicki, J., Godfrey, P., Gryz, J., Liang, D.: Skyline with presorting (2002)
15. Kossmann, D., Ramsak, F., Rost, S.: Shooting stars in the sky: an online algorithm for skyline queries. In: Proc. of the 28th Int. Conf. on VLDB, pp. 275–286 (2002)
16. Papadias, D., Tao, Y., Fu, G., Seeger, B.: An optimal and progressive algorithm for skyline queries. In: Proc. of the 2003 Int. Conf. ACM SIGMOD, pp. 467–478 (2003)
17. Cosgaya-Lozano, A., Rau-Chaplin, A., Zeh, N.: Parallel computation of skyline queries. In: Proc. of the 21st Int. Symp. on HPCS and Applications, p. 12 (2007)
18. Gao, Y., Chen, G., Chen, L., Chen, C.: Parallelizing progressive computation for skyline queries in multi-disk environment. In: Bressan, S., Küng, J., Wagner, R. (eds.) DEXA 2006. LNCS, vol. 4080, pp. 697–706. Springer, Heidelberg (2006)
19. Dellis, E., Seeger, B.: Efficient computation of reverse skyline queries. In: Proc. of the 33rd Int. Conf. on VLDB, pp. 291–302 (2007)

# On the Efficient Construction of Multislices from Recurrences

Romans Kasperovics[1], Michael H. Böhlen[2], and Johann Gamper[1]

[1] Free University of Bozen-Bolzano, Dominikanerplatz 3, 39100 Bolzano, Italy
[2] University of Zürich, Binzmühlestrasse 14, 8050 Zürich, Switzerland

**Abstract.** Recurrences are defined as sets of time instants associated with events and they are present in many application domains, including public transport schedules and personal calendars. Because of their large size, recurrences are rarely stored explicitly, but some form of compact representation is used. Multislices are a compact representation that is well suited for storage in relational databases. A multislice is a set of time slices where each slice employs a hierarchy of time granularities to compactly represent multiple recurrences.

In this paper we investigate the construction of multislices from recurrences. We define the compression ratio of a multislice, show that different construction strategies produce multislices with different compression ratios, and prove that the construction of minimal multislices, i.e., multislices with a maximal compression ratio, is an NP-hard problem. We propose a scalable algorithm, termed `LMerge`, for the construction of multislices from recurrences. Experiments with real-world recurrences from public transport schedules confirm the scalability and usefulness of `LMerge`: the generated multislices are very close to minimal multislices, achieving an average compression ratio of approx. 99%. A comparison with a baseline algorithm that iteratively merges pairs of mergeable slices shows significant improvements of `LMerge` over the baseline approach.

## 1 Introduction

A recurrent event is the association of the same information with multiple time instants, e.g., the departure times of bus 10A from stop P. Domenicani in direction north-west. We call such a set of time instants the *recurrence* of an event. Recurrences might easily become very large. For example, in the city of Bozen-Bolzano with 15 bus routes, the buses are making around 1,000 trips a day, visiting up to 20 stops per trip. In a half year period the corresponding schedule contains approximately 7.5 million departure times. Due to this large size, recurrences are rarely stored explicitly in databases, rather some form of compact representation is used.

*Multislices* [1], defined as sets of *time slices*, are a compact representation formalism with a number of good properties: high compression for common real-world recurrences, scalable relational representation, and easy interpretation and processing. A time slice employs a *hierarchy* of time granularities

M. Gertz and B. Ludäscher (Eds.): SSDBM 2010, LNCS 6187, pp. 42–59, 2010.

to compress a recurrence that follows a regular pattern. For example, slice $\lambda_1 = (yea\{7\}, wee\{0\text{-}25\}, day\{0\text{-}4\}, hou\{7\}, min\{0{,}25{,}55\})$ represents minutes 0, 25, and 55 past 7 from Monday to Friday in the first 26 weeks in 2007. A multislice groups a set of time slices allowing to represent recurrences with more complex patterns.

In order to benefit from the multislice representation we first must construct multislices. In this paper we address the construction of multislices with a given hierarchy from recurrences that are represented explicitly as sets of time instants.

*Example 1.* Figure 1(a) shows a fragment of an explicit representation of a schedule as it is stored in an existing application. The fragment shows the recurrence $P_{10\mathrm{A}}$ of departures of bus no. 10A in direction north-west from "P. Domenicani" which is the first stop on route 10A in that direction. The recurrence contains 3250 departure times in the first 26 weeks in 2007. The attributes of relation BUSEXP are the identifier of a route, a direction, the identifier of a stop, and a departure time. Figure 1(c) shows a compact representation of $P_{10\mathrm{A}}$ as multislice

BUSEXP

| rtid | dir | seq | stid | depti |
|---|---|---|---|---|
| 10A | nw | 1 | P. Domenicani | 2007-01-01 07:00 |
| 10A | nw | 1 | P. Domenicani | 2007-01-01 07:25 |
| 10A | nw | 1 | P. Domenicani | 2007-01-01 07:55 |
| 10A | nw | 1 | P. Domenicani | 2007-01-01 08:25 |
| 10A | nw | 1 | P. Domenicani | 2007-01-01 08:55 |
| 10A | nw | 1 | P. Domenicani | 2007-01-01 09:25 |
| 10A | nw | 1 | P. Domenicani | 2007-01-01 09:55 |
| ⋮ | ⋮ | ⋮ | ⋮ | ⋮ |
| 10A | nw | 1 | P. Domenicani | 2007-07-01 18:55 |

(a)

MSL

| mid | sid |
|---|---|
| 10A | $\lambda_1$ |
| 10A | $\lambda_2$ |

SLI

| sid | lev | gid | xid |
|---|---|---|---|
| $\lambda_1$ | 1 | *yea* | 649 |
| $\lambda_1$ | 2 | *wee* | 650 |
| $\lambda_1$ | 3 | *day* | 651 |
| $\lambda_1$ | 4 | *hou* | 652 |
| $\lambda_1$ | 5 | *min* | 653 |
| $\lambda_2$ | 1 | *yea* | 649 |
| $\lambda_2$ | 2 | *wee* | 650 |
| $\lambda_2$ | 3 | *day* | 651 |
| $\lambda_2$ | 4 | *hou* | 654 |
| $\lambda_2$ | 5 | *min* | 655 |

SEL

| xid | st | en |
|---|---|---|
| 649 | 7 | 7 |
| 650 | 0 | 25 |
| 651 | 0 | 4 |
| 652 | 7 | 7 |
| 653 | 0 | 0 |
| 653 | 25 | 25 |
| 653 | 55 | 55 |
| 654 | 8 | 18 |
| 665 | 25 | 25 |
| 665 | 55 | 55 |

(b)

$$M_{10\mathrm{A}} = \{\lambda_1 = (yea\{7\}, wee\{0\text{-}25\}, day\{0\text{-}4\}, hou\{7\}, \quad min\{0{,}25{,}55\}),$$
$$\lambda_2 = (yea\{7\}, wee\{0\text{-}25\}, day\{0\text{-}4\}, hou\{8\text{-}18\}, min\{25{,}55\})\}$$

(c)

**Fig. 1.** Different representations of recurrence $P_{10\mathrm{A}}$: (a) explicit relational representation, (b) as multislice $M_{10\mathrm{A}}$ in a relational representation, (c) as multislice in a symbolic notation

$M_{10\mathrm{A}}$ that consists of two time slices. Figure 1(b) shows the relational representation of $M_{10\mathrm{A}}$. Relation MSL groups time slices into multislices. Relation SLI stores time slices as sets of tuples ordered by hierarchy levels, where each tuple refers to a time granularity and a set of integers. Relation SEL stores the sets of integers as sets of non-adjacent, non-overlapping intervals.

In this paper we show that a recurrence can be represented with various multislices of different size. Smaller multislices provide higher compression ratios. We establish a two-step process for constructing multislices with a given hierarchy of time granularities from a given recurrence. In the first step we construct a singular multislice where each slice has the required hierarchy and corresponds to a single time instant in the recurrence. In the second step we minimize the singular multislice by merging slices until no further merging is possible. The order in which the merging is done impacts the size of the resulting multislice. We prove that the construction of a minimal multislice representation is an NP-hard problem. We propose an algorithm, called `LMerge`, that merges time slices in an order imposed by the levels of the hierarchy (`LMerge` stands for level-wise merge). `LMerge` runs in $O(d^2 n \log n)$ time, where $d$ is the depth of the hierarchy and $n$ is the size of the recurrence. We analyze the performance of `LMerge` by constructing the worst cases, running experiments on the real-world data, and comparing it with a straightforward baseline algorithm.

The main contributions of this paper can be summarized as follows:

- We propose a two-step bottom-up process for the construction of multislices, where first a singular multislice is constructed followed by an iterative merging of slices.
- We show that different merging strategies produce multislices with different compression ratio, and we prove that the construction of minimal multislices (with maximal compression ratio) is NP-hard.
- We provide `LMerge`, a scalable approximation algorithm for the construction of multislices.
- We show empirically that `LMerge` is scalable and produces multislices that are close to minimal multislices with an average compression ratio of 99%.

The rest of the paper is organized as follows. Section 2 introduces preliminary concepts. In Section 3 we prove that the construction of minimal multislices is NP-hard and we propose `LMerge` algorithm with an analytical evaluation in Section 4. Section 5 reports about an empirical evaluation using real-world recurrences from bus schedules. The paper concludes with related work, conclusions, and future work.

## 2 Preliminaries

### 2.1 Time Domain and Granularities

We assume a *time domain*, $\mathcal{A}$, as a set of time instants equipped with a total order $\leq$ and isomorphic to the integers. A time granularity is a partitioning of a subset of $\mathcal{A}$ into non-empty intervals of time instants, termed *granules*. Examples of time granularities are minutes (*min*), hours (*hou*), days (*day*), weeks (*wee*), months (*mth*), and years (*yea*). We assume a *bottom granularity*, $G_\perp$, such that each granule of $G_\perp$ contains exactly one time instant. In our running example minutes represent the bottom granularity, and we use the ISO 8601:2004 notation to denote time instants, e.g., 2007-02-12 07:15. Granularity *day*, for instance, divides the time domain into granules of 1440 minutes. The granules of each

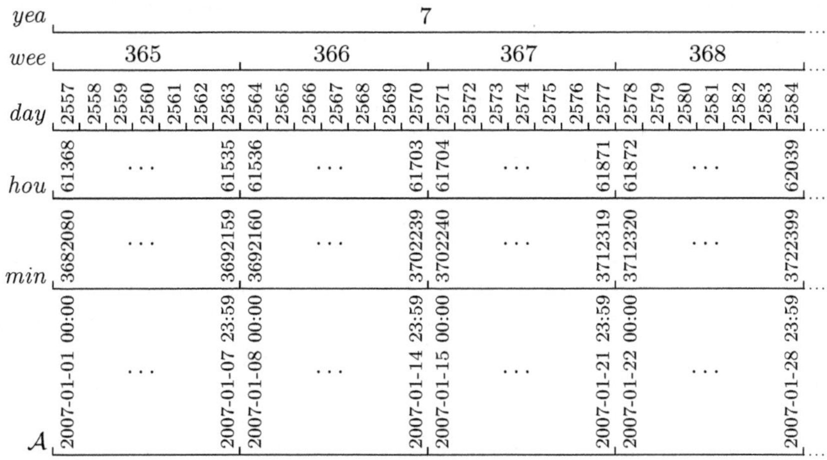

**Fig. 2.** Time domain and time granularities *min*, *hou*, *day*, *wee*, and *yea*

granularity $G$ are ordered according to the time domain order and indexed with a subset of integers, $\mathcal{L}_G$, such that the indexing function $\mathcal{M}_G : \mathcal{L}_G \rightarrow G$ is an isomorphism that preserves the total order $\leq$. For each granularity we assume that the granule with index 0 contains time instant 2000-01-01 00:00. Figure 2 illustrates some correspondences of indexes between different granularities, e.g., $\mathcal{M}_{day}(2568) = $ [2007-01-12 00:00, 2007-01-12 23:59].

We adopt the *bigger-part-inside* [2,3] conversion between time granularities. The bigger-part-inside conversion of a granule $i \in \mathcal{L}_H$ of a granularity $H$ to a granularity $G$, denoted $\lfloor_G^H(i)$, returns (the indexes of) those granules in $G$ that are covered by granule $i$ in $H$ for more than a half or, if exactly half of a granule in $G$ is covered, those with the second half covered, i.e.,

$$\begin{aligned}\lfloor_G^H(i) = \{j \mid & (|\mathcal{M}_G(j) \cap \mathcal{M}_H(i)| > |\mathcal{M}_G(j) \setminus \mathcal{M}_H(i)|) \vee \\ & (|\mathcal{M}_G(j) \cap \mathcal{M}_H(i)| = |\mathcal{M}_G(j) \setminus \mathcal{M}_H(i)| \wedge \max(\mathcal{M}_G(j)) \in \mathcal{M}_H(i))\}\end{aligned}$$

## 2.2 Time Slices and Multislices

A (time) *slice* [4] is a finite list of pairs, $\lambda = (G_1X_1, \ldots, G_dX_d)$, where $G_l$ are granularities and $X_l$ are *selectors* that are defined as sets of integers. Each selector $X_{l+1}$ specifies a set of granules in $G_{l+1}$ with a relative positioning with respect to $G_l$. The sequence of granularities $(G_1, \ldots, G_d)$ is the *hierarchy* of a slice, and we assume that it always ends with the bottom granularity, i.e., $G_d = G_\perp$. Consider the slice $\lambda_1 = (yea\{7\}, wee\{0\text{-}25\}, day\{0\text{-}4\}, hou\{7\}, min\{0,25,55\})$. The hierarchy is (*yea*, *wee*, *day*, *hou*, *min*). Selector {7} selects the year 2007, selector {0-25} selects the first 26 weeks in 2007, selector {0-4} selects the days from Monday to Friday from each of these weeks, etc.

The semantics of a slice $\lambda = (G_1X_1, \ldots, G_dX_d)$ is defined through the following mapping $\mathcal{I}$ to a subset of the time domain:

$$\mathcal{I}(\lambda) = \begin{cases} \bigcup_{k\in X_1} \mathcal{M}_{G_1}(k) & d = 1 \\ \mathcal{I}\left((G_2 \bigcup_{k\in X_1} (\downharpoonleft^{G_1}_{G_2}(k)/X_2), \ldots, G_dX_d)\right) & d > 1 \end{cases}$$

A slice of depth $d = 1$ consists of a single granularity-selector pair and represents all time instants covered by those granules in $G_1$ selected by $X_1$. Otherwise, if $d > 1$, the slice is reduced to a slice of depth $d-1$ with hierarchy $(G_2, \ldots, G_d)$; $\downharpoonleft^{G_1}_{G_2}(k)/X_2$ is defined as $\downharpoonleft^{G_1}_{G_2}(k) \cap \{\min(\downharpoonleft^{G_1}_{G_2}(k)) + i \mid i \in X_2\}$. Consider again the slice $\lambda_1 = (\mathit{yea}\{7\}, \mathit{wee}\{0\text{-}25\}, \mathit{day}\{0\text{-}4\}, \mathit{hou}\{7\}, \mathit{min}\{0{,}25{,}55\})$. First, years are mapped to weeks yielding $\mathcal{I}((\mathit{wee}\{365\text{-}390\}, \mathit{day}\{0\text{-}4\}, \mathit{hou}\{5\text{-}6\}, \mathit{min}\{15{,}35\}))$, then weeks are mapped to days, and so on, returning a total of 390 time instants.

A slice can be split into two slices by splitting one selector into two disjoint subsets [1]. The two slices represent disjoint sets of time instants, and their union is equal to the set represented by the original slice. For example, by splitting the selector of weeks the slice $(\mathit{yea}\{7\}, \mathit{wee}\{0\text{-}25\}, \mathit{day}\{0\text{-}4\}, \mathit{hou}\{7\}, \mathit{min}\{0{,}25{,}55\})$ can be split into $(\mathit{yea}\{7\}, \mathit{wee}\{0{,}2\text{-}25\}, \mathit{day}\{0\text{-}4\}, \mathit{hou}\{7\}, \mathit{min}\{0{,}25{,}55\})$ and $(\mathit{yea}\{7\}, \mathit{wee}\{1\}, \mathit{day}\{0\text{-}4\}, \mathit{hou}\{7\}, \mathit{min}\{0{,}25{,}55\})$.

A slice $\lambda' = (G_1X'_1, \ldots, G_dX'_d)$ is a *subslice* of a slice $\lambda = (G_1X_1, \ldots, G_dX_d)$, denoted $\lambda' \sqsubseteq \lambda$, if they both have the same hierarchy and $X'_l \subseteq X_l$ for all levels $l = 1, \ldots, d$. For example, the slice $(\mathit{yea}\{7\}, \mathit{wee}\{1\}, \mathit{day}\{0\text{-}4\}, \mathit{hou}\{7\}, \mathit{min}\{25{,}55\})$ is a subslice of $(\mathit{yea}\{7\}, \mathit{wee}\{0\text{-}25\}, \mathit{day}\{0\text{-}4\}, \mathit{hou}\{7\}, \mathit{min}\{0{,}25{,}55\})$. The subslice $\lambda'$ represents a subset of the recurrence represented $\lambda$, i.e., $\lambda' \sqsubseteq \lambda \implies \mathcal{I}(\lambda') \subseteq \mathcal{I}(\lambda)$.

A *multislice* $M$ is defined as a set of slices and represents all the time instants represented by the included slices, i.e., $\mathcal{I}(M) = \bigcup_{\lambda\in M} \mathcal{I}(\lambda)$. To simplify the operations on multislices, we require that all slices within a multislice have the same hierarchy. The *compression* of a multislice $M$ is defined as $1 - \frac{|M|}{|\mathcal{I}(M)|}$. Referring to Example 1, recurrence $P_{10\text{A}}$ with 3250 time instants is represented by multislice $M_{10\text{A}}$ with two slices, which gives a compression ratio of $1 - \frac{2}{3250} = 99.94\%$.

## 3 Constructing Multislices from Recurrences

In this section we study the construction of multislices from recurrences. We adopt a bottom-up approach which first constructs a slice for each individual time instant in the recurrence and then iteratively merges these slices.

### 3.1 Basic Concepts

**Definition 1 (Singluar Slice).** *A slice* $\dot{\lambda} = (G_1X_1, \ldots, G_dX_d)$ *is* singular *if for all hierarchy levels* $l = 1, \ldots, d : |X_l| = 1$.

Singular slices have two important properties: (1) they represent exactly one time instant[1] and (2) two different singular slices cannot represent the same time instant. To facilitate reading, we put a dot over the slice symbol for singular slices, e.g., $\dot{\lambda}$.

If a slice represents a time instant it must have as a subslice a singular slice representing the same time instant.

**Lemma 1.** *For slices* $\lambda = (G_1X_1, \ldots, G_dX_d)$ *and* $\dot{\lambda} = (G_1\{x_1\}, \ldots, G_d\{x_d\})$, *if* $t \in \mathcal{I}(\lambda)$ *and* $t = \mathcal{I}(\dot{\lambda})$ *then* $\dot{\lambda} \sqsubseteq \lambda$.

We call a multislice that contains only singular slices a *singular multislice*. For a given hierarchy $(G_1, \ldots, G_d)$, each recurrence $P$ can be represented by a unique singular multislice (provided that empty slices are excluded).

*Example 2.* Consider the input recurrence $P$ = {2007-01-12 05:10, 2007-01-12 05:30, 2007-01-12 06:10, 2007-01-12 06:20, 2007-01-12 06:30, 2007-01-12 06:40, 2007-01-12 06:50, 2007-01-12 07:20, 2007-01-12 07:40, 2007-01-12 07:50, 2007-01-12 08:10, 2007-01-12 08:30} and the hierarchy (*yea*, *wee*, *day*, *hou*, *min*). The corresponding singular multislice is the following multislice $M$ where each of the 12 time instants is represented with a distinct singular slice:

$$\begin{aligned}
M = \{\dot{\lambda}_1 &= (yea\{7\}, wee\{1\}, day\{4\}, hou\{5\}, min\{10\}),\\
\dot{\lambda}_2 &= (yea\{7\}, wee\{1\}, day\{4\}, hou\{5\}, min\{30\}),\\
\dot{\lambda}_3 &= (yea\{7\}, wee\{1\}, day\{4\}, hou\{6\}, min\{10\}),\\
\dot{\lambda}_4 &= (yea\{7\}, wee\{1\}, day\{4\}, hou\{6\}, min\{20\}),\\
\dot{\lambda}_5 &= (yea\{7\}, wee\{1\}, day\{4\}, hou\{6\}, min\{30\}),\\
\dot{\lambda}_6 &= (yea\{7\}, wee\{1\}, day\{4\}, hou\{6\}, min\{40\}),\\
\dot{\lambda}_7 &= (yea\{7\}, wee\{1\}, day\{4\}, hou\{6\}, min\{50\}),\\
\dot{\lambda}_8 &= (yea\{7\}, wee\{1\}, day\{4\}, hou\{7\}, min\{20\}),\\
\dot{\lambda}_9 &= (yea\{7\}, wee\{1\}, day\{4\}, hou\{7\}, min\{40\}),\\
\dot{\lambda}_{10} &= (yea\{7\}, wee\{1\}, day\{4\}, hou\{7\}, min\{50\}),\\
\dot{\lambda}_{11} &= (yea\{7\}, wee\{1\}, day\{4\}, hou\{8\}, min\{10\}),\\
\dot{\lambda}_{12} &= (yea\{7\}, wee\{1\}, day\{4\}, hou\{8\}, min\{30\})\}
\end{aligned}$$

Two slices $\lambda_X = (G_1X_1, \ldots, G_dX_d)$ and $\lambda_Y = (G_1Y_1, \ldots, G_dY_d)$ that have the same hierarchy can be merged into one slice of the same hierarchy iff at all hierarchy levels except one the corresponding selectors are equal, i.e., $X_m \neq Y_m$ for some level $m$ and $X_l = Y_l$ for all levels $l \neq m$. We say also that $\lambda_X$ and $\lambda_Y$ are *mergeable* across level $m$, denoted as mergeable$(\lambda_X, \lambda_Y, m)$.

**Definition 2 (Merge Operation).** *Let* $\lambda_X = (G_1X_1, \ldots, G_dX_d)$ *and* $\lambda_Y = (G_1Y_1, \ldots, G_dY_d)$ *be two slices that are mergeable across level* $m$. *The* merge *operation of* $\lambda_X$ *and* $\lambda_Y$ *returns a slice and is defined as*

$$\lambda_X + \lambda_Y = (G_1X_1, \ldots, G_{m-1}X_{m-1}, G_mX_m \cup Y_m, G_{m+1}X_{m+1}, \ldots, G_dX_d)$$

[1] We assume that the selectors are consistent and exclude the cases when a slice represents the empty set due to inconsistent selectors.

*Example 3.* Consider the multislice $M$ from the previous example. The slices $\dot{\lambda}_1$ and $\dot{\lambda}_2$ are mergeable across the level of *min*, since only at this level the corresponding selectors are different. The result of merging these two slices is $(yea\{7\}, wee\{1\}, day\{4\}, hou\{5\}, min\{10{,}30\})$. As another example, the slices $\dot{\lambda}_1$ and $\dot{\lambda}_4$ are not mergeable because the corresponding selectors for more than one granularity differ, namely *min* and *hou*.

The merge operation is *commutative*, i.e., for two mergeable slices $\lambda_X$ and $\lambda_Y$, we have $\lambda_X + \lambda_Y = \lambda_Y + \lambda_X$, and it is *associative* only for slices that are mergeable across the same level, i.e., if mergeable$(\lambda_X, \lambda_Y, m)$ and mergeable$(\lambda_Y, \lambda_Z, m)$ then $(\lambda_X + \lambda_Y) + \lambda_Z = \lambda_X + (\lambda_Y + \lambda_Z)$.

### 3.2 Baseline Algorithm BMerge

Let $P \subset \mathcal{A}$ be a non-empty finite recurrence and $(G_1, \ldots, G_d)$ be a hierarchy with $G_d = G_\perp$. Our goal is to construct a multislice $M$ with the given hierarchy such that $\mathcal{I}(M) = P$. Algorithm `BMerge` implements a baseline strategy for the bottom-up construction of a multislice and operates in two steps. First, for each time instant in the recurrence $P$ a singular slice is constructed, yielding a singular multislice $M$ that has the same size as the recurrence. The second step iterates over the slices in $M$. In each iteration a pair of mergeable slices is selected and merged into a single slice. The loop terminates when no more mergeable slices exist.

Algorithm `BMerge`

**input**: recurrence $P$, hierarchy $(G_1, \ldots, G_d)$
**output**: multislice $M$
*// Step 1: build a singular multislice*
$M := \varnothing$;
**for each** $t \in P$ **do**
  $M := M \cup \{$singular slice for $t\}$;
*// Step 2: merge slices*
**while** $M$ contains mergeable slices **do**
  Select a pair $\lambda, \lambda' \in M$ such that mergeable$(\lambda, \lambda', m)$;
  $M := M \setminus \{\lambda, \lambda'\} \cup \{\lambda + \lambda'\}$;
**return** $M$;

The result of `BMerge` is a *final* multislice, i.e., a multislice that contains no mergeable slices. Depending on the order in which pairs of mergeable slices are selected in Step 2 of the algorithm, different final multislices are obtained as shown in the following example.

*Example 4.* Consider the recurrence $P$ from Example 2 and the corresponding singular multislice $M$ which `BMerge` constructs in the first step. If in Step 2 the merging is done in the order indicated with parentheses $(\dot{\lambda}_1 + \dot{\lambda}_2) + (\dot{\lambda}_{11} + \dot{\lambda}_{12})$,

$(\dot\lambda_3 + \dot\lambda_4) + (\dot\lambda_5 + \dot\lambda_6)$, $(\dot\lambda_7 + \dot\lambda_{10})$, and $(\dot\lambda_8 + \dot\lambda_9)$, we get a final multislice

$$\begin{aligned} M_{\text{fin}} = \{&(yea\{7\}, wee\{1\}, day\{4\}, hou\{5,8\}, min\{10,30\}),\\ &(yea\{7\}, wee\{1\}, day\{4\}, hou\{6\}, \quad min\{10,20,30,40\}),\\ &(yea\{7\}, wee\{1\}, day\{4\}, hou\{6\text{-}7\}, min\{50\}),\\ &(yea\{7\}, wee\{1\}, day\{4\}, hou\{7\}, \quad min\{20,40\})\}. \end{aligned}$$

If, instead, we merge $((\dot\lambda_1 + \dot\lambda_2) + (\dot\lambda_3 + \dot\lambda_5)) + (\dot\lambda_{11} + \dot\lambda_{12})$ and $((\dot\lambda_4 + \dot\lambda_6) + \dot\lambda_7) + ((\dot\lambda_8 + \dot\lambda_9) + \dot\lambda_{10})$ we get a different final multislice

$$\begin{aligned} M_{\text{min}} = \{&(yea\{7\}, wee\{1\}, day\{4\}, hou\{5\text{-}6,8\}, min\{10,30\}),\\ &(yea\{7\}, wee\{1\}, day\{4\}, hou\{6\text{-}7\}, \quad min\{20,40,50\})\}. \end{aligned}$$

While both multislices are final, they have a different size and hence achieve a different compression ratio.

**Definition 3 (Minimal Multislice).** *Let $P$ be a recurrence and $\mathsf{M} = \{M_1, \ldots, M_n\}$ be the set of all multislices with hierarchy $(G_1, \ldots, G_d)$ that represents $P$. A multislice $M_{min} \in \mathsf{M}$ is* minimal *iff $\forall M \in \mathsf{M}(|M| \geq |M_{min}|)$.*

A multislice representation with a given hierarchy of a recurrence $P$ is minimal if all other multislices for $P$ are of the same size or greater. A recurrence $P$ can have more than one minimal multislice with a given hierarchy, where all have the same size. Minimal multislices provide the best compression ratio. A minimal multislice is always a final multislice, but not vice versa. In the above example, the final multislice $M_{\text{min}}$ is also a minimal, which is not true for $M_{\text{fin}}$. Thus, for a recurrence $P$, a minimal multislice $M_{\text{min}}$, and a final multislice $M_{\text{fin}}$ the following holds: $|M_{\text{min}}| \leq |M_{\text{fin}}| \leq |P|$.

The worst case complexity of `BMerge` is $O(d \cdot |P|^2)$. In this worst case after the first pass through the singular slices of $M$ all mergeable slices are merged and appended at the "end" of the multislice. Further merging is only possible among these appended slices which result in new appended slices, etc.

### 3.3 NP-Hardness of Computing Minimal Multislices

In the following we show that searching for a minimal multislice representation is an NP-hard problem.

**Definition 4 (Decomposition).** *A singular multislice $M$ is a* decomposition *of a slice $\lambda = (G_1X_1, \ldots, G_dX_d)$ if $M$ contains all non-empty singular subslices of $\lambda$, i.e., $M = \{(G_1\{x_1\}, \ldots, G_d\{x_d\}) \mid (G_1\{x_1\}, \ldots, G_d\{x_d\}) \sqsubseteq \lambda\}$.*

For each slice there is a unique decomposition. From Lemma 1 follows that if $M$ is a decomposition of a slice $\lambda$ then $M$ represents the same recurrence as $\lambda$, i.e., $\mathcal{I}(M) = \mathcal{I}(\lambda)$. Lemma 2 states if $M$ is a decomposition of $\lambda$ then the unions of selectors at the corresponding levels in $M$ yield the selectors of $\lambda$.

**Lemma 2.** *If a singular multislice $M = \{\dot\lambda_1, \ldots, \dot\lambda_p\}$ is a decomposition of a slice $\lambda = (G_1X_1, \ldots, G_dX_d)$ and for all $i \in [1, p] : \dot\lambda_i = (G_1\{x_{1,i}\}, \ldots, G_d\{x_{d,i}\})$ then for all $l \in [1, d] : X_l = \bigcup_{i=1}^{p} \{x_{l,i}\}$.*

Consider the slice $\lambda_2 = (yea\{7\}, wee\{1\}, day\{4\}, hou\{6\text{-}7\}, min\{20,40,50\})$. The following multislice $M_{\lambda_2}$ is a decomposition of $\lambda_2$ and represents the same recurrence as $\lambda_2$. The unions of selectors at the corresponding levels give the selectors of $\lambda_2$.

$$\begin{aligned} M_{\lambda_2} = \{&(yea\{7\}, wee\{1\}, day\{4\}, hou\{6\}, min\{20\}),\\ &(yea\{7\}, wee\{1\}, day\{4\}, hou\{6\}, min\{40\}),\\ &(yea\{7\}, wee\{1\}, day\{4\}, hou\{6\}, min\{50\}),\\ &(yea\{7\}, wee\{1\}, day\{4\}, hou\{7\}, min\{20\}),\\ &(yea\{7\}, wee\{1\}, day\{4\}, hou\{7\}, min\{40\}),\\ &(yea\{7\}, wee\{1\}, day\{4\}, hou\{7\}, min\{50\})\} \end{aligned}$$

Let $M$ be a singular multislice representing a recurrence $P$ with a hierarchy $(G_1, \ldots, G_d)$ that contains no empty slices. Let $M_{\min} = \{\lambda_1, \ldots, \lambda_q\}$ be a minimum multislice representation of $P$ with the same hierarchy. From Lemma 1, each singular subslice $\dot{\lambda}$ of each slice $\lambda_i \in M_{\min}$ is in $M$, i.e., $\forall \lambda_i \in M_{\min}(\forall \dot{\lambda} \sqsubseteq \lambda_i(\dot{\lambda} \in M))$. The decomposition $M_{\lambda_i}$ of each slice $\lambda_i \in M_{\min}$ is then a subset of $M$, $M_{\lambda_i} \subseteq M$.

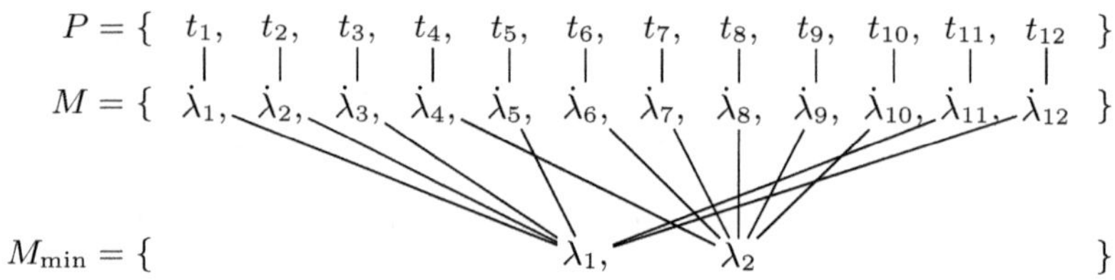


**Fig. 3.** Relationships between $P$, $M$, and $M_{\min}$ from Examples 2 and 4

*Example 5.* Consider the singular multislice $M = \{\dot{\lambda}_1, \ldots, \dot{\lambda}_{12}\}$ from Example 2. Each singular slice in $M$ represents a distinct time instant in $P$. A minimal multislice representation $M_{\min}$ of $P$ with hierarchy (*yea*, *wee*, *day*, *hou*, *min*) consists of two slices $\lambda_1$ and $\lambda_2$:

$$\begin{aligned} M_{\min} = \{&\lambda_1 = (yea\{7\}, wee\{1\}, day\{4\}, hou\{5\text{-}6,8\}, min\{10,30\}),\\ &\lambda_2 = (yea\{7\}, wee\{1\}, day\{4\}, hou\{6\text{-}7\}, \quad min\{20,40,50\})\} \end{aligned}$$

The two corresponding decompositions $\{\dot{\lambda}_1, \dot{\lambda}_2, \dot{\lambda}_3, \dot{\lambda}_5, \dot{\lambda}_{11}, \dot{\lambda}_{12}\}$ and $\{\dot{\lambda}_4, \dot{\lambda}_6, \dot{\lambda}_7, \dot{\lambda}_8, \dot{\lambda}_9, \dot{\lambda}_{10}\}$ are subsets of $M$ and cover all slices in $M$. Figure 3 illustrates the relationships between $P$, $M$, and $M_{\min}$ from Examples 2 and 4.

**Theorem 1.** *Let $P$ be a finite recurrence and let $(G_1, \ldots, G_d = G_\perp)$, $d > 1$, be a hierarchy of time granularities. Finding a minimum multislice representation of $P$ with the hierarchy $(G_1, \ldots, G_d = G_\perp)$ is an NP-hard problem.*

*Proof.* The problem of finding a minimal multislice representation of $P$ with the hierarchy $(G_1, \ldots, G_d = G_\perp)$ can be formulated as the following problem $\Pi_1$ :

Given a singular multislice $M$ which contains no empty slices. Find the minimal number of subsets of $M$ such that each subset is a decomposition of some slice and all subsets cover all slices in $M$.

We prove that $\Pi_1$ is NP-hard by reducing a known NP-complete problem of covering a bipartite graph by complete bipartite subgraphs (appears as the problem GT18 in [5]) to $\Pi_1$. We formulate the problem of covering a bipartite graphs as the problem $\Pi_4$ : Given a bipartite graph $(A, B, E)$, where $A, B$ are disjoint sets of vertexes and $E \subseteq \{\{a, b\} \mid a \in A, b \in B\}$ is a set of edges. Given a natural number $q$, $1 \leq q \leq |E|$. Are there $q$ complete bipartite subgraphs $(A'_1, B'_1, E'_1), \ldots, (A'_q, B'_q, E'_q)$, where $A'_i \subseteq A$, $B'_i \subseteq B$, and $E'_i = \{\{a, b\} \mid a \in A'_i, b \in B'_i\}$, such that they cover all edges in $E$, i.e., $E = \bigcup_{i=1}^{q} E'_i$?

We define intermediate problems $\Pi_2, \Pi_3$, and then prove that $\Pi_4 \leq_T \Pi_3 \leq_T \Pi_2 \leq_T \Pi_1$, where $\leq_T$ stands for Turing reducible. The problem $\Pi_1$ is an optimization problem. Using the fact that the size of a minimal multislice representation is always between 1 and $|M|$, we can formulate the following decision problem $\Pi_2$ : Given a singular multislice $M$ which contains no empty slices, and a natural number $q$, $1 \leq q \leq |M|$. Are there $q$ subsets of $M$ such that each subset is a decomposition of some slice and all subsets cover all slices in $M$?

Having the solution to $\Pi_1$, we can solve the problem $\Pi_2$ in constant time. By proving that $\Pi_2$ is NP-complete we show that $\Pi_1$ is NP-hard. $\Pi_2$ is certainly in NP: if we guess $q$ subsets of $M$ we can check if they are decompositions of some slices in polynomial time using Lemma 2. For $d = 2$ the problem $\Pi_2$ is formulated as the following problem $\Pi_3$ : Given two sets $X_1, X_2$ and a multislice $M \subseteq \{(G_1\{x_1\}, G_2\{x_2\}) \mid x_1 \in X_1 \wedge x_2 \in X_2\}$. Given a natural number $q$, $1 \leq q \leq |M|$. Are there $q$ subsets of $M$ such that each subset is a decomposition of some slice and all subsets cover all slices in $M$?

The problem $\Pi_4$ is equivalent to the problem $\Pi_3$, where every $a \in A$ corresponds to $x_a \in X_1$, every $b \in B$ corresponds to $x_b \in X_2$. Each edge $\{a, b\} \in E$ corresponds to a slice $(G_1\{x_a\}, G_2\{x_b\}) \in M$. A complete bipartite subgraph in $(A, B, E)$ corresponds to a decomposition in $M$. Figure 4(a,b) shows an example of such a correspondence. Note, that the bipartite graph in Fig. 4(a) can be covered by its four complete bipartite subgraphs, and even though the subgraph drawn with bold lines is the largest complete bipartite subgraph in the given graph, it does not belong to these four (see Fig. 4(d)).

We can reduce a problem $\Pi_3$ with $d = 2$ to a problem $\Pi_2$ with $d \geq 2$ just by adding the same pairs granularity-selector to each slice in $M$. For example, we can map the multislice from Fig. 4(b) to the multislice in Fig. 4(c). □

### 3.4 Level-Wise Merge Algorithm `LMerge`

Recall that `BMerge` does not impose any ordering in the merging phase. Here we present the algorithm `LMerge` (Level-wise Merge) which imposes a specific order on the merging process: slices are merged by granularities, that is, for each hierarchy level $l$ the algorithm performs all possible merges across $l$ before it begins to merge across another level. Within a hierarchy level the order in which slices are merged is irrelevant due to the associativity of the merge operation.

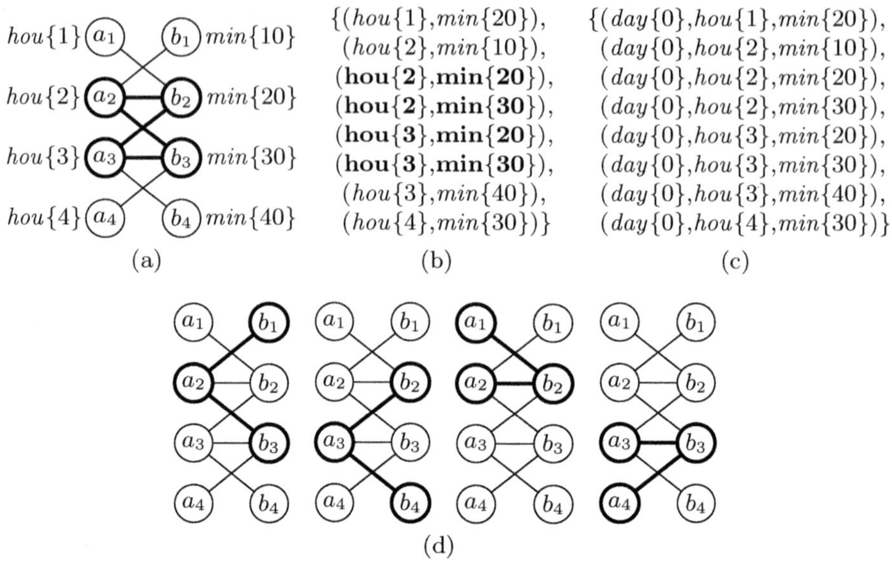


**Fig. 4.** A bipartite graph with a complete bipartite subgraph (a), the corresponding singular multislice with the corresponding decomposition (b), the corresponding multislice with $d = 3$ (c), and the smallest cover of the bipartite graph by complete bipartite subgraphs (d)

The `LMerge` algorithm adopts the same bottom-up strategy as the baseline algorithm: (Step 1) a singular multislice $M$ with the given hierarchy $(G_1, \ldots, G_d)$ is constructed and (Step 2) mergeable slices in $M$ are merged. The main loop in Step 2 iterates through all levels of the hierarchy $(G_1, \ldots, G_d)$ and determines the order in which slices are merged. At each iteration the slices in $M$ are sorted on all selectors except the one that corresponds to level $l$ of the iteration. For instance, if the hierarchy is (*yea*, *wee*, *day*, *hou*, *min*) and the iteration level is of *day*, the slices are sorted on the selectors of *yea*, *wee*, *hou*, and *min*. Such sorting brings the slices that are mergeable across $l$ together into contiguous clusters such that in a single pass through the multislice each cluster can be merged into a single slice. The functions first and next retrieve the first and next slice from $M$, respectively.

`LMerge` runs in $O(d^2 \cdot |P| \cdot \log |P|)$ time, where $O(d \cdot |P| \cdot \log |P|)$ is the time complexity of sorting.

*Example 6.* Consider the singular multislice $M$ from Example 2. The first iteration of the main loop merges across the granularity *min*. The sorting step produces the four clusters $\{\dot\lambda_1, \dot\lambda_2\}$, $\{\dot\lambda_3, \dot\lambda_4, \dot\lambda_5, \dot\lambda_6, \dot\lambda_7\}$, $\{\dot\lambda_8, \dot\lambda_9, \dot\lambda_{10}\}$, and $\{\dot\lambda_{11}, \dot\lambda_{12}\}$, which in a single pass are merged into four slices, yielding

$$\begin{aligned} M = \{&(yea\{7\},\ wee\{1\},\ day\{4\},\ hou\{5\},\ min\{10{,}30\}),\\ &(yea\{7\},\ wee\{1\},\ day\{4\},\ hou\{6\},\ min\{10{,}20{,}30{,}40{,}50\}),\\ &(yea\{7\},\ wee\{1\},\ day\{4\},\ hou\{7\},\ min\{20{,}40{,}50\}),\\ &(yea\{7\},\ wee\{1\},\ day\{4\},\ hou\{8\},\ min\{10{,}30\})\}. \end{aligned}$$

Algorithm `LMerge`

---

**input**: recurrence $P$, hierarchy $(G_1, \ldots, G_d)$
**output**: multislice $M$
*// Step 1: build a singular multislice*
$M := \varnothing$;
**for each** $t \in P$ **do**
  $M := M \cup \{$singular slice for $t\}$;
*// Step 2: merge slices level–wise*
**for** $l \in \{1, \ldots, d\}$ **do**
  Sort $M$ on $X_1, \ldots, X_{l-1}, X_{l+1}, \ldots, X_d$;
  $\lambda :=$ first$(M)$;
  **while** $\lambda \neq null$ **do**
    $\lambda' :=$ next$(M)$;
    **while** mergeable$(\lambda, \lambda', l)$ **do**
      $\lambda := \lambda + \lambda'$;
      $M := M \setminus \{\lambda'\}$;
      $\lambda' :=$ next$(M)$;
    $\lambda := \lambda'$;
**return** $M$;

---

The second iteration merges across the level of *hou*. The slices are sorted on the selectors of the granularities *yea*, *wee*, *day*, and *min*, yielding three clusters, which are merged to get the multislice

$$\begin{aligned} M = \{&(yea\{7\}, wee\{1\}, day\{4\}, hou\{6\}, \ \ min\{10,20,30,40,50\}),\\ &(yea\{7\}, wee\{1\}, day\{4\}, hou\{7\}, \ \ min\{20,40,50\}),\\ &(yea\{7\}, wee\{1\}, day\{4\}, hou\{5,8\}, min\{10,30\})\} \end{aligned}$$

This multislice is final, and the iteration through the granularities of *day*, *wee*, and *yea* does not provide further merging.

**Lemma 3.** *Let $P$ be a recurrence and $(G_1, \ldots, G_d)$ be a hierarchy. The algorithm `LMerge` returns a final multislice $M$.*

*Proof.* To keep the proof simple, we assume the merging is done from level 1 to level $d$ (the lemma holds for any order of levels). After $m$–1 iterations the selectors at levels $m, \ldots, d$ of all slices are still unmodified and consist of single integers. We do a proof by contradiction. Assume the result of `LMerge` is not final and contains two slices $\lambda_X = (G_1X_1, \ldots, G_dX_d)$ and $\lambda_Y = (G_1Y_1, \ldots, G_dY_d)$ that are mergeable across some level $m \in [1, d]$. Then, $X_l = Y_l$ for all levels $l \neq m$, and there is a subslice $\lambda'_X = (G_1X_1, \ldots, G_{m-1}X_{m-1}, G_m\{x_m\}, \ldots, G_d\{x_d\})$ of $\lambda_X$ and a subslice $\lambda'_Y = (G_1Y_1, \ldots, G_{m-1}Y_{m-1}, G_m\{y_m\}, \ldots, G_d\{y_d\})$ of $\lambda_Y$ such that $x_m \neq y_m$ and $x_l = y_l$ for all $l \in [m+1, d]$. Such a situation is impossible, because slices $\lambda'_X$ and $\lambda'_Y$ should already have been merged after iteration $m$, which leads to a contradiction. □

## 4 Analytical Evaluation

Let $P$ be a finite recurrence, $M_{\min}$ be a minimal multislice representation of $P$ with a hierarchy $(G_1, \ldots, G_d)$, and $M$ be a multislice representation of $P$ with the same hierarchy constructed by `LMerge`. We define the worst case of `LMerge` as maximum difference $|M| - |M_{\min}|$. In the following we show that for $d = 2$ in the worst case $|M| < \min\left\{2^{|M_{\min}|}, \frac{2|P|}{|M_{\min}|}\right\}$. This means that in the worst case the multislice produced by `LMerge` can be exponentially larger than a minimum multislice representation of $P$, however, still less than $P$ by the factor of $\frac{|M_{\min}|}{2}$. To give an intuition, for $d = 2$ and $|M_{\min}| = 10$ in the worst case $|M| = 1023$ and $|P|$ is at least 5120. In Section 5 we show that real recurrences from bus schedules are far from this worst case, and the `LMerge` algorithm provides an average compression ratio of 99%.

To show the rationale of these bounds we introduce a geometric visualization of singular multislices. A singular multislice with a hierarchy $(G_1, G_2)$ can be visualized as a set of points in 2D space. Consider the singular multislice in Fig. 5(a). This multislice has hierarchy (*hou*, *min*) and can be visualized in 2D space where one dimension corresponds to the granularity *hou* and the other dimension corresponds to the granularity *min* (see Fig. 5(b)). This geometric visualization allows to observe two properties. First, all slices laying on the same line parallel to the *min* axis are mergeable across the granularity *min*, and all slices laying on the same line parallel to the *hou* axis are mergeable across the granularity *hou*. Second, a subset of slices which fills a rectangle in the geometric visualization is the decomposition of some slice. For example, the subset of slices connected with dotted lines in Fig. 5(b) forms the decomposition of the slice (*hou*{6-7}, *min*{40,50}).

Note, that both segments and points are special cases of a rectangle and visualize the decompositions of some slices. A change of order of values on both axes does not change any of the two properties. This means that a subset of points visualizes a decomposition if there are two permutations of values on both axes for which it fills a rectangle. Figure 5(c) visualizes a multislice with all slices grouped into two decompositions marked with white and black circles. The corresponding slices make up a minimal multislice representation of the recurrence represented by the singular multislice in Fig. 5(a).

Applying `LMerge` to the multislice in Fig. 5(a) the slices are merged iteratively across the two hierarchy levels. For example, in Fig. 5(d) the slices that are merged in the first iteration across the level of *min* are connected into segments (dotted lines). In the second iteration, the mergeable slices are merged across the level of *hou*. In our geometric visualization the mergeable slices would be the segments that fill a rectangle for some permutation of indexes of *hou*. For example, in Fig. 5(d) there are three groups of such segments making up three decompositions that are marked with white circles, white squares, and black circles. For comparison, Fig. 5(e) visualizes 4 decompositions that are found by `BMerge` when the singular slices are chronologically ordered.

{(*hou*{5},*min*{10}),
(*hou*{5},*min*{30}),
(*hou*{6},*min*{10}),
(*hou*{6},*min*{20}),
(*hou*{6},*min*{30}),
(*hou*{6},*min*{40}),
(*hou*{6},*min*{50}),
(*hou*{7},*min*{20}),
(*hou*{7},*min*{40}),
(*hou*{7},*min*{50}),
(*hou*{8},*min*{10}),
(*hou*{8},*min*{30})}
(a)

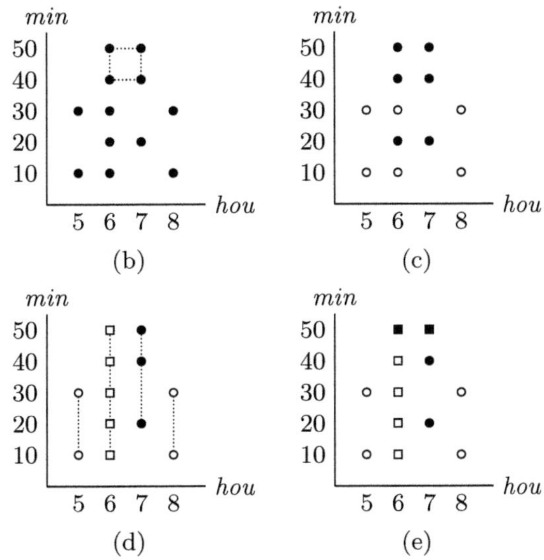


**Fig. 5.** A singular multislice with $d = 2$ (a), its geometric visualization in 2D space (b), grouping into minimal number of decompositions (c), grouping into decompositions by `LMerge` with merging across levels 1,2 (d), grouping into decomposition by `BMerge` (chronological order) (e)

Figure 6(a) shows the worst case for `LMerge` when merging is done first across $G_1$ and then across $G_2$. When merging first across $G_2$, the singular slices visualized in this figure can be merged into 4 slices and it is a minimal multislice representation of the corresponding recurrence. Merging first across $G_1$ would return 15 slices which corresponds to the number of all possible intersections of 4 sets. We can systematically construct recurrences $P$ for which `LMerge`$(P, (G_1, G_2))$ returns $2^{|M_{\min}|} - 1$ slices. We can construct the cases where merging first across $G_1$ or $G_2$ does not avoid the exponential difference. For example, Fig. 6(b) visualizes a singular multislice which can be compressed into 8 slices, however, `LMerge` algorithm would return 19. In such cases `LMerge` would return at least $2^{\frac{|M_{\min}|}{2}} - 1 + |M_{\min}|$ slices.

The singular multislice visualized in Fig. 6(a) contains 32 singular time slices. In order to construct the worst case where $|M| = 2^{|M_{\min}|} - 1$, we need at least $|P| = |M_{\min}| \cdot 2^{|M_{\min}|-1}$ singular slices. From here, $|M| = \frac{2|P|}{|M_{\min}|} - 1$.

## 5 Empirical Evaluation

For the empirical evaluation we implemented `BMerge` and `LMerge` in PostgreSQL. We used the `BMerge` algorithm with two different orderings of the singular multislices: when the singular slices are ordered chronologically (`BMerge`, chronological order), and when the singular slices are ordered randomly (`BMerge`, random

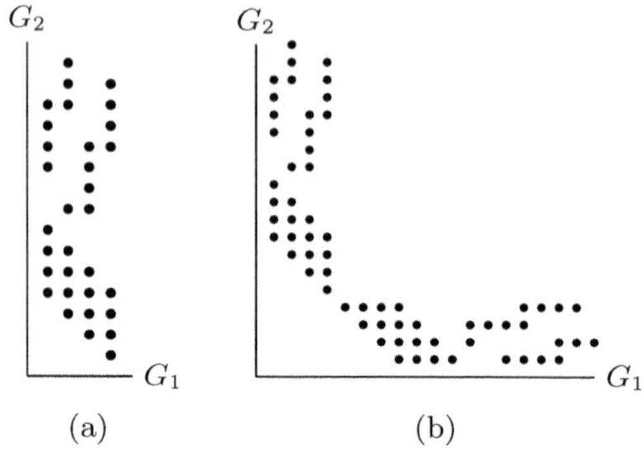


**Fig. 6.** The worst case for `LMerge` with merging across levels 1, 2 (a), and a bad case for `LMerge` for any order of levels (b)

order). The randomization is achieved by reordering the multislice according to a sequence of randomly generated numbers using PostgreSQL system functions. In all experiments we used the hierarchy $(wee, day, hou, min)$[2]. For the `LMerge` algorithm we tried all 24 possible orders in which `LMerge` can iterate through the levels of the hierarchy $(wee, day, hou, min)$. In the plots below for the `LMerge` algorithm we show the average compression ratio and the average running time over all 24 possible orders.

In the first experiment we compare `LMerge` and `BMerge` on the real-world data from the bus network of Bozen-Bolzano from the first half of the year 2007. This data describes 384 different route options grouped into 18 main routes. We selected 20 route options with recurrences of departures with sizes uniformly distributed within the range $[100, 2000]$. The best theoretically possible average compression for these recurrences is 99.64% assuming that each of the recurrences can be represented with a multislice of size 2. Figure 7 shows the results of this experiment. Algorithm `LMerge` provides with an average compression ratio of 98.93% which is very close to the optimal solution (i.e., minimal multislice). Changing the order of levels in the `LMerge` algorithm does not significantly impact the compression ratio for the selected recurrences. The average compression for the best orders is 99.01% and for the worst orders 98.81%. Algorithm `BMerge` with the random order is visibly behind `LMerge` providing on average 78.94% compression. Algorithm `BMerge` with the chronological order is very close to `LMerge` providing an average compression ratio of 98.52%. The running time of both algorithms conforms to our asymptotic bounds: $O(d^2 \cdot |P| \cdot \log |P|)$ for the `LMerge` algorithm and $O(d \cdot |P|^2)$ for the `BMerge` algorithm.

For the second experiment we generated 20 multislices representing recurrences from the first half of the year 2007 with the size varying within the range $[96, 2009]$. The sizes of the generated multislices cover the range $[1, 20]$ and are

[2] Since all recurrences are within the year 2007, the granularity *yea* provides no additional compression, hence we omitted it.

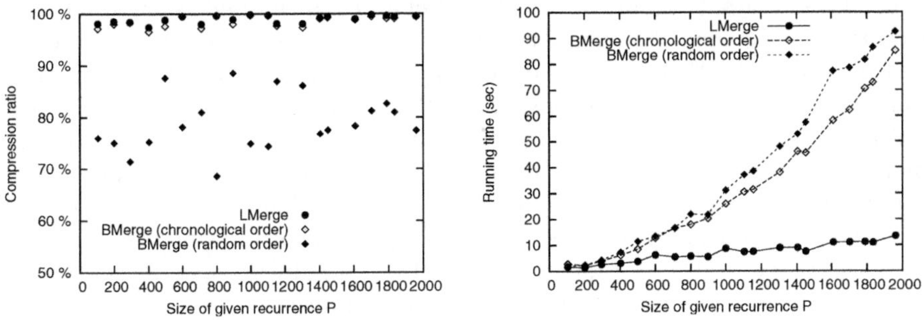


(a) Comparison of compression ratios. (b) Comparison of running time.

**Fig. 7.** Comparison of multislices produced by `LMerge` and `BMerge` for 20 real-world recurrences

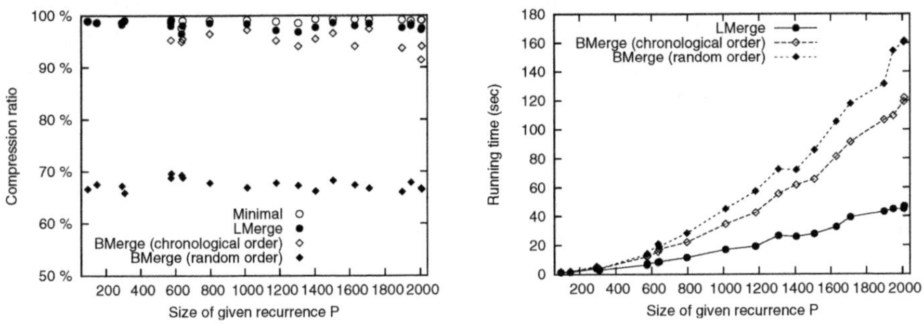


(a) Comparison of compression ratios. (b) Comparison of running time.

**Fig. 8.** Comparison of multislices produced by `LMerge` and `BMerge` for 20 generated recurrences

taken for known minimal representations providing the average compression ratio of 98.94%. Figure 8 shows the results of this experiment. Algorithm `LMerge` provides with an average compression ratio of 98.04%. Changing the order of levels in `LMerge` has a bigger impact than in the previous experiment (more than 1% in compression). The average compression for the best orders is 98.62% and for the worst orders 97.19%. In this experiment the difference between `LMerge` and `BMerge` has increased for both versions of the `BMerge` algorithm. `BMerge` with the random order provides on average 67.50% compression. `BMerge` with the chronological order provides an average compression ratio of 96.23%.

## 6 Related Work

Multislices are based on various formalisms coming from the research community [4,6,7,2] and generalize some known representations used in industry [8,9].

Time slices originate from the works of Leban et al. [6] and Niezette et al. [4]. Niezette et al. coined the term time slice and defined the intersection operation on time slices. In their work the authors used sets of slices to overcome the limitation of expressiveness of single time slices. Kasperovics et al. [1] introduced multislices as a basic object for representing recurrences, defined the difference operation on time slices and multislices, and proposed a scalable representation of multislices in relational databases. There is a number of works improving the expressiveness of time slices (e.g., [10,11,12,2]), or incorporating them into more complex representation formalisms (e.g., [13,7,14]). In this paper we presented an operation that constructs multislice representation for a given recurrence, which was not addressed by the previous works.

There are few works that address constructing compact representations from given recurrences. These representations, however, favor periodic recurrences and do not use time granularities. Behr et al. [15] proposed a compact representation formalism, called periodic moving tree, for periodic moving objects and provided with an algorithm for constructing periodic moving trees from recurrences. Work by Bettini et al. [16] proposed an algorithm for minimizing the representations of periodic sets which can be used for constructing compact representations of periodic recurrences. Multislices provide a high compression for recurrences aligned to the hierarchies of time granularities. Such recurrences are common for many kinds of schedules and are less periodic because of monthly or yearly repetitions, and because of multiple exceptions, such as public holidays. The representation of such recurrences with periodic moving trees or periodic sets would require more space.

## 7 Conclusions and Future Work

In this paper we studied the problem of constructing multislice representations for non-empty finite recurrences. We proved that the construction of a minimal multislice representation is an NP-hard problem and proposed a scalable approximation algorithm `LMerge`. Although in the worst case `LMerge` might produce an exponentially worse compression than the minimal solution, experiments with real-world data show that the multislices computed by the algorithm provide a very high compression ratio of 99%, which is very close to the optimal solution. `LMerge` clearly outperforms a straightforward baseline algorithm `BMerge` both in terms of compression and in terms of time.

The recurrences in public transport schedules, lecture schedules, and personal calendars are often a subject of changes, and so would be their multislice representations. The changes can be resolved using the union and difference operations on multislices [1], which in most would decrease the compression. The ideas presented in this paper can be extended for compressing multislices in more general settings, where multislices are not necessarily singular (e.g., when produced as the result of operations on multislices).

## References

1. Kasperovics, R., Böhlen, M.H., Gamper, J.: Evaluating exceptions on time slices. In: Laender, A.H.F. (ed.) ER 2009. LNCS, vol. 5829, pp. 251–264. Springer, Heidelberg (2009)
2. Ohlbach, H.J.: Periodic temporal notions as 'tree partitionings'. Forschungsbericht/Research Report PMS-FB-2006-11, Institute for Informatics, University of Munich (2006)
3. Dawson, F., Stenerson, D.: Internet calendaring and scheduling core object specification, iCalendar (1998)
4. Niezette, M., Stévenne, J.M.: An efficient symbolic representation of periodic time. In: Proceedings of the First International Conference on Information and Knowledge Management, pp. 161–168
5. Garey, M.R., Johnson, D.S.: Computers and Intractability: A Guide to the Theory of NP-Completeness. W. H. Freeman, New York (1979)
6. Leban, B., McDonald, D.D., Forster, D.R.: A representation for collections of temporal intervals. In: Proceedings of AAAI 1986, August 1986, pp. 367–371 (1986)
7. Terenziani, P.: Symbolic user-defined periodicity in temporal relational databases. IEEE Trans. Knowl. Data Eng. 15(2), 489–509 (2003)
8. Google Inc.: Google Transit Feed Specification (February 2008)
9. Weber, C., Brauer, D., Kolmorgen, V., Hirschel, M., Provezza, S., Hulsch, T.: Fahrplanbearbeitungssystem FBS – Anleitung. iRFP (September 2006)
10. Cukierman, D.R., Delgrande, J.P.: The SOL theory: A formalization of structured temporal objects and repetition. In: Proceedings of TIME, pp. 28–35 (2004)
11. Anselma, L.: Recursive representation of periodicity and temporal reasoning. In: Proceedings of TIME, pp. 52–59 (2004)
12. Kasperovics, R., Böhlen, M.H.: Querying multi-granular compact representations. In: Li Lee, M., Tan, K.-L., Wuwongse, V. (eds.) DASFAA 2006. LNCS, vol. 3882, pp. 111–124. Springer, Heidelberg (2006)
13. Chandra, R., Segev, A., Stonebraker, M.: Implementing calendars and temporal rules in next generation databases. In: Proceedings of ICDE 1994, Washington, DC, USA, pp. 264–273. IEEE Computer Society, Los Alamitos (1994)
14. Ning, P., Wang, X.S., Jajodia, S.: An algebraic representation of calendars. Ann. Math. Artif. Intell. 36(1-2), 5–38 (2002)
15. Behr, T., de Almeida, V.T., Güting, R.H.: Representation of periodic moving objects in databases. In: Proceedings of the 14th International Workshop on Geographic Information Systems (ACM-GIS), pp. 43–50 (2006)
16. Bettini, C., Mascetti, S.: An efficient algorithm for minimizing time granularity periodical representations. In: Proceedings of TIME, pp. 20–25 (2005)

# Optimizing Query Processing in Cache-Aware Wireless Sensor Networks*

Mario A. Nascimento[1], Romulo A.E. Alencar[2], and Angelo Brayner[2]

[1] University of Alberta, Canada
mn@cs.ualberta.ca
[2] Universidade of Fortaleza, Brazil
romulo@assessus.com.br, brayner@unifor.br

**Abstract.** Most models for Wireless Sensor Networks (WSNs) assume the existence of a base station where query results could in principle be cached, however, the opportunity for re-using such cached data for minimizing data traffic in the WSN has not been well explored thus far. Aiming at filling this gap, we propose an approach that first clips the original query into a polygon after selectively choosing a good subset of the cached queries for reuse. Next, this polygon is partitioned into sub-queries that are then submitted to the WSN. These two problems are interconnected and lead to a highly combinatorial problem that justifies the use of efficient and effective heuristics. This paper presents algorithms for each of these problems that are used within a cost-driven optimization search in order to find a set of sub-queries that minimizes the cost of in-network query processing. Experimental results show that our heuristic solution is orders of magnitude faster than an exhaustive search, and yields no more than 10% loss compared to the optimal query processing.

## 1 Introduction

A typical Wireless Sensor Network (WSN) is comprised of a set of several identical sensor nodes with limited CPU and storage capacity plus one base station which is assumed to have more resources, e.g., more CPU power, additional storage space and a relatively large, or possibly continuous, energy supply. All nodes are able to communicate wirelessly within a certain range and are assumed to be aware of its neighbors, i.e., other nodes within its wireless communication range. No node is assumed to have full knowledge of the network, including the location of other nodes. The base station is a partial exception in the sense that it is assumed to have some high-level knowledge of the WSN, e.g., node density, wireless range, etc., which is used in the query cost model. All decisions, such as data packet routing and collision resolution, are to be made locally by the nodes. Each node is capable of observing its surroundings and capturing one or more measures.

* Research partially supported by NSERC (Canada), CBIE (Canada), CAPES (Brazil) and FUNCAP (Brazil).

M. Gertz and B. Ludäscher (Eds.): SSDBM 2010, LNCS 6187, pp. 60–77, 2010.

Many applications for WSN have been proposed and discussed in the literature, e.g., [1,2,3] to name but a few. In general, once the WSN is active and nodes are collecting data, a number of queries can be issued, e.g., spatio-temporal range queries, join queries and aggregate queries, for which a number of algorithms have been proposed, e.g., [4,5,6]. Most algorithms also assume the existence of a base station from where queries are injected into the WSN and to where the queried data is returned. In this scenario, there exists a clear opportunity for reducing query cost by caching query results at the base station and subsequently re-using such data when new queries are posed. While in a traditional database system the use of cache is for maximizing the system's throughput, we aim at minimizing the energy cost of query processing. As well, we do not make any strong assumptions regarding how in-network query processing is done, rather we only assume that a cost model for the adopted technique is available. Typically, algorithms for query processing in WSNs borrow the minimum bound rectangle abstraction from spatial databases and assume that the query is a rectangle within the monitored area; we follow suit and make similar assumptions.

Our main problem in this paper is to *minimize the energy cost of processing a query $Q$ within a WSN that requests the most recent values of (possibly all) sensed attributes of sensor nodes located within $Q$*[1]. While WSNs are of great usefulness in a streaming scenario, that is not the only possible scenario. Consider for instance a remote WSN connected to a satellite link, which is capable to receiving and sending data. In many cases it would be simply too expensive to have the WSN continuously streaming data to the base station. Hence, a possibility would be to have different users querying, at will, the WSN through the base-station, which would then send *optimized* queries to the WSN. The WSN would then process the query and send its results back to the base station. It may also be the case that several independent, and likely physically apart, users are interested in the same WSN. Thus a natural choice would be to have the base station acting as a "portal" to the WSN. In such a scenario, the advantage of having users being able to transparently re-use relevant and valid data from another user's query in a cache at such portal should be quite clear.

To illustrate the potential gain of using cached data consider for instance the scenario depicted in Figure 1(a), where $Q$ is a new query and $\{P_1, P_2, P_3\}$ represents previously processed queries. Assuming the cached data is still valid, it is clear that only nodes located in the "clipped" query region $Q'$, need be contacted. Since, the number of nodes within the area of $Q'$ is bound to be smaller than those within $Q$'s area, the intuition is that processing $Q'$ should be energy-wise less expensive than processing $Q$.

One trivial way to solve this problem is to find the minimum bounding rectangle of $Q'$, denoted by $R(Q')$, and process the query using $R(Q')$ instead of $Q$. Clearly, that would not necessarily minimize query processing cost as $R(Q')$ would often be likely equal to $R(Q)$ (as in Figure 1(a)).

[1] To simplify notation we refer to a *query* as well as to its *spatial attributes* using the same variable.

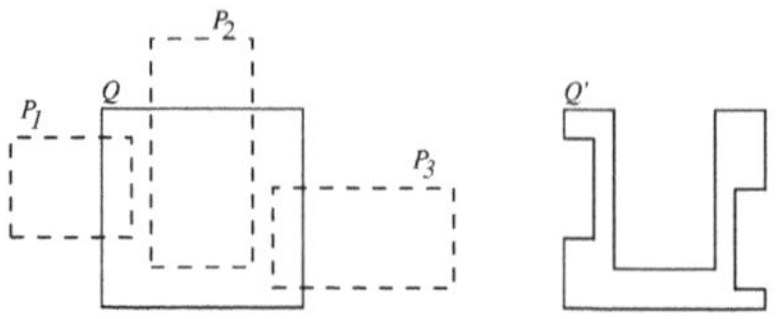


(a) Potential gain from cached queries.

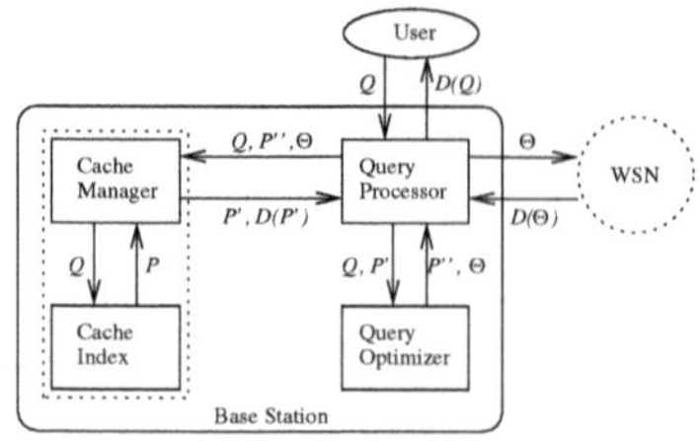


(b) Query processing framework within the base station.

**Fig. 1.** Motivation and optimization framework

Another straightforward way to solve this problem is to "flood" the query area and have only the sensors within the query area respond to the query. There are two main drawbacks in this approach. One is that in order to decide whether it should respond or not to the query, a sensor would need to know whether it is actually inside the query area. Even though efficient algorithms exist to answer the point-in-polygon problem [7], they depend on the size of the polygon description. In general the contour of the clipped query $Q'$ can be very complex and also have holes, that is, its description may be quite large. Another, and more severe, problem is that the query area may contain a large number of nodes, and each one (plus possibly others sufficiently close to the query's boundary) would receive such large description of the query's polygon. This would imply a potentially large number of large messages flowing in the network. Given that the the larger the message the more energy is needed to transmit it, this flooding-based approach is non-practical.

Thus a more sophisticated solution is needed to adequately address the *cache-aware query processing problem in WSN* motivated above. The solution we propose assumes a query processing framework, illustrated in Figure 1(b), located on the WSN's base station, and whose functioning is as follows. The user poses a query $Q$ at the base station. The Query Processor requests from the Cache Manager the set $P$ of previous queries that intersect $Q$. The Cache Manager uses the Cache Index to quickly obtain the set $P$ of relevant (cached) queries. (Although other possibilities could be used, an obvious alternative for the Cache Index would be an R*-tree [8].) The Cache Manager inspects whether any of the queries in $P$ contain stale data. If needed it updates the Cache Index, and returns the set $P'$ of valid relevant queries that intersect $Q$, along with the union respective cached datasets $D(P_i'), \forall P_i' \in P'$. Having $Q$ and $P'$, the Query Processor uses the services of a Query Optimizer[2] for two inter-dependent tasks aiming at reducing the cost of processing $Q$: (1) to determine which set $P'' \subseteq P'$ to use, and thus determine the clipped query $Q'$ and, considering $Q'$ and $P''$, (2) to partition $Q'$ in order to determine a set of sub-queries $\Theta$. Finally, the Query Processor receives $\Theta$ from the Query Optimizer, submits them to the WSN,

[2] We do not claim that this is a full-fledged query optimizer in the usual sense, we use this term simply for the sake of argumentation.

combines their results with the cached datasets of the queries in $P''$ and returns the final query result to the user.

In this paper we focus mainly on the Query Optimizer module, i.e., given a query $Q$ and the set $P'$, we aim at determining the sets $P''$ and $\Theta$ that minimize the energy cost for processing $Q$. To the best of our knowledge this cache-aware query optimization problem has not been investigated yet. In summary, this paper presents the following two main contributions: (1) we define the cache-aware query processing problem and argue that its highly combinatorial nature justifies the development of efficient sub-optimal solutions, and (2) we propose cost-oriented heuristic algorithms that are able to rapidly find good solutions (and often the best one) to the cache-aware query processing problem.

The remainder of the paper is structured as follows. In the next section we discuss in detail the cached data selection problem and its inherently complex nature in the context of in-network query processing. Heuristic algorithms that are combined to find a cost-wise good strategy for solving the cache-aware query processing problem are presented in Section 3. Section 4 follows presenting empirical evidence that our proposed solutions can be both effective and efficient when compared to the obvious alternatives of not using the cache at all or using all of it. Finally, Sections 5 and 6 presents a review of the related work and concludes the paper respectively.

## 2 Cache-Aware Query Processing

Before proceeding further we need to decide on a good model for estimating the cost of processing queries in a WSN to be used within the Query Optimizer module. In the remainder of this paper we re-use the SWIP framework for processing rectangular queries within a WSN [9]. While other query processing algorithms could be used, the main advantage of using the SWIP framework is that it offers an intuitive and accurate cost model that can be used for guiding the optimization problem we have. Due to limited space we skip the details of the cost model and refer the interested reader to [9]. SWIP's query processing approach can be summarized in the following four major tasks, which form the main components of SWIP's cost model:

- S1: The query is sent from the base station node to a coordinator node.
- S2: The query is partially flooded within the query area.
- S3: All nodes in the query area send their data to the coordinator node.
- S4: The coordinator node returns the gathered data to the Base Station node (likely the same path used in step S1).

An interesting issue at this point is the following. Consider a query $Q$ and a possible decomposition of $Q$ into smaller sub-queries $q_i$ such that $\bigcup_i q_i = Q$. Which option is less expensive: processing the larger single query $Q$ or the set of smaller sub-queries $q_i$? The answer is not obvious. In fact, depending on several parameters, the answer could be either one. For instance, the more smaller queries one has, the smaller the combined cost in step S2, but the larger the costs of step S1 and S4, although in S4 each message is smaller. We advocate that the optimal choice depends on how the set of sub-queries is determined, and determining a good (ideally optimal) such a set is our main goal in this paper.

Let $P$ be the set of all cached queries each having a possibly distinct validity period. We assume that all cached queries are pair-wise disjoint. This is a natural assumption because only the most recent data of any sensor needs to be cached. The set $P' = \{P'_1, P'_2, \ldots, P'_M\} \subseteq P$ of queries which are still valid and such that $P'_i \bigcap Q \neq \emptyset, \forall P'_i \in P'$, is the set of relevant valid queries with respect to $Q$. We make the natural assumption that the resulting data set $D(P'_i)$ for each query $P'_i$ is cached in the base station as well.

The following definitions summarizes some of the notation used throughout the rest of the paper. Note that, unless otherwise noted, whenever we refer to a polygon we mean its boundaries as well as its interior points.

**Definition 1.** *Given two polygons $R$ and $T$, $R \bigcup T$ denotes the polygon given by the union of all points interior to $R$ or to $T$ as well all as their boundaries. Similarly, given a set $P$ of polygons $P_i$, their union is denoted as $\mathcal{U}(P) = \bigcup_{P_i \in P} P_i$.*

**Definition 2.** *Given a polygon $R$ and a set of polygons $S$, such that $R \bigcap S_i \neq \emptyset, \forall S_i \in S$, we denote as $R \oplus S$ the clipping of $R$ with respect to $S$. Informally, $R \oplus S$ is the portion of $R$ not overlapped by any $S_i \in S$.*

**Definition 3.** *Given a rectilinear polygon $R$ we denote as its partition a set $\rho(R)$ of rectangles such that their pair-wise intersection is null and their union is equal to $R$.*

We can now state our main problem's definition more formally as follows. We want to to minimize the cost of processing a query $Q$ which requests the *current observations of all sensor nodes within $Q$'s area.* Considering only the set $P'$, this amounts to a request for the current data from the sensors in the area denoted by $Q' = Q \oplus P'$. We can take advantage of previously proposed algorithms for processing rectangular queries in WSN by determining $\Theta = \{\theta_1, \theta_2, \ldots, \theta_T\} = \rho(Q')$ . Once this is done, one can use suitable algorithms to execute each sub-query in $\Theta$, and obtain the answer for $Q$, i.e., $D(Q) = (\bigcup_{\theta_i \in \Theta} D(\theta_i)) \bigcup (\cup_{P'_i \in P} D(P'_i))$. Under the reasonable assumption that data for previous queries can be obtained at no cost within the base station, the cost of processing the original query $Q$ is $C(Q) = \sum_{\theta_i \in \Theta} C(\theta_i)$. Hence, our main problem is to determine the set $\Theta$ that minimizes $C(Q)$.

However, as indicated before, we claim that often one may be better off not using $P'$, due to the overhead that each additional query imposes. For each element $P'_i \in P'$ considered for re-use the query area is reduced but the number of sub-queries in $\Theta$ is further increased. However, each sub-query carries the burden of an inherent overhead, namely that of dispatching and receiving each query, thus adding sub-queries in $\Theta$—an unavoidable consequence of adding $P'_i$ to $P''$—is worth it if and only if the amount of in-network flow saved is larger than the overhead added.

However, the reasoning above assumes one is able to solve two sub-problems in an efficient manner, namely: clipping a polygon with respect to another one and partitioning a rectlinear polygon. We discuss those in the following.

For the polygon clipping problem we use the well-known GPC public implementation[3] which is based on a polygon clipping algorithm presented in [10]. Furthermore, we need to evaluate the query cost yielded by a given set $P''$.

There are many goals one can aim at when partitioning a polygon. As discussed earlier each obtained rectangle in the partitioning of the clipped query will correspond to a sub-query, and in order to minimize the query processing overhead we restrict ourselves to finding a minimum cardinality decomposition of $Q'$. Interestingly, this produces a positive side-effect; it helps to improve query performance from a networking perspective as well, e.g., by minimizing the effect of packet collisions in the network. There exists a $O(v^{1.5} \log v)$ time optimal algorithm for this problem, where $v$ is the number of vertices of the polygon to be partitioned [11]. Unfortunately its implementation is quite complex. An alternative approximative algorithm, with complexity $O(v \log v)$ and much simpler to implement has been presented in [12]. Furthermore it has also been argued in [13] that the partitioning problem has "an $\Omega(v \log v)$ lower bound on the time-complexity. The result holds for any decomposition, optimal or approximative." That is, the algorithm we chose, albeit not guaranteed to provide the optimal partition is as efficient as it can possibly be in terms of time complexity. Considering the fact that base station may not be computationally resourceful, and furthermore that within a WSN environment one should use every chance to save energy as opportunistic as it might be, we consider that settling for a sub-optimal but effective and efficient algorithm is an worthy trade-off.

## 3 The Cache-Aware Query Optimization Problem

In order to address the problems discussed in the previous section, we begin by assuming $Q$ and $P'$ are given. How one determines the set $P' \subseteq P$ bears no impact on the following discussion, for now it suffices to assume that the Cache Manager module (Figure 1(b)) is able to find which previous queries intersect $Q$ and among those, the ones which are still valid.

If $C(X)$ is the cost of processing a query $X$, and assuming the use of cached data at the base station can be done at null cost, the optimization problem at hand is to find the subset $P''$ and the rectangular partitioning $\Theta$ that minimizes $C(Q) = \sum_{\theta_i \in \Theta} C(\theta_i)$. We now have two problems for which we seek effective and efficient solutions. One problem is to find the set $P''$ that yields the optimal query cost assuming a particular polygon rectangular partitioning algorithm, which turns itself out to be the second problem.

Given the arguments above, the main problem is we need to solve is finding which set $P'' \subseteq P'$ of previous queries to use. A trivial but impractical way to solve this problem is by brute-force. In this case one would to consider all elements of $P'$'s powerset, whose cardinality is $2^{|P'|}$, and for each one find a

[3] http://www.cs.man.ac.uk/~toby/alan/software/

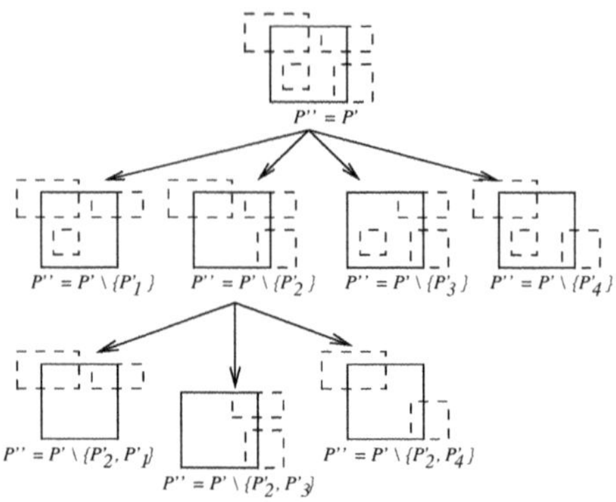

**Fig. 2.** The branch-and-bound search for a good set $P''$ and corresponding set $\Theta$

partition $\Theta$—we discuss how to do this in the next section—and then select the set $P''$ that minimizes $C(Q)$. A more practical approach is to start with an empty (full) set $P''$ and judiciously increase (decrease) its size until no improvement can be achieved, at which point the best solution found so far is adopted. This idea forms the core of the branch-and-bound approach we present in this section.

In our preliminary experiments we rarely saw a case where using no available cache was the best option. This suggests that instead of starting with the original query and incrementally evaluate the solutions obtained by considering more and more intersections, it may be more productive to work the other way around.

We build our search tree by considering $P'' = P'$, i.e., all possible $|P'|$ intersections between $P'$ and $Q$ in the root node; we define the root node's height to be 0. Then at height 1 we consider all possible intersections using $|P'| - 1$ elements from $P'$. In general, at height $K < |P'|$ of the tree, each node represents the intersection between $Q$ and a set $P''$ containing a unique set of $|P'| - K$ elements of $P'$ Furthermore, each such node will branch out yielding $P - K$ subtrees. Clearly, if no branch is pruned *and memoization* is used properly, then all elements of $P''$s powerset will be evaluated, and the one with minimum cost can be chosen as the best solution. It is important to note that for each one of $2^{|P'|}$ possibilities, one needs to compute a $Q'$ as well as its partitioning. While such an exhaustive search is conceptually correct and guaranteed to find the optimal solution, it is not practical. Thus we propose to use a branch-and-bound technique to find a solution, possibly sub-optimal, to this search problem.

The search works as follows (we use Figure 2 to support the explanation). The root node uses $P'' = P'$, we compute its cost $C(Q)$ and save it as the *incumbent cost*. Note that it implies performing both appropriate clipping as well as partitioning operations. Next we "open" the node corresponding to the incumbent solution, i.e., obtain all the possibilities using $|P'| - 1$ intersections and compute their cost. Any un-opened node, i.e., one not yet explored, that has a cost lower than the incumbent is a candidate node to be opened as it indicates a better solution that the current incumbent one. Following a greedy mode, we choose the node with lowest cost, update the incumbent cost to that

**Algorithm 1.** B+B: a branch-and-bound search for $P''$

**Input:** $Q$ and set $P'$
create a node and set it as an open incumbent node
set $P'' = P'$
compute a set of sub-queries $\Theta = \rho(Q \oplus \mathcal{U}(P''))$
compute the incumbent cost $C^* = \sum_{\theta_i \in \Theta} C(\theta_i)$
set the incumbent solution $\langle P'', \Theta \rangle$
**while** there is at least one open incumbent node **do**
  select as incumbent node the node closer to the root and set it as closed
  **for** each element $P_i' \in P''$ **do**
    set $P'' = P'' \setminus \{P_i'\}$
    set $\Theta = \rho(Q \oplus \mathcal{U}(P''))$
    compute the cost $C = \sum_{\theta_i \in \Theta} C(\theta_i)$
    **if** $C \leq C^*$ **then**
      set the incumbent solution to $\langle P'', \Theta \rangle$
      set the current node as an open incumbent node
      set $C^* = C$
    **else**
      set the current node as closed
    **end if**
  **end for**
**end while**
**return** the incumbent solution

of the chosen node, and open it, leading us to one level further down the search tree. In Figure 2, the chosen node is the one corresponding to using $P' \setminus \{P_2'\}$. As long as there are un-opened nodes with cost lower than the current incumbent, the search proceeds down the tree. Once all un-opened nodes fail this test, we return the best solution thus far, i.e., the set $P''$ and partitioning $\Theta$ associated with the node which yielded the current incumbent cost. In the case of Figure 2, if none of the newly opened nodes has a better cost than the current incumbent then the search would stop and report $P'' = P' \setminus \{P_2'\} = \{P_1, P_3, P_4\}$ and the corresponding partition of $Q \oplus \mathcal{U}(P'')$ as the solution for the search.

Algorithm 1. shows the pseudo-code the searching procedure just discussed; in what follows we refer to it as "B+B". As we shall confirm shortly it provides very good solutions at a very small fraction of the exhaustive search cost.

While Algorithm B+B will stop at a locally optimum solution and typically be much faster than the exhaustive search, one can be even more aggressive. Another possibility is to start the search as the branch-and-bound approach does, i.e., using all intersections. Then at each step remove the smallest one, i.e., the intersection that contributes the least to the savings. If this improves the query cost, i.e., the overhead yielded by the removed query was larger than its savings, we proceed removing the next smallest intersection, and so on and so forth as long as the total query cost is not increasing. This greedy approach leads to what we refer to as Algorithm GrF.

With Algorithm GrF in mind, one can think of yet another fairly intuitive alternative. A previous query in set $P'$ is worth using only if it saves more cost than it induces through the overhead of the resulting sub-queries. Then if one uses $P'_i \in P'$ that yields the largest intersection with the current $Q'$ chances are that the gain may be larger than the added overhead. This can be repeated iteratively in a greedy mode. We refer to this alternative as Algorithm GrE.

By the way they start, it is easy to see that the solution by both the B+B and the GrF algorithms above cannot be worse than using all of the cache without any further optimization. Likewise the GrE algorithm cannot deliver a worse solution than not using any cache at all. Furthermore, one can anticipate that a bad (greedy) decision by the GrE algorithm is going to be more costly than a bad decision by the GrF algorithm. In the GrF algorithm the change in the set $P''$ from one iteration to the next is by construction relatively small whereas in the case of the GrE algorithm it is exactly the opposite case, hence yielding a bigger change in the solution. Indeed, this will be confirmed in the experiments we present in Section 4.

Due to space restrictions we do not discuss here the issue of cache maintenance, instead we refer the interested reader to [14]. For now it suffices to say that we do make sure the Cache Manager works effectively by cleaning the cache, i.e., removing stale queries and data in an opportunistic fashion, as well as updating the cache whenever new data is acquired.

## 4 Experimental Results

In order to evaluate the quality of our solutions we considered their efficiency and effectiveness with respect to a number of different parameters. Efficiency is related to query processing time. Query processing time can be divided in time spent at the base station devising the best query scheme, i.e., which (sub-)queries to actually submit to the WSN, and time spent within the WSN forwarding the query and collecting the results. To simplify our analysis we assume the latter is proportional to the query cost, i.e., a higher cost means more traffic in the network which implies more complex scheduling of messages and the like. Thus, we concentrate on the time spent within the base station, which turns out to be dominated by the Query Optimizer module. Since searching for the best configuration $\langle P'', \Theta \rangle$ is the most intensive process during query optimization, we measure efficiency by the number of states explored during the search for the cost-wise optimal (or good) configuration. We also make the simplifying assumption that a query is completely processed much faster than the time elapsed between incoming queries, which we believe could be in the order of a few seconds vs. several minutes, respectively. Likewise we assume that the time interval after which cached data becomes invalid is larger than the time it takes to process a query; otherwise any cached data would be trivially of no use.

Regarding effectiveness we used the estimated energy cost, as per the cost model, as the measure of interest. We first used an exhaustive –hence impractical– search to find the optimum solution, i.e., the configuration $\langle P'', \Theta \rangle$, which yields the least expensive query processing plan. This optimal cost was used throughout as our baseline. Then we obtained the energy cost of the solutions obtained by heuristic approaches presented in Section 3. Even though the cost model estimates the query cost in nJ (nano Joules), in the figures that follow we report the average relative loss in terms of energy cost, for each of our proposed solutions, with respect to energy cost by the baseline configuration.

Given that the search space is relatively large and in order to make the experiments practical we stopped the exhaustive search when it reached $2^{13}$ states, which was typically at least one order of magnitude larger than the number of states explored by the heuristic searches. (In the few cases where this maximum limit was reached the best solution found thus far was adopted as the optimal one.) We compared the cost of all solutions against two straightforward choices: not using any cached data at all (i.e., submitting the original query without any further processing) or using all of the relevant cached data. As expected, only in very rare cases not using cache at all was the best option, and in the interest of space, we do not detail these results any further. Nonetheless, recall that Algorithms GrF and GrE, cannot, by their very design, yield a solution that is worse than using all or using none of the relevant cached data, respectively.

In order to adhere to the cost model's assumptions, in all of our experiments we assume the sensor nodes are uniformly distributed in the monitored area, and so are the centroids of the queries. The location of the base station is fixed in the center of the monitored area. (Experiments not shown here revealed the location of base station does not have a qualitative influence in the results.) For the sake of completeness Table 1 presents the values (borrowed from [9]) which are used in the cost model for the WSN in our experiments.

We focus on studying the impact of the following parameters in our solutions. By varying the number of sensors ($N$) we influence the sensor density of the WSN, and consequently amount of data that flows when a query is processed. The larger the $N$ the more important role of the query optimizer will become and the heavier its workload. Even though the base station can be realistic considered to be less constrained in terms of resources, one must consider a limited amount of storage for cached data. We denote this parameter by $M$ and investigated its effect on the simulated scenarios. The average size of the queries ($S$) play an important role in our scenario. Larger queries will yield a larger number of intersections with cached queries, thus more opportunity for optimization, which, however, comes at a cost (searching process). We assume

**Table 1.** Parameters used in WSN model

| **Parameter** | **Used Values** |
|---|---|
| Monitored area | 1000 m$\times$1000 m |
| Cost to transmit 1 bit over $d$ meters | $50 + 10 \times d^2$ nJ |
| Cost to receive 1 bit | 50 nJ |
| Wireless range radio | 50 m |
| Query message size | 32 bytes |
| Answer tuple size ⟨value, timestamp⟩ | 8 bytes |

**Table 2.** Parameters investigated and respective values (bold face denotes default values)

| Parameter | Used Values |
|---|---|
| $N$ (# of sensors × 1,000) | 1, 2, **3**, 4, 5 |
| $M$ (# of cached queries × 100) | 1, 2, **3**, 4, 5 |
| $S$ (query size as % of total area) | 0.01, 0.25, **1**, 4, 16 |
| $V$ (validity period in timestamps) | 10, 20, **30**, 40, 50 |

that the size (area) of the queries follows an exponential distribution in order to accommodate for eventual relatively larger queries. The last parameter we investigate is the validity period of cached data ($V$), which reflects how dynamic and fresh the cached data is. In order to evaluate how each of those affected the algorithms' performance we adopted a *ceteris paribus* assumption, i.e., when varying one parameter all others were kept constant at their default values. All values used for the parameters above are listed in Table 2.

Before we started accumulating statistics about the algorithms performance we run the experiments for a "cold-start" period where enough queries to fill the cache were posed. Whenever a query was posed, i.e., during the cold-start or afterwards, algorithms for maintaining cache consistency were used [14], and when the cache run out of space the query closest to expiration, along with its respective dataset, was evicted.

In the figures that follow we use the following convention to denote the origin of the data: "FC" denotes results obtained by using the full content of the cache without any optimization, "OPT" denotes results obtained via the exhaustive search, "B+B" denotes results obtained using Algorithm 1., and "GrF" and "GrE" denote results obtained using Algorithms GrF and GrE respectively. The reported figures are average values obtained for each setting during consecutive timestamps, where 10 queries were posed in each such timestamp.

In our first set of experiments we set all parameters to their default values and compared how often the cost obtained by each of the heuristic algorithms was greater to the optimal cost found by the exhaustive search and also how much faster it was. We found that B+B's solution cost was worse than OPT's only 7% of the time, while GrF and GrE were worse about 1/3 of the time respectively. Regarding speedup, all heuristics consumed less than 2% of the time required by OPT's exhaustive search, with B+B being about 1.5% slower than GrF and GrE (which were virtually equally fast).

Looking further into this experiment, Figure 3 shows the histograms of the losses by all heuristics with respect to OPT. B+B's cost advantage is quite clear; it is not only very seldom worse than OPT's but in about half of the (very few) cases where it is worse than OPT it is less than 1% worse. The other approaches are, as one would expect, less robust, in particular GrE—recall our previous discussion on the effect of bad choices by GrE being more pronounced than bad choices by GrF.

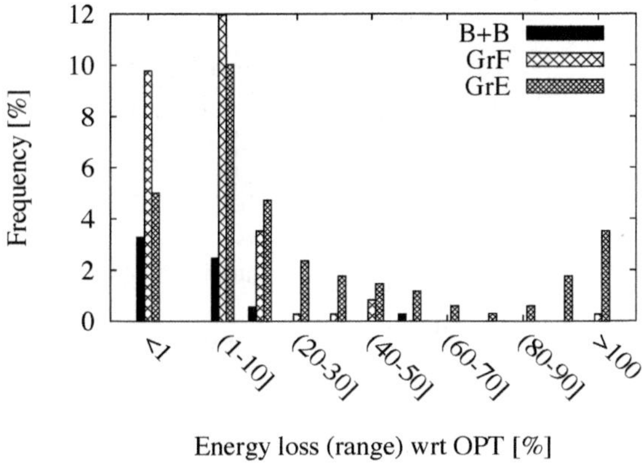


**Fig. 3.** Distribution of all approaches' energy cost losses with respect to the optimal one. (Note the first and last columns have different ranges.)

**Table 3.** How each approach performed with respect to using no cache

| Algorithm | Better | Tied | Worse |
|---|---|---|---|
| B+B | 71% | 28% | 1% |
| GrF | 67% | 30% | 3% |
| GrE | 70% | 30% | N/A |

Next we investigated how the heuristic approaches compare with respect to the two straightforward optimization-free alternatives to process $Q$: using no cache ($P'' = \emptyset$) or using all of it ($P'' = P'$). From Table 3 it is clear that using no cache is very rarely a worthwhile option. For instance, in over 2/3 of the experiments all heuristics found query plans yielding a energy cost often 50% less expensive than processing the full unchanged query. When using all of the cache, Table 4 reveals that none of the heuristics was able to remain as consistently superior as the opposite case. Nonethless B+B was strictly better almost half of the time and over 40% of the time it obtained gains upwards of 20%. Therefore using $P'' = P'$ may be an option that should to be considered depending on the application scenario. However, we observe that in an environment such as WSN, every opportunity to save energy must be seized, and all our experiments seem to indicate that, compared to the two optmization-free alternatives, the B+B heuristic is able to accomplish that at the expense of very minimal overhead.

The main conclusion at this point is that it is clear that there is merit in our claim, i.e., that it is worth performing the optimization search in order to determine good sets $P''$ and $\Theta$. Next, we investigate how robust each of the proposed solutions are with respect to the parameters in Table 2.

The results obtained by varying $N$ are displayed in Figures 4(a) and (b). On average B+B's solution is sub-optimal by a factor smaller than 2% for all values of $N$, and it obtained exploring typically less than 20 states as opposed

**Table 4.** How well each approach performed with respect to using full cache

| Algorithm | Better | Tied | Worse |
|---|---|---|---|
| B+B | 46% | 54% | N/A |
| GrF | 27% | 73% | N/A |
| GrE | 30% | 46% | 24% |

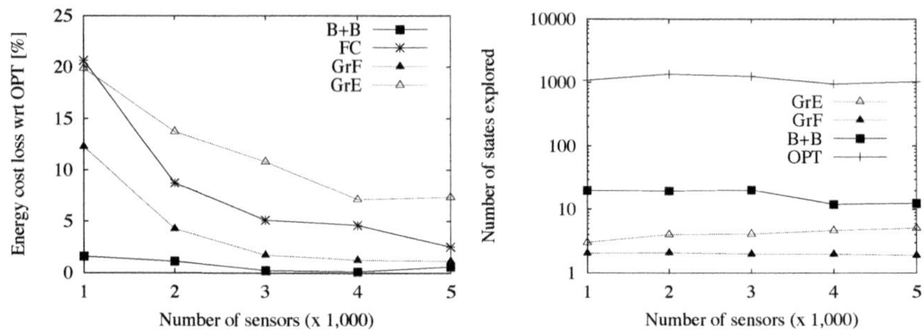


(a) Effectiveness (b) Efficiency

**Fig. 4.** Effectiveness and efficiency when varying number of number of sensors

to over 1,000 ones explored by the exhaustive search. Both greedy algorithms are driven by the size of the intersections only. In scenarios with low sensor densities (lower $N$) this turns out to be somewhat misleading and affects their effectiveness noticeably. Nonetheless they are both faster than B+B, requiring no more than a few states to reach a local optimum. The results also seem to suggest that while B+B is a good compromise in general, for very dense networks (large values of $N$) GrF may actually be a better one (though one must consider that greedy approaches are typically less stable).

In order to simplify our analysis we measure the cache size ($M$) as number of queries. Note that given the values in Tables 1 and 2, it is easy to estimate the average actual size (in Bytes) of queries and their answers. When varying $M$ we observe that while B+B is again stable and very effective, GrE tend to lose more when dealing with larger caches (Figure 5(a)). The reason is that while a larger cache offers more opportunities for optimization it also opens the door to more bad choices due to greedy short-sightedness. More interestingly however, using FC becomes a less attractive alternative with the increase of $M$, confirming our claim that trivially using $P'' = P'$ may often not be worthwhile. Given that ideally one would like to use as much storage as possible (within reason) for the cache, our results suggest that the optimization becomes increasingly important as the cardinality of $P'$ grows. Among the greedy approaches GrF is actually an interesting option, unlike GrE. In terms of efficiency (Figure 5(b)), the number of states explored grows with $M$ since a larger cache yields larger sets of candidates queries for re-use, thus more choices to be evaluated in the

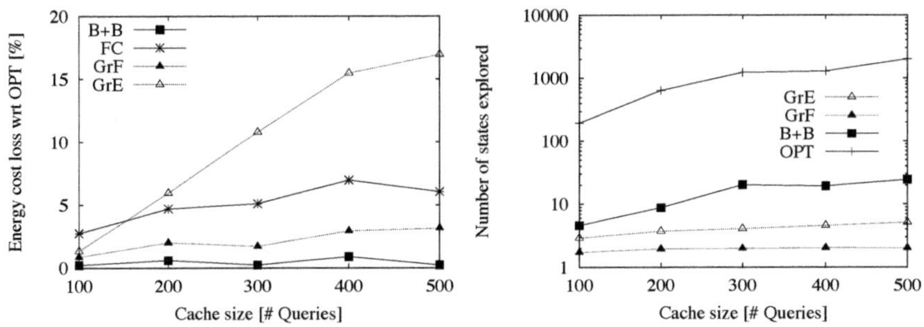


(a) Effectiveness (b) Efficiency

**Fig. 5.** Effectiveness and efficiency when varying number of cached queries

optimization process. As expected the greedy approaches are practically not affected in terms of efficiency.

Figures 6(a) and (b) show the effect of varying the size of the query. As before B+B offers very good effectiveness with best overall efficiency. With the increase of $S$ it is clear that GrE's effectiveness becomes rather unacceptable, due again to poor (greedy) optimization choices. On the other hand, using FC turns out to be a not bad choice. As the size of the queries increase the optimization quickly becomes a harder problem. This is due to a larger number of intersections and a large number of configurations to be considered, and this is clearly reflected in Figure 6(b). One aspect that is not transparent in our experiments is that when queries become very large at some point the monitored area will be eventually fully covered by cached queries (unless they have a very short validity period). Hence, a rather trivial solution to the optimization problem is to use all of the cache the area of the new query will be fully covered by cached data.

Our last experiment was varying the validity period ($V$). Figures 7(a) and (b) do not show a very clear dependence between this parameter and overall performance. This is not unexpected, since while having long lived queries can potentially allow for better optimization, the number of cached queries is limited (by $M$), i.e., queries still valid will eventually need to be evicted, forcefully limiting the search space. (Recall that we assume that the data's validity period is larger than the time it takes to process a query.)

In summary, it is clear that the branch-and-bound optimization process is able to almost always offer identical or very close to optimal query plans at the low cost of exploring only a very small number of configurations $\langle P'', \Theta \rangle$. While on the one hand one cannot deny that using all the relevant valid cached data is often a reasonable compromise, in a domain, such as WSNs, the chance of saving every bit of energy, as opportunistic as it may be, must be taken. Even relatively small savings over the long term are worth the optimization overhead (which incidentally has no impact in the energy budget of the network as it is performed in the base station).

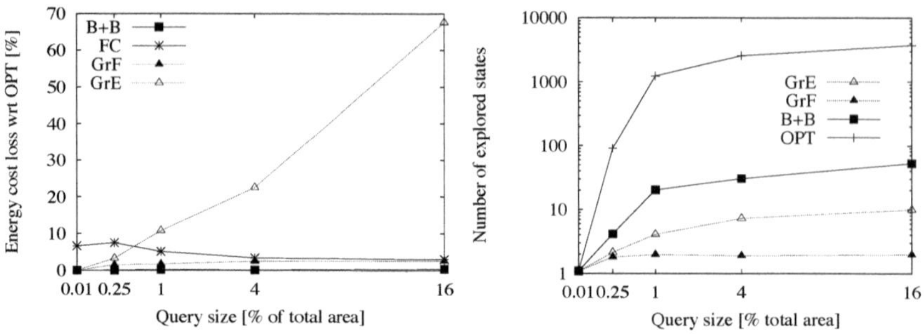


(a) Effectiveness (b) Efficiency

**Fig. 6.** Effectiveness and efficiency when varying query size

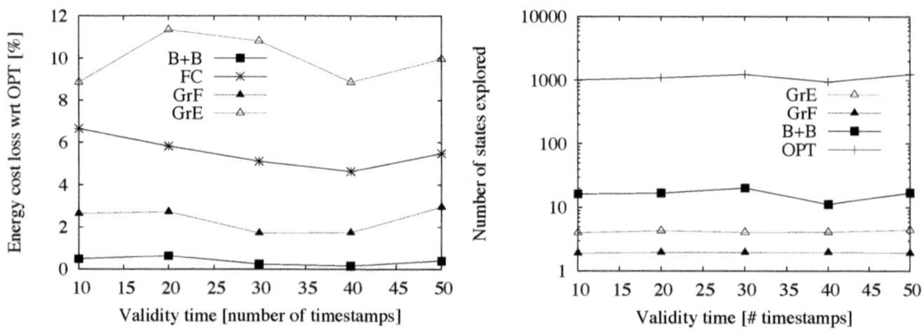


(a) Effectiveness (b) Efficiency

**Fig. 7.** Effectiveness and efficiency when varying queries's validity time

# 5 Related Work

Data caching has been a well-known mechanism for enhancing query throughput in database systems in general for quite some time [15]. In a typical setting, the cache offers much faster access smaller than the main storage, and it is used so that requests to frequently accessed data can performed more efficiently.

Cache strategies can be classified into two groups [16]: physical and logical caching. Physical caching, arguably the most common one, replicates in the (faster) cache pages or tuples identified as hot spots. In order to identify hot spots, heuristics based on access frequency and cost/benefit analyses can be used. Logical caching, on the other hand, replicates data that belong to query results. For example, a logical caching mechanism where the main idea is to use query semantics for organizing the cache was proposed in [17]. Our approach may be likened to that one in the sense that the authors model cached data and queries as "geometric" constraints onto the data space, whereas in our case we deal with queries as actual polygons in the Euclidean space. Another difference is that our approach aims at minimizing data flowing in the WSN using past queries whereas in [17] the authors aim at optimizing cache usage and replacement in data servers using the query semantics.

The context in which we consider the use of cache, namely WSN, is fairly novel itself, and a relatively small number of papers have been published in this area. Most of them are related to the networking rather than the database aspect of the problem. In that context data caching can be applied to minimizing packet transmissions in the network and consequently reducing power consumption. For instance, in [18] the authors propose a strategy that emulates a data caching mechanism by predicting when a sensor's observed data will change. Such a technique aims at avoiding requests to redundant data but it might impact negatively the correctness of query results, because some unpredicted change may not be propagated in the WSN. Another strategy proposed in the same paper is to aggregate the flow of redundant (replicated) values in a single message. Again, this may have an adverse effect on the query result as a single message failure becomes responsible for several values from different nodes being lost. While link failures can always affect query processing in a WSN, we minimize their effect by placing the cache on the base station which needs to relay the query results to the user anyway.

In [19] the authors discuss how to explore a natural hierarchy of entities within a WSN using an XML framework. One of the main focus of that work is on the so-called Query-Evaluate-Gather technique which enables one to not only find relevant queried data within a node but also how to gather the missing parts. We, on the other hand, assume that no data is cached on the (resource-challenged) sensor nodes. More importantly the authors focus only on improving query throughput, ignoring the energy cost factor, whereas in this paper, by virtue of having the cache at the base station, we focus on minimizing the energy cost of query processing in the WSN.

A work that assumes a context closer to ours, i.e., it is database-oriented in nature and geared towards an WSN has been presented in [20]. The authors assume that the WSN uses a tree-based routing protocol and propose that several nodes in the network to be used for caching data. The problem of choosing these so-called cache-nodes reduces to finding a Steiner Minimal Tree (SMT), i.e., a tree that connects all points with minimal length. Since finding an SMT is a NP-Hard problem, the authors propose a sub-optimal solution, called Steiner Data Caching Trees (SDCT). Unfortunately the bottleneck of the proposal is that it is as robust as the cache-nodes, i.e., once they become unavailable (which can happen for a variety of reasons), not only data is lost but also another SDCT needs to be reconstructed from scratch. By relying on the base-station our approach is relatively free from side-effects when individual nodes become unavailable.

Finally, Galpin et al discuss how to compile/optimize queries within a WSN, e.g., employing well-known techniques such operator re-ordering and query re-writing at the network and node level [21]. The main difference between their contributions and ours is that we focus of re-using previously cached data in a (sub-)optimal way and delegate the actual query processing to the in-network query processing engine, whereas in [21] the authors are not concerned with pre-existing data in a cache, rather they focus on optimizing the query from a in-network perspective. Clearly, both proposals are complementary and orthogonal in the sense that one can (and should) first optimize the use of existing data (using our proposal) and then optimize the actual query processing (using the approach in [21]).

## 6 Conclusions

We have investigated the problem of how to effectively exploit a data cache at the base station of a WSN. The problem calls for answers to two sub-problems: (1) how to select which cached queries to use, and depending on those, (2) how to create a query cost-wise good set of sub-queries that will be submitted to the WSN. Given the highly combinatorial nature of the problem we proposed a few heuristic approaches. The best alternative of the one we investigated, which is based on a branch-and-bound optimization search, is (a) very efficient, devising a query plan typically two orders of magnitude faster than an exhaustive search, and (b) quite effective, yielding query energy cose typically less than 2% and no more than 10% over the optimal one. Finally, even though this work re-used the query processing framework presented in [9], the solution we propose does not depend on the same. Rather, any approach can be used as long as it provides the cost model that is used to guide the search for an optimized query "plan". We are currently working on extending the ideas in this paper to address other types of queries, e.g., aggregate queries.

## References

1. Brooks, R., Ramanathan, P., Sayeed, A.: Distributed target classification and tracking in sensor networks. In: Proc. of the IEEE, pp. 1163–1171 (2003)
2. Perrig, A., Stankovic, J., Wagner, D.: Security in wireless sensor networks. Commun. ACM 47(6), 53–57 (2004)
3. Szewczyk, R., et al.: Habitat monitoring with sensor networks. Commun. ACM 47(6), 34–40 (2004)
4. Intanagonwiwat, C., et al.: Directed diffusion for wireless sensor networking. IEEE/ACM Trans. Netw. 11(1), 2–16 (2003)
5. Madden, S., et al.: TAG: A tiny aggregation service for ad-hoc sensor networks. In: Proc. of OSDI (2002)
6. Silberstein, A., Munagala, K., Yang, J.: Energy-efficient monitoring of extreme values in sensor networks. In: Proc. of SIGMOD, pp. 169–180 (2006)
7. Preparata, F., Shamos, M.: Computational Geometry - An Introduction. Springer, Heidelberg (1985)
8. Beckmann, N., et al.: The R*-tree: An efficient and robust access method for points and rectangles. In: Proc. of SIGMOD, pp. 322–331 (1990)
9. Coman, A., Sander, J., Nascimento, M.: Adaptive processing of historical spatial range queries in peer-to-peer sensor networks. Distributed and Parallel Databases 22(2-3), 133–163 (2007)

10. Vatti, B.: A generic solution to polygon clipping. Commun. ACM 35(7), 56–63 (1992)
11. Soltan, V., Gorpinevich, A.: Minimum dissection of a rectilinear polygon with arbitrary holes into rectangles. Discrete & Computational Geometry 9, 57–79 (1993)
12. Tseng, I.L., Postula, A.: An efficient algorithm for partitioning parameterized polygons into rectangles. In: Proc. of GLSVLSI, pp. 366–371 (2006)
13. Gudmundsson, J., Husfeldt, T., Levcopoulos, C.: Lower bounds for approximate polygon decomposition and minimum gap. Inf. Process. Lett. 81(3), 137–141 (2002)
14. Nascimento, M., Alencar, R., Brayner, A.: Optimizing query processing in cache-aware wireless sensor networks. Technical Report TR 09-05, Dept. of Computing Science, Univ. of Alberta (2009)
15. Effelsberg, W., Härder, T.: Principles of database buffer management. ACM Trans. Database Syst. 9(4), 560–595 (1984)
16. Kossmann, D., Franklin, M., Drasch, G.: Cache investment: integrating query optimization and distributed data placement. ACM Trans. Database Syst. 25(4), 517–558 (2000)
17. Dar, S., et al.: Semantic data caching and replacement. In: Proc. of VLDB, pp. 330–341 (1996)
18. Rahman, M., Hussain, S.: Effective caching in wireless sensor network. In: Proc. of AINA Workshops (1), pp. 43–47 (2007)
19. Deshpande, A., et al.: Cache-and-query for wide area sensor databases. In: Proc. of SIGMOD, pp. 503–514 (2003)
20. Prabh, S., Abdelzaher, T.: Energy-conserving data cache placement in sensor networks. ACM Trans. on Sensor Networks 1(2), 178–203 (2005)
21. Galpin, I., et al.: Comprehensive optimization of declarative sensor network queries. In: Proc. of SSDBM, pp. 339–360 (2009)

# Approximate Query Answering and Result Refinement on XML Data

Katja Seidler[1], Eric Peukert[1], Gregor Hackenbroich[1], and Wolfgang Lehner[2]

[1] SAP Research CEC Dresden, Chemnitzer Str. 48, 01187 Dresden, Germany
{firstname.lastname}@sap.com
[2] Technische Universität Dresden, 01062 Dresden, Germany
wolfgang.lehner@tu-dresden.de

**Abstract.** Today, many economic decisions are based on the fast analysis of XML data. Yet, the time to process analytical XML queries is typically high. Although current XML techniques focus on the optimization of query processing, none of these support early approximate feedback as possible in relational Online Aggregation systems.

In this paper, we introduce a system that provides fast estimates to XML aggregation queries. While processing, these estimates and the assigned confidence bounds are constantly improving. In our evaluation, we show that without significantly increasing the overall execution time our system returns accurate guesses of the final answer long before traditional systems are able to produce output.

## 1 Introduction

The data volume and growing rates of today's business systems make approximate query processing an inevitable technique for fast analyses. Online Aggregation (OLA) has been proposed as an approach for analytical processing of relational data. In OLA, the database system quickly returns approximate answers to aggregation queries together with statistical guarantees on the error bounds. This computing paradigm allows users to more flexibly explore data: Query processing may be terminated at any time once sufficient accuracy has been reached; if exact answers are needed, they can be computed with little overhead as compared to traditional systems.

In this paper, we show how OLA can be performed on XML data. We present a novel query processing system—referred to as XML Database Online (XDBO) System—which performs OLA on XML data in a scalable way. We have been faced with the following main challenges: Query processing on XML data is heavily dominated by the evaluation of so called twig patterns. This pattern matching process involves a multitude of structural joins and is a major bottleneck within XML query processing. Compared to relational databases the queries differ in both the number and the kind of joins. Additionally, in current XML processing systems an aggregate cannot be returned until the whole structural join operation is completed. This is a time-consuming task, especially for complex queries and/or queries over large data sets. We address these challenges and make the following contributions:

M. Gertz and B. Ludäscher (Eds.): SSDBM 2010, LNCS 6187, pp. 78–86, 2010.

- We propose novel operators for the random and non-blocking selection and join of query path patterns.
- We show how sideways information passing can be used for fast approximate query answering and introduce the architecture of the XDBO System.
- With an extensive evaluation of a prototypical implementation we demonstrate the feasibility and the efficiency of our approach.

Furthermore, we point out optimization possibilities and present our prototype in the long version of this paper [10].

## 2 Indexing and Pattern Matching

In this section, we introduce the foundations of our proposed XDBO System that are based on the following requirements of OLA: First, for a scalable query processing and for fast first answers the pattern matching must be performed in a *non-blocking fashion*, and second, to guarantee statistical valid estimates and error bounds XML elements have to be processed in *random order*. We now describe two novel pattern matching operators and a special index structure that are designed to meet the given requirements. The operators reflect the general procedure of the approximate query processing in the XDBO System: Instead of processing a query pattern as a whole, we decompose it into a set of query path patterns. We identify all path patterns of the query and remember the positions of branching nodes that connect individual paths. With a novel selection operator (Section 2.2) we search for solutions to query path patterns; a special index structure (Section 2.1) facilitates its efficiency. Finally, a join operator (Section 2.3) connects the solutions of individual path patterns.

Figure 1 illustrates the main steps, starting from the query pattern, all identified query path patterns and the constructed execution plan for a count query over the XPath expression `//a[.//b[c]/d]//e[f]/g`.

### 2.1 Element Path Index

Traditional XML database systems utilize special numbering schemes to speed up query processing: They label all elements of an XML document, often encode the structural relationship into the labels and store them for each element into an index structure. The index is then used to accelerate a pattern matching operation. To support pattern matching in a system that meets the OLA requirements a special index is needed. Based on a thorough state-of-the-art analysis, we decided to utilize the extended Dewey numbering (EDN) scheme [7]. In addition to the encoding of the structural relationship, the EDN scheme encodes—with the help of a Finite State Transducer (FST)—the whole root-to-node path of each element into the label. Therefore, only the labels of the leaf node element of a query pattern need to be accessed during pattern matching. The solutions of the query pattern $//a//b/c$ can be found by examining all labels of $c$ elements and check if they match the query pattern. Hence, only the decoding of EDN labels and the comparison of the retrieved path patterns with the query path pattern have to be done. This enormously speeds up and simplifies pattern matching.

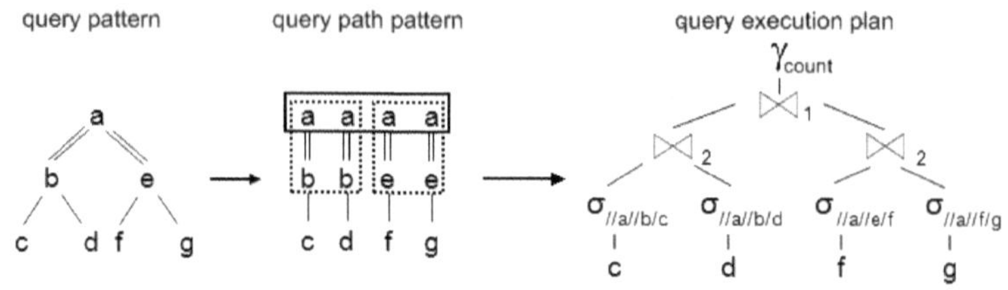


**Fig. 1.** Generation of the execution plan

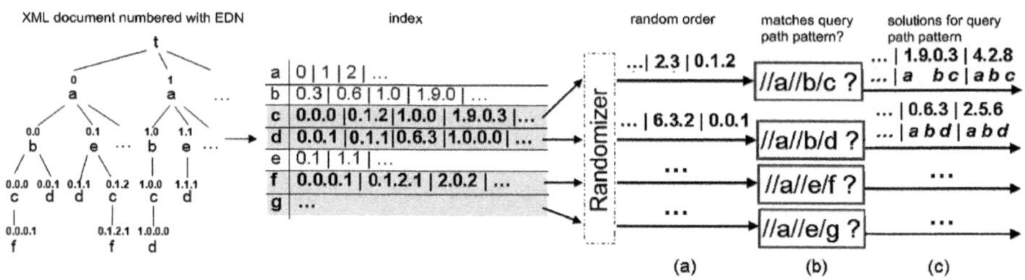


**Fig. 2.** Selection process

### 2.2 Path Pattern Selection Operator

Based on an index that stores EDN labels for each element type, we propose a novel selection operator $\sigma_{XPath}$ (see Figure 1). The characteristic of this operator is the processing of input elements—the EDN labels from the index—in random order. On the right part of Figure 2, we show how this is achieved (the XML document and the corresponding index are given in the left part): The element labels of the leaf nodes of the query are extracted from the index in random order (a). If the index structure does not guarantee randomness a randomizer has to be used. During the selection process (b) the operator translates each label of the random input stream with the FST into a root-to-node path and compares it with the query path pattern. If there is a match a solution is found. For further processing, not only the selected labels but also the positions of the query path pattern elements are memorized (c).

### 2.3 Path Pattern Join Operator

To find solutions for the whole query pattern the results of the individual query path patterns need to be joined at branching nodes. Branching nodes (specifically their position *pos* in the path pattern) are defined by the join operator $\bowtie_{pos}$ (see Figure 1). The join process is much more complex than the relational join operation. Rather than comparing columns of different tuples positions of labels are compared to join the records. Two labels can only be joined if they coincide from root position up to the position of the associated branching node.

# 3 Query Processing

This section describes how the XDBO System effectively uses the presented index and the two pattern matching operations to provide early estimates of the final aggregate of a query. To achieve high scalability we employ the concept of sideways information passing. According to this concept, operations at a single level of a query plan are performed concurrently while allowing to share some of its intermediate results with other operations at the same level. Thereby, preliminary result tuples can be generated on the fly on each layer of the query plan and are used to provide an estimate for the final query answer. Sideways information passing was introduced as a design paradigm for OLA of relational data [5]. Due to space limitations, we will only give an overview how sideways information passing and related design principles can be adapted and combined with EDN to allow scalable OLA of XML data. A detailed description can be found in the long version of this paper [10].

As in [5], we refer to all of the joins at one level of a query plan, i.e., joins that are evaluated concurrently, as a *levelwise step*. The query processing starts at the bottom level and proceeds in ascending order. By passing information among the join operations of a levelwise step $i$ an estimate $N_i$ of the final answer of the aggregation query is maintained. This estimate becomes more and more accurate as the levelwise step progresses. At any time, all available estimates $N_i$ are combined into a single estimate for the answer which will more and more converge to the exact query result.

## 3.1 Levelwise Steps

Each levelwise step is partitioned into two phases: a scan and a merge phase. The scan phase sorts the labels of all individual path solutions and finds early solutions for the whole query pattern. In the merge phase, the actual join is performed. To ensure scalability the set of path pattern solutions that are pipelined into the join operations are divided into equal-sized runs. The size of the runs is adjusted to ensure that the join can be performed in main memory.

Both phases are executed analog to the DBO System [5], but instead of tuples results of path pattern operations are processed. Figure 3 illustrates the start of the scan phase of the first levelwise step. Path pattern solutions are read into memory in a round-robin fashion by the already introduced selection operator ($i = 1$) or by the merge phase of the preceding levelwise step ($i > 1$). Subsequently, they are sorted by a hash function that only takes into account the parts of the labels that are significant for the join operation (specified by *pos*). To guarantee an unbiased label sorting the hash function is initialized with a different seed for each single binary join operation. After each sorting, all records being present in memory are immediately joined, thus, yielding early overall join results to the join conditions specified in the query pattern. Based on these early results, estimates and error bounds for the final result are generated at each step of the query execution. Due to space limitations, we omit the explanation of the estimate computation here and refer to [10].

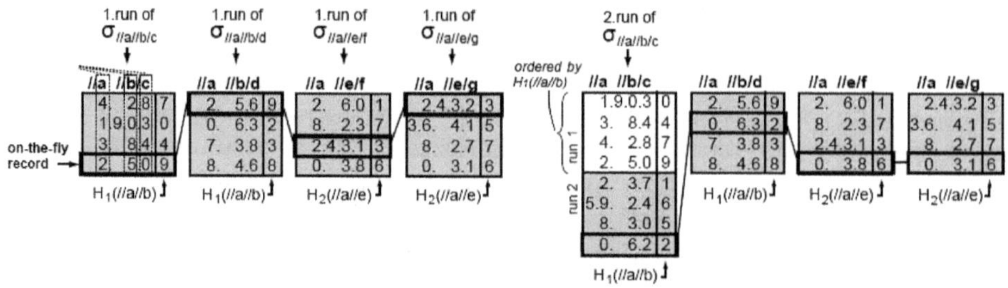


**Fig. 3.** Scan phase of the first levelwise step

The merge phase is directly connected with the scan phase of the subsequent levelwise step. It provides the following two characteristics: (i) it guarantees a (semi-)random output order and (ii) it produces output partitioned into equal-sized runs that fit into main memory. The partitioning is controlled by the values of the hash function from the scan phase. Based on equal-sized hash ranges the merge process produces runs of joined pattern in a round-robin fashion. The results of the join operations are directly streamed into the next levelwise step.

# 4 The XDBO System

We now present the architecture of the XDBO System whose main concepts were implemented in a Java prototype. As shown in the next section, this prototype is able to demonstrate the feasibility and the efficiency of our solution. However, it is designed as proof of concept, and thus, limited in its functionality (see [10] for restrictions). The XDBO System comprises two main parts which are the Import and Indexing Component (Part (I) of Figure 4) and the core XML Database System (Part II). They are supplemented by an underlying index storage.

**Import and Indexing.** The Import and Indexing Component comprises three sub-components: the Data Import Interface, the Numbering Component and a Finite State Transducer (FST) for the EDN. The Data Import Interface is used to load XML data into the system. The Numbering Component creates an element path index based on the FST that is set up for an XML document or a predefined XML schema. For each element type, this index lists the EDN labels of all nodes. Additional text indexes are created for the values of text nodes.

**Database System.** The database system follows a layered architecture with three components: a Query Execution Plan (QEP) Generator, an Execution Component and a Data Access Component. A user interface for posting queries against the system using structural XML query languages can be realized on top of XDBO. The QEP Generator accepts a structured query pattern as input and generates a QEP; it converts the given query pattern into join trees of query paths. The QEP is then handed over to the Execution Component which manages the processing of the given join tree. Joins are executed in a levelwise

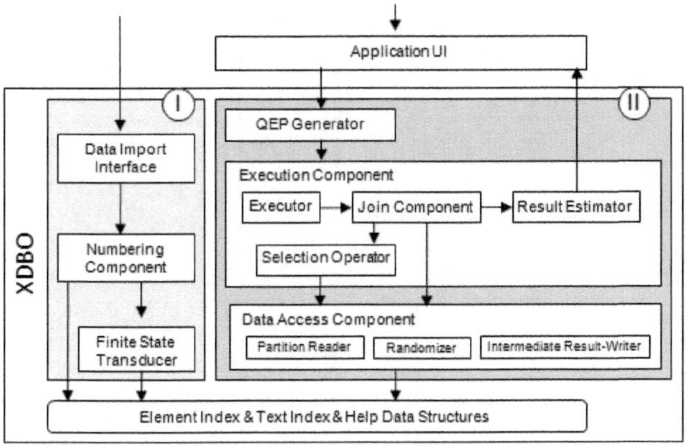


**Fig. 4.** Architecture of the XDBO System

fashion as described in Section 3.1. Additional query optimization is possible but is left for future work. On-the-fly records produced throughout the query execution are used to estimate the final aggregate with the help of the Result Estimator. All operators retrieve and store data via the Data Access Component which offers a randomization and partitioned reading functionality.

## 5 Evaluation

For the evaluation of the XDBO System, we used different sized XML documents (113 MB to 11.1 GB) generated with the XMark [9] data generator (scaling factors 1 to 100) and compared main characteristics of XDBO with a scalable implementation of the TwigStack System [2]. All experiments were conducted on a 2.4 GHz processor with 4 GB RAM running a 32-bit Windows Vista Enterprise operating system. Besides the evaluation of query processing presented as follows we had a look on the index performance, the impact of the document size and the application of the proposed optimizations. These detailed results are skipped here due to space constraints and can be found in [10].

To evaluate the query execution performance we ran several `COUNT` queries with different characteristics (selection rate, size of intermediate results, number of branching nodes) on the different sized XMark documents and picked out three of them for this paper; the respective query patterns Q1-Q3 can be found in [10]. We ran each query three times and—as each execution of a query will result in a different estimation chain which prevents averaging the results—we picked the one with the medial total execution time.

Overall, the evaluation shows that the XDBO Systems generates good estimates with confidence intervals decreasing over time. Furthermore, accurate estimates are produced long before the TwigStack System finishes execution.

**Confidence interval ratio.** First, we analyzed the relative confidence interval width defined as the ratio of the 95% confidence interval width and the query

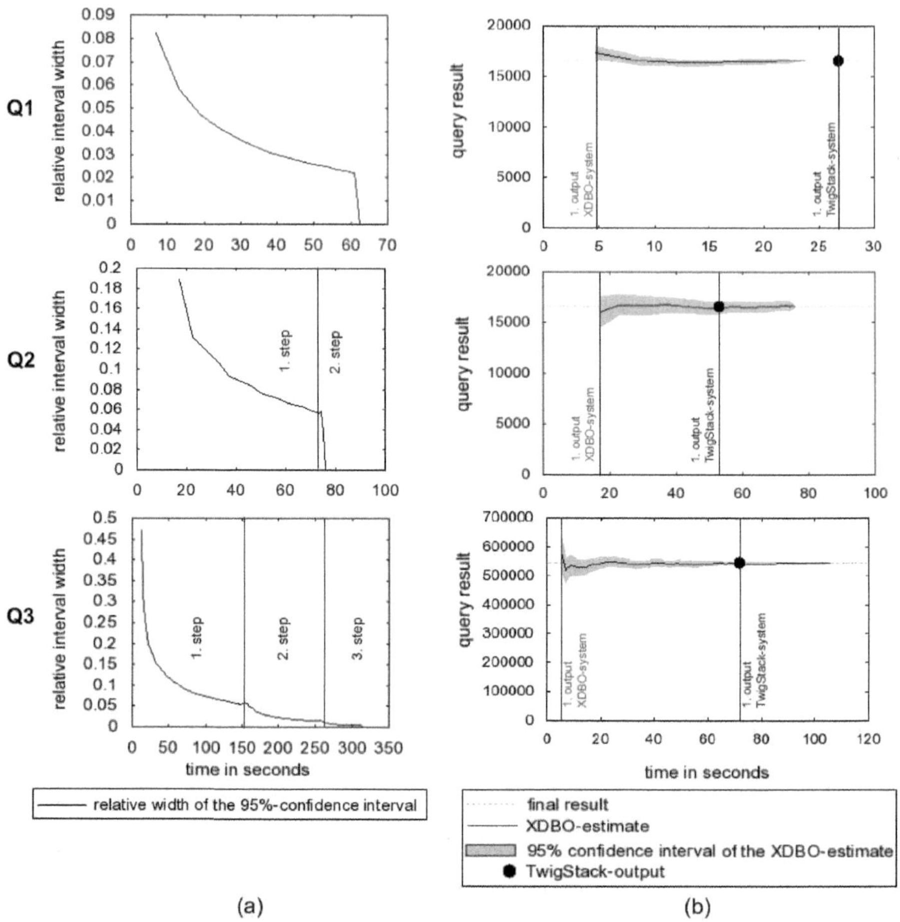


**Fig. 5.** Time evaluation of relative confidence interval width and comparison of XDBO and TwigStack System (for 2.8 GB XMark document)

estimate. Figure 5(a) shows the relative confidence interval width as a function of the processing time for a 2.8 GB XMark document (XMark scaling factor 25). A value of 0.1 implies that the 95% confidence interval equals 10% of the current estimate. The relative interval width decreases with time for all queries. The very small confidence interval of the query Q1 demonstrates very accurate estimates. In comparison, the queries with branching nodes (Q2 and Q3) show larger relative interval widths, especially at the early phase of query processing. However the interval width quickly decreases and therewith estimates are getting accurate soon. First optimization approaches to address the limitations of the relatively wide starting confidence intervals can be found in [10].

**Comparison of XDBO and TwigStack.** Figure 5(b) shows how the XDBO query execution compares with the TwigStack System for the 2.8 GB XMark document. The TwigStack System returns the exact query result while XDBO outputs early estimates and error bounds as well as the exact result at the end of the query evaluation. For all queries the XDBO System was able to give first output before the TwigStack System did. For the query without branching nodes (Q1) the XDBO System not only provided fast accurate estimates but also finished before the TwigStack System was able to generate an answer. Moreover, an aggregate with a relative confidence interval width lower than 10% was produced in less than 20% of the time needed by the TwigStack System to yield the result. The queries with branching nodes required longer total execution time, but still returned accurate guesses long before the TwigStack System produced output.

## 6 Related Work

In this section, we give an overview over the different areas of related work.

**Online Aggregation.** Online Aggregation was introduced by Hellerstein et al. in [4]. A major technical challenge in OLA is to combine efficient join processing with unbiased guaranteed accuracy estimates. To address this task various algorithms such as the Ripple Join [3] or the SMS Join [6] have been proposed. Jermaine et al. [5] observed that the result inaccuracy for these algorithms significantly increases with the number of tables to be joined; their DBO System ensures scalable query processing for OLA by sharing information across relational operations at different levels of the query plan. Especially from the DBO System we adopted some concepts; however, we made significant effort to adapt these concepts to the fairly different style of query processing of XML data.

**Indexing and numbering schemes for XML data.** Indexes are a well-known technique to speed up query processing; clearly, this also holds for XML data as shown in [8]. Additionally, to speed up pattern matching a multitude of numbering techniques and algorithms have been proposed [1,7]. They encode structural relationships into labels for each element. The extended Dewey numbering scheme (EDN) [7], that we incorporate for highly efficient path pattern matching, additionally encodes the complete root-to-node paths into the labels.

**Pattern matching.** Recent algorithms for XML pattern matching exploit the characteristics of various numbering schemes to significantly improve the processing speed of structural joins. The first proposed structural join operations [1,2] focus on binary and query path patterns, but suffer from the need of additional stitching steps when applied to more complex query patterns. To process query patterns as a whole several holistic twig join algorithm had been presented [2,7]. While some of the proposed pattern matching algorithms are non-blocking they generally rely on the processing of labels in a sorted order. Like our solution, TJFast [7] exploits the features of the EDN, but does not meet the OLA requirements. Accordingly, none of these algorithms supports early result feedback and processing with guaranteed statistical error bounds.

## 7 Conclusion

In this paper, we presented the concepts and the architecture of a system capable of performing Online Aggregation over XML data. This XDBO System is able to give fast feedback to aggregation queries by approximating and refining the final answer throughout query processing. Additionally, it provides accuracy guarantees by attaching confidence information to the estimates. We introduced a novel query processing approach that splits query patterns into query path patterns; efficient query processing is realized by novel operators for selecting and joining path patterns in combination with an appropriate index structure. For accurate estimates we adapted principles of the DBO engine to the XML query processing. We prototypically implemented the XDBO System to demonstrate the efficiency of our solution. Within our extensive evaluation, we have shown that our system returns accurate guesses of the final answer long before traditional systems are able to produce output. Furthermore, good estimates are gained very fast for query patterns without branching nodes. We identified some limitations for more complex queries, but presented and demonstrated first optimization approaches to address these limitations in the long version of this paper [10].

## References


1. Al-Khalifa, S., Jagadish, H.V., Koudas, N., Patel, J.M., Srivastava, D., Wu, Y.: Structural Joins: A Primitive for Efficient XML Query Pattern Matching. In: ICDE 2002, pp. 141–152 (2002)
2. Bruno, N., Koudas, N., Srivastava, D.: Holistic twig joins: optimal XML pattern matching. In: SIGMOD 2002, pp. 310–321 (2002)
3. Haas, P.J., Hellerstein, J.M.: Ripple joins for online aggregation. ACM SIGMOD Record 28(2), 287–298 (1999)
4. Hellerstein, J.M., Haas, P.J., Wang, H.J.: Online Aggregation. In: SIGMOD 1997, pp. 171–182 (1997)
5. Jermaine, C., Arumugam, S., Pol, A., Dobra, A.: Scalable approximate query processing with the DBO engine. TODS 33(4), 1–54 (2008)
6. Jermaine, C., Dobra, A., Arumugam, S., Joshi, S., Pol, A.: A disk-based join with probabilistic guarantees. In: SIGMOD 2005, pp. 563–574 (2005)
7. Lu, J., Ling, T.W., Chan, C.-Y., Chen, T.: From region encoding to extended dewey: on efficient processing of XML twig pattern matching. In: VLDB 2005, pp. 193–204 (2005)
8. McHugh, J., Widom, J.: Query Optimization for XML. In: VLDB 1999, pp. 315–326 (1999)
9. Schmidt, A., Waas, F., Kersten, M., Carey, M.J., Manolescu, I., Busse, R.: XMark: a benchmark for XML data management. In: VLDB 2002, pp. 974–985 (2002)
10. Seidler, K., Peukert, E., Hackenbroich, G., Lehner, W.: Approximate Query Answering and Result Refinement on XML Data (Full Version). Technical report (2010), `http://wwwdb.inf.tu-dresden.de/publications`

# Efficient and Scalable Method for Processing Top-k Spatial Boolean Queries*

Ariel Cary[1], Ouri Wolfson[2], and Naphtali Rishe[1]

[1] School of Computing and Information Sciences,
Florida International University, Miami, FL 33199, USA
{acary001,rishen}@cis.fiu.edu
[2] Department of Computer Science,
University of Illinois at Chicago, Chicago, IL 60607, USA
wolfson@cs.uic.edu

**Abstract.** In this paper, we present a novel method to efficiently process *top-k* spatial queries with conjunctive Boolean constraints on textual content. Our method combines an R-tree with an inverted index by the inclusion of spatial references in posting lists. The result is a disk-resident, dual-index data structure that is used to proactively prune the search space. R-tree nodes are visited in best-first order. A node entry is placed in the priority queue if there exists at least one object that satisfies the Boolean condition in the subtree pointed by the entry; otherwise, the subtree is not further explored. We show via extensive experimentation with real spatial databases that our method has increased performance over alternate techniques while scaling to large number of objects.

**Keywords:** Geographic databases, spatial keyword query, scalability.

## 1 Introduction

Today's Internet applications typically offer users the ability to associate geographical information to Web content, a process known as "geotagging". For example, Wikipedia has standardized geotagging of their encyclopedia articles and images via templates [6]. Furthermore, technological advances in digital cameras and mobile phones allow users to acquire and associate geospatial coordinates, via built-in GPS devices or Wi-Fi triangulation, to media resources. Additionally, Web content can be automatically paired with geographical coordinates, for instance, exploiting content features, such as place names or street addresses, in combination with gazetteers. Thus, the powerful combination of Internet applications, GPS-enabled devices, and automatic geotagging can potentially generate large amounts of georeferenced content. On the structured end, spatial databases usually contain rich textual descriptions, stored in non-spatial attributes. For example, a database of property parcels may store property's owner name, description, and street address in addition to its coordinates.

* Research was partially supported by NSF DGE-0549489, IIS-0957394, and IIS-0847680.

M. Gertz and B. Ludäscher (Eds.): SSDBM 2010, LNCS 6187, pp. 87–95, 2010.

A key problem recently tackled by the academia and industry is spatial searches with text constraints in geographical collections [3] [7] [11] [9] [10]. For example, in a database of parcels, we may be interested in finding nearby houses to Miami Beach (spatial constraint) that have backyard and are located on Collins Avenue (text constraint). Typically, query keywords are assumed to be conjunctively connected. That is, records containing all query keywords are retrieved. In the general case, text constraints may involve complex combinations of keywords with logical connectives beyond the conjunctive semantics. For instance, in the database of parcels, fire fighters traveling in a truck may want to quickly determine the nearest parcels that have swimming pool and are *not* located in buildings for water replenishment in an emergency.

As geospatial collections increase in size, the demand of efficient processing of spatial queries with text constraints becomes more prevalent. In this paper, we propose a method for efficiently processing top-k nearest neighbor queries with text constraints where keywords are combined with the three basic Boolean operators $AND$, $OR$, and $NOT$. Our method uses an R-tree to guide the spatial search and an inverted file for text content retrieval, which are combined in a novel hybrid spatial–keyword index. The specific contributions of this paper are:

1. We define a *top-k* spatial Boolean (*k-SB*) query that finds nearest neighbor objects satisfying Boolean constraints on keywords combined with conjunctive ($\wedge$), disjunctive ($\vee$), and complement ($\neg$) logical operators.
2. We propose a novel hybrid Spatial-Keyword Index (*SKI*) to efficiently process *k-SB* queries. A salient feature of *SKI* is that it only searches subspaces that do contain objects satisfying the query Boolean predicate.
3. We execute extensive experimentation on an implementation of our method over large spatial databases. Experimental results show that the proposed method has excellent performance and scalability.

Section 2 discusses related work to our research. Section 3 formally defines the problem. Section 4 presents the proposed hybrid indexing approach and query processing algorithms. Experimental study on an implementation of our hybrid index is conducted in Section 5. Section 6 presents our concluding remarks.

## 2 Related Work

The R-tree traversal method in our work is inspired in Hjaltason and Samet's [5] incremental top-k nearest neighbor algorithm using R-trees [1]. Performance improvements on the original R-tree work have been proposed, e.g. R*-tree [13] , R+-tree [14], and Hilbert R-tree [15]. Any of these variants can replace the R-tree index used in the proposed hybrid spatial keyword index without modifying our search algorithms. In information retrieval, inverted files are arguably the most efficient index structure for free-text search [2] [12].

The problem of retrieving spatial objects satisfying non-spatial constraints has been studied in the recent past. Park and Kim [10] proposed RS-trees, a combination of R-trees and signature trees for attributes with controlled cardinality;

signature chopping is suggested to mitigate *combinatorial errors* [8] (database overrepresentation) of superimposed signatures. Harinharan et al. [9] proposed to include a list of terms in every node of an R-tree. De Felipe et al. [11] augmented signature files in R-tree nodes with similar constraints as [10]. Recently, Cong et al. [3] augmented an inverted file in every node of an R-tree, and used a ranking function that combines spatial proximity and text relevancy. Our work differs in that we assume distance as ranking score, and we focus on efficiently processing Boolean constraints on textual data. Further, none of the previous works offer efficient processing of the complement logical operator, which limits their applicability to the *k-SB* queries we considered in this work. Likewise, modern Web search engines, like Google and Yahoo!, offer *Local Search* services. Advanced querying options are provided to include and exclude certain terms from the search result. These are similar to the *k-SB* queries we consider. However, specific search algorithms are kept confidential by their owning companies.

## 3 Problem Definition

A spatial database $D = \{o_1, o_2, ..., o_N\}$ is a set of objects such that every $o \in D$ has a pair of attributes $< p, T >$, where: $p \in E$ is a point in a metric space $E$ with distance $dist(p_1, p_2)$, and $T = \{t_1, t_2, ...\}$ is a document as a set of terms.

A *top-k* spatial Boolean (*k-SB*) query $Q$ is a triple $< l, k, B >$, where: $l \in E$ is the query location (*spatial constraint*), $k$ is the desired output size, and $B$ is the conjunctive Boolean predicate (*text constraint*). $B$ is a set of keywords prefixed with Boolean operators $\{\wedge, \vee, \neg\}$, conjunctively connected as follows:

$$B = \Big[\wedge(A = \{a_1, a_2, ...\}) \bigwedge \vee(C = \{c_1, c_2, ...\}) \bigwedge \neg(G = \{g_1, g_2, ...\})\Big] \quad (1)$$

$A$ (*AND*-semantics), $C$ (*OR*-semantics), $G$ (*NOT*-semantics) are subsets of terms prefixed with $\wedge$, $\vee$, and $\neg$, respectively. An object $o \in D$ *satisfies* $B$ if:

$$[(\forall a \in A : o.T \cap a \neq \emptyset) \wedge (\exists c \in C : o.T \cap c \neq \emptyset) \wedge (\forall g \in G : o.T \cap g = \emptyset)] \quad (2)$$

The result of the *k-SB* query $Q$ is the list:

$$L = \{o_i \in D, i = 1, ..., n_L | o_i \; satisfies \; B \wedge n_L \leq k\}, \text{ such that:}$$
$$\forall o \in (D \setminus L) \; : \; [dist(o.p, l) \geq arg\,max_{r \in L} dist(r.p, l) \vee \neg(o \; satisfies \; B)] \quad (3)$$

Objects in $L$ are sorted by distance to $l$ in non-decreasing order. In other words, a *k-SB* query $Q$ returns the $k$ nearest neighbor objects to the query location $l$ that satisfy the conjunctive Boolean predicate $B$. In this work, we assume $E$ is the Euclidean space. The problem is how to efficiently compute $L$.

**Example:** In database $D_1$ of Table 1, the query "Find *top-10* houses nearby Miami that have masterbed with bathtub, have a pool or backyard, and are not located in a building" translates to the following *k-SB* query: $Q_1 = \{Miami, 10, [\wedge(masterbed, bathtub) \bigwedge \vee(pool, backyard) \bigwedge \neg(building)]\}$ and retrieves $L_1 = \{o_3, o_8\}$.

**Table 1.** Property parcel database $D_1 = \{o_1, o_2, ..., o_{12}\}$. For every textual term ($t$), the list of objects containing $t$ is shown.

| Term | Object List | Term | Object List |
|---|---|---|---|
| backyard ($t_1$) | $\{o_2, o_3, o_6, o_8\}$ | collins ($t_4$) | $\{o_2, o_6, o_{10}\}$ |
| bathtub ($t_2$) | $\{o_3, o_5, o_8, o_9\}$ | masterbed ($t_5$) | $\{o_3, o_8, o_{11}\}$ |
| building ($t_3$) | $\{o_1, o_5, o_7, o_{12}\}$ | miami ($t_6$) | $\{o_1, o_3, o_4, o_{10}\}$ |

## 4 Hybrid Spatial-Keyword Indexing

In designing the hybrid index, we pursue the following objectives. First, we want to attain fast retrieval even when matching objects are located far away from one another. Second, we want to efficiently filter objects not satisfying the query Boolean constraints on keywords. A key challenge is to perform small number of computations to eliminate as many non-candidate objects as possible. In particular, *NOT*-semantics constraints may substantially shrink the output size and lead to unnecessary scans. Third, we want to maintain low storage requirements while keeping high query performance. With these objectives in mind, our indexing approach leverages the strengths of R-trees [1] in spatial search, and modifies an inverted file [2] for efficient processing of Boolean constraints. The combination of indexing techniques yields the hybrid data structure: *Spatial-Keyword Index* (*SKI*). We next introduce two important definitions in *SKI*.

**Definition 1.** *Given an R-tree R with fanout m, a super node s is the list of m leaf (level 1) nodes that have the same parent node. The universe of super nodes of R is* $S(R) = [s_1, s_2, ...]$, *where* $s_1$ *references the left-most leaf nodes of R.*

**Definition 2.** *The term bitmap of term t at super node s is a fixed-length bit sequence* $I(t, s)$ *of size* $m^2$, *where the i–th bit is computed as follows:*

$$I(t,s)[i] = \begin{cases} 1 & \text{if } s[i] \text{ points to object } o : t \in o.T \\ 0 & \text{otherwise} \end{cases} \quad (4)$$

For an R-tree with $L$ levels, a *super node* $s$ contains $O(m)$ leaf nodes, or equivalently $O(m^2)$ object pointers, and $|S(R)| = O(m^{(L-2)})$ for $L > 1$. A single-level R-tree has no super nodes. Figure 1 shows super node $s_1$ of an R-tree built on $D_1$, and term bitmap for "miami" keyword at $s_1$.

### 4.1 Spatial Keyword Index

The hybrid spatial keyword index ($SKI$) is composed of two building blocks:

**a) R-tree Index** ($R$): A modified R-tree built with spatial attributes of $D$. Entries in $R$'s inner nodes are augmented with index ranges $[a, b]$, where $s_a$ and $s_b$ are the left-most and right-most, respectively, super nodes contained in the subtree rooted at node entry. Ranges in leaf-node entries contain a single value, the index of the super node containing the leaf node.

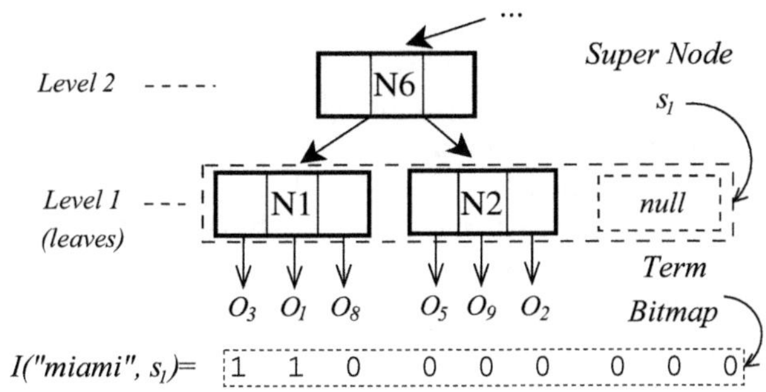


**Fig. 1.** Super node $s_1$ composed of leaf nodes $[N_1, N_2]$, and term bitmap for *"miami"*

**b) Spatial Inverted File** $(SIF)$: A modified inverted file constructed on the vocabulary $V = \{\bigcup_{o \in D} o.T\}$. The Lexicon contains terms in $V$ and their document frequencies (*df*). Posting lists are modified to include spatial information from $R$. Specifically, the posting list of term $t$ contains all its *term bitmaps* (rather than documents) sorted by super node index as follows:

$$Posting(t) = [I(t, s_1), I(t, s_2), ...] \text{ where } s_i \in S(R) \quad (5)$$

Efficiency Considerations. We organize posting elements in a B+tree to allow fast random and range retrieval. Keys are $< t, i >$ pairs while values are bitmaps $I(t, s_i)$. In order to reduce storage requirements, we compress $I(t, s_i)$ using the Word-Aligned Hybrid bitmap compression method (*WAH*) [4]. *WAH* method allows fast bitwise computations with logical operators $AND$, $OR$, and $NOT$ on uncompressed bitmaps, which is capitalized during query processing.

Figure 2 shows $R$ and $SIF$ structures for database $D_1$ in Table 1.

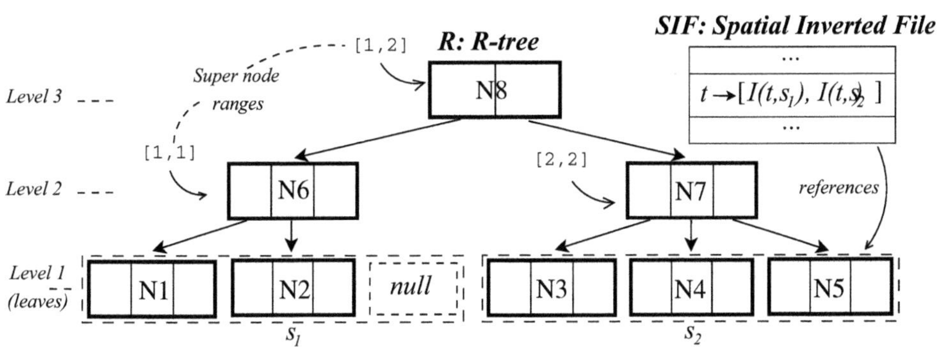


**Fig. 2.** Hybrid Spatial-Keyword Index for database $D_1$ in Table 1

### 4.2 Processing *k-SB* Queries

In order to process query $Q = < l, k, B >$, R-tree $R$ is traversed from the root node following the best-first traversal algorithm proposed in [5]. That is, node entries are visited in order of proximity of their *minimum bounding rectangles* ($MBR$) to location $l$. A node entry $e$ is placed in a priority queue, with priority equal to $dist(MBR, l)$, if at least one object within $e$'s subtree satisfies Boolean predicate $B$. The $SIF$ structure is used to qualify $e$. A powerful feature of the previous filter is that unnecessary subtree traversals are eliminated altogether.

Algorithm 1 shows the steps involved in processing *k-SB* queries using $SKI$. The algorithm starts by resorting query keywords by documents frequency (line 1) in such a way that as many object candidates as possible are eliminated with few posting list merges. For instance, infrequent terms have large number of 0*s* in their term bitmaps, and possibly short $Posting()$ lists, which are adequate to be processed first for $AND$-semantics terms. In line 2, the priority queue, result list, and a globally accessible hash map $M$ are initialized. $M$ caches merged term bitmaps of previously evaluated super nodes during query execution. Next, $R$ is traversed in best-first order starting from its root in lines 4–9. A node entry $e$ is evaluated w.r.t. $B$ by the function $isSubtreeCandidate$ (line 8). Only when $e$'s subtree has at least one object that satisfies $B$ is it pushed into the queue.

**Algorithm 1.** Process *k-SB* Query

```
Input. k-SB query Q =< l, k, B >
Output. A list of objects satisfying Q (see Equation 3)
begin
1     Sort term subsets in B by document frequency (df) as follows:
        A (AND) in ascending order, and C, G (OR, NOT) in descending order
2     Initialize: priority Queue ← R.root; list L ← ∅; global hash map M ← ∅
3     r ← 0          /* number of B-satisfying objects retrieved so far */
4     while (Queue ≠ ∅ and r < k) do
5         Node n ← Queue.pop()
6         if (n is obj. pointer) then r ← r + 1
            L.add(getObject(D, n))          /* retrieve o ∈ D pointed by n */
7         else for (every entry e in node n) do
8             if (isSubtreeCandidate(B, n, [e's position in n])) then
9                 Queue.push(e.ptr) with priority dist(e.MBR, l)
10    return L
```

$isSubtreeCandidate$ function, described in Algorithm 2, evaluates $B$ predicate by merging query term bitmaps on a range of super nodes, one super node at a time, until one candidate is found (lines 4–9). This processing style is similar to Document-At-A-Time processing in inverted files [2], except that postings are not exhausted. Logical bitwise operations are performed on term bitmaps

**Algorithm 2.** isSubtreeCandidate

**Input.** $B$: query predicate; $n$: node; $i$: positional index
**Output.** *True* if $\exists\ o$ that satisfies $B$ within subtree at $n[i]$, *false* otherwise

```
begin
1   if (n is leaf node) then
2       if (The i-th bit in M(n[i].a) is set) then return true
3       else return false
4   else for (j ← n[i].a to n[i].b) do
5       pe ← ∧_{t∈B.A} I(t, j)                    /* execute bitwise operations */
6       pe ← pe ∧ [∨_{t∈B.C} I(t, j)]              /* on term bitmaps over */
7       pe ← pe ∧ [∧_{t∈B.G} flip(I(t, j))]        /* super node range in n[i] */
8       if (cardinality(pe) > 0) then M.add(key = j, value = pe)
9           return true
10  return false
```

(lines 5–7) according to term semantics. Complement operator requires term bitmaps to be flipped (converting 1*s* into 0*s* and vice versa), which is accomplished by the *flip* function (line 7). Next, if the merged bitmap has at least one bit set (line 8), meaning there is a candidate, then it is cached in $M$ (line 8), and the function returns *true*. Otherwise, $B$ is evaluated at the next super node in the range until a candidate is found, or the range is exhausted. In the latter worst case, the subtree is discarded in its entirety. Since a super node references $O(m^2)$ objects, a range $[a, b]$ can potentially filter out $O(m^2 \times |a - b|)$ objects. The $I/O$ cost is remarkably only $O(|B| \times \log(|V|) \times |a - b|)$, where $|B|$ is the number of query terms, $|V|$ the vocabulary size, and $\log(|V|)$ the cost of term bitmap retrievals from a B+tree (see Section 4.1).

## 5 Experiments

We conducted a series of querying experiments with three real spatial datasets explained in Table 2. Records contain geographical coordinates, and between 30 and 80 text attributes (concatenated in a term set). $SKI$ was implemented in Java, and experiments ran on an Intel Xeon E7340 2.4GHz machine with 8GB of RAM. We measured average number of random $I/Os$ and response times in processing *k-SB* queries and compared performance with two baselines:

Baseline 1 (IFC). An inverted file containing object coordinates in addition to object pointers. Queries are processed in two phases. First, term postings are merged according to $B$ semantics. Second, satisfying objects are sorted by proximity to query location. The top-k objects in the sorted list are returned.

Baseline 2 (RIF). An R-tree with every node augmented with an inverted file on keywords within its subtree. This baseline is inspired by arts [3] [9]. At query time, R-tree nodes are visited in best-first order w.r.t. spatial attributes. $B$ is evaluated with the inverted file at every node, except for $NOT$-semantics terms.

Workload. Every vocabulary was sorted by document frequency (*df*) and divided in three quantiles: **S**: Terms with *df* $<$ 1–quantile (infrequent terms), **M**: Terms with *df* $<$ 2–quantile, **L**: Terms with *df* $<$ 3–quantile (entire vocabulary). In each quantile, *k-SB* queries were composed by randomly picking between 3 and 8 terms and prefixing them with $\{\wedge, \vee, \neg\}$ operators to form $B$. $k$ was fixed to 20.

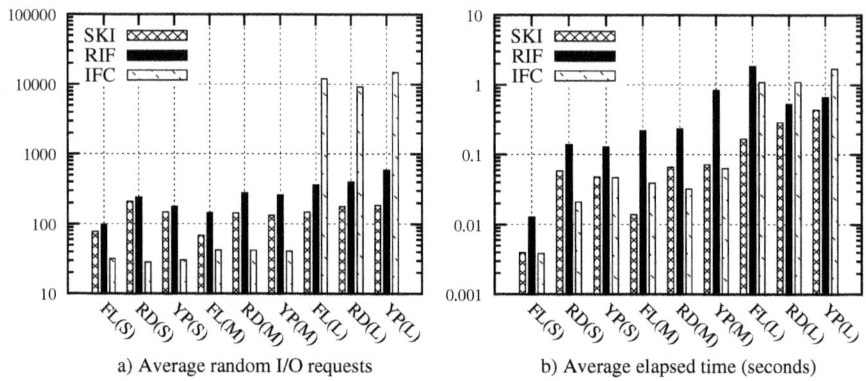


**Fig. 3.** Performance metrics on 50 *k-SB* query runs. *Y-axis* is in logarithmic scale.

Figure 3 shows the average number of $I/O$s and elapsed time over 50 *k-SB* queries of each workload type $\{S, M, L\}$ for every dataset. $IFC$ shows performance advantage when query terms are relatively infrequent ($S$). Short posting lists can be quickly evaluated to compute query result, whereas $SKI$ and $RIF$ spend additional R-tree traversals. When query terms become more frequent ($M$ and $L$), $IFC$ incurrs in expensive long posting list merges, which is observed in peaks of Figure 3.a for $L$ queries. $RIF$ performs acceptably for $S$ queries but degrades for $M$ and $L$ queries. This may be due to filtering limitations in R-tree upper levels. Eventually, subtrees known (via inverted file) to contain query terms are traversed. However, terms may belong to different objects, i.e. no single object satisfies $B$ predicate. In the same vein, $RIF$ must wait until objects are retrieved to apply $NOT$-semantics filters, which can also degrade its performance. In summary, we observed consistent enhanced retrieval performance using the proposed hybrid indexing and query processing methods.

**Table 2.** Experimental spatial datasets. Dataset and vocabulary sizes are in millions.

| D | $\|D\|$ | $\|V\|$ | Subject |
|---|---|---|---|
| FL | 10.8 | 21.2 | Property parcels in the Florida state. |
| YP | 20.4 | 40.8 | Yellow pages of businesses in the United States. |
| RD | 23.0 | 64.8 | Road segments in the United States. |

## 6 Conclusions

In this paper, we proposed a disk-resident hybrid index for efficiently answering $k$-NN queries with Boolean constraints on textual content. We combined modified versions of R-trees and inverted files to achieve effective pruning of the search space. Our experimental study showed increased performance and scalability on large, 10M and 20M sized, spatial datasets over alternate methods.

**Acknowledgment.** This research was supported in part by NSF grants IIS-0837716, CNS-0821345, HRD-0833093, IIP-0829576, IIP-0931517, DGE-0549489, IIS-0957394, and IIS-0847680.

## References

1. Guttman, A.: R-trees: A dynamic index structure for spatial searching. In: SIGMOD, pp. 47–57. ACM, New York (1984)
2. Zobel, J., Moffat, A.: Inverted files for text search engines. ACM Comput. Surv. 38(2) (2006)
3. Cong, G., Jensen, C.S., Wu, D.: Efficient retrieval of the top-k most relevant spatial web objects. Proc. VLDB Endow. 2(1), 337–348 (2009)
4. Wu, K., Otoo, E.J., Shoshani, A.: Optimizing bitmap indices with efficient compression. ACM Trans. Database Syst. 31(1), 1–38 (2006)
5. Hjaltason, G., Samet, H.: Distance browsing in spatial databases. ACM Trans. Database Syst. 24(2), 265–318 (1999)
6. WikiProject on geographical coordinates, `http://en.wikipedia.org/wiki/Wikipedia:WikiProject_Geographical_coordinates`
7. Xin, D., Han, J.: P-Cube: Answering preference queries in multi-dimensional space. In: ICDE, pp. 1092–1100. IEEE Computer Society, Los Alamitos (2008)
8. Chang, W.W., Schek, H.J.: A signature access method for the Starburst database system. In: VLDB, pp. 145–153 (1989)
9. Hariharan, R., Hore, B., Li, C., Mehrotra, S.: Processing spatial-keyword (SK) queries in geographic information retrieval (GIR) systems. In: SSDBM, p. 16 (2007)
10. Park, D.J., Kim, H.J.: An enhanced technique for k-nearest neighbor queries with non-spatial selection predicates. Multimedia Tools and Apps., 79–103 (2004)
11. De Felipe, I., Hristidis, V., Rishe, N.: Keyword search on spatial databases. In: ICDE, pp. 656–665. IEEE Computer Society, Los Alamitos (2008)
12. Zobel, J., Moffat, A., Ramamohanarao, K.: Inverted files versus signature files for text indexing. ACM Trans. Database Syst. 23(4), 453–490 (1998)
13. Beckmann, N., Kriegel, H.P., Schneider, R., Seeger, B.: The R*-tree: An efficient and robust access method for points and rectangles. In: SIGMOD, pp. 322–331 (1990)
14. Sellis, T.K., Roussopoulos, N., Faloutsos, C.: The R+-tree: A dynamic index for multi-dimensional objects. In: VLDB, pp. 507–518 (1987)
15. Kamel, I., Faloutsos, C.: Hilbert R-tree: An improved R-tree using fractals. In: VLDB, pp. 500–509 (1994)

# A Framework for Moving Sensor Data Query and Retrieval of Dynamic Atmospheric Events*

Shen-Shyang Ho[1], Wenqing Tang[1], W. Timothy Liu[1], and Markus Schneider[2]

[1] Jet Propulsion Laboratory, California Institute of Technology,
Pasadena CA 91109, USA
{sho,Wenqing.Tang,w.t.liu}@jpl.nasa.gov

[2] Department of Computer & Information Science & Engineering,
University of Florida, Gainesville, FL 32611, USA
mschneid@cise.ufl.edu

**Abstract.** One challenge in Earth science research is the accurate and efficient ad-hoc query and retrieval of Earth science satellite sensor data based on user-defined criteria to study and analyze atmospheric events such as tropical cyclones. The problem can be formulated as a spatio-temporal join query to identify the spatio-temporal location where moving sensor objects and dynamic atmospheric event objects intersect, either precisely or within a user-defined proximity. In this paper, we describe an efficient query and retrieval framework to handle the problem of identifying the spatio-temporal intersecting positions for satellite sensor data retrieval. We demonstrate the effectiveness of our proposed framework using sensor measurements from QuikSCAT (wind field measurement) and TRMM (precipitation vertical profile measurements) satellites, and the trajectories of the tropical cyclones occurring in the North Atlantic Ocean in 2009.

**Keywords:** data retrieval, satellite data, atmospheric events, spatio-temporal join.

## 1 Introduction

The Earth Observing System Data and Information System (EOSDIS)[1] is a comprehensive data and information system which archives, manages, and distributes Earth science data from the EOS spacecrafts (a.k.a. satellite sensors) [1]. A challenge of EOSDIS is how to "help users find the data that they need and how to get it to them" [2]. The Warehouse Inventory Search Tool (WIST)[2] is the primary search and order tool for Earth Science data sets for EOSDIS. It

* This work was partially carried out at the Jet Propulsion Laboratory, California Institute of Technology and was funded by the National Aeronautics and Space Adminstration (NASA) Advanced Information Systems Technology (AIST) Program under grant number AIST-08-0081.

[1] http://esdis.eosdis.nasa.gov

[2] https://wist.echo.nasa.gov/~wist/api/imswelcome/

M. Gertz and B. Ludäscher (Eds.): SSDBM 2010, LNCS 6187, pp. 96–113, 2010.

allows users to browse and retrieve satellite measurements based on user-defined spatial and temporal conditions. This type of data query and retrieval is known in the Earth science community as data "subseting". One important use of the retrieved satellite sensor data is the improvement of weather forecasting such as the use of QuikSCAT wind measurements to accurately depict the initial conditions of air and sea states for tropical cyclone forecast model [3].

In the mid-nineties, there was an ambitious project to develop a "flexible, extensible, and seamless SCF [Scientific Computing Facilities] for scientific data analysis, knowledge discovery, visualization, and collaboration" called the Open Architecture Scientific Information System (OASIS) to support EOSDIS based on the Common Object Request Broker Architecture (CORBA) [4]. The OASIS was not embraced by the scientific community which could have been the result of serious technical, complexity, and security issues related to CORBA [5].

Currently, there is still a lack of capabilities that support flexible data retrieval in the EOSDIS. One non-existent capability is the accurate and efficient ad-hoc query and retrieval of Earth science satellite sensor data for dynamic atmospheric events such as tropical cyclones based on ad-hoc user-defined criteria and event trajectories. In this paper, we describe a fast data query and retrieval framework based on a spatio-temporal partitioning scheme driven by the partitioning of the moving satellite trajectory so that the positions which the satellite trajectory and an atmospheric event trajectory intersect, either precisely or within close proximity, are used for satellite data retrieval. We demonstrate the feasibility of our framework on the tropical cyclone event which is a "non-frontal synoptic scale low-pressure system over tropical or sub-tropical waters with organized convection and definite cyclonic surface wind circulation"[3]. Experimental results are used to show the effectiveness of our proposed framework using sensor measurements from QuikSCAT (wind field measurement) and TRMM (precipitation vertical profile measurements) satellites, and the tropical cyclones occurring in the North Atlantic Ocean in 2009.

From published scientific journal papers [6,7,8,9,10], one observes that such a capability is extremely important to scientists who retrieve specific sensor data of specific atmospheric events for statistical analysis. Some query examples derived from these published scientific papers that require search, retrieval, and analysis of satellite data containing cyclone features, are listed below:

1. Retrieve TRMM precipitation data for tropical cyclones that attained tropical storm intensity or higher over western North Pacific and the South China Sea between longitudes $100^{o}E$ and $180^{o}$. 138 sensor datasets from 61 tropical cyclones retrieved [6].
2. Retrieve TRMM precipitation data for tropical cyclones from December 1997 to December 2003. 3703 sensor datasets from 563 tropical cyclones retrieved [7].
3. Retrieve QuikSCAT wind data for tropical cyclones in western North Pacific from September 1999 to December 2004 which formed west of $160^{o}E$ and south of $26^{o}N$. Datasets containing 124 tropical cyclones retrieved [8].

[3] `http://www.aoml.noaa.gov/hrd/tcfaq/A1.html`

Our problem is fundamentally different from previous research to discover and track cyclones from either sea-level pressure fields [11] or from heterogeneous satellite data [12]. For our problem, the cyclone tracks are known. Our main contribution is an efficient framework that enables the retrieval of satellite data based on known cyclone tracks, an approach to fuse two databases with widely different characteristics.

The paper is organized as follows. In Section 2, we briefly review previous research and systems developed for satellite data query and retrieval, in particular, for the tropical cyclone events. In Section 3, the satellite sensor data query and retrieval problem is defined. In Section 4, the satellite data and tropical cyclone event trajectory data are briefly described. In Section 5, the satellite sensor trajectory data partitioning scheme and partition search algorithm are described in detail. In Section 6, the satellite data retrieval algorithm is described in detail. In Section 7, experimental results are presented to demonstrate the feasibility of our proposed framework for both QuikSCAT and TRMM satellite sensor data. Some visualizations of the retrieved satellite data sets from a queried hurricane trajectory are also shown.

## 2 Related Work

Existing state-of-the-art publicly available web-based tropical cyclone data and information portals[4,5], data archives[6], and forecast services[7] provide excellent visualizations and information of tropical cyclones and satellite sensor measurements.

However, comfortable data access (e.g., ad-hoc data retrieval for specific weather events) is not provided, and users only have limited, simple, and hard-coded query and request capabilities. Examples of such queries are:

1. Provide specific satellite data of a specified region at a specific date and time. [EOSDIS]
2. Provide the static dataset for a specific tropical cyclone event. [Physical Oceanography DAAC: Hurricane/Typhoon Tracker]

Users are not able to perform own queries to retrieve satellite data based on arbitrary trajectory information and retrieval parameters.

Many spatio-temporal access methods (for indexing historical spatio-temporal data) have been developed [13,14] (and references therein) to support certain query types or to support efficiently as many query types as possible. Some of the common query types are

[4] Navy/NRL Tropical Cyclone, `http://www.nrlmry.navy.mil/tc_pages/tc_home.html`

[5] NASA GSFC Hurricane Portal, `http://daac.gsfc.nasa.gov/hurricane/`

[6] Physical Oceanography DAAC Hurricane/Typhoon Tracker, `http://podaac.jpl.nasa.gov/hurricanes/`

[7] NOAA National Hurricane Center, `http://www.nhc.noaa.gov/pastall.shtml`

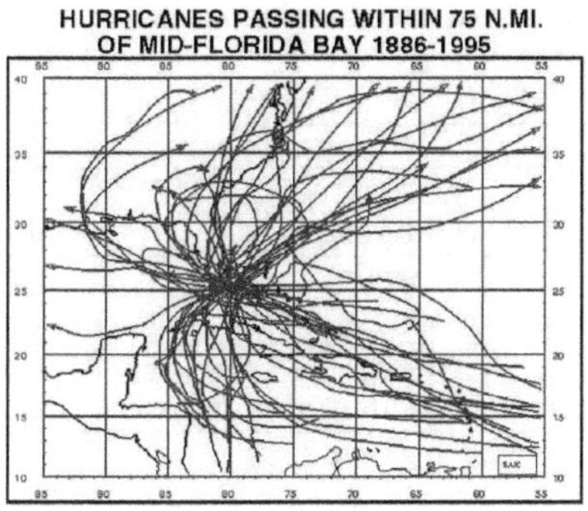


**Fig. 1.** Visualization of the output from the query "Find all hurricanes from 1886 to 1996 within 75 nautical miles of mid-Florida Bay" (http://www.aoml.noaa.gov/hrd/Storm_pages/fl_track_red.html)

1. Selection: Find all objects within a specific region and/or during a specific time interval.
2. Join: Find all objects that are spatially close during a specific time interval.
3. Nearest Neighbor: Find the k-closest objects with respect to a specific region and/or time interval.

These queries are of interest to scientists studying tropical cyclones An example of a selection query is "Find all hurricanes[8] from 1886 to 1996 within 75 nautical miles of mid-Florida Bay" and its output shown in Fig. 1.

In this paper, we are, however, interested in exploring the intersection of two different object classes (hurricanes and satellite trajectories) by a query such as "Find the spatial region(s) $R$ and time interval(s) $I$ such that the hurricane path is either in the satellite sensor scanning region or within some user-defined distance outside the boundary of the satellite sensor scanning region" and then to use its output for data retrieval.

## 3 Problem Definition

Consider the set of satellite sensors, $O_s = \{O_{s1}, O_{s2}, \ldots, O_{sk}\}$, and the set of atmospheric events, $O_c = \{O_{c1}, O_{c2}, \ldots, O_{cm}\}$ such as the set of tropical cyclones. In particular, the query and retrieval problem of interest is "Find all *unique* satellite sensor measurements from $O_{si}$ that is at most $x$ kilometers from the tropical cyclone path $P$ of $O_{cj}$ and in the time interval $I$." It can be generalized to "Find all *unique* satellite sensor measurements from satellite $O_{s1}, \ldots, O_{sk}$ that are at most $x$ kilometers from the tropical cyclone paths $p_1, \ldots, p_m$ in region $R$ at time interval $I$." This is closely related to the *spatio-temporal join* which retrieves all pairs of objects $< o_1, o_2 >$ with $o_1 \in O_s$ and $o_2 \in O_c$, $|o_1(t_q) - o_2(t_q)| \leq d$

[8] Hurricanes are tropical cyclones with sustained surface wind intensity equal or more than 119km/h.

**Table 1.** Differences in the characteristics between the satellite sensor objects and the tropical cyclone objects

| Characteristics | $O_s$ | $O_c$ |
|---|---|---|
| Temporal Length | long (several years) | short (unlikely to be several months) |
| Temporal Resolution | fine grain (order of $10^{-1}$ seconds) | course grain (several hours) |
| Motion Speed | high (a full orbit is about 100 minutes) | low |
| Representation | line segments | points (can be extended to a region) |
| Spatial Position | continuous motion (orbiting; not geostationary satellites) | unlikely to be stationary, but possible |
| Data Updates/ Modifications | No delete; most current | No delete; historical, most current |

where $t_q$ is a time-stamp and $d$ is an upper-bound threshold. Our problem goes further by querying for the positions and time instances where and when the join condition is satisfied. This condition is likely to be satisfied at multiple positions and time instances. An orbiting satellite sensor trajectory consists of many years of continuous spatio-temporal information. Hence, one needs to construct an efficient partitioning scheme to handle the lengthy data sequence. We construct the partitions by treating time as another dimension for a satellite sensor object. The tropical cyclone objects are stored in an index structure since there are some fundamental differences between the two object types. The differences in the characteristics between the two object types are shown in Table 1. For selection and nearest neighbor queries for objects in $O_c$, one can use an index structure such as TB-tree [15] or SEB-tree [16].

Let $S$ be the spatial bound (latitude[min, max], longitude[min, max]) and $T$ be the temporal bound time(start, end). Queries that return sensor objects and their intersecting spatio-temporal information such as

$$O_q = \{o_{si} \in O_s | O_s \cap_{ST} O_s \neq \emptyset \text{ within spatial bound } S \text{ and temporal bound } T\}$$
$$TS = \{(t,s) | t \in T, s \in S \text{ and } O_s \cap_{ST} O_s \neq \emptyset \text{ within spatial bound } S \text{ and temporal bound } T\}$$

are not the focus of this paper as the intersections ($\cap_{ST}$[9]) of satellite sensor trajectories *alone* are not useful information for atmospheric, ocean, and weather event research. One is interested in

$$O_q = \{o_{si} \in O_s | O_c \cap_{ST} O_s \neq \emptyset \text{ within spatial bound } S \text{ and temporal bound } T\}$$
$$TS = \{(t,s) | t \in T, s \in S \text{ and } O_c \cap_{ST} O_s \neq \emptyset \text{ within spatial bound } S \text{ and temporal bound } T\} \quad (1)$$

[9] $\cap_{ST}$ denotes the operation that returns the set of elements from the bigger set (usually $O_c$, if the two sets are different) when the trajectories of objects in $O_c$ and $O_s$ intersect. The simplest case is when $|O_c| = |O_s| = 1$.

The first one is a "Which" query such as a selection or nearest neighbor query. The latter one is a query which determines the positions and time instances where and when the trajectories of the objects in the two sets intersect, either precisely or within a certain proximity. In this paper, we focus on the latter query which can be derived from the first one and its outputs are applicable to our satellite data retrieval problem.

# 4 Data Description

In this paper, we use the Level 2B QuikSCAT wind field swath data and the Level 2A12 TRMM precipitation swath data stored in hierarchical data format (HDF)[10] to demonstrate the feasibility and efficiency of the partitioning scheme and the data retrieval framework. In Section 4.1, we give a brief description of the satellite data. In Section 4.2, we give a brief description of the tropical cyclone trajectories.

## 4.1 Satellite Data

**QuikSCAT.** One QuikSCAT satellite full polar orbiting revolution takes about 101 minutes. The Level 2B data are grouped by rows of wind vector cells (WVC) which are squares of dimension 25 km or 12.5 km. A complete coverage of the earth circumference requires 1624 WVC rows at 25 km spatial resolution, and 3248 rows at 12.5 km spatial resolution. The width of the swath is 1800 km which amounts to seventy-two 25 km WVCs or one hundred and forty-four 12.5 km WVCs.

**Table 2.** Relevant QuikSCAT data fields. nrow: number of rows; ncol: number of columns.

| Field | matrix size | Unit | Minimum | Maximum |
|---|---|---|---|---|
| wvc_lat | [nrow, ncol] | degree | -90.00 | 90.00 |
| wvc_lon | [nrow, ncol] | degree E | 0.00 | 359.99 |
| selected speed | [nrow, ncol] | meter per second | 0.00 | 50.00 |
| selected direction | [nrow, ncol] | degree from North | 0.00 | 359.99 |
| wvc_row_time | [nrow] | Coordinated Universal Time (UTC) | 1993-001 T00:00.000 | 2009-365 T23:59:59.999 |

There are 25 fields in the data structure for Level 2B data [17]. We are, however, only interested in the latitude, longitude, time, and the most likely wind speed and direction for the WVCs. The fields that we are interested in are summarized in Table 2 and used in Algorithm 1 and 2. The QuikSCAT Level 2B data is obtained from the JPL Physical Oceanography DAAC (PO.DAAC)

[10] `http://www.hdfgroup.org/`

**Table 3.** Relevant TRMM spatio-temporal data field. nscan: number of rows in the data matrix; npixel: number of column in the data matrix.

| Field | Structure | Size |
|---|---|---|
| Scan Time | Table | 9 $bytes \times nscan$ |
| Geo-location | Array | $2 \times npixel \times nscan$ |

**Table 4.** Scan Time

| Name | Format | Description |
|---|---|---|
| Year | 2-byte integer | 4-digit year |
| Month | 1-byte integer | The month of the Year |
| Day of Month | 1-byte integer | The day of the Month |
| Hour | 1-byte integer | The hour (UTC) of the Day |
| Minute | 1-byte integer | The minute of the Hour |
| Second | 1-byte integer | The second of the minute |
| Day of Year | 2-byte integer | The day of the Year |

**Table 5.** Geo-location. Off-Earth is represented by -9999.9.

| Name | Minimum | Maximum |
|---|---|---|
| Latitude | -90.00 | 90.00 |
| Longitude | -179.99 | 180.00 |

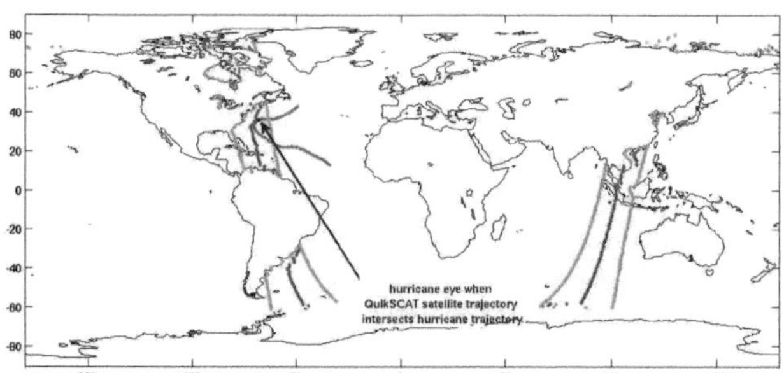


**Fig. 2.** One QuikSCAT swath intersecting path of Hurricane Irene in 2005

FTP server[11]. In Fig. 2, the two outer curves are the boundaries of the satellite observations and the middle curve represents the median of the observation boundaries. The median approximates the satellite trajectory when sensor takes measurements above the ocean. However, it is impossible to estimate the QuikSCAT satellite trajectory accurately from the Level 2B data when the

[11] `ftp://podaac.jpl.nasa.gov/ocean_wind/quikscat/L2B12/data`

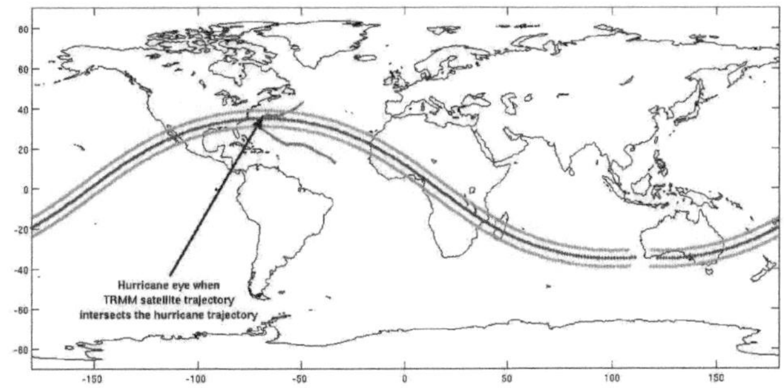


**Fig. 3.** One TRMM swath intersecting path of Hurricane Irene in 2005

satellite is above or near land due to the satellite sensor measurement constraints above or near land.

**TRMM.** The Tropical Rainfall Measurement Mission (TRMM) is a joint mission between NASA and the Japan Aerospace Exploration Agency (JAXA) designed to monitor and study tropical rainfall. TRMM satellite orbits between 35 degrees north and 35 degrees south of the equator. It takes measurements between 50 degrees north and 50 degrees south of the equator. All TRMM products are archived and distributed to the public by the Goddard Distributed Active Archive Center (GES DISC DAAC).[12]

For TRMM, we use the Level 2A12 data product, "TMI Profiling" which contains vertical hydrometeor profiles on a pixel by pixel basis. For each pixel, cloud liquid water, precipitation water, cloud ice water, precipitation ice, and latent heating are given at 14 vertical layers [18]. The TRMM Level 2A12 data is obtained from the Goddard Earth Sciences and Information Services Center[13].

There are 15 fields in the SDS (Science Data Set) in the TRMM Level 2A12 HDF data file. We use the scan time and geo-location shown in Table 3 to estimate the satellite motion. These fields are summarized in Table 4 and 5. Fig. 3 shows a TRMM swath intersecting path of Hurricane Irene in 2005. One notes that TRMM satellite takes measurements over land unlike the QuikSCAT satellite. Hence, the median of the observation boundaries approximates the TRMM satellite trajectory well.

## 4.2 Tropical Cyclone Event Trajectory

A trajectory is the path a moving object follows through space and time. Consider a time-stamped $d$ dimensional data sequence defining a trajectory $Tr$ as follows.

$$Tr = \langle (t_1, \boldsymbol{x}_1), \ldots, (t_i, \boldsymbol{x}_i), \ldots, (t_N, \boldsymbol{x}_N) \rangle$$

[12] `http://disc.sci.gsfc.nasa.gov/`

[13] `ftp://disc2.nascom.nasa.gov/ftp/data/s4pa/TRMM_L2/TRMM_2A12`

**Fig. 4.** Cyclone track for Hurricane Ike 2008 from NHC best track data

where $N$ is the length of the data sequence $Tr$, $t_1 < \cdots < t_i < \cdots < t_N$ are the timestamps, and the vector $\boldsymbol{x}_i$ containing spatial information can have cardinality $d = 1, 2$, or 3; A tropical cyclone trajectory is described by (i) spatial attributes (latitude and longitude), and (ii) temporal attributes (year, day, time). Fig. 4 shows the trajectory of Hurricane Ike 2008 based on National Hurricane Center (NHC) best track information.

Historical tropical cyclone trajectories are obtained from the NOAA Coastal Services Center (Atlantic and North Eastern Pacific)[14]. The eleven tropical cyclone trajectories in North Atlantic Ocean in 2009 are used in our experiments.

## 5 Satellite Sensor Object Partitioning Scheme

Since (i) the temporal resolution of the satellite observations is relatively high, and (ii) the satellite orbiting speed is also relatively high compared to the atmospheric event objects, a large amount of data is generated in a relatively short time. Hence, one partition tree structure is used for each satellite object. The partitioning scheme is based on the time segmentation of the satellite trajectory, defined by the boundaries of the satellite sensor measurements.

We use the QuikSCAT satellite swath data (see Table 2) as an example to illustrate the partitioning scheme for satellite sensor objects. One notes that satellite measurements and their positions in an arbitrary row $i$ in a data matrix (e.g., selected speed[$i$, 1:ncol]) have a fix timestamp in QuikSCAT, TRMM, and other satellites. Hence, the satellite sensor object at a fix time instance $t$ (e.g., wvc_row_time[$i$]) can be represented by a spatial line segment or curve defined by the latitude and longitude values in row $i$ in the position matrices (e.g., wvc_lat[$i$,1:ncol] and wvc_lon[$i$,1:ncol]).

The QuikSCAT satellite data swath is divided into partitions such that each partition is a spatial region within a time interval defined by a fixed $n$ number of consecutive wvc_row_time elements (see Fig. 5). These partitions form the leave nodes in the partition tree. Each partition time interval varies slightly due to the non-uniform measurement sampling. Each leave node (partition) contains (i) the temporal information consisting of the start of the time interval wvc_row_time[$i$]

[14] `http://csc-s-maps-q.csc.noaa.gov/hurricanes/`

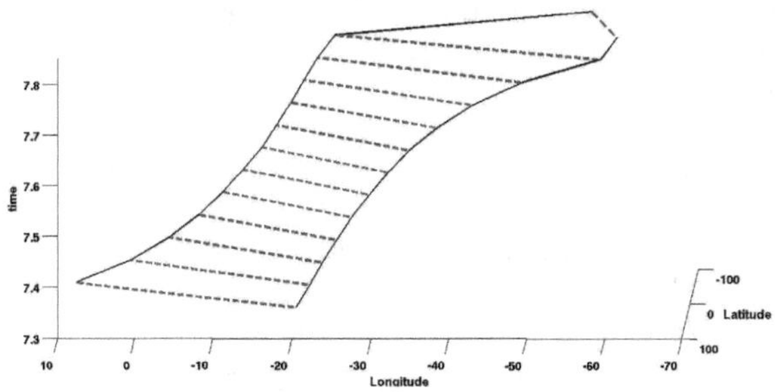


**Fig. 5.** A segment of the QuikSCAT satellite data swath divided into partitions

```
Root Node:                              [Year, Y]
                                            |
Non-Leave Nodes:                [Year, Y; Julian Day, D]
                                            |
Non-Leave Nodes:      [Year, Y; Julian Day, D; Rev. Number, Rn]
                                            |
Non-Leave Nodes:         [Rev. No., Rn; time: s_time, e_time]
                                            |
Leave Nodes: [p_id; Rev. No., Rn; Partition, P; time: Ps_time, Pe_time]
```

**Fig. 6.** Partition tree scheme for the moving satellite trajectory

$= t_s$, and the end of the time interval wvc_row_time$[i + n - 1] = t_e$, and (ii) the spatial information for a swath data partition defined by the first and last non-zero elements in wvc_lat[$i$,1:ncol] and wvc_lon[$i$,1:ncol] at $t_s$, and wvc_lat[$i + n - 1$,1:ncol] and wvc_lon[$i + n - 1$,1:ncol] at $t_e$. In other words, a leave node partition is a quadrilateral region defined by the four corners of the data swath partition approximating the data swath partition. One notes that as $n$ increases, some measurements in a data swath partition nearer to one of the swath data boundaries fall outside the leave node partition. If $n$ is too high, one may fail to identify the data swath partitions that intersect a tropical cyclone trajectory.

The partition tree structure for a satellite sensor object is shown in Fig. 6. Revolution numbers (Rev. No) are unique incremental numbers tagging the orbits. *p_ids* are unique numbers tagging the partitions shown in Fig. 5. For the QuikSCAT satellite object, there are either 365 or 366 Julian days each year, 14 unique revolution numbers per day, and each swath defined by a revolution number is divided into segments containing $n$ consecutive time instances. For the TRMM satellite object, the only difference is that there is either 15 or 16 unique revolution numbers per day.

Algorithm 1 is used to search the partition tree structure (for QuikSCAT swath data) for partitions that intersect a path defined by two consecutive trajectory points and the user-defined radius $R$ in degree. In Lines 2 to 3, spatio-temporal points between the two consecutive trajectory points and their

**Input**: Two consecutive trajectory points, $(t_s, \boldsymbol{x}_s)$ and $(t_e, \boldsymbol{x}_e)$; Radius, $R$ (in degree)
**Output**: $RI_s, RI_e, Rn, TS$
1: $TS := \{\}; I := \{\}$ ;
2: Generate a set of interpolated points, $P = \{p_1, \ldots, p_k\}$, using $(t_s, \boldsymbol{x}_s)$ and $(t_e, \boldsymbol{x}_e)$;
3: Generate a set of circumference points, $C_i$ for each $p_i \in P$ based on $R$;
4: **for** interpolated point $p_i = (t_i, \boldsymbol{x}_i)$ **do**
5: Identity $Rn$ and leave-node partitions within time interval $T$ =[s_time, e_time] in the partition tree based on $t_i$;
6: **if** $Rn \neq \emptyset$ **then**
7: $C_i := C_i \bigcup \{p_i\}$;
8: **for** partition, $Q_j$ in $T$ of $Rn$ **do**
9: $I_i := \{Q_j | Q_j \bigcap C_i \neq \emptyset\}$;
10: **if** $I_i \neq \emptyset$ **then**
11: $I := I \bigcup I_i$ ;
12: $TS := TS \bigcup \{p_i\}$ ;
13: **end if**
14: **end for**
15: **end if**
16: **end for**
17: **if** $I = \emptyset$ **then**
18: $RI_s := RI_e := Rn := \emptyset$;
19: **end if**
20: Use $I$ to identify the start row number, $RI_s$ and end row number, $RI_e$ for wvc_lat, wvc_lon, and wvc_row_time in $Rn$.

**Algorithm 1.** Partition tree search to locate the tropical cyclone event in satellite swath data

corresponding circumference points are computed. For each interpolated spatio-temporal point, the partition tree structure is searched to locate the Revolution number $Rn$ which the spatio-temporal point may be in (Line 5). When a $Rn$ is located, the partitions which may contain the interpolated point will be searched (Lines 8 to 14). If the interpolated point and its circumference points are found in a partition, $I$ and $TS$ are updated (Lines 10 to 13). $I$ contains information related to the start time instances and the end time instances of the spatio-temporal partitions that the interpolated points and their circumference points intersect. The goal of Line 20 is to locate the earliest start time and the latest end time from $I$ and also the start row number $RI_s$ and the end row number $RI_e$ in the swath $Rn$. $TS$ is the set defined in (1). Algorithm 1 can be generalized to other satellite sensor data.

## 6 Retrieval Algorithm

Next, we describe the algorithm that retrieves all satellite measurements within a specified radius $R$ from $TS$ defined in (1). In practice, we want a unique set of

**Input**: $Rn$, $RI_s$, $RI_e$, $R$ (in degree), $TS$.
**Output**: Point Sets: $PS_{ws}$, $PS_{wd}$
Retrieve QuikSCAT HDF Data with Rev. No., $Rn$;
$p_y := \{\text{wvc\_lat}[i, 1 : ncol],\ i \in [RI_s, RI_e]\}$;
$p_x := \{\text{wvc\_lon}[i, 1 : ncol],\ i \in [RI_s, RI_e]\}$;
$ws := \{\text{selected\_speed}[i, 1 : ncol],\ i \in [RI_s, RI_e]\}$;
$wd := \{\text{selected\_direction}[i, 1 : ncol],\ i \in [RI_s, RI_e]\}$;
Compute $\hat{\boldsymbol{x}}$ using (3) OR Cyclone Eye Locator (see Algorithm 3);
**for** $p(j) := (p_y(j), p_x(j))$ **do**
  $dist(j) := \| p(j) - \hat{\boldsymbol{x}} \|_2$;
**end for**
$PS_{ws} := \{ws(k) \mid dist(k) < R\}$;
$PS_{wd} := \{wd(k) \mid dist(k) < R\}$;

**Algorithm 2.** Retrieval algorithm for wind direction and speed measurements

**Input**: QuikSCAT L2B Data with rev. no, $Rn$; $(t_s, \boldsymbol{x}_s)$ and $(t_e, \boldsymbol{x}_e)$.
**Output**: $S$, Cyclone Eye
Subset the L2B data based on $(t_s, \boldsymbol{x}_s)$ and $(t_e, \boldsymbol{x}_e)$;
Grid the L2B subseted data;
**for** Pixel $i$ from the gridded L2B subseted data **do**
  Compute the normal vector $\hat{n}_i$ to the direction vector $\hat{d}_i$;
  Calculate which 8-neighbors $\hat{n}_i$ is pointing;
  Update the neighbor count $N_k$ of the pixel $k$ $\hat{n}_i$ is pointing;
  Update $l_k$, list of neighbor pixels, pointing at $k$ ;
**end for**
$MaxNeighbor := \max_{1 \le k \le m} N_k$;
$VC := \{i \mid N_i \ge MaxNeighbor - 1\}$;
**for** $j \in VC$ **do**
  $root := j$;
  $Count[j] := SizeOfSpanningTree(root, l_{root})$;
**end for**
$S := \arg\max_{j \in VC} Count[j]$;

**Algorithm 3.** Cyclone eye locator

retrieved satellite sensor measurements, $\mathcal{M} = \{M_1, \ldots, M_s\}$ from the satellite sensor data set $S$ such that

$$M_i \bigcap M_j = \emptyset, i \neq j, \forall i, j \in \{1, \ldots, s\} \tag{2}$$

with each $M_i$ defined by $M_i = \{m | m \in S, |m - tp_i| < R\}$ and represented by a unique $tp_i \in TS$ and a user-defined radius $R$. However, one is likely to match more than one (interpolated) trajectory point $tp_i \in TS$ to a specific satellite measurement partition. This may result in $M_i \bigcap M_j \neq \emptyset$ with $M_i$ corresponding to $tp_i$ and $M_j$ corresponding to $tp_j$, $tp_i \neq tp_j$, and $i \neq j$. One needs to identify the best time interpolated trajectory position $\hat{\boldsymbol{x}}$ that corresponds to the satellite measurement set $M_{\hat{\boldsymbol{x}}}$ such that (2) is satisfied. We compute the best time interpolated trajectory position $\hat{\boldsymbol{x}}$ as follows.

$$\hat{\boldsymbol{x}} = \underset{\boldsymbol{x} \in X}{\operatorname{argmin}} \{\bar{\boldsymbol{s}} - \boldsymbol{x}\} \text{ for } \bar{\boldsymbol{s}} \in T \tag{3}$$

where

$$\begin{aligned} T &= \left\{ \boldsymbol{s} \mid \boldsymbol{s} = \frac{\boldsymbol{x}_e - \boldsymbol{x}_s}{t_e - t_s}(t - t_s) + \boldsymbol{x}_s \text{ for } t \in [t_s, t_e] \right\}, \\ X &= \{\boldsymbol{x} = (x_1, x_2) \mid x_1 = \text{wvc\_lat}[i,j], x_2 = \text{wvc\_lon}[i,j], \\ &\quad \forall (i,j), j = 1, \cdots, ncol \text{ and } \text{wvc\_row\_time}(i) \in [t_s, t_e]\}, \end{aligned} \tag{4}$$

such that $(t_s, \boldsymbol{x}_s)$ and $(t_e, \boldsymbol{x}_e)$ are two consecutive (interpolated) trajectory points and $M_s \bigcap M_e \neq \emptyset$.

Algorithm 2 retrieves wind direction and speed measurement sets from the QuikSCAT HDF data files based on user-defined radius and outputs from Algorithm 1. Assuming that $Rn$ is a single revolution number, a single HDF data file is retrieved (Line 1). To improve the accuracy of a tropical cyclone eye position $\hat{\boldsymbol{x}}$ and data retrieval, a cyclone eye locator algorithm (see Algorithm 3 [19]) based on the vortex feature of a tropical cyclone can be used instead of computing $\hat{\boldsymbol{x}}$ using (3) (Line 6). Then, the distances between all the spatial points in the partition located using outputs from Algorithm 1 and $\hat{\boldsymbol{x}}$ are computed (Line 7-9). The point sets containing wind speed and direction measurements within the user-defined radius, $R$, are created (Lines 10 to 11). Algorithm 2 can be generalized to data retrieval for any satellite HDF file.

A simple query and retrieval system for QuikSCAT L2B swath data is shown in Fig. 7. The user inputs consist of arbitrary trajectory information and the retrieval parameter $R$. First, Algorithm 1 searches the partition tree structure. The retrieval parameter $R$ and the outputs from Algorithm 1 are then used by Algorithm 2 to retrieve the satellite data for analysis.

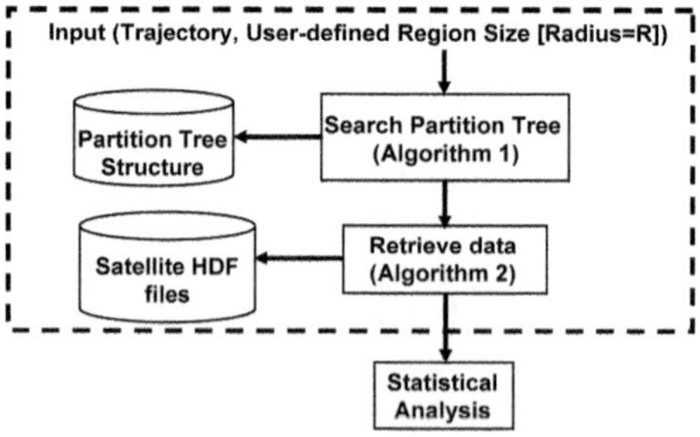


**Fig. 7.** QuikSCAT data search and retrieval system

One notes that using Algorithm 3 increases the computation cost of Algorithm 2. Algorithm 3 works as follows. First, the satellite data is gridded (Line 2). Then, one computes the normal vector to the wind direction at each gridded pixel and compute the number of pixels pointing to each gridded pixels (Lines 3 to 8). The most likely cyclone eye position is the one which creates the largest spanning tree from among the pixels (Lines 11 to 14) with the largest number of pixels pointing to them (Line 15). For TRMM measurements, one can use the characteristics discussed in [6] to improve the cyclone eye positions.

## 7 Experimental Results

In our experiments, we used QuikSCAT L2B data and TRMM 2A12 data from Day 182 (July 1) to 325 (November 21) in 2009. There are 2623 uncompressed QuikSCAT L2B HDF data files (32.1M each and a total size of 84.2G) and 2245 uncompressed TRMM 2A12 HDF data files (98.4M each and a total size of 220.9G). All eleven tropical cyclones occurring in North Atlantic Ocean in 2009 are used in the experiments.

First, we look at the effect of partition size to the partition tree search time, data retrieval time, and the number of vectors returned to users. The number of consecutive instances, $n$, in the time interval for each partition is varied from 1 to 200 with $R = 1$. When $n = 1$, it represents the standard approach where each row in a measurement position matrix has to scan through to decide whether there is an intersection between a tropical cyclone trajectory and a satellite object. As $n$ increases, the partition size increases and the number of partitions decreases. One observes from Fig. 8 that as $n$ increases, the mean search time (MST) drops exponentially and stabilizes after $n = 50$ for both the QuikSCAT and TRMM satellite data. The number of vectors returned to the user query decreases as $n$ increases. We pointed out earlier in Section 5 that a bigger $n$ value decreases the accurate approximation of the data swath partition which in turns affects the data retrieval accuracy by failing to return the data vectors based on the tropical cyclone trajectory. While the number of HDF files (NRtr) that need to be opened in Algorithm 2 remains almost the same, the mean retrieval time (MRT) increases due to the decrease in the number of returned vectors (NRtn). The mean retrieval time for TRMM data is much higher than QuikSCAT data as much more data is retrieved for each HDF data file.

Next, we query for QuikSCAT and TRMM measurements for all the North Atlantic Ocean tropical cyclones in 2009 with user-defined radius $R = 1, 2,$ and 3. The data query and retrieval performance statistics for each tropical cyclone for QuikSCAT and TRMM data are presented in Table 6 and 7, respectively. Based on results shown in Fig 8, we set $n$ to 25 for QuikSCAT and 50 for TRMM satellite data so that it has identical returned vectors as standard approach ($n = 1$). Some observations from the experimental results in Table 6 and 7 are as follows.

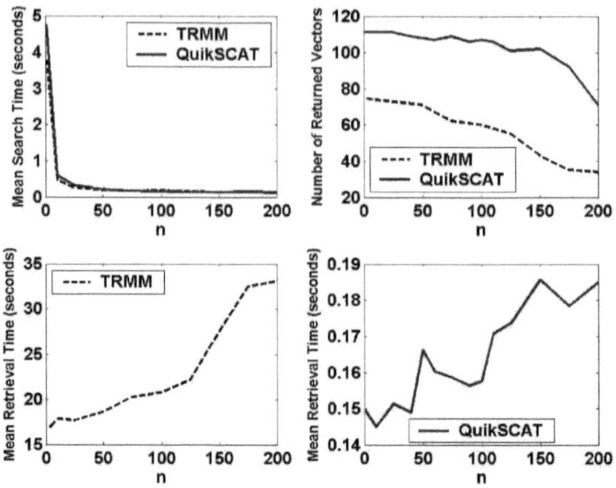


**Fig. 8.** Effect of partition size, $n$, on the mean search time (MST), number of vectors returned (NRtn) and mean retrieval time (MRT) for QuikSCAT and TRMM satellite data

**Table 6.** Query and Retrieval Performance: QuikSCAT data query and retrieval for North Atlantic tropical cyclones in 2009

| | | Radius = 1 | | | | | Radius = 2 | | | | | Radius = 3 | | | | |
|---|---|---|---|---|---|---|---|---|---|---|---|---|---|---|---|---|
| Name | NS | TST | MST | NRtr | NRtn | TRT | TST | MST | NRtr | NRtn | TRT | TST | MST | NRtr | NRtn | TRT |
| 01L | 13 | 3.27 | 0.27 | 0 | 0 | 0.00 | 3.19 | 0.27 | 0 | 0 | 0.00 | 3.22 | 0.27 | 0 | 0 | 0.00 |
| Ana | 31 | 9.39 | 0.31 | 11 | 11 | 1.01 | 9.38 | 0.31 | 12 | 12 | 1.11 | 9.44 | 0.31 | 14 | 14 | 1.43 |
| Bill | 49 | 14.82 | 0.31 | 21 | 21 | 1.90 | 14.79 | 0.31 | 21 | 21 | 1.91 | 14.91 | 0.31 | 23 | 23 | 2.19 |
| Claudette | 5 | 1.22 | 0.30 | 2 | 2 | 0.30 | 1.22 | 0.31 | 2 | 2 | 0.18 | 1.22 | 0.31 | 2 | 2 | 0.18 |
| Danny | 22 | 6.60 | 0.31 | 8 | 8 | 0.72 | 6.58 | 0.31 | 8 | 8 | 0.72 | 6.63 | 0.32 | 9 | 9 | 1.28 |
| Erika | 32 | 9.67 | 0.31 | 11 | 11 | 0.97 | 9.70 | 0.31 | 12 | 11 | 1.10 | 9.73 | 0.31 | 14 | 13 | 1.35 |
| Fred | 34 | 10.43 | 0.32 | 14 | 14 | 1.22 | 10.49 | 0.31 | 15 | 15 | 1.37 | 10.48 | 0.32 | 16 | 16 | 1.64 |
| 08L | 8 | 2.31 | 0.33 | 4 | 4 | 0.35 | 2.33 | 0.33 | 4 | 4 | 0.37 | 2.34 | 0.33 | 4 | 4 | 0.37 |
| Grace | 37 | 11.57 | 0.32 | 20 | 20 | 1.84 | 11.67 | 0.32 | 20 | 20 | 1.94 | 11.69 | 0.33 | 20 | 20 | 1.91 |
| Henri | 21 | 6.71 | 0.34 | 9 | 8 | 1.67 | 6.75 | 0.34 | 10 | 10 | 0.90 | 6.76 | 0.34 | 12 | 11 | 1.35 |
| Ida | 29 | 9.29 | 0.33 | 13 | 12 | 1.74 | 9.32 | 0.33 | 15 | 15 | 1.43 | 9.28 | 0.33 | 15 | 15 | 1.53 |

**Table 7.** Query and Retrieval Performance: TRMM data query and retrieval for North Atlantic tropical cyclones in 2009

| | | Radius = 1 | | | | | Radius = 2 | | | | | Radius = 3 | | | | |
|---|---|---|---|---|---|---|---|---|---|---|---|---|---|---|---|---|
| Name | NS | TST | MST | NRtr | NRtn | TRT | TST | MST | NRtr | NRtn | TRT | TST | MST | NRtr | NRtn | TRT |
| 01L | 13 | 1.76 | 0.15 | 0 | 0 | 0.00 | 1.75 | 0.15 | 0 | 0 | 0.00 | 1.74 | 0.14 | 0 | 0 | 0.00 |
| Ana | 31 | 5.86 | 0.20 | 24 | 13 | 230.20 | 5.87 | 0.20 | 24 | 15 | 225.32 | 5.89 | 0.20 | 25 | 18 | 236.71 |
| Bill | 49 | 8.93 | 0.19 | 26 | 14 | 214.87 | 8.87 | 0.18 | 27 | 20 | 212.05 | 8.87 | 0.18 | 27 | 21 | 211.55 |
| Claudette | 5 | 0.75 | 0.19 | 2 | 2 | 13.32 | 0.74 | 0.18 | 2 | 2 | 13.23 | 0.74 | 0.19 | 2 | 2 | 14.41 |
| Danny | 22 | 3.99 | 0.19 | 9 | 6 | 81.61 | 3.97 | 0.20 | 9 | 8 | 81.77 | 3.94 | 0.19 | 9 | 8 | 81.15 |
| Erika | 32 | 5.98 | 0.19 | 22 | 10 | 186.13 | 6.00 | 0.20 | 22 | 13 | 176.35 | 5.99 | 0.19 | 22 | 17 | 180.55 |
| Fred | 34 | 6.40 | 0.19 | 22 | 6 | 197.97 | 6.35 | 0.20 | 22 | 9 | 195.58 | 6.43 | 0.19 | 22 | 11 | 200.66 |
| 08L | 8 | 1.43 | 0.20 | 5 | 2 | 63.88 | 1.46 | 0.21 | 5 | 3 | 62.47 | 1.48 | 0.21 | 5 | 3 | 63.82 |
| Grace | 37 | 6.59 | 0.18 | 9 | 6 | 58.47 | 6.71 | 0.19 | 11 | 6 | 69.76 | 6.71 | 0.19 | 14 | 7 | 93.15 |
| Henri | 21 | 4.08 | 0.20 | 11 | 7 | 148.06 | 4.20 | 0.21 | 11 | 8 | 156.24 | 4.13 | 0.21 | 11 | 8 | 157.68 |
| Ida | 29 | 5.52 | 0.20 | 14 | 5 | 123.21 | 5.59 | 0.20 | 14 | 9 | 126.56 | 5.50 | 0.20 | 14 | 11 | 126.71 |

**Table 8.** Abbreviation Definitions

| Abbreviation | Definition |
|---|---|
| NS | Number of line segments = Number of trajectory points - 1 |
| TST | Total time for partition tree searching (seconds) |
| MST | Mean search time for each segment= $\frac{TST}{NS}$ (seconds) |
| NRtr | Number of HDF files opened. |
| NRtn | Number of sensor measurement vectors returned to user |
| TRT | Total time for data retrieval (seconds) |

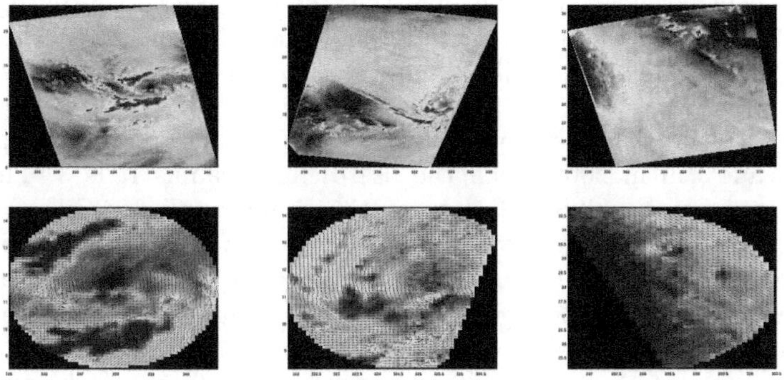

**Fig. 9.** QuikSCAT examples of retrieved partition and output vector when $R = 3$ for Hurricane Bill in 2009

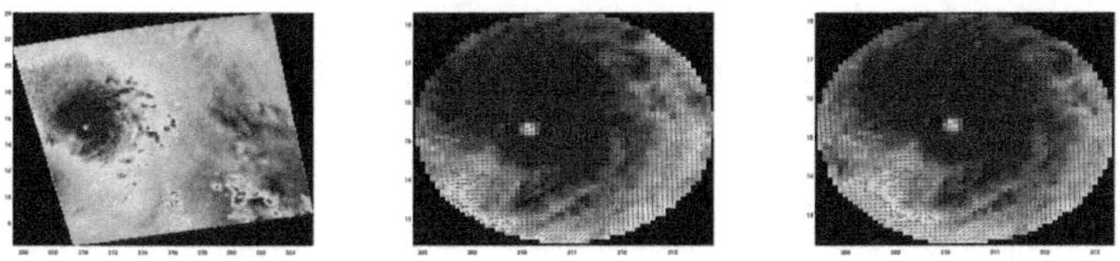

**Fig. 10.** A fully developed Hurricane Bill from QuikSCAT measurements. Left: Retrieved Partition; Middle: Output vector with $R = 3$ using interpolated eye location; Right: Output vector with $R = 3$ using Algorithm 3

1. The mean search time (MST) for each tropical cyclone for a particular satellite is similar. The MST for TRMM satellite is lower than QuikSCAT satellite as there are more leave nodes (partitions) for each QuikSCAT non-leave node (revolution number).
2. User-defined radius does not affect the MST as the number of sampling points is fixed. It only affects the number of HDF files opened and measurement vectors returned to user, which in turn affects the total retrieval time (TRT).
3. The total retrieval time (TRT) is related to (i) the number of HDF opened (Nrtr), (ii) the number of data features retrieved from the HDF files and their matrix size, and (iii) the number of measurement vectors to be returned to user. For each retrieved QuikSCAT data file, four 2-D matrices, namely speed, direction, latitude, and longitude, are retrieved. For each retrieved

TRMM data file, six 3-D (fourteen data points for each spatial location) matrices for five features, and the spatial location (two data points for spatial location) are retrieved. Hence, TRMM data retrieval takes longer time.
4. Even though Hurricane Grace consists of thirty-seven segments, only six to seven TRMM measurement vectors are returned compared to the twenty QuikSCAT measurement vectors since Hurricane Grace occurred close to Europe which is near and beyond the edge of TRMM orbiting latitude.
5. 01L occurred near and beyond the edge of TRMM orbiting latitude. QuikSCAT also did not registered any measurement when three degrees from its eye. Hence, no related data is retrieved or returned.

Fig. 9 shows examples of retrieved QuikSCAT partitions and their output vectors for Hurricane Bill in 2009 when the user-defined radius $R$ is 3. The top row shows the retrieved QuikSCAT data partitions for Hurricane Bill at three time instances. The bottom row shows the output vectors at the three time instances. One notes that the satellite sensor captured the hurricane partially at the later two time instances. In the right column, the example shows a case when the interpolated hurricane eye location is beyond the sensor data boundaries.

Fig. 10 shows a fully developed hurricane. The middle image shows the output vector based on the interpolated hurricane eye location at 15.33N, 310.83E which is slightly East of the hurricane eye. The right image shows the output vector using the eye position computed from Algorithm 3. The hurricane eye is at 15.20N, 310.40E. The right image appears to be the more accurate output vector. Again, one notes that the retrieval time (TST) increases with the application of a cyclone eye location algorithm such as Algorithm 3.

## 8 Conclusions and Future Work

In this paper, we describe an efficient framework to handle ad-hoc query and retrieval of satellite sensor data for dynamic atmospheric events such as tropical cyclones based on ad-hoc user-defined criteria. This approach provides Earth science researchers the capability to retrieve and manipulate satellite data to study dynamic atmospheric events. Future work include (i) integrating the current framework into a moving objects database for both satellite sensor objects and dynamic atmospheric (also earth and ocean) event objects, and (ii) the design and implementation of a spatio-temporal query language that enables users to pose ad-hoc satellite data retrieval queries (see query examples in Section 1). One also foresees the possibility of integrating our query and retrieval framework into a scientific workflow system to support flexible scientific analysis.

## References

1. Esfandiari, M., Ramapriyan, H., Behnke, J., Sofinowski, E.: Earth observing system (EOS) data and information system (EOSDIS) - evolution update and future. In: IEEE Inter. Geoscience and Remote Sensing Symposium, pp. 4005–4008 (2007)

2. Behnkre, J., Watts, T.H., Kobler, B., Lowe, D., Fox, S., Meyer, R.: EOSDIS petabyte archives: tenth anniversary. In: Proc. 22nd IEEE/13th NASA Goddard Conference on Mass Storage Systems and Technologies (MSST 2005), pp. 81–93 (2005)
3. Yueh, S.H., Stiles, B.W., Liu, W.T.: QuikSCAT Wind Retrievals for Tropical Cyclones. IEEE Transactions on Geoscience and Remote Sensing 41(11), 2616–2628 (2003)
4. Mesrobian, E., Muntz, R., Shek, E.C., Nittel, S., Rouche, M., Kriguer, M., Fabbrocino, F.: OASIS: An EOSDIS science computing facility. In: Proc. SPIE, vol. 2820, pp. 284–298 (1996)
5. Henning, M.: The Rise and Fall of CORBA. ACM Queue 4(5), 28–34 (2006)
6. Kodama, Y.M., Yamada, T.: Detectability and Configuration of Tropical Cyclone Eyes over the Western North Pacific in TRMM PR and IR Observations. Monthly Atmospheric Review 133, 2213–2226 (2005)
7. Yokoyama, C., Takayabu, Y.N.: A Statistical Study on Rain Characteristics of Tropical Cyclones using TRMM Satellite Data. Monthly Atmospheric Review 136, 3848–3862 (2008)
8. Lee, C.S., Cheung, K.W., Hui, S.N., Elsberry, R.L.: Mesoscale Features Associated with Tropical Cyclone Formations in the Western North Pacific. Monthly Atmospheric Review 136, 2006–2022 (2008)
9. Rodgers, E.B., Pierce, H.F.: A Satellite Observational Study of Precipitation Characteristics in Western North Pacific Tropical Cyclones. Journal of Applied Meteorology 34, 2587–2599 (1995)
10. McTaggart-Cowan, R., Deane, G.D., Bosart, L.F., Davis, C.A., Galarneau Jr., T.J.: Climatology of Tropical Cyclogenesis in the North Atlantic (1948-2004). Monthly Weather Review 136, 1284–1304 (2008)
11. Shek, E.C., Muntz, R., Mesrobian, E.: Extensible Parallel Query Processing for Exploratory Geoscientific Data Mining. Data Min. Knowl. Discov. 5(4), 277–304 (2001)
12. Ho, S.-S., Talukder, A.: Automated Cyclone Discovery and Tracking using Knowledge Sharing in Multiple Heterogeneous Satellite Data. In: Proc. 14th ACM SIGKDD Int. Conf. on Knowledge Discovery and Data Mining, pp. 928–936 (2008)
13. Guting, R.H., Schneider, M.: Moving Objects Databases. Morgan Kaufmann, San Francisco (2005)
14. Mokbel, M.F., Ghanem, T.M., Aref, W.G.: Spatio-Temporal Access Methods. Bullentin of the IEEE Computer Society Technical Committee on Data Engineering 26(2), 40–49 (2003)
15. Pfoser, D., Jensen, C.S., Theodoridis, Y.: Novel Approaches to the Indexing of Moving Object Trajectories. In: Proc. 26th Int. Conf. on Very Large Databases, pp. 395–403 (2000)
16. Song, Z., Roussopoulos, N.: SEB-tree: An Approach to Index Continuously Moving Objects. In: Chen, M.-S., Chrysanthis, P.K., Sloman, M., Zaslavsky, A. (eds.) MDM 2003. LNCS, vol. 2574, pp. 340–344. Springer, Heidelberg (2003)
17. Lungu, T., et al.: QuikSCAT Science Data Product User's Manual, Version 3.0, D-18053-Rev A (2006)
18. Tropical Rainfall Measuring Mission Science Data and Information System, File Specifications for TRMM Products - Level 2 and Level 3, Release 6.09, vol. 4 (2007)
19. Ho, S.-S., Talukder, A.: Utilizing Spatio-Temporal Text Information for Cyclone Eye Annotation in Satellite Data. In: Proc. IJCAI Workshop on Cross-media Information Access and Mining, pp. 25–32 (2009)

# Client + Cloud: Evaluating Seamless Architectures for Visual Data Analytics in the Ocean Sciences

Keith Grochow[1], Bill Howe[1], Mark Stoermer[2], Roger Barga[3], and Ed Lazowska[1]

[1] University of Washington, Computer Science Department, Seattle, Washington, USA 98195
{keithg,billhowe,lazowska}@cs.washington.edu
[2] Center for Environmental Visualization, Ocean Sciences Building, 1492 N.E. Boat Street, Seattle, Washington, USA 98195
mstorm@u.washington.edu
[3] Microsoft Research, Microsoft Corporation
PO Box 91017, Redmond, WA, USA, 98073
barga@microsoft.com

**Abstract.** Science is becoming data-intensive, requiring new software architectures that can exploit resources at all scales: local GPUs for interactive visualization, server-side multi-core machines with fast processors and large memories, and scalable, pay-as-you-go cloud resources. Architectures that seamlessly and flexibly exploit all three platforms are largely unexplored. Informed by a long-term collaboration with ocean scientists, we articulate a suite of representative visual data analytics workflows and use them to design and implement a multi-tier immersive visualization system. We then analyze a variety of candidate architectures spanning all three platforms, articulate their tradeoffs and requirements, and evaluate their performance. We conclude that although "pushing the computation to the data" is generally the optimal strategy, no one single architecture is optimal in all cases and client-side processing cannot be made obsolete by cloud computing. Rather, rich visual data analytics applications benefit from access to a variety of cross-scale, seamless "client + cloud" architectures.

## 1 Introduction

Science in every field is becoming data-intensive, motivating the use of a variety of data management, analysis, and visualization platforms and applications. This is particularly true for the Earth sciences that involve a host of observational and numeric modeling systems. A comprehensive infrastructure addressing this need requires cooperation between desktop Graphics Processing Units (GPUs) for immersive, interactive visualization, server-side data processing, and massive-scale cloud computing. The requirement that applications seamlessly span all three platforms, leveraging the benefits of each, is becoming the norm rather than the exception. Moreover, application components cannot be statically assigned to these resources — specific use cases motivate specific provisioning scenarios. For example, in "small data" conditions, local processing is ideal for simplicity, to reduce latency, to reduce load on shared resources, and — in the era of "pay-as-you-go" computing — to reduce cost in real

M. Gertz and B. Ludäscher (Eds.): SSDBM 2010, LNCS 6187, pp. 114–131, 2010.

currency. However, as data is increasingly deposited in large shared resources, and as data sizes grow, reliance on local processing incurs significant transfer delays and may not be feasible. We advocate *seamlessness*, where data analysis pipelines transparently span a variety of platforms — client, server, cloud — and can be reconfigured dynamically as the situation warrants — either manually as with our current system or automatically based on estimated cost.

Remarkably, there is little research on architecture, principles, and systems for seamless visual data analytics. Existing workflow systems are dataflow-oriented [1-5]; they do not subsume client-side interactive visualization applications such as Google Earth. Existing visualization systems [6-8] lack data integration capabilities to access and manipulate data from different sources.

In this paper, we explore the design space for architectures spanning client, server, and cloud for visual data analytics in the ocean sciences. Our technology includes the Collaborative Ocean Visualization Environment (COVE) [9], the Trident Scientific Workflow Workbench [1] running on both client and server, and the Microsoft Azure cloud computing platform [10]. We compare various design choices, model their performance, and make recommendations for further research.

To inform the analysis, we defined 9 visual data analytics scenarios gleaned from a multi-year collaboration with ocean scientists. From these scenarios we distilled a set of common sub-tasks and then implemented a selection of the scenarios as representative visualization workflows in Trident and COVE.

We model these visual data analytics workflows as instances of a Data-Workflow-Visualization-Client pipeline, and use this abstraction to derive a simple cost model based on data transfer costs and computation time. We then use this cost model to design a set of experiments testing each workflow in a variety of multi-tier architecture scenarios using typical resources, measuring both computation and data transfer costs at each step.

We find that the role of the client remains critical in the era of cloud computing as a host for visualization, local caching, and local processing. The network bandwidth limitations found in practice frequently dominate the cost of data analytics, motivating the need for pre-fetching and aggressive caching to maintain interactive performance necessary for immersive visualization applications. We also confirm that a GPU is crucial for efficient visual data analytics, suggesting that the generic hardware configurations found in many cloud computing platforms are not a complete solution. Finally, we show that there is no "one size fits all" architecture that is satisfactory in all cases, motivating further research in dynamic provisioning and seamless computing.

**Summary of contributions.** We evaluate potential architectures for *seamless, multi-platform* visual analytics using a representative benchmark of workflows in the ocean sciences. We implemented these workflows in an integrated visualization and workflow system using COVE and Trident, and tested them on several candidate architectures involving client, server, and cloud resources. We make the following specific contributions:

- We present a test suite of representative visual data analytics tasks derived from a multi-year collaboration with ocean scientists;
- We describe a comprehensive visual data analytics system based on COVE, an immersive visualization environment, Trident, a scientific workflow workbench

to support seamless multi-platform computing, and Microsoft Azure, a cloud computing platform that we use for serving data and limited computation;

- We implement the test suite on the complete system across a variety of different architectures spanning client, server, and cloud;
- We experimentally compare these architectures using the test suite, report and analyze their performance, and conclude that seamless "Client + Cloud" architectures — as opposed to cloud-alone or client-alone — are an important consideration for visual data analytics applications.

## 2 Background and Related Work

**Visualization.** McCormick et al provide an early and influential call to arms for the importance of visualization [11] in the face of large scientific datasets. Stemming from this need, computer visualization researchers articulated a standard data visualization pipeline architecture around which the majority of visualization systems today are designed [12]. This architecture consists of three logical steps: *Filter* (selection, extraction, and enrichment of data), *Map* (production of a spatial representation of the data using visualization algorithms), and *Render* (generation of a series of images from the spatial representation). Today, the Map and Render steps are typically performed together using high-performance GPUs; we refer to these two steps together as simply "visualization."

Visual Data Analytics pipelines, in contrast to pure visualization pipelines, must incorporate more than just "Filtering"; they must perform arbitrary data processing, restructuring, manipulation, and querying — the capabilities associated with data management and workflow systems as opposed to pure visualization systems [2].

The requirements of visualization systems, analytics engines, and data retrieval systems are converging. The scientific visualization community is recognizing that visualization systems must do more than just "throw datasets" through the rendering pipeline — that data restructuring, formatting, query, and analysis cannot be relegated to an offline "pre-processing" phase [13, 14]. Simultaneously, the data management community is recognizing the importance of incorporating visualization capabilities into data management systems, for two reasons. First, visualization is a critical method of interpreting large datasets, thanks to the acuity and bandwidth of the human visual cortex — humans cannot quickly "see" the patterns in a million data points without a visual representation. Second, since visualization pipelines typically reduce large datasets to relatively small images or sequences of images, requiring the client to be solely responsible for visualization creates a significant data transfer cost.

Some proposed systems provide optimization and control of distributed visualization pipelines [15, 16], but are restricted to specialized visualization algorithms rather than a general purpose framework, as our collaboration with ocean scientists mandates.

**Workflow.** Workflow systems [1-5] provide a significant step forward in this regard, striving for several goals simultaneously. First, workflow systems attempt to raise the level of abstraction for scientist-programmers, allowing them to reason about their computational tasks visually as data flow graphs instead of syntactically as scripts. Second, workflow systems aim to provide reproducible research. Perhaps paradoxically, computational tasks are often more difficult to reproduce than laboratory protocols, due to diversity of languages, platforms, user skills, and usage scenarios. Expressed as a workflow (assuming agreement on the workflow system!), these protocols are easier to share, reuse, and compose than are raw scripts. Third, and most relevant to our discussion, workflow systems help to abstract away the execution environment, allowing workflow tasks to be executed on a variety of different platforms. For example, Kepler and Trident systems allow workflows to be submitted to a cluster for execution or be evaluated directly in the desktop environment [1, 4].

However, these tools do not provide for interactive visualization on the client — workflows are typically executed as batch jobs. More recently, the VisTrails system [2], adopting the VTK visualization library [8] as a core plugin, has added richer support for visualization. VisTrails also provides a powerful caching mechanism to support repeated execution and exploratory analysis. However, VisTrails does not consider visual analysis pipelines that span multiple platforms in one execution.

Workflow execution and optimization is a well-studied problem [3, 17-19], but these approaches typically ignore client-side processing and interactive visualization. We demonstrate that the local client remains an important resource. Further, since optimization of workflow execution over heterogeneous environments is NP-complete [19], we adopt a simpler model and experimentally verify its accuracy.

## 3 Ocean Science Requirements

The goal of our requirements analysis was to obtain a representative suite of real ocean data visualization and analysis scenarios, then measure the effectiveness of different visualization architectures on their performance. This was part of a multi-year study to determine requirements for more effective science visualization tools. We met with groups of scientists on multiple occasions to collect examples of datasets, visualizations, and workflows. We also interviewed eleven members of the teams in depth to glean detailed requirements. This close collaboration was instrumental to our success, as many of the workflows were not documented and were often problematic for the scientists to recall from memory.

Our work took place at two different ocean science institutions: the Monterey Bay Aquarium Institute (MBARI) [20], and the University of Washington College of Ocean and Fisheries Sciences [21]. MBARI is the largest privately funded oceanographic organization in the world and acquires data through fixed and mobile instruments, ship based cruises, and occasional large-scale multi-institute projects. We worked with MBARI on two such projects: The Autonomous Ocean Sampling Network (AOSN), which is a program to design and build an adaptive, coupled observation/modeling system. This program involved a series of multi-month activities to measure the effectiveness of adaptive sampling in Monterey Bay. A second MBARI effort involves the preparation for a multi-organization program in 2010 to study the interaction of typhoons with the ocean surface. At the University of Washington College of Ocean and Fisheries Sciences, we worked with one group building the Regional Scale Nodes (RSN) portion of the NSF-funded Ocean Observatories Initiative, and another group generating regional-scale simulations of the Puget Sound. Both of these institutions consist of primarily desktop system users who connect to a local network to share data when necessary. Both also expressed interest in how cloud computing could help them on current and future projects.

### 3.1 Abstract Use Scenarios

A key result of this interaction with ocean scientists was a set of 16 data analysis scenarios spanning a wide range of requirements in oceanographic data visualization and analysis. To make our investigation more tractable, we focused on 9 scenarios that had relatively similar workflow needs based on our analysis and discussions with the scientists. These scenarios are listed in Table 1 along with a short description.

**Table 1.** Use case scenarios for visual data analytics in oceanography

| Scenario | Description |
|---|---|
| 1) *Data Archive Analysis* | Analyze existing collections of observed and simulated data |
| 2) *Ocean Modeling* | Generate more accurate and denser ocean simulations |
| 3) *Observatory Simulation* | Simulate ocean observatory data collection from existing data |
| 4) *PCA Sensor Placement* | Determine optimal sensor placement using PCA modeling |
| 5) *Hydrographic Analysis* | Estimate larger ocean effects based on limited observed data |
| 6) *Data Comparison* | Compare observed and simulated data sets for integrity |
| 7) *Flow Field Analysis* | Measure changes over time based on ocean currents |
| 8) *Hydrographic Fluxes* | Measure changes over time in a specific ocean volume |
| 9) *Seafloor Mapping* | Generate detailed terrain maps from collected sensor points |

What we observe in our study is that even though the scenarios shared very similar underlying tasks, they are difficult to categorize as data-intensive, computation-intensive, or visualization-intensive. This difficulty is due in some part to the heterogeneous nature of oceanographic data. Simulations of the ocean are very data-intensive, producing multiple terabytes of simulated output. Most observed data, in contrast, is significantly smaller since it is expensive to obtain and usually sparse, requiring aggressive extrapolation and interpolation to determine ocean effects. Therefore data sizes in a scenario often show extreme variability from task to task. We also find that while large datasets increase computation time as expected, analytics are not usually inherently compute-bound in these scenarios. Visualization needs vary from simple 2D plots up to animations of geographically located datasets with multiple 3D iso-surfaces of ocean parameters. The choice of visualization primarily depends more on a current research need rather than the specific scenario category, making it difficult to build specialized applications.

### 3.2 Concrete Workflows

From this suite of scenarios, we derive 43 re-usable components (called *activities*) in order to recreate the scenario visualizations. These activities are linked together to carry out filtering of the raw datasets to create visualization ready data products. Some of the activities supported were subsampling, supersampling, cropping, filtering, masking, scaling, merging, and resampling data to match other data sample points. Some of these activities are not compute-intensive while others, such as resampling of simulations, can be quite compute-intensive due to the use of irregular grids in ocean simulation and the size of the simulated datasets. We also provide more ocean-science-specific activities such as *particle advection* to map currents or the projection of instrument collected data onto *vertical sections* by supersampling data points. For details on the complete activity set and usage, please see the standard oceanographic library included with Microsoft's Trident Workflow system [1], which was created as a direct result of this collaboration.

Based on these activities, we created a set of 12 visualization-based workflows that provide a representative cross-section of visualization workflows we observed or collected. These workflows each consisted of from 8 to 20 activities and comprised the test cases for our visualization architecture described in the next section. Each workflow loads the necessary inputs from a data store, transforms the input datasets into a new dataset, and then outputs the data to the COVE visualization engine to create a time series visualization of the data. These set of workflows are listed in Table 2 along with the primary scenarios they apply to and a broad measure of how data-intensive, computation-intensive, and visualization-intensive they were relative to the other workflows in the sample.

**Table 2.** Representative workflows tested based on ocean science scenarios

| Workflow | Scenarios | Data | Computation | Visualization |
|---|---|---|---|---|
| *Advect Particles* | 1,2,3,6,7 | Medium | Medium | High |
| *Combine Data* | 1,4,5,9 | Low | Low | Low |
| *Combine Models* | 1,2,3,6 | High | Low | Medium |
| *Compare Models* | 1,2,6 | High | High | High |
| *Compare Data to Model* | 1,2,6,7 | Medium | Medium | Low |
| *Filter Model* | 1,2,8 | Medium | Low | Medium |
| *PCA Projection* | 2,4 | Medium | High | Medium |
| *Regrid Model* | 1,2,7,8 | Medium | Medium | Medium |
| *Subsample Terrain* | 3,9 | Medium | Low | High |
| *Supersample Data* | 1,3,5 | Medium | Low | Medium |
| *Verify Model* | 2,6 | High | Low | Medium |
| *Vertical Section* | 1,5,6 | Low | Low | High |

The overall result of this effort suggests that there are no obvious or simple patterns in the workload of oceanographic analytics, and therefore no obvious or simple system that can be built to satisfy the requirements. Informed by this effort, we have designed a general platform for visual data analytics that spans these requirements, incorporating workflow, visualization, and cloud-based data access.

### 3.3 Cost Model

Informed by the basic Data, Filter, Map, Render visualization pipeline, we model visual analysis tasks in terms of four logical software components: *Data Store*, *Workflow*, *Visualization*, and *Client* arranged linearly according to dataflow. The *Data Store* component may be a remote query service: a database, an OPeNDAP server

[22], or an Open Geospatial Consortium web service [23]. These services are typically outside the scope of a workflow system, though calls may be issued from the context of a workflow. We model the *Visualization* component as distinct from the *Workflow* component for two reasons: First, there are a variety of stand-alone visualization systems found in practice [6-8]. Second, the visualization step occurs last and benefits from access to a GPU, and is therefore often evaluated independently from the rest of the workflow. The *Client* component is responsible for processing user interaction and issuing calls to the upstream pipeline. This model allows us to seamlessly move the Visualization component from platform to platform based on current graphic processing needs; it can be tightly bound with the client for interactivity, tightly bound with the workflow system to minimize data transfer, or run independently to leverage external graphics resources.

We map these components onto a physical architecture consisting of three resources: Cloud, Server, and Client. An *architecture configuration*, or simply *configuration*, is a mapping from components {Data Store, Workflow, Visualization, Client} to {Local, Server, Cloud} that respects data flow order. For example, Fig. 1 illustrates a configuration that maps the Data Store to the Cloud, and the Trident Workflow Service, Visualization Engine, and COVE Client to the local computer.

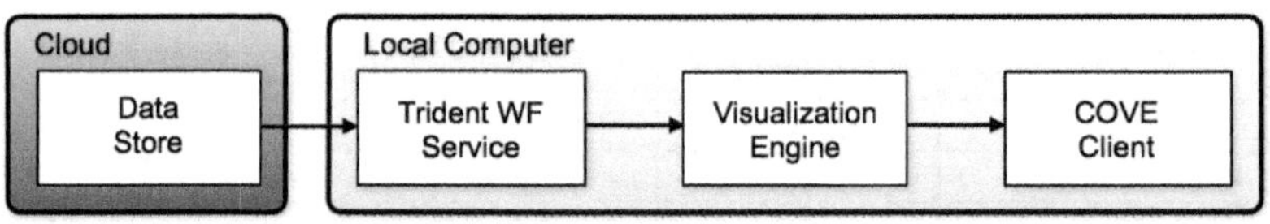


**Fig. 1.** An example of an architectural configuration mapping software components to resources. In this case the data is provisioned in the cloud and all other tasks are local.

We express the cost of each scenario as the sum of the workflow execution time, the visualization execution time, and the total data transfer cost between each pair of adjacent steps. That is:

$$\text{COST} = \text{RAW\_TX} + \text{WF\_COMP} + \text{WF\_TX} + \text{VIS\_COMP} + \text{VIS\_TX} \tag{1}$$

where

$$\begin{aligned}
\text{RAW_TX} &= \text{RAW_SIZE} / \text{BANDWIDTH_DATA_WF} \\
\text{WF_COMP} &= \text{WF_WORK (RAWSIZE)} / \text{PROCESSOR_WF} \\
\text{WF_TX} &= \text{WF_SIZE (RAWSIZE)} / \text{BANDWIDTH_WF_VIZ} \\
\text{VIS_COMP} &= \text{VIZ_WORK (WF_SIZE)} / \text{PROCESSOR_VIZ} \\
\text{VIS_TX} &= \text{VIZ_SIZE (WF_SIZE)} / \text{BANDWIDTH_VIZ_CLIENT}
\end{aligned}$$

RAW_SIZE is the size in bytes of the input dataset. BANDWIDTH_DATA_WF, BANDWIDTH_WF_VIZ, and BANDWIDTH_VIZ_CLIENT are the bandwidth between the data source/workflow system, the workflow system/visualization system, and the visualization system/client respectively. WF_SIZE and VIZ_SIZE are functions of the final output size based on the input data size for the pipeline step. PROCESSOR_WF and PROCESSOR_VIZ are the processor speeds for the respective machines, accounting for the potentially significant difference between server and client machines. WF_WORK and VIZ_WORK are functions of data size and return the (approximate) number of instructions required to process their input. These functions can be estimated precisely through curve fitting, sampling, or provided by the user directly [24]. These functions are typically polynomial in the size of the input data, but we find that even rough linear estimates of the workflows often provide a reasonable estimate.

Although this model captures the cost of the pipeline, it is not directly useful for prediction or optimization because the parameters are too difficult to estimate *a priori*. Therefore, we retain this model as a reasoning tool in Section 5, but experiment with a simpler proxy model based *only* on data transfer overhead. This proxy model, although simple, frequently captures the relative cost between different architecture configurations, as we will see. In this case, the model is

$$\mathrm{COST} = \mathrm{RAW\_TX} + \mathrm{WF\_TX} + \mathrm{VIS\_TX} \tag{2}$$

In Section 5, we will show experiments that justify this simplification for certain configurations.

# 4 System Design

To implement a system to measure the cost components over our workflow set, we leverage three existing systems: the COVE visualization system, the Microsoft Trident workflow system, and Microsoft Windows Azure cloud computing service. Communication between the components is provided through system I/O services if the components are co-located or by RESTful HTTP interfaces when distributed. Each component is described in more detail below.

## 4.1 Visualization with COVE

The Collaborative Ocean Visualization Environment (COVE), shown in Fig. 2, is a system designed in close collaboration with scientists to provide support for oceanographic data visualization and planning. For ease of use, the interface is based on the Geo-browser interface applied successfully for data visualization in applications such as Google Earth and Microsoft's Virtual Earth. COVE provides all the essential features of these commercial geo-browser systems, as well as enhancements designed in cooperation with ocean scientists.

In particular, COVE incorporates better support for the time and depth dimensions of ocean data sets. Visualizations can be animated and synchronized in time. COVE also provides extensive terrain visualization support, as each scientist may require a different set of terrain information. To provide more visual cues for the underwater terrain there are depth-based color gradients and contour lines as well as user adjustable shading and terrain detail to enhance visualization of seafloor features.

To enable experiment planning, asset deployment and tracking, and observatory design, enhanced interactive layout facilities are provided. To support vessel track routing and cable layout, COVE provides a large selection of smart cable and track types. These conform to the terrain, and positioning handles are available for maneuvering the cable around obstacles such as trenches. To provide instant feedback (e.g., budget and current cost), heads-up displays are provided during editing sessions.

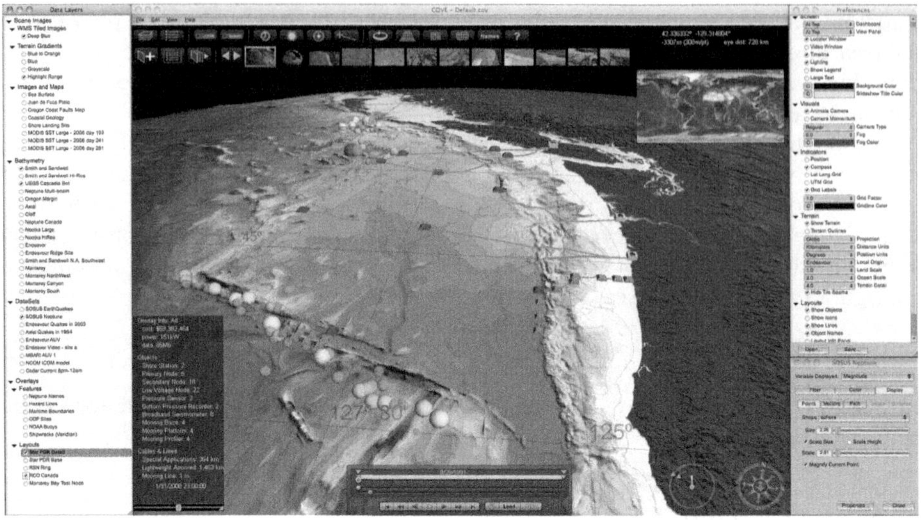

**Fig. 2.** COVE displays a geo-positioned scientific data, seafloor terrain, images, and instrument layout with selectable layers on the left and rich visualization controls on the right

To help share visualizations throughout the team, anything created in COVE can be uploaded to a server to be viewed by other members of the team. Other users can then download the visualization script and datasets to jumpstart derivation of new visualizations for their own needs.

COVE has been successfully deployed for a variety of tasks. It was a key tool in the design of a planned deep-water ocean observatory off the northwest coast of the United States, and has also been a part of two ocean expeditions. The first expedition mapped sites for the deep-water observatory and the second explored ways to support deep ocean navigation while exploring volcanic sites on the Juan de Fuca plate. While quite successful in these deployments, limitations became apparent. The geo-browser interface was empowering to novices, but expert users required extensibility for data manipulation. Also, as datasets grew in size, scalability problems associated with a desktop-only deployment of COVE emerged. To meet these needs, we integrated the Trident workflow system for data analysis and pre-processing.

### 4.2 Workflow with Trident

The Trident Workflow system, developed at Microsoft Research, is a domain-independent workbench for scientific workflow based on Microsoft's Windows Workflow Foundation. The system supports a high level component based view of scientific tasks that offers a number of advantages over traditional script-based approaches including visual programming, improved reusability, provenance, and execution in heterogeneous environments. In addition to these features common to many workflow systems, it also provides automated provenance capture, "smart" re-execution of different versions of workflow instances, on-the-fly updateable parameters, task monitoring, and support for fault-tolerance and failure recovery.

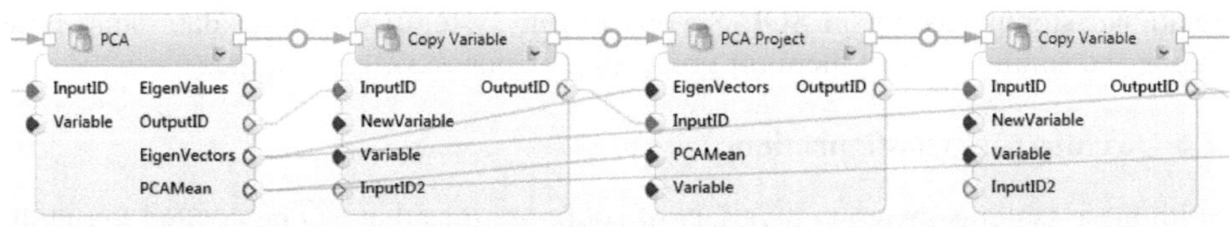


**Fig. 3.** This image displays an example of the interactive workflow editing interface of Trident

Trident can be executed on the local desktop, on a server, or on a High Performance Computing (HPC) cluster. It currently runs on the Windows OS using the .NET API, with SQL Server for data storage and provenance capture. Interactive editing and management of workflows is available through a set of programs that are part of the Trident suite (Fig. 3). Trident provides cross-platform support using Silverlight, a downloadable cross-browser, cross-platform, and cross-device plug-in for delivering .NET-based applications over the Web.

Cross platform support is also available through a web service interface developed as part of this effort. This interface allows execution and job control through a RESTful API. For example, a user can login, select a desired workflow, monitor its progress, poll for created data products, and retrieve data products for local use using HTTP GET and POST calls. This is the communication interface used by COVE to provide cross-platform access to Trident.

### 4.3 Cloud Services with Azure

Azure is a cloud computing platform offering by Microsoft. In contrast to Amazon's suite of "Infrastructure as a Service" offerings (c.f., EC2, S3), Azure is a "Platform as a Service" that provides developers with on-demand compute and storage for web applications through Microsoft datacenters. A primary goal of Windows Azure is to be a platform on which ISVs can implement Software as a Service (SaaS) applications. Amazon's EC2, in contrast, provides a host for virtual machines, but the user is entirely responsible for outfitting the virtual machine with the needed software.

Windows Azure has three components: a Compute service that runs applications, a Storage service, and a Fabric that supports the Compute and Storage services. To use the Compute service, a developer creates a Windows application consisting of *Web Roles* and *Worker Roles* using the .NET API or the Win32 API. A Web Role package responds to user requests and may include an ASP.NET web application. A Worker Role, often initiated by a Web Role, runs in the Azure Application Fabric to implement parallel computations. Unlike other parallel programming frameworks such as MapReduce or Dryad, Worker Roles are not constrained in how they communicate with other Worker Roles.

For persistent storage, Windows Azure provides three storage options: *Tables*, *Blobs*, and *Queues*, all accessed via a RESTful HTTP interface. A table is a scalable key-value store, a Blob is a file-like object that can be retrieved, in its entirety, by name, and a Queue simplifies asynchronous inter-communication between workers. The Windows Azure platform also includes SQL Azure Database offering standard relational storage based on SQL Server. In our system, we model data sources as Blobs and simply retrieve them for processing by our workflow engine.

## 4.4 Architecture Configurations

With these systems there are a variety of configurations that can be created to run the visualization workflows enumerated in Table 2. Fig. 4 illustrates the six architectures we evaluate.

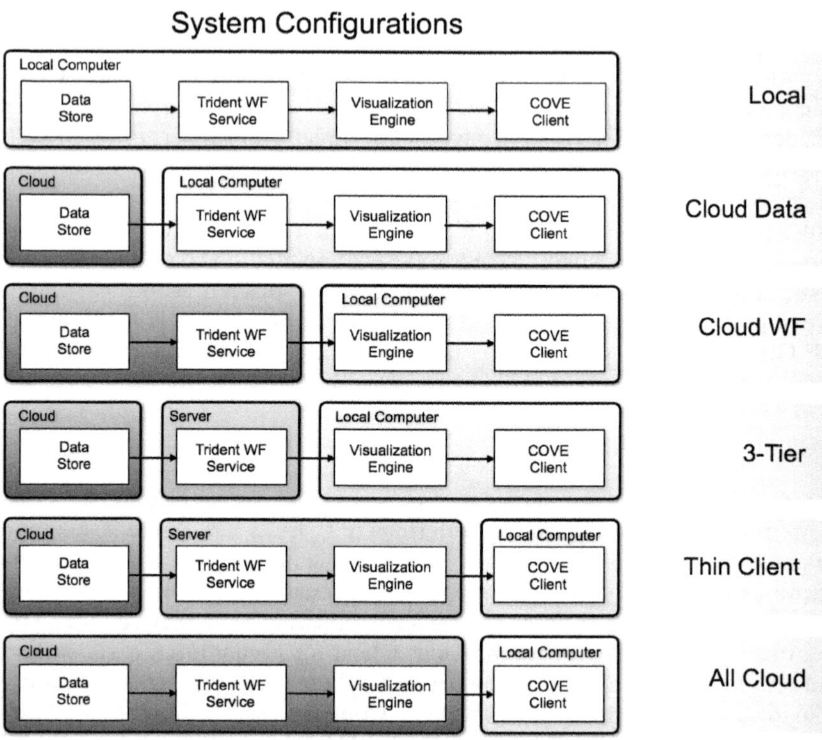


**Fig. 4.** The 6 evaluated configurations of the COVE + Trident + Azure system

In the *Local* configuration, all the data and visualization is handled locally. This is the most common visualization mode we noted with the scientists. It avoids network latency or cross platform communication issues. The disadvantage is that computation and data size are limited by available cores and local storage capacity.

In *Cloud Data,* the data has been moved to the cloud. This configuration allows larger data sizes and also allows sharing of the data with other researchers, but with the overhead of downloading all necessary data to the local system.

In *Cloud Workflow,* the computation has been moved to the cloud and co-located with the data. This leverages the computational and storage capabilities of the remote platform and removes the overhead of moving raw data. However, this configuration still incurs the cost of downloading the filtered data.

In *3-Tier*, the computation has been moved remotely to a server and the data stored on in cloud storage. This allows the most flexibility to optimize the choice of platform based on cost and needs. It also is the most sensitive to network speeds, since raw and filtered data are both transferred to a remote location.

*3-Tier Thin* provides the ability to move the data and visualization handling to a server, possibly with fast graphics capability, and place the data on cloud storage. This configuration is useful for a thin client environment such as a browser or phone interface, but requires a fast connection between the cloud and the server.

Finally, the *All Cloud* configuration allows all the data to be handled in the cloud, with a minimum of network overhead since only the visual product is transferred over the network. The drawback is that the environment is usually unspecialized. In particular, the cloud typically does not provide graphics support for fast visualization.

## 4.5 Data Model

Our data model is essentially file-oriented. On Azure, each file is stored as a Blob. On the Server and Local platforms, each file is stored on local disk and referenced with standard filename conventions. In either case, we access non-local files using HTTP.

Files are downloaded by the workflow system from the data store and cached on the workflow system. The workflow system then accesses them from the local cache. This transfer mechanism could be optimized to reduce the overhead of local disk IO, but the local storage also allows for re-use of cached files in future workflows. Further, we observe in Section 5 that the local IO overhead is small relative to the overall cost of the workflow.

Similarly, the resulting data products are cached locally by the workflow service and made available through HTTP using a RESTful API. Although Trident provides access to SQL server for data storage, we found the current implementation for serializing and de-serializing large files to the database to be prohibitively slow. Instead, we implemented a multi-threaded file-based data storage solution that significantly improved IO performance. All experiments were conducted using the file-based storage solution.

Trident by default loads all data into memory to allow pointer-based access. This means large files can exceed physical memory and lead to thrashing. For our Trident workflow activities, we instead use a lazy loading strategy. We load only a descriptive header when opening a file, and read in sections of the file on demand. This technique reduces the memory footprint and prevents thrashing.

The data files we access are taken directly from our collaborators. Each dataset is represented as a NetCDF [25] file or in simple binary and textual table data formats. NetCDF files are a very common format in the ocean sciences and allow us to use publicly available libraries for data access. We also use the NetCDF CF-Metadata naming conventions to standardize identification of position and time variables.

## 4.6 Programming Model

The Trident activities are written in C and deployed to a dynamic library for increased performance. The object interface for the library is then wrapped by a set of .NET managed C# Trident activities. Each activity typically accesses a single method in the library. This design also made it easy to expose the same functionality available to the workflow system to other systems. For example, since Trident was not yet available natively on the Windows Azure service, we created a substitute workflow shell on Azure that executed our workflow activities.

Each activity has a set of inputs and outputs that can be declared explicitly by the user or implicitly through composition with another activity (e.g., the output of the file load activity may connect to the input of the resample activity.) The activities may be linked together interactively using the Trident Workflow Composer or by editing the XML based workflow description. While the activities may execute either serially or in parallel according to the instructions in the workflow specification, all our workflows operate serially to simplify performance monitoring.

# 5 Experimental Analysis

We tested the 12 benchmark workflows in Table 2 on each of our 6 architectural configurations in Fig. 4 to record the 5 cost components of Eq. 1. Since the final dataset is too large to visualize effectively in this paper, we show a summary of the overall performance results in Fig. 7. This figure displays the average time of each of the cost components across the entire workflow set for each configuration.

**Setup.** We instrumented COVE and all of the Trident activities to record wall clock time for each of the components of the cost model: network transmission (RAW_TX, WF_TX, VIZ_TX), workflow computation (WF_COMP), and visualization creation (VIZ_COMP). We used the three systems described in Table 3 as the Local Machine, Web Server, and Azure Web Role in our architecture configurations.

**Table 3.** Physical Specification of Experimental Systems

| Machine | Description |
|---|---|
| Local Machines | Apple Macbook Pro Laptop running Windows 7 (32 bit)<br>Intel Core Duo T2600 CPU 2.16 GHz, 2GB RAM,<br>Radeon X1600, 256 Mb memory<br>Internet Connection: 11.43 Mb/Sec in, 5.78 Mb/Sec out |
| Web Server | HP PC running Windows Server 2008 R2 Enterprise<br>Intel Core Duo E6850 CPU @ 3.00 GHz, 4 GB RAM<br>Internet Connection: 94.58 Mb/Sec in, 3.89 Mb/Sec out |
| Azure Web Role | Intel PC running Windows Server 2008 R2 Enterprise<br>Intel 1.5-1.7 GHz, 1.7 GB RAM, No Video System<br>Internet Connection: .85 Mb/Sec in, 1-2 Mb/Sec out |

**Data sizes.** The data sizes used for each workflow appear in Fig. 5, averaging around 150MB per task. Typical datasets include time steps of an ocean simulation, a set of "glider tracks" from an Autonomous Underwater Vehicle (AUV), or a terrain model for a region. All datasets pertain to the Pacific Northwest or Monterey Bay region and are "live" in the sense that they are actively used by scientists.

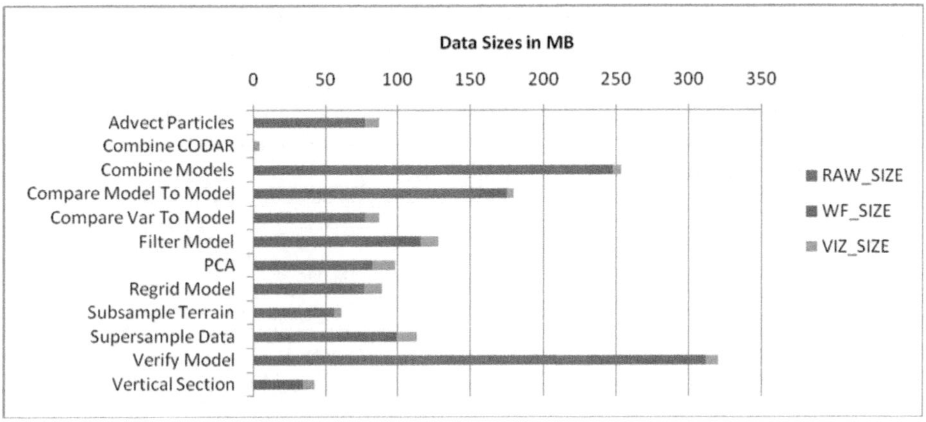


**Fig. 5.** Data sizes used in the experiments. Each bar is broken into three sections: the Raw data size (RAW_SIZE), the filtered data size generated by the workflow (WF_SIZE), and the size of the final result generated by the visualization (VIZ_SIZE).

**Summary of Findings.** We answer the following questions: (1) Is one architecture preferable for all of our visual analytics benchmarks? (2) What role does client-side processing have in cloud and server oriented analytics? (3) Does access to a GPU strongly affect performance for visual analytics workflows? (4) Does the simple cost model derived in Section 3 accurately capture performance?

Our results show that: (1) There is no "one size fits all" architecture — the appropriate configuration depends on workflow characteristics (Fig. 7); (2) client-side processing is a crucial resource for performance, assuming data can be pre-staged locally to minimize transfer costs (Fig. 8); (3) access to a GPU strongly affects the performance of visual data analytics workflows, meaning that generic, virtualized cloud-based resources are not ideal (Fig. 9); (4) the simple cost model is sufficient to capture the behavior of these workflows, and that the cost is generally dominated by data transfer times.

### 5.1 There Is No "One Size Fits All" Architecture

The diversity of workflows in the benchmark illustrates that multiple architecture configurations must be supported in practice. Although local processing outperforms other configurations due to data transfer overhead, this configuration is not always viable. Among the alternatives, no one configuration is best in all cases. In the Vertical Section workflow, for example, the output of the filter step is larger than its input, motivating an architecture that pulls data down from remote locations before processing; contradicting the conventional wisdom that one should "push the computation to the data". In terms of the cost model, this distinction is captured by the ratio of data output to data input in the workflow or WF_RATIO = WF_SIZE / RAW_SIZE. In Fig. 6, the time profile for two workflows is displayed: one with WF_RATIO $<$ 1, and the other with WF_RATIO $>$ 1. For WF_RATIO $<$ 1, the preferred (non-local) configuration to minimize transfer overhead is *Cloud WF*, where the data is processed on the same machine where it resides, however, when WF_RATIO > 1, the preferred configuration is *Cloud Data*, where data is sent to the local computer for processing.

The 3-tier configuration in these examples appears to be universally bad, but asymmetric processing capabilities between server and client can make up the difference. For example, the PCA workflow is highly compute bound, and therefore benefits from server-side processing at the middle tier.

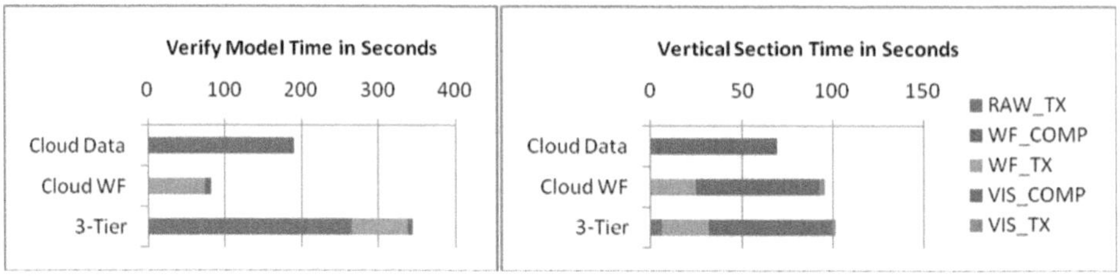


**Fig. 6.** Time profile comparison of a workflow with WF_RATIO < 1 on the left and WF_RATIO > 1 on the right. When WF_RATIO < 1, the preferred (non-local) strategy is to push the computation to the data using the *Cloud WF* configuration. When WF_RATIO > 1, the better strategy is to bring the data to the computation using the *Cloud Data* configuration.

## 5.2 Client-Side Processing Improves Efficiency

At these modest data sizes, the local data configuration performed well in all cases. Fig. 7 shows the average performance across all benchmark workflows. The performance benefits are perhaps not surprising — desktop computers are increasingly powerful in terms of CPU speed and memory size, and are typically equipped with GPU to accelerate visualization. However, local processing is only appropriate for small datasets that are either private or have been pre-staged on the user's machine. Since the trend in ocean sciences (and, indeed, in all scientific fields) is toward establishing large shared data repositories, we believe that aggressive pre-fetching and caching on user's local machines will become increasingly important.

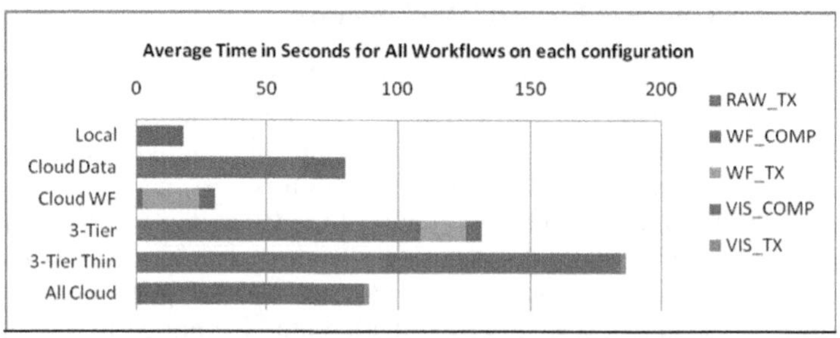


**Fig. 7.** The average runtime of all 12 workflows for each of the 6 architecture configurations is dominated by data transfer overhead. The *Local* configuration, although not necessarily feasible in practice, eliminates this overhead and therefore offers the best performance. This result suggests that aggressive caching and pre-fetching methods should be employed to make best use of local resources.

### 5.3 Visual Analytics Benefit from GPU-Based Processing

Tasks involving significant visualization processing benefit from having access to GPUs. Although GPUs are becoming popular for general computation due to their vector processing capabilities, they can of course be used for visualization tasks with no change to the application. Using the instrumented COVE and Trident platform, we tested whether having access to a GPU would improve performance for the visual data analytics tasks. In particular, in the *Thin Client* and *All Cloud* configurations, the visualization engine ran in the cloud and performed rendering in software using the Mesa 3D library, a state-of-the-art OpenGL software renderer. On average, the workflow set ran 5x faster overall with access to a GPU (Fig. 7). The visualization portion of the work ran 9x faster. This result suggests that the generic environment typically found on cloud computing platforms may be insufficient for visual data.

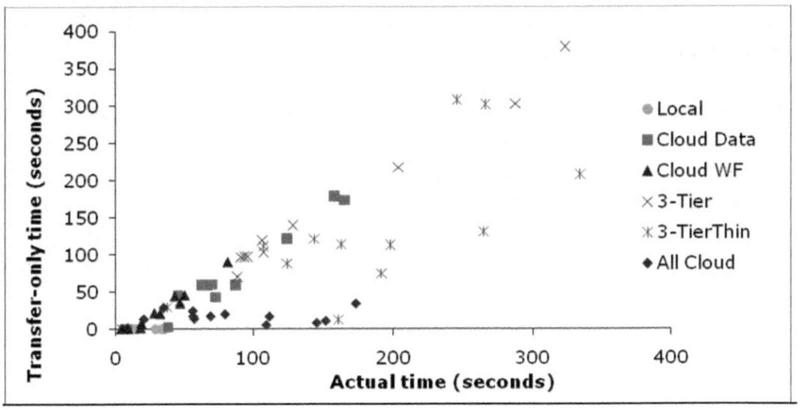


**Fig. 8.** Scatter plot of estimated results from Eq. 2 compared to actual results

### 5.4 A Simple Cost Model Informs Architecture Decisions

The proxy cost model presented in Section 3 is very simple, capturing only the data transfer costs between each step. We allow the source data and each of these two steps to be located on any of the three tiers in the client-server-cloud pipeline, subject to technical constraints. Despite its simplicity, we find that this cost model adequately describes several of the computations, suggesting that a very simple "architecture optimizer" could be based on it.

In Fig. 8, we plot the estimated running time against the actual measured times using a model that ignores everything except for transfer times. A linear relationship is clear, though of course it underestimates CPU and Visualization-heavy workflows, as well as fully local configurations that do not require any data transfer. For these cases, we are exploring an incrementally more sophisticated model based on parameters that can be estimated by the scientists ad hoc.

## 6 Conclusions and Future Work

Overall, we conclude that cloud-based platforms must be augmented with significant local processing capabilities for maximum performance. Due to the overhead of data transfer, access to GPUs for high-performance visualization, and the interactive nature of interactive visual data analytics, "Client + Cloud" architectures are appropriate for maximizing resource utilization and improving performance.

We base our conclusions on 1) a comprehensive, multi-year collaboration with ocean scientists from which we gleaned a suite of representative workflows, 2) a complete visual ocean analytics system involving immersive visualization capabilities in COVE and a flexible workflow environment in Trident, and 3) a set experiments testing each workflow in a variety of client, server, and cloud configurations.

Based on these results, we are pursuing an architecture optimization framework that will dynamically distribute computation across the client-server-cloud pipeline to maximize utilization and improve performance. We distinguish this work from the heterogeneous resource scheduling problem by focusing on visualization and a domain-specific and realistic suite of workflows.

**Acknowledgments.** The authors wish to thank Microsoft's Technical Computing Initiative, University of Washington School of Oceanography, and Monterey Bay Aquarium Research Institute for data and technical advice. This work was supported in part by grants from Microsoft Corporation, the National Science Foundation (Cluster Exploratory Award # 0844572 and MREFC Award # 1005697, through a subcontract from the Ocean Observatories Initiative through Woods Hole Oceanographic Initiative [26]).

## References

[1] Barga, R.S., Jackson, J., Araujo, N., Guo, D., Gautam, N., Grochow, K., Lazowska, E.: Trident: Scientific Workflow Workbench for Oceanography. In: IEEE Congress on Services, pp. 465–466 (2008)

[2] Bavoil, L., Callahan, S.P., Scheidegger, C.E., Vo, H.T., Crossno, P.J., Silva, C.T., Freire, J.: VisTrails: Enabling Interactive Multiple-View Visualizations. In: IEEE Symposium on Visualization, p. 18 (2005)

[3] Deelman, E., Singh, G., Su, M.-H., Blythe, J., Gil, Y., Kesselman, C., Mehta, G., Vahi, K., Berriman, G.B., Good, J., Laity, A., Jacob, J.C., Katz, D.S.: Pegasus: A framework for mapping complex scientific workflows onto distributed systems. Scientific Programming 13, 219–237 (2005)

[4] Ludäscher, B., Altintas, I., Berkley, C., Higgins, D., Jaeger, E., Jones, M., Lee, E.A., Tao, J., Zhao, Y.: Scientific workflow management and the Kepler system. Concurrency and Computation: Practice and Experience 18, 1039–1065 (2006)

[5] The Triana Project, `http://www.trianacode.org`

[6] MayaVi, `http://mayavi.sourceforge.net/`

[7] ParaView, `http://www.paraview.org/`

[8] The Visualization Toolkit, `http://www.vtk.org`

[9] Grochow, K., Stormer, M., Kelley, D., Delaney, J., Lazowska, E.: COVE: A Visual Environment for ocean observatory design. Physics Conference Series 125, 012092–012098 (2008)

[10] Windows Azure Platform, `http://www.microsoft.com/windowsazure/`
[11] McCormick, B.H., DeFanti, T.A., Brown, M.D.: Visualization in Scientific Computing. Computer Graphics 21 (1987)
[12] Abram, G., Treinish, L.: An Extended Data-Flow Architecture for Data Analysis and Visualization. In: IEEE Symposium on Visualization, p. 263 (1995)
[13] Bethel, E.W., Campbell, S., Dart, E., Shalf, J., Stockinger, K., Wu, K.: High Performance Visualization Using Query-Driven Visualization and Analytics. Lawrence Berkeley National Laboratory (2009)
[14] Ma, K.-L., Wang, C., Yu, H., Moreland, K., Huang, J., Ross, R.: Next-Generation Visualization Technologies: Enabling Discoveries at Extreme Scale. SciDAC Review, 12–21 (2009)
[15] Brodlie, K., Duce, D., Gallop, J., Sagar, M., Walton, J., Wood, J.: Visualization in Grid Computing Environments. Presented at the Proceedings of the conference on Visualization 2004 (2004)
[16] Wu, Q., Gao, J., Zhu, M., Rao, N.S.V., Huang, J., Iyengar, S.: Self-Adaptive Configuration of Visualization Pipeline Over Wide-Area Networks. IEEE Trans. Comput. 57, 55–68 (2008)
[17] Bright, L., Maier, D.: Efficient scheduling and execution of scientific workflow tasks. In: Scientific and Statistical Database Management, pp. 65–74 (2005)
[18] Langguth, C., Ranaldi, P., Schuldt, H.: Towards Quality of Service in Scientific Workflows by Using Advance Resource Reservations. In: IEEE Congress on Services, vol. 0, pp. 251–258 (2009)
[19] Wu, Q., Gu, Y., Bao, L., Jia, W., Dai, H., Chen, P.: Optimizing Distributed Execution of WS-BPEL Processes in Heterogeneous Computing Environments. Quality of Service in Heterogeneous Networks, 770–784 (2009)
[20] Monterey Bay Aquarium Research Institute, `http://www.mbari.org`
[21] College of Ocean and Fishery Sciences, University of Washington, `http://www.cofs.washington.edu/`
[22] OPeNDAP: Open-source Project for a Network Data Access Protocol, `http://opendap.org/`
[23] OGC Web Map Service, `http://portal.opengeospatial.org/standards/wms`
[24] Boulos, J., Ono, K.: Cost estimation of user-defined methods in object-relational database systems. ACM SIGMOD Record. 28, 22–28 (1999)
[25] Jenter, H., Signell, R.: NetCDF: A public-domain software solution to data-access problems for numerical modelers. Preprints of the American Society of Civil Engineers Conference on Estuarine and Coastal Modeling, 72 (1992)
[26] Woods Hole Oceanographic Institution Submersibles, `http://www.whoi.edu/`

# Scalable Clustering Algorithm for N-Body Simulations in a Shared-Nothing Cluster

YongChul Kwon, Dylan Nunley, Jeffrey P. Gardner,
Magdalena Balazinska, Bill Howe, and Sarah Loebman

University of Washington, Seattle, WA
{yongchul,dnunley,magda,billhowe}@cs.washington.edu,
gardnerj@phys.washington.edu,
sloebman@astro.washington.edu

**Abstract.** Scientists' ability to generate and collect massive-scale datasets is increasing. As a result, constraints in data analysis capability rather than limitations in the availability of data have become the bottleneck to scientific discovery. MapReduce-style platforms hold the promise to address this growing data analysis problem, but it is not easy to express many scientific analyses in these new frameworks. In this paper, we study data analysis challenges found in the astronomy simulation domain. In particular, we present a *scalable*, *parallel* algorithm for *data clustering* in this domain. Our algorithm makes two contributions. First, it shows how a clustering problem can be efficiently implemented in a MapReduce-style framework. Second, it includes optimizations that enable *scalability*, even in the presence of skew. We implement our solution in the Dryad parallel data processing system using DryadLINQ. We evaluate its performance and scalability using a real dataset comprised of 906 million points, and show that in an 8-node cluster, our algorithm can process even a highly skewed dataset 17 times faster than the conventional implementation and offers near-linear scalability. Our approach matches the performance of an existing hand-optimized implementation used in astrophysics on a dataset with little skew and significantly outperforms it on a skewed dataset.

## 1 Introduction

Advances in high-performance computing technology are changing the face of science, particularly in the computational sciences that rely heavily on simulations. Simulations are used to model the behavior of complex natural systems that are difficult or impossible to replicate in the lab: subatomic particle dynamics, climate change, and, as in this paper, the evolution of the universe. Improved technology — and improved access to this technology — are enabling scientists to run simulations at an unprecedented scale. For example, by the end of 2011, a single astrophysics simulation of galaxy formation will generate several petabytes of data, with individual snapshots in time ranging from 10s to 100s of terabytes. The challenge for scientists now lies in how to analyze the massive datasets output by these simulations. In fact, further increases in the scale and resolution of these simulations — to adequately model, say, star formation — are constrained not by limitations of the simulation environment, but by limitations of the data analysis environment. That is, data analysis rather than data acquisition has become the bottleneck to scientific discovery.

M. Gertz and B. Ludäscher (Eds.): SSDBM 2010, LNCS 6187, pp. 132–150, 2010.

Ad hoc development of data analysis software to efficiently process petascale data is difficult and expensive [1]. As a result, only relatively few science projects can afford the staff to develop effective data analysis tools [2,3]. An alternate strategy is to use either a parallel database management system (DBMS) or a MapReduce-style parallel processing framework [4,5]. Both types of systems provide the following benefits: (1) they run on inexpensive shared-nothing clusters; (2) they provide quick-to-program, declarative interfaces [6,7,8]; and (3) they manage all task parallelization, execution, and failure-handling challenges. These frameworks thus hold the promise to enable cost-effective, massive-scale data analysis. However, porting complex scientific analysis tasks to these platforms is far from trivial [9,10] and therefore remains relatively rare in practice.

Clustering algorithms in particular have been difficult to adapt to these shared nothing parallel data processing frameworks, for two reasons.

First, both parallel DBMSs and MapReduce-type systems support a dataflow style of processing where data sets are transformed by a directed acyclic graph of operators that do not otherwise communicate with each other. Additionally, the system controls the data placement and movement. In this setting, it is difficult to efficiently track clusters that span machine boundaries because such tracking typically requires frequent communication between nodes, especially when clusters may be arbitrarily large, as is the case in astronomy. Previous work on distributed clustering used a space-filling curve to partition the data, then built and queried a global distributed spatial index such that only adjacent partitions needed to communicate [11]. However, the same approach is difficult to implement in a MapReduce-style system that constrains communication patterns and controls data placement.

Second, the varying data density causes significant skew (i.e., inter-node load imbalance) in processing-times per partition. Significant skew can counteract the benefit of using a parallel system [12]. We find this effect to be significant in the astronomy simulation domain (see Section 6). Previous research proposed to use approximation to handle such dense regions [13,14]. This approach, however, yields a different result than an exact serial computation.

In this paper, we address the above two challenges by describing dFoF, an algorithm for scalable, parallel clustering of N-body simulation results in astrophysics. Our algorithm is designed to run efficiently in a MapReduce-style data processing engine and is also optimized to deliver high performance even in the presence of skew in the data. We implement dFoF on the shared-nothing parallel data processing framework Dryad [15], and evaluate it on real data from the astronomy simulation domain. Dryad can be described as a generalization and refinement of MapReduce [4] allowing arbitrary relational algebra expressions and type-safe language integration [16].

The contributions of this paper are threefold. First, we develop dFoF, the first density-based parallel clustering algorithm for MapReduce-type platforms. Second, we show how to leverage data-oriented (rather than space-oriented) partitioning and introduce a spatial index optimization that together enable dFoF to achieve near-linear scalability even for data sets with massive skew. Third, we implement the proposed algorithm using DryadLINQ [16] and evaluate its performance in a small-scale eight-node cluster using two real world datasets from the astronomy simulation domain. Each dataset comprises over 906 million objects in 3D space. We show that our approach can cluster a massive-scale 18 GB simulation dataset in under 70 minutes (faster than the naïve version by a factor of 17) and offers near-linear scaleup and speedup. We also show that

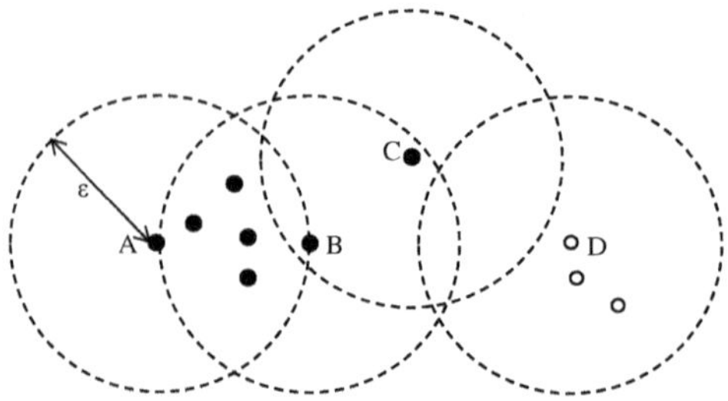


**Fig. 1. Friends of Friends clustering algorithm.** Two particles are considered *friends* if the distance between them is less than a threshold $\epsilon$: $A$ and $B$ are friends and $B$ and $C$ are friends, but $A$ and $C$ are not. The friend relation is symmetric if the distance is symmetric. The Friend of Friend relation (FoF) is defined between two points if they are friends or if they are contained in the transitive closure of the friend relation (e.g., $A$ and $C$ are a friend of friend pair via $B$). In the figure, the FoF relation induces a partition on the particles: all black points are in one cluster and all white points are in another.

our approach matches the performance of an existing hand-optimized implementation used in the astrophysics community on a dataset with little skew and improves running time by a factor of 2.7 on a skewed dataset.

## 2 Background and Related Work

**Application domain.** Cosmological simulations serve to study how structure evolves in the universe on distance scales ranging from a few million light-years to several billion light-years in size. In these simulations, the universe is modeled as a set of particles. These particles represent gas, dark matter, and stars and interact with each other through gravitational force and fluid dynamics. Particles may be created or destroyed during the simulation (e.g., a gas particle may spawn several star particles). Every few simulation timesteps, the program outputs a snapshot of the universe as a list of particles, each tagged with its identifier, location, velocity, and other properties. The data output by a simulation can therefore be stored in a relation with the following schema:

$$Particles(id, x, y, z, v_x, v_y, v_z, mass, density, \cdots)$$

State of the art simulations (e.g., Springel *et al.* 2005 [17]) use over 10 billion particles producing a dataset size of over 200 GB per snapshot. When the NCSA/IBM Blue Waters system [18] comes online in late 2010, it will support astrophysical simulations that generate 100 TB per snapshot and a total data volume of more than 10 PB per run.

**Friends of Friends Clustering Algorithm.** The Friends-of-Friends (FoF) algorithm (c.f.Davis *et al.* 1985 [19] and references therein) has been used in cosmology for at least 20 years to identify interesting objects and quantify structure in simulations [17,20]. FoF is a simple clustering algorithm that accepts a list of particles $(pid, x, y, z)$ as input and returns a list of cluster assignment tuples $(pid, clusterid)$. To compute the clusters, the algorithm examines only the distance between particles. FoF defines two particles as friends if the distance between them is less than $\epsilon$. Two particles are *friends-of-friends* if they are reachable by traversing the graph induced by the friend relationship. To compute the clusters, the algorithm computes the transitive closure of the friend relationship for each unvisited particle. All particles in the closure are marked as visited and linked as a single cluster. Figure 1 illustrates this clustering algorithm.

**Related work.** Thanks to its simplicity, FoF is one of only two algorithms to have been implemented in a distributed parallel fashion in the astrophysics community [21,22] using the *N*tropy library [21,22]. *N*tropy is an application-specific library that supports parallel kd-trees by combining "distributed shared memory" (DSM), a popular parallel data-management paradigm, with "remote procedure call" for workload orchestration.

FoF is a special case of the DBSCAN algorithm [23] corresponding to a $MinPts$ parameter of zero; there exists a large body of work on distributed DBSCAN algorithms [11,13,14,24]. This prior work can be categorized into two groups. The first category of approaches is similar to Ntropy. These algorithms build a distributed spatial index on a shared-nothing cluster and use this index when merging local clustering results [11,24]. The second category of approaches is to perform approximate clustering by using clustering on local models [13] or using samples to reduce the size of data or the number of spatial index lookups [14].

In contrast to these prior techniques, dFoF does not require any approximations. More importantly, it is designed and implemented to run on a data analysis platform such as Dryad [15] or MapReduce [4] rather than as a stand-alone parallel or distributed application. By leveraging an existing platform, dFoF automatically benefits from fault-tolerance, task scheduling, and task coordination. Further, dFoF does not rely on a global shared index but rather incrementally merges large clusters detected by different compute nodes.

Additionally, previous work on parallelizing DBSCAN has been evaluated against relatively small and often synthetic datasets [11,13,14,24]. Their datasets have, at most, on the order of one million objects in two dimensions. In this paper, we evaluate the performance and scalability with real datasets of substantially larger scale.

Programming shared-nothing clusters has been gaining increased attention. Several distributed job execution engines have been proposed [5,4,15,25], and several high-level job description languages have been defined [7,16,26,27,28]. However, complex scientific analysis tasks are only just beginning to be ported to these new platforms. In particular, Chu *et al.* investigated how to leverage such emerging platforms to run popular machine-learning algorithms and gain linear scalability [29]. There are several efforts to implement scalable machine learning algorithms in MapReduce-style framework [30,31,32]. Papadimitriou *et al.* implemented a co-clustering algorithm [31]. Panda *et al.* implemented a decision tree learning algorithm using MapReduce [32]. The Mahout project, inspired by Chu *et al.*, implements many machine learning algorithms in Hadoop including k-means and other clustering algorithms, but there is no density-based algorithm yet [30].

## 3 Basic Distributed Friends of Friends

In this section, we introduce dFoF, our distributed FoF algorithm for MapReduce-style shared-nothing clusters. We discuss critical optimizations that make this algorithm truly scalable in the following section.

The basic idea behind any distributed clustering algorithm is to (1) partition the space of data to be clustered, (2) independently cluster the data inside each partition, and

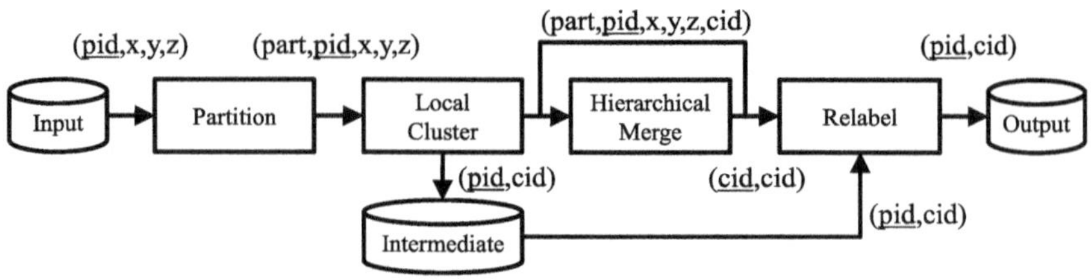


**Fig. 2. Dataflow in dFoF algorithm.** dFoF runs in four phases. Each phase exchanges data in the form of a standard relation or set of key-value pairs. Underlined attributes are the primary keys of the corresponding relations. part represents a partition id. pid represents a particle ID. x, y, and z correspond to the particle coordinates. cid is a cluster id. Phases execute in series but with intra-phase parallelism.

finally (3) merge clusters that span partition boundaries. There are several challenges related to implementing this type of algorithm on a MapReduce-style platform and in the context of astronomy data.

**Challenges.** First, in astrophysical applications, there is no characteristic cluster size or mass. The clustering of matter in the universe is largely scale-invariant at the size represented by the simulation. This means a cluster can be arbitrarily large and span arbitrarily many partitions. To identify such arbitrarily-large clusters from locally found ones, one cannot simply send to each compute node its own data plus a copy of the data at the boundary of adjacent partitions. Indeed, nearly all data would have to be copied to merge the largest clusters. Alternatively, one could try to use a global index structure, but this approach requires extensive inter-node communication and is therefore unsuitable for the dataflow-style processing of MapReduce-type platforms. In this paper, we investigate a radically different approach. Instead of trying to use a distributed index, we redesign the algorithm to better follow the shared-nothing, parallel query processing approach and not require a global index at all. In this section, we present this algorithm, which we call dFoF.

Second, the uncharacteristic clusters pose a challenge for load balancing — each node needs to hold a contiguous region of space but there is no *a priori* spatial decomposition that is likely to distribute the processing load evenly. Load imbalances can negate the benefits of parallelism [12]. To achieve load balance and improve performance, we must ensure that each partition of the same operation processes its input data in approximately the same amount of time. This requirement is more stringent than ensuring each node processes the same amount of data. Indeed, in the FoF algorithm, execution times depend not only on the number of particles in a partition but also their distribution: small dense regions are significantly slower to process than large sparse ones. We discuss extensions to our algorithm that address these challenges in Section 4.

**Approach.** Our basic dFoF algorithm follows the typical distributed clustering approach in that the data is first partitioned, then clustered locally, and finally the local clusters are reconciled into large ones. Our algorithm differs from earlier work primarily in the way it handles the last phase of the computation. Instead of relying on a distributed index, dFoF reconciles large clusters through a *hierarchical merge process* that resembles a parallel aggregate evaluation [33]. To keep the cost of merging low, only the *minimum amount of data* is propagated from one merge step to the next.

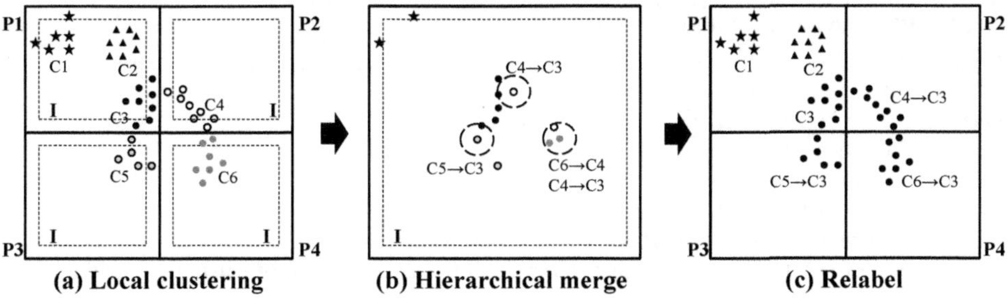


**Fig. 3. Illustration of the dFoF algorithm.** (a) shows the first local clustering phase. Data is partitioned into four cells. Points with the same shape are in the same global cluster. Particles with different shades but with the same shape are in different local clusters. Each $P_i$ shows the cell boundary and each $I$ shows the interior region that is excluded during the *Hierarchical Merge* phase. (b) demonstrates *Hierarchical Merge* phase. Note that only boundary particles in (a) are considered during the merge phase. After the merge, three cluster mappings are generated: (C4,C3), (C5,C3), and (C6,C3). Such mappings are used to relabel local clusters during the *Relabel* phase as illustrated in (c).

The rest of the data is written to disk before the merge. A final *relabeling* phase takes care of updating this data given the final merged output. dFoF thus runs in four phases: *Partition*, *Local cluster*, *Hierarchical merge*, and *Relabel*. Figure 2 shows the overall data flow of the algorithm, with each step labeled with the type of its output. We now describe the four phases in more detail using a simple 2D example.

**Partition.** During partitioning, we assign each node a contiguous region of space to improve the probability that particles in the same cluster will be co-located on the same node. Figure 3 illustrates a 2D space split into four partitions $P_1$ through $P_4$. To determine these uniform regions, dFoF recursively bisects the space, along all dimensions, until the estimated number of particles per region is below the memory threshold of a node, such that local processing can be performed entirely in memory. We call the hierarchical regions *cells*, and the finest-resolution cells — the leaves of the tree — *unit cells*. The output of this phase is a partition of all data points (i.e., particles).

**Local Cluster.** Once the data is partitioned, the original FoF algorithm runs within each unit cell. As shown in Figure 2, the output of this phase is written to disk and consists of a set of pairs: `(pid, cid)`, where `pid` is a particle ID and `cid` is a globally-unique cluster ID. Each input particle is labeled with exactly one cluster ID. Particles within distance $\epsilon$ of the boundary of each cell continue on to the next phase. They will serve to identify locally found clusters that need to be merged into larger ones.

**Hierarchical Merge.** To identify clusters that span multiple cells, particles at cell boundaries must be examined. If particles in adjacent partitions are within distance threshold $\epsilon$ of each other, their clusters must be merged. Figure 3 illustrates the merge step for four partitions P1 through P4. The outer boxes, $P_i$, represent the cell boundaries. The inner boxes, $I$, are distance $\epsilon$ away from the corresponding edge of the cell. In Figure 3(a), the local clustering step identified a total of six clusters labeled C1 through C6. Each cluster comprises points illustrated with a different shape and shade of gray. However, there are only three global clusters in this dataset. These clusters are identified

**Algorithm 1.** Merge result of FoF (`mergefof`)

**Input:** $D \leftarrow \{(pid, cid, x, y, z)\}$ // output from *Local Cluster* or *Hierarchical merge*
$\epsilon \leftarrow$ distance threshold
**Output:** $\{(old\ cid, new\ cid)\}$
1: $M \leftarrow \emptyset$ // nested set to store cluster ids of merged clusters
2: $R \leftarrow \emptyset$ // output mappings
3: $sidx \leftarrow$ `build_spatial_index`$(D)$
4: **for all** unvisited $p \in D$ **do** // compute cluster ids to merge
5: $N \leftarrow$ `friendclosure`$(p, \epsilon, sidx)$ // find all friends of friends of $p$ using the spatial index
6: mark all $q \in N$ as visited
7: $C \leftarrow \{x.cid \mid x \in N\}$ // set of all cluster ids found in N
8: $M \leftarrow M \cup \{C\}$ // All cluster ids in N must be merged
9: **end for**
10: **repeat** // find additional clusters to merge
11: **for all** $C \in M$ **do**
12: $C^+ \leftarrow \{X | X \in M, C \cap X \neq \emptyset\}$
13: **if** $|C^+| > 1$ **then**
14: $M \leftarrow M - C^+$
15: $C' \leftarrow \{x | x \in X, X \in C^+\}$
16: $M \leftarrow M \cup \{C'\}$
17: **end if**
18: **end for**
19: **until** $M$ does not change
20: **for all** $C \in M$ **do** // produce output
21: $newCid \leftarrow \min C$ // select the lowest identifier in $C$
22: $R \leftarrow R \cup \{(cid, newCid) | cid \in C\}$
23: **end for**
24: **return** $R$

during the hierarchical merge process. Clusters C3, C4, C5, and C6 are merged because the points near the cell boundaries are within distance $\epsilon$ of each other. Only points inside each $P_i$ but outside each region $I$ are needed to determine that these clusters must be merged. Figure 3(b) shows the actual input to the hierarchical merge following local clustering phase. This data reduction is necessary to enable nodes to process hierarchically larger regions of space efficiently and without running out of memory.

Algorithm 1, which we call `mergefof`, shows the detailed pseudocode of the merge procedure. At a high-level, the algorithm does two things. First, it re-computes the clusters in the newly merged space. Second, it relabels the cluster ids of those clusters that have been merged. The input is a set of particles, each labeled with a cluster id. The output is a set of pairs $(oldcid, newcid)$ providing a mapping between the pre-merge cluster ids and the post-merge cluster ids.

Lines 1-8 show the initial cluster re-computation whose output, $M$, is a nested set of clusters that must be merged. For example, for the dataset in Figure 3, $M$ will have three elements, $\{\{C1\}, \{C3, C4, C5\}, \{C4, C6\}\}$. This set $M$, however, is not yet quite correct, as there are potentially members of $M$ that should be further combined. To see why, recall that some particles — those in the interior of the merged regions — were set aside to disk before the merge process began. These set-aside particles may connect two otherwise disconnected clusters. In our example, C6 should be merged with C3,

C4, and C5 but is not because the particles of C4 bridging C6 to C3 were set aside to disk before merging. We can infer such missing links by examining the pairwise intersections between sets of merged cluster identifiers. For example, since $\{C3, C4, C5\}$ and $\{C4, C6\}$ both contain C4, we infer that C3, C4, C5, and C6 are all part of the same cluster and can be assigned a single cluster id. The second step of `mergefof` (lines 10-19) performs this inference. In the last step, the algorithm simply chooses the lowest cluster id as the new id of the merged cluster (lines 20-23).

Algorithm `mergefof` executes every time a set of child cells under the same parent are merged as we proceed up the cell hierarchy. After each execution, the mappings between clusters that are found are saved to disk. They will be reused during the final *Relabel* phase.

**Relabel.** In dFoF, there are two occasions for relabeling, *intermediate* and *global*. Intermediate relabeling assigns each particle used during the merge process a new cluster id based on the output of `mergefof`. This operation occurs once for each cell in the merge hierarchy. Global relabeling occurs at the end of dFoF. This operation first determines the final cluster ids for each local cluster id based on the accumulated output of `mergefof`. It then updates the local cluster assignments from the first phase with the final cluster id information by reprocessing the data previously set aside to disk as shown in Figure 2.

# 4 Scalable Distributed Friends of Friends

The dFoF algorithm presented thus far is parallel but not scalable due to skew effects. Some compute nodes during *Local clustering* phase may run significantly longer than others, negating the benefits of parallelism. In this section, we discuss this problem and present two optimizations that address it. The first optimization significantly improves the performance of both local `fof` and `mergefof` algorithms. The second optimization improves load balance.

## 4.1 Pruning Visited Subtrees

With an ordinary spatial index implementation, each partition can spend a significantly different amount of time processing its input during the local clustering phase (i.e., FoF), despite having approximately the same amount of input data. We demonstrate this effect in Section 6, where we measure the variance in task execution times (in Figure 7, all plots except for non-uniform/optimized exhibit high variance). This imbalance is due to densely populated regions taking disproportionately longer to process than sparsely populated regions, even when both contain the same number of points.

To understand the challenge related to dense regions, recall that the serial FoF algorithm computes the transitive closure of a particle using repeated lookups in a spatial index. The average size of the closure, and therefore of the traversed part of the index, are proportional to the density of the region. These lookups dominate the runtime. Astronomy simulation data is especially challenging in this respect, because the density can vary by several orders of magnitude from region to region. To address this challenge, we optimize the local cluster computation as follows.

The original FoF algorithm constructs a spatial index over all points to speed up friend lookups. We modify this data structure to keep track of the parts of the subtree

**Algorithm 2.** Range search with pruning visited subtree

```
Input: root ← search root node
    query ← center of the range search (i.e., querying object)
    ϵ ← distance threshold
Output: set of objects within distance ϵ of query
1: if root.visitedAll is true then
2:     return ∅ // skip this subtree
3: end if
4: R ← ··· // normal range search for root
   // update bookkeeping information
5: if entire branch under root marked visited then
6:     root.visitedAll ← true
7: end if
8: return R
```

where all data items have already been visited. For each node in the tree (leaf node and interior node), we add a flag that is set to *true* when all points within the subtree rooted at the node have been returned as a result of previous friends lookups. The algorithm can safely skip such flagged subtrees because all data items within them have already been covered by previous lookups. By the nature of spatial indexes, points in a dense region are clustered under the same subtree and are therefore quickly pruned. With this approach, the index shrinks over time as the previously visited subtrees are pruned.

Because this optimization requires only one flag per node in the spatial index, it imposes a minimal space overhead. Furthermore, the flag can be updated while processing range lookups. In Algorithm 2, we show the modified version of the range search using this modified index structure. Line 5 is dependent on the type of spatial index. For a kd-tree, the condition can be evaluated by checking the flags of the child nodes and the data item assigned to the *root* node. For an R-tree, the condition can be evaluated similarly by checking child nodes and data items in a leaf node.

We apply this optimization both during the local clustering and the merging phases.

### 4.2 Non-uniform Data Partitioning

While the above optimization solves the problem of efficiently processing dense regions, it does not solve all load imbalance problems. Indeed, with the uniform space-based partitioning described in Section 3, some nodes may be assigned significantly more data than others and may delay the overall execution or even halt if they run out of memory when the data is not uniformly distributed. The only way to recover is for the system to restart the job using a smaller unit cell. On the other hand, unit cells that are unnecessarily fine-grained add significant scheduling and merging overheads.

To address this challenge, we use a variant of Recursive Coordinate Bisection (RCB) scheme [34] to ensure that all partitions contain approximately the same amount of data (i.e., same number of particles). The original RCB repeatedly bisects a space by choosing the median value along alternating axis to evenly distribute input data across multi-processors. Since the input data does not fit in memory, we first scan the data, collect a random sample, and run RCB over the sample until the estimated size of the data for each bucket fits into the memory of one node. We use RCB because its spatial partitioning nature is well-suited to the underlying shared-nothing architecture (i.e., it

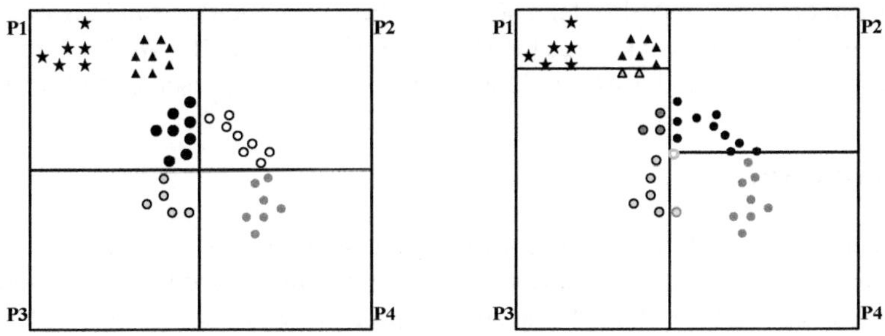


**Fig. 4. Uniform partitioning and Non-uniform partitioning.** Uniform partitioning would generate uneven workloads: $P_1$ contains 22 points while $P_3$ have only 5 points in it. Data-oriented partitioning, however, produces an even workload: each partition is assigned 10 or 11 points.

generates non-overlapping regions that are also easy to merge compared to space filling curve). In Figure 4, we compare the uniform and data partitioning schemes. Because we use a sample instead of the entire dataset, there is some small discrepancy in the size of the partitions. Also, sampling requires an extra scan over the data, thus adding overhead to the entire job. However, it effectively reduces load skew, especially with the first optimization, and improves the job completion time as we show in Section 6.

## 5 Implementation

We implemented dFoF in approximately 3000 lines of C# code using DryadLINQ [16] the programming interface to Dryad [15]. Dryad is a massive-scale data processing system that is similar to MapReduce but offers more flexibility because its vertices are not limited to map or reduce operations. DryadLINQ is a Language-Integrated Query (LINQ) interface provider for Dryad. The LINQ offers relational-style operators such as filters, joins, and groupings and users can write complex data query succinctly and seamlessly in C#. At runtime, DryadLINQ automatically translates and optimizes the task written in LINQ expressions into a Dryad job which is a directed acyclic graph of operators with one process per operator. If possible, connected vertices communicate through shared memory pipes. Otherwise, they communicate through compressed files stored in a distributed file system. The job is then deployed and executed in the Dryad cluster.

We wrote the core `fof()`, `mergefof()` functions as user-defined operators. Because both functions have to see all data in the input data partition, we used DryadLINQ's `apply` construct which exposes the entire partition to the operator rather than a single data at a time. Other than the user defined operators, we used standard LINQ operators not only for the initial data partitioning and relabeling but also for the post-processing output of each phase. We also used the lazy evaluation feature of the LINQ framework to implement the iterative hierarchical merge phase. Thus, we only submit a single Dryad job for the entire dFoF task. Using MapReduce, we would have to schedule one MapReduce job for the local clustering, and also one for each iteration of the iterative hierarchical merge process. The entire job coordination is written in only 120 lines out of a total of 3000 lines. The final Dryad plan to process dataset in Section 6 consists of 1227 vertices with three hierarchical merges.

For the node-local spatial index used in the FoF computation (and also partitioning the data), we chose to use a kd-tree [35] because of its simplicity. We implemented both a standard version of the kd-tree and the optimized version presented in Section 4.1.

# 6 Evaluation

In this section, we evaluate the performance and scalability of the dFoF clustering algorithm using two real world datasets. We execute our code on an eight-node cluster running Windows Server 2008 Datacenter edition Service Pack 1. All nodes are connected to the same gigabit ethernet switch. Each node is equipped with dual Intel Xeon E5335 2.0GHz quad core CPU, 8GB RAM, and two 500GB SATA disks configured as RAID 0. Each Dryad process requires 5GB RAM to be allocated, or it is terminated. This constraint helps quickly detect unacceptable load imbalance. Note that we tuned neither the hardware nor software configurations other than implementing the algorithmic optimizations that we described previously. Our goal is to show improvements in the relative numbers rather than try and show the best possible absolute numbers.

We evaluate our algorithm on data from a large-scale astronomy simulation currently running on 2048 compute cores of the Cray XT3 system at the Pittsburgh Supercomputing Center [36]. The simulation itself was only about 20% complete at the time of submission. Therefore we use two relatively early snapshots: S43 and S92 corresponding respectively to 580 million years and 1.24 billion years after the Big Bang. Each snapshot contains 906 million particles occupying 43 GB in uncompressed binary format. Each particle has a unique identifier and 9 to 10 additional attributes such as coordinates, velocity vector, mass, gravitational potential stored as 32-bit real numbers. The data is preloaded into the cluster and is hash partitioned on the particle identifier attribute. Each partition is also compressed using the GZip algorithm. Dryad can directly read compressed data and decompresses it on-the-fly as needed.

For this particular simulation, astronomers set the distance threshold ($\epsilon$) to 0.000260417 in units where the size of the simulation volume is normalized to 1. Both datasets require at least two levels of hierarchical merging.

As the simulation progresses, the Universe becomes increasingly structured (i.e., more stars and galaxies are created over time). Thus, S92 has not only more clusters (3496) than S43 (890) but also has denser regions than S43. The following table shows the distribution of the number of particles within distance threshold (i.e., density of data):

| Percentile | 25 | 50 | 75 | 90 | 99 | 99.9 | 100 |
|---|---|---|---|---|---|---|---|
| S43 | 6 | 16 | 97 | 373 | 1,853 | 8,322 | 10,494 |
| S92 | 8 | 44 | 1,370 | 41,037 | 350,140 | 386,577 | 387,136 |
| S92:S43 | 1.33 | 2.75 | 14.12 | 110.02 | 188.96 | 46.45 | 36.89 |

Ideally, the structure of data should not affect the runtime of the algorithm so that scientists can examine and explore snapshots taken at any time of simulation in a similar amount of time.

**Evaluation summary.** In the following subsections, we evaluate our dFoF Dryad implementation. First, we process both snapshots using an eight-node Dryad cluster while varying the partitioning scheme and the spatial index implementation. These experiments enable us to measure the overall performance of the algorithm and the impact of

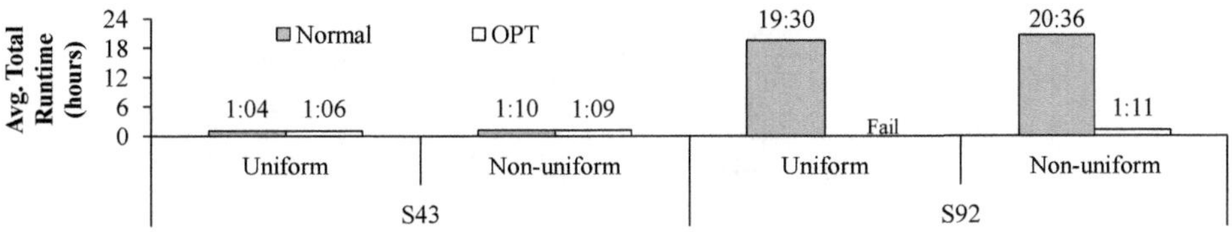


**Fig. 5. Average time to cluster entire snapshot.** Average of three executions except for jobs that took longer than 20 hours. Missing bar is due to a failure caused by an out-of-memory error. As the figure shows, with both optimizations enabled, both snapshots are processed within 70 min.

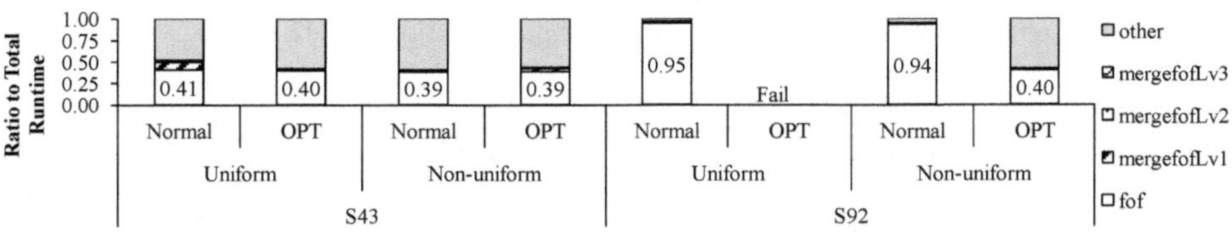


**Fig. 6. Runtime breakdown across phases.** Average of three executions except jobs that take longer than 20 hours. The initial `fof()` takes more than 40% of total runtime. The three-level hierarchical merges, `mergefof()`, took less than 4% of total runtime. "Other" represents time to take to run all standard vertices such as filter, partition, joins to glue the phases. Overall, `fof()` is the bottleneck and completely dominates when the data is highly skewed and an ordinary kd-tree is used.

our two optimizations. Second, we evaluate dFoF's scalability by varying the number of nodes in the cluster and the size of the input data. Finally, we compare dFoF to the existing OpenMP implementation that the astronomers use today. Overall, we find that dFoF exhibits a near linear speedup and scaleup even with suboptimal hardware and software configurations. Additionally, dFoF shows consistent performance regardless of skew in the input data thanks to the optimization in Section 4.

### 6.1 Performance

In this section, we use the full eight-node cluster, varying the partitioning scheme and spatial index implementation. For the partitioning scheme, we compare deterministic uniform partitioning (Uniform) described in Section 3 and dynamic partitioning (Non-uniform) described in Section 4.2. We also compare an ordinary kd-tree implementation (Normal) to the optimized version (OPT) described in Section 4.1. We repeat all experiments three times except for Uniform partitioning using the Normal kd-tree because it took over 20 hours to complete. For Non-uniform partitioning, we use a sample of size 0.1%. We show the total runtime including sampling and planning times. There is no special reason for using a small sample except to avoid a high overhead of planning. As the results in this section show, even small samples work well for this particular dataset.

Figure 5 shows the total run times for each variant of the algorithm and each dataset. For dataset S43, which has less skew in the cluster-size distribution, all variants complete within 70 minutes. However, when there is high skew (i.e., more structures as in S92), the normal kd-tree implementation takes over 20 hours to complete while the

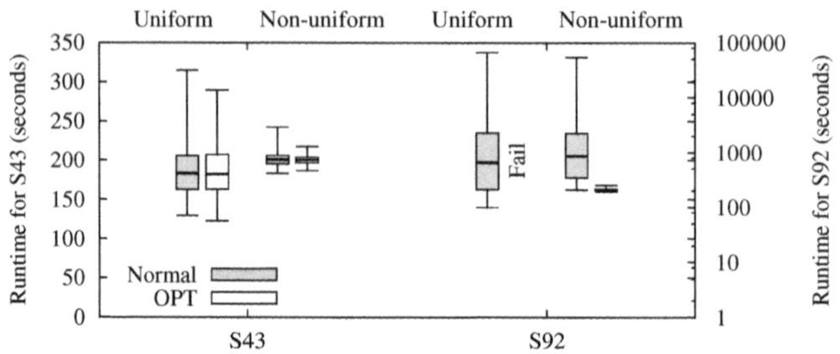


**Fig. 7. Distribution of FoF runtime per partition.** Uniform partitioning yields higher variance in per partition runtime than Non-uniform partitioning. FoF with optimized index traversal runs orders of magnitude faster than FoF with normal implementation in S92 dataset. Note that the y-axis for S92 is in log scale.

optimized version still runs in 70 minutes. Uniform-OPT over snapshot S92 did not complete because it reached full memory capacity while processing a specific data partition, causing the failure of the entire query plan as we discuss in more detail below.

Figure 6 shows the average relative time taken by each phase of the algorithm. The hierarchical merge occurs in order of mergeLv1, mergeLv2, and mergeLv3. As the figure shows, local clustering, `fof`, takes more than 40% of total runtime in all cases and completely dominates when there is high-skew in the data and a normal kd-tree is used. All other user-defined functions account for less than 4% of total runtime. All other standard operators account for over 50% of total runtime, but the total is the sum of more than 30 operators including repartitions, filters, and joins to produce intermediate and final result for each level of the hierarchical merge. In the following subsections, we report results only for the dominant `fof` phase of the computation and analyze the impact of different partitioning schemes and different spatial index implementations.

In Figures 7 and 8, we measure the *per-node* runtime and peak memory utilization of the local `fof` phase. We plot the quartiles and minimum and maximum values. Low variance in runtime represents a balanced computational load, and low variance in peak memory represents balance in both computation and data across different partitions. In both Figures 7 and 8, Non-uniform partitioning shows a tighter distribution in runtime and peak memory utilization than uniform partitioning. With uniform partitioning, the worst scenario happens when we try the optimized kd-tree implementation. Due to high data skew, one of the partitions runs out of memory causing the entire query plan to fail. This does not happen with normal kd-tree and uniform partitioning because the optimized kd-tree has a larger memory footprint as discussed in Section 4.1. Non-uniform partitioning is therefore worth the extra scan over the entire dataset.

As Figure 7 shows, dFoF with the optimized index (Section 4.1) significantly outperforms Normal implementation especially when there is significant skew in the cluster-size distribution. Thanks to the pruning of visited subtrees, the runtime for S92 remains almost the same as that for S43. However, the optimization is not free. Due to the extra tracking flag, the optimization requires slightly more memory than the ordinary implementation as shown in Figure 8. The higher memory requirement could be alleviated by a more efficient implementation such as keeping a separate bit vector indexed per node identifier or implicitly constructing a kd-tree on top of an array rather than keeping

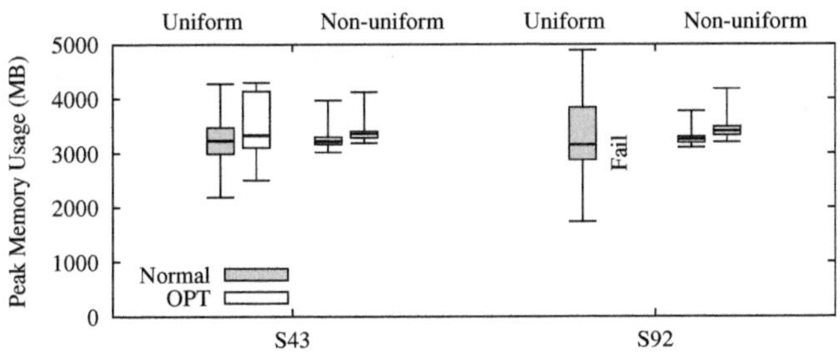


**Fig. 8. Distribution of FoF peak memory utilization per partition.** Uniform partitioning yields a higher variance in peak memory utilization per partition than Non-uniform partitioning. This high variance caused the crash of one of the partitions with optimized index traversal. The optimized kd-tree index traversal has a higher memory footprint than the normal implementation.

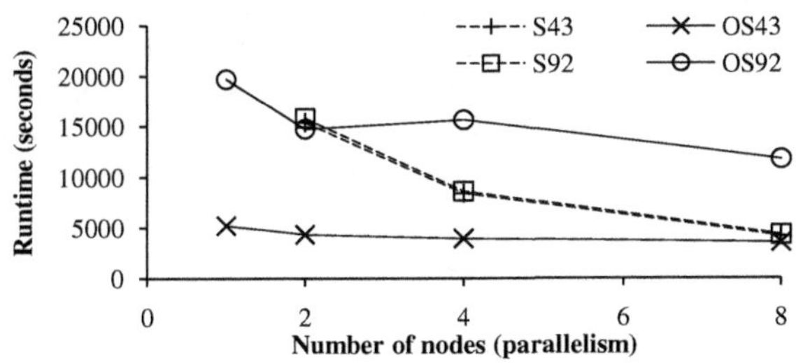


**Fig. 9. Speedup.** dFoF runtime for each dataset with varying number of nodes. dFoF speedup is almost linear. OS43 and OS49 are the result of OpenMP implementation of FoF with varying degree of parallelism. Note that S43 overlaps with S92.

pointers to children in each node. Overall, however, the added memory overhead is negligible compared with the order-of-magnitude gains in runtime.

### 6.2 Scalability

In this section, we evaluate the scalability of the dFoF algorithm with non-uniform data partitioning and the optimized kd-tree. In these experiments, we vary the number of nodes in the cluster and redistribute the input data only to the participating nodes. All reported results are the average of three runs. The standard deviation is less than 1%.

Figure 9 shows the runtime of dFoF for each dataset and increasing number of compute nodes. *Speedup* measures how much faster a system can process the same dataset if it is allocated more nodes [12]. Ideally, speedup should be linear. That is, a cluster with $N$ nodes should process the same input data $N$ times faster than a single node. For both datasets, the runtime of the dFoF is approximately half as long as we double the number of nodes, showing a close-to perfect linear speedup. We do not present the number for the single-node case due to an unknown problem in the Dryad version we use; the system did not schedule remaining operators if currently running operator takes too long to complete.

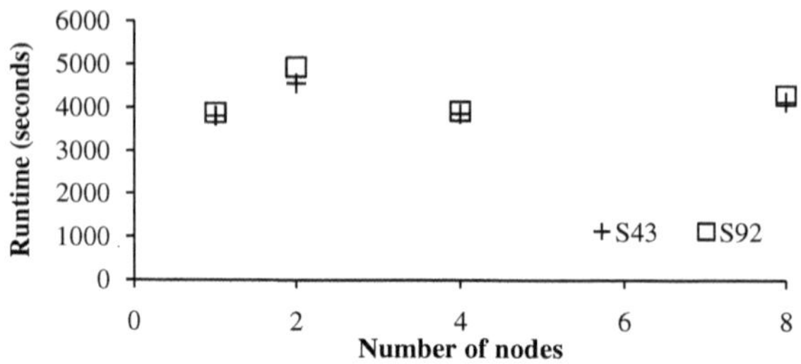


**Fig. 10. Scaleup.** Runtime of dFoF with increasing data size proportional to the number of nodes. Except for the two node case where scheduling overhead pronounced, dFoF scales up in linear.

Figure 10 shows the scaleup results. Scaleup measures how a system handles data size that has increased in proportion to the cluster size. Ideally, as the data and cluster size increase proportionally to each other, the runtime should remain constant. To vary the data size, we subsample the S43 and S92 datasets. For 4-node and 8-node configurations, the scaleup is close to ideal: the ratio of runtimes to the single-node case are 0.99 and 0.91 respectively. The 2-node experiment showed a scaleup of only 0.83 and 0.78. We investigated the 2-node case and found that the size of the subsampled dataset was near the borderline of requiring one additional hierarchical merge. Thus, each partition was underloaded and completed quickly, overloading the job scheduler and yielding a poorer scaleup.

Overall, considering our suboptimal hardware configuration, the scalability of dFoF is excellent.

### 6.3 Compared to OpenMP Implementation

Astronomers currently use a serial FoF implementation that has been moderately parallelized using OpenMP [37] as a means of scheduling computation across multiple threads that all share the same address space. OpenMP is often used to parallelize programs that were originally written serially. The two biggest drawbacks of OpenMP are (1) non-trivial serial portions of code are likely to remain, thereby limiting scalability by Amdahl's Law; (2) the target platform must be shared memory. The serial aspects of this program are state-of-the-art in terms of performance — they represent an existing program that has been performance-tuned by astrophysicists for over 15 years. It uses an efficient kd-tree implementation to perform spatial searches, as well as numerous other performance enhancements. The OpenMP aspects are not performance-oriented, though. They represent a quick-and-dirty way of attempting to use multiple processing cores that happen to be present on a machine with enough RAM to hold a single snapshot.

The shared-nothing cluster that we used for the previous experiments represents a common cost-efficient configuration for modern hardware: roughly 8 cores per node and one to two GB of RAM per core. Our test dataset is deliberately much larger than what can be held in RAM of a single one of these nodes. The astrophysics FoF application must therefore be run on an unusually large shared-memory platform. In our case, the University of Washington Department of Astronomy owns a large shared-memory system with 128 GB of RAM, 16 Opteron 880 single-core processors running at 2.4 GHz, and 3.1 TB of RAID 6 SATA disks.

At the scale of 128 GB of RAM, it is now cheaper to buy a single shared-memory system than to distribute the same 128 GB across 16 nodes. However, this cost-savings breaks down at the scales beyond 128 GB. For example, it is not possible to find symmetric multiprocessing systems (SMPs) with 1TB of RAM. At this scale, certain vendors offer systems with physically distributed memory that share a global address space ("Non-Uniform Memory Access" or "NUMA" systems), but these are generally more expensive than building a cluster of distributed-memory nodes from commodity hardware. Furthermore, the ostensible advantage of the shared-nothing architecture over a large, shared-memory system is the scalability of I/O.

Consequently, our goal is to achieve competitive performance with the astrophysics FoF running on the shared-memory system with our Dryad version running on the shared-nothing cluster (i.e., 64 GB of total RAM — just barely large enough to fit the problem in memory). If we do this, then we have demonstrated that the MapReduce paradigm is an effective means of utilizing cheaper distributed-memory platforms for clustering calculations at scales large enough to have economic impact.

In order to normalize serial performance, we ran the existing astrophysics FoF application on a smaller dataset on both the shared-memory system and our cluster. The dataset was small enough to fit completely into RAM on a single cluster node. The shared-memory platform took 61.4 seconds to perform the same analysis that required 34.8 seconds on a cluster node excluding I/O. We do not include I/O in our normalization because the system's storage hardware is still representative of the current state-of-the-art; only its CPUs are dated. In the following results, we normalize the timings of the CPU portion of the test on shared-memory system to the standard of the Dryad cluster hardware.

Running the astronomy FoF algorithm in serial on the shared-memory system for our test dataset S43 (with the same parameters as our cluster runs) took 5202 seconds in total — only 1986 of this was actual FoF calculation, the rest was I/O. In comparison, our Dryad version would likely have taken an estimated 30,000 seconds, as extrapolated from our optimized Dryad 2-node run assuming ideal scalability. However, since we do not actually know the serial runtime of Dryad on this dataset, it is difficult to compare a parallel Dryad run directly to our serial FoF implementation, since there is undoubtedly parallel overhead induced by running Dryad on more than one node.

The runtime comparisons are much more interesting for S92. The particle distribution in S92 is more highly clustered than S43, meaning that the clusters are larger on average, and there are more of them. In this case, the astrophysics FoF takes quite a bit longer: 16763 seconds for the FoF computation itself and 19721 for the entire run including I/O, compared to roughly 30,000 seconds for a serial Dryad run of the same snapshot. The OpenMP implementation still wins, but the difference is smaller than for S43.

One can also see the effect of S92's higher clustering on the OpenMP scalability. The OpenMP version is not efficient for snapshots with many groups spanning multiple thread domains. This limitation is because multiple threads may start tracking the same group. When two threads realize they are actually tracking the same group, one gives up entirely but does not contribute its already-completed work to the survivor. While this is another optimization that could be implemented in the OpenMP version, astronomers have not yet done so. This effect can be seen in Figure 9.

Since our Dryad version performed similarly on both snapshots, we conclude that our methodology achieves scalability in both computational work and I/O. The advantage of our implementation can be seen when we run on more nodes. This advantage allows us to match the performance of the astrophysics code on S43 (3513 seconds vs. 4141 seconds) and to substantially outperform it for S92 (11763 seconds vs. 4293 seconds). This idea is in keeping with the MapReduce strategy: We employ a technique that may be less than optimally efficient in serial, but that scales very well. Consequently, we have achieved our goal of reducing time-to-solution on platforms that offer an economic advantage over current shared-memory approaches at large scales.

## 7 Conclusion

Science is rapidly becoming a data management problem. Scaling existing data analysis techniques is very important to expedite the knowledge discovery process. In this paper, we designed and implemented a standard clustering algorithm to analyze astrophysical simulation output using a popular MapReduce-style data analysis platform. Through experiments on two real datasets and a small eight-node lab-size cluster, we show that our proposed dFoF algorithm achieves near-linear scalability and performs consistently regardless of data skew. To achieve such performance, we leverage non-uniform data partitioning based on sampling and introduce an optimized spatial index approach. An interesting area of future work, is to extend dFoF to the DBSCAN algorithm.

## Acknowledgment

It is a pleasure to acknowledge the help we have received from Tom Quinn, both during the project and in writing this publication. Simulations "Cosmo25" and "Cosmo50" were graciously supplied by Tom Quinn and Fabio Governato of the University of Washington Department of Astronomy. The simulations were produced using allocations of advanced NSF–supported computing resources operated by the Pittsburgh Supercomputing Center, NCSA, and the TeraGrid. We are also grateful to the Dryad and DryadLINQ teams, MSR-SV, and Microsoft External Research for providing us with an alpha release of Dryad and DryadLINQ and for their support in installing and running this software. This work was funded in part by the NASA Advanced Information Systems Research Program grants NNG06GE23G, NNX08AY72G, NSF CAREER award IIS-0845397, CNS-0454425, and gifts from Microsoft Research. Magdalena Balazinska is also sponsored in part by a Microsoft Research New Faculty Fellowship.

## References

1. Becla, J., Lim, K.T.: Report from the SciDB meeting (a.k.a. extremely large database workshop) (2008), `http://xldb.slac.stanford.edu/download/attachments/4784226/sciDB2008_report.pdf`
2. Sloan Digital Sky Survey, `http://cas.sdss.org`
3. The Large Hadron Collider, `http://lhc.web.cern.ch/lhc/`
4. Dean, J., Ghemawat, S.: MapReduce: simplified data processing on large clusters. In: Proc. of the 6th OSDI Symp. (2004)

5. Hadoop, http://hadoop.apache.org/
6. Hadoop Hive, http://hadoop.apache.org/hive/
7. Olston, C., Reed, B., Srivastava, U., Kumar, R., Tomkins, A.: Pig latin: a not-so-foreign language for data processing. In: Proc. of the SIGMOD Conf., pp. 1099–1110 (2008)
8. ISO/IEC 9075-*:2003: Database Languages - SQL. ISO, Geneva, Switzerland
9. Cohen, J., Dolan, B., Dunlap, M., Hellerstein, J.M., Welton, C.: Mad skills: new analysis practices for big data. Proc. VLDB Endow. 2(2), 1481–1492 (2009)
10. Stonebraker, et al.: Requirements for science data bases and SciDB. In: Fourth CIDR Conf., perspectives (2009)
11. Xu, X., Jäger, J., Kriegel, H.P.: A fast parallel clustering algorithm for large spatial databases. Data Min. Knowl. Discov. 3(3), 263–290 (1999)
12. DeWitt, D., Gray, J.: Parallel database systems: the future of high performance database systems. Communications of the ACM 35(6), 85–98 (1992)
13. Januzaj, E., Kriegel, H.P., Pfeifle, M.: Scalable density-based distributed clustering. In: Boulicaut, J.-F., Esposito, F., Giannotti, F., Pedreschi, D. (eds.) PKDD 2004. LNCS (LNAI), vol. 3202, pp. 231–244. Springer, Heidelberg (2004)
14. Aoying, Z., Shuigeng, Z., Jing, C., Ye, F., Yunfa, H.: Approaches for scaling dbscan algorithm to large spatial databases. Journal of Comp. Sci. and Tech., 509–526 (2000)
15. Isard, M., Budiu, M., Yu, Y., Birrell, A., Fetterly, D.: Dryad: Distributed data-parallel programs from sequential building blocks. In: Proc. of the 2007 EuroSys Conf., pp. 59–72 (2007)
16. Yu, et al.: DryadLINQ: A system for general-purpose distributed data-parallel computing using a high-level language. In: Proc. of the 8th OSDI Symp. (2008)
17. Springel, et al.: Simulations of the formation, evolution and clustering of galaxies and quasars. Nature 435, 629–636 (2005)
18. About the Blue Waters project, http://www.ncsa.illinois.edu/BlueWaters/
19. Davis, M., Efstathiou, G., Frenk, C.S., White, S.D.M.: The evolution of large-scale structure in a universe dominated by cold dark matter. Astrophysical Journal 292, 371–394 (1985)
20. Reed, et al.: Evolution of the mass function of dark matter haloes. Monthly Notices of the Royal Astronomical Society 346, 565–572 (2003)
21. Gardner, J.P., Connolly, A., McBride, C.: Enabling rapid development of parallel tree search applications. In: Proc. of the 2007 CLADE Symp. (2007)
22. Gardner, J.P., Connolly, A., McBride, C.: Enabling knowledge discovery in a virtual universe. In: Proc. of the 2007 TeraGrid Symp. (2007)
23. Ester, M., Kriegel, H.P., Sander, J., Xu, X.: A density-based algorithm for discovering clusters in large spatial databases with noise. In: Proc. of the 2nd KDD Conf., pp. 226–231 (1996)
24. Arlia, D., Coppola, M.: Experiments in parallel clustering with dbscan. In: Sakellariou, R., Keane, J.A., Gurd, J.R., Freeman, L. (eds.) Euro-Par 2001. LNCS, vol. 2150, pp. 326–331. Springer, Heidelberg (2001)
25. DeWitt, et al.: Clustera: an integrated computation and data management system. In: Proc. of the 34th VLDB Conf., pp. 28–41 (2008)
26. Chaiken, et al.: Scope: easy and efficient parallel processing of massive data sets. In: Proc. of the 34th VLDB Conf., pp. 1265–1276 (2008)
27. Cascading, http://www.cascading.org/
28. Pike, R., Dorward, S., Griesemer, R., Quinlan, S.: Interpreting the data: Parallel analysis with Sawzall. Scientific Programming 13(4) (2005)
29. Chu, et al.: Map-reduce for machine learning on multicore. In: Schölkopf, B., Platt, J., Hoffman, T. (eds.) NIPS, vol. 19 (2007)
30. Apache Mahout, http://lucene.apache.org/mahout/

31. Papadimitriou, S., Sun, J.: Disco: Distributed co-clustering with map-reduce: A case study towards petabyte-scale end-to-end mining. In: Proc. of the 8th ICDM Conf., pp. 512–521 (2008)
32. Panda, B., Herbach, J., Basu, S., Bayardo, R.: Planet: massively parallel learning of tree ensembles with mapreduce. Proc. of the VLDB Endowment 2(2) (2009)
33. Yu, Y., Gunda, P.K., Isard, M.: Distributed aggregation for data-parallel computing: interfaces and implementations. In: Proc. of the 22nd SOSP Symp. (2009)
34. Berger, M., Bokhari, S.: A partitioning strategy for nonuniform problems on multiprocessors. IEEE Transactions on Computers C-36(5) (1987)
35. Gaede, V., Günther, O.: Multidimensional access methods. ACM Comput. Surv. 30(2), 170–231 (1998)
36. Bigben, `http://www.psc.edu/machines/cray/xt3/`
37. Dagum, L., Menon, R.: Openmp: An industry-standard api for shared-memory programming. Computing in Science and Engineering 5(1), 46–55 (1998)

# Database Design for High-Resolution LIDAR Topography Data*

Viswanath Nandigam, Chaitan Baru, and Christopher Crosby

San Diego Supercomputer Center, University of California San Diego

**Abstract.** The advent of high-resolution mapping technologies such as airborne Light Detection and Ranging (LIDAR) has revolutionized the study of processes acting on the earth's surface. However, the massive volumes of data produced by LIDAR technology pose significant technical challenges in terms of the management and web-based distribution of these datasets. This paper provides a case study in the use of relational database technology for serving large airborne LIDAR "point cloud" datasets, as part of the National Science Foundation funded OpenTopography facility. We have experimented with the use of spatial extensions in the database as well as implementation solutions from a single partition database on a supercomputer resource to a multi-partition implementation on a shared-nothing commodity cluster for management of these terabyte scale datasets. We also describe future directions being pursued to support binary data formats and for scaling to larger system configurations.

## 1 Introduction

High-resolution topography data acquired with LIDAR (Light Detection and Ranging) are revolutionizing the study of geomorphic processes acting along the Earth's surface. These data are emerging as a fundamental tool for research on a variety of topics ranging from earthquake hazards to ice sheet dynamics. LIDAR topography data allow earth scientists to study the processes that contribute to landscape evolution at resolutions not previously possible and provide new insights into many geologic phenomena, e.g. [1,2,3].

LIDAR data are currently being acquired by local, state, and federal agencies across the United States for a wide range of applications, from earthquake hazard studies (including for recent earthquakes in Haiti and Mexicali, near the California/Baja California border) to mapping utility corridors and other vital infrastructure.

Although high-resolution topographic data collection is burgeoning for research, planning, and regulatory activities, the volume of data generated by the technology currently impedes wider utilization. On the one hand, many organizations that acquire LIDAR topography struggle to manage the datasets due

* This research is supported by US National Science Foundation grants: EAR-0930731, EAR-0744229, CluE-0844530.

M. Gertz and B. Ludäscher (Eds.): SSDBM 2010, LNCS 6187, pp. 151–159, 2010.

to their relatively large size and the fact that most organizations do not have the necessary disk capacity and bandwidth, nor the in-house expertise, to make these data available via the Internet for community access. On the other hand, these acquisitions are often undertaken with public funding by federal, state, and local agencies at a cost of a few hundred dollars per square kilometer, thus it is important to maximize the utilization of such data by providing easy online access to a range of potential users.

The NSF-funded OpenTopography facility (www.opentopography.org) provides a cyberinfrastructure-based platform to improve web-based access to high-resolution LIDAR topography data, online processing tools, and derivative products. The OpenTopography effort began as a research and development activity within the GEON project [4], and has since been funded as an NSF facility with an active user community of thousands of scientists, educators, students, and government agency users. The central component of the OpenTopography Facility is the OpenTopography Portal, which provides access to LIDAR data in various formats to serve LIDAR users at various levels of expertise. These include "raw" LIDAR point cloud data emphasized here, standard LIDAR-derived digital elevation models (DEMs), and easily accessible KMZ-based Google Earth products [7].

The sections that follow describe the design of the OpenTopography LIDAR database, its evolution since the early phases of the project, lessons learned and future directions.

## 2 The LIDAR Point Cloud Data Management System

The primary focus of this paper is on the management of the raw LIDAR "point cloud" datasets representing discrete measurements of the earth's surface using IBM's DB2 database.

### 2.1 LIDAR Point Cloud Data Format

LIDAR point cloud data are a collection of the individual geographic coordinates (e.g. Universal Transverse Mercator projection, UTM [9]) of each individual return of the outgoing pulse of the laser scanning system. Each return is represented as a record in the point cloud data file and includes the horizontal coordinates of the return (x, y) and the elevation (z), as well as other attributes that provide additional information about that data point. For example, each data point in the Northern San Andreas Fault point cloud dataset [8] includes information about the number of returns recorded by the laser scanner (*noreturns*), orientation of the scanner at the time of the shot (*offnidar*), the intensity of the return as a 256 grey scale value (*returnint*), a classification parameter that designates whether the return came from the ground, vegetation, or a structure (*classification*), and date and time of collection tied to a high-precision GPS time stamp (*time*), as shown in this data row extract:
[x, y, z, date, time, returnnumber, noreturns, offnidar, returnint, classification]

```
6048776.74, 2240379.76, 4.43, 1204, 515158.764, 1.00,5,12.62,12,G
```

The dataset contains approximately 1.2 billion point returns and was originally organized in groups of files corresponding to USGS Quarter Quadrangles [10].

The attributes associated with each data point are critical to applications of the data. For example, a user can query on the classification attribute to perform "*virtual deforestation*" by selecting only points classified as "ground return", thereby revealing the ground structure beneath a vegetation canopy. While the NSAF dataset attributes are typical of most LIDAR data, the list of attributes can vary among datasets and the database must be designed to accommodate such variations.

## 2.2 Data Preparation and Loading

As shown in Figure 1, the raw LIDAR point cloud data needs go through a pre-processing and transformation phase before it can be loaded into the database. A typical dataset may contain billions of point returns and range anywhere from 100's of GB to a few TB depending on its extent and attributes. They are usually shipped to the OpenTopography facility on hard drives or transfered via an FTP server and arrive organized into numerous hetrogenous files of varying point densities and spatial extents.

Since the raw LIDAR data are collected by a variety of vendors, datasets may also arrive in different formats, with different compression schemes, and different attributes. In some cases, even within the same dataset, different files may contain data recorded in different geographic projections. A pre-processing step is required to convert all data into the same projection system. The first phase of data preparation involves extracting data, error checking, and converting data into a target projection system, as necessary. This initial *validation phase* is then followed by a *transformation phase* where the data are reorganized to create a set of output files with more uniform data distribution across files. We have found that for large datasets usually in excess of a billion rows, it is more efficient to distribute the data across multiple tables in the database rather than storing all data in a single very large table.

Each LIDAR dataset is first analyzed based on its spatial extent and average point density to determine the number of tables across which it should be distributed in the database. For example, in the case of the Northern San Andreas (NSAF) dataset, all files within a USGS Quarter Quadrangle were aggregated into a single file, which was then implemented as a single table in the database. Thus, the dataset comprising of approximately 1 billion records is distributed uniformly across 45 tables, with an average of about 25 million rows per table. The specific implementation, including the number of tables and size of each table, will vary for each LIDAR dataset.

Data access can be further speeded up by using a *metadata table*, which serves as an additional index layer. The metadata table stores information including the table name, the spatial extent corresponding to the data in that table, number of rows in the table, and geographic projection for the data in the table. A user query in the form of a bounding box is first applied to the metadata table

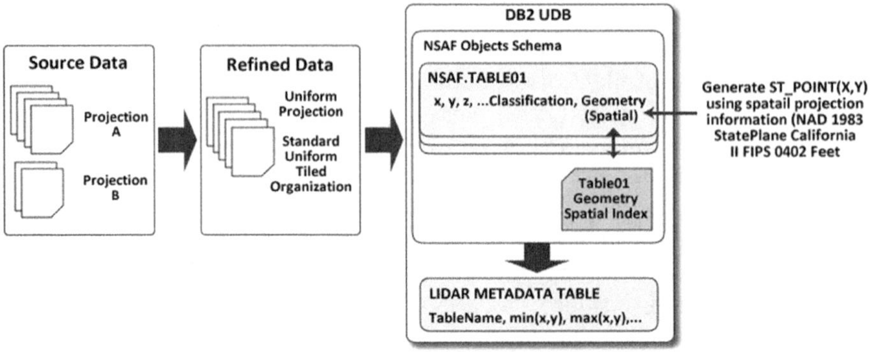


**Fig. 1.** Data preparation and loading workflow

to obtain a subset of tables whose extents intersect with the bounding box. Occassionaly, there may be additional data appended to an existing LIDAR dataset. This is done with logging turned off, to improve performance.

### 2.3 Spatial Database Implementation

We use IBM's DB2 database for storing the LIDAR point cloud data. We use standard regular data types to store all information including coordinates, elevation and related attributes. The DB2 Spatial Extender enables storage, SQL-based access and management of spatial data in DB2 by supporting a set of spatial data types, viz. points, lines and polygons, along with related spatial functions that interoperate with these data types [11,12,13]. The spatial extender also supports a standard set of spatial reference systems in which the LIDAR data may be encoded, with the ability to create new custom ones.

The DB2 spatial data type ST_Point constructs a geometry point ("spatial column") from the X and Y coordinates (latitude, longitude) in the LIDAR data set. Prior to populating the spatial column, it is necessary to define the *Spatial Reference System (SRS)* to be used to interpret the coordinates. All spatial queries and functions on a table then operate on this spatial data column. Continuing with our example of the NSAF dataset, which was collected in the *California State Plane Zone II* coordinate system [9], we define the appropriate spatial reference system (SRS) as follows:

```
db2se create_srs LIDARDB -srsName "NSAF" -srsID 1001 -xScale 1
-coordsysName "NAD_1983_STATEPLANE_CALIFORNIA_II_FIPS_0402_FEET"
```

In the above command, LIDARDB is the name of the database, NSAF is the name of the SRS being created and 1001 is the id associated with the SRS. One can then register the spatial column in the table to this SRS. The ST_Point user defined function (UDF) is then used to populate the spatial column using the X, Y coordinates and SRS id as follows:

```
update NSAF.TABLE01 set SPATIALPOINT = ST_POINT(X, Y, 1001)
```

Once the spatial column is populated, it needs to be indexed using a *grid index*, optimized for two-dimensional queries and created on the X and Y dimensions of a geometry [12]. The spatial index scan is done in "strips" the width of a grid cell with the height of the actual query window. If a small grid size is set compared to the average size of the query window, there may be an excessive number of index entries scanned. If the grid size is set too large, there may be an inordinate number of geometry data examinations. The grid size can be optimized by either utilizing the index advisor that is provided or by studying the spatial query window patterns and using that information to modify grid size though performance testing. We first arrived at our index grid sizes via a series of synthetic query performance tests on the dataset. Over a period of time, we were also able to measure the average actual query size for the NSAF dataset, which is about 1, 454, 000 points (rows) per query. In cases where query window size estimates and patterns are not available, it is more efficient to make the spatial index grid size larger rather than smaller. With a larger grid size, a large number of points may be assigned the same grid key value but the filtering is fast during the index scan because the actual point coordinates are also stored in the key. If the grid size is small, there may be a large number of "strips" corresponding to the query window, resulting in numerous restarts of the index scan [14].

The command to create a spatial index for the SPATIALPOINT column is:

```
create index SPI on NSAF.TABLE01 (SPATIALPOINT) extend using
SPATIAL_INDEX (1000,0,0)
```

The typical LIDAR spatial query calls the comparison function *EnvelopesIntersect*, since it utilizes the spatial grid index to provide improved query performance. A spatial query that returns all ground (G) classified LIDAR points within a specified bounding box coordinates is as follows:

```
select SPATIALPOINT..ST_X, SPATIALPOINT..ST_Y, Z from NSAF.TABLE01
where EnvelopesIntersect (SPATIALPOINT, 6048700.00, 2240300.00,
6048900.00, 2240700.00, 1001) = 1 and CLASSIFICATION='G'
```

### 2.4 Single Partition Implementation

In the initial stages, efficient LIDAR data management and concurrent access to these massive volumes was provided by leveraging the high-end hardware infrastructure and software resources provided by DataStar, a TeraGrid cluster computing resource located at the San Diego Supercomputer Center [15]. We utilized one of the nodes in the DataStar cluster, which was a 32-way SMP node with P690 processors, each running at 1.7 GHz, and with 128 GB of node memory. The node was connected to a storage area network (SAN) disk via a fibre channel link for fast data movement at a rate of approximately 4 GB/sec. Eight terabytes of SAN disk were allocated for hosting the LIDAR database, which were configured in RAID 5. DataStar ran AIX 5.2, IBM's 64-bit version of the Unix OS. The powerful hardware with a 64-bit OS and large real memory and large capacity fault tolerant disk space made this an ideal system for hosting the LIDAR database.

The 64-bit version of DB2 UDB Enterprise Server Edition (ver.8.2) along with the Spatial Extender component was installed on DataStar. The storage configuration was optimized by creating eight large logical disks using disk striping to spread the I/O load across multiple physical disks, while maintaining reliability using RAID-5 in case of individual disk failures. The set of tables corresponding to each LIDAR dataset is stored in its own, separate tablespace with a dedicated buffer pool. Since each dataset has its own "hot zone" or area of interest, frequently accessed rows in each dataset can remain in memory. The tablespace is spread across all available disks by creating a tablespace container in each disk. All queries involve processing sequential subsections of the dataset. Thus, prefetching and parallel I/O significantly improve overall query performance.

Apart from providing fast query response times, DataStar also provided improved data loading and spatial index generation times. When compared to a LIDAR database installed on a Dell PowerEdge 2650 server, load times on the LIDAR database on DataStar were approximately four and half times faster and spatial data generation was eight times faster.

However running a database on a shared TeraGrid resource had its disadvantages. There were other applications utilizing the same processors and shared memory, leading to poor database performance at times of heavy shared usage. Thus, repeatability and scaling of performance is an issue, since it is difficult to achieve isolation of an individual subsystem in a shared, supercomputing environment. In the next section we describe our approach based on the use of commodity clusters and IBM DB2's "partitioned database" (*aka* shared nothing) feature.

### 2.5 Partitioned Database Implementation

A key reason for using the partitioned implementation is to take advantage of the processing power and distributed memory across multiple systems at reasonable costs (lower costs than a large multiprocessor system). In a partitioned database, the data are stored across multiple partitions or nodes that function together as a single database engine. Each partition has an independent database manager, each with its own data, indexes, logs and configuration files. Tables can be created on single or multiple partitions and the data (rows) are distributed across partition using range or hash partitioning on a "partitioning key". The query optimizer utilizes properties of the data partitioning scheme to optimize query performance.

**Partitioned Database Optimizations.** For the LIDAR database, we create four partition groups to account for the variations in the database table sizes. Small tables, like the *metadata table* mentioned before, are created on a single node partition group, while larger tables are created in medium or other larger partition groups. This organization scheme gives us the maximum performance to overhead ratio.

An important consideration in a partitioned environment is the choice of a partitioning key for each table. We employ hash partitioning: for each row in a table, the hash algorithm is applied to the specified partitioning key. The result of the hash is a number between 0 and 1023, called the *partition number.* At the time of creation of a nodegroup, the 1024 partitions are distributed across all the nodes of the nodegroup in round-robin fashion. This mapping between the partition and the node is stored in a *partitionmap.* For a given row, the hash value obtained from the hash function, which is used to lookup the partitionmap to determine which node the row will reside on [16]. Ideally, the data should be evenly distributed across all the nodes in a nodegroup to maximize parallelism and performance. For LIDAR datasets, the choice of partitioning key depends on a number of factors including the geographical orientation of the dataset and the available attributes that are candidate partitioning key attributes. For example the NSAF dataset extends in a narrow North-South swath along the coast. In this dataset, the $y$ attribute will have many distinct values, compared to $x$, and choosing this as the partitioning key results in a better distribution of the data across nodes. In other datasets, other attributes like a GPS timestamp column, may serve better as the partitioning key due to the many distinct values.

**Spatial Extender in a Partitioned Environment.** DB2 Spatial Extender functionality works in a similar manner in a partitioned database as it does in a regular single partition environment. However, when spatially enabling the database in a partitioned environment, we need to specify that the spatial catalog tables also reside on the same node as the main DB2 catalog. We also need to alter the spatial data generation phase. The ST_Point UDF queries the SRS definition tables to get the values of the SRS offsets and multipliers needed to construct a geometry, which it then passes to the *GsePoint* which is an internal UDF. By using the *GsePoint* UDF directly we can avoid the additional table access which force table queue broadcasts in a partitioned environment [14]. Using this internal UDF also significantly improves the performance of the spatial point generation process as the DB2 optimizer executes this update query in parallel.

While the primary additional cost in a partitioned environment is the increase in the one time data partitioning and load phase, this is overshadowed by the benefits in terms of improved performance. This partitioned database architecture provides better scalability and lower costs. New commodity machines can be added to the cluster and the database can be expanded across them.

**Spatial Overhead and Data Growth Implications.** One disadvantage of using spatial data types in the database is a significant increase in storage overhead. The ST_Point data type is in binary format and causes inflation on database disk to approximately six times the size of the original data. For hosting seven datasets with 27.2 billion LIDAR returns, the database size grew to approximately 10.4 TB including spatial indexes. The other hidden overhead is the time taken to generate the spatial data and the corresponding spatial grid indexes. As the number of LIDAR datasets increase and more data is loaded, disk space also becomes a major issue.

The switch to a partitioned environment allowed us to experiment with dropping the spatial index and replacing it with "regular" (B-tree) indexes on $X$ and $Y$ attributes. A typical bounding box query can still run quite efficiently using the X and Y columns indexes (using B-tree indices). This switch in implementation saves significant amount of disk space and also eliminates the spatial generation and grid index creation phases that were necessary after loading the data into the database. With this modification, the current LIDAR database is now about 3 TB in size and hosts about 31 billion LIDAR returns from eight distinct datasets including EarthScope Northern California, Intermountain Seismic Belt, Southern and Eastern California and Alaska Denali Totschunda LIDAR projects.

The binary LAS format is gaining popularity as a standard for LIDAR data exchange. The data sizes are significantly smaller compared with ASCII data and the format includes a built-in header for recording metadata [6]. We plan to extend the capabilities of OpenTopography to incorporate the ability to ingest and serve data in LAS format. The database will thus need to provide the capability to support queries to the LAS-based datasets as well as the existing LIDAR ASCII data. We plan to take advantage of DB2's object-relational features that will allow programs written in various languages like C and Java to be bound to the database as "external" user defined functions (UDFs). With the LAS metadata stored in regular tables, these UDFs can then be used along with standard SQL to query and subset the LAS files.

## 3 Future Work

One of the challenges arising from incorporating the LAS format is the management of these binary files in a partitioned enviroment. The binary files themselves could be reorganized to support range-partitioning or hash-partitioning of the data within the files. We will investigate different techniques for optimally distributing the files, and hence the workload, across the nodes of a partitioned database.

We also plan to investigate other RDBMS offerings including ORACLE Spatial, which provides some packaged solutions for management of LIDAR data. This includes new data types to support point cloud data as well as spatial functions to generate topological data models from this data [17].

Another key direction is associating more processing capabilities closer to the data. For example, we plan to integrate digital elevation model (DEM) processing capability, which involves generation of different types of grids from point cloud data, within the database itself in the form of stored procedures and UDFs.

## References

1. Carter, W.E., Shrestha, R.L., Tuell, G., Bloomquist, D., Sartori, M.: Airborne Laser Swath Mapping Shines New Light on Earth's Topography. Eos, Transactions, American Geophysical Union 82, 549–550, 555 (2001)

2. Sallenger, A.H., Krabill, W., Swift, R., Brock, J., List, J., Hansen, M., Holman, R.A., Manizade, S., Sontag, J., Meredith, A., Morgan, K., Yunkel, J.K., Frederick, E., Stockdon, H.: Evaluation of airborne scanning lidar for coastal change applications. J. Coastal Research 19(1), 125–133 (2003)
3. Prentice, C.S., Crosby, C.J., Whitehill, C.S., Arrowsmith, J.R., Furlong, K.P., Phillips, D.A.: Illuminating Northern California Active Faults. Eos 90(7), 55–56 (2009)
4. Keller, R., Seber, D., Sinha, A.K., Baru, C.: The Geosciences Network (GEON): one step towards building cyberinfrastructure for the geosciences,European Geophysical Union, Vienna (November 2004), `http://www.geongrid.org`
5. Carter, W.E., Shrestha, R., Slatton, K.C.: Geodetic Laser Scanning. Physics Today 60(12), 41–47 (2007)
6. American Society for Photogrammetry & Remote Sensing, LAS 1.3 Specification, `http://www.asprs.org/society/committees/standards/lidar_exchange_format.html`
7. Crosby, C.J., Nandigam, V., Arrowsmith, J.R., Blair, J.L.: Visualization of High-Resolution LiDAR Topography in Google Earth. In: American Geophysical Union, Fall Meeting 2009, abstract IN33A-1034 (2009)
8. Northern San Andreas Dataset, OpenTopography Facility, `http://www.opentopography.org/data`
9. Snyder, J.P.: Map Projections - A Working Manual. U.S. Geological Survey Professional Paper 1395. United States Government Printing Office, Washington, D.C (1987)
10. USGS National Mapping Program Technical Instructions, Standards or Digital Orthophotos, `http://rockyweb.cr.usgs.gov/nmpstds/acrodocs/doq/2DOQ1296.PDF`
11. DB2 Spatial Extender for Linux, UNIX and Windows, `http://www-01.ibm.com/software/data/spatial/db2spatial/`
12. Adler, D.W.: DB2 Spatial Extender - Spatial data within the RDBMS. In: Proceedings of the 27th International Conference on Very Large Data Bases, September 11-14, pp. 687–690 (2001)
13. DB2 Spatial Extender User's Guide and Reference, `ftp://ftp.software.ibm.com/ps/products/db2/info/vr8/pdf/letter/db2sbe80.pdf`
14. Personal communications with David Adler, IBM Spatial Database Technology
15. SDSC DataStar, `http://www.sdsc.edu/us/resources/datastar/`
16. DB2 Information center, `http://publib.boulder.ibm.com/infocenter/db2luw/v8/index.jsp`
17. Oracle Spatial, `http://www.oracle.com/technology/products/spatial/index.html`

# PetaScope: An Open-Source Implementation of the OGC WCS Geo Service Standards Suite

Andrei Aiordăchioaie and Peter Baumann

Jacobs University Bremen, Germany
Campus Ring 12
Bremen, Germany
{a.aiordachioaie,p.baumann}@jacobs-university.de

**Abstract.** A growing number of scientific data archives set up Web interfaces for researchers and sometimes for the general public. While these services often deploy sophisticated search facilities, these are constrained to metadata level where conventional SQL/XML technology can be leveraged; no comparable retrieval support is available on original observation or simulation data.

For raster data in the earth sciences, this is overcome by the 2008 Open GeoSpatial Consortium (OGC) Web Coverage Processing Service (WCPS) standard. It defines a retrieval language on multi-dimensional raster data for ad-hoc navigation, extraction, aggregation, and analysis. WCPS is part of the Web Coverage Service (WCS) suite which additionally contains a simple retrieval service and a upload and update service for raster data.

In this contribution we present *PetaScope* , an open-source implementation of the complete WCS suite. Most of the suite's functionality is available already, and a first code version has been released. An online showcase is being built, and the system will soon undergo real-life evaluation on mass data. After briefly introducing the WCPS language concept we discuss the architecture of the service stack based on examples publicly available on the demo website.

## 1 Introduction

Demand for unlimited availability of scientific data is rapidly increasing, be these collected as observations and simulation results. This goes far beyond the traditional ftp archives where files with some cumbersome names had to be downloaded as a whole, buried in directory hierarchies with similarly cumbersome names. Dynamic subsetting is a must today, based on a variety of individual criteria. To this end, sophisticated metadata catalogs with powerful retrieval capabilities are being built; ontologies, controlled vocabularies and other techniques help to guide search.

This search, however, usually is based on the metadata alone; selection criteria based on the ground truth data themselves are not supported well, in particular when these data are of high volume and difficult to represent in SQL-supported relational databases. For example, on a three-dimensional hyperspectral satellite time series cube with axes $x$, $y$, and $t$ questions like *"when did summer ice coverage fall below 50% in some given area?"* and *"a vegetation timeline for some given area and time period"* are important for climate change research questions. They require significant processing of the ground truth data.

M. Gertz and B. Ludäscher (Eds.): SSDBM 2010, LNCS 6187, pp. 160–168, 2010.

Service providers prefer to pre-calculate such data and provide them for plain download for several reasons. One reason is the fear that naive users or denial-of-service attacks might misuse processing capabilities to block the service as such. Another is that there is no generally accepted request language on multi-dimensional raster data which can do a job comparable to SQL in metadata search. The net effect is that only very selected, predefined queries can be answered by such services, which constitutes a severe lack of flexibility and hinders exploitation significantly.

Recognizing this shortcoming, the Open GeoSpatial Consortium (OGC), which develops and maintains open, interoperable geo service standards, in 2008 has adopted the Web Coverage Processing Service (WCPS) which offers a high-level raster query language suitable for Web-based retrieval from large, multi-dimensional sensor, image, and statistics data archives. WCPS is part of the Web Coverage Service (WCS) standards suite. WCS, as a base service, allows for simple subsetting, scaling, reprojection, and format encoding requests. WCS-T, a WCS extension like WCPS, defines an open interface for manipulating coverages [22]. The term "coverage", in OGC and ISO speak, means "space-time varying phenomenon" [13], in current practice: spatio-temporal raster data.

In this contribution we present *PetaScope* , an implementation of the complete WCS suite, encompassing WCS, WCS-T, and WCPS. As the latter constitutes the most complex functionality we put particular emphasis on this part. The next section gives a brief introduction to the standards addressed and their core functionality. Section 3 presents addresses the *PetaScope* architecture, related work is discussed in Section 4. Section 5 describes the demo, and Section 5 gives a conclusion.

## 2 The OGC WCS Standards Suite

In this section we give a brief overview on the WCS suite of geo raster standards; the official website is [15]. ISO 19123 [13] defines a coverage as "a function from a spatio-temporal domain to an attribute domain". This is adopted by WCS [23], which currently only considers regular rasters (arrays in a programming sense). Simplified, a WCS coverage consists of a multi-dimensional array described by an axis-parallel bounding box (its *domain*), one or more coordinate reference systems (CRSs) in which it can be queried (one of which must allow addressing in integer array coordinates), and a locally unique title (i.e., identifier). The array cell type (its *range type*) consists of a list of named atomic components ("bands"). For each range component its null values can be indicated, plus the interpolation methods applicable to this component.

All coverage service protocols share two initialization request types. If information about a service is not known otherwise, the client will issue a *GetCapabilities* request to obtain data and service information like specification version supported, protocols supported, and coverages offered. Further details about selected coverages can be obtained via a *DescribeCoverage* request; the response contains all relevant metadata about the coverages inquired, such as coverage domain extent and range ("pixel", "voxel") type and CRSs in which the coverage can be addressed.

Further request types are service specific. WCS itself defines the *GetCoverage* request for subsetting, scaling, reprojecting, and encoding a coverage [23]. WCS-T adds the *Transaction* request which serves to add a new coverage, update an existing coverage partially or completely with new data, or to delete a coverage from a WCS repository [22]. WCPS, finally, adds a *ProcessCoverages* request [1]. In the remainder we will focus on WCPS queries.

A WCPS expression iterates over lists of server-side stored coverages. A variable is bound to each element inspected; several variables, each iterating over one list, can be indicated, thereby emulating nested loops. During each iteration, an optional filter predicate is applied which can suppress the current item combination in the result list. The result of each iteration is generated according to a processing clause using the coverage variables. Among the processing operators available are

- *spatio-temporal subsetting operations*, in particular cutout (*trim*) and slicing;
- *induced operations* which apply an operation available on the cell type simultaneously to all cell values; these include unary and binary arithmetic, exponential, trigonometric, and boolean operations;
- *condensers* allow to derive summary information (such as *count, avg, some, all*);
- a *general array constructor* to derive completely new arrays (such as histograms);
- *reprojection* of the coverage into another coordinate reference system;
- auxiliary functions, such as metadata extraction.

To convey the flavor of the language, whose syntax tentatively has been designed close to XQuery, consider derivation of the Normalized Difference Vegetation Index (NDVI). This is a mathematical measure to discover whether an earth observation image contains live green vegetation. The mathematical definition, $NDVI = \frac{nir-red}{nir+red}$, takes into account the red ($red$) and near-infrared ($nir$) measurements from a satellite, and yields an index in $[-1, 1]$, where values close to $+1$ suggest presence of vegetation.

The WCPS request that computes the NDVI of a coverage object *rgb* implements the mathematical definition in a straightforward manner: This request binds variable $\$s$ to satellite images ("scenes") $Landsat1$, $Landsat2$, and $Landsat3$ in turn. Only those assignments are considered where, in the red channel, average intensity exceeds a value of 127. Such objects are processed in the $return$ clause where the NDVI is computed and thresholded with a value of $0.6$ in our case. The result image is encoded in JPEG for delivery to the client:

```
for    $s in ( LandSat1, Landsat2, Landsat3 )
where  avg( $s.red ) > 127
return encode((($s.nir-$s.red)/($s.nir+$s.red))>0.6,"png")
```

Figure 1 shows on the left side a false-color image consisting of the near infrared, read, and green bands of a 7-band Landsat scene. On the right side, the NDVI result can be seen for a threshold value of $0.6$; white pixels denote vegetation detected and black pixels indicate vegetation-free locations.

A complete presentation of the WCPS language, including a formal treatment as well as a discussion of the design decisions made, is given in [2]. The expressive power of this language allows to perform a range of statistics, imaging, and signal processing operations, such as aggregation or roll-up, modes, convolutions, filter kernels and the Fast Fourier Transform [17]. Still, it is *safe in evaluation*: every possible request will terminate after a finite number of steps.

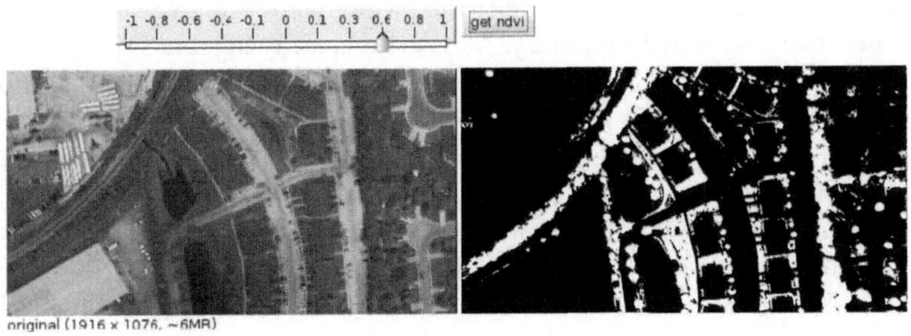


**Fig. 1.** Slider for scalar query parameter input; false-color image (left), threshold selector (top), and thresholded NDVI (right)

# 3 *PetaScope* Architecture

## 3.1 Overview

The *PetaScope* architecture follows a model-driven architecture: service functionality is orthogonally offered via different protocols. For example, WCPS requests can be sent using the abstract syntax shown in the above example, or alternatively employing an equivalent XML encoding specified in the standard. Figure 2 illustrates the overall system architecture, together with the tools used. On server side, two main layers can be distinguished. The *service layer* provides the Web service interfaces. It is mainly concerned with marshalling and unmarshalling of requests according to the different protocol specifications. Incoming requests are translated, with the help of service metadata stored in the PostgreSQL database, into queries of the rasdaman array DBMS. The *data management layer* encapsulates two database management systems that store all information. Next, we discuss the layers.

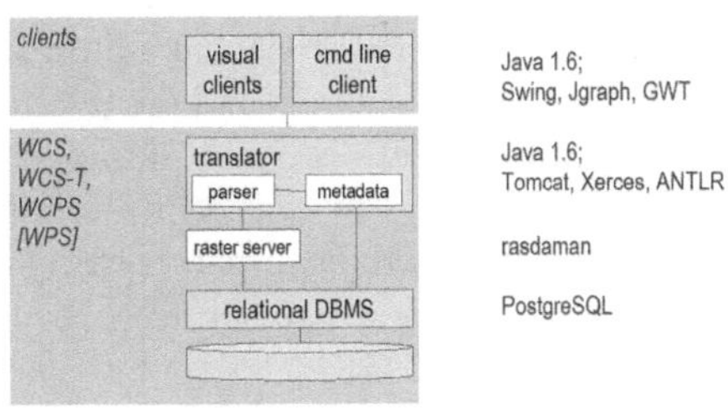


**Fig. 2.** *PetaScope* overall architecture (left), including tools used (right)

## 3.2 Data Processing and Management Layer

The data processing and management layer consists of the rasdaman array DBMS middleware and the PostgreSQL relational DBMS. Rasdaman ("raster data manager") allows to store multi-dimensional arrays of unlimited size in standard relational databases while offering a declarative query language, rasql, which extends SQL with raster operations. Such raster objects are partitioned (*tiled*), and each tile is stored in a BLOB of the underlying relational DBMS. Incoming queries are transformed into a parse tree and then undergo a series of optimizations, including algebraic rewriting with currently 150 rules, just-in-time compilation for CPU and GPU, pre-aggregation, and several more.

Query tree execution relies on *tilestreaming* which allows to process objects significantly larger than server main memory. As rasdaman array algebra [3], query language [14], engine architecture [24], the R+-tree indexing used in rasdaman [8], query optimization [19] including just-in-time compilation [11] and graphics processors [20], parallelization [10], and application in earth [9], space [4], and life [18] sciences has been described elsewhere we omit further details.

The dynamic type system of rasdaman allows definition of new raster types at runtime; the following statement[1] defines a five-band 3-D Landsat satellite image time series stack of unlimited extent in x and y (assumed as first and second dimensions) and a fixed lower bound and variable upper bound for time (assumed as third dimension):

```
typedef marray<
  struct{ char band1, band2, band3, band4, band5; },
  [ *:*, *:*, 0:* ]
> LandsatTimeseries;
```

This schema definition functionality is not passed through to PetaScope, as the WCPS standard currently only supports read access. WCS-T, while offering simple update functionality, does not allow schema modification either. However, it is planned to develop a Web-based tool for local administrators to set up and maintain the geo service schema using the rasdaman and the relational base DBMS's facilities.

Said relational DBMS comes into play as raster data, their metadata, and *PetaScope* metadata ultimately are stored in a relational database, in our case PostgreSQL. The rasdaman/PostgreSQL layer part is being used under operational conditions since about five years, with object sizes up to a dozen TB. The *EarthLook* database currently encompasses about 70 GB.

## 3.3 Service Layer

The service layer contains the three service components mentioned previously: WCS for simple data access, WCPS for complex retrieval, and WCS-T for updating.

WCPS accepts queries written in Abstract Syntax as well as in XML. We have used ANTLR [16] to construct the Abstract Syntax parser and Xerces to handle incoming XML. Both query representations ultimately are transformed into a query tree from which subsequently a rasdaman query is generated.

Since WCS functionality (concretely: the *GetCoverage* request type) is a subset of WCPS, WCS queries can be relayed to WCPS.

## 3.4 Networks Transport

Sometimes it is argued that Web transport is inefficient for large data sets. While this may hold for comparatively small chunks of data where the http header occupies a significant part this is certainly not the case for raster transport – any header and eventual

[1] This also demonstrates why multi-dimensional arrays cannot be modelled adequately by object-relational databases: the n-D array constructor, `marray`, is a template and not a data type, similar to stacks, lists, etc. Object-relational systems allow injection of new data types, but not of type constructors.

metadata are negligible against the multi-Megabyte payload. This actually can be experimentally verified in the system demonstration as the rasdaman system comes with three carrier protocols: SUN RPC, http, and RNP (rasdaman networks protocol) which maps to http. In tests where identical query workloads are run over the different protocols there is no significant response time difference.

That said, server-side optimizations have reached an effectiveness where data transfer takes up a large part of the overall response time. Therefore, transfer data compression has been introduced additionally [7].

Still, however, the main gain in bandwidth saving is simply through the query language approach itself which allows users to specify the desired outcome, rather than downloading the ingredients for a client-side evaluation. A factor of 10 can be obtained on the average [12], but the following example demonstrates much higher peak rates. A Hyperion satellite image has 250 bands of which two are used to compute the NDVI. If this is thresholded like in Figure 1 then ultimately a binary image is sent to the client. Not only is this a 1-bit image as compared to 250 8-bit channels, but this binary image also compresses excellently. The *EarthLook* demo case allows to monitor Internet response times of both situations in real time.

## 3.5 User Interface

Unleashing the power of the query language to the end user presents a GUI design challenge. The construction of *EarthLook* turned out representative for many projects we had done earlier in one particular aspect: the large variety of data combined with the use case variability makes user interface design a major task in the overall project effort. Roughly, three categories of use cases can be distinguished:

- Static, unparametrized queries. Such WCPS queries are completely prefabricated, and the client will simply submit them upon a user mouse click. One example is presented in Figure 3 where the histogram is displayed for an 8-bit image.
- Queries requiring a (usually numeric) parameter provided by the user. For example, computing the Normalized Difference Vegetation Index (NDVI) requires a threshold parameter between -1 and +1 to be chosen by the user. Figure 1 shows an

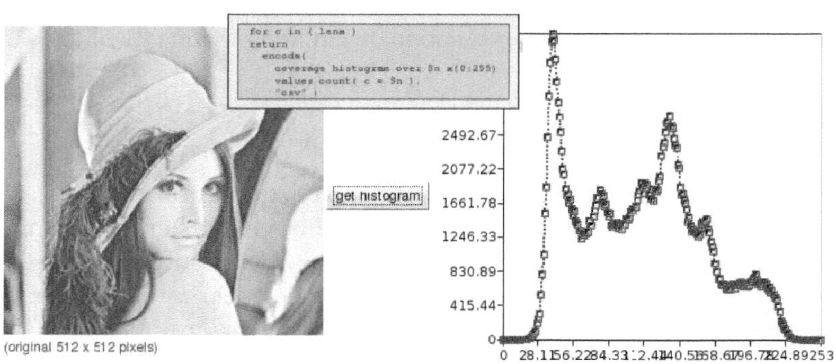


**Fig. 3.** Unparametrized query submission

*EarthLook* screenshot with a false color image, a slider to choose the threshold value, and the result image where white represents a vegetation guess.
- Queries expecting query fragments from the user. In particular expert users often want to choose and vary evaluation functions, but without having to write the whole query on their own. Such a situation was encountered, for example, when designing an experimental interface for astrophysical data analysis [4].

Several tasks, like spatio-temporal subsetting, are conveniently solved via sliders and other guiding input devices, wrong input is impossible by construction. For more complex expressions, however, the client needs to perform syntactic and even semantic analysis to ensure an error free input query, something which is difficult to accomplish. Currently, therefore, we are experimenting with visual programming techniques.

For the screenshots shown, a prototype of a GUI design tool for query construction and multi-dimensional result display has been developed. Based on the experiences made we are investigating into a design methodology which will allow to compose manipulation (i.e., query generating) widgets with display (query execution and result presentation) widgets into a custom Web interface.

## 4 Related Work

Matlab and Mathematica are popular computing environments that support importing scientific data (reading NetCDF and HDF formats, among others), but they target desktop environments. Further, working with data volumes which exceed main memory capaity by several orders of magnitude is not efficient.

In Web world, various WCS implementations exist [6] [21], yet WCS alone is unsuitable for ad-hoc exploration and analysis of high-volume data (such as earth observation satellitei image streams). To the best of our knowledge, *PetaScope* is the first implementation of standardized web services that allow retrieval, data management and remote query evaluation. Furthermore, we are not aware of any package which combines WCS 1.1 (the current version), WCS-T, and WCPS.

NASA is developing, with our collaboration, an on-board satellite interface which allows to task WCPS queries in an ad-hoc fashion [5]. Based on an own implementation independent from *PetaScope* , NASA's plan is to significantly enhance quality and intelligence of service for the next generation of earth observation satellites.

## 5 Demonstration

The *PetaScope* demonstration will make use of a variety of earth science use cases to explain issues in query language design, optimizability, GUI design, as well as application specifics. Demonstration data will cover the complete spectrum of spatio-temporal dimensions, ranging from 1-D timeseries over 2-D remote sensing and seafloor imagery to 3-D geophysics and 4-D climate model data. Among the operations performed are spatio-temporal subsetting; band extraction and recombination; ad-hoc sensor fusion; processing derivation of various aggregates, such as min/max, histogram; and further processing, like convolution. In addition to the prefabricated demo cases, a "sandbox" allows to visually experiment with the queries. All this functionality is additionally permanently made available on the *EarthLook* site, www.earthlook.org.

These queries challenge the engine in different ways. Subsetting speed is mainly driven by disk access (and the fit of the tiling structure) and to some lesser extent by agglomerating the result from the tiles read, data format encoding, and shipping to the client. The other operations mentioned above are mostly CPU-bound, except when just-in-time compilation of query fragments comes in. By using the command line query interface, timing of requests can be tested under both RPC and http based transport protocols to explore protocol performance overhead as discussed in Section 3.4.

Similar scenarios have been applied successfully in Computer Science courses recently and at OGC's Climate Change Integration Plugfest at the FOSS4G "Free and Open Source for Geospatial" Conference in Fall 2009. Depending on the Internet connection, either a local notebook server or Jacobs University's server will be acessed. Visitors can simultaneously exercise prefabricated and ad-hoc queries via *EarthLook* .

## 6 Conclusion

Serving rapidly growing amounts of data to both public audiences and expert communities at hitherto unknown qualities is one of the main current challenges arising in geo-scientific data management. The immense data volumes potentially addressed in queries, spanning multi-Terabyte and soon multi-Petabyte object sizes, lead to new dimensions of I/O bandwidth, CPU processing, and network capacity requirements.

*PetaScope* constitutes a flexible, multi-dimensional, multi-purpose geo raster server which is available in open source. Its components have been tested on all spatio-temporal dimensions and with multi-Terabyte object sizes. This system constitutes the reference implementation of the OGC WCPS standard and, at the same time, incorporates the currently most comprehensive collection of OGC's geo raster service standards.

Among our research avenues are further server-side query optimizations, addressing both software measures (like further heuristic query rewriting and cost-based optimization) and hardware (such as GPU support and distributed query processing). Collaboration with NASA continues towards on-board WCPS services, and the European Space Agency (ESA) has awarded two contracts for the further development of *PetaScope* for use in value-adding services on their satellite mission results. Further, we envisage application of the *PetaScope* technology in domains beyond the earth sciences, such as human brain imaging and gene expression analysis.

## References

1. Baumann, P. (ed.): Web Coverage Processing Service (WCPS) Implementation Specification. Number 08-068. OGC, 1.0.0 edn. (2008)
2. Baumann, P.: The ogc web coverage processing service (wcps) standard. Geoinformatica (2009)
3. Baumann, P.: A database array algebra for spatio-temporal data and beyond. In: Tsur, S. (ed.) NGITS 1999. LNCS, vol. 1649, pp. 76–93. Springer, Heidelberg (1999)
4. Calori, L., Gheller, C., Rossi, E., Amati, G.: Astrotool: Data management and visualisation in astrophysics. In: IST 2002, November 4 - 6 (2002)

5. Cappelaere, P.: Nasa wcps for ground-space interoperability, http://www.geobliki.com/2009/08/11/nasa-wcps-for-ground-space-interoperability (seen 22-01-2010)
6. Deegree. Deegree-free software for spatial data infrastructures (2009), http://www.deegree.org/ (seen 22-01-2010)
7. Dehmel, A.: A Compression Engine for Multidimensional Array Database Systems. Phd thesis, TU Muenchen (2001)
8. Furtado, P.: Storage Management of Multidimensional Arrays in Database Management Systems. Phd thesis, TU Muenchen (1999)
9. Gutierrez, A.G., Baumann, P.: Modeling fundamental geo-raster operations with array algebra. In: IEEE International Workshop in Spatial and Spatio-Temporal Data Mining, pp. 607–612 (2007)
10. Hahn, K., Reiner, B.: Intra-query parallelism for multidimensional array data. In: 28th International Conference on Very Large Data Bases, VLDB 2002 August 20 (2002)
11. Jucovschi, C.: Precompiling Queries in a Raster Database System. Bachelor thesis, Jacobs University Bremen (2008)
12. Kleese, K., Baumann, P.: Intelligent support for high i/o requirements of leading edge scientific codes on high-end computing systems - the estedi project. In: Proc. Sixth European SGI/Cray MPP Workshop, September 7-8 (2000)
13. n.n. Geographic Information - Coverage Geometry and Functions. Number 19123:2005. ISO (2005)
14. n.n. rasdaman query language guide, 8.1 edn. (2009)
15. OGC. Wcs. (2010), http://www.opengeospatial.org/standards/wcs (seen 22-01-2010)
16. Parr, T.J., Parr, T.J., Quong, R.W.: Antlr: A predicated-ll(k) parser generator (1995)
17. Buneman, P.: The Fast Fourier Transform as a Database Query. Technical Report MS-CIS-93-37, University of Pennsylvania (1993)
18. Pisarev, A., Poustelnikova, E., Samsonova, M., Baumann, P.: Mooshka: a system for the management of multidimensional gene expression data in situ. Information Systems 28, 269–285 (2003)
19. Ritsch, R.: Optimization and Evaluation of Array Queries in Database Management Systems. Phd thesis, TU Muenchen (1999)
20. Stancu-Mara, S.: Using Graphic Cards for Accelerating Raster Database Query Processing. Bachelor thesis, Jacobs University Bremen (2008)
21. THREDDS. Thematic realtime environmental distributed data services (2009), http://www.unidata.ucar.edu/projects/THREDDS/ (seen 22-01-2010)
22. Whiteside, A. (ed.): Web Coverage Service (WCS) Transaction Operation Extension. Number 07-068r4. OGC (2008)
23. Whiteside, A., Evans, J. (eds.): Web Coverage Service (WCS) Implementation Specification, Number 07-067r5. OGC, 1.1.2 edn. (2008)
24. Widmann, N.: Efficient Operation Execution on Multidimensional Array Data. Phd thesis, TU Muenchen (2000)

# Towards Archaeo-informatics: Scientific Data Management for Archaeobiology

Hans-Peter Kriegel[1], Peer Kröger[1], Christiaan Hendrikus van der Meijden[2], Henriette Obermaier[3], Joris Peters[2,3], and Matthias Renz[1]

[1] Institute for Informatics, Ludwig-Maximilians-Universität München, Germany
{kriegel,kroeger,renz}@dbs.ifi.lmu.de
[2] Faculty of Veterinary Medicine,
Ludwig-Maximilians-Universität München, Germany
v.d.Meijden@it.vetmed.uni-muenchen.de
[3] State Collection of Anthropology and Palaeoanatomy Munich, Germany
{henriette.obermaier,joris.peters}@palaeo.vetmed.uni-muenchen.de

**Abstract.** In this short paper we outline a novel and rich application domain for scientific data management: Archaeobiology. We give a short introduction to the key quests and issues in this research domain and derive a list of data management and data analysis tasks that requires original contributions from the Computer Science community and can initiate the birth of a new research discipline which we call Archaeo-Informatics. Furthermore, we describe a prototype for scientific data management called OSSOBOOK that meets many of the identified requirements of this application domain. In particular, OSSOBOOK is a distributed database system specially designed for Archaeobiology data management and analysis. Finally we give some future perspectives which is intended to serve as input for novel challenges for the Computer Science community.

## 1 Introduction

Archaeobiology basically deals with the historic evolution of the relationships between human, plants, and animals. For that purpose, Archaeobiologists maintain excavations all over the world to explore historic findings of humans, plants, animals, housings, grave yards, etc. The amount of data derived from these findings has reached a critical point: manual management, i.e. storage, analysis, and retrieval, as it is still common practice among Archaeobiology researchers is no longer feasible. The domain experts have realized that Computer Science methods for managing scientific data is urgently needed in order to avoid drowning in the flood of relevant data produced. Unfortunately, Computer Scientists are not really aware of this situation nor do they usually know details about the application and its specific problems. This is a pity since Archaeobiology provides a rich origin of novel challenges for Computer Scientists touching most aspects of scientific data management.

In this paper, we claim the following two key contributions. First, we introduce Archaeobiology as a highly interesting and challenging application domain

M. Gertz and B. Ludäscher (Eds.): SSDBM 2010, LNCS 6187, pp. 169–177, 2010.

for Computer Science in general and the scientific data management research community in particular. Based on this description, we also detail our vision of a new interdisciplinary research field called Archaeo-Informatics by identifying a list of application specific needs and deriving potential research issues for Computer Scientists. Second, we propose a demo of a first prototype system called OSSOBOOK that offers an integrated database system for managing Archaeobiological data that meets many of the identified requirements. We describe the system architecture and scientific workflow of OSSOBOOK as well as the first set of data analysis tools provided by OSSOBOOK, including methods for similarity search and data mining of scientific data. In addition, we sketch a case study that demonstrates the use of OSSOBOOK in a real Archaeobiological project.

The remainder is organized as follows. Section 2 introduces our vision of Archaeo-Informatics. In Section 3 we present details of our demonstration of the OSSOBOOK system. Section 4 rounds up the paper with some concluding remarks.

## 2 A Vision of Archaeo-informatics

### 2.1 A Brief Introduction to Archaeobiology

In the following, we will give a brief introduction to Archaeobiology. We will focus on Archaeozoology as a prototype research branch of research of Archaeobiology. Other branches, including Archaeobotany and Anthropology, deal with similar problems.

Archaeozoology evaluates bone findings of domestic and wild animals and other faunal remains from prehistoric and historical times. Most of these findings come from archaeological excavations. Whereas palaeontology explores previous geological eras, archaeozoology deals with the Holocene, the actual era. Archaeozoological research focuses on the cultural history of mankind and the relationship between humans and animals from Mesolithic periods to early modern times. Key issues are the history of domestication, geographical expansion of domesticated animals, relevance of stock-keeping and hunting, ecological changes, interaction of different cultural groups, burial rituals.

Fundamental methods of archaeozoology are macroscopic investigations of the faunal remains. Important precondition is their taxonomical identification. This has to be learned by long-time practice and is done in comparative collections. Identification work includes the determination of skeletal elements, manner of dissection, sex, age at death for humans or slaughter age for animals as well as the size by measuring the bones. On the molecular biological level stable isotopes and ancient DNA are investigated. Research on stable isotopes aims at recognizing vertebrate food-webs and subsistence strategies ($^{13}C$ and $^{15}N$). The analysis of stable isotopes of strontium and oxygen ($^{88}Sr$ and $^{16}O$) reveals migration phenomena. Ancient DNA is a reliable technique, if properly used, for phylogenetic investigations.

Projects in Archaeobiology maintain archaeological excavations all over the world, producing a tremendous amount of information that can no longer be analyzed by any human manually. Rather, the information on individual findings, e.g. descriptions of osseous parts, should be stored in a database system and should be available for analysis purposes like information retrieval and data mining via a central portal. Since the findings can usually not be transferred to other locations due to regional legal restrictions or high transportation costs, the information on these findings need to be recorded on-site.

### 2.2 Towards Archaeo-informatics

The situation of Archaeobiology nowadays can be compared with the situation of Molecular Biology in the 1980's that led to the birth of a new interdisciplinary research field: Bioinformatics. In particular, the researchers in Archaeobiology face an ever increasing amount of data but the use of IT to store, manage, retrieve, and analyze this amount is not widespread at all. Individual researchers all have their own way to record data (usually in Excel spreadsheets or even old fashioned on paper) and use only very limited tools for data analysis, e.g. the limited tools of Excel or SPSS).

The domain of Archaeobiology urgently needs some wake-up call in order to realize the wealth of Computer Science technology for managing and analyzing scientific data. In fact, many researchers from this domain currently are aware that they need informatics methods in order to not drown in the flood of data they currently produce. Any help from the Computer Science community is usually highly appreciated. However, Archaeobiology researchers do not have a clue how this help could look like and what Computer Science methods could provide. On the other hand, Archaeobiology represents a rich origin of interesting and novel challenges for the Computer Scientists. Thus, establishing Archaeo-Informatics as a discipline where researchers from Archaeobiology and Computer Science strongly collaborate, would obviously create a win-win situation.

In the following, we try to list some of the major requirements for Archaeobiology data management and data analysis and try to derive challenges for Computer Science research thereof.

**Requirements for Managing Archaeobiology Data.** The first step towards Archaeo-Informatics is to establish an environment to store and manage Archaeobiology data that considers domain specific constraints. Only if such an infra-structure is built, data is available in a standardized way that allows concise analysis. This leads to the following challenges for Computer Scientists.

In general, Archaeobiologists produce data of quite different types including the following.

- Structured data that can originally be stored in tables of a relational database system (e.g. numerical features of bones like metrics, weight, etc.). However, structured data items are often incomplete, i.e., some of the features are missing, because the findings may be fragmentary.
- Interval data and uncertain data consisting of features that cannot be measured precisely.

- Temporal data: individual projects consisting of findings from different time epochs need to be correlated to explore the evolution of the relationship between humans and animals.
- Spatial data (such as 2D and 3D images of findings) and location data (such as the location of a given finding, e.g. in terms of GPS coordinates).
- Spatio-temporal data consisting of the combination of temporal and location data, e.g. data recording the movement of (sets of) animals or humans.
- Set-valued data, e.g. a project (excavation) basically consists of a set of findings of different types.

The produced data is usually very heterogeneous, i.e. different classes of findings have varying features of different types. For example, two bones having a different position within the skeleton of the same species usually have different features and two bones from two different species may also have dissimilar features. These heterogeneous data featuring different data types need to be managed adequately. This challenge also relates to the question of how to define similarity models for such data types for efficient and accurate similarity search and data mining (see below).

In order to avoid redundant and error-prone data recording including a manual and *ad hoc* on-site documentation at the location of each excavation followed by a successive input of this documentation into a central database at some institute, advanced and integrated database systems for managing Archaeobiology data need to be provided. These database systems particularly need to provide intuitive user interfaces for data input and also advance visualization techniques to display and browse the data.

Any database system for Archaeobiology data is required to be capable of dealing with the application specific obstacles, in particular with the fact that internet access may not be available during long field sessions all the time. Thus, dedicated synchronization concepts need to be explored and developed that allow consistent online access to the central database even if internet access cannot be guaranteed persistently at the location of a given excavation.

Ideally, Archaeobiology data from different institutions all over the world working in different projects should be shared. Therefore, the methods for advanced project management as well as meta data management need to be employed. In addition, advanced methods for integrating data from distributed heterogeneous sources need to be applied and developed.

**Requirements for Analyzing Archaeobiology Data.** Once the envisioned infrastructure for storing Archaeobiology data is established and researchers begin to use it to archive their findings, they need powerful tools for analysis and retrieval.

*Similarity Models.* The foundation of data analysis and retrieval is the development of accurate and efficient similarity models for the data types listed above. In particular, Computer Scientists are required to design similarity models for

- incomplete data, i.e., objects with missing features,
- set-valued data,
- temporal, spatio-temporal, and location (GPS) data,
- 2D and 3D spatial data,
- interval data and uncertain data.

Each similarity model must consider domain specific constraints in order to meet the domain experts' intuitions.

A general approach which is applicable for most types of objects, even for those having a complex structure, is to extract a set of features, each represented by a numerical value. For example, the shape of a bone can be represented by features like weight, size, further attributes specifying the curvature of the bone surface, etc. In this way, each object can be represented as a vector in a $d$-dimensional space and the distance between the vectors reflects the dissimilarity of the corresponding objects. As a distance function, the Euclidean distance is most commonly used. This model works well for most types of objects (e.g. see [1,2,3], if we assume that we extracted the most significant features from the objects. However, the identification of suitable features is challenging and the applicability highly depends on the particular application.

Sequence data including time series and spatio-temporal trajectories require more advanced similarity measures coping with distortion in time, gaps and different sequence lengths [4,5,6]. Dynamic programming based methods like Dynamic Time Warping (DTW) [4] and variants can adequately handle such problems but are very expensive [5]. The design of suitable approximation techniques and access methods which can be used for multi-step query processing methods are mandatory for these types of data.

Another important issue is the effective handling of uncertainty in the data. Most of the existing data analysis and retrieval tools are designed for certain data. However, efforts in reconstructing certain data from uncertain sources, e.g. by applying aggregation methods, would yield loss of potentially relevant information. As a consequence, analysis and retrieval of uncertain data call for new, more advanced definitions of similarity models [7]. Thereby, problems like efficient handling of similarity distributions and dependencies between object similarities have to be solved.

*Similarity Search.* Similarity search is the most important tool for retrieval of Archaeobiology data. This includes standard query types like distance range, nearest-neighbor and ranking queries as well as more advanced types like finding the furthest neighbor of a given query object, skyline queries, and reverse-nearest neighbor queries. A variety of applications including digital mock-up and partial similarity search is also needed, the latter e.g. when search for incomplete or fragmentary data. Since the amount of data is ever increasing and similarity search deals with complex objects, novel performance issues such as multi-step querying approaches are also very important.

*Data Mining.* For an advanced data analysis, new data mining methods need to be explored. Major challenges include the development of algorithms for trend mining in spatial as well as in temporal data, data methods that are capable of handling uncertain data and high dimensional data. Again, due to the large amount of raw data, high performance issues also need to be solved. In general, the data basis is highly dynamic, i.e. updates of the raw data frequently occur. Thus, data mining methods should be incremental to efficiently adjust the derived patterns when the underlying data changes.

*Visualization.* Since Archaeobiology researchers have only little knowledge about Computer Science, new methods for visualizing data and mined patterns need to be designed. This includes data browsing capabilities, the visualization of spatial and temporal trends, visual integration of data from different features (e.g. map overlay, temporal and spatial joins), etc.

## 3 OSSOBOOK: A First Solution for Archaeobiology Data Managament

In the following, we will sketch a first prototype of a system for managing and analyzing Archaeobiology data that was designed to meet as many requirements identified above as possible. The system is called OSSOBOOK and provides an integration of database technology with state-of-the-art similarity search and data mining methods.

### 3.1 System Architecture and Data Management Workflow

OSSOBOOK implements a distributed client/server database system using the concept of intermittently synchronized databases [8] to handle the application specific problem that users may have no persistent access to the central system due to network constraints but may still want to update certain parts of the database. A client-server architecture ensures that each client (usually a particular researcher equipped with a laptop) manages its own local database that is schema-equivalent to the central database at the server. This way, each client can make its updates locally, independently, and—most important—offline. At a given time, e.g. when a network connection to the server is established, the client and the server synchronize, i.e. the updates of the client are inserted into the central database at the server and the updates of the server (e.g. originating from other clients that have already synchronized) are sent to the client. The application scenario of the OSSOBOOK system is visualized in Figure 1. The central database is located at some institute. Within the institute, clients can connect to this central database system. On the field, each client has its own local copy of the central database and can connect from time to time to the central repository via a network for synchronization.

OSSOBOOK is implemented as a MySQL DB with a JAVA GUI. For the purpose of collaboration between different institutes in different countries, the central database has a user management which allows the institutes to manage there own projects independently from each other. Research results stay related to the institute. Each cooperating institute can maintain its own database which

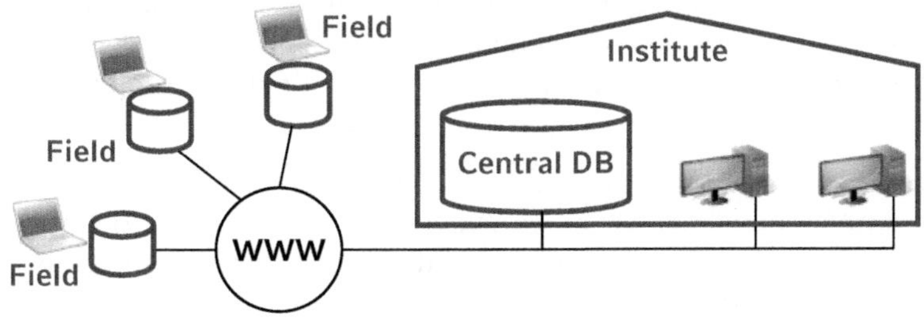


**Fig. 1.** The architecture of the mobile OSSOBOOK database system

will synchronize with the central database. Within an institute, clients connect either directly to a project on the local institute database or they log into the related project on the central database. In case of field work, the researcher has a copy of the project on a locally installed OSSOBOOK database on the notebook. The researcher therefore can use and alter all the project related data directly on the field. As soon as the researcher has internet access, he or she can synchronize the local database with the institute database which then will synchronize with the central database. On the central database all the research data is stored in the different projects of the different institutes. Here, the data mining algorithms are provided to all participants. These data mining methods use the complete data set of all collaborating institutes. This is the main scientific advantage of the OSSOBOOK database. Similarities in data collected in different parts of the world, on different time periods, by different institutes can be displayed independently from the internal use of the data.

The synchronization of OSSOBOOK operates in double depth. First stage is the synchronization of the local databases of the field clients to the local institute's database. The second stage is the synchronization of the institute database to the central database. Within these stages data input can be done at the field clients and at the local institute clients. The data mining concepts can be used from the local institute clients at the central database without direct access to the underlying central data.

From 2010, OSSOBOOK is used as the common primary database system by eight laboratories from Europe that have founded the BioArch [9] initiative. To protect unpublished data that should not yet shared among the partners to be seen by unauthorized users, OSSOBOOK also implements dedicated project management methods.

### 3.2 Data Analysis Capabilities

OSSOBOOK not only provides a database system for storing data of archaeological findings. It also offers facilities for retrieving and mining this data.

*Similarity Search.* Beside the standard retrieval capabilities of relational database systems, OSSOBOOK provides the possibility to perform similarity queries on more complex objects like entire projects. Conceptually, we implemented a method for searching for similar projects using $k$NN ranking queries. The underlying similarity model for projects, i.e., sets of findings, represents projects as sets of feature vectors and uses a minimum matching distance that can be computed e.g. by the Kuhn-Munkres algorithm.

*Data Mining.* The data mining unit of OSSOBOOK provides algorithms for standard data mining tasks such as clustering, outlier detection, classification and association rule mining to do specialized, domain-driven analysis of the entire database. For example, association rule mining based on the *Apriori* algorithm [10] is used for rating archaeological excavations. Every excavation can be treated as a market basket, the items are the found objects. From the application, it is now interesting to find rules like "If item $A$ has been found, item $B$ will also be found with a probability of $x\%$". This gives the local excavation manager a list of items to look for.

### 3.3 OSSOBOOK Demo – A Case Study

The Institute for Palaeoanatomy of the Ludwig-Maximilians-Universität München (LMU), Germany, participates at an archaeological excavation in Göbekli Tepe, Turkey. About 30,000 bones of different animals are analyzed. Originally, these data have been recorded manually. Now the OSSOBOOK system is used for data input and data storage. A demo prototype can be provided that exemplarily shows how archaeological data from the Göbekli excavation is input into a local client and then synchronized with the central database at the LMU. The data consists of classical relational data as well as complex data like images and 3D spatial objects. We will also show how the data mining capabilities of OSSOBOOK can give a rating of the current findings in the site, taking other projects all over the world into account. In particular, OSSOBOOK can derive a list of items, each associated with a probability that it can be found in Göbekli Tepe.

### 3.4 Availability

The complete source code of the current OSSOBOOK system is accessible via SOURCEFORGE.NET at `http://sourceforge.net/projects/ossobook`.

## 4 Conclusion

This paper is a mixture of a vision paper and a demo paper. It sketches the vision of a new interdisciplinary research field which we call Archaeo-Informatics that deals with the requirements of managing and analyzing Archaeobiological data using Computer Science methods. A list of domain specific requirements for managing Archaeobiological data is identified and research challenges for the Computer Science domain are derived thereof.

We further present a demonstration of the OSSOBOOK system for Archaeobiology applications that explores current concepts and strives state-of-the-art research issues in the field of scientific data management. The demo provides first-hand experiences with research prototype systems from these areas that are integrated into OSSOBOOK. We show how the synchronization of multiple users in a client-server environment can be performed by using the concept of intermittently synchronized database systems. Furthermore, we demonstrate how specialized data mining techniques can provide important application specific services like the rating of archaeological excavations, etc.

For the future, we would like to establish Archaeo-Informatics as new and rich origin of research challenges in the area of scientific data management serving a fascinating application domain. In addition, we want to extend the OSSOBOOK system by further capabilities for analyzing and visualizing Archaeobiology data, in particular focusing on 2D and 3D spatial data originating from images and 3D models of findings, e.g. methods for partial similarity search on spatial data and methods for the digital mock-up of skeletons.

## References


1. Jagadish, H.V.: A retrieval technique for similar shapes. In: Proc. SIGMOD, pp. 208–217 (1991)
2. Agrawal, R., Faloutsos, C., Swami, A.: Efficient similarity search in sequence databases. In: Lomet, D.B. (ed.) FODO 1993. LNCS, vol. 730. Springer, Heidelberg (1993)
3. Ankerst, M., Kastenmüller, G., Kriegel, H.P., Seidl, T.: 3d shape histograms for similarity search and classification in spatial databases. In: Güting, R.H., Papadias, D., Lochovsky, F.H. (eds.) SSD 1999. LNCS, vol. 1651, pp. 207–226. Springer, Heidelberg (1999)
4. Berndt, D., Clifford, J.: Using dynamic time warping to find patterns in time series. In: KDD Workshop (1994)
5. Keogh, E.: Exact indexing of dynamic time warping. In: Proc. VLDB (2002)
6. Vlachos, M., Kollios, G., Gunopulos, D.: Discovering similar multidimensional trajectories. In: Proc. ICDE (2002)
7. Aggarwal, C., Yu, P.: A survey of uncertain data algorithms and applications. IEEE TKDE 21(5), 609–623 (2009)
8. Mahajan, S., Donahoo, M., Navathe, S., Ammar, M., Malik, S.: Grouping techniques for update propagation in intermittently connected databases. In: Proc. ICDE (1998)
9. BioArch: A description of the bioarch initiative, `http://www2.mnhn.fr/archeozoo-archeobota/?Presentation,210`
10. Agrawal, R., Srikant, R.: Fast algorithms for mining association rules. In: Proc. SIGMOD (1994)

# DESSIN: Mining Dense Subgraph Patterns in a Single Graph

Shirong Li, Shijie Zhang, and Jiong Yang

EECS Dept., Case Western Reserve University, Cleveland OH 44106
{shirong.li,shijie.zhang,jiong.yang}@case.edu

**Abstract.** Currently, a large amount of data can be best represented as graphs, e.g., social networks, protein interaction networks, etc. The analysis of these networks is an urgent research problem with great practical applications. In this paper, we study the particular problem of finding frequently occurring dense subgraph patterns in a large connected graph. Due to the ambiguous nature of occurrences of a pattern in a graph, we devise a novel frequent pattern model for a single graph. For this model, the widely used Apriori property no longer holds. However, we are able to identify several important properties, i.e., *small diameter*, *reachability*, and *fast calculation of automorphism*. These properties enable us to employ an index-based method to locate all occurrences of a pattern in a graph and a depth-first search method to find all patterns. Concluding this work, a large number of real and synthetic data sets are used to show the effectiveness and efficiency of the DESSIN method.

## 1 Introduction

With the emergence of bioinformatics and social network applications, many data can be naturally represented as graphs. Thus, graph analysis and mining are of great research interests. The following are some example applications: (1) Biological Networks. Many types of biological data can be represented as graphs, e.g., protein interaction network. Each vertex is a protein while an edge represents the interaction between two proteins. There are usually tens of thousands of vertices and more edges. By discovering the frequently occurring dense substructure in a protein interaction network, the corresponding protein complex can be discovered. [1]. (2) Social Networks. The power of social networks lies in large-scale connectivity. As mentioned in [17], the extended effects of social networks are clear considering the spread of diseases that have crossed the globe (mainly) through an intimate but far-reaching social network. A tradition of work on the small-world problem similarly rests on large-scale connectivity, which has been shown to have potentially important consequences for information and large scale coordination. (3) Procedural Dependency Networks. Each graph represents a procedure augmented with special edges linking callers and callees. There may be thousands of vertices and tens of thousands of edges. By using the commonly occurring patterns as rules, any violator of these rules could be a candidate of bugs or neglected conditions (e.g., missing paths, missing conditions, and missing cases) in software programs. Useful results have been generated and reported in [3].

M. Gertz and B. Ludäscher (Eds.): SSDBM 2010, LNCS 6187, pp. 178–195, 2010.

All above applications share some similar characteristics. (1) A single large database graph has hundreds and thousands to millions of vertices. (2) The average degree can be high, e.g. tens or more. (3) It is necessary to find dense frequent subgraph patterns (with a large number of edges) in a single large graph. Thus in this paper, we study the problem of mining frequent dense subgraph patterns in a single large graph.

There are two main challenges in mining frequent subgraph patterns in a single graph: the definition of occurrence and the high computational complexity. First, it is difficult to define the number of occurrences of a pattern in a graph. Let's consider the occurrences of pattern $g$ in graph $G$ in Figure 1. In this example, one may consider $g$ occurs five times in $G$. However, the occurrences overlap. It is ambiguous whether a pair of overlapping occurrences should be counted as one or two. There are two extremes in the occurrence definition. One extreme is that as long as two occurrences differ by at least 1 edge, they are considered **two** occurrences. This solution suffers from the following shortcoming. If a pattern of 100 edges occurs 1000 times in a graph and all these occurrences share 99 edges in common and only 1 edge is different, then we will consider it occurs 1000 times under this definition, which may not be a good assessment. The other extreme is that we consider a pattern occurs twice only if the two occurrences are entirely non-overlapping. This may not work well either. If a pattern of 100 edges occurs 1000 times in a graph, all these occurrences share only 1 common edge, and all other edges' occurrences are different, then this pattern is still considered to occur only once in the graph. Therefore, a new definition that lies somewhere between the two extremes is needed.

In most previous frequent subgraph models, the problem setting is that there are a large number of database graphs, the goal is to find patterns that occur in many of these graphs. It only needs to determine whether a pattern occurs in a graph or not and does not consider the number of occurrences. In recent years, some researchers have considered the problem of finding patterns occurring many times in a single graph[6,16]. These solutions mostly use the maximum independent set concept. However, the maximum independent set problem itself is NP-hard. Therefore, this model may not be practical especially in large graphs.

In this paper, we propose a new definition of frequent pattern in a single graph. Any pattern is frequent if and only if both of its minimum and maximum vertex supports are higher than some given thresholds. There are two advantages in this new definition, efficiency and flexibility. First, we can calculate whether a pattern is frequent or not in the polynomial time, given all its occurrences in hand. Second, when the database graph has an abundance of patterns of many automorphisms, the number of generated patterns can be reduced by varying parameters.

The second challenge of mining frequently occurring patterns in a single large graph is the high computational complexity. The subgraph isomorphism test is generally accepted to be an NP-complete problem. As a result, the computation time could be very high especially when the pattern grows. As mentioned before, most previous work only considers whether a graph contains a pattern, but not all occurrences of a pattern in a graph. However, in this work, we need to locate all occurrences of a pattern in a graph. Thus, it is natural to use some indexing method with the following two properties for the purpose of mining. (1) The indexing structure should be able to locate all occurrences of a pattern in a graph efficiently compared to performing isomorphism tests. (2) It should be relatively more efficient in terms of space and time to construct the index than the entire mining process. Fortunately, the GADDI indexing structure [26] satisfies both requirements. For a graph of tens of thousands of edges, it takes around twenty minutes to construct the indexing structure, which is much less than the mining time (often in the range of hours). The query (pattern locating) time is in the range of 100ms, which is much less than the isomorphism tests. The advantages of employing an indexing structure is more significant when the discovered patterns are large.

Furthermore, based on our definition, the Apriori property no longer holds. Fortunately, we have identified the reachable property, i.e., for any non-trivial frequent dense pattern $g$, there exists at least one proper subgraph $g'$ of $g$, such that $g'$ is frequent and dense. This enables us to use a depth-first search algorithm (namely, DESSIN) to find all frequently occurring dense patterns. DESSIN proceeds as the following. (1) A preprocessing step is performed for constructing the GADDI indexing structure. (2) We mine the frequent vertex sets via a method similar to the depth-first frequent itemset mining. (3) For each frequent vertex set $S$, we generate the candidate patterns composed of vertices in $S$ in a depth-first manner. (4) The number of occurrences of a candidate pattern is computed via the graph indexing structure. The frequent patterns are finally outputted.

The following are the main contributions of this paper:

1. We propose a definition for counting the number of occurrences of a pattern in a graph.
2. We devise an efficient algorithm, DESSIN, to find the frequent dense subgraphs in a large single graph. This algorithm has the following novelties.
   (a) The DESSIN algorithm first constructs an indexing structure for the mining process. This is used to locate all occurrences of a pattern in the graph.
   (b) Based on the reachability property, frequent vertices sets are identified via a depth-first manner.
   (c) For a set of frequent vertices $S$, we find all frequent dense patterns involving all vertices in $S$.
3. A large set of real and synthetic data sets are employed to show the effectiveness and efficiency of our proposed model and method.

The remainder of this paper is organized as follows. Related work is discussed in Section 2 while preliminaries are presented in Section 3. Section 4 and 5 introduces the properties and algorithms of DESSIN, respectively. We show the empirical studies in Section 6. Finally, the conclusions are drawn in Section 7.

## 2 Related Work

Regarding the problem studied in this paper, one category of related work is mining frequent subgraph patterns in a set of database graphs [4,10,11,12,13,14,15,18,19]. A subgraph pattern is defined to be frequent if it occurs in a substantial number of graphs. These algorithms focused on mining all frequent subgraph patterns from the graph databases. In [5,8,21,24,27], the searching process was optimized by focusing on those more discriminative and hence more important patterns. $M^bT$ [5] used a decision tree based algorithm to partition data and select patterns. In ORIGAMI [8], a new representative graph mining method was proposed to find $\alpha$ - orthogonal, $\beta$ - representative set of graphs. MARGIN [21] found maximal patterns, while LEAP [24] extracted those distinct patterns with two novel concepts, structural leap search and frequency descending mining, both of which are proposed to support leap search in the graph pattern space. RING [27] integrated a representative pattern selection process into the pattern mining procedure.

There is also quite a significant amount of work related to finding dense graph patterns. [7] used a randomized approach to find large dense subgraphs in massive networks. [23] proposed CSV, which maps edges and vertices to a multi-dimensional space to help extracting dense subgraphs. However, the discovered dense subgraph is not necessarily frequent, and it is not guaranteed that all frequent patterns will be enumerated. [9,20,22,28] mined coherent dense patterns, quasi-cliques, closed cliques, and coherent closed quasi-clique over a set of graphs. However, as these algorithms are designed for mining arbitrary subgraph patterns over a set of database graphs, they may not work equally well on the problem we try to solve in this paper.

Compared to the large amount of work on mining frequent subgraph patterns in multiple graphs, there is not much work on either frequent pattern mining in a single graph. The underlying reason is that defining "frequency" in a single graph is not as straightforward as it is in a set of graphs, as occurrences of a pattern may overlap with each other. To solve this problem, [16] proposed a maximum independent set based support definition which successfully removed the ambiguity introduced by overlapping. [6] proved the anti-monotone property of a slightly modified maximum independent set based support and improved it by taking into account the harmful overlapping. However, as calculating maximum independent set itself is NP-hard, the algorithm performs less efficiently when it deals with dense and large database graphs. In [2], a minimum vertex support definition based on the most restrictive node was proposed.

## 3 Preliminaries

In this section, we introduce the fundamental definitions used in this paper and give the formal problem statement.

**Definition 1.** *A* **labeled graph** *G is a five element tuple* $G = \{V, E, \Sigma_V, \Sigma_E, L_G\}$ *where V is a set of vertices and* $E \subseteq V \times V$ *is a set of edges.* $\Sigma_V$ *and* $\Sigma_E$ *are the sets of vertices and edge labels, respectively. The labeling function* $L_G$ *defines the mappings* $V \rightarrow \Sigma_V$ *and* $E \rightarrow \Sigma_E$. *A graph G′ is defined as a* **subgraph** *of G, denoted as* $G' \subseteq G$, *if the graph vertices and graph edges of G′ form subsets of the graph vertices and graph edges of G. A graph* $G = \{V, E, \Sigma_V, \Sigma_E, L_G\}$ *is defined to be* **dense** *if and only if* $|E| \geq |V|(|V|-1)/2 - (|V|-2)$, *i.e., the average degree of the graph is close to* $|V|-1$.

**Definition 2.** *A labeled graph* $G = (V, E, \Sigma_V, \Sigma_E, l)$ *is* **isomorphic** *to another graph* $G' = \{V', E', \Sigma'_V, \Sigma'_E, l'\}$, *denoted by* $G \approx G'$, *if and only if there exists a bijection* $f : V \rightarrow V'$ *s.t. (1)* $\forall\, u \in V$, $l(u) = l'(f(u))$, *(2)* $\forall\, u, v \in V$,$(u, v) \in E$

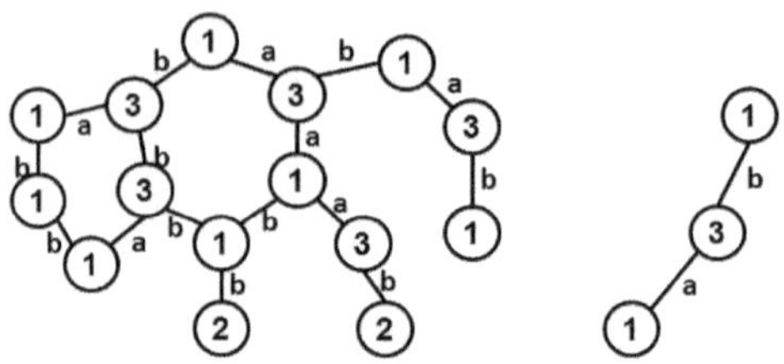
(a) Database graph $G$ (b) Pattern $g$

**Fig. 1.** Example Database Graph and Pattern

*$\Leftrightarrow$ $(f(u), f(v)) \in E'$, and (3) $\forall$ $(u, v) \in E$, $l(u, v) = l'(f(u), f(v))$. We denote $G(v) \approx G'(v')$ if $f(v) = v'$. $S$ is* **subgraph isomorphic** *to $G'$, if $S$ is isomorphic to at least one subgraph $G''$ of $G'$. $G''$ is an* **occurrence** *of $S$ in $G'$. Two occurrences overlap with each other if and only if they share at least one vertex.*

**Definition 3.** *Let $O$ model the relationships among occurrences of $g$ in $G$, in which each occurrence is modeled as a vertex, and an edge is created between two overlapping occurrences. Then the* ***maximum independent set support*** *of $g$ in $G$, denoted as $Sup_{MIS}(g, G)$, is the size of any maximum independent vertex set of $O$.*

As an example, the maximum independent support of the pattern graph in Figure 1(b) is 3 in the database graph in Figure 1(a), while there are 5 distinct occurrences.

The maximum independent set support is first proposed by [15], and served as a benchmark for subgraph pattern mining in a single graph. As calculating the maximum independent set is NP-hard, this support definition will not be adopted in our mining algorithm, but serves as a standard method to evaluate our support definition.

**Definition 4.** *The* ***minimum vertex support*** *of a pattern graph $g$ in database graph $G$, denoted as $Sup_{minV}(g, G)$, is defined as the minimum number of distinct database graph vertices that a pattern graph vertex mapped to. Formally, $Sup_{minV}(g, G) =$*

$$min_{v \in g} |\{v' | v' \in m, m \subseteq G, m \approx g, g(v) \approx m(v')\}|$$

*Similarly, the* ***maximum vertex support****, denoted as $Sup_{maxV}(g, G)$, is the maximum number of distinct database graph vertices that a pattern graph vertex mapped to. Formally $Sup_{maxV}(g, G) =$*

$$max_{v \in g} |\{v' | v' \in m, m \subseteq G, m \approx g, g(v) \approx m(v')\}|$$

Let's assume that a pattern $g$ occurs 100 times in a graph $G$. All these occurrences share one vertex and all other vertices are not overlapped at all. The minimum vertex support of $g$ in $G$ is 1 while the maximum vertex support is 100. Intuitively, the minimum vertex support reflects the case that overlapping occurrences are considered as a single occurrence. On the other hand, the maximum vertex support represents the scenario that overlapping occurrences are considered as distinct occurrences. By varying these two thresholds, users can find desired frequent patterns.

**Definition 5.** *Given a database graph G and threshold parameters $\gamma_{max}$ and $\gamma_{min}$, a subgraph g of G is defined to be* ***frequent*** *if and only if the minimum vertex support of g is no less than $\gamma_{min}$ and the maximum vertex support of g is no less than $\gamma_{max}$, i.e., $Sup_{minV}(g, G) \geq \gamma_{min}$ and $Sup_{maxV}(g, G) \geq \gamma_{max}$.*

**Problem Statement:** Given a large database graph $G$ and threshold parameters $\gamma_{max}$, $\gamma_{min}$, we aim to find all frequent subgraphs of $G$ which are also dense.

## 4 Properties

In this section, we introduce some important properties of the dense frequent subgraph patterns, which are small diameter, reachability, and fast calculation of automorphisms. In the next section, we design mining algorithms by taking advantage of these properties.

### 4.1 Small Diameter

The diameter is defined as the largest shortest distance among all pairs of vertices in the given graph. It is expected that the diameter of any dense graph is small. Apparently, if the graph is not complete, the diameter of the graph will be at least two, which is achieved by any pair of non-adjacent vertices. And clearly, the diameter of a dense subgraph is at most two since at least k-1 edges have to be removed from a k-clique to remove all paths of length one and two between any two vertices.

### 4.2 Reachability

In [6], the frequent patterns defined by the maximum independent set were proved to meet the anti-monotone property. So were the frequent patterns defined by minimum vertex support in [2]. The anti-monotone property guarantees that any frequent pattern can be found by a graph mining algorithm based on enumeration. In contrast to the anti-monotone property which requires that every subgraph of any frequent pattern be frequent, the property of reachability is proposed in this paper.

The reachability property states that for every non-trivial frequent dense pattern $g$, there exists at least one subgraph $g'$ of $g$, such that $g$ has one more vertex than $g'$ and $g'$ is frequent and dense. If the reachability property is satisfied, then any frequent pattern could be found by a graph mining algorithm where candidate patterns are generated by adding one vertex to existing frequent patterns. Next we prove that for any non-trivial frequent dense pattern we defined satisfies the reachability property.

When $g$ is composed of fewer than four vertices, the reachability property is easy to prove by a simple enumeration. There exist two situations for $g$ with four or more vertices. Let us assume that $v$ is connected to $v'$ and vertex $v_{max}$ achieves the maximum vertex support (maps to the maximum number of distinct vertices in among embedding of $g$ in the database graph $G$). In the first case, there exists one and only one vertex $v$ in $g$, such that the degree of $v$ is one. It is allowable for $v_{max}$ to be either $v$ or $v'$. After any of the vertices other than $v'$ and $v_{max}$ is removed from $g$, the induced subgraph of the remaining vertices, denoted as $g'$, is a frequent dense subgraph of $g$, because(1)

$g'$ is connected by definition; (2) $g'$ is dense as the removal of the vertex will delete at most $|V_g| - 2$ edges where $V_g$ is the vertex set of $g$; and (3) $g'$ is frequent as each occurrence of $g$ corresponds to an occurrence of $g'$ in the database graph, indicating that $Sup_{minV}(g', G) \geq Sup_{minV}(g, G)$. Besides, $v_{max}$ is mapped to no less than $Sup_{maxV}(g, G)$ of vertices. In the second case, if there does not exist any vertex in $g$ with degree one, then, we simply remove any vertex from $g$ other than $v_{max}$. We can prove that the induced subgraph of $g$ composed of the remaining vertices is a connected frequent dense pattern. Thus, we prove the property of reachability of frequent dense patterns.

### 4.3 Fast Calculation of Automorphisms

An automorphism of a graph is a graph isomorphism with itself, i.e., a bijection from the vertices of the given graph $g$ back to vertices of $g$ such that the resulting graph is isomorphic with $g$. To compute all automorphisms of any given graph can be computationally expensive.

Since we focus on dense patterns in this paper, it is very likely for a vertex in the graph to be adjacent to most of the other vertices. We denote a vertex that is adjacent to all other vertices as a *complete* vertex. We have the following observations regarding to automorphisms. If in a graph $g$ vertices $v_a$ and $v_b$ have the same vertex label and are (1) adjacent to every vertex other than $v_a$ and $v_b$ with the same edge label, or (2) adjacent to a set of complete vertices of same vertex labels and with the same edge labels, then we can find at least one automorphism of $g$ that maps $v_a$ to $v_b$ and $v_b$ to $v_a$.

We briefly prove our conclusion. In the first case, we can simply construct a bijection function $f_1$ in which $v_a$ is mapped to $v_b$ while all the other vertices map to themselves. $f_1$ is an automorphism by definition. This leads to the proof for the second case. In the second case, we can construct a bijection function $f_2$ that maps each adjacent vertex of $v_a$ to an adjacent vertex of $v_b$ and $v_a$ to $v_b$. It is obvious that $f_2$ is the production function of a set of automorphism. Thus $f_2$ is also an automorphism.

For example, in Figure 2, assuming all labels are the same, $v_c$ and $v_d$ can be mapped to each other by an automorphism as both of them are complete vertices; $v_a$ and $v_b$ can also be mapped to each other by an automorphism as they are adjacent to the same set of complete vertices.

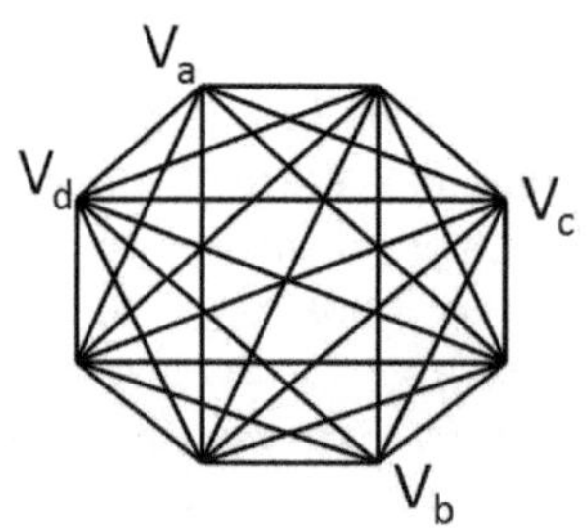


**Fig. 2.** Fast Calculation of Automorphisms

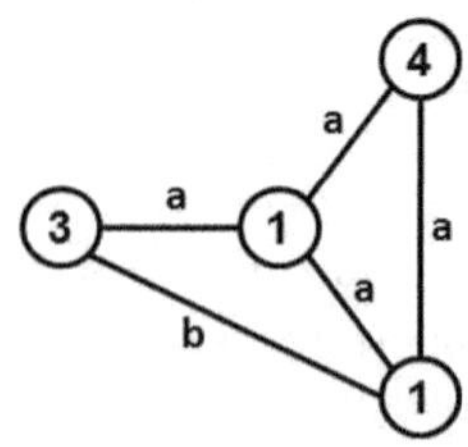


**Fig. 3.** An Example of Inequality Property

# 5 The Mining Algorithm

In this section, we introduce our mining algorithm for searching frequent dense subgraph patterns. The mining algorithm is composed of three components, preprocessing the database graph, generating the candidate patterns, and finding the occurrences.

## 5.1 Preprocessing the Database Graph

The matching process will be extensively invoked during the search for frequent patterns. The most straightforward method to accelerate this process may be to keep the matches of the predecessors in the matching process, where predecessors are the set of vertices that have been matched already. Since the database graph is quite large, of thousands or tens of thousands of vertices and edges, the memory tends to be exhausted if the occurrences are saved.

Before proceeding to any mining process, we first preprocess the database by constructing a series of indices, which greatly facilitates the discovery of the occurrences of any candidate pattern. To the best of our knowledge, few existing graph mining algorithms pre-process the database graph before starting the searching process.

As shown in the previous section, the diameter of any dense pattern is at most two. The information on any database vertex within distance two is of crucial importance. There are two types of index structures to be constructed in our method, the shortest distance based index and sharing vertex based index. For the shortest distance based index, we keep the information of whether the distance between any pair of database vertices is exactly two. For the sharing vertex based index, the number of mutually shared adjacent vertices is extracted for any pair of vertices.

The following are two inequalities for a graph $G$ and its subgraph $g$. (1) The shortest distance between any two vertices $v_a$ and $v_b$ in $g$ is always larger than or equal to that between their counterparts in $G$. (2) Similarly, the number of commonly shared adjacent vertices of $v_a$ and $v_b$ in $g$ is always less than or equal to that of their counterparts in $G$.

For example, let's assume the database graph is the graph in Figure 3, the pattern graph is the one in Figure 1(b), and $v_a$ and $v_b$ are the two vertices with label 1. There is exactly one occurrence of the pattern graph in the database graph. The shortest distance between $v_a$ and $v_b$ is 1 in the database graph, while it is 2 in the pattern graph. Similarly, the number of commonly shared adjacent vertices between $v_a$ and $v_b$ is 2 in the database graph, while it is 1 in the pattern graph.

The time complexity to construct the shortest distance based index is $O(d^2|V|)$, $d$ the average degree and $V$ the vertex set of the database graph. On the other hand, the time complexity to construct the sharing vertex based index based index is $O(d^3|V|)$, since we only need to process the pair of vertices whose shortest distance is no greater than 2. The space complexity of both indices is $O(d^2|V|)$.

## 5.2 Generating Candidate Patterns

In this subsection, we introduce a scheme of generating candidate patterns. The candidate patterns are generated in a hybrid fashion. Since only dense patterns are going to be searched, the total number of possible dense graph patterns with the same vertex set is relatively small. We take advantage of this fact and use a frequent itemset mining algorithm to assist the generation process.

First all labels with no less than $\gamma_{min}$ occurrences are discovered in the database graph. These labels are denoted as frequent labels and used as the initial frequent label set candidates. At this time, we have an initial set of frequent label sets. Each label set contains one label only. After that, a frequent label set is extended by iteratively including one more frequent label. To qualify as a frequent label set, each newly generated label set should have at least $\gamma_{max}$ vertex set instances whose induced subgraphs are dense. A vertex set instance of a label set is a set of vertices whose labels are exactly the same as the label set. It is not necessary to enumerate all the vertex set instances of a given label set. We keep records of all the vertex set instances of a frequent label set, whose induced subgraphs are dense. When a new label is added into a label set, we merely join the vertex set instances and the vertices of the new label.

For example, suppose $\gamma_{max} = 2$ and a frequent label set $\sigma$ has two vertex set instances $\{v_1, v_2, ..., v_i\}$ and $\{u_1, u_2, ..., u_i\}$. Next $\sigma$ is expended to a label set $\sigma'$ with one more label $l'$. There are two vertices, $v'$ and $u'$, with label $l'$ in database graph $G$. Therefore, four vertex set instances of $\sigma'$ are generated by joining two vertex set instances of $\sigma$ and two vertices with label $l'$, which are $\{v_1, v_2, ..., v_i, v'\}$, $\{v_1, v_2, ..., v_i, u'\}$, $\{u_1, u_2, ..., u_i, v'\}$, and $\{u_1, u_2, ..., u_i, u'\}$. If there is only one vertex set with dense induced subgraph, then there is no way that frequent dense graph with the same labels in $\sigma'$ exists. Therefore, $\sigma'$ is not included as the candidate label set.

After obtaining a frequent label set $\sigma$ based on the label set mining described above, instead of starting from a sparse graph, we start from a complete graph composed of vertices in $\sigma$, then remove one edge at a time. As long as the search of the successor vertex set of $\sigma$ has not been done, all maximal frequent dense patterns composed of $\sigma$ are stored. For each ongoing candidate graph, we check (1) if the ongoing graph has already been examined, and (2) whether it is frequent. If the graph has not been examined and is not frequent at the same time, we continue to shrink it by removing one more edge from the candidate graph. Otherwise, the current pattern is frequent and thus we go back to the predecessor of this graph and generate another candidate graph by removing another edge to that graph. The process terminates when we have explored all possible dense subgraphs composed of $\sigma$. All frequent dense graphs are outputted.

To check whether the graph has already been reached or not, two types of canonical forms are used: the regular canonical adjacency matrix [10] and tree canonical forms [25]. Since the frequent patterns of interest are dense, their complement graphs are very likely to be trees. For example, in Figure 4, the complement graph of the left dense

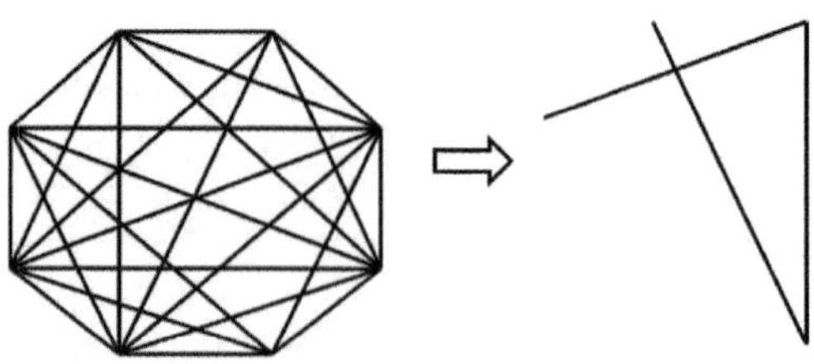

**Fig. 4.** An Example of Complement Graph

graph is a single tree. Thus, if the complement graph of the candidate graph is a tree or a forest, we use the tree canonical forms to represent the candidate graph as it is asymmetrically easy to calculate. Otherwise, we use the canonical adjacency matrix for the representation of the candidate graph.

**Algorithm 1.** *DESSIN*

**Input:** Database graph $G$, minimum vertex support $\gamma_{min}$, and max vertex support $\gamma_{max}$
**Output:** A set of frequent dense pattern $\Pi$

```
Π ← ∅.
Preprocess G and construct the index.
Find all frequent labels, add them into the set SFL.
Initialize a stack of candidate label set Σ.
for each label l in SFL do
   Create an label set σ containing l only.
   Push σ into Σ.
end for
while Σ is not empty do
   σ ← Σ.pop().
   Start searching from the complete graph composed of vertices with labels in σ.
   for each candidate pattern g composed of vertices with labels in σ do
      if g is dense and has not been reached then
         Find all occurrences of g by index based matching.
         if g is frequent then
            Add g into Π.
            Continue to process other subgraphs of g's predecessor.
         else
            Generate a candidate pattern by removing 1 edge from g.
         end if
      end if
   end for
   for each label l in SFL do
      Add l into σ.
      Support of σ, s ← 0.
      Obtain the set of vertex set Ψ, each of which has the same label set as σ.
      for each vertex set ψ in Ψ do
         Create an induce subgraph g using vertices in ψ.
         if g is dense then
            s ← s + 1.
         end if
      end for
      if s ≥ γ_max then
         Create a copy of σ and push it into Σ.
      end if
      Remove l from σ.
   end for
end while
Return Π.
```

### 5.3 Occurrence Discovery

In order to check whether any candidate pattern is frequent, we need find out all the occurrences of this pattern in the database graph. With all the occurrences in hand, we will be able to count the minimum/maximum vertex support of the pattern by a simple enumeration.

In [26], a depth first matching algorithm GADDI was proposed for graph querying in a single database graph. GADDI is used to find all occurrences of candidate patterns. GADDI adopts a two-way pruning. First, a database graph vertex $v_g$ is matched to a candidate graph vertex $v_c$ if and only if the following condition is true. For any neighboring vertex $v_{nc}$ of $v_c$, we can find a corresponding neighboring vertex $v_{ng}$ of $v_g$ with the same label as $v_{nc}$. Besides, the distance between $v_{nc}$ and $v_c$ is no larger than that between $v_{ng}$ and $v_g$. Second, after a database graph vertex is matched, all vertices that cannot appear in the occurrence based on the restriction composed by the matching of $v_c$ and $v_g$ are pruned. In addition, GADDI also applied a dynamic matching scheme, in which it temporarily records the relationships between database and candidate graph vertices in order to avoid redundant calculation.

Since only the dense patterns are of interest, this matching scheme can be improved by taking advantage of the property of dense patterns. As shown in the previous section, some pair of vertices can be easily found as equivalent because of automorphisms. Let us suppose that vertex $v_a$ can be mapped to $v_b$ by an automorphism in a candidate graph vertex, if we can find one occurrence in which $v_a$ is mapped to database graph vertex $v_g$, then $v_b$ can also be mapped to $v_g$ and we do not need to check it anymore.

Having introduced all three essential parts of DESSIN, we summarize it in Algorithm 1.

## 6 Experimental Results

In this section, we empirically analyze the performance of DESSIN against SIGRAM [16], which is designed for finding all frequent patterns in a very large sparse graph. We cannot find an existing algorithm that finds frequent dense patterns only in a single graph, which is very important in many applications. So SIGRAM is employed here for the comparison. DESSIN and SIGRAM are both implemented with C++ code. They were all run on a Dell PowerEdge 2950, with two 3.0GHZ dual-core CPUs and 16GB main memory, using Linux 2.6.16.21-0.8-smp.

For SIGRAM, there are actually two methods, HSIGRAM and VSIGRAM, proposed in [16]. HSIGRAM follows a horizontal approach and discovers the vertices in a breadth-first fashion, whereas VSIGRAM follows a vertical approach and discovers the vertices in a depth-first fashion. SIGRAM also has three formulations of frequent subgraph discovery in a single large graph. They are exact discovery, approximate discovery, and upper bound discovery. We choose exact discovery to do the comparison since DESSIN does exact discovery only. Also, we choose VSIGRAM instead of HSIGRAM as it performs better in most parts of exact discovery tests from the experiment in [16].

The definition of support in SIGRAM is the number of embeddings that have no overlap, which is based on the maximum independent set. SIGRAM mines all frequent patterns first and then finds those without overlaps. However, to facilitate comparison, we modified it to find only dense patterns which satisfy the minimum and/or maximum vertex support requirement. There is no difference between minimum and maximum vertex support for SIGRAM since it first mines all frequent patterns and then finds those that satisfy dense and support requirements. The execution time of SIGRAM only depends on the value of support threshold.

In experiments with DESSIN and SIGRAM, both minimum vertex and maximum vertex supports, $\gamma_{min}$ and $\gamma_{max}$, are used except those experiments that are designed for minimum vertex support or maximum vertex support only. We can then see which definition can find bigger patterns in a reasonable time. Users can decide to use minimum or maximum vertex support based on their requirements.

The experiment is divided into two parts. First we compare the performance of DESSIN with SIGRAM on two real data sets, a protein interaction network and a social network. Then, a large number of synthetic data sets are employed to show the efficiency and scalability of these two methods. The performance of DESSIN and SIGRAM is measured using the following three criteria, the execution time, the number of patterns found and the size of largest pattern found, which is measured in the number of edges.

### 6.1 Real Data Sets

In this set of experiments, two graphs generated from real data sets are utilized. They are both non-directed graphs. The first graph is generated from a subset of the protein-protein interaction networks for homo sapiens. There are 6,410 vertices, 22,408 edges, and the average degree of a vertex is around 7. Each vertex represents a protein and the label of the vertex is its gene ontology term from [29]. There are a total of 632 distinct labels. An edge in the graph represents an interaction between the two proteins it connects. We also compare DESSIN with SIGRAM in a social network graph, where the average degree is much higher. The social network graph is obtained from a social network in [30]. There are 297 vertices, 2148 edges, and the average degree of a vertex is 14. It has 40 different labels in total. Each vertex represents a person (with a unique vertex label), and an edge corresponds to communication between two persons.

For the protein interaction network, we vary the threshold and test both minimum vertex support and maximum vertex support mentioned in section 3. As a result, we show the execution time in figure 5, the number of found patterns and the size of the largest found pattern of DESSIN and SIGRAM in Table 1. SIGRAM crashed when the vertex support was set lower than 20.

For the social network graph, we also vary the threshold and test both minimum vertex support and maximum vertex support. Figure 6 shows the execution time and Table 2 shows the number of found patterns and the size of the largest found pattern. SIGRAM crashed when support was set to 3 due to a too lengthy execution time and memory exhaustion.

From the results of the real data sets, we can see that as expected, for both methods, the running time, number, and largest size of found patterns increases as the threshold decreases. DESSIN is much more efficient than SIGRAM since SIGRAM intends to find all patterns while DESSIN finds only dense patterns. The running time of SIGRAM

**Table 1.** Pattern found in PPI network

| $\gamma_{min}$ | largest size | NO. of Pattern | $\gamma_{max}$ | largest size | NO. of Pattern |
|---|---|---|---|---|---|
| 10 | 24 | 2,311 | 15 | 33 | 12,721 |
| 15 | 17 | 936 | 20 | 25 | 3,342 |
| 20 | 6 | 504 | 30 | 18 | 1,013 |
| 25 | 5 | 310 | 40 | 11 | 434 |
| 30 | 4 | 208 | 50 | 7 | 236 |

**Table 2.** Pattern found in social network

| $\gamma_{min}$ | largest size | NO. of Pattern | $\gamma_{max}$ | largest size | NO. of Pattern |
|---|---|---|---|---|---|
| 3 | 22 | 25,539 | 10 | 46 | 49,864 |
| 5 | 13 | 2,450 | 15 | 30 | 3,017 |
| 8 | 9 | 555 | 20 | 24 | 1,020 |
| 10 | 6 | 232 | 25 | 6 | 11 |
| 15 | 5 | 72 | 30 | 4 | 8 |
| 20 | 3 | 23 | 40 | 0 | 0 |

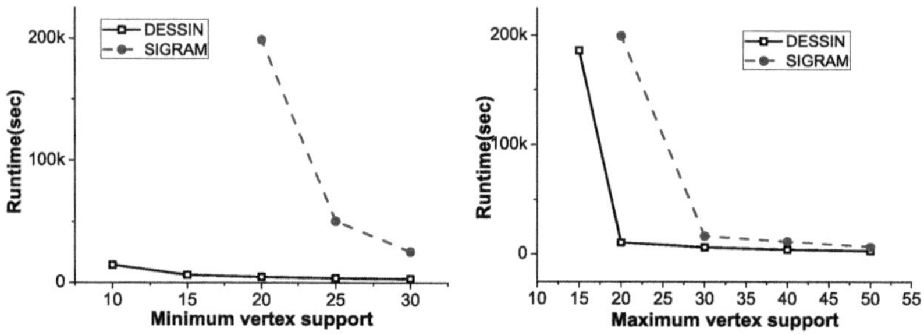


(a) Min. Vertex Support (b) Max. Vertex Support

**Fig. 5.** Runtime for PPI network

increases much faster than DESSIN. When the threshold was set low, SIGRAM was aborted because of either the excessively long runtime or memory exhaustion. However, if SIGRAM can finish running, DESSIN could still find all dense patterns as SIGRAM did.

## 6.2 Synthetic Data Sets

We analyze the performance of the two methods from various aspects based on a set of synthetically generated graphs. To systematically analyze the performance of DESSIN and SIGRAM, we vary one parameter at a time. The default parameter values are in Table 3. We test all graphs using both maximum vertex support and minimum vertex support. The default threshold is set to 30 for maximum vertex support while 10 for minimum vertex support.

The first aspect is the number of vertices in $G$. We test DESSIN and SIGRAM from 500 vertices to 6,000 vertices. Query time of DESSIN is less than SIGRAM regardless of the size of $G$. When the size of $G$ is large, SIGRAM was aborted due to an excessively long runtime. DESSIN was still able to finish the mining process in a reasonable amount of time when $G$ has 6,000 vertices. The runtime of both methods grows as the number of vertices increases, but SIGRAM grows much faster, because the number of patterns increases much faster than the number of dense patterns with more vertices in $G$. Figure 7 shows the execution time of both methods with both support thresholds

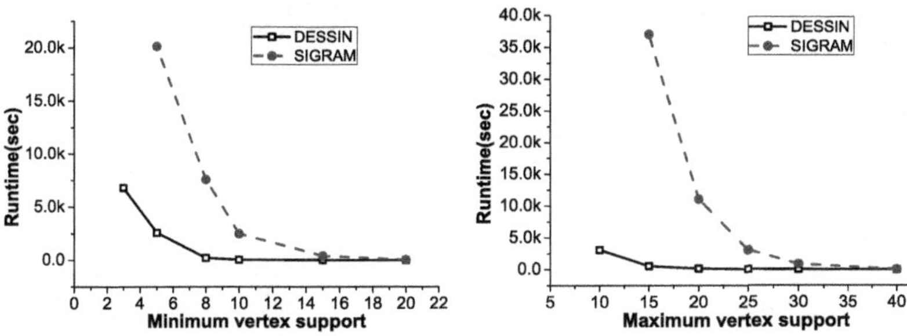


(a) Min. Vertex Support (b) Max. Vertex Support

**Fig. 6.** Runtime for social network

**Table 3.** Default Param. Value

| Param. | Default Value |
|---|---|
| Num. of Vertices in $G$ | 2,000 |
| Avg. Degree in $G$ | 8 |
| Num. of Labels | 500 |
| $\gamma_{min}$ | 10 |
| $\gamma_{max}$ | 30 |

and Table 4 shows the number and largest size of found patterns. When the minimum vertex support threshold was set to 10, SIGRAM can finish the execution only with 500 and 1,000 vertices $G$. However, if it was set to 30, SIGRAM is able to finish most experiments except for the largest $G$ which has 6,000 vertices.

The second aspect is the average degree of a vertex in $G$. We tested both methods with average degree 4, 6, 8, 10 and 12. SIGRAM crashes when the average degree is greater than 8. It is easy to imagine that the number of patterns in $G$ increases exponentially as the average degree grows, which is also true for dense patterns. This is the reason why SIGRAM crashes when average degree of $G$ is higher than 6 or 8 with the vertex support threshold of 10 or 30. Figure 8(a) and (b) show the execution time for both support thresholds for both methods. Table 5 shows the number and largest size of found patterns.

**Table 4.** Various size of $G$

| Vertices in $G$ | largest size | | NO. of Pattern | |
|---|---|---|---|---|
| | min | max | min | max |
| 500 | 6 | 6 | 243 | 8 |
| 1,000 | 17 | 33 | 3,675 | 9,866 |
| 2,000 | 24 | 46 | 9,637 | 49,864 |
| 4,000 | 32 | 48 | 18,765 | 56,234 |
| 6,000 | 34 | 49 | 35,982 | 69,875 |

**Table 5.** Various average degree of $G$

| Degree of $G$ | largest size | | NO. of Pattern | |
|---|---|---|---|---|
| | min | max | min | max |
| 4 | 13 | 22 | 2,560 | 6,894 |
| 6 | 18 | 38 | 4,986 | 17,456 |
| 8 | 24 | 46 | 9,637 | 49,864 |
| 10 | 31 | 48 | 24,579 | 67,841 |
| 12 | 39 | 490 | 78,415 | 89,638 |

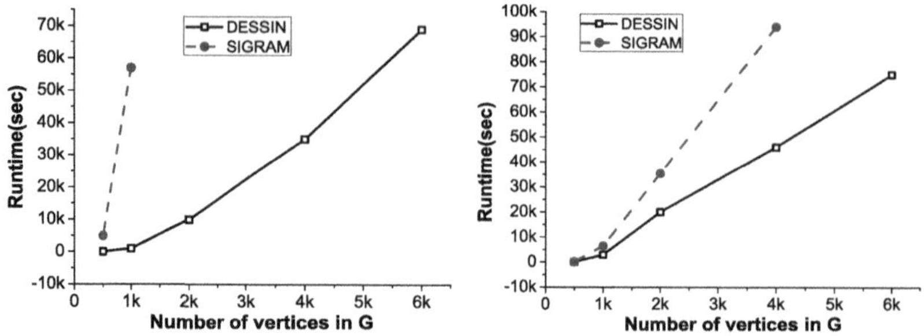


(a) Min. Vertex Support (b) Max. Vertex Support

**Fig. 7.** Runtime with various size of $G$

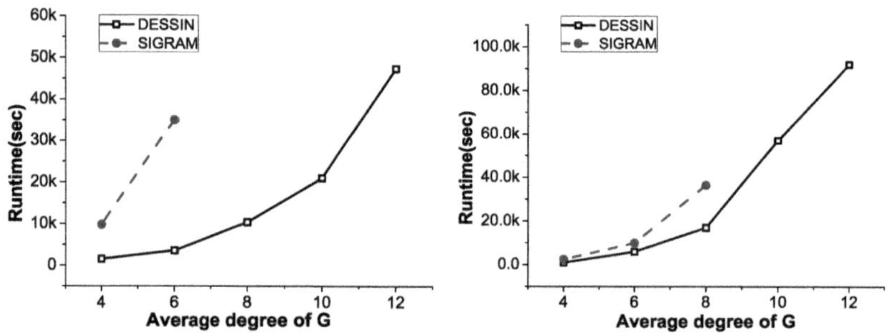


(a) Min. Vertex Support (b) Max. Vertex Support

**Fig. 8.** Runtime with various average degree of $G$

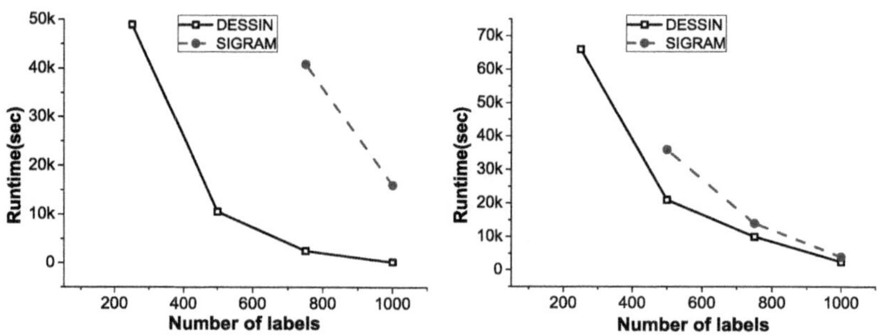


(a) Min. Vertex Support (b) Max. Vertex Support

**Fig. 9.** Runtime with various # of labels

The third aspect is the number of distinct label types. We test a 2000-vertex graph with the number of distinct labels from 250 to 1,000. With more labels in $G$, the number of frequent patterns is reduced significantly. Figure 9 shows the execution time of both methods with two support thresholds SIGRAM also crashes due to the long execution time and memory exhaustion when number of distinct labels is too small.

The fourth and fifth aspects are the minimum and maximum vertex support of patterns in $G$. The number and largest size of patterns found by both methods grow very fast as $\gamma_{min}$ and $\gamma_{max}$ decrease. SIGRAM cannot finish the execution when $\gamma_{min}$ is set lower than 12. Figure 10(a) and 10(b) show the runtime with various vertex support for both methods. Table 6 and 7 shows the number and largest size of patterns found.

**Table 6.** Various Min. vertex support

| $\gamma_{min}$ | largest size | NO. of Pattern |
|---|---|---|
| 8 | 37 | 44,652 |
| 9 | 29 | 22,021 |
| 10 | 24 | 9,637 |
| 12 | 22 | 7,812 |
| 15 | 16 | 3,403 |

**Table 7.** Various Max. vertex support

| $\gamma_{max}$ | largest size | NO. of Pattern |
|---|---|---|
| 20 | 47 | 90,610 |
| 25 | 46 | 56,721 |
| 30 | 46 | 49,864 |
| 35 | 30 | 19,312 |
| 40 | 25 | 8,547 |

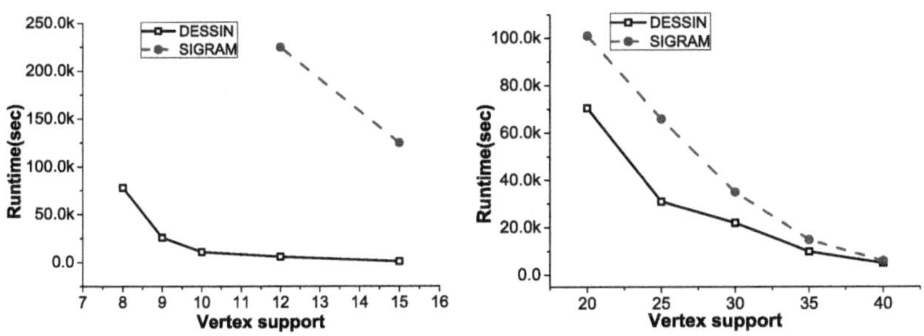


(a) Min. Vertex Support

(b) Max. Vertex Support

**Fig. 10.** Runtime with various vertex support

We experimented two methods on various real and synthetic data sets. SIGRAM was modified to find all frequent dense patterns which satisfy the minimum and maximum vertex support requirements. Both DESSIN and SIGRAM were able to find all frequent dense patterns, as long as they can finish the mining process. However, SIGRAM performs less efficiently when it deals with dense and large database graphs than DESSIN does since it is not designed for them. DESSIN is faster in all tests than SIGRAM which sometimes crashes due to either excessively long runtime or memory exhaustion. For DESSIN, we have two thresholds of support, minimum vertex and maximum vertex support thresholds. The maximum vertex support is much looser than the minimum vertex support. Using the maximum vertex support, the algorithm could find more patterns than the minimum vertex support even when it is set much higher. It is possible that a frequent pattern has a very high maximum vertex support but a low minimum vertex support if the vertex is heavily shared by most embeddings of the pattern in $G$. In conclusion, if the database graph $G$ is relatively sparse, e.g., a degree of 2, SIGRAM can be employed to mine frequent patterns in it. On the other hand, if $G$ has a higher degree and dense patterns are intended to be found, then DESSIN should be deployed.

## 7 Conclusion

In this paper, we propose the frequent dense patterns model for a single large connected graph. The DESSIN algorithm is devised to mine these patterns. There are two main characteristics of DESSIN. (1) To find these patterns efficiently, a preprocessing step is employed to build an indexing structure. By employing the indexing structure, it is shown be much faster in locating all occurrences of a pattern. (2) A depth-first pattern generation method is utilized based on the reachability property. Last but not least, a large number of real and synthetic data sets are employed to show the effectiveness and efficiency of DESSIN.

## References

1. Bader, G., Hogue, C.: An automated method for finding molecular complexes in large protein interaction networks. BMC Bioinformatics 4(2) (2003)
2. Bringmann, B., Nijssen, S.: What is Frequent in a Single Graph? In: Washio, T., Suzuki, E., Ting, K.M., Inokuchi, A. (eds.) PAKDD 2008. LNCS (LNAI), vol. 5012, pp. 858–863. Springer, Heidelberg (2008)
3. Chang, R., Podgurski, A., Yang, J.: Finding what's not there: a new approach to revealing neglected conditions in software. In: International symposium on software testing and analysis (2007)
4. Dehaspe, L., Toivonen, H., King, R.: Finding frequent substructures in chemical compounds. In: Proc. of KDD, New York, NY, USA (1998)
5. Fan, W., Zhang, K., Cheng, H., Yan, X., Han, J., Yu, P., Verscheure, O.: Direct mining of discriminative and essential frequent patterns via model-based search tree. In: Proc. of KDD, Las Vegas, Nevada, USA, pp. 230–238 (2008)
6. Fiedler, M., Borgelt, C.: Subgraph support in a single large graph. In: Proc. of ICDMW, pp. 399–404 (2007)
7. Gibson, D., Kumar, R., Tomkins, A.: Discovering Large Dense Subgraphs in Massive Graphs. In: Proc. of VLDB, Trondheim, Norway, pp. 721–732 (2005)
8. Hasan, M., Chaoji, V., Salem, S., Besson, J., Zaki, M.: ORIGAMI: Mining Representative Orthogonal Graph Patterns. In: Proc. of ICDM, pp. 153–162 (2007)
9. Hu, H., Yan, X., Huang, Y., Han, J., Zhou, X.: Mining coherent dense subgraphs across massive biological networks for functional discovery. In: Proc. of ISMB (Supplement of Bioinformatics), pp. 213–221 (2005)
10. Huan, J., Wang, W., Prins, J.: Efficient mining of frequent subgraphs in the presence of isomorphism. In: Proc. of ICDM, Melbourne, Florida, USA, pp. 549–552 (2003)
11. Huan, J., Wang, W., Prins, J., Yang, J.: SPIN: mining maximal frequent subgraphs from graph databases. In: Proc. of SIGKDD, Seattle, WA, USA, pp. 581–586 (2004)
12. Inokuchi, A., Washio, T., Motoda, H.: An apriori-based algorithm for mining frequent substructures from graph data. In: Proc. of Principles of Data Mining and Knowledge Discovery, pp. 13–23 (2000)
13. Ketkar, N., Holder, L., Cook, D.: Subdue: compression-based frequent pattern discovery in graph data. In: Proc. of the 1st international workshop on open source data mining: frequent pattern mining implementations, Chicago, Illinois, USA, pp. 71–76 (2005)
14. Koyuturk, M., Grama, A., Szpankowski, W.: An efficient algorithm for detecting frequent subgraphs in biological networks. Bioinformatics 21(16), 3401–3408 (2004)
15. Kuramochi, M., Karypis, G.: Frequent subgraph discovery. In: Proc. of ICDE, pp. 313–320 (2001)

16. Kuramochi, M., Karypis, G.: Finding Frequent Patterns in a Large Sparse Graph. DMKD 11(3), 243–271 (2005)
17. Moody, J.: Peer Influence Groups: Identifying Dense Clusters in Large Networks. Social Networks 23, 261–283 (2001)
18. Nijssen, S., Kok, J.: A quick start in frequent structure mining can make a difference. In: Proc. of KDD, Seattle, WA, US, pp. 647–652 (2004)
19. Palmer, C., Gibbons, P., Faloutsos, C.: ANF: A fast and scalable tool for data mining in massive graphs. In: Proc. of KDD, Edmonton, Alberta, Canada, pp. 81–90 (2002)
20. Pei, J., Jiang, D., Zhang, A.: On mining cross-graph quasi-cliques. In: Proc. of KDD, Chicago, Illinois, USA (2005)
21. Thomas, L., Valluri, S., Karlapalem, K.: MARGIN:Maximal Frequent Subgraph Mining. In: Proc. of ICDM, pp. 1097–1101 (2006)
22. Wang, J., Zeng, Z., Zhou, L.: CLAN: An Algorithm for Mining Closed Cliques from Large Dense Graph Databases. In: Proc. of ICDE, vol. 73 (2006)
23. Wang, N., Parthasarathy, S., Tan, K., Tung, A.: CSV: Visualizing and Mining Cohesive Subgraphs. In: Proc. of SIGMOD (2008)
24. Yan, X., Cheng, H., Han, J., Yu, P.: Mining significant graph patterns by leap search. In: Prof. of SIGMOD, Vancouver, Canada, pp. 433–444 (2008)
25. Zhang, S., Hu, M., Yang, J.: TreePi: a novel graph indexing method. In: Proc. of ICDE (2007)
26. Zhang, S., Li, S., Yang, J.: GADDI: Distance index base subgraph matching in biological networks. In: Proc. of EDBT (2009)
27. Zhang, S., Yang, J., Li, S.: RING: an integrated method for frequent representative subgraph mining. In: Proc. of ICDM (2009)
28. Zeng, Z., Wang, J., Zhou, L., Karypis, G.: Coherent closed quasi-clique discovery from large dense graph databases. In: Proc. of KDD, Philadelphia, PA, USA, pp. 797–802 (2006)
29. Gene Ontology, `http://www.geneontology.org/`
30. Social Network, `http://www-personal.umich.edu/~mejn/netdata/`

# Discovery of Evolving Convoys

Htoo Htet Aung and Kian-Lee Tan

School of Computing, National University of Singapore

**Abstract.** Traditionally, a convoy is defined as a set of moving objects that are close to each other for a period of time. Existing techniques, following this traditional definition, cannot find evolving convoys with dynamic members and do not have any monitoring aspect in their design. We propose new concepts of dynamic convoys and evolving convoys, which reflect real-life scenarios, and develop algorithms to discover evolving convoys in an incremental manner.

## 1 Introduction

Object identification and tracking technologies as well as triangulation techniques enable to monitor and archive movement data of objects. For example, in an urban setting, pedestrian and vehicle movement can be recorded at high temporal resolutions using a combination of GPS, cellular networks, Wi-Fi hotspots and other radio frequency (RF) sensor networks. These data can be used to find interesting spatial-temporal movement patterns including convoys.

Discovering and monitoring convoys have many practical applications ranging from traffic planning to wild-life research. Traffic planners can use the knowledge of groups of trucks moving between factories, warehouses and stores. Convoy discovery can be also used to extract complex herding behaviour of wild animals.

**Definition 1.** *A convoy can be defined as a set of $m$ or more objects, which are within proximity of each other for a duration $dur \geq w$, where $m > 1$ and $w > 1$ are user-defined parameters.*

Convoys were traditionally defined as in Def. 1 using arbitrary spatial proximity – in a circle [1,2], in a clique [3,4] or in a density-connected cluster [5]. The primary focus of this paper is on convoys formed from density-connected objects as it is more relevant for real-world objects.

Although Def. 1 is intuitive, it cannot be applied directly in real-life. Figure 1(a) shows movement of five college students ($a$, $b$, $c$, $d$ and $e$). Circles with time-stamps show spatial proximity. An administrator, trying to find convoys of size $m = 2$ and duration $w = 5$, will be overwhelmed by a result containing seven convoys as listed in Fig. 1(b).

From the above example, we made the following observations on the nature of real-life convoys that Def. 1 cannot cope with :

1. Some members of the convoy may temporarily leave the group. Actually, $a$, $b$, $c$ and $e$ formed a convoy from $t_6$ to $t_{22}$ as they were literally moving

M. Gertz and B. Ludäscher (Eds.): SSDBM 2010, LNCS 6187, pp. 196–213, 2010.

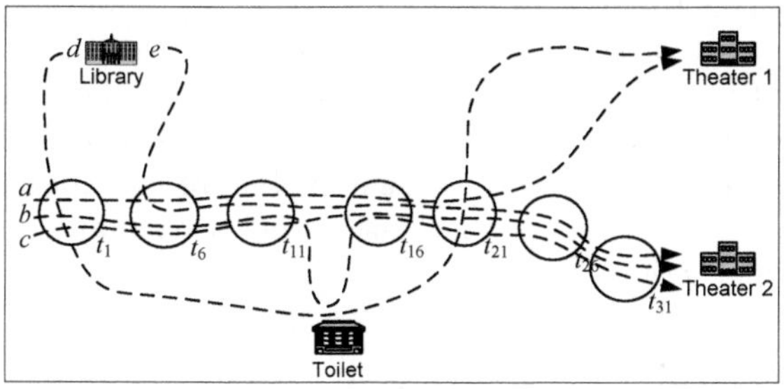


(a) Movement Trajectories.

| Convoys | Life-span |
|---|---|
| $C_1 = \{a, c\}$ | $t_1$-$t_{22}$ |
| $C_2 = \{c, e\}$ | $t_6$-$t_{31}$ |
| $C_3 = \{a, b, c\}$ | $t_1$-$t_{13}$ |
| $C_4 = \{a, c, e\}$ | $t_6$-$t_{22}$ |
| $C_5 = \{b, c, e\}$ | $t_{15}$-$t_{31}$ |
| $C_6 = \{a, b, c, e\}$ | $t_6$-$t_{13}$ |
| $C_7 = \{a, b, c, e\}$ | $t_{15}$-$t_{22}$ |

(b) Convoys and Life-spans.

**Fig. 1.** Movement of Five College Students and Corresponding Convoys

together. However, according to Def. 1, there were three convoys (see $C_4$, $C_6$ and $C_7$ in Fig. 1(b)) for their movement because $b$ was not detected together with the rest ($a$, $c$ and $e$) at a single time-stamp $t_{14}$ resulting in a short gap that eventually creates three overlapping convoys. We will refer to a convoy that allows its members to be briefly absent as a *dynamic convoy.*

2. In reality, it is also possible that convoys may evolve into larger (smaller) convoys. In our example, the convoy $\{a, b, c\}$ was joined by $e$ and evolved into a larger convoy $\{a, b, c, e\}$ (at $t_6$), which, in turn, evolved into a smaller convoy $\{b, c, e\}$ (at $t_{23}$). Representing this evolving convoy as seven overlapping convoys is not intuitive and hard to comprehend. It is also difficult to order or establish relationship among the overlapping convoys. It will be more useful if it is represented as three stages of a single *evolving convoy.*

Many existing works do not have a satisfactory mechanism to handle the convoys' behaviour we observed above. Algorithms proposed in [5] report only two convoys – $\{a, c\}$ from $t_1$ to $t_{22}$ and $\{b, c, e\}$ from $t_{23}$ to $t_{31}$ – omitting the longest-duration convoy $C_2$[1] while those in another work [6] report different number of cluster sequences for different values of similarity threshold, $\theta$.[2] For example, two cluster sequences will be reported for similarity threshold $\theta = 0.70$.

In this paper, we made the following contributions :

1. **Introduce novel concepts of dynamic convoys and evolving convoys** – In contrast to traditional persistent-members-only definitions, a dynamic convoy (DC) allows dynamic members under constraints imposed by user-defined parameters. An evolving convoy (EC) captures the relationship between different stages of convoys such that a convoy in a stage has more (fewer) members than its previous stage.
2. **Three algorithms to discover evolving convoys** – All proposed algorithms are incremental, and can be used in both off-line and streaming datasets. All dynamic convoys can be derived from the evolving convoys.

[1] Personal communications with the authors confirmed this claim.

[2] For detailed description of parameter $\theta$ and its effects, please refer to Sec. 2.2.

To the best of our knowledge, this is the first work that addresses dynamic convoys and evolving convoys. The rest of the paper is organized as follows : the next section outlines related works and is followed by a section on formal definitions of dynamic convoys and evolving convoys. In the subsequent section, the proposed algorithms to find evolving convoys are presented. Before concluding our work, we report the results of experiments that assess the performance of the algorithms on real-life and synthetic datasets.

## 2 Related Works

### 2.1 Clustering of Spatial Points

Existing works on spatial clustering consist of hierarchical [7,8] and partitioning [9] algorithms but they need domain-specific parameters in advance. These parameters cannot be pre-determined in convoy discovery, where grouping behaviour of the objects should not be assumed. Ng and Han [10] proposed an efficient partition algorithm CLARANS and suggested running it multiple times to determine the best number of targeted clusters. In convoy discovery, clustering of points for each time-stamp is required and, hence, this may be expensive.

Ester et al. [11] suggested density-based clustering, DBSCAN, which does not need any domain-specific parameters and is scalable. DBSCAN distinguishes each object in a density-connected clusters into two categories: core and border. A core object has at least $min\_pts$ objects within its $\varepsilon$-proximity and is used to expand the clusters. An object, which has fewer than $min\_pts$ objects within its $\varepsilon$-proximity and has a core object as its $\varepsilon$-neighbours is a border objects. For example, in Fig. 2, (for $min\_pts = 3$) black circles like $c$ are core objects while white circles like $b$ are border objects. DBSCAN can handle clusters of arbitrary shape and is tolerant to noise. Dynamic clustering, to cope with insertion and deletions, in spatial databases can be performed by incremental DBSCAN [12].

### 2.2 Moving Clusters, Flocks, Groups and Convoys

Kalnis et al. [6] proposed algorithms to find moving clusters. A sequence of clusters is defined to be a moving cluster if Jaccard index between each cluster and its immediate predecessor is not lower than a user-defined threshold, $\theta$. It

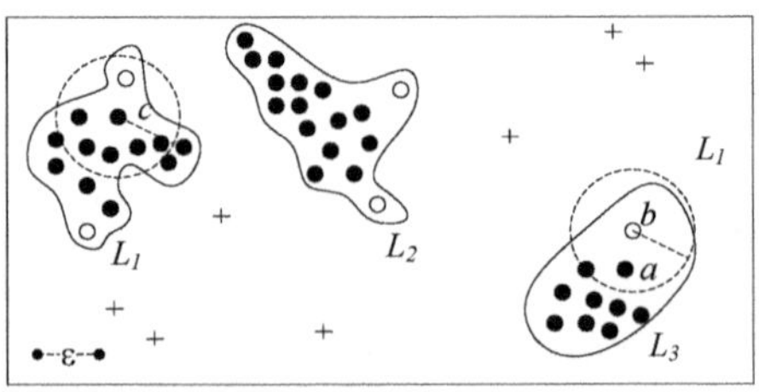


**Fig. 2.** An Example of Density-based Clustering

permits clusters to be completely different (larger, smaller etc.) in a short time, especially for lower $\theta$ values. Using higher $\theta$ values, however, cluster transitions (merge, split etc.) tend to break moving clusters into shorter episodes. MONIC [13] models and monitors cluster transitions: survival, split, absorbed, disappear and emerge.

A fixed flock is defined as a set $F$ of $m$ or more objects, which are within a circle of radius $r > 0$ in $w$ or more consecutive time-stamps ($r$, $m$ and $w$ are given). Gudmundsson and Kreveld [1] reported computing longest-duration fixed flock is NP-Hard and gave various approximations. Benkert et al. [2] described a method that transforms $d$ dimensional trajectories (containing $\tau$ points) into $d\tau$ dimensional points and performs range-query to find flocks. Vieira et al. [14] reported polynomial-time algorithms to find flocks of fixed duration $dur = w$.

Hwang et al. [3] described a definition of moving groups. A moving group is a set of objects $G$, whose members must be within $min\_dis$ away from each other for $min\_dur$ or more consecutive time-stamps. They proposed an Apriori based algorithm and VG-growth based algorithm to find all such groups of moving objects. These algorithms are extended to find maximal groups in [4].

Jeung et al [5] defined a convoy, which can occupy a spatial region of arbitrary size and shape in its lifetime, as a group of at least $m$ objects being density-connected with each other throughout $w$ consecutive time-points, where $m$, $w$ and DBSCAN parameters are provided by the user. They proposed a filter-refinement scheme called CuTS. Although CuTS is better than the simple refinement step alone, it cannot produce a complete list of convoys.

## 3 Dynamic Convoys and Evolving Convoys

**Definition 2.** *For a given set of objects $O = \{o_1, o_2, ..., o_n\}$, time-stamps $T = \{t_1, t_2, ..., t_\tau\}$ and a spatial-space $\mathbb{R}^d$, a moving object dataset $\mathcal{R}$ is a set of records of the form $\langle o, t, loc\rangle$ where $o \in O, t \in T$ and $loc \in \mathbb{R}^d$.*

In a moving object dataset, $o$ and $t$ form a composite key that uniquely determines $loc$. However, a given moving object dataset ($\mathcal{R}$) can be incomplete – i.e. for all $\{o, t\} \in O \times T$, there may not be $\langle o, t, loc\rangle \in \mathcal{R}$ – since, in reality, some objects may be untraceable in certain time-stamps due to hardware limitations. Although time is assumed as a discrete sequence with an equal intervals between each pair of consecutive points, generality of Def. 2 is not undermined since any application can set an arbitrarily small interval.

**Definition 3.** *For given parameters: $m$, $k$ and $w$ ($m > 1$, $1 \leq k \leq w$), a set of moving objects $D$ forms a dynamic convoy from $t_{\text{start}}(D)$ to $t_{\text{end}}(D)$ if it :*

- *Contains at least $m$ persistent-members (denoted by $PM_D$), all of which are density-connected in each time-stamp $t$ in $[t_{\text{start}}(D), t_{\text{end}}(D)]$ and*
- *Contains zero or more dynamic members (denoted by $DM_D$), each of which must be density-connected with the persistent-members at least $k$ times for any $w$ sliding window in $[t_{\text{start}}(D), t_{\text{end}}(D)]$.*

Under Def. 3, members of a convoy are density-connected and, hence, a dynamic convoy can assume arbitrary spatial size and shape in its life-time. The first condition ensures a fixed set of persistent members ($PM_D$) forms its main body. The second condition requires each dynamic member $o \in DM_D$ to stay close with the persistent members at least $k$ times in any $w$ sliding window in its life-span. For smaller $k$ values, a dynamic-member can move away from the convoy longer while larger $k$ values prohibit a dynamic-member from being away for a long time ($k = w$ means no dynamic-member and, hence, a traditional convoy). For example, with $m = 2$, $w = 5$ and $k = 4$, in Fig. 1(a), $\{a, b, c, e\}$ forms a dynamic convoy from $t_6$ to $t_{22}$.

It is clear that, for a dynamic convoy $D$, $PM_D$ forms a traditional convoy. Therefore, for a given dataset, we can have as many dynamic convoy as we have traditional convoys. It is also difficult for a human user to establish relationship between overlapping dynamic convoys. For $m = 2$, $k = 4$ and $w = 5$, in the scenario described in Fig. 1(a), $D_1 = \{a, b, c\}$ in $[t_1, t_{22}]$, $D_2 = \{b, c, e\}$ in $[t_6, t_{31}]$, $D_3 = \{a, b, c, e\}$ in $[t_6, t_{22}]$ and many of their subsets are all dynamic convoys. From the usability point of view, reporting all convoys, whose members and life-spans are overlapped, may be confusing. Selecting a representative from overlapping convoys is also application-dependent. For example, some administrators may be interested in longer-duration convoys (like $D_2$) while others may be interested in larger convoys (like $D_3$). A more comprehensive approach is to report each set of overlapping convoys as an evolving entity with stages.

**Definition 4.** *A dynamic convoy of duration* $dur = w$ *is called a* $w$*-convoy.*

For given $m$, $k$ and $w$, a dynamic convoy $D$ of duration $dur \geq w$ has $dur - w + 1$ $w$-convoys $D_1, D_2, ..., D_{(dur-w+1)}$ of duration $w$, each of which has the same persistent-members and dynamic-members as $D$. For example, the convoy $D_1 = \{a, b, c\}$ (see above paragraph) that exists from $t_1$ to $t_{22}$ has 18 convoys of duration $w$, each having the same set of members as $D_1$.

**Definition 5.** *A* $w$*-convoy* $D$ *that exists from* $t$ *to* $t+w-1$ *evolves into another* $w$*-convoy* $D'$ *that exists from* $t+1$ *to* $t+w$ *if they have at least* $m$ *common persistent-members, i.e* $|PM_D \cap PM_{D'}| \geq m$.

Definition 5 defines how a $w$-convoy can evolve into the next $w$-convoy of duration $w$. It ensures that a convoy evolves only into a related convoy (not to a convoy with totally different members). The $w$-convoys formed by $a$, $b$, $c$ and $e$ in the scenario in Fig. 1(a), for parameters $m = 2$, $k = 4$ and $w = 5$, is shown in Fig. 3. $D_1 = \{a, b, c\}$ that exists from $t_1$ to $t_5$ evolves into $D_2 = \{a, b, c\}$ that exists from $t_2$ to $t_6$, which in turn evolves into $D_3$, $D_4$ and $D_5$. Then, $D_5 = \{a, b, c\}$ evolves into $D_6 = \{a, b, c, e\}$ as they share $\{a, b, c\}$ as persistent members. The evolution continues until $D_{18}$, which evolves into smaller $D_{19}$ and so on.

**Definition 6.** *A sequence of* $w$*-convoy* $D_1, D_2, ..., D_z$ *such that each* $D_i$ *evolves into* $D_{(i+1)}$ *for* $1 \leq i < z$ *is maximal if there is no* $w$*-convoy* $D'$*, which evolves into* $D_1$ *or into which* $D_z$ *evolves into.*

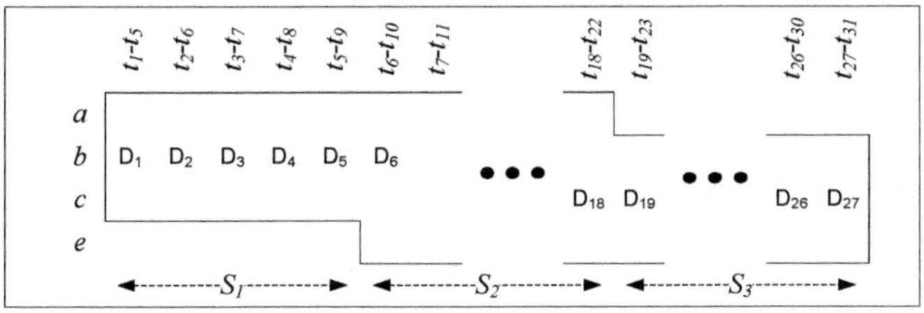


**Fig. 3.** The Concept of Convoy Evolution

Following Def. 6, we can see that in Fig. 3, there is a single maximal sequence of 27 $w$-convoys, from $D_1 = \{a, b, c\}$ to $D_{27} = \{b, c, e\}$. Informally, for each maximal sequence of $w$-convoys in a dataset, there is a corresponding evolving convoy (defined below) that covers all related convoys (even longer ones).

**Definition 7.** *For given parameters $m$, $k$, $w$ and a maximal sequence of $w$-convoys, $D_1, D_2, ..., D_z$ such that each $D_i$ evolves into $D_{(i+1)}$ for $1 \leq i < z$, the corresponding evolving convoy $V$ contains $z' \leq z$ stages. Each stage $S_j$, for $1 \leq j \leq z'$, is defined as a continuous sequence of $w$-convoys $[D_s, D_e]$ having the same set of members.*

Definition 7 ensures a sequence of related dynamic convoys to be covered in an evolving convoy with stages. The members at each stage $S_{[s,e]}$ that covers $w$-convoys $[D_s, D_e]$ are the members of $D_s$ ($D_e$). The start-time and end-time of a stage $S_{[s,e]}$ can be derived from the start-time and end-time of participating $w$ convoys. For example, in Fig 3, the evolving convoy corresponding to the maximal sequence of $w$-convoys has three stages – stage $S_1 = \{a, b, c\}$, stage $S_2 = \{a, b, c, e\}$ and stage $S_3 = \{b, c, e\}$. The period of the first stage $S_1$ of the evolving convoy $V$ is from $t_1$ to $t_5$, while the period of the last stage $S_3$ of $V$ is from $t_{22}$ to $t_{31}$. Each stage corresponds to at least a dynamic convoy and, from an evolving convoy, the dynamic convoys it covers can be easily derived.[3]

By Def. 7, an evolving convoy can gain (lose) new (existing) dynamic members throughout its life. For instance, stage $S_1 = \{a, b, c\}$ of evolving convoy $V$ in Fig. 3 evolves to the next stage $S_2 = \{a, b, c, e\}$ by obtaining $e$ as a new member. They also allow a persistent member in the current stage to become a dynamic member in subsequent stages (and vice versa) and impose no hard differentiation on a member's role. Any member can become a dynamic member (persistent member) and leave (form) the main body of the convoy. This property agrees with real-life scenarios. Consider a group of five soldiers each, in turn, taking a point-duty, i.e to walk ten meter ahead of the group looking for anomalies, depicted in Fig. 4. Although this is a convoy moving for 50 time-stamps, there is no fixed set of persistent-members defining the main body from $t_1$ to $t_{50}$ for any $m > 1$. However, with parameters $w = 20$, $k = 10$ and $m = 2$, we can have an evolving convoy as the soldiers returning from point-duty will take the role

[3] The detailed process is omitted to conserve space.

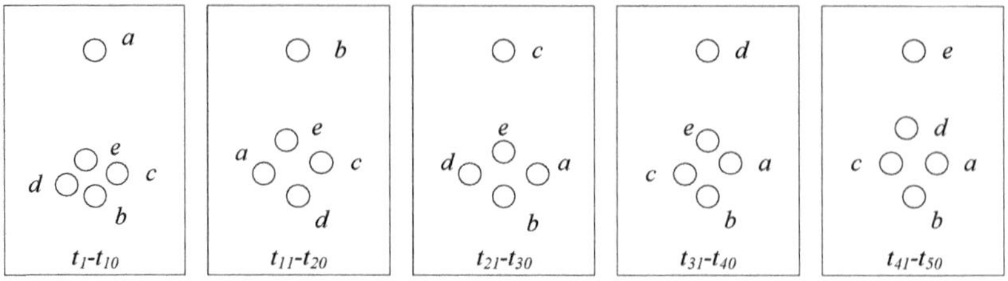


**Fig. 4.** Movement of Five Soldiers

of persistent-member and form the main body of the convoy. For example, $b$ is a dynamic-member earlier and, eventually, a persistent-member at $t_{21}$ onwards.[4] Thus, $a$ and $b$ together formed the main body of the evolving convoy during $[t_{41}, t_{50}]$.

To summarize, following the traditional notions of convoys, there are many overlapping convoys in a moving object dataset and the relationship among them is hard to establish. Therefore, the new concept of evolving convoys, which allows a convoy to evolve from a stage to the next, can provide a better picture of the real-life groups of moving objects than the traditional definitions.

## 4 Discovery of Evolving Convoys

We developed three algorithms to discover evolving convoys from a moving object dataset. The first algorithm is a straight-forward implementation while the next two algorithms mitigate the performance bottlenecks of their predecessors.

### 4.1 Simple Slice-by-Slice Algorithm

The Simple Slice-by-Slice algorithm $S^3$ is directly obtained from the problem definition and is similar to MC2 in [6] and CMC in [5]. It obtains density-connected clusters in each time-stamp in the dataset. Each cluster is treated as a potential candidate and $S^3$ tries to verify if it actually forms a convoy by checking clusters in subsequent time-stamps.

Details of $S^3$ is shown in Fig. 5. If the moving object dataset $\mathcal{R}$ has missing records, the function SNAP performs linear interpolation to fill the gaps in $\mathcal{R}'$. EXTEND is a function that tracks *count* or the number of times an object $o \in O$ is found with the $PM_V$ for each convoy $V$ and assigns different role to each member $o$ for a convoy. EXTEND maintains a log of stages for each convoy.[5] The internals of EXTEND is shown in Fig. 6

For each time-stamp $t$, $S^3$ obtains a complete snapshot $\mathcal{R}'$ using SNAP and all the objects in $\mathcal{R}'$ are clustered using DBSCAN (line 3). $S^3$ tries to match

[4] This, however, can be inferred only after movement information up to $t_{40}$ is available.

[5] Information on role transitions between persistent-members and dynamic-members can be also tracked to provide the list of all the dynamic convoys if desired.

**Algorithm:** $S^3$
**Input:** $\mathcal{R}$, $\varepsilon$, $min\_pts$, $m$, $k$ and $w$.
**Output:** A set of **Evolving Convoys** $\mathcal{V}$.
1: Set $\mathcal{V} \leftarrow \phi$ and $\mathcal{V}_{\text{cur}} \leftarrow \phi$
2: **for** $t = 1$ to $\tau$ **do**
3: Set $\mathcal{R}' \leftarrow \text{SNAP}(\mathcal{R}, t)$ and $\mathcal{L} \leftarrow \text{DBSCAN}(\mathcal{R}', \varepsilon, min\_pts)$
4: Set $match(L) \leftarrow$ **false** for all $L \in \mathcal{L}$
5: **for all** $V \in \mathcal{V}_{\text{cur}}$ **do**
6: Set $extended \leftarrow$ **false**
7: **for all** $L \in \mathcal{L}$ such that $|L \cap PM_V| \geq m$ **do**
8: EXTEND($V$, $L$) and Set $match(L) \leftarrow$ **true** and $extended \leftarrow$ **true**
9: **if** $extended =$ **false then**
10: Set $t_{\text{end}}(V) \leftarrow (t-1)$ and $\mathcal{V}_{\text{cur}} \leftarrow \mathcal{V}_{\text{cur}} - \{V\}$
11: **if** $t_{\text{end}}(V) - t_{\text{start}}(V) + 1 \geq w$ **then**
12: Set $\mathcal{V} \leftarrow \mathcal{V} \cup \{V\}$
13: **for all** $L \in \mathcal{L}$ such that $match(L) =$ **false** and $|L| \geq m$ **do**
14: Create new convoy $V$ with $PM_V \leftarrow L$ and $t_{\text{start}}(V) \leftarrow t$
15: Set $\mathcal{V}_{\text{cur}} \leftarrow \mathcal{V}_{\text{cur}} \cup \{V\}$
16: **for all** $V \in \mathcal{V}_{\text{cur}}$ such that $\tau - t_{\text{start}}(V) + 1 \geq w$ **do**
17: Set $t_{\text{end}}(V) \leftarrow \tau$ and $\mathcal{V} \leftarrow \mathcal{V} \cup \{V\}$

**Fig. 5.** Algorithm $S^3$ for DEC

**Function:** EXTEND($V$, $L$, $m$, $k$, $w$)
**for all** $o \in O$ **do**
Set $count \leftarrow$ no. of times $o$ is density-connected to $PM_V$ in $[t - w + 1, t]$
**if** $count = w$ **then**
Set $PM_V \leftarrow PM_V \cup \{o\}$ and $DM_V \leftarrow DM_V - \{o\}$
**else**
**if** $count \geq k$ **then**
Set $PM_V \leftarrow PM_V - \{o\}$ and $DM_V \leftarrow DM_V \cup \{o\}$
**else**
Set $PM_V \leftarrow PM_V - \{o\}$ and $DM_V \leftarrow DM_V - \{o\}$

**Fig. 6.** Function EXTEND for $S^3$

each of the current convoys maintained in $\mathcal{V}_{\text{cur}}$ with the clusters found in the current time-stamp (lines 5 - 8). If $m$ or more persistent-members of a convoy $V$ is found in a cluster $C$, $V$ is matched to $C$ – we say $V$ "*extends*" to $C$. For each evolving convoy $V$ matched to a cluster $L$, its member objects are tracked by EXTEND$(V, L)$ (line 8). When a matching cluster cannot be found, the convoy is put in the results if its life-span is at least $w$ (lines 9-12). Those clusters $L$, into which no convoy has extended, are made potential convoys and placed in $\mathcal{V}_{\text{cur}}$(lines 13-15).

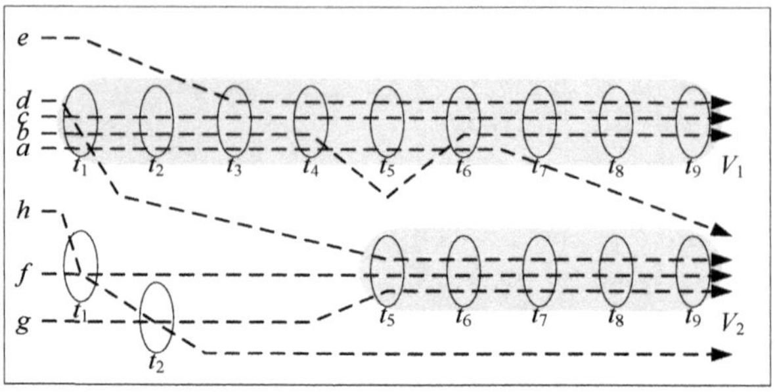


**Fig. 7.** Movement of Eight Objects

The $S^3$ algorithm reports a split when it detects a convoy $V$ extends to more than one clusters. It can also detect merges using a test – conducted in each time-stamp – which checks whether two convoys, $V$ and $V'$, have the same set of persistent-members.

Figure 7 shows movement of eight objects in nine time-stamps. For $min\_pts = 2$, $m = 2$, $k = 3$ and $w = 4$, this dataset contains two evolving convoys, shown in shaded areas, namely $V_1$ and $V_2$. A partial trace following convoy $V_1$ is listed in Tab. 1. At $t = t_1$, $S^3$ found a cluster $C_{1,1} = \{a, b, c, d\}$, which is made as a potential convoy $V1$ and put into $\mathcal{V}_{\text{cur}}$. In subsequent time-stamp $t = t_2$, DBSCAN returns a cluster $C_{2,1} = \{a, b, c\}$, into which the potential convoy $V1$ extends to because $C_{2,1}$ has $3 \geq m$ objects common with $PM_{V1}$. Now, $PM_{V1}$ becomes $\{a, b, c\}$. For each object $o$, EXTEND tracks *count* or the number of times it appeared with $PM_{V1}$ in $[t - w + 1, t]$, thus, for example, at $t_2$, *count* for $a = 2$ and *count* for $d = 1$. In this way, at $t = t_4$, the existence of convoy $V1$ starting from $t_1$ is confirmed ($d$ and $e$ are not included as *count* for $d = 1 < k$ and *count* for $e = 2 < k$). In time-stamp $t = t_5$, DBSCAN returns two clusters $C_{5,1} = \{a, c, e\}$ and $C_{5,2} = \{d, f, g\}$. $V1$ extends to cluster $C_{5,1}$, and, since *count* for $e = 3 \geq k$, $e$ is noted to be joining the convoy. Since no convoy extends to cluster $C_{5,2}$, a potential convoy $V2 = \{d, f, g\}$ is put into $\mathcal{V}_{\text{cur}}$.

### 4.2 Interleaved DEC Algorithms (ID Family)

In $S^3$, all objects in each time-stamp are clustered using DBSCAN, which is an expensive operation. Therefore, for better performance, we need to minimize DBSCAN calls. TRAJ-DBSCAN (DBSCAN for trajectories) proposed in [5] uses the closest distance between each pair of trajectories as their distance. It has a property that if objects $o_1$ and $o_2$ are density-connected at $t$ ($t \leq t \leq t + \lambda - 1$), their trajectories $j_1$ and $j_2$ for $[t, t + \lambda - 1]$ are in the same trajectory-cluster returned by TRAJ-DBSCAN. Therefore, in order to prune objects which may not form a cluster in a given time-stamp $t$ ($t \leq t \leq t + \lambda - 1$), we borrowed TRAJ-DBSCAN to check the trajectory-clusters for trajectories in $[t, t + \lambda - 1]$.

**Table 1.** A Partial Trace of $S^3$

| $t$ | $PM_{V1}$ | $DM_{V1}$ | *count* of | | | | | | $log(V1)$ |
|---|---|---|---|---|---|---|---|---|---|
| | | | $a$ | $b$ | $c$ | $d$ | $e$ | $f$ | |
| $t_1$ | $\{a,b,c,d\}$ | - | 1 | 1 | 1 | 1 | 0 | 0 | |
| $t_2$ | $\{a,b,c\}$ | - | 2 | 2 | 2 | 1 | 0 | 0 | |
| $t_3$ | $\{a,b,c\}$ | - | 3 | 3 | 3 | 1 | 1 | 0 | |
| $t_4$ | $\{a,b,c\}$ | - | 4 | 4 | 4 | 1 | 2 | 0 | Stage $S_1 = \{a,b,c\}$. |
| $t_5$ | $\{a,c\}$ | $\{b,e\}$ | 4 | 3 | 4 | 0 | 3 | 0 | Stage $S_2 = \{a,b,c,e\}$. $b$ became DM. |
| $t_6$ | $\{a,c,e\}$ | $\{b\}$ | 4 | 3 | 4 | 0 | 4 | 0 | $e$ became PM. |
| $t_7$ | $\{c,e\}$ | $\{a,b\}$ | 3 | 3 | 4 | 0 | 4 | 0 | $a$ became DM. |
| $t_8$ | $\{c,e\}$ | $\{b\}$ | 2 | 3 | 4 | 0 | 4 | 0 | Stage $S_3 = \{b,c,e\}$ |
| $t_9$ | $\{b,c,e\}$ | - | 1 | 4 | 4 | 0 | 4 | 0 | $b$ became PM. |

For better performance, TRAJ-DBSCAN works on trajectories simplified by DP-simplification [5]. DP-simplification uses a parameter $\delta$ to reduce the number of points to represent a trajectory by allowing an error less than $\delta$.

Our proposed, Interleaved-DEC (ID) algorithms divide the dataset into partitions, each containing $\lambda$ consecutive time-stamps. For each partition, the Interleaved-DEC (ID) algorithms operate in two steps – the first is to get the set of objects which are likely to form convoys while the second is the actual clustering of objects and extending of the convoys. The ID algorithms, therefore, interleave the two steps (hence their name) as they progress. The length of each partition ($\lambda$) and trajectory simplification parameter ($\delta$) can be set independently.

**ID-1.** The first interleaving algorithm, ID-1, is a simple extension of $S^3$. A sketch of ID-1 is shown in Fig. 8. The function PARTITION($\mathcal{R}, p, \lambda$) returns the $p^{\text{th}}$ $\lambda$-length partition from moving object dataset $\mathcal{R}$. Selective SNAP – S_SNAP($\mathcal{P}, J, t$) – returns the data of the given set of objects $J$ at $t$. For each partition $\mathcal{P}$, the trajectories are clustered using TRAJ-DBSCAN (lines 3-5). For each trajectory-cluster $J$ found in current partition, only its members are clustered in each-time-stamp $t$ (lines 6-7) saving clustering efforts. Matching the clusters found in each time-stamp against the set of current convoys and initiating unmatched clusters as potential convoys are the same as $S^3$(lines 8-9).

ID-1 brings performance improvement over $S^3$ by clustering a handful of objects each time-stamp. For example, in Fig. 7, if we set $\lambda = 2$, in partition $[t_3, t_4]$, only trajectories of $a$, $b$, $c$ and $e$ will form trajectory-clusters while those of $d$, $f$, $g$ and $h$ will not. Therefore, in time-stamps $t_3$ and $t_4$, ID-2 needs to cluster only four objects in contrast to $S^3$ clustering eight objects each time-stamp.

**ID-2.** Although ID-1 is expected to have better performance than $S^3$, it is still costly because the pruning is not tight enough and have false positives, which must be checked and removed by the slice-by-slice loop that follows. For

**Algorithm:** ID-1

**Input:** $\mathcal{R}$, $\varepsilon$, *min_pts*, $m$, $k$ and $w$.

**Output:** A set of **Evolving Convoys** $\mathcal{V}$.

Set $\mathcal{V} \leftarrow \phi$ and $\mathcal{V}_{\text{cur}} \leftarrow \phi$

**for** $t = 1$ to $\tau$ **do**

  **if** $mod(t-1, \lambda) = 0$ **then**

    Set $p = t/\lambda + 1$ and $\mathcal{P} \leftarrow$ PARTITION($\mathcal{R}, p, \lambda$)

    Set $\mathcal{J} \leftarrow$ TRAJ-DBSCAN($\mathcal{P}, \varepsilon, min\_pts, \delta$)

  **for all** $J \in \mathcal{J}$ **do**

    Set $\mathcal{R}' \leftarrow$ S_SNAP($\mathcal{P}$, $J$, $t$) and $\mathcal{L} \leftarrow \mathcal{L} \cup$ DBSCAN($\mathcal{R}', \varepsilon, min\_pts$)

  Set $match(L) \leftarrow$ **false** for all $L \in \mathcal{L}$

  {The rest is the same as lines 5 - 15 in $S^3$}

**for all** $V \in \mathcal{V}_{\text{cur}}$ such that $\tau - t_{\text{start}}(V) + 1 \geq w$ **do**

  Set $t_{\text{end}}(V) \leftarrow \tau$ and $\mathcal{V} \leftarrow \mathcal{V} \cup \{V\}$

**Fig. 8.** Algorithm ID-1 for DEC

**Algorithm:** ID-2

**Input:** $\mathcal{R}$, $\varepsilon$, *min_pts*, $m$, $k$ and $w$.

**Output:** Set of **Realistic Convoys** $\mathcal{V}$.

1: Set $\mathcal{V} \leftarrow \phi$, $\mathcal{V}_{\text{cur}} \leftarrow \phi$ and $N \leftarrow w/\lambda$

2: **for** $p = 1$ to $\tau/\lambda + 1$ **do**

3:   Set $\mathcal{P}_p \leftarrow$ PARTITION($\mathcal{R}, p, \lambda$)

4:   Set $\mathcal{V} \leftarrow \mathcal{V} \cup$ S_VERIFY($\mathcal{P}_p$, $\mathcal{V}_{\text{cur}}$, $\varepsilon$, *min_pts*, $m$, $k$, $w$)

5:   Set $\mathcal{V}_{\text{cur}} \leftarrow \mathcal{V}_{\text{cur}} \cup$ NEW_CONVOY($p$, $\mathcal{V}_{\text{cur}}$, $\varepsilon$, *min_pts*, $m$, $k$, $w$)

6: **for all** $V \in \mathcal{V}_{\text{cur}}$ such that $\tau - t_{\text{start}}(V) + 1 \geq w$ **do**

7:   Set $t_{\text{end}}(V) \leftarrow \tau$ and $\mathcal{V} \leftarrow \mathcal{V} \cup \{V\}$

**Fig. 9.** Algorithm ID-2 for DEC

instance, in the scenario shown in Fig. 7, trajectories of objects $f$, $g$ and $h$ form a trajectory cluster in partition $[t_1, t_2]$ as the closest distance between $h$ and $f$ ($g$) was small as they meet in $t_1$ ($t_2$). ID-1 must, therefore, try to cluster them for 2 time-stamps ($t_1$ and $t_2$) without finding a single cluster (and convoy) they form. We also noted that if a convoy is verified to exist from $t_i$ to $t_{i+\lambda-1}$, its members can be excluded from TRAJ-DBSCAN, i.e. clustering the trajectories of $a$, $c$ and $e$ in partition $[t_5, t_6]$ is a waste if their convoy is verified to exist up to $t_6$.

We developed another interleaving algorithm ID-2 to have tighter pruning than ID-1 and exploit the fact we noted to save trajectory-clustering efforts. The skeleton of the second interleaving algorithm, ID-2, is given in Fig. 9. For each partition $\mathcal{P}_p$, ID-2 first tries to extend the current convoys in $\mathcal{V}_{\text{cur}}$ and those which failed to extend until end of $\mathcal{P}_p$ are put into results (line 4). Objects which are not persistent-members of any current convoy (verified up to end of $\mathcal{P}_p$) can

**Function:** S_VERIFY($\mathcal{P}_p$, $\mathcal{V}_{\text{cur}}$, $\varepsilon$, $min\_pts$, $m$, $k$, $w$)

1: **for** $t = t_{\text{start}}(\mathcal{P}_p)$ to $t_{\text{end}}(\mathcal{P}_p)$ **do**
2:   Set $\mathcal{L}_t \leftarrow \phi$
3:   **for all** $V \in \mathcal{V}_{\text{cur}}$ **do**
4:     Set $\mathcal{L}_t \leftarrow \mathcal{L}_t \cup$ S_DBSCAN($\mathcal{R}, PM_V, t, \varepsilon, min\_pts$)
5:   Set $match(L) \leftarrow$ **false** for all $L \in \mathcal{L}_t$
6:   **for all** $V \in \mathcal{V}_{\text{cur}}$ **do**
7:     Set $extended \leftarrow$ **false**
8:     **for all** $L \in \mathcal{L}_t$ such that $|L \cap PM_V| \geq m$ **do**
9:       Extend($V$, $L$) and Set $match(L) \leftarrow$ **true** and $extended \leftarrow$ **true**
10:     **if** $extended =$ **false then**
11:       Set $t_{\text{end}}(V) \leftarrow t-1$, $\mathcal{V}_{\text{cur}} \leftarrow \mathcal{V}_{\text{cur}} - \{V\}$ and $\mathcal{V} \leftarrow \mathcal{V} \cup \{V\}$
12: Return $\mathcal{V}$

**Fig. 10.** Function S_VERIFY for ID-2

form new convoys. Therefore, new convoys are formed out of them and put into the list of current evolving convoys $\mathcal{V}_{\text{cur}}$ (line 5).

Since, a current convoy $V$ can only extend to a cluster $L$ containing at least $m$ of its persistent members ($PM_V$), S_VERIFY, shown in Fig. 10, uses the persistent-members of the convoy $PM_V$ as a guide to build the clusters it can extend. In each time-stamp $t$ in the given partition $\mathcal{P}_p$, clusters containing persistent-members of evolving convoy $V \in \mathcal{V}_{\text{cur}}$ are formed by S_DBSCAN (lines 3 - 4). Then, the convoys are extended to the clusters found (lines 6-9) and those convoys, which cannot extend any more are returned (lines 10-11).

S_DBSCAN is a modified version of DBSCAN that returns all the valid clusters in $\mathcal{R}$ at $t$ containing all objects $o \in PM_V$ according to DBSCAN parameters $\varepsilon$ and $min\_pts$. S_DBSCAN is built around the fact that any object $o$ can be either a core point or a border point in a density cluster (or a noise). Since a density-cluster can be built starting with any of its core points, the given object will be used as the seed to recursively expand its cluster if it is a core point. On the other hand, if it is a border point, one of its $\varepsilon$-neighbour must be a core point. Therefore, its $\varepsilon$-neighbours are used as seeds to build the clusters containing them. For example, if we ask S_DBSCAN to find clusters containing $\{b, c\}$, in Fig. 2, it will return $L_1$ and $L_3$ (but not $L_2$). While $c$ can be directly used as the seed to build $L_1$, $a$, a neighbour of $b$ is used to construct $L_3$ as $b$ is not a core-point.

Since it is possible that new convoy formed from the clusters that S_DBSCAN leaves to build (for example $L_2$ from Fig. 2), NEW_CONVOY (see Fig. 11) uses a filter-refinement scheme to initiate new convoys. In order to avoid finding convoys already verified to exist, only trajectories of objects, which are not persistent-members of any existing convoys, are clustered (lines 1-2). Trajectory-clusters are verified if they can form a set of persistent members across $N = w/\lambda$ partitions (or $w$ time-stamps) to get convoy-candidates (lines 3 - 9). The set of convoy candidates $\mathcal{D}$ is used as a guide to find the set of convoys $\mathcal{V}'_{\text{cur}}$, whose start-time

**Function:** NEW_CONVOY($p$, $\mathcal{V}_{\mathrm{cur}}$ $\varepsilon$, $min\_pts$, $m$, $k$, $w$)

1: Set $\mathcal{P}'_p \leftarrow \mathcal{P}_p - \{\langle o, t, loc\rangle |$ there is $V \in \mathcal{V}_{\mathrm{cur}}$ such that $o \in PM_V\}$
2: Set $\mathcal{J}_p \leftarrow$ TRAJ-DBSCAN($\mathcal{P}'_p, \varepsilon, min\_pts, \delta$)
3: Set $\mathcal{D} \leftarrow \mathcal{J}_{(p-N+1)}$
4: **for** $T = p - N + 1$ to $p$ **do**
5:    Set $\mathcal{D}' \leftarrow \phi$
6:    **for all** $D \in \mathcal{D}$ **do**
7:       **for all** $J \in \mathcal{J}_T$ such that $|J \cap D| \geq m$ **do**
8:          Set $\mathcal{D}' \leftarrow \mathcal{D}' \cup \{J \cap D\}$
9:    Set $\mathcal{D} \leftarrow \mathcal{D}'$
10: Set $\mathcal{V}'_{\mathrm{cur}} \leftarrow \phi$ and Call VERIFY($\mathcal{P}_{(p-N+1)}$, $\mathcal{D}$, $\mathcal{V}'_{\mathrm{cur}}$, $\varepsilon$, $min\_pts$, $m$, $k$, $w$)
11: **for** $T = p - N + 2$ to $p$ **do**
12:    Call S_VERIFY($\mathcal{P}_T$, $\mathcal{V}'_{\mathrm{cur}}$, $\varepsilon$, $min\_pts$, $m$, $k$, $w$)
13: Return $\mathcal{V}'_{\mathrm{cur}}$

**Fig. 11.** Function NEW_CONVOY for ID-2

is in partition $\mathcal{P}_{(p-N+1)}$ (line 10). VERIFY is a similar to S_VERIFY except it uses $\mathcal{D}$ to find cluster instead of $\mathcal{V}_{\mathrm{cur}}$ to find density-connected cluster (see line 3 of S_VERIFY) and it initiates the unmatched clusters as potential convoys (which S_VERIFY does not). Convoys in $\mathcal{V}'_{\mathrm{cur}}$ are extended by S_VERIFY until the end of partition $\mathcal{P}_{(p)}$ (lines 11 - 12).

Here is an illustration of ID-2 on dataset in Fig. 7. For the first two partitions $[t_1, t_2]$ and $[t_3, t_4]$, there is no existing convoys in $\mathcal{V}_{\mathrm{cur}}$. To find new convoys of at least $w = 4$ period, trajectory-clusters from those partitions are examined. In the first partition, there are two trajectory-clusters, $\{a, b, c\}$ and $\{f, g, h\}$. However, the second partition has only one trajectory cluster $\{a, b, c, e\}$. Thus, slice-by-slice verification is done only for the convoy containing persistent-members $\{a, b, c\}$ and put it into the set of existing convoys. In the third partition $[t_5, t_6]$, the existing convoy $\{a, b, c\}$ is extended until $t_6$ ($e$ became a persistent-member, $b$ became dynamic-member). Since the convoy containing $\{a, b, c, e\}$ is verified to exist up to $t_6$, trajectories of its members are left in TRAJ-DBSCAN operation and a trajectory cluster containing $d$, $f$ and $g$ is formed. In the fourth partition $[t_7, t_8]$, existing convoy is extended up to $t_8$ and a new convoy $\{d, f, g\}$ is formed.

# 5 Experimental Evaluations

## 5.1 Experiment Set-Up

We implemented the algorithms in C++ and evaluated their performance on a Windows XP-Professional workstation equipped with Intel Core 2 Duo E6500 processor and 4GB RAM. Two real-life datasets and a synthetic dataset used to evaluate the performance of the algorithms are:

- **Mob** contains human movement in five different sites [15]. In order to obtain more moving objects, we merge data from five sites by aligning their reference

points. We further divide the dataset into five-hour-periods and merge them to obtain 559 trajectories. It is notable that the update rate of each trajectory is strictly 30 seconds.
- **Bus** contains bus movements during peak hours (0800-1600 hours) in Seattle from 30-Oct-2001 to 05-Oct-2001 [16]. We merge the data into a single day to obtain a large dataset of 4,471 bus movement.
- **Synth** is a synthetic dataset, in which we maintain a total of ten thousand moving objects at any time by spawning a new object for each one leaving the map (total unique objects is 13,635). The initial positions and velocities of the objects are randomly determined. The mean location update rate of 30% of the objects is 3 while that of the rest is 5. Moreover, there is 1% missing records introduced randomly. Based on a random variable, new convoys of random durations are artificially built from existing objects.

For all sets of experiments, the interval between each consecutive time-stamps is set at 10 seconds but no pre-processing is done for missing records. The parameters used for the experiments are selected intuitively. For example, the distance between walking humans in the same convoy is 3 meter while that of moving buses is 30 feet. The range query operation heavily used in DBSCAN is supported by dividing the map into 100 equal-sized grids, i.e. 10 rows and 10 columns. This is a fair assumption in real-time setting (like streaming data), where building a high-performance spatial-index is out of the question. More information of the datasets and experiment settings are summarized in Tab. 2.

**Table 2.** Datasets and Experiment Settings

| Dataset | Time-stamps | Records | Unit | Map | $m$ | $w/k$ | $\varepsilon$ | $min\_pts$ | $\lambda/\delta$ |
|---|---|---|---|---|---|---|---|---|---|
| Mob | 1,800 | 267,459 | meter | $(40\text{K})^2$ | 3 | 90/54 | 3 | 3 | 10/1 |
| Bus | 2,880 | 1,000,579 | feet | $(300\text{K})^2$ | 5 | 90/54 | 30 | 5 | 10/5 |
| Synth | 720 | 2,046,112 | meter | $(10\text{K})^2$ | 5 | 90/54 | 3 | 3 | 10/3 |

Since each evolving convoy starts with a dynamic convoy, for comparison, we extend CuTS [5] into X-CuTS to find dynamic-convoys and include it in the first set of experiments. However, to prevent its pruning mechanism from pruning dynamic members, $\lambda$ values for X-CuTS must be greater than $w - k$. We run X-CuTS with $\lambda = w/2$ when $k = 0.60 \times w$. Moreover, MC2 [6] is also run on Mob and Bus datasets, with $\theta = 0.67$, in order to compare the results.

### 5.2 Results and Analysis

Table 3 shows a comparison of running time (in seconds) of the algorithms to find evolving convoys for each dataset. The ID family (ID-1 and ID-2) always out-performs $S^3$ and X-CuTS as they prune many of the objects from clustering, which $S^3$ must inadvertently perform. In general, ID-2 is better than ID-1 since

**Table 3.** Running Time Comparison of Algorithms for Different Datasets

| Dataset | No. of Convoys | $S^3$ | ID-1 | ID-2 | X-CuTS |
|---|---|---|---|---|---|
| Mob | 10 | 174.39 | 137.41 | 113.00 | 156.959 |
| Bus | 153 | 1843.88 | 1765.95 | 1423.24 | 2470.83 |
| Synth | 6 | 1932.61 | 1852.75 | 1607.44 | 5127.87 |

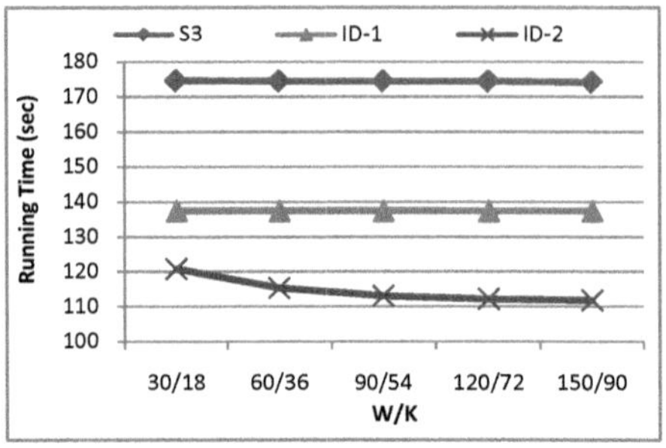


(a) $k$ is fixed at 60% of $w$.

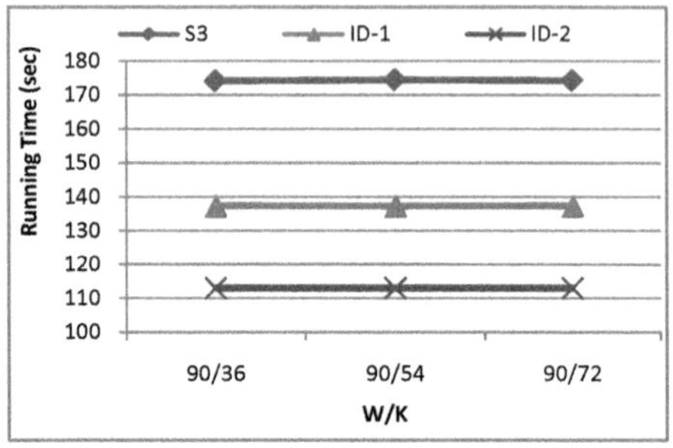


(b) $w$ is fixed at 90.

**Fig. 12.** Effect of Parameters $w$ and $k$ on Performance in Mob Dataset

ID-2 has a tighter pruning and saves clustering and verification efforts for objects, which accidentally came close for a short period of time. X-CuTS performed worse than $S^3$ in Bus and Synth datasets. Although X-CuTS performs better than $S^3$ in Mob dataset, it does not return a complete answer in Bus and Synth datasets. Therefore, we omit its results in further discussions.

Figure 12 shows how the parameters $w$ and $k$ affect the performance of the algorithms in Mob dataset. Algorithm $S^3$ is not affected by changing $w$ and $k$ values. The ID family is not affected by changing $k$ value but ID-2 performs better for larger $w$ value since it can prune evolving convoys of short-duration while $S^3$ and ID-1 cannot.

Figure 13 shows how the DBSCAN parameters $\varepsilon$ and $min\_pts$ affect the performance of the algorithms in Mob dataset. All algorithms are affected by changing $\varepsilon$ and $min\_pts$ values. Increasing $\varepsilon$ means more clusters and/or larger clusters are found in each time-stamps. This, in turn, increases pruning, clustering and joining time. However, the ID family benefits from the pruning steps while $S^3$ does not. Increasing $min\_pts$ means fewer and/or smaller clusters and, hence, shorter running time. The ID family out-performs $S^3$, with ID-2 being the best.

Parameters $\delta$ and $\lambda$ do not affect the correctness of the ID family but may have impact on performance. Although $\delta$ can be set independently, our preliminary studies show that $\delta$ should be lower than half of $\varepsilon$ to have a tighter bound. Otherwise, higher $\delta$ values will increase the running time.

However, $\lambda$ is not an independent variable as it determines how often the user gets the reports as all information of convoys in a $\lambda$-partitions $\mathcal{P}$ are reported in bulk only after $\mathcal{P}$ has been read in. Therefore, setting $\lambda$ as low as possible would

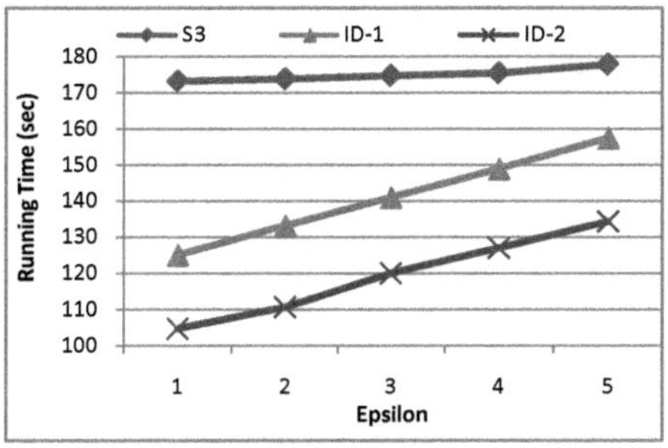


(a) *min_pts* is fixed at 3.

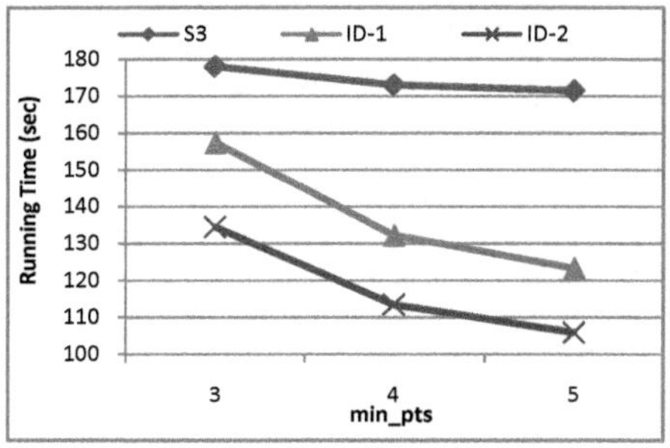


(b) $\varepsilon$ is fixed at 3.0

**Fig. 13.** Effect of DBSCAN Parameters $\varepsilon$ and *min_pts* on Performance in Mob Dataset

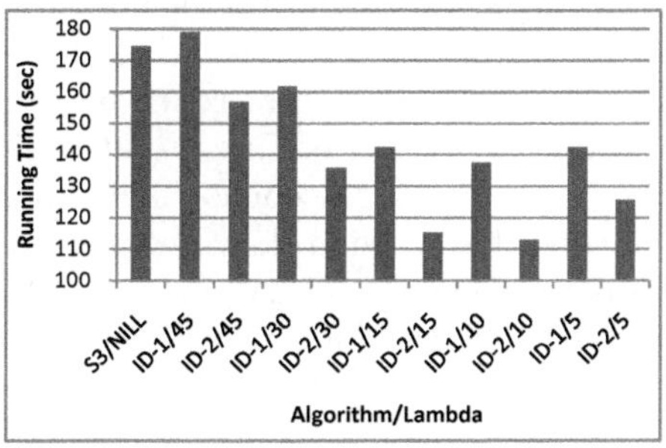


**Fig. 14.** Effect of Parameter $\lambda$ on Performance

be preferred. Figure 14 shows the performance of the algorithms with different $\lambda$ values. We observed that the lower the value of $\lambda$, the better the ID algorithms perform. The running time rises when $\lambda$ is set to 5 because the update rate for Mob dataset is 3 (30 seconds), thus each partition includes 1-2 movement record for each object, putting more overheads in TRAJ-DBSCAN operations. Therefore, from our studies, we recommend setting a low $\lambda$ value as long as each object reports its location 3 or more times in a given length of partition ($\lambda$).

In order to assess how the algorithms would perform when given more/less complete data, more experiments are conducted. Objects in Synth dataset is modified to have higher/lower update frequencies. Performance of $S^3$, ID-1 and ID-2 are plotted in Fig. 15(a). In general, lower update rates introduce lower I/O costs. However, this forces $S^3$ to perform more linear interpolation to predict locations of all the objects, reducing the saving in I/O. However, the ID algorithms benefit as trajectory clustering time is reduced and they can prune much interpolation and clustering efforts.

To assess how the algorithms scale, they are evaluated on more synthetic datasets. Figure 15(b) shows the running time of each algorithm. The ID algorithms outperform $S^3$ when the dataset contains more than 7,500 objects. ID-1

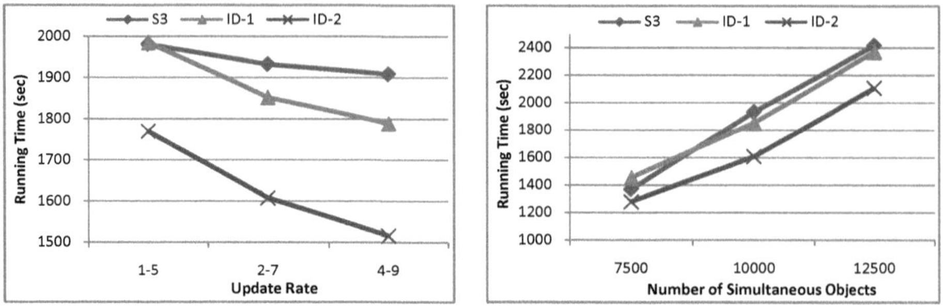


(a) With varying update frequencies. (b) With varying number of objects.

**Fig. 15.** Performance of the Algorithms on Synthetic Datasets

performs slightly better than $S^3$ as its pruning power is limited. It is found that ID-2 performs best and scales better than $S^3$ and ID-1.

Finally, we compare the moving clusters reported by MC2 [6] against the convoys our algorithms report. MC2 often finds a set of shorter moving clusters instead of a single evolving convoy as the convoy's members are often found in a cluster not similar to the one they were in the previous time-stamp (for example, merge). In Mob and Bus datasets, 9 and 248 moving clusters (compared to 10 and 153 evolving convoys), which last for 90 time-stamps, are found respectively. Yet, they do not cover all the evolving convoys with the same duration because some convoys correspond to a set of disjoint moving clusters, some of whose duration are shorter than 90 time-stamps.

To summarize the experiment results, $S^3$ cannot scale well with the size of dataset. ID-1 can be used when we want convoys of short-duration or when few false positives are expected. ID-2 is suitable for many scenarios. By definition, evolving convoys are more compact and more expressive than moving clusters.

## 6 Conclusion

In this paper, we presented and proposed new and practical convoy definitions and proposed algorithms to find them. Dynamic convoys allow members to briefly move away under user's constraints. Evolving convoys present a more comprehensive result for human users. All three proposed algorithms can report details of evolving convoys, from which dynamic convoys can be extracted. They work in an incremental manner suitable for both off-line discovery and on-line monitoring. The ability to work with continuous-valued time-stamps and awareness of deadlines for real-time monitoring are left as future extension.

## References

1. Gudmundsson, J., van Kreveld, M.: Computing longest duration flocks in trajectory data. In: GIS 2006: Proceedings of the 14th annual ACM international symposium on Advances in geographic information systems, pp. 35–42. ACM, New York (2006)

2. Benkert, M., Gudmundsson, J., Hübner, F., Wolle, T.: Reporting flock patterns. Comput. Geom. Theory Appl. 41(3), 111–125 (2008)
3. Hwang, S.Y., Liu, Y.H., Chiu, J.K., Lim, E.P.: Mining mobile group patterns: A trajectory-based approach. In: Ho, T.-B., Cheung, D.W.L., Liu, H. (eds.) PAKDD 2005. LNCS (LNAI), vol. 3518, pp. 713–718. Springer, Heidelberg (2005)
4. Wang, Y., Lim, E.P., Hwang, S.Y.: Efficient algorithms for mining maximal valid groups. The VLDB Journal 17(3), 515–535 (2008)
5. Jeung, H., Yiu, M.L., Zhou, X., Jensen, C.S., Shen, H.T.: Discovery of convoys in trajectory databases. Proc. VLDB Endow. 1(1), 1068–1080 (2008)
6. Kalnis, P., Mamoulis, N., Bakiras, S.: On discovering moving clusters in spatio-temporal data. In: Bauzer Medeiros, C., Egenhofer, M.J., Bertino, E. (eds.) SSTD 2005. LNCS, vol. 3633, pp. 364–381. Springer, Heidelberg (2005)
7. Guha, S., Rastogi, R., Shim, K.: CURE: an efficient clustering algorithm for large databases, pp. 73–84 (1998)
8. Karypis, G., Han, E.H.S., Kumar, V.: Chameleon: A hierarchical clustering algorithm using dynamic modeling (1999)
9. Alsabti, K., Ranka, S., Singh, V.: An efficient k-means clustering algorithm. In: Proceedings of IPPS/SPDP Workshop on High Performance Data Mining (1998)
10. Ng, R.T., Han, J.: Clarans: A method for clustering objects for spatial data mining. IEEE Trans. on Knowl. and Data Eng. 14(5), 1003–1016 (2002)
11. Ester, M., peter Kriegel, H., Sander, J., Xu, X.: A density-based algorithm for discovering clusters in large spatial databases with noise, pp. 226–231. AAAI Press, Menlo Park (1996)
12. Ester, M., Kriegel, H.P., Sander, J., Wimmer, M., Xu, X.: Incremental clustering for mining in a data warehousing environment. In: VLDB 1998: Proceedings of the 24th International Conference on Very Large Data Bases, pp. 323–333. Morgan Kaufmann, San Francisco (1998)
13. Spiliopoulou, M., Ntoutsi, I., Theodoridis, Y., Schult, R.: Monic: modeling and monitoring cluster transitions. In: KDD 2006: Proceedings of the 12th ACM SIGKDD international conference on Knowledge discovery and data mining, pp. 706–711. ACM, New York (2006)
14. Vieira, M.R., Bakalov, P., Tsotras, V.J.: On-line discovery of flock patterns in spatio-temporal data. In: Agrawal, D., Aref, W.G., Lu, C.T., Mokbel, M.F., Scheuermann, P., Shahabi, C., Wolfson, O. (eds.) GIS, pp. 286–295. ACM, New York (2009)
15. Rhee, I., Shin, M., Hong, S., Lee, K., Kim, S., Chong, S.: CRAWDAD data set ncsu/mobilitymodels (v. 2009-07-23), `http://crawdad.cs.dartmouth.edu/ncsu/mobilitymodels` (July 2009)
16. Jetcheva, J.G., Hu, Y.C., PalChaudhuri, S., Saha, A.K., Johnson, D.B.: CRAWDAD data set rice/ad_hoc_city (v. 2003-09-11), `http://crawdad.cs.dartmouth.edu/rice/ad_hoc_city` (September 2003)

# Finding Top-k Similar Pairs of Objects Annotated with Terms from an Ontology

Arnab Bhattacharya[1], Abhishek Bhowmick[1], and Ambuj K. Singh[2]

[1] Computer Science and Engineering, Indian Institute of Technology, Kanpur, India
[2] Computer Science, University of California, Santa Barbara, USA
{arnabb,bhowmick}@iitk.ac.in, ambuj@cs.ucsb.edu

**Abstract.** With the growing focus on semantic searches, an increasing number of standardized ontologies are being designed to describe data. We investigate the querying of objects described by a tree-structured ontology. Specifically, we consider the case of finding the top-$k$ best pairs of objects that have been annotated with terms from such an ontology when the object descriptions are available only at runtime. We consider three distance measures. The first one defines the object distance as the minimum pairwise distance between the sets of terms describing them and the second one defines the distance as the average pairwise term distance. The third and most useful distance measure—earth mover's distance—finds the best way of matching the terms and computes the distance corresponding to this best matching. We develop lower bounds that can be aggregated progressively and utilize them to speed up the search for top-$k$ object pairs when the earth mover's distance is used. For the minimum pairwise distance, we devise an algorithm that runs in $O(D + Tk \log k)$ time, where $D$ is the total information size and $T$ is the number of terms in the ontology. We also develop a best-first search strategy for the average pairwise distance that utilizes lower bounds generated in an ordered manner. Experiments on real and synthetic datasets demonstrate the practicality and scalability of our algorithms.

## 1 Introduction

We are witnessing an unprecedented growth in annotated information. This growth has been motivated by a need to share information and, more recently, by a need to search and analyze objects based on their structure and semantics. Annotated objects occur in multiple application domains including language (http://wordnet.princeton.edu/), biology (http://www.geneontology.org), medical documents (http://www.nlm.nih.gov/mesh/), web content (http://www.semanticweb.org/), etc. In all these cases, annotations are derived from a structured vocabulary or ontology.

This paper investigates the analysis of large sets of objects that have been annotated with terms from a common ontology. The analysis is useful in many practical situations. For example, consider a reviewer assignment scenario for a conference. There is a set of reviewers along with interest areas in which they have expertise, and a set of submitted papers described using keywords. The set of keywords and interest areas are organized as an ontology (e.g., http://www.academia.edu/ maintains a detailed hierarchy of research interests). An efficient algorithm should rank a paper-reviewer pair high if the

M. Gertz and B. Ludäscher (Eds.): SSDBM 2010, LNCS 6187, pp. 214–232, 2010.

keywords in them match, as then, the reviewer is likely to review this paper. Thus, this can act as a guide to the reviewers by showing more interesting papers earlier. In short, we need to perform an efficient join (may be self-join) of two sets of objects described using terms in a hierarchy. Therefore, the basic problem we consider in this paper is as follows: Given two sets of objects annotated with terms from an ontology, how to find the top-$k$ pairs of objects from the two sets that are most similar.

The above problem statement requires us to formalize the notion of distance *between two terms* in a given ontology and then to extend this notion to distance *between two annotated objects*. The distance between two terms can be measured by the shortest path distance on the ontology. There are a number of definitions for distance (or conversely, similarity) between objects. Two obvious definitions are based on the minimum pairwise distance and the average pairwise distance. The third one is the earth mover's distance [1] that takes into account the relative positions of the terms in the hierarchy that describes the objects. We investigate querying based on these three distances.

In this paper, we consider that the object descriptions are available *only* at run-time. As such, *no* pre-processing or index construction or any other offline processing can be used, and all the computation costs are paid at run-time. Even if the distance function used is a metric, the online nature of the problem renders the use of index structures (such as M-tree [2]) infeasible due to their high index construction times. In a way, this is reminiscent of the problem of spatial joins on objects in the Euclidean space: the spatial datasets are delivered online and we need to compute the best spatial matches [3]. Only that, in the case of ontologies, the distance is not Euclidean, but computed on a hierarchy.

The problem can be easily extended when objects are annotated with multiple independent ontologies. We can compute the per-ontology distance and combine them using an aggregate ranking technique [4]. The problem of querying with a particular object similar to a given query object (i.e., the $k$-NN problem) reduces to the special case of a join of the database with a singleton set (the query object). Similarly, range queries can be solved by choosing only those pairs having a distance less than the query range. While these and other kinds of queries can also be considered, the problem of top-$k$ join exposes the computational and data management complexities of this domain the best.

Formally, our problem can be stated as:

*Problem 1.* Given a set of objects each of which is defined by a set of terms from an ontology and a distance function $d(O_i, O_j)$ between two objects $O_i$ and $O_j$, find $k$ pairs of objects $P$ such that for any $(O_i, O_j) \in P$ and $(O_g, O_h) \notin P$, $d(O_i, O_j) \leq d(O_g, O_h)$.

Fig 1(a) illustrates a particular instance of the problem. The ontology tree consists of 10 terms. There are 4 objects that are described using these terms. An inverted index, i.e., mapping of a term to a set of objects can be maintained on the ontology itself (as shown in the figure). Thus, each node in the tree maintains a list $L$ of its associated objects. For example, the list of objects for $t_1$ is ($O_1$,$O_2$). We use *term* and *node* interchangeably to denote the node in which the term resides.

We denote the number of objects by $N$, the number of terms by $T$, the total information size (i.e., the total number of describing terms for all the objects) by $D$, and the number of object pairs queried by $k$. In Fig 1(a), $N = 4$, $T = 10$, and $D = 11$.

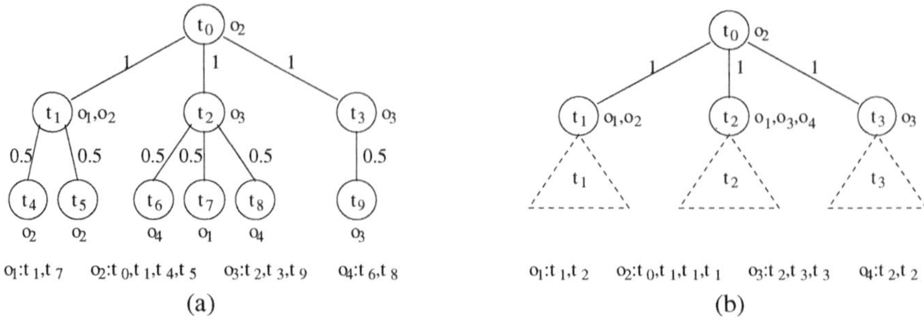

**Fig. 1.** (a) Example of an ontology tree with objects. (b) The tree after reduction.

Our contributions in this paper are as follows:

1. First, we propose the problem of finding top-$k$ most similar object pairs that are annotated with terms in a *hierarchy* in an online fashion.
2. Then, we define and motivate three different distance functions that can be used to describe the dissimilarity between a pair of objects (Sec 3). The *minimum pairwise distance* is useful for searching objects sharing a similar term (concept). The *average pairwise distance* can be used to query objects that are described using multiple attributes. The *earth mover's distance* (EMD) finds the best way of matching the terms from two objects and finds the distance corresponding to this best matching.
3. Finally, we develop efficient algorithms to solve the problem using the above distances. We use lower bounds based on $L_1$ on reduced number of terms for EMD. The $L_1$ distance, in turn, is computed progressively using a modified version of the threshold algorithm (Sec 4). For the minimum pairwise distance, we show that the top-$k$ query runs in $O(D + Tk \log k)$ time (Sec 5). For the average pairwise distance, we devise an efficient best-first search algorithm that avoids distance computations by generating lower bounds in an ordered manner (Sec 6). Experiments demonstrate the scalability and practicality of our algorithms (Sec 7).

## 2 Related Work

Heterogeneous and high-throughput data is becoming commonplace in the sciencesand there is consensus that integration of this information is needed for newbreakthroughs. In all these cases, annotations are derived from a structured vocabulary or ontology. The Semantic Web (http://www.semanticweb.org/) has defined a specific language, OWL (http://www.w3.org/2004/OWL/), for describing ontologies. In biology, genes are described using Gene Ontology (GO) (http://www.geneontology.org/) that annotates genes and gene products by three kinds of terms reflecting molecular functions, biological processes, and cellular components. Millions of abstracts in Pubmed (http://www.pubmed.gov/) are indexed using MESH terms (http://www.nlm.nih.gov/mesh/). WordNet (http://wordnet.princeton.edu/) is a lexical database that groups English words into cognitive synonyms (or *synsets*). A good compendium of different ontologies is maintained at http://www.ontologyonline.org/. A given ontology uses different hierarchical relationships to organize concepts. Of these, "is-a" and "is-part-of" are the most prevalent. Both of these lead to structures in which the proximity between terms (concepts) grows as one descends into the hierarchy.

There have been numerous works on gene ontology ranging from gene function prediction using information theory [5] to defining similarity among genes using the full graph structure of GO [6]. In [7], a comparison of three different gene similarity measures were presented. Probabilistic approaches have also been used [8]. Biologists have used average and minimum pairwise distances between genes based on GO for comparing co-evolutionary rates of yeast genes [9] and for co-clustering with gene expression data [10] respectively. There are a number of similar efforts in the area of information retrieval where the similarity between documents is measured by considering the overlap of terms. Work on text matching showed that hierarchy-based measures using tf-idf [11] outperform lexical similarity measures [12]. EMD has been shown to be better than others in finding document similarities using the WordNet ontology [13].

Embedding an ontology into Euclidean space [14] and then processing the queries is another alternative. However, an object description will then span multiple points leading to possibly large MBRs. Further, the embedding may suffer from high distortion.

## 3 Distance Definitions

### 3.1 Distance between Terms

The distance $d(t_i, t_j)$ between two terms $t_i$ and $t_j$ is defined as the length of the path between them on the ontology tree. Since there is only one path between two terms in a tree, from the properties of the shortest path, this distance is a metric [15].

In an ontology, concepts closer to the root are less similar than concepts that share some common ancestors. For example, broader concepts such as "sports" and "politics" should be more dissimilar than relatively narrower concepts such as "football" and "cricket". Exponentially decreasing edge weights capture this notion. An interesting and important point to note in such cases is that the distance between two terms at the leaves of two subtrees can be approximated by the distance between the roots of the subtrees. For example, in Fig 1(a) where the edge distances are halved at each level, the distance between $t_4$ and $t_6$ (= 3) can be approximated by that between $t_1$ and $t_2$ (= 2). We emphasize the fact that our algorithms are general enough to work correctly with all edge weights, and not just the exponential function.

We next define the three object distance measures—$d_{min}$, $d_{avg}$ and $d_{emd}$. We use the terms $d_{min}$ and MinDist, $d_{avg}$ and AvgDist, $d_{emd}$ and EMD interchangeably.

### 3.2 Minimum Pairwise Distance

**Definition 1 (Minimum Pairwise Distance).** *The minimum pairwise distance between two objects $O_i$ and $O_j$, denoted by* MinDist, *is defined as:*

$$d_{min}(O_i, O_j) = \min_{t_i \in O_i, t_j \in O_j} \{d(t_i, t_j)\} \qquad (1)$$

This distance is useful for searching objects that have similar terms. It is of particular use in keyword searching, where a single keyword is queried, and all documents having that keyword are returned with a distance of 0. MinDist, in general, extends this idea by finding additional documents that contain terms most similar to the queried keyword. The MinDist measure is heavily used in hierarchical bottom-up clustering methods where in each step, two clusters with the minimum pairwise distance are merged. It has also been successfully used for finding the distance between two genes, where a gene is annotated with a set of terms from GO [10].

**Table 1.** (a) MinDist, (b) AvgDist, and (c) EMD for example in Fig 1(a)

| Min | $O_1$ | $O_2$ | $O_3$ | $O_4$ |
|---|---|---|---|---|
| $O_1$ | 0.0 | 0.0 | 0.5 | 1.0 |
| $O_2$ | | 0.0 | 1.0 | 1.5 |
| $O_3$ | | | 0.0 | 0.5 |
| $O_4$ | | | | 0.0 |

(a)

| Avg | $O_1$ | $O_2$ | $O_3$ | $O_4$ |
|---|---|---|---|---|
| $O_1$ | 1.25 | 1.50 | 2.08 | 1.75 |
| $O_2$ | | 0.75 | 2.17 | 2.50 |
| $O_3$ | | | 1.11 | 2.00 |
| $O_4$ | | | | 0.50 |

(b)

| EMD | $O_1$ | $O_2$ | $O_3$ | $O_4$ |
|---|---|---|---|---|
| $O_1$ | 0.00 | 1.25 | 1.75 | 1.75 |
| $O_2$ | | 0.00 | 2.17 | 2.50 |
| $O_3$ | | | 0.00 | 2.00 |
| $O_4$ | | | | 0.00 |

(c)

Table 1(a) shows the MinDist measures among the objects in Fig 1(a). MinDist is *not* a metric distance as it does not maintain the triangular inequality. For example, $d_{min}(O_1, O_4) + d_{min}(O_1, O_2) = 1.0 + 0.0 < 1.5 = d_{min}(O_2, O_4)$.

### 3.3 Average Pairwise Distance

**Definition 2 (Average Pairwise Distance).** *The average pairwise distance between two objects $O_i$ and $O_j$, denoted by* AvgDist, *is defined as:*

$$d_{avg}(O_i, O_j) = \frac{1}{|O_i|.|O_j|} \sum_{t_i \in O_i, t_j \in O_j} d(t_i, t_j) \qquad (2)$$

*where $|O_i|$ and $|O_j|$ denote the number of terms describing $O_i$ and $O_j$ respectively.*

The AvgDist is useful in cases where the objects are not precisely defined. For example, it has been successfully used for gene function prediction using GO terms for yeast genes [9] as well as in the domain of web services [16].

Table 1(b) shows the AvgDist measures among the objects in Fig 1(a). AvgDist is not a metric, as it fails to satisfy the identity property (e.g., $d_{avg}(O_1, O_1) = 1.25$). However, since it follows symmetry and triangular inequality[1], it is a *pseudo-metric*.

### 3.4 Earth Mover's Distance

AvgDist suffers from the fact that each term of an object is matched with all terms of the other object. Consider two documents with the terms {war, sports} and {war, football}.

[1] See extended version of the paper [17] for the proof.

Even though it is obvious that the distance between these two documents should be small, AvgDist unnecessarily compares "war" in the first document with "football" in the other. The earth mover's distance (EMD) [1] rectifies this shortcoming by comparing only the similar terms by finding the best matching among them. For this example, EMD will match "war" with "war" and "sports" with "football" and aggregate these distances only. Consequently, EMD performs better than other distances (e.g., in finding similar documents using the WordNet ontology [13]).

Formally, each object is considered to be composed of "mass" at the specific nodes in the ontology (corresponding to the terms that describe the object). The total mass of each object is 1, i.e., the mass at each node is inverse of the number of terms describing the object (e.g., $O_1$ in Fig 1(a) has mass $\frac{1}{2}$ corresponding to terms $t_1$ and $t_7$). The EMD between two objects $A$ and $B$ is the *minimum* work required to transform $A$ to $B$, where one unit of work is equal to moving one unit of mass through one unit of distance in the ontology (called "ground distance"). Finding the best "flows" (i.e., how much mass needs to be moved from one term in $A$ to another term in $B$) is a linear programming (LP) problem.

**Definition 3 (Earth Mover's Distance).** *The earth mover's distance between two objects $O_i$ and $O_j$, denoted by* EMD, *is defined as:*

$$d_{emd}(O_i, O_j) = \min_f \sum_{t_p \in O_i} \sum_{t_q \in O_j} c_{pq} f_{pq} \tag{3}$$

$$\text{s.t., each } f_{pq} \geq 0, \quad \forall_{t_p \in O_i}, \sum_{t_q \in O_j} f_{pq} = O_{i_p}, \text{ and } \forall_{t_q \in O_j}, \sum_{t_p \in O_i} f_{pq} = O_{j_q}$$

*where $c_{pq}$ is the distance between terms $t_p$ and $t_q$ and $O_{i_p}$ is the mass of $t_p$ in $O_i$, etc.*

EMD is a metric when the term distance is a metric (proof in [1]). Table 1(c) shows the EMDs among the objects in Fig 1(a).

### 3.5 Comparison of the Distance Measures

To compare the usefulness of the three distance measures, we performed the following experiment. We used WordNet (http://wordnet.princeton.edu/) as the ontology and the "bag-of-words" dataset from the UCI repository (http://archive.ics.uci.edu/ml/datasets/Bag+of+Words) as the set of objects. We chose the first 59 documents from the categories *enron* and *kos* of the bag-of-words dataset. Each document was described using nouns from the WordNet ontology, and the ontology was converted into a tree. The top-50 and top-10 pairs were obtained using all the three distances. For EMD, on an average, there were 45 and 10 pairs respectively where both the objects were from the same category. The corresponding numbers for AvgDist distance were 23 and 6 respectively. The MinDist returned 505 object pairs with distance 0 as many objects shared one or more terms. Consequently, the top-$k$ lists returned were arbitrary and precision was poor. This established the quality of the EMD and its usefulness in finding the top-$k$ similar pairs of objects. Nevertheless, the two other distance measures have been proved to be useful in specific contexts (e.g., [9,10,16]).

We next design algorithms to efficiently compute the top-$k$ pairs using these distances. We start with EMD as it is the most interesting and useful measure.

## 4 The Algorithm for EMD

When the two sets contain $N$ objects each, the problem of finding top-$k$ pairs of objects can be solved by computing and sorting $O(N^2)$ EMD distances. However, the prohibitive time required by each EMD computation makes the entire running time $(O(N^2) \times O(EMD) + O(N^2 \log N))$ impractical.

### 4.1 Lower Bound Using Reduced Number of Terms

When the ontology tree has a size $T$, the ground distance matrix is of size $T^2$. However, we need not consider all the terms as we can prune those that are absent in both the object descriptions.[2] This is still impractical: the average time taken to compute $d_{emd}$ for objects of size 7 was 54 ms.[3]

Since the complexity of EMD depends mainly on the number of flow variables, which is quadratic in the number of terms in each object, the running time can be reduced if the size of the object descriptions is reduced. Fig 1(b) shows how such reduction can be accomplished. The ontology tree is pruned at height 1; only the root term and its immediate children remain. When a term thus deleted appears in an object description, it is replaced by its ancestor that is retained. Hence, all the terms in the dashed subtrees in the figure are removed and replaced by the root of the subtrees. The size of an object description is now upper bounded by the branching factor of the root. Table 2 shows the reduced object descriptions.

**Table 2.** Reduction of terms using Fig 1(b) for example in Fig 1(a)

| | Before reduction | After reduction |
|---|---|---|
| Object | $\{t_0, t_1, t_2, t_3, t_4, t_5, t_6, t_7, t_8, t_9\}$ | $\{t_0, t_1, t_2, t_3\}$ |
| $O_1$ | $\{0, \frac{1}{2}, 0, 0, 0, 0, 0, \frac{1}{2}, 0, 0\}$ | $\{0, \frac{1}{2}, \frac{1}{2}, 0\}$ |
| $O_2$ | $\{\frac{1}{4}, \frac{1}{4}, 0, 0, \frac{1}{4}, \frac{1}{4}, 0, 0, 0, 0\}$ | $\{\frac{1}{4}, \frac{3}{4}, 0, 0\}$ |
| $O_3$ | $\{0, 0, \frac{1}{3}, \frac{1}{3}, 0, 0, 0, 0, 0, \frac{1}{3}\}$ | $\{0, 0, \frac{1}{3}, \frac{2}{3}\}$ |
| $O_4$ | $\{0, 0, 0, 0, 0, 0, \frac{1}{2}, 0, \frac{1}{2}, 0\}$ | $\{0, 0, 1, 0\}$ |

The EMD between two objects calculated using the reduced ontology is a lower bound of the EMD using the full ontology [1][4]. If the number of terms in the reduced ontology is $t$ (generally $t \ll T$), the number of flow variables are reduced to at most $t^2$. Since the complexity of linear programming is super-linear in the number of flow variables, the running time of EMD decreases by at least a (large) factor of $T^2/t^2$. The number of distance computations, however, still remains $O(N^2)$. Next, we show how to reduce that.

[2] The row and column sums corresponding to these terms in the flow matrix will be 0 and, hence, all the flows will be 0 individually as well.

[3] All the times reported in the paper are based on Java implementation on a 3 GHz machine with 2 GB of RAM running Linux Fedora 11.

[4] A lower bound can be obtained by pruning the tree at any height. However, there is a trade-off between the tightness and computational efficiency of the lower bound.

### 4.2 $L_1$ Lower Bound

The $L_1$ distance, when scaled by the sum of the total mass, can be used as a lower bound for EMD [18]. Hence, the $L_1$ distance between two objects computed using all $T$ terms, when divided by 2, serves as a lower bound for EMD. From now on, whenever we mention $L_1$, we mean the scaled version of it which is a lower bound. $L_1$ on all terms, in turn, is lower bounded by $L_1$ on reduced number of terms. The proof uses the fact that $|a_i - b_i| + |a_j - b_j| \geq |(a_i + a_j) - (b_i + b_j)|$. Since $L_1$ is much faster to compute (for 3 terms, it takes only 0.002 ms), we can calculate a $L_1$ lower bound on EMD for each object pair and then use it as a filtering step to prune object pairs.

The $L_1$ distance between two objects is a sum of the distances between the corresponding values in each dimension; therefore, if the distances for all the object pairs are obtained and sorted for each dimension, an aggregate ranking technique such as the threshold algorithm (TA) [4] can generate in a progressive manner the object pairs with the least sum of distances (i.e., the least $L_1$ distance). The increasing order of generated $L_1$ distances can then guide the order of EMD computations.

TA can avoid sorting of object pairs when the *next* object pair in the list can be output in a sorted manner whenever asked for. This avoids the $O(N^2)$ computations. Hence, now our problem is reduced to delivering the next smallest pairwise distance whenever asked for in a particular list (or dimension).

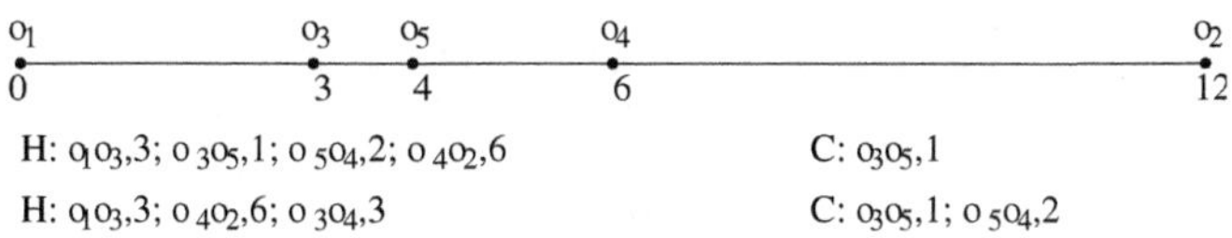


**Fig. 2.** Example of ordered generation of object pairs for one dimension

For this, we maintain two data structures for each dimension: (i) a min-heap $H$ that outputs the next best pair, and (ii) a list $C$ that stores all the pairs that have been output from $H$. Initially, the $N$ objects are sorted and all $N - 1$ consecutive object pairs (not necessarily $O_iO_{i+1}$) corresponding to $N - 1$ differences are inserted into $H$. Fig 2 shows an example. The 5 objects are sorted according to their values for the dimension that is being processed. Initially, $H$ contains the 4 object pairs corresponding to the 4 differences in the sorted list. Whenever the next pair is asked for by TA, the minimum object pair from $H$ is extracted and returned. It is also inserted into $C$. In this example, after the first call, $O_3O_5$ is extracted from $H$ and inserted into $C$. Proceeding similarly, in the next call, $O_5O_4$ is extracted.

Extracting just the initial pairs is not enough as there may be a non-initial pair with a value (e.g., $O_3O_4$ with 3) less than that of an initial pair ($O_4O_2$ with value 6). The important point to note, however, is that any non-initial pair is a *combination* of some of the initial pairs. Two pairs having an overlapping object can be fused together to generate a new pair. For example, $O_3O_4$ can be generated by fusing $O_3O_5$ and $O_5O_4$. Further, a pair can *never* be the least pair until and unless the pairs from which it has been generated have been chosen (i.e., output from $H$). Therefore, in the example,

$O_3O_4$ is added to $H$ only after both $O_3O_5$ and $O_5O_4$ have been chosen. In general, when a pair $O_xO_y$ is chosen, the contents of $C$ are scanned and new pairs are generated if possible. If $C$ has pairs of the form $O_wO_x$ and $O_yO_z$, new pairs $O_wO_y$ and $O_xO_z$ are generated respectively, and are inserted into $H$. The value of this new pair is the sum of the values of the fused pairs.

### 4.3 Algorithm

The EMD algorithm[5] uses the lower bounds to find the top-$k$ pairs. It uses a priority queue to list the top-$k$ pairs. When the size of $P$ is less than $k$, $P.dist$ is $\infty$; otherwise, it is maintained as the $k^{\text{th}}$ largest distance in $P$. It examines the object pairs in sorted order of the $L_1$ lower bound on reduced number of terms by using the heap as explained earlier. If it is less than $P.dist$, the bound is improved by computing $L_1$ on all terms. If it is still less, the exact EMD is computed and the top-$k$ list is modified, if necessary. For each such $L_1$-reduced computation, the threshold distance $R$ of TA is increased. When $R > k^{\text{th}}$ distance in $P$, no other object pair can have $L_1$-reduced distance less than the top-$k$ pairs already found. Therefore, the EMDs will also be greater. Hence, the algorithm halts correctly.

### 4.4 Analysis of Time Complexity

For each of the reduced number of dimensions $t$, the algorithm incurs the following costs. Initial sorting takes $O(N \log N)$ time. Thereafter, inserting the $N-1$ elements in the heap takes $O(N)$ time. At the $i^{\text{th}}$ iteration, at most $i$ elements are added to the heap again. This takes $O(i \log N)$ time. Thus, if we have $k'$ calls (this $k'$ is generally larger than $k$ as many object pairs with low lower bound but high EMD are examined), the time per dimension is $O(k'^2 \log N)$ which leads to a total time of $\sum_{j=1}^{t} O(k_j'^2 \log N)$ or $O(tk_{max}'^2 \log N)$ where $k_{max}$ is the maximum of all $k_j'$s.
**Space Complexity:** Heap $j$ requires $O(N + k_j'^2)$ space where $k_j'$ is the number of calls made on column $j$. Hence, the total space required is $O(t(N + k_{max}'^2))$.

## 5 The Algorithm for MinDist

Unlike EMD, the MinDist for an object pair can be estimated whenever two terms corresponding to two objects are encountered, If it is better than the current estimate, it is retained; otherwise, it is *never* needed again. We next explain the MinDist algorithm that exploits this property.

Any object pair $(O_i, O_j)$ having a lesser distance than $(O_g, O_h)$ must have a term pair $(t_i \in O_i, t_j \in O_j)$ which has a lesser distance than all term pairs $(t_g \in O_g, t_h \in O_h)$. Hence, we only need to identify such term pairs $(t_i, t_j)$ that are close and process their inverted lists of objects.

Initially, an inverted index is built for MinDist and AvgDist but not EMD. For each object $O_i$, when a term $t_j$ appears in it, $O_i$ is inserted into the inverted list of $t_j$. The list is accessed using hashing, and the object is inserted at the top of the list.

[5] The pseudocode for the entire algorithm is provided in full version of the paper [17].

Algorithm **MinDist**
**Input:** Node $t$
**Output:** Pair list $P$ of size $k$; Object list $B$ of size $O(\sqrt{k})$
1. $TB$ := list of objects in $t$ of size $O(\sqrt{k})$
2. $c$ := number of children of $t$
3. **for** $i$ = 1 to $c$
4. $\quad CB[i], CP[i]$ := MinDist($t.child[i]$)
5. $\quad$ Add $t.edge[i]$ cost to each object in $CB[i]$
6. **end for**
7. $B$ := Merge($CB[1], \ldots, CB[c], TB$)
8. $TP$ := GenPairs($B$)
9. $P$ := Merge($CP[1], \ldots, CP[c], TP$)

**Fig. 3.** The MinDist algorithm

Fig 3 describes the MinDist algorithm that computes the top-$k$ object pairs in a node. Any such object pair must either be in the top-$k$ list of the children, or contains terms from different children. The recursive definition of the first kind allows us to employ a divide-and-conquer approach. For the second kind, we need a list of objects that are close to the subtree of the children nodes. The lists can then be joined to generate the necessary object pairs. The MinDist algorithm called at the root of the ontology returns the top-$k$ pairs.

Each node $t$ maintains two lists: (i) a list of pairs of objects $P$ ordered by their $d_{min}$ distances; and (ii) a list of objects $B$ ordered by their minimum distances $d_i$ to the node $t$. The length of $P$ is at most $k$. The length of $B$ is $k' = O(\lceil\sqrt{k}\rceil)$ which is enough to ensure that $k$ distinct pairs of objects can be generated from $B$.[6]

When MinDist is called on a node $t$, it selects $k'$ objects from its list of associated objects $L$ into $TB$. MinDist is then called on each of its $c$ children. The cost of the edge from $t$ to its child is added to the objects in the corresponding child's object list (line 5) to ensure that the distances are maintained correctly. The $c$ sorted object lists and the list of objects in $t$ are then merged to produce the sorted list $B$.

The merging (line 7) is done using a heap. The heap is initialized with $c+1$ elements (from position 1 of each of the child lists and the list $TB$). The minimum element is then extracted into $B$. Since all the individual lists are sorted, the properties of heap guarantee that the object extracted has the least $d_{min}$ distance from this node. The object at the next position of the list from where this minimum object was obtained is then inserted into the heap. This is repeated $k'$ times.

All the possible $k$ pairs are then generated from the $k'$ objects in $B$ (method GenPairs in line 8). This list $TP$ computes the $k$ best distances of the object pairs which are not in any of the subtrees. $TP$ is finally merged with the pair lists $CP[i], i = 1 \ldots c$ from the children to produce the final pair list $P$ using a heap in the same manner as above (line 9).

[6] Since $k'(k'-1)/2 \geq k$, the actual number of terms required is $k' = \lceil 1/2 + \sqrt{1/4 + 2k}\rceil$.

### 5.1 Analysis of Time Complexity

We first analyze the time required to compute the inverted index. The object descriptions are read once, and for each term in an object, the corresponding list is accessed in $O(1)$ time using hashing, and the object is inserted at the top of the list in another $O(1)$ time. The total time required for this phase is, therefore, $O(D)$ where $D$ is the total size of the description.

We next analyze the running time for the main phase of the algorithm. Selecting $k'$ objects in $TB$ requires $O(k')$ time. Adding the child edge costs to each object in $CB$ lists takes $O(k'c)$ time. At every step of the merging operation, the object with the minimum distance is extracted from the heap and another object is inserted. The size of the heap is, therefore, never more than $O(c)$ for $c$ children. Extracting the minimum element and inserting another object into the heap takes $O(\log c)$ time. Since the operation is repeated $k'$ times, the total running time of the merging procedure is $O(k' \log c)$.

If, however, the objects in the child lists are not unique, $k'$ operations may not be enough to select $k'$ different objects. Thus, a hashtable is used to ensure that an object is inserted into the heap only once. The hashtable maintains only a single copy of an object, the one with the smallest distance. The other copies are never required. This limits the number of heap operations to $O(k')$. Assuming that the hashtable operations take constant time, the running time is $O(k' \log c)$. Scanning the $c$ lists require an initial $O(k'c)$ time.

Sorting $k$ local object pairs requires $O(k \log k)$ time. The sorted pair lists at the node and the children are merged in $O(kc + k \log c)$ time using a heap and a hashtable in a similar manner as before. Thus, the total running time of the MinDist algorithm at a node with $c$ children is $O(kc + k \log k)$.

The algorithm is run once at each node of the ontology. Assuming that there are $T$ terms in the ontology, the total number of children for *all* the nodes is $O(T)$. Hence, the amortized cost is $O(Tk + Tk \log k) = O(Tk \log k)$.

The total running time of the MinDist algorithm is, therefore, $O(D + Tk \log k)$.

**Space Complexity:** Each node in the ontology contains an object list of size $O(k')$ and a pair list of size $O(k)$. Once these lists are sent to the parent, they are no longer required. Thus, at any time, the space requirement at a node is $O(c(k' + k))$. The total space complexity, therefore, is $O(c_{max}(k + k'))$ where $c_{max}$ is the largest branching factor of a node in the tree. The inverted index requires $O(D)$ space for storage.

## 6 The Algorithm for AvgDist

Unlike the MinDist algorithm that needs to maintain only one term pair for each object pair, the $d_{avg}$ distance needs to remember *all* term-pair distances. Consequently, the AvgDist algorithm runs in two phases: (i) the *Build* phase, when pertinent information about objects are collected at the root in a bottom-up manner, and (ii) the *Query* phase, when such information is used to identify the top-$k$ pairs in a top-down order.

For any object pair, two types of costs need to be accumulated: (i) *across-tree* costs, i.e., the distances between terms that occur in different subtrees of the root, and (ii) *within-tree* costs, i.e., the distances between terms that are within the same child of the root. For example, in Fig 1(a), the total pairwise term distances for $(O_1, O_4)$ can be broken into 2 parts: (i) the across-tree distances between $t_1$ of $O_1$ and $t_6$, $t_8$ of $O_4$ in the different subtrees under $t_1$ and $t_2$ respectively, and (ii) the within-tree distances between $t_7$ of $O_1$ and $t_6$, $t_8$ of $O_4$ in the same subtree under $t_2$.

To estimate the across-tree distances for object pairs at a node, the following information need to be calculated for each object $O_i$: (i) the *number of terms*, $n_i$, in the subtree that describe the object, and (ii) the *total distance*, $w_i$, of all such terms to this node. This information is accumulated at the root of the ontology by the build phase AvgDist-Build, which we describe later (in Sec 6.4).

We next explain how lower bounds for the across-tree costs of an object pair can be computed and generated in an *ordered* manner.

### 6.1 Lower Bounds for Across-Tree Costs

The estimates of the across-tree distances of a pair of objects $O_i$ and $O_j$ at a node $t$ depend on the distribution of their describing terms. The *span* of an object is defined to be the number of subtrees of the root where its constituent terms occur. It can be either single (terms occur in only one subtree), or multiple (terms occur in multiple subtrees). Based on these, 3 different cases need to be considered. In each case, we would like to write the bounds at a node in terms of the parameters maintained for $O_i$ and $O_j$ at the node, i.e., in terms of $(O_i, n_i, w_i)$ and $(O_j, n_j, w_j)$ only.

**Case 1:** Both objects have single spans. Two sub-cases need to be considered.

**Sub-case 1(a):** The objects are in the same subtree. The across-tree cost is 0 and nothing can be concluded about their distance in the subtree without descending deeper into it. Hence, the lower bound is

$$d_{lb} = 0 \tag{4}$$

**Sub-case 1(b):** The objects are in different subtrees. The distance between two terms $t_i \in O_i$ and $t_j \in O_j$ at node $t$ is $d(t_i, t) + d(t_j, t)$. The *total* across-tree distance is obtained by adding all such combinations of terms:

$$\sum_{j=1}^{|O_j|}\sum_{i=1}^{|O_i|} d(t_i, t) + \sum_{i=1}^{|O_i|}\sum_{j=1}^{|O_j|} d(t_j, t) = n_j \sum_{i=1}^{|O_i|} d(t_i, t) + n_i \sum_{j=1}^{|O_j|} d(t_j, t) = n_j w_i + n_i w_j \tag{5}$$

Thus, the average distance is

$$d_{lb} = d = w_i/n_i + w_j/n_j \tag{6}$$

Since the within-tree distance for this pair is 0, this is the *exact* distance.

**Case 2:** Both objects have multiple spans. The minimum across-tree distance can be estimated in a manner similar to that in Case 1(b). There are at least two pairings of terms of $O_i$ and $O_j$ that are in different subtrees. Using Eq. (5), the *total* across-tree costs for these pairings are $w_{i_1} n_{j_2} + w_{j_2} n_{i_1}$ and $w_{i_2} n_{j_1} + w_{j_1} n_{i_2}$, where $n_{i_1}$, $w_{i_1}$ etc.

are the number of terms of $O_i$ in one subtree and its total distance to $t$ from that subtree. Each of $n_{i_1}$, $n_{i_2}$, $n_{j_1}$, and $n_{j_2}$ is at least 1. Thus, the total across-tree distance is at least $w_{i_1} + w_{i_2} + w_{j_1} + w_{j_2} = w_i + w_j$. The lower bound, then, is

$$d_{lb} = (w_i + w_j)/(n_i n_j) \tag{7}$$

**Case 3:** One object $O_i$ has a single span, and the other object $O_j$ has a multiple span. Similar to Case 2, there is at least one subtree containing terms of $O_j$ but not containing terms of $O_i$. The *total* across-tree cost is then the minimum of $w_i n_{j_1} + w_{j_1} n_i$ and $w_i n_{j_2} + w_{j_2} n_i$. Again, similar to Case 2, there is at least one term of $O_j$ that is not in the same subtree of $O_i$. Thus, $n_{j_1}$ and $n_{j_2}$ are at least 1. However, without knowing where the terms of $O_j$ occur, nothing can be concluded about $w_{j_1}$ and $w_{j_2}$. Since the terms may occur at the node itself, the estimates for $w_{j_1}$ and $w_{j_2}$ are 0. Hence, the total distance is at least $w_i$ producing a lower bound of

$$d_{lb} = w_i/(n_i n_j) \tag{8}$$

### 6.2 Generating Ordered Pairs

Though the above mentioned lower bounds can be computed for a given pair, the cost of computing them for every pair is $O(N^2)$. We would like to avoid that. The trick is to separate the parameters of $O_i$ and $O_j$ in each lower bound such that they can be systematically generated in an ordered manner whenever needed. The order of generation will guarantee that at any point of time, the lower bounds of the pairs not examined will be greater than or equal to the lower bounds of the pairs already generated. In this section, we discuss ways to achieve this for each of the cases mentioned above.

To identify pairs of objects in the same subtree (Case 1(a)), $c + 1$ different lists are maintained at the root corresponding to itself and its $c$ children.

To handle Case 1(b), each of these $c + 1$ lists of objects are sorted by the average distance $w_i/n_i$. Given two such sorted child lists, the lower bound (which is the sum of the distances) for an object pair at positions $p_i$ in the first list and $p_j$ in the second list is lower than the estimate of every pair whose positions are $> p_i$ and $> p_j$. Thus, every time a pair at positions $(p_i, p_j)$ is inspected, only its immediate successors $(p_i + 1, p_j)$ and $(p_i, p_j + 1)$ need to be considered next. Since there are $c+1$ child lists, the number of possible ways of generating object pairs is $c(c + 1)/2$.

The lower bound for Case 2 is not easily separable in terms of parameters of $O_i$ and $O_j$. It is, however, separable, if for an object pair, the number of terms for the objects (i.e., $n_i$, $n_j$) are known a priori. For that, objects with multiple spans is partitioned such that each partition only contains objects with a particular $n_i$. Pairing $O_i$ and $O_j$ and knowing which partitions they come from immediately defines the denominator of the lower bound. Thus, if there are $r$ partitions, sorting each partition by $w_i$ and performing $r^2$ pairings in the same way as done for Case 1(b) orders the pairs.

Case 3 is handled similarly. The single-span objects are partitioned into $c + 1$ lists and the multiple-span objects into $r$ partitions. Generating all $r(c+1)$ pairings produces the lower bounds in an ordered manner.

We next describe how the Query phase of the algorithm uses these lower bounds.

### 6.3 Query Phase

The AvgDist-Query procedure is run at the root of the ontology.[7] Initially, the list $L$ of objects at the root is partitioned into $c + 1 + r$ lists corresponding to single and multiple spans as explained in the earlier section. From these lists, the initial pairs with the lower bounds are generated and put into a heap $H$.

The algorithm progresses by extracting the current *best pair* from the heap, i.e., the pair $p$ with the current best lower bound. If the lower bound is an estimate for $p$ and not an exact distance as in Case 1(b), the bound can be improved in two ways. First, the within-tree costs at the subtrees in the next level can be estimated again using Eq. (4) to Eq. (8) by descending into the subtree (denoted as AvgDist-NextEstimate). The descent is made in a breadth-first order on the tree.[8] The second way is to compute the term-wise distances exhaustively without resorting to recursion (denoted as AvgDist-Complete). This, however, disregards the structure of the ontology.

When the exact distance of $p$ is computed, the top-$k$ list $P$ is updated with $p$. If, however, the lower bound of $p$ is still an estimate, $p$ is re-inserted back into the heap $H$. The next pairs are generated from the $c + 1 + r$ lists and inserted into the heap as well.

In the next iteration, the pair which is now the *best* is examined. If this pair has a distance more than $P.dist$ (i.e., the $k^{\text{th}}$ largest distance in $P$), it is guaranteed that all pairs currently in the heap and all pairs that have not yet been generated will have a greater distance. This is due to the ordered nature of generating the pairs from the $c + 1 + r$ lists. Thus, the algorithm is then terminated correctly.

The top-down searching for object pairs proceeds in a manner where at every stage, only the current "best" pair is examined [19]; hence, this is called the *best-first search*.

### 6.4 Build Phase

In this section, we describe how AvgDist-Build computes the information $(O_i, n_i, w_i)$ for an object.[9] Each node $t$ maintains an inverted list $L$ of objects $O_i$ (with $n_i = 1$ and $w_i = 0$) described using $t$. It calls AvgDist-Build for each of its children. For each object $O_j$ in list $CL$ that it receives from a child, it modifies $w_j$ by adding to it the distance to the child node to ensure that the total distance from $t$ is maintained correctly. The distance is accumulated for all terms and, therefore, $w_j$ is modified as $w_j + dist \times n_j$, where $dist$ is the edge distance from $t$ to its child.

**Analysis of Space and Time Complexities:** Each object's information is stored at the terms describing it. The information stored in a term is repeated along all its ancestors. Since the size of the description is $D$, and there are $O(\log T)$ ancestors (assuming the ontology to be balanced), the storage cost is $O(D \log T)$.

The inverted index requires $O(D)$ time for construction. At the leaf level of the tree, there are $D$ describing terms. When this $O(D)$ information is sent up to the next level, the time required to combine the information is still $O(D)$ since each object description

---

[7] The pseudocode of the entire algorithm is provided in [17].

[8] Any other order, e.g., depth-first order, will also work. However, if the edge distances decrease exponentially, breadth-first ordering produces better bounds.

[9] The pseudocode is provided in [17].

is read only once and is matched using a hashtable to the information already computed. Assuming the height of the tree to be $O(\log T)$, the total running time is $O(D \log T)$.

# 7 Experiments

In this section, we describe the experiments. Due to space constraints, we show only the most interesting results. Please refer to full version of the paper [17] for more details.

## 7.1 Datasets

We have experimented with real as well as synthetic datasets. The real dataset is that of Gene Ontology (GO, http://www.geneontology.org/). There are three ontologies in GO, corresponding to biological process, molecular function, and cellular component (localization), containing 13762, 7803 and 1990 terms respectively. The number of unique genes described using the ontologies are 3437, 1958 and 645 respectively.

The synthetic datasets were generated by controlling the number of objects, the number of terms, the average branching factor of the ontology tree and the average number of terms per object. The details of how the object descriptions were obtained are in [17].

## 7.2 Experiments on EMD

When the distance function between the objects is defined as the *earth mover's distance* the following schemes were evaluated:

- $L_1$-reduced: In this scheme (Sec 4), the $L_1$ on reduced number of terms is used.
- $L_1$-full: In this scheme, the $L_1$ on all terms is used. The tree is not pruned.
- EMD-reduced: All the $O(N^2)$ EMDs on reduced number of terms are computed. These are then used to prune those object pairs for which the reduced EMD is greater than the $k^{\text{th}}$ best EMD already found.
- Brute-force: In this scheme, all the $O(N^2)$ pairs are computed and then the top-$k$ pairs are returned.

The performance of the brute-force scheme (267 s for $N = 100$ objects) is too impractical to be of any use and are, therefore, not reported. Also, the times of $L_1$-full are not reported since, in the best case, it can only save $L_1$-reduced computations, which are very fast anyway. In all the experiments, it was actually worse than $L_1$-reduced.

When the number of retrieved object pairs, $k$, increases, more number of $L_1$ computations are needed before the TA can halt. Consequently, more number of EMD calculations are also required. However, for small $k$, the effect is minimal (graph not shown).

Fig 4(a) shows that the scalability of our algorithm with $N$ is better than quadratic. Due to $L_1$ lower bounding, many of the object pairs are pruned. As a result, the number of full EMD computations increases by a lower factor. Also, even for $N = 350$ which translates to $6 \times 10^4$ object pairs, our algorithm finishes in only 55 s. To further understand the effect of increasing $N$, we measured the ratio of object pairs for which full EMD computation was done. The ratio was measured as number of pairs investigated to

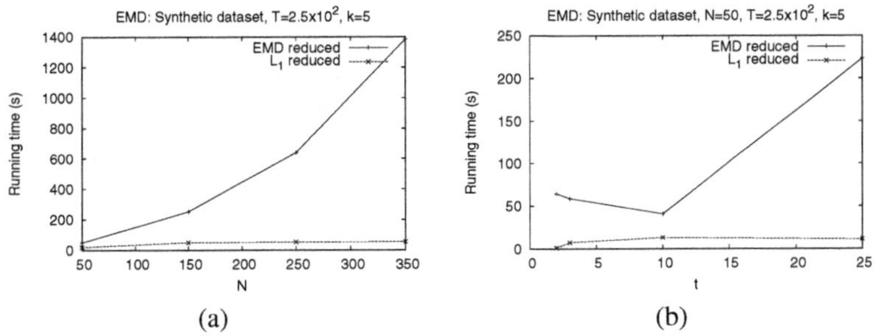


**Fig. 4.** (a) Effect of $N$ on EMD. (b) Effect of $t$ on EMD.

the total number of possible pairs $(N(N-1)/2)$ and is denoted by $\eta$. As $N$ increased, $\eta$ decreased which explained why the scalability was better. For $N > 250$, $\eta < 0.1$.

We next measure the effect of the total number of terms, $T$, on the EMD computations. Since both $L_1$ and EMD-reduced depends only on the reduced number of terms, the effect is minimal (graph not shown).

However, as the number of children of root, i.e., $t$ increases, the complexity of the TA increases linearly. Fig 4(b) shows the running times for varying $t$. The size of each object description is limited to 10. When $t \leq 10$, the time increases. EMD-reduced behaves in the opposite manner. This is due to the interaction of two opposing effects: as $t$ increases, each computation takes more time, but the lower bound gets tighter as more number of terms are taken into account resulting in less number of full EMD computations. However, when $t > 10$, since there are at most 10 terms in each object, the object description size do not get reduced and each EMD-reduced computation takes as much time as the full EMD computation. Since $O(N^2)$ of these computations are performed, the running time shoots up. The $L_1$-reduced, on the other hand, shows only a little increase.

### 7.3 Experiments on MinDist

When the distance function between the objects is defined as the *minimum pairwise distance* between the terms, the following schemes were considered:

- MinDist: This scheme has a running time of $O(D + Tk \log k)$.
- Brute-force: In this scheme, all the $O(N^2)$ pairs are computed and then the top-$k$ pairs are returned. Maintaining a heap of size at most $k$ reduces the running time of this scheme to $O(N^2 \log k)$.

For $N = 10^4$, the top-$k$ computation using the brute-force algorithm finishes in $\sim$300 s. Since MinDist has a better running time, we report the experiments for MinDist only.

The first experiment on MinDist measures the effect of the number of top pairs queried, $k$, on the running time. As shown in Fig 5(a), the scalability with $k$ is linear. The analysis in Sec 5.1 shows that for small values of $k$, this is the expected behavior. The largest real dataset—GO process—finishes in less than 1 s for $k \leq 50$, demonstrating the effectiveness of the algorithm.

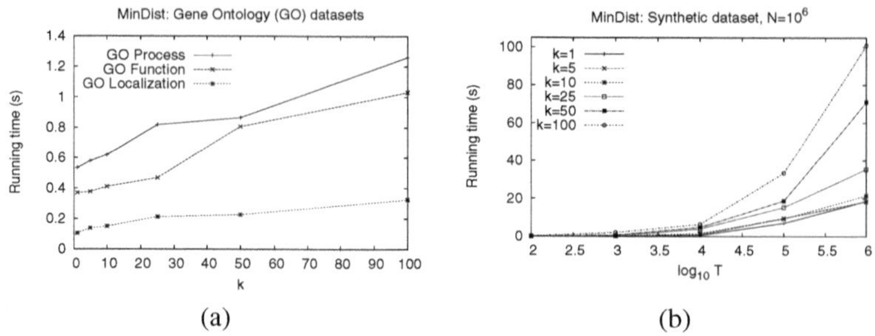


**Fig. 5.** (a) Effect of $k$ on MinDist. (b) Effect of $T$ on MinDist.

Fig 5(b) shows that increasing $T$ increments the running time of MinDist linearly, independent of the value of $k$. We also note the practicality of the MinDist algorithm. Even for a very large dataset of size $N = 10^6$ (translating to $10^{12}$ pairs) and a very large tree of size $T = 10^6$, a top-100 query finishes in about 100 s.

When the number of terms, $T$, is kept constant, experiments confirm that the running time increases only slightly with $N$ (graph not shown).

### 7.4 Experiments on AvgDist

When the distance function between the objects is defined as the *average pairwise distance* between the terms, the following schemes were evaluated:

- AvgDist-NextEstimate: In this variant of AvgDist, the estimate for the best-pair is improved by progressively descending into the subtrees and estimating the across-tree costs at the roots of those subtrees.
- AvgDist-Complete: This is the other variant of AvgDist where the exact distance is computed at one go by computing all the pairwise term distances.
- Brute-force: In this scheme, all the $O(N^2)$ pairs are computed and then the top-$k$ pairs are returned.

The performance of the brute-force scheme (300 s for $10^4$ dataset) is much higher than that for AvgDist schemes. Consequently, it is not discussed any further.

The first experiment on AvgDist measures the effect of $k$ on the running time of the Build phase and the two different variants—NextEstimate and Complete—for the two larger GO datasets. Intuitively, the running time of AvgDist depends on the actual number of object pairs investigated. For the GO datasets, even for large $k$'s up to 100, this remains almost constant (graph not shown). Moreover, the Build phase takes negligible time in comparison to the Query phase.

To analyze further, we measured the number of object pairs that are examined in the Query phase for $k$ up to 10000. Fig 6(a) shows that $\eta$ (i.e., the ratio of object pairs examined to the total number of possible pairs) increases very slowly with $k$. The results are robust across different values of $T$ (as shown in the figure) and $N$ (not shown). This is the reason why the running time is almost constant across $k$.

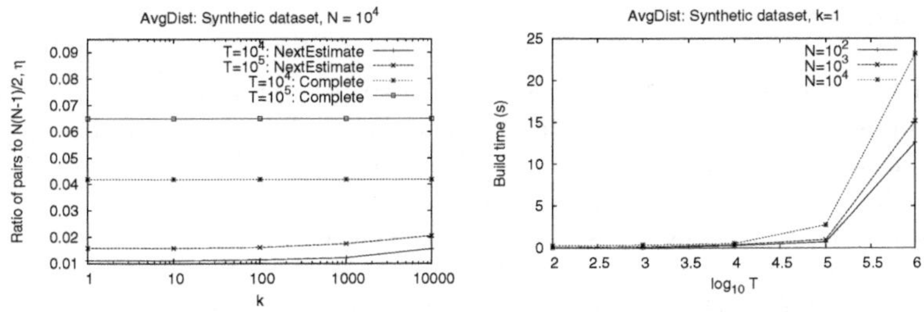


(a) (b)

**Fig. 6.** (a) Effect of $k$ on number of pairs examined. (b) Effect of $T$ on Build phase of AvgDist.

The NextEstimate method examines less than 2% of the total number of pairs. The Complete method investigates more object pairs (about 7%) than the NextEstimate method. Computing a distance for the current best-pair guarantees that only those pairs which have a bound lower than this distance will be analyzed. For the NextEstimate method, the distance of the best-pair is computed progressively, thereby saving on full AvgDist computations as compared to the Complete method, which directly finds the actual distance of the best-pair. Consequently, AvgDist-NextEstimate is faster.

We next discuss the results when the number of objects, $N$, is varied. From the analysis done in Sec 6.4, we expect the running time of the Build phase to grow linearly with the size of the input information. Assuming that the number of describing terms for an object is constant, the size of the information is directly proportional to the number of objects. Experiments confirm that the scalability with $N$ is indeed linear (graph not shown). The number of object pairs and, hence, the running time of the Query phase, grows at most quadratically with $N$ (graph not shown).

The next experiment measures the effect of the number of terms, $T$, on the different components of the AvgDist algorithm. Fig 6(b) shows the time required for the Build phase. Since the build procedure is run at each node, the effect of $T$ is linear. Further, when the number of objects increase, more information needs to be processed at each node and the running time increases linearly (graph not shown).

The number of pairs examined depends primarily on the span of the objects—mainly the number of objects in the single span lists—and not on the size of the tree. As a result, the size of the tree, $T$, has no appreciable effect on $\eta$ (graph not shown).

## 8 Conclusions

In this paper, we proposed the problem of finding top-$k$ most similar object pairs annotated with terms from an *ontology*. The terms represent concepts and the objects are described using these concepts. We then defined and motivated three object distances, *minimum pairwise distance*, *average pairwise distance*, and *earth mover's distance*. Finally, we designed algorithms to efficiently solve the join problem using the above distance measures. Range and $k$-NN queries should be simple extensions of the proposed algorithms.

## References


1. Ljosa, V., Bhattacharya, A., Singh, A.K.: Indexing spatially sensitive distance measures using multi-resolution lower bounds. In: Ioannidis, Y., Scholl, M.H., Schmidt, J.W., Matthes, F., Hatzopoulos, M., Böhm, K., Kemper, A., Grust, T., Böhm, C. (eds.) EDBT 2006. LNCS, vol. 3896, pp. 865–883. Springer, Heidelberg (2006)
2. Ciaccia, P., Patella, M., Zezula, P.: M-tree: An efficient access method for similarity search in metric spaces. In: VLDB, pp. 426–435 (1997)
3. Patel, J.M., DeWitt, D.J.: Partition based spatial-merge join. In: SIGMOD, pp. 259–270 (1996)
4. Fagin, R., Lotem, A., Naor, M.: Optimal aggregation algorithms for middleware. In: PODS, pp. 102–113 (2001)
5. Tao, Y., Sam, L., Li, J., Friedman, C., Lussier, Y.A.: Information theory applied to the sparse gene ontology annotation network to predict novel gene function. Bioinf. 23(13), i529–i538 (2007)
6. Couto, F.M., Silva, M.J., Coutinho, P.M.: Measuring semantic similarity between gene ontology terms. Trans. Data & Knowledge Engg. 61(1), 137–152 (2007)
7. Guo, X., Liu, R., Shriver, C.D., Hu, H., Liebman, M.N.: Assessing semantic similarity measures for the characterization of human regulatory pathways. Bioinf. 22(8), 967–973 (2006)
8. Lord, P.W., Stevens, R.D., Brass, A., Goble, C.A.: Investigating semantic similarity measures across the gene ontology: the relationship between sequence and annotation. Bioinf. 19(10), 1275–1283 (2003)
9. Mariño-Ramírez, L., Bodenreider, O., Kantz, N., Jordan, I.K.: Co-evolutionary rates of functionally related yeast genes. Evolutionary Bioinf. 2, 271–276 (2006)
10. Brameier, M., Wiuf, C.: Co-clustering and visualization of gene expression data and gene ontology terms for Saccharomyces cerevisiae using self-organizing maps. J. Biomed. Inf. 40(2), 160–173 (2007)
11. Salton, G., Buckley, C.: Term-weighting approaches in automatic text retrieval. Inf. Proc. & Mgmt. 24(5), 513–523 (1988)
12. Mihalcea, R., Corley, C.: Corpus-based and knowledge-based measures of text semantic similarity. In: AAAI, pp. 775–780 (2006)
13. Wan, X., Peng, Y.: The earth mover's distance as a semantic measure for document similarity. In: CIKM, pp. 301–302 (2005)
14. Gupta, A.: Embedding tree metrics into low dimensional euclidean spaces. In: STOC, pp. 694–700 (1999)
15. Cormen, T.H., Leiserson, C.E., Rivest, R.L., Stein, C.: Introduction to Algorithms. MIT, Cambridge (2001)
16. Johnston, E., Kushmerick, N.: Web service aggregation with string distance ensembles and active probe selection. Inf. Fusion 9, 481–500 (2008)
17. Bhattacharya, A., Bhowmick, A., Singh, A.K.: Finding top-k similar pairs of objects annotated with terms from an ontology. arXiv:1001.2625v1 [cs.DB] (2010)
18. Assent, I., Wenning, A., Seidl, T.: Approximation techniques for indexing the earth mover's distance in multimedia databases. In: ICDE, pp. 11–22 (2006)
19. Hjaltason, G.R., Samet, H.: Distance browsing in spatial databases. ACM Trans. Database Syst. 24(2), 265–318 (1999)

# Identifying the Most Influential User Preference from an Assorted Collection

Hua Lu[1] and Linhao Xu[2]

[1] Department of Computer Science, Aalborg University, Denmark
luhua@cs.aau.dk
[2] IBM China Research Lab, China
xulinhao@cn.ibm.com

**Abstract.** A conventional skyline query requires no query point, and usually employs a MIN or MAX annotation only to prefer smaller or larger values on each dimension. A relative skyline query, in contrast, is issued with a combination of a query point and a set of preference annotations for all involved dimensions. Due to the relative dominance definition in a relative skyline query, there exist various such combinations which we call as *user preferences*. It is also often interesting to identify from an assorted user preference collection the most influential preference that leads to the largest relative skyline. We call such a problem *the most influential preference query*. In this paper we propose a complete set of techniques to solve such novel and useful problems within a uniform framework. We first formalize different preference annotations that can be imposed on a dimension by a relative skyline query user. We then propose an effective transformation to handle all these annotations in a uniform way. Based on the transformation, we adapt the well-established Branch-and-Bound Skyline (BBS) algorithm to process relative skyline queries with assorted user preferences. In order to process the most influential preference queries, we develop two aggregation R-tree based algorithms. We conduct extensive experiments on both real and synthetic datasets to evaluate our proposals.

## 1 Introduction

Given a $d$-dimensional point set $P$, a skyline query [4] returns a subset of points that are not dominated by any other points. Point $p_1$ *dominates* $p_2$ (termed as $p_1 \prec p_2$), if $p_1$ is better than $p_2$ in at least one dimension and no worse than $p_2$ in all other dimensions. The skyline operator plays an important role in multi-criteria user decision making applications [2, 4, 10, 12, 18–20]. In the conventional skyline computation, no query point but MIN or MAX annotations on different dimensions are required [4]. Here the MIN (or MAX) annotation indicates that smaller (or larger) values are preferred on each dimension.

Given a same point set $P$, different users may issue skyline queries with different annotations, which produce different skylines. Refer to Figure 1(a) as an example, which shows a set of hotels with two attributes: room price and distance to the beach. Suppose a skyline query is issued with the MIN annotation

M. Gertz and B. Ludäscher (Eds.): SSDBM 2010, LNCS 6187, pp. 233–251, 2010.

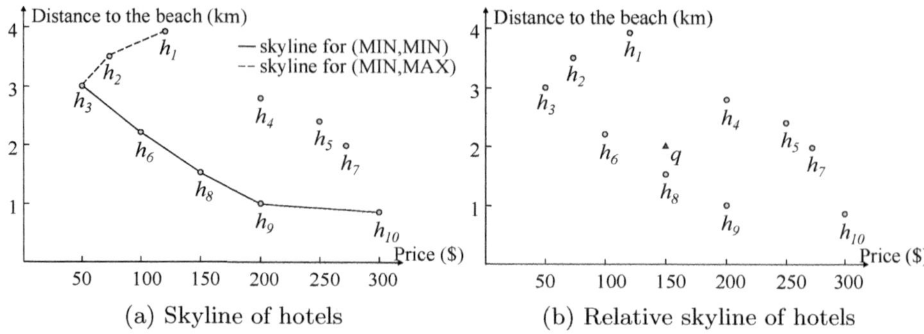


**Fig. 1.** Example of hotels

on both attributes, then the skyline is $\{h_3, h_6, h_8, h_9, h_{10}\}$. Sometimes, however, a user may prefer hotels far away from the beach for reasons like quietness and easy transportation to downtown. In that case, the MAX annotation instead can be used on the distance attribute. As a result, the skyline is $\{h_1, h_2, h_3\}$.

Different from conventional skyline queries, a relative skyline query is issued with a query point and preference annotations on the involved dimensions. The consequent relative skyline is formed by all those points that are not dominated by others with respect to the given query point and preference notations. For example, Figure 1(b) displays the same set of hotels with a query point $q$, where $q$ corresponds to a (virtual) hotel that is priced to \$150 and 2km to the beach. A user with specific preferences is interested in finding those hotels that are the most similar to $q$.

In such relative skyline queries, users have more flexibility in the sense that there are more options for preference in hotel selection. Specifically, users who do not care much about the price are interested in any hotel absolutely close to the given query point $q$ on the price dimension (preference I). Other users may prefer hotels that are cheaper and close to the price of $q$ (preference II). Also, users may prefer those hotels that have the similar (no matter longer or shorter) distance to the beach as does $q$ (preference III).

Consequently, if preference I is combined with preference III, the relative skyline is $\{h_6, h_7, h_8\}$; if II is combined with III, the relative skyline is $\{h_6, h_8\}$. Note that even more preference types can be involved in this example. For instance, those who do not like the beach may require hotels close to $q$ but having longer distance to the beach.

When more dimensions are involved (e.g., *star*, *rating* for hotels), more flexible preference types can be defined according to various user needs. However, only the absolute close annotation (preference I in the above example) has been studied in the literature [7, 9, 22]. This single and simple annotation is unable to cope with various user needs. For example in Figure 1(b), this annotation does not differentiate hotels $h_6$ and $h_9$ on the price dimension because both of them have an absolute price difference \$50 with the query point $q$. Whereas, preferring $h_6$ to $h_9$ makes sense as $h_6$ has a lower price than $h_9$.

We call such a combination of a query point and a set of annotations a *user preference*. When there is a set of assorted user preferences, it is often interesting to identify the one that leads to the largest skyline. We call such a one *the most influential* user preference. Refer to the hotel example again. Different customer requirement types can be captured as a set of user preferences (e.g., from user generated data online [1]). Identifying the most influential user preference will disclose the customer requirement type that can be easily satisfied by the available hotel resources. As a result, promotions and advertisements targeting such requirements are expected to boost the business in the corresponding market.

Motivated by the above observations, we in this paper formally study assorted user preferences, support them in relative skyline queries, and develop algorithms to identify efficiently the most influential user preference from an assorted collection. We make the following contributions in this paper:

- To the best of our knowledge, we are the first to systematically define and study assorted user preference annotations for relative skyline queries.
- We propose an effective transformation that equivalently converts an arbitrary relative user preference annotation to a conventional MIN annotation. Based on the transformation, we develop branch-and-bound skyline (BBS [18]) based algorithm for processing relative skyline queries with assorted user preferences.
- We define the *most influential preference query* to return from a set of user preferences the one leading to the largest relative skyline.
- We design two aggregate R-tree based algorithms for processing the novel and useful most influential preference queries; we also discuss the complexity and extensibility of the proposed algorithms.
- We conduct extensive experimental studies to evaluate our proposals and the results demonstrate that our approaches are efficient and scalable.

The remainder of this paper is organized as follows. Section 2 gives a brief review of related work. Section 3 defines a set of user preference annotations and formulates our problems. Section 4 elaborates on how to represent assorted user preferences in a uniform way, and exploits such a representation in processing relative skyline queries. Section 5 details and discusses the algorithms for processing most influential preference queries. Section 6 presents the experimental studies. Section 7 concludes and discuss directions for future work.

## 2 Related Work

Two categories of algorithms exist for conventional skyline queries. Those in the first category, namely BNL [4], D&C [4], SFS [8], LESS [10], LS [15], and SaLSa [3], require no index on the dataset. Those in the second category require specific indexes. *Bitmap* requires bitmap [20], *Index* [20] and ZSearch [13] require $B^+$-tree or its variant, NN [12] and BBS [18] require $R^*$-tree. Recent work [26] proposes a dynamic indexing tree to organize skyline points in sort-based algorithms (SFS, LESS and SaLSa), in order to reduce the CPU costs (not the IO costs) in skyline computation.

Skyline queries can be issued in subspaces [16, 21, 23, 24] of a multi-dimensional data set. For high dimensionality, skylines can be unmanageably large. Techniques [5, 6, 14, 18, 25] have been proposed to narrow down the large results.

Given a point set $P$ and a query point $q$, the reverse skyline query [9] on $P$ returns the points whose dynamic skylines contain $q$. In other words, $p \in P$ is included in the reverse skyline if the dynamic skyline with $p$ as the query point contains $q$. The dynamic skyline query in [9] is the same as the relative skyline query in this paper.[1] However, only the absolute close preference annotation is allowed by dynamic skyline queries in [9], which falls short in real-life scenarios as we have pointed out in Section 1.

The bichromatic reverse skyline query [7, 22] extends the above monochromatic definition that involves only one dataset to a setting with two datasets. A basic bichromatic reverse skyline algorithm [7] is proposed for uncertain data. An improved algorithm [22] is proposed for certain data.

Two important points distinguish this work from previous ones [7, 9, 22]. First, this work is focused on supporting assorted user preference annotations in relative skyline queries, whereas previous ones deal with reverse skyline queries with the single absolute close preference annotation. Second, compared to previous ones, this work offers users more flexibility in defining their preferences. The binary dimension classification in [22] differentiates dimensions in two cases that may have different user preferences (e.g., users always prefer lower car price but higher car capacity). However, its binary nature and aforehand differentiation fail to capture various possible user needs. For example, some users may prefer low car capacity because they only drive alone. In contrast, our proposed preference annotations offer more options for users to choose from, such that they are able to issue relative skyline queries according to their personalized needs.

## 3 Problem Formulation

We first study preference annotations that can be used in a relative skyline query, and then formalize our problem definitions based on these annotations. Let $P$ be a $d$-dimensional dataset, where each dimension is on a domain of numerical values. Without loss of generality, we assume that each dimension domain is $\mathcal{R}$, the set of real numbers. The domain of the $i$-th dimension is denoted by $\mathcal{D}_i$. For any $d$-dimensional point $p$, we use $p[i]$ to denote its value on the $i$-th dimension.

### 3.1 Preference Annotations

A conventional skyline can have a specific preference annotation attached on each dimension [4]. For example, the MIN annotation indicates that smaller

[1] A slightly different dynamic skyline query definition in [18] may involve a derived dimension obtained from a function on original dimensions, e.g., the distance $\sqrt{(x_i - x_q)^2 + (y_i - y_q)^2}$ between data location $(x_i, y_i)$ and the query location $(x_q, y_q)$. For simplicity, we assume that a relative skyline query involves only original dimensions but no such derived dimensions. The techniques proposed in this paper can be applied to the definition in [18].

values are preferred on each dimension; whereas the MAX annotation chooses larger values. In reality, for a relative skyline query on the dataset $P$ with the query point $q$, more preference annotations can be defined by a user.

**Absolute Close annotation (ABC).** The Absolute Close annotation is intended to minimize the distance between the query point $q$ and a data point $p$ on a particular dimension. Specifically, the ABC annotation on the $i$-th dimension indicates that small values $|q[i] - p[i]|$ are preferred in the relative dominance relationship. For example, users can use this annotation to select the hotels with similar prices as the given query hotel.

**MIN Close annotation (MIC).** The MIN Close annotation picks the closest value that is smaller than $q$ on a particular dimension. If all values are larger than $q$, the MIC annotation picks the smallest value. Notice that the ABC annotation does not differentiate whether $p[i]$ is larger or lower than $q[i]$ in a similarity comparison. While the MIC annotation prefers a similar value lower than the counterpart of $q$. Refer to the example of retrieving similar hotels in Figure 1(b). The MIC annotation prefers hotel $h_6$ to $h_9$ as $h_6$ has a lower price than the query point $q$, although $h_6$ and $h_9$ have the same absolute price distance to $q$.

**MAX Close annotation (MAC).** Contrary to the MIN Close annotation, the MAX Close annotation chooses the closest value larger than $q$ on a particular dimension. If all values are smaller than $q$, then the MAC annotation picks the largest value. In the example of retrieving hotels similar to a given query hotel $q$, the MAC annotation can be used to select those with more stars from all candidates having the same absolute star difference with $q$.

**Absolute Far annotation (ABF).** Contrary to the ABC annotation, the Absolute Far annotation is intended to maximize the distance between the query point $q$ and a data point $p$ on a particular dimension. Specifically, the ABF annotation on the $i$-th dimension prefers large values $|q[i] - p[i]|$ in the relative dominance relationship. The ABF annotation reflects the powerful differential competition strategy. For a company to market a new product, for example, the ABF annotation can be used to identify those most different products from a set of competitive products. It is in turn beneficial to compete with those products, by advertising the new product within the same space or time slot.

**MIN Far annotation (MIF).** The MIN Far annotation picks the farthest value that is smaller than $q$ on a particular dimension. If all values are larger than $q$, then the MIF annotation selects the smallest value. Given a new mobile phone type, for example, the MIF annotation can be used to identify the competitive product with shortest standby time.

**MAX Far annotation (MAF).** Contrary to the MIC annotation, the MAX Far annotation is intended to pick the farthest value that is larger than $q$ on a particular dimension. If all values are smaller than $q$, then the MAF annotation picks the largest value. Given a new mobile phone type, for example, the MIF annotation can be used to identify the competitive product with highest price.

### 3.2 Problem Definitions

A relative skyline query on dataset $P$ is issued together with a query point $q$. In addition, we can specify a preference annotation from the set {ABC, MIC, MAC, ABF, MIF, MAF} on an arbitrary dimension. Let $v_1$ and $v_2$ be two arbitrary values on the arbitrary $i$-th dimension. If there is an annotation $ant_i \in$ {ABC, MIC, MAC,ABF, MIF, MAF} imposed on the $i$-th dimension, $v_1$ and $v_2$ will be compared accordingly to decide if one is preferred to the other. If neither value is preferred to the other according to the definition of the annotation $ant_i$, or no annotation is imposed on the corresponding dimension, we say $v_1$ and $v_2$ are *incomparable* with respect to $q$.

**Definition 1 (User Preference).** *In a d-dimensional space, a* user preference *$\psi$ is defined as a 2-tuple $\psi = \langle p, ants \rangle$, where $p$ is a d-dimensional point and ants is a list of d preference annotations. Specifically, $\psi.ants = \langle ant_1, \ldots, ant_d \rangle$, where for $1 \leq i \leq d$ each $ant_i \in \{ABC, MIC, MAC, ABF, MIF, MAF, null\}$. A null $ant_i$ indicates that no annotation is imposed on i-th dimension.*

**Definition 2 (Relative Dominance).** *Let $p_1$ and $p_2$ be two d-dimensional points, and $\psi$ be a user preference. Point $p_1$* relatively dominates *$p_2$ with respect to $\psi$, if $\forall 1 \leq i \leq d$, $p_1[i]$ is preferred to or incomparable with $p_2[i]$ according to $\psi.p[i]$ and $\psi.ants[i]$, but $\exists 1 \leq i \leq d$, $p_1[i]$ is preferred to $p_2[i]$ according to $\psi.p[i]$ and $\psi.ants[i]$.*

**Definition 3 (Relative Skyline Query).** *Given a d-dimensional point set $P$, a relative skyline query with a user preference $\psi$, termed as $RSQ_\psi$, returns from $P$ all points that are not relatively dominated by any others with respect to $\psi$.*

It is noteworthy that the set of preference annotations defined in Section 3.1 offers to users convenience and flexibility when they need to retrieve interesting and meaningful objects from a complex data set. For example, a music database may contain enormous song samples that are represented as vectors of specific attributes (e.g., melody, rhythm, tempo, pitch, etc.). Without defining any complex distance function within the vector space, one can issue relative skyline queries with appropriate preference annotations to retrieve from the database those samples that are most similar (or most dissimilar) to a given sample.

We use $RSky(P, \psi)$ to denote the relative skyline query result on $P$, i.e., the relative skyline of $P$ with respect to $\psi$.

**Definition 4 (Most Influential Preference Query).** *Given a d-dimensional point set $P$, and a user preference set $\Psi$ within the d-dimensional space, a most influential preference (MIP) query returns a user preference $\psi$ from $\Psi$ such that $\forall \psi' \in \Psi, |RSky(P, \psi')| \leq |RSky(P, \psi)|$.*

The definition above can be easily extended to return the top-$k$ most influential preferences. Such MIP queries are very useful in various applications. In customer relationship management (CRM) systems, for example, MIP queries can identity very important customers who are interested in the largest number of products.

As another example,it is often interesting for composers and music researchers to know which types of music are the most influential in a music database. By capturing different music types in the preference set $\Psi$, a MIP query against the music database $P$ retrieves the type that leads to the largest skyline of $P$, i.e. the most frequent music type in $P$.

## 4 Supporting Assorted User Preferences

In this section, we address how to efficiently support assorted user preferences that can be used in relative skyline queries and MIP queries. Section 4.1 develops a transformation mechanism through which various preference annotations can be represented in a uniform way. Based on the necessary uniform representation, Section 4.2 adapts the branch-and-bound skyline (BBS) algorithm [18] to process relative skyline queries with various preference annotations.

### 4.1 Uniform User Preference Annotation Representation

It is desirable that we unify the presentations of all those annotations aforementioned, as this will give us convenience in the query processing. In our approach, we convert all preference annotations into the conventional MIN annotation. The key point of this transformation is a function $f_{ant}$ for each annotation type, from a dimension domain $\mathcal{D}_i$ to $\mathcal{R}$.

For the ABC annotation, $f_{ABC}$ is defined as:

$$f_{ABC}(q[i], p[i]) = |q[i] - p[i]| \tag{1}$$

For the MIC annotation, $f_{MIC}$ is defined as:

$$f_{MIC}(q[i], p[i]) = \begin{cases} (q[i] - p[i])/(\mathcal{D}_i.MAX - \mathcal{D}_i.MIN), & \text{if } q[i] \geq p[i] \\ 1 + (p[i] - q[i])/(\mathcal{D}_i.MAX - \mathcal{D}_i.MIN), & otherwise \end{cases} \tag{2}$$

For the MAC annotation, $f_{MAC}$ is defined as:

$$f_{MAC}(q[i], p[i]) = \begin{cases} (p[i] - q[i])/(\mathcal{D}_i.MAX - \mathcal{D}_i.MIN), & \text{if } q[i] \leq p[i] \\ 1 + (q[i] - p[i])/(\mathcal{D}_i.MAX - \mathcal{D}_i.MIN), & otherwise \end{cases} \tag{3}$$

For the ABF annotation, $f_{ABF}$ is defined as:

$$f_{ABF}(q[i], p[i]) = -|q[i] - p[i]| \tag{4}$$

For the MIF annotation, $f_{MIF}$ is defined as:

$$f_{MIF}(q[i], p[i]) = p[i] - q[i] \tag{5}$$

For the MAF annotation, $f_{MAF}$ is defined as:

$$f_{MAF}(q[i], p[i]) = q[i] - p[i] \tag{6}$$

Using these functions, any preference annotation $ant_i$ on the $i$-th dimension in a relative skyline query can be transformed to a conventional MIN annotation on a dynamic dimension $f_{ant_i}(q[i], p[i])$. Thus, given a relative skyline query $RSQ = (q, \langle ant_1, ant_2, \ldots, ant_d \rangle)$, we have the following corollary.

**Corollary 1 (Dominance Equivalence).** *Let $P$ be a d-dimensional point set, and $RSQ = (q, \langle ant_1, ant_2, \ldots, ant_d \rangle)$ be a relative skyline query. For two points $p_1, p_2 \in P$, $p_1$ relatively dominates $p_2$ with respect to $RSQ$ if and only if $\forall 1 \leq i \leq d, f_{ant_i}(q[i], p_1[i]) \leq f_{ant_i}(q[i], p_2[i])$ and $\exists 1 \leq i \leq d, f_{ant_i}(q[i], p_1[i]) < f_{ant_i}(q[i], p_2[i])$.*

Corollary 1 tells that, with our proposed transformation, a relative skyline query with arbitrary annotations can be processed by adapting the dynamic skyline query approach [18]. We proceed to detail the adaptation and algorithms.

### 4.2 Processing Relative Skyline Queries with Assorted Preferences

We adapt the *Branch-and-Bound Skyline* (BBS) algorithm [18] for our skyline computation. The BBS algorithm is based on the best-first nearest neighbor [11] via R-tree. Given a dataset $P$ indexed by an R-tree $R_P$, BBS employs a min-heap $H$ to keep all R-tree entries that contain skyline points. For an entry $e$ in $R_P$, we use $e.min$ ($e.max$) to denote its minimum (maximum) corner. Initially, BBS enheaps all entries in the root of $R_P$. Subsequently, BBS accesses all entries via $H$. At each step, the entry $e$ with the smallest $L_1$ distance between $e.min$ and the origin is deheaped from $H$ and expanded. The expansion eliminates all $e$'s subentries dominated by any current skyline point, and enheaps the remaining subentries to $H$. It repeats the aforementioned expansion until $H$ becomes empty.

Our choice is justified by the three desirable properties of the BBS algorithm. First, it requires no specialized index but the popular R-tree; neither does it require any specific data transformation before specialized indexes can be created [13, 20]. Second, it never expands an entry that does not contain a skyline point (IO-optimality). Third, at any moment, all points in the current skyline are in the final skyline (progressiveness). Therefore, it is interesting to adapt BBS to process relative skyline queries with assorted user preferences.

Specifically, the essence of BBS is its ability to prune R-tree entries (and their nodes) by checking whether an entry is dominated by any current skyline point. In order to retain this beneficial feature, we need to address how to check whether a given R-tree entry $e$ is relatively dominated by any current skyline point with respect to a given user preference $\psi$. The crucial step for that check is to derive from $e$ a *virtual minimum corner* in the transformed space, which is then compared with the skyline points according to Corollary 1. We use $VMBB(e, \psi)$ to denote the virtual minimum bounding box derived from $e$ and $\psi$. The virtual minimum corner is then denoted as $VMBB(e, \psi).min$. It is noteworthy that $VMBB(e, \psi).min$ is not necessarily the same as the result of transforming $e$'s minimum corner $e.min$.

**Deriving virtual minimum corners.** Now let us elaborate how to derive the virtual minimum corner $VMBB(e, \psi).min[i]$ on an arbitrary dimension $\mathcal{D}_i$. The results are listed in Table 1. In general, for each annotation, if it is the cases that $q[i] < e.min[i]$ or $q[i] > e.max[i]$, the appropriate entry boundary is used in the corresponding transformation function, which calculates the

**Table 1.** Construction of $VMBB(e, \psi).min$

| | $q[i] < e.min[i]$ | $q[i] > e.max[i]$ | $e.min[i] \leq q[i] \leq e.max[i]$ |
|---|---|---|---|
| ABC | $f_{ABC}(q[i], e.min[i])$ | $f_{ABC}(q[i], e.max[i])$ | 0 |
| MIC | $f_{MIC}(q[i], e.min[i])$ | $f_{MIC}(q[i], e.max[i])$ | 0 |
| MAC | $f_{MAC}(q[i], e.min[i])$ | $f_{MAC}(q[i], e.max[i])$ | 0 |
| ABF | $f_{ABF}(q[i], e.max[i])$ | $f_{ABF}(q[i], e.min[i])$ | $min\{f_{ABF}(q[i], e.min[i]), f_{ABF}(q[i], e.max[i])\}$ |
| MIF | $f_{MIF}(q[i], e.min[i])$ | $f_{MIF}(q[i], e.min[i])$ | $f_{MIF}(q[i], e.min[i])$ |
| MAF | $f_{MAF}(q[i], e.max[i])$ | $f_{MAF}(q[i], e.max[i])$ | $f_{MAF}(q[i], e.max[i])$ |

expected $VMBB(e, \psi).min[i]$. If $q[i]$ is (inclusively) between $e.min[i]$ and $e.max[i]$, $VMBB(e, \psi).min[i]$ is derived differently.

For all Close annotations (ABC, MIC and MAC), the transformation functions in Section 4.1 always produce non-negative values. Therefore, when $q[i]$ is between $e.min[i]$ and $e.max[i]$, $VMBB(e, \psi).min[i]$ is 0 which indicates that entry $e$ is likely to contain points that dominate others on the $i$-th dimension.

For ABF annotations, the transformation function $f_{ABF}$ always produces non-positive values. Whereas, when $q[i]$ is between $e.min[i]$ and $e.max[i]$, $VMBB(e, \psi).min[i] = min\{f_{ABF}(q[i], e.min[i]), f_{ABF}(q[i], e.max[i])\}$ indicates that the distance from $q[i]$ to the farther boundary determines the likelihood that entry $e$ contains potential preferred values on the $i$-th dimension.

For the MIF (MAF) annotation, the same preferred entry boundary $e.min[i]$ ($e.max[i]$) is used, according to the preference definition.

Note that for a leaf entry $e$ (i.e., $e$ corresponds to a point), the above construction still works with $e.min[i] = e.max[i]$.

**Algorithm.** We now present the algorithm for processing relative skyline queries with assorted preference annotations. We call it *branch-and-bound relative skyline algorithm*, or BBRS for short. Its pseudo code is shown in Algorithm 1. Here, the $L_1$ distance metric is used at line 4 and line 14 to prioritize the R-tree node access. For an entry $e$, however, its virtual minimum corner $VMBB(e, \psi).min$ is used rather than its original minimum corner $e.min$.

Function *isDominated* used in Algorithm 1 checks whether an entry is relatively dominated by any current skyline point (lines 7 and 12). It is shown in Algorithm 2, where only the virtual minimum corner $VMBB(e, \psi).min$ is compared with the transformed skyline points.

## 5 Processing Most Influential Preference Queries

We proceed to present two algorithms for processing most influential preference queries. Both algorithms require that the point set $P$ is indexed by an aggregate R-tree [17], where each node entry $e$ stores in *e.count* the count of points in its subtree. We make use of that count to prune unqualified user preferences.

### 5.1 The Probing-with-Pruning Algorithm

The first algorithm is Probing-with-Pruning (PwP for short), as shown in Algorithm 3. The PwP algorithm takes two inputs: a user preference list $\Psi$ and an

**Algorithm 1. BBRS**(R-tree $R_P$ for dataset $P$, User preference $\psi$)

initialize a min-heap $H$; $S \leftarrow \emptyset$
**for** each entry $e$ in $R_P$'s root **do**
  $mindist(\psi.p, e) \leftarrow \sum_{i=1}^{d} VMBB(e, \psi).min[i]$
  enheap$(H, \langle e, mindist(\psi.p, e)\rangle)$
**while** $H$ is not empty **do**
  $e \leftarrow$ deheap$(H)$
  **if** $isDominated(e, S, \psi)$ **then**
    **continue**
  **else**
    **if** $e$ is a non-leaf entry **then**
      **for** each child $e_j$ of $e$ **do**
        **if** $!isDominated(e_j, S, \psi)$ **then**
          $mindist(\psi.p, e_j) \leftarrow \sum_{i=1}^{d} VMBB(e_j, \psi).min[i]$
          enheap$(H, \langle e_j, mindist(\psi.p, e_j)\rangle)$
    **else**
      insert $e$ to $S$
**return** $S$

**Algorithm 2. isDominated**(R-tree entry $e$, Current skyline $S$, User preference $\psi$)

**for** each skyline point $s \in S$ **do**
  **if** $\forall 1 \leq i \leq d, f_{\psi.ants[i]}(\psi.p[i], s[i]) \leq VMBB(e, \psi).min[i]$ **and**
  $\exists 1 \leq i \leq d, f_{\psi.ants[i]}(\psi.p[i], s[i]) < VMBB(e, \psi).min[i]$ **then**
    **return** true
**return** false

aggregate R-tree $R_P$ for point set $P$. Using $R_P$ as the index, PwP processes a relative skyline query in the similar way as BBRS(Algorithm 1) for each user preference $\psi \in \Psi$, and the one leading to the largest query size is maintained and finally returned.

The PwP algorithm employs two variables to maintain the most influential preference ($mip$) and the relevant skyline result size ($max$) (line 1). Before popping the heap and expanding an $R_P$ entry, it checks whether all current $R_P$ entries in the heap contain enough points to make the current candidate $\psi$ exceed the existing result $mip$ (lines 8–9). If the sum of the total number of points in the heap and the cardinality of the current skyline $S$ is not larger than $max$ (line 8), then $\psi$ cannot lead to a larger skyline even if all points in the heap enter skyline $S$. As a result, $\psi$ is pruned and the further processing on it is avoided (line 9). When the processing for the current preference $\psi$ ends, PwP checks whether it is necessary to update the current result (lines 21–22).

### 5.2 The Prioritized Probing Algorithm

The second algorithm is Prioritized Probing (PP for short), as shown in Algorithm 4. It takes the same inputs as the PwP algorithm but works with a different philosophy. Instead of continuing the relative skyline query processing for each

**Algorithm 3. PwP**(User preference list $\Psi$, Aggregate R-tree $R_P$ for point set $P$)

```
max ← 0; mip ← null
for each user preference ψ ∈ Ψ do
  initialize a min-heap H; S ← ∅
  for each entry e in R_P's root do
    mindist(ψ.p, e) ← Σ_{i=1}^{d} VMBB(e, ψ).min[i]
    enheap(H, ⟨e, mindist(ψ.p, e)⟩)
  while H is not empty do
    if Σ_{e_i∈H} e_i.count + |S| ≤ max then
      break
    e ← deheap(H)
    if isDominated(e, S, ψ) then
      continue
    else
      if e is a non-leaf entry then
        for each child e_j of e do
          if !isDominated(e_j, S, ψ) then
            mindist(ψ.p, e_j) ← Σ_{i=1}^{d} VMBB(e_j, ψ).min[i]
            enheap(H, ⟨e_j, mindist(ψ.p, e_j)⟩)
      else
        insert e to S
  if |S| > max then
    max ← |S|; mip ← ψ
return mip
```

user preference until either the query is done or the query is terminated because of pruning, the PP algorithm at each step only selects the most promising user preference $\psi$ and pushes forward the relative skyline query processing for that particular $\psi$.

Specifically, the PP algorithm employs a max-heap to prioritize the processing for all user preferences (line 1). In the max-heap, each user preference $\psi$ is attached with a list of $R_P$ tree entries that may contain relative skyline points for $\psi$. In addition, a variable *count*, the total number of points that may be in the relative skyline for $\psi$, is used as the key to prioritize all user preferences in the max-heap. Initially, each user preference $\psi$ in the input gets its list based on all entries in the root of $R_P$ tree (lines 2–5). Its *count* is initialized as the total number of all points contained in the list, by referring to the aggregate values stored in the child node entries; then each $\psi$ is enheaped with its *count* as the key (line 6). The selection of the promising $R_P$ tree entries into a $\psi$'s list is done by the procedure *addEntry* (we will discuss it later).

The subsequent processing is prioritized by the max-heap. Each time, the user preference $\psi$ attached with the largest *count* is deheaped (line 8). If $\psi$'s list is empty, which means that its relative skyline query has been processed and the corresponding skyline is the largest (due to the property of a max-heap), $\psi$ is returned as the result (lines 9–10).

**Algorithm 4. PP**(User preference list $\Psi$, Aggregate R-tree $R_P$ for point set $P$)

```
1: initialize a max-heap H
2: for each user preference ψ ∈ Ψ do
3:    list ← ∅
4:    for each entry e in R_P.root do
5:       addEntry(e, list, ψ)
6:    count ← Σ_{e∈list} e.count; enheap(H, ⟨ψ, list, count⟩)
7: while H is not empty do
8:    ⟨ψ, list, count⟩ ← deheap(H)
9:    if list is empty then
10:      return ψ
11:   else
12:      repeat
13:         count1 ← count; flag ← true
14:         for each entry e in list do
15:            if e is a non-leaf entry then
16:               flag ← false; remove e from list
17:               for each subentry e_i in e do
18:                  addEntry(e_i, list, ψ)
19:         if flag then
20:            list ← ∅
21:         else
22:            count ← Σ_{e∈list} e.count
23:      until flag or (count1 − count) = 0
24:   enheap(H, ⟨ψ, list, count⟩)
```

Otherwise, $R_P$ tree entries in $\psi$'s list will be expanded and processed to eliminate unpromising subentries and maintain promising ones (lines 12–23). Each non-leaf entry $e$ in the list is moved out, and all its promising child entries will be added back to the list by calling addEntry (lines 14–18). The expansion is repeated until all entries in the list are leaf entries, or the expansion does not reduce $\psi$'s list (line 23). The latter case is indicated by the unchanged *count* value. The variable *flag* indicates whether all entries are leaf entries or not. If positive, the list attached to $\psi$ will be set to empty (line 19–20); otherwise, the count value is updated to the total number of points contained in the current list (lines 21–22). After the processing for $\psi$ stops, it is enheaped again with updated list and count (line 24).

The selection of the promising $R_P$ tree entries into a user preference $\psi$'s list is done through the procedure *addEntry*, shown in Algorithm 5. Given a new entry $e$ and all candidate entries in *list*, it performs a mutual dominance check between $e$ and *list* to eliminate the dominated entries (including $e$). Given two entries $e_1$ and $e_2$ and a user preference $\psi$, if $VMBB(e_1, \psi).max \prec VMBB(e_2, \psi).min$ in the transformed space, every point in $e_2$ must be dominated (with respect to $\psi$) by some point(s) in $e_1$. As a result, $e_2$ can be safely pruned.

**Algorithm 5. addEntry**(Aggregate R-tree entry $e$ from $R_P$, Candidate entry list $list$, User preference $\psi$)

**for** each entry $e_i$ in $list$ **do**
  **if** $VMBB(e_i, \psi).max \prec VMBB(e, \psi).min$ **then**
    **return**
  **else if** $VMBB(e, \psi).max \prec VMBB(e_i, \psi).min$ **then**
    remove $VMBB(e, \psi)$ from $list$
add $e$ to $list$

**Table 2.** Construction of $VMBB(e, \psi).max$

| | $q[i] < e.min[i]$ | $q[i] > e.max[i]$ | $e.min[i] \leq q[i] \leq e.max[i]$ |
|---|---|---|---|
| ABC | $f_{ABC}(q[i], e.max[i])$ | $f_{ABC}(q[i], e.min[i])$ | $max\{f_{ABC}(q[i], e.min[i]), f_{ABC}(q[i], e.max[i])\}$ |
| MIC | $f_{MIC}(q[i], e.max[i])$ | $f_{MIC}(q[i], e.min[i])$ | $f_{MIC}(q[i], e.max[i])$ |
| MAC | $f_{MAC}(q[i], e.max[i])$ | $f_{MAC}(q[i], e.min[i])$ | $f_{MAC}(q[i], e.max[i])$ |
| ABF | $f_{ABF}(q[i], e.min[i])$ | $f_{ABF}(q[i], e.max[i])$ | $max\{f_{ABF}(q[i], e.min[i]), f_{ABF}(q[i], e.max[i])\}$ |
| MIF | $f_{MIF}(q[i], e.max[i])$ | $f_{MIF}(q[i], e.max[i])$ | $f_{MIF}(q[i], e.max[i])$ |
| MAF | $f_{MAF}(q[i], e.min[i])$ | $f_{MAF}(q[i], e.min[i])$ | $f_{MAF}(q[i], e.min[i])$ |

The construction of $VMBB(e, \psi).max$ for an entry $e$ is detailed in Table 2. It follows the same line of reasoning as we construct $VMBB(e, \psi).min$. Due to the space limitation, we omit the detailed explanation here.

### 5.3 Discussions

We now provide a brief estimation on the worst-case IO costs for the two algorithms proposed above. Let $N_P$ be the number of nodes in the aggregate R-tree $R_P$ on $P$, $L_P$ be the number of leaf nodes in $R_P$, and $f$ be the fan-out of $R_P$. In the worst-case, PwP processes a relative skyline query for each user preference in $\Psi$; and such a skyline query processing visits all tree nodes in the aggregate R-tree $R_P$ on $P$. As a result, the worst-case IO cost of PwP is $|\Psi| \cdot N_P$.

On the other hand, PP always conducts a complete relative skyline query processing only for one user preference in $\Psi$. However, in the worst-case, it may reach the leaf node level of the aggregate R-tree $R_P$ on $P$ for all other preferences in $\Psi$. As a result, the worst-case IO cost of PP is $N_P + (|\Psi| - 1) \cdot (N_P - L_P) \leq N_P + (|\Psi| - 1) \cdot (N_P - \frac{|P|}{f})$.

When it is necessary to return the top-$k$ most influential user preferences from $\Psi$, both PwP and PP algorithms need very slight change, i.e., a list instead of a variable to keep the temporary and/or final results.

In addition, it is noteworthy that both PwP and PP algorithms are able to handle special input formats, e.g., a fixed query point with a list of preference annotations, or a list of query points with a common set of annotations for all dimensions. Neither PwP nor PP needs major changes to handle such cases. Due to the space limitation, we leave for future work the possible specialized subtle optimizations for such cases.

# 6 Experimental Studies

All algorithms were implemented in Java and run on a Windows XP PC with a 2.8GHz Intel Pentium D CPU and 1GB RAM. We used both real and synthetic datasets, all normalized to space $[0,1]^d$ ($d$ is the data dimensionality). For synthetic datasets, both anti-correlated (AC) and independent (IN) distributions were generated according to methods in previous work [4]. For each algorithm, we set the page size to 4K and used an LRU memory buffer whose size is set to 1% of the sum of the input data size. We mainly report the results of IOs since they are dominant in query processing.

## 6.1 Experiments on Assorted User Preferences

In the first set of experiments, we investigate the performance of relative skyline queries with assorted preference annotations. In each experiment, 50 relative skyline queries were executed. The user preference $\psi$ in each query was generated as follows unless stated otherwise. Its query point $p$ was a random point within the space $[0,1]^d$; the annotation on each dimension was randomly chosen from the set {ABC, MIC, MAC, ABF, MIF, MAF}. In addition, we also imposed each annotation type on all $d$ dimensions and ran 50 queries accordingly.

We first fixed the dimensionality $d$ to 2 and varied $P$ cardinality from 100K to 1000K. The results are reported in Figures 2(a) and 3(a), on AC and IN datasets respectively. Overall, all queries perform steadily and scalably as the cardinality increases. The AC datasets have large skylines, which offers enough room to make the differences more visible among various preference annotations.

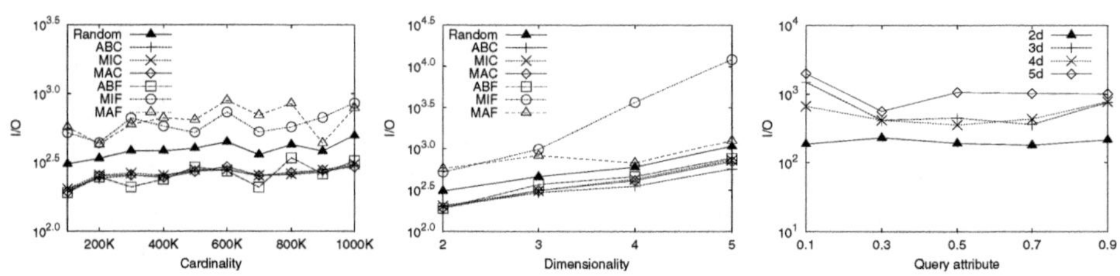


(a) Effect of Cardinality (b) Effect of Dimensionality (c) Effect of Query

**Fig. 2.** Relative Skyline Query Performance on AC Data Sets

We then fixed $P$ cardinality to 100K and varied the dimensionality $d$ from 2 to 5. The results are reported in Figures 2(b) and 3(b). For most annotation types on both distributions, a higher dimensionality incurs a modest cost increase less than one order of magnitude. The exception of MIF on the AC datasets is attributed to the very large corresponding skylines. This is because the MIF transformation (see Equation 5) is actually a parallel translation, which makes the relative skyline as large as the conventional skyline.

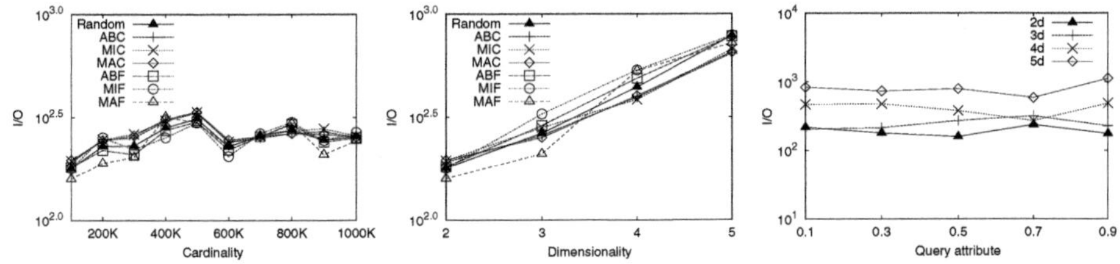


**Fig. 3.** Relative Skyline Query Performance on IN Data Sets

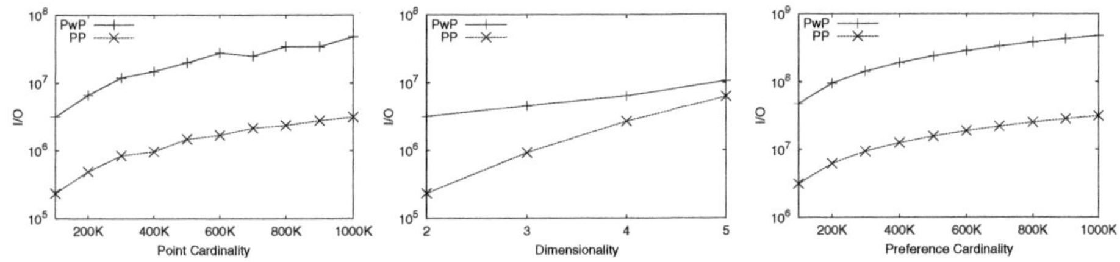


(a) Point Cardinality (b) Dimensionality (c) Preference Cardinality

**Fig. 4.** Performance of Most Influential Preference Query on AC Data Sets

Finally we investigated the effect of the variations of the query point $p = \{v, \ldots, v\}$ in $\psi$, by varying $v$ from 0.1 to 0.9. We used random annotations. The results are shown in Figures 2(c) and 3(c). For each dimensionality, the change of the query point does not affect the query performance much.

In summary, the performance of relative skyline queries with assorted user preference annotations is efficient and scalable under various settings. This indicates that our preference annotation transformation is effective, and the adapted query algorithm is efficient.

## 6.2 Experiments on Most Influential Preference Queries

We also conducted extensive experiments on most influential preference queries. We first report the results on the synthetic datasets. The default settings were used: 100K points in $P$, 10K user preferences with random query points and random annotations in $\Psi$, and 2 as the dimensionality.

We compared the query processing efficiency of PwP and PP algorithms, and the results are reported in Figures 4 and 5. Figure 4(a) and Figure 5(a) describe the effect of varying $P$ cardinality. As $P$ becomes larger, all cases incur more IO costs. The PP algorithm outperforms the PwP algorithm by more than one order of magnitude on both distributions, because the PP algorithm completes relative skyline query processing for only one user preference.

Figure 4(b) and Figure 5(b) show the effect of varying dimensionality. Higher dimensionality incurs more IO costs in every case, whereas the PP algorithm is better than the PwP algorithm. Figure 4(c) and Figure 5(c) reports on the

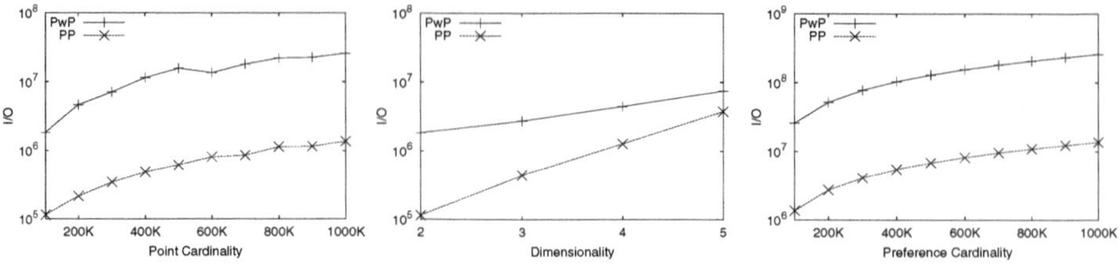


(a) Point Cardinality (b) Dimensionality (c) Preference Cardinality

**Fig. 5.** Performance of Most Influential Preference Query on IN Data Sets

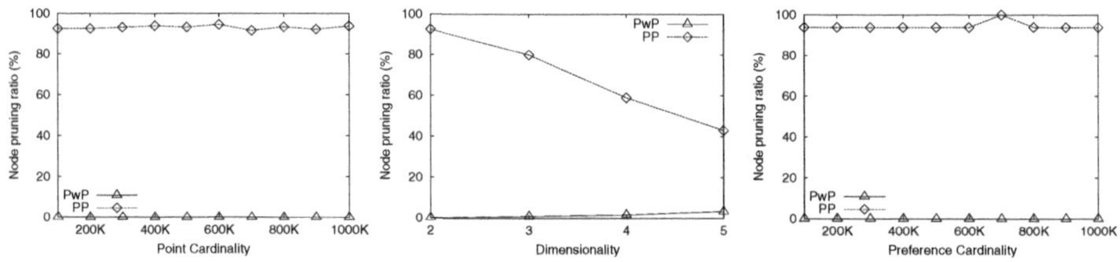


(a) Point Cardinality (b) Dimensionality (c) Preference Cardinality

**Fig. 6.** Pruning Effectiveness on AC Data Sets

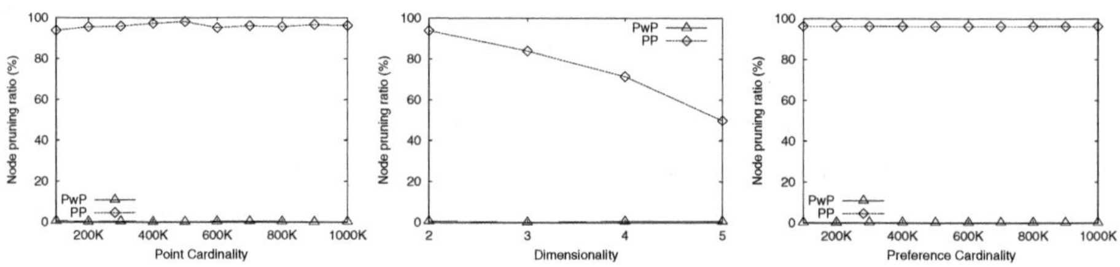


(a) Point Cardinality (b) Dimensionality (c) Preference Cardinality

**Fig. 7.** Pruning Effectiveness on IN Data Sets

effect of varying $\Psi$ cardinality. Again, the PP algorithm outperforms the PwP algorithm as the former avoids considerable unnecessary computations.

We also investigated the R-tree node pruning effectiveness of PwP and PP algorithms, by comparing them to a baseline approach that executes a complete relative skyline query for each user preference in the input preference list $\Psi$. We measure the node pruning ratio, i.e., the ratio between the number of tree node accesses PwP or PP saves and that the baseline approach incurs.

The results are reported in Figures 6 and 7. It is seen that PP always has a significantly higher pruning ratio than PwP does. This indicates that the prioritized probing strategy is very effective in avoiding accessing unnecessary tree nodes in query processing. This also explains why PP outperforms PwP markedly.

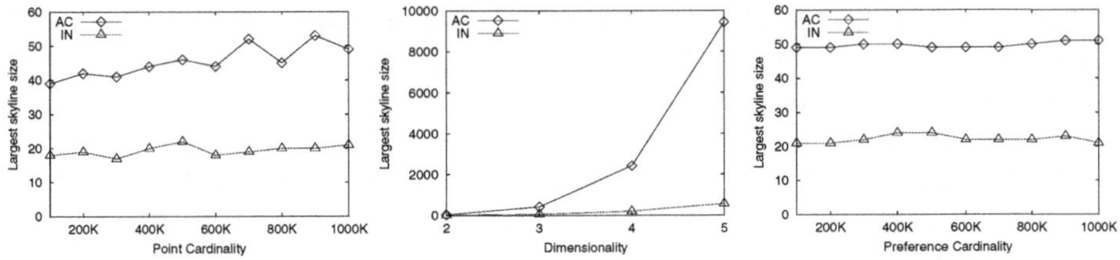


(a) Point Cardinality (b) Dimensionality (c) Preference Cardinality

**Fig. 8.** Skyline Size of the Most Influential User Preference

An interesting phenomenon is seen from Figure 6(b) and Figure 7(b), where the pruning ratio of PP decreases apparently as the dimensionality increases. The reason behind is as follows. A higher dimensionality leads to a larger skyline size for all user preferences, which makes the counting based pruning employed by PP less discriminative and thus less effective. Consequently, PP has to execute more steps in the prioritized relative skyline query processing for all user preferences, which incurs considerably more node accesses.

Sometimes it is also interesting to know the size of the skyline of the most influential user preference. Figure 8 reports such results. As expected, the skyline size is larger on AC data distributions than that on IN distributions. As dimensionality increases, referring to Figure 8(b), the skyline size increases especially on AC distributions. This is consistent with what we have observed above.

In the final experiment, we used the US hotel dataset (USH) from AllStays.com to compare our PwP and PP algorithms. After data cleaning, we had 30,918 hotel records of three attributes: *review*, *stars*, and *price*. The dataset approximately follows a correlated distribution. Each attribute was normalized to the range [0, 1]. Two thirds (20,612 records) were randomly picked as the $P$ dataset, and all others (10,306 records) formed the query points in $\Psi$ dataset.

We used different quality attribute combinations and obtained four variants of $P$ dataset: *review* and *stars* (denoted as rs), *review* and *price* (denoted as rp), *stars* and *price* (denoted as sp), and all three attributes (denoted as rsp). The corresponding $\Psi$ dataset variants were obtained similarly, except that each query point got random preference annotations on all attributes.

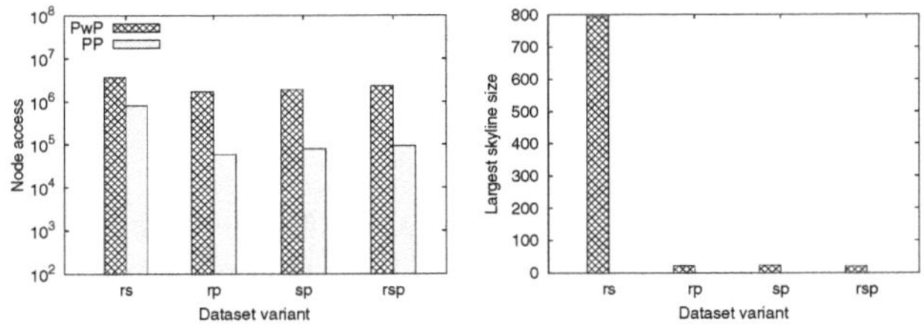


(a) Node access (b) Skyline Size

**Fig. 9.** Results on USH

The experimental results are shown in Figure 9. Figure 9(a) reports on the node access costs of PwP and PP algorithms. Due to its prioritized nature of tree node expansion and query processing, the PP algorithm outperforms the PwP algorithm on all dataset variants. Figure 9(b) reports on the size of the skyline of the most influential user preference. The significantly large skyline size on the rs dataset contributes to the corresponding relatively very high node access cost of PP seen in Figure 9(a).

## 7 Conclusion and Future Work

A relative skyline query is issued with a user preference that is the combination of a query point and a set of preference annotations on dimensions. Various user preferences are expected to be supported when relative skyline queries are to be issued. It is also interesting to identify from an assorted user preference collection the most influential preference that leads to the largest skyline. This paper offers a complete set of techniques to solve such interesting problems within a uniform framework.

As a basis, different preference annotations that can be imposed on a dimension are formalized. An effective transformation is then proposed to handle all these annotations in a uniform way. Using the transformation, the well-established BBS algorithm is neatly adapted to process relative skyline queries with assorted user preferences. Furthermore, the most influential preference query is introduced, which returns from an assorted collection of user preferences the one leading to the largest relative skyline. In order to process such novel and useful queries, two aggregation R-tree based algorithms are designed and discussed. Extensive experiments are conducted on both real and synthetic datasets. The informative experimental results demonstrate that our proposals are efficient and scalable.

Several directions for future work exist. First, it is relevant to apply the formalization of user preferences defined in this paper to existing relative dominance based reverse skyline queries [7, 9, 22]. Second, it is interesting to explore the possibility to adapt other skyline algorithms than BBS to support the user preferences and the most influential preference queries defined in this paper. Third, it is possible to define other useful query types by using the assorted user preferences defined in this paper, e.g., by applying them to the relative versions of conventional skyline query variants [5, 6, 14, 19].

## References

1. TripAdvisor, `http://www.tripadvisor.com/`
2. Balke, W.-T., Guentzer, U., Zheng, J.X.: Efficient distributed skylining for web information systems. In: Bertino, E., Christodoulakis, S., Plexousakis, D., Christophides, V., Koubarakis, M., Böhm, K., Ferrari, E. (eds.) EDBT 2004. LNCS, vol. 2992, pp. 256–273. Springer, Heidelberg (2004)
3. Bartolini, I., Ciaccia, P., Patella, M.: Efficient sort-based skyline evaluation. ACM Trans. Database Syst. 33(4) (2008)

4. Borzonyi, S., Kossmann, D., Stocker, K.: The skyline operator. In: Proc. ICDE, pp. 421–430 (2001)
5. Chan, C.-Y., Jagadish, H., Tan, K.-L., Tung, A.K., Zhang, Z.: Finding k-dominant skylines in high dimensional space. In: Proc. SIGMOD, pp. 503–514 (2006)
6. Chan, C.-Y., Jagadish, H., Tan, K.-L., Tung, A.K., Zhang, Z.: On high dimensional skylines. In: Ioannidis, Y., Scholl, M.H., Schmidt, J.W., Matthes, F., Hatzopoulos, M., Böhm, K., Kemper, A., Grust, T., Böhm, C. (eds.) EDBT 2006. LNCS, vol. 3896, pp. 478–495. Springer, Heidelberg (2006)
7. Chen, L., Lian, X.: Dynamic skyline queries in metric spaces. In: Proc. EDBT, pp. 333–343 (2008)
8. Chomicki, J., Godfrey, P., Gryz, J., Liang, D.: Skyline with presorting. In: Proc. ICDE, pp. 717–719 (2003)
9. Dellis, E., Seeger, B.: Efficient computation of reverse skyline queries. In: Proc. VLDB, pp. 291–302 (2007)
10. Godfrey, P., Shipley, R., Gryz, J.: Maximal vector computation in large data sets. In: Proc. VLDB, pp. 229–240 (2005)
11. Hjaltason, G., Samet, H.: Distance browsing in spatial database. ACM TODS 24(2), 265–318 (1999)
12. Kossmann, D., Ramsak, F., Rost, S.: Shooting stars in the sky: An online algorithm for skyline queries. In: Proc. VLDB, pp. 275–286 (2002)
13. Lee, K.C.K., Zheng, B., Li, H., Lee, W.-C.: Approaching the skyline in Z order. In: Proc. VLDB, pp. 279–290 (2007)
14. Lin, X., Yuan, Y., Zhang, Q., Zhang, Y.: Selecting stars: The k most representative skyline operator. In: Proc. ICDE, pp. 86–95 (2007)
15. Morse, M.D., Patel, J.M., Jagadish, H.V.: Efficient skyline computation over low-cardinality domains. In: Proc. VLDB, pp. 267–278 (2007)
16. Pei, J., Jin, W., Ester, M., Tao, Y.: Catching the best views of skyline: A semantic approach based on decisive subspaces. In: Proc. VLDB, pp. 253–264 (2005)
17. Papadias, D., Kalnis, P., Zhang, J., Tao, Y.: Efficient OLAP operations in spatial data warehouses. In: Jensen, C.S., Schneider, M., Seeger, B., Tsotras, V.J. (eds.) SSTD 2001. LNCS, vol. 2121, pp. 443–459. Springer, Heidelberg (2001)
18. Papadias, D., Tao, Y., Fu, G., Seeger, B.: An optimal and progressive algorithm for skyline queries. In: Proc. SIGMOD, pp. 467–478 (2003)
19. Pei, J., Jiang, B., Lin, X., Yuan, Y.: Probabilistic skylines on uncertain data. In: Proc. VLDB, pp. 15–26 (2007)
20. Tan, K.L., Eng, P.K., Ooi, B.C.: Efficient progressive skyline computation. In: Proc. VLDB, pp. 301–310 (2001)
21. Tao, Y., Xiao, X., Pei, J.: Subsky: Efficient computation of skylines in subspaces. In: Proc. ICDE, p. 65 (2006)
22. Wu, X., Tao, Y., Wong, R.C.-W., Ding, L., Yu, J.X.: Finding the influence set through skylines. In: EDBT, pp. 1030–1041 (2009)
23. Xia, T., Zhang, D.: Refreshing the sky: the compressed skycube with efficient support for frequent updates. In: Proc. SIGMOD, pp. 491–502 (2006)
24. Yuan, Y., Lin, X., Liu, Q., Wang, W., Yu, J.X., Zhang, Q.: Efficient computation of the skyline cube. In: Proc. VLDB, pp. 241–252 (2005)
25. Yiu, M.L., Mamoulis, N.: Efficient processing of top-k dominating queries on multi-dimensional data. In: Proc. VLDB (2007)
26. Zhang, S., Mamoulis, N., Cheung, D.W.: Scalable skyline computation using object-based space partitioning. In: SIGMOD Conference, pp. 483–494 (2009)

# MC-Tree: Improving Bayesian Anytime Classification

Philipp Kranen, Stephan Günnemann, Sergej Fries, and Thomas Seidl

Data management and data exploration group, RWTH Aachen University, Germany
{kranen,guennemann,fries,seidl}@cs.rwth-aachen.de

**Abstract.** In scientific databases large amounts of data are collected to create knowledge repositories for deriving new insights or planning further experiments. These databases can be used to train classifiers that later categorize new data tuples. However, the large amounts of data might yield a time consuming classification process, e.g. for nearest neighbors or kernel density estimators. Anytime classifiers bypass this drawback by being interruptible at any time while the quality of the result improves with higher time allowances. Interruptible classifiers are especially useful when newly arriving data has to be classified on demand, e.g. during a running experiment. A statistical approach to anytime classification has recently been proposed using Bayes classification on kernel density estimates.

In this paper we present a novel data structure called MC-Tree (Multi-Class Tree) that significantly improves Bayesian anytime classification. The tree stores a hierarchy of mixture densities that represent objects from several classes. Data transformations are used during tree construction to optimize the condition of the tree with respect to multiple classes. Anytime classification is achieved through novel query dependent model refinement approaches that take the entropy of the current mixture components into account. We show in experimental evaluation that the MC-Tree outperforms previous approaches in terms of anytime classification accuracy.

## 1 Introduction

Classification is one of the most frequently used data mining techniques in scientific processes. The classifier is trained on data repositories that often comprise large data bases. A common application is continuous online classification or monitoring, e.g. during a running experiment, using measured sensor data. Examples from chemistry, physics or biology include the monitoring of concentrations or mixing ratios, temperature, pressure, intensity, velocity (movement), and so forth. Rather than simply checking values against thresholds, classification using multiple measurements simultaneously can exploit correlations among attributes and build more sophisticated classifiers.

The data stream resulting from the consecutive measurements differs depending on the application. In mechanical engineering for example, one might be

M. Gertz and B. Ludäscher (Eds.): SSDBM 2010, LNCS 6187, pp. 252–269, 2010.

interested in measurements including pressure, temperature, etc. at a certain position of the piston of an engine. Taking these measurements at varying revolutions per minute results in a varying data stream, i.e. the data tuples arrive in varying time intervals (e.g. every 60 ms at 1000 rpm and every 20 ms at 3000 rpm). In chemistry or biology, measuring concentrations or movements is often done in fixed intervals. Hence, these processes yield constant data streams, where the time interval between two arriving data tuples is constant. Advanced sensors, however, only send measurements if the actual value changed resulting once again in varying data streams.

Algorithms, such as classification algorithms, traditionally had either no time limitation or they got a fixed time budget for a certain task. The budget was known in advance, i.e. they were tailored to the specific application. These budget algorithms can neither provide a result in less time nor exploit additional time to improve their result. In contrast, anytime algorithms can provide a result after a very short initialization, improve their result incrementally when more time is available and hold the most recent result ready at any time. In data mining anytime solutions have been proposed for many tasks such as clustering [13] and classification [6,8,21].

Anytime algorithms are the natural choice for varying data streams since they flexibly exploit all available time to improve the quality of their result. Recently it has been shown in [14] that also on constant data streams anytime classifiers can improve the classification accuracy over that of traditional budget approaches. With their superiority on varying and constant data streams, applications for anytime classifiers are numerous and range from science over industrial applications to robotics and health applications.

In this paper we propose a novel approach to Bayesian anytime classification called MC-Tree. It can provide a very fast first result after evaluating just one Gaussian normal distribution per class at the root level and it can improve the classification accuracy as long as time permits by refining its current model incrementally. On the finest level a kernel density estimator is evaluated for each object in the training set (database). In between, the MC-Tree stores a hierarchy of mixture models that allows effective and query adaptive anytime density estimation. The mixture components contain objects from several (potentially all) classes. During tree construction data transformations are used that take both the locality of the data and the class distribution into account. Our novel descent strategies, which exploit the entropy information available through the MC-Tree, achieve parallel model refinement for several classes. Our experiments confirm the effectiveness of the MC-Tree and show significant improvements over previous approaches in terms of anytime classification accuracy.

## 2 Related Work

Traditional classification aims at determining the class label of unknown objects based on training data. Different classification approaches are discussed in the literature including nearest neighbor classifiers [17], decision trees [18] or support vector machines [4]. Bayes classifiers constitute a statistical approach that has been successfully used in numerous application domains [2,7]. The naive Bayes classifier uses a simple model to estimate the data distribution by assuming strong statistical independence of the dimensions. Other models do not make this strong independence assumption, but estimate the density for each class by taking the dependencies of the dimensions into account. Another approach to Bayesian classification is represented by kernel density estimation [12]. Especially for huge data sets the estimation error using kernel densities is known to be very low and even asymptotically optimal [3].

Anytime classification is classification up to a point of interruption. In addition to high classification accuracy as in traditional classifiers, anytime classifiers have to make best use of the limited time available, and, most notably, they have to be interruptible at any given point in time. This point in time is usually not known in advance and may vary greatly [23]. Anytime classification has for example been discussed for decision trees [8], support vector machines [6] or nearest neighbor classification [21]. While decision trees, and often also support vector machines (SVM), provide a classification result after very short time, classification using a nearest neighbor approach (NN) might take considerably longer, especially with growing training set size. In [21] an anytime version of the NN classifier is achieved by ordering the items of the training set during the training phase and processing the items in that fixed order during classification as long as time permits. The ordering is done based on a leave-one-out cross validation on the training data, where an item is given one point if it contributes to the correct decision. Otherwise it gets subtracted $2/(m-1)$ points, where $m$ is the number of classes. Besides a recent approach to Bayesian anytime classification from [19], we compare our approach against the anytime NN from [21] as well as the decision tree and SVM implementation from Weka [22].

For Bayesian classification based on kernel densities an anytime algorithm called Bayes tree has been proposed in [19]. The Bayes tree is a balanced tree structure and is basically an extension of the R-tree [10]. It stores in each entry a pointer and a minimum bounding rectangle and additionally a cluster feature representing the corresponding subtree. In [19] one tree structure is build per class using the standard R-tree insert, i.e. no optimization is done with respect to overlapping or effectiveness in terms of density estimation. For anytime classification several heuristics are proposed that first have to determine a class, i.e. a tree (out of all trees), whose model is refined in the next step. As a consequence, for $m$ classes, $m$ steps are necessary to reach one refinement per class model.

Our novel approach takes up on the Bayes tree idea, removes its drawbacks and shows significantly better anytime classification performance. More precisely, we improve the tree construction by a top down approach that tries to optimize the construction with respect to the eventual classification task. Also, we combine all classes in one Multi-Class tree whereby we only need one step to refine all class models simultaneously. Finally we introduce novel improvement strategies that exploit the MC-tree structure by incorporating the class distribution of the mixture components into the descent decision.

## 3 The MC-Tree

Our Multi-Class Tree (MC-Tree) is a generative model that tries to find a good representation of the underlying data distribution for a classification with high accuracy. We do not analyze each class on its own, but we describe several classes simultaneously if their objects show similar characteristics. At the same time we present a data transformation approach to consider the class information. By this we reach a stronger discrimination between the classes. The structure and construction of our MC-Tree is presented in Section 3.2. Also, within the classification and refinement process, which is necessary for the anytime behavior of our algorithm, the possible mixing of classes is considered. The classification process is described in Section 3.3. Section 3.4 concludes with our novel refinement techniques for anytime classification to improve the classification accuracy.

### 3.1 Preliminaries

Given a set of classes $C$ and an object $x$ a classifier is a function $G$ that assigns to $x$ the class label $G(x)$. Based on a statistical model of the distribution of class labels the Bayes classifier assigns to an object the class $c_i$ with the highest posterior probability $P(c_i|x)$. With Bayes rule it holds:

$$G(x) = \underset{c_i \in C}{argmax}\{P(c_i|x)\} = \underset{c_i \in C}{argmax}\{P(c_i) \cdot p(x|c_i)\}$$

Estimating the class-conditional density $p(x|c_i)$ is the challenging task. One method is to assume a certain distribution of the data, e.g. a unimodal Gaussian. In general this approach yields no good representation of the true distribution. An improvement of this model is realized by the mixture of densities, i.e. a combination of several probability density functions (pdfs). In our work we use Gaussian mixture densities $p(x|c_i) = \sum_{j=1}^{k} w_j \cdot g(x, \mu_j, \Sigma_j)$ with

$$g(x, \mu_j, \Sigma_j) = \frac{1}{\sqrt{(2\pi)^d \cdot det(\Sigma_j)}} e^{\left(-\frac{1}{2}(x-\mu_j)^T \Sigma_j^{-1}(x-\mu_j)\right)}$$

where $\mu_j$ is the mean of the $j$-th Gaussian component, $w_j$ its weight and $\Sigma_j$ its covariance matrix. For a valid model the weights $w_j$ must sum up to 1. Another approach is kernel density estimation that defines an influence function for each object separately. The pdf is obtained by replacing the Gaussians $g$ with the kernels of each object. We use Gaussian kernels, i.e. $K(x) = \frac{1}{(2 \cdot \pi)^{d/2}} e^{-\frac{x^2}{2h_i}}$, where $h_i$ is the bandwidth corresponding to the variance of a Gaussian component. To set the bandwidth for our kernel estimators we use a common data independent method according to [20]. Kernel density estimation is known to perform well for traditional classification [3] and anytime classification [19].

### 3.2 Tree Structure and Construction

The general idea of our Multi-Class Tree (MC-Tree) is to store a hierarchy of mixture densities. The hierarchical structure allows us to represent data in more

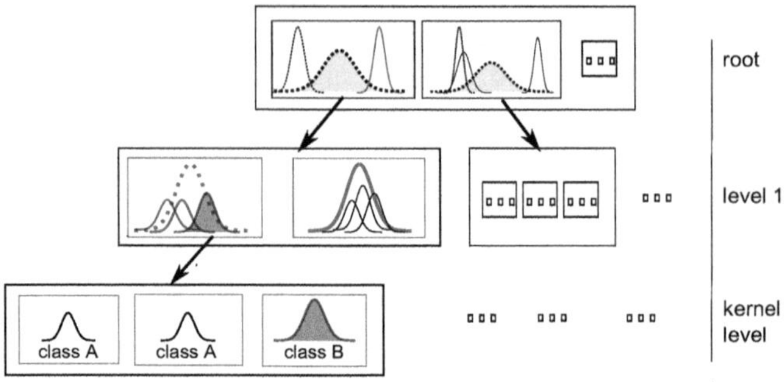


**Fig. 1.** Example of an MC-Tree. Gaussian components of an entry may represents entities from various classes.

or less detail. Figure 1 shows an exemplary MC-tree structure with three levels. The root node of the tree consists of two entries and represents the coarsest data model. The grey depicted Gaussians in these entries represent the aggregated statistical information of the points in the subtrees. They are constructed from the Gaussians in the level below. For better illustration these lower-level components are shown once again in the entries of the root node but are actually not stored twice in our MC-Tree. The Gaussians of the first level on their part are constructed from kernel based Gaussian components in the leaves, which represent the finest data model. As one can see at the left most entry in level 1, our MC-Tree permits to represent objects from different classes (A and B) in one Gaussian component. This is beneficial if the spatial similarity of the underlying objects is high and thus our model remains compact. Gaussians that comprise objects from several classes are represented by dotted lines in the figure.

Furthermore, unbalanced MC-Trees are possible. If an area of the data space needs a more detailed representation, paths can get longer than for other areas. Hence the level of detail in our object representation is adjusted to the actual data set.

Our MC-Tree consists of interlinked nodes, where each node contains a set of entries. We develop and analyze two types of entries for our MC-Tree. In the first version, we store the necessary information for calculating the mean and variance for each class contained in an entry separately. Thus if $O(e, c)$ is the set of objects from class $c$ in the entry $e$ we can derive the corresponding Gaussian. This can be done for each class in the entry individually. Furthermore we can calculate the mean and variance of the overall entry, i.e. independent to which classes the objects belong.

**Definition 1.** *MC-Tree node entry (type A)*
*Let $O(e)$ be the objects that are represented by an entry $e$ of the MC-Tree and $O(e, c) \subseteq O(e)$ the objects belonging to the class $c \in C$. The entry $e$ of type A stores the following information:*

- *A pointer to its subnode* $Sub_e$ *(set of entries)*
- *For each class* $c \in C$ *a cluster feature* $CF_c = (n_{e,c}, LS_{e,c}, SS_{e,c})$ *representing the objects* $O(e,c)$ *with their number* $n_{e,c} = |O(e,c)|$, *their linear sum* $LS_{e,c}$ *and their squared sum* $SS_{e,c}$

The algebraic measures mean and variance can be calculated out of the linear and squared sums. For class $c$ and entry $e$ we get the mean via $\mu_{e,c} = \frac{1}{n_{e,c}} \cdot LS_{e,c}$ and the variance by $\sigma_{e,c} = \frac{1}{n_{e,c}} \cdot SS_{e,c} - (\frac{1}{n_{e,c}} \cdot LS_{e,c})^2$. Accordingly, we can calculate these values for the overall entry.

In our second approach we use a technique called variance pooling. Instead of storing the squared sum for each class we only use the squared sum of all objects in the entry. By this we assume for all classes the same variance within the entry, but we use less space. Please note that the linear sum, the number of objects and hence the mean are still used for each class on its own.

**Definition 2.** *MC-Tree node entry (type B)*
*The entry* $e$ *of type B stores the following information:*

- *A pointer to its subnode* $Sub_e$ *(set of entries)*
- *For each class* $c \in C$ *a cluster feature* $CF_c = (n_{e,c}, LS_{e,c})$ *representing the objects* $O(e,c)$ *with their number* $n_{e,c} = |O(e,c)|$ *and their linear sum* $LS_{e,c}$
- *The squared sum* $SS_e$ *for all objects* $O(e)$

An *inner* node of our MC-Tree is a set of the beforehand introduced entries. As in [19] a *leaf* node of our tree is a set of kernels. Thus a kernel can be regarded as a special kind of entry that is only possible in leaf nodes. This special entry $e$ represents only one object and hence $O(e)$ is just a single object. The overall definition of our MC-Tree is:

**Definition 3.** *MC-Tree*
*Let* $DB$ *be a database of objects. An MC-Tree with a fanout of* $\theta$ *is a tree that fulfills the following properties:*

- *each inner node is a set of maximally* $\theta$ *entries (type A or B)*
- *each leaf node is a set of maximally* $\theta$ *kernels*
- *the objects* $O(e)$ *represented by an entry* $e$ *correspond to the objects of its subnode* $Sub_e$, *i.e.* $O(e) = \bigcup_{e_i \in Sub_e} O(e_i)$
- *the entries of a single node* $N$ *represent disjoint object sets, i.e.* $\forall e_i, e_j \in N: \; O(e_i) \cap O(e_j) = \emptyset$
- *the root-node* $R$ *represents the whole database, i.e.* $\bigcup_{e_i \in R} O(e_i) = DB$

*Tree construction.* With the definition of the tree structure we know how to represent a certain subset of objects. In the next step we have to determine which objects should be grouped together to get a high classification accuracy based on our MC-Tree. We use a top-down approach to divide the whole database $DB$ in smaller subsets $S_i$. For each subset one entry $e_i$ is constructed that represents the objects $S_i$. All the entries together represent an inner node of the MC-Tree.

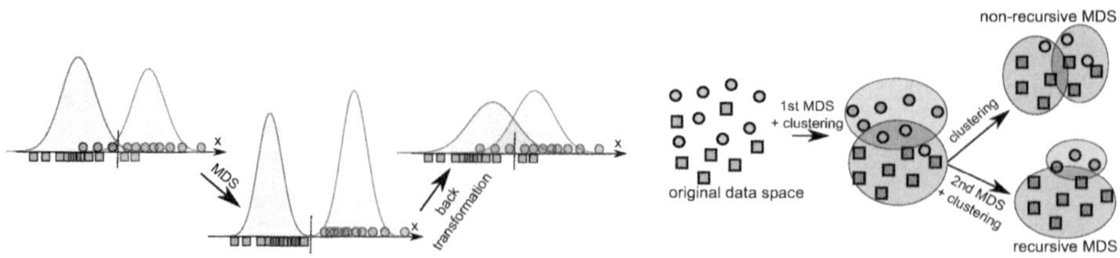


(a) Transformation for better cluster detection; Gaussians in original space

(b) Recursive vs. non-recursive MDS

**Fig. 2.** Multidimensional scaling (MDS) for class discrimination

The subsets are recursively divided in smaller subsets and hence further inner nodes are constructed until the kernel level is reached.

One aspect for a good partitioning of the objects is using their spatial order. The mixture of densities calculated from the entries should represent the underlying data distribution well. For dividing a set of objects in reasonable subsets we use the EM clustering algorithm [16]. The EM algorithm tries to represent objects with the best possible Gaussians. Similar to our approach it is a generative model, so we can directly use its clusters as our division of objects in entries. Because both models, our MC-Tree and the EM algorithm, use Gaussians to describe the data the clustering results of EM are well suited for our index construction. Other methods like the density-based clustering paradigm [9] optimize different criteria to obtain the clusters. Thus, a subsequent description of these clusters by Gaussians in our MC-Tree might result in poor results. The number of clusters used in the EM algorithm determines the branching factor of our MC-Tree (explicit branching factors are given in Section 4).

Using this clustering method, our MC-Tree is able to mix up several classes in one entry and we can achieve compact representations of the data. However, very impure clusters with respect to their class labels could result in low classification accuracy even if the underlying objects show a similar spatial relationship. In an impure cluster we cannot discriminate between the classes and thus a precise class prediction is problematic. Hence its preferable to find pure clusters with respect to their class labels if they also show good spatial compactness/similarity. The MC-Tree has to form a trade-off between pure entries with respect to the class labels and compact spatial clusters.

The EM algorithm does not consider the classes in the clustering process. It simply gets all objects neglecting their labels and hence pure clusters cannot be expected. To take care of this fact, objects from the same class must be considered as more similar than objects from different classes. Hence we use a new distance function that combines the spatial similarity of the objects and their class similarity:

$$d_\delta(x,y) = \begin{cases} \delta \cdot ||x-y||_2 & \text{if } class(x) \neq class(y) \\ ||x-y||_2 & else \end{cases}$$

where $||x-y||_2$ is the Euclidean distance between the objects $x$ and $y$ and $\delta > 1$. However, EM cannot work on arbitrary distance functions and requires a vector space.

Our approach is to transform the data space, such that the desired similarity/distance between the objects results. After the transformation the class information should also be reflected by the spatial similarity, i.e. the Euclidean distance between $x$ and $y$ in the new space is approximately the value $d_\delta(x, y)$. As an advantage, we still have a vector space on which EM can work but we also implicitly use the class information.

We make use of multi-dimensional scaling (MDS [5]) to transform the data space. MDS is a non-linear transformation technique for representing or visualizing objects in any $d$-dimensional vector space. Given the original distances between the objects, MDS iteratively tries to find a mapping into the new $d$-dimensional space such that the distances match best. In our technique we do not transform our objects to a lower-dimensional space but we use the same dimensionality as our original objects and change the distances to $d_\delta(x, y)$. Furthermore, the initial coordinates which are used for the MDS algorithm are the original coordinates of the objects. By this we keep to the most parts the original spatial structure of the objects and achieve by selective adjustments the consideration of the class information.

In Figure 2(a) (left) we see two classes (squares/circles) which are mixed together in the 1d space. Its not possible for the EM to identify pure clusters, i.e. both clusters contain squares and circles. The clusters are marked in red and blue, respectively. After transformation with $\delta > 1$ the situation in the middle is obtained, for which EM gets the two marked clusters. Keep in mind that the transformation is only performed for the detection of clusters, i.e. which subsets should be grouped together. The Gaussians of the corresponding entries in the MC-Tree are still calculated in the original space. An object to be classified (cf. Sec. 3.3) cannot be transformed because of its unknown class. The resulting clusters/entries are presented in Figure 2(a) (right). Both clusters represent only objects from one class. Hence, Gaussians could overlap in the original space if by this we get purer clusters.

We do not employ our MDS technique only once at the beginning of the tree construction, but recursively for each subtree. By application of MDS only for a subset of objects a better discrimination of the classes in further steps is possible. An example is depicted in Figure 2(b), where it is not possible to separate all objects from class 1 to those from class 2 with the first transformation. If we do not perform MDS recursively (right upper case) the clusters are still impure. However, if we apply MDS on the remaining smaller subset (right lower case), we can further discriminate the classes. Thus Gaussians which represent only objects from one class are more likely to show in higher levels of our MC-Tree with this recursive application.

With our method we can generate clusters and thus entries which account for the trade-off between compact spatial representations and pure cluster with respect to the class labels. Due to the flexibility of the MC-Tree construction we can use any other method that also considers this trade-off.

### 3.3 Classification

Given our MC-Tree we are able to perform classification of objects with unknown labels based on the mixture of densities. We distinguish two steps in the classification process which are alternately performed. First, given a mixture of models, i.e. in our MC-Tree a set of entries, we have to determine the probability of a class a novel objects belongs to. Second, to realize the anytime property, in each step we refine our mixture to get a more fine-grained model. For this we have to replace an entry with the entries in its subtree. In the following we discuss the first step, the second step is presented in Section 3.4.

Each entry represents a Gaussian, which is associated to a set of objects. Not every set of entries is a valid mixture of densities for our classification task. We have to make sure that each object in our training set is represented by exactly one Gaussian, i.e. we need a complete model. Representing objects multiple times would favor some objects in the classification process. Objects which are not represented by Gaussians consequently are not considered for the classification. We call a set of entries $\mathcal{F} = \{e_1, \ldots, e_r\}$ a frontier if it is a complete model. Formally:

**Definition 4.** *Frontier*
*Let $O(e)$ be the set of objects represented by the entry $e$ and $DB$ the whole training set. A set of entries $\mathcal{F} = \{e_1, \ldots, e_r\}$ is a frontier iff*

1. $\bigcup_{i=1}^{r} O(e_i) = DB$
2. $\forall\ e_i, e_j \in \mathcal{F} :\ O(e_i) \cap O(e_j) = \emptyset$

The idea of the frontier is demonstrated in Figure 3. In this example you see a frontier (highlighted entries) which consists of two entries in the root node, one entry in the level 1 and three kernels. Obviously the set of all entries from the root-node is a valid frontier. It corresponds to the coarsest model. The same holds for the set of all leaf nodes, which is the finest model. The example in Figure 3 shows a case in between these extremes. This frontier results from refinement of the most left entry in the root node and the most left entry in the level 1 and represent a data model where one area is represented in a higher resolution. The mentioned refinement step is discussed in the Section 3.4. Given the frontier we can calculate the density of an object with respect to one class. Keep in mind that our MC-Tree can store objects from different classes in one entry. Hence, given an entry we must use only the class-specific information.

**Definition 5.** *Probability density query pdq in MC-Tree*
*Given a frontier $\mathcal{F} = \{e_1, \ldots, e_r\}$ and a class $c$. Let $n_{e,c}$ be the number of objects from class $c$ in the entry $e$. The pdq returns the density of an object $x$ with respect to $c$ and $\mathcal{F}$, i.e.*

$$pdq(x|c, \mathcal{F}) = \sum_{e \in \mathcal{F}} \frac{n_{e,c}}{|DB|} \cdot g(x, \mu_{e,c}, \sigma_{e,c})$$

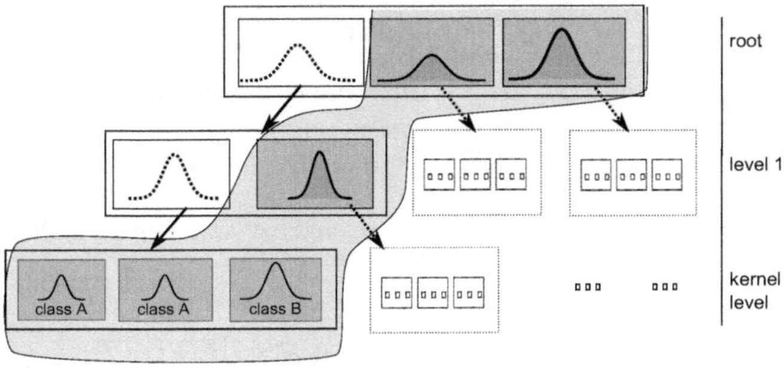


**Fig. 3.** Example of a frontier. The gray entries contribute to the current mixture model for the density estimation and can be refined in further steps.

*where* $\mu_{e,c}$ *and* $\sigma_{e,c}$ *are calculated based on the stored information within the entries (cf. Def. 1 or Def. 2).*

This is a weighted mixture of densities according to distribution of number of objects from the current class. For the leaf entries a kernel estimator is used. By our two different types of entries we have also two versions of our pdq depending on the beforehand chosen entry type.

Let $n_{c_i}$ be the total number of objects from class $c_i$ and let the a priori probability $P(c_i)$ be estimated from the training data as the relative frequency of each class. Then it holds:

$$\begin{aligned} pdq(x|c_i, \mathcal{F}) &= \sum_{e \in \mathcal{F}} \frac{n_{e,c_i}}{|DB|} \cdot g(x, \mu_{e,c_i}, \sigma_{e,c_i}) \\ &= \frac{n_{c_i}}{|DB|} \cdot \sum_{e \in \mathcal{F}} \frac{n_{e,c_i}}{n_{c_i}} \cdot g(x, \mu_{e,c_i}, \sigma_{e,c_i}) \\ &= P(c_i) \cdot p(x|c_i) \end{aligned}$$

The term $p(x|c_i)$ is a valid probability density function because the weights associated to the Gaussians sum up to 1. With our MC-Tree the class-specific weighting $P(c_i)$ is directly integrated in the pdq. According to Bayes classification the class label assigned to an object can be calculated by the rule:

$$\underset{c_i \in C}{argmax}\{P(c_i) \cdot p(x|c_i)\} = \underset{c_i \in C}{argmax}\{pdq(x|c_i, \mathcal{F})\}$$

### 3.4 Refinement

Given a frontier $\mathcal{F}$ we are able to determine the class of a new object. For anytime processing we have to generate a chain of such frontiers, starting with the coarsest model from the root, down to the leaf nodes. In each step we replace one entry $e \in \mathcal{F}$ with the entries in the subnode of $e$. By this we perform a refinement of the underlying spatial data distribution and hence a refinement of the probability density query pdq.

**Definition 6.** *Anytime pdq processing in MC-Tree*
*Given a frontier $\mathcal{F}_i$. Let $e \in \mathcal{F}_i$ and $\{e_1, \ldots, e_m\}$ the entries of the subnode of e. We refine $\mathcal{F}_i$ to $\mathcal{F}_{i+1}$ by removing e and inserting the child entries:*

$$\mathcal{F}_{i+1} = (\mathcal{F}_i \setminus \{e\}) \cup \{e_1, \ldots, e_m\}$$

*The pdq of an object $x$ with respect to a class $c$ and the new frontier $\mathcal{F}_{i+1}$ is calculated by:*

$$pdq(x|c, \mathcal{F}_{i+1}) = pdq(x|c, \mathcal{F}_i) - \frac{n_{e,c}}{|DB|} \cdot g(x, \mu_{e,c}, \sigma_{e,c}) + \sum_{i=1}^{m} \frac{n_{e_i,c}}{|DB|} \cdot g(x, \mu_{e_i,c}, \sigma_{e_i,c})$$

Calculating the new density for $x$ is based on the previous result and hence the cost is low. At the beginning of the anytime processing ($i = 1$) we initialize $\mathcal{F}_1$ to the entries of the root node. From each time step $i$ to $i + 1$ we have to decide which $e \in \mathcal{F}_i$ should be replaced. This decision is important for the performance in terms of anytime classification. If an entry with low information with respect to the current query is refined, the classification result may change only slightly but we have wasted time which could be spend for an improvement with more useful entries. We present different strategies for choosing the next entry in the following. Because we perform only local refinements during our anytime processing, it is very unlikely that we reach the leaf level for all objects in the available time. Overfitting is mitigated because we generalize huge parts of the data via aggregated information.

*Quality measure.* During our anytime processing the result is not only incrementally improved but our model is refined individually based on the current object to be classified. The classification is based on densities. A high density increases the probability of a class being selected. Hence a first approach, as presented in [19], is to refine the entry $e \in \mathcal{F}$ with the highest density to hopefully increase the density further. Doing this in our MC-Tree is not straightforward. Each entry subsumes several classes and densities of each class could vary. The question is, how to decide which entry is the best for refinement without favoring single classes. To make a fair selection, we use the density resulting from all objects by disregarding their class labels. The next entry to refine is defined by

$$\underset{e \in \mathcal{F}}{argmax}\{\frac{n_e}{|DB|} \cdot g(x, \mu_e, \sigma_e)\}$$

with the mean $\mu_e$, variance $\sigma_e$ and number of objects $n_e$ based on all objects in the entry $e$.

Similar to the tree construction this first approach only considers the spatial order of the data. During construction we had to consider the trade-off between pure clusters with respect to their class labels and the spatial similarity of the objects. A similar observation can also used for our refinement method. Consider an entry $e$ with several classes that splits up in the subtree in complete pure clusters, i.e. each sub-entry of $e$ contains only objects from one class. If we refine $e$ we can make a clear decision in the following steps and hence our accuracy could increase. This entry $e$ should be preferred to an entry whose sub-entries are still impure. Based on this intuition we need a measure that assesses the skew of the class label distribution in an entry and the possible gain if we refine it.

We use the well known information gain that is already used for decision trees [15,18]. The information gain for an entry $e$ with sub-entries $\{e_1, \ldots, e_m\}$ is defined as:

$$IG(e) = entropy(e) - \sum_{i=1}^{m} \frac{n_{e_i}}{n_e} \cdot entropy(e_i)$$

where $entropy(e)$ measures the entropy of the class label distribution in $e$:

$$entropy(e) = \sum_{c \in C} \left( -\frac{n_{e,c}}{n_e} \cdot \log \left( \frac{n_{e,c}}{n_e} \right) \right)$$

The information gain measures the reduction of the entropy, i.e. the reduction of the class label skew, if we replace the entry $e$ by the entries in its subnode. This information can be calculated before the query processing because it is independent of the actual query object $x$.

The higher the information gain the better is the refinement of $e$ with respect to the class purity of the subtree. The higher the beforehand defined density measure the better is the refinement of $e$ with respect to the spatial similarity. Both measures are important for our MC-Tree and hence we realize this trade-off by building a linear combination of these terms for our quality measure.

**Definition 7.** *Refinement quality of an entry*
*Given a query $x$ and a frontier $\mathcal{F}$. The refinement quality of an entry $e \in \mathcal{F}$ with respect to $x$ and $\mathcal{F}$ is defined as:*

$$quality_\alpha(e, x) = \alpha \cdot \frac{IG(e)}{\log |C|} + (1 - \alpha) \cdot \frac{n_e \cdot g(x, \mu_e, \sigma_e)}{\max_{w \in \mathcal{F}} n_w \cdot g(x, \mu_w, \sigma_w)}$$

We normalize both measures to the range $0 - 1$, so that a fair comparison is possible. The information gain is at most $\log |C|$ if $C$ is the set of all possible classes in our database. The user can control the influence of both measures by changing $\alpha$.

*Meta strategies.* Formally our quality measure defines a ranking of the entries in the current frontier. We select the first entry out of this ranking, i.e. the entry resulting out of

$$\underset{e \in \mathcal{F}}{argmax}\{quality_\alpha(e, x)\}$$

and we perform our refinement step. Afterwards the ranking is adapted based on the newly inserted entries and we can select the next best entry after updating our pdq. We call this method *first-best*, as in each step the best entry is refined.

One possible problem of this approach is that only a small local area around the query object is refined. We can stick to one path of refined entries, while other entries that could show a strong influence on the query in later steps are not refined. This problem is related to greedy algorithms which choose at each step the best local solution and hence can run into local optima and not resulting to a global optimal solution. To avoid this we present two further meta strategies for the selection of entries.

The *k-best* method is a direct extension of *first-best*. Instead of choosing the best entry we mark the $k$ best entries in the current frontier. While there are marked entries in the frontier we select the best out of these and perform our refinement step and pdq update. Other non-marked entries are ignored even if they show better quality values. Only when all marked entries are processed for refinement, we again consider all entries in the frontier for marking the $k$ currently best ones based on their quality measures. By this method we widen the search space because a currently second best entry is refined and can advance to a top choice for the following steps. If we set $k = 1$ we get the *first-best* method.

The *k-best* method simply chooses the $k$ best entries based on their quality measures. The method does not consider the classes within the entries which is the important characteristic of the MC-Tree. Hence for *k-best* it is possible to select $k$ entries all belonging to one class. This single class is favored in the classification process and all remaining classes are neglected. If the true class of the query object belongs to one of the neglected classes its unlikely to reach a correct classification. Therefore our last method tries to consider all classes equally within the refinement steps, i.e. in $k$ successive refinement steps we favor $k$ different classes. Similar to k-best we mark the $k$ best entries with respect to the quality measure, but now with the additional constraint that the strongest represented class of each marked entry is always different among the $k$ entries. This method is similar to the *qbk* heuristic, which yielded the best results in [19]. Formally we select for each class $c_i$ the entry with the highest quality and for which $c_i$ is also the strongest representative:

$$e^*_{c_i} = \underset{e \in \mathcal{F}}{argmax}\{quality_\alpha(e, x) \mid c_i = \underset{c \in C}{argmax}\{n_{e,c}\}\}$$

Out of the set $\{e^*_{c_i}\}_{c_i \in C}$ we mark the $k$ best entries for the next refinement steps. Note that the strongest represented class of each entry can be calculated before the actual query processing. This method, called *k-class*, accounts for different classes in each refinement step and hence our classification decision is more likely to be changed to the correct class if it is underestimated so far.

## 4 Experiments

To evaluate the performance of the MC-Tree we ran experiments on different real world data sets with varying dimensionality, cardinality and number of classes. Table 1 summarizes their characteristics (Covtype = Forest Covertype). All experiments were run on Windows machines with 3 GHz and 2 GB RAM using

**Table 1.** Data sets used in the experiments

| name | size | classes | features | ref. |
|---|---|---|---|---|
| Vowel | 990 | 11 | 10 | [11] |
| Pendigits | 10,992 | 10 | 16 | [11] |
| Letter | 20,000 | 26 | 16 | [11] |
| Gender | 189,961 | 2 | 9 | [1] |
| Covtype | 581,012 | 7 | 10 | [11] |

Java 6.0. Mostly we will use an implementation invariant time measure (as used e.g. in [21]), i.e. in the graphs we report the classification accuracy over the number of Gaussians that have been evaluated. When comparing against anytime nearest neighbor [21], SVM [22] and C4.5 [22] we report the actual time on the x-axis. Please note that our goal is to improve the accuracy of anytime Bayesian classification rather than showing statistical evidence for the superiority of one or the other classifier in different domains. We perform 4-fold cross validation on the data sets and report the average accuracy value. The tree structures are constructed once using all training data of the current fold. For updates of the trees using additional new training data one can employ the incremental insertion proposed in [19] or adapt other split strategies. Since we focus on the anytime classification performance, we do not study these aspects here. In the next section we first evaluate the influence of the parameters on the anytime classification accuracy of the MC-Tree and in Section 4.2 we show the improvement of anytime Bayesian classification that is gained through our novel approach over previous results from [19].

### 4.1 MC-Tree Parameter Evaluation

To find a good parameter setting for the MC-Tree we start by evaluating the influence of the entropy level during descent by varying the parameter $\alpha$ in Figure 4 (left). We use the *k-class* strategy because in primary experiments it performs best among all meta strategies. In addition, we use zero penalty for the MDS ($\delta = 1$) and the classification decision is based on $\mu_{e,c}$ and $\sigma_{e,c}$. The maximal number of entries in a node and hence the number of clusters for the EM algorithm is set to the number of classes in the respective data set.

We find a clear winner in the results indicating that $\alpha = 0$ yields the best results. This means that the local density of the individual Gaussian components in the frontier is sufficient to best determine the next entry for a refinement. Deprecating the importance of entries that yield a high probability density with respect to the query object by promoting other entries due to their higher entropy obviously delays beneficial model refinements and thereby reduces the anytime accuracy performance. Hence we only use the entry's probability density and set $\alpha$ to zero in the following.

In Figure 4 (right) we evaluate the influence of the penalty for the construction using MDS on the Gender data set. The purple line corresponding to $\delta = 1$

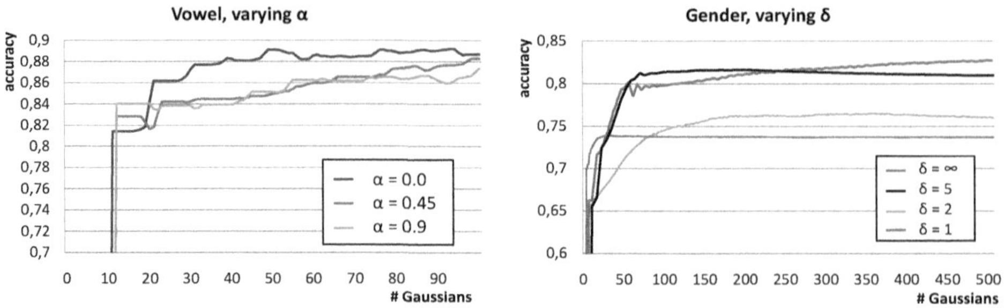


**Fig. 4.** Left: Varying the influence of entropy during descent via the parameter $\alpha$. Right: Varying the penalty for MDS construction via the parameter $\delta$.

(zero penalty) rises quickly to an accuracy of around 74%, but does not improve it afterwards. We found similar results, i.e. steep increase early on and little improvement in later stages, for most data sets when using the same parameter setting.

Increasing the penalty through a higher $\delta$ yields continuous improvement in terms of anytime accuracy. While the curve for $\delta = 1$ shows better performance for the first Gaussians that are read, the other settings can soon improve the accuracy significantly. The tree build with $\delta = \infty$ penalty shows an accuracy that is up to 9% higher for this data set. The superior performance for this setting was confirmed on the other data sets. Moreover, the stagnating behaviour disappeared throughout as will be shown in the next section.

$\delta = \infty$ constitutes a special case, since this transformation can be considered as dividing our database in subsets, such that all objects with the same class label are in the same subset. Afterwards we perform clustering only on the separated classes. Hence we do not need the actual transformation but can directly cluster in the original space on these subsets. This special case is more similar to the Bayes tree, but the resulting hierarchy is still very different due to the top down clustering instead of the balanced R-tree split as in [19]. We will see in the next section that the MC-tree shows significantly better anytime accuracy.

As a consequence of the high penalty and the resulting tree structure, all classification options provided by the different node types (cf. Def. 1 and 2) yield the same results and are therefore not displayed here.

## 4.2 Comparison: Improvement of Anytime Bayesian Classification

We compare our novel MC-Tree to a recent anytime Bayes classifier described in [19] (Bayes tree). For the Bayes tree we use the global best descent strategy and the *qbk* refinement strategy as they were reported to yield the best results. For the MC-Tree we set the fanout, i.e. the maximal number of entries per node, to the same amount as in the Bayes tree where it is dictated through the page size (2KB pages for all experiments as was used in [19]). Note that eventually the results of both approaches will be equal, i.e. if the entire leaf level has been read the decision of both classifiers is based on the same model. However, in the graphs we focus on the interesting part, i.e. the anytime performance in the beginning of the classification process. On the right hand side of the Figures we show the corresponding accuracy reached by the SVM and C4.5 implementation from Weka [22]. These methods do not constitute an anytime approach. Clearly, for each individual application there will be a best performing classifier, but no single classification approach will be the best choice for all application domains. Our goal in this paper is to improve anytime Bayesian classification, hence we focus our comparison on the Bayes tree [19].

Figure 5 (left) shows the results for the Pendigits data set. The Bayes tree performs only slightly better than the anytime nearest neighbor in the beginning before it falls behind. The MC-tree shows a steep increase in the very beginning and outperforms the other two anytime classifiers throughout. While the accuracy of the MC-tree is similar to the nearest neighbor in later stages, it quickly shows a performance gain over the Bayes tree of three to four percent accuracy. Support vector machine (SVM) and decision tree (C4.5), which are considered very fast classifiers, perform well with 97.9% and 96.3% accuracy respectively. These approaches, however, can not improve their accuracy once they computed their result while the anytime classifiers will use additional time for further computations.

Similar results can be seen for the letter data set in Figure 5 (right). For this domain C4.5 (86.8%) performs better than the SVM (81.8%). The results of the

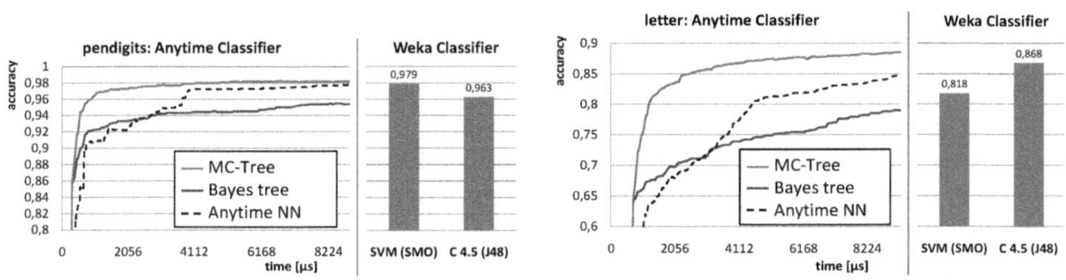


**Fig. 5.** Classification accuracy on pendigits (left) and letter (right) for anytime classifiers and static classifier

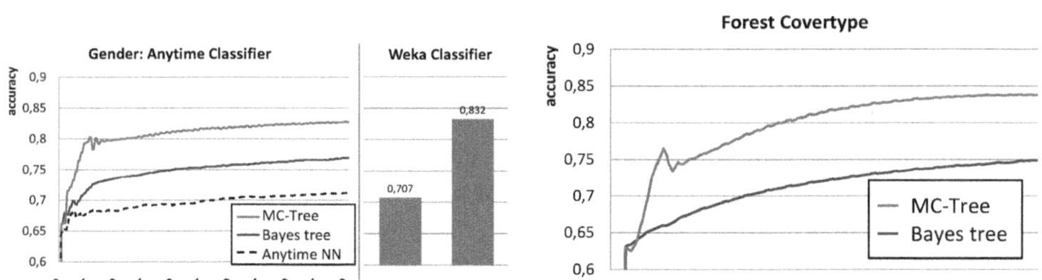


**Fig. 6.** Classification accuracy on gender (left) and Forest Covertype (right)

anytime NN and the Bayes tree are again similar, after a short time the nearest neighbor bypasses the accuracy of the Bayes tree. The MC-tree outperforms both approaches and reaches accuracy values which are up to 15% higher as compared to the Bayes tree constituting a major performance gain. Moreover, it soon reaches higher accuracy than both SVM and C4.5.

On the gender data set (cf. Figure 6 (left)) the Bayes tree shows constantly better performance than anytime NN. Once more, the MC-tree constantly outperforms both approaches by roughly 6% compared to the Bayes tree and 10% compared to anytime NN. As was the case for the letter data set, the decision tree (83.2%) reaches higher accuracy than the support vector machine (70.7%). This performance is once again met by the MC-tree after short time and additional time can be used for further improvement. More importantly, as was our mayor goal, the new concepts of the MC-tree prove to be effective through constantly better performance in comparison with the Bayes tree.

In Figure 6 (right) we show our results for the MC-tree and Bayes tree on the Forest Covertype data set. The results for the anytime nearest neighbor, SVM and C4.5 could not be computed due to memory issues. We report in this Figure the number of Gaussians that have been evaluated until classification. As stated above, the goal in this paper was to improve the performance of Bayesian anytime classifiers, which is again clearly reached in this experiment.

Theoretically, the accuracy curve of an anytime approach corresponds to a non-decreasing function. In Figure 6 we observe a slight up and down in the anytime curves for the MC-tree. Note that in both cases $k = 2$, i.e. the two most probable classes are refined in turns. Obviously the classification decision changes for some queries after each node that is evaluated. The amplitude of the oscillation indicates the percentage of queries behaving as just described. Those query points fall into a region of the data space where two classes overlap and where a correct decision is difficult to find. Refining the one class' model by reading an additional node increases its probability in that step, while in the next refinement the other class' model is refined (due to $k = 2$) and its corresponding probability prevails. However, the slight oscillation of the anytime curves does not diminish the dominance of the MC-Tree in terms of anytime accuracy.

## 5 Conclusions

Anytime algorithms and in particular anytime classification received a lot of attention over the last years. Different classification approaches are proposed in the literature which all have certain domains where they perform best. In this paper we focused on Bayesian classification and proposed a novel data structure called MC-Tree that significantly improves the anytime classification performance over previous approaches. We investigated various strategies for tree construction, descent and classification. In experimental evaluation on real world data sets we showed that the MC-Tree outperforms previous Bayesian anytime classifiers and that it improves the accuracy constantly by up to 15%.

**Acknowledgments.** This work has been supported by the UMIC Research Centre, RWTH Aachen University, Germany and the Federal Ministry of Economics and Technology on the basis of a decision by the German Bundestag.

## References

1. Andre, D., Stone, P.: Physiological data modeling contest In: ICML 2004 (2004), http://www.cs.utexas.edu/users/pstone/workshops/2004icml/
2. Bayes, T.: An essay towards solving a problem in the doctrine of chances. Philosophical Transactions of the Royal Society 53, 370–418 (1763)
3. Bouckaert, R.: Naive Bayes Classifiers that Perform Well with Continuous Variables. In: AI (2004)
4. Burges, C.J.C.: A tutorial on support vector machines for pattern recognition. DMKD Journal 2(2), 121–167 (1998)
5. de Leeuw, J.: Applications of convex analysis to multidimensional scaling. In: Recent Developments in Statistics, pp. 133–146 (1977)
6. DeCoste, D.: Anytime interval-valued outputs for kernel machines: Fast support vector machine classification via distance geometry. In: ICML, pp. 99–106 (2002)
7. Duda, R., Hart, P., Stork, D.: Pattern Classification, 2nd edn. Wiley, Chichester (2000)
8. Esmeir, S., Markovitch, S.: Anytime induction of decision trees: An iterative improvement approach. In: Proc. of the 21st AAAI (2006)
9. Ester, M., Kriegel, H.-P., Sander, J., Xu, X.: A density-based algorithm for discovering clusters in large spatial databases. In: ACM KDD (1996)
10. Guttman, A.: R-trees: A dynamic index structure for spatial searching. In: SIGMOD, pp. 47–57 (1984)
11. Hettich, S., Bay, S.: The UCI KDD archive (1999), http://kdd.ics.uci.edu
12. John, G., Langley, P.: Estimating continuous distributions in bayesian classifiers. In: UAI. Morgan Kaufmann, San Francisco (1995)
13. Kranen, P., Assent, I., Baldauf, C., Seidl, T.: Self-adaptive anytime stream clustering. In: Proc. of the 9th IEEE ICDM (2009)
14. Kranen, P., Seidl, T.: Harnessing the strengths of anytime algorithms for constant data streams. DMKD Journal, ECML PKDD Special Issue 19(2), 245–260 (2009)
15. Kullback, S.: Information Theory and Statistics. Wiley, New York (1959)
16. Lauritzen, S.: The EM algorithm for graphical association models with missing data. Comp. Statistics & Data Analysis 19, 191–201 (1995)
17. Patrick, E., Fischer, F.: A generalized k-nearest neighbor rule. Information and Control 16(2), 128–152 (1970)
18. Quinlan, J.R.: Induction of decision trees. Machine Learning 1(1), 81–106 (1986)
19. Seidl, T., Assent, I., Kranen, P., Krieger, R., Herrmann, J.: Indexing density models for incremental learning and anytime classification on data streams. In: EDBT, pp. 311–322 (2009)
20. Silverman, B.: Density Estimation for Statistics and Data Analysis. Chapman & Hall/CRC, Boca Raton (1986)
21. Ueno, K., Xi, X., Keogh, E.J., Lee, D.-J.: Anytime classification using the nearest neighbor algorithm with applications to stream mining. In: ICDM (2006)
22. Witten, I.H., Frank, E.: Data Mining: Practical machine learning tools and techniques, 2nd edn. Morgan Kaufmann, San Francisco (2005)
23. Zilberstein, S.: Using anytime algorithms in intelligent systems. The AI magazine 17(3), 73–83 (1996)

# Non-intrusive Quality Analysis of Monitoring Data

Mark Brightwell[1], Anastasia Ailamaki[2], and Anna Suwalska[1]

[1] European Organization for Nuclear Research, 1211 Geneva 23, Switzerland
[2] Ecole Polytechnique Fédérale de Lausanne, 1015 Lausanne, Switzerland

**Abstract.** Any large-scale operational system running over a variety of devices requires a monitoring mechanism to assess the health of the overall system. The Technical Infrastructure Monitoring System (TIM) at CERN is one such system, and monitors a wide variety of devices and their properties, such as electricity supplies, device temperatures, liquid flows etc. Without adequate quality assurance, the data collected from such devices leads to false-positives and false-negatives, reducing the effectiveness of the monitoring system. The quality must, however, be measured in a non-intrusive way, so that the critical path of the data flow is not affected by the quality computation. The quality computation should also scale to large volumes of incoming data. To address these challenges, we develop a new statistical module, which monitors the data collected by TIM and reports its quality to the operators. The statistical module uses Oracle RDBMS as the underlying store, and builds hierarchical summaries on the basic events to scale to the volume of data. It has built-in fault-tolerance capability to recover from multiple computation failures. In this paper, we describe the design of the statistical module, and its usefulness for all parties involved with TIM: the system administrators, the operators using the system to monitor the devices, and the engineers responsible for attaching them to the system. We present concrete examples of how the software module helped with the monitoring, configuration and design of TIM since its introduction last year.

## 1 Introduction

Monitoring the status of large numbers of devices across a scientific installation is vital to assuring the operational quality and accuracy of the experiments. The Technical Infrastructure Monitoring System (TIM) at CERN monitors hardware devices and allows the operators to control them if necessary. TIM is responsible for collecting the data from the devices, storing the values in the database, and presenting them through a graphical interface.

TIM itself requires a system to monitor its own quality. For example, a faulty device can generate many spurious events in the monitoring system to create false-positives and waste valuable operator time. Similarly, over aggressive filtering of the events can create false-negatives and consequently reducing

M. Gertz and B. Ludäscher (Eds.): SSDBM 2010, LNCS 6187, pp. 270–278, 2010.

the operator control over the devices. Since TIM may be stretched by the incoming events from the devices, the self-monitoring part of TIM should be as non-intrusive as possible and by-pass the critical path followed by the device events. It should also scale to the high volume of incoming events (≈80 million a day).

To address these challenges, we develop a *statistics module* to monitor the events entering TIM. The module monitors the filtering activity to report substantial loss of events, and reports the quality of the incoming events for each device. The module resides away from the critical path of the main data flow, so that the operators are not inconvenienced by any delay introduced by the quality computation.

The design of the database underlying this module is vital to address the scaling challenges. All incoming updates (filtered or not) are written to the database. To account for short database outages or bursts in the incoming events, the module keeps a FIFO queue of the incoming events. Several processes consume events from these queues and append them to the database. The database is horizontally partitioned by the event's origin date, and older partitions are discarded to keep the database size at a manageable level. To scale the statistics computation to the large volume of events, the module avoids using complex statistical measures, and employs several simple aggregation computations over multiple time windows. The module monitors itself, by identifying the failed aggregation jobs, and restarts the jobs on detecting a failed job. The configuration parameters are held within the database itself, allowing for easy modification of the archival settings. It is also extensible, i.e., can automatically create new aggregation summaries using the configuration parameters, as users typically change the requirements as they become more familiar with the system.

The module is now in production at CERN and is used by system administrators and engineers to monitor the performance of the system. It has already led administrators to reconsider certain aspects of the design of TIM and helps engineers tweak the configuration of the devices they are responsible for. More generally, this running implementation demonstrates the importance of a self-monitoring quality control module for achieving the full potential of any monitoring system.

The rest of the paper is organized as follows: Section 2 provides an overview of TIM, Section 3 discusses the design decisions behind the statistics module. We provide the use cases for the module in Section 4, and discuss the related work in Section 5.

## 2 The Technical Infrastructure Monitoring System (TIM)

The *Technical Infrastructure Monitoring system* (TIM) is a large-scale system currently being used to monitor a variety of infrastructure at CERN (see [2][4][6] for details on TIM). TIM is an example of a *Supervisory Control And Data Acquisition system* (SCADA) [3].

### 2.1 TIM Architecture

The devices monitored by TIM are spread across the site and very diverse in nature: temperatures, flows, the status of doors, access point procedures are all monitored by the system. Control functionality is also supported, with certain devices accepting commands sent via TIM. Figure 1 gives an overview of the TIM architecture.

The system is made up of 5 main components: the **Data Acquisition Layer** is the interface with the monitored devices (or *equipment*); a number of Java modules have been written for connecting to different kinds of hardware (e.g. Siemens PLCs). The **TIM Viewer** is the client side of the system providing a graphical interface for observing the monitored devices. The **database (Oracle)** stores both configuration data and updates received for each monitored point; in general, updates are kept for 2 weeks. The final two components are the **application server (Oracle oc4j)** and **message-oriented middleware (Sonic MQ)**.

*Quality codes in TIM:* Each monitored point in TIM has a associated quality code, reflecting the status of the currently held value and sensor. The value

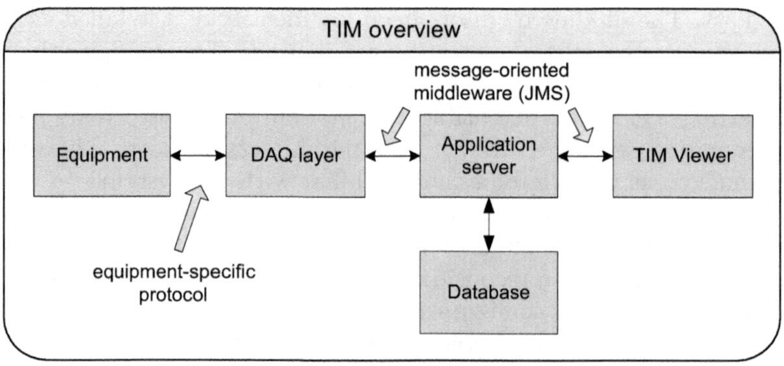


**Fig. 1.** Overview of TIM

**Table 1.** DAQ filtering mechanisms

| | |
|---|---|
| REPEATED VALUE | updates representing the same value as the previous value are filtered out |
| REPEATED INVALID | updates with the same invalid quality code as the previous value are filtered out |
| VALUE DEADBAND | for numeric values, updates inside the value deadband are filtered out (that is, the new value is too close to the current one) |
| TIME DEADBAND | if a time deadband $t$ is set, a single update will be forwarded every $t$ seconds (the most recent will be forwarded, with the others filtered out) |

will either be considered *valid*, or given one of the following invalidity codes: *uninitialised*, *inaccessible*, *value-expired*, *value-out-of-bounds*, *invalid-tag*, *value-undefined*, *unknown* (the meaning of most of these codes should be quite clear; see appendix B in [2] for further details)

*Filtering at TIM's data acquisition layer:* One particularity of TIM is that a number of filtering mechanisms are applied to the updates by the DAQ processes. Filtered updates are not forwarded to the application server and are invisible to the rest of system. There are four such filters at work: we list them in table 1, together with a brief explanation of each mechanism.

### 2.2 TIM Usage

TIM is primarily used in the CERN Control Center, where operators monitor the devices attached to the system. The operators use the monitoring system both to detect potential hazards on the CERN site, and to identify faulty equipment that needs attention. The operators are interested in the current value of a data tag, its most recent changes, and the current status of the sensor (that is, the quality of the values that are arriving, as described above).

### 2.3 TIM Shortcomings

The key purpose of TIM is *real-time monitoring* of the equipment sensor readings and the system provides ample functionality in this respect. Having said that, the original design failed to provide for any significant *monitoring of the monitoring system*. More precisely, we identify two deficiencies of the original system:

1. Firstly, no record is kept of the filtering taking place at the DAQ layer. More generally, the system provides no mechanism for monitoring the activity of the DAQ processes.
2. Secondly, no statistics on the performance of the system are readily available. In the original design, only the last 2 weeks of incoming updates are kept, and these can only be analyzed using SQL by system administrators.

These deficiencies illustrate a general lack of monitoring features in the original design. As a consequence of this deficiency, significant information, useful to both users and administrators of the system, is lost. In particular, administrators are lacking the necessary information for correctly managing the DAQ processes: there is no systematic analysis or archiving of the performance and load of the various parts of the system. Similarly, engineers are not given adequate tools for monitoring the performance of the equipment they have connected to the system: information useful for detecting equipment malfunctions and fine tuning configuration choices, is being lost (for example, indications of badly configured value deadbands). Finally, operators are deprived of useful information for detecting equipment malfunctions (for example, operators will generally fail to identify devices sending only invalid updates, since these statistics are not systematically created and accessible).

The module developed in this project seeks to address the shortcomings outlined above: a mechanism is developed for recording the filtering activity of the DAQ layer and an archival system is set up for storing, displaying and monitoring performance statistics.

## 3 Design Aspects

In this section we present an overview of the design of the new statistics module. Details of all the issues touched on below can be found in [2].

Figure 2 shows the three (sub-)modules in the design of the statistics module: the *filter module*, the *database module* and the *display module*.

The critical path up the left side is the original path taken by sensor updates in TIM; updates filtered at the DAQ layer are redirected down the newly implemented *filter path*. Implementing independent paths prevents the performance of the critical path being affected by the filtering. Both paths rely on JMS middleware for transmitting the updates. The heart of the filter path is a *Consumer process*, responsible for reading the updates from JMS and writing them to the database. The design remains highly scalable, since several Consumer processes can be started up on different machines, and extra JMS brokers can be added as needed. A number of design choices ensure that the critical path remains unaffected by failures in the filter path (see [2] for details).

The *database module* is an archival system, managing the process of summarizing the raw data arriving from the filter module using a number of aggregate functions. The database module design can be split into four layers, as illustrated in Figure 3. The first layer is made up of the raw updates received from the critical and filter paths. The second layer consists in a unique table storing counts of the different types of updates received for each tag. The third layer manages

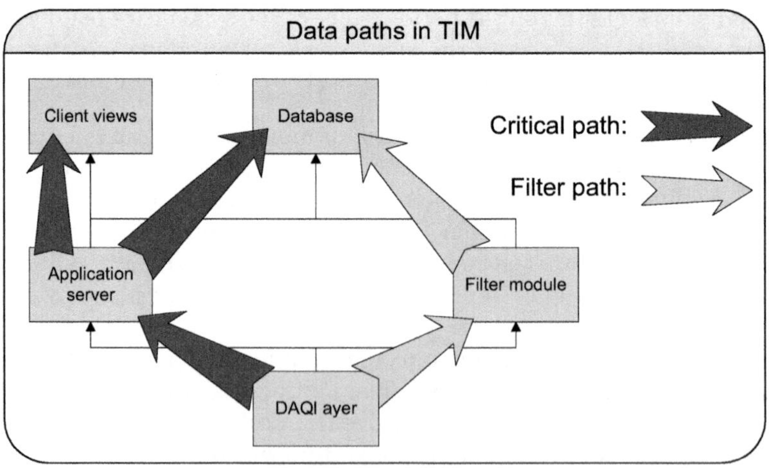


**Fig. 2.** The paths taken by sensor updates in TIM

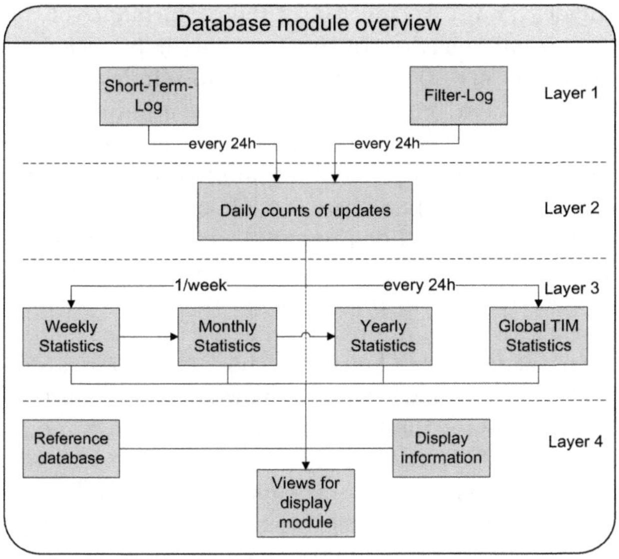


**Fig. 3.** The database module design

the longer-term storage of the information using weekly, monthly and yearly aggregations. Finally, the fourth layer is the interface to the display module, and consists of specific-format views integrating any necessary external information about the tags. The database module is optimized for dealing with large numbers of incoming updates (currently runs in operation at around 700 updates per second). It runs as an Oracle database job and the job status is always checked to restart the job in case of failures.

The *display module* manages the process of displaying the statistics in graphical form through a web interface. It accesses the database once every 24 hours to generate the required charts (specified in an XML configuration file), which can then be accessed by the web application.

## 4 Module Use Cases

The new module has now been in operation for several months at CERN. In this section, we examine how it is being used and the benefits that have been observed since its introduction. We address the perspectives of all three parties interacting with TIM: the administrators, the CERN operators and the engineers responsible for the hardware devices.

### 4.1 Administrators' Perspective

So far, the administrators of TIM are those making the most use of the features provided by the new module. They are employing it in three different ways, which we address in the paragraphs below.

Firstly, it provides a daily perspective of the performance of the system, helping identify any unusual behavior. In this way, the high-level charts provided by the module complement other standard performance indicators, such as CPU usage and load average. On arriving at their desk, the administrators are presented with the last 24 hours of data and the trend over the last few days.

Secondly, the new module presents the administrators with detailed statistics of the behavior of the DAQ processes (and hence attached devices); unusual behavior is documented and can be presented to the responsible engineers, with a view of improving the overall performance. As a concrete example, the new module has revealed that a very small number of devices (the first three out of roughly 120 attached to TIM) are responsible for the vast majority of updates, both those arriving at the DAQ layer and those being forwarded to the application server. This precise knowledge has allowed the administrators to contact the engineers responsible for these devices. It is likely that the configuration of this equipment will need reassessing. It may also prove necessary to split the DAQ processes in question into several smaller ones running on different machines. As an illustration of the charts used in this process, Figure 4 provides a breakdown of the activity of the DAQ layer over the last 24 hours: it shows the DAQs contributing the most updates to TIM, split into filtered values and values forwarded to the application server. Further examples of useful charts can be found in [2].

Thirdly, the new module is stimulating further design efforts, both to address newly-observed potential weaknesses in the system and to enhance the available monitoring information. For instance, one significant surprise when the module was put into operation was the very large proportion of values being filtered out at the DAQ layer. This has raised questions about excessive network usage by the system, since updates transit over the network from the devices to the DAQ processes. Moreover, it is now clear that a badly configured device could endanger the system as a whole, by flooding the application server. As a result, new design efforts are focusing on a *dynamic filtering mechanism*, which would pro-actively configure time deadbands on individual sensors as soon as excessive data rates are observed. The statistics module has also pushed the developers to revisit the *quality code framework*. Indeed, the statistical tool has created

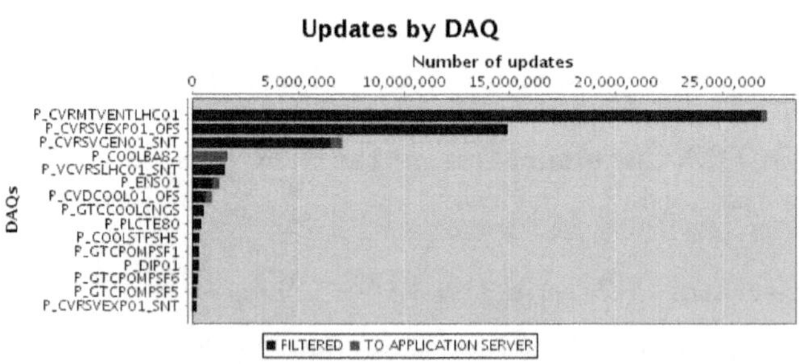


**Fig. 4.** Number of updates by DAQ (only top contributors are shown)

an interest in adding additional quality measures to the system, which could then also be monitored via the module web interface. In this way, the software is moving towards providing statistical overviews of any "data events" taking place in the system.

### 4.2 Operators' Perspective

Operators in the CERN Control Center are concerned with both identifying potential hazards on the site (through alarms for instance), and detecting faulty devices. They are currently informed of equipment malfunction by an associated "alive" signal. The new software provides additional pointers to problems in the form of an *overview* of the quality of the values received. Moreover, it can provide sensor-specific information (a device consists of a set of sensors). For example, a sensor constantly feeding values out of the acceptable range (i.e. with quality code "out-of-bounds") may indicate sensor malfunction. Other invalidity codes can be used to the same effect. A useful chart for identifying problematic devices is a ranking of sensor points according to the proportion of invalid values received. Such charts can be monitored by the operators, who are able to notify the responsible engineers.

### 4.3 Engineers' Perspective

All equipment connected to TIM must initially be configured by the responsible engineer. The configuration process consists in fixing a number of parameters for each sensor, such as intervals of valid values, or value and time deadbands. Ensuring correct configurations and the smooth connection of new equipment to TIM, is a major concern of the administrators.

Prior to this project, TIM provided feedback to the engineers on the connected devices only via the CERN operators, who detect equipment malfunction

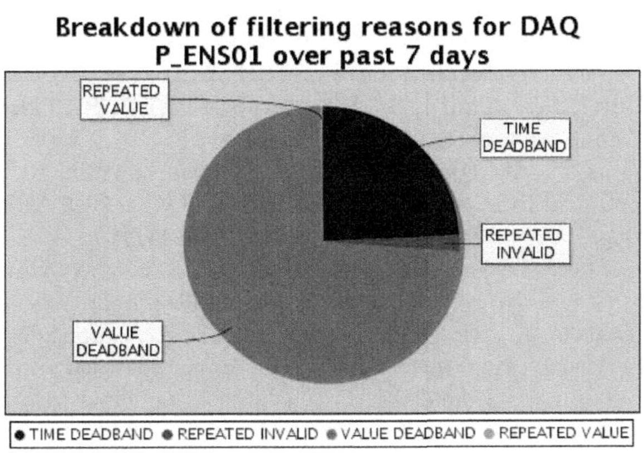


**Fig. 5.** Breakdown of filtering mechanisms over last 7 days for a DAQ

through the CERN alarm system. In addition, only standard checks were run before validating a newly configured device. With the new software, the engineers are now able to access equipment-specific charts to help them with both the configuration process and longer-term monitoring. More concretely, once the initial configuration parameters have been decided on, and the system has been running for a short period of time, the engineer is able to gain an overview of the effectiveness of his choices. Both the effect of the value and time deadbands can be measured, and the chosen min-max intervals can be given an initial assessment. For example, the chart in Figure 5 provides a breakdown of the filtering mechanisms used by a particular DAQ. The engineer can return to these charts over time and refine the configuration if necessary, as well as monitor the overall behavior of the equipment he is responsible for.

## 5 Related Work

Using statistical analysis of incoming data in establishing equipment failures is already used in the context of Supervisory Control and Data Acquisition (SCADA) systems, notably in wind turbine applications [7]. Together with fault detection, these techniques are often aimed at ensuring system security [1]. Similarly, filtering incoming data using a variety of mechanisms is a recurrent theme in the literature: see for instance [5]. As far as the authors are aware, the approach taken in this work has not been looked at before.

**Acknowledgments.** The authors would like to warmly thank Dash Debabrata (EPFL) for his help in preparing this paper.

## References

1. Bigham, J., Gamez, D., Lu, N.: Safeguarding SCADA Systems with Anomaly Detection. LNCS, pp. 171–182. Springer, Heidelberg (2003)
2. Brightwell, M.: Data acquisition statistics and filtering mechanisms for technical infrastructure monitoring. Master's thesis, Ecole Polytechnique Fédérale de Lausanne (2009), https://edms.cern.ch/document/1018821/1
3. Daneels, A., Salter, W.: What is SCADA. In: ICAPLEPCS 1999, Trieste (1999), https://accelconf.web.cern.ch/accelconf/
4. Epting, U., Ninin, P., Martini, R., Sollander, P., Vercoutter, R.B.B., Morodo, C.: CERN LHC technical infrastructure monitoring (TIM). In: ICAPLEPCS 1999, Trieste (1999), https://edms.cern.ch/document/394483/1
5. Llombart, A., Simon, W., Arancha, P., Enrique, T., Javier, R.: Robust data filtering in wind power systems. In: EWEC 2006, Athens (2006), http://www.ewec2006.info
6. Sowisek, J., Suwalska, A., Riesco, T.: Technical infrastructure monitoring at CERN. In: EPAC 2006, Luzern (2006), https://edms.cern.ch/document/750284
7. Zaher, A., McArthur, S., Infield, D., Patel, Y.: Online wind turbine fault detection through automated SCADA analysis. Wind Energy (2009), http://dx.doi.org/10.1002/we.319

# Visual Decision Support for Ensemble Clustering

Martin Hahmann, Dirk Habich, and Wolfgang Lehner

Dresden University of Technology, Database Technology Group
dbinfo@mail.inf.tu-dresden.de

**Abstract.** The continuing growth of data leads to major challenges for data clustering in scientific data management. Clustering algorithms must handle high data volumes/dimensionality, while users need assistance during their analyses. *Ensemble clustering* provides robust, high-quality results and eases the algorithm selection and parameterization. Drawbacks of available concepts are the lack of facilities for result adjustment and the missing support for result interpretation. To tackle these issues, we have already published an extended algorithm for ensemble clustering that uses soft clusterings. In this paper, we propose a novel visualization, tightly coupled to this algorithm, that provides assistance for result adjustments and allows the interpretation of clusterings for data sets of arbitrary size.

## 1 Introduction

Advanced scientific applications, e.g., gene expression analyses in biology and medical science, come with increased amounts of input data and performance requirements. This leads to two major challenges for data clustering. On the one hand, appropriate algorithms must be developed, while on the other hand, users require assistance with the application of such algorithms and the interpretation/perception of the vast data sets involved in the clustering process.

Fundamentally, clustering is defined as the problem of partitioning a set of objects into groups, so-called clusters [1,2], where objects in the same cluster are similar, while objects in different clusters are dissimilar. In order to create a clustering, the user has to complete three steps: (i) algorithm selection, (ii) algorithm execution (including parameterization), and (iii) result interpretation. Each of these steps has critical impact on the clustering process/result. The selection of the best-fitting clustering algorithm and parameters is a non-trivial task, additionally complicated by the multitude of available algorithms [2,3]. Therefore, the most common workflow for clustering in practice is found in the constant iteration over the mentioned three steps until a user-satisfying result is created. However, this iterative approach—corresponding to a 'trial and error' procedure—is tedious work and wastes time and resources.

To overcome this issue, *ensemble clustering* has been proposed [3,4,5,6]. This approach aggregates several partitionings of a data set—the cluster ensemble—into a final clustering result. The aggregate shows increased quality and robustness in comparison with the single input clusterings [3,4,5,6]. While the creation

M. Gertz and B. Ludäscher (Eds.): SSDBM 2010, LNCS 6187, pp. 279–287, 2010.

of a robust result is eased, existing methods lack instruments to enable the user to adjust/refine the obtained clustering result. Our algorithm proposed in [7] helps overcome this issue. A user is now able to modify a result, not by supplying 'technical' parameters but by choosing an intended *effect*, namely: *merge* if fewer clusters are desired or *split* if more clusters are needed.

For an effective refinement, the interpretation of the result and the derivation of corresponding adjustments are important. Our novel visualization concept proposed in this paper, which is tightly coupled with our extended ensemble clustering, assists the user in identifying the optimal *effects* for result refinement. In addition, our approach simplifies the interpretation of clustering results for data sets of arbitrary size. We start by introducing our ensemble-clustering scenario in Sec. 2. Subsequently, an in-depth description of our visualization is given in Sec. 3. In Sec. 4, we propose our software demonstration, before we end this paper with a conclusion and some remarks on future work.

## 2 Overview

The overall goal of our research project AEGIS is to enable users to conduct clustering processes in a simplified and efficient way, regardless of their background knowledge in the area of data mining. We want to achieve this goal by assisting the user during the mentioned three steps: (i) selection, (ii) execution, and (iii) interpretation. Our scenario is illustrated in Fig. 1, where two domains face each other. The *user domain* on top contains the data that is to be analyzed, the user's context knowledge about the data, and the clustering result. The *algorithm domain* at the bottom incorporates all existing algorithms for the clustering analysis, including their parameters. At the center, we find the three-step clustering cycle, during which the input data is passed to the algorithm domain for analysis, from where the clustering result is returned to the user domain for interpretation. The separated domains exemplify the average user's lack of knowledge in the area of algorithms and parameters. We have already introduced the ensemble-clustering concept as an effective way to support the

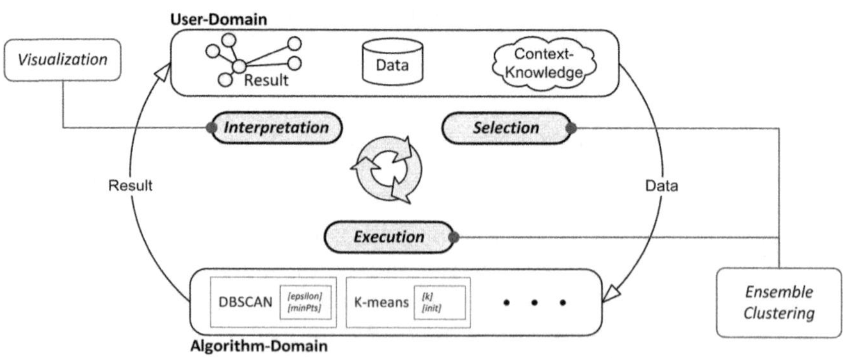


**Fig. 1.** The clustering scenario

user during algorithm selection and execution. Currently, most aggregation algorithms use a set of hard clustering results as basic input. Such hard clusterings are, e.g., obtained with k-means or DBSCAN, and they assign each object exclusively to the one cluster with the highest similarity to it. Based on this mapping, a pairwise assignment is determined for each object pair in every input clustering. Two cases of pairwise assignments are known: a pair of objects can either be located (i) in the same cluster or (ii) in different clusters. Using these assignments, the final aggregate is constructed by selecting the most frequent of both cases for each object pair and setting it in the aggregation result.

***Influence of Input.*** The major drawback of all existing aggregation approaches is their lack of controllability. Suppose an aggregate does not satisfy the user, then the user's only option for result adjustment is the modification of the input clusterings. In this case, the actual benefits regarding user support are lost, since algorithm and parameter adjustments now need to be made for a whole set of clusterings. In addition, the modified input must be re-computed, which costs time and resources, especially for large cluster ensembles. With the enhanced aggregation concept we proposed in [7], both of these issues are tackled. The key of our technique is to change the aggregation input from hard to soft clusterings. Such clusterings assign to each object its relative degree of similarity with all clusters. They can be obtained via algorithms like *FCM* [8] or via refinement techniques like the a-posteriori approach [4]. The major benefit of soft assignments is the fine-grained information about object-cluster relations they provide. This allows, for example, the identification of undecidable cluster assignments that are found if an object has the same maximal similarity to more than one cluster. This may occur in every clustering but cannot be handled by hard assignments; it is thus ignored or randomly solved, respectively.

***Flexibility of Aggregation.*** To utilize soft clusterings to the full extent, we expand pairwise assignment cases by adding an undecidable case that represents object pairs with undecidable assignments. Based on this, we propose a significance measure for pairwise assignments, including the intra-pair similarity and decidability for the respective object assignments. The range for decidability is defined as follows: zero decidability (meaning a decision is impossible) is given to objects with a maximal degree of similarity with more than one cluster. The maximum decidability is given if one of the object's degrees of similarity approaches 1 while all others approach 0. The decidability values for all objects are inside this range.

Based on our significance score, we define a filter that classifies all pairwise assignments not exceeding a certain significance threshold as undecidable. With this, actual aggregation control becomes possible. The mentioned result adjustments are achieved via such control and the handling of the undecidable pairwise assignments during aggregate construction. Since *undecidable* is no valid option for a final object assignment, we propose two handling strategies: one assumes that undecidable pairs are part of the same cluster, while the other assumes just the opposite. Our evaluation shows that these two strategies allow to merge or split clusters without modifying the original cluster ensemble, thus saving time and resources. Now, one could argue that there are still parameters burdening the user, which would normally be true, but our control parameters have a novel character. In general, the relation between parameters and the clustering result is one of cause and effect. With common 'technical' parameters like $k$ for k-means or $\varepsilon$ for DBSCAN, the user modifies the *cause* and awaits the effect regarding the cluster number and size. In our approach, the user simply chooses the desired *effect*, namely: *merge* for fewer clusters or *split* for more clusters.

Until now, merging and splitting have been mutually exclusive and had to be set for the whole clustering. This is sufficient if the bulk of clusters requires the same operation, but it effectively prevents an individual handling of clusters. In tight coupling with our extended aggregation approach, our developed visualization shall enable the user to interpret the obtained clustering and assist in the decision on whether or not clusters are stable and should be merged or split. With this, the result quality can be iteratively refined, whereas the provided support keeps the iteration count low.

## 3 Augur Visualization

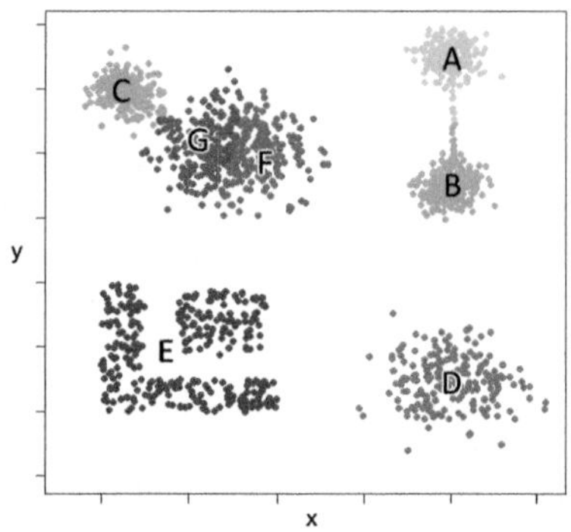


**Fig. 2.** Example aggregate

This section introduces our visualization by describing its input, its single views, the information visualized, and its interpretation. The input consists of the clustering aggregate provided by our algorithm [7], offering access to cluster centroids and sizes, soft cluster assignments, and significance scores for object pairs. From this input, additional information is computed for certain views, which will be explained during the description of the respective view. On the basis of Shneiderman's mantra, *'overview first, zoom and filter, then details-on-demand'* [9], our visualization features three views: overview, cluster composition and relations, and the attribute view. With this, we want to enable the user to determine the clusters that need no adjustment and to decide which ones should be merged or split, with the goal to improve the quality of the result. In this section, the clustering aggregate depicted in Fig. 2 is used as an example. It has been generated with ensemble clustering and its already good partitioning still needs adjustments. In all figures, clusters are identified via color.

***Overview.*** The overview is the first view presented to the user and depicted in Fig. 3. This view is completely result-driven, i.e., only characteristics of the clustering aggregate are shown. The dominant circle represents the clusters of the aggregate, whereas each circle segment corresponds to a cluster whose percental size correlates with the segment's size. The radar-like gauge located on the left shows

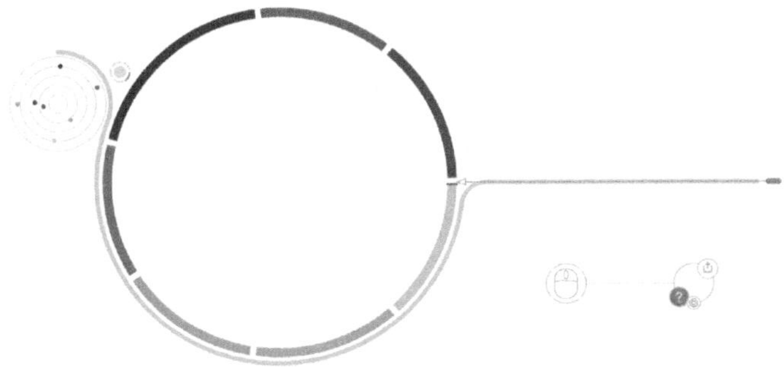

**Fig. 3.** AUGUR overview showing clusters and inter-cluster distances

the distances between the prototypes (centroids) of all clusters. The mapping between centroids in the radar and circle segment is done via color. The radar shows a distance graph, where vertices represent centroids, and edges—invisible in our visualization—represent the Euclidean distance between centroids in the full dimensional data space. Therefore, the radar is applicable for high-dimensional data. Since all our views are basically result-driven, we can also handle high-volume datasets without problems. The overview provides the user with a visual summary of the clustering result, allowing a first evaluation of the number of clusters and relations between clusters expressed by distance and size.

***Cluster Composition and Relations.*** If the user identifies clusters of interest in the overview, e.g., two very close clusters like the pink (F) and red (G) ones in Fig. 2, they can be selected individually to get more information about them, thus performing *'zoom and filter'*. Cluster selection is done by rotation of the main circle. As soon as a cluster is selected, the composition and relations (c&r) view depicted in Fig. 4 (for cluster F) is displayed. The selected cluster's composition is shown by the row of histograms on the right. All histograms feature the interval $[0, 1]$ with ten bins of equal width. From the left to the right, they show the distribution of: (i) fuzzy assignment values, (ii) significance scores for all object-centroid pairs, and (iii) significance scores for all object-object pairs in the selected cluster. For details concerning these scores, refer to [7]. Certain histogram signatures indicate certain cluster states, e.g., a stable and compact cluster is given if all three histograms show a unimodal distribution with the mode—ideally containing all objects—situated in the right-most (highest significance) bin.

Let us regard the signature of the example depicted in Fig. 4. The histograms show that many of the object-centroid and pairwise assignments are not very strong. This indicates that there are other clusters (G in the example) that strongly influence the selected cluster objects, which leaves the chance that these clusters could be merged. To support such assumptions, the relations between clusters have to be analyzed. For this, the two 'pie-chart' gauges and arcs inside the main circle are used. The smaller gauge shows the degree of 'self-assignment' of the selected cluster, while the other one displays the degree of 'shared assignment' and its distribution among the remaining clusters. These degrees are

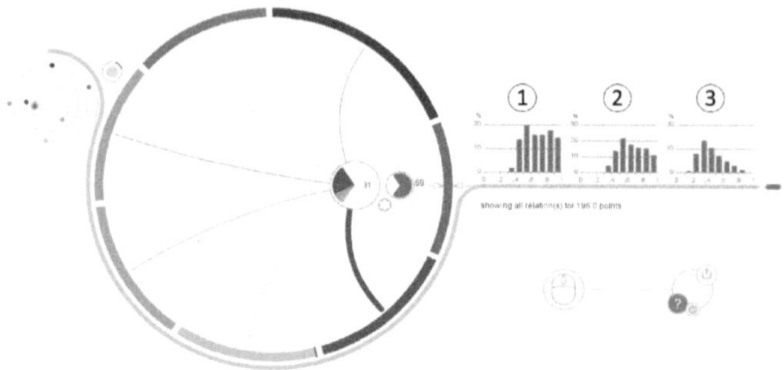


**Fig. 4.** AUGUR c&r view showing composition and relations for the pink cluster

calculated as follows: each fuzzy object assignment is a vector with a sum of 1, consisting of components ranged between 0 and 1, indicating the relative degree of assignment to a certain cluster, i.e., each vector-dimension corresponds to a cluster. The degree of self-assignment is calculated by summing up all components in the dimension corresponding to the selected cluster. This sum is then normalized and multiplied with 100 to get a percental score. The shared assignment is generated in the same fashion for each remaining cluster/dimension. The target and strength of relations between the selected cluster and others is described by the color and size of the shared-assignment slices. For easy identification, the displayed arcs show these cluster-to-cluster relations by connecting clusters, where the stroke width shows the strength of the relation.

If a cluster is not influenced by others, it shows a very high degree of self-assignment with no outstanding relations to other clusters. In contrast, the example in Fig. 4 shows that the selected cluster has a noticeable relation to the red cluster. This supports the merge assumption and furthermore indicates which other cluster should be part of a possible merge. To get additional information, the inter-cluster distances can be analyzed. For this, the user can employ the 'radar', showing that both clusters in our example are relatively close to each other (the selected cluster is encircled), or switch on additional distance indicators (*'details-on-demand'*), as shown in Fig. 5. These display the ratio of centroid-to-centroid distances—like the radar—and minimum object-to-object distances between the selected and the remaining clusters. If this ratio approaches 1, the respective clusters are well separated and the colored bars are distant. In our example, this is the case for all clusters except for the red one, where both bars nearly touch each other, showing that the minimal object distance between the clusters is much smaller than the centroid distance. With this, the user can now savely state that the pink and the red cluster should be merged. To double-check, the red cluster can be selected and should show similar relations to the pink one.

With the c&r view, it is also possible to evaluate whether or not a cluster should be split. Candidates for a split show the following: In all three histograms, the mode of the distribution is located in one of the medium-significance bins. Additionally, they feature a reduced degree of self-assignment, but in contrast to

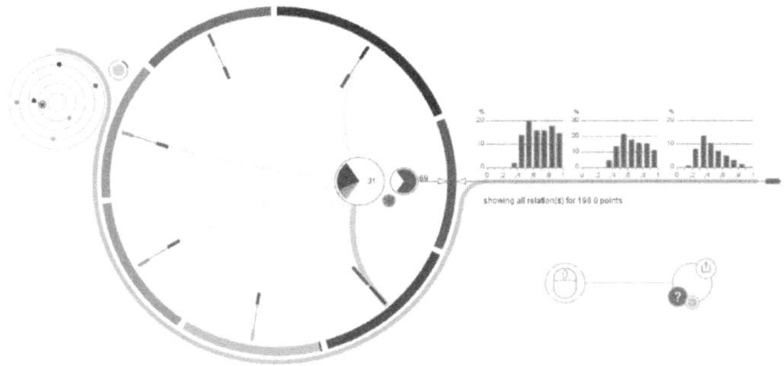

**Fig. 5.** AUGUR c&r view with activated distance indicators

the merge case, they have equally strong relations to the remaining clusters and are well separated in terms of the radar and distance indicators. Unfortunately, these characteristics are no clear indication for a split, e.g., non-spherical clusters can exhibit the same properties. To gain more certainty in decisions for split candidates, the attribute view has been developed.

***Attribute View.*** When we look at attributes in terms of clustering, we can state the following: If an attribute has a uniform or unimodal distribution (in the following $\Phi$), it is not useful for clustering because the objects of the dataset cannot be clearly separated in this dimension. In contrast, bi- or multi-modal distributions are desired, since they can be used for object separation. When we look at attributes on the cluster level, this is inverted. Regarding a cluster, it is desirable that all of its attributes have unimodal distributions, since this shows high intra-cluster homogeneity. A multimodal-distributed attribute would imply that the cluster could be further separated in this dimension. Generally, we desire the following: On the dataset level, attributes should be dissimilar to $\Phi$, while on the cluster level, they should resemble it as closely as possible. These are the basics for our attribute view.

To calculate the similarity to $\Phi$, we use a straightforward approach. We generate histograms, on the dataset and cluster level, for each attribute. From the histogram bins, those that are local maxima are selected. From each maximum, we iterate over the neighboring bins. If a neigboring bin contains a smaller or equal number of objects, it is counted and the next bin is examined; otherwise, the examination stops. With this, we can determine the maximum number of objects and bins of this attribute that can be fitted under $\Phi$. This is the value we display in the attribute view. In Fig. 6, the attribute view is depicted for the violet cluster E from our example. There are two hemispheres and a band of numbers between them. The band shows the attributes of the dataset, ordered by our computed values, and is used to select an attribute for examination (selection has a darker color). The small hemisphere on the right shows the global behavior of attributes. Each curve represents an attribute, while for the selected attribute, the area under its curve is colored. The hemisphere itself consists of two 90-degree scales, the upper for the percentage of objects and the lower for

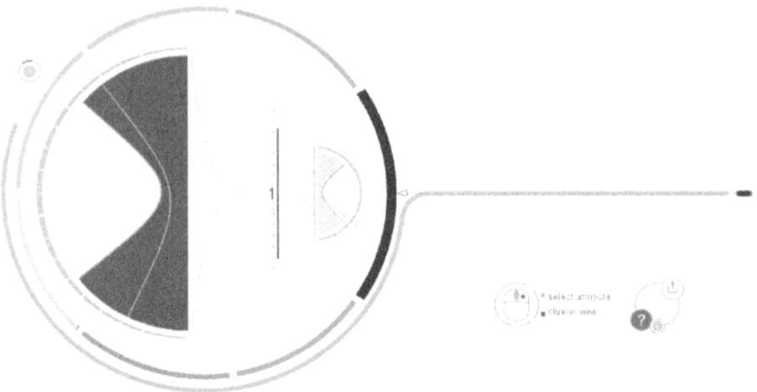

**Fig. 6.** AUGUR attribute view indicating a split for the violet cluster

the percentage of bins that can be fitted under $\Phi$. The start and end point of each curve show the values for the attribute on these scales. If all objects and bins fit under $\Phi$, a vertical line is drawn and there is no color in the hemisphere. All this also applies to the left hemisphere showing the attribute in the selected cluster. For our example in Fig. 6, we selected attribute 1.

We can see a large colored area, showing that more than 50% of the objects and bins do not fit under $\Phi$. If, in addition, the selected cluster shows split characteristics in the c&r view, the user may assume that this cluster should be split. The benefit of this view lies in the fast and easy interpretability. More color in the left hemisphere indicates a higher split possibility, while the amount of color in the right hemisphere acts as a measure of confidence for the left. In terms of Shneiderman's mantra, this view can either be considered as *'details-on-demand'* or as an *'overview'* and *'zoom and filter'* for the attribute space.

## 4 Demo Details

The demo at SSDBM comprises an in-depth explanation of all necessary concepts and the demontration of the AUGUR prototype, in which we will show how our visualization and interaction concepts, in tight combination with our flexible aggregation approach, can be used to conduct a visually-driven exploration of scientific data sets. To distinguish our work, we will try to apply some basic and well-known visualization techniques like, among others, scatterplots and parallel coordinates [10] in our described scenario and show their limitations.

We will demonstrate how non-clustering experts are able to efficiently utilize our proposed concepts to determine clustering results with high quality. For this purpose, we will prepare a set of different artificial and realistic data sets (biological domain) to show the applicability of our approach. The artificial data sets will have different degrees of complexity regarding cluster shapes, density of clusters, and outliers. With these data sets, we will simulate different tough situations for data clustering. For the demonstration of the realistic data sets, we will have results being determined by the corresponding data set owner. Using these results, we will show how we can derive the results in a non-expert-oriented way with our AUGUR prototype.

## 5 Conclusion and Future Work

In this paper, we introduced our AUGUR visualization, which focuses on enabling the user to evaluate an ensemble clustering result and on providing decision support for result refinement with our extended aggregation algorithm proposed in [7]. There already exist a multitude of cluster visualization techniques [10], which mostly try to visualize all objects of the dataset and are thus limited if data sets exceed a certain size. Furthermore, some of these techniques use complex visual concepts, which can hinder interpretation. In contrast, our visualization is tightly coupled to our aggregation method [7]. We do not try to visualize all objects of the data set but concentrate on the presentation of clusters as well as cluster-cluster and cluster-object relations, derived from soft cluster assignments. This result- and relation-oriented approach allows the interpretation of data sets with arbitrary volume/dimensionality and supports the user in making decisions concerning result refinement via the mentioned *split* and *merge* actions. In addition, focusing on *'what'* to visualize, namely clusters and relations, allows the use of well-known and simple visual elements, e.g., pie charts and histograms, when it comes to *'how'* to visualize.

Future work for our AUGUR approach includes the development and integration of a recommender system, additional views on the *details-on-demand* level, and scalability. At the moment, AUGUR can display up to 360 clusters in WXGA resolution.

## References


1. Ester, M., Kriegel, H.P., Sander, J., Xu, X.: A density-based algorithm for discovering clusters in large spatial databases with noise. In: Proc. of KDD (1996)
2. Jain, A.K., Murty, M.N., Flynn, P.J.: Data clustering: a review. ACM Comput. Surv. 31(3) (1999)
3. Jain, A., Law, M.: Data clustering: A users dilemma. In: Pal, S.K., Bandyopadhyay, S., Biswas, S. (eds.) PReMI 2005. LNCS, vol. 3776, pp. 1–10. Springer, Heidelberg (2005)
4. Zeng, Y., Tang, J., Garcia-Frias, J., Gao, G.R.: An adaptive meta-clustering approach: Combining the information from different clustering results. In: Proc. of CSB (2002)
5. Gionis, A., Mannila, H., Tsaparas, P.: Clustering aggregation. In: Proc. of ICDE (2005)
6. Strehl, A., Ghosh, J.: Cluster ensembles — a knowledge reuse framework for combining multiple partitions. Journal of Machine Learning Research 3 (2002)
7. Hahmann, M., Volk, P., Rosenthal, F., Habich, D., Lehner, W.: How to control clustering results? flexible clustering aggregation. In: Adams, N.M., Robardet, C., Siebes, A., Boulicaut, J.-F. (eds.) IDA 2009. LNCS, vol. 5772, pp. 59–70. Springer, Heidelberg (2009)
8. Bezdek, J.C.: Pattern Recognition with Fuzzy Objective Function Algorithms. Plenum, New York (1981)
9. Shneiderman, B.: The eyes have it: A task by data type taxonomy for information visualizations. In: VL 1996: Proceedings of the 1996 IEEE Symposium on Visual Languages, Washington, DC, USA, p. 336. IEEE Computer Society, Los Alamitos (1996)
10. Hinneburg, A.: Visualizing clustering results. In: Encyclopedia of Database Systems, pp. 3417–3425 (2009)

# An Indexing Scheme for Fast and Accurate Chemical Fingerprint Database Searching

Zeyar Aung and See-Kiong Ng

Institute for Infocomm Research
A*STAR (Agency for Science, Technology and Research)
1 Fusionopolis Way, #21-01 Connexis, Singapore 138632
zeyarag@gmail.com, skng@i2r.a-star.edu.sg

**Abstract.** Rapid chemical database searching is important for drug discovery. Chemical compounds are represented as long fixed-length bit vectors called fingerprints. The vectors record the presence or absence of particular features or substructures of the corresponding molecules. In a typical drug discovery application, several thousands of query fingerprints are screened for similarity against a database of millions of fingerprints to identify suitable drug candidates. The existing methods of full database scan and range search take considerable amounts of time for such a task. We present a new index-based search method called "ChemDex" (**Chem**ical fingerprint in**Dex**ing) for speeding up the fingerprint database search. We propose a novel chain scoring scheme to calculate the Tanimoto (Jaccard) scores of the fingerprints using an early-termination strategy. We tested our proposed method using 1,000 randomly selected query fingerprints on the NCBI PubChem database containing about 19.5 million fingerprints. Experimental results show that ChemDex is up to 109.9 times faster than the full database scan method, and up to 2.1 times faster than the state-of-the-art range search method for memory-based retrieval. For disk-based retrieval, it is up to 145.7 times and 1.7 times faster than the full scan and the range search respectively. The speedup is achieved without any loss of accuracy as ChemDex generates exactly the same results as the full scan and the range search.

## 1 Introduction

Chemical database searching plays a crucial role in drug discovery. A group of chemical compounds of interest for a drug are screened (searched) through a database of millions of known compounds to find similar compounds with the desired chemical properties. These compounds can then serve as candidates for the drug to be further analyzed in details. Typically, several thousands of compounds are screened routinely through chemical databases containing millions of fingerprints in developing a single drug [1].

A chemical compound can be represented in three formats: 1-dimensional fingerprint, 2-dimensional structure, and 3-dimensional structure. In the fingerprint representation, a chemical compound is encoded as a fixed-length bit vector (an array of 0's and 1's). Each bit corresponds to the presence (or absence) of a

M. Gertz and B. Ludäscher (Eds.): SSDBM 2010, LNCS 6187, pp. 288–305, 2010.

particular chemical feature such as the existence of certain type of atoms or substructures (e.g. rings). Fingerprint encoding schemes of various lengths are used in the popular chemical databases such as PubChem (881 bits) [2], ChemDB (512 or 1024 bits) [3], and Daylight (2048 bits) [4].

Comparing a pair of 1-dimensional chemical fingerprints is clearly much faster (though less detailed) than comparing a pair of 2- or 3-dimensional chemical structures. As such, screening using fingerprints is routinely used as a first-stage filtering step before going into more comprehensive analysis using 2- or 3-dimensional structures. A number of scoring schemes such as Tanimoto (also known as Jaccard), Tversky, Pearson, Dice, and Kulczynski are available [5,6] for comparing two given fingerprints. Among them, Tanimoto scoring scheme is the most popular and widely used among the chemists [6].

The time incurred for screening thousands of query fingerprints against a database of millions of chemical fingerprints can become quite considerable if each fingerprint is linearly scanned through the chemical database. For instance, while it takes only about 730 nanoseconds to retrieve and compare a single pair of fingerprints on a PC, it takes about 14 seconds to scan a single fingerprint query though the the NCBI PubChem database [2] of 19.5 million fingerprints. For 1,000 queries, it takes about 14,200 seconds (about 4 hours) if the database is to be read repeatedly for every query, and still 4,500 seconds (1 hour and 15 minutes) about even if the database is read only once for all queries. Since a total of tens or even hundreds of thousands of fingerprints may need to be screened against the database in a drug discovery exercise (sometimes interactively), it is important to keep search times to a minimum.

A number of fast search schemes [7,5,8,9,10] have been proposed to reduce the fingerprint screening time (see Section 2 for details). However, all of these methods have their limitations either in terms of accuracy or speed. Among the existing methods, Swamidass and Baldi's range search [5] is the most promising one because it achieves a sub-linear search system with a 100% accuracy.

Our objective is to further reduce the retrieval time of the state-of-the-art Swamidass and Baldi's range search without sacrificing any accuracy. In our approach, we opt to use an indexing scheme, which has been typically used for speeding up the retrievals of various kinds of databases [11].

We propose a novel indexing scheme using an early-termination strategy named "ChemDex" (**Chem**ical fingerprint in**Dex**ing) for rapid searching of chemical fingerprint database. First, we horizontally rearrange (sort) the fingerprints in the database by the total number of 1's they contain. Then, we vertically rearrange (shuffle) the bit order in each fingerprint so that the start region of the fingerprint is generally more populated with 1's than its end region. After the re-arrangements, we sub-divide the fingerprints vertically into $k$ equal-size slices. We then build a two-tier index based on the number of 1's in the whole fingerprint and its fragments in the slices.

When a new fingerprint of a chemical compound (or a family of compounds) is screened against a database, the objective is to rapidly retrieve all the previously characterized compounds contained in the database that are similar to the query within a user-specified similarity threshold based on a given similarity measure. In this work, we use the industry-standard Tanimoto score [6] to measure the similarity of the fingerprints. Given the user-specified similarity threshold, the search range (lower and upper bounds) is first established. Then, we use a slice-by-slice chain scoring scheme to filter out the unpromising answers. First, all the fingerprint fragments from the first slice within the search range are accessed, and the partial score for each fingerprint is evaluated with the help of the information in the index. For the second slice, only the fragments whose first slice's partial scores are greater than the similarity threshold are accessed. Then, the second slice's partial scores of the accessed fragments are evaluated, and only the qualifying fragments from the third slice are accessed, and so on.

Filtering the fragments slice-by-slice reduces the number of fragments being accessed as we laterally traverse the slices. The total time taken is thus significantly decreased as compared to processing fingerprints in full within the search range. We will formally prove that the partial score for each slice is the upper bound for the final score. In other words, our approach does not leave out any good answer and there is therefore no loss in accuracy with our approach to speed up the search.

As evaluation, we have conducted an experiment of searching 1,000 queries against the NCBI PubChem database [2] of about 19.5 millions fingerprints. For memory-based retrieval, where the whole database is read from disk into memory just once and maintained there throughout all queries, our proposed ChemDex scheme is up to 109.9 times faster than the full database scan, and up to 2.1 times faster than the state-of-the-art Swamidass and Baldi's range search [5] that retrieves the full-length fingerprints within lower and upper bounds. For the traditional disk-based retrieval, where the required portions of the database are read one or more times from disk into memory upon request by the program, ChemDex is up to 145.7 and 1.7 times faster than the full database scan and the range search respectively. As mentioned, ChemDex is 100% accurate as it generates exactly the same result as the full database scan and the range search.

In addition to chemical fingerprint database searching, our proposed bit vector indexing and chain scoring schemes can potentially be used in a range of other applications [12,13,14,15,16] where a large volume of fixed-length bit vectors is involved and Tanimoto score is used to compare them.

## 2 Related Works

Pairwise sequence comparison methods such as Blast [17] and index-based sequence retrieval methods such as [18] are used in the searching of DNA and protein sequence databases. These methods may be extended to cater for chemical fingerprint bit vectors when they are encoded as character sequences. However, they are primarily designed to deal with variable-length sequences rather than fixed-length ones like chemical fingerprints, and thus are not much suited to handle the latter.

The inverted index search method has been successfully used for searching the fixed-length text document vectors for information retrieval [10]. Since chemical fingerprints are also fixed-length bit vectors, one can use the inverted index search for the problem of chemical fingerprint retrieval. However, though very effective in processing the text document vectors, our experimental results shows that inverted index search performs poorly for the chemical fingerprint vectors which are relatively much denser with the number of 1's. The performance of the inverted index search for the NCBI PubChem database is reported in Section 4.

Speed is clearly a major concern when designing algorithms for searching chemical databases as we are dealing with large databases. Several researchers have proposed algorithms that traded speed for accuracy. For example, Lim *et al.* [9] suggested a search scheme using an inverted index built on the selected features in the fingerprints. While the method is faster than the full database scan, it is not 100% accurate as only limited set of features are considered. Daylight Inc. [7] has developed a lossy compression method to generate the smaller fingerprints by means of fingerprint folding. Scanning the compressed fingerprint database is faster than scanning the original database. But, this speedup is again achieved with a loss of accuracy.

Baldi *et al.* [8] proposed a lossless compression method to generate the smaller fingerprints and use them for faster database searching. Because the compression is lossless, uncompressed similarity between molecules can be computed exactly from their compressed representations. However, the retrieval time remains linear since all the compressed fingerprints in the database still need to be scanned through.

Swamidass and Baldi [5] have then invented a method that achieves a sub-linear retrieval system without any loss of accuracy. Their method reduces the search space by establishing the lower and the upper bounds of the search range. It can be applied either on the original fingerprints or the compressed ones proposed in [8,7]. Yet, even after defining the search range, the number of fingerprints to scan through still remains considerably high. In our proposed ChemDex method, we will further reduce the retrieval time of the Swamidass and Baldi's scheme without sacrificing any accuracy. The performance comparison of the two methods is given in Section 4.

# 3 Method

## 3.1 Fingerprint Similarity Measure

We use the most popular industry-standard Tanimoto (also known as Jaccard) similarity score [6] to determine the similarity of two given chemical fingerprints. Tanimoto score $S$ for two fingerprints $A$ and $B$ is calculated as:

$$S(A, B) = \frac{|A \cap B|}{|A \cup B|} \tag{1}$$

where $|A \cap B|$ is the number of 1 bits that are common to both $A$ and $B$, and $|A \cup B|$ is the number of 1 bits that occur in both or either of $A$ and $B$. For two 16-bit fingerprints $A$ and $B$ in Figure 1, their Tanimoto score $S(A, B) = 6/11 = 0.5454$. The possible range for a Tanimoto score is from 0 to 1.

```
      A = 1 0 1 0 1 0 0 1 1 1 0 1 0 0 1 1
      B = 1 0 1 1 1 1 0 0 1 0 0 1 0 0 0 1
      -----------------------------------
  A ∩ B = 1 0 1 0 1 0 0 0 1 0 0 1 0 0 0 1 =  6
  A ∪ B = 1 0 1 1 1 1 0 1 1 1 0 1 0 0 1 1 = 11
```

**Fig. 1.** Calculating Tanimoto score of two fingerprints

In real-life implementations, a bit vector is usually encoded as an array of integers. For example, a 512-bit fingerprint is encoded as an array of 16 32-bit integers. In this case, $|A \cap B|$ can be easily computed using bitwise AND operations on integers and obtaining the number of 1's by a fast bit counting method such as pre-computed bit counting [19]. $|A \cup B|$ can be simply calculated as $|A| + |B| - |A \cap B|$.

Note that in addition to chemical fingerprint comparison, Tanimoto score is also widely used to compare various types of fixed-length binary feature vectors in other applications such as data cleaning [12], all-against-all document similarity [13], stereo image matching [14], video sequence matching [15], embedded software error detection [16], etc. As such, our approach can also be potentially used for speeding up database retrieval in these applications.

### 3.2 Rearranging Fingerprints Horizontally

In the first step, we rearrange (sort) the order of fingerprints in the database according to the numbers of 1's they contain. This is achieved by an external (disk-based) sorting of fingerprints. The purpose of the horizontal rearrangement is to make the fingerprints ready to be indexed in the future (see Section 3.5). Figure 2 depicts an example of horizontally rearranging fingerprints.

### 3.3 Rearranging Fingerprints Vertically

Next, we rearrange (shuffle) the bit order of the fingerprints so that the start region of the fingerprint is generally denser with 1's than its end region. In this second step, we first count the frequency of 1's for each bit position (column), and rearrange the order of columns so that the column with the highest frequency of 1's comes first. The purpose of this vertical rearrangement is to improve the filtration power of the lower-order slices — after the database is partitioned into slices as discussed in the next section. (Vertical rearrangement is an indispensable step in our ChemDex method. Without it, the search efficiency of the method is found to be greatly reduced. However, we are not able to show the statistics here because of the space limitation.) An example of vertically rearranging bits is demonstrated in Figure 3.

### 3.4 Dividing Fingerprints into Slices

After rearranging the fingerprints both horizontally and vertically, we partition them into $k$ equal-size slices vertically. The purpose of partitioning is to enable

**Original Fingerprints**

| | | | | | | | | | | | | | | | | | No. of 1's |
|---|---|---|---|---|---|---|---|---|---|---|---|---|---|---|---|---|---|
| Fingerprint #1 | 1 | 0 | 1 | 0 | 1 | 0 | 0 | 1 | 1 | 1 | 0 | 1 | 0 | 0 | 1 | 1 | 9 |
| Fingerprint #2 | 1 | 0 | 1 | 1 | 1 | 1 | 0 | 0 | 1 | 0 | 0 | 1 | 0 | 0 | 0 | 1 | 8 |
| Fingerprint #3 | 1 | 0 | 0 | 1 | 0 | 1 | 0 | 1 | 1 | 0 | 0 | 0 | 1 | 0 | 1 | 1 | 8 |
| Fingerprint #4 | 1 | 0 | 0 | 0 | 1 | 0 | 0 | 1 | 1 | 0 | 0 | 1 | 0 | 0 | 0 | 0 | 5 |
| Fingerprint #5 | 0 | 0 | 1 | 0 | 0 | 0 | 1 | 1 | 1 | 1 | 1 | 0 | 0 | 0 | 0 | 0 | 6 |
| Fingerprint #6 | 1 | 0 | 0 | 1 | 1 | 0 | 0 | 1 | 1 | 0 | 0 | 1 | 1 | 0 | 0 | 0 | 7 |
| Fingerprint #7 | 0 | 1 | 1 | 1 | 0 | 1 | 1 | 1 | 1 | 1 | 1 | 0 | 1 | 0 | 1 | 1 | 12 |
| Fingerprint #8 | 1 | 0 | 1 | 1 | 0 | 0 | 1 | 1 | 1 | 1 | 0 | 1 | 0 | 0 | 1 | 1 | 10 |

**Horizontally Rearranged Fingerprints**

| | | | | | | | | | | | | | | | | | No. of 1's |
|---|---|---|---|---|---|---|---|---|---|---|---|---|---|---|---|---|---|
| Fingerprint #4 | 1 | 0 | 0 | 0 | 1 | 0 | 0 | 1 | 1 | 0 | 0 | 1 | 0 | 0 | 0 | 0 | 5 |
| Fingerprint #5 | 0 | 0 | 1 | 0 | 0 | 0 | 1 | 1 | 1 | 1 | 1 | 0 | 0 | 0 | 0 | 0 | 6 |
| Fingerprint #6 | 1 | 0 | 0 | 1 | 1 | 0 | 0 | 1 | 1 | 0 | 0 | 1 | 1 | 0 | 0 | 0 | 7 |
| Fingerprint #2 | 1 | 0 | 1 | 1 | 1 | 1 | 0 | 0 | 1 | 0 | 0 | 1 | 0 | 0 | 0 | 1 | 8 |
| Fingerprint #3 | 1 | 0 | 0 | 1 | 0 | 1 | 0 | 1 | 1 | 0 | 0 | 0 | 1 | 0 | 1 | 1 | 8 |
| Fingerprint #1 | 1 | 0 | 1 | 0 | 1 | 0 | 0 | 1 | 1 | 1 | 0 | 1 | 0 | 0 | 1 | 1 | 9 |
| Fingerprint #8 | 1 | 0 | 1 | 1 | 0 | 0 | 1 | 1 | 1 | 1 | 0 | 1 | 0 | 0 | 1 | 1 | 10 |
| Fingerprint #7 | 0 | 1 | 1 | 1 | 0 | 1 | 1 | 1 | 1 | 1 | 1 | 0 | 1 | 0 | 1 | 1 | 12 |

**Fig. 2.** Rearranging fingerprints horizontally

**Original Fingerprints**

| Original Bit Order | 1 | 2 | 3 | 4 | 5 | 6 | 7 | 8 | 9 | 10 | 11 | 12 | 13 | 14 | 15 | 16 |
|---|---|---|---|---|---|---|---|---|---|---|---|---|---|---|---|---|
| Fingerprint #4 | 1 | 0 | 0 | 0 | 1 | 0 | 0 | 1 | 1 | 0 | 0 | 1 | 0 | 0 | 0 | 0 |
| Fingerprint #5 | 0 | 0 | 1 | 0 | 0 | 0 | 1 | 1 | 1 | 1 | 1 | 0 | 0 | 0 | 0 | 0 |
| Fingerprint #6 | 1 | 0 | 0 | 1 | 1 | 0 | 0 | 1 | 1 | 0 | 0 | 1 | 1 | 0 | 0 | 0 |
| Fingerprint #2 | 1 | 0 | 1 | 1 | 1 | 1 | 0 | 0 | 1 | 0 | 0 | 1 | 0 | 0 | 0 | 1 |
| Fingerprint #3 | 1 | 0 | 0 | 1 | 0 | 1 | 0 | 1 | 1 | 0 | 0 | 0 | 1 | 0 | 1 | 1 |
| Fingerprint #1 | 1 | 0 | 1 | 0 | 1 | 0 | 0 | 1 | 1 | 1 | 0 | 1 | 0 | 0 | 1 | 1 |
| Fingerprint #8 | 1 | 0 | 1 | 1 | 0 | 0 | 1 | 1 | 1 | 1 | 0 | 1 | 0 | 0 | 1 | 1 |
| Fingerprint #7 | 0 | 1 | 1 | 1 | 0 | 1 | 1 | 1 | 1 | 1 | 1 | 0 | 1 | 0 | 1 | 1 |
| Frequency | 6 | 1 | 5 | 5 | 4 | 3 | 3 | 7 | 8 | 4 | 2 | 5 | 3 | 0 | 4 | 5 |

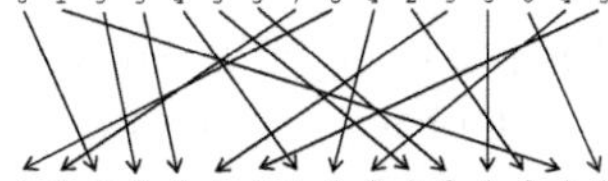

**Vertically Rearranged Fingerprints**

| | | | | | | | | | | | | | | | | |
|---|---|---|---|---|---|---|---|---|---|---|---|---|---|---|---|---|
| Fingerprint #4 | 1 | 1 | 1 | 0 | 0 | 1 | 0 | 1 | 0 | 0 | 0 | 0 | 0 | 0 | 0 | 0 |
| Fingerprint #5 | 1 | 1 | 0 | 1 | 0 | 0 | 0 | 0 | 1 | 0 | 0 | 1 | 0 | 1 | 0 | 0 |
| Fingerprint #6 | 1 | 1 | 1 | 0 | 1 | 1 | 0 | 1 | 0 | 0 | 0 | 0 | 1 | 0 | 0 | 0 |
| Fingerprint #2 | 1 | 0 | 1 | 1 | 1 | 1 | 1 | 1 | 0 | 0 | 1 | 0 | 0 | 0 | 0 | 0 |
| Fingerprint #3 | 1 | 1 | 1 | 0 | 1 | 0 | 1 | 0 | 0 | 1 | 1 | 0 | 1 | 0 | 0 | 0 |
| Fingerprint #1 | 1 | 1 | 1 | 1 | 0 | 1 | 1 | 1 | 1 | 1 | 0 | 0 | 0 | 0 | 0 | 0 |
| Fingerprint #8 | 1 | 1 | 1 | 1 | 1 | 1 | 1 | 0 | 1 | 1 | 0 | 1 | 0 | 0 | 0 | 0 |
| Fingerprint #7 | 1 | 1 | 0 | 1 | 1 | 0 | 1 | 0 | 1 | 1 | 1 | 1 | 1 | 1 | 1 | 0 |
| Rearranged Bit Order | 9 | 8 | 1 | 3 | 4 | 12 | 16 | 5 | 10 | 15 | 6 | 7 | 13 | 11 | 2 | 14 |

**Fig. 3.** Rearranging fingerprints vertically

retrieval and processing of smaller fingerprint fragments rather than the full-length fingerprints.

### 3.5 Building Index

For fast retrieval, a two-tier index is constructed. The entries in the first tier correspond to the number of 1's in the fingerprints. For an $m$-bit fingerprint, the dimension of the first tier is $m + 1$ (0 to $m$). Each entry in the first tier points to the records in the second tier having that number of 1's. Since the number of fingerprints in large databases (usually millions or more) is much larger than the number of bits in a fingerprint (hundreds to thousands), a majority of first tier entries each points to multiple records in the second tier.

Each record in the second tier contains an abstract of the information of an individual fingerprint: its ID, the number of 1's in the full-length fingerprint, and the number of 1's in the fingerprint fragments in each of its slices. The number of records in the second tier is the same as the number of fingerprints in the database. Each second tier record points to the fingerprint fragments in the slice files which are stored on disk or in memory.

On an average modern PC, both the first and the second tiers of the index for a large database (like the NCBI PubChem database of 19.5 million fingerprints) can be stored in memory. Although the second tier stores the information for every fingerprint in the database, its record size is much smaller than that of an actual fingerprint. For example, while the size of an 881-bit PubChem fingerprint is 112 bytes, the size of a second tier entry for a 2-slice partitioning is only 10 bytes, and that for a 4-slice partitioning is only 14 bytes. Thus, for the PubChem database, the size of the second tier for a 2-slice (4-slice respectively) partitioning will be 186 MB (260 MB respectively), which can be conveniently stored in a modern PC with a memory capacity of 1 GB or above.

A small example of the two-tier index with 2-slice partitioning is illustrated in Figure 4.

### 3.6 Query Evaluation

When a query fingerprint $Q$ is submitted together with a similarity threshold $t$, its bit order is rearranged in the same way as the fingerprints in the database (see Section 3.3), and it is divided into $k$ fragments as those in the database (see Section 3.4). Then, the number of 1's in it, $|Q|$, is counted, and the lower and the upper bounds of the number of 1's for the database's fingerprints to match with the query are calculated. We can compute these bounds based on the equations given in Swamidass and Baldi [5].

$$Lower(Q, t) = ceiling(|Q| \times t) \tag{2}$$

$$Upper(Q, t) = floor(|Q| \,/\, t) \tag{3}$$

For example, if the number of 1's in the query is 7 and the similarity threshold is 0.75, its lower bound is $ceiling(7{\times}0.75) = 6$, and its upper bound is $floor(7 \,/\, 0.75) = 9$. That means we only have to look at the database's fingerprints with their numbers of 1's between 6 and 9, and simply ignore the others.

Now, let us further reduce the amount of data to be accessed within the upper and the lower bounds using an early-termination approach. We propose a chain scoring scheme that incrementally calculates a fingerprint's partial score for each slice up to the final score in the last slice. If the partial score at a certain slice is less then the given similarity threshold, this fingerprint is discarded without having to access the remaining slices any further.

First, we access the fingerprint fragment from Slice #1, and calculate its partial score with the help of the information stored in the index second tier. For a query fingerprint $Q$ and a target fingerprint $F$, their partial score $S_1(Q, F)$ for Slice #1 is calculated as:

$$S_1(Q, F) = \frac{|Q_1 \cap F_1| + \sum_{j=2}^{k} \min(|Q_j|, |F_j|)}{|Q_1 \cup F_1| + \sum_{j=2}^{k} \max(|Q_j|, |F_j|)} \tag{4}$$

where $Q_1$ and $F_1$ are Slice #1's fingerprint fragments of the query and the target respectively, and $|Q_j|$ and $|F_j|$ are the number of 1's in their remaining slices $2..k$ respectively. $|Q_j|$ and $|F_j|$ can be readily obtained from the index's second tier.

Since Slice #1's partial score assumes the maximum possible matches in each of the remaining slices $2..k$, it is the upper bound of the actual final score. (We will prove this in Lemma 1.) Consequently, if a partial score of a fingerprint is less than the similarity threshold, its final score can never be greater than or equal to that threshold. This means that accuracy is maintained as we will not be losing any of the good answers. (We will prove this in Theorem 1.)

Thus, when we access the fingerprint fragments from Slice #2, only the qualified ones with their partial scores greater than or equal to the similarity threshold need to be examined. The unqualified ones can be discarded immediately without having to look at its fingerprint fragments in Slice #2 and the later slices. For the qualified ones, their Slice #2's partial scores are calculated, and the process is carried on only for those qualified ones to Slice #3, and so on. In this way, we repetitively reduce the number of fingerprint fragments to be retrieved from each slice as we laterally traverse the slices. The partial scores for the slices $2..k-1$ are calculated in the same manner as that for Slice #1.

$$S_i(Q,F) = \frac{|Q_{1..i} \cap F_{1..i}| + \sum_{j=i+1}^{k} \min(|Q_j|, |F_j|)}{|Q_{1..i} \cup F_{1..i}| + \sum_{j=i+1}^{k} \max(|Q_j|, |F_j|)} \tag{5}$$

where $2 \le i \le k-1$.

The partial score $S_k(Q,F)$ for the last slice $k$ is the essentially the final score $S(Q,F)$ of the fingerprint $F$.

$$S(Q,F) = S_k(Q,F) = \frac{|Q_{1..k} \cap F_{1..k}|}{|Q_{1..k} \cup F_{1..k}|} \tag{6}$$

Let us now prove the upper bound property of the partial scores.

**Lemma 1.** *For a query fingerprint $Q$ and a target fingerprint $F$, their partial score $S_i(Q,F)$ for any slice $i$ ($1 \le i \le k-1$, where $k$ is the total number of slices a fingerprint is partitioned) is the upper bound for the final score $S(Q,F)$.*

$$S_i(Q,F) \ge S(Q,F)$$

*Proof.* Without loss of generality, let us take $i = 1$ and look at the partial score $S_1(Q,F)$ for Slice #1.

Since the size of the intersection of two sets is at most that of the smaller set, for some non-negative integer $x_j$ ($2 \le j \le k$), we have:

$$\min(|Q_j|, |F_j|) \ge |Q_j \cap F_j| \Leftrightarrow \min(|Q_j|, |F_j|) = |Q_j \cap F_j| + x_j$$

Again, since the size of the union of two sets is at least that of the larger set, for some non-negative integer $y_j$ ($2 \le j \le k$), we have:

$$\max(|Q_j|, |F_j|) \le |Q_j \cup F_j| \Leftrightarrow \max(|Q_j|, |F_j|) = |Q_j \cup F_j| - y_j$$

We can then rewrite Equation 4 as:

$$S_1(Q,F) = \frac{|Q_1 \cap F_1| + \sum_{j=2}^{k} (|Q_j \cap F_j| + x_j)}{|Q_1 \cup F_1| + \sum_{j=2}^{k} (|Q_j \cup F_j| - y_j)}$$

$$= \frac{|Q_1 \cap F_1| + \sum_{j=2}^{k} |Q_j \cap F_j| + \sum_{j=2}^{k} x_j}{|Q_1 \cup F_1| + \sum_{j=2}^{k} |Q_j \cup F_j| - \sum_{j=2}^{k} y_j}$$

But, since $x_j$ and $y_j$ $(2 \leq j \leq k)$ are non-negative integers, we have:

$$\sum_{j=2}^{k} x_j \geq 0 \text{ and } \sum_{j=2}^{k} y_j \geq 0$$

Again, since subtracting a non-negative integer from the quotient and adding another non-negative integer to the divisor of a non-negative fractional number makes the resultant number smaller than or equal to the original number, we finally have:

$$S_1(Q,F) \geq \frac{|Q_1 \cap F_1| + \sum_{j=2}^{k} |Q_j \cap F_j|}{|Q_1 \cup F_1| + \sum_{j=2}^{k} |Q_j \cup F_j|} = \frac{|Q_{1..k} \cap F_{1..k}|}{|Q_{1..k} \cup F_{1..k}|} = S(Q,F)$$

Similarly, $S_i(Q,F) \geq S(Q,F)$ for the other slices $i = 2$ to $k-1$.

Now, we will prove the accuracy property of the filtration by the partial scores.

**Theorem 1.** *Any filtration using the partial scores* $S_i(Q,F)$ $(1 \leq i \leq k-1)$ *does not discard any good answer.*

*Proof.* Given the similarity threshold $t$, at any slice $i$, we filter out a fingerprint $F$ which satisfies the condition:

$$S_i(Q,F) < t$$

From Lemma 1 we have:

$$S(Q,F) \leq S_i(Q,F)$$

Thus, we finally have:

$$S(Q,F) \leq S_i(Q,F) \wedge S_i(Q,F) < t \Rightarrow S(Q,F) < t$$

This means if the partial score of a fingerprint is less than the similarity threshold, its final score will also be less than this threshold, and we can safely reject it. Thus, filtration using the partial scores will not discard any good answer whose final score is greater than or equal to the similarity threshold. In other words, a 100% accuracy is guaranteed.

An example of evaluating a query is demonstrated in Figure 4. The records that are accessed are highlighted in gray. The fragments for Fingerprint IDs #5, #6, #2, #3, and #1 are accessed from Slice #1, and those for Fingerprint IDs #2 and #1 are accessed from Slice #2. Only Fingerprint ID #2 is returned as the answer as its score is greater than 0.75.

Suppose the size of a full-length fingerprint is $l$ bytes. For our example, if the full database scan is used, $8l$ bytes will be processed (i.e. accessed from memory/disk and compared to the query). If the range search method [5] is used, $5l$ bytes will be processed. Using our ChemDex method, only 7 half-length fingerprint fragments of size $7 \times 0.5l = 3.5l$ bytes are processed. Thus, we have improved the speed by 8 / 3.5 = 2.29 times compared to the full database scan, and 5 / 3.5 = 1.43 times compared to the range search in this example.

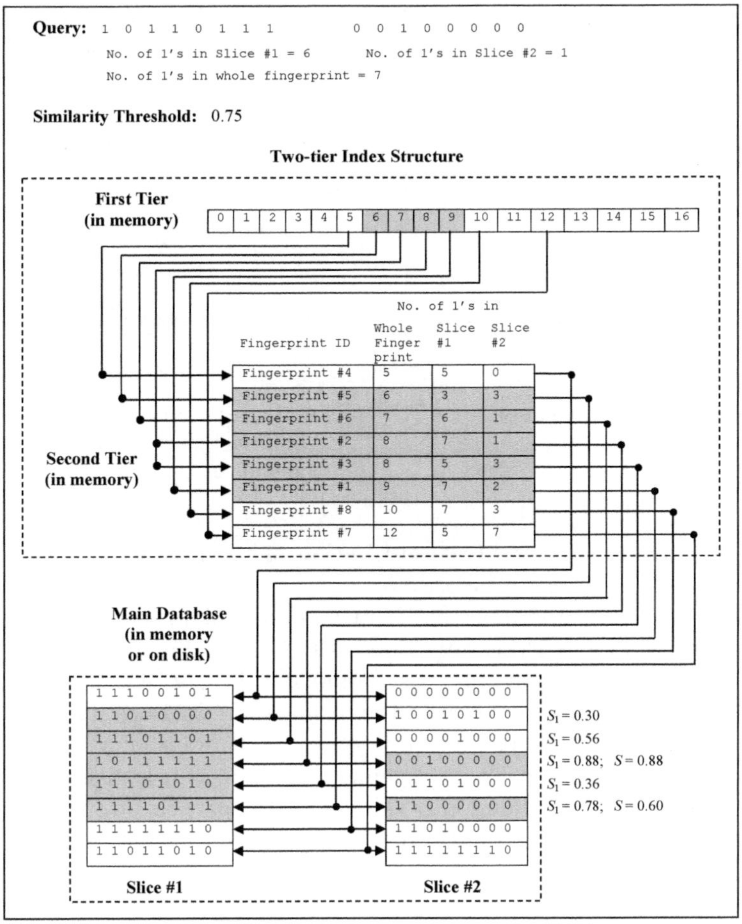


**Fig. 4.** ChemDex's two-tier index and evaluation of a query using it. The records that are accessed are highlighted in gray.

## 4 Results and Discussions

### 4.1 Experimental Setup

We use the PubChem [2] database from NCBI (National Center for Biotechnology Information, USA) downloaded in November 2008. It contains 19,501,867 (about 19.5 millions) fingerprints. The length of a fingerprint is 881 bits. We encode the fingerprint into an array of 28 32-bit integers. ($28 \times 32 = 896$. Since we only have 881 bits, the last 15 bits of the last integer are used as padding.)

The statistics of the number of 1's among the PubChem fingerprints is as follows: the minimum is 0 (i.e. some fingerprints have no 1's at all), the maximum is 290, the median is 146, the mode is 156, the mean is 139.71, and the

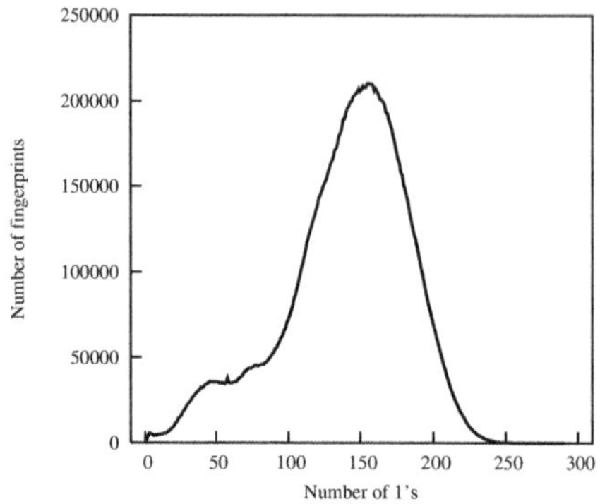


Fig. 5. Distribution of the number of 1's in the PubChem database

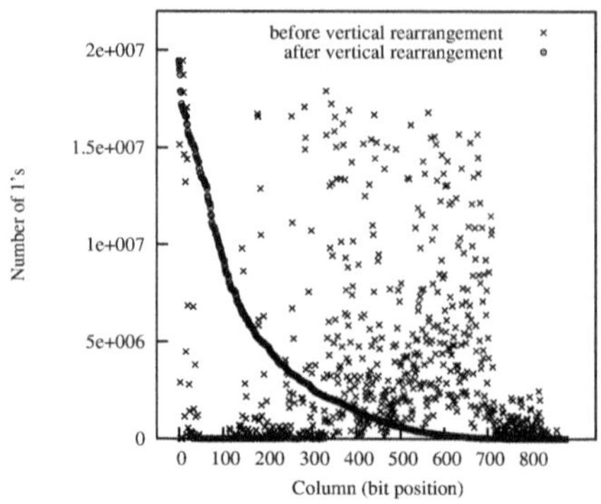


Fig. 6. Distribution of the number of 1's in columns before and after vertical rearrangement

standard deviation is 42.58. The distribution of the number of 1's in the PubChem fingerprints is given in Figure 5.

The statistics of the number of 1's in different bit positions (columns) is as follows: the minimum is 1 (i.e. only 1 out of 19,501,867 bits is set to 1 in the least populated column), the maximum is 19,450,390 (i.e. 99.74% of the bits are set to 1 in the most populated column), the mean is 3,092,714.87, and the standard deviation is 4,431,637.98. The distribution of the number of 1's in the columns before and after the vertical rearrangement (Section 3.3) is given in Figure 6.

From the database, we randomly select 1,000 fingerprints to serve as queries. As the mean of number of 1's in the query fingerprints is 138.69 and the standard deviation is 42.90, we can say that the query data set has a similar distribution of the number of 1's as the entire database.

We search these 1,000 queries against the PubChem database of 19,501,867 fingerprints using 7 different Tanimoto similarity thresholds: 1.00, 0.95, 0.90, 0.85, 0.80, 0.75, and 0.70. We do not include the similarity thresholds lower than 0.70 in our experiments. The lower thresholds are not useful for real-life drug discovery applications as they tend to generate large volumes of results which are impractical to be further analyzed in a meaningful way. For reference, the PubChem's search website [20] uses an even higher value of 0.80 as the lowest possible threshold value.

We run our experiments on a standard PC with Intel Pentium D 2.8 GHz CPU, 4 GB RAM, and 300 GB SATA2 disk drive, running the 32-bit version of Windows Vista. All the programs are written in C++ and compiled with Microsoft Visual C++ 2008 Express Edition using the maximize speed (`/O2`) optimization. We execute the programs with high system priority (using `start /high` command), and make sure that no background service such as anti-virus or Windows file indexing is running during the executions of the programs. We also make certain that every data file involved in the experiment is in a single disk fragment by using JKDefrag [21].

We will consider the problem of fingerprint database retrieval in two scenarios: memory-based and disk-based. For each scenario, we search the 1,000 query fingerprints against the PubChem database using five methods: (1) full database scan (baseline), (2) inverted index search [10], (3) Swamidass and Baldi's range search [5], (4) ChemDex with 2-slice partitioning, and (5) ChemDex with 4-slice partitioning.

## 4.2 Memory-Based Retrieval

In the memory-based scenario, we have enough memory to hold all the data file(s) that are required to evaluate the queries. When processing multiple queries as a batch, all the required data files are loaded from disk into memory only once, and are maintained there throughout the processing of all queries.

For the full database scan method, the whole PubChem database (2,083 MB) is loaded into memory. This takes an average of 9 seconds.

For the Swamidass and Baldi's range search method [5], the whole fingerprint database plus an index file indicating the the number of 1's in the fingerprints (a total of 2,194 MB) are loaded. This takes an average of 10 seconds.

For ChemDex with 2-slice partitioning, 2 half-length fingerprint fragment files plus the first tier and the second tier index files (a total of 2,269 MB) are loaded. This takes an average of 10 seconds.

For ChemDex with 4-slice partitioning, 4 quarter-length fingerprint fragment files plus the first tier and the second tier index files (a total of 2,343 MB) are loaded. This takes an average of 10 seconds.

For the inverted index search method, the size of the inverted index for the entire PubChem database is 10,394 MB, which is too big to be held in our PC with 4,096 MB (4 GB) of memory. Thus, we split the original database into 4 smaller databases of approximately equal sizes, build 4 smaller inverted indexes, load each index at a time and use it for the processing of all the 1,000 queries, and finally consolidate the results form 4 inverted indexes. The total time taken to load the four inverted indexes into memory is 47 seconds. (In fact, we have also tried variable-byte encoding [22] to compress the inverted index into 2,609 MB which can be fit into the memory. However, because of the overhead of decompression incurred when accessing the compressed index, the searching time is even longer by a factor of 1.5. We do not show the results of the compressed index for the sake of clarity.)

The running times of the five methods for this memory-based retrieval exercise are presented in Figure 7. Note that each time figure does not include the one-time cost of loading the relevant data file(s) from disk into memory. For all the five methods, care was taken such that none of the data is read more than once from disk, even in the case of the inverted index search method where we had to split the database into 4 smaller databases.

For each method, the average volume of data processed (accessed from memory and compared with their respective counterparts in the query to calculate the Tanimoto score) for a query is shown in Figure 8.

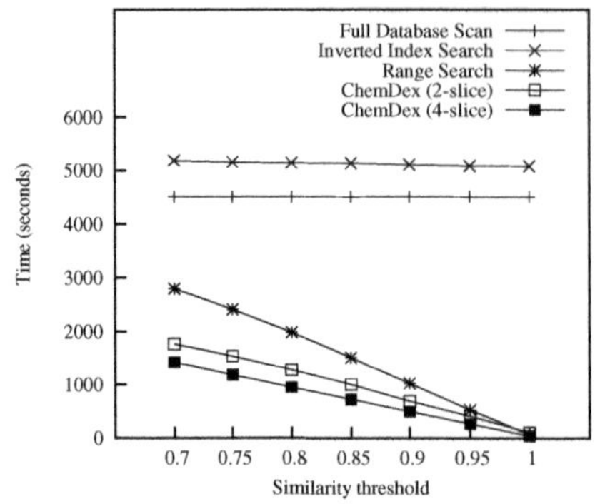


**Fig. 7.** Running times for searching 1,000 queries though the PubChem database for memory-based retrieval

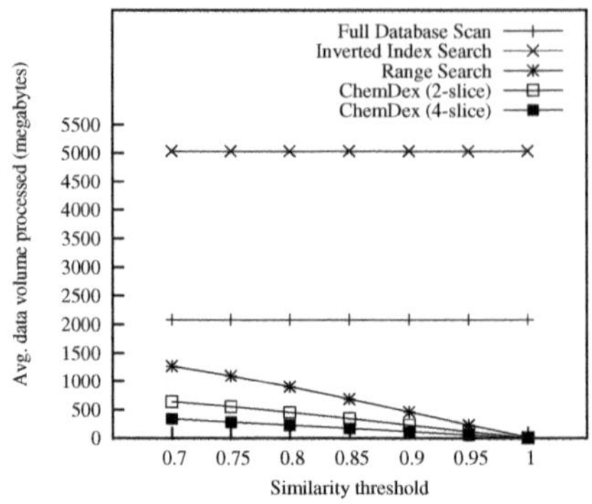


**Fig. 8.** Average volumes of data to be processed for a query

Except for the inverted index search, the distribution of the times taken for memory-based retrieval (Figure 7) is more or less proportionate to the distribution of the data volumes that is processed (Figure 8). This is because the time taken to access any fingerprint (or a fragment of it) from memory is virtually constant. As such, the 4-slice version of ChemDex gives consistently better results than its 2-slice version does, since a smaller data volume needs to be accessed and processed in the former. Therefore, the best strategy for ChemDex in memory-based retrieval is to always use the 4-slice partitioning.

When compared with the full database scan, ChemDex (4-slice version) is clearly much faster in all cases. In the best case, it is 109.88 times faster than the full scan (for the similarity threshold $t = 1.00$). In the worst case, it is still 3.18 times faster (for $t = 0.70$).

In comparison with the range search, ChemDex (4-slice version) is 2.09 times faster than it in the best case (for $t = 0.80$), and still 1.66 time faster than it (for $t = 1.00$) in the worst case.

In relation to the inverted index search, ChemDex (4-slice version) is 123.93 times faster than it in the best case (for $t = 1.00$), and still 3.65 time faster than it (for $t = 0.70$) in the worst case.

It is interesting to learn here that the performance of the inverted index search is even worse than that of the full database scan. While inverted index search was reported to perform well in other areas like text database retrieval [10], our experiments have revealed it to be unsuitable for the task of chemical fingerprint retrieval. This is due to the relatively dense nature of the chemical fingerprints. The average density of 1's in PubChem's fingerprints with respect to their length is $139.71/\ 881 = 0.1586 = 15.86\%$, whereas the average densities of the document vectors in text databases are normally much lower (for example 0.86% for MEDLINE medical abstract database and 1.82% for Time Magazine's news abstract database [23]). Thus, a large volume of information needs to be accessed from all the inverted lists corresponding to the 1's in the query. For one query,

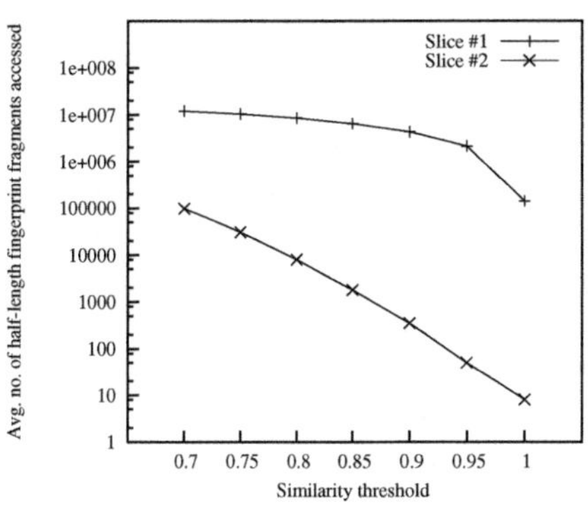


**Fig. 9.** Average number of half-length fingerprint fragments accessed from Slices #1 and #2 in 2-slice version of ChemDex

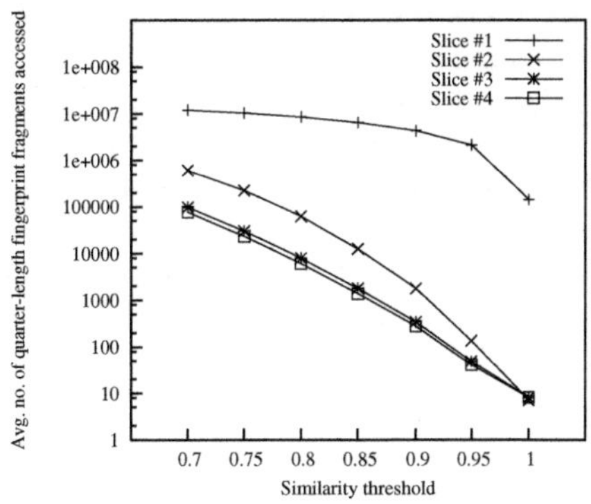


**Fig. 10.** Average number of quarter-length fingerprint fragments accessed from Slices #1, #2, #3 and #4 in 4-slice version of ChemDex

the average amount of inverted list information required to be accessed from memory is 5,035 MB, which is 2.4 times of the 2,083 MB fingerprint information needed to be accessed for the full database scan (The overall difference in their running times is less than 2.4 times because the full database scan involves a relatively expensive operation of bit counting, whereas the inverted index search does not.)

Let us investigate the filtration power of ChemDex. Figures 9 and 10 show the average numbers of half-length and quarter-length fingerprint fragments accessed from the different slices for the 2-slice and the 4-slice versions of ChemDex respectively (do note that the Y-axis in each figure is in log-scale). It can be observed in Figure 9 that the number of fingerprint fragments accessed from Slice #2 is only a small fraction of that of Slice #1. This means that a large number disqualified fingerprints have been filtered out from the processing of Slice #1. Similarly, the numbers of fragments accessed from Slice #2, #3, #4 are only small fractions of that of Slice #1 in Figure 10. As a result, the total volumes of data required to be accessed by ChemDex (both for 2-slice and 4-slice versions) is much lower that of Swamidass and Baldi's range search which needs to access all the full-length fingerprints within the specified search range.

### 4.3 Disk-Based Retrieval

Since the size of a chemical database can potentially grow up to $10^{60}$ compounds [24], it is possible in the future that the growth of the database size outpaces the amount of memory that is generally affordable. When the size of the database becomes too large to fit into memory, we have to employ a traditional disk-based retrieval approach. In disk-based retrieval, all the data file(s) are primarily stored on disk, and only the required pieces of data are read from disk into memory as requested by the program. For example, in the full database scan, for a particular query, a database fingerprint at a time is read from disk into memory to compare with the query. For another query, the same fingerprint will have to be read again from disk.

In addition to the limited memory situation, the disk-based scenario is also applicable to a situation in which queries are necessary to be processed one-by-one due to their different arrival times (as opposed to the batch processing of the queries as discussed in the above Section 4.2). This is particularly important if the fingerprint database search program is to be run on a general office PC or laptop rather than on a dedicated server. It is obviously not desirable to hold a large database in memory when not in use, since this can adversely affect the performances of the other applications running on the same machine.

Their running times the four different methods are presented in Figure 11. (The result of the inverted index search again turns out to be even worse than that of the full database scan, and hence is excluded for the sake of clarity.)

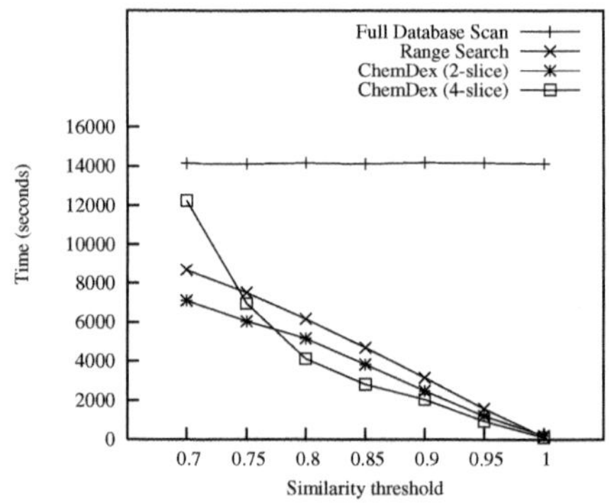


**Fig. 11.** Running times for searching 1,000 queries though the PubChem database for disk-based retrieval

ChemDex achieves the best results using the 4-slice partitioning for the similarity thresholds of 0.80–1.00, and with the 2-slice partitioning for the thresholds of 0.70–0.75. Thus, the optimization of ChemDex for the disk-based retrieval can be achieved by keeping the indexes and database files for both the 2-slice and the 4-slice versions, and using the 2-slice one if the user-specified similarity threshold is less than 0.8, and the 4-slice one otherwise.

ChemDex, using the above optimization, is clearly much faster the full database scan in all cases. In the best case, it is 145.71 times faster than the full scan (for the similarity threshold $t = 1.00$). In the worst case, it is still 1.99 times faster (for $t = 0.70$).

In comparison with the range search, ChemDex (using the optimization) is 1.69 times faster than it in the best case (for $t = 0.95$), and still 1.22 times faster than it (for $t = 0.70$) in the worst case.

It can be noticed from Figure 8 that the volume of data to be processed for ChemDex (for both the 2-slice and 4-slice versions) is much lower than that of the range search. However, unlike memory-based retrieval, the time incurred in processing the data here is not as proportionately reduced. (Compare Figure 8 with Figure 11.) This is because the range search can read in all data blocks containing the full-length fingerprints from disk consecutively, whereas ChemDex can only read in Slice #1 in the consecutive manner. For the remaining slices, the fingerprint fragments to be read in can be sparsely located, and ChemDex cannot benefit from the effect of disk buffering in accessing them. As a result, the time taken to access the fingerprint fragments in the later slices can be relatively high compared to that for accessing the sequential fragments in Slice #1.

The uptick in the response time observed on the curve for ChemDex (4-slice) in Figure 11 is because of the dramatic surge in the number of sparse quarter-length fragments to be read from Slices #2, #3, and #4 for the lower thresholds of 0.70–0.75. (See Figure 10 whose Y-axis is in log-scale.)

### 4.4 Preprocessing Costs

The proposed ChemDex method requires some preprocessing steps to rearrange the fingerprints and to build the index. Table 1 shows the preprocessing times for the PubChem database using 2-slice and 4-slice partitionings.

**Table 1.** ChemDex's preprocessing times for the PubChem database

| Step | Procedure | Time (seconds) | |
|---|---|---|---|
| | | 2-slice | 4-slice |
| 1 | Rearranging fingerprints horizontally (Section 3.2) | 835 | 835 |
| 2 | Rearranging fingerprints vertically (Section 3.3) | 1,937 | 1,937 |
| 3 | Dividing fingerprints into slices (Section 3.4) | 205 | 316 |
| 4 | Building Index (Section 3.5) | | |
| | (a) First tier | 84 | 84 |
| | (b) Second tier | 78 | 126 |
| | **Total** | **3,139** | **3,298** |

Although the full database scan does not require any preprocessing and the range search method requires only Steps #1 and #4(a) of preprocessing, it should be noted that ChemDex's preprocessing costs are only one-time costs. So, when thousands of queries are evaluated routinely and/or interactively, the time savings by ChemDex overrides the time spent in the preprocessing.

## 5 Conclusion

In this paper, we have presented a chemical fingerprint database search system named "ChemDex". ChemDex uses an index-based early-termination approach in which the large chemical fingerprint database is both horizontally and vertically rearranged, partitioned into slices, and then indexed. A chain scoring scheme is then used for query evaluation: the fingerprint fragments from the initial slices are retrieved and their partial scores (upper bounds of their respective final scores) are calculated with the information stored in the index; the process continues into the subsequent slices only if the computed partial score is greater than or equal to the given similarity threshold. This chain scoring scheme enables the search space to be pruned effectively without any loss of accuracy.

We have tested our proposed method using the NCBI PubChem database with about 19.5 million fingerprints and 1,000 randomly selected queries. Our experimental results show that in the memory-based scenario, ChemDex is up to 109.9 times faster than the full database scan and up to 2.1 times faster than the state-of-the-art range search. In the traditional disk-based scenario, ChemDex is up to 145.7 times and 1.7 times than the full database scan and the range search respectively. ChemDex is able to achieve these speedups while maintaining the same level (100%) of accuracy as the slower methods.

Methods such as ChemDex is important for drug discovery as the chemical compound database search space can potentially grow considerably beyond its current typical value of a few million molecules towards the estimated $10^{60}$ size of the virtual space of small organic molecules [24]. In addition, the proposed bit vector indexing and chain scoring schemes in ChemDex can also be applicable in other domains whereby very large databases of fixed-length bit vectors are involved. As future work, we will explore some such other applications as document processing, image and video processing, error detection, etc., where the proposed techniques can also be exploited.

## References


1. Alvarez, J., Shoichet, B. (eds.): Virtual Screening in Drug Discovery. CRC Press, Boca Raton (2005)
2. The PubChem Project, `http://pubchem.ncbi.nlm.nih.gov/`
3. ChemDB.com Chemistry Databases, `http://cdb.ics.uci.edu/`
4. Daylight Chemical Information Systems Inc., `http://www.daylight.com/`
5. Swamidass, S.J., Baldi, P.: Bounds and algorithms for fast exact searches of chemical fingerprints in linear and sub-linear time. J. Chem. Info. Model. 47, 302–317 (2007)
6. Willett, P.: Similarity-based virtual screening using 2D fingerprints. Drug Discov. Today 11, 1046–1053 (2006)
7. Daylight User Manual, `http://www.daylight.com/dayhtml/doc/theory/index.html`
8. Baldi, P., Benz, R.W., Hirschberg, D.S., Swamidass, S.J.: Lossless compression of chemical fingerprints using integer entropy codes improves storage and retrieval. J. Chem. Info. Model. 47, 2098–2109 (2007)
9. Lim, C., Chua, S.L., Bong, X.F., Lim, C.G., Lau, S.Y.H., Wang, E.P., Chung, K.Y., Wong, V.P.Y., Aung, Z.: Rapid chemical database search: a filter-and-refine approach. In: Poster Proceedings of the 18th International Conference on Genome Informatics, pp. 90–91 (2007)

10. Manning, C.D., Raghavan, P., Schütze, H.: Introduction to Information Retrieval. Cambridge University Press, Cambridge (2008)
11. Samet, H.: Foundations of Multidimensional and Metric Data Structures. Morgan Kaufmann Publishers, San Francisco (2006)
12. Xiao, C., Wang, W., Lin, X., Yu, J.X.: Efficient similarity joins for near duplicate detection. In: Proceedings of the 17th International World Wide Web Conference, pp. 131–140 (2008)
13. Bayardo, R.J., Ma, Y., Srikant, R.: Scaling up all pairs similarity search. In: Proceedings of the 16th International World Wide Web Conference, pp. 131–140 (2007)
14. Cyganek, B.: Comparison of nonparametric transformations and bit vector matching for stereo correlation. In: Klette, R., Žunić, J. (eds.) IWCIA 2004. LNCS, vol. 3322, pp. 534–547. Springer, Heidelberg (2004)
15. Ren, W., Singh, S.: Video sequence matching with spatio-temporal constraints. In: Proceedings of the 17th International Conference on Pattern Recognition, pp. 834–837 (2004)
16. Zoeteweij, P., Abreu, R., Golsteijn, R., van Gemund, A.J.C.: Diagnosis of embedded software using program spectra. In: Proceedings of the 14th Annual IEEE International Conference & Workshops on Engineering of Computer-Based Systems, pp. 213–220 (2007)
17. Altschul, S.F., Gish, W., Miller, W., Meyers, E.W., Lipman, D.J.: Basic local alignment search tool. J. Mol. Biol. 215, 403–410 (1990)
18. Hunt, E., Atkinson, M.P., Irving, R.W.: Database indexing for large DNA and protein sequence collections. The VLDB J. 11, 256–271 (2002)
19. Fast Bit Counting Routines, `http://gurmeetsingh.wordpress.com/2008/08/05/fast-bit-counting-routines/`
20. PubChem Structure Search, `http://pubchem.ncbi.nlm.nih.gov/search/search.cgi`
21. JkDefrag Harddisk Defragger and Optimizer, `http://www.kessels.com/jkdefrag/`
22. Büttcher, S., Clarke, C.L.A.: Index compression is good, especially for random access. In: Proceedings of the 16th ACM Conference on Information and Knowledge Management, pp. 761–770 (2007)
23. Zhang, X., Berry, M.W., Raghavan, P.: Level search schemes for information filtering and retrieval. Info. Proc. & Mgt. 37, 313–334 (2001)
24. Baldi, P.: Chemoinformatics, drug design, and systems biology. Genome Info. 16, 281–285 (2005)

# BEMC: A Searchable, Compressed Representation for Large Seismic Wavefields

Julio López[1,⋆], Leonardo Ramírez-Guzmán[2], Jacobo Bielak[2], and David O'Hallaron[1]

[1] Parallel Data Laboratory, Carnegie Mellon University
[2] Computational Seismology Laboratory, Carnegie Mellon University

**Abstract.** State-of-the-art numerical solvers in Earth Sciences produce multi terabyte datasets per execution. Operating on increasingly larger datasets becomes challenging due to insufficient data bandwidth. Queries result in difficult to handle I/O access patterns. BEMC is a new mechanism that allows querying and processing wavefields in the compressed representation.

This approach combines well-known spatial-indexing techniques with novel compressed representations, thus reducing I/O bandwidth requirements. A new compression approach based on boundary integral representations exploits properties of the simulated domain. Frequency domain representation further compresses the data by eliminating temporal redundancy found in wave propagation data.

This representation enables the transformation of a large I/O workload into a massively-parallel CPU-intensive computation. Queries to this representation result in largely sequential I/O accesses. Although, decompression places heavy demands on the CPU, it exhibits parallelism well-suited for many-core processors. We evaluate our approach in the context of data analysis for the Earth Sciences datasets.

## 1 Introduction

Massive datasets representing multi-dimensional *fields* are common in many disciplines of science [16]. Fields describe N-dimensional continuum spaces by assigning scalar or vector quantities to each point in the space. Field datasets found in computational sciences correspond to discrete representations of continuum fields. Advances in simulation methodologies coupled with enabling technological trends, such as faster multi-core processors and increased storage capacity, allow scientists and engineers to collect, generate and store increasingly larger fields. As a result, we have become very good at generating gigantic datasets. For example, computations running on current high-performance computing platforms generate datasets with sizes in the order of tens of terabytes (TB) and soon petabytes (PB) [3].

On the downside, we have outstripped our capacity for analyzing these datasets. The main goal of high-resolution numerical simulation is to provide insight about physical phenomena. As the resolution and dataset sizes increase, it becomes difficult to store

⋆ This work was sponsored in part by NSF under grant IIS-0429334; in part by a subcontract from the Southern California Earthquake Center (SCEC) as part of NSF ITR EAR-0122464; and in part by a grant from the Moore Foundation.

M. Gertz and B. Ludäscher (Eds.): SSDBM 2010, LNCS 6187, pp. 306–321, 2010.

these datasets at simulation time. Similarly, moving, querying, processing and analyzing these datasets becomes extremely hard. To work around some of these challenges, often a large portion of the data is discarded and instead just a few selected data points or small regions are stored by the simulation for later analysis and publication.

We propose a new mechanism, named *BEMC*, for compactly representing, storing and querying large simulation-generated seismic wavefields. Wavefields are four dimensional vector fields that describe wave propagation phenomena. BEMC is specifically designed to support and enable new data analytic applications in Earth Sciences. The aim is two-fold. First, reduce the I/O bandwidth and storage capacity requirements at simulation time through a compact wavefield representation. Second, facilitate post-simulation analysis through efficient queries and reconstructions of subsets of the wavefield, especially for analytics performed in the frequency domain. Many analysis operations only require portions of a large wavefield at a time. A user might be interested in studying a phenomenon confined to a region of interest. BEMC represents large wavefields as compressed data structures that support spatial queries. Only a relatively small portion of the compressed dataset needs to be accessed and decompressed when analyzing a subset of the wavefield.

BEMC is a domain-specific compression scheme that takes advantage of spatial redundancy present in many wavefields. BEMC uses a novel approach based on boundary integral equations and their corresponding discretization into the boundary element method (BEM) [9,24]. It is coupled with a frequency-based encoding method to further push the limits of wavefield compression while keeping the ability to perform spatial searches on the wavefield.

The basic idea behind BEMC is to only store the computed solution (wave displacement values) for carefully chosen points in the wavefield. These points lie at the boundary of various regions in the simulation input model. In a 3D domain, the region boundaries are the 2D surfaces that wrap each of the 3D regions. At query time a *BEM microsolver* performs a numerically intensive computation to reconstruct the data for a query point from the solutions at the boundary of the region that contains the query point.

The BEM microsolver computation is highly parallel and the compressed data is laid out to exploit the sequential streaming bandwidth of storage systems. The result of the combined approach is that I/O intensive analysis tasks become highly-parallel compute-intensive tasks. With the advent of many-core processors, with hundreds of processing elements per chip, we believe this compression approach will be extremely useful in alleviating I/O bandwidth constraints.

BEMC yields up to 3:1 data size reduction when applied to wavefields based on unstructured octree meshes. Combining BEMC with a frequency-based wave compression results in up to 10:1 factors on these datasets. The location of boundary points is known prior to the simulation. This results in a 66% reductions in the I/O bandwidth requirements at simulation time, since the simulation needs to output values for boundary points only. A post-simulation step transforms the boundary values to a frequency-domain compressed representation to achieve the final 10X compression ratio.

BEMC is independent of the simulation method used in the generation of the synthetic wavefield. It can be used to represent wavefields produced by simulation approaches such as Finite Differences Methods (FD) [25], octree-based Finite Element Methods (FEM) [3], unstructured tetrahedral FEM [7] and Boundary Element Methods (BEM) [24]. BEMC can be applied to other wave propagation problems, and in general to other domains where the problem can be formulated in terms of boundary integral equations. For explanation purpose and without loss of generality, we present BEMC in the context of wavefields generated by octree-based FEM numerical solver.

## 2 Seismic Wavefield Analysis

The goal of large-scale ground-motion simulations is to enhance our understanding of how the ground shakes during strong earthquakes. Simulating physical processes, such as seismic wave propagation during strong earthquakes, involves computing the solution to a set of governing equations. Non-trivial scenarios have no closed-form solution and the solution is obtained through numerical methods such as FD [25] and FEM [6]. These simulations take as input a model of the ground (material model), construct a discrete simulation *mesh* from the material model and solve a set of partial differential equations on the mesh (See Fig. 1). The simulation produces a large 4-dimensional wavefields and a corresponding mesh. Wavefields are spatio-temporal datasets that describe wave propagation processes by assigning a quantity to each point in space. In the context of ground-motion simulations, a seismic wavefield describes ground properties such as displacement, velocity and acceleration of points in the ground at different moments in time during an earthquake [3]. The analysis of these wavefields has great value for scientists and the community in general. Data analysis produce derived data for applications such as: verification and validation of the simulation process; analysis of interaction with buildings and other man-made structures; real-time damage estimation; material model inversion; and, visualization. Efficient access to these wavefields is key for such analysis applications. The mechanisms presented here help alleviate the I/O requirements needed to store the wavefield (Dataset 3 in Fig. 1) at simulation time and provide a searchable representation for the data analysis tasks.

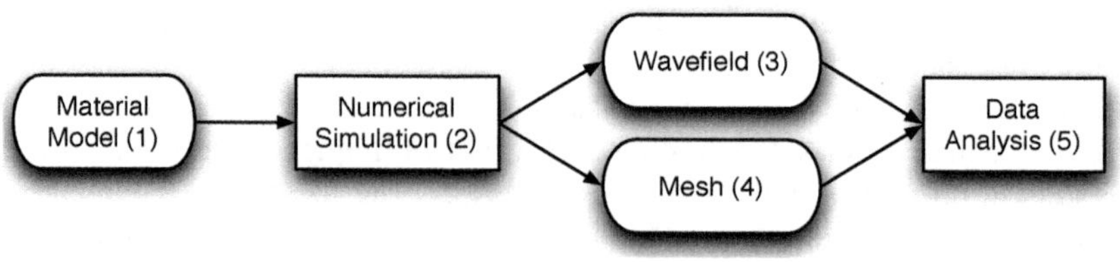


**Fig. 1.** Physical simulation process. A material model (1) is the input to a numerical simulation process (2), which produces an output wavefield (3) and a corresponding simulation mesh (4). The produced datasets (3) and (4) are used for post-simulation data analysis (5).

## 3 Compactly Storing Wavefields

Many datasets from various domains in computational sciences exhibit spatial coherence. The values represented by the field vary in a smooth manner across points in space and time. This is certainly the case for simulation-generated ground-motion wavefields where displacement values vary smoothly in a volume of the wavefield. Despite their spatial coherence, wavefields generated by FEM numerical simulations are difficult to compress since they contain floating point (FP) values associated with the nodes of an irregular mesh. Compressing FP values is challenging because small differences in absolute value yield large changes in the FP bit representation. Moreover, unstructured meshes used in FEM simulations adapt to variations in the properties of the input model parameters, thus greatly eliminating spatial redundancy in the corresponding output wavefield. FEM octree-based meshes and corresponding output wavefields commonly require 1/8 of the space needed to represent a FD mesh for the same problem. It is hard to use image compression techniques in this case due to the irregular nature of the meshes used to generate the wavefields, as many image compression approaches operate on regularly spaced grids. The question is then: How can spatio-temporal coherence be exploited to compress massive wavefields? BEMC exploits wavefield spatial coherence through domain-specific formulation based on Boundary Integral Equations and Green's functions. This approach can be used to compress datasets generated using FEM, FDs or other method. The main idea is to make use of a property of the input material model (Dataset 1 in Fig. 1) to compress the output wavefield (Dataset 3). This is based on the observation that the *input* material models used in simulation (Dataset 1) have large homogeneous regions. Then, for any point inside a homogeneous region in the input (Dataset 1), we can compute the corresponding output displacement values (in Dataset 3) in terms of the (output) displacement values of the points that lie on the region boundary.

### 3.1 Model Homogeneity

Material models used for simulations comprise large homogeneous regions. This is depicted in Fig. 2 (a), where 5 homogeneous regions (different shades of gray) make up a simulation domain. Simulating physical phenomena in complex structures requires the use of full-domain methods such as FEM and FD. Meshes for these methods divide the domain into small discrete mesh elements depicted by dotted squares in the figure. The element corners are referred to as mesh nodal points or simply nodes. Homogeneous regions in the input model are also divided into small mesh elements to satisfy numerical stability requirements for the simulation. Finer resolution meshes increase simulation accuracy. For example, simulating higher wave frequencies requires finer meshes. As a mesh becomes finer, more elements are needed to fill up the same homogeneous region. In the simulation output wavefield (Dataset 3 in Fig. 1), the wave displacement values at mesh nodal points inside homogeneous regions vary relatively smoothly within each region. Although the values have small differences from node to node, the variations are significant enough and thus need to be explicitly stored.

BEMC reduces wavefield storage requirements by exclusively keeping values for nodes located on region boundaries, i.e., lying on the thick lines in Fig. 2 (a). A discrete

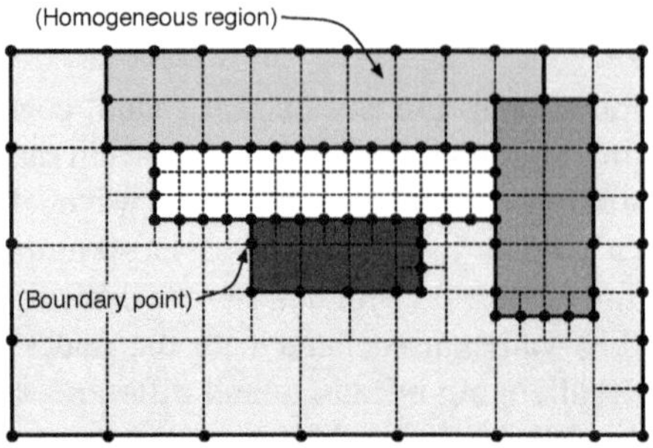


(**a**) Material model homogeneity.

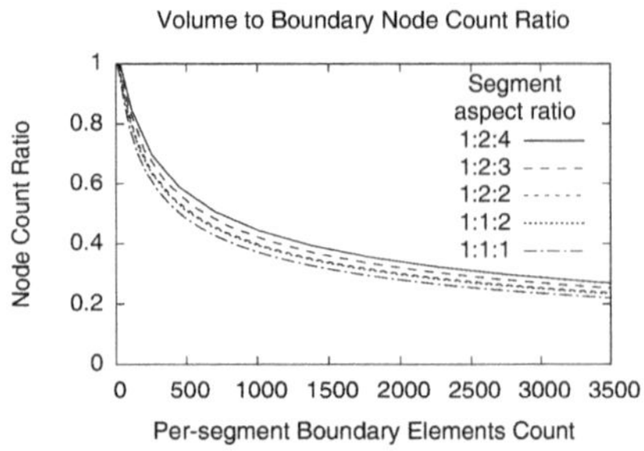


(**b**) Node Count Reduction Ratio.

**Fig. 2.** (**a**) Material model homogeneity. This 2D sketch shows the composition of a hypothetical material model for ground-motion simulation. This corresponds to Dataset 1 in Fig. 1. It contains various homogeneous regions (different shades of gray), separated by boundaries (thick lines). The size and properties of these regions can vary by various orders of magnitude.
(**b**) Node Count Ratio. This is the achievable compression for regions of different sizes and aspect ratios. The X axis is the number of boundary elements needed to wrap the segment. The Y axis shows the reduction in the number of mesh nodes compared to a regular volume mesh with the same resolution as the boundary mesh.

representation of region boundaries is made up of 2D *boundary elements* (BE) embedded in a 3D space. In the 2D illustration in Fig. 2 (a), the BEs correspond to the thick lines between two mesh points at the boundary of the regions.

A boundary mesh representation only requires nodes at the boundary. Values for nodes inside a region can be safely discarded. Figure 2 (b) shows the storage reduction obtained by only storing boundary node values. The X axis is the boundary mesh size in number of elements. The Y axis shows the ratio of boundary node count to volume node count for a boundary mesh of the given size. Different lines show the ratio for hexahedral regions for various 3D aspect ratios — 1:1:1, 1:1:2, etc. Compression ratios below 0.3 are possible for regions with more than 1500 boundary elements.

### 3.2 Compression Steps

The BEMC comprises the steps shown in Figure 3: Model Segmentation (6), Boundary mesh generation (7) and Wavefield data extraction (8). These steps are explained below. The inputs for BEMC are: the full domain wavefield to be compressed (3), the input material model used to generate the wavefield (1) and the full 3D domain simulation mesh (4). The BEMC process produces a compact output representation comprised of a segment index (9), a boundary mesh (10) and the wave data associated with nodes along the boundaries of homogeneous regions (11). The segment index and boundary mesh are used to support spatial range queries. The segment index is used as a spatial index, and the boundary mesh provides the mapping from the segment boundary to wave data associated with points along the boundary for the segments. At query time, the data for a query point inside a segment is reconstructed from the data associated with the boundary nodes.

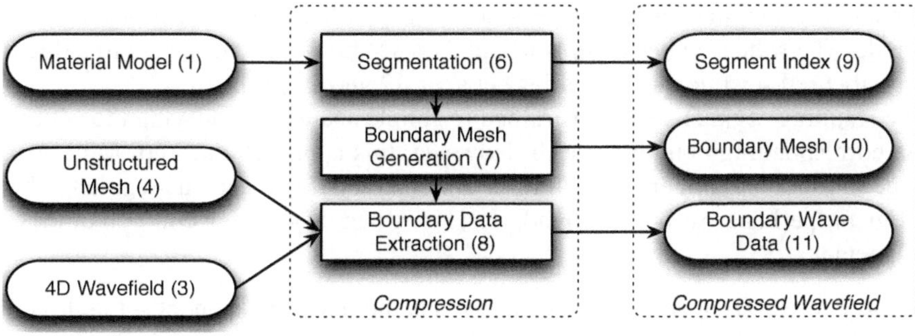


**Fig. 3.** Steps for the BEMC compression phase. Its inputs are a wavefield (3), the corresponding unstructured mesh (4) and the material model (1) for the region covered by the wavefield. This phase consists of the following processes: Segmentation (6), Boundary Mesh Generation (7) and Boundary Data Extraction (8). They produce a compressed boundary wavefield with three components: a segment index (9), a boundary mesh (10) and associated wave data (11).

**Model Segmentation.** The goal of this step is to find a set of homogeneous regions or *segments* in the input model and produce a spatially-indexed segment set. A region is considered to be homogeneous if all of its material properties remain constant in its volume. Extracting homogeneous regions becomes challenging due to the large model sizes, currently in the order of tens to hundreds of gigabytes. Segmentation is an active area of research with applications to medical imaging and computer vision [31]. Most readily available implementations of algorithms for image segmentation target the case where the image fits in main-memory [13]. Researchers in the area of scientific visualization have proposed methods for iso-surface extraction [11], model simplification [12] and near real-time rendering [18] of large spatial datasets.

In order to deal with large 3D material models, we developed a simplified out-of-core segmentation procedure [19] that leverages the internal representation of material models and octree meshes used in FEM ground-motion simulation [3,27]. The general idea is to use an octree FEM mesh as a segmentation template, and check the mesh against the material model to eliminate any over-segmentation –whenever possible coarsen the mesh where it is too fine. These octree-based meshes are stored on disk as indexed *linearized octrees* using the CMU etree library [26]. The mesh elements are cubes that correspond to nodes of the octree. The order for the elements' on-disk representation corresponds to a *pre-order traversal* of the corresponding octree. The segmentation process performs a pre-order traversal of the octree mesh elements and checks the homogeneity of a set of 8 sibling octants elements by querying to the material model. If the octants are homogeneous they are coalesced into a single parent octant. If the octants cannot be coalesced, they are output as individual segments.

This algorithm has complexity $O(n)$ and requires little in-memory state. This approach requires a single pass over the mesh elements. It uses the streaming bandwidth of storage devices very efficiently, as the pre-order traversal of the octree structure results in sequential I/O accesses. The implementation has a very small footprint. It only requires state for eight siblings octree nodes[1] in the path from the tree root to the current leaf node. The state size has an upper bound of $8 \times$ `tree_depth`. The octree depth for commonly used seismic meshes varies between 12 and 20 [19].

The resulting segments are constrained to simple shapes, simplifying the generation of the corresponding boundary mesh. However, this approach does not fully take advantage of model homogeneity as it does not coalesce homogeneous segments that do not align properly across octree boundaries, i.e., when they are not children of the same parent octant.

**Boundary Mesh Generation.** This stage reads the material segment set and the full-domain mesh in order to generate discrete *boundary meshes* (BM) for the homogeneous regions. The resulting BMs discretize the segment boundaries such that they can be later used to reconstruct any point inside using a numerical computation. A BM comprises a set of 2D boundary elements (BE) embedded in a 3D space. The corresponding element corners are the boundary mesh nodes (BN).

This procedure reads each segment and subdivides each segment face into smaller rectangular boundary elements according to the material properties of the segments on both sides of the face. The size of the BE is chosen such that it satisfies the numerical requirements for the numerical computation in the reconstruction process. Whenever possible, the BE size is the same as the size of the faces of the elements in the unstructured mesh. Matching the BE size to the one of the FEM elements can be done based on two simulation parameters (points per wavelength and maximum wave frequency), thus access to the complete unstructured FEM mesh is not needed. Boundary mesh nodes are generated in a second pass over the generated boundary mesh elements. This is an involved process that assigns two identifiers to each node: a segment-local id and a mesh global id. The corresponding mapping is stored as part of the boundary mesh output. The global node identifiers are used for laying out and addressing the wave data associated with boundary nodes.

**Wavefield Data Extraction.** This process extracts the actual wave data associated with boundary nodes. It accounts for the bulk of the data size reduction. The first step is to build an auxiliary structure for mapping between boundary mesh node ids and full-domain mesh node ids. If the BM generation above produces meshes with BEs that are aligned with the FEM elements, then there is a one-to-one mapping between boundary mesh nodes and nodes in the full domain mesh. Additional interpolation operations on the associated boundary data are avoided when the boundary mesh nodes are aligned with full domain mesh nodes. This process iterates over the boundary nodes and uses the node mapping structure to locate and extract the corresponding data from the 4D wavefield.

The wave data is transposed from the *space domain* to the *time domain*. Popular ground-motion solvers produce wave data one time step at a time and store it in a space domain representation (space $\times$ time), where the dataset is a collection of volumes each corresponding to a snapshot in time [3,21]. Given a time step $t$, values for all the mesh nodes are adjacently stored, then all the values for time step $t+1$, and so on. To further compress the data and facilitate its reconstruction at query time, the wave data is stored

[1] Child nodes with the same common parent.

in a time domain representation (time × space). In the time domain, the data is stored as a sequence of time series. The extracted wave data is transposed with an efficient out-of-core scheme optimized for matrices with extremely large aspect ratios, e.g., 1000:1 [19].

Simulation-generated seismic wavefields often are *band-limited*, i.e., they contain useful wave data in a limited frequency range. In particular, the numerical solver produces wave data up to a specified maximum frequency for the simulation. This offers an opportunity to achieve higher compression. We developed a frequency-based compression scheme named *effective-zero* encoding. First, the wave data is transformed to the *frequency domain* using an available FFT implementation. Then, an *effective zero* value is independently computed for each node wave spectrum [19]. In the frequency spectrum, a wave number has an effective-zero value if its magnitude is below a user defined threshold relative to the cummulative energy of the spectrum. Only non-zero values are stored in the frequency spectrum for a boundary node.

# 4 Wavefield Reconstruction

Wavefield reconstruction is formulated as queries for a point $q$ in the wavefield. The query set can include arbitrary points in the domain–it is not limited to points in the original full-domain mesh. Spatial range queries are possible due to the chosen storage representation and can be satisfied by reading only the portion of the dataset covered by the query range. The first step involves looking up $q$ in the segment index to find the homogeneous region containing $q$ (See Fig. 4). Reconstructing the data for $q$ is achieved through one of the following methods:

1. If *$q$ coincides* with a boundary mesh node, then return the data associated with the mesh node.
2. When $q$ is *on* or *near* the boundary, interpolate from the data associated with the corners of the closest boundary element.
3. When $q$ is *far* from the boundary, execute a *microsolver* to compute the wave data from the values at the region boundary.

A query point is near the boundary if its distance to the closest BE is less than a user specified parameter, which by default is $1/4$ of the BE edge length. In all the cases above, satisfying the query only requires access to small subsets of the compressed wavefield, thus reducing I/O bandwidth usage and computation. The compressed layout is such that it induces sequential I/O accesses.

## 4.1 Microsolver Computation

For cases where $q$ is far from the region boundary, the answer is computed by applying the Boundary Element Method (BEM) [9,24]. A microsolver carries out the required numerical computation using as input the compressed boundary wavefield. This process is divided into two steps: Phi computation (13) and Wave data computation (14). The BEM mathematical formulation and the corresponding steps are explained below.

**BEM Formulation.** Without loss of generality, assume we have a query point $q \in \Omega, \Omega \subset \Re^3$, where $\Omega$ is a homogeneous 3D region with a boundary $S$ (See Fig. 5 for

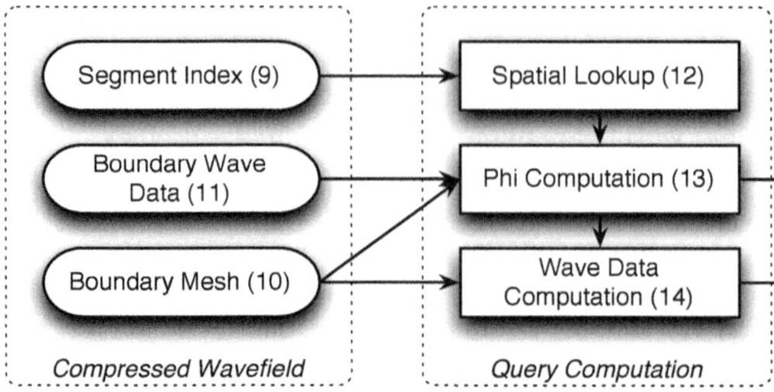


**Fig. 4.** BEM decompression phase. At query time, the data for query points is reconstructed from the boundary wavefield representation. The computation involves three steps: Spatial Index Lookup (12), Phi Computation (13) and Query Wave Data Computation (14).

an illustration in two dimensions). Reconstructing the displacement values for a point inside $\Omega$ involves numerically computing the boundary integral shown in Eq. 1.

$$u(q) = \int_S \phi(\xi)G(q,\xi)dS_\xi \tag{1}$$

The discrete approximation is shown in Equation 2. This is roughly equivalent to dividing the boundary $S$ into discrete boundary elements $\xi_i$ and summing the contributions of all boundary elements $\xi_i$ along the boundary $S$ as shown in Fig. 5.

$$u(q) = \sum_{k=0}^{n-1} \phi(\xi_k)G(q,\xi_k) \times A(\xi_k) \tag{2}$$

Here, $u(q)$ is a vector containing the displacement in the frequency domain for a point $q$, $\phi(\xi_k)$ weights the contribution to $u(q)$ from $\xi$ relative to other points (or BEs) on the surface $S$. $A(\xi_k)$ is the area of the BE $\xi_k$. $G(q,\xi_k)$ is the Green's function [5] between $q$ and a boundary element $\xi_k$. $G(q,\xi_k)$ can be analytically computed based on the material properties of the region $\Omega$ and the coordinates of $q$ and $\xi$. See Appendix A for details.

**Phi Computation.** The phi values $\phi(\xi)$ in equations 1 and 2 are initially unknown. The first phase of the microsolver computes the $\phi(\xi)$ terms for the $\Omega$ region. The computed $\phi(\xi)$ depend exclusively on the region material properties and boundary displacement values. Once the phi values are computed, they can be reused across other query points in the same region.

Equation 1 also holds for boundary points as shown in Fig. 6. Thus, computing the phi values is achieved by using Eq. 2 with points at the boundary, by letting $q = \xi_i$. In this case, $u(\xi_i)$ are known values stored in the boundary wavefield (Dataset 11 in Fig. 4) and $G(\xi_i,\xi_j)$ can be analytically computed. This enables setting up a system of $N$ linear equations with $N$ unknown $\phi(\xi_i)$ values, where $N$ is the number of boundary elements.[2]

[2] More precisely, the number of equations and unknowns is $3N$ once $u(\xi_i)$, $\phi(\xi_i)$ and $G(\xi_i,\xi_j)$ are expanded into their individual 3D components.

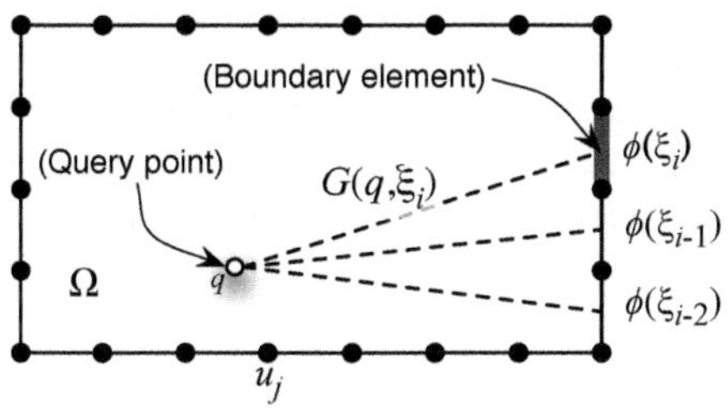


**Fig. 5.** Query point computation. Computing values associated with a query point $q$, in a homogeneous region $\Omega$, from the $\phi(\xi_i)$ values associated with boundary elements $\xi_i \in S$ (outer line).

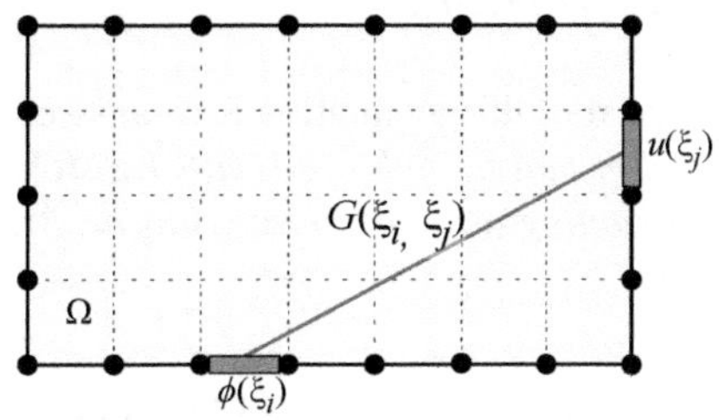


**Fig. 6.** Phi computation. The $\phi(\xi_i)$ values are unknown. They are computed from the known displacement values at the boundary $u(\xi_j)$ by solving a system of linear equations.

$$\overbrace{\begin{bmatrix} G(\xi_0\xi_0) & \cdots & G(\xi_0\xi_i) & \cdots & G(\xi_0\xi_{n-1}) \\ G(\xi_1\xi_0) & \cdots & G(\xi_1\xi_i) & \cdots & G(\xi_1\xi_{n-1}) \\ \vdots & & \vdots & & \vdots \\ G(\xi_j\xi_0) & \cdots & G(\xi_j\xi_i) & \cdots & G(\xi_j\xi_{n-1}) \\ \vdots & & \vdots & & \vdots \\ G(\xi_{n-1}\xi_0) & \cdots & G(\xi_{n-1}\xi_i) & \cdots & G(\xi_{n-1}\xi_{n-1}) \end{bmatrix}}^{\xi_i} \times \overbrace{\begin{bmatrix} \phi_{\xi_0} \\ \phi_{\xi_1} \\ \vdots \\ \phi_{\xi_i} \\ \vdots \\ \phi_{\xi_{n-1}} \end{bmatrix}}^{\phi} = \overbrace{\begin{bmatrix} u(\xi_0) \\ u(\xi_1) \\ \vdots \\ u(\xi_i) \\ \vdots \\ u(\xi_{n-1}) \end{bmatrix}}^{u}$$

**Fig. 7.** Matrices representing the linear system of equations corresponding to the $\mathcal{G}_\omega \times \Phi_\omega = U_\omega$ equation. This system is solved to obtain the unknown $\phi$ values for a frequency $\omega$. $\mathcal{G}_\omega$ contains the (known) coefficients of the Green's tensors, $\Phi_\omega$ is the vector of unknown variables and $U_\omega$ is the vector of known displacement values obtained from the simulation wavefield.

Figure 7 shows the matrix system resulting from these equations. The discretization details can be found elsewhere [19,24]. Equation 1 is undefined for the entries along the matrix diagonal, more precisely $G(\xi_i, \xi_i)$ is undefined. These singularities are resolved through numerical integration using quadratures of odd order [22]. All these computations are carried out in the frequency domain. A system of equations needs to be solved for each frequency (wave number) that has a non-zero $u(\xi)$ value. The last step in the compression phase eliminates frequencies with effective zero values. This also reduces the number of systems of equations that need to be resolved at query time.

**Query Value Computation.** After computing the phi values, the data for $q$ is obtained from Eq. 2. The data for $q$ is the sum of the products between the $\phi(\xi_i)$ and the corresponding Green's tensor $G(q, \xi_j)$. Figure 5 illustrates the process.

## 5 Evaluation

The goal of this evaluation is to answer the following questions: (1) *What level of compression can be achieved with BEMC?* and (2) *What is the computational cost of reconstructing a query point with the BEM microsolver?* These questions are answered below.

### 5.1 Quake Unstructured Wavefields

Table 1 shows the characteristics of the wavefields used in the experiments. These are seismic wavefields generated using a state-of-the-art numerical solver for seismic wave propagation problems. They cover a 100 km × 100 km × 37.5 km region in Southern California that includes Los Angeles and San Fernando basins. The first table column contains the dataset name, which corresponds to the maximum resolved wave frequency. The second and third columns respectively show the number of mesh elements and nodes. The fourth column displays the wavefield size in Gigabytes.

**Table 1.** Unstructured 4D Wavefields

| Wavefield Name | Mesh Elements | Mesh Nodes | Size (GB) |
|---|---|---|---|
| LA 0.50 Hz | 8,026,868 | 8,634,452 | 116 |
| LA 0.70 Hz | 17,970,403 | 19,372,567 | 260 |
| LA 1.00 Hz | 64,128,816 | 66,548,707 | 893 |

**Table 2.** BEMC Compression Ratio

| Wavefield | BEMC | BEMC + freq. |
|---|---|---|
| LA 0.50 Hz | 0.71 | 0.14 |
| LA 0.70 Hz | 0.51 | 0.13 |
| LA 1.00 Hz | 0.27 | 0.07 |

### 5.2 BEMC Compression

In order to find out the effectiveness of BEMC, we applied the method on the wavefields shown in Table 1. We constructed boundary meshes for these wavefields and compared the number of mesh nodal points versus the number of nodes in the FEM hexahedral mesh for the same wavefield. The boundary mesh is constructed using the approach described in Section 3. Remember that this approach might not capture all the homogeneity of the model, thus not allowing the BEMC compression to take advantage of all the spatial redundancy.

The compression ratio (`output_size / input_size`) for the different wavefields is shown in Table 2. Column 2 contains the compression ratio achieved exclusively from the dimensionality reduction –storing only values at the boundary. As the wavefield simulation frequency increases, BEMC produces better compression. This is expected as an FEM mesh needs to subdivide a homogeneous region with higher resolution as the maximum simulation frequency increases. Compressing the LA-0.5Hz wavefield with BEMC produces only 30% storage savings, however for the LA-1.0Hz the savings are 73%, this is a 3.7:1 compression factor. The implication is that the number of boundary elements per region is larger for the LA-1Hz wavefield, which has an effect on computation performed by the BEM microsolver at query time.

The third column in Table 2 shows the compression ratio obtained when applying the frequency-based encoding technique (described in Section 3.2) to the boundary wavefields. The combined scheme achieves a compression ratio of 0.07 (14.3:1 factor) in the best case on the LA-1Hz wavefield, and a 0.14 ratio (7:1 factor) in the worst case for the LA-0.5Hz wavefield.

Combining these two approaches, not only reduces storage requirements, but also computation requirements. At query time, the BEM microsolver only needs to compute values for frequencies that are non-zero. This represents a 5X reduction of computation for the best case (LA-0.5Hz) and a 4X reduction for the worst case (LA-0.7Hz).

### 5.3 BEM Microsolver Computation Cost

The following micro-benchmark was used to determine the computational cost of the BEM microsolver. For regions of different sizes (measured in the number of elements along the boundary), we measured the time needed to compute the data for a query point inside the region. The boundary mesh and wave data were already in memory, allowing to measure the actual compute cost. The microsolver is implemented as a library of C++ classes. In the phi computation phase, the system of linear equations is solved by calling LAPACK [4] functions with low-level BLAS [8] routines provided by ATLAS [29]. Theses experiments were carried out on dual SMP machines with 3.6 GHz x86_64 processors, 2 MB L2 cache per processor and 8 GB of memory running version 2.6.15 of the Linux™kernel. The numerical libraries were configured to use 2-processors. The system setup and query phases are done sequentially on a single processor.

Figure 8 shows the microsolver compute time per frequency. The X axis indicates the region size in number of boundary elements, the Y axis contains the elapsed time in seconds. Each bar is divided into the following BEM microsolver phases: Setup, Solve, and Query computation. The table in Fig 8 shows the corresponding values in seconds.

Not surprisingly, the query time grows linearly with the region size, setup time is $O(n^2)$ and solving time is $O(n^3)$. This puts a practical limit on the achievable

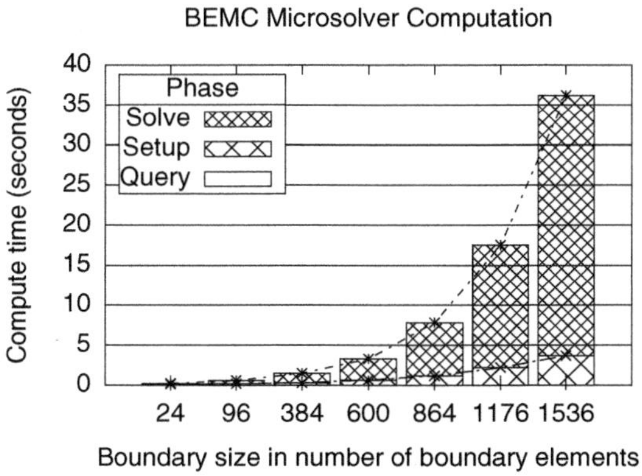


BEMC Microsolver Time (s)

| BE count | Setup | Solve | Query | Total |
|---|---|---|---|---|
| 24 | 0.13 | 0.12 | 0.002 | 0.25 |
| 96 | 0.20 | 0.40 | 0.005 | 0.60 |
| 384 | 0.30 | 1.19 | 0.008 | 1.50 |
| 600 | 0.66 | 2.61 | 0.011 | 3.29 |
| 864 | 1.19 | 6.61 | 0.014 | 7.81 |
| 1176 | 2.19 | 15.29 | 0.019 | 17.50 |
| 1536 | 3.67 | 32.51 | 0.024 | 36.20 |

**Fig. 8.** BEMC microsolver compute time in seconds

compression ratio, in the sense that homogeneous regions cannot grow too large, otherwise the query computation time becomes too high.

A typical homogeneous region contains in the order of a 100 wave numbers in its frequency spectrum. Thus the total required computation is about 100X larger. However, with the increase in the number of available processor cores, the solving time for the system of equations can be reduced. Moreover, the computation for different frequencies (wave numbers) can proceed independently in parallel in separate chips or compute nodes. The setup and compute phases are performed once per region, introducing a one-time cost. Subsequent query points for the same region can be computed from the already obtained solution in linear time, thus amortizing the setup and solving costs.

We can trade off the achieved compression ratio to reduce the query latency by precomputing the phi values and storing them on disk. The raw size of the phi set is 2X the size of the compressed displacement field for the boundary points. However, both additional storage size and computational reductions can be obtained by devising a multi-resolution scheme for storing the phi set, such that the representation for lower frequencies has a coarser boundary element mesh (i.e., fewer phi values) and higher frequencies have finer-resolution boundary meshes.

## 6 Related Work

The goal of data compression is to reduce the number of bits needed to represent the data. Compression techniques exploit data features such as redundancy. Clever encoding schemes reduce the number of bits required to represent a data symbol. Such techniques include arithmetic coding, Huffman coding, Golomb-Rice codes among others [1]. Lelewer and Hirschberg present a good survey of these and other techniques [17]. Run-length encoding (RLE) is commonly used in many applications, including the compression of non-photographic images, that is, diagrams produced using drawing tools. BEMC employs a form of implicit RLE encoding to avoid storing the effective zero values of a frequency spectrum.

There are various approaches that exploit data features commonly found in text files. These include Lempel-Ziv-Welch (LZ and LZW) and the Burrows-Wheeler transform (BWT) [10]. The LZW and BWT methods are respectively used in the popular `gzip` and `bzip2` compression tools. These approaches work well on text data and binary executable programs.

Lossy compression schemes achieve higher compression factors at the cost of some information loss. Upon decompression, the output is an approximation of the input. Image formats such as JPEG [28] use lossy compression methods based on a discrete cosine transform [2]. JPEG compression takes advantage of the fact that photographic images have smooth variations from one pixel to the next one. Audio compression techniques exploit the fact that the stream of data to compress corresponds to sound waves [20,30]. Approaches for compressing floating-point values have been recently developed [14,15,23]. These approaches are complementary to BEMC, as they could be used as a post-processing pass to effectively encode the residual floating point data for points at the boundary.

# 7 Conclusion

Generating, querying and otherwise analyzing simulation-generated wavefield datasets becomes difficult as their data size increases. We presented BEMC, a novel approach for compactly representing large seismic wavefields. A key feature of BEMC is that it enables spatial range queries in the compressed domain, only a small portion of the data needs to be retrieved from storage at query time. BEMC uses a domain-specific approach based on the boundary element method (BEM) to reconstruct the wave data. A query-time microsolver is used to carry out the BEM numerical computation. We believe that this approach can be generalized and applied to other wave propagation problems and in general to other domains that can be formulated in terms of boundary integral equations.

Our evaluation shows that dimensionality reduction alone offers up to a 3.7X compression factor when applied to large seismic wavefields. The combined BEMC approach yields compression factors up to 14X. The frequency-based encoding used in BEMC contributes to the reduction of both storage and query-time computational requirements.

# A Boundary Integral Equations

$$u_i(p) = \int_S \sum_{j=0}^{2} \phi_j(\xi) G_{ij}(p,\xi) dS_\xi \tag{3}$$

$$G_{ij}(x,\xi) = [f_2\delta_{ij} + (f_1 - f_2)\gamma_i\gamma_j]/4\pi\mu r \tag{4}$$

The following is the corresponding expansion for the terms in the Green's function ($G_{ij}(x,\xi)$). The parameters involved in the equations are shown as well.

$$\begin{aligned}
f_1 &= \frac{\beta^2}{\alpha^2}\left[1 - \frac{2i}{qr} - \frac{2}{(qr)^2}\right]e^{-iqr} + \left[\frac{2i}{kr} + \frac{2}{(kr)^2}\right]e^{-ikr} \\
f_2 &= \frac{\beta^2}{\alpha^2}\left[\frac{i}{qr} + \frac{1}{(qr)^2}\right]e^{-iqr} + \left[1 + \frac{i}{kr} - \frac{1}{(kr)^2}\right]e^{-ikr} \\
\gamma_j &= (p_j - \xi_j)/r \\
r^2 &= (p_0 - \xi_0)^2 + (p_1 - \xi_1)^2 + (p_2 - \xi_2)^2 \\
\mu &= \rho\beta^2 \\
q &= \omega/\alpha = \text{P-wave number} \\
k &= \omega/\beta = \text{S-wave number} \\
\delta_{ij} &= 1 \text{ if } i = j; 0 \text{ otherwise}
\end{aligned}$$

| | Description |
|---|---|
| $p$ | Point (3D coordinates) |
| $u(p)$ | 3D displacement at $p$ |
| $\phi(\xi)$ | Phi vector for BE $\xi$ |
| $\delta_{ij}$ | Kronecker's delta |
| $q$ | P-wave number |
| $\alpha$ | P-wave velocity |
| $k$ | S-wave number |
| $\beta$ | S-wave velocity |
| $\rho$ | Region's mass density |

## References


1. Abramson, N.: Information Theory and Coding. McGraw-Hill, New York (1963)
2. Ahmed, N., Natarajan, T., Rao, K.R.: Discrete cosine transform. Trans. on Computers (TOC) C(23), 90–93 (1974)
3. Akcelik, V., Bielak, J., Biros, G., Ipanomeritakis, I., Fernandez, A., Ghattas, O., Kim, E., López, J., O'Hallaron, D., Tu, T., Urbanic, J.: High resolution forward and inverse earthquake modeling on terascale computers. In: Proc. Supercomputing SC 2003 (2003)
4. Anderson, E., et al.: LAPACK Users' Guide, 2nd edn. SIAM, Philadelphia (1995)
5. Arfken, G.: Nonhomogeneous Equation–Green's Function. In: Mathematical Methods for Physicists, 3rd edn., pp. 480–491. Academic Press, London (1985)
6. Babuska, I., Strouboulis, T.: The Finite Element Method and Its Reliability, 1st edn. Oxford University Press, USA (December 2001)
7. Bao, H., et al.: Large-scale simulation of elastic wave propagation in heterogeneous media on parallel computers. Computer Methods in Applied Mechanics and Engineering 152 (1998)
8. Blackford, L., et al.: An updated set of basic linear algebra subprograms (BLAS). ACM Trans. Math. Soft. 28(2), 135–151 (2002)
9. Bonnet, M.: Boundary Integral Equation Methods for Solids and Fluids, 1st edn. John Wiley & Sons, Chichester (June 1999) ISBN:0-471-97184-7
10. Burrows, M., Wheeler, D.J.: A block-sorting lossless data compression algorithm. Tech. Rep. 124, Digital Equipment Corporation (December 1994)
11. Chiang, Y.J., Farias, R., Silva, C.T., Wei, B.: A unified infrastructure for parallel out-of-core isosurface extraction and volume rendering of unstructured grids. In: Proc. Symp. on Parallel and Large-data Visualization and Graphics, pp. 59–66. IEEE Press, Los Alamitos (2001)
12. Hoppe, H.: Smooth view-dependent level-of-detail control and its application to terrain rendering. In: Proc. Int. Conf. Visualization, VIS 1998, October 1998, pp. 35–42. IEEE, Los Alamitos (1998)
13. Ibáñez, L., Schroeder, W., Ng, L., Cates, J.: The ITK Software Guide, Kitware, Inc. (November 2005) ISBN: 1930934157
14. Ibarria, L., Lindstrom, P., Rossignac, J., Szymczak, A.: Out-of-core compression and decompression of large n-dimensional scalar fields. In: Proc. Eurographics (2003)
15. Isenburg, M., Lindstrom, P.: Fast and efficient compression of floating-point data. IEEE Transactions on Visualization and Computer Graphics (TOVCG) 12(5), 1245–1250 (2006)
16. Landau, L.D., Lifshitz, E.M.: Classical Theory of Fields, The Course of Theoretical Physics, 3rd edn., vol. 2. Pergamon, London (1976)
17. Lelewer, D.A., Hirschberg, D.S.: Data compression. ACM Comput. Surveys (CSUR) 19(3), 261–296 (1987), doi:10.1145/45072.45074
18. Lindstrom, P.: Out-of-core construction and visualization of multiresolution surfaces. In: Proceedings of the 2003 ACM Interactive 3D Graphics Conference (2003)
19. López, J.: Methods for Querying Compressed Wavefields. Ph.D. thesis, Department of Electrical and Computer Engineering, Carnegie Mellon University (May 2007)
20. (MPEG), I.J.M.P.E.G.: ISO/IEC-11172 MPEG-1 standard, Coding of Moving Pictures and Audio. International Organisation For Standardisation (ISO), 1st edn. (1996)
21. Olsen, K.: Three-dimensional ground motion simulations for large earthquakes on the san andreas fault with dynamic and observational constraints. Comp. Acoust. 9(3), 1203–1215 (2001)
22. Press, W.H., Teukolsky, S.A., (Contributor), W.T.V.: Numerical Recipes in C: The Art of Scientific Computing, p. 1020. Cambridge University Press, Cambridge (1992)
23. Ratanaworabhan, P., Ke, J., Burtscher, M.: Fast lossless compression of scientific floating-point data. In: Proc. Data Compression Conference (DCC), March 2006, pp. 133–142 (2006)

24. Sanchez-Sesma, F.J., Luzon, F.: Seismic response of three-dimensional alluvial valleys for incident p, s, and rayleigh waves. Bulletin of the Seismological Society of America 85(1), 269–284 (1995)
25. Smith, G.D.: Numerical Solution of Partial Differential Equations: Finite Difference Methods, 3rd edn. Oxford University Press, New York (1985)
26. Tu, T., López, J., O'Hallaron, D.: The Etree library: A system for manipulating large octrees on disk. Tech. Rep. CMU-CS-03-174, Carnegie Mellon, Computer Science Dept. (2003)
27. Tu, T., O'Hallaron, D., López, J.: Etree – a database-oriented method for generating large octree meshes. In: Proc. 11th Int. Meshing Roundtable, Ithaca, NY, September 2002, pp. 127–138 (2002)
28. Wallace, G.K.: The JPEG still picture compression standard. Communications of the ACM (CACM) 34(4), 30–44 (1991)
29. Whaley, R.C., Dongarra, J.: Automatically Tuned Linear Algebra Software (ATLAS). In: Ninth SIAM Conference on Parallel Processing for Scientific Computing (1999)
30. Yang, D., Moriya, T., Liebchen, T.: A lossless audio compression scheme with random access property. In: Proc. Int. Conf. on Acoustics, Speech, and Signal Processing (ICASSP 2004), May 2004, vol. 3, pp. iii:1016–1019. IEEE, Los Alamitos (2004)
31. Yoo, T.S. (ed.): Insight into Images: Principles and Practice for Segmentation, Registration, and Image Analysis. AK Peters, Ltd., Wellesley (July 2004) ISBN:1568812175

# Dynamic Data Reorganization for Energy Savings in Disk Storage Systems

Ekow Otoo, Doron Rotem, and Shih-Chiang Tsao

Lawrence Berkeley National Laboratory,
University of California
1 Cyclotron Road
Berkeley, CA 94720

**Abstract.** High performance computing (HPC) systems utilize parallel file systems that are striped over large number of disks to address the I/O performance requirement of data intensive applications. These large number of disks are typically configured into RAID groups for resiliency. Such arrangements of on-line disk storage systems constitutes one of the major consumers of power in HPC centers. Many disk power management (DPM) schemes have been suggested where by the power consumed by these disks is reduced by spinning them down after they experience long idle periods. Spinning the disks down and up results in additional energy and response time costs. For that reason, DPM schemes are effective only if the disks experience relatively long idle periods and the scheme does not introduce a severe response time penalty. In this paper we focus on RAID storage systems where by, depending on the RAID level, a group of disks are formed into RAID units. We introduce a dynamic block exchange algorithm which switches data between such units based on the observed workload such that frequently accessed blocks end up residing on a few "hot" units thus allowing the majority of RAID groups to experience longer idle periods. We validated the effectiveness of the algorithm with several real-life and synthetic traces showing power savings of up to 50% with very small response time penalties.

**Keywords:** Energy Saving, RAID System Configuration, Energy-aware storage.

## 1 Introduction

Large scale scientific computing research and applications are generating and exploring information contents of extremely large datasets most of which are maintained online for easy accessibility to a community of researchers. These large datasets are retained and managed on thousands of traditional rotating disks and sometimes supported by mass storage systems when the data is to be migrated to deep archive.

As prices of disks are getting cheaper in terms of dollars per gigabyte, the prediction is that the energy costs for operating and cooling these rotating disks will eventually outstrip the cost of the disks and the associated hardware needed to control them [1]. As a result, there are now many research programs in industry, government and academia, which address reducing energy costs at data centers. Disk storage vendors are introducing more energy efficient hard disks drives with rotating platters (HDD) [2] as well

M. Gertz and B. Ludäscher (Eds.): SSDBM 2010, LNCS 6187, pp. 322–341, 2010.

as Solid State Drives (SSDs)[3] whose energy consumption is only a fraction of that of HDDs. Examples of such initiatives and programs for energy efficient computing currently underway include:

- The Green Grid Consortium that include such companies as IBM, Microsoft, Google, NetApps, $EMC^2$, etc.
- DiskEnergy at Microsoft Research [4].
- The GreenLight project at UC San Diego,
- The Leadership in energy Efficient Computing (LEEC) at LBNL,
- The Green-NET Project in INRIA

Currently it is estimated that disk storage systems consume about 25–35 percent of the total power used in data centers [5]. This percentage of power consumption by disk storage systems will only continue to increase, as data intensive applications demand fast and reliable access to on-line data resources. This in turn requires the deployment of power hungry faster (high rpm) and larger capacity disks.

Reducing the energy consumption of the disk storage system has been addressed in many recent research works. Research efforts are directed at several levels such as *physical device* level, *systems* level and dynamic power management (DPM) algorithms. At the physical device level, disk manufacturers are developing new energy efficient disks [6] and hybrid disks (i.e., disks with integrated flash memory caches). At the system level, a number of integrated storage solutions such as MAID [7], PARAID [8], PERGAMUM [9] and SEA [10] have emerged all of which are based on the general principle of transitioning the disks automatically to a low-power state (standby) after they experience some pre-determined period of inactivity. This period of inactivity is also called *idleness threshold* in the literature.

Disks cannot service any I/O requests when they are in the standby state. For that reason, a read or write I/O request targeted to a standby disk causes it to spin-up and return to the active state before it can service it. This of course comes at the expense of a longer response time to satisfy the I/O request as well as a penalty in terms of energy costs incurred by the transitioning from the standby to the active state.

In this paper we focus on algorithms for conserving energy in storage systems configured as RAID. These are commonly found in many high performance scientific computing centers where applications require parallel access to disks as well as fault-tolerance. We compare our results with another technique used to conserve energy in RAID environments called PARAID.

Dynamic power management (DPM) algorithms have been proposed to make decisions in real time when disks should be transitioned to a lower power dissipation state while experiencing an idle period. Analytical solutions to this online problem have been evaluated in terms of their competitive ratio. This ratio is used to compare the energy cost of an online DPM algorithm to the energy cost of an optimal offline solution which knows the arrival sequence of disk access requests in advance. It is well known [11] that for a two state system where the disk can be in either standby or in idle mode there is a tight bound of 2 for the competitive ratio of any deterministic algorithm. This ratio is achieved by setting the idleness threshold, $T_\tau$, to $\frac{\beta}{P_\tau}$ where $\beta$ is the energy penalty (in joules) for having to serve a request while the disk is in standby mode, (i.e., spinning the disk down and then spinning it up in order to serve a request) and $P_\tau$ is the rate of energy consumption of the disk (in watts) in the idle mode. We call this value the *competitive idleness threshold*. This work however, addresses only independent disks and not when disks are configured into units of RAID groups where for example to maintain RAID-5 storage configuration, a minimum of 3-disks are grouped into a RAID Group (RDG) unit. In this paper we focus on energy savings on configurations of RAID units where the I/Os are mainly for read requests. Figure 1 shows a schematic diagram of the storage configuration for energy efficient resilient storage. We consider write requests to be handled efficiently by using any one of the energy-friendly approaches presented in the literature. For example, in [9] it is recommended that files will be written into an already spinning disk if sufficient space is found on it or written into any other disk (using best-fit or first-fit policy) where sufficient space can be found. The written file may be re-allocated to a better location later during a reorganization process. Another recently proposed strategy for energy saving for writes is called Write Off-Loading [4]. This technique allows write requests to spun-down disks to be temporarily redirected reliably to persistent storage elsewhere in the data center.

Our approach for extending the disk idle period is to exchange data between RAID groups (RDGs) such that the most frequently accessed data ends up residing on a few of the RDGs which are kept almost always spinning (active state) while the rest of the RDGs can be powered down most of the time. Our block exchange algorithm also makes sure that the active disks are not overloaded beyond an acceptable response time threshold.

The general idea is best explained in terms of temperatures of the disks and of Exchange Blocks (XB), where each XB may consist of several physical disk blocks. The temperature of a disk is determined by the arrival rate of requests to it. The higher the arrival rate of requests to an RDG, the hotter it becomes. An XB is designated as *hot* if it is accessed frequently otherwise it is considered *cool*. Our algorithm performs two types of exchanges. First, it exchanges relatively cool XBs from hot disks with hot XBs taken from cool disks. Second, in order to guarantee acceptable response times, hot disks that are overloaded with too many hot XBs are cooled off by removing hot XBs from them to cooler disks.

## 1.1 Contributions of This Paper

In this paper, we propose a new dynamic block exchange algorithm which can save up to 50% of energy consumption while satisfying response time constraints. We use a queuing model and measurements of observed workloads in order to re-distribute the workload among the disks by exchanging blocks such that a small fraction of the disks are kept spinning while the rest can be placed in standby mode. The algorithm is intended to be used with off-the-shelf disk storage systems configured as RAID systems with or without the presence of SSD drives. We present efficient data structures for mapping disk blocks to disks. We then present the results of simulating the performance of our proposed dynamic exchange block algorithms and compare these with those of PARAID [8] using SimPy [12]). Results show that our power saving algorithm achieves over 50% savings in energy with small response time penalties when applied to both real life and synthetic workloads.

The remainder of the paper is organized as follows. More details about related relevant work are provided in Section 2. In Section 3 we present the exchange algorithm and the computations that are needed to determine which RDGs participate in block exchanges and give some details of the data structure to identify hold and cold blocks to be exchanged in Section 4. Experimental results are presented in section 5 and we conclude with Section 6. The details of the exchange algorithms are presented in the Appendix.

## 2 Related Work

The implementation of energy efficient storage systems has received much attention lately from governement, industry and academia. Hardware vendors are now offering energy-efficient hard disk drives (HDD), Solid State Devices (SSD) as alternatives to HDD and also hybrid disks [13] that utilize SSDs as caches to HDDs. SSDs typically use non-volatile flash memory or battery backed RAM which offer great energy savings since there are no mechanical parts involved. However their prohibitively high cost in terms of dollars per gigagabyte makes them an ineffective option for replacing HDDs in large data centers [14].

Energy efficient storage systems including both hardware and software are offered by companies such as COPAN mainly targeting write-once/read-occasionally (WORO) data. Their solution is based on the MAID (Massive Array of Idle Disks) platform which guarantees that only about 25% of the disks in each enclosure are powered at any one time. Another energy efficient prototype storage system for this kind of data, called Pergamum, has been recently reported in [9]. It is based on a distributed network of disk-based storage appliances using the hybrid-disk approach. Pergamum uses a relatively small NVRAM attached to each node, called Tome, to allow storage of data signatures (used in disk recovery) and also metadata.

A different approach is taken by the experimental system Hibernator [15] which assumes the availability of multi-speed disks. The system divides the disks into tiers where disks in different tiers can spin at different speeds. The system dynamically assigns speeds to different tiers based on observed workloads while also automatically migrating data between the disks in order to save energy while satisfying response time constraints. A storage system called PARAID (Power-Aware RAID) presented in [8] introduces a skewed striping pattern that allows RAID devices to use just enough disks to meet the system load. The system "shifts gears" based on the observed workload by varying the number of powered-on disks to meet the response time constraints while conserving energy. We denote by *PARAID(N,M)* a PARAID system based on RAID groups each consisting of $N$ disks where the number of active disks in a group can be shifted down to $M$. The main difference between these systems and the block exchange algorithm in this paper is that both Hibernator and PARAID allow exchange of blocks only within a single RAID group whereas our algorithm exchanges data blocks between different RAID groups (RDGs). We assume block-level striping of the files across the available disks in an RDG. The blocks in a stripe together with the parity block form an *RDG segment of blocks*. As a result we exchange segments of data blocks between RAID groups (see illustration in Figure 5). Nevertheless, we will use the term *Exchange Block (XB)* when we mean a segment of data blocks since the algorithm also applies to non-RAID configuration. For example each RAID group can be configured simply as a single disk.

Other differences between our work and the Hibernator is that the Hibernator assumes multispeed disks which are not currently available whereas in this paper we assume a RAID group can only be in either of two states (active or standby) and a transition state (an idle mode). PARAID needs to reserve extra space on active disks for storing the replicated data from the standby disks.

Concentrating *frequently accessed blocks* on a few disks in this paper, is similar in concept with the *popular data concentration (PDC)* concepts of [16]. However, PDC exchanges popular "files", instead of "data blocks". Exchanging fixed-size blocks is transparent to the file system implemented on top of the storage. The use of low level block exchanges on storage systems and how block table maps are utilized for this purpose are describd in [17,18].

Other algorithmic approaches to conserve energy include power-aware caching policies where replacement is based on minimizing energy consumption rather that minimizing cache misses. Several caching algorithms that use dynamic programming are presented in [19,20]. Several interesting theoretical results have been published during the last decade in the area of Dynamic Power Management (DPM) for disk systems. Many of these results are reviewed in [11]. Most of this work assumes a single disk and attempts to find an optimal idle waiting period (also called idleness threshold time) after which a disk should be moved to a state which consumes less power. Requests can only

**Table 1.** Characteristics of existing studies

| Techniques | Cache | Migration | Placement | Replication | Spin-down | Multi-disk | RAID-based | Evaulation tools | Traces | Storage model | Metrics |
|---|---|---|---|---|---|---|---|---|---|---|---|
| PDC | | Y | | | Y | Y | | Own simulator | Synthetic, Hummingbird, PoP | Seagate Cheetah ST39205LC (SCSI) | Energy saving |
| Hibernator | | Y | | | | Y | | DiskSim | OLTP, Cello99 | IBM Ultrastar 36Z15 (SCSI) | Avg response time, energy saving |
| RIMAC | Y | | | | Y | | Y | DiskSim+own | Cello99, TPC-D, SPC search | IBM Ultrastar 36Z15 (SCSI) | Response time, power consumption |
| PARAID | | | | Y | Y | | Y | Prototype | Web trace, Cello99 | Fujitsu MAP3367 (SCSI) | Response time, power consumption |
| SEA | | | Y | | | Y | Y | Own simulator | Synthetic | Seagate Cheetah ST39205LC (SCSI) | Response time, power consumption |

be served when the disk is at the highest power state (active state) and there is a penalty associated with moving from a lower power state to the active state. The problem is that of devising dynamic on-line algorithms for selecting optimal idleness threshold times, based on observed idle periods between request arrivals, to transition the disk from one power state to another. The most common case has only two states namely, active state (full power) and standby (sleep) state. The quality of these algorithms is measured by their competitive ratio which compares their power consumption to that of an optimal offline algorithm. It has been shown that in the two state case a competitive ratio of 2 is the best possible. Another type of theoretical work uses a probabilistic model checking tool PRISM used to explore DPM using probabilistic models. The main characteristics of related studies in the area of energy efficient disk systems are summarized in Table 1.

# 3 Features of the Exchange Algorithm

## 3.1 The Storage Configuration

Figure 1 illustrates the storage architecture. It consists of an array of conventional disk storage configured into identical *RAID Groups (RDG)*. A RAID (Redundant Array of Inexpensive Disks), is a form of storage system in data centers that provides high performance and fault tolerance at a relatively low cost. Each RDG in our system can be configured as RAID-0, RAID-1, RAID-4 or RAID-5. We will assume, from now on, that each RDG is configured as a RAID-5 unit. A *RAID Group* uses a Solid State Drive (SSD) as a large cache to stage data read from and written into an RDG. Using an SSD for each RDG is attractive since it is fast, durable, noiseless and energy efficient and currently is also available in large capacities of the order 64, 128, 256 GiB [3]. An I/O sub-system, complete with I/O nodes, maintains a large number of RDGs. Clients interact with the I/O subsystems by writing and reading files either as a parallel file system or as Storage Area Network (SAN), with the provision that each block of a file must be entirely contained in an RDG unit. A good conceptual view of our systems is that of nested RAID-5+0 [21] (see Figure 5. We call the set of disk blocks (also termed disk chunks) in an RDG that form a *stripe* an *RDG segment*. Our configuration allows for migrating *RDG segments* (as explained subsequently) of disk blocks from one RDG to another.

Files in each RDG unit are striped according to the configured RAID level of the RDGs. One primary objective of the system is to concentrate active files in a small enough number of active RDG units without compromising the aggregate I/O bandwidth that satisfies the required response time of data accesses. Two approaches to achieving this is by dynamically migrating either entire files or *RDG segments* from an RDG with less I/O requests to others with high I/O activity but with just enough load on the active RDGs that the overall bandwidth is sufficient to meet the response time requirements. In this manner the less active RDGs can be idle long enough for the entire RDG unit to be spun down.

The SSD caches may prolong the idle times of RDG units and extend the shutdown periods of an RDG unit. In this paper the unit of exchange is called an XB (exchange block) which consists of one or more *RDG segments*.

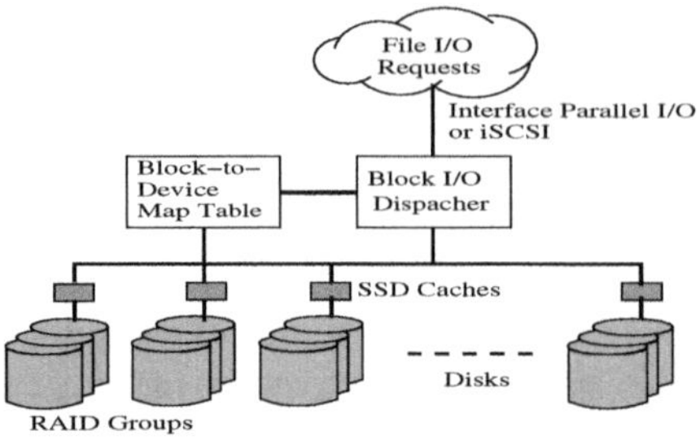


**Fig. 1.** Overview of RAID configured energy smart disk storage

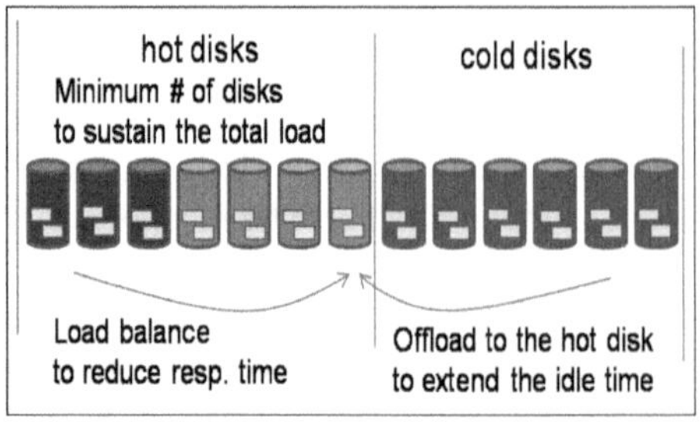


**Fig. 2.** Two ways of XB exchanges

### 3.2 Arrival and Departure Rates

Before introducing the exchange system, we first define the arrival and departure rate for an RDG. The arrival rate for an RDG means the arrival rate of block requests received by the RDG but excluding the requests introduced by the block exchanges. We divide the timeline into epochs of $T$ seconds and predict the mean arrival rate $R$ for the next epoch as a weighted average of our predicted arrival rate $R^{pred}$ and the measured arrival rate $R^{meas}$ of the previous epoch. The rate $R$ is computed by the following equation,

$$R = w \cdot R^{pred} + (1 - w) \cdot R^{meas},$$

where the constant $w$ represents the weight of the previously predicted arrival rate. As shown later, when $R$ exceeds a given threshold the arrival rate of the RDG becomes too high and its requests should be off-loaded to other RDGs. In computing $R$, we intentionally ignore the portion of the arrival rate caused by block exchanges in order to prevent off-loading an RDG whose load is caused only by exchanges and not by real data requests.

The predicted departure rate $D$ includes serviced requests due to either original data requests as well as requests caused by exchanges. To ensure proper update of $D$ under heavy workload, we update $D$ after every $K$ requests are serviced, instead of the fixed time epochs used for computing $R$. We use the following equation to compute $D$,

$$D = w \cdot D^{pred} + (1 - w) \cdot D^{meas},$$

where $D^{pred}$ is our previous prediction and $D^{meas}$ is the average of the measured departure rate over the latest $K$ requests, i.e., $D^{meas} = K/q$ where $q$ is the number of seconds it took to service the last $K$ requests. Using such a definition, the departure rate of a *hot* RDGs reflects whether the disk is still suitable to share more workload from other RDGs immediately, particularly when the RDG becomes busy. Including the exchange workload in the computation of $D$ can stop an RDG from a short term overloading due to exchange. In this work, we set $w$ to 0.875, $T$ to 10 sec, and $K$ to 128 based on analyzing several real workload traces.

### 3.3 Hot and Cool RDGs

We maintain a sorted list $L$ of the $n$ RDGs in decreasing order of their $D$ (departure rate) values. Each time the value of $D$ changes for any RDG, it is moved to its appropriate position in $L$ according to the sort order. As shown in Figure 2, the system divides $L$ into two groups. The first $m$ RDGs in $L$ are characterized as *hot* while the other $n-m$ RDGs are characterized as *cool*.

We refer to the unit of data exchanged between RDGs by the algorithm as XB (exchange block) and this may consist of one or several RAID stripes. We use two types of block exchanges. The first type of exchange is performed after a block is accessed on a *cool* RDG. The algorithm interchanges the XB containing this block with an XB that was not accessed recently residing on a *hot* RDG starting the search for the first such XB with the RDG at position $m$ in $L$ followed by position $m-1$ etc. The logic behind this type of exchange is to "lower" the temperature of *cool* RDGs to further reduce their request arrival rate and thus extend their idle time periods. The second type of exchange is used to avoid overheating of *hot* RDGs that may cause long queuing delays and excessive response times. This exchange is performed after accessing a block on a *hot* RDG at position $j$ in $L$ where $1 \leq j < m$ if it is determined that the RDG is overloaded. In this case, the XB containing the accessed block will be interchanged with an XB that was not accessed recently in RDGs "cooler" than $j$ in the *hot* group. The search for such an XB starts from an RDGs at position $m, m-1, \ldots, j+1$ until a first such XB is found.

The number, $m$, of *hot* RDGs is dynamically determined based on the arrival rate of user requests. If the arrival rate is high, then more RDGs would be included in this group. These *hot* RDGs are never shut down in order to serve the bulk of arriving requests efficiently. On the other hand, the *cool* RDGs are supposed to have long idle time periods allowing greater power saving. The calculation of $m$ is described in the subsequent subsection.

### 3.4 Sustainable Rate of RDGs

As explained above, the goal of the block exchange system is to dynamically balance the load of the *hot* RDGs. By moving out the frequently-accessed XBs from an overloaded one, the arrival rate of the RDG would be reduced and the response time of requests can be efficiently shortened. However, the penalty associated with this exchange is that it can potentially cause more RDGs to move to an active state in order to serve the user requests. Let us denote by $t$ the constraint on expected response time acceptable to users. We now show how to calculate the maximum arrival rate that is sustainable by a hot RDG while still satisfying $t$. In the remainder of this paper, we will call this rate the *sustainable rate* of an RDG and denote it by $S(R)$.

In [22] we analyzed the energy savings and response time trade-offs, and presented an analytical model to estimate the power cost and response time of an RDG under different arrival rates and service times of requests. We now describe how $S(R)$ is computed. From [22], we know that the expected response time, $E[J]$ in the *hot* RDGs is

$$E[J] = \frac{\rho}{1-\rho}\frac{E[S^2]}{2E[S]} + E[S].$$

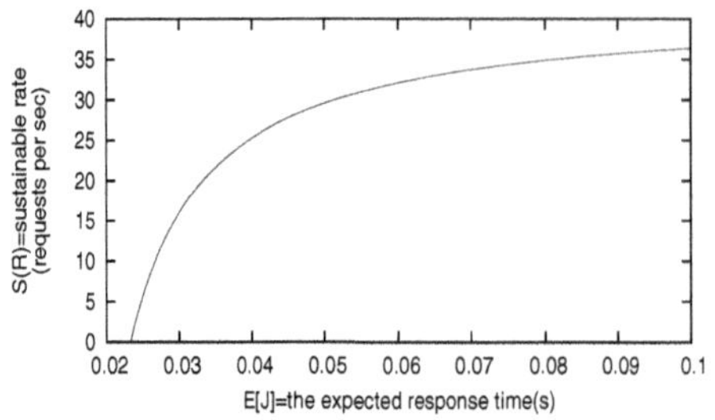


**Fig. 3.** Relationship between expected response time and sustainable rate of an RDG

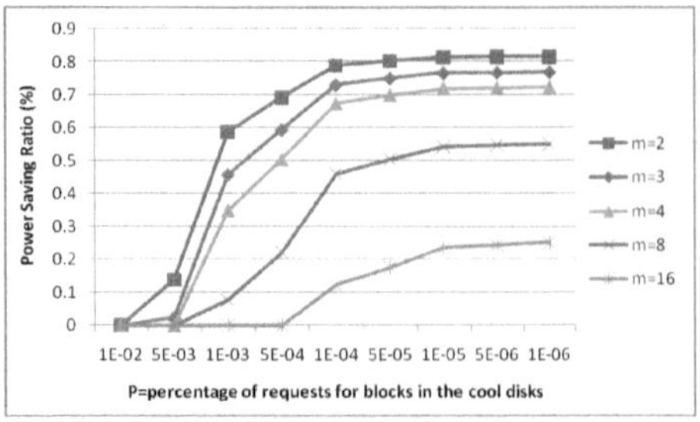


**Fig. 4.** The potential power saving ratio of EXGBLK under different request arrival rates

where ρ is the load, i.e., $\rho = R * E[S]$, $R$ is the arrival rate, and $E[S]$ is the expected service time of requests. In our case, based on the disk characteristics given in Figure 2 and the real life workload of [23], we get E[S]=0.022 and E[S$^2$]=5.24E-4. Figure 3 plots the relationship between the expected response time, $E[J]$ and the arrival rate $S[R]$ for a single *hot* RDG as calculated from the above expression. From the figure, we can see that, to achieve a response time constraint $t = 0.05$, the sustainable rate of an RDG $S(R)$ should be set to 30 requests per second assuming block exchange operations are executed.

Then, after determining $S(R)$, we can calculate the number $m$ of *hot* RDGs as follows,

$$m = \left\lceil \frac{\sum_{i=1}^{n} R_i}{S(R)} \right\rceil$$

where $R_i$ is the arrival rate of the $i^{th}$ RDG.

Also, based on our analysis model, we can estimate the potential power saving by our block exchange algorithm called BLKEXG. For example, in Figure 4 we plot the power saving ratio as a function of $P$ the percentage of requests arrivals (including exchanges) to the cool RDGs for different values of $m$ (the hot RDGs).

Figure 4 shows the normalized power saving of BLKEXG, compared to the NPS (no power saving) case over different $P$ and $m$, respectively. In this figure we assume the system consists of $n = 24$ RDGs with $t = 0.08$, from which we derive $S(R)$ to be 35 based on Figure 3.

### 3.5 Thresholds for Starting Block Exchanges

There are three thresholds, LowTH, TargetTH, and HighTH, applied to each RDG to determine whether to proceed with a block exchange. Since our goal is to keep the arrival rate of each *hot* RDG close to its $S(R)$, sustainable rate of an RDG, we set TargetTH to $S(R)$. Then, as described in *Procedure Recv()* (please see the Appendix), to achieve a load balance among the *hot* RDGs, whenever a request arrives for blocks in a *hot* RDG, ranked $j$ in $L$, we check whether its arrival rate is higher than the high threshold HighTH. If it is, then the RDG is marked as a *hotspot*. For each of the requests arriving to the RDG, after serving the request, the ExgBlk function is called to locate the XB which contains the requested block. Then, the XB is exchanged with an un-accessed XB starting the search from the RDG currently ranked $m$ in $L$ (*hot* RDGs with the lowest departure rates) and proceeding to $m-1$ up to $j+1$. In the search, RDGs marked as *hotspot* will be skipped due to their heavy loads. Note that since the currently accessed RDG is ranked $j$, then the search is stopped after the rank $j+1$ since continuing the search will only encounter RDGs with ranks smaller than $j$ which must have higher $D$ (departure rates).

The procedure to locate an un-accessed block in a selected RDG is called GetUnaccessedXB() and is described in Section 4 and uses a tree data structure. It returns -1 if all blocks on the RDG are accessed.

Such an exchange will proceed whenever a request arrives to the hotspot RDG until the arrival rate of the RDG is lower or equal to the TargetTH. Then, the *hotspot* mark will be removed. Let us now turn to the procedure for extending the idle time of the *cool* RDGs which is similar to the above procedure. Whenever a request arrives for blocks in a *cool* RDG, we examine whether the arrival rate of the RDG is lower than the low threshold LowTH. If it is, after serving the request, we call ExgBlk to locate the XB which covers the requested block and then exchange the XB with an un-accessed XB located at a *hot* RDG starting the search with the RDG with the lowest departure rate (ranked $m$).

Note that here we exchange blocks with a *hot* RDG based on measurements of departure rate (the lowest departure rate), instead of the lowest arrival rate. The reason is that an RDG with low arrival rate may be busy serving the queued requests. Also, since the exchange itself also adds loading to the selected *hot* RDG, by picking the *hot* RDG with the lowest departure rate, we can further avoid the selected RDG from short-term overloading caused by the exchange operations. Also note that due to the dynamic sorting of the RDGs based on their departure rates, the blocks are exchanged with different *hot* RDGs at different times thus leading to load balancing among them.

# 4 Data Structures for Block Mapping

## 4.1 How to Select Blocks for Exchanges

As described in Section 3.3, we need to pick a non-frequently accessed XB from the coolest *hot* disk for the exchange. Thus, we need a method to quickly find such an XB on a disk. To simplify the problem, let's first assume we want to distinguish between the XBs accessed at least once from the ones who have never been accessed called un-accessed XBs. The naïve way to satisfy this goal is to allocate a bit vector (initialized to all 0's) which we call XB-Access-Vector where each bit in the vector corresponds to one XB on the disk. Once an XB is accessed, we turn its corresponding bit to 1 if it is 0. Then, to find an un-accessed XB, one can sequentially search the XB-Access-Vector until encountering a 0 bit. However, this method needs N-bits of space and O(N) search time, where N is the number of XBs in one disk. To reduce the search time, we propose a binary tree structure as shown in Figure 6 which we call double-bit tree (DBT).

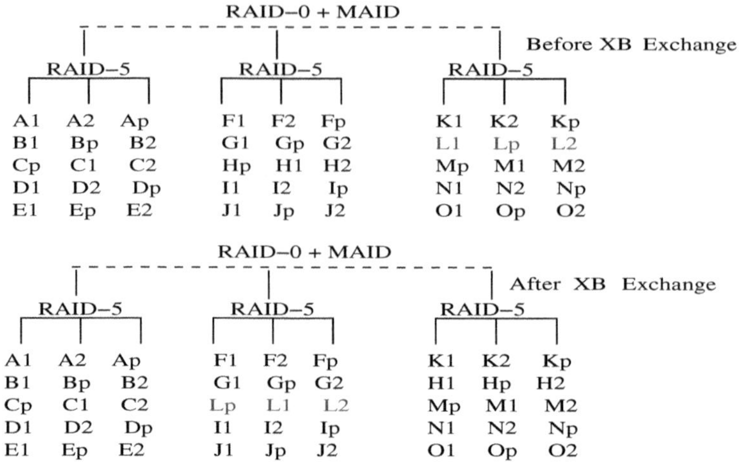


**Fig. 5.** Illustration of XB exchanges in a RAID-0 + MAID configurations

Each internal node of the DBT consists of two bits called the left-bit and the right-bit. The leaves of the DBT are formed from the entries of the XB-Access-Vector, i.e each bit corresponds to an XB and it is set to 0 or 1 according to whether the corresponding XB was accessed or not respectively. The left-bit (right-bit) of an internal node in a DBT is set to 0 if at least one of the leaves in its left (right) sub-tree are 0 otherwise it is set to 1. To find an un-accessed XB, one starts searching from the root of the DBT, if both left and right bits at the root are 1 all XBs at the leaves have been accessed and the search stops. Otherwise we search recursively in the left sub-tree of the root if the left-bit=0 or search in the right sub-tree if left-bit=1. For reference purposes we call this DBT search procedure GetUnaccessedXB. It is easy to see that GetUnaccessedXB operates in $O(logN)$ steps. Updating the DBT once an un-accessed XB gets accessed is done by changing the bit at the leaf corresponding to that XB to 1 and updating the internal nodes on the path from the leaf to the root as necessary. The update procedure simply changes the left-bit (right-bit) of a parent node to 1 if both the left and right bits of its left (right) child are 1. This can also be done in $O(logN)$ steps.

### 4.2 Block Exchange Information

We can now build a slightly more complex data structure that monitors the access frequency of XBs across a time window of $s$ time units and decides whether an XB is frequently accessed during the time window. To do this we maintain a set of XB-Access-Vectors (XAB) called $XAB(T_i)$ for the last $s$ time units $T_1, T_2, ..., T_s$. We then compute an additional vector called Total-XB-Access-Vector where each of its entries is a function $g$ (based on some weighted average) of the corresponding entries in $XAB(T_i)$ for $i = 1, 2, .., s$. The DBT is then built using the Total-XB-Access Vector entries as its leaves. An example of this is given in Figure 7 for $s = 3$. In the formula below we give more weight ($W_i = 2^{i-1}$) to more recent accesses than ones that occurred in the past but

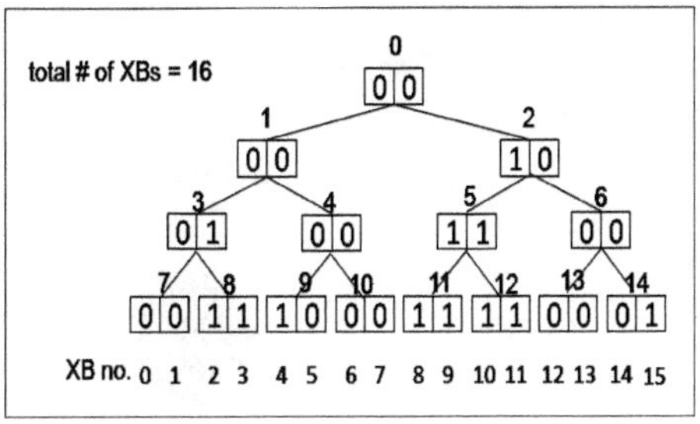


**Fig. 6.** The Tree Structure to locate Block Accesses

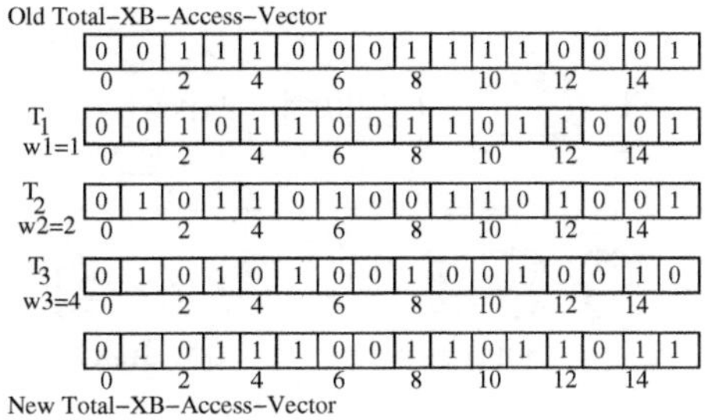


**Fig. 7.** Information retained to track frequently accessed XBs

at the same time our function also gives some fixed weight to the frequency of accesses independent of when they occurred. This is represented by the addition of 1 to each $W_i$ in the expression for $exp(j)$. In this case the function $g(j)$ which determines the value of the $j^{th}$ bit in the New Total-XB-Access-Vector is set as follows

$$\exp(j) = \sum_{i=1}^{3} XAB(T_i)[j](W_i + 1)$$

and

$$g(j) = \begin{cases} 1 & \exp(j) \geq 5 \\ 0 & \text{otherwise} \end{cases}$$

# 5 Experimental Results

## 5.1 Simulation Configuration

We developed a simulation model to examine the block exchange system proposed in Section 3. The simulation environment was developed and tested using SimPy [12], as illustrated in Figure 8. The environment consists of a workload generator, a block dispatcher, and a group of hard disks. Table 1 shows the characteristics of the hard disk used in the simulation. With the specifications taken from [6] and [24] we built our own hard disk simulation modules. A hard disk is spun down and set into standby mode (see Figure 9) after it has been idle for a fixed period which is called idleness threshold [16],[25].

The workload generator supports two different ways to produce block requests. First, the generator can follow a Poisson process to produce requests at a rate $R$ to access disks. Based on the statistics collected from the real workload [23], we set the number of disks to 24 and the data size required by each request to 8, 16, 24, or 32KB with even probabilities. Then, the arrival requests to disks are generated based on a Zipf distribution whose cumulative density function $F(x)$ is given by

$$F(x) = P(x < i) = (i/N)^{\theta}\ \forall 1 \leq i \leq N.$$

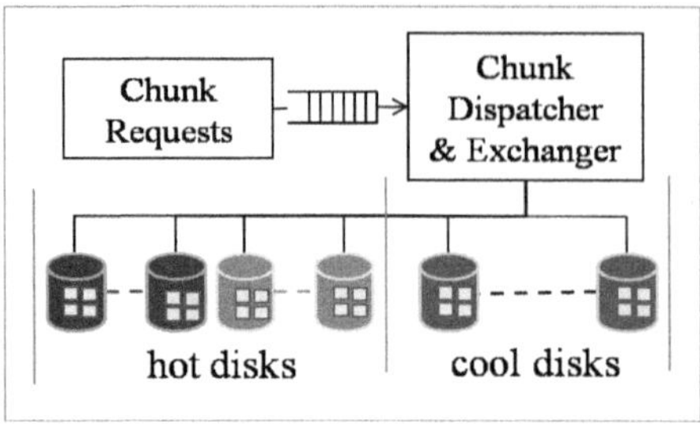


**Fig. 8.** Configuration of disks used in the simulation

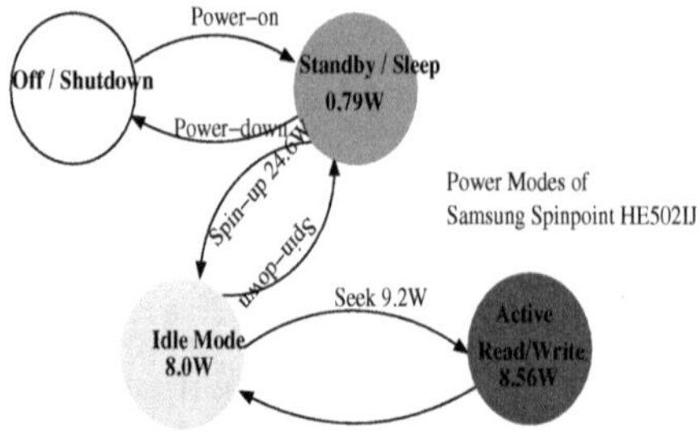


**Fig. 9.** Power usage modes of a disk drive

**Table 2.** The characteristics of the hard disk

| ***Description*** | ***Value*** |
|---|---|
| Disk model | Seagate ST3500630AS |
| Standard interface | SATA |
| Rotational speed | 7200 rpm |
| Avg. seek time | 8.5 msecs |
| Avg. rotation time | 4.16 msecs |
| Disk size | 500GB |
| Disk load (Transfer rate) | 72 MBytes/sec |
| Idle power | 9.3 Watts |
| Standby power | 0.8 Watts |
| Active power | 13 Watts |
| Seek power | 12.6 Watts |
| Spin up power | 24 Watts |
| Spin down power | 9.3 Watts |
| Spin up time | 15 secs |
| Spin down time | 10 secs |

where $N$=24 and its skew parameter $\theta$ is set to log 0.8/log 0.2, which means 80% of all requests would go to 20% of disks. Similarly, we divided the space of a disk into 500 segments. Then, the Zipf distribution is used again to determine the frequency of requests for blocks in each segment, where $N$ is set to 500.

Besides producing workload based on probability model, the workload generator can produce requests based on a log of block access to a storage system. Two realistic workload logs are used in our experimental results. The first log is the I/O trace from OLTP applications running at two large financial institutions [18]. There are 4099352 writes requests interleaved with 1235632 read requests for the blocks distributed on 24 storage devices. The mean rate of arrival requests is 123.5/s. The second log is HP Cello99 trace [HP], collected by the HP Storage Research Lab. Since the whole one-year workload is too large, we consider the trace beginning from 1999-05-01 to

1999-05-12 in the simulation, this period is about 6 times the period that was used in PARAID work. The extracted trace involves 23 storage devices, accessed by 30M write requests and 20M read requests during the time period.

In the experiments, the sustainable rate of a device was set to 35 requests per second. The high threshold (HighTH in Section 3) is 1.3 times of 35, or 45 while the low threshold (LowTH) is half of 35, i.e. 17.5. To compare the effects of the block exchange algorithm on power saving and response time, we also examined the effects of DPM with fixed idleness thresholds and PARAID(5,3) [8], denoted as PARAID in the following results. Dynamic power management (DPM) algorithms have been proposed in [11] to determine on-line when the disk should be transitioned to a lower power dissipation state while experiencing an idle period. Based on the description and configuration in PARAID, we also implemented PARAID(5,3) in our simulation, which provides two tiers of service capacity. When the request load is high, all 5 hard disks would be kept spinning to serve requests as a generic RAID-5 device. However, when the load becomes lower than a threshold, only 3 disks would be active and the other 2 disks would be spun down to save energy. To ensure that all data on the 2 spun-down disks can be accessed during the power-saving tier, PARAID initially has to reserve a specific amount of space in the 3 spinning-always disks to duplicate the data and their corresponding error correction code from the 2 spun-down disks. This reservation implies that deploying more PARAID systems may be necessary to provide the same total free space of the RAID-5 systems. To model this situation, we examine a special case of PARAID, denoted as PARAID* to provide the same free storage space as RAID-5 systems by deploying more PARAID systems. In fact, because a PARAID(5,3) system has to duplicate the data from the 2 inactive disks into the 3 spinning-always disks and in addition generate the error correction code for these data, 3/8 of space in a PARAID(5,3) system is sacrificed. That is, about 38 PARAID(5,3) systems are necessary to provide the same free space of 24 RAID-5 systems.

## 5.2 Power Saving Results for OLTP Workload

Figure 10 shows the power saving ratios of DPM, BLKEXG, PARAID, and PARAID* under the OLTP workload, the ratios are normalized with the power cost of 24 RAID-5 systems with disks that are always spinning. As shown in the figure, for this workload, simply using DPM can save 10% of power only. The reason is that the mean arrival rate for each device in the workload, 123.5/24 or 5.15/s, is too high for DPM to save power. From earlier results of [22,26], DPM can only save power if the arrival rate for a disk is smaller than 0.029/s. Finally, compared to DPM which saves at most 10%, the BLKEXG system can save up to 50% of the power cost.

Figure 11 further displays the power cost for each RAID device. Obviously, by concentrating frequently accessed blocks into the hot devices from the cool devices, only three devices are necessary to be active (always spinning) to serve requests. The other 21 device can have longer idle periods to save power and thus their mean power cost is only 15W. On the other hand, by using DPM, although some devices may have long idle periods which are sufficient to produce beneficial power savings, the other devices are still too busy to save any power.

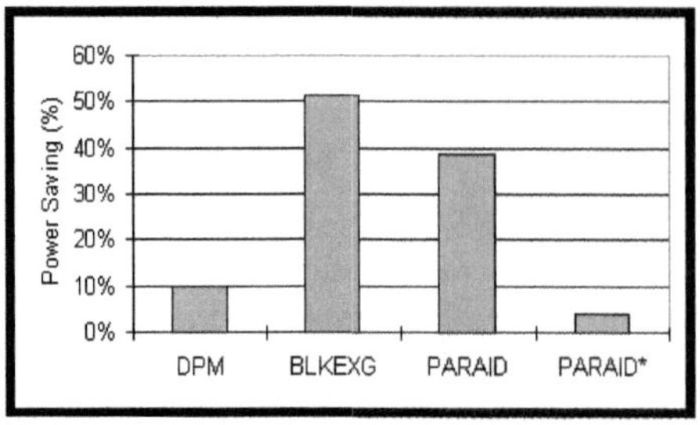


Fig. 10. Power saving ratio of DPM, BLKEXG and PARAID

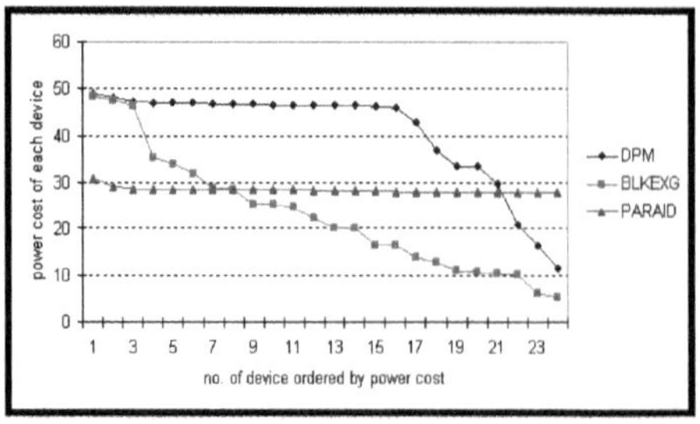


Fig. 11. The power cost of each device under DPM, PARAID, and BLKEXG

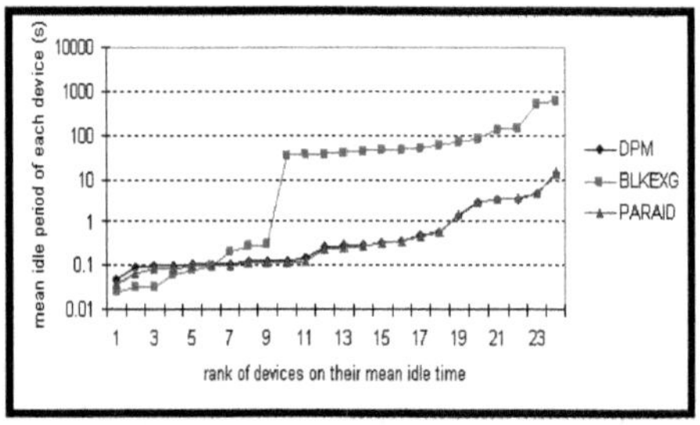


Fig. 12. The mean idle period of each device under DPM, PARAID, and BLKEXG

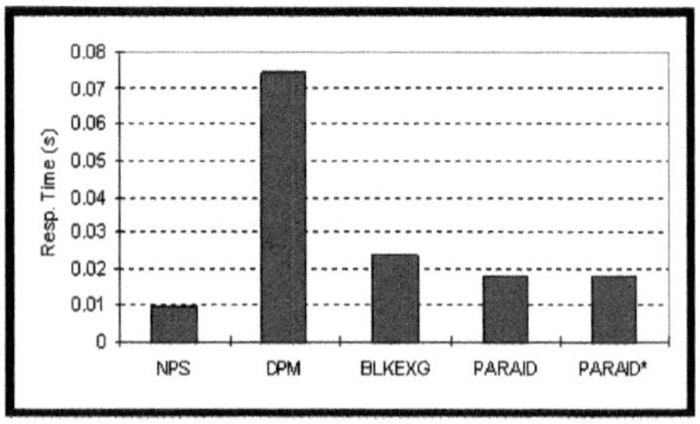


Fig. 13. Comparison of response times for different power saving mechanisms

Figure 12 shows the mean idle period of devices under these power saving mechanisms. Using this figure, we find that BLKEXG can increase the length of the idle period by a factor of almost 100 times of that under DPM or PARAID, by concentrating blocks into the hot devices. The BLKEXG curve shows that the "hottest" devices are chosen to always spin as they have short idle times due to the concentration of frequently accessed blocks on them, this however makes the other devices have long idle periods sufficient to produce power savings.

### 5.3 Response Time Results for OLTP Workload

Saving power often implies an increase in response time. Therefore, it is important to measure the response time penalty due to the power saving policy. Figure 13 shows the response times of requests using DPM, BLKEXG, and PARAID. Again, while DPM only saves 10% of power, it seriously impacts the performance, i.e. increases the response time by a factor of more than 7.5 of that of devices without power saving (NPS), i.e. from 0.01s to 0.07. On the other hand, using BLKEXG only increases the response time to 0.022 while saving 50% of power cost. Obviously, deploying the block exchange system is a preferable option.

### 5.4 Power Saving and Response Time Results for the CELLO99 Workload

We now examine the power saving and response time provided by BLKEXG, DPM, PARAID, and PARAID* under the CELLO99 workload. Figure 14 shows the power saving ratio for each saving mechanisms, compared to the case where power saving modes of devices are disabled. The results display that BLKEXG can save 64% of energy, which is double the savings achieved by simply using the DPM mechanism and 16% more than PARAID. In fact, since PARAID has to keep at least 3 disks spinning, it is hard to save more energy in this case. Moreover, as shown in Figure 14 (the bar corresponding to PARAID*), if the total free space provided by a storage system is considered, then PARAID would save only 12% of energy since more PARAID systems are required to provide the same free space as that by others.

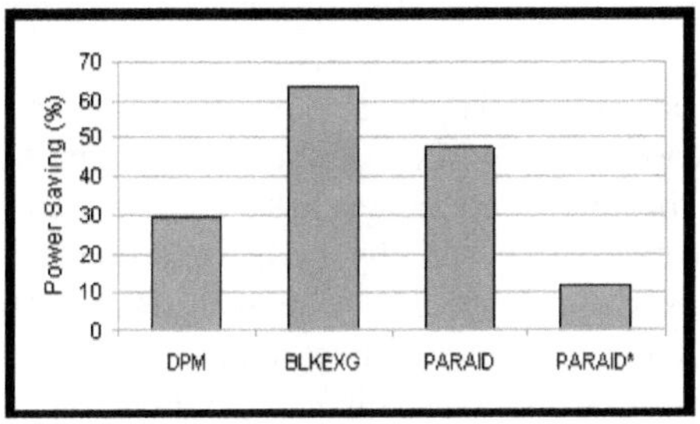


**Fig. 14.** Comparison of power savings of HP Cello99 for different power saving mechanisms

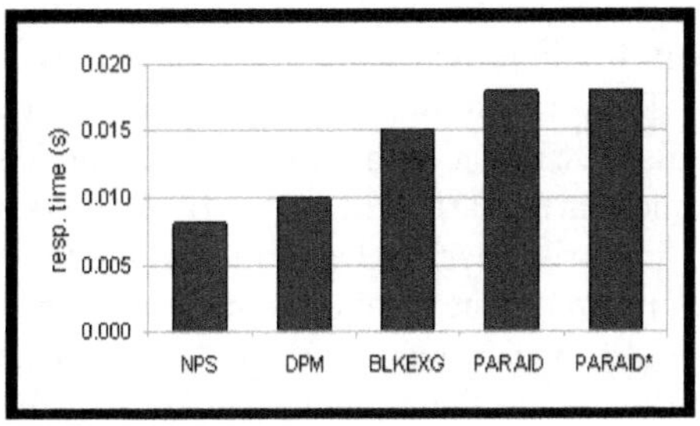


**Fig. 15.** Comparison of response times of HP Cello99 for different power saving mechanisms

Figure 15 shows the response time for each power saving mechanism. Undoubtedly, the devices without power saving mode always provide the shortest response time. Also, BLKEXG provides shorter response time than PARAID while saving more energy. On the other hand, although BLKEXG provides 1.5 times of response time of the DPM mechanism, it saves 2.2 times of energy. Finally, it is surprising that PARAID* does not provide shorter response time as compared with PARAID although PARAID* has more devices to serve requests.

### 5.5 Results for Synthetic Workload

To further verify BLKEXG under different heavy workloads, we used synthetic workloads with different arrival rate of requests and measured the effect on power saving and response time of the BLKEXG system. We also, measured power savings and response times for DPM and PARAID for comparison. Figure 16 shows the power saving ratios of these mechanisms under this workload. The ratios are normalized with the power cost of 24 RAID-5 systems with disks that are always spinning. The results show that

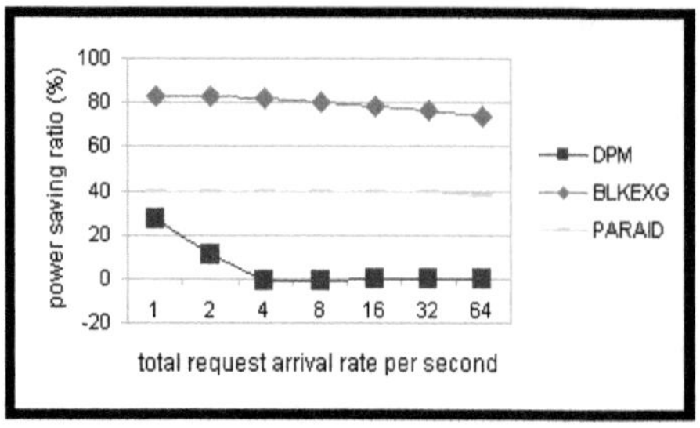


**Fig. 16.** Power saving ratios of different schemes under varying request arrival rates

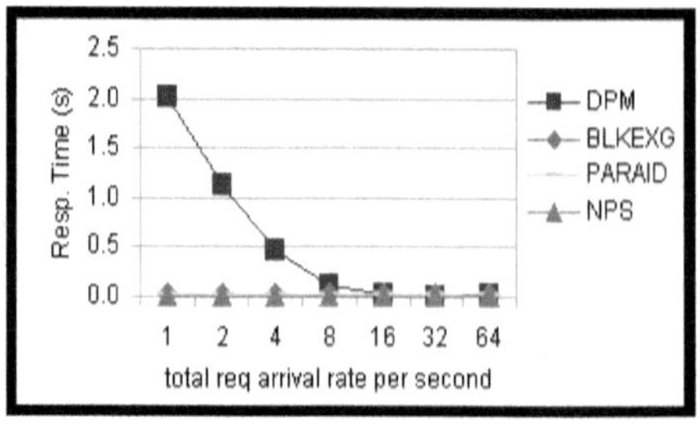


**Fig. 17.** Response times of requests for different schemes under varying arrival rates

BLKEXG can save 80% of power while PARAID provides 40% of power saving and DPM only provides about 5% on average.

Figure 17 shows the response time of requests provided by these power saving mechanisms. Similar to the results under the real workloads, DPM causes very long response times particularly when the arrival rate is low, because each request has a high probability of arrival during the periods where the hard disks are in standby mode and then has to wait a long time for the spinning up of the disks in the device. However, since BLKEXG would concentrate frequently-accessed blocks into hot devices, most requests would be redirected to these devices and only a few requests which are directed to the cool devices may suffer such long response time delays. Therefore, the response time under BLKEXG is much shorter than DPM. On the other hand, although PARAID provides similar short response times as BLKEXG, it saves only 40% of energy, which is just half of BLKEXGs.

## 6 Conclusion

In this paper, we presented a response time sensitive dynamic block exchange algorithm for reducing energy consumption of storage systems configured as RAID-5 systems and compared this with a similar RAID-5 energy saving system given by PARAID. Our algorithm operates by measuring arrival rates at each of the RDG and then dynamically re-distributing the workload by exchanging data segments of RDG blocks when necessary. We also presented the necessary data structures for quickly identifying blocks that need to be exchanged. Using real life workloads we showed that the algorithm leads to the concentration of the bulk of the disk access traffic on a small fraction of the available disks. This allows the remaining disks to experience longer idle periods which in turn makes the DPM (dynamic power management) procedures much more effective.

Extensive experiments with our block exchange algorithm showed that it is much more efficient than simply using known DPM procedures or the PARAID approach. In contrast to PARAID, our algorithm does not need to copy data from stand-by disks within an RDG and therefore more space efficient. For typical workloads, our algorithm is more efficient than PARAID by a factor of 2 in terms of energy savings.

## Acknowledgement

We thank Jinoh Kim for his help in editing this paper. This work was supported by the Director, Office of Science, Office of Advanced Scientific Computing Research, of the U.S. Department of Energy under Contract No. DE-AC02-05CH11231.

## References

1. Harizopoulos, S., Shah, J.M.M.A., Ranganathan, P.: The new holy grail of data management systems research. In: CIDR 2009: Proc. of the 4th Biennial Conf. on Innovative Data Syst. Research. ACM, New York (2009)
2. Deskstar Hard Drives, `http://www.hitachigst.com/portal/site/en/products/deskstar/`
3. SSD: Solid State Drives From Toshiba, `http://www.toshiba.com/taec/catalog`
4. Narayanan, D., Donnelly, A., Rowstron, A.: Write off-loading: Practical power management for enterprise storage. In: Proc. 6th USENIX Conf. on File and Storage Technologies (FAST 2008), San Jose, California, pp. 253–267 (2008)
5. Gurumurthi, S., Sivasubramaniam, A., Kandemir, M., Franke, H.: Reducing disk power consumption in servers with drpm. Computer 36(12), 59–66 (2003)
6. Seagate: Seagate Barracuda 7200.10 Serial ATA Product Manual. Seagate Technology, Scotts Valley, CA (December 2007)
7. Colarelli, D., Grunwald, D.: Massive arrays of idle disks for storage archives. In: Supercomputing 2002: Proc. ACM/IEEE Conference on Supercomputing, pp. 1–11. IEEE Computer Society Press, Los Alamitos (2002)
8. Weddle, C., Oldham, M., Qian, J., Wang, A.: PARAID: A gear shifting power-aware RAID. ACM Trans. on Storage (TOS) 3(3), 28–26 (2007)
9. Storer, M.W., Greenan, K.M., Miller, E.L.: Pergamum: Replacing tape with energy efficient, reliable, disk-based archival storage. In: Proc. 6th USENIX Conf. on File and Storage Technologies (FAST 2008), San Jose, California, February 2008, pp. 1–16 (2008)
10. Xie, T.: SEA: a striping-based energy-aware strategy for data placement in RAID-structured storage system. IEEE Transactions on Computers 57(6), 748–769 (2008)
11. Irani, S., Singh, G., Shukla, S.K., Gupta, R.K.: An overview of the competitive and adversarial approaches to designing dynamic power management strategies. IEEE Trans. VLSI Syst. 13(12), 1349–1361 (2005)
12. SimPy: SimPy Simulation Package in Python, `http://simpy.sourceforge.net/`
13. Wang, A.A., Kuenning, G., Reiher, P., Popek, G.: The conquest file system: Better performance through a disk/persistent-ram hybrid design. ACM Trans. on Storage (TOS) 2(3), 309–348 (2006)
14. Narayanan, D., Thereska, E., Donnelly, A., Elnikety, S., Rowstron, A.: Migrating server storage to ssds: analysis of tradeoffs. In: EuroSys 2009: Proceedings of the 4th ACM European conference on Computer systems, pp. 145–158. ACM, New York (2009)
15. Zhu, Q., Chen, Z., Tan, L., Zhou, Y., Keeton, K., Wilkes, J.: Hibernator: Helping disk arrays sleep through the winter. In: SOSP 2005: Proc. 20th ACM Symp. on Operating Syst., pp. 177–190. ACM Press, New York (2005)
16. Pinheiro, E., Bianchini, R.: Energy conservation techniques for disk array-based servers. In: Proc. Int'l. Conf. on Supercomputing (ICS 2004), Saint-Malo, France, June 26 (2004)
17. Bhadkamkar, M., Guerra, J., Useche, L., Burnett, S., Liptak, J., Rangaswami, R.: BORG: self-adaptive file reallocation on hybrid disk arrays. In: 7th USENIX Conference on File and Storage Technologies (FAST 2009), February 2009, pp. 183–196. USENIX (2009)

18. Xie, T., Sun, Y.: PEARL: performance, energy, and reliability balanced dynamic data redistribution for next generation disk arrays. In: IEEE Int'l. Symp. Modeling, Analysis and Simulation of Computers and Telecommunication Systems, MASCOTS 2008, September 2008, pp. 1–8. IEEE, Los Alamitos (2008)
19. Zhu, Q., David, F.M., Devaraj, C.F., Li, Z., Zhou, Y., Cao, P.: Reducing energy consumption of disk storage using power-aware cache management. In: HPCA 2004: Proc. of the 10th Int'l. Symp. on High Perform. Comp. Arch., Washington, DC, USA, p. 118. IEEE Computer Society, Los Alamitos (2004)
20. Zhu, Q., Zhou, Y.: Power-aware storage cache management. IEEE Trans. Comput. 54(5), 587–602 (2005)
21. Levels, N.R.: `http://www.absoluteastronomy.com/topics/nested_raid_levels`
22. Otoo, E.J., Rotem, D., Tsao, S.C.: Energy smart management of scientific data. In: 21st Int'l. Conf. on Sc. and Stat. Database Mgmnt., New Orleans, Louisiana, USA (June 2009)
23. UMassTraceRepository: `http://traces.cs.umass.edu/index.php/storage/storage`
24. Zedlewski, J., Sobti, S., Garg, N., Zheng, F., Krishnamurthy, A., Wang, R.: Modeling hard-disk power consumption. In: FAST 2003: Proc. 2nd USENIX Conf. on File and Storage Tech., Berkeley, CA, USA, pp. 217–230. USENIX Association (2003)
25. Cunha, C., Bestavros, A., Crovella, M.: Characteristics of www client-based traces. Technical report, Boston University, Boston, MA, USA (1995)
26. Otoo, E.J., Rotem, D., Tsao, S.C.: Workload-adaptive management of energy-smart disk storage systems. In: IASDS 2009: Workshop on Interfaces and Architectures for Scientific Data Storage, New Orleans, Louisiana, USA (September 2009)

## Appendix: Algorithms

The following functions are used in the algorithm, for lack of space we simply explain here what each of them does.

(1) GetMappedDevID(): Get the current ID of the device to be accessed by a request.
(2) GetMappedBlockID(): Get the address of a block on a device.
(3) ForwardToDev(): Forward a request to a device.
(4) GetCorrespondingXB(): Locate the XB (exchange block containing a given block).
(5) GetDevIDWithRank(): Get the ID of a device with a given rank in *L*.
(6) Exchange(): Perform an exchange between two XBs.

---

**Procedure** Recv(Req,HotSpot)

```
begin
    Input: Req: Received Request
    Output: HotSpot: a bit vector where each bit corresponds to a storage device
    id_dev ← GetMappedDevID(req) ;
    id_blk ← GetMappedBlockID(req) ;
    ForwardToDev(id_dev,id_blk) ;
    if (isHot(id_dev)) then
        if Req(id_dev)≥ HighTH then
            HotSpot[id_dev]← 1
        else
            if Req(id_dev) < TargetTH then
                HotSpot[id_dev] ← 0
        if HotSpot[id_dev]=1 then
            ExgBlk(id_dev,id_blk)
    else
        if Req(id_dev) < LowTH then
            ExgBlk(id_dev,id_blk)
```

---

**Function** ExgBlk(id_dev,id_blk)

```
begin
    Input: id_dev: device id, id_blk: block id
    id_XB ← GetCorrespondingXB(id_blk) ;
    for i ← m downto 1 do
        nid_dev ← GetDevIDWithRank(i);
        if HotSpot[nid_dev] = 1 then continue ;
        if nid_dev = id_dev then break ;
        nid_XB ← GetUnaccessedXB(nid_dev) ;
        if nid_XB < 0 then continue ;
        Exchange(id_dev,id_XB,nid_dev,nid_XB) ;
        break ;
```

# Organization of Data in Non-convex Spatial Domains

Eric Perlman[1], Randal Burns[1], Michael Kazhdan[1], Rebecca R. Murphy[2], William P. Ball[2], and Nina Amenta[3]

[1] Dept. of Computer Science, Johns Hopkins University
{eric,randal,misha}@cs.jhu.edu
[2] Dept. of Geography and Environmental Engineering, Johns Hopkins University
{rebecca.murphy,bball}@jhu.edu
[3] Dept. of Computer Science, University of California, Davis
amenta@cs.ucdavis.edu

**Abstract.** We present a technique for organizing data in spatial databases with non-convex domains based on an automatic characterization using the medial-axis transform (MAT). We define a tree based on the MAT and enumerate its branches to partition space and define a linear order on the partitions. This ordering clusters data in a manner that respects the complex shape of the domain. The ordering has the property that all data down any branch of the medial axis, regardless of the geometry of the sub-region, are contiguous on disk. Using this data organization technique, we build a system to provide efficient data discovery and analysis of the observational and model data sets of the Chesapeake Bay Environmental Observatory (CBEO). On typical CBEO workloads in which scientists query contiguous substructures of the Chesapeake Bay, we improve query processing performance by a factor of two when compared with orderings derived from space filling curves.

## 1 Introduction

We present a system that provides efficient disk access when querying spatial structures across multiple, heterogeneous data sets defined over a non-convex spatial domain. Non-convex means that the line segment connecting two points in the domain is not guaranteed to be contained within the domain's interior. We built the system to support data discovery and analysis of environmental data sets from the Chesapeake Bay, which exhibits non-convexity: estuaries are long and skinny with a large number of winding, tendril-like tributaries. Non-convexity arises in many other systems, such as medical applications (the circulatory system), manufactured systems (road networks and indoor air systems), and other natural systems (turbulent structure and flow in porous media).

Querying spatial data has emerged as an important topic in database management systems, for both scientific databases [1,2] and geo-spatial services, such as geotagging, urban computing [3], and collaborative sensing [4]. The Chesapeake is the most intensively studied estuary in the United States. Our databases

M. Gertz and B. Ludäscher (Eds.): SSDBM 2010, LNCS 6187, pp. 342–359, 2010.

include more than 15 observational data sets from buoys, shallow-water sensors, cruises, aircraft observations, etc. alongside high-resolution water-quality and hydrodynamic models. Providing scientists with the ability to compare, correlate, and join data among these data sets has transformed our understanding of critical Bay processes [5], such as hypoxia (oxygen depletion) and the variable influence of flow and nitrogen load on water quality and the benthic community. For example, using high-resolution model output to inform the interpolation of water-quality measurements from 40 measurement sites has produced more accurate maps of salinity and dissolved oxygen over 10 years of data than were previously possible [6].

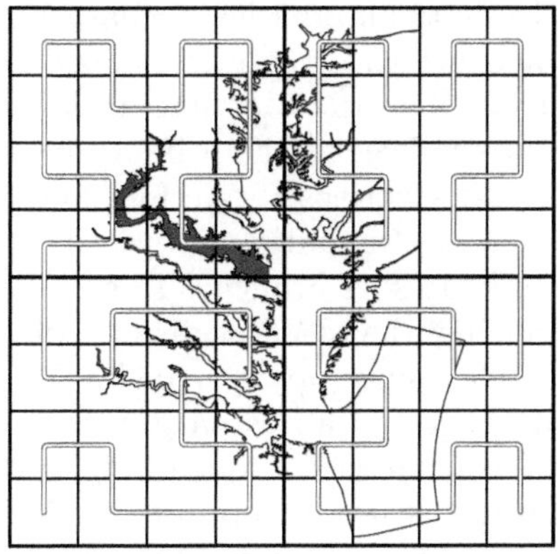

**Fig. 1.** A Hilbert ordering applied to the Chesapeake Bay. The Potomac River is highlighted.

Traditional approaches for organizing spatial data on disk do not meet the requirements of Chesapeake Bay data sets specifically and data drawn from non-convex spatial domains in general. Two aspects make the problem challenging: (1) the non-convex boundaries define a complex notion of spatial proximity among data and (2) the support of queries across multiple, heterogeneous data sets requires a regular decomposition of space.

Data organizations that do not respect the boundaries of non-convex spatial domain lead to poor I/O performance when querying spatial structures. Most decompositions of space, e.g. tessellations, space-filling curves, region trees, and packed R-trees [7], group data by Euclidean distance. However, data points near each other in Euclidean space may have a weak spatial relationship. For example, Figure 1 shows how a Hilbert curve fails to cluster the region of space associated with the Potomac River (shaded). If one uses the linear ordering following the curve to define the address space, the Hilbert curve will break up data from the river into many disjoint regions.

A regular decomposition of the spatial domain creates a global addressing scheme that makes comparing and joining data from different data sets possible [8]. The index value (lookup key) of a data point derives from its location in space alone. For this reason, regular decompositions are called *data independent.* Owing to data independence, data will have an index value that only depends on its spatial position, making it possible to compute joins across multiple data sets. Similarly, spatial properties of the index are preserved and we can compute nearest neighbors and clusters across multiple data sets.

We provide a data organization and indexing system based on a regular-decomposition that captures the complex spatial relationships of non-convex domains. We call this RINGS for regular indexing of non-convex geometric spaces. RINGS employs a computational geometry construct, the medial-axis transform

(MAT), to automatically characterize the domain. Based on the MAT, we partition space and create an index on the partitions. RINGS defines a primary index for our databases in that we lay the data out on disk in index order by using RINGS indices as the primary keys in a sorted relation.

RINGS derives its performance benefits from encoding the geometry of the domain in the index and data layout. It represents the medial-axis as a tree and enumerates its branches to generate the indices. In doing so, all data down any branch of the MAT, regardless of the geometry of the sub-region, are contiguous in index space and on disk. For Chesapeake Bay data, this means that any substructure—an estuary, river, or bay—consists of a contiguous index range and can be read sequentially from disk. RINGS preserves index contiguity at multiple scales in support of self-similar structures, e.g. Rock Creek occupies a contiguous sub-region of the Potomac River's contiguous index range.

We evaluate the performance of RINGS in comparison to indexes derived from space filling curves. On workloads derived from queries submitted to the Chesapeake Bay Environmental Observatory, our implementation improves query processing times by a factor of two for queries of contiguous substructure. An evaluation against randomly generated shapes shows further performance improvements as non-convexity increases.

## 2 Related Work

**The Medial Axis Transform:** Introduced by Blum more than four decades ago, the Medial Axis Transform [9] is a computational geometric structure characterizing the "central skeleton" of a shape. In 2-d, it comprises a network of curves, whereas in higher dimensions it can be made up of surface patches, volume elements, and higher degree manifolds up to co-dimension one. The MAT characterizes the general structure of the shape and has found applications in varied disciplines, such as path planning [10] and image segmentation in medicine [11], studying drainage patterns in watersheds [12], surface reconstruction in computer graphics [13], and routing in sensor networks [14].

The computation of the MAT has proved difficult for all but the simplest of polyhedral models, and numerous approximating methods have been proposed. These have included using morphological thinning [15,16], adapting quadtrees to define the MAT [17], approximating the MAT by the vertices of a Voronoi diagram defined by a dense sampling of the boundary [18], modifying the underlying spatial metric [19], pruning the set of interior edges in a Delaunay triangulation computed from the union of boundary and Voronoi vertices [20], and using the center points of a constrained Delaunay triangulation to define the skeleton [21].

**Regular Decompositions:** The simplest regular decomposition divides space into a grid of square (2-d) or cubic (3-d) cells. To construct an index from a grid, one defines a linear-ordering over the cells. For simplicity, this can be done in a row-major or column-major order. Many applications choose to use space-filling curves, such as the Z-order or Peano-Hilbert curve, which cluster data spatially [8]. Space-filling curves reduce the number of accesses to indexes for query regions that are square, circular, or simple polygons [22].

Region quadtrees in 2-d [23] and region octrees in 3-d [24] recursively partition space into successively smaller squares or cubes. By themselves, the trees are just spatial search structures and do not define a linear ordering. *Locational codes* derive labels for each leaf based on a Z-ordering of the grid implied by the smallest leaf nodes [8].

The Astrophysics community has adopted the Hierarchical Triangular Mesh (HTM) [25] regular decomposition for indexing and data organization. The HTM defines a space-filling curve for spherical coordinates using a quad tree: it approximates a sphere by starting with an octahedron and recursively refining each triangle into 4 sub-triangles.

Space filling curves and locational codes cannot respect non-convex boundaries. Even if the underlying grid identifies the boundary, e.g. a region tree that has small cells along the boundary and bigger cells elsewhere, the linearization remains insensitive to the structure of the domain.

**Other Spatial Indexing Techniques:** R-trees [26] index objects in space by providing navigation paths to minimum-bounding rectangles. While the structure is data defined, one could produce a regular decomposition from R-trees by triangulating the spatial domain and building an R-tree over the triangles. However, when indexing triangles, R-trees have many overlapping minimum bounding rectangles [27], which requires the navigation of multiple tree paths. R+-Trees [28] mitigate this by dividing objects into disjoint bounding boxes. As with other spatial search data structures, R-trees do not order data on disk. The preferred technique for placing R-tree data onto disk, called Hilbert-packing [7], uses space-filling curves to define a linear order on the R-tree's bounding rectangles.

Papadomanolakis et al. describe a system for indexing unstructured tetrahedral meshes [27]. When searching for a point (or nearest neighbors), they use a Hilbert-curve to find a mesh cell near the point and then conduct a local search based on mesh connectivity. We adopt similar search techniques, using a pixelation of all space to identify a nearby point on the MAT and then search the local structure of the MAT to identify a point, neighbor, or range. They do not address data placement on disk.

**The MAT in Geospatial Applications:** The medial-axis transformation has been used for cartographic and hydrological applications, because it preserves topological structure. McAllister and Snoeyink [29] use the medial-axis to characterize rivers, e.g. match shores, calculate width, and estimate volume. Gold et al. [30] use the medial-axis transform to generalize objects while maintaining the spatial relationships between them. Neither previous work applies the MAT to data organization or system design.

## 3 Motivating Applications

Estuarine studies are increasingly data-intensive, pulling in a heterogeneous mix of observational and model-derived data to gain further understanding of hydrological and biochemical processes. The Chesapeake Bay Environmental Observatory (CBEO) provides the infrastructure for developing new methods for interacting with data [5]. Our collaborators have been using the CBEO to query Bay structures for several years [31]. Our goal in this work is to improve the I/O performance of their workloads.

One project studies how changes in the level of dissolved oxygen effect animal species in benthic (bottom) regions. One of the better datasets for this study comes from the tidal region near Calvert Cliffs Nuclear Power Plant, where detailed monitoring has taken place since 1968. This data is combined with other data, both modeled and measured, to gain a better understanding of how the benthic community composition changes with respect to dissolved oxygen.

Individual estuaries are often studied as their own microcosm. The Patuxent River in Maryland is one such tributary. Testa et al. [32] have studied the long-term changes in the water quality with both measured data and a box model that estimates the estuary's time-dependent water circulation. Using these methods, the authors were able to link anthropogenic and environmental events, e.g. identifying how new sewage treatment techniques resulted in nutrient changes.

Spatial interpolation techniques are widely used in estuarine science to estimate the distribution of variables over all space from a discrete number of measurements. Kriging is one such method for generating spatial predictions by using a model of the spatial correlation of the measurements to predict unknown values as a function of location. Murphy et al. [6] have extended traditional kriging techniques to use the output from a water-quality model as a covariate to improve the interpolation of data collected from fixed locations. Ongoing work includes the integration of non-Euclidian cost functions, such as water-distance and hydrodynamic travel time, with these techniques.

The workloads presented by these applications have several common features that inform the design of RINGS. They all perform data fusion, bringing data together from heterogeneous sources to facilitate new scientific discovery. RINGS supports this efficiently through a regular decomposition of space which provides for consistent indexing across multiple data sources. Also, many queries focus on regions of interest that correspond to physical structures. This arises naturally, because the different structures express different properties: hydrodynamics, geochemistry, land-use, etc. RINGS captures structure through the use of the medial-axis transform, which automatically identifies spatial features and clusters data by structure.

## 4 Methodology

In this section, we describe how we generate an index from a shape file. We also outline how to process point, range, region, and water-distance queries using this index. The input to this process is a polygon that describes the spatial domain. We will output a triangulation of the space, a linear ordering of the triangles, and auxiliary data structures to be used for query processing.

**Fig. 2. Finding the MAT:** We take simple polygon (left), subdivide edges to create a Gabriel-conforming graph and construct a Delaunay Triangulation (center), and connect the circumcenters of adjacent triangles to define the approximate MAT (right)

### 4.1 Approximate Medial-Axis

The fundamental principle underlying our approach is the use of the medial-axis transform (MAT) to characterize the spatial domain. The MAT is commonly referred to as the *skeleton*. For 2-d domains, it is a series of curves that represent the "centerline" of the shape. In RINGS, we generate a piece-wise linear approximation of the MAT.

Our approach is to construct a Delaunay triangulation of the vertices and use the edges of the dual Voronoi diagram to define the MAT. However, the Delaunay triangulation does not necessarily preserve the edges of the original polygon. To address this, we subdivide the edges of the polygon to guarantee that each sub-edge has the property of being a *Gabriel edge* [33]. Formally, this means the circle that has a Gabriel edge as its diameter contains no other vertex in the polygon. Using Gabriel edges has several advantages:

1. The edges of the original polygon are a subset of the Delaunay triangulation as the end-points of each edge satisfy the *empty circle property* [34].
2. Each Delaunay triangle is entirely interior or entirely exterior to the bounding polygon.
3. The circumcenters of interior Delaunay triangles and the Voronoi edges connecting two such triangles are interior to the polygon.

As a result, the Delaunay triangulation of the vertices provides a well-defined partition of the spatial domain, and our derived approximate MAT, generated by connecting the circumcenters of adjacent triangles, is guaranteed to be contained within the domain.

Figure 2 illustrates our MAT construction. Starting with an initial polygon, we subdivide the edges to ensure that the sub-edges are Gabriel-conforming and compute the Delaunay triangulation. Then, we obtain the approximate medial axis by connecting the circumcenters of adjacent interior Delaunay triangles.

### 4.2 Linearizing the MAT

Subsequent steps will require the MAT to take the form of a tree with no cycles. This is the case for genus-0 boundaries, i.e. simple, connected, closed polygons.

For non-genus-0 boundaries, we fill in all holes interior to the domain, creating a genus-zero boundary. This approach is simple and appropriate when the interior structures are small. For the Chesapeake Bay, the holes are a series of small islands. Leaving the islands in would produce a MAT that encircles every island and may not represent the outline of the shape well. The issue of holes can also be addressed more generally by building a MAT and breaking the cycles to construct a tree (e.g., computing the minimum spanning tree). Many other tendril-like structures, however, are not easily reducible to trees; for instance, road networks are highly interconnected. Nonetheless, it is always possible to find a spanning tree that covers the entire network, the selection of which may be tuned for a specific application.

### 4.3 Index Generation

Using the MAT to guide the process, we assign a unique index to each triangle. The index serves as a spatial identifier, with data points inside and objects intersecting the triangle labeled by the triangle's index. Using the fact that adjacent vertices in the MAT correspond to adjacent Delaunay triangles in the triangulation of the polygon, we index the triangles using a simple tree traversal. Starting at a leaf of the tree, we traverse the tree in depth-first order and label each triangle we encounter with a unique, consecutive identifier. At branch points, we index all of the vertices on one branch before proceeding to the indexing of triangles on the second branch. (Figure 3 shows an example where the indexing was started at the top-left triangle.)

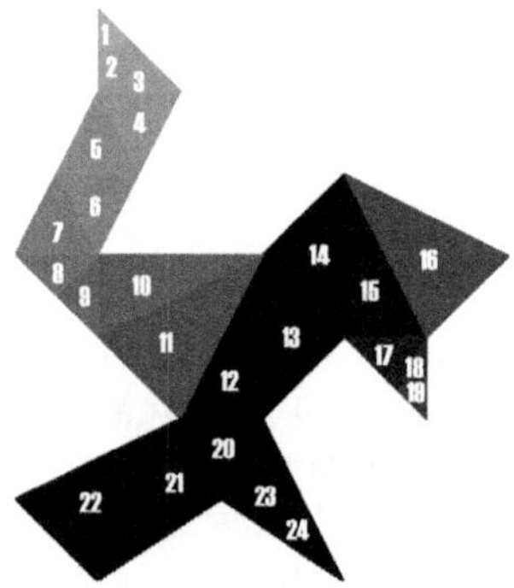

**Fig. 3.** Spatial index generated from the polygon in Figure 2

This generates an indexing in which the triangles within a branch of the MAT are assigned consecutive addresses. Since the branches correspond to logically distinct regions (estuaries, rivers, bays, etc.) we obtain an indexing that characterizes the spatial domain.

**Order of Medial Axis Traversal:** Once a starting node is selected, the indexing of triangles remains deterministic until we reach a branch point. The choice of which branch to traverse first can give rise to markedly different indexing of the domain. We consider two different approaches.

When encountering a branch in the MAT, we select which branch to follow based on the weight of the subtree down that branch, i.e. the sum of the area of the descendant triangles. In the first technique (Figure 4(b)), we traverse the least-weighted subtree first. In the second (Figure 4(c)), we traverse the heaviest subtree first. Traversing the least-weighted subtrees first gives a smoother indexing of the shape, including all of the micro-structure on the sides of each tributary. Smoothness would seem to be best, by our intuition, but does not

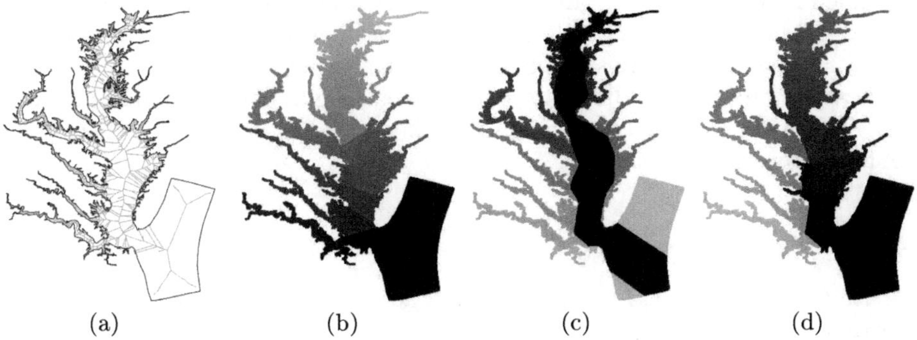


**Fig. 4.** Our primary shape, a union of the Chesapeake Bay outline combined with the outline of the water-quality models with an extra 1 km buffer. The approximate medial-axis is shown in (a). We also show several gray-scale visualizations of the indexes generated by traversing the MAT, including the results of using a least-weight-first ordering for branch traversal (b), using heaviest-weight-first ordering (c), and using heaviest-weight-first with a threshold for minimal area branches (d).

cluster large structure. Traversing the heaviest subtrees first, yields a consecutive "main stem" of the bay and each of the tributaries. However, it introduces discontinuities in the index where small structures break off from larger ones.

We strike a compromise by including small, border areas into the heaviest first policy (Figure 4(d)). Specifically, we choose a threshold weight (area) and use heaviest if both branches are above the threshold and least-weighted otherwise. We choose this approach for the Chesapeake Bay with a threshold of 2.5% of the total weight of the shape, which has the effect of combining the shallows on the boundary of the main stem with the main stem itself.

**Auxiliary Data Structures**

The index encodes spatial locality in a linear ordering of the Delaunay triangulation and defines an organization on disk based on that ordering. However, it does not naturally associate points in space with that index.

We use an additional lookup table to determine the triangle(s) associated with a point or region of space. We generate the lookup table by rasterizing the domain onto a low-resolution pixel grid. For each pixel, we store a list of the triangles that intersect the pixel. The table is generated once for each shape. The resolution process for a point within this pixel traverses the list until it finds the triangle that contains the point.

The size of the lookup table needs to be chosen with consideration. Too fine a pixelation produces an overly large lookup table, which consumes cache space. Too coarse a pixelation would result in too many triangles intersecting each pixel, which could slows query evaluation. For the Chesapeake Bay, we chose a grid of 150,000 (350x500) pixels to render the 22,729 indexed regions (triangles). The data structure consumes only 1.17MB of memory. The domain covers 29.6% of the pixelated area with an average list length of 2.54 triangles per covered pixel.

The maximum length of the list is 54 triangles and only 53 pixels have 25 or more candidates. In practice, these long lists are not a concern as they occur in narrow regions with many small triangles which rarely contain data.

We also maintain an adjacency map that lists the adjacent triangles for each triangle. We use the adjacency map to quickly traverse the local structure of the MAT and the triangulation.

### 4.4 Query Processing

We use the MAT index, lookup table, and adjacency map to implement spatial selection queries.

**Index Lookup/Point Query:** As described in the previous section, this basic operation finds the index value for a coordinate location, and is used most frequently with data ingest.

**Range and Polygon Queries:** Queries in which the user specifies either a Euclidean distance from a point or a polygon of interest are processed by identifying candidate triangles that intersect the query. We consult the lookup table to find pixels that overlap the query. We include all the data from triangles that are entirely inside the query. Additionally, the data from triangles that intersect the query boundary are evaluated to determine if they are inside the range.

**Approximate Water-Distance Range Query:** Users may specify a range query in terms of water distance, i.e. the length of the shortest path between two points that lies entirely inside the shape (domain). This query has real-world implications, e.g. travel time between two points. It also could be a more useful distance metric for interpolation than Euclidean distance [35]. For simplicity, we implement water distance approximately. We sum the length of the medial-axis in the traversal between two points. Having selected the portion of the medial-axis, we process the query as a range query.

The accuracy of approximate water distance depends upon the aspect ratio and size of the triangles. Our value will never be *less* than the actual water distance. In the future, we will consider supporting shortest path queries [36] for obtaining the exact distance.

## 5 Implementation

Our software consists of a utility that generates the spatial index from a shape file and database routines that use the precomputed index to process queries.

The preprocessor was written in C++ and uses triangulation routines from CGAL [37]. Our input files are typically ArcGIS shape files containing a polygon with the region of interest. The index generation process on our Chesapeake Bay outline of 80,000 points takes several seconds to run on a standard PC.

**Compiling map files:** We "compile" all of the generated data into C# class files. This includes all metadata, the pixelated look-up table, triangle vertices,

```
SELECT IndexFromLatLong(@map, 39.46678, -75.87466)
```

(a) Finding the index value for a specific location

```
SELECT data.* FROM MedialRangeWalk(@map, 39.0257, -76.2017, @range)
AS m JOIN wqm57k.dbo.WQM_data AS data ON m.IndexID = data.IndexID
ORDER BY range
```

(b) Table-valued function that performs a water-distance range query.

```
SELECT * FROM DirectionalMedialWalk (@map, 37.97155, -76.330637, +1)
AS m JOIN eotb.EOTB_data WHERE m.IndexID = eotb.IndexID
```

(c) Retrieve all EOTB data upstream from a specified point.

```
SELECT cims.*,MedialDistanceBetweenPoints
(@map, 39.2833, -76.6097, cims.Latitude, cims.Longitude)
AS Distance FROM cims.Station_info AS cims ORDER BY Distance
```

(d) Get the approximate water-distance between Baltimore and each station.

**Fig. 5.** Sample SQL Queries

and adjacency map. We chose these data structures for ease of implementation, requiring only basic array indexing to retrieve the vertices for a triangle. We will explore a winged-edge [38] structure in the future for a more compact storage format.

**Database Implementation:** We implement query processing routines that use these data structures in Microsoft's SQL Server. We use a combination of user-defined scalar and table-value functions (TVFs). All functions are written in C# using SQL's common language runtime interface [39].

We store data in sorted database tables, using the MAT-index value as the primary key for a clustered index. Our largest datasets have a large volume of data output for all data points at regular time intervals. We cluster these datasets first by time and then by index. Queries to these databases tend to select distinct regions of data across specific time-ranges for comparison.

**Range Queries:** Range queries, both regular and water-distance, are implemented as table-valued functions. A list of all candidate regions which overlap the range query are returned. We obtain the requested data by joining the candidate indexes with the data tables. Finally, we apply a filter to the result to eliminate data located within the border index regions yet outside the query range. Water-distance queries are done through a similar interface (Figure 5(b)). Another variation of the range query allows for a complete traversal from a point on the medial-axis. For example, a simple query can be written to select all data contained within the Potomac river (Figure 5(c)) by traversing upstream from the mouth.

**Calculated Columns:** We also implement the water-distance query in a user-defined function. This allows it to be called as a subroutine to a larger query that performs further data analysis. Figure 5(d) shows an SQL query that retrieves a list of CIMS monitoring stations sorted by their approximate water-distance from the Baltimore Inner Harbor.

## 6 Evaluation on CBEO Data

We have implemented RINGS on the Chesapeake Bay Environmental Observatory (CBEO) and evaluate its performance using workloads derived from the queries submitted to the CBEO. We characterize the CBEO's workload by query type and built workloads that cover the entire spatial domain for each query type. The CBEO's users tend to study a specific region. For example, one scientist queries the Patuxent River, an entire estuary. For this, we have generated workloads that randomly select space-constrained water-distance ranges. We also examine the performance of circular range queries that are unconstrained by boundaries, because they are the most fundamental geospatial range query.

We start by looking at the indexes generated on our primary dataset, the Chesapeake Bay. Figure 4 shows the medial-axis and visualizations of the indexes generated on the spatial domain. The shape comprises the union of the outline of the Chesapeake Bay with the cells of the water quality models. We then expand the boundary by 1 km in order to include the stations that take tidal samples.

Our experiments use the CBEO's most popular data set: the 56,920-cell water quality model. The water-quality model has cells of roughly equal surface area that cover the entire bay and major estuaries. We use a 1 month subset of the output totaling 1.7 million rows of 296 bytes each for a total data size of 522MB.

We compare RINGS against other spatial organization techniques. We implement two space filling curves: our implementation of a Z-order curve and the hierarchical triangular mesh (HTM) index [1,25] used widely by the Astronomy community. HTM supports geospatial as well as celestial coordinates. We also provide latitude-longitude addressing (approximately row major ordering).

For each ordering, we create a database table that contain the same data. Tables are sorted by $(time, index)$. For RINGS and HTM, the index is derived from the index address of the triangle containing the data point. For Z-order, it is the locational code of the square containing the data point.

For all results, we measure the time spent reading the data table. For each query, we consult the index in memory and retrieve a list of the index elements that could satisfy the query; triangles for RINGS and HTM, and squares for Z-order that intersect the query region. Our timed operation is the `JOIN` between the list of specific index values and the data tables sorted by spatial index. SQL optimizes this as a `HASH JOIN` between this list and a non-clustered index created on each data table for all $(time, index)$ pairs.

**Range Queries:** This experiment compares the performance of all data organization schemes on circular range queries. The circular range ignores boundaries and returns data points from multiple non-connected water regions. Thus, we expect RINGS to realize no advantage when compared with HTM or space-filling curves. The query geometry more closely matches the shape of the recursive triangle or rectangular decomposition of space used by HTM and space-filling curves respectively than it does the MAT used by RINGS.

The experiment selects 200 points uniformly at random in the interior of the Chesapeake Bay and its tributaries. The same points and ranges are used for all

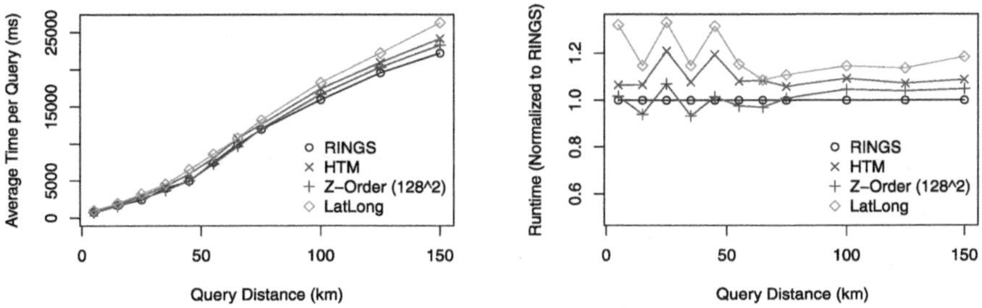


**Fig. 6.** Index performance for range queries on the water-quality model. RINGS' performance is comparable to the other spatial organization techniques.

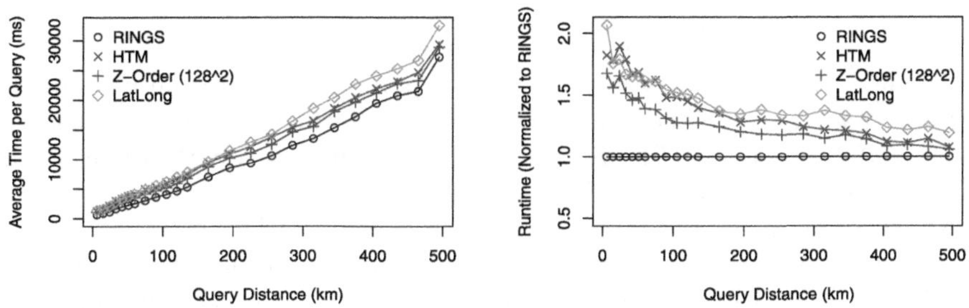


**Fig. 7.** Index performance for water-distance range queries on the water-quality model

indexes. We do this for ranges from 5 km to 250 km in 10-50 km increments. The Chesapeake Bay outline extends roughly 350 km from north to south and 230 km from east to west.

We show both the average runtime per query and the runtime normalized to that of RINGS in Figure 6. Even though these range queries which do not employ the structure of the Bay, RINGS' performance matches the performance of Z-order and exceeds the performance of HTM.

For some queries, RINGS performs more work than the Z-order curve because it has to read more data. It generates a list of candidate triangles, reads all data within those candidate triangles, and filters out data not within the range. This can be problematic when the triangles are as large or larger than the range of the query. This occurs with smaller ranges in the main stem.

In contrast, RINGS benefits when the query region is long and skinny and includes space exterior to the boundary. HTM and Z-order curve grow their index recursively in triangles and squares respectively, which prevents them from indexing long skinny structures contiguously. In contrast, RINGS adapts to the local geometry.

**Water-Distance Range Queries:** When constraining the range by the geometry of the domain, RINGS improves performance. As with the previous experiment, we select 200 points uniformly at random, however this time we use the water-distance instead of the Euclidean distance. That is, the query selects all

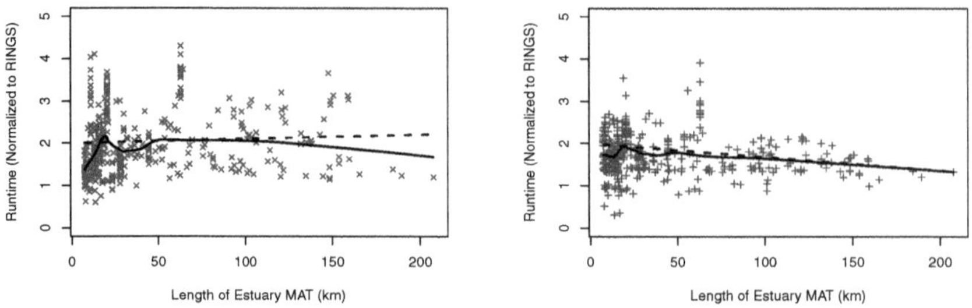


**Fig. 8.** Scatter plots comparing index performance for estuary queries between RINGS and both HTM (left) and Z-Order (right), each with linear regression and locally weighted smooth (lowess) curve. Both plots are normalized to RINGS.

data for which the shortest path to the query point *interior* to the Chesapeake Bay is less than the specified range. We do this for ranges from 5 to 500km in increments of 10-30km. As Figure 7 shows, RINGS improves performance in all cases. The improvement is most dramatic for smaller ranges.

RINGS cuts the query time in half for for ranges up to 50 km. The improvements are most dramatic for queries that select a substantial amount of data from tributaries. It is not uncommon to see an individual query speedup a factor of six when comparing RINGS with the Z-order. For queries in the main stem, the structure of the MAT is less helpful. Similarly, larger ranges reduce the benefit, because the queries are less selective. For a range that covers the entire Bay, the query will result in a table scan. Our results reflect this as the performance of all indexes begin to merge at large ranges.

**Estuary Queries:** Scientists frequently use the CBEO database to query contiguous substructures, e.g. the Potomac or the Patuxtent River (see Section 3). This usage pattern was the original motivation for the design of RINGS.

To evaluate the performance of RINGS when querying such substructures, we create a random workload based on the `DirectionalMedialWalk` query (see Figure 5(c)). In this experiment, we select points from the interior of the domain uniformly at random. If the point is on the main stem or in the ocean region, we discard it. Otherwise, we query all data upstream from that point. Our scientists use this query to select an entire tributary by picking a point on the MAT at the mouth of that tributary. The query is particularly convenient, because the scientist does not need to specify geographic boundaries.

For estuary queries, RINGS reduces the query time in half, on average, when compared with the Z-order or HTM. Figure 8 shows these results as a function of the length of the estuary from the randomly selected point to the farthest point upstream. The length is, in some sense, the query diameter of a water-distance query. The results show a tremendous amount of variance, because performance depends upon the geometry of the query region. The few queries in which HTM and Z-order outperformed RINGS are short queries, most of which were centered near the source of the rivers.

## 7 Evaluation on Random Shapes

In order to demonstrate the applicability of RINGS beyond our prototypical application, we evaluate its performance on randomly generated shapes of varying complexity. We use a $64^2$ (4096-cell) Z-order curve as a basis for comparison. We execute two queries on the random data: (1) a rectangular range query shows that RINGS preserves performance even when the query space matches the index space and (2) a water-distance distance query indicates the performance benefits when the query conforms to the spatial structure.

**Shape Generation:** We generate shapes by splitting boundary segments on a polygon by repeatedly moving their midpoints. We begin with a boundary defined by four points arranged as a square. We create each new edge by selecting a random segment to divide with a new point. We then move that point a random direction and distance (bounded by a defined amplitude). We verify that the new segments do not intersect or coincide with any existing segment, because both would lead to an invalid polygon. If the move fails this test, we try again. This process is repeated until all of the desired points have been inserted. Four sample shapes are shown in Figure 9. We chose to generate square shapes so that they align well the Z-order curve used in comparison.

**Fig. 9.** Shapes with 15, 50, 200 and 500 edges

A metric based on the distance between points in the interior of the shape characterizes the "complexity" of the generated shapes. This metric is defined as the ratio of the Euclidean distance to shortest interior path between the points. The metric captures the distinction between Euclidean distance and water-distance, a distinction that motivated the design of RINGS. We compute this as an average over 2000 points randomly selected from within the interior of the shape. The RINGS medial axis gives an upper bound on point-to-point interior distance, which we use in the calculation.

**Experimental Results:** For both distance queries, we examine the number of non-contiguous ranges of data that the queries access. The number of ranges roughly corresponds with the number of disk seeks needed to read the data. The data set consists of 10,000 points randomly placed within the interior of the shape. For each experiment, we perform 5,000 randomly generated queries. Each range query is centered at a randomly chosen point interior to the shape. The rectangular range queries were restricted to be between 10% and 80% of the shape's bounding box. The range used for water-distance queries was a random value between 5% and 50% of the shape's perimeter.

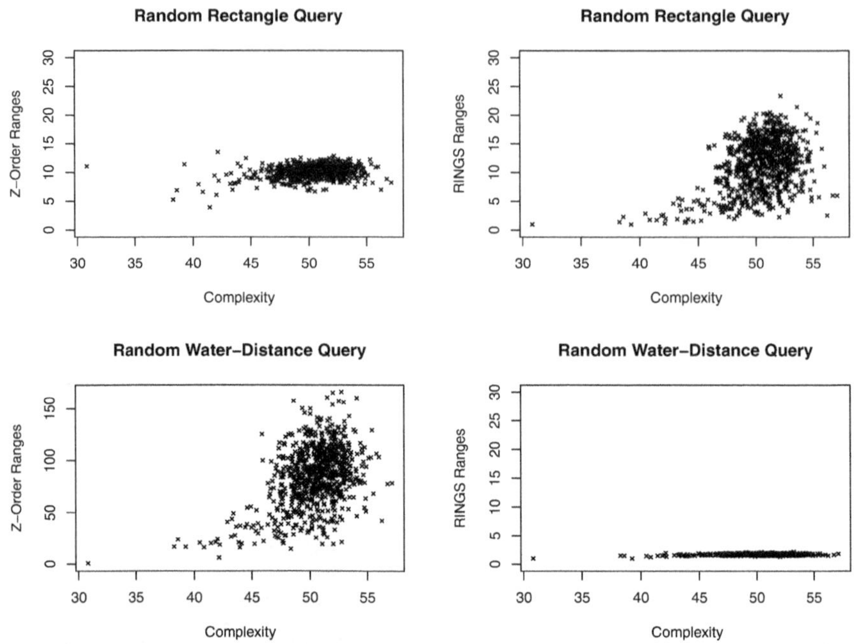


**Fig. 10.** The number of index regions necessary to resolve a query as a function of shape complexity

The rectangular query results show that RINGS provides roughly equivalent performance to the Z-order curve with higher variance (Figure 10). The number of disjoint data regions in the Z-order curve index vary relatively little because the Z-order curve indexes the entire space not the domain. RINGS exhibits similar performance with some increase in the disjoint data regions as the shape becomes more complex. As the shape increases in complexity, each rectangular query region intersects the boundary of the shape more times. But, even for shapes much more complex than the Chesapeake Bay, RINGS compares favorably.

For the water-distances queries for which it was designed, RINGS accesses very few disjoint regions of data. In contrast, the Z-order curve has to access many disjoint regions of data and performance worsens as shape complexity increases. Because the domain defines the query region, the query region has a complex boundary that intersects the Z-order curve many times. For RINGS, the number of disjoint regions increases very little as the shape grows in complexity. Disjoint regions arise only when the query region spans multiple internal structures, i.e. when the tree defined by the MAT forks and the query does not cover both branches in their entirety. Comparing these results with the complexity of the Chesapeake Bay reveals that the Chesapeake lies at the low end of the range for which the non-convex complexity results in marked performance improvements and more complex systems would realize even bigger benefits.

## 8 Conclusions

We have presented RINGS, an organization system for spatial databases based on the automatic characterization of non-convex domains. The key behind our approach is the use of the medial-axis transform for indexing the data and supporting efficient traversal of spatial structures. Our system was designed for environmental data sets and, more specifically, for the Chesapeake Bay Environmental Observatory's (CBEO) heterogeneous collection of observations and models. In empirical evaluation, we have found that RINGS is competitive with traditional indexing methods for general range queries and improves performance substantially on queries that take into account the geometry of the domain. These queries arise naturally in the CBEO, because the users study structures, such as rivers and estuaries, that are contiguous within the interior of the Bay.

## Acknowledgments

We thank Jennifer Bosch, Damian Brady, Jeremy Testa and the other members of CBEO team for their expertise on estuarine science and Chesapeake Bay data. We also thank Damian Coventry for his pseudo-random polygon code. This work was supported by the National Science Foundation award ATM-0618986.

## References

1. Szalay, A., Gray, J., Fekete, G., Kunszt, P., Kukol, P., Thakar, A.: Indexing the sphere with the hierarchical triangular mesh. Technical Report MSR-TR-2005-123, Micrsoft Research (2005)
2. Perlman, E., Burns, R., Li, Y., Meneveau, C.: Data exploration of turbulence simulations using a database cluster. In: SC 2007: Proceedings of the 2007 ACM/IEEE conference on Supercomputing. ACM, New York (2007)
3. Joseph, A.D. (ed.): Urban computing and mobile devices. IEEE Pervasive Computing 6(3), 52–57 (2007)
4. Reddy, S., Burke, J., Estrin, D., Hansen, M., Srivastava, M.B.: A framework for data quality and feedback in participatory sensing. In: SenSys. (2007)
5. Ball, W.P., et al.: A prototype system for multi-disciplinary shared cyberinfrastructure—Chesapeake Bay Environmental Observatory (CBEO). Journal of Hydrological Engineering 13(10), 960–970 (2008)
6. Murphy, R.R., Curriero, F.C., Ball, W.P.: Comparison of spatial interpolation methods for water quality evaluation in the Chesapeake Bay. Journal of Environmental Engineering 136(2), 160–171 (2010)
7. Kamel, I., Faloutsos, C.: On packing r-trees. In: CIKM 1993: Proceedings of the second international conference on Information and knowledge management, pp. 490–499. ACM, New York (1993)
8. Samet, H.: Foundations of Multidimensional and Metric Data Structures. Morgan Kaufmann Publishers Inc., San Francisco (2006)
9. Blum, H.: A transformation for extracting new descriptors of shape. In: Models for the Perception of Speech and Visual Form, pp. 362–380. MIT Press, Cambridge (1967)

10. Ge, Y., Stels, D., Wang, J., Vining, D.: Computing centerline of a colon: A robust and efficient method based on 3d skeletons. Journal of Computer Assisted Tomography 23(5), 786–794 (1999)
11. Joshi, S., Pizer, S., Fletcher, P.T., Yushkevich, P., Thall, A., Marron, J.: Multiscale deformable model segmentation and statistical shape analysis using medial descriptions. IEEE Transactions on Medical Imaging 21(5), 538–550 (2002)
12. TRIM Watershed Atlas, `http://www.barrodale.com/watershed/twapage.htm`
13. Amenta, N., Choi, S., Kolluri, R.: The power crust. In: Sixth ACM Symposium on Solid Modeling and Applications, pp. 249–260 (2001)
14. Bruck, J., Gao, J., Jiang, A.: MAP: medial axis based geometric routing in sensor networks. In: MobiCom 2005: Proceedings of the 11th annual international conference on Mobile computing and networking, pp. 88–102. ACM, New York (2005)
15. Maragos, P., Schafer, R.: Morphological skeleton representation and coding of binary images. IEEE Transactions on Acoustics, Speech and Signal Processing 34, 1228–1244 (1986)
16. Lam, L., Lee, S., Suen, C.: Thinning methodologies: A comprehensive survey. Transactions on Pattern Analysis and Machine Intelligence 14(9), 869–885 (1992)
17. Joan-Arinyo, R., Pérez-Vidat, L., Gargallo-Monllau, E.: An adaptive algorithm to compute the medial axis transform of 2-d polygonal domains. In: CAD Systems Development: Tools and Methods, London, UK, pp. 283–298. Springer, Heidelberg (1997)
18. Brandt, J.W.: Convergence and continuity criteria for discrete approximation of the continuous planar skeletons. Image Understanding 59, 116–124 (1994)
19. Aichholzer, O., Aurenhammer, F., Alberts, D., Gärtner, B.: A novel type of skeleton for polygons. Journal of Universal Computer Science 1(12), 752–761 (1995)
20. Gold, C.: Crust and anti-crust: A one-step boundary and skeleton extraction algorithm. In: Annual Symposium on Computational Geometry, pp. 189–196 (1999)
21. Zou, J.J.: A fast skeletonization method. In: DICTA, pp. 283–288 (2003)
22. Moon, B., Jagadish, H.V., Faloutsos, C., Saltz, J.H.: Analysis of the clustering properties of the Hilbert space-filling curve. IEEE Transactions on Knowledge and Data Engineering 13(1) (2001)
23. Klinger, A.: Patterns and Search Statistics, p. 423. Academic Press, London (1971)
24. Hunter, G.M.: Efficient computation and data structures for graphics. PhD thesis, Dept. of Electrical Engineering and Computer Science, Princeton University (1981)
25. Kunszt, P.Z., Szalay, A.S., Thakar, A.R.: The hierarchical triangular mesh. In: ESO Astrophysics Symposia: Mining the Sky, pp. 631–637 (2001)
26. Guttman, A.: R-trees: a dynamic index structure for spatial searching. In: SIGMOD 1984: Proceedings of the 1984 ACM SIGMOD international conference on Management of data, pp. 47–57 (1984)
27. Papadomanolakis, S., Ailamaki, A., Lopez, J.C., Tu, T., O'Hallaron, D.R., Heber, G.: Efficient query processing on unstructured tetrahedral meshes. In: SIGMOD 2006: Proceedings of the 2006 ACM SIGMOD international conference on Management of data, pp. 551–562 (2006)
28. Sellis, T., Roussopoulos, N., Faloutsos, C.: The R+-tree: A dynamic index for multi-dimensional objects. In: VLDB (1987)
29. McAllister, M., Snoeyink, J.: Medial axis generalization of river networks. CaGIS 27(2), 129–138 (2000)
30. Gold, C., Thibault, D., Liu, Z.: Map generalization by skeleton retraction. In: ICA Workshop on Map Generalization (1999)
31. Chesapeake Bay Environmental Observatory (CBEO), `http://cbeo.communitymodeling.org/`

32. Testa, J.M., Kemp, W.M., Boynton, W.R., Hagy III, J.D.: Long-term changes in water quality and productivity in the Patuxent River estuary: 1985 to 2003. Estuaries and Coasts 31(6), 1021–1037 (2008)
33. Gabriel, K.R., Sokal, R.R.: A new statistical approach to geographic variation analysis. Systematic Zoology 18(3), 259–278 (1969)
34. Amenta, N., Bern, M., Eppstein, D.: The crust and the $\beta$-skeleton: combinatorial curve reconstruction. Graphical Models and Image Processing 60, 125–135 (1998)
35. Rathbun, S.L.: Spatial modelling in irregularly shaped regions: kriging estuaries. Environmetrics 9(2), 109–129 (1998)
36. Guibas, L.J., Hershberger, J.: Optimal shortest path queries in a simple polygon. In: SCG 1987: Proceedings of the third annual symposium on Computational geometry, pp. 50–63. ACM, New York (1987)
37. CGAL, Computational Geometry Algorithms Library, `http://www.cgal.org/`
38. Baumgart, B.G.: Winged edge polyhedron representation. Technical Report CS-TR-72-320, Stanford University (1972)
39. Rathakrishnan, B., Kleinerman, C., Richards, B., Venkatesh, R., Rao, V., Kunen, I.: Using CLR integration in SQL Server 2005. Technical report, Microsoft (2005)

# PrefIndex: An Efficient Supergraph Containment Search Technique

Gaoping Zhu, Xuemin Lin, Wenjie Zhang, Wei Wang, and Haichuan Shang

The University of New South Wales, Sydney, NSW, Australia
{gzhu,lxue,zhangw,weiw,shangh}@cse.unsw.edu.au

**Abstract.** Graphs are prevailingly used in many applications to model complex data structures. In this paper, we study the problem of supergraph containment search. To avoid the NP-complete subgraph isomorphism test, most existing works follow the *filtering-verification* framework and select graph-features to build effective indexes, which filter false results (graphs) before conducting the costly verification. However, searching features multiple times in the query graphs yields huge redundant computation, which leads to the emergence of the *computation-sharing* framework. This paper follows the roadmap of computation-sharing framework to efficiently process supergraph containment queries. Firstly, database graphs are clustered into disjoint groups for sharing the computation cost within each group. While it is shown NP-hard to maximize the computation-sharing benefits of a clustering, efficient algorithm is developed to approximate the optimal solution with an approximation factor of $\frac{1}{2}$. A novel prefix-sharing indexing technique, PrefIndex, is then proposed based on which efficient query processing algorithm integrating both filtering and verification is developed. Finally, PrefIndex is enhanced with multi-level sharing and suffix-sharing to further avoid redundant computation. An extensive empirical study demonstrates the efficiency and scalability of our techniques which achieve orders of magnitudes of speed-up against the state-of-the-art techniques.

## 1 Introduction

Recently, graph structured data have been increasingly adopted in applications such as Bio-informatics, Chemistry, Social Networks, WWW, etc. For instance, graphs are used to model protein interaction networks and chemical compounds in Bio-informatics and Chemistry, respectively. Efficient query processing is thus strongly demanded by graph database.

Graph containment search is defined as *supergraph containment search* [2] and *subgraph containment search* [12]. Given a query graph $q$ and a graph database $D = \{g_1, ..., g_n\}$, supergraph containment search finds all the graphs in $D$ contained by $q$, while subgraph containment search finds all the graphs in $D$ containing $q$. In Chemistry, given a newly found molecule (query graph) and a large number of descriptors (data graphs indicating chemical properties), we can predict its chemical function based on the descriptors it contains. In pattern recognition, given a graph structured background (query graph) and various

M. Gertz and B. Ludäscher (Eds.): SSDBM 2010, LNCS 6187, pp. 360–378, 2010.

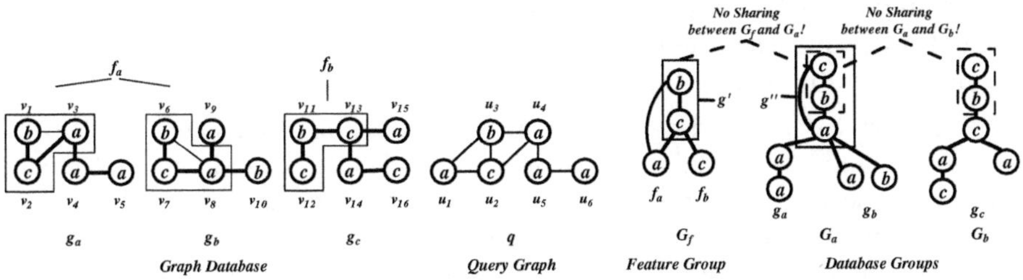


**Fig. 1.** Supergraph Containment Search

objects (data graphs), we may detect the foreground objects contained in the background. More applications can be found in [2, 12]. Regarding Figure 1, the result of supergraph containment search of query graph $q$ is $g_a$.

Since the subgraph isomorphism test is NP-complete [4], most works adopt the *filtering and verification* framework. While a feature-based index filters most false results in the filtering phase, survived candidate graphs are checked in the verification phase. Unlike its extensively studied dual version [3, 5–7, 9, 10, 12, 13, 16, 17], supergraph containment search is comprehensively investigated in only two studies [2, 14]. cIndex, proposed in [2], adopts historical *query-log* to select features for maximizing pruning power. Regarding Figure 1, assume that $f_a$ and $f_b$ are two features. cIndex first tests if $q$ contains $f_a$ and $f_b$. As $f_b$ is not contained by $q$, $g_c$ is filtered; while $g_a$ and $g_b$ survived to be candidates as $f_a$ is contained by $q$. As $f_a$ is a subgraph of $g_a$ and $g_b$, it will be searched for two more times in $q$ for the verifications of $g_a$ and $g_b$. Generally speaking, if a feature $f$ is contained by $n$ candidates, the subgraph isomorphism test on $f$ against $q$ will be repeated $(n + 1)$ times (including one test in the filtering phase).

To avoid redundant subgraph isomorphism test cost, [14] proposes GPTree, a computation-sharing framework. It encodes each graph or feature in a sequence called GVCode. The GVCodes of a group of graphs or features are organized in a tree called GPTree such that a common subgraph of these graphs or features is stored only once as a prefix of the tree. This finally yields a forest structured database or index. GPTreeTest, the proposed subgraph isomorphism algorithm, verifies a group of graphs or features altogether by sharing the computation (subgraph isomorphism test) cost of the common subgraph within the group. For instance, in Figure 1, one feature group $G_f$ (for $f_a$, $f_b$), two database groups $G_a$ (for $g_a$, $g_b$) and $G_b$ (for $g_c$) are built. The computation cost of the common subgraphs $g'$ and $g''$ are shared within $G_f$ and $G_a$, respectively. However, with further observations, GPTree has the following defects: (1)Computation cost can not be shared between filtering and verification, as the common edge $b - c$ of $G_f$ and $G_a$ can not be shared between them; (2)Computation cost can not be shared between database groups, as the common edge $b - c$ of $G_a$ and $G_b$ can not be shared between them; (3)GPTree prefers to select large-sized common subgraphs for sharing, which goes against the fact that large-sized subgraphs are usually infrequent and not likely to be shared by many graphs.

Motivated by the above observations, this paper proposes a novel computation-sharing framework with the aim to maximize the computation-sharing benefits. The main contributions of this paper are summarized as follows.

- We propose to cluster database graphs into disjoint groups such that graphs in each group contain a common feature $f$. While it is shown NP-hard to optimize the computation-sharing benefits, an efficient greedy algorithm is used to approximate the optimal solution with an approximation factor of $\frac{1}{2}$.
- Based on QuickSI traversal technique [9], a novel prefix-sharing indexing technique PrefIndex and a query processing algorithm PrefSearch are developed to share computation cost between filtering and verification.
- A group encoding technique is proposed to efficiently construct PrefIndex for a group of graphs based on the effective ordering of their GVCodes.
- Multi-level sharing and suffix-sharing techniques are proposed to enhance PrefIndex for sharing computation cost among database groups and further sharing computation within each database group, respectively.

**Organization.** The rest of the paper is organized as follows. Section 2 gives preliminaries and formalizes the problem. Section 3 presents the database clustering, feature selection and index construction techniques. Section 4 proposes our sharing-aware query processing algorithm integrating filtering and verification. Section 5 presents our multi-level sharing and suffix-sharing techniques. Experimental results and related work are reported in Section 6 and 7, while Section 8 concludes our study.

# 2 Preliminaries

## 2.1 Problem Statement

For presentation simplicity, our study only focuses on *simple, vertex-labeled* graphs. A *simple* graph is an *undirected* graph with no self-loops nor multiple edges between any two different vertices. From now on, a database graph is called a *data graph*, while a query graph is called a *query*. All data graphs are assumed to be *connected*. Nevertheless, our approach can be immediately extended to *directed* or *edge-labeled* graphs.

Given two sets of labels, $\Sigma_V$ and $\Sigma_E$, a graph $g$ is defined as a triplet $(V(g), E(g), l)$ where $V(g)$ and $E(g)$ denote the vertex set and edge set of $g$, respectively. $l$ is a mapping: $V(g) \rightarrow \Sigma_V$ which assigns a label $l(u)$ to each vertex $u \in V(g)$.

**Definition 1 (Subgraph Isomorphic).** *Given two graphs $g = (V, E, l)$ and $g' = (V', E', l')$, $g$ is subgraph isomorphic to $g'$, denoted by $g \subseteq g'$, if there is an injective function $f : V \rightarrow V'$ such that (1) $\forall v \in V$, $f(v) \in V'$ and $l(v) = l'(f(v))$; (2) $\forall (u, v) \in E$, $(f(u), f(v)) \in E'$ and $l(u, v) = l'(f(u), f(v))$. Under the above conditions, $g$ ($g'$) is a subgraph (supergraph) of $g'$ ($g$).*

**Definition 2 (Induced Subgraph).** *Given a graph $g$, a graph $g'$ is an induced subgraph of $g$, if and only if (1) $g'$ is subgraph isomorphic to $g$ under an injective function $f$; (2) $\forall u, v \in V(g')$, if $(f(u), f(v)) \in E(g)$, $(u, v) \in E(g')$.*

**Definition 3 (Supergraph Containment Search).** *Given a graph database* $D = \{g_1, g_2, ..., g_n\}$ *and a query graph* $q$*, find the answer set* $D_q$ *which consists of each* $g_i \in D$ *such that* $g_i \subseteq q$.

## 2.2 Computation-Sharing Framework

cIndex [2] is the first filtering-verification framework for supergraph containment search. It applies the *exclusive logic* to filter data graphs; namely, if a feature $f \not\subseteq q$, any data graph $g$ such that $f \subseteq g$ can be filtered. However, sequentially testing each feature (candidate graph) against the query involves huge redundant computation cost in the filtering (verification) phase.

GPTree [14], the first computation-sharing framework, directly extends the filtering-verification framework to avoid the redundant computation cost in cIndex. Inspired by DFS code [11] and QISequence [9], GPTree proposes a new graph encoding technique called GVCode. Based on a spanning tree $t$ of a graph $g$, it encodes $g$ into a sequence represented by a regular expression $Code_g = [[S_i E_{ij}^*]^{V(g)}]$. Each entry $S_i$ is the mapped image of a vertex $v$ in $g$. While $S_i.l$ keeps the label of $v$, $S_i.p$ stores the entry corresponding to the parent vertex of $v$ in $t$. Once $S_1$ is fixed, $t$ is viewed as a tree rooted at the vertex corresponding to $S_1$ and thus $S_1.p = 0$. Each edge in $g$ but not in $t$ is recorded as a back edge. If $S_i$ has back edges, they are kept in $\{E_{ij}\}$.

Table 1 gives two GVCodes of $g_a$ and $g_b$ in Figure 1. The corresponding vertex of $S_i$ is in the bracket. The bold lines in Figure 1 show the spanning trees of $g_a$ and $g_b$. As $g''$ in Figure 1 is represented as a three-entry prefix from $S_1$ to $S_3$ in both $Code_a$ and $Code_b$, a tree structured organization of $Code_a$ and $Code_b$, called GPTree, can be built to share the three-entry prefix as a common prefix. Note that a common prefix must be an induced subgraph of all graphs in the group and the GVCode of a graph is not unique.

Based on QuickSI [9], GPTreeTest, a new subgraph isomorphism test algorithm is proposed to verify a group of graphs sharing a common prefix. Regarding Table 1, GPTreeTest first searches in $q$ a subgraph isomorphism mapping of the common prefix from $S_1$ to $S_3$. A found mapping is then extended in a depth first fashion to search a whole mapping for the rest $Code_a$ and $Code_b$ under the common prefix, respectively.

**Table 1.** The GVCodes of $g_a$ and $g_b$

| *Type* | $(S_i.l, S_i.p)$ |
|---|---|
| $S_1(v_2)$ | $(c, 0)$ |
| $S_2(v_1)$ | $(b, S_1)$ |
| $S_3(v_3)$ | $(a, S_2)$ |
| $E_{31}$ | $[edge : S_3]$ |
| $S_4(v_4)$ | $(a, S_3)$ |
| $S_5(v_5)$ | $(a, S_4)$ |

$Code_a$

| *Type* | $(S_i.l, S_i.p)$ |
|---|---|
| $S_1(v_7)$ | $(c, 0)$ |
| $S_2(v_6)$ | $(b, S_1)$ |
| $S_3(v_8)$ | $(a, S_2)$ |
| $E_{31}$ | $[edge : S_3]$ |
| $S_4(v_{10})$ | $(b, S_1)$ |
| $S_5(v_9)$ | $(a, S_1)$ |

$Code_b$

The framework of GPTree can be outlined by four phases: (1) Mine frequent subgraphs from the database and build a feature-based index $\mathcal{F} = \{f_1, ..., f_n\}$. Each $f_i$ is attached a graph-ID list $list_{f_i} = \{g.id | f_i \subseteq g \wedge g \subseteq D\}$. (2) Mine common induced subgraphs from features and data graphs respectively. Greedily select the largest common induced subgraphs and divide features and data graphs into disjoint groups such that each group $G$ shares a common induced subgraph $g'$. Graphs in each group $G$ are encoded to share $Code_{g'}$ as a common prefix, based on which a GPTree is built for $G$. (3) For filtering, each feature group is tested by GPTreeTest to obtain the candidate set $C_q = D - \bigcup_f list_f (f \not\subseteq q \wedge f \in \mathcal{F})$. (4) For verification, each database group is projected on $C_q$ and all non-empty projected database groups are verified by GPTreeTest to obtain the answer set $D_q$.

## 3 PrefIndex

**Our Framework.** We propose a novel computation-sharing framework called PrefIndex, which directly selects a feature as the common subgraph shared by a group of data graphs. Since a feature is encoded as a common prefix of all the data graphs in the group, its test cost can be shared between filtering and verification. The whole framework is outlined as follows.

1. Mine frequent induced subgraphs from the database and cluster all data graphs into disjoint groups $\{(f_i, G_i) | 1 \le i \le k\}$ such that for each graph $g$ in a group $G_i$, $f_i$ is an induced subgraph of $g$ and a selected feature.
2. Encode each graph $g$ in a group $G_i$ into $Code_g$ of which $Code_{f_i}$ is a prefix. Organize all GVCodes of graphs $G_i$ into a PrefIndex tree.
3. Apply our query processing algorithm integrating filtering and verification to process each group $G_i$ by sharing the computation cost of $Code_{f_i}$.

### 3.1 Cost Model and Feature Selection

Given a data graph $g$ and a query $q$, if $f \subseteq g$, the subgraph isomorphism test cost of $g$ may be approximately represented by $cost_f + cost_{(g-f)}$. Given a group $G_i$ of graphs sharing a common induced subgraph $f_i$, if we test all graphs in $G_i$ by sharing the test cost of $f_i$ (to process $f_i$ only once), the cost gain (computation-sharing benefits) approximately equals (1). Assume that no pre-knowledge is given on $q$, (1) may be interpreted as the expected gain for any $q$.

Given a database $D$ and a set $\mathcal{D} = \{(f_i, D_i) | 1 \le i \le m\}$ where each $D_i$ contains all graphs in $D$ which share $f_i$ as a common induced subgraphs, we call $f_i$ and $D_i$ *master feature* and *master group* of $f_i$, respectively.

**Definition 4 (Disjoint Database Cover).** *Given a set $\mathcal{D} = \{(f_i, D_i) | 1 \le i \le m\}$ of master features and master groups and assume that $\bigcup_i D_i = D$, $\mathcal{G} = \{(f'_j, G_j) | 1 \le j \le k\}$ is a disjoint cover of $D$ conforming $\mathcal{D}$ if and only if (1) $\forall (f'_i, G_i)$, $\exists (f_j, D_j) \in \mathcal{D}$ such that $f'_i = f_j$ and $G_i \subseteq D_j$; (2) $\forall G_j \neq G'_j, G_j \bigcap G'_j = \emptyset$; (3) $\forall g \in D$, $\exists G_j \in \mathcal{G}$ such that $g \in G_j$.*

Given a disjoint cover $\mathcal{G}$ of $D$, the total cost gain by sharing the test cost of the master feature within each master group is in (2).

$$gain_{G_i} = cost_{G_i} - cost'_{G_i} = (|G_i| - 1) \times cost_{f_i} \quad (1)$$

$$gain_{\mathcal{G}} = \textstyle\sum_{i=1}^{k}(|G_i| - 1)cost_{f_i} \quad (2)$$

**Definition 5 (Maximized Gain (MG)).** *Given a database $D$ and a set $\mathcal{D} = \{(f_i, D_i)|1 \leq i \leq m\}$ of master features and master groups such that $\forall g \in D$, $\exists D_i \in \mathcal{D}$, $g \in D_i$, find a disjoint cover $\mathcal{G}$ of $D$ such that $gain_{\mathcal{G}}$ is maximized.*

**Theorem 1.** *The problem of Maximized Gain is NP-hard.*

*Proof.* In a special case of MG where each $cost_{f_i}$ equals a constant $c$, $gain_{\mathcal{G}} = c \times (n - k)$. Consequently, solutions of MG in this case aim to minimize $k$, which makes MG exactly a *minimum set cover* problem (NP-hard) [4].

Assume that each data graph contains at least one feature. Algorithm 1 is adopted to approximate the optimal disjoint cover with the maximum $gain_{\mathcal{G}}$. Let $\mathcal{G}$ be a set of already selected disjoint groups ($\mathcal{G}$ is empty at the beginning). Let $g(\mathcal{G})$ be all the data graphs currently covered by $\mathcal{G}$. For each $D_i$ with a master feature $f_i$, let $\frac{cost_{f_i} \times (|D_i - g(\mathcal{G})| - 1)}{|D_i - g(\mathcal{G})|}$ be the average gain from each remaining data graph in $D_i - g(\mathcal{G})$. The greedy algorithm iteratively selects a group $(f_i, D_i - g(\mathcal{G}))$ with the highest average gain, until $\mathcal{G}$ covers all the data graphs.

**Algorithm 1.** ***Clustering***

**Input** . $D$: a graph database $\{g_1, ..., g_n\}$;
$\mathcal{D}$: a set of features and master groups $\{(f_1, D_1)..., (f_m, D_m)\}$;
**Output** . $\mathcal{G}$: a disjoint cover of $D$;

```
𝒢 := ∅; 𝒮 := 𝒟;;
while D − g(𝒢) ≠ ∅ do
    Select (f_i, D_i) ∈ 𝒮 with the maximum cost_{f_i} × (|D_i − g(𝒢)| − 1) / |D_i − g(𝒢)|;
    Insert (f_i, D_i − g(𝒢)) to 𝒢;
    𝒮 := 𝒮 − {(f_i, D_i)};
return 𝒢;
```

*Example 1.* Given $D = \{g_1, ..., g_5\}$ in Figure 2, for each $f_i$, its master group $D_i$ and cost $cost_{f_i}$ are in the left two tables, respectively. Consider clustering (a) of PrefIndex by Algorithm 1. For the first iteration, the average gains from $D_1$ to $D_4$ are 2, 2, $\frac{5}{2}$ and $\frac{8}{3}$, respectively. Consequently, ($f_4$, $\{g_1, g_4, g_5\}$) is selected. Then $g_1$, $g_4$ are removed from $D_1$, while $g_5$ is removed from $D_3$. The average gains of $D_1$ and $D_3$ become 0, while the average gain of $D_2$ remains unchanged. For the second iteration, ($f_2$, $\{g_2, g_3\}$) is selected. Finally, we obtain a disjoint cover $\mathcal{G} = \{(f_4, \{g_1, g_4, g_5\}), (f_2, \{g_2, g_3\})\}$ with a total gain of 12.

**Time Complexity.** Due to the greedy nature of Algorithm 1, the worst case time complexity is $O(n^2 \times m)$ where $n$ and $m$ are the numbers of data graphs and features, respectively.

| | |
|---|---|
| $D_1$ | $g_3, g_5$ |
| $D_2$ | $g_2, g_3$ |
| $D_3$ | $g_4, g_5$ |
| $D_4$ | $g_1, g_4, g_5$ |

| | |
|---|---|
| $cost_{f1}$ | 4 |
| $cost_{f2}$ | 4 |
| $cost_{f3}$ | 5 |
| $cost_{f4}$ | 4 |

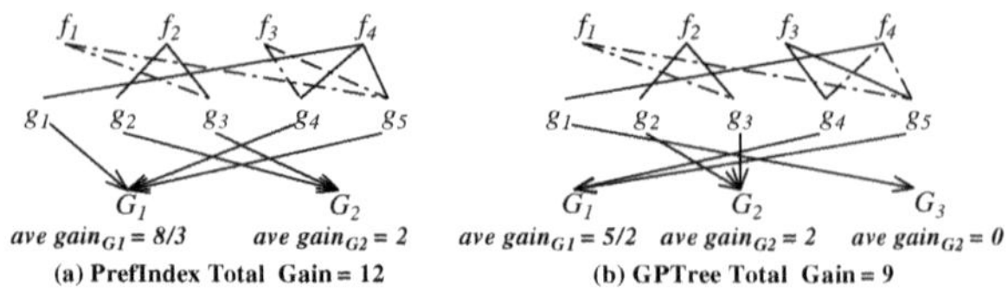


**Fig. 2.** Example of Database Clustering

**Accuracy Guarantee.** Let $OPT$ and $A$ denote the total gains of the optimal solution and Algorithm 1, respectively. The following theorem can be proved.

**Theorem 2.** $A \geq \frac{1}{2}OPT$.

*Proof.* Let $\mathcal{G} = \{(f_i, G_i)|1 \leq i \leq l\}$ be the optimal solution of MG and $OPT_{G_i}$ be the gain of group $G_i$; the total gain $OPT$ of $\mathcal{G}$ is (3). Let the number of graphs in $G_i$ be $n_{G_i}$; the average gain $a_{G_i}$ of $G_i$ is (4).

$$OPT = \sum_{i=1}^{l} cost_{f_i} \times (|G_i| - 1) = \sum_{i=1}^{l} OPT_{G_i} \tag{3}$$

$$a_{G_i} = \frac{cost_{f_i} \times (n_{G_i} - 1)}{n_{G_i}} \tag{4}$$

Since the gain of any group with only one graph is 0, we only consider those groups with at least two graphs. Let $\mathcal{G}' = \{(f'_j, G'_j)|1 \leq j \leq l'\}$ be the greedy solution generated by Algorithm 1 and $A$ be the total gain of $\mathcal{G}'$. Assume $G'_j$ is selected at the $j$th iteration. By removing any graph $g \notin G'_j$ from $G_i$, we obtain $G_i^j = G_i \bigcap G'_j (1 \leq j \leq l')$. By removing any group $G_i^j = \emptyset$, $G_i$ can be partitioned into a set of disjoint subgroups $\{G_i^{j_1}, ..., G_i^{j_k}\}$ such that $(1) \bigcup_{t=1}^{k} G_i^{j_t} = G_i$; $(2) \forall t, t' (1 \leq t < t' \leq k), j_t < j_{t'}$.

Let the average gain of $G_i^{j_t}$ in the greedy algorithm be $a'_t$ and the number of graphs in $G_i^{j_t}$ be $n'_t$ ($\sum_{t=1}^{k} n'_t = n_{G_i}$). Two observations can be made based on the partition of $G_i$. (1) Only the last subgroup $G_i^{j_k}$ may have a gain of 0 in the greedy solution, since $G'_{j_k}$ may have only one graph and $G_i^{j_k}$ is not empty. If another group $G'_{j_t} (j_t < j_k)$ has only one graph and $G_i^{j_t}$ is not empty, a new subgroup $G_i^{j_k} \bigcup G_i^{j_t}$ can be obtained to yield a gain greater than 0. (2) Due to the greedy nature of Algorithm 1, $a'_1$, the average gain of the first subgroup $G_i^{j_1}$ in the greedy solution, must be no less than $a_{G_i}$, Otherwise, $G_i$ instead of $G'_{j_1}$ will be selected for the $j_1$th iteration in the greedy solution. It can be concluded that the gain of $G_i^{j_1} \bigcup G_i^{j_k}$ in the greedy solution is at least $\frac{1}{2}$ of that in the optimal solution. For each rest subgroups $G_i^{j_t}$ $(t \neq 1, k)$, due to the greedy nature of Algorithm 1, (5) can be immediately verified. By replacing $cost_{f_i}$ in (5) with (4), we have (6). Let the gain of $G_i$ in the greedy solution be $A_{G_i}$. By (6), we have (7), which leads us to our conclusion that $A \geq \frac{1}{2}OPT$.

$$a'_{t'} \geq \frac{cost_{f_i} \times (n_{G_i} - \sum_{t=1}^{t'-1} n_t - 1)}{n_{G_i} - \sum_{t=1}^{t'-1} n_t} \tag{5}$$

$$a'_{t'} \geq \frac{n_{G_i} \times (n_{G_i} - \sum_{t=1}^{t'-1} n_{t'} - 1)}{(n_{G_i} - 1) \times \sum_{t=1}^{t'-1} n_t} \times a_{G_i} \geq \frac{1}{2} \times a_{G_i} \quad (6)$$

$$A_{G_i} = \sum_{t=1}^{k} a'_t \times n_t \geq \sum_{t=1}^{k} \frac{a_{G_i} \times n_t}{2} = \frac{1}{2} OPT_{G_i} \quad (7)$$

**Remark.** Generally speaking, the subgraph isomorphism test runs in an exponential time in the worst case and is algorithm, graph topology and graph size dependent. While our algorithm and its analysis apply to any given cost formula, $|V(f)|$ is used to approximate $cost_f$ in our implementation.

### 3.2 Computation-Sharing Comparison

On computation-sharing strategy, PrefIndex differs from GPTree in two ways. Firstly, GPTree selects common induced subgraphs for features and data graphs respectively, while PrefIndex directly selects common induced subgraphs of data graphs as features and shares the computation between filtering and verification. Secondly, GPTree greedily selects common induced subgraphs with the highest cost (largest size). Since larger subgraphs are usually unlikely to be contained by many graphs, PrefIndex uses a more natural heuristic to greedily select features with the highest average gain.

Consider clustering (b) of GPTree in Figure 2, though $f_3$ has the highest cost, it contributes less than $f_4$ as its master group has less data graphs, which only leads to a total gain of 8. In our experiments, PrefIndex outperforms GPTree in all cases on computation-sharing benefits.

### 3.3 Index Structure

In PrefIndex, each feature $f$ is encoded into a common prefix of the GVCode of each graph $g$ in its master group $G_f$. This requires that $f$ must be an induced subgraph of each $g$ in $G_f$. We extend gSpan [11] to mine frequent, discriminative, induced subgraphs. $\mathcal{D}$ is initialized with the mined induced subgraphs and their master groups and then fed into Algorithm 1 for feature selection. Although a feature $f$ may be contained by a data graph $g$ not in $G_f$ as a non-induced subgraph, such information is not recorded in PrefIndex due to mining efficiency.

The index structure of PrefIndex is outlined as follows: (1) Given a disjoint cover $\mathcal{G} = \{(f_i, G_i) | 1 \leq i \leq k\}$ generated by Algorithm 1, encode each $g$ in a group $G_i$ into $Code_g$ by having $Code_{f_i}$ as its prefix. In practice, QuickSI algorithm [9] is used to efficiently identify subgraph isomorphism mappings from $f_i$ to $g$. (2) Each entry $S_i$ of $Code_g$ only stores the label of its corresponding vertex in $g$, its parent vertex in $Code_g$ and its back edge information. Figure 3(a) shows a PrefIndex of graphs $g_a$ and $g_b$ in Figure 1. The effective ordering of common prefixes and suffixes is discussed in the next section.

## 4 PrefIndex Search

This section firstly presents our querying algorithm for a group of graphs based on PrefIndex and then proposes two techniques to further enhance PrefIndex: (1)

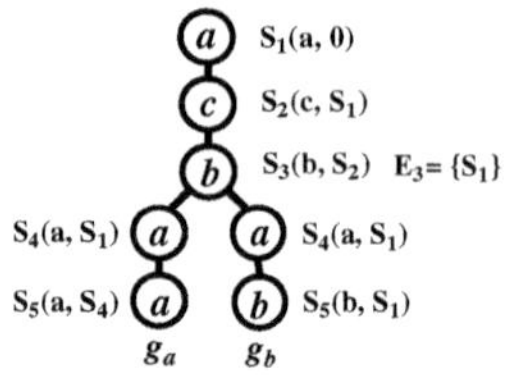


(a) *PrefIndex* $PI_1$ *of* $G_1$

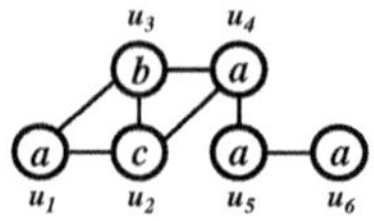


(b) *Query Graph*

| *Type* | $(S_i.l, S_i.p)$ |
|---|---|
| $S_1(v_3)$ | $(a, 0)$ |
| $S_2(v_2)$ | $(c, S_1)$ |
| $S_3(v_1)$ | $(b, S_2)$ |
| $E_{31}$ | $[edge : S_1]$ |
| $S_4(v_4)$ | $(a, S_1)$ |
| $S_5(v_5)$ | $(a, S_4)$ |

$Code_a$

| *Type* | $(S_i.l, S_i.p)$ |
|---|---|
| $S_1(v_8)$ | $(a, 0)$ |
| $S_2(v_7)$ | $(c, S_1)$ |
| $S_3(v_6)$ | $(b, S_2)$ |
| $E_{31}$ | $[edge : S_1]$ |
| $S_4(v_9)$ | $(a, S_1)$ |
| $S_5(v_{10})$ | $(b, S_1)$ |

$Code_b$

**Fig. 3.** PrefIndex

Ordering GVCodes efficiently for PrefIndex; (2) Sharing pruning power among master groups. Given a disjoint cover $\mathcal{G} = \{(f_i, G_i)|1 \leq i \leq k\}$, the PrefIndex of $G_i$ is denoted by $PI_i = \{Code_g|g \in G_i\}$. We aim to share the test cost of $Code_{f_i}$ between filtering and verification. $Code_{f_i}$ is first processed to check whether a subgraph isomorphism mapping exists from $f_i$ to $q$. The test of $Code_{f_i}$ is enforced to be conducted only once for $G_i$, which leads to the following fundamental theorem. The trivial proof is omitted here.

**Theorem 3.** *If a query $q$ contains a data graph $g$, for each prefix $Code'$ of $Code_g$, there must be a subgraph isomorphism mapping from $Code'$ to $g$.*

### 4.1 Algorithm

**Algorithm Sketch.** Based on Theorem 3, for each group $G_i$, our algorithm probes $PI_i$ in a depth first fashion. For each $Code_g$ in $PI_i$, once a mapping $\mathcal{P}'$ is found from a prefix $Code'$ of $Code_g$ to $q$, the algorithm checks if $\mathcal{P}'$ can be extended to cover the next vertex in $Code_g$. If impossible, it backtracks in $PI_i$ to search the next mapping from $Code'$ to $q$. Since $G_i$ may contain many graphs, the last vertex of $Code_{f_i}$ may link to many suffix branches. The algorithm backtracks from the last vertex of $Code_{f_i}$, if all suffix branches under this vertex have been explored in a depth first fashion. The algorithm terminates when no new mapping can be found for the first vertex of $Code_{f_i}$ or all GVCodes in $PI_i$ are detected to be subgraph isomorphic to $q$. The algorithm consists of two parts: PrefixQ and SuffixQ in Algorithm 2 and 3.

*Example 2.* Regarding the example in Figure 1, assume the database is clustered based on disjoint cover $\mathcal{G} = \{(f_a, G_1 = \{g_a, g_b\}), (f_b, G_2 = \{g_c\})\}$. In Figure 3, the two tables show the GVCodes of $g_a$ and $g_b$, while Figure 3 (a) and (b) show the PrefIndex of $G_1$ and the query.

In our algorithm, $S_1$ is first mapped to $u_1$ in $q$ as their labels match. $S_2$ is then mapped to $u_2$ as their labels and parents match; similarly, $S_3$ is mapped to $u_3$ as their labels, parents and back edges match ($S_3.l = b$, $S_3.p = S_2$ and the back edge ($S_3$, $S_1$)). An intermediate mapping $\mathcal{P}_1$ from $Code_{f_a}$ to $q$ is found. This corresponds to the filtering phase.

In verification phase, $\mathcal{P}_1$ is respectively extended for the suffixes of $Code_a$ and $Code_b$. For both $Code_a$ and $Code_b$, $\mathcal{P}_1$ fails to extend to $S_4$ as all adjacent vertices of $u_3$ are either already mapped or unable to meet $S_4.p = S_1$. Consequently, $\mathcal{P}_1$ is abandoned and it backtracks from $S_3$ to search a new mapping. It then finds that no new mapping can be found for $S_3$ while keeping the existing mappings of $S_1$ and $S_2$. After it backtracks for one more depth, no new mapping can be found for $S_2$ while keeping the existing mapping of $S_1$. Finally, it starts from $S_1$ again and finds another intermediate mapping $\mathcal{P}_2$ from $\{S_1, S_2, S_3\}$ to $\{u_4, u_2\ u_3\}$. For $Code_a$, $u_5$ and $u_6$ are mapped to $S_4$ and $S_5$ respectively , which verifies $g_a$ as an answer. For $Code_b$, the extension fails at $S_5$. Since $\mathcal{P}_2$ is the last mapping from $Code_a$ to $q$, the query processing of $G_1$ terminates.

**Algorithm 2.** ***PrefixQ***$(G, Code_f, \mathcal{P}, \mathcal{F}, q, d)$

**Input** . $G$: a group of data graphs represented as GVCodes (PrefIndex);
$Code_f$: the common prefix;
$\mathcal{P}$: a vector, initialized with $\emptyset$;
$\mathcal{F}$: a vector, initialized with 0;
$q$: a query graph;
$d$: the mapping depth;
**Output** . $G_q$: the answer set of $q$ for $G$;

```
if d > |Code_f| then
    for each g ∈ G do
        if SuffixQ(Code_g, P, F, q, d) then
            G_q := G_q ∪ {g};

    G := G − G_q;
    if G = ∅ then
        return G_q;

S := S_d(∈ Code_f); E := E_d(∈ Code_f);
if d = 1 then
    V := {v | v ∈ V(q) ∧ l(v) = S.l ∧ F_v = 0};
else
    V := {v | v ∈ V(q) ∧ l(v) = S.l ∧ (v, P_{S.p}) ∈ E(q) ∧ F_v = 0};
for each v ∈ V do
    for each back edge e ∈ E do
        goto line 13 if e ∉ E(q);
    P_d := v; F_v := 1;
    G_q := G_q ∪ PrefixQ(G, Code_f, P, F, q, d + 1);
    G := G − G_q;
    if G = ∅ then
        return G_q;
    F_v := 0;
return G_q;
```

**PrefixQ** processes the common prefix $Code_f$ of a group $G$ and calls SuffixQ to complete the searching. It is in a recursive, depth first search fashion presented in Algorithm 2. The output $G_q$ is the answer set for $G$. $\mathcal{P} = \{\mathcal{P}_1, \mathcal{P}_2, ...\}$ stores the vertex mappings from $Code_f$ to $q$. $\mathcal{P}_d = v_i$ means $S_d \in Code_f$ is mapped to $v_i$ in $q$. $\mathcal{F} = \{\mathcal{F}_1, ..., \mathcal{F}_{|V(q)|}\}$ stores the vertex state for each $v_i$ in $q$. $\mathcal{F}_i = 1$ means $v_i$ is already mapped to a vertex in $Code_f$. The mapping depth $d$ indicates the current vertex $S_d \in Code_f$ to be mapped. PrefixQ firstly checks if the current mapping $\mathcal{P}$ covers all the vertices of $Code_f$. Condition $d > |Code_f|$ (line 1) implies that a mapping $\mathcal{P}$ from $Code_f$ to $q$ is found. SuffixQ (to process each suffix respectively) is then called (line 3) to extend $\mathcal{P}$. Once a mapping from $Code_g$ to $q$ is successfully extended, $g$ is moved from $G$ to $G_q$. PrefixQ terminates when all GVCodes in $G$ are detected subgraph isomorphic to $q$ (line 7) or all mappings have been exhausted (line 13 and then line 22) for $S_1$ of $Code_f$.

**SuffixQ** processes a suffix under $Code_f$; namely, $Code_g - Code_f$. It has the same input and also follows a recursive, depth first search fashion. The correctness of Algorithm 2 and 3 is immediate from Theorem 3. Although costing exponential time in the worst case, they are very efficient in practice.

**Algorithm 3.** ***SuffixQ***$(Code_g, \mathcal{P}, \mathcal{F}, q, d)$

**Input** . Same as PrefixQ;
**Output** . Boolean: $Code_g$ is a subgraph of $q$;
1 **if** $d > |V(q)|$ **then**
2 | **return** $True$;
3 $S := S_d \in Code_g$; $E := E_d \in Code_g$;
4 $V := \{v | v \in V(g) \wedge l(v) = S.l \wedge (v, \mathcal{P}_{S.p}) \in E(q) \wedge \mathcal{F}_v = 0\}$;
5 **for each** $v \in V$ **do**
6 | **for each** back edge $e \in E$ **do**
7 | | **goto line** 5 **if** $e \notin E(q)$;
8 | $\mathcal{P}_d := v$; $\mathcal{F}_v := 1$;
9 | **if** SuffixQ $(Code_g, \mathcal{P}, \mathcal{F}, q, d + 1)$ **then**
10 | | **return** $True$;
11 | $\mathcal{F}_v := 0$;
12 **return** $False$;

### 4.2 Effectively Ordering GVCode

Given a graph $g$ with $m$ vertices, there are $m!$ different possible GVCodes. As shown in [9], a good ordering of a query $q$ can determine earlier if a subgraph isomorphism mapping from $q$ to a graph $g$ exists. Thus the edges (labels) in $q$ with lower occurrence rates should have a higher priority to be allocated earlier in $Code_q$ to reduce the number of intermediate mappings to be considered. As our problem is the dual problem of that in [9], edges (labels) in a data graph $g$ with lower occurrence rates in the database are "signatures" of $g$ and should be allocated earlier in $Code_g$ for early pruning. When constructing PrefIndex $PI_i$ for a group $G_i$ with a feature $f_i$, QISequence ordering technique is firstly applied on $Code_{f_i}$ and then on each suffix under $Code_{f_i}$ in the same way.

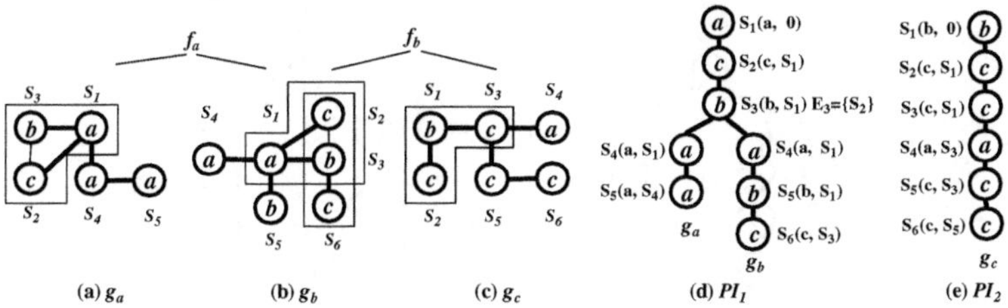


**Fig. 4.** Enhancing Pruning Power

### 4.3 Enhancing Pruning Power

In Figure 4, three graphs are clustered into two groups $G_1 = \{g_a, g_b\}$ with $f_a$ and $G_2 = \{g_c\}$ with $f_b$. Since $g_b$ contains $f_b$, $g_b$ can also be pruned if $f_b$ fails to pass the filtering phase. To share pruning power among different groups, two lists of graph IDs, M(Master)-List and R(Reference)-list are added at the last vertex of $Code_{f_i}$ in $PI_i$. M-list consists of IDs of the graphs in $G_i$, while R-List consists of IDs of the graphs not in $G_i$ but containing $f_i$. Regarding $G_2$, $M\text{-}List_{G_2} = \{g_c\}$ and $R\text{-}List_{G_2} = \{g_b\}$. When PrefixQ detects that $f_b \not\subseteq q$, $g_b$ can be pruned from $G_1$ by not invoking SuffixQ on $g_b$. To realize this, the first SuffixQ call in each $G_i$ is enforced to happen only after PrefixQ calls on all groups are finished and a filtering list $R$ is obtained. In each survived $G_i$, SuffixQ is only invoked on those graphs not in $R$.

PrefixQ can be immediately modified to accommodate the above requirements. If PrefixQ reaches the depth $|Code_f| + 1$ of $G$ for the first time, SuffixQ is not invoked until the depth $|Code_{f'}| + 1$ of all other $G'$ is either reached for the first time (survived groups) or detected impossible to reach (R-lists of pruned groups are added to $R$). The modified algorithm is presented in Algorithm 4.

---

**Algorithm 4.** ***PrefSearch (PS)***

---

**Step 1.** For each $(f_i, G_i)$ $(1 \leq i \leq k)$, probe $Code_{f_i}$ with PrefixQ to check if a subgraph isomorphism mapping $\mathcal{P}_i$ exists from $Code_{f_i}$ to $q$.
If $\mathcal{P}_i$ is found for the first time, we add $(\mathcal{P}_i, PI_i)$ to the verification job list $J$; otherwise, we add the R-List of $f_i$ to the filtering list $R$.

**Step 2.** For each $(\mathcal{P}_i, PI_i) \in J$, conduct verification on $PI_i$ by invoking SuffixQ starting from the end of $Code_{f_i}$ in a depth first search against $q$, while ignoring those $Code_g$ whose IDs are in $R$.

---

## 5 Hierarchical PrefIndex Search

This section explores two further computation-sharing opportunities missed by GPTree: (1) sharing computation among common prefixes of multiple groups; (2) sharing computation among multiple suffixes in each group. We propose to organize the PrefIndexes of multiple groups in a hierarchical structure.

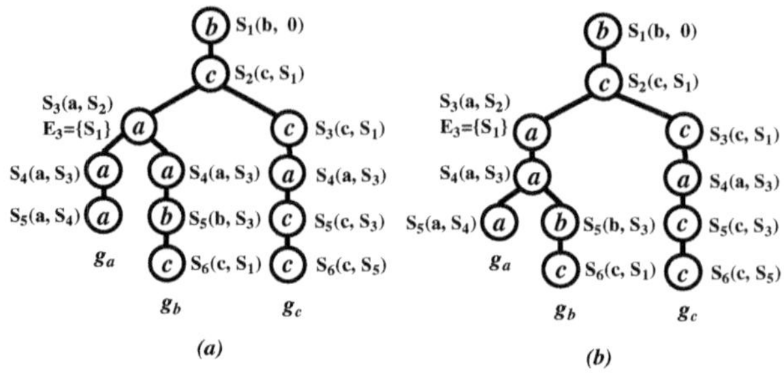


**Fig. 5.** Hierarchical PrefIndex

**Multi-level Sharing.** Regarding Figure 4, assume that (d) and (e) are the PrefIndexes of $G_1 = \{g_a, g_b\}$ and $G_2 = \{g_c\}$. Although $f_a$ and $f_b$ contain the same induced subgraph, an edge $(b, c)$, the chance to share it between $G_1$ and $G_2$ is missed since it is not the prefix of $PI_1$, To address this, a level 2 PrefIndex can be obtained by applying PrefIndex on all selected master features. Generally, a level $n$ PrefIndex can be obtained by applying PrefIndex on all sub-features of level $n - 1$. The procedure can be iteratively performed until no new common subgraphs are identified at the current level.

Regarding Figures 4, we first mine frequent induced subgraphs from $f_a$ and $f_b$ as sub-features and then apply feature selection to construct a 2-level PrefIndex. Figure 5 (a) shows a 2-level PrefIndex where edge $(b, c)$ (sub-feature) is shared.

**Suffix-Sharing.** In PrefixQ, SuffixQ is recursively invoked for each survived suffix. Note that multiple suffixes in a group are still likely to share common entries. As in Figure 5 (a), two entries $Code_a.S_4$ and $Code_b.S_4$ have identical information as well as the common prefix. By sharing them as a common prefix of these two suffixes, the resulted PrefIndex is organized in Figure 5 (b).

Greedy algorithm and PrefIndex technique are adopted to explore the common prefixes of suffixes within each group. All possible next vertices in all suffixes which connects to the common prefix are identified and classified into different types based on label, parent and back edge information. We greedily selecting the vertex contained by the most suffixes and encode the vertex as the next entry of GVCodes of these suffixes. The greedy selection terminates when all types are contained by only one suffix. Frequent induced subgraph mining is not used here since the subgraph graph corresponding to each suffix is not always connected.

**Building HiPrefIndex.** PrefIndex technique is firstly applied on data graphs to build the first level index. Then we iteratively build index on common sub-features identified on each next level. Finally, suffix-sharing is applied within each group to complete the hierarchical PrefIndex which is called HiPrefIndex. If the generated HiPrefIndex is forest structured, a dummy root, which links to the top of each PrefIndex, is inserted into HiPrefIndex.

**Searching HiPrefIndex.** The querying processing on HiPrefIndex starts from the (dummy) root of HiPrefIndex and probes HiPrefIndex in a depth first fashion.

PrefixQ and SuffixQ can be immediately modified to support query processing on HiPrefIndex. For space limits, the details are not presented here.

**Space-Time Efficiency vs Pruning Power.** A branch in HiPrefIndex may correspond to more than one data graph. Regarding Figure 5 (b), the left branch of $(S_3, S_4)$ leads to $g_a$ and $g_b$. Given the query in Figure 1, the prefix corresponding to $f_b$ is not contained by $q$. Since we know $g_b$ also contains $f_b$, in order to remove $g_b$ in the filtering phase, we need to record graph IDs along each edge in HiPrefIndex to share pruning power. This increases not only the storage space but also the computation cost to check graph IDs on each edge. Thus we ignore such information and do not share pruning power in HiPrefIndex.

## 6 Performance Evaluation

We evaluate the performance of our techniques by comparing with GPTree. The following techniques are examined: (1) Indexing techniques PrefIndex and HiPrefIndex in Section 3 and 5. (2) Querying algorithms PrefSearch and HiPrefSearch in Section 4 and 5. (3) Querying algorithms GPTree(A) and GPTree(E) in [14]. GPTree(A) differs from GPTree(E) as it approximately mines frequent closed subgraphs to save index construction cost, which yields an (incomplete) feature set contained by the (complete) feature set of GPTree(E). We obtain the code of GPTree from its authors [14]. All algorithms are implemented in C++ and compiled by GNU GCC. Experiments are conducted on PCs with Intel Xeon 2.4GHz dual CPU and 4G memory under Debian Linux.

**Datasets: AIDS and AIDS10K.** Two real datsets are used. AIDS Antiviral dataset, denoted by AIDS, contains 43,905 graph structured chemical compounds. It is a popular benchmark for studying graph queries downloaded from Development Therapeutics Program. To compare with GPTree based on its experiment settings, a subset of AIDS with 10K graphs, denoted by AIDS10K, is downloaded from **http://www.xifengyan.net/software.htm**.

**Database and Query Set.** For fair comparison, we adopt the experiment settings in [14]. We mine frequent subgraphs from AIDS10K with frequency ranging from 0.5% to 10% and randomly select 10K graphs as the *default database*, while the *default query set* is exactly AIDS10K.

### 6.1 Efficiency on Real Dataset

The default database and query set is used to evaluate the efficiency of our techniques. The default query set is divided into 5 groups from $Q_1$ to $Q_5$. The answer set size of queries in $Q_1$ falls in $[0, 20)$, while those of the rest groups from $Q_2$ to $Q_5$ fall in $[20, 40)$, $[40, 60)$, $[60, 80)$ and $[80, \infty)$. Both techniques mine candidate features from the default database with a minimum frequency of 1%.

**Table 2.** Index Construction

| | PrefIndex | HiPrefIndex | GPTree(A) | GPTree(E) |
|---|---|---|---|---|
| Index Construction (sec) | 311.5 | 313.6 | 129.7 | 697.9 |
| Index Size (# of Features) | 268 | 268 | 1301 | 1278 |

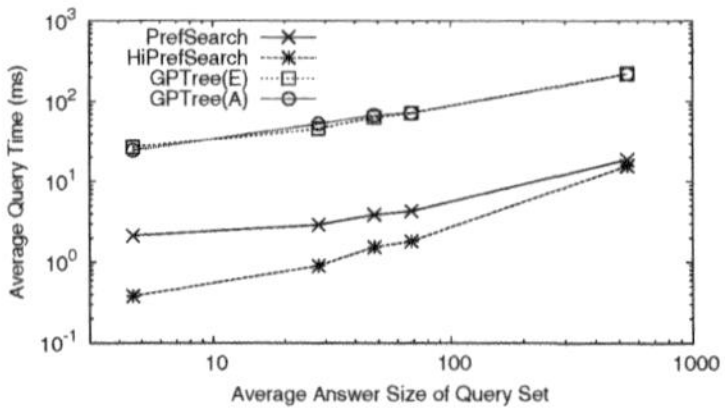


**Fig. 6.** Query Response

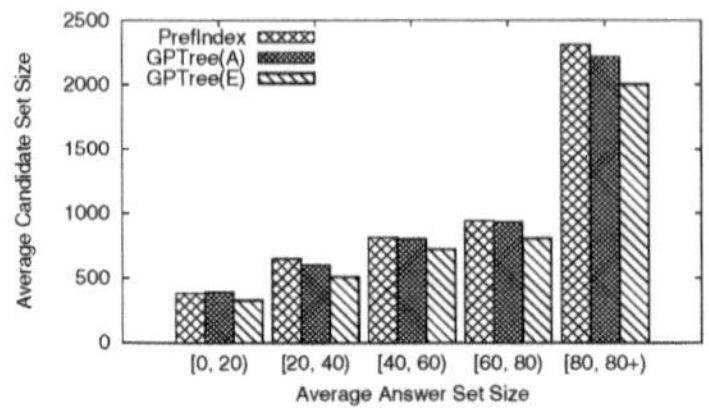


**Fig. 7.** Pruning Power

**Query Processing.** Figure 6 shows average query response time within each query group[1]. PrefSearch and HiPrefSearch outperform GPTree(A) and GPTree(E) for up to 2 orders of magnitudes in query processing, while GPTree(E) slightly outperforms GPTree(A). Although HiPrefSearch disables some of its pruning power, it outperforms other techniques due to its multi-level and suffix-sharing techniques.

**Pruning Power.** Figure 7 shows average pruning power measured by candidate size within each query group. The pruning power of PrefIndex is very similar to that of GPTree(E) and GPTree(A), while GPTree(E) outperforms GPTree(A) due to its complete frequent closed subgraph mining. Since HiPrefIndex disables a part of its pruning power to share more computation as discussed in Section 5, its pruning power is not evaluated here.

**Index Construction.** Table 2 shows index construction cost and index size measured by number of features. While most of the cost for both techniques is spent on the frequent subgraph mining, the effective ordering of GVCode of PrefIndex and HiPrefIndex only consumes less than 0.8% of the total cost. PrefIndex slightly outperforms HiPrefIndex due to the extra cost spent on mining multi-level subgraphs and common suffixes. GPTree(A) costs much less construction time as it approximately mine a small feature set. GPTree(E) costs the most index construction time since it mines not only a complete feature set but also common induced subgraphs from features and data graphs respectively. For fair comparison, we only focus on GPTree(E) for the rest experiments.

## 6.2 Scalability on Real Dataset

**Varying Database Size.** We first evaluate the scalability of our techniques by varying database size. For this reason, AIDS instead of AIDS10K is adopted to generate databases of various size. We first randomly select 10K graphs from

[1] The X-axis represents the average number of answer graphs in each group.

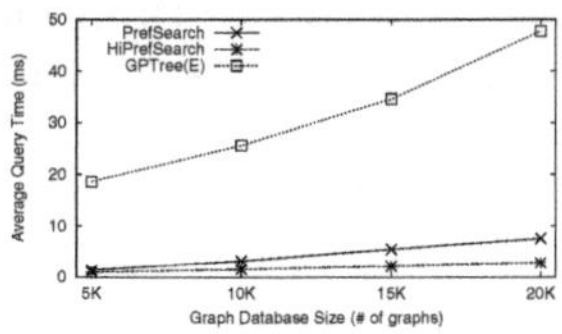


**Fig. 8.** Query Response

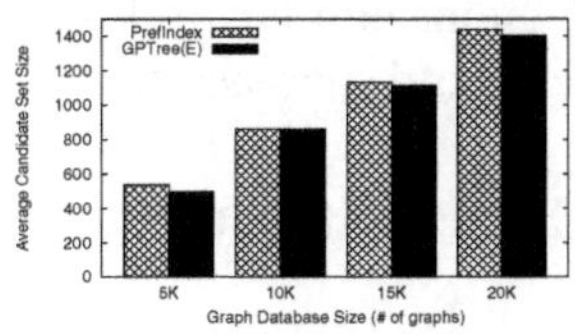


**Fig. 9.** Pruning Power

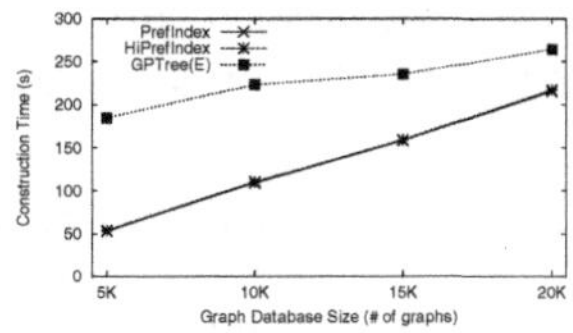


**Fig. 10.** Construction

AIDS as the query set from which we mine frequent subgraphs via the same way as in the overall performance and randomly select 5K, 10K, 15K and 20K frequent subgraphs to form 4 databases from $D_1$ to $D_4$.

Figure 8 shows average query response time for each database. The increment of query response time is almost linear for PrefSearch and HiPrefSearch with increasing database size. HiPrefSearch is still up to an order of magnitude faster than GPTree(E). Figure 9 shows average pruning power for each database. The pruning power of PrefIndex is similar to that of GPTree(E), which confirms the advantage of PrefSearch and HiPrefSearch over GPTree(E) mainly comes from the maximized computation-sharing benefits. Figure 10 shows index construction cost for each database. PrefIndex and HiPrefIndex always needs similar index construction time. It is because HiPrefIndex mines frequent subgraphs from a sequentially decreasing set of sub-features on each level, while common prefixes of suffixes are searched only within each group. GPTree(E) costs the most time due to the extra cost on mining common induced subgraphs.

**Varying Data Graph Size.** We then evaluate the scalability of our techniques by varying data graph size (in # of vertices). We randomly select 10K graphs from AIDS as the query set from which we mine frequent subgraphs via the same way as above and randomly select 5K frequent subgraphs of 10 vertices as database $D_1$. We construct other four database from $D_2$ to $D_5$ by selecting 5K frequent subgraphs of 12, 14, 16, and 18 vertices respectively.

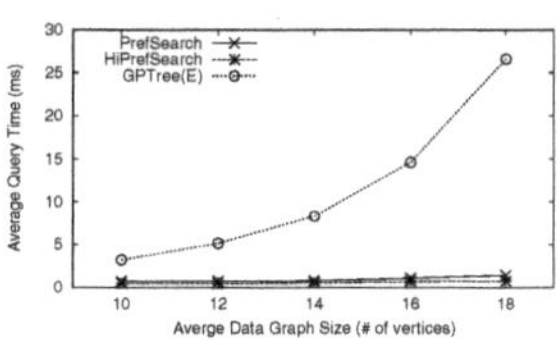


**Fig. 11.** Query Response

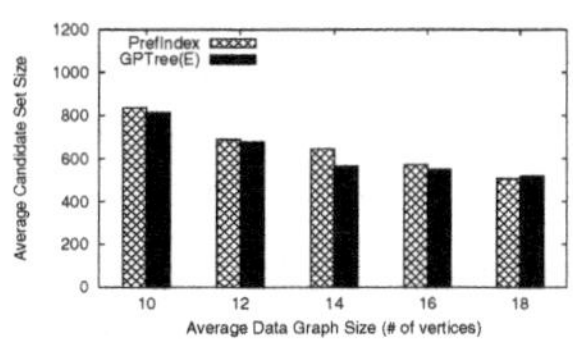


**Fig. 12.** Pruning Power

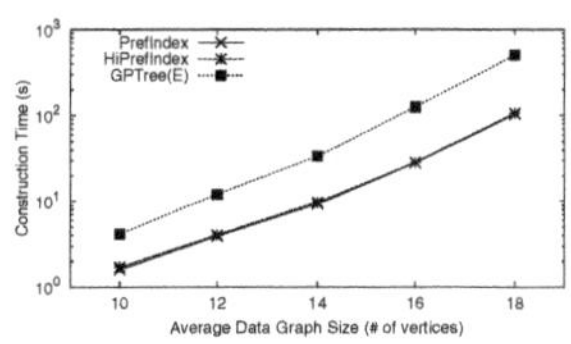


**Fig. 13.** Construction

The query response time, pruning power and index construction time for each database are respectively reported in Figures 11, 12 and 13. Note that the gap on query response time between PrefIndex and GPTree(E) are dramatically furthered with increasing data graph size, since the benefits of multi-level and suffix-sharing are more likely to be obtained on large graphs. While the pruning power for both techniques remains similar, index construction cost of PrefIndex and HiPrefIndex are very close and increase less significantly than GPTree(E).

### 6.3 Scalability on Synthetic Dataset

We evaluate the scalability on synthetic dataset by varying database size. A graph generator from [3] is used. A default query set of 10K graphs is generated by setting the average graph size to 30 vertices, while the average density ($\frac{|V|}{|E|}$) is set to 1.3. The distinct number of labels is set to 10 and distributed uniformly. The default database and 4 databases of 5K, 10K, 15K and 20K graphs are constructed in the same way as above.

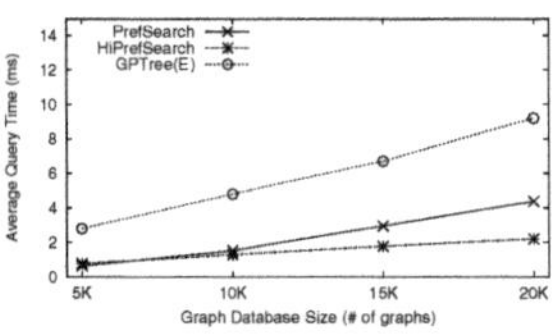


**Fig. 14.** Query Response

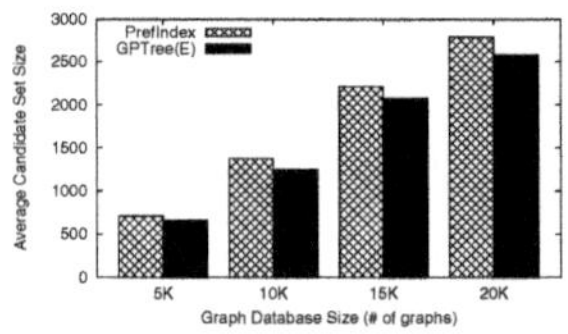


**Fig. 15.** Pruning Power

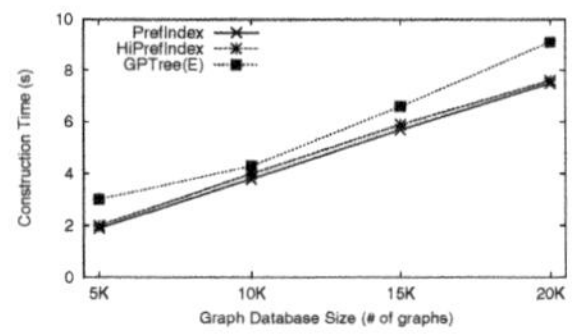


**Fig. 16.** Construction

The query response time, pruning power and index construction time are respectively recorded in Figure 14, 15 and 16. Although PrefSearch and HiPrefSearch outperform GPTree(E) on query response time and index construction cost, the gap between the techniques shortens a lot. Due the uniform distribution of vertex label, the number and size of frequent subgraphs greatly decrease and thus yields limited computation-sharing opportunity. However, PrefIndex still has its advantage over GPTree(E) as expected.

## 7 Related Work

Many studies have been done on graph containment search. While the subgraph containment search has been extensively studied, the supergraph containment search does not draw attentions from database community until most recently.

The filtering-verification framework is popular among most related work on subgraph containment search, which uses effective indexing techniques to filter most false results before the costly verification. Shasha et al. propose a path-based index, GraphGrep [5], which is known as the first feature-based index for subgraph containment search. To enhance the pruning power, frequent subgraph mining techniques such as gSpan [11] and F3TM [15] are developed. Yan et al. develop an effective indexing approach gIndex [12] based on frequent, discriminative subgraphs. Due to the expensive cost of frequent subgraph mining, Zhang et al. and Zhao et al. propose TreePI [13] and (Tree+$\Delta$) [16] independently to index frequent subtrees. Cheng et al. propose a verification-free framework FG-Index [3] to further avoid subgraph isomorphism test. Besides the feature-based index approaches, He et al. propose a clustering-based approach, called C-tree [6], to index graph closures (integration of graphs) in a B-tree like structure. It is the first work to support both exact and similarity subgraph containment search. Other clustering-based approaches include [8] and [1]. Moreover, Williams et al. [10] focus on the efficiency of processing small data graphs, while Jiang et al. [7] convert subgraph containment search to a string search problem. Recently, Shang et al. [9] present an efficient verification algorithm QuickSI.

On supergraph containment search, the first work cIndex proposed by Chen et al. [2] adopts historical query-log information to select features with maximized pruning power. Zhang et al. propose GPTree [14], a computation-sharing framework to share computation cost respectively in the filtering phase and verification phase. To address the defects of GPTree, our techniques propose efficient clustering and query processing algorithm to further share computation cost between filtering and verification, while multi-level and suffix-sharing techniques provide other opportunities to avoid redundant computation.

## 8 Conclusions

In this paper, a novel computation-sharing framework is proposed for supergraph containment search. All data graphs are clustered into disjoint groups for computation-sharing within each group. While the optimization problem MG is shown NP-hard, efficient greedy heuristic is used to approximate the optimal solution with an approximation factor of $\frac{1}{2}$. Based on the compact index structure, PrefIndex, an efficient algorithm PrefSearch integrating filtering and verification is proposed. PrefIndex is enhanced with multi-level sharing and suffix-sharing techniques to explore further sharing opportunities. An extensive empirical study demonstrates the efficiency and scalability of our proposed techniques which achieve orders of magnitudes of speed-up against the state-of-the-art techniques.

## References


1. Berretti, S., Bimbo, A.D., Vicario, E.: Efficient matching and indexing of graph models in content-based retrieval. IEEE Trans. Pattern Anal. Mach. Intell. 23(10), 1089–1105 (2001)
2. Chen, C., Yan, X., Yu, P.S., Han, J., Zhang, D.-Q., Gu, X.: Towards graph containment search and indexing. In: VLDB, pp. 926–937 (2007)
3. Cheng, J., Ke, Y., Ng, W., Lu, A.: Fg-index: towards verification-free query processing on graph databases. In: SIGMOD Conference, pp. 857–872 (2007)
4. Garey, M.R., Johnson, D.S.: Computers and Intractability: A Guide to the Theory of NP-Completeness. W. H. Freeman, New York (1979)
5. Shasha, D., Wang, J.T.-L., Giugno, R.: Algorithmics and applications of tree and graph searching. In: PODS, pp. 39–52, 200
6. He, H., Singh, A.K.: Closure-tree: An index structure for graph queries. In: ICDE, p. 38 (2006)
7. Jiang, H., Wang, H., Yu, P.S., Zhou, S.: Gstring: A novel approach for efficient search in graph databases. In: ICDE, pp. 566–575 (2007)

8. Messmer, B.T., Bunke, H.: A decision tree approach to graph and subgraph isomorphism detection. Pattern Recognition 32(12), 1979–1998 (1999)
9. Shang, H., Zhang, Y., Lin, X., Yu, J.X.: Taming verification hardness: an efficient algorithm for testing subgraph isomorphism. PVLDB 1(1), 364–375 (2008)
10. Williams, D.W., Huan, J., Wang, W.: Graph database indexing using structured graph decomposition. In: ICDE, pp. 976–985 (2007)
11. Yan, X., Han, J.: gspan: Graph-based substructure pattern mining. In: ICDM, pp. 721–724 (2002)
12. Yan, X., Yu, P.S., Han, J.: Graph indexing: A frequent structure-based approach. In: SIGMOD Conference, pp. 335–346 (2004)
13. Zhang, S., Hu, M., Yang, J.: Treepi: A novel graph indexing method. In: ICDE, pp. 966–975 (2007)
14. Zhang, S., Li, J., Gao, H., Zou, Z.: A novel approach for efficient supergraph query processing on graph databases. In: EDBT, pp. 204–215 (2009)
15. Zhao, P., Yu, J.X.: Fast frequent free tree mining in graph databases. In: ICDM Workshops, pp. 315–319 (2006)
16. Zhao, P., Yu, J.X., Yu, P.S.: Graph indexing: Tree + delta $\geq$ graph. In: VLDB, pp. 938–949 (2007)
17. Zou, L., Chen, L., Yu, J.X., Lu, Y.: A novel spectral coding in a large graph database. In: EDBT, pp. 181–192 (2008)

# Supporting Web-Based Visual Exploration of Large-Scale Raster Geospatial Data Using Binned Min-Max Quadtree

Jianting Zhang[1,2] and Simin You[2]

[1] Department of Computer Science
The City College of the City University of New York
138th Convent Avenue, New York, NY 10031
jzhang@cs.ccny.cuny.edu
[2] Department of Computer Science
The Graduate Center of the City University of New York
365 Fifth Avenue, New York, NY 10006
syou@gc.cuny.edu

**Abstract.** Traditionally environmental scientists are limited to simple display and animation of large-scale raster geospatial data derived from remote sensing instrumentation and model simulation outputs. Identifying regions that satisfy certain range criteria, e.g., temperature between [t1,t2) and precipitation between [p1,p2), plays an important role in query-driven visualization and visual exploration in general. In this study, we have proposed a Binned Min-Max Quadtree (BMMQ-Tree) to index large-scale numeric raster geospatial data and efficiently process queries on identifying regions of interests by taking advantages of the approximate nature of visualization related queries. We have also developed an end-to-end system that allows users visually and interactively explore large-scale raster geospatial data in a Web-based environment by integrating our query processing backend and a commercial Web-based Geographical Information System (Web-GIS). Experiments using real global environmental data have demonstrated the efficiency of the proposed BMMQ-Tree. Both experiences and lessons learnt from the development of the prototype system and experiments on the real dataset are reported.

**Keywords:** Binned Min-Max Quadtree, raster geospatial data, Web-GIS, visual exploration.

## 1 Introduction

Advancements in remote sensing technology and instrumentation have generated huge amounts of remotely sensed imagery. It has been estimated that remotely sensed imagery is acquired at the rate of several terabytes per day [1]. In addition to raw imagery data, derived data products targeting at domain-specific applications are fast growing as well. For example, regional and global coverage of Land Cover, Land Surface Temperature, Albedo and Vegetation Indices are among a fraction of MODIS data product table [2]. Still yet, numerous environmental models, such as Weather Research and Forecast

M. Gertz and B. Ludäscher (Eds.): SSDBM 2010, LNCS 6187, pp. 379–396, 2010.

(WRF [3]), have generated even larger volumes of geo-referenced raster model output data with different combinations of parameters, in addition to increasing spatial and temporal resolutions. Traditionally environmental scientists are limited to simple display and animation of raster geospatial data in a desktop computing environment. Very little visual exploration functionality has been provided despite the continuous community software development efforts, such as the Integrated Data Viewer (IDV) from UCAR [4] and WorldWind from NASA [5]. A general purpose, high-performance spatial database backend is highly desirable in supporting visual explorations of large-scale raster geospatial data. Unfortunately, most of existing spatial database research and developments focus on vector geospatial data.

The limited support for binary raster data in the form of quadtree indexing that have been implemented in leading spatial databases, e.g., Oracle Spatial [6] and Microsoft SQL Server Spatial [7], are primarily designed for query filtering on vector spatial data rather than querying numeric raster data natively. We also argue that the pyramid-alike approaches, such as Oracle GeoRaster [8], ArcGIS tiled map services [9] and MapServer[10]/TileCache [11] are mostly designed for fast simple display purposes and are not suitable for supporting interactive visual explorations that involve ad-hoc queries on raster cell values. Efficient data structures, indexing techniques and coordination between browser-based applications and servers are essential to support such queries for interactive visual explorations in a Web environment.

In this study, we propose to use a binned min-max quadtree data structure to index integer or real value rasters to facilitate query-based visualization and visual explorations [12][13][14] [15][16] of large-scale raster geospatial data. By quantizing numeric raster cell values into a set of bins based on the histogram of a raster, the complexity of the resulting quadtree can be greatly reduced. The memory footprint of the quadtree can be sufficiently small to reside in main memory to efficiently answer exploratory queries, such as finding regions whose temperature are between [t1,t2) and precipitation are between [p1,p2). Our work along the direction is largely motivated by the binned bitmap indexing implemented in FastBit [17] with adaptation to more efficient support of finding Regions of Interests (ROIs) in large geo-referenced raster environmental datasets. We term the problem as ROI-finding query which obviously is an extension to finding individual data items as in [12][13]. The problem is similar to the one addressed in [18] and we have adopted a different approach. The data structure can be parallelized across multiple shared-nothing machines to effectively support visual explorations of large-scale geospatial raster data in a Web environment. A prototype that integrates our in-house developed query processing backend based on the proposed data structure and the commercial ArcGIS server software demonstrates the feasibility and effectiveness of the proposed approach. Our technical contributions cover the following three aspects:

- We have proposed a novel binned min-max quadtree data structure to index non-binary rasters. The data structure is efficient for processing queries in support of interactive visual explorations of large-scale raster data by taking advantages of the approximate nature of visualization related queries.
- We have developed a Web-based end-to-end system that allows users interactively and visually explore large-scale raster geo-referenced raster environmental data by coordinating Web clients and query processing backend.

- Experiments using a real environmental data have demonstrated the efficiency of the binned min-max quadtree data structure. The experiments also have provided experiences and lessons to further improve the performance of the Web-based system.

The remainder of the paper is structured as follows. Section 2 introduces related works on visual explorations of raster geospatial data and managing and indexing of raster geospatial data in a database environment. Section 3 presents the binned min-max quadtree data structure. Section 4 provides the architecture and the components of the prototype system to support Web-based visual explorations. Section 5 presents our experiments on the WorldClim global precipitation data at the 30 arc-seconds resolution. We report both experiences and lessons learnt from the development of the prototype system and experiments on the real dataset. Finally, Section 6 concludes the paper and outlines future research directions.

## 2 Background and Related Work

Visual explorations play an important role in seeking casual relationships among environmental factors and the possible relationships between human activities and their environmental consequences. As the majority of environmental data have a geospatial and a temporal component, research on exploratory spatial and spatiotemporal analysis [19] [20][21] can be generally applied. Quite a few research prototypes, such as GeoDa[22] and GeoVista [23] are available for vector geospatial data (including the associated attribute data) and they are quite successful in social, economic and health domains. On the other hand, while numerous image clustering, segmentation and classification algorithms have been applied to satellite imagery, only a handful research on visual explorations of the correspondences between pixel values and class labels have been reported [24][25]. The recently emerging object-oriented classification algorithms and their applications in remote sensing imagery have provided an opportunity for visual explorations of remotely sensed image data [26][27]. On the environmental model output side, most of existing developments focus on overlaybased display, map generation and animation. Little progresses have been evidenced on exploratory analysis with the exception of iso-surface generation. As an example, UCARs IDV[4] is capable of generating iso-surfaces from 3D atmospheric model outputs. However, the capabilities of linking geospatial phenomena (objects or events) with the underlying raster data (sensor observations or model outputs) are still lacking despite the availability of several pioneering theoretical works (e.g. [28]). It is beyond the scope of this paper to provide a comprehensive solution to visual explorations of raster geospatial data. Rather, our focus is on efficient implementation of a few generic operations to facilitate such visual explorations on large-scale raster geospatial data. More specifically, we target at the ROI-finding queries.

A few options are available to manage geospatial raster data in databases based on existing database technologies. First of all, each individual element can be treated as a tuple in relational table and traditional relational database technologies can be applied. Second, the raster data can be treated as multidimensional arrays and subsequently N-Array or nested table techniques can be applied in object-relational databases [29].

Finally, large raster data can be decomposed into small units and stored in databases as Large Binary Objects or BLOBs [30]. While each of the approaches has their suitable application scenarios, none of them can be used to process ROI-finding queries efficiently. Studies also have shown that multidimensional array supports implemented in mainstream databases are far less efficient than using native scientific data formats when scaling up to large datasets [29]. While the recently emerging column-store database techniques optimized for read-only or append only data [31][32] might provide an opportunity to reevaluate the suitability of relational and object-relational database technologies for geospatial raster data, it is likely that extending existing spatial indexing techniques remain to be the most effective way to process the ROI-finding queries.

We note that column-store based database layouts are similar to popular scientific data formats, such as NetCDF[33] and HDF5[34] in many aspects. We believe that one of the biggest problems in handling geo-referenced gridded environmental data in existing databases is the lacking of proper indexing mechanisms that take spatial or spatiotemporal autocorrelations into consideration. In fact, as discovered in [18], while sophisticated bitmap indexing techniques such as those implemented in FastBit [17] are very efficient in finding individual raster cells, it is more computationally expensive to assemble them into regions and return the regions as query results, i.e., assembling tuple IDs into regions. In contrast, our approach is based on spatial indexing that indexes regions and returns regions that satisfy searching criteria directly without incurring expensive post-processing cost. We also note that our work on indexing raster geospatial data complements existing works on array query definition language [35][36][37] and physical data layout of multidimensional data[38][39][40].

The most popular spatial indexing techniques include R-trees, quadtrees, octtrees and kd-trees. We refer readers to the overview papers and books for more detailed information [41][42]. Various quadtrees have been used to index both vector and binary raster data. On the other hand, interval tree [43],octree [44][45] and kd-tree [46][47] techniques have gained considerable popularity in deriving static and time-evolving iso-surfaces with or without ray-tracing. There are two problems in directly applying octree and kd-tree techniques to visual explorations of large scale gridded environmental data. First, techniques developed for iso-surface generation and/or ray-tracing usually have large memory footprints. While they are suitable for fine-scale offline rendering, it may be too costly for online visual explorations in a Web environment. Usually only limited resources are allocated to a Web browser. Data communication overheads between browsers and servers are much higher than those in tightly coupled desktop or cluster computing environments. Second, these techniques are mostly designed for tracing boundaries (iso-surfaces) and intersecting with linear objects (ray-tracing) and it is not straightforward to apply them to identify ROIs.

There are also works trying to extend quadtree techniques for binary rasters to grayscale or color images [48] [49][50]. However, most of existing studies along the direction focused on image encoding or compression with only few of them actually targeted at efficient query processing which are more relevant to visual explorations of scientific data. The difference between image compression and query processing is that the former focuses on the tradeoffs between disk storage and compression computation while the later focuses on the tradeoffs between the filtering and refinement in processing a query using an acceptable memory footprint. Previous research on quadtree based data structures and query processing focused on storage and manipulation of clusters of (overlapped) images. We refer readers to [51][52][53][54][55] and the review article by Manouvrier[56] for more details. These data structures are not tailored for read-only applications and they may not be suitable for supporting visual explorations of large-scale raster data, especially in a Web environment. Furthermore, most of the works utilized or followed a B-Tree indexing approach and assumed portions of the indices are dynamically loaded into memory. In contrast, our approach quantizes raw data into bins and tries to build a memory-resident index with desired memory footprint. The memory-resident index ensures fast filtering in query processing and returns regions that approximate true query results before subsequent refinement.

Our approach is largely motivated by the binned bitmap indexing reported in [57] and the multi-scale bitmap indexing reported in [58]. The binned bitmap indexing approach has been successfully applied to large-scale query-based interactive visualization using techniques such as Parallel Coordinate Plot or PCP [59]. A similar bin-hashing strategy has been applied to query driven visualization before rendering resulting records as point clouds [60]. One drawback of directly applying binned bitmap indexing for visual explorations of geospatial raster data is that when value ranges of a query are wide, it is likely that a large number of cells will be returned independently. It could be very expensive to transport the individual query results from query backend to client machines and paint these cells individually in a Web browser. The rendering speed in Web browsers could be improved by specifying regions instead of individual pixels. The advantages and practical needs of returning regions from a query are also identified by a recent work by Sinha[18] which is based on the FastBit. The authors proposed to identify regions from the bit vector of a query result which had been observed to be very computationally expensive. As such, while we recognize the generality of bitmap indexing that is suitable for both structured and unstructured data items, we argue that our approach is more suitable for ROI-finding queries for visual exploration purposes.

With respect to Web-based visual exploration of geospatial data, previous works focused on the mashup techniques by dynamically compositing images generated at the server sides [61][62]. However, very few of the reported works have taken query efficiency into consideration. Most of them assume that the server side programs are sufficiently fast and the bandwidth is large enough for interactive visualizations. As detailed in Section 3, the hierarchical nature of quadtree data structures allow pruning quadrants that do not intersect with the spatial extents that are under investigations by users. This not only speeds up query response times but also reduce the data volumes of query results need to be transported to clients. In addition, any lower level quadrants whose spatial extents are less than single pixel based on visualization scales at the clients can be pruned as well, which further reduce query response times and query result data volumes.

## 3 Binned Min-Max Quadtree

In this section, we first define the ROI finding queries before presenting the binned min-max quadtree data structure and its construction and query processing algorithms.

Given a set of rasters representing environmental variables $\{F_i|0 \leq i < n\}$ over a spatial domain D whose value ranges are $\{V_i^H\}$ and $\{V_i^L\}$ respectively, a ROI finding query Q identifies regions in D whose cells $C_j$ satisfy the compound condition $\left\{C_j|V_{1j} \in [V_1^{QL}, V_{1j}^{QH}] \,\mathbf{op}\, V_{2j} \in [V_2^{QL}, V_2^{QH}] \ldots \mathbf{op}\, V_{kj} \in [V_k^{QL}, V_k^{QH}]\right\}$ where op can be either conjunctive and disjunctive and $0 < k < n$. $V_i^{QL}$ and $V_i^{QH}$ represent the lower and high bounds of query Q for variable i. While the formulation does not impose any relationships among the resulting raster cells, since we divide domain D into quadrants in quadtree indexing and evaluate the compound condition against relevant quadrants, the resulting cells are naturally reported as a collection of quadrants that satisfy the compound query criteria. Instead of reporting the cells individually from the query result, using a collection of quadrants may significantly save memory consumption and improve query results rendering for visualization purposes. Assuming that a quadtree for each environmental variable has been constructed, it is not difficult to see that evaluating the compound condition can be achieved by synchronized traversal of relevant quadtrees as described in (Manouvrier et al 2002) and will be omitted here due to space constraints. We next focus on the construction of a single quadtree and evaluating a single condition on a quadtree.

The Binned Min-Max Quadtree, or BMMQ-Tree for short, is directly motivated by both binned bitmap indexing [57] for scientific data and min-max octree/kd-tree for isosurface generation and ray tracing[47]. As discussed above, while min-max octrees and kd-trees are efficient in pruning tree branches that do not contain the iso-values being used, building a full octree or kd-tree using the finest resolution data may consume too much memory and slow down index construction and query processing. The binned bitmap indexing is more efficient and more suitable for large scale scientific data when compared with classic bitmap indexing. The downside is that the resulting cells in binned bitmap indexing do not naturally form regions and the post-processing to assemble cells into regions could be very computationally expensive. The proposed BMMQ-Tree combines the advantages of min-max octree/kd-tree indexing and binned bitmap indexing. Furthermore, our empirical studies have shown that, while environmental data are well-known for significant spatial autocorrelation due to the first law of geography [63], neighboring cell values are often slightly different. This makes traditional quadtree-based indexing techniques that require the uniformity of quadrants inappropriate. By binning cell values using proper boundary values, quadrant uniformity can be derived and mature quadtree indexing techniques (such as linearization and query processing in databases) can be applied. In this sense, our BMMQ-Tree data structure is an extension to traditional region quadtrees by associating each quadrant with a min and a max value of a quadrant. The min and max values are bin indices which can be bytes (8 bits for 256 bins) or short integers (16 bits for 65,536 bins), which normally are just a fraction of the storage requirement for a quadtree node. On the other hand, BMMQ-Tree branches can be efficiently pruned if the nodes min/max values do not overlap with the range of the query being evaluated. We next present the tree construction and query processing in more details.

Fig. 1 illustrates the process of constructing a BMMQ-Tree. The process first determines bin boundaries. While quite a few options are available, we decide to use a histogram based quantile approach for simplicity. The open source GDAL package

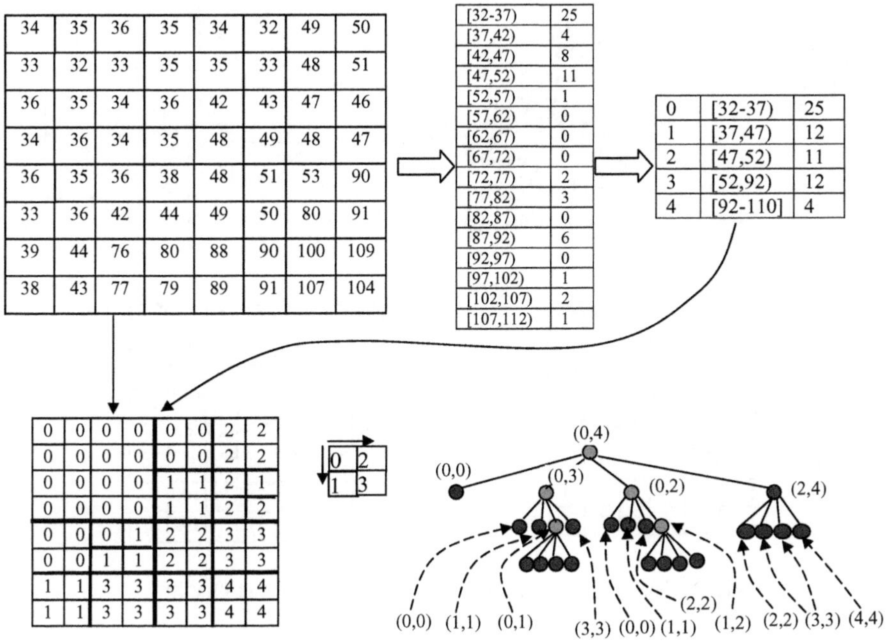


**Fig. 1.** Illustration of Binned Min-Max Quadtree Construction

[64] has provided an API to efficiently generate histograms for major image and raster data formats which further makes the histogram based approach desirable from implementation perspective. After the histogram with desired low/high boundary and bins has been retrieved, we loop through the histogram bins to determine the quadtree bins as the following. For each of the histogram bins, if its count is larger than the average count of the quadtree bins (calculated as the total valid raster cells divided by the desired quadtree bins - denoted as NA), then it is qualified as a quadtree bin; otherwise it will be combined with previous histogram bins until the combined count is larger than NA. Due to the bin formulation policy, the resulting number of bins can be less than the desired bins.

The main process of BMMQ-Tree construction is as the following. First, the 2D raster data being indexed is read into main memory following the sequence of BMMQ-Tree nodes that are being constructed. Each cell value is first quantized based on the bin boundary values. After the four cells that form a quadrant are processed, if their bin indices are exactly the same, then they will be combined to form a quadrant with the same min/max value. The process then moves to the next quadrant based on the quadtree space tessellation (row-major or column-major). The combination is also performed recursively to determine the min/max bin indices for each quadtree node. It is clear that the memory requirement in the BMMQ-Tree construction process is never larger than the size of the constructed quadtree plus four quadtree nodes and the data buffer to hold the values of raster cells being processed. We are in the process of exploring the possibilities of GPGPU based parallel constructions of BMMQ-Trees which is likely to

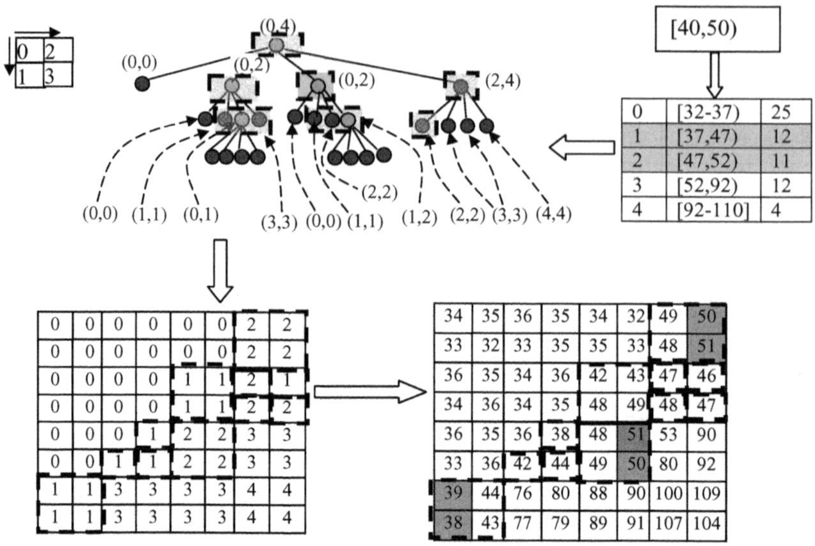


**Fig. 2.** Query Processing Based on Binned Min-Max Quadtree

reduce index construction times significantly. On the other hand, as most georeferred environmental data are read only, offline index creation and online query processing are independent of each other. While it is difficult to compare our approach with approach presented in [18] directly, we consider our approach trades offline index construction times with online query processing times by forming uniform quadrants which are intermediate between connected components and individual raster cells. We next turn to online query processing using BMMQ-Trees.

Query processing using BMMQ-Trees is illustrated in Fig. 2 using an example. First, the low and high boundary values [40,50) are mapped to the low and high ends of bin indices 1 and 2, respectively. The boundary values corresponding to the resulting bin indices [37,52) completely contain the query low and high boundary values to avoid true negatives. Second, starting from the root, each quadrant is recursively visited. If the min-max indices range does not overlap with the indices range corresponding to the query range, then all quadrants under the node corresponding to the current quadrant can be safely pruned. In Fig. 2 (top-left part), non-leaf nodes not in the shaded rectangles have been pruned. The recursive query processing stops under two conditions. First, a leaf node is reached which indicates that either a raster cell at the finest resolution is reached or all the raster cells in the quadrant corresponding to the node have the same bin index. Second, the quadrant corresponding to the node has a spatial extent less than a single pixel based on visualization scales at the client side. Assuming the width and height of visualization canvas at the client side are Wc and Hc and the width and height measured as the real-world coordinate system (e.g., latitude/longitude) are Wr and Hr, respectively, the quadtree level to stop recursive query processing can be easily calculated as $L_{stop} = floor(log_2(min(Wr/Wc, Hr/Hc)))$. It is clear that false positives may be introduced (the shaded cells in the lower-right part of Fig. 2) due to the binning nature of the data structure and the less-than-single-pixel stopping policy. While this may be a problem for querying databases exactly, it turns out that allowing false positives reduces the structural complexities of query results and hence the data volumes to be transported to the clients as well as rendering times at the client side. More discussions are provided in the experiments section.

## 4 System Architecture and Implementation

The primary focus of this research is to develop an end-to-end system that can effectively facilitate environmental scientists to explore large-scale geo-referenced raster data. Compared to desktop applications, a Web-based interface is more preferable. However, normally only limited resources are allocated to a Web browser and graphics rendering accelerators are usually not accessible to browser-based applications. Data communication overheads between browsers and servers are much higher than those in tightly coupled desktop or cluster computing environments. As such, careful design to take the characteristics of both client and server sides into consideration is essential in visual exploration of large-scale raster geospatial data in a Web environment. In our prototype system, the client side is based on the Rich Internet Application (RIA) framework using Adobe Flex programming [65]. The server side is a combination of commercial ArcGIS server technologies [9] and our in-house developed distributed query processing modules that implement the binned min-max quadtree based indexing as described above. The overall architecture is shown in Fig. 3 and more details on each of the components will be provided subsequently. Note that some components in Fig. 3 involve both offline and online parts and both of them will be introduced in the respective subsections.

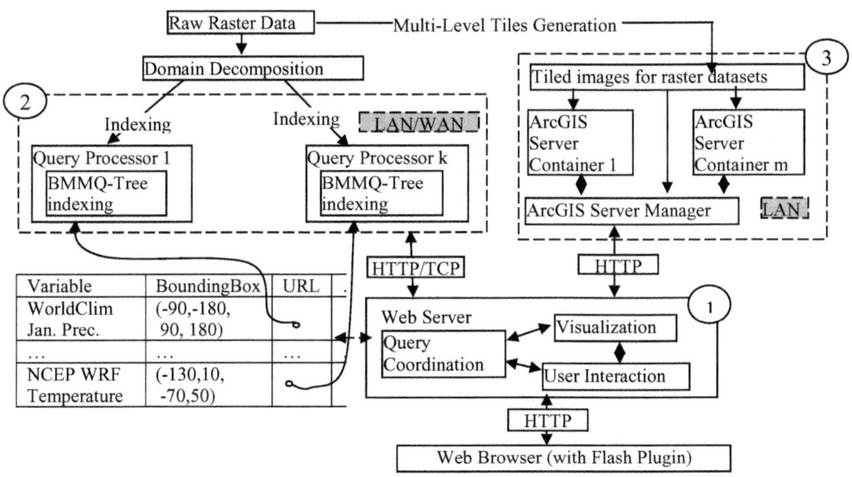


**Fig. 3.** Prototype System Architecture

### 4.1 Visual Exploration Client Module

We have adopted Adobe Flex programming [65] to develop the client module for the following considerations. First, the Flex RIA framework has built-in rich graphics functionality and allows users control rendering canvas at the pixel level which is much more powerful and flexible than traditional Ajax based solutions. Second, it also allows more complex and immediate interactions with users which are crucial in visual explorations. Third, quite a few popular visualization packages, such as ArcGIS [66], have provided Flex APIs which makes the choice very attractive compared to the similar frameworks. Nevertheless, we believe that our design is also applicable to other RIA frameworks, should an alternative be more desirable for practical reasons.

The client module provides graphics user interfaces (GUIs) and interacts with users. Fig. 4 provides a snapshot shows the layout of the GUIs. A tree interface shows the catalog of available raster datasets based on their semantic classifications. Users can search and subsequently select a subset of rasters as the candidates for explorations. For the chosen rasters, histograms can then be visualized to help users determine ranges of values for subsequent visual explorations. The "Query" button serves as the entry point to translate the query criteria represented by GUIs into a query string to be passed to

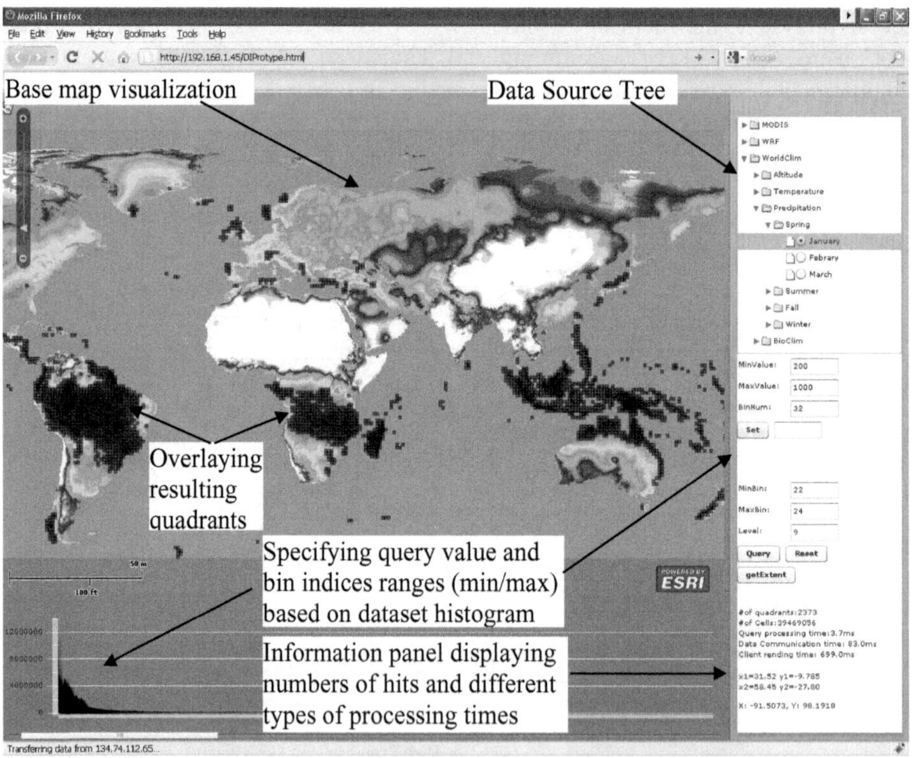


**Fig. 4.** Prototype System Snapshot and Web Client GUI Layout

the appropriate query processing backend. The query string currently includes spatial extent, bin index range and desired level of details. There are different options to visualize query results at the client side. We have chosen to ask the backend to send back the results in the form of a collection of (x, y, level) triples, convert these triples into geographical coordinates and generate polygons so that they can be easily visualized in Flex-enabled runtime engines embedded in Web browsers through ArcGIS Flex API. While this approach is simple to implement and works well when the numbers of resulting quadrants are in the order up to a few thousands, we have found that the performance degrades as the numbers of resulting quadrants increase when the desired levels of details are high in some tests. We are in the process of exploring an image-based option that clients ask servers send back the query results in the form of binary images so that they can be visualized in Web browsers using less memory and computation resources. The visualization module is also responsible for requesting proper tiles from ArcGIS Server Manager and displays the returned images representing raw data with a predefined coloring schema. Note that client requests to the query processing backend and ArcGIS servers are completely independent. More information on this part is provided in Section 4.3.

## 4.2 Distributed Query Processing

As discussed before, the BMMQ-Tree based indices can be distributed across multiple shared-nothing machines to make visual exploration related query processing scalable. While there are quite a few options for workload distribution in facilitating parallel computing, the approach used in this study is based on a combination of spatial and categorical criteria which certainly lefts rooms for further refinements. As an example, the GLCF MODIS data from the University of Maryland comes with five parts [67], namely Africa, EuraAsia, North America, South America and Oceania. Each part has images at about 60 time periods and each image for a single period has 7 bands. Thus it is natural to decompose the spatial domain by the five parts. Depending on the available machines, the raster images in each part can be further decomposed by time and/or by bands. There are advantages and disadvantages of using fine and coarse level parallelization in this context. Using more computer nodes certainly reduces workload per node but also increases monetary costs. Furthermore, for processing conjunctive queries that involve multiple rasters (layers), if these rasters are indexed by a same computer node, query optimization is possible by early termination during synchronized traversals of co-located quadtrees.

## 4.3 Tiled Map Visualization Using ArcGIS

Fast visualizing and examining raw data are among the basic requirements for visual explorations of environmental data. Major Internet map providers, such as Google map and Microsoft Live map use the tile cache technology to speed up map rendering. GIS server software, such as ArcGIS [9] and MapServer+TileCache[10][11] provide similar functions to allow users to publish their own data as tiled maps that can be visualized in a variety of client software. We choose ArcGIS due to its technical maturity and easy of use. Map tiles at the different scales for all rasters have been generated in ArcGIS server. The ArcGIS Flex API [66] has made it easy to use tiled maps hosted by

ArcGIS servers in Web-based client applications. Note that, in our prototype design, visualizing the raw data is completely independent of processing ROI-finding queries. The resulting regions derived from ROI-finding queries can be overlaid on top of base maps to maximize the benefits of visual explorations. For example, users can compare raster cells inside the resulting ROIs with those nearby. While processing ROI-finding queries involves identifying cells from all relevant rasters which can be computationally intensive when sophisticated indexing technqiues are used, displaying base map only involves determining appropriate pre-generated image tiles under the spatial extent of the current active view, which is much less computationally expensive.

# 5 Experiments and Evaluation

## 5.1 Data and Experiments Setup

The experiments are designed for two purposes. First, we would like to examine the efficiency of the proposed binned min-max quadtree. It is clear that the sizes of the resulting quadtrees increase when the numbers of quadtree bins increase. At the same time, the false positives will decrease and the numbers of returned ROIs will increase. There are tradeoffs among disk/memory consumptions of constructed indices, rates of false positives, data communication costs and client visualization rendering costs. The later two are proportional to the number of returned ROIs. As we are not able to provide an analytical cost model for the binned min-max quadtree at this moment, the empirical results are important in understanding the efficiency of the data structure in real applications. Second, we would like to examine the overall performance of the end-to-end prototype system.

The data communication time also includes the overheads of data passing through different protocol stacks in the middleware and Web server in addition to data transport time over the network. To minimize the network traffic instabilities, in our experimens, the client machines and the server machines are co-located within our campus network. The client visualization rendering time includes parsing returned quadrants data of triples (x, y, level), converting the triples to squares in the real-world coordinate system that is being used at the client side and rendering the squares to the client visualization canvas embedded in a Web browser. We plan to use the current climate data published by WorldClim [68][69]. The dataset is the interpolations of observed data from 1950-2000 and includes monthly precipitation, minimum temperature and maximum temperature (12 month) and 18 derived bioclimatic variables at the global 30 arc-seconds ( 1 kilometers) resolution. Thus the number of grid cells is 432000*216000 for each of 12*3+18=54 rasters. Due to space limit, we only report the experiment results using the January precipitation data. For the January precipitation data, the number of cells with valid values is 222,265,892, which is about 23.82% of the total number of cells in the raster dataset. The percentage is slightly less than the percentage of land over the earth surface as there are no data for cells to the south of 60 degrees. The minimum and maximum precipitation values are 0 and 1003 millimeter, respectively. We have set the maximum level of the BMMQ-Tree to 16 as $2^{16} = 65536$ is already larger than 432000. We have used three bin numbers (8, 16 and 32) in our experiments for the reasons discussed above. The numbers of the leaf nodes of the corresponding quadtrees are

8,491,370, 15,036,155 and 25,877,417, respectively. These numbers translate to 110:1, 62:1 and 36:1 compression rates. We have performed extensive tests using different combinations of value ranges, spatial extents and quadtree bin numbers.However, due to space limit, only the results for precipitation range [90,300] with eight different spatial extents are reported in the following subsections. The cell selectivity rates of the eight queries vary from 0.23% to 5.76% using the total number of valid cells as the denominator.

### 5.2 Results of Query Processing

Results show that the query response times for the eight queries measured at the server side using the three bin numbers are 51-160, 42-162 and 47-252 milliseconds, respectively. All the response times are just fractions of a second which clearly shows the efficiency of the proposed BMMQ-Tree data structure in facilitating ROI-finding queries. As discussed previously, queries based on BMMQ-Tree are approximate in nature. Our experiments show that the larger bin sizes the smaller false rates, which is expected. The minimum and maximum false rates for B=32 are 12% and 53%, respectively, with an average of 23%. Visual inspections show that false positives are close to true positives and the resulting quadrants highlights the locations of true positives in a simplified manner which are often desirable in visual explorations.

### 5.3 Results of End-to-End Performance

As discussed before, the end-to-end performance of each query-driven visual exploration operation has three components: server query response time ($T_{Server\_Query}$), data communication time ($T_{Data\_Comm}$) and visualization rendering time ($T_{Vis\_Rendering}$). Due to space limit, we only report the three components for the eight queries using bin size 32 and the queries stop at the quadtree level 12 (determined based on ess-than-single-pixel stopping policy discussed in Section 3). In addition to showing the three categories of times for the eight queries in Table 1, we also report the resulting numbers of quadrants at the first column of the table ($N_Q$).

From Table 1, it is clear that both the data communication times and the visualization rendering times are proportional to the resulting number of quadrants which is expected. Compared with the server query response times, data communication times are generally one order greater and the visualization rendering times are more than one order

**Table 1.** End-to-end Performance Measurements with B=32 and MaxLevel=12 (in milliseconds)

| Query ID | $N_Q$ | $T_{Server-Query}$ | $T_{Data-Comm}$ | $T_{Vis-Rendering}$ |
|---|---|---|---|---|
| Q1 | 13990 | 18.35 | 180.7 | 5329 |
| Q2 | 12941 | 16.39 | 163.7 | 4741 |
| Q3 | 31936 | 36.49 | 340.3 | 21667 |
| Q4 | 13904 | 18.21 | 341.3 | 5790 |
| Q5 | 3771 | 5.35 | 108.7 | 1262 |
| Q6 | 15313 | 18.67 | 300.0 | 6647 |
| Q7 | 21507 | 25.66 | 306.7 | 11705 |
| Q8 | 11143 | 13.82 | 174.7 | 3896 |

greater than the data communication times. While the server query response times are excellent and the data communication times are adequate for visual explorations (less than 1 second), the visualization rendering times may be too large for the purpose.

To further investigate the rendering bottleneck incurred by ArcGIS Flex API, we have performed additional experiments on querying a value range of [200,1000] at the tree level 9 to 12 using the globe as the spatial extent. Note the value range corresponds to bins [22-14] with B=32. The results show that the visualization rendering time is acceptable for level=9 (0.693s) and level=10 (2.238s) while it becomes impractical for level=11 (8.2s) and level=12 (73.9s). We suspect that ArcGIS Flex API may be the bottleneck in rendering tens of thousands of squares. We are in the process of implementing our native square rendering algorithms in Adobe Flex. Another option would be requesting the query processing backend send back compressed images rather than individual quadrants as discussed in Section 4.1. On the other hand, we note that quadrants at level 10 have an approximate spatial resolution of 0.5 degree which is comparable to many datasets being used for global studies.

### 5.4 Discussions

As BMMQ-Tree and binned bitmap indexing [57] share many similarities, it is desirable to compare the two indexing approaches. However we found that direct comparisons are both inappropriate and difficult. First of all, binned bitmap indexing seeks to answer queries exactly at the individual data element (raster cell) level while BMMQ-Tree is primarily designed for visual explorations that allow approximate queries. Second, BMMQ-Tree query results naturally approximates connected components which are more suitable for further analysis of raster geospatial data. In contrast, binned bitmap requires expensive post-processing to find connected component [18]. BMMQ-Tree query results represent an intermediate step between individual raster cells and more complex connected components. Third, binned bitmap may generate large numbers of individual data element identifiers whose data volumes generally are too big to be transported to Web browsers for visualization purposes. Differently, BMMQ-Tree allows specify a maximum query level for a quadtree and thus reduce resulting data volumes at the expenses of higher false positive rates. The feature may be desirable in many visual exploration applications.

We believe exact queries based on FastBit can enhance our prototype system in the following way. For each client query, we first direct the query to FastBit and obtain the exact number of cells in the query result. We then direct the query to our query processing backend based on BMMQ-Tree indexing using a stopping quadrant level determined based on the less-than-single-pixel stopping policy discussed at the end of Section 3 and calculate the false positive ratio. Users then can determine whether to increase the stopping quadrant level based on the false positive rate. When the exact number of cells in a query result set is less than a predefined number (e.g., 10,000), the coordinates of the cells can be transported to the client side and visualized in Web browsers directly. Integrating FastBit with our prototype to allow visualization of exact query results is underway.

## 6 Conclusions and Future Work

Lacking interactive query-driven visualization supports for large-scale raster geospatial data in a Web environment has motivated us to develop a binned min-max quadtree data structure to index raster geospatial data. A prototype system that integrates commercial ArcGIS system with our query processing backed has been developed to demonstrate the feasibility and identify pitfalls. Experiments show a mixture of successes and failures. The BMMQ-Tree data structure is successful in the sense that it takes advantages of the approximate query nature of visual exploration based applications in both spatial and value dimensions. Our experiments show that BMMQ-Tree based indexing is able to process the WorldClim January Precipitation with nearly 1 billion cells in less than a quarter of a second for a query value range across multiple bins using a 32-bin, 16-level BMMQ-Tree. The resulting numbers of quadrants are in the order of a few thousands to a few hundreds of thousands whose data transport delays between servers and Web browsers range from excellent to acceptable. However, our experiment results also revealed that the ArcGIS Flex API that we used to render the resulting quadrants in Web browsers perform poorly for numbers of quadrants beyond a few thousands.

For the future work, our focus would be improving the visualization rendering speed at the client side. We will explore both options discussed in the text. We also want to integrate FastBit exact query with our prototype so that users can be aware of the quality of approximate query based visual explorations and retrieve exact query results when necessary. Finally, we are interested in profiling users queries and select better quadtree bin boundary values, in addition to providing more choices in automatically generating quadtree bin boundary values. We are expecting to work with environmental scientists more closely on this matter.

## References


1. Li, Y.K., Bretschneider, T.R.: Semantic-sensitive satellite image retrieval. IEEE Transactions on Geoscience and Remote Sensing 45(4), 853–860 (2007)
2. USGS: Modis product table, `https://lpdaac.usgs.gov/lpdaac/products/modis_products_table`
3. WRF: Weather research and forecast, `http://www.wrf-model.org`
4. UCAR Unidata: Unidata integrated data viewer (idv), `http://www.unidata.ucar.edu/software/idv/`
5. NASA: Worldwind, `http://worldwind.arc.nasa.gov/java/`
6. Kothuri, R.K.V., Ravada, S., Abugov, D.: Quadtree and r-tree indexes in oracle spatial: a comparison using gis data. In: SIGMOD 2002, pp. 546–557 (2002)
7. Fang, Y., Friedman, M., Nair, G., Rys, M., Schmid, A.E.: Spatial indexing in microsoft sql server 2008. In: SIGMOD 2008, pp. 1207–1216 (2008)
8. Oracle: Georaster, `http://download.oracle.com/docs/html/B10827-01/geor-intro.htm`
9. ESRI: Arcgis server, `http://www.esri.com/software/arcgis/arcgisserver`
10. MapServer: Mapserver open source mapping, `http://mapserver.org/`
11. TileCache: Tilecache - web map tile caching, `http://tilecache.org/`

12. Wu, K., Koegler, W., Chen, J., Shoshani, A.: Using bitmap index for interactive exploration of large datasets. In: SSDBM 2003, pp. 65–74 (2003)
13. Stockinger, K., Shalf, J., Wu, K., Bethel, E.W.: Query-driven visualization of large data sets. In: IEEE Visualization, p. 22 (2005)
14. Glatter, M., Mollenhour, C., Huang, J., Gao, J.Z.: Scalable data servers for large multivariate volume visualization. IEEE TVCG 12(5), 1291–1298 (2006)
15. Kendall, W., Glatter, M., Huang, J., Peterka, T., Latham, R., Ross, R.: Terascale data organization for discovering multivariate climatic trends. In: Bergel, A., Fabry, J. (eds.) SC 2009. LNCS, vol. 5634, pp. 1–12. Springer, Heidelberg (2009)
16. Fuchs, R., Hauser, H.: Visualization of multi-variate scientific data. Computer Graphics Forum 28(6), 1670–1690 (2009)
17. Lawrence Berkeley National Laboratory: Fastbit, `https://sdm.lbl.gov/fastbit/`
18. Sinha, R.R., Winslett, M., Wu, K.: Finding regions of interest in large scientific datasets. In: SSDBM 2009, pp. 130–147 (2009)
19. Maceachren, A.M., Wachowicz, M., Edsall, R., Haug, D., Masters, R.: Constructing knowledge from multivariate spatiotemporal data: integrating geographical visualization with knowledge discovery in database methods. International Journal of Geographical Information Science 13(4), 311–334 (1999)
20. Andrienko, N., Andrienko, G., Gatalsky, P.: Exploratory spatio-temporal visualization: an analytical review. Journal of Visual Languages and Computing 14(6), 503–541 (2003)
21. Guo, D.S., Chen, J., MacEachren, A.M., Liao, K.: A visualization system for space-time and multivariate patterns (vis-stamp). IEEE TVCG 12(6), 1461–1474 (2006)
22. Anselin, L., Syabri, I., Kho, Y.: Geoda: An introduction to spatial data analysis. Geographical Analysis 38(1), 5–22 (2006)
23. Gahegan, M., Takatsuka, M., Wheeler, M., Hardisty, F.: Introducing geovista studio: an integrated suite of visualization and computational methods for exploration and knowledge construction in geography. Computers, Environment and Urban Systems 26(4), 267–292 (2002)
24. Rushing, J., Ramachandran, R., Nair, U., Graves, S., Welch, R., Lin, H.: Adam: a data mining toolkit for scientists and engineers. Computers & Geosciences 31(5), 607–618 (2005)
25. Zhang, J.T., Gruenwald, L., Gertz, M.: Vdm-rs: A visual data mining system for exploring and classifying remotely sensed images. Computers & Geosciences 35(9), 1827–1836 (2009)
26. Benz, U.C., Hofmann, P., Willhauck, G., Lingenfelder, I., Heynen, M.: Multi-resolution, object-oriented fuzzy analysis of remote sensing data for gis-ready information. ISPRS Journal of Photogrammetry and Remote Sensing 58(3-4), 239–258 (2004)
27. Liu, Y., Guo, Q.H., Kelly, M.: A framework of region-based spatial relations for non-overlapping features and its application in object based image analysis. ISPRS Journal of Photogrammetry and Remote Sensing 63(4), 461–475 (2008)
28. Goodchild, M.F., Yuan, M., Cova, T.J.: Towards a general theory of geographic representation in gis. Int. J. of Geographical Information Science 21(3), 239–260 (2007)
29. Cohen, S., Hurley, P., Schulz, K.W., Barth, W.L., Benton, B.: Scientific formats for object-relational database systems: a study of suitability and performance. SIGMOD Rec. 35(2), 10–15 (2006)
30. Stancu-Mara, S., Baumann, P.: A comparative benchmark of large objects in relational databases. In: IDEAS 2008, pp. 277–284 (2008)
31. Abadi, D.J., Madden, S.R., Hachem, N.: Column-stores vs. row-stores: how different are they really? In: SIGMOD 2008 (2008)
32. Pavlo, A., Paulson, E., Rasin, A., Abadi, D.J., DeWitt, D.J., Madden, S., Stonebraker, M.: A comparison of approaches to large-scale data analysis. In: SIGMOD 2009, pp. 165–178 (2009)
33. UCAR Unidata: Netcdf, `http://www.unidata.ucar.edu/software/netcdf/`

34. The HDF Group: Hdf5, http://www.hdfgroup.org/HDF5/
35. Baumann, P., Furtado, P., Ritsch, R., Widmann, N.: The rasdaman approach to multidimensional database management. In: SAC 1997, pp. 166–173 (1997)
36. Marathe, A.P., Salem, K.: Query processing techniques for arrays. The VLDB Journal 11(1), 68–91 (2002)
37. Baumann, P.: Designing a geo-scientific request language - a database approach. In: SSDBM 2009 (2009)
38. Sarawagi, S., Stonebraker, M.: Efficient organization of large multidimensional arrays. In: ICDE 1994, pp. 328–336 (1994)
39. Otoo, E.J., Rotem, D.: Efficient storage allocation of large-scale extendible multidimensional scientific datasets. In: SSDBM 2006, pp. 179–183 (2006)
40. Kim, J., JaJa, J.: Component-based data layout for efficient slicing of very large multidimensional volumetric data. In: SSDBM 2007, p. 8 (2007)
41. Gaede, V., Gunther, O.: Multidimensional access methods. ACM Computing Surveys 30(2), 170–231 (1998)
42. Samet, H.: Foundations of Multidimensional and Metric Data Structures. Morgan Kaufmann Publishers Inc., San Francisco (2005)
43. Cignoni, P., Marino, P., Montani, C., Puppo, E., Scopigno, R.: Speeding up isosurface extraction using interval trees. IEEE TVCG 3(2), 158–170 (1997)
44. Wilhelms, J., Vangelder, A.: Octrees for faster isosurface generation. ACM Transactions on Graphics 11(3), 201–227 (1992)
45. Wang, C., Chiang, Y.J.: Isosurface extraction and view-dependent filtering from time-varying fields using persistent time-octree (ptot). IEEE TVCG 15(6), 1367–1374 (2009)
46. Gress, A., Klein, R.: Efficient representation and extraction of 2-manifold isosurfaces using kd-trees. Graphical Models 66(6), 370–397 (2004)
47. Hughes, D.M., Lim, I.S.: Kd-jump: a path-preserving stackless traversal for faster isosurface raytracing on gpus. IEEE TVCG 15(6), 1555–1562 (2009)
48. Lin, T.W.: Compressed quadtree representations for storing similar images. Image and Vision Computing 15(11), 833–843 (1997)
49. Chan, Y.K., Chang, C.C.: Block image retrieval based on a compressed linear quadtree. Image and Vision Computing 22(5), 391–397 (2004)
50. Chung, K.L., Liu, Y.W., Yan, W.M.: A hybrid gray image representation using spatial- and dct-based approach with application to moment computation. Journal of Visual Communication and Image Representation 17(6), 1209–1226 (2006)
51. Vassilakopoulos, M., Manolopoulos, Y., Economou, K.: Overlapping quadtrees for the representation of similar images. Image and Vision Computing 11(5), 257–262 (1993)
52. Manolopoulos, Y., Nardelli, E., Papadopoulos, A., Proietti, G.: Mof-tree: a spatial access method to manipulate multiple overlapping features. Inf. Syst. 22(9), 465–481 (1997)
53. Nardelli, E., Proietti, G.: An efficient spatial access method for spatial images containing multiple non-overlapping features. Information Systems 25(8), 553–568 (2000)
54. Tzouramanis, T., Vassilakopoulos, M., Manolopoulos, Y.: On the generation of time-evolving regional data. Geoinformatica 6(3), 207–231 (2002)
55. Manolopoulos, Y., Nardelli, E., Proietti, G., Tousidou, E.: A generalized comparison of linear representations of thematic layers. Data & Knowledge Engineering 37(1), 1–23 (2001)
56. Manouvrier, M., Rukoz, M., Jomier, G.: Quadtree representations for storage and manipulation of clusters of images. Image and Vision Computing 20(7), 513–527 (2002)
57. Wu, K., Stockinger, K., Shoshani, A.: Breaking the curse of cardinality on bitmap indexes. In: Ludäscher, B., Mamoulis, N. (eds.) SSDBM 2008. LNCS, vol. 5069, pp. 348–365. Springer, Heidelberg (2008)
58. Sinha, R.R., Winslett, M.: Multi-resolution bitmap indexes for scientific data. ACM Trans. Database Syst. 32(3), 16 (2007)

59. Rubel, O., Wu, K., et al.: High performance multivariate visual data exploration for extremely large data. In: Pautasso, C., Tanter, É. (eds.) SC 2008. LNCS, vol. 4954, pp. 1–12. Springer, Heidelberg (2008)
60. Gosink, L.J., Anderson, J.C., Bethel, E.W., Joy, K.I.: Query-driven visualization of time-varying adaptive mesh refinement data. IEEE TVCG 14(6), 1715–1722 (2008)
61. Wood, J., Dykes, J., Slingsby, A., Clarke, K.: Interactive visual exploration of a large spatio-temporal dataset: Reflections on a geovisualization mashup. IEEE TVCG 13(6), 1176–1183 (2007)
62. Dork, M., Carpendale, S., Collins, C., Williamson, C.: Visgets: Coordinated visualizations for web-based information exploration and discovery. IEEE TVCG 14(6), 1205–1212 (2008)
63. Tobler, W.: A computer model simulating urban growth in the detroit region. Economic Geography 46(2), 234–240 (1970)
64. GDAL: Geospatial data abstraction library, `http://www.gdal.org/`
65. Adobe: Adobe flex api, `http://www.adobe.com/products/flex/`
66. ESRI: Arcgis flex api, `http://www.adobe.com/products/flex/`
67. University of Maryland: Global land cover facility (glcf), `ftp://ftp.glcf.umiacs.umd.edu/modis/500m/`
68. Hijmans, R.J., Cameron, S.E., Parra, J.L., Jones, P.G., Jarvis, A.: Very high resolution interpolated climate surfaces for global land areas. International Journal of Climatology 25(15), 1965–1978 (2005)
69. WorldClim: Worldclim current conditions data 1950-2000, `http://www.worldclim.org/current`

# Bridging Workflow and Data Provenance Using Strong Links

David Koop[1], Emanuele Santos[1], Bela Bauer[2], Matthias Troyer[2], Juliana Freire[1], and Cláudio T. Silva[1]

[1] SCI Institute, University of Utah, USA
[2] Theoretische Physik, ETH Zurich, Switzerland

**Abstract.** As scientists continue to migrate their work to computational methods, it is important to track not only the steps involved in the computation but also the data consumed and produced. While this provenance information can be captured, in existing approaches, it often contains only weak references between data and provenance. When data files or provenance are moved or modified, it can be difficult to find the data associated with the provenance or to find the provenance associated with the data. We propose a persistent storage mechanism that manages input, intermediate, and output data files, strengthening the links between provenance and data. This mechanism provides better support for reproducibility because it ensures the data referenced in provenance information can be readily located. Another important benefit of such management is that it allows caching of intermediate data which can then be shared with other users. We present an implemented infrastructure for managing data in a provenance-aware manner and demonstrate its application in scientific projects.

## 1 Introduction

As the volume of data generated by scientific experiments and analyses grows, it has become increasingly important to capture the connection between the derived data and the processes as well as parameters used to derive the data. Not surprisingly, the ability to capture the provenance of data products has been a major drive for a wide adoption of scientific workflow systems [1,2,3]. By tracking workflow execution, it is possible to determine how an output is derived, be it a data file, an image, or an interactive visualization.

However, the common practice of connecting workflows and data products through file names has important limitations. Consider, for example, a workflow that runs a simulation and outputs a file with a visualization of the simulation results. If the workflow outputs an image file to the filesystem, any future run will overwrite that image file. If different parameters are used, or the simulation code is improved and the updated workflow is run, the original image is lost. If that image file were managed with a version control system, the user could retrieve the old version from the repository. However, if the user reverts the output image to the original version, how does she know how it was created?

M. Gertz and B. Ludäscher (Eds.): SSDBM 2010, LNCS 6187, pp. 397–415, 2010.

Since there is no explicit link between the workflow instance (i.e., the workflow specification, parameters and input files) and the different versions of its output, determining their provenance is challenging. If we examine the provenance logs for the workflow runs, we will see that there are two runs that create the specified image file, one with the older simulation routine and the second with the newer one. We may be able to check timestamps in order to guess, but this is far from ideal. This problem is compounded when computations take place in multiple systems, and recording the complete provenance requires tying together multiple workflows through their outputs and inputs. As files are overwritten, renamed, or moved, provenance information may be lost or become invalid. As a result, maintaining an accurate provenance graph which ties processes and the data they manipulate requires a time-consuming and error-prone process.

While version control systems effectively track changes to files, such systems can only determine that changes have occurred, not how they came about. Provenance-enabled workflow systems, on the other hand, are able to capture how changes came about but do not provide a systematic mechanism for maintaining data provenance in a persistent fashion, i.e., given a file it may not be possible to determine which workflow instance generated it. We posit that a *tighter integration between scientific workflows and file management is necessary to enable the systematic maintenance of data provenance.*

**Contributions.** In this paper, we propose a new framework which, by coupling workflow provenance with the versioning of data produced and consumed by workflows, captures the actual changes to data as well as detailed information about how those changes came about. A persistent store for the data ensures that old inputs and results can be retrieved, and we can tie each version of a result to the provenance that details how the result was generated. We introduce the notion of a *strong link* which reliably captures the connection between a workflow instance and data it derives, and describe an algorithm for generating these links. Instead of relying on the user or ad-hoc approaches to automatically derive file names, strong links are identifiers derived from the file content, the workflow specification, and any parameters. As a result, they accurately and reliably tie a given workflow instance and its input and derived data.

Besides simplifying the process of maintaining data provenance, this approach has several benefits. By automatically capturing versions of data, it seamlessly supports exploratory tasks without requiring users to curate the data (e.g., managing the file names). It also provides a general mechanism for the persistent caching of both intermediate and final results—this is in contrast to previous approaches which supported only in-memory caching [4,5]. The caching mechanism can be used not only to speed up workflow execution, but also to support check-pointing for long-running computations. In addition, the use of a managed data repository allows the creation of workflows that are location agnostic: unlike workflows that point to files in the filesystem, workflows can be shared and run in multiple environments unchanged. Last but not least, our approach is general and can be combined with existing workflow systems. We describe our implementation in the VisTrails system and present a case-study, where the

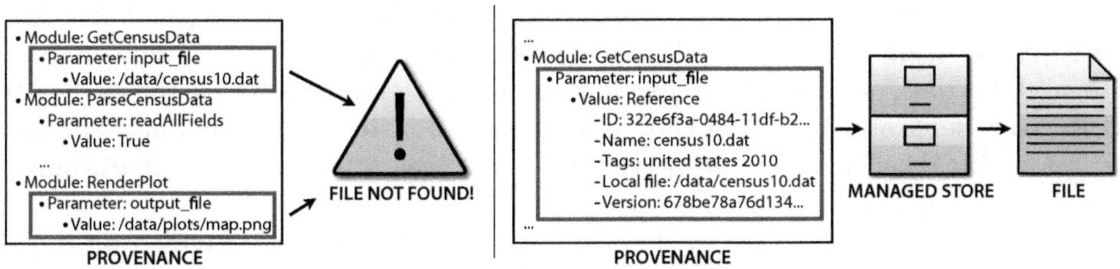


**Fig. 1.** When provenance information references file-system paths, there is no guarantee those files will not be moved or modified. We propose references that are linked to a persistent repository which maintains that data and with hashing and versioning allows for querying, reuse, and data lineage.

persistent data provenance infrastructure was deployed in a real application: managing data products in the context of the ALPS project [6].[1]

**Outline.** We begin by introducing our persistence scheme in Section 2, and then show how it can be applied to support data provenance in Section 3. In Section 4 we describe how our approach can be used to extend workflow caching strategies and for publishing scientific results. In Section 5, we describe how managed repositories can be shared among multiple users for both data access and caching. We describe an implementation of our scheme in Section 6, and describe its use in the ALPS project in Section 7. We highlight related work in Section 8 before concluding with future directions in Section 9.

## 2 Persisting Data Provenance Links

By integrating file management and version control with workflows, we aim to maintain stronger provenance by referencing data in a versioned, managed repository instead of via file paths (see Figure 1). This repository stores input, output, and intermediate data products, and can be used to facilitate caching and data sharing.[2] Similar to version control systems, this repository stores multiple versions of files, but to connect to workflow provenance information, it also contains metadata that represents identity and annotations.

Our approach to this problem is user-driven. As a user designs a workflow, she can specify which results (or input data) should be persisted in the repository. As we describe in Section 6, a possible implementation is to provide special workflow modules that can be connected to the output ports of modules whose results should be persisted (see the `ManagedIntermediateDir` module in Figure 6). When users run workflows using data from the repository, we can ensure that future provenance queries can not only identify the data involved in the computations but also retrieve the actual data. In addition, given provenance of

[1] `http://alps.comp-phys.org`

[2] In the remainder of the text, we use the terms "repository" and "managed store" interchangeably.

a workflow execution, we can reproduce it using the exact versions of the data used in the original execution. In these provenance applications, there is no need to archive data according to specific path-name conventions or remember to keep each separate version of the input data. Also, the automatic and transparent identification and versioning require little user involvement in maintaining these stronger links.

In what follows, we start by describing a scheme to derive reliable and representative ids for linking data products and their provenance. We also present the file-management infrastructure and the attributes we maintain in the managed repository, the differences in our storage depending on the role of the data, and how data should be updated and stored. Note that while we discuss *file* management, the techniques described can be easily extended to directories as well.

### 2.1 Deriving Strong Links

Our approach to deriving strong links was inspired by the in-memory caching mechanism proposed by Bavoil at al. [4] and the content hashing used in version control systems including `git` [7]. We use the signatures of workflows to identify intermediate and output data derived by the workflows, and content hashing to identify input data.

The central idea of caching in workflow systems is that any self-contained piece of a computation can be reused if the computation is deterministic and its structure, input data, and parameters do not change. For dataflows, we can formalize this concept by defining the *upstream subworkflow* of a module $m$ in a workflow $W$ as the subgraph induced by all modules $u \in W$ for which there exists a path from $u$ to $m$ in $W$ (including $m$ itself). Note that the existence of such a path implies that the results of $u$ may have an effect on the computation of $m$. Then, if any module or connection in the upstream workflow of $m$ changes, we must recompute $m$. Conversely, if the upstream workflow does not change, we need not recompute $m$, and can reuse results from a previous execution. Thus, for any other workflow $W'$ that contains an upstream subworkflow $U$ that also exists in $W$, we can reuse the intermediate results of $U$ from $W$ in $W'$.

Caching thus requires the identification of equivalent subworkflows. This would be expensive if we needed to perform graph matching, but we instead use a recursive serialization of the upstream workflow that allows us to quickly check the cache. We define the default *label* of a module $m$, $\ell(m)$, as the serialization of its type and parameter values ordered by parameter name. Note that individual module types can override this default label to better capture module state; for example, a module linked to a specific file would define its label based on the contents of the file—if that file changes, the label changes. Similarly, the *label* of a connection $c$, $\ell(c)$, is the serialization of the types of the ports it connects. Then, a canonical serialization of the upstream subworkflow of a module $m$ is defined recursively as

$$S(m) = \ell(m) + \bigplus_{c \,\in\, \mathrm{UC}(m)} S(source(c)) + \ell(c)$$

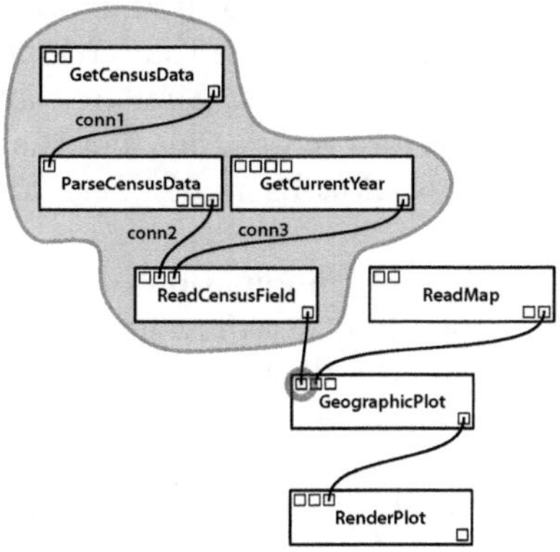


| Module | Serialization |
|---|---|
| S(GetCensusData) | ℓ(GetCensusData) |
| S(GetCurrentYear) | ℓ(GetCurrentYear) |
| S(ParseCensusData) | ℓ(ParseCensusData) + S(GetCensusData) + ℓ(conn1) |
| S(ReadCensusField) | ℓ(ReadCensusField) + S(ParseCensusData) + ℓ(conn2) + S(GetCurrentYear) + ℓ(conn3) |

**Fig. 2.** The *upstream signature* S(M) for a module is calculated recursively as the signature of the module concatenated with the upstream signatures of the upstream subworkflow for each port and the signature of the connection

where UC($m$) is the set of upstream connections into $m$ sorted by $\ell(c)$, *source* returns the source (upstream) module of the given connection, and $+$ is concatenation. The *upstream signature* is the SHA1 hash of this serialization.

Figure 2 shows an example workflow and the serialization of the upstream subworkflow of the `ReadCensusField` module. Note that the upstream subworkflow will not always be a tree, but the recursive serialization always branches like it is. This allows two topologically different upstream subworkflows to have the same signature, but when this happens, the computations must be identical. For example, consider a subworkflow with a single module $m$ that connects upstream to two other modules. Whether those two modules connect upstream to a single module $n$ or to two identical modules that both do the same computation as $n$ will not affect the downstream computation of $m$. In addition, by using memoization, we can keep this computation efficient despite the added branching.

For input files, we define the signature as the hash of its contents. Then, if the file's contents changes, its signature changes even though its path or other identifying information may not. Note that we store the content hash separately as well so a file that is the output of one workflow and the input of another can be identified in both ways. Thus, the signature provides a strong link that contains a precise and accurate representation of the workflow fragment that derived a given result. As we describe in Section 3, we use this signature as the means to link a data product to the computation that derived it.

### 2.2 File Management

We are concerned with three roles for files in workflows: inputs, outputs, and intermediate data. Note that a single file may fill different roles depending on the workflow it is used in; an output from one workflow may be used as the input to another. Thus, the distinction between roles does not affect the use of data in any situation, but rather determines what metadata can be captured, stored, and utilized. An output file can store information about the process that created its contents but an input file selected from the filesystem cannot. Similarly, an intermediate file need not be annotated at all if is used for caching, but files that are to be used again should be named and tagged to allow users to query for them.

Each file in the repository is uniquely identified by a combination of an id and a version string, and annotated with user-defined and workflow-generated information including its signature and content hash. By allowing a collection of files to share the same id, a reference to that id can be configured to always retrieve the latest version. This is helpful to a user who wishes to run a workflow with the latest version of a data set but does not wish to manually configure which is the latest version. On the other hand, reproducing a workflow execution exactly requires a particular version of the data, and thus identifying data by both the id and version guarantees that the exact data will be retrieved.

**Input Files.** An input file must reference an existing file, whether it is already in the managed store or only in the local system. Upon selection, we either use the existing identifier (from the store), or create a new unique identifier for the data. Note that we can detect whether the contents of a file already exists in the repository by computing the hash and checking for that hash in the repository. By default, changing the contents of the file creates a new version while changing the selected file creates a new id and version. Users can configure this behavior if necessary.

**Output Files.** The main difference between output and input files is that input files are not affected by changes in the rest of the workflow. For outputs, any changes to the part of the workflow that is upstream of the output file may affect its contents. In addition, it is less clear when an output is a new entity and when it is a new version of an existing entity. When only parameters change, the output is likely a tweaked version of the original, but when the input files are switched, the output is more likely new. By default, we create new versions for each execution but allow users to change this behavior in order to version the outputs. Like inputs, output files can be both stored in the persistent store for future reference and use and saved to a local file for immediate use or inspection.

**Intermediate Files.** An intermediate file is exactly the same as an output file except that it is not a sink of the workflow; execution continues after the file is serialized and the contents are used in further calculations. Such files can be used as checkpoints for debugging, but they can also be used to cache computational results in order to speed further analyses. Note that an intermediate file need not be manually annotated or named; it is defined by its signature–the serialization of the upstream subworkflow.

**Customization.** It may be necessary for users to configure the behavior of the persistence of files in the store in order to link similar files or maintain separate identities for data products. By selecting an existing reference and linking it to a local file, a user can tie the reference to a new local file. In addition, users can decide whether files are only persisted in the managed store or if they are also saved to local files. If they use a local file, they can configure whether the contents of the file should take precedence or whether a new version should always be obtained from the repository. Similarly, if the local file contents change, a user can choose whether those changes should always be persisted to the managed store.

## 3 Linking Provenance

Below we discuss how we exploit the strong provenance links to answer important queries. We also suggest how stronger links from data to provenance can be accomplished. With the advent of extensible file formats (e.g., HDF5[3]), it is possible to include direct links to provenance or even the provenance itself with the data. Finally, we present an application of the improved results from provenance queries in publishing scientific results.

### 3.1 Algorithms for Querying Linked Provenance

Perhaps the most basic provenance query is one that retrieves the lineage of a data product, specifically what input data and computations contributed to the result [8]. With only the provenance of the execution, a user may find the path to an input but even if a file still exists at that location, there is no guarantee it has not been modified. To protect against such problems, users store the exact data used with the provenance, manually archive all of the data, or add archival as part of the workflow process [9]. With our file management scheme, we can store the id, version, and content hash of any input as part of the provenance. Then, for lineage queries, we can return references that can be accessed from the provenance store using the id and version and verified using the content hash. Most workflow systems that support provenance capture also provide support for determining lineage queries [8].

Note that the content hash also gives us a way to locate the provenance of files that are un-managed and may have been moved to a different location or had their names changed. We begin by hashing the contents of the file, then query the managed store for this content hash. The resulting entries have ids and versions for which we can then search our provenance for. Because the provenance contains these stronger references, we can also identify and return the input data via the managed store. An outline of this algorithm is shown in Figure 3.

Because we abstract workflows from a specific filesystem, the provenance of the workflow executions can be tied directly to the exact inputs and outputs. This ensures better reproducibility because the exact content can be retrieved; with links to the file names, we have no guarantee that the files at those locations were unchanged. To reproduce a workflow execution, we retrieve the workflow

[3] `http://www.hdfgroup.org/HDF5`

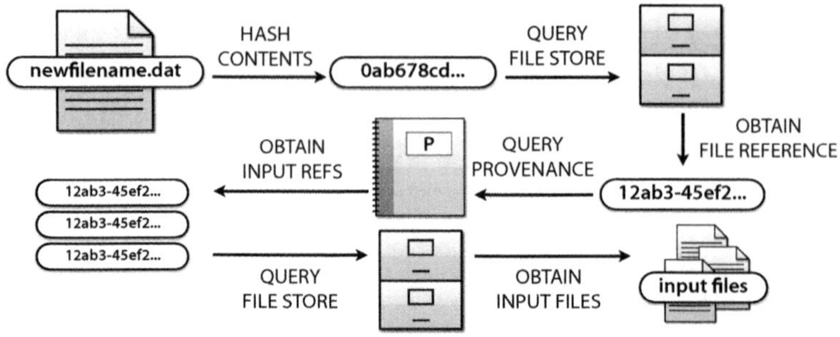


**Fig. 3.** Given a file which has been moved and renamed, we can use the managed file store and provenance to first locate the managed copy, and we can locate the original input files as well

specification and execute it using the data pointed to by the managed file references. Recall, however, that some workflow specifications may include only data identifiers and not the versions of the data used. This allows a user to re-run a workflow with the latest data which is not what we desire for reproduction. Thus, we need to examine the provenance for the execution, retrieve the exact version specified by the provenance and modify the specification.

Another provenance query that our strong links solves is the lineage of data when the input of one workflow is the output of another. In the Second Provenance Challenge [10], teams were asked to answer provenance queries from outputs that were the result of running data through three consecutive workflows. One issue was the identification of data as it was transferred from the output of one workflow to the input of another. With the managed store, we allow users to designate inputs as the output of another workflow by assigning them the same id. Thus, when the first workflow changes, the second workflow will incorporate the changed results. Even if users do not use the same identifiers, we can perform provenance queries using the content hashes to link data across different workflows.

### 3.2 Embedding Provenance with Data

We have demonstrated methods to find the provenance of data by searching a provenance store for the hash of a given file. However, such methods depend on access to the provenance store. An alternative approach is to embed provenance with the data itself. With many file formats including HDF5 supporting annotations, it is possible to embed provenance information or links to provenance with the data. In directories of data, we can add an additional file that contains the same information. Then, verifying data or regenerating a data product can be accomplished by examining the provenance stored with the data.

We have developed a schema that allows a user to either link to or directly encode provenance information in a file. Information represented in this schema can be serialized to XML and embedded in an existing file or saved to a

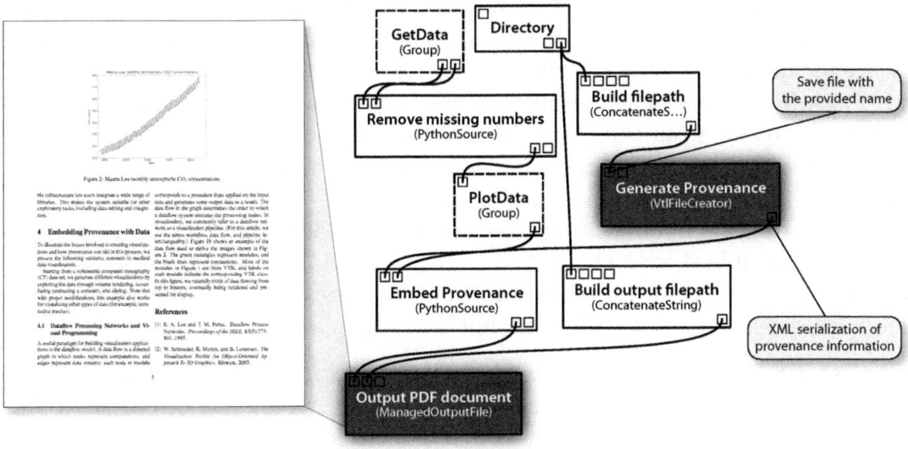


**Fig. 4.** Embedding provenance with data: provenance can be either saved to a separate file or serialized to XML and embedded in an existing file

separate file. Figure 4 shows an example of a workflow using this schema. While a provenance link can refer to a local file, we provide support for accessing a central repository of provenance information. With a central repository, if the file is transferred to a different user or machine, the link remains valid. With a local reference, it will be more difficult to link back to provenance information.

# 4 Using Strong Links

## 4.1 Caching

Caching the intermediate results of workflow computations is useful to avoid redundant computations. If a user executes a workflow, we can reuse any intermediate results from that first execution in future executions [4]. Using our file management for intermediate files, we are able to add support for caching *files* to existing in-memory caching which means that cached data can be persisted across sessions. With this extension, we can also consider how to share cached data between different users as well. We begin by reviewing the in-memory workflow caching algorithm and then introduce an extension for caching across sessions using the managed file store.

**In-memory Caching.** Using the upstream signatures, we build a cache by labeling each intermediate result with its upstream signature. Dataflow computation proceeds in a bottom-up fashion; a sink (a module with no outgoing connections) requests data from all of its inputs which may in turn request data from their inputs and so on. Our caching algorithm works by hijacking this request for data and checking if the upstream subworkflow has already been calculated, returning the result from the cache when it exists instead of doing the computations.

Before executing any workflow, we compute the upstream signatures for each module in the workflow. Note that the recursive computation of all signatures is easily memoized. During workflow execution, before a module is set to execute, we check if that module's upstream signature exists in the cache. If it does, we return the result from the cache. If not, we proceed with the computation, and after the module finishes executing, we store the results of the computation in the cache labeled by the upstream signature.

There are some modules that may not perform deterministic calculations. We allow the module developer to designate such modules as non-cacheable. After a workflow with one or more such modules executes, we immediately remove all modules downstream of such a module from the cache.

**Persistent Caching.** We can extend the in-memory caching techniques to persist results to disk, allowing users to cache results across sessions or share intermediate results. Note that we need a serialization of the results of any module type in order to mirror the entire in-memory cache. In addition, saving every intermediate result to disk can needlessly slow down computation. For these reasons, we have developed persistent caching as a user-driven technique for intermediate files. We allow the user to connect a new module to the workflow that designates that the upstream subworkflow of the module should be cached. For non-cached computation, this module receives a file and passes it downstream. However, when the module finds that the signature associated with needed file exists in the cache, it retrieves the linked file without doing the upstream calculations.

This allows any module with serializable results to be persisted in a disk-based cache, but we can improve this process using the file management scheme described in Section 2.2. Using this scheme, additions to the cache are managed as intermediate files and cache lookup is a simple query to the store. In addition, users need not identify or in any way configure the intermediate files using for caching; the store assigns identity and stores signature information automatically. When the upstream workflow of the caching module changes, the cache lookup fails, and the store adds a new version of the intermediate file. Thus, a user does not lose any intermediate results when exploring different workflow configurations.

### 4.2 Publishing

When publishing scientific results, it is important to describe the lineage of a result. Providing data sets and computer code allows scientists to verify and reproduce published results and to conduct alternate analyses. In the past years, interest in this subject has increased in different communities which led to different approaches for publishing scientific results (see [11] for an overview). Our schema for embedding provenance with data can be combined with these approaches. In particular, it simplifies the process of packaging workflows and results for publication. In addition, we have also implemented a solution that allows users to create documents whose digital artifacts (e.g., figures) include a deep caption: detailed provenance information which contains the specification of the computational process (or workflow) and associated parameters used to produce the artifact [12].

## 5 Sharing Data

We have shown that maintaining workflow data in a managed store allows us to quickly locate existing data, store accurate provenance, and cache intermediate results across sessions. Additional benefits can be gained from having multiple users share the repository. For example, if one user has run a time-intensive step of a calculation, making that result available to other users allows them to proceed with later steps without each re-computing the same result. Similarly, if one user has already added a specific file to the store, other users with access to that store can access the data without locating and copying the same data. Below, we describe both centralized and decentralized approaches for sharing managed data across systems, and note that the advantages and disadvantages mirror those encountered with version control systems.

**Centralized Storage.** With a central store, users may either read and write directly to a common repository or transfer data between a local repository and a central repository. If users have access to a common disk, it may be possible to simply store all managed files and metadata in a single store on that disk. Then, all users will access the same repository and automatically have access to each other's input, output, and intermediate files. However, this solution may become impractical for large numbers of users. A second problem is that whenever users do not have access to that disk, they are unable to access their managed data.

When a central store is added to individual local repositories, a user will always have access to the local repository but can also retrieve from and add to a central repository. This allows a set of geographically distant users to share common data. In addition, it allows users to maintain and access local data even when disconnected from the central store. However, we maintain an extra copy of the data in this case, and there may be overhead in transferring files, especially if the distance from the central store is far. In addition, it requires building and maintaining infrastructure.

**Decentralized Storage.** In a decentralized approach, users would advertise their data and allow other users to transfer data directly from their repository. A search for a particular piece of data by, for example, name or signature, would query individual systems instead of one store. If the desired file is found, it is transferred directly from the source location to the requesting user. Thus, unlike with the central store, data is only transferred when it is needed. Combined with P2P approaches, the transfer may be distributed over several machines. However, if a particular machine is offline, the data generated on that machine may not be available.

A hybrid approach that supports a central table of files but decentralized storage would allow users to locate files even if they were not currently accessible. Users would not push data to or pull files from the repository but rather register the available files as they are added and whenever that data is requested, directly transfer it to the requesting machine.

## 6 Implementation

We added file management to the VisTrails system [13] by introducing a new package that included module types for input, output, and intermediate files and directories. The package also includes code to set up the managed store as well as navigate and update it through configuration dialogs. Our goal was to add this support in a way that changes little in workflow structure while providing ways for users to directly locate and identify data during workflow construction. Thus, users that normally only configure the path of an input file can do exactly the same for a managed input file module. In addition, adding an output file has fewer requirements; a user only needs to connect the data to be persisted to a managed output file module. The system generates unique ids and signatures automatically. At the same time, we provide methods for annotating data and configuring its storage and use.

The interface of our prototype implementation is shown in Figure 5. We define three new module types for files: `ManagedInputFile`, `ManagedOutputFile`, and `ManagedIntermediateFile` and their equivalents for directories. As described in Section 2.2, all share a common set of attributes and options. The key difference between inputs and outputs (or intermediates) is that outputs have a

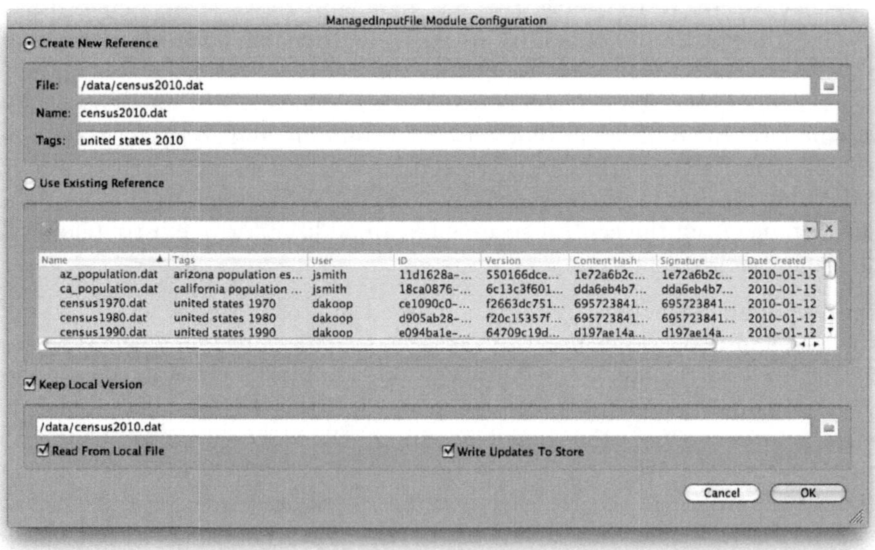


**Fig. 5.** The ManagedInputFile configuration allows the user to choose to create a new reference from a file on his local filesystem or use an existing reference from the managed store

workflow-dependent signature. Thus, an input file needs to be manually identified by the user while an output file can be totally identified by its upstream signature.

A user can select a file by either referencing an existing identifier or by creating a new reference. When referencing a file that already exists in the managed store, the user can search the repository for metadata including name, tags, user id, date added, or a specific id or version. When creating a new reference, the user may provide a name and tagging information, and for input files, the local file that contains the data.

By default, an identifier for an input file changes when a new local path is selected but does not change if the contents of the file changes. In the second case, we maintain versions of the data, but update the "current version" whenever the contents changes. Thus, any user that wishes to use this data in another workflow will always get the latest data by referencing that identifier. Note that users may choose to link data to an existing reference even if that reference was initially linked to different data.

**Storing Data.** We use the `git` version control system [7] to manage files because it stores content independent of filesystem structure, and an `SQLite` database[4] to store its metadata. Thus, when the managed store is initialized for the first time, we create a `git` repository along with a database to store file information. While a reference is created and annotated during workflow design, the data is not persisted until execution. Upon execution, we save the file in the repository with its id (a UUID) as its name. We use `git` to add and commit the version of the file, and retrieve the content hash (`git` uses SHA1) and the version id (a SHA1 hash of the commit). Then, we update the database with the id, version, content hash, signature (if applicable), name, tags, user, and modification date.

**Finding Data.** In order to locate existing data, we provide methods to match content hashes and signatures as well as query the store for specific metadata like name or tag information. When a user selects a file, we can check the repository to see if that content has already been added by querying the database for the selected file's hash. If it does exist, we can prompt the user to reuse the existing reference. Additionally, when we execute a workflow, we can check to see if an intermediate file's signature matches one that already exists; if so, we can reuse that file instead of computing the upstream workflow. Finally, the configuration for managed file selection includes a free-text query field for the managed file database. A user can query for a specific name or tag to locate matching files that can be used as references. This is accomplished by querying the `SQLite` database and retrieving the matching id and, optionally, version.

## 7 ALPS Case Study

We have used the file management solution implementation for VisTrails with the ALPS project[5] (Algorithms and Libraries for Physics Simulations) [6]. ALPS

[4] `http://www.sqlite.org`

[5] `http://alps.comp-phys.org/`

is an open source software package that makes modern, high-performance algorithms for the simulation of quantum systems available to experimental and theoretical condensed-matter physicists. Typically, a simulation with ALPS consists of three steps:

- Preparing the input files describing the model to be simulated.
- Simulating the model using one of the ALPS programs. Such a simulation can take between minutes on a laptop for very small test cases and weeks on large compute clusters or supercomputers for demanding applications.
- Collaboratively evaluating the "raw" simulation output by exploring & analyzing the data, comparing it to experimental data, and creating figures.

In one specific use case, we have simulated a quantum Heisenberg spin ladder, a model for quasi-one-dimensional copper oxide materials where magnetic excitations are suppressed at low temperature by an energy gap $\Delta$ [14]. The purpose of the simulation is to determine this gap $\Delta$ by calculating the magnetic susceptibility $\chi$ as a function of the temperature $T$ and fitting it to the expression $\chi(T) \sim \frac{1}{\sqrt{T}} \exp^{-\Delta/T}$ [15]. We first use the "looper" program [16] of ALPS to calculate $\chi(T)$ and then use the exploration features of VisTrails to explore the data and find the optimal range $[T_{min}, T_{max}]$ for the non-linear fit. The results of this exploration are shown in Figure 6.

Persistent caching and provenance adds a number of important advantages for the ALPS users:

- Caching persistent files on a shared filesystem means that after one physicist runs the simulation, her colleague can modify the evaluation part of the workflow and explore the data without having to redo the time-intensive simulation.
- Identifying the cached files with the workflow signature avoids potentially critical mistakes of using old simulation results when input parameters to the simulation change. In our experience, simulations have often been recomputed only to ensure that the data has been produced with the latest version of codes and input files.
- Embedding provenance information in the data and figures gives immediate access to the provenance including any aspect of the simulation a physicist might wish to know. Since most projects involve collaborations with other scientists—often at different institutions—facilitating the exchange of data is very valuable. A common source of confusion is incomplete documentation of data sent to collaborators. Embedded provenance information has been invaluable in making remote collaborations more efficient.
- Decoupling the executions of different parts of the workflows using persistent data enables physicists to explore data without the need to always rerun the entire workflow—while still having the workflow provenance accessible when needed.

In Figure 6, we show one ALPS workflow along with plots resulting from an exploration of the fitting range parameter. The modules colored in blue, including the time-consuming simulation module "AppLoop", were not run when this

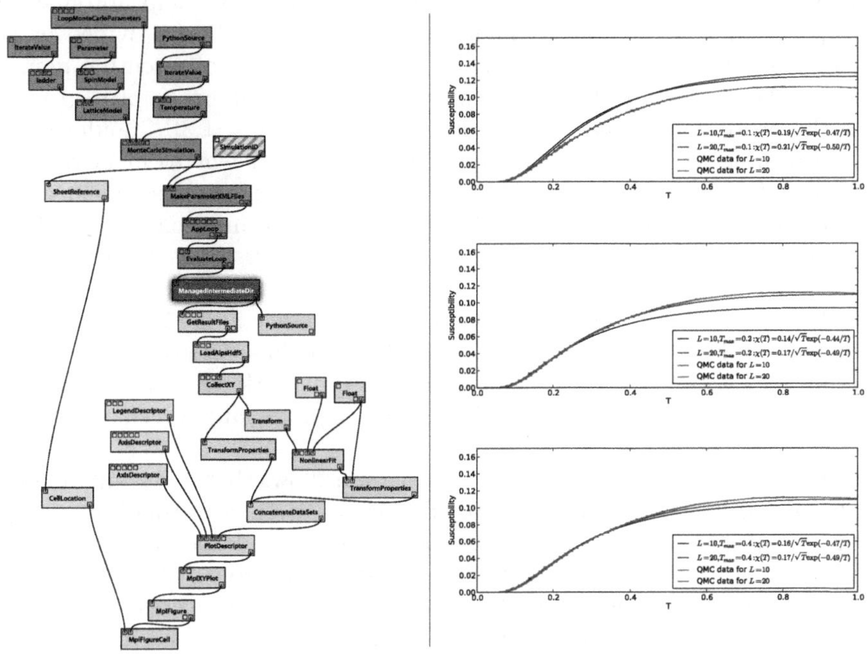


**Fig. 6.** An ALPS workflow colored by execution information and the results of a parameter exploration (i.e., multiple runs of the same workflow with different parameter values) of the fitting range. The colors of the modules indicate their status: blue modules were not executed because the data was found in a persistent directory on disk, yellow modules were cached in memory and green modules were executed.

workflow was executed to create the plots because the output of the simulation had previously been persistently cached. Only the evaluation part of the workflow was re-executed when the fit range $[T_{min}, T_{max}]$ was modified. Note that the `SimulationID` module is striped blue and yellow; this is because it has two outgoing connections, one used in a file stored in the persistent cache and the other as part of a computation using the in-memory cache. Changing its value or structure would thus invalidate both cached results and all others downstream.

## 8 Related Work

Data provenance consists of the trail of processing steps and inputs that led to the creations of a given data object. Tracking changes to files and entire directory structures is well-studied, and version control systems have been developed exactly for this purpose [17,18]. However, such systems can only determine that changes have occurred, not how they came about. More recently, version control systems that focus on tracking content and directory structure separately have been developed (see e.g., [7]). Such systems identify files with hashing, and if duplicate files exist, the content is stored only once in the repository.

A number of workflow systems have been developed to help automate and manage complex calculations. The structure and abstraction provided by such systems have made them appealing to wide assortment of scientific domains. Many of these systems [19,20,13] have included provenance capture to document the process and data used to derive data products [1,3]. Standard provenance captured by these systems, however, is not sufficient to identify exactly which workflow generated a specific file. In fact, in recent exercises to investigate requirements for querying and integrating provenance information, the lack of effective means to identify intermediate and final results of workflows has been identified as an important challenge in provenance management [10,21,22]

Techniques have been developed to track provenance in databases [23]. These track fine-grained provenance, i.e., changes to individual data items. In contrast, our approach is targeted to (whole) files. In future work, we plan to investigate how we can adapt our system to utilize database provenance given encapsulated changes.

There is a significant amount of work with workflows that access and maintain curated data. In these cases, the provided ids or URIs are usually guaranteed to exist, and thus provenance information with them. Plale et al. have examined the issues involved in maintaining and cataloging large meteorological data, and noted the importance of allowing users to search and access this data [24]. Simmhan et al. have proposed data valets as a workflow-based method for facilitating the management of stores on the Cloud [25]. Note that if data for computations comes from or is persisted to a curated source, a separate managed store is not required to ensure access to those files. However, maintaining local copies of these files does allow users to run workflows even when they cannot connect to the store.

For curated scientific data, the identification of that data is important. There are standards for such identification including LSID [26] and DOI [27]. Our primary goal is orthogonal to these: we aim to maintain strong links between data and its provenance. We are not concerned with registering ids for our local persistent stores and use UUIDs to identify data. Identifying data by content hashes is has been accomplished using the MD5 and SHA1 hashes. Hashing has also been used in the context of secure provenance to maintain the confidentiality and integrity of provenance [28]. We use hashing to both identify and search for content as well as compute signatures for upstream subworkflows.

The problem with maintaining the data with workflows has been examined before. Some systems have provided specific modules for file management as part of workflow execution [9]. For example, after generating a data product, the result is not only displayed but also archived in a specific location or disk. This approach works well for static workflows, but for exploratory tasks, archival is not often included. The `cacher` package for R[6] provides a way to export verifiable statistical analysis and data in a tamper-proof scheme that utilizes hashing [29].

While we developed our store to aid users who use local files as data sources, our discussion of sharing the data in these stores overlaps many issues that

---

[6] `http://www.r-project.org`

have been considered. There already exist a number of solutions for managing scientific data on the grid and in cloud environments. GridFTP [30] and storage resource managers [31] have been developed to efficiently access data sets by utilizing networked resources. Such solutions can help provide faster access to data and infrastructure for transferring data across persistent stores.

## 9 Conclusion and Future Work

We have presented file management infrastructure that can be integrated with workflow systems to provide strong links to data in provenance information. In addition, we have discussed how such links can be used to solve provenance queries, facilitate persistent caching, and impact scientific publishing. Finally, we have described our implementation of this system in VisTrails and its use in the ALPS project.

One important aspect that we have not addressed is how the persistent store should be managed. In theory, keeping all of the data manipulated by workflows would ensure full reproducibility, but this is impractical for large amounts of data. In future work, we plan to investigate different strategies for determining when data can be purged from the store; for example, cached data that has not been annotated. While our current implementation supports a rich class of queries over the information in the repository, we would also like to support queries that involve workflow specification and the data involved—for example, finding a workflow with a `ParseCensusData` module that accesses the `census2010.dat` file.

Another area for future study is the automatic identification of intermediate files for caching. While users can identify important way points, it can be tedious to add such modules to a large collection of workflows. By examining the timestamps of module execution in provenance, we may be able to determine which steps are time-intensive and could benefit from caching. Also, the size of the intermediate result may also be important; if a large file is generated by a time-intensive step, but the next step strips unneeded information away, it may be more efficient to store the file after the extra information has been removed.

## References

1. Freire, J., Koop, D., Santos, E., Silva, C.T.: Provenance for computational tasks: A survey. Computing in Science and Engineering 10(13), 11–21 (2008)
2. Davidson, S.B., Freire, J.: Provenance and scientific workflows: challenges and opportunities. In: Proceedings of SIGMOD, pp. 1345–1350 (2008)
3. Davidson, S.B., Boulakia, S.C., Eyal, A., Ludäscher, B., McPhillips, T.M., Bowers, S., Anand, M.K., Freire, J.: Provenance in scientific workflow systems. IEEE Data Eng. Bull. 30(4), 44–50 (2007)
4. Bavoil, L., Callahan, S., Crossno, P., Freire, J., Scheidegger, C., Silva, C., Vo, H.: VisTrails: Enabling interactive multiple-view visualizations. In: Proceedings of IEEE Visualization, pp. 135–142 (2005)

5. Altintas, I., Barney, O., Jaeger-Frank, E.: Provenance collection support in the kepler scientific workflow system. In: Moreau, L., Foster, I. (eds.) IPAW 2006. LNCS, vol. 4145, pp. 118–132. Springer, Heidelberg (2006)
6. Albuquerque, A., Alet, F., Corboz, P., Dayal, P., Feiguin, A., Fuchs, S., Gamper, L., Gull, E., Gürtler, S., Honecker, A., Igarashi, R., Körner, M., Kozhevnikov, M., Läuchli, A., Manmana, S., Matsumoto, M., McCulloch, I., Michel, F., Noack, R., Pawlowski, G., Pollet, L., Pruschke, T., Schollwöck, U., Todo, S., Trebst, S., Troyer, M., Werner, P., Wessel, S.: The alps project release 1.3: open source software for strongly correlated systems. J. Mag. Mag. Mat. 310, 1187 (2007)
7. git, `http://git-scm.com`
8. First provenance challenge (2006), `http://twiki.ipaw.info/bin/view/Challenge/FirstProvenanceChallenge`
9. Mouallem, P., Barreto, R., Klasky, S., Podhorszki, N., Vouk, M.: Tracking files in the kepler provenance framework. In: SSDBM 2009: Proceedings of the 21st International Conference on Scientific and Statistical Database Management, pp. 273–282 (2009)
10. Second provenance challenge (2007), `http://twiki.ipaw.info/bin/view/Challenge/SecondProvenanceChallenge`
11. Fomel, S., Claerbout, J.F.: Guest editors' introduction: Reproducible research. Computing in Science and Engineering 11, 5–7 (2009)
12. Santos, E., Freire, J., Silva, C.: Information Sharing in Science 2.0: Challenges and Opportunities. In: CHI Workshop on The Changing Face of Digital Science: New Practices in Scientific Collaborations (2009)
13. The VisTrails Project, `http://www.vistrails.org`
14. Dagotto, E., Rice, T.M.: Surprises on the Way from One- to Two-Dimensional Quantum Magnets: The Ladder Materials. Science 271(5249), 618–623 (1996)
15. Troyer, M., Tsunetsugu, H., Würtz, D.: Thermodynamics and spin gap of the heisenberg ladder calculated by the look-ahead lanczos algorithm. Phys. Rev. B 50(18), 13515–13527 (1994)
16. Todo, S., Kato, K.: Cluster algorithms for general- $s$ quantum spin systems. Phys. Rev. Lett. 87(4), 047203 (2001)
17. Concurrent Versions System, `http://www.nongnu.org/cvs`
18. Subversion, `http://subversion.tigris.org`
19. The Taverna Project, `http://taverna.sourceforge.net`
20. The Kepler Project, `http://kepler-project.org`
21. Third provenance challenge (2008), `http://twiki.ipaw.info/bin/view/Challenge/ThirdProvenanceChallenge`
22. Moreau, L., Freire, J., Futrelle, J., McGrath, R.E., Myers, J., Paulson, P.: The open provenance model: An overview. In: Freire, J., Koop, D., Moreau, L. (eds.) IPAW 2008. LNCS, vol. 5272, pp. 323–326. Springer, Heidelberg (2008)
23. Cheney, J., Chiticariu, L., Tan, W.C.: Provenance in databases: Why, how, and where. Foundations and Trends in Databases 1(4), 379–474 (2009)
24. Plale, B., Alameda, J., Wilhelmson, B., Gannon, D., Hampton, S., Rossi, A., Droegemeier, K.: Active management of scientific data. IEEE Internet Computing 9(1), 27–34 (2005)
25. Simmhan, Y., Barga, R., van Ingen, C., Lazowska, E., Szalay, A.: Building the trident scientific workflow workbench for data management in the cloud. In: International Conference on Advanced Engineering Computing and Applications in Sciences, pp. 41–50 (2009)

26. Salamone, S.: Lsid: An informatics lifesaver. Bio-ITWorld (2004)
27. Paskin, N.: Digital object identifiers for scientific data. Data Science Journal 4, 12–20 (2005)
28. Hasan, R., Sion, R., Winslett, M.: The case of the fake picasso: preventing history forgery with secure provenance. In: FAST 2009: Proccedings of the 7th conference on File and storage technologies, pp. 1–14 (2009)
29. Peng, R.S., Eckel, S.P.: Distributed reproducible research using cached computations. Computing in Science & Engineering 11, 28–34 (2009)
30. Allcock, W., Bester, J., Bresnahan, J., Chervenak, A., Liming, L., Tuecke, S.: Gridftp: Protocol extensions to ftp for the grid. Global Grid Forum, 3 (2001)
31. Shoshani, A., Sim, A., Gu, J.: Storage resource managers: essential components for the Grid, pp. 321–340. Kluwer Academic Publishers, Dordrecht (2004)

# LIVE: A Lineage-Supported Versioned DBMS

Anish Das Sarma[1], Martin Theobald[2], and Jennifer Widom[3]

[1] Yahoo! Research
[2] Max Planck Institute
[3] Stanford University
{anish,theobald,widom}@cs.stanford.edu

**Abstract.** This paper presents LIVE, a complete DBMS designed for applications with many stored derived relations, and with a need for simple versioning capabilities when base data is modified. Target applications include, for example, scientific data management and data integration. A key feature of LIVE is the use of *lineage* (provenance) to support modifications and versioning in this environment. In our system, lineage significantly facilitates both: (1) efficient propagation of modifications from base to derived data; and (2) efficient execution of a wide class of queries over versioned, derived data. LIVE is fully implemented; detailed experimental results are presented that validate our techniques.

## 1 Introduction

Motivated by scientific data management, data integration, information extraction, and other applications that require storing and processing both base and derived data, we have developed LIVE, a new kind of DBMS. LIVE incorporates a *lightweight versioning capability* and *lineage tracking* in an environment of base and derived relations. There has been considerable past work on data modifications and incremental view maintenance (refer to [15] for a survey) as well as on support for versioning and temporal aspects in databases (refer to [13,20]). LIVE distinguishes itself from this previous work in the following ways:

- Derived data maintenance: Lineage in LIVE generalizes various kinds of information (such as keys [9], pointers [19], and predicate properties [6]) traditionally exploited for incremental view maintenance. LIVE supports the best possible incremental view maintenance algorithms for a wide class of views and modifications.
- Versioning: LIVE provides a lightweight versioning system primarily to support data modifications in our motivating applications. LIVE's versioning system works together with lineage to enable efficient query processing over derived, versioned relations. In the future, LIVE's versioning system together with lineage will also support a seamless combination of propagating and nonpropagating base data modifications; in the nonpropagating case, the lineage of "current" derived data may identify "old" base data. This feature is of particular use in scientific applications.
- Probabilistic data: Some of our motivating applications require managing *probabilistic* (*uncertain*) data. Probabilistic data may arise as a result of imprecise information extraction, for example, or because of uncertain mappings in data integration. LIVE supports probabilistic data without additional mechanisms. Thus, all of the the lineage, versioning, and query processing capabilities of LIVE can be applied to probabilistic as well as conventional data.

M. Gertz and B. Ludäscher (Eds.): SSDBM 2010, LNCS 6187, pp. 416–433, 2010.

LIVE is an offshoot of the *Trio* project at Stanford [23], which is a system for managing data, uncertainty, and lineage. The specific goal of LIVE is to support modifications and versioning in an environment of stored, derived relations. As we shall see, adopting Trio's lineage functionality significantly eases propagating modifications and answering queries in this environment.

We note that *SciDB* [1], a recent proposal outlining the requirements of a general-purpose DBMS for scientific applications, includes derived data, lineage, versioning, and probabilistic data as key features. Similarly, a recent paper [16] laying out challenges in data integration includes derived data, lineage, and probabilities. We believe LIVE's overall combination of capabilities, and how they work together seamlessly and efficiently, is an important step towards supporting these application areas.

In the following, we briefly describe the main contributions made by this paper. Related work is discussed in Section 7, and we conclude in Section 8.

**Unified Data Model (Section 2):** LIVE is based on a unified data model, LDM, which is derived from Trio's ULDB data model [5]. LDM incorporates base and derived relations, probabilistic data, lineage, and versioning. As is typical [8], LDM captures probabilistic data by attaching a *probability* (or *confidence*) in the range [0,1] to each tuple, indicating the likelihood of that tuple being present. As queries are performed, LIVE creates the lineage of derived data items, connecting them to the input data from which they were derived. In the standard versioning fashion, each LDM tuple includes a *start version number* and an *end version number*, between which the tuple is "valid."

**Modifications and Versions (Section 3):** We extend the typical relational modification primitives (insert, delete, and update of tuples) to include modifications of tuple probabilities. We then formalize all of the modifications in the presence of probabilities, based on the accepted *possible-worlds* [3] semantics of probabilistic databases. Finally, we specify how the primitive modification operations create versioned relations. Again, our goal is to incorporate lightweight versioning capabilities whose main function is to support meaningful data modifications in an environment of base and derived relations. We do not support historical modifications, for example; modifications are always applied to the "current version" of the database.

**Query Processing (Section 4):** Also in the interest of supporting only a lightweight versioning capability, we do not support rich constructs for referencing versions or histories. Queries over an LDM database are expressed as regular queries, and they produce a *versioned answer*: the result is an LDM relation representing the query result across all versions. Queries can include a special clause that restricts the result to data valid in the current version—often more useful than the full versioned result, and more efficient to compute. Furthermore, a user can view the *snapshot* of any relation (base or derived) as of any version.

We specify the semantics of query answering in LDM and present detailed algorithms. We will see that the LDM model introduces some subtleties with respect to defining lineage and probabilities on query results, especially in the presence of negation. Determining start and end versions on query results adds little overhead: LIVE's lineage feature enables a clean algorithm to compute versions on result tuples efficiently. In the special case of negation, for which we prove intractability of computing exact version-intervals, lineage enables an efficient approximation.

**Propagating Modifications (Section 5):** Next we address the problem of modifying derived relations automatically when there are modifications to the relations from which they were derived, analogous to the well-known *materialized view maintenance* problem. Lineage provides us with critical information enabling efficient incremental view maintenance techniques for a wide class of modifications and derived relations.

**System and Experiments (Section 6):** LIVE is fully implemented, including the entire suite of data modification and versioning capabilities described in this paper. We believe ours is the first DBMS that incorporates data modifications and a lightweight versioning system for derived relations over ordinary and probabilistic data. Moreover, the lineage feature of LIVE enables elegant algorithms for propagating modifications and query processing. We describe the implementation of LIVE and include performance results.

## 2 LIVE Data Model (LDM)

In this section we describe LDM, the data model on which LIVE is built. We begin by introducing how lineage is represented and created in LIVE (Section 2.1), then we define LIVE's probabilistic data (Section 2.2), and finally we add versioning (Section 2.3). Many of these features are similar to previous work in their respective areas and not particularly novel, but they are a necessary basis for the system and for the new contributions in the remainder of the paper. Our model for lineage is adopted from Trio [5,11], so it is only briefly reviewed here.

### 2.1 Lineage

Whenever a derived relation is created in LIVE, lineage is tracked and stored automatically. Lineage connects derived tuples to the (base or derived) tuples from which they were derived.

Suppose we have two relations: `People(Name,State,Job)` lists people's state and occupation, while `Photo(Num,Name)` identifies the names of people appearing in numbered photos. (We call them `P(Name,S,J)` and `Ph(N,Name)` for short.). We begin with the following sample data, including tuple identifiers (denoted ID)[1]:

| ID | Ph(N, Name) |
|---|---|
| 11 | (1,Amy) |
| 12 | (1,Bob) |
| 13 | (1,Carl) |
| 14 | (1,Dale) |

| ID | P(Name, S, J) |
|---|---|
| 21 | (Amy,CA,Engineer) |
| 22 | (Bob,NY,Analyst) |
| 23 | (Carl,IL,Teacher) |
| 24 | (David,PA,Manager) |

Suppose we join `Photo` and `People`, then project attributes `Number` and `State`. We obtain derived relation `States(Number,State)`, listing the states of the people appearing in photos:

| ID | States(Num, State) | |
|---|---|---|
| 31 | (1,CA) | $\lambda(31) = 11 \wedge 21$ |
| 32 | (1,NY) | $\lambda(32) = 12 \wedge 22$ |
| 33 | (1,IL) | $\lambda(33) = 13 \wedge 23$ |

[1] Our system automatically generates, and manages identifiers. Identifiers are exposed in the paper only for presentation, however, all notions of "tuple values" and duplicates do not consider tuple identifiers.

Lineage, denoted by $\lambda$, is shown alongside each tuple. In general, the lineage of a tuple in a derived relation is a boolean formula over other tuple identifiers. Intuitively, a derived tuple exists because the existence of the tuples in its lineage formula make the formula evaluate to true. Joins generate conjunctions as seen in this example, while other constructs (e.g., duplicate elimination) generate disjunctions, and yet others (difference) generate negation. We will see shortly that lineage is also closely tied with the semantics of derived probabilistic data.

### 2.2 Probabilities

Each tuple in an LDM relation may optionally be annotated with a value in the range $[0, 1]$, denoting the probability that the tuple is present in the relation. (The absence of a probability is equivalent to probability 1.) We adopt the standard *possible-worlds* interpretation for probabilistic databases [8]: The possible-worlds of each base relation $R$ consist of omitting the tuples in $R$ that have probability $< 1$ in all possible combinations. Restricting ourselves to base relations, the possible-worlds of a database combine the possible-worlds of the base relations in all possible ways. Each possible-world has a probability associated with it. The probability of a possible-world is given by the product of the probabilities $p_i$ of each tuple $t_i$ present in the world, and $(1 - p_i)$ for each tuple omitted in the world. The possible-world probabilities are guaranteed to sum to 1.

When a query $Q$ is executed on an LDM database $D$ with probabilities, the result is an LDM relation $R$, including lineage, whose possible-worlds represent the result of applying $Q$ to each possible-world of $D$. When $R$ is added to $D$ as a derived relation, lineage is created as described in Section 2.1. This semantics for derived data with lineage extends the possible-worlds model in a natural way: Possible-worlds for a derived relation are only combined with those possible-worlds for base relations such that the following property holds. A derived tuple is present in a possible-world if and only if its "transitive" lineage formula, i.e., expanded to refer to base tuples only, evaluates to *true* based on the presence (*true*) and absence (*false*) of referenced base tuples. Note in particular that derived relations do not increase the number of possible-worlds.

A very nice property observed elsewhere [5] is that the probability associated with a derived tuple $t$ is the probability of its transitive lineage formula computed using the given probabilities for the base tuples. We will soon see that version intervals for derived tuples also can be computed through lineage, with an even more efficient algorithm.

*Example 1.* Let us add probabilities to the `Photo` relation (indicating uncertainty in identification), but suppose all tuples in the `People` relation still have a probability 1.0.

| ID | **Ph(N, Name)** |
|---|---|
| 11 | `(1,Amy):1.0` |
| 12 | `(1,Bob):0.6` |
| 13 | `(1,Carl):0.3` |
| 14 | `(1,Dale):0.1` |

The data and lineage in our join result `States` remains the same. To compute the probability of one of its tuples, say 32, we evaluate the probability of its lineage formula $\lambda(32) = 12 \wedge 22$; $\Pr(32) = \Pr(12 \wedge 22) = 1 * 0.6$. □

### 2.3 Versioning

Next we add versions to our data model. Most parts of the versioning model are standard, but a few subtleties do arise due to lineage and probabilities.

Each tuple in an LDM relation now includes a *start version* and an *end version*, which are non-negative integers or $\infty$. Suppose a tuple $t$ has start version $s$ and end version $e$, denoted by the interval $[s, e]$. Then, intuitively, the tuple is *valid* for all versions $v$ such that $s \leq v \leq e$. We use start$(t)$ and end$(t)$ to denote the start and end versions of tuple $t$.

The database $D$ maintains a current version $v_D$. Initially, the database starts at version 0, i.e., $v_D = 0$, and all tuples have the interval $[0, \infty]$. ($\infty$ denotes the special version number greater than all integer versions. Intuitively, a tuple valid till $\infty$ means the tuple hasn't expired.) As data modifications are committed to $D$, the current version number $v_D$ is increased, and the intervals of modified tuples are updated. (It is also possible to create an already-versioned database, but that seems to be a less likely scenario.)

We defer until Section 3 a formal definition of how precisely modifications create versioned relations. Section 4 covers (among other topics) more details on how versions interact with derived relations and lineage. In the remainder of this section we define the *snapshot* of an LDM relation, and we use snapshots to define formally the semantics of versioned LDM relations in terms of possible-worlds.

**Definition 1 (Snapshot).** *Given an LDM relation $R$ whose current version is $v_D$, the* snapshot *of $R$ at version $v \leq v_D$ (denoted $R_{@v}$) is a non-versioned LDM relation obtained by eliminating from $R$ all tuples $t$ such that $v <$ start$(t)$ or $v >$ end$(t)$. In the snapshot of a derived relation, the lineage of a tuple $t'$ is obtained by replacing every tuple identifier $i$ in $\lambda(t')$ with* false *if $i$'s version-interval does not include $v$. If now $\lambda(t') \equiv$* false, *$t'$ is not included in the snapshot. The probability of $t'$ in the snapshot is determined by its lineage in the snapshot in the standard fashion.* □

A valid LDM relation $R$ must satisfy some basic properties: Every tuple $t$ in $R$ must have start$(a) \leq v_D$ (recall $v_D$ denotes the current version), and if end$(a) \geq v_D$ then end$(a) = \infty$. Intuitively, all tuples must have come into existence at or before the current version, and any tuple that is valid at the current version is valid at and beyond the current version; i.e., no tuple could already have been deleted after the current version. We then have the following straightforward result, which says that the database is constant from version $v_D$ onwards.

**Theorem 1.** *Given an LDM database $D$ whose current version is $v_D$, for versions $v_1, v_2 \geq v_D$, the snapshot $D_{@v_1}$ is the same as the snapshot $D_{@v_2}$.* □

Just as probabilistic databases encode a set of possible-worlds, LDM databases with versions encode a list of sets of possible-worlds: one set for each version $v \geq 0$.

**Definition 2 (Possible-Worlds).** *Given an LDM database $D$ whose current version is $v_D$, the set of possible-worlds of $D$ at version $v$ is the set of possible-worlds of $D_{@v}$.* □

*Example 2.* Consider the relation `Photo` from our running example extended with versioning (Table 1(a)). Version-intervals for each tuple are marked as superscripts. Suppose the current version of the database is $v_D = 2$. For example, the tuple `(1,Amy)` is

**Table 1.** Table for Example 2

| ID | Ph(N, Name)$^2$ |
|---|---|
| 11 | (1,Amy)$^{[0,1]}$:1.0 |
| 12 | (1,Bob)$^{[0,\infty]}$:0.6 |
| 13 | (1,Carl)$^{[0,0]}$:0.3 |
| 14 | (1,Dale)$^{[1,1]}$:0.1 |

(a)

| Ph$_{@1}$(N, Name) |
|---|
| (1,Amy):1.0 |
| (1,Bob):0.6 |
| (1,Dale):0.1 |

(b)

valid for versions 0 and 1, and the only tuple valid in the current version is `(1,Bob)`. The snapshot of `Photo` at version 1 is shown in Table 1(b). (Tuple identifiers are omitted from the snapshot.) □

Just as the question of *completeness* arises in the theory of non-versioned probabilistic databases [3], the corresponding question arises here: whether LDM is *complete for versioned probabilistic databases*. That is, given some $v_D$ and a set of possible-worlds $P_i$ for $0 \leq i \leq v_D$, is there an LDM database $D$ whose current version is $v_D$, and $\forall i : 0 \leq i \leq v_D$, the possible-worlds of $D_{@i}$ are equal to $P_i$?

**Theorem 2.** *LDM is complete for versioned probabilistic databases.* □

All proofs are omitted in this version of the paper due to space constraints; they appear in the full version available online [12].

## 3 Modifications

Recall that LIVE supports modification of the current version of the database and not historical modifications. In this section, we define LIVE's set of primitive modification operations. We provide a formal semantics based on possible-worlds, and we specify how the modification operations create versioned LDM relations. In this paper we assume modifications are allowed on base relations only, then are propagated to all derived relations using the algorithms to be presented in Section 5.

LIVE supports a declarative SQL-based language for modifying relations. As in SQL, a statement in this language results in a set of primitive modification operations executed by the system. In LIVE the primitive modifications are:

- insert a new tuple
- delete an existing tuple
- update the value of one or more attributes in an existing tuple
- update the probability of an existing tuple

### 3.1 Semantics

We define the semantics of each of the primitive modification operations in terms of their effect on the set of possible-worlds [8]. Consider a relation $R$ with possible-worlds $\{R_1, \ldots, R_n\}$ (for a given version). Let possible-world $R_i$ have probability $p_i$, $i = 1..n$.

**Insert tuple:** Suppose we insert into $R$ a tuple $t$ with probability $p(t)$. The resulting set of $R$'s possible-worlds is $\{R_1^1, R_1^2, R_2^1, R_2^2, \ldots, R_n^1, R_n^2\}$, where for $i = 1 \ldots n$: $R_i^1$ adds tuple $t$ to $R_i$ and has probability $p_i * p(t)$; $R_i^2 = R_i$ and has probability $p_i * (1 - p(t))$. If the new set of possible-worlds contains any *duplicate worlds*, then their probabilities are summed and one world is retained: Duplicate worlds are possible worlds with the identical set of tuples.

**Delete tuple:** Suppose we delete a tuple $t$ from $R$. The resulting set of $R$'s possible-worlds for the new $R$ is $\{R'_1, \ldots, R'_n\}$, where each $R'_i$ deletes $t$ from $R_i$ if it is present. The probabilities remain unchanged, however when tuples are deleted from possible-worlds, duplicate worlds are always created. As with insertion, duplicate worlds are merged and probabilities added. For instance, two possible-worlds differing only in one tuple are merged, when this distinguishing tuple is eliminated.

**Update value:** When one or more values in an existing tuple are updated, $R$'s possible-worlds are modified by replacing the old tuple in every possible-world with the corresponding new tuple. Probabilities remain unchanged, and duplicate worlds are merged.

**Update probability:** Modifying the probability of a tuple does not change the set of possible-worlds, but only changes their probabilities, following the semantics of LDMs.

### 3.2 Execution

Now consider execution of modifications. We assume any number of modification statements may be performed together. A `commit` operation then increments the version number and installs the modifications permanently in the new version. (Note that the much-studied details of versioning systems, such as the interaction between versions and transactions, are neither a focus nor contribution of this paper.)

Consider an LDM relation $R$ whose current version is $v_D$.

1. **Insert Tuple:** When a tuple $t$ is inserted into $R$, $t$ is assigned the version-interval $[v_D + 1, \infty]$.
2. **Delete Tuple:** When a tuple $t$ is deleted from $R$, it is retained in $R$ as is, except $\text{end}(t)$ is modified to be $v_D$.
3. **Update Value:** When a tuple $t$ is updated to $t'$, it is treated as a deletion of $t$ and an insertion of $t'$. That is, $\text{end}(t)$ is modified to be $v_D$, and tuple $t'$ is inserted with version-interval $[v_D + 1, \infty]$.
4. **Update Probability:** When the probability $p$ of a tuple $t$ is modified to be $p'$, it is treated as a deletion of $t$ with probability $p$ and an insertion of $t' = t$ with probability $p'$. That is, $\text{end}(t)$ is modified to be $v_D$, and tuple $t' = t$ is inserted with probability $p'$ and version-interval $[v_D + 1, \infty]$.

*Example 3.* Consider the `People` relation from our running example, but now with probabilities, versions, and slightly modified data, shown on the left below. The database is currently at version $v_D = 0$, indicated by the superscript on the relation name.

| ID | People(Name, State, Job)$^0$ |
|---|---|
| 22 | (Bob,NY,Analyst)$^{[0,\infty]}$:1.0 |
| 23 | (Carl,IL,Teacher)$^{[0,\infty]}$:1.0 |
| 24 | (David,PA,Manager)$^{[0,\infty]}$:0.6 |

| ID | People(Name, State, Job)$^4$ | |
|---|---|---|
| 22 | (Bob,NY,Analyst)$^{[0,3]}$:1.0 | ← (4) |
| 23 | (Carl,IL,Teacher)$^{[0,2]}$:1.0 | ← (3) |
| 24 | (David,PA,Manager)$^{[0,\infty]}$:0.6 | ← (2) |
| 25 | (Frank,CA,Eng.)$^{[1,\infty]}$:0.3 | ← (1) |
| 26 | (David,PA,CEO)$^{[2,\infty]}$:0.3 | ← (2) |
| 27 | (Bob,CA,Student)$^{[4,\infty]}$:1.0 | ← (4) |

On the right we show the `People` relation after the following modifications in sequence, committing after each operation (We mark the modification alongside affected tuples; the final database version is $v_D = 4$.): (1) With probability 0.3 engineer Frank from CA is now known, so a tuple inserted. (2) We decide that David is possibly (30% chance) a CEO as well, so a tuple is inserted. (3) Carl retires, so his tuple is deleted. (4) Bob decides to go to graduate school in California, so his tuple is updated, changing his job from Analyst to Student and his state from NY to CA. □

# 4 Query Evaluation

We now address the problem of query evaluation in LDM. In query results, we are now interested not only in the data, probabilities, and lineage, but also in the version-intervals of each result tuple.

**Definition 3 (Query Answer).** *Given an LDM database $D$ whose current version is $v_D$ and a query $Q$ over relations $R_1, \ldots, R_n$ in $D$, the result of $Q$ is an LDM relation $R$ whose tuples have lineage to tuples in $R_1, \ldots, R_n$. The resulting LDM database $D'$ containing $D$ and $R$ still has current version $v_D$. For each version $v \leq v_D$, the possible-worlds of $D'_{@v}$ are the possible-worlds obtained by executing $Q$ on $D_{@v}$.* □

Intuitively, the versioned possible-worlds of the result of a query correspond to applying the query to the set of possible-worlds at each version of the database. (Recall from Section 2.2 that, further, the result of a query over a set of possible-worlds is defined as logically applying the query to each possible-world.)

In Section 4.1 we specify how version-intervals are computed in query results. Then, in Section 4.2 we consider queries that specifically filter data based on their version-interval. Section 4.3 discusses the subtleties surrounding probability values in query results over LDMs.

## 4.1 Version-Interval Computation

We first address query evaluation for queries that generate "positive" lineage, then extend our algorithm for all queries (i.e., also negative lineage). We then briefly discuss pushing interval computation into the query execution engine.

**Positive Lineage.** We say that a relation $R$ has *positive* lineage if the lineage of every tuple in $R$ contains only positive literals. Results of queries involving select, project, join, union, and duplicate-elimination always have positive lineage.

Consider a query $Q$ over input relations $R_1, \ldots, R_n$ that generates positive lineage. Conceptually we answer $Q$ in two steps:

1. Data Computation: We compute the result $S$ of $Q$ by treating $R_1, \ldots, R_n$ as LDM relations without versions; i.e., we disregard the version-intervals of tuples in this stage. The tuples in $S$ and their lineage can be computed using the query processing algorithms in [5].
2. Version Computation: We use the lineage of each tuple in $S$ to compute its version-interval.

Let us look at performing Step 2. (We discuss performing Steps 1 and 2 together in Section 4.1.) Given a tuple $a$ in the result $S$, we want to know all the versions of $S$ in which $a$ is present in some possible-world. Recall from the semantics of LDMs that $a$ is present only if its lineage $\lambda(a)$ is *true*. Therefore, we need to know all versions in which $\lambda(a)$ can be evaluated to *true*. The following theorem, whose proof follows directly from the discussion below, describes how this set of all versions can be computed.

**Theorem 3 (Version Interval Computation).** *Consider a tuple $a$ in a result relation, with lineage $\lambda(a)$ referring to tuples $a_1, \ldots, a_m$ in the input relations. Let the version-intervals of $a_1, \ldots, a_m$ be $I_1, \ldots, I_m$. The version-interval $I$ of $a$ is computed by evaluating a formula $f$ obtained from $\lambda(a)$ as follows:*

1. *In $\lambda(a)$, replace every instance of each tuple $a_i$ by its version-interval $I_i$.*
2. *In the resulting expression, replace logical AND ($\wedge$) with the intersection operator $\cap$ of intervals, and replace OR ($\vee$) with the union operator $\cup$.* □

**Corollary 1.** *The version-interval of a tuple $a$ with positive lineage $\lambda(a)$ can be computed in PTIME in the number of tuples in $\lambda(a)$.* □

The above theorem translates the boolean lineage formula into an expression over version-intervals of tuples, such that the result of the new expression gives the version-interval of the resulting tuple. If the lineage formula contains $(a_i \wedge a_j)$, replacing it by $I_i \cap I_j$ yields the versions in which $a_i \wedge a_j$ can be true. Similarly, $I_i \cup I_j$ gives the versions in which $a_i \vee a_j$ can be true. In general, replacing each boolean operator by the corresponding set operation and evaluating the formula yields the set of all versions in which $\lambda(a)$ can be true, i.e. all versions in which $a$ appears in some possible-world.

Notice that the original query $Q$ that produced the result relation is not needed for computing version-intervals—they can be computed using just lineage and version-intervals for the input data. Lineage allowed us to decouple the two steps, instead of performing version computation as part of query evaluation.

*Example 4.* Consider `Photo` and `People` modified once again and omitting probabilities for this example:

| ID | Photo(Number, Name) |
|---|---|
| 12 | `(1,Bob)` $^{[2,\infty]}$ |
| 13 | `(1,Carl)` $^{[4,6]}$ |
| 14 | `(2,Frank)` $^{[0,1]}$ |

| ID | People(Name, State, Job) |
|---|---|
| 22 | `(Bob,NY,Analyst)` $^{[0,3]}$ |
| 23 | `(Carl,IL,Teacher)` $^{[0,2]}$ |
| 25 | `(Frank,CA,Eng.)` $^{[1,\infty]}$ |
| 27 | `(Bob,CA,Student)` $^{[4,\infty]}$ |

As before, suppose `States(Number,State)` is obtained by joining the two relations. After Step 1 (data computation), we have the following result tuples and lineage:

| ID | States(Number, State) | |
|---|---|---|
| 41 | (1,NY) | $\lambda(41) = 12 \wedge 22$ |
| 42 | (1,IL) | $\lambda(42) = 13 \wedge 23$ |
| 43 | (2,CA) | $\lambda(43) = 14 \wedge 25$ |
| 44 | (1,CA) | $\lambda(44) = 12 \wedge 27$ |

In Step 2 we compute the version-intervals of each tuple. For example, the interval of tuple 41 is $[2, \infty] \cap [0, 3] = [2, 3]$. We may obtain an empty interval for some tuples, in which case the result tuple is *extraneous*, and is removed. For example, the interval of 42 above is $[4, 6] \cap [0, 2] = \emptyset$. The final result after interval computation is:

| ID | States(Number, State) | |
|---|---|---|
| 41 | (1,NY) $^{[2,3]}$ | $\lambda(41) = 12 \wedge 22$ |
| 43 | (2,CA) $^{[1,1]}$ | $\lambda(43) = 14 \wedge 25$ |
| 44 | (1,CA) $^{[4,\infty]}$ | $\lambda(44) = 12 \wedge 27$ |

Now let us consider a further derived relation `Region(State)`, obtained from relation `States` by projecting onto attribute `State` and eliminating duplicates (which generates disjunctive lineage). The resulting relation after data and version computation is:

| ID | Region(State) | |
|---|---|---|
| 51 | (NY) $^{[2,3]}$ | $\lambda(51) = 41$ |
| 52 | (CA) $^{[1,1] \cup [4,\infty]}$ | $\lambda(52) = 43 \vee 44$ |

As illustrated by Tuple 52 in our example, it is possible that the version-interval computed based on Theorem 3 consists of a set of disjoint intervals as opposed to a single interval. Disjoint sets of intervals are encoded in LIVE by creating multiple tuples, each with a single interval. □

**Arbitrary Lineage.** Now we consider computing version-intervals of result relations with arbitrary lineage. Specifically, the lineage of a tuple may now also contain negation, typically generated by a query involving the difference operator (e.g., $R_1$ EXCEPT $R_2$).

As a first step, we ensure $\lambda(a)$ is a DNF formula with all negations pushed down to literals (using De Morgans laws), which is how lineage formulas are stored in LIVE anyway. Just as before, we replace every conjunction with intersection, disjunction with union, and positive literal $a_i$ with $a_i$'s version-interval $I_i$.

However, we now replace every negated literal $\neg a_j$ with the interval $[0, \infty]$. One would have expected replacing $\neg a_j$ with the complement of the interval $I_j$, but that is incorrect. Consider a tuple $a_j$, whose probability is less than 1. Recall we are trying to find the version-interval in which $\neg a_j$ could be *true*. Clearly for any version $v$ not contained in $I_j$ we could have $\neg a_j$ *true* since $a_j$ is not present at version $v$; in addition, even for some version $v \in I_j$, $a_j$ has some probability of not being present, hence $\neg a_j$ could still be true. Therefore, $\neg a_j$ is replaced by $[0, \infty]$ while constructing the expression over version-intervals. After that, the version-interval of each tuple is computed as before. If we know $a_j$ has probability 1 in $I_j$, then we can make the intuitive replacement of $\neg a_j$ with $I'_j$, the complement of $I_j$, to compute the exact version-interval. However, the following theorem shows that the hardness of checking for probability 1 in probabilistic databases [10] makes exact version-interval computation also intractable. Further, it shows that the algorithm described above correctly computes version-intervals in PTIME when probabilities are known, i.e., computed.

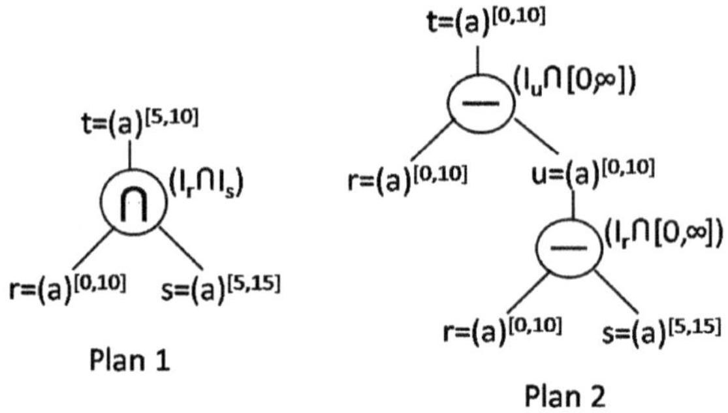


**Fig. 1.** Pushing version-interval computation into query plans with negation

**Theorem 4.** *Computing the version-interval of a tuple* $a$ *with arbitrary lineage* $\lambda(a)$ *referring to tuples* $a_1, \ldots, a_m$ *is:*

- *PTIME when all* $a_i$*'s probabilities are known.*
- *NP-hard when probabilities of* $a_i$*'s are unknown (i.e., not computed).* □

Despite this "negative" theorem, in the absence of negation our algorithm can always compute version-intervals in linear time. In the presence of negation, if probabilities are known then our algorithm is still linear. If probabilities are not known, our algorithm finds the best conservative interval based purely on lineage and input version-intervals.

**Pushing Interval Computation into Query Plans.** Lineage enables version-interval computation to be performed as a separate step, but we may also wish to perform version-interval computation during query execution. In the absence of negation, we can do so in a standard fashion: `select` and `project` operators retain the version-interval of the input, the `duplicate-elimination` operator takes the union of the version-intervals of the input tuples, and the `join` operator intersects the version-intervals of the input tuples. If the version-interval of an intermediate tuple in the query plan is empty (for instance, as a result of a join), the tuple is dropped.

When a query includes negation, computing version-intervals within a query plan is not always possible, as shown in the following example.

*Example 5.* Consider performing an intersection of relations $R$ and $S$, each containing one tuple $(a)$ with probability $< 1$, using two query plans: (1) $(R \cap S)$, and (2) $(R - (R - S))$. (Assume $R$ and $S$ have no duplicates so the two query plans are equivalent.)

Let the tuples in $R$ and $S$ be denoted $r$ and $s$ and let their version-intervals be $[0, 10]$ and $[5, 15]$ respectively. Figure 1 shows the operator-by-operator interval computation based on both the query plans. The lineage formulas for the final result tuple are equivalent: $r \wedge s$ for the first plan and $r - (r - s) \equiv r \wedge \neg(r \wedge \neg s)$ for the second plan. Plan 1 produces the correct output version-interval $[5, 10]$. However, in the second plan an incorrect version-interval of $[0, 10]$ is produced. □

In the above example, intuitively the reason the interval computation is incorrect is that the same tuple is involved in multiple levels of negation, not taken into account in operator-by-operator interval manipulations. Even without double-negations, interval computations within a query plan with negation may be incorrect. Hence, for such queries it is necessary to support some "lineage-like" method for decoupling data and interval computation.

LIVE pushes version-interval computation into the query plan whenever possible. We have also built suitable indexes on start and end version columns to enable efficiently combining and intersecting version-intervals in the query plan.

### 4.2 Filtering Based on Versions

LIVE provides two constructs that enable filtering data based on their version.

**1. Valid-At Queries:** The clause "`valid at <version-number>`" can be added to any regular LIVE query, to filter out input tuples not valid at a particular version. For example, "`Select * from People valid at 3`" selects from `People` all tuples whose version-interval contains 3. Note that while valid-at queries filter out data based on a specified version, their result is still a versioned LDM relation.

**2. Snapshot Viewing:** Our system allows users to view snapshots of LDM relations using the command: "`View <table-name> at <version-number>`", e.g., "`View People at 4`" displays `People@4`. The result is a non-versioned LDM relation.

### 4.3 Probabilities

An important subtlety arises when combining derived relations, probabilities, and versioning. The subtlety occurs only in query results with disjunctive lineage, typically due to duplicate elimination. While a tuple can be present in multiple versions of data, its probability may vary across versions.

A simple example illustrates the issue. Consider a modified `States` base relation.

| ID | States(Number, State) |
|---|---|
| 41 | (1,NY)$^{[0,3]}$: 1.0 |
| 43 | (1,CA)$^{[0,\infty]}$: 0.5 |

If we perform a duplicate-eliminating projection onto `Number`, the result contains a single tuple `[1]`. The probability of `[1]` from versions 0 to 3 is 1.0, because tuple 41 is present with probability 1.0. However, the probability from versions 4 onwards is 0.5, because from version 4 onwards only tuple 43 is present.

All information needed to determine probabilities for any version is included in result lineage, but there is a question of presentation and clarity. One possibility would be to split tuples based on probabilities, remembering somehow that duplicate-elimination has been performed so the result is a set. For example, in the query result above we could have two result tuples with value `[1]`, the first having version-interval $[0, 3]$ and probability 1.0, the second having version-interval $[4, \infty]$ and probability 0.5. LIVE does not use this approach. Rather, LIVE displays the probability for the current version $v_D$ as default, and historical probability values can be shown on request.

## 5 Propagating Modifications

Next we address the problem of propagating the modifications on base data described in Section 3 to derived relations that are dependent on the modified data. It suffices to consider propagating modifications to derived relations that are derived directly from modified base data. Modifications can be propagated to an entire LDM database in topological order: Once the set of relations, say $I(R)$, derived from a modified base relation $R$ are modified, then relations derived from $I(R)$ are modified, and so on.

As we worked on the propagation component of data modifications, and studied the considerable body of related previous work on materialized view maintenance, we realized that most algorithms for incremental view maintenance (particularly to handle deletions) exploit some technique or extra information that, if one looks carefully, is really a type of lineage. Thus, the lineage maintained by LIVE allows us to apply the most efficient propagation techniques, without requiring, gathering, or maintaining additional information. Specifically, we are able to identify data in derived relations that refers to modified data easily. Furthermore, we are able to propagate deletions for all types of queries, including negation, incrementally and without using the original query. (Deletions from the right side of a difference operator have traditionally been a particularly difficult case.) Next we give one example of how our propagation algorithm handles deletions. Detailed algorithms for propagating all types of modifications are given in the full version of our paper available online [12].

**Deletion with EXCEPT:** Consider derived relation $T$ obtained by executing "$R_1$ EXCEPT $R_2$", where $R_1$ and $R_2$ are base relations. Deleted tuples in $R_1$ are again propagated to $T$ by recomputing the version-intervals of affected tuples in $T$. The only case when recomputation of version-intervals in $T$ doesn't give the correct answer is when we delete tuples from $R_2$: Suppose there's a tuple $a$ in $R_1$ that also appears in $R_2$ with version-interval $[0, \infty]$ and probability 1.0. Then when $R_1 - R_2$ is executed, since the tuple $a$ is certainly present in $R_2$, it does not appear in the result relation. However, if the tuple gets deleted from $R_2$, then $a$ needs to be included in the result.

If a set $S$ of tuples is deleted from $R_2$, we modify $T$ as follows. For each distinct tuple value $a$ in $S$, check whether $T$ contains tuples with value $a$:

1. If yes, recompute the version-intervals of the tuples in $T$ with value $a$.
2. If not check whether any tuple in $R_1$ has value $a$. For each such tuple $a_1$ in $R_1$:
   (a) Insert a new tuple $a_1$ in $T$.
   (b) Let $s_1, \ldots, s_k$ be all $R_2$ tuples with $a_1$'s value. Set lineage of the newly added tuple in $T$ to $(a_1 \wedge \neg s_1 \wedge \ldots \wedge \neg s_k)$, and then compute its version-interval.

Effectively, we only need to insert tuples into $T$ that were not included because $R_2$ contained certain tuples with the same value. For remaining tuples in $T$, if they refer to modified tuples, we recompute their version-intervals; else, they are unchanged. Again, the task of determining which tuples in $T$ refer to modified tuples is eased by lineage.

## 6 System and Experiments

### 6.1 System Description and Setup

Like Trio [23], LIVE is layered on top of a conventional DBMS. It encodes LDM relations in standard relational tables, and lineage of each derived LDM relation is materialized into a separate table. In addition to data columns, each tuple in the encoding has a column for the probability, two system columns—`start` and `end`—corresponding to start and end versions respectively, and some extra columns to encode lineage. (Details of the exact encoding are omitted due to space constraints.)

LIVE uses the PostgreSQL 8.2 open-source DBMS as its relational back-end. Experiments were conducted on a Quad-Xeon server with 16 GB RAM and a large SCSI RAID. For all queries, we report actual wall-clock runtimes (in seconds) to execute the query and place the result in a new LDM relation. Lineage and version-intervals (but not probabilities) are computed and stored. Query execution time is measured over a "hot" cache, i.e., by running a query once and then reporting the average runtime over three subsequent, identical executions. Our experiments focus on investigating the overhead of modifications and version management in LIVE and its effects on query processing, compared to a non-versioned LIVE implementation.

Our dataset is based on a synthetically created set of TPC-H [22] tables using a scale-factor of 1. For modifications and queries, we consider different subsets of the `Lineitem` and `Orders` tables, by varying the selectivity of selections over the `Orderkey` attribute from 0.1% to 1% of the input table size. To make the TPC-H data probabilistic, we independently and randomly assigned a probability in $[0, 1]$ to each tuple. In our dataset, `Lineitem` contained 6,000 (at a selectivity of 0.1%) to 60,000 (at a selectivity of 1%) tuples, and `Orders` contained between 1,500 and 15,000 tuples respectively. We note that other recent work [4,10,11] on probabilistic databases has used similarly generated synthetic data sets based on TPC-H for experimental studies.

In addition to indexes over data columns, to facilitate answering predicates over the version columns, we create a multi-attribute B+ tree index over the concatenation of $(start, end)$ and a B+ tree index over $end$ for each input table in LIVE. Ensuring nonempty intersection of a set of version-intervals $[s_1, e_1]$, ..., $[s_n, e_n]$ then translates to the predicates $\mathtt{max}_i(s_i) \leq \mathtt{min}_i(e_i)$. For valid-at and snapshot queries referring to a given version $v$, we include predicates $s_i \leq v \leq e_i$ for each table in the `FROM` clause. Hence, queries may use range scans over the B+ tree indexes, in addition to other indexes that may be involved in the data-related part of the query processing. Unless mentioned otherwise, all versioned query executions in our experiments combine data and version computation using the predicates above, as described in Section 4.1.

### 6.2 Experimental Results

**Baseline Runs Without Modifications.** We start by comparing the performance of LIVE with versioning turned off against version-enabled LIVE. In Figure 2(a) we use a join of `Lineitem` and `Orders` on `Orderkey`, varying join selectivity from 0.1% to 1%. No modifications have been performed at this point. As expected, Figure 2(a) shows join query executions as linear functions of the join selectivity (the join multiplicity is constant at 1). The gap between the two plots indicates the overhead of processing the two system columns for $start$ and $end$ intervals in the encoding: We notice only a small (10-12%) overhead in the execution times.

**Scalability.** Next we study the same join query, but when an increasing number of tuples that go into the join have been modified in both the `Lineitem` and `Orders` tables. Each modification performs a tuple update, whose effect is to close one interval and create a new tuple as described in Section 3.2. Figure 2(b) displays runtime as a function of the number of tuples that have been modified, varying modification selectivity from 0.1% to 1%. The join selectivity is fixed at 1. We see that our versioning

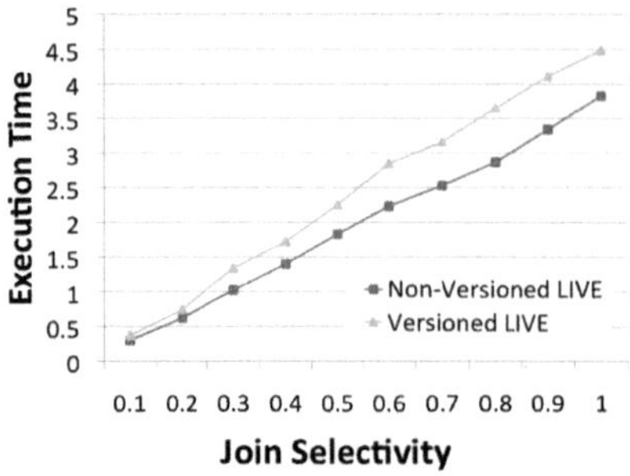


(a) Overhead of join query processing with versions enabled, no modifications.

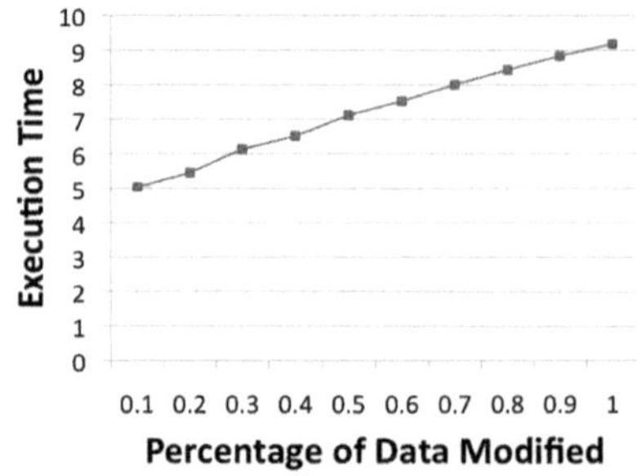


(b) Scalability of query processing for varying amounts of modified data.

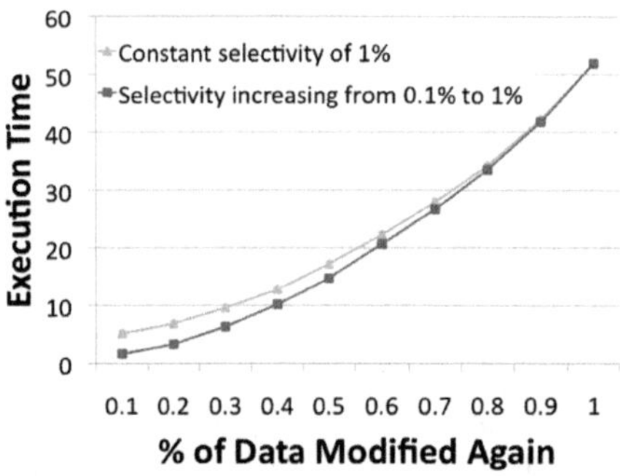


(c) Query execution time when the amount of modified data increases non-linearly.

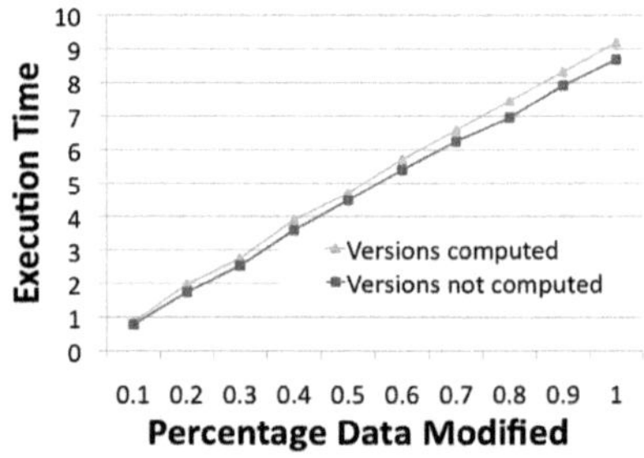


(d) Overhead of version computation in join query processing.

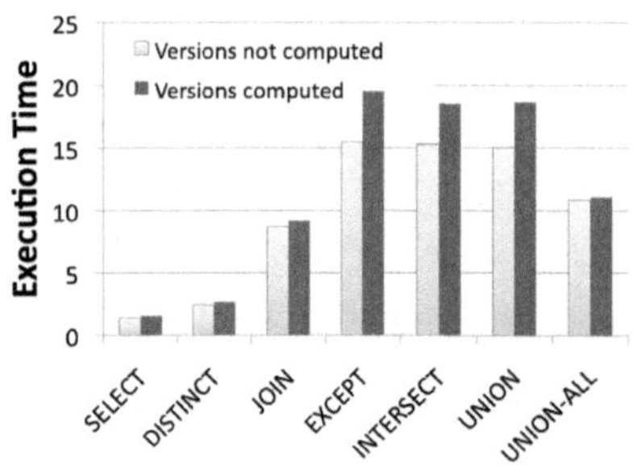


(e) Overhead of version computation for different operators.

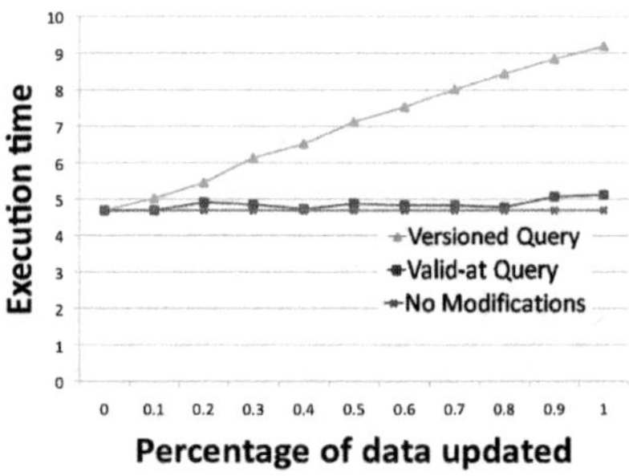


(f) Valid-at query execution time compared to versioned and non-versioned queries.

**Fig. 2.** Experimental results (execution time measured in `ms`)

algorithm clearly scales linearly with the amount of data modified. Figure 2(b) also shows that query execution time almost exactly doubles when all tuples that go into the join have been modified once (at a modification selectivity of 1%), compared to executing the same join query without modified data as depicted before in Figure 2(a). This conforms to the best-possible case, since for each modified (and hence expired) tuple, a new tuple with a different version-interval is inserted into each of the input tables, which also exactly doubles the amount of versioned tuples in the result at 1% update selectivity.

Figure 2(c) addresses query processing behavior when different fractions of tuples are modified progressively, i.e., more than once. The first point corresponds to 0.1% of the data being modified, the second point reflects performance when the initial 0.1% plus an additional 0.2% of data has been modified, and so on. The figure plots two lines: one for a constant join query with selectivity 0.1%, and the other for varying the selectivity of the join from 0.1% to 1%, thus corresponding to the number of tuples being modified. As expected, we notice a nonlinear increase in execution time for both cases, because the total amount of data modified and hence the number of versioned tuples, is increasing nonlinearly.

**Overhead of Version Computation.** In Figure 2(d) we study the overhead of computing version-intervals in query results, again when increasing fractions of data are modified. It turns out almost no overhead is induced by processing tuples with both overlapping and non-overlapping versions, because we are able to push the version predicate into the query. In Figure 2(d), one plot refers to the execution time when version-intervals are computed on result tuples, and the other refers to the execution time to obtain the same result but without version computation. For the former plot, each tuple that goes into the join has been modified exactly once, while for the latter plot, the same number of tuples were inserted (but not modified), so that version computation was not necessary.

Figure 2(e) depicts the overhead of version computation for different query operators, with 1% of the data being modified and queried in each case. As we can see, for all types of operators the overhead of version computation remains very small. Moreover, the plots show that the trend is similar for joins and other queries; hence our focus on join queries for the major part of our experiments.

**Versioned vs. Valid-at Queries.** Recall LIVE supports restriction of queries to specific versions, called "valid-at" queries. Figure 2(f) compares the execution time of the versioned join query with selectivity 1%, with the corresponding valid-at query, which only selects data valid at the current version. The fraction of data modifications is varied from 0.1% to 1%. The execution time of the versioned query grows linearly with the amount of data modified. However, the execution time of the valid-at query remains almost the same as the execution time of the join query when no data is modified (marked by the horizontal line in Figure 2(f)). Hence modifications and versioning in LIVE adds little overhead when we want to query only the current (or any fixed) version: The execution time primarily depends on the amount of data valid at the specified version.

## 7 Related Work

Due to space constraints, we provide a compressed related-work discussion and an abbreviated bibliography; extensive discussion and a full bibliography appear in the online full version [12]. To the best of our knowledge, LIVE is the first implemented DBMS with unified support for lightweight versioning, probabilistic data, and lineage, in an environment of stored derived relations over base data that is modified over time. Broadly, related work falls into four categories:

**Probabilistic and uncertain data.** Despite the significant amount of research on uncertain and probabilistic databases, little work has focussed on modifications, and none on versioning. Moreover, the few papers on modification [2,17,18,24] primarily consider language issues, but unlike our paper, don't focus on the problems of query answering, propagation and systems issues.

**Lineage.** We do not make a new contribution to the great deal of work in lineage (see [21,14]). Rather, we adopt Trio's model and algorithms for lineage [5], and we use them to support efficient management of modifications and versioning in our system, including update propagation and query processing.

**Versioning.** Incorporating versions and notions of time in databases has been studied a great deal (refer to [13,20]). Recently, [7] developed techniques for archiving (through versioning) of scientific data represented as XML. Our paper is different from [7] in several respects: While [7] works with XML data, we are interested in relational data (with probabilities and lineage). The focus of our paper is SQL query answering over versioned relations, with a lightweight versioning capability primarily to support data modifications; however, the focus of [7] is to "merge" newer versions of XML data with an existing versioned data for archival, and to support evolutionary queries. We note that, to the best of our knowledge, no versioning system has been closely integrated with data lineage, derived relations, and probabilistic data.

**View Maintenance.** A large body of work studies incremental view maintenance in traditional relational databases (see [15]), and is devoted to exploiting additional information and features to enable incremental computation. For instance, reference [9] exploits information about keys, [19] uses pointers to base data, while [6] analyzes predicates in queries and properties of modified data. Lineage generalizes the kinds of information exploited by previous work, and thus enables applying similar propagation techniques for a wider class of queries and modifications.

## 8 Conclusions

This paper describes LIVE, a fully implemented DBMS designed for applications requiring base and derived relations that are modified over time. LIVE incorporates a lightweight versioning system and it supports probabilistic data, for both base and derived relations. The key feature integrating LIVE's variety of capabilities is *lineage*: lineage supports efficient propagation of modifications from base to derived data, and efficient processing of a wide variety of queries on versioned data. The suite of capabilities supported by LIVE are of particular interest in scientific data management (as well as other application domains discussed earlier), as evidenced by the recent *SciDB* proposal [1]. Several directions for future work arise, including handling modifications to derived data, "partial propagation" of modifications, and lineage updates.

## References


1. SciDB, `http://confluence.slac.stanford.edu/display/XLDB/SciDB`
2. Abiteboul, S., Grahne, G.: Update semantics for incomplete databases. In: Proc. of VLDB (1985)
3. Abiteboul, S., Kanellakis, P., Grahne, G.: On the Representation and Querying of Sets of Possible Worlds. Theoretical Computer Science 78(1) (1991)
4. Antova, L., Jansen, T., Koch, C., Olteanu, D.: Fast and simple relational processing of uncertain data. In: Proc. of ICDE (2008)
5. Benjelloun, O., Das Sarma, A., Halevy, A., Widom, J.: ULDBs: Databases with uncertainty and lineage. In: Proc. of VLDB (2006)
6. Blakeley, J.A., Larson, P., Tompa, F.W.: Efficiently updating materialized views. In: Proc. of ACM SIGMOD (1986)
7. Buneman, P., Khanna, S., Tajima, K., Tan, W.-C.: Archiving scientific data. ACM TODS 29(1) (2004)
8. Cavallo, R., Pittarelli, M.: The theory of probabilistic databases. In: Proc. of VLDB (1987)
9. Ceri, S., Widom, J.: Deriving production rules for incremental view maintenance. In: Proc. of VLDB (1991)
10. Dalvi, N., Suciu, D.: Efficient Query Evaluation on Probabilistic Databases. In: Proc. of VLDB (2004)
11. Das Sarma, A., Theobald, M., Widom, J.: Exploiting lineage for confidence computation in uncertain and probabilistic databases. In: Proc. of ICDE (2008)
12. Das Sarma, A., Theobald, M., Widom, J.: LIVE: A Lineage-Supported Versioned DBMS. Technical report, Stanford InfoLab. (2009), `http://ilpubs.stanford.edu:8090/926/`
13. Date, C., Darwen, H.: Temporal Data and the Relational Model. Morgan Kaufmann Publishers, San Francisco (2002)
14. Green, T.J., Karvounarakis, G., Tannen, V.: Provenance semirings. In: Proc. of ACM PODS (2007)
15. Gupta, A., Mumick, I.S.: Maintenance of materialized views: Problems, techniques, and applications. IEEE Data Engineering Bulletin 18(2) (1995)
16. Haas, L.: The theory and practice of information integration. In: Schwentick, T., Suciu, D. (eds.) ICDT 2007. LNCS, vol. 4353, pp. 28–43. Springer, Heidelberg (2006)
17. Hegner, S.J.: Specification and implementation of programs for updating incomplete information databases. In: PODS (1987)
18. Keller, A.M., Winslett, M.: Approaches for updating databases with incomplete information and nulls. In: Proc. of ICDE (1984)
19. Roussopoulos, N., Economou, N., Stamenas, A.: ADMS: A testbed for incremental access methods. IEEE TKDE 5(5) (1993)
20. Snodgrass, R.T.: Developing time-oriented database applications in SQL. Morgan Kaufmann Publishers, San Francisco (2000)
21. Tan, W.-C.: Provenance in Databases: Past, Current, and Future. IEEE Data Engineering Bulletin (2008)
22. Transaction Processing Council (TPC). TPC Benchmark H: Standard Specification (2006), `http://www.tpc.org/tpch`
23. Widom, J.: Trio: A System for Integrated Management of Data, Accuracy, and Lineage. In: Proc. of CIDR (2005)
24. Winslett, M.: A model-based approach to updating databases with incomplete information. ACM TODS 13(2) (1988)

# Optimizing Resource Allocation for Scientific Workflows Using Advance Reservations*

Christoph Langguth and Heiko Schuldt

Databases and Information Systems Group
Department of Computer Science, University of Basel, Switzerland
firstname.lastname@unibas.ch

**Abstract.** Scientific applications are more and more faced with very large volumes of data and complex, resource-intensive workflows that process or analyze these data. The recent interest in web services and service-oriented architectures has strongly facilitated the development of individual workflow activities as well as their composition and the distributed execution of complete workflows. However, in many applications concurrent scientific workflows may be served by multiple competing providers, with each of them offering only limited resources. At the same time, these workflows need to be executed in a predictable manner, with dedicated Quality of Service guarantees. In this paper, we introduce an approach to Advance Resource Reservation for service-oriented complex scientific workflows that optimize resource consumption based on user-defined criteria (e.g., cost or time). It exploits optimization techniques using genetic algorithms for finding optimal or near-optimal allocations in a distributed system. The approach takes into account the locality of services and in particular enforces constraints imposed by control or data flow dependencies within workflows. Finally, we provide a comprehensive evaluation of the effectiveness of the proposed approach.

**Keywords:** Scientific Workflows, Advance Resource Reservation, Quality of Service.

## 1 Introduction

Service-Oriented Architectures (SOA) have become widely adopted both in industry and research environments: standardized messages and message exchange formats such as WSDL and SOAP facilitate loose coupling, thus enabling service consumers and providers to interact in a much more flexible fashion than previously. One particularly interesting aspect of these SOAs is the possibility to combine several services into workflows (also known as "programming in the large").

Beyond the pure provisioning (or using) of functionality, however, both service providers and consumers usually have other interests: providers will strive for

* This work has been partly supported by the Hasler Foundation within the project COSA (Compiling Optimized Service Architectures).

M. Gertz and B. Ludäscher (Eds.): SSDBM 2010, LNCS 6187, pp. 434–451, 2010.

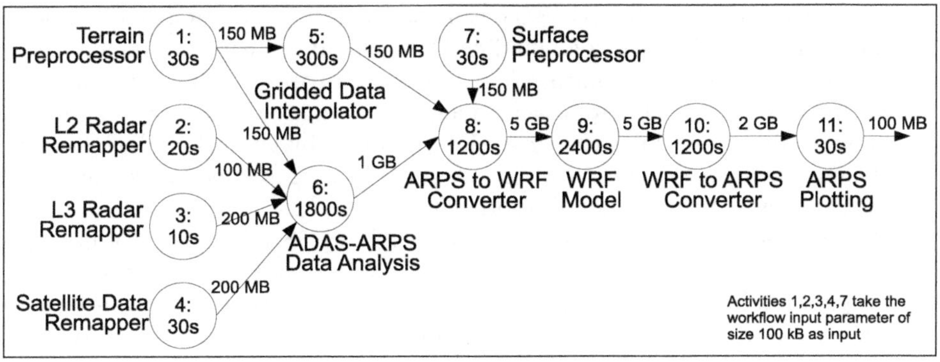


**Fig. 1.** Sample Weather Forecast Workflow

the best possible usage of their provided resources in order to maximize profit; conversely, consumers may want to execute an entire workflow as fast as possible, or as cheap as possible (or combinations thereof).

Consider the sample workflow given in Figure 1, which is a simplified version of an actual scientific workflow presented in [5] and is used for producing weather forecasts. Reasonable non-functional criteria that an end user might specify for the execution (of the entire workflow) could be "as fast as possible", or "as cheap as possible, but with a deadline so that the results are available for the evening news". All of the operations are available as Web Services (WS) and may be provided by one or more service providers. Assume that details on timing and data quantities of individual operations are as indicated in Figure 1. This implies that the overall execution of a single instance of this workflow is in the range of several hours – the exact duration strongly depends on the available resources. Thus, in this constellation, we consider that workflow as a good example of a Scientific Workflow, as it is characterized by large volumes of data and contains long-running, CPU-intensive operations [17,21].

To meet the aforementioned non-functional requirements, we propose a workflow engine (called DWARFS: Distributed Workflow engine with Advance Reservation Functionality Support) that is capable of providing Quality of Service (QoS) guarantees to the end users. When multiple independent clients run workflows concurrently, these clients are generally competing for the limited resources that providers have available. Our approach is based on the notion of Advance Resource Reservations (AR for short), which, in simple terms, reserves all required resources for running a workflow before the actual workflow execution.

The goal of the AR component of the DWARFS workflow engine is to find a combination of resource reservations at the providers of the individual operations that can satisfy the client's needs in terms of QoS, and to set up the required reservations, using negotiations based on WS-Agreement, so that the following execution of the workflow is guaranteed to meet these requirements. While we have presented an overview of the DWARFS system in [11], this paper focuses in detail on the planning phase. In particular, the contribution of this paper is an approach to make the execution of Scientific Workflows predictable by exploiting genetic algorithms for finding the optimal or near-optimal allocation of all resources needed at runtime (e.g., CPU, storage, specialized instruments, network bandwidth). The approach takes into account the locality of services and also enforces the different constraints imposed by control or data flow dependencies within a workflow. Finally, we provide a comprehensive evaluation of the effectiveness of the proposed approach.

The rest of this paper is structured as follows: Section 2 introduces the DWARFS system model. The optimization task is specified in Section 3. Section 4 presents in detail the application of genetic algorithms for advance reservation of resources. The results of a comprehensive evaluation of the DWARFS approach to AR is given in Section 5. Section 6 discusses related work and Section 7 concludes.

## 2 System Model and Assumptions

In this section, we shortly describe our overall approach, including basic assumptions. First and foremost, we assume that the operations that the workflow uses are provided in a SOA, i.e., that there are (possibly many) competing service providers that offer the required operations. We suppose that for the planning, we have the required knowledge about the infrastructure (such as which operation providers and workflow engines exist, network connectivity characteristics, etc.).[1]

### 2.1 Resources

Any operation invocation is assumed to require some resources for its execution. The most obvious case is that operation invocations require processing power (i.e., CPU cycles). However, "almost anything" involved in an operation can be considered a resource that needs to be taken into account when invoking an operation.

As an example, Figure 2 shows a more complete case of the resources that may need to be (co-)allocated for a particular operation execution at a specific service provider P: The actual operation requires reservations for CPU (2) and some hardware instrument (5). As the invocation takes place over the network, the system also considers reservations for bandwidth, required for the data upload (pre-invocation, (1)), and the download of the computed result (post-invocation, (3)), between the workflow engine E and the provider P. Finally, the provider specified that the client needs to reserve a certain amount of storage (4) for the entire duration of the operation call. Thus, even in this simple example, there are five resources involved, including dependencies on the timing of their allocation requirement. Note that the need for co-allocating multiple resources using such dependencies is the rule, not the exception. Requirements to only allocate a

[1] That information could for example be acquired using registries such as UDDI, or by any other means – an in-depth discussion is out of scope in this context.

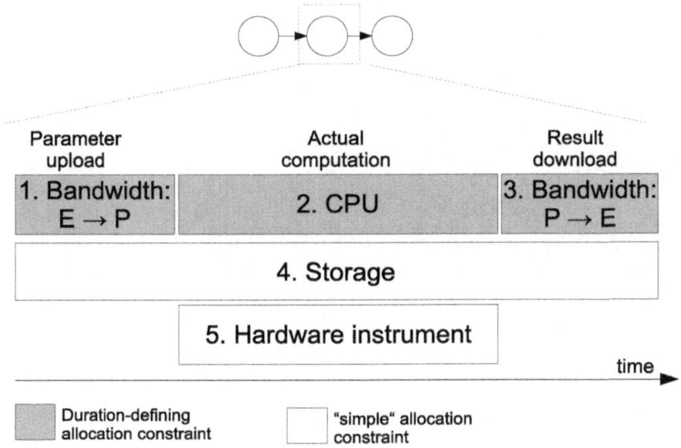


**Fig. 2.** Required Resource Allocations for Operation Call

single resource are rare, and are simply treated as the most elementary case of a co-allocation.

The information about which resources need to be allocated for a particular operation invocation is made available by the service provider. Staying with the example shown in Figure 2, a simplified form of these co-allocation constraints could look as follows:

- **CPU:** This invocation requires 25 billion CPU cycles and may use a maximum of 50% of the available computing power (for instance because this is a single-threaded operation deployed on a dual-core machine).
- **Hardware:** For the duration of the computation, you must reserve one mass spectrometer.
- **Storage:** For the duration of the invocation, you must reserve an amount of storage equal to twice the sum of the expected input and output sizes.

Finally, in addition to this information, every provider also makes available information about the current usage of each resource it provides (i.e., the amount of committed allocations already reserved by other clients; an example is shown in Figure 3), and the cost function for the respective resource. In the spirit of a SOA, all of this information is made available using standardized formats and usual mechanisms, e.g., embedded in, or referenced from, the service's WSDL or other public metadata.

These items also illustrate the relation between resource requirements and the actual duration of the resulting allocation: The duration is actually determined dynamically by the allocation request itself, and the available resources. While the provider specifies a maximum of 50% for the CPU allocation, clients may want to acquire less (say, a maximum of 20%, but a guaranteed minimum of 10% at all times), thus making the call take longer, but become cheaper. For more in-depth information about the calculation, provision, and usage of these data, please refer to [11].

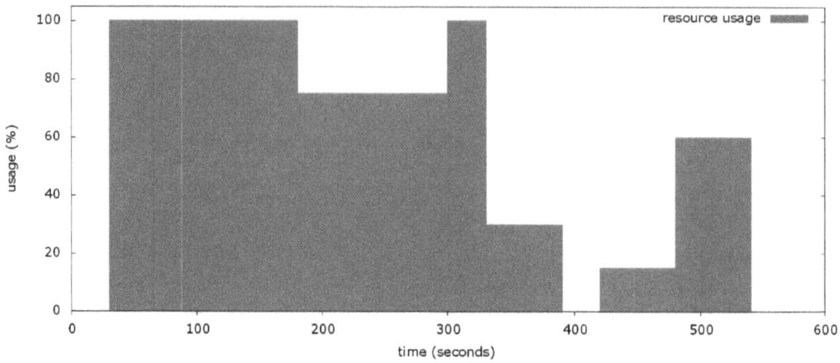


**Fig. 3.** Example of Resource Usage Representation

### 2.2 Distributed Workflow Engine

While the discussion so far has mostly presented provider-side aspects, it has also touched one system-wide issue: the flow of data between the operation provider and the invoking workflow engine. Essentially, bandwidth capacity within the system is modeled as "just another resource" – so clearly, the network locations of the provider and the engine also influence the execution, especially when very large amounts of data are to be transmitted.

As opposed to traditional centralized workflow engines, DWARFS is meant to be a distributed workflow orchestration engine, which means that there are actually several co-operating workflow engines that can orchestrate a single workflow, and "move along" the network as the process execution evolves. Besides avoiding possible single hot-spots, this helps in leveraging operation locality – e.g., in the simplest case, choosing an execution engine that is close (in terms of network) to two consecutive operations in the workflow for invoking them will usually yield faster throughput. Finally, another advantage of executing long-running, resource-intensive Scientific Workflows by a set of distributed workflow engines is the possibility to seamlessly parallelize the orchestration of concurrent workflow instances across several engines.

## 3 The DWARFS Approach to Advance Reservation

As we have discussed, any workflow execution within DWARFS is subject to some user-defined QoS constraints. In order to meet these constraints, the resources that will be required at runtime need to be reserved in advance at the respective providers. In simple words, the question is thus: which combination of reservations fulfills the user's requirements best?

There are a multitude of variables that influence how suitable a particular combination is:

- **Chosen providers for operations:** There are possibly many providers offering the operations required for every single activity within the workflow, differing in the resulting cost, and execution time.
- **Operation providers' resource availability:** Every operation invocation needs to be able to reserve the required resources, as specified by the provider. However, because every provider keeps track of already allocated resources, not all theoretically possible reservation requests are actually feasible (or are only feasible at a later time, thus delaying the execution).
- **Resource allocation requests:** While providers state which resources are required and give bounds on their usage, this information may allow for flexibility. As shown in the previous section, some allocation requests may be modified to weigh execution time against cost.
- **Workflow Engine instance for activity:** Since we are dealing with a distributed execution engine, every workflow activity may be handled by any available workflow engine in the system. This choice again affects the overall planning, as for example network throughput (and availability) between different engines and operation providers differ.
- **Timing:** Because of the abovementioned aspects – especially those on the availability of resources – even small changes in the planned timing may substantially influence the overall outcome. As an example, starting the workflow execution a few seconds later may be able to use resources at a provider that was previously fully loaded, and thus result in a faster overall execution time.

Given the above discussion, it becomes clear that there is an extremely vast space of potential solutions to explore. For instance, the comparatively small experimental setup we used (see Section 5) has over 180 billion combinations of merely choosing a workflow engine and a provider for all activities – not yet counting the additional, essentially infinite, factor of possible resource allocation variations and timing offsets.

On the other hand, the inherent unpredictability of the system (caused by pre-existing provider-side resource allocations) makes it impossible to use traditional (precise) optimization techniques such as linear or non-linear optimization. Rather, this class of problem suggests using a metaheuristic approach.

We have investigated a number of possible metaheuristic approaches; in the end, we have decided to use Genetic Algorithms (GA), mainly because of three factors [4,1]: i) in general, they avoid getting trapped in local optima as good as, or better than, other approaches; ii) a GA usually converges relatively fast; iii) GAs are a relatively simple and easy-to-understand, yet powerful concept.

## 4 The DWARFS Planner Implementation: Optimizing Allocations Using a Genetic Algorithm

Genetic algorithms use an optimization approach that mimics natural selection as it happens in the real world: Each possible solution to the problem to be solved is represented as a genotype (or individual), represented by a single chromosome. The chromosome consists of a number of genes which can have different values (allele). Finally, a population consists of a number of individuals with different gene expressions. A fitness function is used to assign each individual within the population a value which determines its suitability in reaching the optimization goal.

The actual optimization then takes place by evolving the population into a new generation of individuals. For finding new problem solutions, two approaches are generally employed: mutation (i.e., randomly changing the value of a random gene), and crossover (mating of two individuals by recombining their genes). As these operations increase the value of genotypes, the fitness function is used to select the best individuals – considering both the originally existing individuals, and the newly created ones – and carry them over to the next generation (survival of the fittest).

### 4.1 Chromosome Layout

In trying to use a GA for our goal, the first question to be answered is: how can one represent a specific (possible) workflow instance, along with the required resource reservations, as a combination of genes that can be mutated and that form a chromosome? Because of the structure of a workflow definition, using a simple array of genes seemed too limiting. Rather, we use a feature of the JGAP framework [14] called SuperGene, which allows to build tree-like structures of genes. The actual allele values are then only stored in the leaf nodes (real genes in the GA sense) of the tree, but all internal tree nodes can be considered genes as well and as such mutated (delegating the actual mutation to child nodes).

Figure 4 shows an example of such a chromosome, representing a trivial workflow that consists of a single activity. Note that the representation of a workflow as a chromosome is directly derived from the workflow definition itself – there is no "one size fits all" chromosome representation suitable for all workflows. For instance, the sample process introduced in Section 1 results in a chromosome containing a total of 126 genes.

In the following, we will shortly walk through the example and explain the chromosome layout. For the genes that actually mutate (the leaf nodes of the tree), we provide a description of the values the allele can take. Note that many of the issues that have been mentioned in Section 3 have a direct correspondence with one of the presented genes.

- **WorkflowActivityGene:** This is the root gene of an entire workflow and essentially acts as a container for the other genes. It is also planned to be usable as a nested gene in order to represent sub-workflows (similar to the InvokeActivityGene), however this is left for future work.
- **StartActivityGene** and **EndActivityGene:** These genes represent explicit entry and exit points of the process. For example, all workflow activities that do not have at least one predecessor are represented by genes that will depend on the StartActivityGene, and the EndActivityGene depends

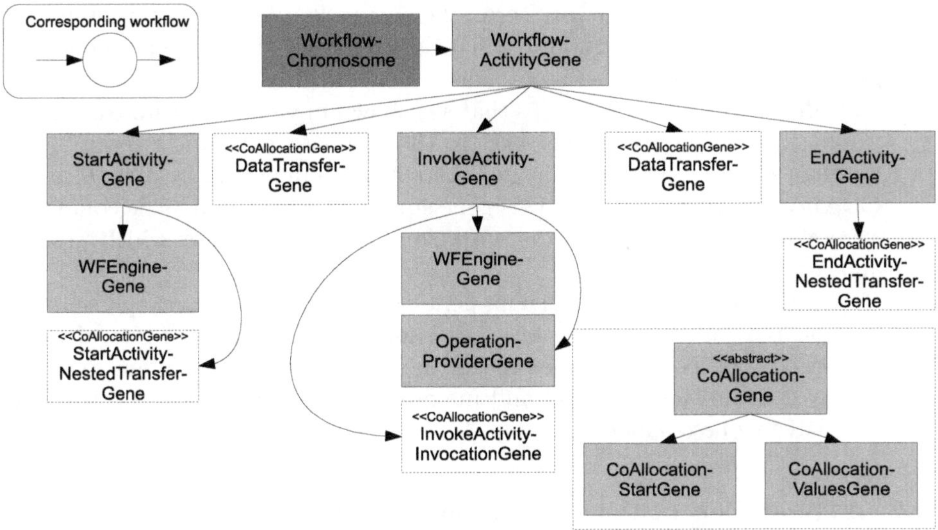


**Fig. 4.** Chromosome Layout for a trivial Process

on all activities not having successors. In addition, these genes make sure that the workflow start and end are actually scheduled at the same workflow engine, so that the SOA semantics of "a workflow invocation is perceived as just another web service" can be maintained.

- **WFEngineGene:** This gene represents the workflow engine executing the activity denoted by its parent gene. The possible allele values are in principle all workflow engines known to exist in the infrastructure.
- **StartActivityNestedTransferGene** and **EndActivityNestedTransfer-Gene:** these genes represent the transfer of the input/output data from/to the end user, and the resources that are required for these transfers.
- **DataTransferGene:** These genes are inserted whenever data produced by one activity is required as input by another activity. In other words, they represent the data edges in the workflow graph[2]. Note that the actual resources that are affected depend on the source and target of the data transfer – i.e., if the source and target are actually the same workflow engine, this activity results in zero overhead, whereas physical network transmissions will require real allocations and influence the timing.
- **InvokeActivityGene:** This is a gene that models a remote operation invocation.
- **OperationProviderGene:** This gene represents the chosen provider for the operation represented by its parent gene. Possible allele values are all providers known to offer the operation.

[2] For mere control flow edges, a (simpler) **ControlTransferGene** implementation exists (not used in the example).

- **InvokeActivityInvocationGene:** This gene represents the actual invocation (and required allocations). It has dependencies on its parent and sibling genes for determining the allocations.
- **CoAllocationGene:** All genes that are shown in white dotted boxes are actually subclasses of this gene. The CoAllocationGene itself is responsible for finding the required allocations for the resources indicated by its subclasses.
- **CoAllocationStartGene:** This gene simply consists of an allele containing a number which influences the start timestamp at or after which possible allocations are to be found.
- **CoAllocationValuesGene:** This gene contains an allele that represents the variable part of the coallocation to be found. It is actually an array of values (so strictly speaking, contains more than one mutable part). For example, it may contain the minimum and maximum values to request for resources that have to be co-allocated.

### 4.2 Exploitation of the Information Represented in the Chromosome

Every gene within the chromosome can be mutated independently, and every possible allele combination results in an – in principle – valid schedule (even if it may still be considered unsuitable with regard to the envisaged QoS constraints, e.g., because it takes longer than a user-specified deadline).

However, the alleles only denote the most basic information that is required to deduce the characteristics of the schedule that the individual represents. In fact, the interpretation of the genotype (answering questions such as: "when does it terminate, how much does it cost, which resources do I need to reserve?") is rather complex.

Figure 5 presents a close-up look into the inner structure of the InvokeActivityGene, and its relation with its predecessor and successor genes. The gray boxes with bold text represent the actual alleles as introduced previously, while

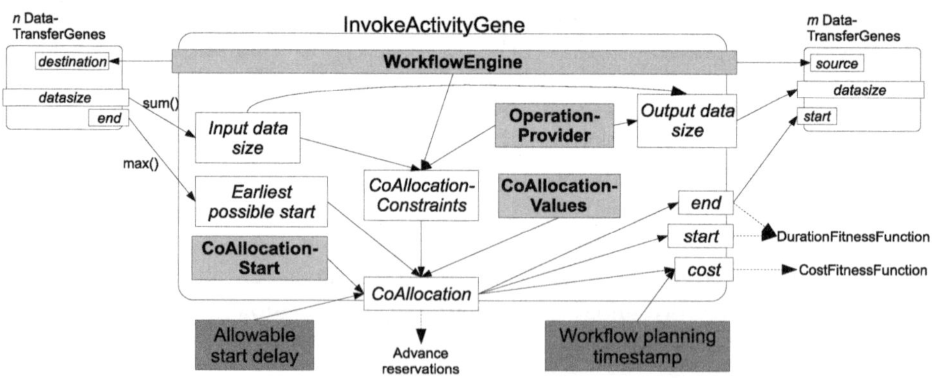


**Fig. 5.** Chromosome Interpretation and Interdependencies

white boxes stand for computed values. The two dark gray boxes at the bottom can be considered static: they are given as input parameters for the optimization run. The arrows depict dependencies.

It is relatively straightforward to see that those dependencies are reflecting the structure, as well as integrity constraints, of the workflow. For example, the earliest possible start for an activity is the maximum of the timestamps when all of its predecessor activities have finished. All other genes have a similar structure, which in fact yields a directed acyclic graph of dependencies, when looking at the chromosome as a whole. This graph is spanning all of the alleles within the genotype: in order to determine e.g., the end timestamp of the EndActivityGene, all of the alleles of the entire workflow have to be inspected, and essentially all computations within the graph need to be performed. The computationally most expensive operation is to determine feasible co-allocations.

In order to reduce the computational overhead, we are caching already calculated results. When an allele is mutated, only the depending calculations are notified and re-performed, stopping whenever no further changes occur. This may still mean a considerable amount of re-calculations if an allele early in the workflow is mutated.

### 4.3 Fitness Functions

A fitness function assigns each chromosome a fitness value representing its suitability for solving the envisaged optimization criteria, and allows the algorithm to evolve towards better solutions.

We have implemented two straightforward fitness functions that represent the most sensible QoS requirements: A *CostFitnessFunction* which considers the total cost of all allocations generated by an individual, and a *DurationFitnessFunction* which considers the total runtime. Both functions have "smaller is better" semantics. While the raw values of cost or duration are easily understandable, they are not ideal as fitness measures. We rather perform the same multi-step transformation for both cost and duration, which results in normalized values. The fitnesses are calculated for the entire population at once, thus resulting in *relative* fitness values (i.e., how does the individual perform within this generation). The resulting values are such that each individual $i$ of a population $P$ is assigned a fitness value $f_i$, where $f_i \in [0, 1]$, and $\sum_{i \in P} f_i = 1$. Larger values indicate a better fitness.

Even though this transformation results in the fitness values losing the clearly defined semantics the absolute values provide, they still remain correctly ordered and maintain the fitness proportions. However, this distribution offers two important advantages: i) the values are directly suitable for realistic crossover candidate selection, and ii) the values are combinable. While the first item is left for future work, the second can readily be used to formulate *combining fitness functions* such as "the cost is 10 times as important as the duration", thus allowing for essentially arbitrary combinations (and weighing) of otherwise incomparable QoS domains. We are also using the possibility of combining fitness functions for defining constraints like "Optimize for cost, but be ready by a certain deadline". In the latter example, as long as the deadline is not met by any individual (i.e., all would have a fitness of 0), the original weight factors of 1 and 0 are reversed, thus resulting in an (initial) optimization for deadline only until at least one individual meets the deadline constraints.

## 5 Evaluation

For evaluating the planner, we have used the workflow presented in Figure 1. For simplicity, the parameters (and thus the characteristics of the data and the operation runtimes) remain fixed for every workflow invocation, unlike the dynamic behaviour discussed in [11]. The workflow is scheduled 50 times on an initially empty infrastructure (i.e., no ARs exist before the first planning). The intervals between the planning runs are randomly chosen from a normal distribution between 0 (directly after the last planning run) and 3 hours later; additionally, the planned earliest start of the execution is uniformly distributed between 0 (directly after planning) and 5 hours after planning. The client that starts the invocation is randomly selected for each run. The QoS criteria that were used as optimization goal were also randomly chosen according to the following scheme (actual absolute numbers for the test run are in parentheses):

1. 30 % duration only (10)
2. 10 % cost only (8)
3. 20 % duration, but respecting a given budget (9)
4. 20 % cost, but respecting a given deadline (14)
5. 10 % weighing cost 80% over duration 20% (5)
6. 10 % weighing duration 20% over cost 80% (4)

### 5.1 Experimental Setup

The infrastructure that we simulated for all evaluations consists of 9 hosts that act as service providers, 3 available workflow engines, and 3 client hosts (from which the workflow instances are to be started). This setup is small enough to eventually saturate some hosts' resources, but large enough to induce a search space which is too large for naïve optimizations such as exhaustive search. All hosts in the system have a network capacity of 100 MB/s both for incoming and outgoing bandwidth, however the hosts are located in three separate networks which differ in available bandwidth between them. The networks and machines are shown in Figure 6.

The hosts acting as operation providers have been set up as shown in Table 1. This setup and deployment has been randomly auto-generated, so as to avoid any possible form of "human bias". We have knowingly refrained from using any kind of exact numbering (GHz, FLOPs or the like) for the CPU classes, but rather classified them as slow, medium, and fast; however, there is a linear relationship between these classes: medium is twice as fast as slow, and fast is three times faster. On the other hand, if the optimization goal is cost only (and

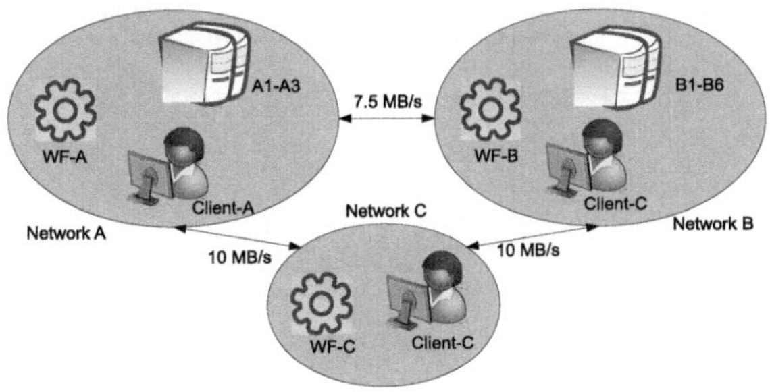


**Fig. 6.** Experimental Setup: Networks and Hosts

**Table 1.** Operation Provider and Host Specifications

| *Host* | *A1* | *A2* | *A3* | *B1* | *B2* | *B3* | *B4* | *B5* | *B6* |
|---|---|---|---|---|---|---|---|---|---|
| CPU class | medium | fast | fast | medium | medium | slow | medium | slow | fast |
| Storage | 200GB | 100GB | 300GB | 100GB | 400GB | 400GB | 400GB | 400GB | 200GB |
| Op. 1 | 100% | 100% | 100% | 100% | | | | | |
| Op. 2 | | 25% | 25% | | 50% | | | | 100% |
| Op. 3 | 25% | | | 25% | | | | 25% | |
| Op. 4 | 25% | 100% | 50% | 25% | | | | | |
| Op. 5 | | | 25% | | 50% | | | | |
| Op. 6 | | 100% | | | | | 50% | | 100% |
| Op. 7 | 50% | | 100% | | 50% | 50% | | | 50% |
| Op. 8 | 50% | | 50% | | | | | 25% | |
| Op. 9 | 25% | 50% | 50% | | | 100% | 100% | | |
| Op. 10 | | 25% | | | | 25% | 50% | | |
| Op. 11 | 25% | 25% | 25% | | | | | 50% | |

only CPU is considered), it could be beneficial to use a slower host, as the "unit cost" for CPU are 0.25, 0.5, and 1.0 for slow, medium, and fast, respectively[3].

For a concrete example of how to interpret the table, consider operation 8 (ARPS to WRF Converter) of the sample workflow, which states 1200 seconds as its runtime. This number is to be interpreted as "If running on a fast host and at 100% of the CPU, it would take 1200 seconds". From the table, we can deduce that the fastest actually possible invocations for operation 8 are i) 3600 seconds if run on host A1 at 50%[4], ii) 2400 seconds if run on host A3 at 50%, or iii) 14400 seconds if run on host B5 at 25%.

All operations require reservations for storage exactly equal to the sum of the input and output sizes; all providers have the same cost function for storage, and all hosts have the same cost function for bandwidth. Please note that we

[3] The cost advantage may be outweighed by having to reserve other resources for the correspondingly longer time, though.

[4] $3600 = 1200 * 1.5$ (downgrade from fast to medium) $* 2$ (downgrade from 100% to 50%).

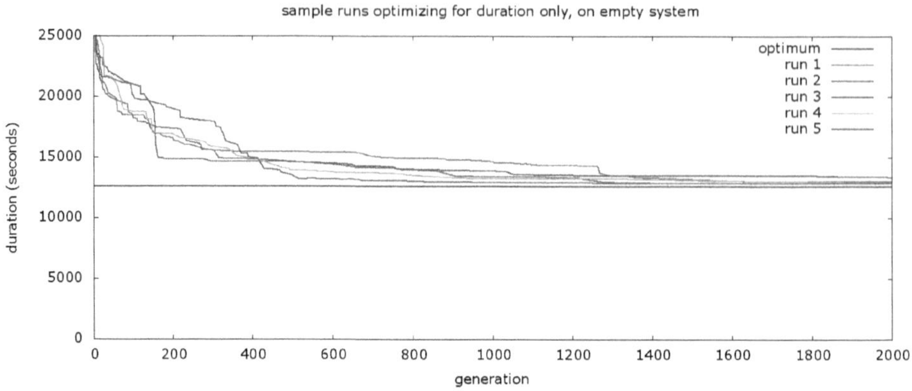


**Fig. 7.** Quality of the Evolution of the Planning using known Optimum

**Table 2.** Qualitative Analysis of 100 Scheduling Runs with known Optimum

| *criteria* | *average* | *standard dev.* | *min.* | *max.* | *90th perc.* | *95th perc.* |
|---|---|---|---|---|---|---|
| duration | 13116.88 | 228.26 | 12758 | 13865 | 13415 | 13606 |
| % of optimum | 104.1 | 1.8 | 101.3 | 110.1 | 106.5 | 108.0 |
| effectiveness (%) | 96.1 | 1.6 | 90.9 | 98.7 | 93.9 | 92.3 |
| *Minimum generation to reach effectiveness of:* | | | | | | |
| 75% | 159.77 | 87.71 | 28 | 498 | 263 | 321 |
| 90% | 538.62 | 302.20 | 87 | 1892 | 942 | 1080 |
| 95%[a] | 1073.38 | 392.74 | 400 | 1985 | 1643 | 1867 |

[a] Not all runs reached 95% effectiveness; the statistics are for the 79 runs that did.

currently apply a virtual unit for the costs. In future work, we plan to consider the exact costs incurring at the providers' sites by exploiting an economic model for ARs.

### 5.2 Evaluation: Result Quality of ARs for a Single Run

Because of the reasons outlined in Section 3, it is generally not possible to analytically calculate how close the found solution is to the actual absolute optimum. However, we have manually calculated the absolute optimum for a feasible case, namely an optimization for duration only on an empty system, with the client being fixed to Client-C. The absolute achievable optimum in this case is 12597 seconds (approximately 3.5 hours). Figure 7 graphically shows how the algorithm evolved in 5 test runs, while Table 2 presents a more detailed analysis of 100 runs.

Figure 8 shows the CPU reservations that one of those runs has made at different providers. Note that at the beginning of the process, there are indeed overlapping boxes, representing parallel execution of activities on multiple hosts. The gaps between the shown reservations correspond to data transfers (we have

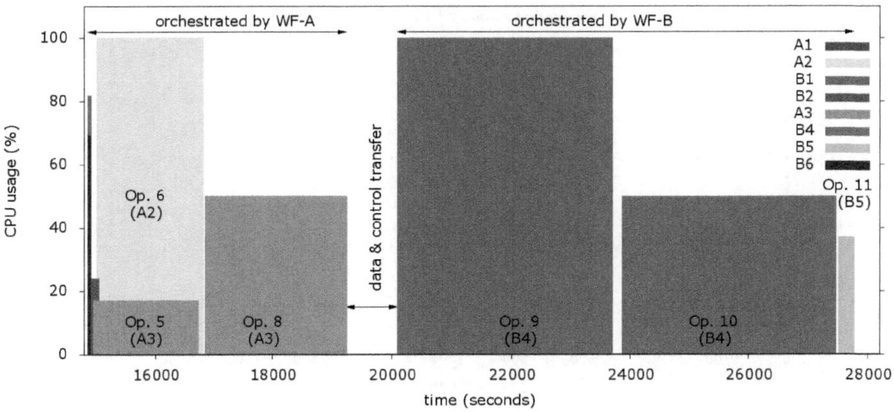


**Fig. 8.** Combined Usages of one single Process

not depicted bandwidth reservations, as those would clutter the figure). Finally, it is worth mentioning that the workflow is scheduled to be run by two different workflow engines: Activities 1 through 8 are executed by WF-A, then control (and data) is handed over to WF-B for executing activities 9 through 11. This is one example of how multiple engines may leverage network locality to the target providers.

### 5.3 Evaluation of Resource Allocations after 50 Runs

Of the 50 planning runs, two did not achieve the required QoS criteria; both were optimizations for duration, with a minimal possible budget that was set too low. All other runs were successfully finished and made the resulting reservations in the system.

Figure 9 shows the evolution of cost and duration for one sample workflow scheduling. In this case, the goal was to optimize for cost, while keeping the duration of the process under a given deadline (120,000 seconds, which is roughly 10 times higher than the minimum that can be achieved when scheduling a single run on an empty system). The convergence rate of the criteria to be optimized is similar to the ones shown in Figure 7. Since cost is the primary optimization goal (which is achieved by using fewer resources and thus "traded" for runtime), and because resources are already partly allocated by previous runs, the duration is significantly higher than in the case depicted in Figure 7. In fact, the duration generally stays close to the deadline, as this allows to achieve the best cost.

As each successfully scheduled workflow reserves resources, the initially unallocated infrastructure is gradually getting filled. Figures 10 shows how the reservations of CPU at hosts B4 and B3 are evolving as new workflows are scheduled. The graphs are simple three-dimensional extrusions of the resource representation shown in Figure 3, where the added dimension (towards the "back" of the graph) is the number of already scheduled workflows.

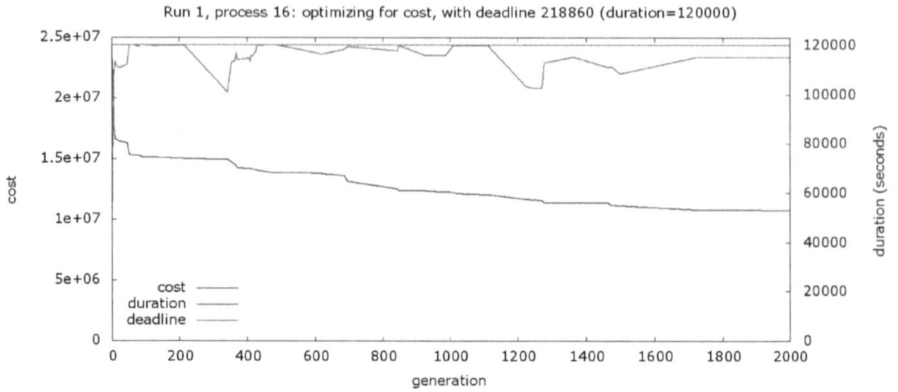


**Fig. 9.** Sample Process Optimization: Evolution of Cost and Duration

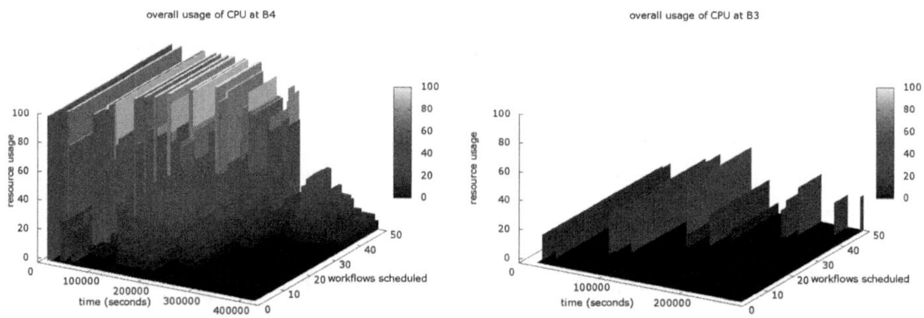


**Fig. 10.** CPU Reservations of Hosts B4 and B3 during Evaluation Run

We have chosen to present these two hosts because they exhibit an interesting case: B4 is much more heavily loaded than B3. The explanation lies in the setup of the infrastructure: B4 provides the fastest available alternative for the (long-running) operations 9 and 10, whereas B3 is slow. B3 is thus being used mostly by processes which prefer a cheap execution – which in turn means that even the slow CPU is not used up to its capacity –, or as an emergency alternative when all faster alternatives are booked out for so long that the slow host becomes the fastest available one.

### 5.4 Performance Evaluation

The experiment was run on a normal modern laptop. Each optimization run evolved a population of 32 individuals over 2000 generations. All runs took about 35 ms to evolve one generation, resulting in a total runtime of around 70 seconds per optimization.

Since the biggest share of the complexity of the calculations is in finding possible co-allocations, we also decided to evaluate a worst-case scenario, in which all clients (all 50 runs) would want to start the workflow at the same time, optimizing for duration only. This naturally results in the system usage rapidly evolving towards a state where almost all resources are fully loaded almost all of the time. This in turn means that finding "free spots" for allocations should take longer and longer with every scheduled workflow. Our measurements have confirmed this expectation: the worst-case behaviour shows a relatively linear increase in the time required for planning that starts at the 6th schedule attempt – i.e., once the infrastructure is "booked out" by the previously scheduled processes. The 50th run took around 11 minutes, i.e., 10 times longer than the average.

The AR approach presented in this paper explicitly addresses complex, long-running Scientific Workflows. For clients of these workflows, planning and advance reservation is a significant qualitative benefit that leads to predictable executions. In particular, due to the long execution time of a single workflow instance, the planning phase itself is not considered time-critical, and an overhead of several seconds up to a few minutes seem absolutely acceptable – especially since in the worst-case scenario with longest planning time due to already booked resources, possible allocations – and thus possible execution times – will be delayed anyhow (e.g., since a workflow cannot be started immediately due to lack of resources).

## 6 Related Work

Scientific Workflows have received considerable attention in the last years; this has among others resulted in complete production-ready systems like Kepler [13], Taverna [15], JOpera [16], Trident [19], VIEW [12] or VisTrails [7]. While they provide sophisticated support for the execution of Scientific Workflows or for analyzing the provenance of workflow results, none of them address the predictability of the execution.

To provide such predictability, several proposals have been made. For instance, [3] shows how QoS criteria for a workflow can be computed based on attributes of the contained services; in contrast to DWARFS, it does not attempt to actually enforce those criteria. In fact, most of the research to give QoS guarantees comes from the related field of Grid computing: [6] and [20] propose using ARs for pre-allocating resources to Grid jobs. The GridCC project presents an approach that combines workflow execution with Advance Reservations [9]; our work differs in one important aspect: whereas in Grid environments, the user is supposed to know the resources that are required, we argue that in a truely service-oriented architecture, this is dynamic information that differs between – and must be obtained from – the service providers.

The actual optimization problem we presented is closely related to classical scheduling problems. Many publications have demonstrated that GAs are indeed an effective approach to solving scheduling problems at various levels of complexity, e.g., for scheduling jobs for multiprocessor systems [10] or in the Grid [8]. The work presented in [2], similarly to our proposal, uses GAs to find optimal workflow schedules according to QoS criteria; however, they do not explicitly consider the involvement of (limited) resources. Conversely, [18] presents how GAs can be used to schedule scientific workflows in an ASKALON Grid environment. Resource availability is taken into account by migrating tasks at runtime if resource shortage occurs, whereas DWARFS explicitly addresses the limitation of resources at planning time by using Advance Reservations, in an attempt to limit such rescheduling operations.

## 7 Conclusion and Future Work

In this paper, we have presented the DWARFS approach that employs Advance Resource Reservations to enable the predictable execution of Scientific Workflows with user-definable QoS criteria. Based on the providers' specifications of the resources needed for executing the operations they offer, DWARFS supports the definition and usage of reservations. To that end, we have devised a Genetic Algorithm that can be used to find near-optimal combinations of the required resource allocations to meet the requested QoS, and provided an evaluation of its qualitative and quantitative performance.

Our current and future work includes some further improvement of the GA implementation, with the two main topics being the addition of a crossover operator (which may increase the convergence rate), and an exploration of possible performance improvements in situations where the infrastructure is heavily loaded. While this optimization phase results in a plan of resource reservations to be made, the actual integration of these reservations with the SOA (i.e., the providers), using the WS-Agreement protocol, lacks an implementation and is part of our future work, as is the integration with the actual execution and enforcement of the resource reservations. We also plan to include more sophisticated strategies for shipping data within the workflow, and partial re-planning and re-negotiation of reservations during the execution of a workflow. The latter is of high practical relevance when, for instance, a provider fails to meet the QoS level that it committed to.

## References

1. Affenzeller, M., Winkler, S., Wagner, S., Beham, A.: Genetic Algorithms and Genetic Programming: Modern Concepts and Practical Applications (Numerical Insights). Chapman & Hall, Boca Raton (2009)
2. Canfora, G., Di Penta, M., Esposito, R., Villani, M.L.: An approach for QoS-aware service composition based on genetic algorithms. In: GECCO 2005: Proceedings of the 2005 conference on Genetic and evolutionary computation (2005)
3. Cardoso, J., Sheth, A., Miller, J., et al.: Quality of Service for Workflows and Web Service Processes. J. Web Sem. 1(3), 281–308 (2004)
4. Collette, Y., Siarry, P.: Multiobjective Optimization: Principles and Case Studies (Decision Engineering). Springer, Heidelberg (2004)
5. Droegemeier, K., et al.: Service-Oriented Environments for Dynamically Interacting with Mesoscale Weather. Computing in Science and Eng. 7(6), 12–29 (2005)
6. Foster, I., Kesselman, C., Lee, C., et al.: A Distributed Resource Management Architecture that supports Advance Reservations and Co-Allocation. In: Proceedings of the International Workshop on Quality of Service, pp. 27–36 (1999)

7. Freire, J., Silva, C., Callahan, S., et al.: Managing Rapidly-Evolving Scientific Workflows. In: Int'l Provenance and Annotation Workshop, pp. 10–18 (2006)
8. Gao, Y., Rong, H., Huang, J.Z.: Adaptive grid job scheduling with genetic algorithms. Future Gener. Comput. Syst. 21(1), 151–161 (2005)
9. Guo, L., McGough, A., Akram, A., et al.: QoS for Service Based Workflow on Grid. In: UK 2007 e-Science All Hands Meeting (August 2007)
10. Hou, E.S.H., Ansari, N., Ren, H.: A genetic algorithm for multiprocessor scheduling. IEEE Trans. Parallel Distrib. Syst. 5(2), 113–120 (1994)
11. Langguth, C., Ranaldi, P., Schuldt, H.: Towards Quality of Service in Scientific Workflows by using Advance Resource Reservations. In: IEEE 2009 Third International Workshop on Scientific Workflows, SWF 2009 (2009)
12. Lin, C., Lu, S., Lai, Z., et al.: Service-Oriented Architecture for VIEW: A Visual Scientific Workflow Management System. In: IEEE SCC, pp. 335–342 (2008)
13. Ludäscher, B., Altintas, I., Berkley, C., et al.: Scientific workflow management and the Kepler system. In: Concurrency and Computation: Practice and Experience (2006)
14. Meffert, K., et al.: Java Genetic Algorithms Package, `http://jgap.sourceforge.net`
15. Oinn, T., Greenwood, R., Addis, M., et al.: Taverna: Lessons in Creating a Workflow Environment for the Life Sciences. Concurrency and Computation: Practice and Experience 18(10), 1067–1100 (2006)
16. Pautasso, C., Heinis, T., Alonso, G.: JOpera: Autonomic Service Orchestration. IEEE Data Eng. Bull. 29(3), 32–39 (2006)
17. Plale, B.: Workload Characterization and Analysis of Storage and Bandwidth Needs of LEAD Workspace. In: Linked Environments for Atmospheric Discovery (2007)
18. Prodan, R., Fahringer, T.: Dynamic scheduling of scientific workflow applications on the grid: a case study. In: SAC 2005: Proceedings of the 2005 ACM symposium on Applied computing, pp. 687–694. ACM, New York (2005)
19. RogerBarga, Fay, D., Guo, D., et al.: Efficient Scheduling of Scientific Workflows in a High Performance Computing Cluster. In: Proc. CLADE, pp. 63–68 (2008)
20. Siddiqui, M., Villazón, A., Fahringer, T.: Grid Allocation and Reservation - Grid Capacity Planning with Negotiation-based Advance Reservation for Optimized QoS. In: Supercomputing, p. 103 (2006)
21. Simmhan, Y.L., Plale, B., Gannon, D.: A Framework for Collecting Provenance in Data-Centric Scientific Workflows. In: ICWS 2006: Proceedings of the IEEE International Conference on Web Services (2006)

# A Fault-Tolerance Architecture for Kepler-Based Distributed Scientific Workflows

Pierre Mouallem[1], Daniel Crawl[2], Ilkay Altintas[2], Mladen Vouk[1], and Ustun Yildiz[3]

[1] North Carolina State University, 890 Oval Drive, Raleigh NC 27695
{pmouall,vouk}@ncsu.edu
[2] San Diego Supercomputer Center, University of California San Diego, 9500 Gilman Drive, La Jolla, CA 92093
{crawl,altintas}@sdsc.edu
[3] University of California Davis, 1 Shields Ave, Davis, CA 95616
yildiz@cs.ucdavis.edu

**Abstract.** Fault-tolerance and failure recovery in scientific workflows is still a relatively young topic. The work done in the domain so far mostly applies classic fault-tolerance mechanisms, such as "alternative versions" and "checkpointing", to scientific workflows. Often scientific workflow systems simply rely on the fault-tolerance capabilities provided by their third party subcomponents such as schedulers, Grid resources, or the underlying operating systems. When failures occur at the underlying layers, a workflow system typically sees them only as failed steps in the process without additional detail and the ability of the system to recover from those failures may be limited. In this paper, we present an architecture that tries to address this for Kepler-based scientific workflows by providing more information about failures and faults we have observed, and through a supporting implementation of more comprehensive failure coverage and recovery options. We discuss our framework in the context of the failures observed in two production-level Kepler-based workflows, specifically XGC and S3D. The framework is divided into three major components: (i) a general contingency Kepler actor that provides a recovery block functionality at the workflow level, (ii) an external monitoring module that tracks the underlying workflow components, and monitors the overall health of the workflow execution, and (iii) a checkpointing mechanism that provides smart resume capabilities for cases in which an unrecoverable error occurs. This framework takes advantage of the provenance data collected by the Kepler-based workflows to detect failures and help in fault-tolerance decision making.

**Keywords:** Scientific Workflows, Fault-tolerance, Distributed Computation, Scientific Data Management.

## 1 Introduction

Scientific Workflow Management Systems *(S-WfMS)* have proven to be a valuable tool in designing and managing scientific simulations as well as integrating data analysis and visualizations [1]. As workflows become more complex, they also

M. Gertz and B. Ludäscher (Eds.): SSDBM 2010, LNCS 6187, pp. 452–460, 2010.

become more vulnerable to internal and external failures. In tun, this calls for fault-tolerance during workflow execution [2].

Classical fault-tolerance solutions can operate well in the context of modern scientific workflow systems, e.g., Pegasus [3]. However, some limitations arise from the nature of the scientific workflow engines, characteristics of workflow models, and the failure rates and bounds that an application domain is willing to tolerate. Scientific workflows may include long-running, loosely coupled and repetitive computational steps that require the tolerance of failures during run-time with minimal impact on the overall execution. Fault-tolerance approaches to scientific workflows should provide run-time failure avoidance and/or mitigation within workflow models and at different levels of an execution infrastructure. They also should be able to adapt to workflow evolution and to changes in its operational environments.

In this paper, we discuss fault-tolerance (FT) challenges observed for some of the high-end scientific workflows studied by the Scientific Process Automation group (SPA) of the Department of Energy (DOE) Scientific Data Management Center (SDM) [4]. The workflows, and FT framework we are discussing, are implemented using the Kepler workflow management system [5]. The ultimate goal of the FT framework is to provide an appropriate end-to-end support for detecting and recovering from failures during execution of scientific workflows.

We organized the remainder of the paper as follows. In Section 2, we discuss two typical simulation workflows and analyze their vulnerabilities. In Section 3, we show a classification of failures arising in the context of these two use-cases. Section 4 presents our FT framework that addresses the issues we have identified; we also discuss the advantages and limitations of our solutions. In Section 5, we discuss some of the related work, and finally Section 6 concludes the paper and discusses future work.

## 2 Use Cases: XGC and S3D Workflows

XGC [6] and S3D [7] are numerical simulation codes that scientists at the Oak Ridge National Laboratory and Sandia National Laboratory use to study fusion plasma effects and combustion phenomena, respectively. Kepler-based workflows, e.g., [8], have been developed for both automating the processing steps involved in deploying these codes on supercomputers and analyzing the outcomes of the runs.

Both workflows are part of a family of workflows involving similar steps known as *deployment* and *monitoring* workflows. After computational codes have been launched on a supercomputer, these workflows monitor and manage outputs from long-running computations. Tasks include movement of data files to an analysis computer, archiving the data, and generation of visualizations based on the progress of the computations. Due to their similarity, these workflows also exhibit similar categories of failures. Below, we provide scenarios that highlight possible failures within these workflows.

In a Kepler workflow a computational step is called an actor. Actors are interconnected by communication channels through which the data flow in the form of tokens. Execution of the whole workflow is controlled by one of a number of special schedulers called *Directors*. In addition, our environment includes a provenance framework [9], and a web-based GUI called dashboard [10], both developed as part of the DOE's SDM initiative.

# 3 Failure Classification

In order to understand the problem better, we have developed a classification of run-time failures that have been observed for the previously described workflows.

Our analysis of workflow failures shows the range of issues that fault-tolerance mechanisms need to handle in our case. Based on a log analysis of more than 1000 production runs, the failures and error-states encountered are summarized in Table 1. Note that many failures, in a sense, are transparent to the workflow, and thus do not interrupt normal workflow execution; unfortunately, in that case, even if the workflow finished successfully the underlying simulation results would be invalid.

The problems listed in Table 1 can be classified based on which layer of the execution environment in which they originate. We have three execution layers: the *Workflow Layer* provides control, directs execution, and tracks the progression of the simulation; the *Middleware Layer* provides all services required for executing the simulation; and the *Hardware/OS Layer* is where the simulation codes run, data are stored, etc. A failure or an error-state occurring at one layer can propagate causing additional issues. For simplicity, we only list descriptions of what we consider was the root-cause for different failure groups shown in Table 1.

Run-time failures can be quite expensive. For XGC [6] the workflow runtime can vary between two and six hours depending on the simulation, with about 2/3 of the time being spent on supercomputers. We found that on average XGC workflows fail about 8% of the time. Wasting up to 5% of allocated supercomputing recourses is probably

**Table 1.** Root-cause analysis. Uncaught exceptions occur mostly during the early stages of the workflow; and deadlocks are usually caused by underlying faults.

| Description | Failure Frequency |
|---|---|
| Uncaught Exception | 3% |
| Deadlock | 10% |
| Missing Modules/Libraries | 3% |
| Data Movement Failure | 10% |
| Incorrect Input | 5% |
| Incorrect Output | 10% |
| Authentication Failed | 10% |
| Job Submission Failed | 5% |
| Service not Reachable / Responding | 10% |
| Machine Crash / Down | 3% |
| Network Down | 3% |
| Out of Disk Space | 3% |
| CPU time limit exceeded | 10% |
| File Not found | 10% |
| Other (Out of Memory, Job Stuck…) | ~5% |
| | 100.00% |

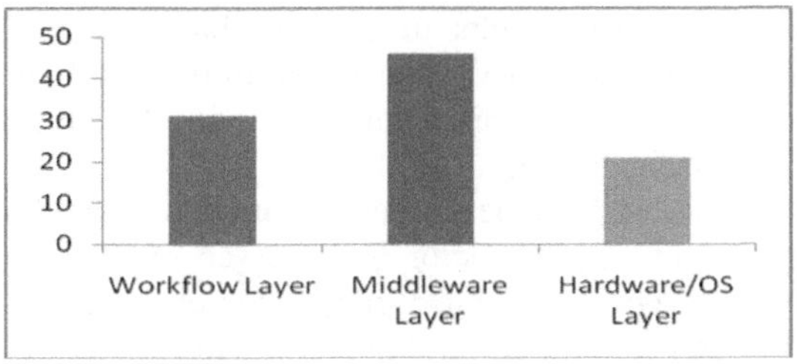


**Fig. 1.** Failure percentages by "Layer"

not good. When one considers more complex situations, such as coupled workflows [8] where one workflow controls both the simulation and the analysis, and the runtime can be as long as two days, workflow failures becomes even more of an issue.

Figure 1 provides a layer-oriented analysis of the data in Table 1. We see that nearly 70% of the originating issues occur either at the Hardware/OS layer or the Middleware layer. These error-states/failures can be difficult to detect. Also, in our experience, most of the time they do not propagate to the workflow layer in time, or with sufficient information attached, for the workflow to actively address the impact and resume execution. Therefore, workflow-level fault-tolerance mechanisms need to be supplemented with methods that actively monitor lower layers and communicates adequate information to the workflow-layer in time for a recovery action to take place.

# 4 Fault-Tolerance Framework

As already mentioned, the environment in which SDM workflows execute can be divided into three layers: The Workflow layer, the Middleware layer, and the OS/Hardware layer. The Workflow layer is the driver behind the wheel providing control, directing execution, and progress tracking. The framework we are proposing has three complementary mechanisms: a) a forward recovery mechanism that offers retries and alternative versions at the workflow level, b) a checkpointing mechanism, also at the workflow layer, that resumes the execution in case of a failure at the last saved good state, and c) an error-state and failure handling mechanisms to address issues that occur outside the scope of the Workflow layer.

## 4.1 Forward Recovery

Forward recovery mechanisms attempt to compensate for failures and keep the workflow execution going without a major externally visible interruption such as re-execution of the whole workflow. To confine failures, a system must automatically recognize error-states, for example by checking execution results for correctness. There are two main approaches to detecting error-states caused during execution: a) acceptance testing of the results via executable assertions [11], and b) use of alternate version(s) [11, 12].

Results they deliver then need to be compared to determine which one is correct, and then either the correct result is passed on to the rest of the workflow, or a "graceful" failure exit needs to be taken. The best-documented techniques and most commonly used for tolerating faults in software-based systems are the Recovery Block (RB) approach [12] and N-version programming (NVP) [13] In either case, there needs to be a decision mechanism that deals with the situation where it may not be possible to recover from a failure.

To implement our strategy, we developed a **Contingency actor**. Its early predecessor – a fault-tolerant web-services actor is discussed in [2] along with performance gains that can be achieved. The Contingency actor executes in the Workflow layer and provides an RB framework. Several sub-workflows may be associated with this actor: one sub-workflow represents the primary set of tasks to execute. When a failure occurs, this sub-workflow can be re-executed with the original inputs if we believe that the failure is a transient one, or an alternative sub-workflow can be executed instead. Furthermore, the actor may pause execution between sub-workflow executions if some other action needs to be taken.

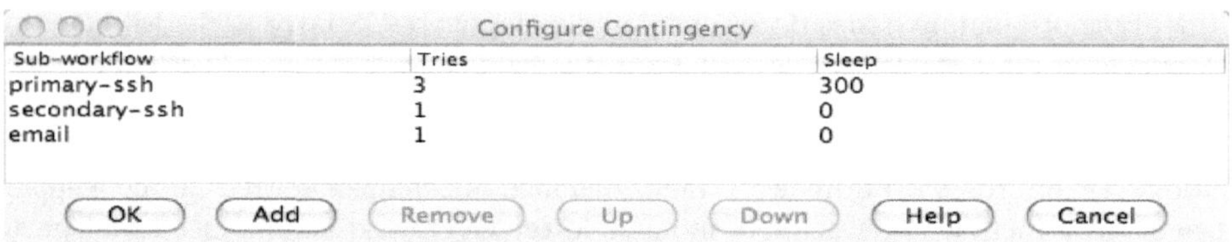


**Fig. 2.** Example Contingency configuration

Figure 2 shows an example configuration of the Contingency actor. The primary task, implemented in a sub-workflow, called "primary-ssh", is to *ssh* to a server and execute a script. When the Contingency actor receives new input from upstream actor(s) for the first time, it executes the primary sub-workflow. The user chooses the first (primary) sub-workflow to execute: it may either be the same sub-workflow each time, or the last successfully executed sub-workflow. In the previous example, "primary-ssh" should always be tried first since the script runs faster on that server. However, if this server is perhaps unreachable for a long period of time, then it may be faster to skip retrying the primary server, and (immediately) go to the secondary server. In this case, Contingency can be configured such that if "primary-ssh" fails but "secondary-ssh" succeeds, subsequent input will execute "secondary-ssh."

### 4.2 Checkpointing

Another approach for providing fault tolerance is checkpointing. Checkpointing is a widely used technique. It consists of storing a snapshot of the current application state, and using it for restarting the execution in the case of a failure [14]. There are many ways for achieving application checkpointing.

If a workflow uses checkpointing, tasks that were successfully completed before the workflow abnormally stopped may not have to be re-executed. This results in a smaller subset of the original workflow. For example, Pegasus [3] provides this capability with Rescue DAGs. However, care must be taken when deciding which successfully completed tasks do not need to be repeated. Unlike Rescue DAGs in which each task is stateless, a workflow actor may have accumulated information during the course of many invocations before the workflow stopped.

### 4.3 Watchdog Process

A watchdog process is a common tool used with computer hardware. It consists of a hardware-timing device that triggers a system reset if the main program, due to some fault condition, neglects to regularly service the watchdog (writing a "service pulse" to it) [15].

We apply this concept to Scientific Workflows and extend it. A watchdog process monitors different components used by our system and alerts the system (typically the workflow), or the end-user, when an issue is detected. We call the proposed solution shown in Figure 3 the *Error Handling Layer*, which acts like a watchdog process.

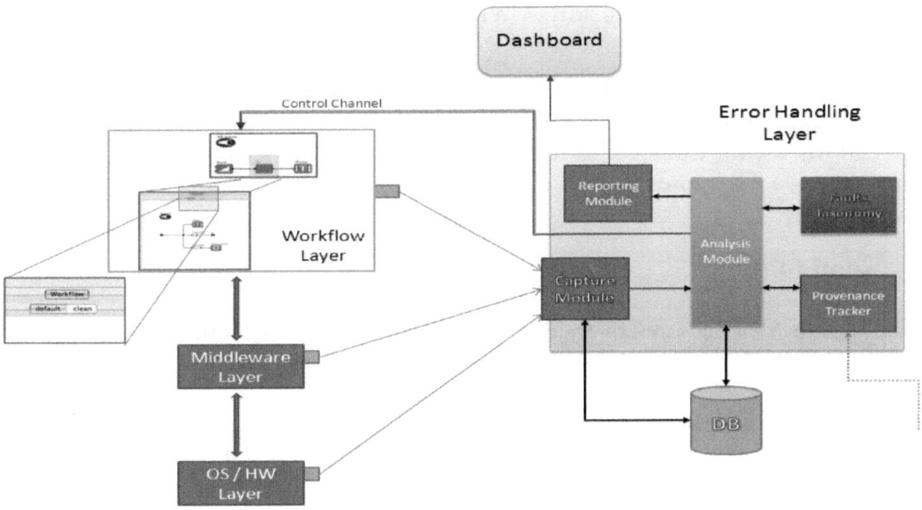


**Fig. 3.** Error Handling Layer

The *Error Handling Layer* is a module that runs separately from the normal execution environment. Its primary task is to monitor the components and processes on which the Workflow Layer depends but cannot monitor. For example, visualization applications that reside in the Middleware Layer are tracked to check their availability and serviceability. If a problem is detected, the Error Handling Layer analyzes it based on previous data, and sends an appropriate signal and possible course of action to the Workflow Layer to handle it.

The Error Handling Layer is made of several interacting components. It is designed to allow other layers to simply "plug" in without the need to modify or extend the Error Handling Layer itself. The following is a brief description of the different components and how they interact:

- ***Faults Taxonomy module:*** This module contains XML descriptions of the warnings and errors that occur in the different layers.
- ***Provenance Tracker:*** This module reads information from the provenance database [9] relating to previous runs, failures and error-states. This information is useful to determine the best way to handle an error.
- ***Capture Module:*** This module listens to the different problem reporting modules embedded in different layers, and forwards that information to the *Analysis Module* along with saving it to a database.
- ***Analysis Module:*** This is the kernel of the Error Handling Layer. It processes the errors recorded by the *Capture Module,* and based on the error taxonomy and provenance data decides on the best solution to address an issues. Once a solution is decided upon, the *Analysis Module* informs the Workflow Layer of the corrective measures that needs to be taken.
- ***Reporting Module:*** This module reports the failures, interrupts, error-states and warnings detected to the Workflow Monitoring Dashboard to allow the end-user to track the problems that are occurring during a run.

One possible extension for the architecture presented above is adding control flows from the Error Handling Layer to all other layers instead of just the workflow layer. This allows us, for example, to restart modules and components in other layers that might have become unresponsive.

## 5 Related Work

This section provides an overview of fault-tolerance capabilities of several well known S-WfMS.

**Pegasus.** Pegasus (Planning for Execution in Grids) [3] relies on Condor [16] for task scheduling and resource management, and uses DAGMan [16], as the underlying execution engine. Pegasus relies heavily on DAGMan for FT support.. It recovers from most failures with the help of DAGMan's Rescue DAG [17]. Workflow level redundancy is also used and light-weight checkpoints are supported.

**Taverna.** Fault-tolerance support in Taverna [18] is limited to retries and alternative versions [19] at both the services level and the workflow level. Several retry types are supported such as exponential back-off of retry times.

**Triana.** Support for fault tolerance in Triana [20] is generally user driven and interactive in Triana. For example, faults will generally cause workflow execution to halt, display a warning or dialog, and allow the user to modify the workflow before continuing execution. Machine crashes, network errors, missing files and deadlocks are recognized, but recovering from or preventing them is not supported.

**Other.** There are several other Scientific Workflow Management Systems, such as VisTrails [21], Escogitare [22] and Swift [23]. They present similar capabilities to other WFMS and offer partial or no fault tolerance support, and each is adapted to a particular science niche and depends on different types of infrastructure.

## 6 Conclusion and Future Work

This paper has presented a Fault-Tolerance framework for dataflow-based scientific workflows. We identified a number of failure scenarios that are not handled well, or at all, at the workflow level. We developed a hybrid fault-tolerance approach that provides fault tolerance for workflow, middleware and hardware layers of an infrastructure collectively. Although it was implemented for Kepler-based workflows, the methodology can be applied to a variety of scientific workflow management systems. The key aspect of the framework is its capability to bridge the gap between the different layers of a scientific workflow execution infrastructure by propagating sufficient information about the failures at different layers, thus allowing the workflow layer to either compensate for those failures or gracefully terminate. We plan to work on the implementation of new design primitives and patterns for different scenarios related to fault-tolerance in order to allow the modular use of the developed strategies by workflow designers.

## Acknowledgments

We would like to thank our colleagues in the SDM center for their useful input and interactions, including Norbert Podhorszki and Scott Klasky from ORNL, and Bertram Ludaescher from UC Davis. This research is funded in part by DOE grants DE-FC02-ER25809 and DE-FC02-ER25811, and by the IBM Shared University Research program.

## References

1. Taylor, I., Deelman, E., Gannon, D., Shields, M.: Workflows for e-Science (2007) ISBN: 978-1-84628-519-6
2. Vouk, M., et al.: Automation of Network-Based Scientific Workflows. In: Gaffney, P.W., Pool, J.C.T. (eds.) Grid-Based Problem Solving Environments. IFIP, vol. 239, pp. 35–61. Springer, Boston (2007)
3. Deelman, E., Singh, G., Su, M., Blythe, J., Gil, Y., Kesselman, C., Mehta, G., Vahi, K., Berriman, G., Good, J., Laity, A., Jacob, J., Katz, D.: Pegasus: A Framework for Mapping Complex Scientific Workflows onto Distributed Systems. Scientific Programming J. 13(3), 219–237 (2005)
4. Scientific Process Automation (SPA), `http://sdm.lbl.gov/sdmcenter/` (visited December 2009)
5. Kepler Project, `http://kepler-project.org/` (Visited December 2009)
6. Chang, C., Ku, S., Weitzner, H.: Numerical study of neoclassical plasma pedestal in a tokamak geometry. Phys. Plasmas 11, 2649–2667 (2004)
7. Chen, J., et al.: Terascale direct numerical simulations of turbulent combustion using S3D. Computational Science & Discovery 2(015001), 31 Pages (2009)
8. Cummings, J., et al.: Plasma Edge Kinetic-MHD Modeling in Tokamaks Using Kepler Workflow for Code Coupling, Data Management and Visualization. Communications in Computational Physics 4(3), 675–702 ISSN 1815-2406

9. Altintas, I., Barney, O., Jaeger-Frank, E.: Provenance Collection Support in the Kepler Scientific Workflow System. In: Moreau, L., Foster, I. (eds.) IPAW 2006. LNCS, vol. 4145, pp. 118–132. Springer, Heidelberg (2006)
10. Klasky, S., Barreto, R., Kahn, A., Parashar, M., Podhorszki, N., Parker, S., Silver, D., Vouk, M.: Collaborative visualization spaces for petascale simulations. In: International Symposium on Collaborative Technologies and Systems, 2008, May 2008, pp. 203–211 (2008)
11. McAllister, D.F., Vouk, M.A.: Software Fault-Tolerance Engineering. In: Handbook of Software Reliability Engineering, ch. 14, January 1996, pp. 567–614. McGraw Hill, New York (1996)
12. Randell, B.: Design-Fault Tolerance. In: The Evolution of Fault-Tolerant Computing, pp. 251–270. Springer, Vienna (1987)
13. Avizienis, A.: The N-Version Approach to Fault-Tolerant Systems. IEEE Trans. Software Engineering SE-11(12), 1491–1501 (1985)
14. Yibei, L., Jie, M., Xiaola, L.: A Variational Calculus Approach to Optimal Checkpoint Placement. IEEE Trans. Computers 50(7), 699–708 (2001)
15. Barr, M.: Introduction to Watchdog Timers, `http://www.embedded.com/story/OEG20010920S0064` (Visited January 2010)
16. Tain, D., Tannenbaum, T., Livny, M.: Distributed Computing in Practice: The Condor Experience. Concurrency and Computation: Practice and Experience 17(2-4), 323–356 (2005)
17. The Condor Project: Job Recovery with Rescue DAG, `http://www.cs.wisc.edu/condor/manual/v6.2/2_10Inter_job_Dependencies.html` (visited December 2009)
18. Oinn, T., Addis, M., Ferris, J., Marvin, D., Senger, M., Greenwood, R., Carver, T., Glover, K., Pocock, M., Wipat, A., Li, P.: Taverna: A Tool for the Composition and Enactment of Bioinformatics Workflows. Bioinformatics 20(17), 3045–3054 (2004)
19. Oinn, T., et al.: Taverna: Lessons in Creating a Workflow Environment for the Life Sciences. J. Concurrency and Computation: Practice and Experience 18(10), 1067–1100 (2002)
20. Taylor, Shields, M., Wang, I., Harrison, A.: The Triana Workflow Environment: Architecture and Applications. In: Workflows for e-Science, pp. 320–339. Springer, New York (2007)
21. Callahan, S., Freire, J., Santos, E., Scheidegger, C., Silva, C., Vo, H.: VisTrails: Visualization Meets Data Management. In: Proc. Special Interest Group on Management of Data Conf. (SIGMOD 2006), pp. 745–747 (2006)
22. Laforenza, D., et al.: Biological Experiments on the Grid: A Novel Workflow Management Platform. In: Twentieth IEEE International Symposium on Computer-Based Medical Systems (CBMS 2007), pp. 489–494 (2007)
23. Zhao, Y., et al.: Swift: Fast, Reliable, Loosely Coupled Parallel Computation. In: Proc. IEEE Int'l. Workshop Scientific Workflows (SWF 2007), pp. 199–206 (2007)

# Provenance Context Entity (PaCE): Scalable Provenance Tracking for Scientific RDF Data

Satya S. Sahoo[1], Olivier Bodenreider[2], Pascal Hitzler[1], Amit Sheth[1], and Krishnaprasad Thirunarayan[1]

[1] Kno.e.sis Center, Computer Science and Engineering Department, Wright State University, Dayton, OH, USA
[2] Lister Hill National Center for Biomedical Communications, National Library of Medicine, NIH, Bethesda, MD, USA
{sahoo.2,pascal.hitzler,amit.sheth,t.k.prasad}@wright.edu, obodenreider@mail.nih.gov

**Abstract.** The Resource Description Framework (RDF) format is being used by a large number of scientific applications to store and disseminate their datasets. The provenance information, describing the source or lineage of the datasets, is playing an increasingly significant role in ensuring data quality, computing trust value of the datasets, and ranking query results. Current provenance tracking approaches using the RDF reification vocabulary suffer from a number of known issues, including lack of formal semantics, use of blank nodes, and application-dependent interpretation of reified RDF triples. In this paper, we introduce a new approach called Provenance Context Entity (PaCE) that uses the notion of *provenance context* to create provenance-aware RDF triples. We also define the formal semantics of PaCE through a simple extension of the existing RDF(S) semantics that ensures compatibility of PaCE with existing Semantic Web tools and implementations. We have implemented the PaCE approach in the Biomedical Knowledge Repository (BKR) project at the US National Library of Medicine. The evaluations demonstrate a minimum of 49% reduction in total number of provenance-specific RDF triples generated using the PaCE approach as compared to RDF reification. In addition, performance for complex queries improves by three orders of magnitude and remains comparable to the RDF reification approach for simpler provenance queries.

**Keywords:** Provenance context entity, Biomedical knowledge repository, Context theory, RDF reification, Provenir ontology.

## 1 Introduction

An increasing number of scientific applications are storing and disseminating their datasets using the Resource Description Framework (RDF) format [1] [2] [3]. The Biomedical Knowledge Repository (BKR) project at the U.S. National Library of Medicine is creating a comprehensive repository of integrated biomedical data from a variety of sources such as biomedical literature, structured data sources (for example

M. Gertz and B. Ludäscher (Eds.): SSDBM 2010, LNCS 6187, pp. 461–470, 2010.

the NCBI Entrez system [4]), and terminological knowledge sources (for example, the Unified Medical Language System (UMLS) [5]) [6]. BKR represents the integrated information in RDF, for example, the RDF statement "`lipoprotein→affects →inflammatory_cells`"[1] was extracted by a text mining tool from a journal article (with PubMed identifier PMID: 17209178) and states that `lipoprotein` (denoted as "subject" of the RDF triple) `affects` (denoted as "property" of the triple) `inflammatory_cells` (denoted as the "object" of the triple).

In addition to the biomedical data, BKR also records and uses provenance metadata describing the history or lineage of the RDF statements. The provenance information identifies the source of an extracted RDF triple, temporal information (for example, the date of publication of a source article), version information for a database, and the confidence value associated with a triple (indicated by a text mining tool). The provenance information is essential in the BKR project to ensure the quality of data and associate trust value with an RDF triple. It has specific applications in the four services offered by the BKR namely, enhanced information retrieval (search based on the named relationship linking two entities), multi document summarization, question answering, and knowledge discovery.

The RDF reification vocabulary [7] has been traditionally used by Semantic Web applications to track provenance in RDF documents. The RDF reification vocabulary consists of the four terms `rdf:Statement`,[2] `rdf:subject`, `rdf:predicate`, and `rdf:object`. A variety of problems have been identified in the use of RDF reification vocabulary for provenance tracking in Semantic Web applications.

The RDF specification [8] states that the RDF formal semantics does not extend to the reification vocabulary, and the intended interpretation of an RDF document using reification is application dependent (i.e., it may vary across applications) [7]. Further, the RDF specification states that entailment rules do not hold between an RDF triple and its reification [8]. The use of blank nodes, which have no "global meaning" outside a particular RDF graph [8], makes it difficult to use reasoning [9] and increases the complexity of query patterns since the queries have to explicitly take into account an extra entity. In addition to the limited formal semantics, use of RDF reification approach leads to a disproportionate increase in the total size of the RDF document without corresponding enhancement in information content of the RDF document. This adversely affects the scalability of large projects, such as BKR, that track provenance of hundreds of millions of RDF triples. A detailed discussion of the limitations of RDF reification and related approaches such as RDF named graph is given in [10].

In this paper, we introduce a new approach for RDF provenance tracking called Provenance Context Entity (PaCE). PaCE is part of a broader framework for provenance management in scientific applications called PrOM [10].

### 1.1 Contributions and Overview

The contributions of this paper are three-fold:

---

[1] We use the courier new font to represent RDF and OWL statements.

[2] The rdf namespace represents the http://www.w3.org/1999/02/22-rdf-syntax-ns Internationalized Resource Identifier (IRI).

1. Define the PaCE approach to track provenance in RDF-based Semantic Web applications without use of reification vocabulary and blank nodes (Section 2),
2. Define the formal semantics of PaCE, using model theory, by extending the existing RDF and RDFS formal semantics to ensure compatibility with existing RDF tools and implementations (Section 2),
3. Demonstrate the practical feasibility of PaCE through implementation in the BKR project (Section 3), and evaluate the advantages of PaCE in terms of storage and query performance as compared to the RDF reification approach.

# 2 Foundations of Provenance Context Entity

The intuition for the PaCE approach is that the provenance associated with RDF statements provides the necessary contextual information for applications to interpret two RDF statements to be equivalent or distinct. Contexts as formal objects have long been used in Artificial Intelligence (AI) applications, such as Cyc [11] and also to a limited extent in the Semantic Web, to facilitate processing of information that do not have a global frame of reference [12]. A detailed discussion of the existing work in context theory is given in [10].

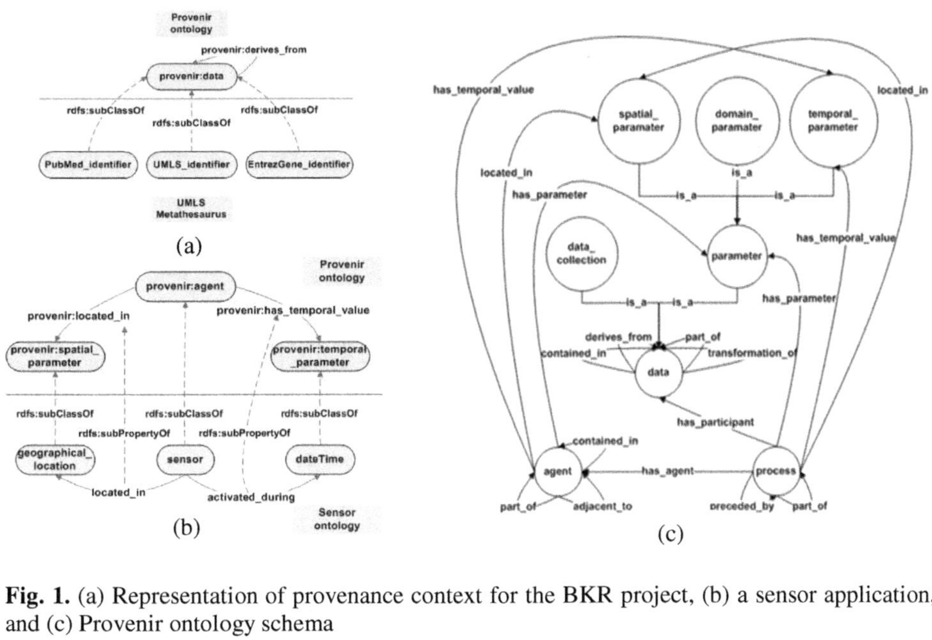


**Fig. 1.** (a) Representation of provenance context for the BKR project, (b) a sensor application, and (c) Provenir ontology schema

## 2.1 Provenance Context and RDF Generation

The contextual information in the BKR project consists of the provenance information about the source of an RDF statement, that is, the journal identifier or the UMLS identifier or the Entrez Gene identifier. In other words, this *provenance context* is a formal object instantiated in the form of set of concepts and relationships that capture the necessary contextual provenance information to enable application to correctly interpret RDF statements. Similar to the provenance context defined in the BKR project (Figure 3(a)), other Semantic Web applications can also define a relevant provenance context for interpreting their RDF dataset. For example, an application in the sensor domain can define its provenance context to consist of sensor used to collect data readings, the geographical location of the sensor, and the timestamp value associated with a data reading (Figure 3(b)). To formalize the notion of provenance context, we define it in terms of the foundational model of provenance called provenir ontology (Figure 3 (c)) [10]. The provenir ontology is a upper-level provenance ontology representing a minimum set of provenance concepts common across domains and is modeled using the description logic profile of the W3C Web Ontology Language (OWL-DL) [13].

The provenir ontology consists of three primary concepts of "`data`", "`agent`" and "`process`" linked by ten relationships adapted from the upper-level Relation Ontology [14] (Figure 3 (c)). An application can define its provenance context either in terms of the provenir ontology or in terms of a domain-specific provenance ontology, which extends provenir ontology. The use of the provenir ontology to define a provenance context has several advantages including the flexibility to model domain-specific provenance at a fine level of granularity, while ensuring consistent modeling and the support for RDF and OWL inferencing [8].

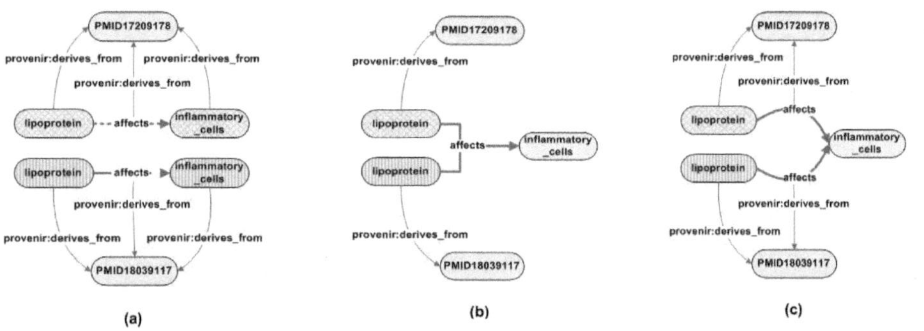


**Fig. 2.** Implementation of the PaCE mechanism to track provenance of RDF triples extracted from two journal articles

The PaCE approach allows an application to decide the level of granularity in modeling provenance of an RDF triple. For example, Figure 2 illustrates the three possible implementations of the PaCE approach in the BKR project that create distinct RDF triples extracted from two separate journal articles (though they share the same S, P, and O). The first implementation (Figure 2 (a)) is an exhaustive approach and explicitly links the S, P, and O to the source journal article and the second implementation (Figure 2 (b)) is a minimalist approach that links only the S of a RDF triple to the source article. The second implementation, on the other hand, requires the application to make additional assumption while processing the RDF triples, that the whole triple is extracted from the same source as the source of S.

The third implementation (Figure 2(c)) takes an intermediate approach that creates two additional provenance-specific triples but requires the application to assume that the source of the O is the same as the S, and the P. The choice to associate explicit "`derives_from`" property with one particular RDF component (S or P or O) in the minimalist (Figure 2 (b)) and the intermediate (Figure 2(c)) is arbitrary and has minimal impact on the provenance tracking functionality of the application.

It is important to note that, in contrast with the reification approach, none of the three variants of the PaCE approach requires the use of RDF reification vocabulary or the use of blank nodes. Further, the reification approach creates a total of six RDF triples (Figure 1) for each RDF triple, while the exhaustive implementation of the PaCE approach creates a total of four triples for one RDF triple. Overall, the PaCE approach is an incremental and simple mechanism that does not define additional vocabulary or require changes to existing RDF data stores. We now introduce the model theoretic semantics of PaCE inferencing.

## 2.2 Model Theoretic Semantics of PaCE Inferencing

The primary motivating factor for defining the formal semantics of PaCE is to provide a way to determine the validity of the inferencing process for Semantic Web applications that use the PaCE approach to track provenance. The definition of the model-theoretic semantics of PaCE is a straightforward modification of the existing RDFS semantics and allows us to infer additional provenance information for triples by virtue of having similar source. Let provenance context pc of an RDF triple $\alpha$ (= (S, P, O)) be the common object of the predicate `provenir:derives_from` associated with the triple. We define an *RDFS-PaCE-interpretation* I of a vocabulary V to be an RDFS-interpretation of the vocabulary $V \cup V_{PaCE}$ that satisfies the following additional condition (meta-rule):

- For RDF triples $\alpha = (S_1,P_1,O_1)$ and $\beta = (S_2,P_2,O_2)$, (provenance-determined) predicates $p$ and entities $v$, if $pc(\alpha) = pc(\beta)$ then $(S_1, p, v) = (S_2, p, v)$ and, $(P_1, p, v) = (P_2, p, v)$ and, $(O_1, p, v) = (O_2, p, v)$

Provenance-determined predicates and entities are specific to an application domain.

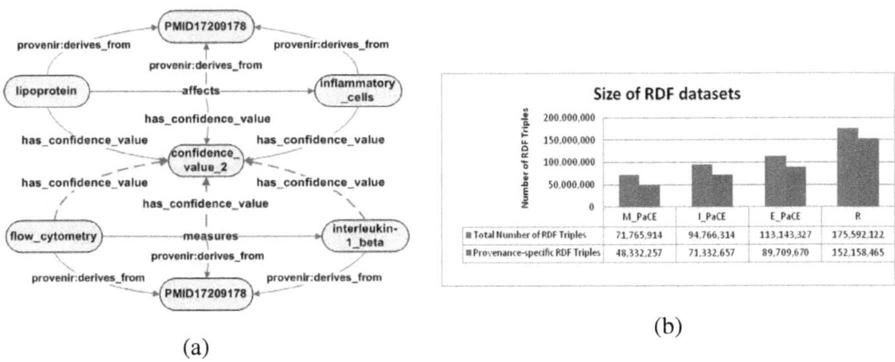


**Fig. 3.** (a) PaCE inferencing, (b) The relative number of provenance-specific triples created using PaCE and RDF reification

Furthermore, a graph $R_1$ PaCE-entails a graph $R_2$ if every *RDFS-PaCE-interpretation* that is a model of $R_1$ is also a model of $R_2$. To illustrate the PaCE inference process, we consider two RDF statements in the BKR project (Figure 3). Given that the two RDF statements have equal provenance contexts (PubMed identifier: PMID17209178) additional provenance information, such as the confidence score (formalized via provenance-related predicate `has_confidence_value` and value `confidence_value_2`), associated with one of the triples can be inferred for the other RDF triple (`flow_cytometry→measures→interleukin-1_beta`) denoted by dotted arrows in Figure 3. We note that PaCE-entailment is strictly stronger than RDFS-entailment in the sense that all inferences which can be drawn using simple, RDF, or RDFS-entailment are also PaCE entailments. This is a deliberately conservative step on top of the existing Semantic Web recommendations that enables PaCE to be compatible with existing OWL and RDF tools and applications, and also allows implementing the PaCE-semantics by making reference to RDF reasoners as black boxes. In the next section, we describe the implementation of the PaCE approach in the context of the BKR project.

## 3 Implementation and Evaluation

A practical challenge for implementing the PaCE approach in the BKR is to formulate an appropriate provenance context-based URI ($URI_p$) scheme that also conforms to best practices of creating URIs for the Semantic Web, including support for use of HTTP protocol [15]. The design principle of $URI_p$ is to incorporate a "provenance context string" as the identifying reference of an entity and is a variation of the "reference by description" approach that uses a set of description to identify an entity [15]. The syntax for $URI_p$ consists of the `<base URI>`, the `<provenance context string>`, and the `<entity name>`. This approach to create URIs for RDF entities also enables BKR (and other Semantic Web applications using the PaCE approach) to group together entities with the same provenance context. For example,

- `http://mor.nlm.nih.gov/bkr/PUBMED_17209178/lipoprotein`
- `http://mor.nlm.nih.gov/bkr/PUBMED_17209178/affects`
- `http://mor.nlm.nih.gov/bkr/PUBMED_17209178/inflammatory_cells`

are entities extracted from the same journal article. Using this URI scheme, RDF statements were generated for the original triples (extracted from the biomedical literature by a text-mining application or found in the UMLS Metathesaurus).

The base dataset (B) used in the evaluation comprises of 23,433,657 RDF triples extracted from two sources: the biomedical literature (PubMed) and the UMLS Metathesaurus. The open source Virtuoso RDF store version 06.00.3123 was used for the experiments running on a Dell 2950 server (Dual Xeon processor) with 8GB of memory. A total of 500,000 9kB buffers were allocated to Virtuoso RDF store.

### 3.1 Provenance-Specific RDF Triples

To evaluate the number of provenance-specific RDF triples generated using the two approaches, we augment the base dataset B with provenance information representing the source information of each triple. For the PaCE approach, we create three datasets representing the exhaustive (E_PaCE), minimalist (M_PaCE), and intermediate (I_PaCE) approaches illustrated in Figure 2 (a), (b) and (c), respectively. For the RDF reification dataset (R), we use the standard method (presented in Section 1). Figure 3(b) shows that the reification approach requires twice as many RDF triples (~152 million) for the representation of provenance information compared to the E_PaCE approach (~89 million). This 49% difference between E_PaCE and R represents a significant reduction in storage requirements (~85 million fewer triples) for the BKR project. Analogously, the M_PaCE and I_PaCE approaches create 72% and 59% fewer provenance-specific triples compared to the reification approach.

### 3.2 Performance of Provenance Queries

We use four representative categories of provenance queries in the BKR project to evaluate the query performance on the four datasets (E_PaCE, M_PaCE, I_PaCE and Reification). We describe the *pattern* of the four queries and their significance in the BKR project:

**Query Pattern 1:** List all the RDF triples extracted from a given journal article (e.g., journal article identified by PMID17209178). This query is used to retrieve all the triples from a given source.

**Query Pattern 2:** List all the journal articles from which a given RDF triple was extracted (e.g., `lipoprotein→affects→inflammatory_cells`). This query identifies the source(s) of a given triple.

**Query Pattern 3:** Count the number of triples in each source (biomedical literature and UMLS Metathesaurus) for the therapeutic use (predicate = treats) of a given drug (e.g., Thalidomide). This complex query illustrates the use of the BKR as a knowledge base for a query answering application (e.g., which diseases are treated by a particular drug?).

**Query Pattern 4:** Count the number of journal articles published between two dates (e.f., 2000-01-01 and 2000-12-31) for a given triple (e.g., `thalidomide → treats → multiple myeloma`). This typical information retrieval query leverages the provenance information associated with each triple. A more complex version of this query is used in Section 3.3 for time series analysis.

We conducted the query performance evaluation in two phases. In the first phase the four queries are evaluated for fixed values, namely, the value underlined in the query description above. In the second phase, queries are evaluated using a larger set of values. The queries are expressed in SPARQL syntax, the RDF query language [16]. The queries are not listed in the paper due to space constraints and are available online along with the result set.[3] The numbers reported for the "fixed" value queries (first phase) are the average of last 5 of a total of 20 runs. The first phase of the evaluation starts with a "cold" cache for each query pattern. The results in Figure 4 demonstrate that query performance for PaCE is generally better than or similar to reification. As expected, M_PaCE generally performs better than I_PaCE, and I_PaCE better than E_PaCE. However, reification performs better than I_PaCE for

[3] Query and result set available at: http://wiki.knoesis.org/index.php/ProvenanceContextEntity.

*Query 1* and better than both I_PaCE and E_PaCE for *Query 3*. *Query 4* is a complex query that uses the SPARQL FILTER to restrict publication dates to a particular range (January 1 to December 31, 2000). In this query, the query performance for E_PaCE is more than two orders of magnitude better than for R.

In the second phase of the evaluation, we aim to reflect the real-world requirements of the BKR project. Toward this end, each of the four query patterns is executed with different values, as if by different users. In practice, we use sets of 100 values for each query pattern. The resulting set of 100 queries is run 5 times (immediately following the first phase of evaluation for each dataset) and the average of the 100 queries for the last run is presented (Figure 5). The results confirm the trend seen in the first phase of evaluation, with the added observation that for *Query Pattern 3* the difference between E_PaCE and R has decreased (R no longer outperforms E_PaCE significantly). In contrast, for the complex *Query Pattern 4*, the query performance for E_PaCE has further improved and is more than three orders of magnitude better than for R. The second phase of evaluation also confirms that in a real-world scenario the query performance of PaCE is comparable to reification for simple provenance queries and significantly better for complex provenance queries. We now evaluate the query performance for an analytical query in the BKR project.

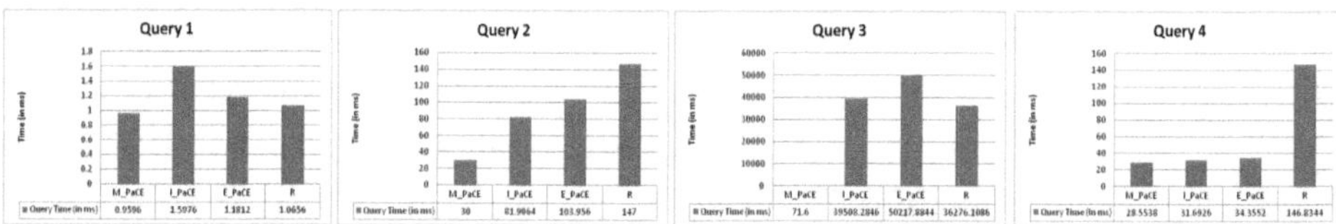


**Fig. 4.** Query performance for fixed values

**Fig. 5.** Query performance for query patterns using a set of 100 values

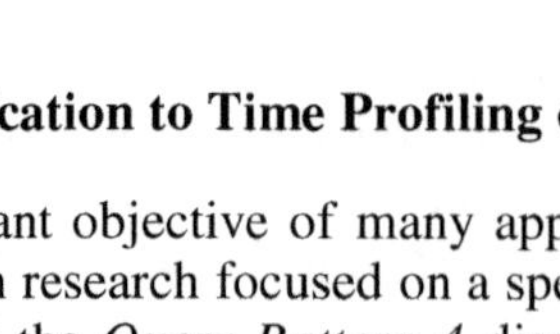


**Fig. 6.** (a)

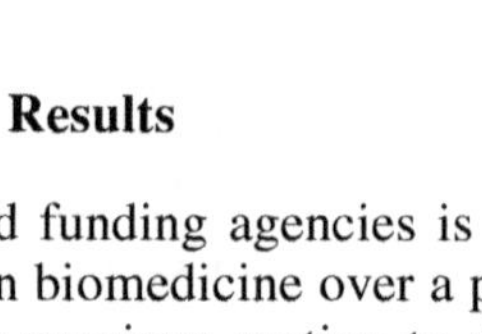


**Fig. 6.** (b)

### 3.3 Application to Time Profiling of Scientific Results

An important objective of many applications and funding agencies is to understand the trend in research focused on a specific topic in biomedicine over a period of time. We extend the *Query Pattern 4* discussed in the previous section to define a query that collates the number of journal articles published over a period of 10 years for mentions of the therapeutic use of the drug Thalidomide over time. Figure 6 (a) shows a histogram created directly from the query results. The query performance is similar to what was observed for *Query Pattern 4*, that is, E_PaCE is three orders of magnitude faster than R (Figure 6(b)). This example query demonstrates the feasibility representing and exploiting provenance information in large triple stores serving real-world applications.

## 4 Conclusion

We show that that challenge of provenance tracking in RDF datasets can be effectively and efficiently addressed by using the PaCE approach in place of the RDF reification vocabulary. The PaCE approach uses the formal objects called provenance contexts that are defined in terms of the provenir upper-level provenance ontology to create provenance-aware RDF triple. The evaluations demonstrate that using the PaCE approach to create provenance-specific RDF triples not only reduces the number of triples by at least 49% but also improves the performance of complex provenance queries by three orders of magnitude.

**Acknowledgments.** This research was supported in part by the Intramural Research Program of the NIH, U.S. NLM and NIH RO1 Grant# 1R01HL087795-01A1. The authors would like to thank Tom Rindflesch, Marcelo Fiszman, Genaro Hernandez and Ramez Ghazzaoui for their extensive help. The open source version of the Virtuoso triple store is made available by OpenLink Software.

## References

1. Protein knowledgebase: Uniprot, `http://www.uniprot.org/` (Retrieved January 10, 2010)
2. Kanehisa, M., Goto, S., Kawashima, S., Okuno, Y., Hattori, M.: The KEGG resources for deciphering the genome. Nucleic Acids Res. 32, D277–D280 (2004)
3. Reactome, `http://www.reactome.org/` (Retrieved January 10, 2010)
4. Entrez, `http://www.ncbi.nlm.nih.gov/Database/` (Retrieved January 10, 2010)
5. Bodenreider, O.: The Unified Medical Language System (UMLS): integrating biomedical terminology. Nucleic Acids Res. 32, 267–270 (2004)
6. Bodenreider, O., Rindflesch, T.C.: Advanced library services: Developing a biomedical knowledge repository to support advanced information management applications. In: Lister Hill National Center for Biomedical Communications, National Library of Medicine, Bethesda, Maryland (2006)
7. Manola, F., Miller, E. (eds.): RDF Primer. W3C Recommendation (2004)
8. Hayes, P.: RDF Semantics. W3C Recommendation (2004)
9. ter Horst, H.J.: Completeness, decidability and complexity of entailment for RDF Schema and a semantic extension involving the OWL vocabulary. Journal of Web Semantics 3, 79–115 (2005)

10. Sahoo, S.S., Barga, R.S., Sheth, A.P., Thirunarayan, K., Hitzler, P.: PrOM: A Semantic Web Framework for Provenance Management in Science. Kno.e.sis Center, Wright State University (2009)
11. Guha, R.V.: Contexts: A Formalization and Some Applications. PhD Thesis, Stanford University (1991)
12. Guha, R.V., McCarthy, J.: Varieties of Contexts. In: Blackburn, P., Ghidini, C., Turner, R.M., Giunchiglia, F. (eds.) CONTEXT 2003. LNCS, vol. 2680, pp. 164–177. Springer, Heidelberg (2003)
13. Hitzler, P., Krötzsch, M., Parsia, B., Patel-Schneider, P.F., Rudolph, S.: OWL 2 Web Ontology Language Primer. W3C (2009)
14. Smith, B., Ceusters, W., Klagges, B., Kohler, J., Kumar, A., Lomax, J., Mungall, C., Neuhaus, F., Rector, A.L., Rosse, C.: Relations in biomedical ontologies. Genome Biol. 6, R46 (2005)
15. Ayers, A., Völkel, M.: Cool URIs for the Semantic Web. In: Sauermann, L., Cyganiak, R. (eds.) Woking Draft. W3C (2008)
16. Prud'hommeaux, E., Seaborne, A.: SPARQL Query Language for RDF. W3C Recommendation (2008)

# Taverna, Reloaded

Paolo Missier[1], Stian Soiland-Reyes[1], Stuart Owen[1],
Wei Tan[2], Alexandra Nenadic[1], Ian Dunlop[1], Alan Williams[1],
Tom Oinn[3], and Carole Goble[1]

[1] School of Computer Science, The University of Manchester, UK
[2] Mathematics and Computer Science Division,
Argonne National Laboratory, Argonne., IL., USA
[3] European Bioinformatics Institute, UK

**Abstract.** The Taverna workflow management system is an open source project with a history of widespread adoption within multiple experimental science communities, and a long-term ambition of effectively supporting the evolving need of those communities for complex, data-intensive, service-based experimental pipelines. This short paper describes how the recently overhauled technical architecture of Taverna addresses issues of efficiency, scalability, and extensibility, and presents performance results based on a collection of synthetic workflows, as well as a concrete case study involving a production workflow in the area of cancer research.

## 1 Introduction

Taverna [7] is a workflow language and computational model designed to support the automation of complex, service-based and data-intensive processes. Although Taverna has been successfully applied in domains as diverse as bioinformatics, astronomy, medical research, and music, it is perhaps best known for its application to the Life Sciences [4], where it has been used to support experimental investigation into a variety of research areas, including gene and protein sequence and structure annotation, proteomics, microarray analysis, text mining, systems biology, and more. The first version, launched in 2004 [13], has enjoyed broad adoption over the years[1], owing in part to a fairly intuitive model for service composition, and to a growing number (in the order of tens of thousands) of available services, mostly community-provided and free to use, and to Taverna's ability to invoke ad hoc scripts and Java object methods.

Taverna combines a dataflow model of computation, whereby a workflow consists of a set of processors (representing software components such as Web Services) that are connected through data dependencies links, with a functional model that accounts for collection-oriented processing. This hybrid model is designed to strike a balance between expressivity and simplicity, with the ultimate goal of empowering users, who may have only a rudimentary understanding of programming, to assemble complex workflows. While the model and its theoretical underpinnings [16] have remained largely stable over the years, the evolving

[1] In 2008 there were over 4000 active users of Taverna, for over 57,000 downloads total.

M. Gertz and B. Ludäscher (Eds.): SSDBM 2010, LNCS 6187, pp. 471–481, 2010.

requirements of e-science applications have recently prompted a radical re-design of the architecture, which we will refer to as "Taverna 2" (T2 for short) to distinguish it from the previous version, T1.x.

This paper presents the salient features of the new architecture[2]. The new architecture has two main goals. Firstly, to improve the scalability of workflow execution, both in terms of data volume and execution times, over its predecessor. Secondly, to provide third-party developers with clear configuration points for performance tuning, and with extensibility points for adding new high-level constructs, such as a while-loop, to the dataflow model, in order to facilitate workflow design in paradigmatic scenarios. More specifically, the following architectural requirements have inspired the design of the T2 architecture:

*Parallelism.* Models of computation that combine dataflow and functional models are known to facilitate parallel execution [10], making the exploitation of the parallelism provided implicitly by the workflow specification a realistic goal. Potential parallelism can be found both amongst processors (*inter-processor*), by statically determining data dependencies amongst processors in the dataflow graph, as well as amongst multiple invocations of the same processors (*intra-processor* data parallelism), i.e., on individual elements of an input collection.

*Configurability.* Each processor may have different operational requirements, for example regarding its tolerance to transient error conditions in the underlying service invocation. Thus, it should be possible to fine-tune the behaviour of each processor independently from that of the others.

*Openness.* It should be possible for third party contributors to extend the functionality of the execution model in a principled way. For example, interacting with asynchronous services that require periodic polling to check on result availability, does not fit the data-driven model well. While in T1.x the model can be "stretched" to simulate polling processors, T2 accommodates this requirement by implementing a limited form of while-loop construct by exploiting a generic extensibility mechanism, called the *dispatch stack*.

*Separation of data and process spaces.* For data-centric computing to scale to arbitrary data volumes, the data space should be managed separately from the process space, and, whenever possible, data should be passed from one processor to the next by reference rather than by value.

This paper describes how the design principles listed above have been translated into a coherent architectural design for T2, and presents performance results for the current implementation.

Workflow modelling for data-intensive scientific applications is, of course, not new. One of the recognized challenges of scientific workflow management systems is to provide abstract modelling constructs that are then automatically instantiated as an orchestration of concrete tasks that execute on an underlying

[2] More details can be found in a complete techreport, available online at `http://bit.ly/9RglCZ`

parallel architecture [2,6]. This is the approach taken for example by the Pegasus system [3], with the goal of decoupling the logical specification of the workflow from the pool of resources required to execute it. In this paradigm, resources are allocated by the scheduler incrementally and dynamically. In a similar fashion, Chimera [5] provides a dedicated language (VDL) for the partial specification of logical workflows. A complementary, bottom up approach, is to start with a job management system, like Condotr, and then provide users with a model for building complex workflows from a pool of individual jobs [1]. Another example of concrete and well-known mechanism used for the specification of complex dataflows is *shell pipes*, proposed in [19].

In Sec. 2 we briefly present the dataflow computation model that underpins parallel and pipelined workflow computation, describe the configurable and extensible processor execution model, and present the main architectural solutions for parallelism. Sec. 3 provides performance figures for the current implementation, and finally in Sec. 4 we present the architecture in action on a concrete case study from the caGrid project.

## 2 Workflow Processing Model and Architecture

We now describe some of the architectural solutions used to realize the principles enunciated in the introduction. The overview architectural diagram is shown in Fig. 1.

A Taverna workflow, described in detail in [16] is specified by a directed graph where nodes, called *processors*, represent software components, typically Web Services or local scripts. A processor node consumes data that arrives on its *input ports* and produces data on its *output ports*. Each arc in the graph connects a pair of ports, and denotes a data dependency from the output port of the *source* processor to the input port of the *sink* processor. In this model, data items are either of a simple type (string, number, etc.), or are lists of items, nested to arbitrary levels.

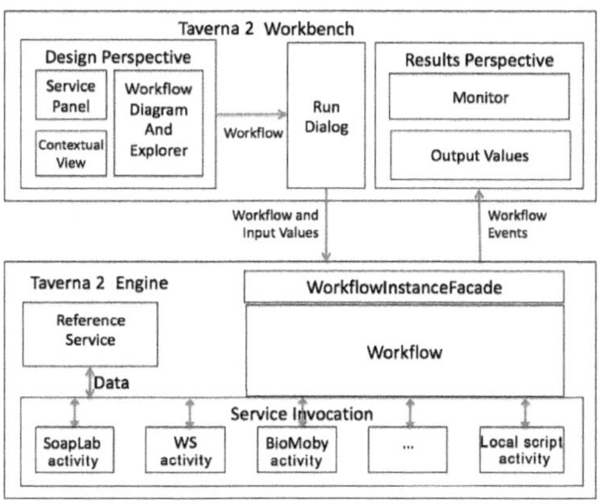


**Fig. 1.** Overview block diagram of Taverna 2 architecture

Conceptually, a workflow computation proceeds by pushing data through the directed data links from one processor to all of its successors, starting with the items that are presented on the workflow inputs. A processor is ready to execute when all of its inputs ports are populated with a data item. A processor's execution consists of the invocation of an associated *activity*, for example a Web Service or a local script, and produces new data items on its output ports. These are then propagated along the outgoing arcs.

A workflow specification is compiled into a multi-threaded object model (implemented in Java), where processors are represented by objects, and data transfers from output to input ports of downstream processor objects are realized using local method invocations between objects. Data-driven computation is realised by mapping each processor to an object, which independently starts its own execution in a separate thread, as soon as all of its (connected) input ports are populated with a data item, and it transfers its output along the arcs upon completion.

In T2, data elements are only loaded into the execution process space on demand, when required by some processor's input port, and are swapped out again to a separate persistent storage when they are no longer needed. Thus, while the same data may be transferred back and forth from storage multiple times, the total amount of main memory required by an execution is bounded. The max memory footprint is determined by the size of each data item and the number of concurrent threads that require in-memory data at any given time. As shown in the use case presented in Sec. 4, the max number of active threads, a parameter that can be configured independently for each processor, can be used to control the total amount of memory required.

Such separation of the data from the workflow execution space is achieved by registering all values that are produced during a computation with a new Data Manager (DM). The DM's main function is to index the values by assigning to them a unique data reference (a URI) and store them into a database, from where a processor that requires the values as part of its input can retrieve them using the reference.

### 2.1 Configurable Processing

The exact sequence of operations that occurs upon invocation of an activity associated to a processor is configurable, making for a flexible and extensible workflow execution model. The *interceptor* design pattern is used to configure each individual processor. Specifically, a *dispatch stack* consisting of an extensible set of *layers* is associated to each processor. Each layer is responsible for a particular feature, typically associated with Quality of Service. In the standard configuration, the stack consists of the following layers, as shown in Fig. 2(a):

**Parallelise:** this layer ensures that, when iterations over lists are involved, independent concurrent threads are created to process each list element;

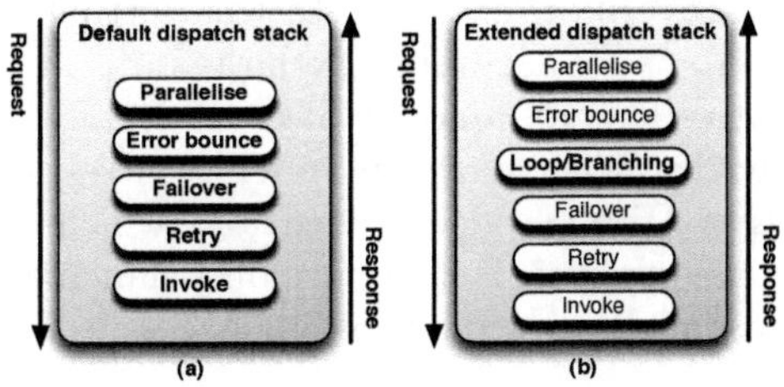


**Fig. 2.** Processor dispatch stack

**Error Bounce:** is responsible for immediately terminating an execution when any of the inputs are in an error state. This protects the underlying activities from being invoked on invalid input;

**Failover:** detects the failure of an activity associated to the processor, and is responsible for selecting an alternate activity, if available (recall that activities can be added and removed dynamically);

**Retry:** provides tolerance to transient errors in the underlying activity, by repeatedly attempting the same invocation for a configurable number of times.

Each of these layers exposes a set of configuration parameters to the workflow designer. The stack is activated by a request message to the processor, consisting of the data on the input ports. The message is pushed down the stack, where each layer performs its function and, if needed, forwards a new version of the request to the next layer. At the bottom of the stack, the *Invoke* layer performs the actual invocation of an activity; in the case of a Web Service invocation, for instance, this layer is a Web Service client that maps the incoming request to a SOAP message, and manages the interaction with the service. The result is mapped to a response message, which finds its way back up along the stack, where it is intercepted by each layer, possibly transformed, and forwarded. Ultimately, the processor invocation terminates and the response is forwarded to downstream processors along the data links.

In this architecture, a private instance of the dispatch stack is associated to each processor, making it configurable independently of the others. Also, the interceptor pattern naturally allows new layers to be added to the standard stack shown in Fig. 2(a). Useful additional layers that are already available as part of the current release include the *while-loop* layer, shown in Fig. 2(b), as well a *Provenance layer*, designed to generate audit events from the processor's execution as a basis for collecting workflow provenance [12].

## 2.2 Parallelism and Pipelining

The majority of Taverna workflows, for the most part in the bioinformatics domain, are rather more data-intensive than compute-intensive. Typically, these workflows perform some form of "on-the-fly data integraton" on large collections of data values retrieved from a variety of databases through their Web service interfaces, exposed as Taverna processors. In this setting, each of the available parallel threads tends to carry a potentially large data item, such as an image, while involving a relatively small amount of computation. Thus, in general the workflow engine has to deal with a large number of intra-processor threads, each typically representing a Web Service invocation, which is likely to dominate the execution time. The emphasis is therefore on balancing the amount of intra- and inter-processore parallelism, while avoiding excessive load on the third-party services.

Inter-processor parallelism, which is available for processors that have no data dependency amongst them, is achieved by letting those processors begin execution in a new thread as soon as they receive their input data. The stack execution model also ensures intra-processor parallelism, by exploiting a model of *implicit iteration on collections*. The model is described extensively in [16]. Briefly, when a list value appears on a port where a simple type is expected, each element of the list is processed independently from the others[3]. This is a case of SPMD parallel processing [8], where the same function is applied concurrently to multiple data elements, and potentially results in multiple independent pipelines (see also the "Multiple instances with a priori runtime knowledge" pattern described in [17]), and is achieved in T2 by having the *Parallelise* layer allocate one thread to each element in the input collection, with an appropriate setting for the max number of threads. Since this layer is at the top of the stack, this has the effect of activating the processor on multiple concurrent requests (which may succeed or fail independently of one another). The collection of all the corresponding responses is then collated into a new output list, which is forwarded to the next processor. Since the requests may be served at different speeds, the elements of the response collection may be produced in arbitrary order. The *Parallelise* layer deals with this by simply waiting for the last element to arrive, before emitting the entire output list, with its order preserved. Additionally, however, a chain of processors which both iterate on their inputs, say P1 and P2, provide an opportunity for pipelining, as follows. The *Parallelise* layer of P1 forwards each response element *as soon as it arrives*, without waiting for the others and regardless of its position in the collection. In P2, each such element is again independent of the rest of the list, so the *Parallelise* layer of P2 can consume it immediately as part of a new thread. When extended to a chain of iterating processors, this strategy results in multiple, parallel pipelines, where both intra- and inter-processor parallelism is maximized. Clearly, any processor that requires to see the entire input before starting its processing represents a serialization point in the pipeline.

This form of *superscalar* and *streaming* pipelining [14] provides the basis for efficiently supporting workflow processing over streams of data, i.e., sequences of discrete input elements of unbounded length that are continuously produced by a source. Biomart[4][15] is an example of a service that supplies its output in a streamed fashion.

[3] The cited paper describes a much more general model that accounts for iterations on the cross product of multiple list-valued inputs.

[4] `www.biomart.org`

## 3 Performance Evaluation

In this section we compare T2's execution times and memory usage with those of T1.x, under a variety of experimental conditions. Focusing on intra- and inter-parallelism, we have programmatically generated a test workflow for performance analysis. The workflow consists of a linear chain of processors, each of which is made to iterate over elements of an input list of varying size. This simple workflow is sufficient to test the effect of both intra-processor parallelism, i.e., concurrent processing of the list elements, and pipelining through the chain of processors, as explained in Sec. 2.2. We have used this workflow to assess the execution times and memory usage for both T1.x and T2, with varying length of the input list and sizes of the list elements (strings). All experiments were conducted using a Taverna workbench running on a Java 6 JVM on a PC with 2GB of RAM and 2.3GhZ dual core processor. The workflows and source code used for all measurement are publicly available[5]. All processors invoke the same *echo* remote Web service, deployed on a concurrent server on a dual core machine on the same local network.

The experiments support the intuition that, when the workflow is structured in a way that makes pipelining available, T2 exploits it effectively, at the cost of an increase in memory usage, while T1.x must rely solely on intra-processor parallelism. Furthermore, the T2 Data Manager with a database back-end (as opposed to an in-memory data model) make the engine scalable over large data inputs. In the rest of the section we analyse these results in detail.

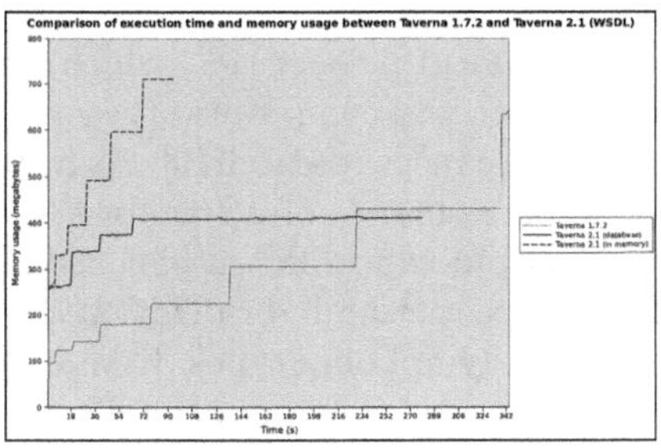


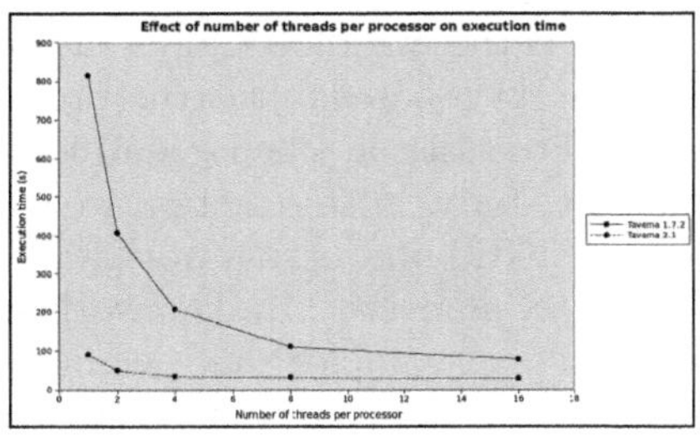


**Fig. 3.** Comparison of memory usage and execution times between T1.X and T2 with varying thread limits

Fig. 3 compares the T1.x memory usage with that of T2 in two Data Manager configurations, namely (a) using a database (embedded Derby) or (b) in-memory data (in the latter, intermediate values are kept in memory throughout the entire execution). For these measurements, the workflow iterates over a list of 1,000 strings, each 10,000 characters in length, using 1 thread for each processor. The charts illustrate the trade-off between overall parallelism and memory usage. In

[5] `http://code.google.com/p/ws-menagerie/`

particular, configuration T2(a) provides a "safe" option in that it guarantees bounded memory usage, at the cost of increased execution time over the faster T2(b). The shorter execution time of T2 over T1.x is due to pipelining, which is not available in T1. In this case, although each processor runs a single thread, each processor in the chain is activated as soon as the previous processor has produced *one element* of the output list. Thus, up to 10 concurrent threads exist in the system, each requiring a string to be loaded into memory. In T1, however, setting the max number of threads to 1 results in a serial computation through the entire chain.

Next, varying the max thread setting on each processor when comparing T1.x vs T2 reveals the impact of inter-processor parallelism, available only in T2, on overall memory usage and execution times. This is illustrated in Fig. 3, where the times are measured across different settings of the max number of threads. The plot for T2 suggests that, for this test workflow, this setting is not as critical as it is in T1.x. One reason is that, even with a small number of threads available for intra-processor parallelism, in T2 pipelining provides substantial inter-processor parallelism, resulting in lower overall execution times. A similar performance in T1.x requires 16 threads per processor or more.

Finally, Fig. 4 confirms that the T2 Data Manager ensures bounded memory usage that scales well with the size of the input and intermediate values. Not only does memory allocation stabilizes as the execution progresses, but, importantly, this is true across a range of data sizes that vary by an order of magnitude.

## 4 Case Study: Performance of a caGrid Workflow

Taverna is the workflow model of choice for the caGrid project [18], which provides a service-based infrastructure consisting of data and computation resources designed to assist in-silico scientific investigation in cancer research [9]. As a specific case study, in this section we compare the performance of T2 against T1.x using a caGrid production workflow[6] used to carry out cancer diagnosis based on microarray analysis [11]. The workflow begins by extracting hybridization data, obtained from samples that belong to two different lymphoma types, from a microarray database. The data is then normalized and used to learn a classification model for lymphoma type prediction, using the Support Vector Machine (SVM) and K-Nearest Neighbour (KNN) algorithms. The model can then be used to classify lymphoma types from an unknown microarray dataset.

Our observations confirm the insight provided by the results presented in the previous section, regarding the time/memory trade-off available in T2. Specifically, Fig. 5 shows similar execution times (380sec. for T1.x and 450sec for T2 with a similar total number of threads, 40 vs 47), but better memory management for T2. The main difference between the two execution models is that T2 resolves references to microarray datasets, each about 10MB in size, on demand, transferring them from disk to process space and flushing them after use.

[6] The workflow, not reproduced here due to space constraints, is available from the myExperiment web site, at `http://www.myexperiment.org/workflows/746`

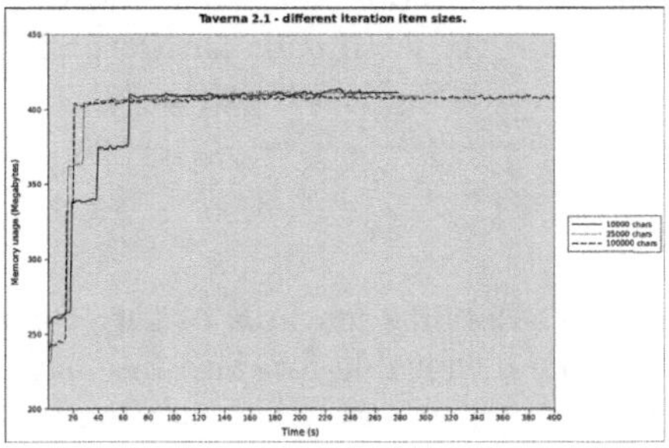


**Fig. 4.** Memory usage in T2 for different input strings lengths

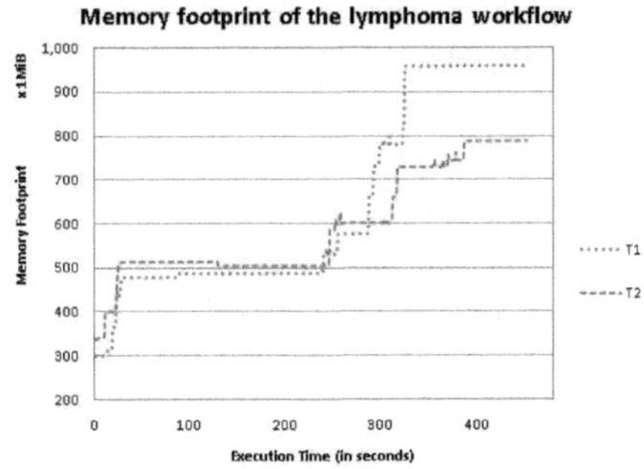


**Fig. 5.** Memory footprints for the lymphoma workflow in T1.X and T2

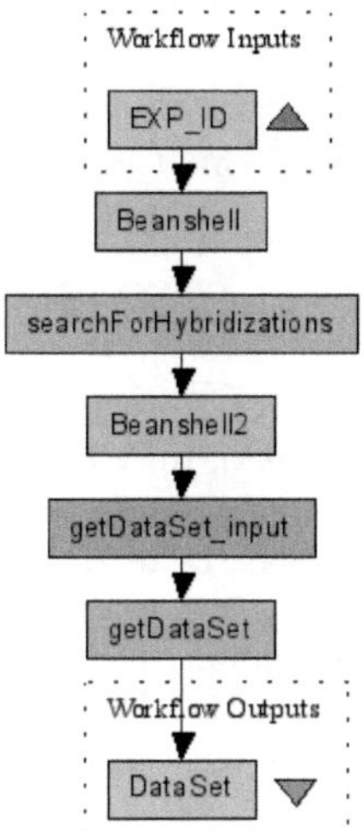


**Fig. 6.** Pipelined portion of the lymphoma workflow

| thread pool size | exec time (sec) | max memory (MB) | max thread count |
|---|---|---|---|
| 1 | 41 | 317 | 47 |
| 2 | 29 | 355 | 49 |
| 5 | 24 | 383 | 55 |
| 10 | 21 | 442 | 56 |

**Fig. 7.** Execution times and memory usage by thread pool size

This makes better use of memory but involves additional disk transfers. The in-memory model of T1.x saves transfer time but results in unbound memory usage.

As a second experiment aimed at showing the effect of pipelining, we have monitored the execution time and memory usage under different settings of max threads per processor, for a portion of the same caGrid workflow consisting of a linear chain of processors (Fig. 6), which are made to iterate over an input list of 10 experiment IDs. The results, shown in Fig. 7, indicate a near-linear correlation between max-thread setting on the processors and execution time, up to 10 threads per processor. A higher number of threads would bring diminishing returns, however, since the amount of real concurrency available on the

Java-based workflow engine is limited by the number of cores that the JVM can use (2, in this experiment), and at the same time those threads saturate the concurrent server where the Web services execute, making it a bottleneck.

## 5 Conclusions

We have presented the salient scalability and extensbility features of the Taverna 2 workflow management system, which make it suitable for data-intensive scientific applications. These features include, among others: (i) a runtime environment in which the available intra- and inter-processor parallelism that are implicit in the dataflow model are exposed as multiple execution threads, and (ii) extensibility and configurability points based on the interceptor pattern.

Our performance results, measured on a suite of programmatically generated workflows that exhibit both processor iteration and pipelining, indicate that T2 with RDBMS-based data storage offers good control of workflow execution memory while exhibiting competitive execution time.

Finally, we have presented a concrete case study that highlights the memory usage / execution time trade-offs on a production workflow from the caGrid project.

## References


1. Couvares, P., Kosar, T., Roy, A., Weber, J., Wenger, K.: Workflow M. In: Workflows for e-Science, Springer, Heidelberg (2007)
2. Deelman, E., Chervenak, A.L.: Data Management Challenges of Data-Intensive Scientific Workflows. In: CCGRID, pp. 687–692 (2008)
3. Deelman, E., Singh, G., Su, M.-H., Blythe, J., Gil, Y., Kesselman, C., Mehta, G., Vahi, K., Bruce Berriman, G., Good, J., Laity, A.C., Jacob, J.C., Katz, D.S.: Pegasus: A framework for mapping complex scientific workflows onto distributed systems. Scientific Programming 13(3), 219–237 (2005)
4. Fisher, P., Hedeler, C., Wolstencroft, K., Hulme, H., Noyes, H., Kemp, S., Stevens, R., Brass, A.: A systematic strategy for large-scale analysis of genotype phenotype correlations: identification of candidate genes involved in trypanosomiasis. Nucleic Acids Research 35, 5625–5633 (2007)
5. Foster, I.T., Vöckler, J.-S., Wilde, M., Zhao, Y.: Chimera: A Virtual Data System for Representing, Querying, and Automating Data Derivation. In: SSDBM, pp. 37–46. IEEE Computer Society, Los Alamitos (2002)
6. Gil, Y., Deelman, E., Ellisman, M., Fahringer, T., Fox, G., Gannon, D., Goble, C., Livny, M., Moreau, L., Myers, J.: Examining the Challenges of Scientific Workflows. Computer 40, 24–32 (2007)
7. Hull, D., Wolstencroft, K., Stevens, R., Goble, C.A., Pocock, M.R., Li, P., Oinn, T.: Taverna: a tool for building and running workflows of services. Nucleic Acids Research 34, 729–732 (2006)
8. Hwang, K., Briggs, F.A.: Computer architecture and parallel processing. McGraw-Hill, New York (1986)
9. Joel, S., Tahsin, K., Shannon, H., Stephen, L., Scott, O., et al.: e-Science, caGrid, and Translational Biomedical Research. Computer 41, 58–66 (2008)

10. Lee, E.A.: Dataflow Process Networks. Memorandum, UC Berkeley EECS Dept. (1994)
11. Shipp, M.A., Ross, K.N., Tamayo, P., Weng, A.P., Kutok, J.L., Aguiar, R.C.T.: Diffuse large B-cell lymphoma outcome prediction by gene-expression profiling and supervised machine learning. Nature Medicine 8, 68–74 (2002)
12. Missier, P., Paton, N., Belhajjame, K.: Fine-grained and efficient lineage querying of collection-based workflow provenance. In: Procs. EDBT, Lausanne, Switzerland (2010)
13. Oinn, T., Addis, M., Ferris, J., Marvin, D., Senger, M., Greenwood, M., Carver, T., Glover, K., Pocock, M.R., Wipat, A., Li, P.: Taverna: A tool for the composition and enactment of bioinformatics workflows. Bioinformatics, 3045–3054 (November 2004)
14. Pautasso, C., Alonso, G.: Parallel Computing Patterns for Grid Workflows. In: Proc. of the HPDC 2006 Workshop on Workflows in Support of Large-Scale Science (WORKS 2006), Paris, France (2006)
15. Smedley, D., Haider, S., Ballester, B., Holland, R., London, D., Thorisson, G., Kasprzyk, A.: BioMart – biological queries made easy. BMC Genomics 10 (2009)
16. Turi, D., Missier, P., De Roure, D., Goble, C., Oinn, T.: Taverna Workflows: Syntax and Semantics. In: Proceedings of the 3rd e-Science conference, Bangalore, India (December 2007)
17. van der Aalst, W.M.P., ter Hofstede, A.H.M., Kiepuszewski, B., Barros, A.P.: Workflow Patterns. Distributed and Parallel Databases 14, 5–51 (2003)
18. Foster, W.T.I., Madduri, R.: Combining the Power of Taverna and caGrid: Scientific Workflows that Enable Web-Scale Collaboration. IEEE Internet Computing 12, 61–68 (2008)
19. Walker, E., Xu, W., Chandar, V.: Composing and executing parallel data-flow graphs with shell pipes. In: WORKS 2009: Proceedings of the 4th Workshop on Workflows in Support of Large-Scale Science, pp. 1–10. ACM, New York (2009)

# Can Shared-Neighbor Distances Defeat the Curse of Dimensionality?

Michael E. Houle[1], Hans-Peter Kriegel[2], Peer Kröger[2], Erich Schubert[2], and Arthur Zimek[2]

[1] National Institute of Informatics
2-1-2 Hitotsubashi, Chiyoda-ku, Tokyo 101-8430, Japan
meh@nii.ac.jp
[2] Ludwig-Maximilians-Universität München
Oettingenstr. 67, 80538 München, Germany
{kriegel,kroegerp,schube,zimek}@dbs.ifi.lmu.de
http://www.dbs.ifi.lmu.de

**Abstract.** The performance of similarity measures for search, indexing, and data mining applications tends to degrade rapidly as the dimensionality of the data increases. The effects of the so-called 'curse of dimensionality' have been studied by researchers for data sets generated according to a single data distribution. In this paper, we study the effects of this phenomenon on different similarity measures for multiply-distributed data. In particular, we assess the performance of shared-neighbor similarity measures, which are secondary similarity measures based on the rankings of data objects induced by some primary distance measure. We find that rank-based similarity measures can result in more stable performance than their associated primary distance measures.

## 1 Introduction

Effective solutions for data indexing and data mining tasks often require that an appropriate measure of object-to-object similarity be provided. Operations such as the retrieval of objects similar to a query object are facilitated using a nearest-neighbor search with an appropriate distance measure. Any use of a similarity measure involves the implicit assumption that the data objects naturally form groups that can be regarded as arising from different generation mechanisms, and sharing common statistical characteristics. In the context of unsupervised learning, these groups can be clusters that follow some local 'natural' distribution. Sometimes, the learning process seeks to model the generation mechanism by fitting the data to known distributions; in other cases, only the groups themselves are sought. In outlier detection, the similarity measure is used to distinguish those objects that are conspicuously dissimilar from the majority of objects. In the context of classification, each class of the training set may be composed of one or more natural clusters, possibly together with outlier objects. In all contexts, we expect that a nearest-neighbor query based at an object from a particular natural grouping should rank objects from the same grouping ahead

M. Gertz and B. Ludäscher (Eds.): SSDBM 2010, LNCS 6187, pp. 482–500, 2010.

of other objects in the data set. In real-valued feature spaces, $L_p$ norms or the cosine of the angle between the pair of vectors are commonly used to express similarities between vectors.

In general, similarity measures based on distances are sensitive to variations within a data distribution, or the dimensionality of a data space. These variations can limit the quality of the solution, the efficiency of the search, or both. For $L_p$ norms in high dimensions, questions have been raised by several researchers, including Beyer et al. in [1], as to whether the concept of the nearest neighbor is meaningful. Intuitively, the key result of [1] states that if the ratio of the variance of the length of any point vector (denoted by $\|X_d\|$) with the length of the mean point vector (denoted by $E[\|X_d\|]$) converges to zero with increasing data dimensionality, then the proportional difference between the farthest-point distance $D_{max}$ and the closest-point distance $D_{min}$ (the *relative contrast*) vanishes:

$$\text{If } \lim_{d\to\infty} \text{var}\left(\frac{\|X_d\|}{E[\|X_d\|]}\right) = 0, \quad \text{then } \frac{D_{max} - D_{min}}{D_{min}} \to_p 0.$$

For a broad range of data distributions and distance measures, the relative contrast does diminish as the dimensionality increases. This *concentration effect* of the distance measure reduces the utility of the measure for discrimination. This phenomenon — recognized as one aspect of the *curse of dimensionality* — is quite general, and occurs for a broad range of data distributions and distance measures. In [2], the behavior of integer $L_p$ norms in high dimensional spaces has been studied. The authors showed by means of an analytic argument that $L_1$ and $L_2$ are the only integer norms useful for higher dimensions. In addition, they studied the use of projections for discrimination, the effectiveness of which depended on localized dissimilarity measures that did not satisfy the symmetry and triangle inequality conditions of distance metrics. In [3], fractional $L_p$ distance measures (with $0 < p < 1$) have been studied in a similar context. The authors provide evidence supporting the contention that smaller values of $p$ offer better results in higher dimensional settings. These well-known studies generally assumed that the full data set followed a single data distribution, subject to certain restrictions. In fact, when the data follows a mixture of distributions, the concentration effect is not always observed; in such cases, distances between members of different distributions may not necessarily tend to the global mean as the dimensionality increases. As briefly noted in [1], if a data set is composed of many natural groupings or clusters, each following their own distribution, then the concentration effect will typically be less severe for queries based on points within a cluster of similar points generated according to the same mechanism, especially when the clusters are well-separated.

The fundamental differences between singly-distributed data and multiply-distributed data are discussed in detail in [4]. The authors demonstrate that nearest-neighbor queries are both theoretically and practically meaningful when the search is limited to objects from the same cluster (distribution) as the query point, and other clusters are well separated from the cluster in question. The key concept is that of *pairwise stability* of clusters, which is said to hold whenever the mean distance between points of different clusters dominates the mean distance between points belonging to the same cluster. When the clusters are pairwise stable, for any point belonging to a given cluster, its nearest neighbors tend to belong to the same cluster. Here, a nearest-neighbor query of size on the order of the cluster size *can* be considered meaningful, whereas differentiation between nearest and farthest neighbors within the same cluster may still be meaningless. Note that for many common distributions these considerations may remain valid even as the dimension $d$ tends to infinity: for example, two Gaussian distributions with widely separated means may find that their separability improves as the data dimension increases. However, it should also be noted that these arguments are based on the assumption that all dimensions bear information relevant to the different clusters, classes, or distributions. Depending on the ratio of relevant versus irrelevant attributes, and on the actual separation of sets of points belonging to different distributions, irrelevant attributes in a data set may impede the separability of different distributions and thus have the potential for rendering nearest neighbor query results less meaningful.

The observations of [4], and the important distinction between the effects of relevant and irrelevant attributes, both seem to have received little if any attention in the research literature. Despite the demonstrated deficiency of conventional $L_p$ norms for high-dimensional data, a plethora of work based on the Euclidean distance has been dedicated to clustering strategies, which appear to be effective in practice to varying degrees for high-dimensional data [5]. Many heuristics have recently been proposed or evaluated for clustering [6, 7, 8, 9, 10, 11, 12, 13, 14], outlier detection [15, 16, 17, 18], and indexing or similarity search [6, 19, 20, 21, 22, 23] that seek to mitigate the effects of the curse of dimensionality. While some of these strategies, such as projected or subspace clustering, do recognize implicitly the effect of relevant versus irrelevant attributes for a cluster, all these papers (as well as others) abstain from discussing these effects, let alone studying them in detail. In particular, the concept of pairwise stability of clusters as introduced in [4] has not been taken into account in any of these papers. Although their underlying data models do generally assume (explicitly or otherwise) different underlying mechanisms for the formation of data groupings, they motivate their new approaches with only a passing reference to the curse of dimensionality. Indeed, it has been observed recently that many questions regarding these effects remain open [24]. Thus, a more detailed study of the effects of the curse of dimensionality on such heterogeneously distributed data sets in the presence of both relevant and irrelevant features is needed. One main objective of this paper is to attempt to address this need.

An interesting alternative to traditional similarity measurement is the definition of secondary measures based on the rankings induced by a specified primary similarity measure (such as an $L_p$ norm, or the cosine measure). The simplest and most common of these methods involves the use of *shared nearest-neighbor* (SNN) information, in which the similarity value for an object pair $(x, y)$ is a function of the number of data objects in the common intersection of fixed-sized neighborhoods centered at $x$ and $y$, as determined by the primary measure. The primary similarity measure can be any function that determines a ranking of the data objects relative to the query. It is not even necessary for the data objects to be represented as vectors.

The most basic form of shared nearest-neighbor similarity measure is that of the 'overlap'. Given a data set $S$ consisting of $n = |S|$ objects and $s \in \mathbb{N}^+$, let $NN_s(x) \subseteq S$ be the set of $s$-nearest-neighbors of $x \in S$ as determined using some specified primary similarity measure. The overlap between objects $x$ and $y$ is defined to be the intersection size

$$SNN_s(x, y) = |NN_s(x) \cap NN_s(y)|. \tag{1}$$

Other similarity measures have been proposed based on the overlap, such as the *cosine measure*:

$$simcos_s(x, y) = \frac{SNN_s(x, y)}{s}, \tag{2}$$

so called as it is equivalent to the cosine of the angle between the zero-one set membership vectors for $NN_s(x)$ and $NN_s(y)$. This was used in [25,26] as a local density measure for clustering.

For computing the nearest neighbors in high dimensional data, SNN measures have been reported to be effective in practice, and supposedly less prone to the curse of dimensionality than conventional distance measures. SNN measures have found use in the design of merge criteria of agglomerative clustering algorithms [25,27,28], in approaches for clustering high-dimensional data sets [26,29], and in finding outliers in subspaces of high dimensional data [30]. However, in all of these studies, no systematic investigation has been made into the advantages of SNN measures over conventional distance measures for high-dimensional data.

The main contributions of this paper are as follows: (i) We present the first study of the effects of high data dimensionality for the more realistic scenario of data mixture models (as opposed to data following a single distribution), for a number of popular distance measures. (ii) We evaluate the performance of secondary similarity measures based on SNN information, as compared to the primary distances from which the rankings are derived. We demonstrate empirical evidence for the claim that SNN is more robust in higher dimensions than primary distances in widely varying settings of data set characteristics. (iii) We also provide interpretations for this observation: since the ranking of points is usually still meaningful in high dimensions, the overlap of the neighborhoods of two points in a common natural grouping can be expected to be substantially large, leading to a high SNN similarity value. The size of the overlap of neighborhoods of points from different groups is expected to be rather small, resulting in a low SNN similarity value. (iv) We derive several SNN-based secondary distance measures with the potential for good results for distance-based applications even when the curse of dimensionality limits the discrimination power of the underlying primary distance functions. In such situations, the distance-based implementation most likely performs worse than the SNN-based application for most choices of a primary distance function.

In the following section, we explore different aspects of the curse of dimensionality, and distinguish between the truth and myths surrounding this phenomenon. We present the framework for our experimentation in Section 3. In Section 4, we evaluate how dimensionality affects the performance of SNN similarity, in contrast to that of the underlying primary similarity. In Section 5, we validate our findings on several real world data sets. This will motivate the formalization and discussion of possible distance measures based on the SNN dissimilarity, in Section 6. The results of the study are summarized in Section 7.

The data sets studied, the plots shown throughout this paper, as well as further information and experimental results and plots, are all available online via `http://www.dbs.ifi.lmu.de/research/SNN/`.

## 2 The Curse of Dimensionality Reconsidered

As mentioned earlier, previous studies of the effects of the curse of dimensionality on $L_p$ norms mainly assume a common data distribution for all attributes of a given data set. Here, we investigate the effects of the curse in the presence of heterogeneous data distributions (for a more detailed discussion, see [5]):

**Problem 1: Poor Discrimination of Distances**

*Concepts such as proximity, distance, or neighborhood become less meaningful with increasing dimensionality due to a loss of contrast of distances.*

This is the fundamental problem studied in [1, 2, 3]. For any data mining, indexing, or similarity search application, this effect is a serious impediment to the successful treatment of high-dimensional data.

**Problem 2: Presence of Irrelevant Attributes**

*Among the features of a high dimensional data set, for any given query object, many attributes can be expected to be irrelevant to that object. Irrelevant attributes can interfere with the performance of similarity queries for that object.*

The relevance of any particular attribute may vary across different groups of objects within the same data set. Since natural clusters of the data are determined only by some subset of the available attributes, the presence of many irrelevant attributes may impede the efforts to identify these groups. The performance of distance measures may be seriously compromised even by a relatively small number of irrelevant attributes. As the total number of dimensions increases, one would expect more and more features to be irrelevant to a given query object. Many publications seem to confuse the problem of irrelevant attributes with that of Problem 1, but they are in fact different — it is not impossible to have poor discrimination of distances even when all attributes are relevant, and good discrimination even when many attributes are irrelevant.

**Problem 3: Presence of Redundant Attributes**

*Similarly as with Problem 2, in a data set containing many attributes, there may be correlations or redundancies among subsets of attributes that also lead to special difficulties for data mining, indexing, or similarity search applications.*

This issue relates to the concept of 'intrinsic dimensionality' of a data set. For spatial queries, the observation that the intrinsic dimensionality of a data set in many cases is lower than the representational dimensionality (due to interdependencies among attributes) is often presented as a justification of strategies for obviating the curse of dimensionality [31,32,33,34]. It should be noted that there are scenarios where correlations among attributes do exist, but the problem of discrimination of distances still applies [1]. The correlations among attributes may be different within differing natural groups of a data set.

Since Problems 1 and 2 are often not well-differentiated in the literature, in our experimental studies, we will take care to demonstrate the differences in their natures and effects. In contrast with the earlier studies in [1,2,3], we limit our investigation here to mixtures of data distributions (as in [4]) as a realistic scenario for data mining or indexing or other similarity search applications.

## 3 Experimental Framework

### 3.1 Data Sets

To study the effects of the curse of dimensionality, we require a series of data sets that scale in dimensionality without introducing bias. After controlling for dimensionality, each of the sets in the series must be constructed so as to share common characteristics to the greatest degree possible. This is difficult to achieve with real world data, as the different attributes often vary in their scales and expressivity. When generating low-dimensional examples from a high-dimensional data set, it is not always clear how to select the projective dimensions fairly. In addition, well-defined ground truth sets necessary for assessing the expressiveness of query results are typically unavailable for large real data sets. The use of synthetic data allows us to study individual effects separately, while real data sets usually prevent the isolation of different influences. For these reasons we construct several series of artificial data sets using pseudo-random generators with largely fixed parameters, avoiding those parameter choices leading to data sets with groupings that are either too difficult or too easy to discriminate. Unless stated otherwise, the synthetic data sets were constructed with the following characteristics: $n = 10,000$ points grouped into $c = 100$ clusters in up to $d_{max} = 640$ dimensions. Cluster sizes are randomized with a mean of $\frac{n}{c} = 100$ and standard deviation $\frac{n}{10 \cdot c} = 10$, with the size of the last generated cluster adjusted so that the total number of points is $n$. When generating data sets for a series, those sets with dimensionality $d < d_{max}$ were generated so that their attributes coincided with the first $d$ attributes of all other data sets having dimensionality greater than $d$.

For each object, attribute values were generated depending on whether the attribute is to be considered 'relevant' or 'irrelevant' for the formation of the cluster to which the object belongs. If the $i$-th attribute is deemed relevant to the $j$-th cluster, the value of this attribute for all members of $c$ are normally distributed with a standard deviation in the range $\sigma_{j,i} \in [0.05 : 0.8]$, and a mean in the range $\mu_{j,i} \in [\frac{\sigma_{j,i}}{2} : 1 - \frac{\sigma_{j,i}}{2}]$. These ranges were chosen to avoid overly compact or overly wide distributions, as well as boundary effects, while still providing a wide variety of distributions and overlaps. No additional clipping or normalization was applied. Any attributes irrelevant to the cluster were assigned noise values uniformly distributed in the interval [0 : 1].

For the experimentation, 6 synthetic data series were created, each consisting of 7 sets of differing dimensionality $d = 10, 20, 40, 80, 160, 320, 640$: (i) *All-Relevant*: in this series, all attributes were generated so as to be relevant for all clusters. (ii) *10-Relevant*: in this series, the first 10 attributes are relevant for all clusters, the remaining attributes are irrelevant. (iii) *Cyc-Relevant*: in this series, the $i$-th attribute is relevant for the $j$-th cluster when $i \bmod c = j$; otherwise, the attribute is irrelevant. This series has $n = 1,000$ and $c = 10$. (iv) *Half-Relevant*: in this series, for each cluster, an attribute was chosen to be relevant with probability $\frac{1}{2}$, and irrelevant otherwise. The selection of attributes was consistent within a cluster, and performed independently of the selection for other clusters. (v) *All-Dependent*: this series is derived from *All-Relevant* introducing correlations among attributes. (vi) *10-Dependent*: this series is derived from *10-Relevant* introducing correlations among attributes.

For the correlated data sets *All-Dependent* and *10-Dependent*, the $i$-th attribute value $X_i$ was generated by computing $X_i = Y_i$ for $1 \leq i \leq 10$, and $X_i = \frac{1}{2}(X_{i-10} + Y_i)$ for $i > 10$, where $Y_i$ is the attribute of the corresponding uncorrelated data set *All-Relevant* or *10-Relevant*. This way of introducing correlations is inspired by Example 3 in [1].

These 6 series provide us with the means to study different aspects of the curse of dimensionality. Data series *All-Relevant* is the basic setting referred to in the statement of Problem 1. However, the sets differ from those considered in other studies [1, 2, 3], and conforms with [4] in that the data objects are partitioned into clusters (as are all our data sets). Data sets *10-Relevant* and *Cyc-Relevant* relate exclusively to Problem 2 in different settings. The clusters are further distinguished in the data set *Cyc-Relevant*, where every attribute is relevant for exactly one cluster. In the series *Half-Relevant*, we give up control of the number and choice of relevant attributes. Half the attributes are expected to be relevant to a given cluster, but the selection of relevant attributes varies (independently) from cluster to cluster.

Our synthetic data sets do not satisfy the IID (independent and identically-distributed) assumptions used in the proofs of [1], as the sets are composed of multiple clusters that overlap in some dimensions and are well-distinguished in others. However, the analysis of [24] applies when dimensional values are comparable in their extent and exhibit the same properties as for normalized data.

As intended, our synthetic data sets show the typical behavior ascribed to the curse of dimensionality. Figure 1 plots the numerator and denominator of the contrast formula $\frac{D_{max} - D_{min}}{D_{min}}$ for individual data sets, to demonstrate that $D_{min}$ (the solid symbols) indeed grows much faster than the difference $D_{max} - D_{min}$ (the hollow symbols). The plots indicate that $D_{min}$ grows exponentially faster than $D_{max} - D_{min}$. Plots for the correlated data series and other distance functions can be found on our web page, as well as plots showing the contrast directly.

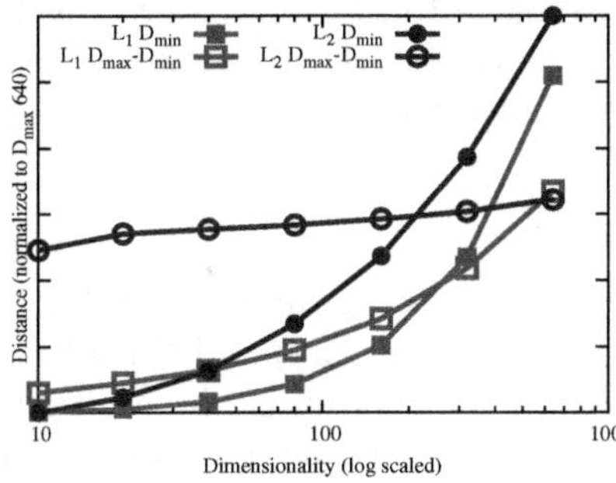


(a) *All-Relevant*

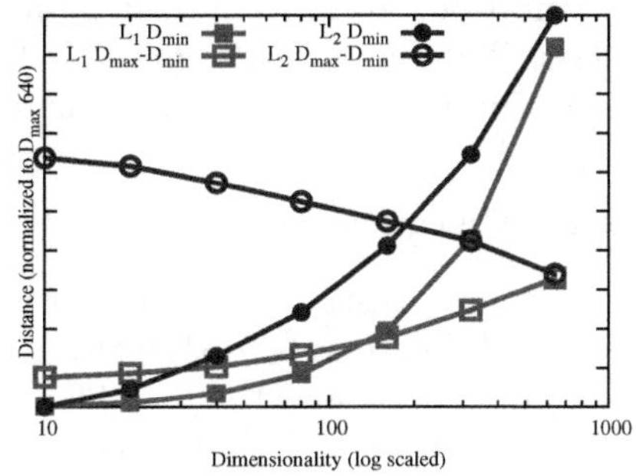


(b) *10-Relevant*

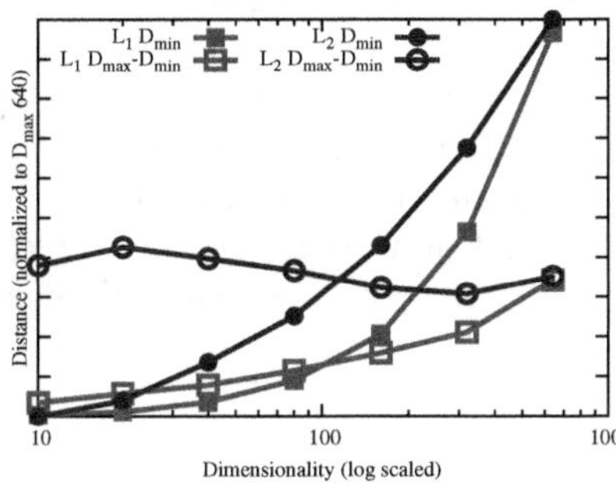


(c) *Cyc-Relevant*

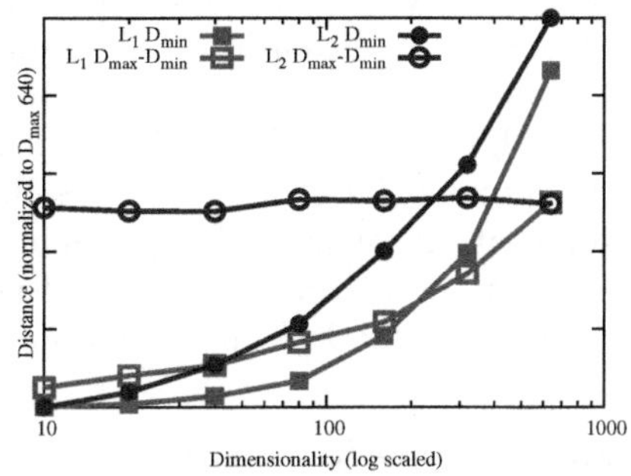


(d) *Half-Relevant*

**Fig. 1.** Curse of dimensionality: $D_{max} - D_{min}$ compared to $D_{min}$

In addition to the synthetic data sets described above, we also considered real-world data sets for our study. Real-world data sets suitable for this study are difficult to obtain, since they should have a reasonable size, number of classes, dimensionality, comparable dimensions and of course a solid ground truth. Results for real data can be difficult to interpret due to a lack of knowledge of the underlying data distributions, even when ground-truth class knowledge is available. Nevertheless, we report experimental results for 3 real data sets. The first real data set we used is the *Multiple Features* data set [35]. It consists of 2000 instances from 10 classes (corresponding to the digits 0 to 9). There are two variants, one with 649 dimensions (coming from multiple feature extraction algorithms and giving the data set its name), and another with 240 dimensions (the pixel averages features, which is the largest subset of directly comparable features). The second set considered is the *Optical Recognition of Handwritten Digits* data set [35]. It consists of 5620 instances from 10 classes (also corresponding to the digits 0 to 9) in 64 dimensions, in the form of an $8 \times 8$ grid of integer values in the range of 0 to 16 obtained by downsampling from a larger $32 \times 32$ grid. The third real data set comes from the *ALOI* image database [36], each image being described by 641 dense features based on color and texture histograms (for a detailed description of how the vectors were produced, see [37]). The full *ALOI* database consists of 110,250 images of 1,000 objects taken from different orientations and in different lighting conditions, each object being treated as a class. We used only the first 22,050 instances of the data set, covering the first 205 objects, with an average class size of approximately 107 objects.

### 3.2 Distance Measures

As primary distance measures we considered for our experimental evaluation a range of different $L_p$ distances, in particular the Manhattan ($L_1$) and Euclidean ($L_2$) distances, and the $p = 0.6$ and $p = 0.8$ fractional $L_p$ distances. In addition, we used also the cosine distance, referred to here as *arccos*, as it is computed as the arc of the cosine similarity. All these distance measures can be used as the primary distance for the computation of a secondary similarity $simcos_s$, as defined in Equation 2. For our experiments, we use the distance measure $1 - simcos_s$, and compare the performance of this secondary distance measure with the corresponding primary distance measure to assess whether the accuracy is improved. There are other possibilities for constructing distance measures from similarity measures. The particular choice of method, however, does not affect the ranking of query results, although it may influence the contrast. We will discuss this further, in Section 6.

### 3.3 Evaluation Criteria

The purpose of a distance function is to facilitate the separation of data objects similar to the query from those objects which are not similar. The discriminative ability of a given distance function can best be evaluated by computing a nearest-neighbor ranking of all data points with respect to a given query point. Ideally, at the top positions of the ranking, we would find all objects drawn from the same natural cluster as the query object, followed by the objects from outside the cluster. To evaluate the discriminative ability of dissimilarity functions without referring to the actual values, we compute Receiver Operating Characteristic (ROC) curves that compare the true positive rate with the false positive rate. For each query, the objects are ranked according to their similarity to the query point. We can compute the matching ROC curve and the corresponding area under the curve (AUC) for each ranking result. An AUC of 1.0 indicates perfect discrimination — all relevant objects are ranked ahead of all other objects. An AUC of 0.5 indicates a total lack of discriminative ability, as this value is what would be expected with a uniform random permutation of the query result set. An AUC significantly less than 0.5 indicates a reversed ordering. The ROC curve and its AUC value provide a summary for a single ordering of points — that is, for a single query object. By generating a ROC curve and AUC value for each data object, the mean AUC value and standard deviation could then be used to rate the quality for a particular distance function. However, we expect points near the center of a cluster (the mean of the generating distribution) to discriminate well for many distance functions. On the other hand, for points near the border of a cluster or in the overlap of clusters, values of the dissimilarity measure will most likely perform less well. Therefore, at data generation time, we assign to each point a centrality rank, based on both its deviation from the mean and the size of the cluster, so as to normalize across clusters of differing sizes. The point generated for cluster $M$ that is closest to the mean of $M$ is assigned a centrality of 1, and the point of $M$ that is farthest from the mean of $M$ is assigned a centrality of 0. To obtain readable graphs, the ROC AUC values then are aggregated into bins based on their centrality values. This allows us to plot the degradation of the distance function with respect to the centrality of a point within its distribution. For the plots shown in this paper, we will be using three bins for the central 20%, outer 20% and middle 60%. In the online material, 20 bins are used (each representing 5% of the data). In these plots we will also show the standard deviation along with the mean ROC AUC value.

## 4 Effects of the Curse of Dimensionality

At first glance, the fact that our synthetic data sets exhibit the typical symptoms of the curse of dimensionality would seem to indicate that these data series are not amenable to indexing or mining. However, such a conclusion would be unnecessarily pessimistic. Especially for data sets with many relevant attributes (such as the *All-Relevant* series), any given number of clusters should become distinguishable when the number of relevant attributes becomes sufficiently large. This intuition is justified by examples such as the combination of kernels and support vector machines (SVM): the number of dimensions is increased in order to be able to separate classes linearly by hyperplanes. In fact, what is stated as a condition for the pairwise stability of clusters in [4], we would expect to hold for any two clusters where the number of discriminative attributes dominates. This is not an essentially original contribution of our study but confirms prior results. We provide, however, evidence for this effect in the online material.

One point that must be stressed is that while the curse of dimensionality tells us not to rely on the absolute values of distances, it is still viable to use distance values to derive a ranking of data objects. An $\varepsilon$-range query is dependent upon the choice of an appropriate value of $\varepsilon$, and thus suffers from the lack of contrast, whereas a $k$-nearest neighbor query will retrieve the top $k$ neighbors independently of their absolute distance values. Hence, the computation of $k$-nearest neighbor queries and rankings has the potential to be viable in higher dimensions, whereas that of $\varepsilon$-range queries likely does not. Furthermore, although the curse of dimensionality contrast formula holds for all our data sets, the ranking results are not tied solely to the data dimensionality, and can in certain situations improve significantly with increasing dimensionality, as reported in [1]. The conclusion we draw is supported by the research literature as well as by our experiments on our synthetic data sets:

**Conclusion 1: Relevant vs. Irrelevant Attributes**
*The quality of the ranking – and thus the separability of the different generating mechanisms – may not necessarily depend on the data dimensionality, but instead on the number of relevant attributes in the data set.*

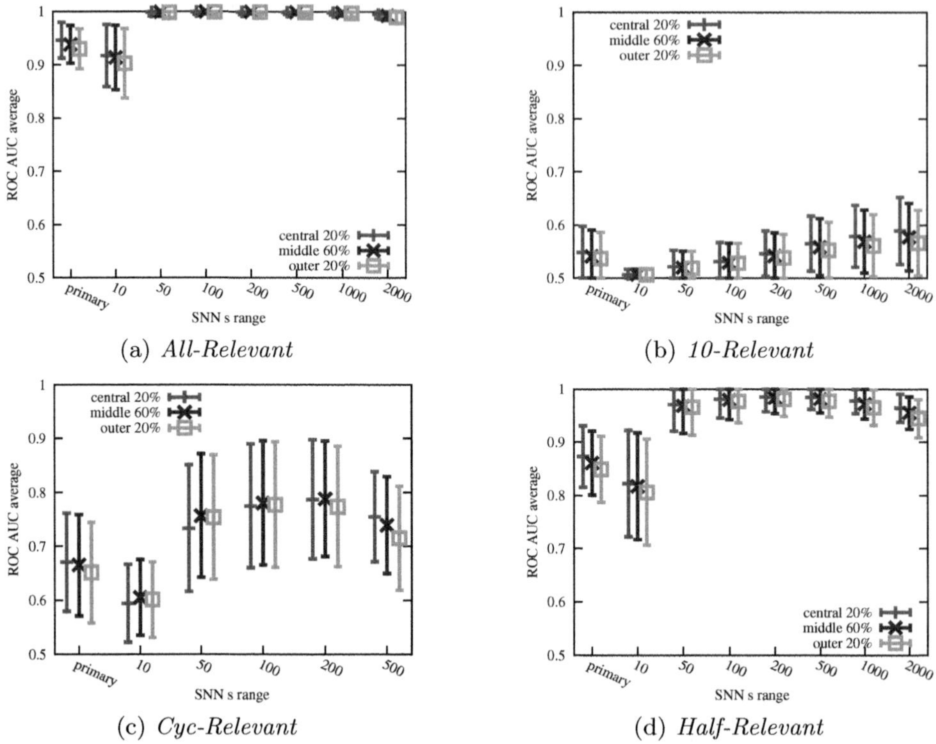


**Fig. 2.** Ranking quality with different SNN distances based on Euclidean distance at 640 dimensions

More specifically, there are two contrary effects of an increase in dimensionality when the number of relevant attributes is high: the relative contrast between points tends to decrease, but the separation among different generating mechanisms can increase. On the other hand, if the data dimensionality is high and the number of relevant dimensions is rather low, the curse of dimensionality fully applies, and hampers any analysis task. In retrospect, this is an important yet unsurprising conclusion to draw. Nevertheless, as mentioned in Section 1, it has not gained much recognition in the research literature to date.

As a further original contribution of this study, we evaluate the behavior of SNN as a secondary similarity measure. Motivated by the findings sketched above, an improved performance can be expected for a rank-based similarity measure such as SNN, whenever the ranking provided by the primary similarity measure is meaningful. Figure 2 compares results for the secondary distance measure with different SNN reference sizes $s$, based on Euclidean distance as the primary distance measure, for dimension $d = 640$. The performance of the corresponding primary distance is given on the left side of each diagram as a reference. Results for lower dimensionalities are comparable, and are shown in

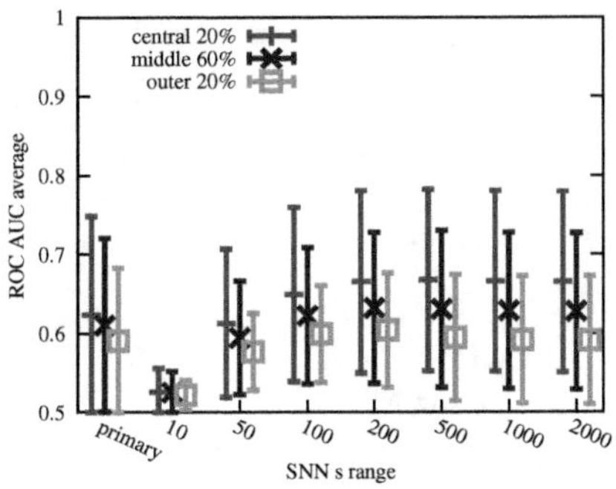


(a) $d = 10$

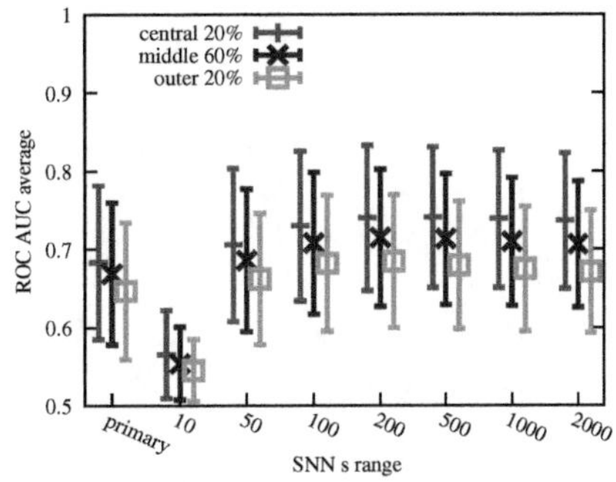


(b) $d = 40$

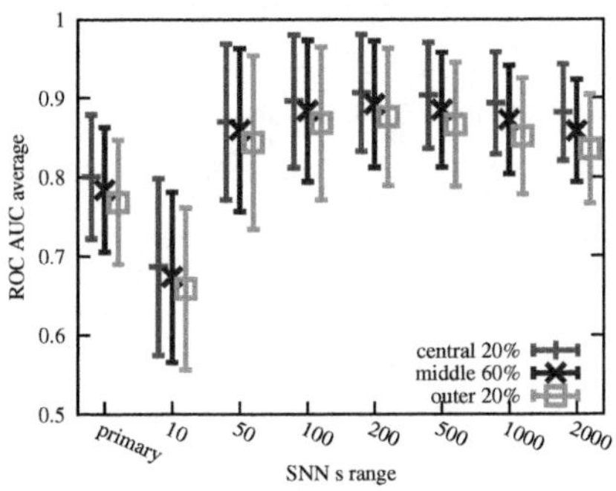


(c) $d = 160$

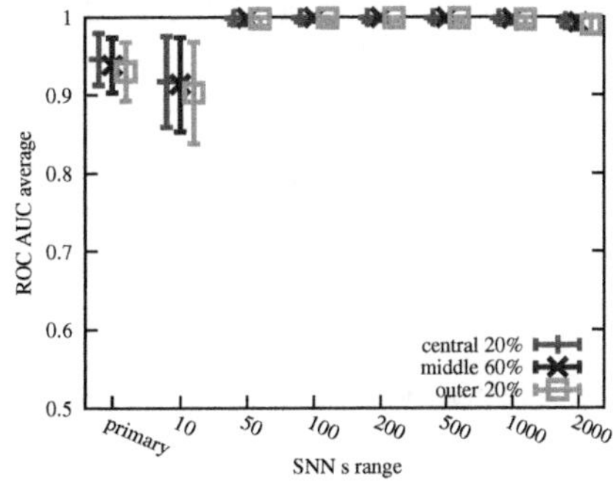


(d) $d = 640$

**Fig. 3.** Ranking quality for the *All-Relevant* set with different SNN distances based on $L_2$

the following figures. For easily separable data sets such as *All-Relevant*, most choices of $s$ yield excellent results. On *Half-Relevant* and *Cyc-Relevant*, the best results are achieved for choices of $s$ of the same order as the cluster size (100). This can also be seen for *All-Relevant* on lower dimensionality, where the contrast between the results is better. On the barely separable *10-Relevant* data set, even larger values of $s$ seem to be needed, although the average ROC AUC score is not significant, being below 0.6. Figure 3 shows the same plots for different dimensionalities of the *All-Relevant* data set. It can be seen that by using an SNN distance, a considerable improvement can be achieved given that the data set is sufficiently separable, and that the parameter $s$ is chosen roughly in the range of the cluster size. In particular, the secondary distance performs very well at high dimensionalities, and is reasonably robust with respect to the choice of $s$. The observations on the correlated data sets (given in the supplementary material) are quite similar. To summarize, we can draw the following conclusion from our experiments (see `http://www.dbs.ifi.lmu.de/research/SNN/` for the complete results with all distance functions on all data sets).

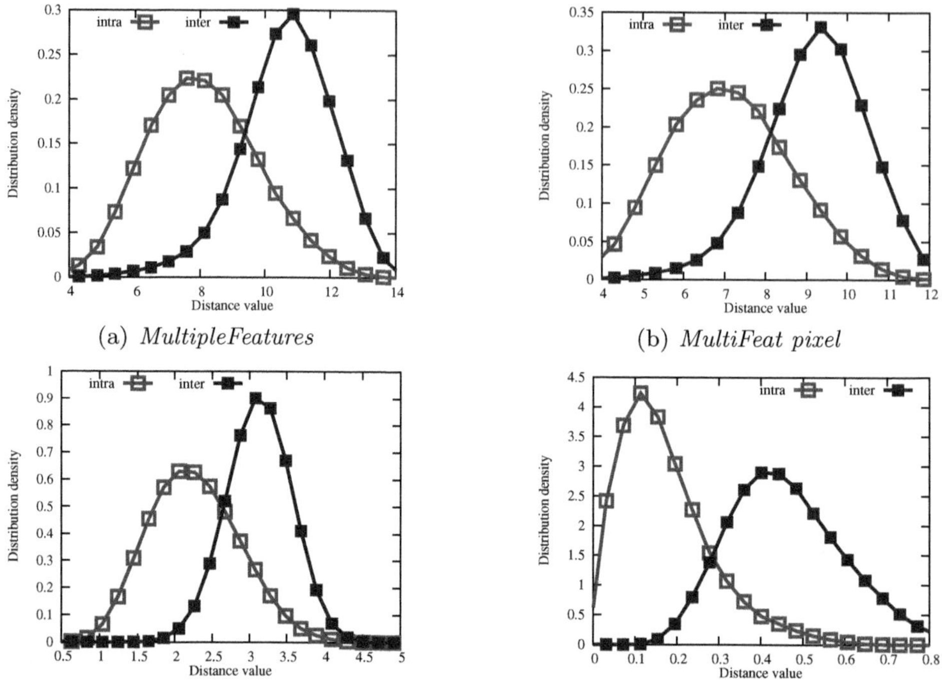


(a) *MultipleFeatures* (b) *MultiFeat pixel*

(c) *Optdigits* (d) *ALOI*

**Fig. 4.** Distributions of intra-class and inter-class distances (Euclidean distance)

**Conclusion 2: Ranking Quality Improvement**
*Our experiments suggest that the use of an SNN similarity measure can significantly boost the quality of a ranking compared to the use of the primary distance measure alone, provided that the primary distance already provides some degree of distinguishability of clusters.*

The experimental results confirm that although the discrimination of primary distances worsens with increasing data dimensionality, the natural data groupings may still be separable and, if so, the neighborhoods of query points would contain many points from the same grouping. Clearly, for two points from a common data grouping, when increasing the value of $s$, the probability that their neighborhoods have significant overlap increases as well. On the other hand, if $s$ is substantially larger than the size of the grouping, many objects from different groups are contained in the neighborhoods of the two points, and the performance of secondary distance measures become less predictable.

## 5 Experiments on Real Data

Experiments on artificial data allow more control over parameters such as the data dimension, and are more amenable to studying effects on the performance

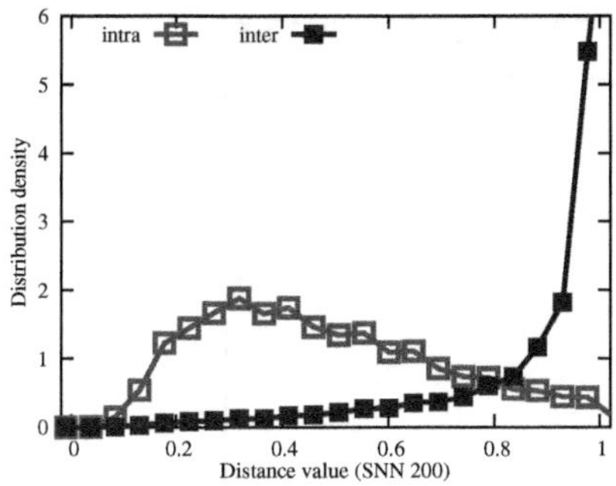


(a) *MultiFeat* $s = 200$

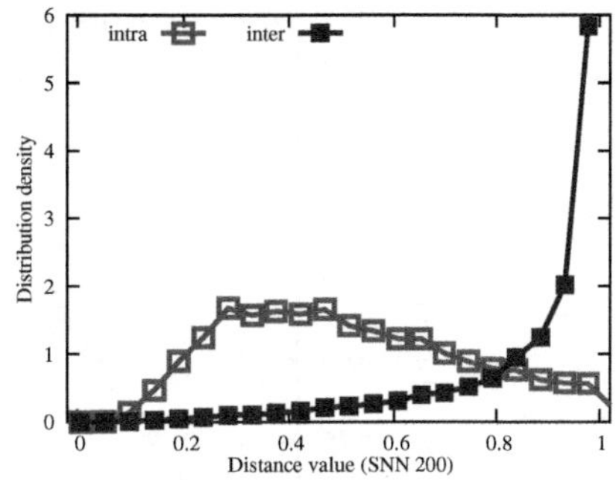


(b) *MultiFeat pixel* $s = 200$

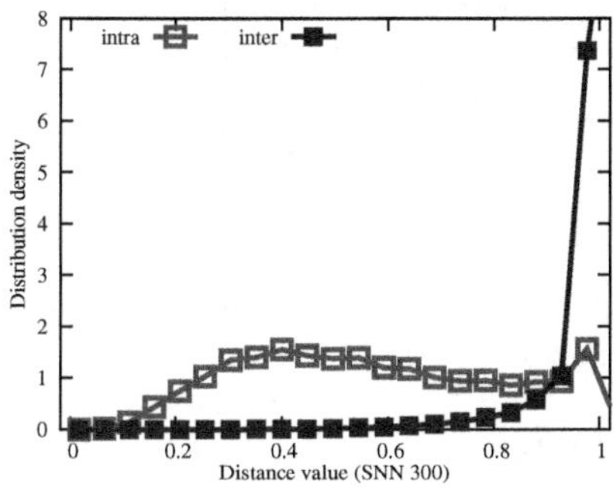


(c) *Optdigits* $s = 300$

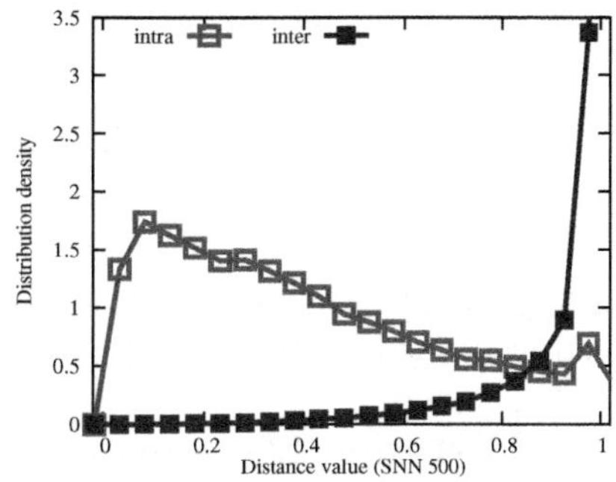


(d) *ALOI* $s = 500$

**Fig. 5.** Distributions of intra-class and inter-class SNN distances (based on Euclidean distance)

of distance measures in isolation. Real-world data, on the other hand, is considerably more difficult to control in this way. Nevertheless, in this section we offer experimental results for real-world data sets in order to validate and confirm some of the effects observed for artificial data. As seen in Figure 4, on all the real data sets considered, the distance distributions are approximately Gaussian (which is to be expected in high dimensionalities for the $L_p$ norms, due to the central limit theorem). It is also apparent that these data sets will be reasonably separable, as the overlap of the distance distributions is not very large. The results for other primary distances are comparable. Figure 5 shows the histogram results when using an SNN-based distance. The data set groupings have become very well separable. The effects of $s$ on the results for real-data are as one would expect from the experiments on artificial data: Figure 6 displays the results for various sizes of $s$. Choosing $s$ to match the class size gives reasonable results; however, the best performances are achieved with even larger values of $s$. Only when $s$ approaches the full data set size does performance drop. The benefits of using SNN on the *ALOI* data set are minimal, as the groupings of that set are already very well separable for primary distances.

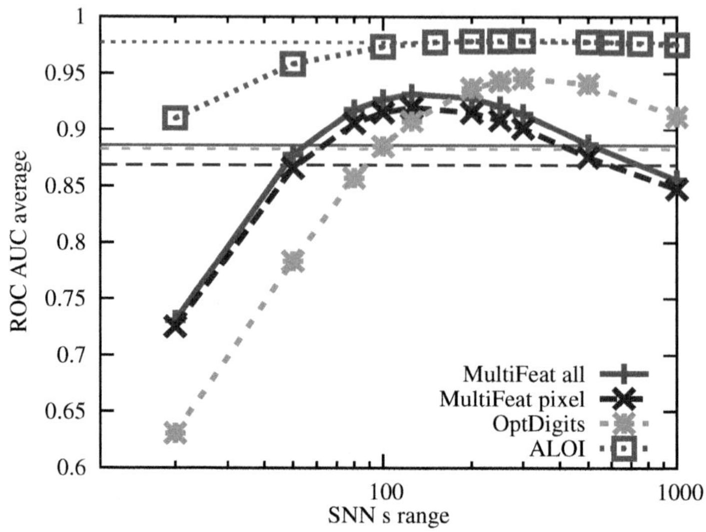


**Fig. 6.** Ranking quality with different SNN distances based on Euclidean distance (straight lines: ranking quality with primary distance)

## 6 Distance Measures Based on SNN

Let us recall, as described in Section 1, the observations reported by previous studies on the behavior of distance measures: (i) The relative contrast in Euclidean distances between nearest and farthest neighbor decreases with increasing dimensionality of the data [1]. (ii) This effect is stronger for $L_p$ distances with higher values of $p$, while it remains weaker for the Manhattan distance $L_1$ [2]. (iii) Fractional distances — $L_p$ distances with $p \in (0:1)$ — may even increase the relative contrast compared to $L_p$ norms with $p \in \mathbb{N}^+$ [3]. The results of our experiments have not only confirmed these observations, but they also dispel some incorrectly held beliefs regarding the effects of dimensionality, through the investigation of data sets drawn from a mixture of distributions, each with varying relevance of attribute subsets.

Despite the performance limitations due to the presence of irrelevant attributes and due to the curse of dimensionality, our experimentation shows that traditional similarity measures can still serve as the basis of effective secondary similarity measures.

**Conclusion 3: Stability of SNN**

*As an alternative to traditional distance measures such as $L_p$ norms or the cosine distance, the performance of similarity search and its applications in data mining or indexing can be stabilized by using SNN secondary distance measures in preference to primary distances.*

There are several common ways to convert a similarity measure into a dissimilarity measure. For the SNN similarity *simcos* (Equation 2) with a given number of neighbors $s$ considered, we propose as possible distance measures:

$$dinv_s(x,y) = 1 - simcos_s(x,y) \tag{3}$$
$$dacos_s(x,y) = \arccos\left(simcos_s(x,y)\right) \tag{4}$$
$$dln_s(x,y) = -\ln simcos_s(x,y) \tag{5}$$

While *dinv*, which has been used throughout our experiments, is simply a linear inversion of the values, *dacos* penalizes slightly suboptimal similarities more strongly, whereas *dln* is more tolerant than *dinv* for a broad range of higher similarity values but approaches infinity for very low similarity values. In general, any function $f$ that is monotonically decreasing on the interval $[0:1]$ with $f(1)=0$ can be used to transform the SNN similarity measure into a dissimilarity measure. The functions only differ in their contrast at different ranges. All of these functions are symmetric (since *simcos* is symmetric) and maintain the same ranking. However, it should be noted that of the three, only *dacos* satisfies the triangle inequality. While most retrieval results (based simply on rankings) remain unaffected by different formulations of these secondary distances, the effects on indexing and clustering may vary from formulation to formulation. For example, the separation of clusters in terms of absolute distances depends on the concrete choice of the distance measure and on the secondary distance measure as well.

## 7 Conclusion

With the ever-increasing capabilities of automatic data generation, the demand is rising for analysis methods that can cope with high dimensional data. The notorious curse of dimensionality and its implications for similarity measurement have been the subject of several recent studies; however, these studies have evaluated only data sets generated according to a single distribution mechanism. Moreover, a number of myths surrounding the effects of the curse of dimensionality have been supported by too loose interpretations of these studies. Seemingly in contradiction to these studies, the SNN similarity measure has been reported to be able to alleviate the effects of the curse for clustering.

In light of these considerations, this paper has made the following contributions. We have presented the first study of the effects of high data dimensionality on a range of popular distance measures, for the more realistic scenario of data mixture models as opposed to data following a single distribution. We exposed some of the myths involving the curse of dimensionality, and partly confirmed previously reported truths. We demonstrated that although the contrast of pairwise distances diminishes with increasing dimensionality (severely hampering all distance-based algorithms), for realistic data sets with a mixture of local distributions, the discrimination power of a distance measure depends more strongly on the number of relevant dimensions, and can actually rise as the dimensionality increases. On the other hand, simultaneously increasing the data dimensionality and decreasing the number of relevant dimensions dramatically decreases the separability of local distributions. In such a scenario, it seems to be more suitable to separate the groupings by means of projection into subspaces.

In addition, we evaluated the performance of secondary similarity measures based on SNN information, as compared to the primary distances from which the rankings are derived. We empirically confirmed that SNN is more robust in higher dimensions than primary distances in all settings. We also provided explanations for this observation: since the ranking of points is typically still meaningful in high dimensions, the overlap of the neighborhoods of two points in a common natural grouping can be expected to be substantially large, leading to a high SNN similarity value; the size of the overlap of neighborhoods of points from different groups is expected to be rather small, resulting in a low SNN similarity value.

Last but not least, we derived several SNN-based secondary distance measures with the potential for good results for distance-based applications even when the curse of dimensionality limits the discrimination power of the underlying primary distance functions. In such situations, the distance-based implementation most likely performs worse than the SNN-based application for most choices of a primary distance function.

In summary, for high dimensional applications, despite a deteriorating contrast in the chosen primary distance measure, we expect the incorporation of ranking information to enhance the quality of rankings and query results.

## References


1. Beyer, K., Goldstein, J., Ramakrishnan, R., Shaft, U.: When is "nearest neighbor" meaningful? In: Beeri, C., Bruneman, P. (eds.) ICDT 1999. LNCS, vol. 1540, pp. 217–235. Springer, Heidelberg (1998)
2. Hinneburg, A., Aggarwal, C.C., Keim, D.A.: What is the nearest neighbor in high dimensional spaces? In: Proc. VLDB (2000)
3. Aggarwal, C.C., Hinneburg, A., Keim, D.: On the surprising behavior of distance metrics in high dimensional space. In: Van den Bussche, J., Vianu, V. (eds.) ICDT 2001. LNCS, vol. 1973, p. 420. Springer, Heidelberg (2000)
4. Bennett, K.P., Fayyad, U., Geiger, D.: Density-based indexing for approximate nearest-neighbor queries. In: Proc. KDD (1999)
5. Kriegel, H.P., Kröger, P., Zimek, A.: Clustering high dimensional data: A survey on subspace clustering, pattern-based clustering, and correlation clustering. ACM TKDD 3(1), 1–58 (2009)
6. Aggarwal, C.C.: Re-designing distance functions and distance-based applications for high dimensional data. SIGMOD Record 30(1), 13–18 (2001)
7. Domeniconi, C., Papadopoulos, D., Gunopulos, D., Ma, S.: Subspace clustering of high dimensional data. In: Proc. SDM (2004)
8. Woo, K.G., Lee, J.H., Kim, M.H., Lee, Y.J.: FINDIT: a fast and intelligent subspace clustering algorithm using dimension voting. Inform. Software Technol. 46(4), 255–271 (2004)

9. Parsons, L., Haque, E., Liu, H.: Subspace clustering for high dimensional data: A review. SIGKDD Explorations 6(1), 90–105 (2004)
10. Yiu, M.L., Mamoulis, N.: Iterative projected clustering by subspace mining. IEEE TKDE 17(2), 176–189 (2005)
11. Liu, G., Li, J., Sim, K., Wong, L.: Distance based subspace clustering with flexible dimension partitioning. In: Proc. ICDE (2007)
12. Kriegel, H.P., Kröger, P., Schubert, E., Zimek, A.: A general framework for increasing the robustness of PCA-based correlation clustering algorithms. In: Ludäscher, B., Mamoulis, N. (eds.) SSDBM 2008. LNCS, vol. 5069, pp. 418–435. Springer, Heidelberg (2008)
13. Moise, G., Sander, J.: Finding non-redundant, statistically significant regions in high dimensional data: a novel approach to projected and subspace clustering. In: Proc. KDD (2008)
14. Achtert, E., Böhm, C., David, J., Kröger, P., Zimek, A.: Global correlation clustering based on the Hough transform. Stat. Anal. Data Min. 1(3), 111–127 (2008)
15. Aggarwal, C.C., Yu, P.S.: Outlier detection for high dimensional data. In: Proc. SIGMOD (2001)
16. Zhu, C., Kitagawa, H., Faloutsos, C.: Example-based robust outlier detection in high dimensional datasets. In: Proc. ICDM (2005)
17. Kriegel, H.P., Schubert, M., Zimek, A.: Angle-based outlier detection in high-dimensional data. In: Proc. KDD (2008)
18. Müller, E., Assent, I., Steinhausen, U., Seidl, T.: OutRank: ranking outliers in high dimensional data. In: Proc. ICDE Workshop DBRank (2008)
19. Katayama, N., Satoh, S.: Distinctiveness-sensitive nearest-neighbor search for efficient similarity retrieval of multimedia information. In: Proc. ICDE (2001)
20. Aggarwal, C.C., Yu, P.S.: Finding generalized projected clusters in high dimensional space. In: Proc. SIGMOD (2000)
21. Berchtold, S., Böhm, C., Jagadish, H.V., Kriegel, H.P., Sander, J.: Independent Quantization: An index compression technique for high-dimensional data spaces. In: Proc. ICDE (2000)
22. Jin, H., Ooi, B.C., Shen, H.T., Yu, C., Zhou, A.Y.: An adaptive and efficient dimensionality reduction algorithm for high-dimensional indexing. In: Proc. ICDE (2003)
23. Aggarwal, C.C., Yu, P.S.: On high dimensional indexing of uncertain data. In: Proc. ICDE (2008)
24. Francois, D., Wertz, V., Verleysen, M.: The concentration of fractional distances. IEEE TKDE 19(7), 873–886 (2007)
25. Ertöz, L., Steinbach, M., Kumar, V.: Finding clusters of different sizes, shapes, and densities in noisy, high dimensional data. In: Proc. SDM (2003)
26. Houle, M.E.: Navigating massive data sets via local clustering. In: Proc. KDD (2003)
27. Guha, S., Rastogi, R., Shim, K.: CURE: An efficient clustering algorithm for large databases. In: Proc. SIGMOD, pp. 73–84 (1998)
28. Jarvis, R.A., Patrick, E.A.: Clustering using a similarity measure based on shared near neighbors. IEEE TC C-22(11), 1025–1034 (1973)
29. Houle, M.E.: The relevant-set correlation model for data clustering. Stat. Anal. Data Min. 1(3), 157–176 (2008)
30. Kriegel, H.P., Kröger, P., Schubert, E., Zimek, A.: Outlier detection in axis-parallel subspaces of high dimensional data. In: Proc. PAKDD (2009)

31. Faloutsos, C., Kamel, I.: Beyond uniformity and independence: Analysis of R-trees using the concept of fractal dimension. In: Proc. SIGMOD (1994)
32. Belussi, A., Faloutsos, C.: Estimating the selectivity of spatial queries using the 'correlation' fractal dimension. In: Proc. VLDB (1995)
33. Pagel, B.U., Korn, F., Faloutsos, C.: Deflating the dimensionality curse using multiple fractal dimensions. In: Proc. ICDE (2000)
34. Korn, F., Pagel, B.U., Falutsos, C.: On the "dimensionality curse" and the "self-similarity blessing". IEEE TKDE 13(1), 96–111 (2001)
35. Asuncion, A., Newman, D.J.: UCI Machine Learning Repository (2007), `http://www.ics.uci.edu/~mlearn/MLRepository.html`
36. Geusebroek, J.M., Burghouts, G.J., Smeulders, A.: The Amsterdam Library of Object Images. Int. J. Computer Vision 61(1), 103–112 (2005)
37. Boujemaa, N., Fauqueur, J., Ferecatu, M., Fleuret, F., Gouet, V., Saux, B.L., Sahbi, H.: IKONA: Interactive generic and specific image retrieval. In: Proc. MMCBIR, pp. 25–28 (2001)

# Optimizing All-Nearest-Neighbor Queries with Trigonometric Pruning

Tobias Emrich, Franz Graf, Hans-Peter Kriegel, Matthias Schubert, and Marisa Thoma

Ludwig-Maximilians-Universität München
Oettingenstr. 67, Munich, Germany
{emrich,graf,kriegel,schubert,thoma}@dbs.ifi.lmu.de

**Abstract.** Many applications require to determine the $k$-nearest neighbors for multiple query points simultaneously. This task is known as all-($k$)-nearest-neighbor (A$k$NN) query. In this paper, we suggest a new method for efficient A$k$NN query processing which is based on spherical approximations for indexing and query set representation. In this setting, we propose trigonometric pruning which enables a significant decrease of the remaining search space for a query. Employing this new pruning method, we considerably speed up A$k$NN queries.

## 1 Introduction

Similarity search in databases is an important problem in content-based multimedia retrieval. Additionally, similarity queries are a useful database primitive for speeding up multiple data mining algorithms on large databases. In the majority of approaches for similarity search, the objects are described as points in a high-dimensional data space, where each dimension describes the object value w.r.t. a given characteristic or feature. These feature vectors are compared via metric distance functions such as the Euclidean distance or other $L_p$-norms. Thus, the distance between two feature vectors $v_1$ and $v_2$ models the similarity between the corresponding objects. One of the most important types of similarity queries in this setting are $k$-nearest-neighbor ($k$NN) queries, retrieving the $k$ objects in the database which have the smallest distance to a given query vector $q$. The majority of the approaches developed so far focus on the efficient processing of a single query at a time. However, in many applications like data mining and similarity search, it is previously known that it is necessary to process a large number of $k$NN queries to generate a result. More precisely, an A$k$NN query retrieves the $k$-nearest neighbors in the inner set or database $\boldsymbol{S}$ for each object in the outer or query set $\boldsymbol{R}$. Let us note that the same type of query is also known as $k$NN join [1].

Multiple computational problems use A$k$NN queries: In multimedia retrieval, many recent approaches model the image content as a set of local descriptors [2] or point clouds [3]. An A$k$NN query efficiently retrieves the best matches for a set of local descriptors in a given image database. Another area of application is data mining: [1] surveys multiple data mining algorithms that can be accelerated by efficient methods for A$k$NN computation like parallel $k$NN classification and $k$-means clustering. Furthermore, it is possible to employ A$k$NN processing for deriving outlier factors like [4].

In this paper, we propose a new approach for processing A$k$NN queries. As our method uses spherical page regions it employs an SS-Tree [5]. To define the pruning

M. Gertz and B. Ludäscher (Eds.): SSDBM 2010, LNCS 6187, pp. 501–518, 2010.

area around the approximations, we introduce trigonometric pruning which accounts for the fact that the relevant search space is not necessarily symmetric around the query approximation. Since this pruning method is based on trigonometric relationships, we refer to it as trigonometric pruning. One of its advantages is its capability to calculate pruning areas which are based on query approximations and to considerably decrease the remaining search space employed by other approaches like [3,6].

The rest of the paper is organized as follows. Section 2 surveys related work for processing A$k$NN queries and $k$NN joins. In Sect. 3, we specify the problem and describe the methods and data structures our solution is based on. Section 4 introduces our new pruning method and Sect. 5 then describes our new query algorithms. A performance evaluation is presented in Sect. 6. The paper concludes with a summary and some directions for future work in Sect. 7.

## 2 Related Work

There already exist several approaches for processing A$k$NN queries. The initial and most simple approach is the computation of a separate $k$NN query on the inner set $\boldsymbol{S}$ for each point in the outer set $\boldsymbol{R}$. This method is often referred to as nested loop join and can be accelerated by various search methods for $k$NN query processing. A comprehensive survey can be found in [7]. Since this basic approach obviously is not optimal w.r.t. the number of page accesses and distance computations, several dedicated approaches for processing A$k$NN queries have been proposed. We first of all have to distinguish index-based from scan-based solutions. In a scan-based solution, we assume that both data sets are not organized in any form of index and thus, we have to scan the complete data set for join processing. Examples for processing $k$NN joins without the use of index structures are GORDER [8] and HANN [9].

In this paper, we assume that at least $\boldsymbol{S}$ is already organized in an index structure. It is shown in the experiments in [6,9] that the use of an index structure can considerably speed up $k$NN join processing. One of the first publications discussing $k$NN join algorithms was [1]. In this paper, Böhm et al. demonstrate that $k$NN joins are useful database primitives that can be employed to speed up various data mining algorithms like $k$-Means clustering. The proposed algorithm is based on a new data structure called multipage index (MuX) which introduces larger pages for fast I/O accesses which are further organized into memory pages aiming at minimizing distance calculations. The proposed join algorithm first retrieves the current page of $\boldsymbol{R}$ and then queries $\boldsymbol{S}$ with the set of all query points. For each query point, the algorithm maintains its own active page list. The current pruning distance is considered as the maximum element of any query of these queues, and pages are refined w.r.t. the minimal distance to any query element. A drawback of this approach is that it has an overhead of distance computations because each object in $\boldsymbol{S}$ has to be compared to all elements in the query page. In [9] the authors discuss two methods for A$k$NN queries that assume that $\boldsymbol{S}$ is organized in a spatial index structure like the $\boldsymbol{R}$-Tree [10]. The first index-based approach discussed in [9] aims at improving the use of a disk cache when posing a separate NN query for each query point. The second proposed method, called *batched nearest neighbor* search (BNN), groups query points based on a Hilbert curve and poses one query for each group of points. The method considers the distance to the $k$-nearest neighbor $\delta_{k,x}$ for each element $x$ in the current query set. The maximum of these distances is now used to extend the minimum bounding rectangle around the query set and thus, describes the current pruning area. In [11], a $k$NN join algorithm based on the similarity search method iDistance [12] is proposed. The paper describes a basic algorithm called iJoin extending iDistance to the $k$NN join problem. Furthermore, two extensions are proposed that employ MBR-approximations to reduce distance computations and a dimensionality reduction approach to improve the performance on higher dimensionalities. Recently, two approaches have been published which reduce distance calculations by not considering the particular elements in the current set of query points. Instead, the pruning area is established on a minimum bounding rectangle around the query set. [3] presents an approach for applications on large point clouds in image processing. In this method, the set of query points is approximated by a minimum bounding rectangle (MBR) which is posed as a query to an $\boldsymbol{R}$-Tree organizing $\boldsymbol{S}$. The authors propose to employ the maximum distance that two points in two compared MBRs might have to determine the current pruning range. This criterion is named MaxMaxDist. The authors prove that their algorithm is optimal w.r.t. the number of pages that intersect a query area spanned by the MaxMaxDist. The experiments are focused on the problem of point clouds and thus, are directed at rather low dimensional settings. In [6], the authors propose NXNDIST which is based on the observation that at each side of an MBR, there must be exactly one contained data point which realizes the minimum distance. Thus, NXNDIST decreases the MaxMaxDist by allowing the use of the minimal MaxDist for exactly one dimension. The result is a closer bound for MBRs that is guaranteed to contain at least one nearest neighbor to any query point in the query MBR in the intersecting pages of $\boldsymbol{S}$. In their solution, the authors additionally propose to employ MBR-quadtrees as an index structure for $\boldsymbol{S}$ instead of R-Trees.

In contrast to all discussed approaches, our method uses spherical page approximations instead of MBRs. We employ the SS-Tree [5] for indexing $\boldsymbol{S}$. Our main pruning method, trigonometric pruning, describes the remaining search space based on the query approximations only. However, opposed to previous approaches, the pruning area is not built by symmetrically extending the query approximation in each direction. Instead, we propose the use of an asymmetric pruning area to further limit the search space. Finally, we show how our new approach can be effectively combined with existing pruning methods to achieve a general improvement on data sets of varying characteristics.

## 3 All-$k$-Nearest-Neighbors Using Spherical Index Structures

In this section, we will formalize our task of A$k$NN queries and describe the index structure used for our approach.

### 3.1 All-$k$-Nearest-Neighbors

As mentioned before, A$k$NN queries aim at retrieving the $k$-nearest neighbors for each element of a given query or outer set $\boldsymbol{R}$ in the inner data set $\boldsymbol{S}$. The set of the $k$-nearest neighbors of point $X$ in a set $\boldsymbol{X}$ is defined as follows:

**Definition 1** **($k$-nearest neighbors).** *Let $X \in \mathbb{R}^n$ be a query vector, let $\boldsymbol{X} \subset \mathbb{R}^n$ be a database of feature vectors and let $d : \mathbb{R}^n \times \mathbb{R}^n \rightarrow \mathbb{R}$ be a distance metric on $\mathbb{R}^n$. Then, the set $NN_k(X, \boldsymbol{X})$ of the k-nearest neighbors of $X$ in $\boldsymbol{X}$ for any $k \in \mathbb{N}$ is defined as follows:*

$$(i)\ |NN_k(X, \boldsymbol{X})| = k$$
$$(ii)\ \forall\, Y \in NN_k(X, \boldsymbol{X}),\ \hat{Y} \in \{\boldsymbol{X} \setminus NN_k(X, \boldsymbol{X})\} : d(X, Y) \leq d(X, \hat{Y})$$

**Definition 2** **(A$k$NN Query).** *Let $\boldsymbol{R}, \boldsymbol{S} \subset \mathbb{R}^n$ be two data sets and $d : \mathbb{R}^n \times \mathbb{R}^n \rightarrow \mathbb{R}$ a distance metric on $\mathbb{R}^n$. An all-k-nearest-neighbor (AkNN) query retrieves the result set $ANN_k(\boldsymbol{R}, \boldsymbol{S}) \subseteq \boldsymbol{R} \times \boldsymbol{S}$ for any $k \in \mathbb{N}$ for which the following condition holds:*

$$\forall\, R \in \boldsymbol{R},\ S \in \boldsymbol{S} \colon (R, S) \in ANN_k(\boldsymbol{R}, \boldsymbol{S}) \Rightarrow S \in NN_k(R, \boldsymbol{S}) \tag{1}$$

Our algorithm for efficiently processing A$k$NN queries is built on trigonometric functions, which need to be valid in the underlying featurespace. In this paper we use the Euclidean metric, the most popular distance metric for this kind of applications. Furthermore, we assume that the inner set $\boldsymbol{S}$ is organized in an index structure which is based on spherical page regions. A spherical page region is specified by a centroid $C \in \mathbb{R}^n$ and a radius $r \in \mathbb{R}^+ \setminus \{0\}$ and thus, it describes a hypersphere around $C$, containing all points $P_i$ with distance $d(C, P_i) \leq r$. Although approximating page regions using minimum bounding rectangles is more common for spatial index structures, there have been several successful index structures employing spherical page regions [5,13].

### 3.2 The SS-Tree

As mentioned above, our method employs the SS-Tree [5], an efficient index structure for similarity search based on spherical page regions. In the following, we will shortly review the characteristics of the SS-Tree.

**Definition 3** **(SS-Tree).** *An SS-Tree in the vector space $\mathbb{R}^n$ is a balanced search tree having the following properties:*

- *All nodes besides the root store between $m$ and $M$ entries. The root is allowed to store between 1 and $M$ entries.*
- *The entries of a leaf node are feature vectors in $\mathbb{R}^n$. The entries of an inner node are nodes, i.e. roots of subtrees.*
- *Each entry is bounded by a spherical page region containing all son entries.*
- *For a leaf node $\mathcal{L}$, the center $C_{\mathcal{L}}$ of the containing hypersphere $B_{\mathcal{L}}$ is the centroid of all contained feature vectors. The radius of $B_{\mathcal{L}}$, $r_{\mathcal{L}}$, is the maximum distance between any entry vector $L \in \mathcal{L}$ and $C_{\mathcal{L}}$.*
- *For an inner node $\mathcal{P}$, the center $C_{\mathcal{P}}$ of the containing hypersphere $B_{\mathcal{P}}$, is the centroid of the centroids $C_{\mathcal{Q}}$ of the contained son pages $\mathcal{Q} \in \mathcal{P}$. The radius $r_{\mathcal{P}}$ is chosen as $\max_{\mathcal{Q} \in \mathcal{P}} (d(C_{\mathcal{P}}, C_{\mathcal{Q}}) + r_{\mathcal{Q}})$.*

In general, the structure of the SS-Tree is quite similar to the structure of the R-Tree [10]. However, the page approximations are spherical instead of rectangular. Additionally, the split heuristics for creating the tree are different. Instead of minimizing the overlap between two pages, the SS-Tree tries to minimize the variance within the entries of its pages. Thus, when splitting a node, the split heuristics determines the dimension having the largest variance. In this dimension, the partition is selected, which minimizes the variance of the resulting pages and for which both new pages contain at least $m$ entries.

### 3.3 Principles of A$k$NN Algorithms

Given two data sets $\boldsymbol{R}$ and $\boldsymbol{S}$, where $\boldsymbol{S}$ is organized in an index structure. We want to find the $k$NN of all elements $R \in \boldsymbol{R}$. The most trivial approach would be to retrieve the $k$NN for each element $R_i$ separately by using the index structure organizing $\boldsymbol{S}$. Obviously this is not very efficient, e.g. for two query points (in $\boldsymbol{R}$) with a close proximity the same pages of the index have to be read twice. An efficient algorithm needs to group the points in $\boldsymbol{R}$ so that spatially close points fall into the same group. Afterwards these groups, containing distinct subsets of $\boldsymbol{R}$, are used as query sets.

For the ensuing step, it is important to decide which pages of $\boldsymbol{S}$ need to be examined for finding the $k$NN of each element contained in a subset $\mathcal{R} \subseteq \boldsymbol{R}$. Therefore, the search space, i.e. the space which could contain $k$NNs of an element $R \in \mathcal{R}$, needs to be defined. To successively minimize the search space, most algorithms start with the search space containing $\boldsymbol{S}$. Defining a pruning area has the opposite intention: define the space which does not have to be further examined. This means, that all pages of $\boldsymbol{S}$ lying completely in the pruning area can be discarded as candidates for the subset $\mathcal{R}$. Keep in mind that pages not completely covered by the pruning area can potentially contain points lying in the search space and therefore need to be resolved. Since all elements in the search space have to be considered in the further processing of $\mathcal{R}$, the goal is to minimize the search space as strongly and quickly as possible.

Minimizing the search space, respectively maximizing the pruning area, is the task of a pruning criterion. The optimal search space would only contain the $k$NNs of all $R \in \mathcal{R}$. Therefore, a pruning criterion should try to estimate this optimum as well as possible with low effort.

## 4 Pruning Criteria

In the following section, we describe MaxDist pruning and trigonometric pruning for the case of a 1-nearest neighbor query for a query set $\mathcal{R}$, using its bounding sphere $B_{\mathcal{R}}$. In Sect. 4.2 we will then explain how to extend the pruning criteria to a $k$NN query with $k > 1$. The notation used in the course of these analyses is summarized in Table 1.

### 4.1 MaxDist Pruning

**Definition 4 (MaxDist, MinDist).** *Given a point $P$ and a spherical region $B_{\mathcal{R}}$ with radius $r_{\mathcal{R}}$ and center $C_{\mathcal{R}}$, the* MaxDist *of $P$ to $B_{\mathcal{R}}$ is defined as: $MaxDist(B_{\mathcal{R}}, P) = d(C_{\mathcal{R}}, P) + r_{\mathcal{R}}$. The* MinDist *of $P$ to $B_{\mathcal{R}}$ is: $MinDist(B_{\mathcal{R}}, P) = d(C_{\mathcal{R}}, P) - r_{\mathcal{R}}$.*

Given a spherical region $B_{\mathcal{R}}$ and an arbitrary data point $S_0 \in \boldsymbol{S}$, we need to distinguish the points of the inner set $\boldsymbol{S}$ which can potentially be the nearest neighbors of any of the

**Table 1.** Definition of Parameters

| | |
|---|---|
| $n$ | The dimension of the feature space |
| $\boldsymbol{R}$ | The outer set ($\subseteq \mathbb{R}^n$) |
| $\boldsymbol{S}$ | The inner set ($\subseteq \mathbb{R}^n$) |
| $\mathcal{R} \subseteq \boldsymbol{R}$ , $\mathcal{S} \subseteq \boldsymbol{S}$ | Subsets of the outer set or the inner set |
| $R \in \boldsymbol{R}$ , $S \in \boldsymbol{S}$ | Points from the outer set or the inner set ($\in \mathbb{R}^n$) |
| $B_{\mathcal{R}}$ , $B_{\mathcal{S}}$ | Spheres $\equiv$ blocks around the sets $\mathcal{R}$, or $\mathcal{S}$, respectively ($\in \mathbb{R}^n$) |
| $\mathcal{P}_{\text{cand}}$ | Candidate set of points of the inner set ($\subseteq \boldsymbol{S}$) |
| $r_{\mathcal{R}}$ , $r_{\mathcal{S}}$ | Radius of sphere $B_{\mathcal{R}}$ or $B_{\mathcal{S}}$ around set $\mathcal{R}$ or $\mathcal{S}$ |
| $C_{\mathcal{R}}$, $C_{\mathcal{S}}$ | Center point of sphere $B_{\mathcal{R}}$ or $B_{\mathcal{S}}$ around set $\mathcal{R}$ or $\mathcal{S}$ |
| $I_i$ | Some intersection point on the surface of a sphere |

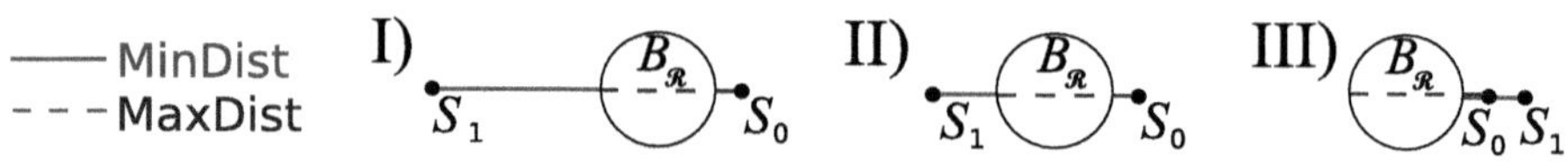


**Fig. 1.** Example for Min-/MaxDist pruning depending on the spatial position of $S_0$ and $S_1$

points enclosed by $B_{\mathcal{R}}$ from the points which do not have to be examined. All points $S_i$ with $\text{MinDist}(B_{\mathcal{R}}, S_i) > \text{MaxDist}(B_{\mathcal{R}}, S_0)$ can be pruned.

Fig. 1 gives an example of comparing $\text{MaxDist}(B_{\mathcal{R}}, S_0)$ with $\text{MinDist}(B_{\mathcal{R}}, S_1)$. In case I), $S_1$ cannot be the nearest neighbor for any point contained in $B_{\mathcal{R}}$, because any point in $\mathcal{R}$ is closer to $S_0$ than to $S_1$. In case II), there may be points in $B_{\mathcal{R}}$ (e.g. points lying on the leftmost side of the sphere) which have $S_1$ as their nearest neighbor and thus $S_1$ cannot be pruned. Case III) reveals the shortcoming of the pruning criteria mentioned above: Although neither $\text{MaxDist}(B_{\mathcal{R}}, S_0)$ nor $\text{MinDist}(B_{\mathcal{R}}, S_1)$ have changed in comparison to case II), it is clear that $S_1$ cannot be the nearest neighbor of any point contained in $B_{\mathcal{R}}$ and could thus be pruned.

This example shows that not only the distances to a query region but also the spatial relations between points of the outer set can play an important role for an optimal pruning criterion.

### 4.2 Trigonometric Pruning

Hence, we propose to consider the spatial relations of points in order to reduce the search space and thus avoid unnecessary page accesses. Therefore, a point $S_i$ close to the query region $B_{\mathcal{R}}$ is picked as pruning candidate. By exploiting the trigonometric properties of the spatial relation of $S_i$ and $B_{\mathcal{R}}$, the search space is reduced.

In order to generalize the correctness of our approach in an $n$-dimensional space, we will first show the correctness in 2D and afterwards extend the approach to $n$ dimensions. To illustrate our approach, we will use the terms and variable declarations corresponding to Fig. 2. Afterwards, we show that the distances between a point $S$ and a query region follow the function described in Definition 5 and thus, define a pruning area. Next, we demonstrate how to combine these functions in order to decide whether or not any of the points in $\boldsymbol{S}$ can be pruned (Sect. 4.2). Then, we extend the pruning

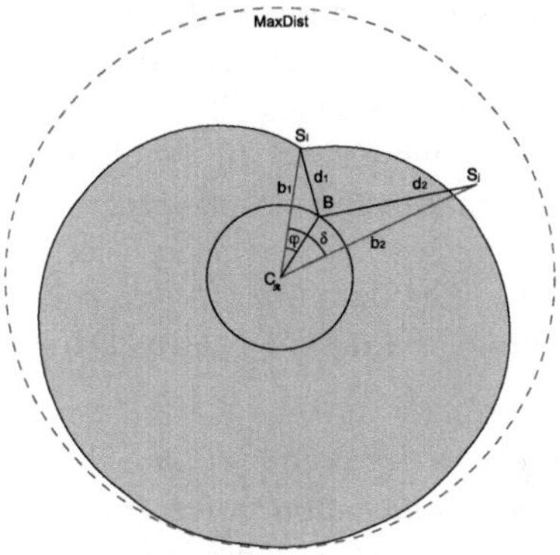


**Fig. 2.** Trigonometric pruning with active region $A_{\mathcal{R}}(S)$ in comparison with MaxDist pruning

criterion such that it also holds for pages, meaning it is possible to prune pages and to use pages as pruning candidates. Finally, we give a geometric interpretation of the approach that allows faster calculation of the pruning area.

**Defining the Pruning Area.** The following definition follows directly from the law of cosines, using the triangle $\triangle SC_{\mathcal{R}}I$ between a pruning candidate $S$, the center of the page $C_{\mathcal{R}}$ and an arbitrary point $I$ on the surface of the page $\mathcal{R}$. This situation is illustrated in Fig. 2. In the following, we will define the Surface Distance describing the distance of $S$ to an arbitrary surface point $I$:

**Definition 5 (Surface Distance $d_\varphi(S, B_{\mathcal{R}})$).** *Let $B_{\mathcal{R}}$ be a sphere around the center point $C_{\mathcal{R}}$ with radius $r_{\mathcal{R}}$, containing all elements $R \in \mathcal{R} \subseteq \mathbf{R}$ of a subset of the outer set. Let $I$ be a point on the surface of $B_{\mathcal{R}}$, i.e. $\overline{C_{\mathcal{R}}I} = r_{\mathcal{R}}$ and let $S$ be a point from the inner set $\mathbf{S}$. The* surface distance *$\overline{SI}$ follows the function*

$$d_\varphi(S, B_{\mathcal{R}}) = \sqrt{\overline{C_{\mathcal{R}}S}^2 + r_{\mathcal{R}}^2 - 2\,\overline{C_{\mathcal{R}}S}\,r_{\mathcal{R}}\,\cos(\varphi)}\ , \tag{2}$$

*where $\varphi = \measuredangle SC_{\mathcal{R}}I$ is the angle between $\overrightarrow{C_{\mathcal{R}}S}$ and $\overrightarrow{C_{\mathcal{R}}I}$. If $S$ is equal to the center $C_{\mathcal{R}}$, $\varphi$ is not defined, thus we set $d_\emptyset(S, B_{\mathcal{R}}) = r_{\mathcal{R}}$ for $S = C_{\mathcal{R}}$.*

As illustrated in Fig. 2, the distance between a candidate $S$ and a point $I$ on the surface of the circle around $C_{\mathcal{R}}$ fulfills Equation (2). Thus, we can define the *active region* $A_{\mathcal{R}}(S)$ as the remaining search space after considering $S$, because any point inside the active region is closer to any position in $\mathcal{R}$ than $S$ is.

**Definition 6 (Active Region $A_{\mathcal{R}}(S)$).** *Let $B_{\mathcal{R}}$ and $S \in \mathbf{S}$ be defined as above. The region $A_{\mathcal{R}}(S)$ contains all points $P$ for which the distance to any point $I$ on the surface of $B_{\mathcal{R}}$ is less than or equal to the distance of $S$ to $I$:*

$$A_{\mathcal{R}}(S) = \{P \in \mathbb{R}^2 \mid \exists\, I \text{ on } B_{\mathcal{R}} : d(P, I) \le d(S, I)\} \tag{3}$$

$$= \{P \in \mathbb{R}^2 \mid \exists\, \varphi \in [0; 2\pi] : d_{\varphi-\delta}(P, B_{\mathcal{R}}) \le d_\varphi(S, B_{\mathcal{R}})\}\ , \tag{4}$$

*where $\delta = \measuredangle PC_{\mathcal{R}}S$ is the angle between $\overrightarrow{C_{\mathcal{R}}S}$ and $\overrightarrow{C_{\mathcal{R}}P}$.*

This definition is equivalent to the union of all circles starting at an intersection point $I$ of $B_{\mathcal{R}}$ with radius $d(S, I)$. $A_{\mathcal{R}}(S)$ is visualized as the gray shaded area in Fig. 2. Since the distance condition of (3) automatically holds for points $I'$ *within* $B_{\mathcal{R}}$, $A_{\mathcal{R}}(S)$ contains only the points $P \in \boldsymbol{S}$ which can still be closer or equally close to any point $R \in B_{\mathcal{R}}$ than $S$ and thus it forms a valid search space.

**Extension to $n$ Dimensions.** The definition for the active region can be extended to $n > 2$ dimensions. The points $S_i$, $S_j$ and $C_{\mathcal{R}}$ span a 2D hyperplane $H$ in any dimension.

**Lemma 1.** *Let $A_{\mathcal{R}}(S_i)$ be the active region of an $S_i \in \boldsymbol{S}$ for a data sphere $B_{\mathcal{R}}$ with $\mathcal{R} \subseteq \boldsymbol{R}$ and let $S_j \in \boldsymbol{S}$ be another data point. If $S_j \in \boldsymbol{S}$ is not in $A_{\mathcal{R}}(S_i)$ in the hyperplane H spanned by $S_i$, $S_j$ and $C_{\mathcal{R}}$, there cannot be any $R \in B_{\mathcal{R}}$ s.t. $d(R, S_j) \leq d(R, S_i)$ and $S_j$ can be pruned.*

The proof is omitted due to space limitations. The idea is to reduce the test on whether or not $S_j$ is within the active region of $S_i$ to the test of (3), which implicitly takes place on the common 2D hyperplane $H$.

**Pruning Points.** Given two candidate points $S_i$, $S_j$ and a query region $B_{\mathcal{R}}$ with center $C_{\mathcal{R}}$ and radius $r_{\mathcal{R}}$. Let $\delta$ be the angle $\measuredangle S_i\, C_{\mathcal{R}}\, S_j$. Then $S_j$ can be pruned if

$$d_{\varphi}(S_i, B_{\mathcal{R}}) < d_{\varphi-\delta}(S_j, B_{\mathcal{R}}); \forall \varphi \in [0; 2\pi[\,. \tag{5}$$

If

$$d_{\varphi}(S_i, B_{\mathcal{R}}) > d_{\varphi-\delta}(S_j, B_{\mathcal{R}}); \forall \varphi \in [0; 2\pi[ \tag{6}$$

holds, $S_i$ can be pruned. If none of the conditions hold, neither $S_i$ nor $S_j$ can be pruned. W.l.o.g. $\varphi$ can be limited to $[0; 2\pi[$. If neither (5) nor (6) holds, there is at least one $\varphi$, where $d_{\varphi}(S_i, B_{\mathcal{R}}) = d_{\varphi-\delta}(S_j, B_{\mathcal{R}})$ and thus both $S_i$ and $S_j$ are NN candidates for the outer set $\mathcal{R}$ (see Fig. 3). This condition can be transformed to finding the roots of function $g_{S_i,S_j,B_{\mathcal{R}}}(\varphi) = d_{\varphi}(S_i, B_{\mathcal{R}}) - d_{\varphi-\delta}(S_j, B_{\mathcal{R}})$. A root of $g_{S_i,S_j,B_{\mathcal{R}}}(\varphi)$ indicates that $d_{\varphi}(S_i, B_{\mathcal{R}})$ and $d_{\varphi-\delta}(S_j, B_{\mathcal{R}})$ intersect such that neither of the points can be pruned safely. In the case of $C_{\mathcal{R}} = S_i$ or $C_{\mathcal{R}} = S_j$, we only need to compare the according MinDists.

As the computation of the roots of $g_{S_i,S_j,B_{\mathcal{R}}}(\varphi)$ is quite expensive, we calculate the extrema by examining the roots of $g'_{S_i,S_j,B_{\mathcal{R}}}(\varphi)$ as defined in Equation (7) and test them on opposite signs.

$$g'_{S_i,S_j,\mathcal{R}}(\varphi) = 2\,\overline{C_{\mathcal{R}}S_i}\,r_{\mathcal{R}}\,\sin(\varphi) - 2\,\overline{C_{\mathcal{R}}S_j}\,r_{\mathcal{R}}\,\sin(\varphi - \delta) \tag{7}$$

$$g'_{S_i,S_j,\mathcal{R}}(\varphi) = 0 \Rightarrow \varphi_{1,2} = \arctan\left(\frac{\overline{C_{\mathcal{R}}S_i}\,\sin(a\pi + \delta)}{\overline{C_{\mathcal{R}}S_j}\,\cos(a\pi + \delta) - \overline{C_{\mathcal{R}}S_i}}\right) \tag{8}$$

$$\text{with } a = 0, 2$$

Obviously, there are only two possible roots $\varphi_1$ and $\varphi_2$ in the domain $[0; 2\pi[$ for $g'_{S_i,S_j,\mathcal{R}}$ because the numerator can only be zero if $\sin(a\pi + \delta) = 0$. Using the signum function, we can now differ between the following cases:

1. $\text{sgn}(g_{S_i,S_j,B_{\mathcal{R}}}(\varphi_1)) = \text{sgn}(g_{S_i,S_j,B_{\mathcal{R}}}(\varphi_2))$ :
   $\Rightarrow \forall\varphi\colon g_{S_i,S_j,B_{\mathcal{R}}}(\varphi) \neq 0$ and thus $\forall\varphi\colon d_{\varphi}(S_i, B_{\mathcal{R}}) \neq d_{\varphi-\delta}(S_j, B_{\mathcal{R}})$.

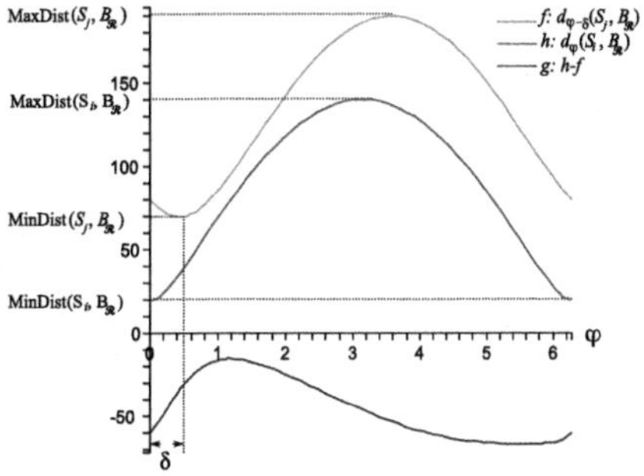


**Fig. 3.** Distance functions $d_\varphi(S_i, B_\mathcal{R})$, $d_\varphi(S_j, B_\mathcal{R})$ of two candidate points $S_i$ and $S_j$ with $\delta = \measuredangle S_i\, C_\mathcal{R}\, S_j$

2. $\text{sgn}(g_{S_i,S_j,B_\mathcal{R}}(\varphi_1)) \neq \text{sgn}(g_{S_i,S_j,B_\mathcal{R}}(\varphi_2))$ :
   $\Rightarrow \exists \varphi \in [0; 2\pi[: d_\varphi(S_i, B_\mathcal{R}) = d_{\varphi-\delta}(S_j, B_\mathcal{R})$.

Only case 1 allows one of the points to be pruned. If $g_{S_i,S_j,B_\mathcal{R}}(\varphi) > 0$ for all $\varphi$, $S_i$ can be pruned since its active region $A_\mathcal{R}(S_i)$ completely contains the active region of $S_j$. Analogously, $S_j$ can be pruned if $g_{S_i,S_j,B_\mathcal{R}}(\varphi) < 0$ holds.

**Pruning Pages.** In order to reduce page accesses, we now extend trigonometric pruning to prune pages without accessing the page itself.

**Lemma 2.** *Let $B_\mathcal{R}$ be a query region, $B_\mathcal{S}$ a page from the inner set, let $S_0$ be a pruning candidate for the query region $B_\mathcal{R}$ and let $\delta$ be the angle $\measuredangle S_0\, C_\mathcal{R}\, C_\mathcal{S}$. Then, $B_\mathcal{S}$ can be pruned if $d_\varphi(S_0, B_\mathcal{R}) < d_{\varphi-\delta}(C_\mathcal{S}, B_\mathcal{R}) - r_\mathcal{S}, \forall \varphi \in [0; 2\pi[$.*

*Proof.* According to Sect. 4.2, a point $S$ can be pruned if $g_{S,S_0,B_\mathcal{R}}(\varphi) > 0\ \forall \varphi \in [0; 2\pi[$. Since every point $S \in \mathcal{S}$ is at most $r_\mathcal{S}$ away from the center $C_\mathcal{S}$, the following condition holds because of the triangle inequality:

$$d_{\varphi-\delta}(C_\mathcal{S}, B_\mathcal{R}) - r_\mathcal{S} \leq d_{\varphi-\delta}(S, B_\mathcal{R}), \forall S \in \mathcal{S}.$$

Therefore, all points $S \in \mathcal{S}$ and thus the page bounded by $B_\mathcal{S}$ can be pruned if

$$d_\varphi(S_0, B_\mathcal{R}) < d_{\varphi-\delta}(C_\mathcal{S}, B_\mathcal{R}) - r_\mathcal{S}, \forall \varphi \in [0; 2\pi[ \tag{9}$$

□

Figure 4 illustrates the initial situation with a query region $B_\mathcal{R}$, a pruning candidate $S_0$ and a page $B_\mathcal{S}$ containing points of the inner set. $I$ is a point on the surface of $B_\mathcal{R}$. The page $B_\mathcal{S}$ can be safely pruned if its distance to any point $I$ is larger than $\overline{S_0 I}$. Since we have a region $B_\mathcal{S}$ rather than a point $S$, we use MinDist($I, B_\mathcal{S}$). The decision whether a page $B_\mathcal{S}$ can be pruned, is based on the existence of at least one $\varphi$ for which $d_\varphi(S_0, B_\mathcal{R}) \geq d_{\varphi-\delta}(C_\mathcal{S}, B_\mathcal{R}) - r_\mathcal{S}$. As in the previous section, we compute the maxima of the difference of the two functions:

$$g_{S_0,B_\mathcal{S},B_\mathcal{R}}(\varphi) = d_\varphi(S_0, B_\mathcal{R}) - (d_{\varphi-\delta}(C_\mathcal{S}, B_\mathcal{R}) - r_\mathcal{S}) \tag{10}$$

$$\Rightarrow g_{S_0,B_\mathcal{S},B_\mathcal{R}}(\varphi) = g_{S_0,C_\mathcal{S},B_\mathcal{R}}(\varphi) + r_\mathcal{S} \tag{11}$$

$$\Rightarrow g'_{S_0,B_\mathcal{S},B_\mathcal{R}}(\varphi) = g'_{S_0,C_\mathcal{S},B_\mathcal{R}}(\varphi) \tag{12}$$

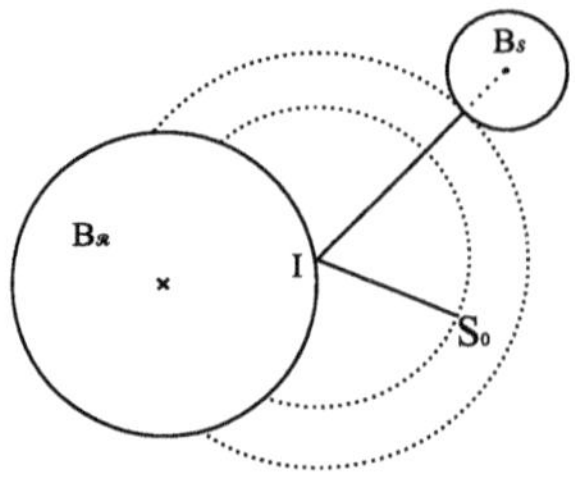


**Fig. 4.** Distances of the candidates $S_0$ and $B_S$ to $I$ for $B_{\mathcal{R}}$

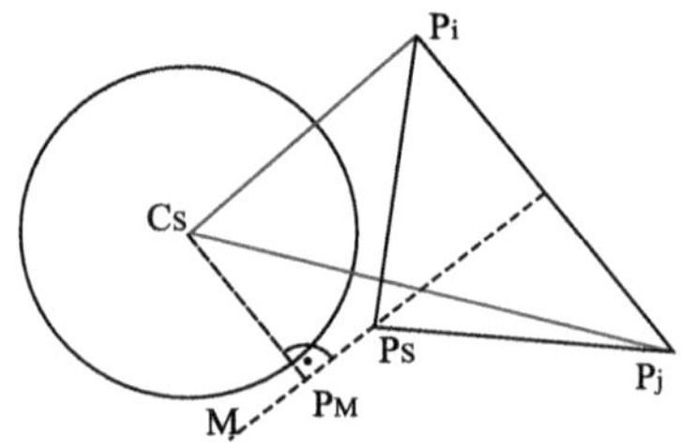


**Fig. 5.** Geometric interpretation of the pruning criterion. $P_j$ can be pruned, if $M$ does not intersect the circle around $C_S$.

Subtracting $r_S$ from $d_{\varphi-\delta}(C_S, B_{\mathcal{R}})$ causes the distance of $C_S$ to the intersection point $I$ to be translated along the y-axis by $-r_S$ units. Hence, the locations of the extrema of $g_{S_0,B_S,B_{\mathcal{R}}}(\varphi)$ are not different from the extrema of $g_{S_0,C_S,B_{\mathcal{R}}}(\varphi)$ such that $g'_{S_0,B_S,B_{\mathcal{R}}}(\varphi)$ can be used for calculating the values of $\varphi$ for testing (9) on whether or not the page $B_{\mathcal{R}}$ can be pruned.

**Geometric Interpretation.** A computationally cheaper and thus faster result can be achieved by using the following geometric interpretation which is illustrated in Fig. 5: Let $P_i$ be a pruning candidate, let $C_S$ be the center of a page $B_S$ with radius $r_S$ and let $P_j$ be a point to be tested on whether it can be pruned or not. Then, $P_j$ can be pruned if $d_\varphi(P_i, B_S) < d_\varphi(P_j, B_S)$ (as shown in 4.2). This condition is fulfilled if $P_i$, $P_j$ and $P_S$ build an isosceles triangle $\triangle P_i\, P_j\, P_S$, with $[P_i, P_S]$ and $[P_j, P_s]$, representing the two sides with equal length, so that $P_S$ is located on the perpendicular bisector $M$ of $[P_i, P_j]$. If $M$ does not intersect the circle around $C_S$, there is no $P_S$ for which $\overline{P_iP_S} = \overline{P_jP_S}$ holds. Thus, $P_j$ can be pruned if $\overline{C_SP_M} > r_S$ with $P_M$ being the orthogonal projection of $C_S$ onto $M$ (cf. Fig. 5). $\overline{C_SP_M}$ can be calculated by Equation (13). Obviously, no additional coordinates than the ones given by $P_i$, $P_j$ and $C_S$ are needed.

$$\overline{C_SP_M} = \frac{-\overline{C_SP_i}^2 + \overline{C_SP_j}^2}{2\overline{P_iP_j}} \tag{13}$$

**Picking Pruning Candidates.** In this section, we explain which points should be selected as pruning candidates. Generally, points close to the query region result in a smaller active region, so that these points are preferable. The active region is further reduced by comparing a point $S_j$ to all pruning candidates $S_i \in \mathcal{S}_{cand}$, since the resulting active region is equivalent to an intersection of the active regions of all $S_i$. Hence, more candidate points result in fewer page accesses at the price of an increasing number of distance calculations. The largest benefit is achieved if the pruning candidates are equally distributed around $C_S$ because the resulting active region is minimized in this case.

Extending the idea of trigonometric pruning from ANN to A$k$NN is very simple: A point or page can be pruned if it is pruned by at least $k$ pruning candidates. Hence, at least $k$ pruning candidates have to exist before defining a search space smaller than the whole space $\mathbb{R}^n$. Resulting from these findings, we define the parameter $\epsilon$, which controls the maximum number of pruning candidates that should be considered for pruning elements from $\boldsymbol{S}$, by setting this number to $k \cdot \epsilon$.

# 5 The Trigonometric Pruning Algorithm

Algorithm 1 gives an overview of our query algorithm. In the following, we explain the employed data structures and describe the complete algorithm. Finally, we propose an extension for employing multiple pruning techniques.

## 5.1 Data Structures

Algorithm 1 requires the following data structures:

**PQ:** A priority queue handling all yet unconsidered pages for a query set $\mathcal{R} \subseteq \boldsymbol{R}$. PQ is organized as a heap with the element with the smallest MinMinDist (extension of MinDist for two pages) to the query region on top.

**RES_HT:** A hash table storing one priority queue for each query point. Each queue has a capacity of $k$ and maintains the $k$-nearest neighbors for its query point. The call RES_HT.add($\mathcal{R}$, $S_i$) adds $S_i$ to the priority queue of $\mathcal{R}$.

**PCLIST:** A list containing the pruning candidates, ordered by their MinDist to the query region. The maximum size of the list is defined by $\epsilon \cdot k$ with $k$ being the amount of nearest neighbors that should be computed and $\epsilon \geq 1$ being an adjustable parameter. The larger $\epsilon$ is chosen, the more pages can be pruned (as PCLIST grows and provides more pruning power) which saves time consuming I/O-accesses at the cost of distance calculations.

## 5.2 The A*k*NN Algorithm

Our algorithm starts with grouping the query set $\boldsymbol{R}$ into compact spherical approximations. We use BIRCH [14] to produce a list of compact regions in linear time and organize them in a list. This way, the resulting query regions can be described by compact hyper spheres having a given maximum radius. Since the pruning area also decreases with the radius of a query region, we use the algorithm proposed in [15] to calculate the approximate smallest enclosing ball (SEB) for the data content of each region. Computing SEBs costs extra CPU time, but it pays off fast with growing $|\boldsymbol{S}|$, as the resulting SEBs' radii are about 10% - 20% smaller than the radii of the original spheres.

The main algorithm now receives a list of query regions from $\boldsymbol{R}$ and the number of nearest neighbors $k$ as input and proceeds as follows:

The query regions are processed successively and independently from each other. First, a new query region is taken from the list. Afterwards, a list for storing pruning candidates (PCLIST) and a priority queue (PQ) are initialized and the root of the SS-Tree storing $\boldsymbol{S}$ is put into the page list PQ. The pages in PQ are ordered by the MinMinDist to the currently processed query region ($B_{\mathcal{R}}$). The SS-Tree is then traversed in a best-first manner, as proposed by Hjaltason and Samet [16]. This is done by always removing the first node from the priority queue PQ processing it and putting all

**Algorithm 1.** The A$K$NN algorithm

```
AkNN(LIST_queryRegions, SSTREE_innerSet, k, RES_HT)
forall R ∈ LIST_queryRegions do
    PCLIST          := new PCLIST(ε · k)
    PQ              := new PQ()
    PQ.add(SSTREE_innerSet.root, -1)
    while PQ.hasElements() do
        if PCLIST.size = ε · k and PQ.smallestDistance > PCLIST.MaxDist_k
            break
        node := PQ.removeFirst()
        if not canBePruned(node, R, PCLIST)
            forall child ∈ node
                if child is an inner node                    // i.e. a B_S from the SS-Tree
                    PQ.add(child, MinDist(child, R))
                else                                         // i.e. an S_i ∈ S
                    if not canBePruned(child, R, PCLIST)
                        PCLIST.add(child)
                        forall queryPoint ∈ R                // i.e. an R_i ∈ R
                            RES_HT.add(queryPoint, child)
```

child nodes (if available) back to PQ, as long as the queue is not empty or the stopping criterion is triggered: The search for other $k$NN-candidates can be stopped if the MinMinDist of the current node to $\mathcal{R}$ is larger than the MaxDist of the $k$-th pruning candidate. In that case, the node and all its successors in the PQ can be pruned (cf. Sect. 4.1).

If the algorithm cannot be terminated in this way, it tests whether the current node can be pruned. This is done by the canBePruned() function, which prunes the node or point w.r.t. the pruning techniques introduced in Sect. 4.2. If the node cannot be pruned and its children are nodes of the SS-Tree, they are all added to the page list PQ. If the children are data points, another test on whether or not they can be pruned ensues. If the test is negative, they are added to the PCLIST and to all priority queues (via RES_HT) of query points contained in $\mathcal{R}$. Let us note that it is possible that the points will be eliminated from both data structures at a later point of time.

### 5.3 Combining Trigonometric Pruning with Other Criteria

In this section, we will discuss the use of different pruning criteria to further increase the performance. Even if employing additional pruning techniques causes additional computational cost, the cost is negligible if the combination yields a significant decrease of the search space and thus saves page accesses. In order to maximize the effect of combining different pruning criteria, it is important that the combined criteria perform always at least as well as one criterion alone. In our case, this can be achieved when trigonometric pruning (TP) is combined with a pruning criterion that also defines

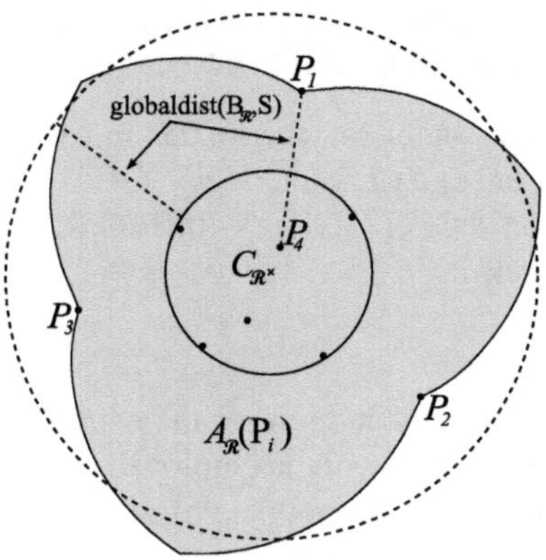


**Fig. 6.** The gray shaded area shows the active region used by trigonometric pruning (see Definition 6) which results from the intersection of the three pruning areas of $P_1, P_2, P_3$. The dashed line $[P1, P4]$ indicates the GlobalDist$(B_{\mathcal{R}}, S)$ which defines the pruning area (dashed outer circle) used by BNN in case of a 1NN query.

a pruning region so that the intersection of both regions can be used as a new pruning region.

In our experiments, we combine TP with BNN [9] which turned out to be one of the best pruning criteria we examined. The fact that the original BNN algorithm is proposed to be applied on rectangular page regions is not a problem, as it can be transferred to spherical page regions, such that BNN can be applied to the SS-Tree as well. The authors of BNN propose to query the inner set $\mathcal{S}$ with compact groups $B_{\mathcal{R}i} \in \mathcal{R}$ whereas each $R_i \in B_{\mathcal{R}i}$ organizes its NNs and according maximum-NNDist$(R_i, \boldsymbol{S})$. The largest value of NNDist$(R_i, \boldsymbol{S})$ of all $R_i \in B_{\mathcal{R}i}$ defines the GlobalDist$(B_{\mathcal{R}i}, \boldsymbol{S})$ of $B_{\mathcal{R}i}$. Pages $\mathcal{S}$ can then be pruned if MinDist$(B_{\mathcal{R}i}, \mathcal{S}) >$ GlobalDist$(B_{\mathcal{R}i}, \boldsymbol{S})$ as $\mathcal{S}$ cannot contain a NN for any $R_i \in B_{\mathcal{R}i}$. The disadvantage of the BNN algorithm compared to TP is that the spatial relation to other NN candidates is ignored. This can lead to the case shown in Fig. 6 where GlobalDist$(C, S)$ degenerates and converges to MaxDist in the worst case.

## 6 Experimental Evaluation

In the following, we outline the evaluation process of the methods suggested in this paper. We compare them w.r.t. to I/O cost to the state-of-the-art methods BNN [9] and MBA [6]. In order to make the approaches competitive for data sets of larger dimensionality, we adapted the algorithm to the X-Tree [17] and the SS-Tree [5] instead of using an R-Tree [10]. We display results for the following algorithmic settings:

- MP: A$k$NN-algorithm, using MaxDist on the SS-Tree
- XBNN: BNN, using **S** indexed in an X-Tree
- SSBNN: BNN, using **S** indexed in an SS-Tree
- TP: A$k$NN-algorithm, using TP (see Algorithm 1)
- TP+SSBNN: A$k$NN-algorithm combining TP and BNN in an SS-Tree
- MBA: MBA algorithm [6]

We have evaluated the algorithms on the following three real-world data sets, which were also used in the evaluation of [6]:

- TAC: Twin Astrographic Catalog Version 2 [18]: a library of stellar coordinates resulting in a set of 705 099 two-dimensional star representations.
- FC: Forest Cover Type data set, retrieved from the UCI KDD repository [19]: 581 012 data points with 10 real-valued attributes, each representing a 30x30 meter square of a forest region.

- COREL: Corel color histograms, which are also available at the UCI KDD repository [19]. They consist of 32-dimensional color histograms for 68 040 images.

For all experiments we used a third of the data sets as outer set, the rest as inner set. The page size was set to 1KB for TAC and 4KB for FC and COREL.

All experiments were run on a 64bit Intel® Xeon™CPU (3GHz) with 16G RAM, under Microsoft Windows 2003 R2, with Service Pack 1.

### 6.1 Results

In this section, we present the results of our experimental evaluation for the named algorithms and data sets. Additionally, we will describe the effect of the employed parameters on the query performance. Due to space limitations, we cannot display all settings for all data sets, but we give representative examples of the parameters involved.

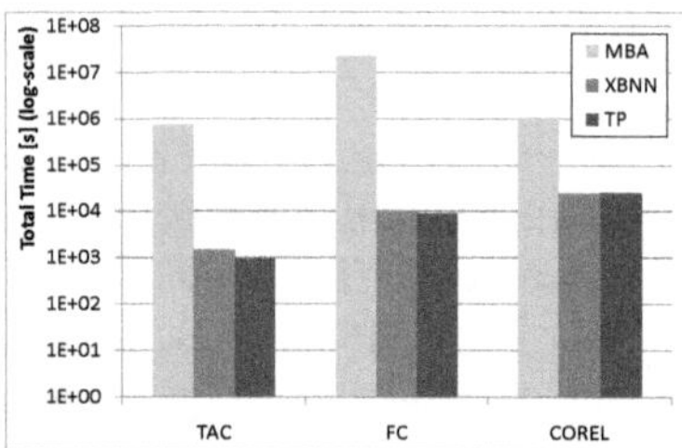


**Fig. 7.** Comparison of MBA, XBNN and TP for $k = 10$. The figure displays the sum of IO and CPU times for one A$k$NN query.

**Comparison to Other Approaches.** In order to compare the different approaches, we performed all-10-NN queries with the mentioned A$k$NN-algorithms on the three data sets and measured the CPU-time and the number of page accesses. To combine these two measures, we considered each logical page access with 8ms. Fig. 7 illustrates that TP and BNN perform orders of magnitudes better than MBA on all used data sets in matters of the overall runtime. Similar results were obtained with the parametric settings used for the experiments described in the following paragraphs. Therefore, we excluded the results of MBA in the further diagrams because the required scaling would conceal interesting effects.

**Dependency on $k$.** In Fig. 8 we compare the named algorithm w.r.t. the number of retrieved neighbors $k$ on all three data sets. Though most methods compare their performance on rather small values of $k$, larger values of $k$ are often of large practical relevance. In the context of search engines, it is quite common to provide large result sets which are ordered with respect to the similarity to the query. Since the performance mainly relies on the I/O operations, only page accesses are measured. While TP and BNN perform comparable for smaller values of $k$, TP clearly shows a better performance for larger values of $k$. For all data sets, our new combined approach (TP + SSBNN) performed significantly better than all compared approaches.

**Dependency on the Choice of $\epsilon$.** The $\epsilon$ parameter regulates the number of pruning candidates and thus, it is the most important parameter for tuning the A$k$NN-algorithm based on TP. Larger $\epsilon$ cause a smaller search space by the price of an increased number of distance calculations. In Fig. 10, we summarize the effect of $\epsilon$ on the performance. As expected, the number of distance calculations grows with increasing $\epsilon$ due to the larger number of pruning candidates. Contrarily, more pruning candidates lead to a tighter pruning effect, and thus the number of page accesses is reduced when increasing $\epsilon$. For all experiments in this paper we set $\epsilon = 5$.

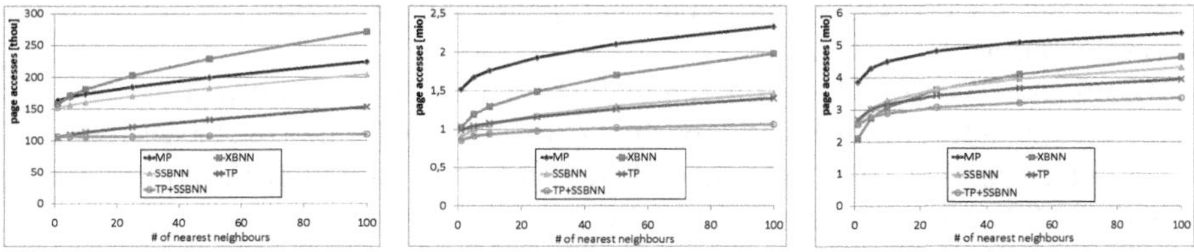


(a) A$k$NN on TAC (b) A$k$NN on FC (c) A$k$NN on COREL

**Fig. 8.** Page accesses for A$k$NN queries on different data sets by all algorithms increasing $k$

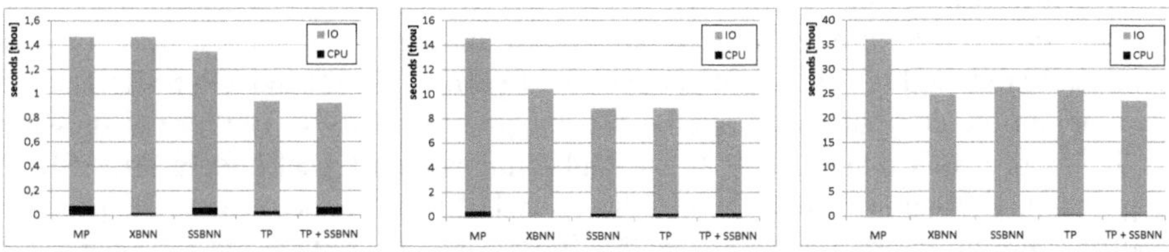


(a) A-10-NN on TAC (b) A-10-NN on FC (c) A-10-NN on COREL

**Fig. 9.** Performance of 10-NN queries on the different dataset with all mentioned algorithms

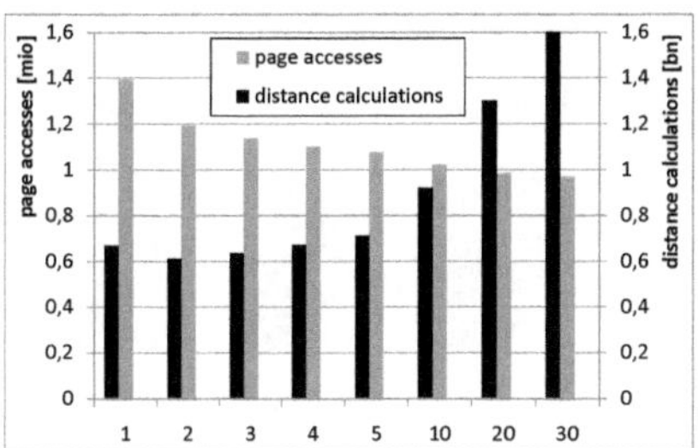


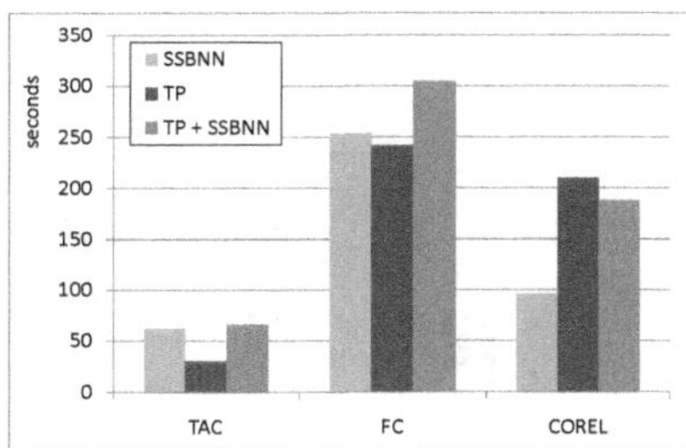


**Fig. 10.** $\epsilon$ of TP for an A-10-NN query on FC

**Fig. 11.** CPU-times on different data sets

**Overall Runtime Performance.** The direct comparison in matters of runtime is shown in Fig. 9 and yields the following insights:

As most operations in the field of databases, the A$K$NN operation is I/O bound, as CPU time is mainly consumed by distance calculations and represents only a small portion of the overall performance.

Comparing MP and TP shows that TP reduces the page accesses by 30% - 40% in contrast to MP. This is a consequence of the reduction of the search space as shown in Fig. 2. This effect is very stable over all data sets, suggesting its independence from the amount of dimensions.

The implementations of BNN on different underlying index structures (XBNN and SSBNN) show that the SS-Tree is at least comparable to the X-Tree in the performed experiments. Only for the 32-dimensional COREL data set, the X-Tree leads to a slightly better performance. Considering that the SS-Tree is not as suitable for large dimensions as the X-Tree, these results demonstrate that spherical page regions are well-suited for the A$k$NN problem.

The effect of TP compared to BNN is dependent on the data set. On the TAC data set, TP clearly outperforms SSBNN by about 30%. On the FC and the COREL data set, both pruning criteria perform similar and are both outperformed by the combination of TP and SSBNN which reduces the costs by $8\% - 15\%$.

This demonstrates that the proposed combination nicely compensates the additional computation costs and that the better approximation of the search space can significantly decrease the amount of page accesses.

**CPU Consumption.** As seen in Sect. 6.1, all A$k$NN-algorithms are clearly I/O bound. However, through the use of buffers and caching strategies, the page accesses can be dramatically reduced. Therefore, it is important to show that TP and TP+SSBNN apply only a negligible computational overhead compared to SSBNN. The results shown in Fig. 11 support this claim. Only at the high-dimensional COREL data set, SSBNN is significantly faster with respect to CPU-time. Let us note that also in the presence of buffers, the main challenge for A$k$NN-algorithms is to reduce the I/O operations. Therefore, it is often beneficial for the overall runtime to reduce I/O operations by the cost of CPU-time.

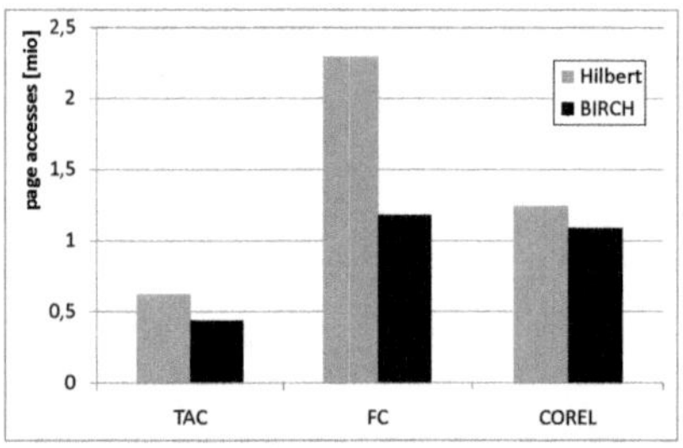


**Fig. 12.** Grouping procedures of the outer set, validated via XBNN

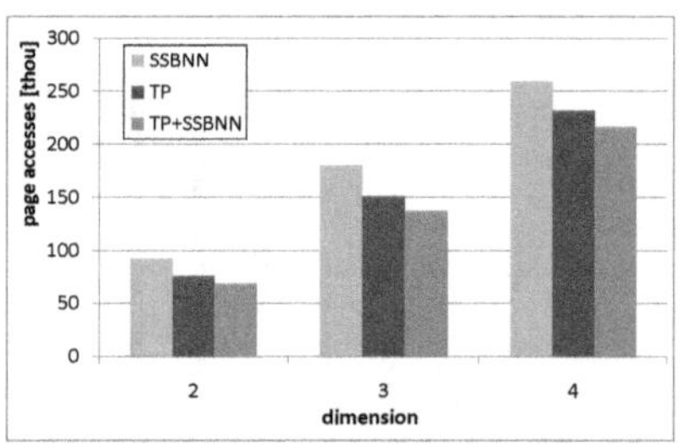


**Fig. 13.** A-10-NN queries for synthetic clustered data sets of varying dimensions

For all our compared methods it is necessary to group the outer set $\boldsymbol{R}$ into compact query regions. In [9], the authors use a grouping approach based on a bulk-load using the Hilbert order with a maximum threshold for the MBR volume and group size. They argue that this procedure runs in linear time and leads to better page approximations than, for instance, the data pages resulting from indexing $\boldsymbol{R}$ like $\boldsymbol{S}$. This grouping procedure can also be transferred to spherical page approximations. However, we chose BIRCH [14], which is a clustering algorithm with linear runtime. Even though this procedure uses spherical page approximations, we experienced that the groupings resulting from BIRCH show a better suitability even for the A$k$NN-algorithm based on the X-Tree (XBNN) than those resulting from Hilbert grouping. Fig. 12 shows the experiments on the three data sets for the two grouping algorithms. The Hilbert groups have been created by limiting the group volume to the average data page size of the inner set's X-Tree. The parametric setting of BIRCH has been chosen such that the number of groups is comparable to the Hilbert grouping. For the algorithms based on spherical page approximations, the results showed even more evidence for using BIRCH as grouping algorithm.

**Synthetic Data Sets.** We have also compared SSBNN, TP and TP+SSBNN on several synthetic data sets. Fig. 13 displays the results of A-10-NN queries on clustered datasets of varying dimensions. The 3000 clusters in the example data set of size 600,000 have been generated using a Gauss-like process: For each cluster a centroid has been sampled from a uniform distribution. The standard deviation used for generating the cluster points was chosen uniformly for each dimension. The experiments show that the combination of TP and SSBNN outperforms TP by approximately 10% and that it outperforms SSBNN by 20 to 30%. We note that this effect is stable for all dimensions – also for dimensions not displayed here due to space limitations.

## 7 Conclusions

In this paper, we introduced a novel approach for processing A$k$NN queries. Unlike previous approaches, our method is based on spherical page regions and thus, we apply it using an SS-Tree. To exclude pages from the search as early as possible, our algorithm introduces trigonometric pruning which allows to consider an asymmetric pruning area around a given query approximation. We propose a new A$k$NN algorithm which is based on this new pruning method. Afterwards, we further extend A$k$NN processing to employ multiple pruning criteria. Thus, it is possible to construct even tighter bounds around the remaining search space and thus to further decrease the number of necessary page accesses. In our experimental evaluation, we demonstrate that our proposed methods decrease the all-over runtime as well as the page accesses necessary to process A$k$NN queries on three real-world data sets. Especially for larger values for $k$, our new method considerably improves the query times.

The application of our pruning principle on spherical page regions allows a simple computation. In future work, we aim at extending the principle of trigonometric pruning to non-spherical page regions. We believe that transferring the principle to other approximations, such as MBRs, will open up new possibilities. Additionally, we investigate the transfer of our approach to other problems involving similarity search.

## Acknowledgements

This research has been supported in part by the THESEUS program in the MEDICO and CTC projects. They are funded by the German Federal Ministry of Economics and Technology under the grant number 01MQ07020. The responsibility for this publication lies with the authors.

## References


1. Böhm, C., Krebs, F.: The k-nearest neighbor join: Turbo charging the KDD process. KAIS 6(6), 728–749 (2004)
2. Lowe, D.: Object recognition from local scale-invariant features. In: International Conference on Computer Vision, Corfu, Greece, pp. 1150–1157 (1999)
3. Sankaranarayanan, J., Samet, H., Varshney, A.: A fast all nearest neighbor algorithm for applications involving large point-clouds. Comput. Graph. 31(2), 157–174 (2007)
4. Breunig, M.M., Kriegel, H.P., Ng, R., Sander, J.: LOF: Identifying density-based local outliers. In: Proc. SIGMOD (2000)
5. White, D.A., Jain, R.: Similarity indexing with the SS-tree. In: Proc. ICDE, pp. 516–523 (1996)
6. Chen, Y., Patel, J.: Efficient evaluation of all-nearest-neigbor queries. In: Proc. ICDE (2007)
7. Samet, H.: Foundations of Multidimensional and Metric Data Structures. The Morgan Kaufmann Series in Computer Graphics. Morgan Kaufmann, San Francisco (2006)
8. Xia, C., Lu, H., Ooi, B.C., Hu, J.: GORDER: An efficient method for KNN join processing. In: Proc. VLDB (2004)
9. Zhang, J., Mamoulis, N., Papadias, D., Tao, Y.: All-nearest-neighbors queries in spatial databases. In: Proc. SSDBM (2004)
10. Guttman, A.: R-Trees: A dynamic index structure for spatial searching. In: Proc. SIGMOD, pp. 47–57 (1984)
11. Yu, C., Cui, B., Wang, S., Su, J.: Efficient index-based KNN join processing for high-dimensional data. Information and Software Technology 49(4) (2007)
12. Jagadish, H.V., Ooi, B., Tan, K.L., Yu, C., Zhang, R.: iDistance: An adaptive B+-tree based indexing method for nearest neighbor search. ACM TODS 30(2) (2005)
13. Ciaccia, P., Patella, M., Zezula, P.: M-Tree: an efficient access method for similarity search in metric spaces. In: Proc. VLDB (1997)
14. Zhang, T., Ramakrishnan, R., Livny, M.: BIRCH: An efficient data clustering method for very large databases. In: Proc. SIGMOD, pp. 103–114 (1996)
15. Bâdoiu, M., Clarkson, K.L.: Smaller core-sets for balls. In: SODA 2003: Proceedings of the fourteenth annual ACM-SIAM symposium on Discrete algorithms, pp. 801–802. Society for Industrial and Applied Mathematics, Philadelphia (2003)
16. Hjaltason, G.R., Samet, H.: Ranking in spatial databases. In: Egenhofer, M.J., Herring, J.R. (eds.) SSD 1995. LNCS, vol. 951, Springer, Heidelberg (1995)
17. Berchtold, S., Keim, D.A., Kriegel, H.P.: The X-Tree: An index structure for high-dimensional data. In: Proc. VLDB (1996)
18. Zacharias, N., Zacharias, M.I.: The twin astrographic catalog on the hipparcos system. The Astronomical Journal 118(5), 2503–2510 (1999)
19. Hettich, S., Bay, S.D.: The UCI KDD archive (1999), `http://kdd.ics.uci.edu`

# Prefix Tree Indexing for Similarity Search and Similarity Joins on Genomic Data

Astrid Rheinländer, Martin Knobloch, Nicky Hochmuth, and Ulf Leser

Humboldt-Universität zu Berlin
Department of Computer Science
Berlin, Germany

**Abstract.** Similarity search and similarity join on strings are important for applications such as duplicate detection, error detection, data cleansing, or comparison of biological sequences. Especially DNA sequencing produces large collections of erroneous strings which need to be searched, compared, and merged. However, current RDBMS offer similarity operations only in a very limited and inefficient form that does not scale to the amount of data produced in Life Science projects.

We present PETER, a prefix tree based indexing algorithm supporting approximate search and appoimate joins. Our tool supports Hamming and edit distance as similarity measure and is available as C++ library, as Unix command line tool, and as cartridge for a commercial database. It combines an efficient implementation of compressed prefix trees with advanced pre-filtering techniques that exclude many candidate strings early. The achieved speed-ups are dramatic, especially for DNA with its small alphabet. We evaluate our tool on several collections of long strings containing up to 5,000,000 entries of length up to 3,500. We compare its performance to *agrep*, *nrgrep*, and user-defined functions inside a relational database. Our experiments reveal that PETER is faster by orders of magnitudes compared to the command-line tools. Compared to RDBMS, it computes similarity joins in minutes for which UDFs did not finish within a day and outperforms the built-in join methods even in the exact case.

## 1 Introduction

Similarity search and similarity join on string data has become a topic of interest in the past years [4,10]. Applications arise in duplicate detection [15], error correction [13] and data cleansing [5], to name only a few. They are also of uttermost importance in the Life Sciences. The characteristics of all organisms are coded in their genomes, which can be represented as a very large string over an alphabet of four letters. Approximately searching DNA sequences is important in virtually all fields of modern genomics. In this paper, we will use ESTs as our running example. *ESTs(Expressed Sequence Tags)* are short DNA sequences with lengths mostly in the region of 300 to 800 bases that are commonly used to identify genes and their localization on a chromosome. However, to be cost-effective,

M. Gertz and B. Ludäscher (Eds.): SSDBM 2010, LNCS 6187, pp. 519–536, 2010.

ESTs are obtained by a single sequencing pass which yields in an estimated error rate of 1% [9]. Thus, few differences in ESTs often are simply due to errors created by the sequencing process, which implies that searching and joining EST data sets should always be carried out approximately rather than exactly. Since the EST sets that are considered go in the millions[1], efficient execution of such similarity operations is crucial.

A large number of tools has been developed by the bioinformatics community to speed-up similarity search [2,20]. Almost all of them focus on computing local alignments [6] and use heuristics to achieve performance – at the cost of accuracy. In contrast, we aimed at developing an algorithm that supports global alignment (i.e., comparison of entire strings and not of substrings) and that is exact. Furthermore, we want our algorithms to be operations inside a relational database. The reason for this decision is that advanced analysis of sequences often depends on the availability of additional information (such as gene function, genomic annotation, biological pathways etc.), which nowadays is mostly maintained in RDBMS [11]. Furthermore, our intention is to provide a universal data structure for similarity operations not restricted to the Life Sciences.

In this paper, we present PETER, an indexing algorithm for scalable approximate search and approximate join operations based on Hamming distance or edit distance. PETER builds on a compressed prefix tree. One advantage of prefix tree indexing is that the complexity of search queries only depends on the depth of the tree, i.e., the maximal length of the indexed strings, and not on the number of indexed strings. Joins between sets of trees can be implemented efficiently by computing the intersection of two prefix trees. However, it is not trivial to sustain these advantages when moving from exact to similarity operations [16]. To this end, we refine algorithms for similarity search in prefix trees with various pruning and filtering techniques. Since we focus on retrieving very similar strings, these reduce the search space significantly; this focus also allows us to use a special alignment method (k-banded alignment) which is much faster than normal edit distance computation. We show that our tool outperforms the Unix command line tools `agrep` and `nrgrep` by magnitudes and also show that it enables efficient similarity based search and join queries on large string collections inside a RDBMS. At the downside, a restriction of our tool is that it is only efficient for searching highly similar strings; however, this is the predominant requirement in most applications we are aware of.

Compressed prefix trees [16], k-banded alignment [3] and the filtering techniques we apply [1,4,16] have been published before. However, this is the first work that combines these different ideas to speed up similarity search into a single, homogeneous algorithm supporting both similarity search and similarity joins. It is also the first work we are aware of that persistently integrates such a method into an RDBMS, thus offering its capabilities to SQL users.

[1] The largest collection of publicly available EST sequences is dbEST [14] with more than 60 million EST sequences from 1745 organisms as of May 2009.

Our paper is structured as follows. Chapter 2 contains an introduction to our data structures and to similarity search in general. In Chapt. 3 we describe our techniques for efficient similarity operations on compressed prefix trees. Chapter 4 gives details on the implementation. We present experimental results in Chapt. 5. Related work is discussed in Chapt. 6 and Chapt. 7 concludes the paper.

## 2 Preliminaries

Let $\Sigma$ be an alphabet (we will usually use $\{a, c, g, t\}$). We use $s$, with subscripts if required, to denote strings in $\Sigma^*$. Let $n = |s|$ be the length of $s$. A substring of $s$, denoted by $s[i \ldots j]$, starts at position $i$ and ends at position $j$. We call $s[1 \ldots j]$ prefix, $s[k \ldots |s|]$ suffix and $s[i..j], (1 \leq i \leq j \leq |s|)$, infix of $s$. Any infix of length $q$ is called $q$-gram. For a fixed $q$, $s$ contains $m = n - q + 1$ $q$-grams. A pair $(i, s[i, \ldots, i + q - 1])$ is called *positional* $q$-gram [18].

### 2.1 Similarity Measures

Similarity-based operations must be based on a concrete similarity measure. PETER supports Hamming distance and edit distance.

**Definition 1 (Hamming distance).** *The Hamming distance $d_{hd}(s_1, s_2)$ of two strings $s_1, s_2$ of equal length is the number of mismatching characters in $s_1$ and $s_2$: $d_{hd}(s_1, s_2) = |\{i|s_1[i] \neq s_2[i]\}|$. We say two strings are within Hamming distance $k$ if $d_{hd}(s_1, s_2) \leq k$.*

Obviously, computing the Hamming distance of two strings with $|s_1| = |s_2| = n$ is possible in $O(n)$. However, Hamming distance is only defined for strings of equal length, and also an inappropriate measure in most bioinformatics applications. There, we are mostly interested in the minimal number of operations that turn one string into the other, called the edit distance (or Levenshtein distance).

**Definition 2 (Edit distance).** *The edit distance $d_{ed}(s_1, s_2)$ of two strings $s_1, s_2$ with $|s_1| = n, |s_2| = m$ is the minimal number of insertions, deletions, or replacements of single characters needed to transfrom $s_1$ into $s_2$. We say two strings are within edit distance $k$, if $d_{ed} \leq k$.*

Using dynamic programming, the edit distance can be computed $O(|s_1| * |s_2|)$ [13,19]. However, faster computation is possible when one is only interested in highly similar strings. The *k-banded alignment* algorithm finds the edit distance of two strings with edit distance of at most $2k$ in $O(k * max\{|s_1|, |s_2|\})$.

**Definition 3 ($k$-banded alignment).** *The $k$-band of an edit distance matrix $M$ is defined as: $M[i, j] \in k\text{-band} \Leftrightarrow |i - j| \leq k$. If $s_1$ and $s_2$ are within edit distance $k$, their optimal alignment path must lie in the $k$-band of $M$. Thus, all cells of $M$ that are not in the $k$-band can be ignored [3].*

### 2.2 Similarity Operators

There are various forms of defining similarity operator [13]. We support two such operations: similarity search and similarity join.

**Definition 4 (Similarity search).** *Given a string s, a set S of strings, and a threshold k, ssearch(s, S) returns all* $s' \in S$ *for which* $d(s, s') \leq k$.

**Definition 5 (Similarity join).** *Given two sets* $S_1, S_2$ *of strings and a threshold k,* $sjoin(S_1, S_2)$ *returns all pairs* $(s_1, s_2), s_1 \in S_1, s_2 \in S_2$ *for which* $d(s_1, s_2) \leq k$.

As described before, we support Hamming and edit distance as distance function. Note that both operations naturally also support exact search and exact joins, simply by setting $k = 0$ for either distance measure. We will see in Chapt. 5 that even exact joins on large collections of long strings are considerably faster with PETER than using hash or merge joins.

### 2.3 Compressed Prefix Trees

Our fundamental data structure are compressed prefix trees [12], built on top of a set of strings. Let $R$ be a set of tuples $(s, ID)$ where $s \in \Sigma^*$ and $ID$ is a unique identifier for $s$.

**Definition 6 (Prefix tree index).** *A compressed prefix tree index T for R is a rooted, directed tree that meets the following conditions:*

1. *Every node x is labeled with a sequence of characters* $c_i \in \Sigma$ *of length* $l \geq 1$. *The labels of any two children y, z of the same node x start with a different character.*
2. *Every string* $s \in R$ *maps to some node* $x \in T$ *such that the concatenation of all labels from T's root to x exactly is s. We call x string node and assign the corresponding ID to x. If a particular string occurs several times in R, all corresponding IDs are assigned to x.*
3. *(Compression of suffixes). Let x be the root of a subtree formed by a linear chain of children* $x_1, \ldots, x_m$*, where solely* $x_m$ *is a string node and has no further children. Then,* $x, x_1, \ldots, x_m$ *are merged to a single node* $x'$ *whose label is the concatenation of their labels. The ID of* $x_m$ *is assigned to* $x'$.
4. *(Compression of infixes). Let x be the root of a subtree formed by a linear chain of children* $x_1, \ldots, x_m$*, where no node is a string node and only* $x_m$ *has more than one child. Then,* $x, x_1, \ldots, x_{m-1}$ *are merged to a single node* $x'$ *whose label is the concatenation of their labels.* □

Conceptually, nodes may have labels of arbitrary length. Technically, we store labels of string nodes without children (e.g., unique suffixes in R) in two parts: A small part (usually 16 characters) is stored inside the node. The rest of the suffix is stored in an extra file (see Sect. 4.2 for details). Furthermore, we attach further information to every node, namely minimum/maximum string lengths and a frequency vector (see Sects. 3.2 and 3.3).

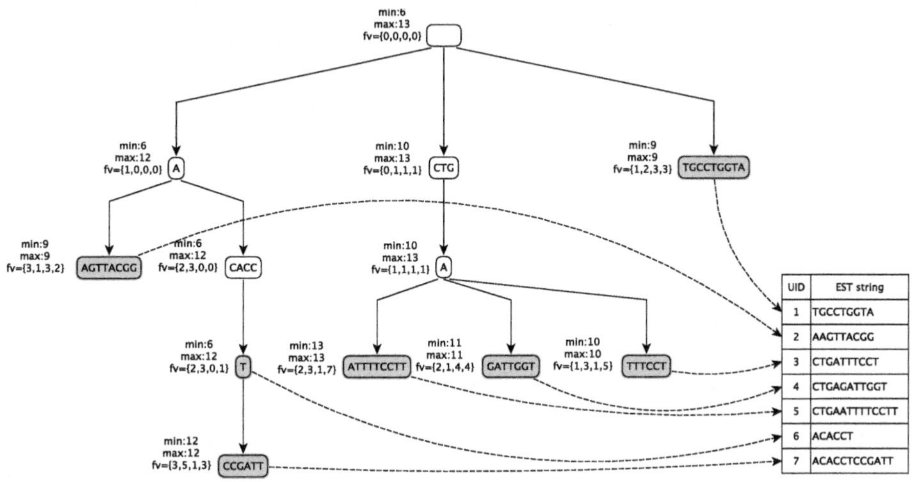


**Fig. 1.** Compressed prefix tree. Grey nodes are string nodes. Min/max specify minimum and maximum string lengths, fv denotes the frequency vector (see text).

Figure 1 shows an example of a compressed prefix tree. It has simple nodes (e.g., "A"), a compressed infix node ("CTG"), and a compressed suffix node ("TGCCTGGTA").

## 3 Similarity Operations on Prefix Trees

To our knowledge, similarity search in prefix trees based on pre-order traversal was first studied in [16]. This method computes the similarity for a given pattern $p$ to all strings indexed in a prefix tree $T$ while traversing $T$. While this does not change the worst-case complexity of searching, large savings are achieved when the indexed strings share many prefixes as these prefixes need to be compared only once to a prefix of the pattern. Thus, the method is very well suited for small alphabets and for very large string collections, as these properties increase the number and average lengths of shared prefixes.

Shang et al. described shared prefix analysis in [16]. In the following, we very briefly repeat the general idea but concentrate on our various extensions which greatly increase effectiveness: switch from global alignment to k-banded alignment, addition of filtering techniques for further search space pruning, and extension of the method to also allow similarity joins. Filtering is performed at two stages. For edit distance, we use a combination of length and frequency filtering to prune whole subtrees. Whenever we reach a leaf, we apply a $q$-gram pre-selection to suffixes. For Hamming distance, we only use length and frequency filtering.

All extensions are described below. For space reasons, we focus on similarity search and only briefly mention changes necessary to compute similarity joins.

Consider a compressed prefix tree $T$ for a set of strings $R$. Let $p$ be a search pattern and $S$ another indexed set of strings. Let $t$ be a node in $T$. By slight abuse of notation, we use $t$ both for the node and for the concatenation of labels from root to the node $t$. Let $k$ be a user-defined threshold for similarity operations.

### 3.1 Shared Prefix Pruning

Clearly, $t$ represents the shared prefix $s[1 \ldots |t|]$ of a set of strings all of which must be descendants of $t$. Note that both Hamming and edit distance to $p$ can only grow with growing prefix length. Thus, the following holds:

1. Hamming-search: If $d_{hd}(t, p[1 \ldots |t|]) > k$, then all strings below $t$ can be pruned. Thus, traversal does not descend further from $t$.
2. Hamming-join: Both trees, $T$ and $S$, are traversed simultaneously. Only nodes with $|s| = |t|$ need to be compared to each other. Let $s \in S$ have the same label length as $t$. If $d_{hd}(t, s) > k$, then the subtrees starting at $t$ in $T$ and $s$ in $S$ can be pruned.
3. Edit-search: Let $p$ be aligned horizontal and $t$ vertical in the $k$-banded distance matrix. All strings in the subtree below $t$ share the same prefix $t$ and thus also share rows 0 to $|t|$ in the matrix. If row $|t|$ contains only values larger than $k$, then no string below $t$ can have a smaller edit distance to $p$. This subtree can be ignored for further search.
4. Edit-join: Again, all strings below $s$ share the same prefix. The same arguments as for search hold, except that now we compare to a shared prefix in $S$ instead of a single $p$. Additionaly, the subtree also can be pruned if any row contains only values larger than $k$.

### 3.2 Length Filtering

Trivially, $t$ is a candidate for $p$ regarding Hamming distance only if it is of equal length as $p$. With respect to edit distance, $t$ and $p$ are worth examining only if $|t| - |p| \leq k$. To quickly check this property, we store two additional attributes at every node - the minimum ($min$) and maximum ($max$) string length of all strings below that node. If $(|max(t)+k| < |p|) \vee (|min(t)-k| > |p|)$ holds, then no string below $t$ can be edit-similar to $p$. Similarly, if $(|max(t)| < |p|) \vee (|min(t)| > |p|)$ holds, no string below $t$ can be Hamming-similar to $p$. Thus, traversal will not descend further. The same argument applies conceptionally to similarity join, when $p$ is replaced with a shared prefix in the joined tree $S$.

### 3.3 Frequency Distance Filtering

Aghili et al. [1] proposed frequency distance based filtering to reduce candidate sets in similarity searching on strings. Consider a string $s \in \Sigma^*$. The corresponding frequency vector $fv(s)$ of $s$ consists of $|\Sigma|$ components, where component $i$ counts the number of occurrences of $x_i \in \Sigma$ in $s$.

**Definition 7 (Frequency distance).** *For* $\{s_1, s_2\} \in \Sigma^*$*, the frequency distance* $fD(s_1, s_1)$ *is the minimum of the necessary number of applications of* $+1$ *or of* $-1$ *needed to transform* $fv(s_1)$ *into* $fv(s_2)$*.*

*Example 1.* Consider $s_1$ = acacctccgatt, $s_2$ = acacatccgaaa with Hamming distance $d_{hd} = 3$ and edit distance $d_{ed} = 3$. The corresponding frequency vectors for $s_1, s_2$ are $fv(s_1) = [3, 5, 1, 3]$ and $fv(s_2) = [6, 4, 1, 1]$. To transform $fv(s_1)$ into $fv(s_2)$, we need to add $3*(+1)$ for character a, $1*(-1)$ for c, and $2*(-1)$ for t. The frequency distance sums up to $fD(s_1, s_2) = min(|3*(+1)|, |3*(-1)|) = 3$.

Actually, frequency distance is a lower bound to Hamming and to edit distance [1]. Thus, evaluation of frequency vectors gives a third method to stop traversal of the index tree. We prune a subtree starting at $t$, if $fD(t, p) - (|t| - |p|) > k$ on both similarity search settings. Extension to join is straight-forward.

### 3.4 Q-Gram Filtering

Indexing methods based on $q$-grams are well-known to restrict search spaces efficiently for edit distance operations. They take advantage of the observation that two strings are within a small edit distance if they share a large number of $q$-grams [17]. Actually, the number of matching $q$-grams acts as another bound to edit distance [4].

**Definition 8 (Mismatching $q$-grams).** *Let* $Q_{s_1}$*,* $Q_{s_2}$ *be sets of positional q-grams of* $s_1$ *and* $s_2$*, respectively.* $s_1$ *and* $s_2$ *are within edit distance k, iff* $|Q_{s_1} \cap Q_{s_2}| \geq max(|s_1|, |s_2|) - 1 - (k-1)*q$*. A string* $s_1$ *is not within edit distance k to* $s_2$*, if* $Q_{s_1}$ *contains at least* $|Q_{mis}| = (|s_1| - q + 1) - (max(|s_1|, |s_2|) - 1 - (k-1)*q)$ *positional q-grams that are not contained in* $s_2$*.*

The choice of $q$ commonly depends on the average string length $l$. In this work, we follow [13] and use $q = log_{|\Sigma|}(l)$. Unlike [4], we do not use $q$-grams for indexing, but for suffix pre-selection. As shown in Fig. 2, nearly 90% of all indexed strings in our evaluation data set have large, unique suffixes. Determining the k-banded edit distance for the whole string needs $m * (2k + 1)$ computations for the suffix (with $m$ smaller, but often not much smaller than $|s|$), whereas the computation of positional $q$-grams for that suffix takes only $m - q + 1$ operations. Thus, the costs for comparing mismatching $q$-grams are on average smaller than computing the edit distance immediately. Therefore, when a leaf with suffix $s[x \ldots |s|]$ of length $m$ is reached, we compute all positional $q$-grams for this suffix. For similarity searches, we also extract the suffix of length $m$ from the search pattern and evaluate $Q_{mis}$ on both sets. For approximate joins, we evaluate $Q_{mis}$ only if we have reached a suffix leaf in both relations. We do not apply $q$-gram filtering to Hamming distance queries as the costs for building and evaluating $q$-grams are higher than comparing the suffixes directly.

## 4 Implementation

In this section, we describe implementation details on the primal functions of PETER. All algorithms can be executed standalone from the command line, as operators inside a database, or as a library in other C++ programs. Our implementation allows for both indexing database relations and flat files. We provide functionality for index building, searching, and insertion, deletion or modification of indexed strings. PETER also contains an index optimization routine that physically rearranges the trees and the suffix files in order to decrease the number of disk page accessions during tree traversal. This method should be called after extensive changes to the index and the string set to prevent index degradation. Next to approximate search and join operations, we support exact searches and joins as well as range queries, the SQL 'LIKE'-operator and prefix-based searches.

### 4.1 Algorithms

**Search.** Algorithm 1 shows the pseudocode for similarity searching in a prefix tree index. PETER essentially performs a depth-first traversal of the prefix tree applying all pruning techniques presented in Chapt. 3. Before descending from a node, we apply length and frequency filters. We also prune if we exceed the allowed distance threshold. In case of edit distance searches, we check for every reached string node whether the number of mismatching positional $q$-grams exceeds $Q_{mis}$. The function *getDistance* checks a flag whether a Hamming or edit distance search is performed and computes the new distance. When a match was found, the pair of matching EST objects (each pair consists of the ESTs and their UIDs) is added to the result set. Finally, the result set is returned to the user and by default printed to `stdout`.

**Join.** When using the join operator (see Algorithm 2) on two relations, conceptionally the intersection of two trees is computed. Both index trees $T$ and $S$ are traversed concurrently, such that the tree with less nodes is traversed first. Tree sizes are checked at startup. Length and frequency filtering are applied as in the search algorithm. Global variables are used to store the number of processed characters for the currently expanded strings in both trees. If we reach a string node in tree $T$ (or $S$, respectively), we fetch the complete string represented by this node and perform a call to the search function, with the string as pattern, the remaining subtree $S'$ of $S$ ($T'$ of $T$) and the current distance value as parameters. We continue the distance computation for the next untreated characters in the string and $S'$ ($T'$). The result set contains all pairs of matching EST objects and is constructed through the search algorithm. Finally, it is returned to the user and printed to `stdout`.

### 4.2 Index Structure

Our index structure is physically stored in two files, the prefix tree and a suffix file. In the prefix tree file, all nodes are stored contiguously in pre-order arrangement. Nodes may have variable size. Each one consists of a node id, information on the node type (string node or not), its label, references to all children, max. and min. lengths, and a frequency vector. If a node is a string node, it also

**Algorithm 1.** searchTree(Node $x$, EST $p$, int $k$, int $d$)

**if** $isLeaf(x) \wedge getEditDistance() \wedge !passesQGramFilter(x)$ **then**
    **return**
**end if**
$newDistance \leftarrow getDistance(x, p, d)$
**if** $newDistance > k$ **then**
    **return**
**end if**
**if** $hasID(x)$ **then**
    $addMatchingESTsToResultSet(s[1 \dots x], p)$
**end if**
**for all** children y of x **do**
    **if** $passesLengthFilter(y, p, k) \wedge passFrequencyFilter(y, p, k)$ **then**
        $searchTree(y, p, k, newDistance)$
    **end if**
**end for**

**Algorithm 2.** joinTree(Node $x$, Node $y$, int $k$, int $d$)

$newDistance \leftarrow getDistance(x, y, d)$
**if** $hasID(x)$ **then**
    $pattern \leftarrow getString(1, x)$
    $searchTree(y, pattern, k, newDistance)$
**else if** $hasID(y)$ **then**
    $pattern \leftarrow getString(1, y)$
    $searchTree(x, pattern, k, newDistance)$
**end if**
**for all** children x' of x **do**
    **for all** children y' of y **do**
        **if** $passesLengthFilter(x', y', k) \wedge passesFrequencyFilter(x', y', k)$ **then**
            $joinTree(x', y', k, newDistance)$
        **end if**
    **end for**
**end for**

contains the respective ID; if the node maps to more than one ID, we store a reference to an index-sequential file that contains all IDs instead.

String nodes also store the length of the remaining suffix and its prefix (of the suffix). As explained previously, this suffix can be quite large; actually, those suffixes form the bulk of the size of the entire data structure. We therefore decided to store all but short prefixes of the suffixes in an extra file, which allows us to keep the prefix tree itself in main memory even for very large string collections. Actually, the tree file for $TX$ (5,000,000 strings, see Fig. 2) has a size of 549 MB on disk and 943 MB when the prefix tree is kept in main memory. Suffixes of the suffixes are stored in an external file referenced from string nodes. Suffix accession follows the *lazy evaluation* paradigm both for $q$-gram evaluation and character comparison: if a suffix node is reached, the internal suffix is examined first. External suffixes are only loaded when needed. Very often, this method allows to take decisions without accessing the suffix file.

Insert operations to the index are executed sequentially. First, our insert algorithm searches by depth-first traversing the index tree the appropriate insert position for the new EST string. We update the values for $min/max$ for all ancestors while descending. Existing nodes might be modified, all newly created nodes are appended to the end of the index file. In case the index file gets too fragmented, we manually launch an optimizing routine that rearranges the index and suffix file in preorder accession.

### 4.3 Integration into RDBMS

We integrated our programs as a shared library into a commercial RDBMS (name omitted) using its built-in extension capabilities. These include user-defined indexes (used for prefix tree) and user-defined table functions necessary to implement similarity joins. Integrating user-defined functions and indexes consists of two parts: The first part is the program code, compiled as a shared library and saved at a specific position in the file system. The second part involves declarations and definitions directly executed on the server, including a reference to the library.

When index and query functions are accessed for the first time in a session, the server determines the location of the shared library. A listener process invokes a session-specific agent and passes over the call including procedure and library name and any parameters, if present. The agent loads the library and runs the desired function, that, in our case, in turn opens the index (and later on the suffix file if required). Any return values are passed back via the agent. Throughout the session, this agent remains alive, which implies that initialization costs for the agent emerge only once.

However, only the code is kept in memory, while any data loaded during executing of the call are discarded by the agent. Caching or buffering of user-loaded data is not supported. This is a severe drawback of the extension mechanism, since it implies that, in our case, the entire prefix tree is loaded again for every single call of a similarity search. As we will see in the next Chapter, this method incurs a large penalty on any user-defined index compared to the server's build-in methods.

## 5 Experiments

We use ESTs (see Introduction) to evaluate the performance of PETER both for similarity and for exact operations ($k = 0$). To this end, we extracted a subset from dbEST as of 28.05.2009. We fixed $|\sigma| = 4$ and removed all sequences containing characters other than A,C,G or T. Figure 2 shows properties of the sets we used during the evaluation. $T_i$ consists of EST sequences from the $i$-th dbEST archive, $T_{ij}$ consists of a subset $j$ of randomly chosen EST strings from $T_i$, $TX$ consists of randomly chosen EST strings from the dbEST archives 20 to

| Set | # EST strings | avg. string length | min/max length | # tree nodes | # ext. suffixes |
|---|---|---|---|---|---|
| $T_1$ | 307,542 | 348 | 14/3,615 | 589,062 | 293,764 |
| $T_2$ | 736,305 | 387 | 12/3,707 | 1,482,709 | 689,590 |
| $T_{2a}$ | 368,152 | 382 | 12/2,774 | 711,632 | 352,872 |
| $T_{2b}$ | 184,076 | 385 | 22/2,774 | 349,329 | 177,846 |
| $T_{2c}$ | 92,038 | 383 | 25/2,774 | 171,964 | 89,198 |
| $T_{2d}$ | 46,019 | 381 | 28/2,774 | 84,954 | 44,716 |
| $T_{2e}$ | 23,009 | 373 | 31/ 878 | 42,375 | 22,366 |
| $T_3$ | 10,000 | 536 | 16/3,707 | 16,310 | 8,774 |
| $TX$ | 5,000,000 | 359 | 14/3,247 | 10,478,214 | 4,834,231 |

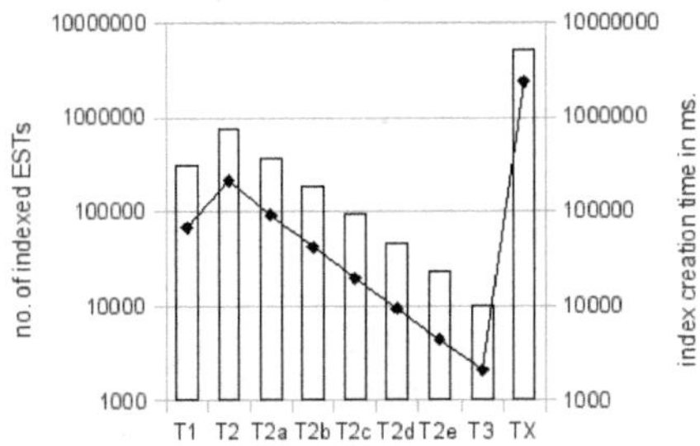


**Fig. 2.** Left: Properties of EST sets. Right: Index creation (line) wrt. set size (bar).

26. We show results for varying numbers of indexed strings,for varying $k$, and for each filter technique (see Chapt. 3) in isolation. Index creation and optimization was performed in advance and is not included in the measured times (but see Fig.2). We observed that the time for index creation grows, as expected, linear with the number of indexed strings.

We compare the performance of PETER against two competitors: The Unix tools command line tools `grep`, `agrep`, and `nrgrep`, and build-in or user-defined functions inside the RDBMS. We also tried to compare to other recently published methods, such as [5,21], but none of these is available for download. In particular, we acknowledge that comparison against Unix command line tools are not completely satisfactory, as our method first builds an index of the set to be searched. Therefore, it is more suited for searching the same set of strings multiple times. However, we will show that index creation time is leveraged already for very few searches (see Section 4.3). Note that [16] also compared against `agrep`.

All experiments were performed on a Pentium-M 740 processor with 2 GB RAM. For each experiment, we report the average of ten runs.

### 5.1 Effect of Pruning Strategies

We evaluated the effects of length, frequency, and $q$-gram filtering individually and in all possible combinations using sets $T_1$ and $T_3$. For search queries, we performed searches for all EST strings taken from $T_3$ in $T_1$ with different similarity thresholds. For joins, we computed $T_1 \bowtie T_3$.

Search results are shown in Fig.3. Overall, frequency filtering did not lead to significant runtime improvements. We suppose that this is caused by the small alphabet which makes the compared vectors very small. Length filtering leads to improvements for Hamming distance searches in the range of 5% for $k = 1$ growing up to 76% for $k = 8$. Looking at edit distance searches, length filtering performed even better, with improvements in the range of 10% for $k = 1$ growing up to 86% for $k = 8$. Interestingly, $q$-gram filtering in edit distance searches improved the execution time significantly only for $k = 1$ (10%) and $k = 3$ (13%). But combining length and $q$-gram filtering for small $k$ improves average execution times in the range of 18% for k=1, for $k = 2$ up to 58% and 81%

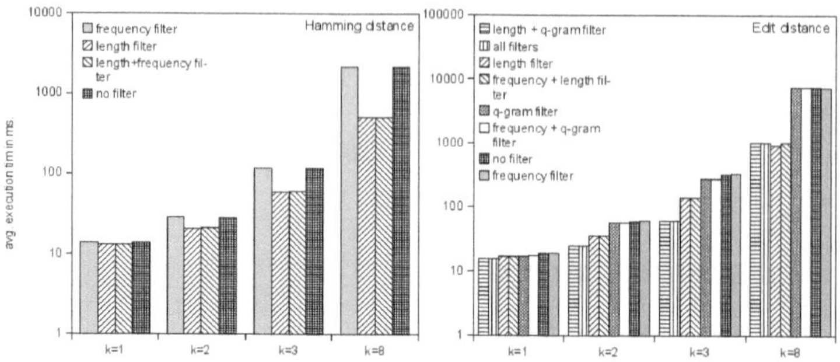


**Fig. 3.** Search execution time of $p \in T_3$ with $k \in \{1, 2, 3, 8\}$ in $T_1$ wrt. filters (log-scale)

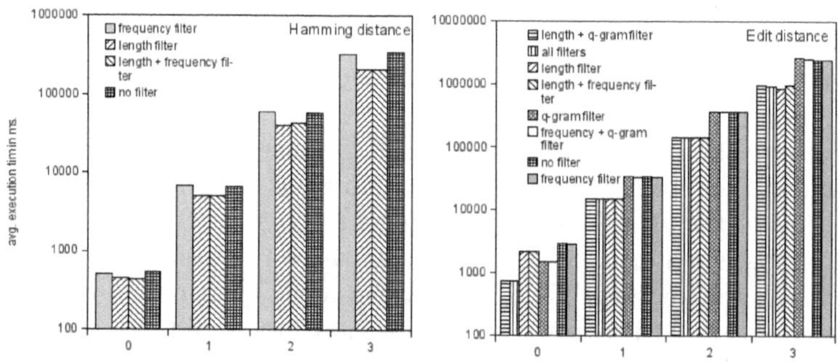


**Fig. 4.** Join execution time of $T_1 \bowtie T_3$ with $k \in \{0, 1, 2, 3, 8\}$ wrt. filters (log-scale)

for $k = 3$. There is also a clear tendency that runtime improvements achieved by filtering increase with increasing similarity thershold, i.e., they are the more effective, the more differences are allowed.

In terms of join algorithms, frequency filtering again only has a neglible impact(see Fig.4). For joins on Hamming distance, we observed that length filtering improved the join execution time from 18% ($k = 0$) up to 40 % ($k = 3$). For edit distance joins, single $q$-gram filtering leads to improvements in the range of 50% for $k = 0$. For growing $k$, standalone length filtering was more effective. Again, speed-ups roughly correlate with allowed differences.

Overall, a combination of length and $q$-gram filtering seems to be the best configuration. Therefore, in all following experiments with PETER we always used length filtering for Hamming distance and a combination of length and $q$-gram filtering for edit distance.

## 5.2 Performance of Search

We compared the execution times of PETER for Hamming and edit distance for various tresholds to Unix command line tools. We used `grep` for $k = 0$, and `agrep` and `nrgrep` for $k \in \{1, 2, 3, 8\}$, respectively. First, we performed individual searches for each pattern $p \in T_3$ in the indexed EST set $T_1$. When searching with the Unix tools all searches were started to match only complete strings to the given pattern. As **agrep** is bounded with a maximum pattern length of 32 characters, we used **nrgrep** to handle longer patterns.

For exact search, we outperform **grep** significantly with a factor of 63 for Hamming distance and a factor of 50 for edit distance scoring enabled. As shown in Fig.6(a), the impact of the pattern length was negligible for exact searches in all tested methods. Figure 5 contrasts the average execution times of inexact searches to **agrep** and **nrgrep**. For very short patterns, we outperform **agrep** with factors in the range of 640 for $k = 1$ up to 1063 for $k = 8$ on Hamming distance and a factor up to 450 for edit distance constraints. When searching with patterns of arbitrary length, we are up to 60 times faster than **nrgrep** for Hamming distance and up to 45 times faster for edit distance.

We observed a small influence of pattern lengths with growing tresholds (data not shown). Searching for patterns of lengths 200 to 600 took slightly longer than searching for shorter or longer patterns. This is not surprising as strings with lengths in this range make up most of all strings in $T_1$. Searching with Hamming distance constraints has always better response times than edit distance, in the range of 5% ($k = 0$) to 65 % with growing $k$. This is caused by costs for initializing and computing the edit distance matrix.

Even if we add the costs for index creation to the evaluation, PETER amortizes quite fast. For example, if we run multiple Hamming distance (edit distance, respectively) searches in $T_1$ with $k = 1$, it takes only 10 (15) searches to outperform the cumulated runtimes of **agrep**. Compared to **nrgrep**, it takes 125 (105) Hamming distance (edit distance) queries until PETER is profitable.

## 5.3 Performance of Similarity Join

We compared the execution time of a natural join on $T_1 \bowtie T_{2i}$ in PETER to the Unix command `join`. All joins were highly selective even for large tresholds as indicated in Fig.7. Since `join` expects sorted flat-files as input, we performed a preprocessing step on the corresponding EST sets that is not included in the execution time of `join`. We thought this to be fair, as index creation times also are not included in the measurements with PETER. `Join` almost always

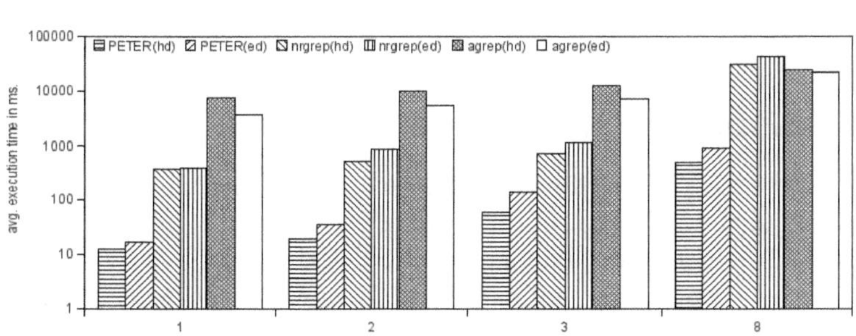


**Fig. 5.** Search in PETER vs. Unix tools for $p \in T_3$, $k \in \{1, 2, 3, 8\}$ (log-scale)

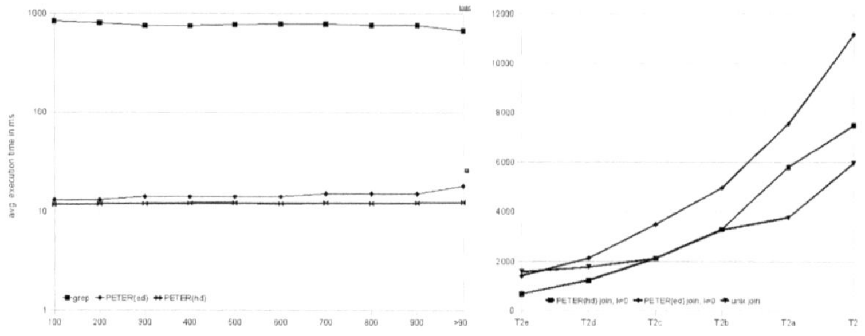

(a) Search $p \in T_3$ in $T_1$  (b) Join $T_1 \bowtie T_{2i}$, $i \in \{a, b, c, d, e\}$

**Fig. 6.** Avg. execution times for exact searches (log-scale) and joins, k=0

| Join | $\|A \times B\|$ | $\|A \bowtie B\|$ $k = 0$ | $\|A \bowtie_{hd} B\|$ $k = 1$ | $\|A \bowtie_{hd} B\|$ $k = 3$ | $\|A \bowtie_{ed} B\|$ $k = 1$ | $\|A \bowtie_{ed} B\|$ $k = 3$ |
|---|---|---|---|---|---|---|
| $T_1 \bowtie T_2$ | 226,444,712,310 | 299 | 514 | 841 | 941 | 2,552 |
| $T_1 \bowtie T_{2a}$ | 113,222,202,384 | 187 | 326 | 374 | 239 | 463 |
| $T_1 \bowtie T_{2b}$ | 56,611,101,192 | 128 | 214 | 236 | 152 | 301 |
| $T_1 \bowtie T_{2c}$ | 28,305,550,596 | 78 | 127 | 178 | 75 | 232 |
| $T_1 \bowtie T_{2d}$ | 14,152,775,298 | 42 | 71 | 91 | 46 | 165 |
| $T_1 \bowtie T_{2e}$ | 7,076,233,878 | 28 | 41 | 55 | 33 | 106 |
| $T_1 \bowtie T_3$ | 3,075,420,000 | 1,048 | 1,053 | 1,059 | 1,058 | 1,082 |
| $T_{2e} \bowtie T_3$ | 230,090,000 | 54 | 70 | 106 | 94 | 258 |
| $T_1 \bowtie TX$ | 1,537,710,000,000 | 37 | 115 | 372 | 354 | 992 |

**Fig. 7.** Join cardinalities for Hamming distance ($\bowtie_{hd}$) and edit distance ($\bowtie_{ed}$) join

outperforms our algorithm with $d_{ed} = 0$. For Hamming distance $d_{hd} = 0$ PETER beats `join` if the joined sets differ in size with a factor of at least 1.7, as presented in Fig.6(b). Both observations are not surprising since an exact join on sorted input only requires to linearly scan both files. For approximate joins, we are not aware of any Unix command line tool that could handle this problem. Comparing edit distance to Hamming distance joins, the latter always performed in a range of 30% to 60 % better, mostly dependent on the given treshold (see Fig.8). We observe an exponential growth of join execution times with respect to the treshold although the result sets don't grow exponentially. The reason for this is that the search space increases exponentially with growing $k$. While tree traversal, PETER descends further as $k$ grows and for every additional node, that is reached in $T$, there are $|\sigma|$ additional subtrees examined in $S$.

### 5.4 Performance of PETER Inside a RDBMS

We compared PETER's performance against exact and similarity-based search and joins inside the RDBMS. For searching, we performed single `SELECT` queries on the B*-indexed relation $T_1$ for each EST string in $T_3$. At all times and for different pattern length, the built-in `SELECT`-operator achieves better runtimes than a prefix tree based search, see Fig.9(a). Factors vary dependent on the pattern length, in a range of 2 ($|p| \leq 400$) to 1.3 ($|p| \geq 800$). There are mostly two reasons for this result. First, the operations in the prefix tree index are handled

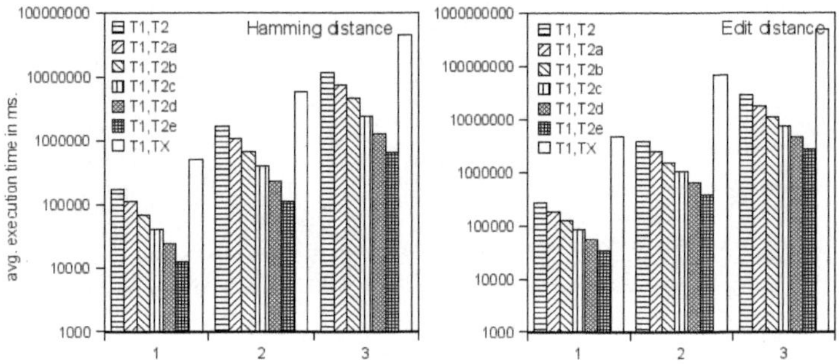


**Fig. 8.** Similarity join in PETER for $k \in \{1, 2, 3\}$ on $T_1 \bowtie T_{2i}$, $T_1 \bowtie TX$ (log-scale)

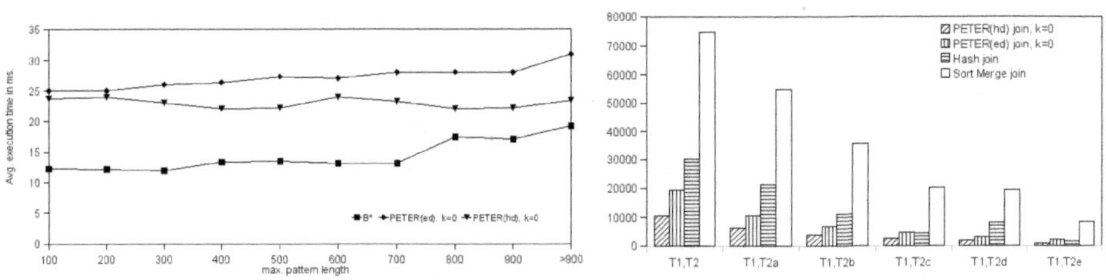


(a) Search (b) Join

**Fig. 9.** PETER vs. RDBMS built-in operators for $k = 0$. For result sizes see Fig.7

via the extension interface which produces overhead for every call. Second, the extension interface does not allow caching of data. While the internal implementation uses the internal buffer pool of the database to cache the most important parts of the B*-index, this is not possible for user-defined indexing. Given these severe drawbacks, it is noteably that PETER is only so little slower. Although the page cache of the OS significantly speeds up the response times of subsequent queries on the command-line (25–30% speedup on avg.), we could not observe this effect inside the RDBMS (5–8% speedup on avg.). This indicates that a more tight integration into the database kernel could give a data structure like PETER significant advantages over B*-indexes (for large sets of long strings).

Regarding joins, we computed $T_1 \bowtie T_{2i}$ as a Hash join and as a Sort-Merge join and compared these results to PETER. Joins on the prefix tree index always outperformed both Hash join (with factors between 1.5 and 4) and Sort-Merge join (with factors 3.8 to 10), see Fig. 9(b). Note that the problem of caching is not a severe one here, as computing the join requires to load both indexes only once. We find PETER's performance for exact strings quite remarkable as they – for large sets of long strings – beat the highly-tuned joins of a commercial database system.

As there are no built-in functions for similarity operations inside the database, we implemented them as user-defined functions (UDF) in the database's

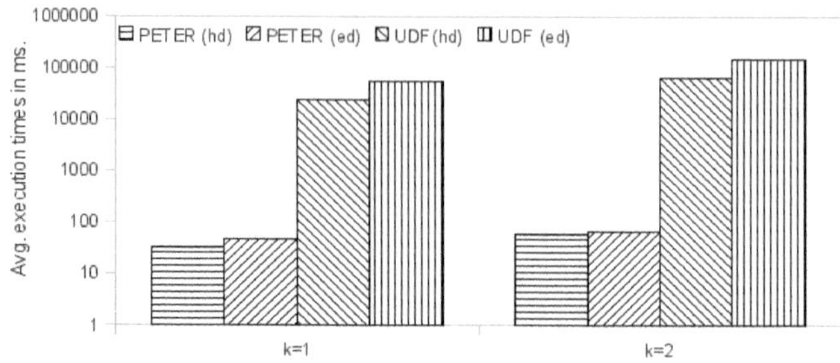


**Fig. 10.** Comparison of prefix tree search to UDFs (log-scale)

programming language. The edit distance function computes the $k$-banded alignment score for two strings. Length filtering is included in both UDFs. We compared the execution time of UDF-based similarity search and joins to PETER. Fig.10 shows that PETER for similarity searches performs better by an order of magnitude than using just UDFs. For Hamming distance search, prefix tree indexing leads to a runtime improvement factor of about 520, for edit distance searches of about 890. We also tried to perform similarity joins for $k = 1$ with UDFs on $T2_e \bowtie T3$, but as the join operations did not finish within a day, we aborted the execution. Similarity joins with prefix trees finished for $k \in \{1, 2\}$ in less than one minute.

## 6 Related Work

Prefix trees, compressed or uncompressed, have applications in many areas. They are well known for representing multiple search patterns in exact pattern matching [6], but have also been shown to perform well in frequent itemset mining algorithms [7] or set joins [8].

Shang et al. [16] were the first that extended prefix trees with dynamic programming techniques to perform inexact string matching. They have shown that searches with one or no error perform several times better than `agrep`, but as they do not apply any filtering techniques, `agrep` outperforms their implementation for larger $k$. Schallehn et al. [15] describe a prefix trie based index for similarity search, joins and group operations for Oracle DB. The authors introduce operators, all based on depth-first traversal, for duplicate detection in heterogenous integration scenarios that outperform non-indexed similarity operators. They did not consider any pruning. Furthermore, prefix trees are generated on-the-fly, while PETER computes them only once.

The filtering techniqes we use are contained in several other algorithms. Gravano et al. [4] introduced an efficient similarity join algorithm that uses a $q$-gram index to preselect similar strings. We could not compare PETER with this algorithm as there is no implementation available. The benefit of using positional $q$-grams was shown in [5]. As the authors implemented a sampling-based approximation for similarity string joins, one cannot directly compare PETER to their tool. Furthermore, the system was specifically designed for use in Microsoft SQL Server, whereas PETER is built on top of another RDBMS.

Xiao et al. [21] proposed to analyze mismatching $q$-grams for candidate preselection in near-duplicate detection. They derived two new lower bounds for edit distance, one of which we also use for suffix filtering. A direct comparison between PETER and this method would be difficult, as it directly targets duplicate detection within one relation, while we have a far more general data structure.

Aghili et al. [1] use frequency filtering as part of a vector transformation. They apply discrete wavelet and discrete fourier transformation for pre-filtering approximate join candidates in biological databases. We could not compare PETER with Aghili et al. since no implementation is available.

## 7 Conclusion

We presented PETER, an efficient data structure for similarity search and similarity joins on large sets of long strings. We showed that PETER outperforms all other methods we compared to, either inside or outside a RDBMS, in all performed similarity operations. Interestingly, it also outperforms exact joins inside a RDBMS.

## References

1. Aghili, S.A., Agrawal, D., Abbadi, A.E.: Bft: Bit filtration technique for approximate string join in biological databases. In: Nascimento, M.A., de Moura, E.S., Oliveira, A.L. (eds.) SPIRE 2003. LNCS, vol. 2857, pp. 326–340. Springer, Heidelberg (2003)
2. Altschul, S.F., Madden, T.L., Schäffer, A.A., Zhang, J., Zhang, Z., Miller, W., Lipman, D.J.: Gapped blast and psi-blast: a new generation of protein database search programs. Nucleic acids research 25(17) (September 1997)
3. Fickett, J.W.: Fast optimal alignment. Nucleic Acids Research 12 (1984)
4. Gravano, L., Ipeirotis, P.G., Jagadish, H.V., Koudas, N., Muthukrishnan, S., Srivastava, D.: Approximate string joins in a database (almost) for free. In: VLDB (2001)
5. Gravano, L., Ipeirotis, P.G., Koudas, N., Srivastava, D.: Text joins in an rdbms for web data integration. In: WWW 2003 (2003)
6. Gusfield, D.: Algorithms on Strings, Trees and Sequences: Computer Science and Computational Biology. Cambridge University Press, Cambridge (1997)
7. Han, J., Pei, J., Yin, Y., Mao, R.: Mining frequent patterns without candidate generation: A Frequent-Pattern tree approach. Data Mining and Knowledge Discovery 8(1) (2004)
8. Jampani, R., Pudi, V.: Using Prefix-Trees for efficiently computing set joins. In: Zhou, L.-z., Ooi, B.-C., Meng, X. (eds.) DASFAA 2005. LNCS, vol. 3453, pp. 761–772. Springer, Heidelberg (2005)
9. Kalyanaraman, A., Alaru, S.: Expressed sequence tags: Clustering and applications. In: Handbook of Computational Molecular Biology. Chapman & Hall CRC computer information science, Boca Raton (2006)

10. Koudas, N., Marathe, A., Srivastava, D.: Flexible string matching against large databases in practice. In: VLDB 2004 (2004)
11. Lee, T., Pouliot, Y., Wagner, V., Gupta, P., Calvert, D.S., Tenenbaum, J., Karp, P.: Biowarehouse: a bioinformatics database warehouse toolkit. BMC Bioinformatics 7 (2006)
12. Morrison, D.R.: PATRICIA - practical algorithm to retrieve information coded in alphanumeric. Journal of the ACM (JACM) 15(4) (1968)
13. Navarro, G.: A guided tour to approximate string matching. ACM Computing Surveys 33(1) (2001)
14. NCBI. dbEST (1992), `http://www.ncbi.nlm.nih.gov/dbest`
15. Schallehn, E., Sattler, K.-U., Saake, G.: Efficient similarity-based operations for data integration. Data & Knowledge Engineering 48 (2004)
16. Shang, H., Merrett, T.: Tries for approximate string matching. IEEE TKDE 8(4) (1996)
17. Sutinen, E., Tarhio, J.: Filtration with q-Samples in approximate string matching. In: Hirschberg, D.S., Meyers, G. (eds.) CPM 1996. LNCS, vol. 1075. Springer, Heidelberg (1996)
18. Sutinen, E., Tarhio, J.: On using q-Gram locations in approximate string matching. In: Spirakis, P.G. (ed.) ESA 1995. LNCS, vol. 979, Springer, Heidelberg (1995)
19. Wagner, R.A., Fischer, M.J.: The String-to-String correction problem. Journal of the ACM (JACM) 21(1) (1974)
20. Williams, H.E., Zobel, J.: Indexing and retrieval for genomic databases. IEEE TKDE 14(1) (2002)
21. Xiao, C., Wang, W., Lin, X.: Ed-Join: an efficient algorithm for similarity joins with edit distance constraints. In: VLDB 2008 (2008)

# Similarity Estimation Using Bayes Ensembles

Tobias Emrich, Franz Graf, Hans-Peter Kriegel,
Matthias Schubert, and Marisa Thoma

Ludwig-Maximilians-Universität München
Oettingenstr. 67, Munich, Germany
{emrich,graf,kriegel,schubert,thoma}@dbs.ifi.lmu.de

**Abstract.** Similarity search and data mining often rely on distance or similarity functions in order to provide meaningful results and semantically meaningful patterns. However, standard distance measures like $L_p$-norms are often not capable to accurately mirror the expected similarity between two objects. To bridge the so-called semantic gap between feature representation and object similarity, the distance function has to be adjusted to the current application context or user. In this paper, we propose a new probabilistic framework for estimating a similarity value based on a Bayesian setting. In our framework, distance comparisons are modeled based on distribution functions on the difference vectors. To combine these functions, a similarity score is computed by an Ensemble of weak Bayesian learners for each dimension in the feature space. To find independent dimensions of maximum meaning, we apply a space transformation based on eigenvalue decomposition. In our experiments, we demonstrate that our new method shows promising results compared to related Mahalanobis learners on several test data sets w.r.t. nearest-neighbor classification and precision-recall-graphs.

**Keywords:** similarity estimation, distance learning, supervised learning.

## 1 Introduction

Learning similarity functions is an important task for multimedia retrieval and data mining. In data mining, distance measures can be used in various algorithms for classification and clustering. To improve classification, the learned distance measure can be plugged into any instance-based learner like $k$NN classification. Though clustering is basically an unsupervised problem, learning a similarity function on a small set of manually annotated objects is often enough to guide clustering algorithms to group semantically more similar objects. For similarity search, adaptive similarity measures provide a powerful method to bridge the semantic gap between feature representations and user expectations. In most settings, the similarity between two objects cannot be described by a standardized distance measure fitting all applications. Instead, object similarity is often a matter of application context and personal preference. Thus, two objects might be similar in one context while they are not very similar in another context. For example, assume an image collection of various general images of

M. Gertz and B. Ludäscher (Eds.): SSDBM 2010, LNCS 6187, pp. 537–554, 2010.

persons, vehicles, animals, and buildings. In this context, a picture showing a red Ferrari will be considered as quite similar to a picture of a red Volkswagen. Now, take the same images and put them into a different context like a catalogue of rental cars. In this more specialized context, both pictures will most likely be considered as dissimilar. An important assumption in this paper is that there is no exact value specifying object similarity. Instead, we consider object similarity as the probability that a user would label the objects as similar.

Learning a distance or similarity function requires a general framework for comparing objects. In most established approaches to similarity learning, this framework is provided by using Mahalanobis distances or quadratic forms. In general, a Mahalanobis distance can be considered to be the Euclidean distance in a linear transformation of the original feature space. Thus, Mahalanobis distances are metric distance functions guaranteeing reflexivity, symmetry and the triangular inequality. Furthermore, the computed dissimilarity of two objects might be increased infinitely. In this paper, we argue that these mathematical characteristics are unnecessarily strict and sometimes even against intuition when trying to construct a similarity measure. For example, it is known from cognition science that humans do not distinguish dissimilar objects to an infinite degree. Thus, a human would not care whether object $o_1$ is more dissimilar to the query object $q$ than object $o_2$ after having decided that both objects $o_1, o_2$ have nothing in common with the query object $q$. Furthermore, it is questionable if characteristics such as strictness are necessary for successful similarity search. In most feature transformations, it is possible that two different objects are mapped to the same feature representation. Thus, even if we can guarantee that two objects having a zero distance are represented by the same feature description, we have no guarantee that the corresponding objects should be considered to be maximally similar as well.

In this paper, we describe similarity in a different way by considering it as the probability that an object $o$ is relevant for a similarity query object $q$. The core idea of our similarity estimation approach is to consider each feature as evidence for similarity or dissimilarity. Thus, we can express the implication of a certain feature $i$ to the similarity of objects $o$ and $q$ as a probability $p(\text{SIMILAR}(o, q) \mid (o[i] - q[i]))$. To calculate this probability, we employ a simple one-dimensional Bayes estimate (BE). However, to build a statement comprising all available information about object similarity, we do not build the joint probability over all features. We argue that in most applications considering a single feature it is not sufficient to decide either similarity or dissimilarity. Thus, to derive a joined estimation considering all available features, we average the probabilities derived from each BE. Our new estimate is basically an Ensemble of weak Bayesian learners. Therefore, we call our new dissimilarity function Bayes Ensemble Distance (BED). A major benefit of BED is that dissimilarity is very insensitive to outlier values in a single dimension which is a drawback of classical $L_p$-norm based measures. The major factors to successfully employing an Ensemble of learners are the quality and the independence of the underlying weak classifiers. Therefore, we will introduce a new optimization problem that derives a linear transformation of the feature space, allowing the construction of more descriptive BEs. To conclude, the contributions of this paper are:

- A discussion about $L_p$-norms and Mahalanobis distances for modelling object similarity.
- A new framework for similarity estimation that is built on an Ensemble of Bayes learners.
- An optimization method for generating a linear transformation of the feature space that is aimed at deriving independent features which are suitable for training high quality weak classifiers.

The rest of the paper is organized as follows. In Sect. 2, we discuss $L_p$ norm and Mahalanobis distances for modeling object similarity. Our new framework for modeling object similarity is described in Sect. 3. In Sect. 4, we introduce an optimization problem to derive an affine transformation that allows the training of more accurate Bayes estimates. Section 5 briefly reviews related similarity learners. Afterwards, Sect. 6 illustrates the results of our experimental evaluation comparing our new method with related metric learners on several UCI classification datasets and two image retrieval data sets. Finally, Sect. 7 concludes the paper with a summary and some directions for future work.

## 2 $L_p$-Norms and Problem Definition

The task of similarity learning is to find a function mapping a pair of objects $o_1, o_2$ to a similarity value $\text{SIM}(o_1, o_2)$ describing how strongly the first object resembles the other one in the best possible way. To train this function, it is necessary to have training examples representing the notion of similarity which underlies the given application. Let us note that there might be various notions of similarity on the same data set depending on the application context or even the current user.

Basically, there are two categories of examples used for learning similarity functions. The first type is providing class labels to a training set indicating that objects with equal labels are similar and objects with different labels are considered as dissimilar. Most machine learning approaches in metric learning use class labels because most of the proposed methods in this area aim at improving the accuracy of instance-based learners. One important advantage of this type of labeling is that there is a large variety of classification data sets available. Additionally, having $n$ labeled objects results in $\frac{n\cdot(n-1)}{2}$ labeled object pairs. Finally, in classification data sets the labeling is usually quite consistent because the classes are usually reproducible by several persons. As a drawback of this approach, it is required to find an universal set of classes before learning a similarity function. Thus, this type of user feedback is difficult to use when learning similarity measures for similarity search. The second type of user feedback is direct relevance feedback providing a similarity value for a set of object pairs. Using relevance feedback allows to determine a degree of similarity for each pair and thus, the similarity information is not necessarily binary. Additionally, relevance feedback does not require to define explicitly known classes and is thus more attractive for similarity search systems. A drawback of relevance feedback is that labelling a sufficiently large set of object pairs with similarity scores is usually much more strenuous than labelling objects with classes. Furthermore, it is often much more difficult to generate a consistent labelling because there usually are no well-defined criteria for object similarity.

After describing the labels of our examples, we will now formalize our object descriptions, i.e. the feature vectors. A feature is a type of observation about an object and the corresponding feature value describes how an object behaves w.r.t. this type of observation. Mathematically, we will treat a feature $F$ as a numerical value $x_F \in \mathbb{R}$. Considering a predefined number of features $d$ leads to a feature vector $x \in \mathbb{R}^d$. Formally, a training example in our setting is a triple $(x_1, x_2, y)$ where $x_1, x_2 \in \mathbb{R}^d$ are two $d$-dimensional feature vectors and $y \in [0, \dots, l]$ is a dissimilarity score, i.e. a 0 represents maximum similarity whereas $l$ describes maximum dissimilarity. In case of class labels, we assign 1 to dissimilar and 0 to similar objects. The most common approach for describing object similarity is to sum up the differences of feature values which is the basis of $L_p$-norm-based similarity. Given two feature vectors $x_1, x_2 \in \mathbb{R}^d$, the $L_p$-norms are defined as:

$$L_p(x_1, x_2) = \left( \sum_{i=1}^{d} |x_{1,i} - x_{2,i}|^p \right)^{\frac{1}{p}}$$

For $p = 2$, the $L_p$-norm is called Euclidean distance which is the most common distance metric in similarity search and distance-based data mining. Semantically, we can interpret the $L_p$-norm as an evidence framework. Each feature represents an observation about an object and the difference of feature values determines how similar two objects behave with respect to this observation. Since a single observation is usually not enough to decide similarity, all observations are combined. By summing up over the differences for each observation, the $L_p$-norm describes the degree of dissimilarity of two objects. The parameter $p$ determines the influence of large difference values in some dimensions to the complete distance. For $p \to \infty$, the object distance is completely determined by the largest object difference in any dimension. Let us note that the exponent $\frac{1}{p}$ is used for normalization reasons only. Therefore, it is not required in algorithms that require a similarity ranking.

Given a specialized application context, the standard $L_p$-norms have several drawbacks:

1. Correlated features are based on the same characteristics of an object and thus, they implicitly increase the impact of this characteristics when calculating the dissimilarity.
2. Not each observation is equally important when deciding about object similarity. When, for instance, deciding between large and small people, the *height* parameter will be more significant than the *weight* parameter.
3. In order to have a large distance w.r.t. an $L_p$-norm, it is sufficient to have a considerably large difference in any single feature. Correspondingly, a small

dissimilarity requires that both vectors display small difference values in each feature. On the other hand, to decide dissimilarity, any single feature is sufficient. This effect is a serious drawback because object similarity might not necessarily always depend on the same set of features. Having an extraordinarily large difference w.r.t. a single rather unimportant feature, could thus prevent two otherwise identical objects from being found in a similarity query. Thus, we argue that dissimilarity as well as similarity should be decided based on a combination of several features.

To solve the problems (1) and (2), the Euclidean distance has been extended to the Mahalanobis distance or quadratic form. The idea of this approach is to employ an affine transformation of the original feature space which is applied within the distance measure itself:

$$D_{\text{Mah}}(x_1, x_2) = \left((x_1 - x_2)^T \cdot A \cdot (x_1 - x_2)\right)^{\frac{1}{2}}$$

In order to make $D_{\text{Mah}}$ a metric, the transformation matrix $A$ has to be positive definite. In this case, $A$ implies an affine transformation of the vector space $B$ where the Euclidean distance is equivalent to $D_{Mah}$ in the original space.

$$\begin{aligned}\left((x_1 - x_2)^T A (x_1 - x_2)\right)^{\frac{1}{2}} &= \left((x_1 - x_2)^T B^T B (x_1 - x_2)\right)^{\frac{1}{2}} \\ &= \left((Bx_1 - Bx_2)^T (Bx_1 - Bx_2)\right)^{\frac{1}{2}}\end{aligned}$$

When properly derived, this matrix $A$ can achieve that the directions in the target space are uncorrelated. Additionally, the directions are weighted by their importance to the given application. There are multiple methods to learn a proper Mahalanobis distance like Fisherfaces [2], RCA [1], ITML [7] or LMNN [21] which are described in Section 5.

However, the Mahalanobis distance does not adequately solve the third problem named above because the feature values are only linearly scaled. Thus, all observed difference values are decreased by the same factor. Therefore, when decreasing a very large difference value to limit its too strong impact in a comparison, the impact of the feature is limited in all other comparisons as well. Thus, by preventing a too large impact in some distance calculations, we would generate too small distance values in others. To conclude, Mahalanobis distances are still equivalent to an Euclidean distance in a transformed data space and thus, these methods are no solution to the third problem mentioned above.

## 3 Ensembles of Bayes Estimates

In the following, we formally describe our method. We start with the definition of Bayes Estimates (BE) and Bayes Ensemble Distance (BED) on the original feature dimensions. Afterwards, we introduce our solution to the problem of correlated features and provide a new way to derive an affine transformation of the feature space that allows the training of a meaningful BED.

### 3.1 Bayes Estimates and Bayes Ensemble Distance

As mentioned above, we want to learn a function having a pair of feature vectors as input and returning a similarity score as output. Similar to the $L_p$-norm, we describe the comparison between two feature vectors $x_1, x_2 \in \mathbb{R}^d$ by their difference vectors $(x_1 - x_2)$, or $(x_2 - x_1)$. Thus, our method assigns a similarity score to each difference vector. Since both difference vectors should provide the same dissimilarity score, we have to make sure that our similarity function is symmetric with respect to the direction of the input difference vector. As mentioned before, our approach treats each dimension of the input space separately. Thus, we define the Bayes Estimates (BE) for feature dimension $i$ as simple Bayes classifier receiving a difference value $x_{1,i} - x_{2,i}$ as input. This classifier distinguishes object comparisons of similar objects (SIM) from comparisons of dissimilar objects (DIS). Thus, we learn two distribution functions over the difference values for similar objects and dissimilar objects. Additionally, we employ a prior distribution describing whether similarity is less likely than dissimilarity. As a result, we can calculate the conditional probability $P(\text{DIS} \mid x_{1,i} - x_{2,i})$ describing the dissimilarity likelihood for two objects under the condition of the observed difference value in dimension $i$. Correspondingly, $P(\text{SIM} \mid x_{1,i} - x_{2,i})$ expresses the likelihood that two objects are similar and can be used as similarity function. Formally, the Bayes Estimate (BE) for comparing two vectors $x_1, x_2 \in \mathbb{R}^d$ w.r.t. dimension $i$ is defined as:

**Definition 1 (Bayes Estimate).** *Let $x_1, x_2 \in \mathbb{R}^d$ be two feature vectors. Let $p_s$ and $p_d$ represent a prior distribution describing the general likelihood that objects are considered to be similar. Then, the* Bayes Estimate (BE) *for $x_1$ and $x_2$ w.r.t. dimension $i$ is defined as follows:*

$$\text{BE}_i(x_1, x_2) = \frac{p_d \cdot P((x_{1,i} - x_{2,i}) \mid \text{DIS})}{P_{total}(x_{1,i}, x_{2,i})} \quad ,$$

*where $p_{total}(x_{1,i}, x_{2,i})$ is the sum of the similarity and the dissimilarity probabilities ($p_s \cdot P\left((x_{1,i} - x_{2,i}) \mid \text{SIM}\right)$ and $p_d \cdot P\left((x_{1,i} - x_{2,i}) \mid \text{DIS}\right)$) in the $i^{th}$ dimension.*

To combine these probabilities, we take the average estimates over all dimensions. Thus, we employ an Ensemble approach combining the descriptiveness of all available features. Let us note that this approach is different from building the joint probability for class DIS like in an ordinary naïve Bayes classifier. This approach would imply that in order to be similar, two objects have to be sufficiently similar in each dimension. Correspondingly, dissimilarity would require a sufficiently large difference value in all dimensions. Thus, the joint probability could again be determined by a single dimension. By building the average, our method underlies the more flexible understanding of similarity. Thus, neither a very large difference nor a very small difference in a single dimension can imply similarity or dissimilarity on its own. Formally, we define the Bayes Ensemble Distance (BED) in the following way:

**Definition 2 (Bayes Ensemble Distance).** *Let $x_1, x_2 \in \mathbb{R}^d$ be two feature vectors. Let $p_s$ and $p_d$ represent a prior distribution describing the general likelihood that objects are considered to be similar. Then, the* Bayes Ensemble Distance (BED) *for $x_1$ and $x_2$ is defined as follows:*

$$\text{BED}(x_1, x_2) = \frac{1}{d} \cdot \sum_{i=1}^{d} \text{BE}_i(x_1, x_2)$$

From a data mining point of view, the BED is an Ensemble of $d$ weak Bayesian learners, each deriving a probabilistic statement from the corresponding feature. Each learner distinguishes two classes, i.e. similarity and dissimilarity. Let us note that our method does not directly distinguish degrees of similarity. Instead, a quantitative view on object similarity is provided by the average probability that both objects are similar.

An open issue to the use of BED is the type of probability distribution being used to model the Bayes estimate. To select a well-suited probability density function, we examined several data sets with respect to their difference vector distribution for similar and dissimilar objects. Therefore, we built histograms on the observed difference values in each dimension. Remember that the all distributions have to be symmetric to the origin because of the pairwise appearance of positive and negative distance values. An example for the histograms derived from two image retrieval data sets is displayed in Fig. 1. In this and all other examined data sets, we observed a normal distribution for similar objects. Very similar or identical objects will usually display almost identical feature values. For the distributions describing dissimilarity, we sometimes observed distributions that also resemble a normal distribution but displayed a larger variance. In cases having well separated classes, the dissimilarity distribution often is split into two components, one for positive and one for negative difference values. Thus, the dissimilarity resembled a mixture model having two symmetric components of equal weight where the first has a positive mean value and the second component has a negative mean value. In our experiments, we employed Gaussians as basis distribution. However, the general method is applicable for any other type of distribution function, e.g. exponential power distributions.

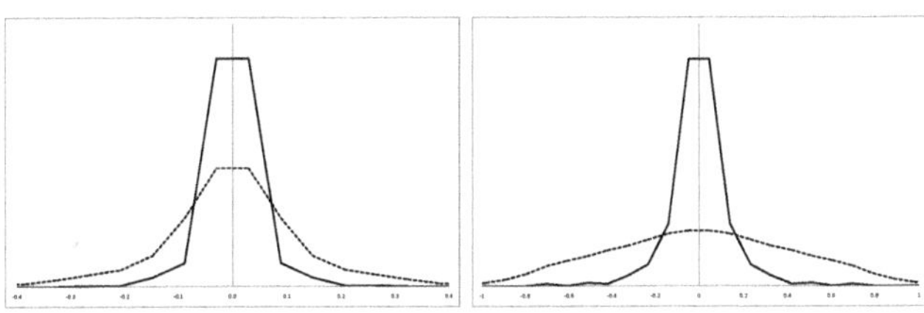

(a) Conf-hsv (10D) (b) Conf-hsv (29D)

**Fig. 1.** Difference distributions for similar (solid lines) and dissimilar (dashed lines) objects in a retrieval data set in dimension 10 and 29

### 3.2 Training BEs

Training BEDs consists of determining the distribution parameters for each dimension, e.g. mean and variance for a Gaussian. Furthermore, it is often useful to determine prior probabilities for similarity and dissimilarity.

In the case that the examples are provided with class labels, it is easy to decide whether an object comparison is counted for the similar class (SIM) or for the dissimilarity class (DIS). If both objects belong to the same class, the observed difference value contributes to the SIM distribution. If both objects belong to different classes, the observed difference vector contributes to the distribution describing DIS. For small data sets, it is possible to consider all possible difference vectors occurring in the training set. However, this approach is not feasible for large data sets because the number of difference vectors is increasing with the squared number of training vectors. Thus, it is often advisable to select a subset of the difference vectors instead of employing all available samples. To find this subset, random sampling is applicable. In our experiments, we adapt the idea of target neighbors from [21] and select the difference vectors corresponding to the $k$-nearest neighbors of the same class and the $k$-nearest neighbors belonging to any other class for each training object. We employed the Euclidean distance to determine the target neighbors.

In case of labeled pairs, selecting examples is usually not an option because each object comparison has to be manually labeled and thus, it is rather unlikely that there will be too many examples for efficient training. However, labeling object pairs allows to distinguish several degrees of similarity $y \in [0..1]$, e.g. the label could indicate a similarity of 0.8 or 0.1. To employ these more detailed labels, we propose to proceed in a similar way as in EM clustering and let the training example contribute to both distributions. However, to consider the class labels, we weight the contribution to the similar distribution by $y$ and the contribution to the dissimilar distribution by $1-y$. This way, undecidable comparisons having a label of 0.5 would equally contribute to both distribution functions, whereas a comparison having a label of 1.0 would exclusively contribute to the similar distribution.

In many applications, using a prior distribution can improve the accuracy of similarity search and object classification. Especially when using BED for nearest neighbor classification, we can assume that we know how many objects belong to the same class and how many objects belong to any other class. In these cases, we can determine the frequency $|c_i|$ of examples for each class $c_i \in C$ in the training set and easily derive the prior probability for similarity:

$$p_s = \frac{\sum_{c_i \in C} |c_i|^2}{(\sum_{c_i \in C} |c_i|)^2} \qquad\qquad p_d = 1 - p_s$$

In other words, we know that there are $|c_i|^2$ comparisons of similar objects within each class $c_i$. Dividing the amount of these comparisons by all possible comparisons computes the relative frequency of $p_s$. Since we only distinguish two cases, we can calculate $p_d$ as $1 - p_s$.

In case of relevance feedback, directly determining the relative portion of similarity in the training objects is also easily possible. However, depending on the selection of the object pairs to be labeled it is often very unlikely that the label distribution is representative for the distribution on the complete database. Thus, it is often more useful to manually assign a value for the occurrence of each class.

## 4 Optimizing the Feature Space for BEs

Employing BED on the original dimensions ensures that neither similarity nor dissimilarity can be decided based on the difference value in a single dimension. Additionally, the importance of each dimension is indicated by the distinction of both distribution functions. However, correlated features still pose a problem for the performance of BED. First of all, the advantage of using an ensemble of learners strongly depends on their statistical independence. Additionally, it might occur that the single BEs in the original dimension might be very informative. However, there often exist dimensions in the data space allowing a good separation of the distribution function. An example is illustrated in Fig. 2. In the displayed case, the distributions of similar and dissimilar objects are modeled as multivariate Gaussians. If we consider the projection of both distributions onto the x-axis, we cannot decide between the two distributions at all. Projecting the Gaussians onto the main diagonal enables a clear separation. In this example, it can be assumed that the BE on the main diagonal has a much stronger predictive quality. To conclude, analogously to the Euclidean distance, BED can be improved by a linear transformation of the input space which decreases feature dependency and provides features allowing meaningful similarity estimation.

Formally, we want to find a set of base vectors $W = [w_1, \ldots, w_d]$ for transforming each original vector $x \in \mathbb{R}^{d'}$ into another $d$-dimensional feature space where each new dimension allows to build a better BE. Since we want to have independent learners, we additionally require that $w_i \perp w_j$ for $i \neq j$.

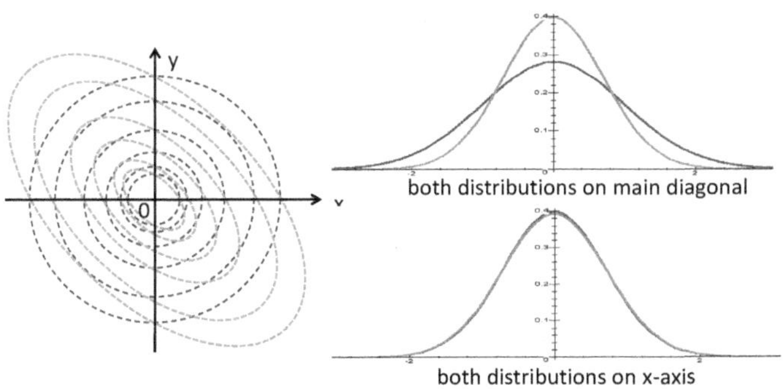


**Fig. 2.** Distributions of similar (green) and dissimilar (red) objects. Top view of multivariate Gaussians (left) and projections onto different dimensions (right).

To determine the suitability of a dimension to train a useful BE, we need to find a criterion that is independent of the used type of distribution function. A certain dimension in the feature space is useful in the case that the distance values between similar objects are in average smaller than the distance values of dissimilar objects. Let us note that the mean value for both distributions has to be zero regardless of the underlying density function. Since distance values always occur in pairs of negative and positive values, the mean is always zero in each dimension. Now, a direction is well-suited if the distance values being observed for similar objects are grouped closer to the origin than the values being observed for dissimilar objects. To quantify this intuition, we calculate the variance of the samples for both distributions SIM and DIS in dimension $i$ and build the difference between both values:

$$q_i = \frac{1}{n} \cdot \left( \sum_{x_d \in \text{DIS}}^{n} (x_{d,i}^2 - 0) - \sum_{x_s \in \text{SIM}}^{n} (x_{s,i}^2 - 0) \right) = \frac{1}{n} \cdot \left( \sum_{x_d \in \text{DIS}}^{n} x_{d,i}^2 - \sum_{x_s \in \text{SIM}}^{n} x_{s,i}^2 \right)$$

If $q_i$ is large, the difference values between similar objects are generally grouped more closely around zero than the difference values between dissimilar objects in dimension $i$. If $q_i$ converges to zero, dimension $i$ will usually not allow the training of a useful BE.

To describe the variance along all possible dimensions in the space of distance values, we can build the covariance matrix for similar and dissimilar difference vectors.

$$(\Sigma_{\text{SIM}})_{i,j} = \sum_{x_s \in \text{SIM}} (x_{s,i} - 0) \cdot (x_{s,j} - 0) = \sum_{x_s \in \text{SIM}} x_{s,i} \cdot x_{s,j}$$

$\Sigma_{\text{DIS}}$ is built correspondingly on the difference vectors of dissimilar objects.

Our task is to find a set of orthogonal dimensions for which the difference between the variance of the dissimilar distribution and the variance of the similar distribution is as large as possible. Formally, we can define the following optimization problem:

$$\begin{aligned} &\text{Maximize } L(w_i) = w_i^T \Sigma_{\text{DIS}} w_i - w_i^T \Sigma_{\text{SIM}} w_i = w_i^T \cdot (\Sigma_{\text{DIS}} - \Sigma_{\text{SIM}})\, w_i \\ &\text{s.t. } w_i \perp w_j \end{aligned}$$

The following eigenvalue equation solves this problem:

$$\lambda w = (\Sigma_{\text{DIS}} - \Sigma_{\text{SIM}}) \cdot w \ .$$

To integrate the learned affine transformation into the training of BED, we can either transform all feature vectors before training and testing by $W$ or integrate the transformation directly into the BE distance by rotating each difference vector before it is processed. To conclude, the training of a BED is performed as follows:

1. Determine $\Sigma_{\mathrm{SIM}}$ and $\Sigma_{\mathrm{DIS}}$ from the labeled data.
2. Calculate $W$ by solving the corresponding eigenvalue problem.
3. Rotate $\Sigma_{\mathrm{SIM}}$ and $\Sigma_{\mathrm{DIS}}$ by $W$.
4. Derive the variance values of the similarity and dissimilarity distributions for each $w_i \in W$.

Let us note that it is necessary to rotate the compared objects or their distance vector using $W$ before calculating BED.

A final aspect of this space transformation is that it allows to reduce the number of considered dimensions. This can be done by selecting a fixed number of features and keep only the top $k$ dimensions w.r.t. the quality $q_i$. Another alternative is to determine a threshold $\tau$ and keep only those dimensions offering a quality $q_i$ which is better than $\tau$.

# 5 Related Work

## 5.1 Metric Distance Learning

Most distance learning methods use the Mahalanobis distance, represented by a semi-definite matrix. The shared principle among all of those approaches is to ensure that the relations among a dataset's objects are transformed such that they best represent an underlying characteristic of the data.

In the following, we give a short summary of existing metric learning approaches. For detailed surveys, see [24,23]. The main idea of unsupervised approaches is to reduce the feature space to a lower-dimensional space in order to eliminate noise and enable a more efficient object comparison. The criteria for selecting such a subspace are manifold. Principal Component Analysis (PCA) [10] builds an orthogonal basis aimed at best preserving the data's variance, Multidimensional Scaling (MDS) [6] seeks the transformation which best preserves the geodesic distances and Independent Component Analysis (ICA) [5] targets a subspace that guarantees maximal statistical independence. ISOMAP [19] by Tenenbaum et al. is a non-linear enhancement of the MDS principle, in identifying the geodesic manifold of the data and preserving its intrinsic geometry. Other unsupervised approaches (e.g. [16,3]) try to fulfill the above criteria on a local scale.

Among supervised approaches, the first to be named is Fisher's Linear Discriminant (FLD) [8]. It maximizes the ratio of the between-class variance and the within-class variance using a generalized eigenvalue decomposition. This method has been extended by Belhumeur et al. [2] to the Fisherfaces approach. It precedes FLD with a reduction of the input space to its principal components and can thus filter unreliable input dimensions. BED and especially the target function $L$ share several important ideas with Fisherfaces. However, FLD assumes that the data is partitioned into classes which are modeled using the Gaussian distribution function, whereas BED does not require explicit object classes. Furthermore, the BED is not determined to the use of Gaussian functions. Instead BEDs employ the difference vectors and always try to distinguish the two basic statements of object similarity and object dissimilarity which can be modeled by an arbitrary symmetric density function. Both methods generate covariance matrices of difference vectors representing similarity (in FLD: the within-class scatter matrix) and dissimilarity (in FLD: the between-class scatter matrix). However, in FLD the matrices are built based on the difference vectors w.r.t. a mean value whereas BED directly employs object-to-object comparisons. Where FLD tries to find dimensions where the ratio between the variances of dissimilarity and similarity are as large as possible, BED maximizes the difference between the variances of the dissimilarity and the similarity distributions.

With RCA [1], Bar-Hillel et al. focus on the problem of minimizing within-*chunklet* variance. They argue that between-class differences are less informative than within-class differences and that class assignments frequently occur in such a way that only pairs of equally-labelled objects can be extracted. These pairs are extended into chunklets (sets) of equivalent objects. The inverse chunklet covariance matrix is used for calculating the Mahalanobis distance. This step should usually be preceded by dimensionality reduction. The main difference between BED and RCA is that RCA does not build a distribution function for object comparison corresponding to dissimilarity. Correspondingly, RCA only requires examples for comparison between the objects of the same class. As a result, the optimization which is provided by RCA is not aimed at distinguishing both classes of difference vectors. Instead, RCA is mostly based on a whitening transformation of the matrix which is similar to the within-class-scatter-matrix of FLD.

NCA [9] proposed by Goldberger et al. optimizes an objective function based on a soft neighborhood assignment evaluated via the leave-one-out error. This setting makes it more resistant against multi-modal distributions. The result of this optimization is a Mahalanobis distance directly aimed at improving nearest-neighbor classification. The objective function is, however, not guaranteed to be convex.

With Information-Theoretic Metric Learning (ITML) [7], Davis et al. propose a low-rank kernel learning problem which generates a Mahalanobis matrix subject to an upper bound for inner-class distances and a lower bound to between-class distances. They regularize by choosing the matrix closest to the identity matrix and introduce a way to reduce the rank of the learning problem.

LMNN (Large Margin Nearest Neighbor) [21] by Weinberger et al. is based on a semi-definite program for directly learning a Mahalanobis matrix. They require *$k$-target neighbors* for each input object $x$, specifying a list of objects, usually of the same class as $x$, which should always be mapped closer to $x$ than any object of another class. These $k$-target neighbors are the within-class $k$-nearest neighbors. Hence, the loss function consists of two terms for all data points $x$: the first penalizes the distance of $x$ to its $k$-target neighbors and the second penalizes close objects being closer to $x$ than any of its target neighbors. In [22], they propose several extensions, involving a more flexible handling of the $k$-target neighbors, a multiple-metric variant, a kernelized version for datasets of larger dimension than size and they deal with efficiency issues arising from the repeated computation of close objects. Nonetheless, LMNN requires a specialized solver in order to be run on larger data sets.

### 5.2 Non-metric Distance Learning

In order to be metric, a distance has to fulfill the metric axioms (i.e. self-similarity, symmetry, triangle inequality). In fact, several recent studies have shown that these axioms (triangle inequality above all) are often not conform with the perceptual distance of human beings [17,20] and thus not suitable for robust pattern recognition [12]. Most of the approaches learning a non-metric function as distance function only use fragments of the objects for the similarity calculation between them (e.g. [18,12]). This can be useful for image retrieval and classification, where only small parts (not a subset of features) of two images can yield to perception of similarity, but is not applicable for object representations in general. Another class of non-metrical distance learners are Bayesian Learners as used in [13], which are also designed for the special case of object recognition in images. In this work, we do not want to restrict similarity to images, but rather present a more general view applicable for a broad range of applications.

## 6 Experimental Evaluation

In this section, we present the results of our experimental evaluation. As comparison partner we selected the methods that are closest to our approach: Relevant Component Analysis (RCA) and Fisher Faces (FF). Let us note that RCA requires only chunks of data objects having the same class and no explicit class set. However, since we used datasets having class labels, we provided RCA the complete set of training objects for each class as a chunk. Furthermore, we compared Bayes Estimate Distance (BED) to the standard Euclidean distance to have baseline method. We evaluated all methods on several real-world datasets to test their performance for classification and retrieval tasks. All methods were implemented in Java 1.6 and tests were run on a dual core (3.0 Ghz) workstation with 2 GB main memory.

### 6.1 Nearest Neighbor Classification

As mentioned before, our similarity learner can be applied for different applications. A first, well-established method is improving the quality of nearest neighbor classification. For the classification task, we used several datasets from the UCI Machine Learning Repository [14]. Evaluation on the datasets was performed using 10-fold cross-validation and all 4 distance measures were used for basic nearest neighbor classification. To train BED, we employed sampling based on the target neighbors. In other words, we took the difference vectors of all training objects to the $k$-nearest neighbors within the same class and the $k$-nearest neighbors in all other classes. To find out a suitable value for $k$, we screened over a small set of suitable values between 5 and 20.

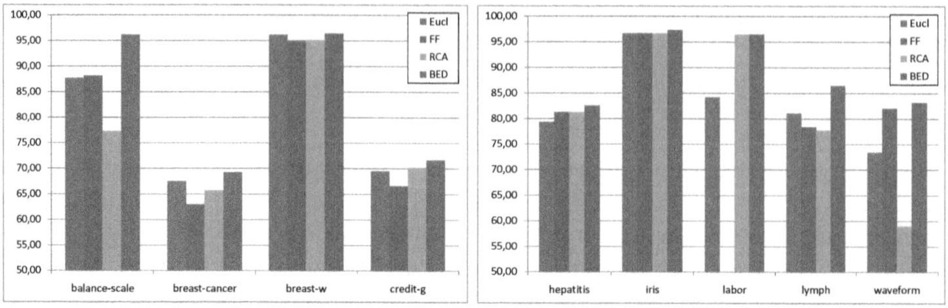


(a) Results on 4 UCI datasets (b) Results on 5 UCI datasets

**Fig. 3.** NN-Classification results on several UCI datasets

**Table 1.** Image Retrieval Data Sets

| Dataset | Instances | Attributes | Classes |
|---|---|---|---|
| Conf-hsv | 183 | 32 | 35 |
| Conf-facet | 183 | 24 | 35 |
| Conf-har | 183 | 65 | 35 |
| Flowers-hsv | 1360 | 32 | 17 |
| Flowers-facet | 1360 | 24 | 17 |
| Flowers-har | 1360 | 65 | 17 |

The results for NN classification are shown in Fig. 3. BED displays the largest accuracy in all 9 datasets. Though RCA achieves the same result on the labor dataset, it impairs the Euclidean distance on data sets like waveform or balance scale. The same observation can be made for FF. Though the accuracy is comparably good in all data sets, there also exist datasets where FF does not yield an advantage even against Euclidean distance (breast-w). On the labor dataset, it was not possible to learn a distance using FF due to a matrix singularity. To conclude, BED leads to an up to 8% better classification of objects on the tested datasets compared to the best of Eucl, FF and RCA. Thus, we can state that BED can be employed to improve the results of instance-based learners.

### 6.2 Precision and Recall Graphs

We employed two image datasets for testing the performance of our new distance measures for retrieval applications. The *Conf* dataset was created by ourselves and contains 183 images of 35 different motives. The *Flowers* dataset was introduced in [15] and consists of 1360 images of 17 different types of flowers. From these two datasets, we extracted color histograms (based on the HSV color space), facet features [4] and haralick features [11]. The characteristics of the resulting feature datasets can be seen in Table 1. On these datasets, we measured the retrieval performance using precision-recall-graphs. We posed a ranking query for each image and measured the precision of the answer resulting

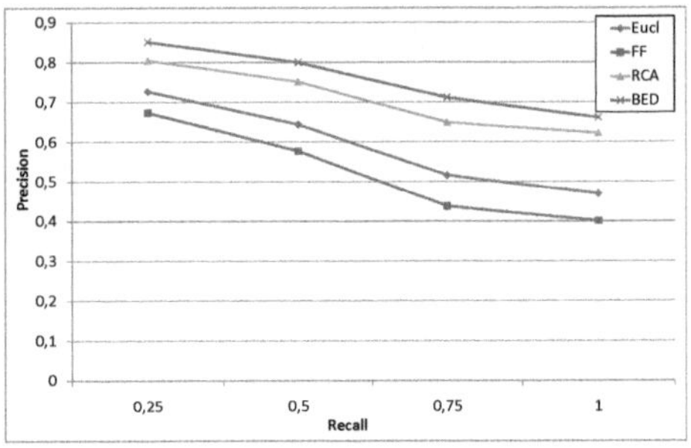


(a) Conf-hsv

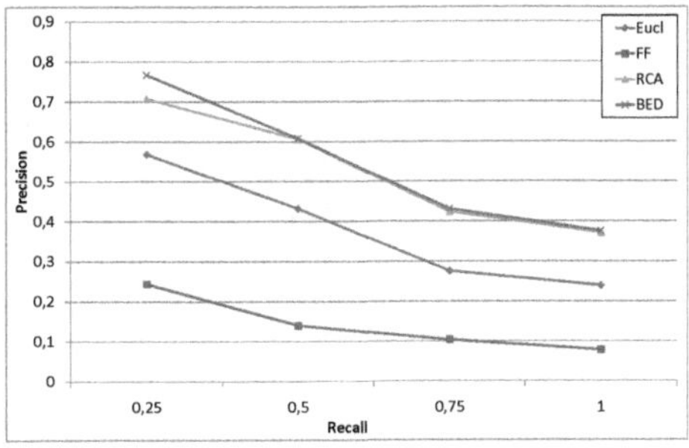


(b) Conf-facet

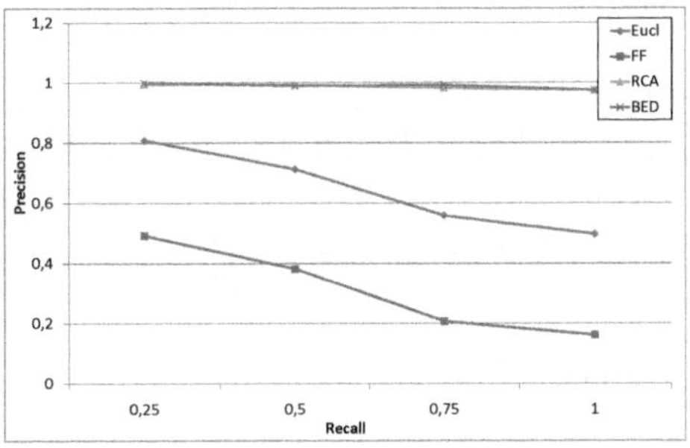


(c) Conf-har

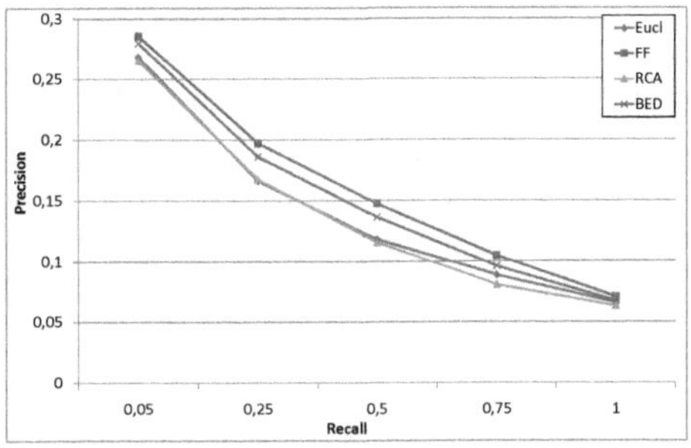


(d) Flowers-hsv

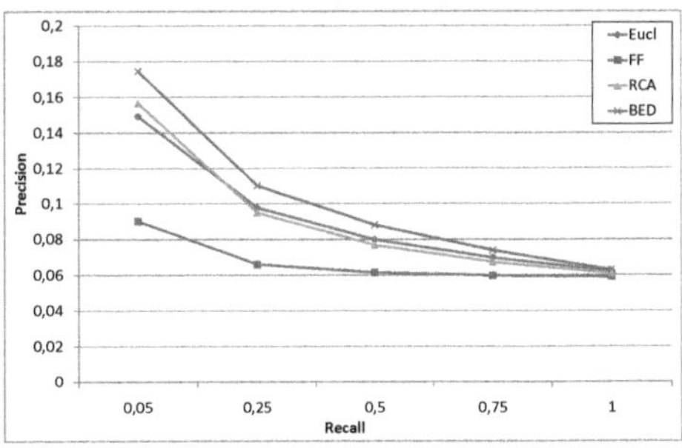


(e) Flowers-facet

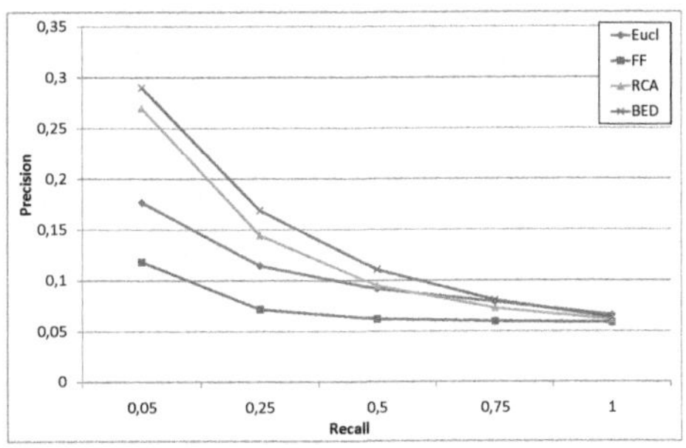


(f) Flowers-har

**Fig. 4.** Precision-Recall Graphs on the Conf and Flowers dataset

from the remaining database for several levels of recall. In the retrieval task, we employed very large numbers of difference vectors for training, to adjust BED to achieving reasonable precision values for large levels of recall.

On the *Conf* dataset, BED shows an impressive boost of the retrieval quality using hsv-color-histograms (Fig. 4(a)), while it still leads to slightly better results using facet or Haralick features (see Figures 4(b) and 4(c)) in contrast to RCA. FF does not appear to be well-suited for these datasets, as it performs even worse than the Euclidean Distance. On the Flowers dataset, retrieval quality can again be improved by BED when using Facet and Haralick features

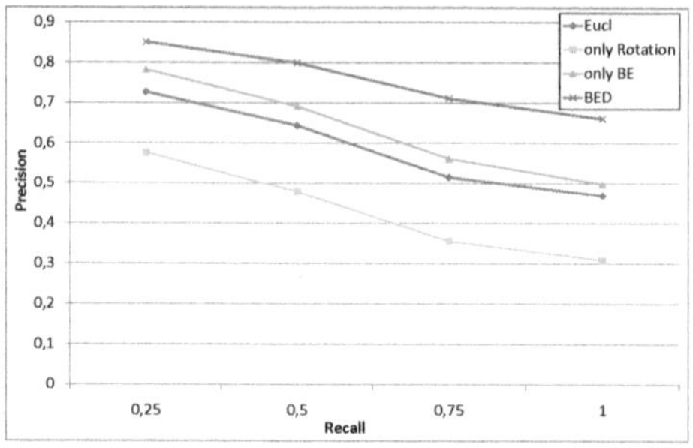


**Fig. 5.** Different versions of BE on Conf-hsv

respectively (see Figures 4(e) and 4(f)). On the feature dataset consisting of the hsv-color-histograms of *Flowers*, Fisherfaces lead to a better Precision-Recall-Graph (Fig. 4(d)) than the other approaches, but note that this is the only retrieval experiment where FF performed better than the Euclidean distance. Thus, we can state the BED is suitable for retrieval tasks as well as for data mining tasks.

### 6.3 Comparison to Its Components

In our last experiment, we examine the performance of BEDs compared to their separated components. We trained BEs on the original dimensions (only BE) of the feature space. Furthermore, we wanted to find out whether the learned eigenvalue decomposition can be used for learning a Mahalanobis distance improving classification results. To create such a transformation, we additionally multiplied each eigenvector $w$ by its inverse eigenvalue. The comparison was performed for several retrieval datasets which all displayed similar results. An example precision-recall graph of the *Conf-hsv* data set is presented in Fig. 5. Using the BED without the rotation still increases the retrieval performance compared to the plain Euclidean distance on the same feature space. Thus, even without an affine transformation, the BED is capable of improving the retrieval quality. A second very interesting result is that the rotation component of BEDs does not yield any performance advantage when used as Mahalanobis learner. Though the learned directions do optimize the BEs being observed in the new dimensions, they seem to be unsuitable for improving the results obtained by the Euclidean distance.

## 7 Conclusion

In this paper, we have introduced Bayes Ensemble Distance (BED) as new adaptable dissimilarity measure. BED is applied to the difference vector of two feature vectors. For each dimension, BED independently determines the likelihood that both objects are dissimilar employing a simple Bayesian learner called

Bayes Estimate (BE). The results of the BEs are combined by computing the average prediction. Thus, the derived similarity score is less dependent on outlier values in some of the dimensions. Since BED is dependent on the spatial rotation of the data space, it is possible to optimize the vector space in order to derive a feature space allowing the training of more descriptive and independent BEs. In our experimental evaluation, we have demonstrated that BEDs can largely increase the classification accuracy of instance-based learning. Additionally, we have demonstrated the suitability of BED for retrieval tasks. For future work, we plan to investigate efficiency issues when using BED for information retrieval. Furthermore, we plan to apply the idea of BEs to structured objects like graphs.

## Acknowledgements

This research has been supported in part by the THESEUS program in the MEDICO and CTC projects. They are funded by the German Federal Ministry of Economics and Technology under the grant number 01MQ07020. The responsibility for this publication lies with the authors.

## References

1. Bar-Hillel, A., Hertz, T., Shental, N., Weinshall, D.: Learning distance functions using equivalence relations. In: Proceedings of the 20th International Conference on Machine Learning (ICML), Washington, DC, USA, pp. 11–18 (2003)
2. Belhumeur, P.N., Hespanha, J.P., Kriegman, D.J.: Eigenfaces vs. Fisherfaces: Recognition using class specific linear projection. IEEE Transactions on Pattern Analysis and Machine Intelligence 19(7), 711–720 (1997)
3. Belkin, M., Niyogi, P.: Laplacian eigenmaps for dimensionality reduction and data representation. Neural Computation 15(6), 1373–1396 (2003)
4. Chinga, G., Gregersen, O., Dougherty, B.: Paper surface characterisation by laser profilometry and image analysis. Journal of Microscopy and Analysis 84, 5–7 (2003)
5. Comon, P.: Independent component analysis, a new concept? Signal Processing 36(3), 287–314 (1994)
6. Cox, T.F., Cox, M.A.A.: Multidimensional Scaling, 2nd edn. Chapman & Hall/CRC, Boca Raton (2001)
7. Davis, J., Kulis, B., Sra, S., Dhillon, I.: Information-theoretic metric learning. In: NIPS 2006 Workshop on Learning to Compare Examples (2007)
8. Fisher, R.A.: The use of multiple measurements in taxonomic problems. Annals of Eugenics 7, 179–188 (1936)
9. Goldberger, J., Roweis, S., Hinton, G., Salakhutdinov, R.: Neighborhood component analysis. In: Advances in Neural Information Processing Systems, pp. 513–520. MIT Press, Cambridge (2004)
10. Gonzalez, R.C., Woods, R.E.: Digital Image Processing. Addison-Wesley Longman Publishing Co., Inc., Boston (2001)
11. Haralick, R.M., Shanmugam, K., Dinstein, I.: Textural features for image classification. IEEE Transactions on Speech and Audio Processing 3(6), 6103–6623 (1973)
12. Jacobs, D.W., Weinshall, D., Gdalyahu, Y.: Classification with non-metric distances: Image retrieval and class representation. IEEE Trans. Pattern Analysis and Machine Intelligence 22(6), 583–600 (2000)

13. Moghaddam, B., Pentland, A.: Probabilistic visual learning for object representation. IEEE Trans. Pattern Analysis and Machine Intelligence 19(7), 696–710 (1997)
14. Newman, D.J., Hettich, S., Blake, C.L., Merz, C.J.: UCI repository of machine learning databases (1998)
15. Nilsback, M.E., Zisserman, A.: A visual vocabulary for flower classification. CVPR 2, 1447–1454 (2006)
16. Roweis, S.T., Saul, L.K.: Nonlinear dimensionality reduction by locally linear embedding. Science 290(5500), 2323–2326 (2000)
17. Santini, S., Jain, R.: Similarity measures. IEEE Trans. Pattern Analysis and Machine Intelligence 21, 871–883 (1999)
18. Tan, X., Chen, S., Zhou, Z.H., Liu, J.: Learning non-metric partial similarity based on maximal margin criterion. In: Proceedings of the IEEE Computer Society Conference on Computer Vision and Pattern Recognition, pp. 138–145 (2006)
19. Tenenbaum, J.B., Silva, V., Langford, J.C.: A global geometric framework for nonlinear dimensionality reduction. Science 290(5500), 2319–2323 (2000)
20. Tversky, A.: Features of similarity. Psychological Review 84(4), 327–352 (1977)
21. Weinberger, K.Q., Blitzer, J., Saul, L.K.: Distance metric learning for large margin nearest neighbor classification. In: Advances in Neural Information Processing Systems. MIT Press, Cambridge (2006)
22. Weinberger, K.Q., Saul, L.K.: Distance metric learning for large margin nearest neighbor classification. Journal of Machine Learning Research 10, 207–244 (2009)
23. Yang, L.: An overview of distance metric learning. Technical report, Department of Computer Science and Engineering, Michigan State University (2007)
24. Yang, L., Jin, R.: Distance metric learning: A comprehensive survey. Technical report, Department of Computer Science and Engineering, Michigan State University (2006)

# Subspace Similarity Search: Efficient k-NN Queries in Arbitrary Subspaces

Thomas Bernecker, Tobias Emrich, Franz Graf, Hans-Peter Kriegel,
Peer Kröger, Matthias Renz, Erich Schubert, and Arthur Zimek

Institut für Informatik, Ludwig-Maximilians-Universität München
{bernecker,emrich,graf,kriegel,kroeger,renz,schube,zimek}@dbs.ifi.lmu.de
http://www.dbs.ifi.lmu.de

**Abstract.** There are abundant scenarios for applications of similarity search in databases where the similarity of objects is defined for a subset of attributes, i.e., in a subspace, only. While much research has been done in efficient support of single column similarity queries or of similarity queries in the full space, scarcely any support of similarity search in subspaces has been provided so far. The three existing approaches are variations of the sequential scan. Here, we propose the first index-based solution to subspace similarity search in arbitrary subspaces.

## 1 Introduction

In the last decade, similarity search in high-dimensional data has gained special interest. Several studies for research on data structures [1, 2, 3, 4, 5] showed that the suitability of the sequential scan [6] compared to methods using partitioning or clustering based data structures is dependent of the characteristics of the data distributions. However, this key message has been neglected in many research contributions [7,8,9,10,11,12]. Thus, it still appears to be well worth noting that nearest neighbor search is meaningful if and only if the nearest neighbor of the arbitrary query object is sufficiently different from its farthest neighbor. This is in general the case whenever a data set exhibits a natural structure in clusters or groupings of subsets of data.

While much effort has been spent on studying possibilities to facilitate efficient similarity search in high-dimensional data, scarcely ever the question arose how to support similarity search when the similarity of objects is based on a subset of attributes only. Aside from fundamentally studying the behavior of data structures in such settings, this is a practically highly relevant question. It could be interesting for any user to search, e.g., in a database of images represented by color-, shape-, and texture-descriptions, for objects similar to a certain image where the similarity is related to the shape of the motifs only but not to their color or even the color of the background. An online-store might like to propose similar objects to a customer where similarity can be based on different subsets of features. While in such scenarios, meaningful subspaces can be suggested beforehand [13, 14], in other scenarios, possibly any subspace could be interesting.

M. Gertz and B. Ludäscher (Eds.): SSDBM 2010, LNCS 6187, pp. 555–564, 2010.

For example, for different queries, different regions of interest in a picture may be relevant. Since there are $2^D$ possible subspaces of a $D$-dimensional data set, it is practically impossible to provide data structures for each of these possible subspaces in order to facilitate efficient similarity search. Another application where efficient support of subspace similarity queries is required are many subspace clustering algorithms [15] that rely on searching for clusters in a potentially large number of subspaces (starting with all 1D subspaces, many combinations of 1D subspaces to 2D subspaces etc.). If efficient support of subspace range queries or subspace nearest neighbor queries were available, virtually all subspace cluster approaches could be accelerated considerably. Note that this problem is essentially different from the feature selection problem [15, 16].

In this paper, we facilitate efficient *subspace similarity search* in large and potentially high-dimensional data sets where the user or the application can define an interesting subspace for each query independently (that is, similarity is defined ad hoc based on an arbitrary subset of attributes only). To this end, we extend our preliminary approach addressed in [17] with more thorough experimental evaluation and we propose a top-down indexing method to support subspace similarity search.

In the remainder, we formally define the problem of subspace similarity search in Section 2. We discuss related work and the algorithmic sources of inspiration to our new solution in Section 3. We propose an index-based top-down approach as an adaptation of the R-tree in Section 4 and, additionally, give a general and theoretical comparison of this approach with [17]. An experimental evaluation of all methods is presented in Section 5. Section 6 concludes the paper.

## 2 Subspace Similarity Search

A common restriction for the small number of approaches tackling subspace similarity search (see Section 3) is that $L_p$-norms are assumed as distance measures. Hence we will also rely on this restriction in the problem definition. In the following, we assume that $\mathcal{DB}$ is a database of $N$ objects in a $D$-dimensional space $\mathbb{R}^D$ and the distance between points in $\mathcal{DB}$ is measured by a distance function $dist : \mathbb{R}^D \times \mathbb{R}^D \rightarrow \mathbb{R}_0^+$ which is one of the $L_p$-norms ($p \in [1, \infty)$). In order to perform subspace similarity search, a $d$-dimensional query subspace will be represented by a $D$-dimensional bit vector $S$ of weights, where $d$ weights are 1 and the remaining $D - d$ weights are 0. Formally:

**Definition 1 (Subspace).** *A* subspace *$S$ of the $D$-dimensional data space is represented by a vector $S = (S_1, \ldots, S_D) \in \{0, 1\}^D$, where $S_i = 1$, if the $i$th attribute is an element of the subspace, and $S_i = 0$, otherwise. The number $d$ of 1 entries in $S$, i.e., $d = \sum_{i=1}^{D} S_i$ is called the* dimensionality *of $S$.*

For example, in a 3D data space, the 2D subspace representing the projection on the first and third axis is represented by $S = (1, 0, 1)$.

A distance measure for a subspace $S$ can then be figured as weighted $L_p$-norm where the weights can either be 1 (if this particular attribute is relevant to the query) or 0 (if this particular attribute is irrelevant to the query), formally:

**Definition 2 (Subspace Distance).** *The distance in a subspace $S$ between two points $x, y \in \mathcal{DB}$ is given by $dist_S(x, y) = \sqrt[p]{\sum_{i=1}^{d} S_i \, |x_i - y_i|^p}$, where $x_i$, $y_i$, and $S_i$ denote the values of the* i*th component of the vectors $x$, $y$, and $S$.*

Thus, a subspace $k$-nearest neighbor ($k$-NN) query can be formalized as:

**Definition 3 (Subspace $k$-NN Query).** *Given a query object $q$ and a $d$-dimensional ($d \leq D$) query subspace represented by a corresponding vector $S$ of weights, a subspace $k$-NN query retrieves the set $NN(k, S, q)$ that contains $k$ objects from $\mathcal{DB}$ for which the following condition holds: $\forall o \in NN(k, S, q), \forall o' \in \mathcal{DB} \setminus NN(k, S, q) : dist_S(o, q) \leq dist_S(o', q)$.*

Some of the rare existing approaches for subspace similarity search focus on $\varepsilon$-range queries. This is a considerable lack because choosing the number $k$ of results that should be returned by a query is usually much more intuitive than selecting some query radius $\varepsilon$. Furthermore, the value of $\varepsilon$ needs to be adjusted to the subspace dimensionality in order to produce meaningful results. This is a non-trivial task since recall and precision of an $\varepsilon$-sphere become highly sensitive to even small changes of $\varepsilon$ depending on the dimensionality of the data space. In addition, many applications like data mining algorithms that further process the results of subspace similarity queries require to control their cardinality [15].

## 3 Related Work

Established index structures (such as [18,19,20,21]) are designed and optimized for the complete data space where all attributes contribute to partitioning, clustering etc. For these data structures, the space of queries facilitated by the index structure must be fixed prior to the construction of the index structure. While the results of research on such index structures designed for one single query space are abundant [22], so far there are some variations of the sequential scan addressing the problem of *subspace similarity search*, implicitly or explicitly.

The *Partial VA-File* [23] as an adaptation of the VA-file [6] is the first approach addressing the problem of subspace similarity search *explicitly*. The basic idea of this approach is to split the original VA-file into $D$ *partial* VA-files, where $D$ is the data dimensionality, i.e. we get one file for each dimension containing the approximation of the original full-dimensional VA-file in that dimension. Based on this information, upper and lower bounds of the true distance between data objects and the query are derived. Subspace similarity queries are processed by scanning only the relevant files in the order of relevance, i.e. the files are ranked by the selectivity of the query in the corresponding dimension. As long as there are still candidates that cannot be pruned or reported using the upper and lower distance bounds, the next ranked file is read to improve the distance approximations or (if all partial VA-files have been scanned) the exact information of the candidates accessed to refine the exact distance.

Another approach to the problem is proposed in [24], although only $\varepsilon$-similarity range queries are supported. The idea of this multi-pivot-based method is to derive lower and upper bounds for distances based on the average minimal and maximal impact of a possible range of $d$ dimensions, $d \in [d_{\min}, d_{\max}]$. The bounds are computed in a preprocessing step for a couple of pivot points. To optimize the selection of pivot points, also a distribution of possible values for $\varepsilon$ is required. The lower and upper bounds w.r.t. all pivot points are annotated to each database object. Essentially, this approach allows to sequentially scan the database reading only the information on lower and upper bounds and to refine the retrieved candidates in a postprocessing step.

The solution to subspace similarity search we are proposing in this paper is based on the ad hoc combination of 1D index structures. The combination technique is algorithmically inspired by top-$k$ queries on a number of different rankings of objects according to different criteria. Let us assume that we have a set of objects that are ranked according to $m$ different score functions (e.g. different rankings for $m$ different attributes). The objective of a top-$k$ query is to retrieve the $k$ objects with the highest combined (e.g. average) score. In our scenario, if we assume the objects are ranked for each dimension according to the distance to the query object, respectively, we can apply top-$k$ methods to solve subspace $k$-NN queries with the rankings of the given subspace dimensions. For the top-$k$ query problem, there basically exist two modes of access to the data given by the $m$ rankings, the sequential access (SA) and the random access (RA) [25]. While the SA mode accesses the data in a sorted way by proceeding through one of the $m$ rankings sequentially from the top, the RA mode has random access to the rank of a given object w.r.t. a given ranking.

## 4 Index-Based Subspace Similarity Search – Top-Down

In this section, we propose the *projected R-tree*, a redefinition of the R-tree to answer subspace queries. Let us note, though, that our solution can be integrated into any hierarchical index structure and is not necessarily restricted to R-trees.

The idea of the top-down approach is to apply one index on the full-dimensional data space. The key issue is that for a subspace similarity query, the minimum distance between an index page $P$ and the query object $q$ in subspace $S$ is properly defined because then, we can just use the best-first search algorithm without any changes. The minimum distance between an index page $P$ and the query object $q$ in subspace $S$ can be computed as

$$mindist_S(q, P) = \sqrt[p]{\sum_{i=1}^{D} s_i \cdot \begin{cases} P_i^{\min} - q_i & \text{if} \quad P_i^{\min} > q_i \\ q_i - P_i^{\max} & \text{if} \quad P_i^{\max} < q_i \\ 0 & \text{else} \end{cases}}, \qquad (1)$$

where $P_i^{\min}$ and $P_i^{\max}$ are the lower and upper bound of the page $P$ in the $i$th dimension, respectively. It should again be noted that Eq. 1 is designed for the rectangular page region of R-trees. For the implementation in this paper we used an R*-tree [19] as underlying tree index.

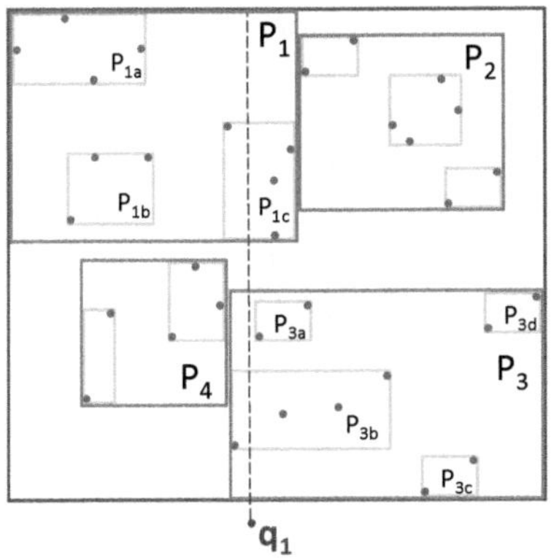


(a) 1D subspace query on 2D space.

| Iteration | APL | max1nnDist |
|---|---|---|
| 0 | (0.0, root) | ∞ |
| 1 | (0.0, $P_1$), (0.0, $P_3$), (0.7, $P_4$), (1.6, $P_2$) | ∞ |
| 2 | (0.0, $P_{1c}$), (0.0, $P_3$), (0.7, $P_4$), (1.6, $P_2$), (3.0, $P_{1b}$), (3.2, $P_{1a}$) | ∞ |
| 3 | (0.0, $P_3$), (0.7, $P_4$), (1.6, $P_2$), (3.0, $P_{1b}$), (3.2, $P_{1a}$) | 0.8 |
| 4 | (0.0, $P_{3b}$), (0.2, $P_{3a}$), (0.7, $P_4$), (1.6, $P_2$), (3.0, $P_{1b}$), (3.2, $P_{1a}$) | 0.8 |
| 5 | (0.2, $P_{3a}$), (0.7, $P_4$), (1.6, $P_2$), (3.0, $P_{1b}$), (3.2, $P_{1a}$) | 0.5 |
| 6 | (0.7, $P_4$), (1.6, $P_2$), (3.0, $P_{1b}$), (3.2, $P_{1a}$) | 0.2 |

(b) Processing of a sample query.

**Fig. 1.** Subspace query using a projected R-Tree

### 4.1 Query Processing

When a query $q$ arrives, it is processed in a best-first manner. The algorithm maintains an active page list (APL) which contains pages of the index structure ordered ascending by their *mindist* to the query. Note that since a subspace query is processed, only the dimensions defined by the query are taken into account for the calculation of the *mindist*. The algorithm starts inserting the root of the index structure into the APL. In each iteration, the first page from the APL is processed. If it is a directory node, its children are inserted into the APL. If it is a leaf node, the distance of each point contained in the page to the query is computed. Each point may therefore update the *maxKnnDist*, which is the distance of the $k$th-nearest point found so far. The process stops if the *mindist* of the first entry of the APL is larger than the *maxKnnDist*. In this case none of the pages in the APL can contain an object being part of the $k$-nearest neighbors of the query. Figure 1 illustrates an example of a subspace query.

### 4.2 Discussion

The top-down approach is a relatively straightforward adaptation and can be regarded as complementary to the bottom-up approach discussed in [17]. In contrast to the bottom-up approach using one index per dimension, the top-down approach just needs one index applied to the full-dimensional data space. As a result, the top-down approach does not need to merge the partial results of the rankings performed for each dimension in the corresponding subspace. Relying on the full-dimensional indexing of a data set, the top-down approach can be expected to perform better than the bottom-up approach where the dimensionality of the query subspace is approaching the dimensionality of the data set, if the latter does not disqualify methods based on full-dimensional indexing. On the other hand, as the index used in the top-down approach organizes the data w.r.t. the full-dimensional space, the locality property of a similarity query which might hold for the full-dimensional space does not necessarily hold for the subspace the query relates on. Generally, the more the dimensionality of the original data space differs from that of the query subspace, the smaller is the expected effectiveness of the index for a given subspace query. In summary, depending on the dimensionality of the query subspace, both indexing approaches qualify for subspace similarity search. While the bottom-up method is more appropriate for lower-dimensional subspace queries, the top-down approach should be used when the dimensionality of the query subspace approaches that of the data space.

# 5 Evaluation

In this section, we evaluate the proposed methods. In particular, Section 5.1 compares the different algorithms for subspace indexing on real-world data sets, whereas Section 5.2 focuses on the performance of the different heuristics for the bottom-up approach proposed by the authors in [17] on synthetic data sets having different characteristics (cf. Table 1).

**Table 1.** Data sets

| Data set | Type | Size | Dims |
|---|---|---|---|
| CLOUD | meteorological data | $> 1,000,000$ | 9 |
| ALOI-8/ALOI-64[1] | color histograms | 110,250 | 8/64 |
| UNIFORM | synthetic, uniform | 100,000 | 20 |
| CLUSTERED | synthetic, multivariate Gaussian clusters | 100,000 | 20 |

## 5.1 Evaluation of Methods for Subspace Indexing

In this section, we compare the approaches **DMI** (Dimension-Merge-Index [17]), **PT** (Projected R-Tree proposed in Section 4), **PVA** (Partial VA-File [6]) and **MP** (Multi-Pivot-Based algorithm [24]) for subspace indexing. Unless stated otherwise, we compare the different approaches on a data set with $k = 1$ and $k = 10$ with increasing subspace dimension displayed on the $x$-axis.

In order to compare the different approaches, we performed between $1,000$ and $10,000$ $k$-NN queries for each data set. For DMI, PT and MP, we measured all page accesses that could not be served by the LRU-cache. PVA does not only perform random page accesses for reading data, but also implements a heuristic that switches to a block read of pages if it turns out that multiple subsequent pages have to be read. Therefore, we measured block read pages and randomly accessed pages of PVA separately. In order to make the results of PVA comparable to the results of the other approaches, we combined the amount of block read pages with the amount of randomly accessed pages and calculated an estimated read time. To achieve this, we assumed a seek time of 8 ms and a transfer rate of 60 MB/s.

[1] Amsterdam Library of Object Images.

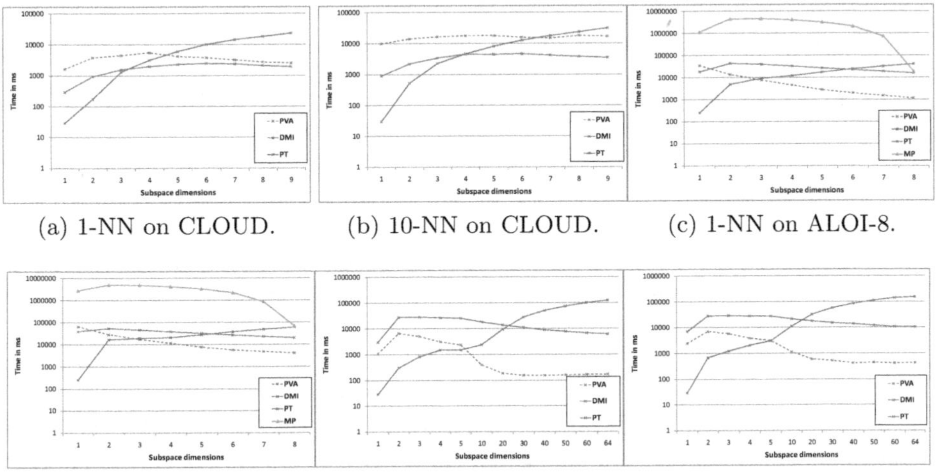


(a) 1-NN on CLOUD. (b) 10-NN on CLOUD. (c) 1-NN on ALOI-8.

(d) 10-NN on ALOI-8. (e) 1-NN on ALOI-64. (f) 10-NN on ALOI-64.

**Fig. 2.** Queries with different subspace dimensions. Due to the long runtime and due to the high amount of disc accesses of MP, we only executed tests on ALOI-8 and omitted MP from the remaining experiments.

In Figure 2, we compare the proposed methods on real-world data sets. For CLOUD (cf. Figures 2a and 2b) it can be seen clearly that DMI is superior or equal to the other approaches up to a subspace size of 4 dimensions. For ALOI-8, DMI is better or equal for a subspace size of up to 3 dimensions. In ALOI-64, DMI outperforms PVA and PT up to 4 dimensions until it reaches a break even point with PVA at a subspace size of 5 dimensions. Regarding the dimensionality of the data set and the subspace dimensions where DMI is better or equal to one of the other methods (3 on ALOI-8, 4 on CLOUD (9D) and 5 on ALOI-64), we can state that DMI - such as PVA - performs better on data sets with higher dimensionality, depending on the parameter $k$ (exemplarily shown in Figure 3a for ALOI-64). The obtained results confirm the discussion from Section 4.2. In all tested settings DMI performs best as long as the dimensionality of the subspace query is moderate. When the dimension increases, PT becomes superior to DMI. PVA is a scan-based approach and well suited if a data set is hard to index (e.g. very high-dimensional). CLOUD seems to be well indexable by the R*-Tree, therefore PT performs better than PVA. The ALOI data sets in contrast are rather hard to index (in particular ALOI-64 having a very high dimensionality).

### 5.2 Evaluation of Heuristics

The proposed heuristics for the bottom-up approach (cf. [17]) address different problems of the data distribution. To accurately show their behavior we tested the heuristics Round-Robin (RR), Global-MinDist (GMD) and MinScore (MS)

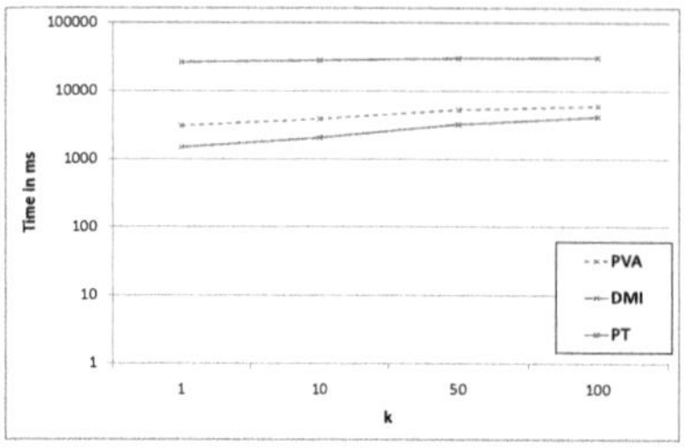


(a) $k$-NN queries on ALOI-64 (4 subspace dimensions, increasing $k$).

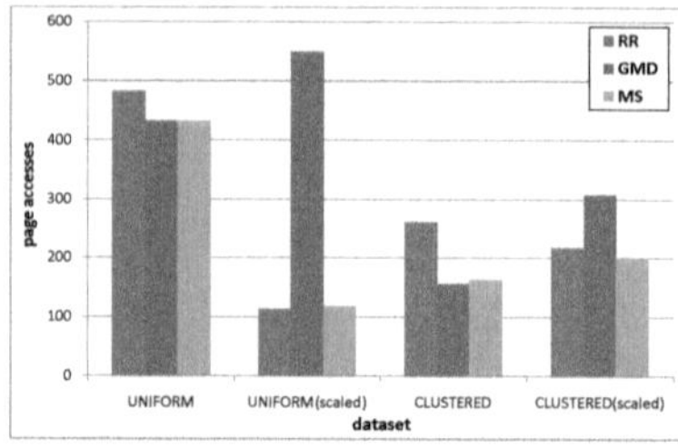


(b) Heuristics on data sets with different characteristics.

**Fig. 3**

on synthetic data sets with different characteristics. We performed 1,000 10NN queries on a 3D subspace and measured the page accesses needed by each dimension using our bottom-up approach and averaged the outcomes. The results are illustrated in Figure 3b. On UNIFORM and CLUSTERED the more sophisticated heuristics (GMD and MS) are superior to the naïve RR method, since they try to find a better dimension instead of more or less randomly picking one. If the dimensions are scaled randomly, the GMD heuristics favors the dimension with the minimal scale factor. However, this dimension does only increase the minimum distance of all other objects by a small value. Therefore it can stop the filter step very late, which results in many unnecessary page accesses.

## 6 Conclusions

In this paper, we proposed and studied new, index-based solutions for supporting $k$-NN queries in arbitrary subspaces of a multi-dimensional feature space. Therefore, we studied two different approaches. One of the main problems we addressed is how to schedule the rankings from the various dimensions in order to get good distance approximations of the objects for an early pruning of candidates. The evaluation shows that our solutions perform superior to the most recent competitors. As future work, we plan to study further heuristics based on our results and to perform a broad evaluation to study the impact of different data characteristics on all existing approaches for subspace similarity search.

## Acknowledgements

This research has been supported in part by the THESEUS program. They are funded by the German Federal Ministry of Economics and Technology under the grant number 01MQ07020. The responsibility for this publication is with the authors.

## References


1. Beyer, K., Goldstein, J., Ramakrishnan, R., Shaft, U.: When is "nearest neighbor" meaningful? In: Beeri, C., Bruneman, P. (eds.) ICDT 1999. LNCS, vol. 1540, pp. 217–235. Springer, Heidelberg (1998)
2. Bennett, K.P., Fayyad, U., Geiger, D.: Density-based indexing for approximate nearest-neighbor queries. In: Proc. KDD (1999)
3. Hinneburg, A., Aggarwal, C.C., Keim, D.A.: What is the nearest neighbor in high dimensional spaces? In: Proc. VLDB (2000)
4. Aggarwal, C.C., Hinneburg, A., Keim, D.: On the surprising behavior of distance metrics in high dimensional space. In: Van den Bussche, J., Vianu, V. (eds.) ICDT 2001. LNCS, vol. 1973, p. 420. Springer, Heidelberg (2000)
5. Francois, D., Wertz, V., Verleysen, M.: The concentration of fractional distances. IEEE TKDE 19(7), 873–886 (2007)
6. Weber, R., Schek, H.J., Blott, S.: A quantitative analysis and performance study for similarity-search methods in high-dimensional spaces. In: Proc. VLDB (1998)
7. Aggarwal, C.C.: Re-designing distance functions and distance-based applications for high dimensional data. SIGMOD Record 30(1), 13–18 (2001)
8. Katayama, N., Satoh, S.: Distinctiveness-sensitive nearest-neighbor search for efficient similarity retrieval of multimedia information. In: Proc. ICDE (2001)
9. Berchtold, S., Böhm, C., Jagadish, H.V., Kriegel, H.P., Sander, J.: Independent Quantization: An index compression technique for high-dimensional data spaces. In: Berchtold, S., Böhm, C., Jagadish, H.V., Kriegel, H.P., Sander, J. (eds.) Proc. ICDE (2000)
10. Jin, H., Ooi, B.C., Shen, H.T., Yu, C., Zhou, A.Y.: An adaptive and efficient dimensionality reduction algorithm for high-dimensional indexing. In: Proc. ICDE (2003)
11. Dittrich, J., Blunschi, L., Salles, M.A.V.: Dwarfs in the rearview mirror: How big are they really? In: Proc. VLDB (2008)
12. Aggarwal, C.C., Yu, P.S.: On high dimensional indexing of uncertain data. In: Proc. ICDE (2008)
13. Koskela, M., Laaksonen, J., Oja, E.: Use of image subset features in image retrieval with self-organizing maps. In: Enser, P.G.B., Kompatsiaris, Y., O'Connor, N.E., Smeaton, A., Smeulders, A.W.M. (eds.) CIVR 2004. LNCS, vol. 3115, pp. 508–516. Springer, Heidelberg (2004)
14. He, X.: Incremental semi-supervised subspace learning for image retrieval. In: Proc. ACM MM (2005)
15. Kriegel, H.P., Kröger, P., Zimek, A.: Clustering high dimensional data: A survey on subspace clustering, pattern-based clustering, and correlation clustering. ACM TKDD 3(1), 1–58 (2009)
16. Guyon, I., Elisseeff, A.: An introduction to variable and feature selection. J. Mach. Learn. Res. 3, 1157–1182 (2003)
17. Bernecker, T., Emrich, T., Graf, F., Kriegel, H.P., Kröger, P., Renz, M., Schubert, E., Zimek, A.: Subspace similarity search using the ideas of ranking and top-k retrieval. In: Proc. ICDE Workshop DBRank (2010)
18. Guttman, A.: R-Trees: A dynamic index structure for spatial searching. In: Proc. SIGMOD (1984)
19. Beckmann, N., Kriegel, H.P., Schneider, R., Seeger, B.: The R*-Tree: An efficient and robust access method for points and rectangles. In: Proc. SIGMOD, pp. 322–331 (1990)

20. Berchtold, S., Keim, D.A., Kriegel, H.P.: The X-Tree: An index structure for high-dimensional data. Proc. VLDB (1996)
21. Katayama, N., Satoh, S.: The SR-tree: An index structure for high-dimensional nearest neighbor queries. In: Proc. SIGMOD (1997)
22. Samet, H.: Foundations of Multidimensional and Metric Data Structures. Morgan Kaufmann, San Francisco (2006)
23. Kriegel, H.P., Kröger, P., Schubert, M., Zhu, Z.: Efficient query processing in arbitrary subspaces using vector approximations. In: Proc. SSDBM (2006)
24. Lian, X., Chen, L.: Similarity search in arbitrary subspaces under Lp-norm. In: Proc. ICDE (2008)
25. Fagin, R., Lotem, A., Naor, M.: Optimal aggregation algorithms for middleware. JCSS 66(4), 614–656 (2003)

# Continuous Skyline Monitoring over Distributed Data Streams

Hua Lu[1], Yongluan Zhou[2], and Jonas Haustad[2]

[1] Dept. of Computer Science, Aalborg Uni., Denmark
luhua@cs.aau.dk

[2] Dept. of Mathematics and Computer Science, Uni. of Southern Denmark, Denmark
zhou@imada.sdu.dk, johau05@student.sdu.dk

**Abstract.** To monitor skylines over dynamic data, one needs to continuously update the skyline query results in order to reflect the new data values. This paper tackles the problem of continuous skyline monitoring on a central query server over dynamic data from multiple data sites. Simply sending the updates of tuple values to the server is cost-prohibitive. Therefore, we propose an approach where the central server collaborates with the data sites to monitor the possible skyline changes. By doing so, the processing load is distributed over all the nodes instead of only on the central server. Furthermore, the approach can minimize the bandwidth consumption between the server and the data sites, which is often critical in a widely distributed environment. Extensive experiments demonstrate that our proposal is efficient and effective.

## 1 Introduction

A skyline query [4] returns from a multi-dimensional data set those points that are not dominated by others. A point is said to *dominate* the other, if it is not worse than the other in every single dimension and better in at least one dimension. Because of the power in retrieving interesting data according to multiple criteria, skyline queries can be used in many decision making applications.

In many applications, multi-dimensional data are often generated from multiple dynamic data sites (e.g., base stations managing sensors or web sites on the Internet). Due to the dynamic nature of data sites, snapshot skyline queries in such environments make little sense for data interpretation and decision making. Instead, continuous skyline monitoring is necessary in such environments.

By capturing the continuous query result changes as time elapses, such continuous skyline monitoring is able to detect potential significant events. For example, geologists, oceanographers and seismologists are able to conduct in tsunami forecast and forewarning by analyzing continuous multiple measures including *water level*, *earthquake wave*, *fall*, etc. An efficient skyline monitoring over relevant data sites can determine a successful warning of a deadly tsunami, which as a result may save millions of lives.

Another example is avalanche monitoring. The occurrence of avalanche is closely related to the weather conditions, e.g., rapid rise of temperature, a strong wind, heavy snowfall, as well as the strong solar radiation at the day. Consider that a large number of weather stations with multiple sensors are installed in the mountain areas to monitor

M. Gertz and B. Ludäscher (Eds.): SSDBM 2010, LNCS 6187, pp. 565–583, 2010.

the conditions of different places. Continuous skyline monitoring over such stations is able to maintain the locations having the most avalanche-favoring conditions.

Continuous skyline monitoring can also be interesting in geographically distributed environments. Within a trade day, for example, a stock trader needs to be continuously aware of which stocks worldwide are worth investing, based on multiple attributes like last sale price, last buy price, volume, etc. Apparently, a continuous skyline monitoring over multiple dynamic stock information sources at different places (e.g., the US market and the Europe market overlap in trading hours) will serve that purpose well.

Motivated by the aforementioned observations, we, in this paper, tackle the problem of efficient continuous skyline monitoring in a distributed environment characterized by a central server that acts as the query interface and multiple data sites each maintaining a large number of dynamic data tuples.

Our solution for continuous skyline monitoring mainly consists of two phases: *initialization* and *maintenance*. In the initialization phase, the initial query result, i.e. the global skyline, is obtained by correctly merging local skyline from all data sites. Based on the initial skyline, all data tuples are categorized with respect to their membership in local skyline and global skyline. Such a categorization is maintained in an efficient way on both server and data sites.

To support accurate and efficient skyline monitoring under dynamic data updates, a comprehensive case study for individual data updates is performed, which reveals the minimal skyline changes that can happen as time elapses. Consequently, in the maintenance phase, possible skyline changes are captured accordingly via efficient collaboration between the server and the data sites. In this way, unnecessary processing on server or data sites, and unnecessary communications between server and data sites are avoided. Furthermore, the processing load are distributed over the server and the data sites to avoid the server becoming the bottleneck.

In summary, we make the following major contributions in this paper. First, we formalize the continuous skyline monitoring problem in a generic two-tier distributed computing environment, and propose a two-phase solution for such an important problem. Second, we conduct a thorough case study on the possible incremental changes of continuous skyline results. Third, we develop an efficient two-tier continuous skyline maintenance approach based on the case study. Fourth, we evaluate our proposal through extensive experimental study.

The remainder of this paper is organized as follows. Section 2 briefly review the related work on skyline queries. Section 3 formalizes the problem statement. Sections 4 and 5 details respectively the initialization and maintenance phases of continuous skyline monitoring. Section 6 presents the experimental results. Finally, Section 7 concludes the paper.

## 2 Related Work

*Skyline queries in the centralized data storage.* Borzonyi et al. [4] introduced two algorithms *Block Nested Loop* (BNL) and *Divide-and-Conquer* (D&C). Chomicki et al. [5] proposed a *Sort-Filter-Skyline* (SFS) algorithm as BNL's variant. Tan et al. [18] proposed *Bitmap* and *Index* algorithms. Kossmann et al. [10] proposed a *Nearest Neighbor* (NN) method. Papadias et al. [16] proposed a *Branch-and-Bound Skyline* (BBS) method. Godfrey et al. [7] did a comprehensive analysis of previous skyline algorithms without indexing supports.

Yiu and Mamoulis [22] proposed efficient algorithms to retrieve top-$k$ points that dominate the largest number of points [16]. Lin et al. [13] proposed to select skyline points such that the total number of dominated points is maximized.

Dellis and Seeger [6] defined the reverse skyline query that returns the points whose dynamic skyline [16] contains the query point. Morse et al. [14] proposed a lattice based skyline algorithm for data on low cardinality domains. Lee et al. [11] proposed to access points in Z-order in order to compute/update skylines more efficiently. Pei et al. [17] defined probabilistic dominance for uncertain data where each record has several instances.

*Skyline queries in distributed and dynamic environments.* Balke et al. [3] addressed skyline operation over web databases where different dimensions are stored on different data sites. Wu et al. [21] proposed a parallel execution of constrained skyline queries in an overlay network. Huang et al. [8] proposed techniques for efficient distributed skyline query processing in MANETs. Zhu et al. [24] proposed a feedback-based skyline algorithm for geographically distributed servers on the Internet.

Huang et al. [9] defined continuous skyline query in a moving setting where dynamic distance between a moving object and all static data point is yet another dimension in the skyline computation. Lin et al. [12] proposed an efficient skyline computation method over sliding window data stream model. Tao and Papadias [19] addressed the similar problem differently by lazy updates and pre-computation. Wu et al. [20] proposed to efficiently maintain skyline with point deletions. Handling point insertion and deletion are also addressed in [24]. Our setting in this paper is different in that updates change point values continuously rather than inserting or deleting points.

Recently, Zhang et al. [23] studied the frequent skyline query over a sliding window on continuous objects from dynamic data sites. Given a window $W_t^s$ (of size of $s$ timestamps until $t$) and a threshold $\theta$ ($0 < \theta \leq 1$), such a query returns all objects that appear in at leat $\theta \cdot s$ snapshot skylines of all the $s$ ones within $W_t^s$. This paper differs from [23] in several important ways. First, each data site in our setting maintains a number of dynamic data tuples/records; while each client in [23] is a dynamic record. Second, our work maintains the real continuous skyline over the dynamic data; while [23] actually looks at several snapshot skylines within the given sliding window. In other words, the query in [23] is still executed one-time, rather than being maintained continuously as in our setting. Third, sampling based approximation is employed in [23] to reduce communication cost; while our continuous skyline query always maintains the exact skyline result efficiently. As a result, the solution in [23] cannot be applied directly to our problem in this paper.

*Monitoring of distributed dynamic data.* Streaming data are often generated from distributed sites. Hence there are much recent research effort devoted to studying continuously monitor over distributed dynamic data. Various query types have been studied. For instance, Babcock et al. [2] studied how to monitor top-$k$ data items efficiently by adaptively setting filters at the data sites. Mouratidis et al. [15] adopted a similar approach to solve the problem of monitoring $k$ nearest neighbors. Zhou et al. [25] studied the problem of multi-join queries over distributed streams. In this paper, we target a much different type of queries, skylines, where we have to consider multiple ranking criteria at the same time. Hence, a much different solution is needed.

## 3 Problem Setting

We consider a typical distributed setting adopted by existing literature, such as [2]. There is a central server responsible for returning the global skyline results. In addition, there are a number of remote $N$ data sites, namely $S_1, S_2, \ldots, S_N$. Each site maintains a set of dynamically changing tuples each of which, for example, can be readings from sensors at a particular weather station. The data sites will communicate with the server for data update and perform local filtering to minimize the communication cost.

At any time $t$, the tuple set on data site $S_i$ ($1 \leq i \leq N$) is captured in a *local relation* $R_i(t)$ with the scheme $\langle id_{tuple}, p_1, p_2, \ldots, p_d, t^* \rangle$, where $p_i$ ($1 \leq i \leq d$) is a value of the corresponding attribute of interest, $id_{tuple}$ is the tuple identifier, and $t^*$ is the time when the tuple is obtained from the corresponding data site. Note that $id_{tuple}$ practically serves as the primary key of a local relation. In other words, only the latest instance of any dynamic tuple is kept in a local relation. For a specific tuple $tp_{id}$ with identifier $id$, we use $tp_{id}(t)$ to denote its instance at timestamp $t$. For simplicity, we also use $tp.attrs$ to denote tuple $tp$'s all attributes from $p_1$ to $p_d$.

Accordingly, we have a dynamic (virtual) *global relation* $R_g(t)$ that basically is the union of all local relations at time $t$, i.e., $R_g(t) = \bigcup_{1 \leq i \leq N} R_i(t)$. For the simplicity of representation, we alter the global scheme to $\langle id_{site}, id_{tuple}, p_1, p_2, \ldots, p_d, t^* \rangle$, where $id_{site}$ indicates the site from which the tuple comes. As a result, $\langle id_{site}, id_{tuple} \rangle$ serves as the primary key of the global relation.

In environmental monitoring applications, weather stations attached with several different types of sensors are deployed to monitor the meteorological conditions [1]. Each station, responsible for its own proximity, continuously reports a dynamic tuple of values, such as *temperature*, *solar radiation*, and *wind speed*. To ease management, several stations will be grouped together and their data would be collected and relayed by a common base station, which we call a data site in this paper. For example, Table 1 shows three local relations and the corresponding global relation.

Given two tuples $tp_1$ and $tp_2$, we define the dominance relationship between them in terms of all their $p_i$ ($1 \leq i \leq d$) attributes. We say that $tp_1$ *dominates* $tp_2$, termed as $tp_1 \succ tp_2$, if $\forall 1 \leq i \leq d$, $tp_1.p_i$ is no worse than $tp_2.p_i$; and $\exists 1 \leq i \leq d$, $tp_1.p_i$ is better than $tp_2.p_i$. Note that "better" and "worse" are generic in the sense that they have different indications in different contexts.

Refer to the example in Table 1. Intuitively, a higher value in any of the three reading attributes indicates a higher chance of avalanche. A reading tuple $tp_i$ dominates another one $tp_j$, if $tp_i$'s all attribute values are no smaller than $tp_j$'s but at least one of $tp_i$'s attribute values is higher than $tp_j$'s. As a result, the local skylines and the global skyline are shown in Table 1(e) and (f) respectively.

The dominance definition above also applies to the different instances of the same tuple at different timestamps. For example, if $tp_1$ at site 1 is updated to $\langle -1.005, 365.292, 5.283 \rangle$ at 16:20, we say the new instance dominates the old one.

**Table 1.** Snapshots of local/global relations and local/global skylines

| $id_{tuple}$ | **temp.** | **solar radi.** | **wind speed** | $t^*$ |
|---|---|---|---|---|
| $tp_1$ | -1.150 | 365.292 | 4.282 | 16:15 |
| $tp_2$ | -4.713 | 146.223 | 2.556 | 16:18 |
| $tp_3$ | -6.900 | 194.078 | 6.646 | 16:18 |
| $tp_4$ | -1.280 | 363.165 | 2.548 | 16:18 |

(a) local relation #1

| $id_{tuple}$ | **temp.** | **solar radi.** | **wind speed** | $t^*$ |
|---|---|---|---|---|
| $tp_1$ | -8.588 | 82.417 | 3.763 | 16:18 |
| $tp_2$ | -1.087 | 309.46 | 1.592 | 16:17 |
| $tp_3$ | -9.713 | 337.642 | 2.573 | 16:18 |

(b) local relation #2

| $id_{tuple}$ | **temp.** | **solar radi.** | **wind speed** | $t^*$ |
|---|---|---|---|---|
| $tp_1$ | 8.787 | 267.455 | 2.866 | 16:18 |
| $tp_2$ | -5.588 | 156.858 | 1.383 | 16:18 |
| $tp_3$ | -14.338 | 247.250 | 2.662 | 16:18 |

(c) local relation #3

| $id_{site}$ | $id_{tuple}$ | **temp.** | **solar radi.** | **wind speed** | $t^*$ |
|---|---|---|---|---|---|
| $site_1$ | $tp_1$ | -1.150 | 365.292 | 4.282 | 16:15 |
| $site_1$ | $tp_2$ | -4.713 | 146.223 | 2.556 | 16:18 |
| $site_1$ | $tp_3$ | -6.900 | 194.078 | 6.646 | 16:18 |
| $site_1$ | $tp_4$ | -1.280 | 363.165 | 2.548 | 16:18 |
| $site_2$ | $tp_1$ | -8.588 | 82.417 | 3.763 | 16:18 |
| $site_2$ | $tp_2$ | -1.087 | 309.46 | 1.592 | 16:17 |
| $site_2$ | $tp_3$ | -9.713 | 337.642 | 2.573 | 16:18 |
| $site_3$ | $tp_1$ | 8.787 | 267.455 | 2.866 | 16:18 |
| $site_3$ | $tp_2$ | -5.588 | 156.858 | 1.383 | 16:18 |
| $site_3$ | $tp_3$ | -14.338 | 247.250 | 2.662 | 16:18 |

(d) global relation

| $id_{site}$ | **local skyline** |
|---|---|
| $site_1$ | $\{tp_1, tp_3\}$ |
| $site_2$ | $\{tp_1, tp_2, tp_3\}$ |
| $site_3$ | $\{tp_1\}$ |

(e) local skylines

| $id_{site}$ | **global skyline tuples** |
|---|---|
| $site_1$ | $\{tp_1, tp_3\}$ |
| $site_2$ | $\{tp_2\}$ |
| $site_3$ | $\{tp_1\}$ |

(f) global skyline

As all tuples are dynamic in our setting, the local skylines and the global skyline are also dynamic. Our goal is to monitor the global skyline continuously in a distributed environment as described above.

**Problem:** ***(Continuous Skyline Monitoring Query).*** A *continuous skyline monitoring query*, termed as $CSMQ$, is issued against the global relation $R_g$. It is activated at some time $t_s$, the start time of the query, and terminated at some later time $t_e$, the end time of the query. The query result is maintained from time $t_s$ to time $t_e$ in the following set:

$$\forall t \in [t_s, t_e], CSMQ(R_g) = \{tp \mid tp \in R_g(t) \ \wedge \ \nexists tp' \in R_g(t), tp' \succ tp\}.$$

Our solution in this paper consists of two phases. The initialization phase, to be presented in Section 4, obtains the initial query result for a $CSMQ$ query, and initializes necessary settings to facilitate continuous query processing. The maintenance phase, to be presented in Section 5, continuously updates the query result according to the dynamic changes of relevant tuples.

## 4 Query Initialization

When a $CSMQ$ query is activated at time $t_s$, the initialization is conducted in the system as follows. The server first sends query requests to all data sites. Each data site $S_i$ in turn sends to the server its local skyline $SK_i(t_s)$ that is a subset of its local relation. The server initializes the global skyline $SK_g$ according to the global scheme. When the server receives the local skyline from a data site, the incoming skyline will be merged into the current global skyline. After all local skylines are received and merged, the server obtains the initial global skyline and sends necessary control information back to all data sites.

The merging procedure (shown in Algorithm 1) is intended to eliminate unqualified temporary skyline points from both the temporary skyline result that is stored in $SK_g$, and the incoming skyline stored in $SK_{in}$. Given a local skyline $SK_{in}$ from data site $S_i$, portion of $SK_{in}$ may not participate the final global skyline. We call that portion *false*

**Algorithm 1. merge** (Incoming local skyline $SK_{in}$, data site identifier $id_{site}$, current global skyline $SK_g$)

$SK_{fp}[id_{site}] \leftarrow \emptyset$
**for** each tuple $tp_i$ in $SK_{in}$ **do**
  $tp_i \leftarrow \langle tp_i.attrs, tp_i.id_{tuple}, id_{site}, tp_i.t^* \rangle$
  **for** each tuple $tp_j$ in $SK_g$ **do**
    **if** $tp_i \succ tp_j$ **then**
      move $tp_j$ from $SK_g$ to $SK_{fp}[tp_j.id_{site}]$
    **else if** $tp_j \succ tp_i$ **then**
      move $tp_i$ from $SK_{in}$ to $SK_{fp}[id_{site}]$
      **break**
$SK_g \leftarrow SK_g \cup SK_{in}$

*positive skyline*. We use an array $SK_{fp}[1..N]$ to store all such false positive skylines for all data sites.

At any timestamp, a tuple $tp$ can be in one and only one state of three possibilities. First, $tp$ can be a non-skyline point. We term this state *NS*. Second, $tp$ can be a local skyline point on its data site but not a global skyline point with respect to all data sites. We term this state *FS*, according to the aforementioned false-positive skyline definition. Third, $tp$ can be a global skyline point. We term this state *GS*.

Our goal in this paper is to efficiently maintain the set of all tuples in the *GS* state when tuples are under possible updates. For that purpose, we are interested in the possible state switching for a single tuple. Figure 1 shows the state diagram of a single tuple.

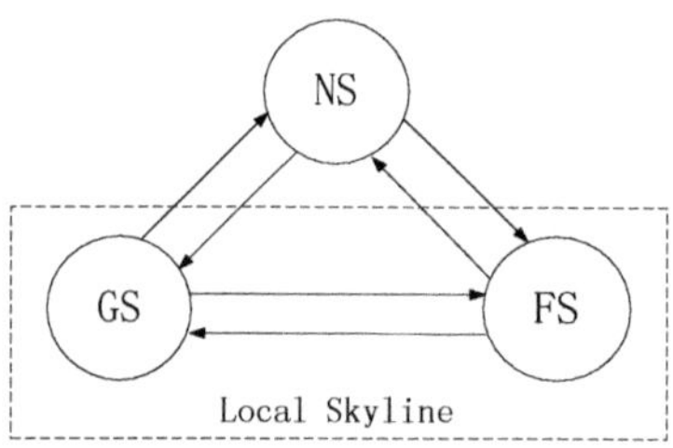


**Fig. 1.** Tuple State Diagram

**Table 2.** $SK_{lg}$ and $SK_{fp}$

| $id_{site}$ | $SK_{lg}$ | $SK_{fp}$ |
|---|---|---|
| $site_1$ | $\{tp_1, tp_3\}$ | $\emptyset$ |
| $site_2$ | $\{tp_2\}$ | $\{tp_1, tp_3\}$ |
| $site_3$ | $\{tp_1\}$ | $\emptyset$ |

On each data site $S_i$, we maintain the following structures: (1) Local skyline $SK_l$, the set of local skyline tuple identifiers. (2) Local global skyline $SK_{lg}$, the set of local skyline tuple identifiers that participate the global skyline. This corresponds to the tuple state *GS*. (3) False-Positive skyline $SK_{fp} = \{tp.id_{tuple} \mid tp \in SK_l\} \setminus SK_{lg}$, the set of local skyline tuple identifiers that do not participate the global skyline. This corresponds to the tuple state *FS*.

On the server side, we maintain the following structures: (1) Global skyline $SK_g$, the set of global skyline tuples. (2) An array of false-positive skyline tuples $SK_{fp}[1..N]$. Here, $\forall 1 \leq i \leq N, SK_{fp}[i] = S_i.SK_{fp}$.

**Table 3.** Change cases from time $t$ to $t'$ $(t' > t)$

| | $tp(t) \in NS$ | $tp(t) \in FS$ | $tp(t) \in GS$ |
|---|---|---|---|
| $tp(t') \sim tp(t)$ | Case 1 (Q1, Q2) | Case 4 (Q1, Q2, Q4) | Case 7 (Q1, Q2, Q3) |
| $tp(t) \succ tp(t')$ | Case 2 (–) | Case 5 (Q4) | Case 8 (Q1, Q3) |
| $tp(t') \succ tp(t)$ | Case 3 (Q1, Q2) | Case 6 (Q1, Q2) | Case 9 (Q2) |

Refer to the running example. The local data structures $SK_{lg}$ and $SK_{fp}$ are shown in Table 2. After all local skylines are merged, the server initializes the relevant data structures, and sends to each data site all its false-positive skyline tuple identifiers. When a data site receives that identifier set, it initializes local data structures accordingly. Note that the server and the sites will make use of their initializations subsequently in continuous skyline monitoring, as to be detailed in Section 5.

# 5 Continuous Skyline Monitoring

In this section we elaborate how the result of a *CSMQ* query is continuously maintained in the presence of dynamic updates from data sites. To be able to design concrete algorithms for the maintenance phase, we first proceed to discuss the cases of possible skyline changes caused by dynamic tuples from data sites.

## 5.1 Cases of Possible Skyline Changes

As tuples get updated continuously, the global skyline also needs to be maintained accordingly and correctly. The initial skyline $SK_g(t_s)$ obtained in Section 4 will serve as the starting point of the continuous maintenance.

Suppose the correct skyline at time $t \geq t_s$ is $SK_g(t) = \{tp \mid tp \in R_g(t) \land \nexists tp' \in R_g(t), tp' \succ tp\}$, and data site $S_i$ gets an updated tuple as $tp(t')$ at a later time $t' > t$, we need to determine the correct skyline $SK_g(t')$ at time $t'$. For that purpose, we need to consider for $tp(t')$ all or part of the three particular questions as follows.

*Question 1.* Is $tp(t')$ dominated by no skyline point in $SK_g(t)$ (or $SK_l(t)$)? If positive, $tp(t')$ will be in $SK_g(t')$ (or $SK_l(t)$).

*Question 2.* Does $tp(t')$ dominate any skyline point in $SK_g(t)$ (or $SK_l(t)$)? If positive, relevant old skyline points will expire and be out of $SK_g(t')$ (or $SK_l(t)$).

*Question 3.* Does $tp(t')$, a global skyline point at time $t$, stop dominating any non-skyline point solely dominated by $tp(t)$ at time $t$? If positive, relevant old non-skyline points will enter $SK_g(t')$.

In addition, it is also of interest to know the answer to the following question, so that the local and global structures for false positive skyline will be correctly updated. This is necessary for facilitating further continuous query processing.

*Question 4.* Does $tp(t')$ stop being a false-positive global skyline point because it is now dominated by some local skyline point? If positive, $tp(t')$ should be removed from local $SK_{fp}$ and server side $SK_{fp}[1..N]$.

These questions, on the other hand, are closely related to two aspects: the membership of $tp(t)$ in $SK_g(t)$, and the dominance relationship between $tp(t)$ and $tp(t')$. All possible cases with respect to these two aspects are listed in Table 3. In this table, each case is attached with questions that can have positive answers, which indicates possible skyline changes. We proceed to explain how $SK_g(t)$ will evolve to $SK_g(t')$ in each case.

**Case 1.** In this case, it is possible that $tp(t')$ at time $t$ is no longer dominated by any skyline point in $SK_g(t)$ (Question 1), which makes it become a new skyline point and $SK_g(t') = SK_g(t) \cup \{tp(t')\}$. It is also possible that $tp(t')$ dominates a subset $SK \subseteq SK_g(t)$ (Question 2), which drives any point in $SK$ out of the skyline. It is noteworthy that Question 2 can have positive answer only if the answer to Question 1 has been proved positive. As a result, the skyline will be $SK_g(t') = (SK_g(t) \setminus SK) \cup \{tp(t')\}$.

Whereas the answer to Question 3 is negative in this case. Since $tp(t)$ is not a skyline point at time $t$, it must be dominated by some skyline point $p \in SK_g(t)$. As a result, any non-skyline point dominated by $tp(t)$ at time $t$ must also be dominated by $p$, because of the transitivity of dominance [4]. It is therefore impossible for $tp(t)$ to solely dominate any non-skyline point at time $t$.

**Case 2.** In this case, we have negative answers to all three questions. The answer to Question 1 is negative, because $tp(t')$ must be dominated by some skyline point $p \in SK_g(t)$ that dominates $tp(t)$ at time $t$. The answer to Question 2 is also negative, because otherwise the skyline point $q \in SK_g(t)$ would also be dominated by $p$ aforementioned and cannot be a skyline point at all. The answer to Question 3 is negative for the same reason in Case 1. As a consequence, the skyline in this case will not change from time $t$ to $t'$, i.e. $SK_g(t') = SK_g(t)$.

**Case 3.** This case is similar to Case 1.

**Case 4.** This case is similar to Case 1, except that Question 4 should be checked because $tp$ may no long be a false positive global skyline point. The answer can be decided locally as we only need to check the updating $tp$ with all other local skyline points.

**Case 5.** This case is similar to Case 2, except that we need to check the answer to Question 4.

**Case 6.** This case is similar to Cases 1 and 3. Here, $tp(t')$ dominates its old instance $tp(t)$ which was a local skyline point. Therefore, $tp(t')$ cannot be dominated by any local skyline point, and it is unnecessary to check the answer to Question 4.

**Case 7.** In this case, answers to all three questions can be positive, because $tp(t)$ is a skyline point at time $t$. If the answer to Question 1 is positive, the skyline keeps unchanged from time $t$ to $t'$, i.e. $SK_g(t') = SK_g(t)$. Otherwise, the skyline will be $SK_g(t') = SK_g(t) \setminus \{tp(t)\}$.

It is still true that Question 2 can have positive answer only if Question 1 does. If the answer to Question 2 is positive, the new skyline becomes $SK_g(t') = SK_g(t) \setminus SK$, where $SK$ is defined the same as in Case 1.

If the answer to Question 3 is positive, which guarantees a set $P \subseteq R_g(t) \setminus SK_g(t)$ of all those non-skyline points that are solely dominated by $tp(t)$ at time $t$ but not by $tp(t')$

at time $t'$, the skyline will become $SK_g(t') = SK_g(t) \cup P$. Here, checking Question 3 does not depend on the answer to Questions 1 or 2.

**Case 8.** This case is similar to Case 7, except that it is not necessary to check the answer to Question 2. In this case, $tp(t)$ dominates its new instance $tp(t')$, which makes it impossible for $tp(t')$ to dominate any local/global skyline points. Because otherwise $tp(t)$ would have already dominated such skyline points.

**Case 9.** In this case we have positive answer to Question 1 and negative answer to Question 3. Since $tp(t)$ is a skyline point, $tp(t')$ with a higher dominating capability must stay in the skyline and still dominate all those non-skyline points dominated by $tp(t)$. The answer to Question 2 can be positive, because $tp(t')$ may dominate some old skyline points. Consequently, the new skyline becomes $SK_g(t') = SK_g(t) \setminus SK$, where $SK$ is defined the same as in Case 1.

With the case study on skyline changes, we are ready to design an efficient solution to dynamically maintain skylines in the distributed environment.

## 5.2 Processing on the Updating Data Site

When an update for tuple $tp$ comes to data site $S_i$ at time $t'$, the site needs to decide the change case type. This requires availability of two pieces of information: the dominance relationship between $tp(t)$ and $tp(t')$, and whether $tp(t)$ belongs to $SK_g(t)$ or not. The former is obtained by comparing $tp(t)$ and $tp(t')$; the latter is obtained by checking the reduced local skyline signature $SK_{lg}$. Both are done locally at data site $S_i$. After deciding the change case, site $S_i$ sends to the server a specific update message together with corresponding information.

Cases 1, 3 and 6 are processed according to Algorithm 2. Here, Question 2 is only checked when the answer to Question 1 is positive. Therefore, the process of checking Question 2 continues only if $tp(t_c)$ is not dominated by any local skyline point (line 1). Particularly, $tp(t_c)$ is added into the local skyline if the case type is not 6 (lines 2–3). Furthermore, the old local/global skyline points that are dominated by $tp(t_c)$ are eliminated accordingly (lines 4–8). Then, a specific update message is sent to the server (line 9). Otherwise, $tp(t_c)$ is dominated and removed from $SK_{fp}$ (lines 10–11).

Case 4 is processed according to Algorithm 3. If the updating tuple $tp(t_c)$ now is dominated by some local skyline point (line 1), it is removed from the local false-positive skyline $SK_{fp}$ if its old instance is there (lines 2–3), and then a specific message is sent to the server to remove $tp$ from $SK_{fp}$ there (line 4). Otherwise, $tp(t_c)$ is not dominated by any local skyline. Similar to the procedure for cases 1, 3 and 6, Question 2 is to be checked (lines 5–11).

Case 5 is processed according to Algorithm 4, which is similar to the first part of the procedure for case 4.

Case 7 is processed according to Algorithm 5. Its first part (lines 1–6) is similar to the counterpart in Algorithm 2. Next, it continues to check the answer to Question 3, by obtaining those tuples that stop being dominated by their sole dominator $tp$ at the updating time (lines7–10). Here, $DR(tp)$ denotes the dominating region [8] of a tuple $tp$. All such tuples are added into the local skyline (line 11). Finally, a specific message is sent to the server (line 12).

**Algorithm 2. updateCase136** (Updating tuple $tp$, current timestamp $t_c$, local global skyline $SK_{lg}$)

**if** $\nexists tp' \in SK_l$ s.t. $tp' \succ tp(t_c)$ **then**
  **if** the case type is not 6 **then**
    add $tp(t_c)$ to $SK_l$
  $SK_{exp} \leftarrow \{id \in SK_{lg} \mid tp(t_c) \succ R_i[id]\}$
  $SK_{lg} \leftarrow SK_{lg} \setminus SK_{exp}$
  $SK_{expf} \leftarrow \{id \in SK_{fp} \mid tp(t_c) \succ R_i[id]\}$
  $SK_{fp} \leftarrow SK_{fp} \setminus SK_{expf}$
  $SK_l \leftarrow \{tp' \in SK_l \mid tp'.id_{tuple} \notin SK_{exp} \cup SK_{expf}\}$
  send $\langle$UPT_MSG_CASE_136, $tp, SK_{exp}, SK_{expf}\rangle$ to the server
**else if** $tp.id_{tuple} \in SK_{fp}$ **then**
  remove $tp.id_{tuple}$ from $SK_{fp}$

**Algorithm 3. updateCase4** (Updating tuple $tp$, current timestamp $t_c$, local global skyline $SK_{lg}$)

**if** $\exists tp' \in SK_l$ s.t. $tp' \succ tp(t_c)$ **then**
  **if** $tp.id_{tuple} \in SK_{fp}$ **then**
    remove $tp.id_{tuple}$ from $SK_{fp}$
  send $\langle$UPT_MSG_CASE_4_Q4, $tp.id_{tuple}\rangle$ to the server
**else**
  $SK_{exp} \leftarrow \{id \in SK_{lg} \mid tp(t_c) \succ R_i[id]\}$
  $SK_{lg} \leftarrow SK_{lg} \setminus SK_{exp}$
  $SK_{expf} \leftarrow \{id \in SK_{fp} \mid tp(t_c) \succ R_i[id]\}$
  $SK_{fp} \leftarrow SK_{fp} \setminus SK_{expf}$
  $SK_l \leftarrow \{tp' \in SK_l \mid tp'.id_{tuple} \notin SK_{exp} \cup SK_{expf}\}$
  send $\langle$UPT_MSG_CASE_4, $tp, SK_{exp}, SK_{expf}\rangle$ to the server

Case 8 is processed according to Algorithm 6. In this case, it is impossible for the disadvantaged new instance of the updating tuple to dominate any local/global skyline points. However, it is still possible that the new instance is dominated by some local/global skyline points. It is also possible that such a local skyline point dominating the $tp(t_c)$ may be dominated by $tp$'s old instance. Therefore, we here check the answer to Question 3 first (lines 1–5), followed by steps of checking that to Question 1 (lines 6–10).

**Algorithm 4. updateCase5** (Updating tuple $tp$, current timestamp $t_c$, local global skyline $SK_{lg}$)

**if** $\exists tp' \in SK_l$ s.t. $tp' \succ tp(t_c)$ **then**
  **if** $tp.id_{tuple} \in SK_{fp}$ **then**
    remove $tp.id_{tuple}$ from $SK_{fp}$
  send $\langle$UPT_MSG_CASE_5, $tp.id_{tuple}\rangle$ to the server

**Algorithm 5. updateCase7** (Updating tuple $tp$, current timestamp $t_c$, local global skyline $SK_{lg}$)

**if** $\nexists tp' \in SK_l$ s.t. $tp' \succ tp(t_c)$ **then**<br>
    $SK_{exp} \leftarrow \{id \in SK_{lg} \mid tp(t_c) \succ R_i[id]\}$<br>
    $SK_{lg} \leftarrow SK_{lg} \setminus SK_{exp}$<br>
    $SK_{expf} \leftarrow \{id \in SK_{fp} \mid tp(t_c) \succ R_i[id]\}$<br>
    $SK_{fp} \leftarrow SK_{fp} \setminus SK_{expf}$<br>
    $SK_l \leftarrow \{tp' \in SK_l \mid tp'.id_{tuple} \notin SK_{exp} \cup SK_{expf}\}$<br>
$P_c \leftarrow \{tp \in R_i \mid tp \in DR(R_i[tp.id_{tuple}]) - DR(tp(t_c))\}$<br>
**for** each tuple $tp' \in P_c$ **do**<br>
    **if** $\exists tp'' \in SK_l \setminus \{tp(t)\}$ s.t. $tp'' \succ tp'$ **then**<br>
        remove $tp'$ from $P_c$<br>
$SK_l \leftarrow SK_l \cup P_c$<br>
send $\langle$UPT_MSG_CASE_7, $tp, SK_{exp}, SK_{expf}, P_c\rangle$ to the server

**Algorithm 6. updateCase8** (Updating tuple $tp$, current timestamp $t_c$, local global skyline $SK_{lg}$)

$P_c \leftarrow \{tp \in R_i \mid tp \in DR(R_i[tp.id_{tuple}]) - DR(tp(t_c))\}$<br>
**for** each tuple $tp' \in P_c$ **do**<br>
    **if** $\exists tp'' \in SK_l \setminus \{tp(t)\}$ s.t. $tp'' \succ tp'$ **then**<br>
        remove $tp'$ from $P_c$<br>
$SK_l \leftarrow SK_l \cup P_c$<br>
**if** $\exists tp' \in SK_l$ s.t. $tp' \succ tp(t_c)$ **then**<br>
    $SK_{exp} \leftarrow \{tp.id_{tuple}\}$<br>
    $SK_l \setminus SK_{exp}$<br>
**else**<br>
    $SK_{exp} \leftarrow \emptyset$<br>
send $\langle$UPT_MSG_CASE_8, $tp, SK_{exp}, P_c\rangle$ to the server

**Algorithm 7. updateCase9** (Updating tuple $tp$, current timestamp $t_c$, local global skyline $SK_{lg}$)

$SK_{exp} \leftarrow \{id \in SK_{lg} \mid tp(t_c) \succ R_i[id]\}$<br>
$SK_{lg} \leftarrow SK_{lg} \setminus SK_{exp}$<br>
$SK_{expf} \leftarrow \{id \in SK_{fp} \mid tp(t_c) \succ R_i[id]\}$<br>
$SK_{fp} \leftarrow SK_{fp} \setminus SK_{expf}$<br>
$SK_l \leftarrow \{tp' \in SK_l \mid tp'.id_{tuple} \notin SK_{exp} \cup SK_{expf}\}$<br>
send $\langle$UPT_MSG_CASE_9, $tp, SK_{exp}, SK_{expf}\rangle$ to the server

Case 9 is processed according to Algorithm 7, which is similar to its counterparts in Algorithms 2 and 3.

### 5.3 Update Processing on the Server

Upon the receipt of an upstream update message from an updating data site, the server processes the message according to the procedure described in Algorithm 8. If the message type is UPT_MSG_Case_4_Q4 or UPT_MSG_Case_5, the updating tuple will be moved out of the false positive skyline array since it is no longer a false positive global skyline point (lines 1–2). Otherwise, the server needs to check the answers to Questions 1, 2 and 3 locally, and send corresponding downstream messages to involved data sites (lines 3–37).

Specifically, other message types are processed as follows. First, a temporary array is initialized to contain possible expiring global skyline points (line 4). Second, those global skyline points that are no longer local skyline points on the updating site are removed from the global skyline (line 6). Next, if the message type is not UPT_MSG_Case_8, those false positive global skyline points that are no longer local skyline points on the updating site are removed from the false positive skyline array (lines 7–8).

After that, all tuples that may enter the global skyline are added into set $gs$ (lines 9–11), including the updating tuple and those sent by the site if it is a UPT_MSG_Case_7 or UPT_MSG_Case_8 message.

Subsequently, Question 1 is checked by comparing the updating tuple with the current global skyline points not coming from the updating site (lines 12–24). If the updating tuple is dominated, the process will stop immediately (lines 15–20). Those existing global skyline points that come from the updating site but are dominated by the updating tuple are removed (line 17–18). Otherwise, all invalid global skyline points are moved to the temporary array for later use (lines 21–22). After that, it is confirmed that the updating tuple is not dominate and it is (still) a global skyline point. All remaining tuples in $gs$ are added into the global skyline, and a corresponding downstream message is sent to the updating site (lines 23–24).

Furthermore, invalid global skyline points, which are still local skyline points on their own data sites, are moved from the temporary array to the false positive skyline array, and a corresponding downstream message is sent to each involved data site for local update (lines 25–28).

Finally, in the case of a UPT_MSG_Case_7 or UPT_MSG_Case_8 message, Question 3 is checked for each particular data site, in order to identify those current false positive skyline tuples that are no longer dominated (lines 29–37). All such tuples are obtained by dominance comparison with the updating tuple and all current global skyline tuples (line 33). If they do exist, they are moved from the false positive skyline to the global skyline (lines 35–36), and a corresponding downstream message is sent to the involved site for local update (line 37).

### 5.4 Passive Update Processing on Data Sites

When the server processes an update message, some data sites may receive downstream messages from the servers. Such data sites (including the updating site) also need to do

**Algorithm 8. serverUpdate** (Update message $msg$, data site identifier $id$)

**if** $msg.type \in \{$UPT_MSG_Case_4_Q4, UPT_MSG_Case_5$\}$ **then**
  remove the tuple identified by $msg.tp.id_{tuple}$ from $SK_{fp}[id]$
**else**
  **for** $i$ from 1 to $N$ **do**
    $SK_{exp}[i] \leftarrow \emptyset$
  $SK_g \leftarrow \{tp \in SK_g \mid tp.id_{site} \neq id \vee tp.id_{tuple} \notin msg.SK_{exp}\}$
  **if** $msg.type \neq$ UPT_MSG_Case_8 **then**
    $SK_{fp}[id] \leftarrow SK_{fp}[id] \setminus msg.SK_{expf}$
  $gs \leftarrow msg.tp$
  **if** $msg.type \in \{$UPT_MSG_Case_7, UPT_MSG_Case_8$\}$ **then**
    $gs \leftarrow gs \cup \{tp \in msg.P_c \mid \nexists tp' \in SK_g \setminus \{msg.tp(t)\}$ s.t. $tp' \succ tp\}$
  **for** each tuple $tp$ in $SK_g$ **do**
    **if** $tp.id_{site} = id$ **then**
      **continue**
    **if** $msg.type \neq$ UPT_MSG_Case_9 **and** $tp \succ msg.tp$ **then**
      $SK_{exp}[id] \leftarrow SK_{exp}[id] \cup \{msg.tp\}$
      **if** $\exists tp' \in SK_g$ s.t. $tp'.id_{tuple} = msg.tp.id_{tuple} \wedge tp'.id_{site} = id \wedge msg.tp \succ tp'$ **then**
        $SK_g \leftarrow SK_g \setminus \{tp'\}$
      remove $msg.tp$ from $gs$
      **break**
    **if** $msg.tp \succ tp$ **then**
      move $tp$ from $SK_g$ to $SK_{exp}[tp.id_{site}]$
  $SK_g \leftarrow SK_g \cup gs$
  send $\langle$UPT_MSG_GS, $\{tp.id_{tuple} \mid tp \in gs\}\rangle$ to data site $S_{id}$
  **for** $i$ from 1 to $N$ **do**
    **if** $SK_{exp}[i] \neq \emptyset$ **then**
      $SK_{fp}[i] \leftarrow SK_{fp}[i] \cup SK_{exp}[i]$
      send $\langle$UPT_MSG_GS2FS, $SK_{exp}[i]\rangle$ to data site $S_i$
  **if** $msg.type \in \{$UPT_MSG_Case_7, UPT_MSG_Case_8$\}$ **then**
    **for** $i$ from 1 to $N$ **do**
      **if** $i = id$ **then**
        **continue**
      $fps \leftarrow \{tp \in SK_{fp}[i] \mid msg.tp(t) \succ tp \wedge msg.tp(t_c) \not\succ tp \wedge (\nexists tp' \in SK_g \setminus \{msg.tp(t)\}$ s.t. $tp' \succ tp)\}$
      **if** $fps \neq \emptyset$ **then**
        $SK_{fp}[i] \leftarrow SK_{fp}[i] \setminus fps$
        $SK_g \leftarrow SK_g \cup fps$
        send $\langle$UPT_MSG_FS2GS, $\{tp.id_{tuple} \mid tp \in fps\}\rangle$ to data site $S_i$

passive updates on their local data structures accordingly. The passive update processing on a relevant data site is described in Algorithm 9.

If the downstream message type is UPT_MSG_GS, it is sent to the updating data site to indicate that the updating tuple and/or some other local points (sent in the $P_c$ set in a UPT_MSG_CASE_7 or UPT_MSG_CASE_8 message) are global skylines now. Therefore, the corresponding tuple identifiers are added to the local global skyline (lines 1–2).

**Algorithm 9. psvSiteUpdate** (Update message $msg$)

1: **if** $msg.type =$ UPT_MSG_GS **then**
2: $SK_{lg} \leftarrow SK_{lg} \cup msg.id\_set$
3: $P_x \leftarrow P_x \setminus msg.id\_set$
4: $SK_{fp} \leftarrow SK_{fp} \cup P_x$
5: $P_x \leftarrow \emptyset$
6: **else if** $msg.type =$ UPT_MSG_FS2GS **then**
7: $SK_{fp} \leftarrow SK_{fp} \setminus msg.id\_set$
8: $SK_{lg} \leftarrow SK_{lg} \cup msg.id\_set$
9: **else if** $msg.type =$ UPT_MSG_GS2FS **then**
10: $SK_{lg} \leftarrow SK_{lg} \setminus msg.id\_set$
11: $SK_{fp} \leftarrow SK_{fp} \cup msg.id\_set$

However, not all local skyline tuples sent to the server become global skyline points. Some may be eliminated by the server. Accordingly, we need to put the identifiers of such false positive skyline tuples to the local $SK_{fp}$ structure. To ease the processing, we maintain on the updating site a local variable $P_x = \{tp.id_{tuple} \mid tp \in P_c$ or $tp$ is the updating tuple$\}$. Particularly, $P_x$ is set after each local update is done. When processing a UPT_MSG_GS message, the identifiers of those new false positive skyline tuples are obtained by the difference between $P_x$ and the returned identifier set in the message (line 3). Those tuples are merged to $SK_{fp}$ and $P_x$ is reset to empty (lines 4–5).

If the downstream message type is UPT_MSG_FS2GS, the involved tuple identifiers will be moved from the local $SK_{fp}$ to $SK_{lg}$, as such tuples are promoted into the global skyline (lines 6–8). If the message type is UPT_MSG_GS2FS, the involved tuple identifiers will be moved from the local $SK_{lg}$ to $SK_{fp}$, because such tuples are no longer global skyline points (lines 9–11).

It is noteworthy that a downstream message cannot force a tuple in the local $SK_{lg}$ or $SK_{fp}$ to move out to enter the non-skyline set. For the local skyline membership to expire, no matter the tuple is in the global skyline or not, the update causing the change must come from the same data site. Such a change is processed before the data sites sends a upstream message to the server, as described in Section 5.2.

### 5.5 Brief Analysis on Algorithm Costs

In this section, we briefly analyze the costs of those algorithms proposed above. Table 4 lists the notations used in this section. Table 5 lists the worst-case costs of main updating algorithms, where we regard the dominance comparison between two tuples as the crucial operation.

Algorithms 2, 3, 4, and 7 need to compare the updating tuple $tp$ with each local skyline tuple in the worst case, which incurs the cost of $\mathcal{O}(s_i)$. In the worst case, Algorithms 5 and 6 need to compare the updating tuple $tp$ with all local tuples in order to find all possible new local skyline points that used to be dominated by the old instance of $tp$, i.e., set $P_c$ in the algorithms. Furthermore, set $P_c$ is compared against the local skyline to find all those points that used to be dominated solely by the old instance of $tp$. Therefore, their worst-case cost is $\mathcal{O}(r_i) + \mathcal{O}(|P_c| \cdot s_i)$.

**Table 4.** Notation

| Nota. | Description |
|---|---|
| $S$ | Cardinality of $SK_g$ |
| $F$ | Total number of false positive skyline points |
| $r_i$ | Cardinality of $R_i$ on the $i$-th data site |
| $s_i$ | Cardinality of $SK_{lg}$ on the $i$-th data site |
| $f_i$ | Cardinality of $SK_{fp}$ on the $i$-th data site |

**Table 5.** Worst-Case Costs

| Algorithms | Worst-Case Cost |
|---|---|
| Alg. 2 | $\mathcal{O}(s_i)$ |
| Alg. 3 | $\mathcal{O}(s_i)$ |
| Alg. 4 | $\mathcal{O}(s_i)$ |
| Alg. 5 | $\mathcal{O}(r_i) + \mathcal{O}(\|P_c\| \cdot s_i)$ |
| Alg. 6 | $\mathcal{O}(r_i) + \mathcal{O}(\|P_c\| \cdot s_i)$ |
| Alg. 7 | $\mathcal{O}(s_i)$ |
| Alg. 8 | $\mathcal{O}(S \cdot F)$ |

The cost of Algorithm 8 mainly comes from two parts. It needs to compare the updating tuple with all global skyline points, which incurs $\mathcal{O}(S)$ in the worst case. Also, in the worst case for a UPT_MSG_Case_7 or UPT_MSG_Case_8 message, it needs to compare each false positive skyline point with all global skyline points in order to decide whether a false positive skyline point should be promoted into the global skyline or not. This incurs the cost of $\mathcal{O}(S \cdot F)$. As a result, the worst case cost of Algorithm 8 is $\mathcal{O}(S) + \mathcal{O}(S \cdot F) = \mathcal{O}(S \cdot F)$.

## 6 Experimental Studies

### 6.1 Experimental Settings

We call the solution proposed in this paper the *Global* approach, and compare it with two alternatives. In the *Naive* approach, each data site maintains its relation of up-to-date tuples, and the server maintains the global relation $R_g$ and the global skyline $SK_g$. A data site sends each tuple update to the server, which in turn triggers the global skyline update accordingly. The update is done in two aspects: removing dominated points from $R_g$, and adding qualified points from $R_g \setminus SK_g$ to $SK_g$. In the initialization phase, the server only computes the initial global skyline without obtaining any other information.

In the *Local* approach, each data site maintains its relation of up-to-date tuples and its local skyline, and the server maintains the global skyline only. A data site only sends to the server a tuple update that changes its local skyline. When the server receives a tuple update, it updates the global skyline by checking the answers to Questions 1, 2, and 3 defined in Section 5.1. Note that as no auxiliary information is maintained on the server, it has to send necessary messages to relevant data sites to answer Question 3. We claim the local approach as our contribution in the sense that it is a weakened version of the global approach.

We consider three performance metrics in the experiments. (1) bandwidth consumption, where we we count the total sizes of tuples and identifiers sent between the server and the data sites, (2) server processing time, where we measure the average time spent on performing the updates the results at the server, and (3) site processing time, i.e. the average processing time on all the data sites for maintaining the updates over the simulation period. All the algorithms are implemented with Java 1.6 and the experiments are run on a Linux desktop with an Intel Core 2 Duo CPU @1.86GHz and 2G RAM.

**Table 6.** Parameter Settings

| Parameter | Settings |
|---|---|
| Dimensionality | 2, **3**, 4, 5 |
| # of data sites | 100, 200, ..., **500**, ..., 800 |
| Data distribution | Random (Indep.), Anti-corr. |

We fix the local cardinality of each site at 100 tuples, and update all tuples for 100 rounds. All tuple values on each dimension are normalized to the range $[0, 1]$. At each round, the ratio of tuples that really get updated by default set to 1%, which will be varied. The other experimental parameters are varied according to Table 6. Default setting values are shown in bold. In the whole period of experiment, updates of each particular tuple are generated according to a Gaussian distribution with a standard deviation of 0.05 and a mean of the tuple's old value.

### 6.2 Experimental Results

Figure 2 reports the results on the effect of site number on anti-correlated data sets. As the number of data site increases, all approaches degrade. Regarding the bandwidth consumption, referring to Figure 2(a), the global approach is the best as it reduces a considerable parts of tuples and messages that otherwise would be sent via the network. Referring to Figure 2(b), the global approach incurs the least server processing time, as it maintains the continuous skyline incrementally and updates the result only when it is necessary. Referring to Figure 2(c), the global approach incurs slightly more site processing time than the naive approach. This is merely because the latter actually does no local processing at all but sending an updated tuple to the server whenever an update happens locally.

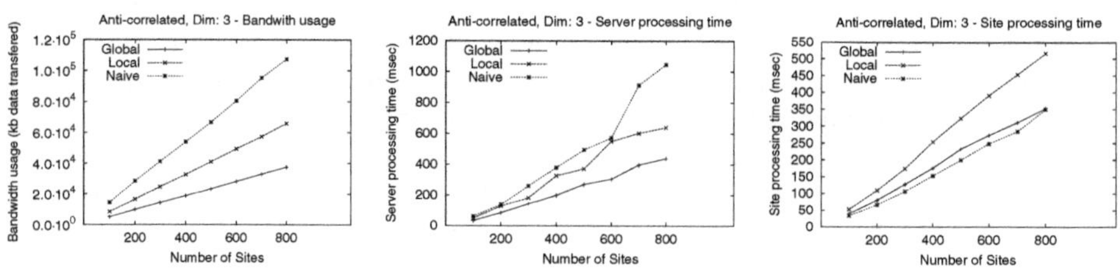


(a) Bandwidth consumption (b) Server processing time (c) Site processing time

**Fig. 2.** Effect of Site Number on Anti-correlated Data Sets

Figure 3 reports the results on the effect of tuple dimensionality on anti-correlated data sets. Higher dimensionality increases the costs of all approaches. The global approach still has the lowest bandwidth consumption and server processing time. Its gap between the naive approach regarding the site processing time becomes apparent, because the local skyline sizes become larger as dimensionality increases.

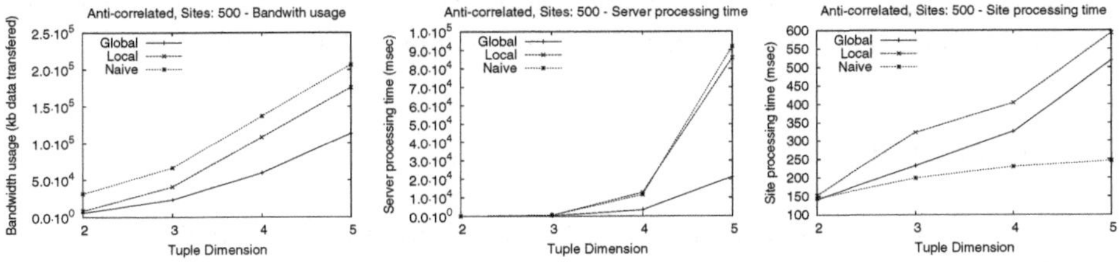


(a) Bandwidth consumption (b) Server processing time (c) Site processing time

**Fig. 3.** Effect of Dimensionality on Anti-correlated Data Sets

The same kinds of results on random data sets are reported in Figures 4 and 5. Regarding bandwidth consumption, as shown in Figures 4(a) and 5(a), The global approach is still the best. Whereas the local approach catches up and outperforms it with even less server processing time, according to Figures 4(b) and 5(b). Local skyline sizes become smaller on random data sets, and therefore fewer updating tuples sent to the server, which favors the local approach that updates the global skyline directly on the server side.

Referring to Figures 4(c) and 5(c), the global approach reclaims its advantage by short site processing time. This is because the smaller local skyline sizes reduce the local processing cost by the global approach; whereas the naive approach still needs to report each updating tuple to the server.

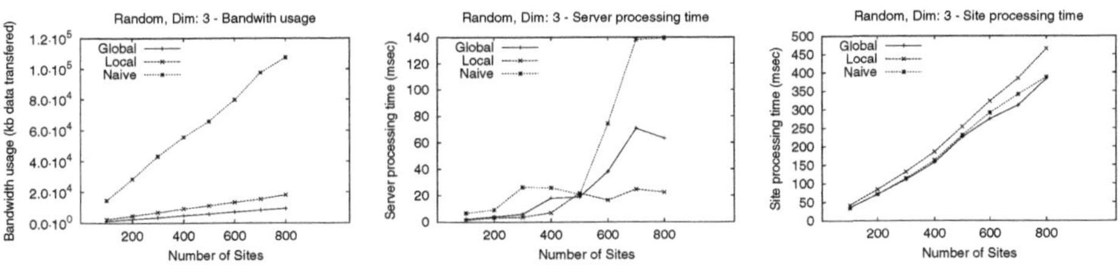


(a) Bandwidth consumption (b) Server processing time (c) Site processing time

**Fig. 4.** Effect of Site Number on Random Data Sets

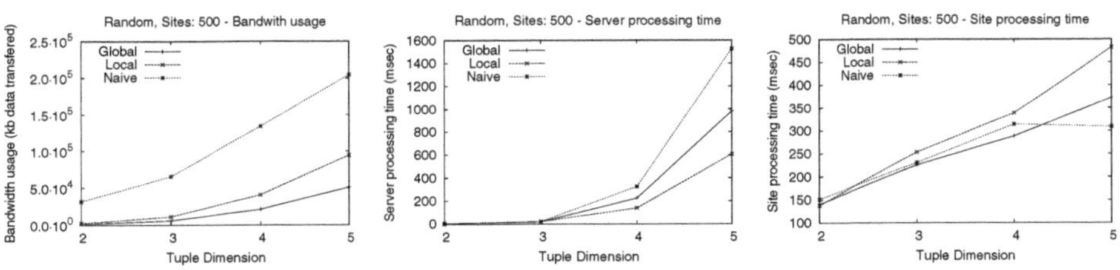


(a) Bandwidth consumption (b) Server processing time (c) Site processing time

**Fig. 5.** Effect of Dimensionality on Random Data Sets

We also varied the tuple updating ratio from 0.1% to 1%, and observed similar trends for various ratios. Due to the space limitation, we omit such results here.

## 7 Conclusion

In this paper we address continuous skyline monitoring in distributed environments. We target a generic type of computing environments with two-tiers: a server as query interface and multiple data sites each managing a number of dynamic data tuples. Our solution consists of two phases: *initialization* and *maintenance*. We propose a complete set of techniques in order to maintain the continuous skyline results efficiently. First, in the initialization phase, the initial query result is obtained and necessary membership information is initialized on both tiers. Second, a comprehensive case study is conducted to disclose the minimal skyline changes under dynamic data updates. Third, an effective two-tier collaboration is proposed to process possible skyline changes and to update the query results continuously in an incremental manner. The results of extensive experiments demonstrate that our proposal is efficient and scalable in terms of both communication costs and processing costs.

**Acknowledgments.** Yongluan Zhou is partially supported by research grant 09-073281 from the Danish Council for Independent Research — Natural Sciences (FNU).

## References

1. SensorScope Project, `http://sensorscope.epfl.ch/`
2. Babcock, B., Babcock, B., Olston, C.: Distributed top-k monitoring. In: Proc. SIGMOD, pp. 28–39 (2003)
3. Balke, W.-T., Guentzer, U., Zheng, J.X.: Efficient distributed skylining for web information systems. In: Bertino, E., Christodoulakis, S., Plexousakis, D., Christophides, V., Koubarakis, M., Böhm, K., Ferrari, E. (eds.) EDBT 2004. LNCS, vol. 2992, pp. 256–273. Springer, Heidelberg (2004)
4. Borzonyi, S., Kossmann, D., Stocker, K.: The skyline operator. In: Proc. ICDE, pp. 421–430 (2001)
5. Chomicki, J., Godfrey, P., Gryz, J., Liang, D.: Skyline with presorting. In: Proc. ICDE, pp. 717–719 (2003)
6. Dellis, E., Seeger, B.: Efficient computation of reverse skyline queries. In: Proc. VLDB, pp. 291–302 (2007)
7. Godfrey, P., Shipley, R., Gryz, J.: Maximal vector computation in large data sets. In: Proc. VLDB, pp. 229–240 (2005)
8. Huang, Z., Jensen, C.S., Lu, H., Ooi, B.C.: Skyline queries against mobile lightweight devices in MANETs. In: Proc. ICDE, p. 66 (2006)
9. Huang, Z., Lu, H., Ooi, B.C., Tung, A.K.H.: Continuous skyline queries for moving objects. TKDE 18(12), 1645–1658 (2006)
10. Kossmann, D., Ramsak, F., Rost, S.: Shooting stars in the sky: An online algorithm for skyline queries. In: Proc. VLDB, pp. 275–286 (2002)
11. Lee, K.C.K., Zheng, B., Li, H., Lee, W.-C.: Approaching the skyline in z order. In: Proc. VLDB, pp. 279–290 (2007)

12. Lin, X., Yuan, Y., Wang, W., Lu, H.: Stabbing the sky: Efficient skyline computation over sliding windows. In: Proc. ICDE, pp. 502–513 (2005)
13. Lin, X., Yuan, Y., Zhang, Q., Zhang, Y.: Selecting stars: The k most representative skyline operator. In: Proc. ICDE, pp. 86–95 (2007)
14. Morse, M.D., Patel, J.M., Jagadish, H.V.: Efficient skyline computation over low-cardinality domains. In: VLDB, pp. 267–278 (2007)
15. Mouratidis, K., Hadjieleftheriou, M., Papadias, D.: Conceptual partitioning: An efficient method for continuous nearest neighbor monitoring. In: Proc. SIGMOD, pp. 634–645 (2005)
16. Papadias, D., Tao, Y., Fu, G., Seeger, B.: An optimal and progressive algorithm for skyline queries. In: Proc. SIGMOD, pp. 467–478 (2003)
17. Pei, J., Jiang, B., Lin, X., Yuan, Y.: Probabilistic skylines on uncertain data. In: Proc. VLDB, pp. 15–26 (2007)
18. Tan, K.L., Eng, P.K., Ooi, B.C.: Efficient progressive skyline computation. In: Proc. VLDB, pp. 301–310 (2001)
19. Tao, Y., Papadias, D.: Maintaining sliding window skylines on data streams. TKDE 18(3), 377–391 (2006)
20. Wu, P., Agrawal, D., Egecioglu, Ö., Abbadi, A.E.: Deltasky: Optimal maintenance of skyline deletions without exclusive dominance region generation. In: Proc. ICDE, pp. 486–495 (2007)
21. Wu, P., Zhang, C., Feng, Y., Zhao, B.Y., Agrawal, D., Abbadi, A.E.: Parallelizing skyline queries for scalable distribution. In: Ioannidis, Y., Scholl, M.H., Schmidt, J.W., Matthes, F., Hatzopoulos, M., Böhm, K., Kemper, A., Grust, T., Böhm, C. (eds.) EDBT 2006. LNCS, vol. 3896, pp. 112–130. Springer, Heidelberg (2006)
22. Yiu, M.L., Mamoulis, N.: Efficient processing of top-k dominating queries on multi-dimensional data. In: Proc. VLDB, pp. 483–494 (2007)
23. Zhang, Z., Cheng, R., Papadias, D., Tung, A.K.H.: Minimizing the communication cost for continuous skyline maintenance. In: SIGMOD Conference, pp. 495–508 (2009)
24. Zhu, L., Tao, Y., Zhou, S.: Distributed skyline retrieval with low bandwidth consumption. TKDE 21(3), 384–400 (2009)
25. Zhou, Y., Yan, Y., Yu, F., Zhou, A.: PMJoin: Optimizing Distributed Multi-way Stream Joins by Stream Partitioning. In: Li Lee, M., Tan, K.-L., Wuwongse, V. (eds.) DASFAA 2006. LNCS, vol. 3882, pp. 325–341. Springer, Heidelberg (2006)

# Propagation of Densities of Streaming Data within Query Graphs

Michael Daum, Frank Lauterwald, Philipp Baumgärtel, and Klaus Meyer-Wegener

Dept. of Computer Science, University of Erlangen-Nuremberg, Germany
{md, frank, snphbaum, kmw}@i6.cs.fau.de

**Abstract.** *Data Stream Systems* (DSSs) use cost models to determine if a DSS can cope with a given workload and to optimize query graphs. However, certain relevant input parameters of these models are often unknown or highly imprecise. Especially selectivities are stream-dependent and application-specific parameters.

In this paper, we describe a method that supports selectivity estimation considering input streams' attribute value distribution. The novelty of our approach is the propagation of the probability distributions through the query graph in order to give estimates for the inner nodes of the graph. For most common stream operators, we establish formulas that describe their output distribution as a function of their input distributions. For unknown operators like *User-Defined Operators* (UDOs), we introduce a method to measure the influence of these operators on arbitrary probability distributions. This method is able to do most of the computational work before the query is deployed and introduces minimal overhead at runtime. Our evaluation framework facilitates the appropriate combination of both methods and allows to model almost arbitrary query graphs.

## 1 Introduction

Over the past few years, the field of data stream research has matured, and first commercial products have appeared. There is still a lot of need of and potential for research in distributing, estimating, and optimizing of queries.

Estimation of costs of data processing in data streams is crucial, especially if data stream processing is distributed over battery-powered sensor nodes. This estimation needs to know the data rates and the distribution of values. In our project *Data Stream Application Manager* (DSAM) [1], we distribute queries over a network of heterogeneous *Stream Processing Systems* (SPSs) and *Wireless Sensor Network* (WSN) nodes. This paper presents some of the theoretical results regarding the cost estimator of DSAM.

Like in a *Database System* (DBS), a query in a *Data Stream System* (DSS) consists of a graph of operator instances (nodes) that are connected by inner streams. Each operator in a query may manipulate both the data rate and the distribution of values in a data stream. The outgoing data rate of an operator is often influenced by the distribution of values. In order to achieve good estimates for the whole query, characteristics of intermediate data streams between operators are also relevant. This requires the propagation of estimates through the entire graph. The manipulation of these characteristics (change of variables' formula) can be either measured, computed by analytic methods or it can be approximated by numerical methods. Basically, an analytic method is preferable as

M. Gertz and B. Ludäscher (Eds.): SSDBM 2010, LNCS 6187, pp. 584–601, 2010.

it is more precise and less computationally intensive. Some operators are unfortunately not manageable with analytic methods. For the support of complex query graphs, however, it will be necessary to combine analytic and numerical propagation methods.

In simple cases, each data element of a data stream consists of one value. There are some approaches that support density estimation of one-dimensional data stream items. Heinz and Seeger present approaches that use kernels and wavelets to estimate densities of one-dimensional data streams [2, 3]. These approaches use measurements in order to determine the density estimators.

To our knowledge, this is the first work addressing the propagation of densities within query graphs of DSSs by using analytic or numerical methods. Further, it supports multi-dimensional data stream elements. Our contribution to the problem of estimating multi-dimensional densities operates on two levels: First, we propose both analytic and numerical propagation of densities for relevant streaming operators and argue which method is appropriate for each operator. Second, we propose a method for combining these approaches as each operator has a best fitting method for propagating densities, but a query graph may contain both kinds of operators.

We address related work in more detail in the next section. The core of this paper starts with basic explanations and definitions for the estimation of *Probability Density Functions* (PDFs) in Sect. 3. In the following two sections, we present the analytic propagation method and the numerical propagation method. We make a synthesis of these two methods using *Kernel Density Estimator*s (KDEs) that includes some experimental results before we conclude.

## 2 Related Work

There are several "historical" approaches that use probabilities for the estimation of databases' statistics. In [4], multi-dimensional histograms model attribute value distributions. There are several formulas for the impact of operators on distributions. We could not adopt these formulas directly for data streams as on the one hand they only consider densities represented as histograms and on the other hand they postulate discrete probability distributions. As they consider databases, e.g. the projection operator uses duplicate elimination.

The *Detailed Database Statistics Model* (DDSM) [5] considers one-dimensional discrete distributions, but with additional matrices that represent dependencies between subdomains of attributes. This paper also describes statistics for estimating join sizes. The influence of operators is evaluated for selection and join.

A survey [6] gives an overview of estimation of statistical profiles in database systems. This paper discusses the influence of statistical methods on cost estimation in different database systems. Further, it discusses different methods of density estimation and the influence of database operators on probability densities without giving concrete formulas.

As mentioned in the introduction, [2] and [3] investigated density estimators over data streams. These papers only consider measuring densities of existing streams. The densities of intermediate streams are still unknown, if there is no actual system executing the respective query.

**Table 1.** Comparison between modeling and simulation

| | Modeling | Simulation |
|---|---|---|
| Method | estimating | measuring |
| Complexity | complex cost model | no cost model required |
| Effort | lean implementation | full system for simulation |
| Impediments | imprecise a high load | impossible at high load |
| Calculation Time | fast results | time for simulation |
| Optimizability | high potential for optimizations | simulation hardly optimizable |

Simulating a query on a second system allows to estimate the costs of a query graph [7]. This circumvents the need to estimate densities of intermediate streams, but requires a second system only for simulation purposes. We summarize the benefits and drawbacks of our approach (modeling) and the simulation approach in Table 1.

The usefulness of density estimates for the selectivity estimation of range queries is described in [8]. This usefulness is further detailed in [9].

In [10], the cost model uses join and filter selectivities to estimate the rate of intermediate streams in a DSS. This work assumes already known selectivities. Our contribution allows to estimate the unknown selectivities.

Meyerhöfer [11] introduces a method to estimate the performance of software assemblies that is based on [12]. This is done by partitioning the range of a method's input variables by certain characteristics into input subdomains that are mapped to output subdomains. We use query graphs analogously to the software assemblies.

## 3 Basics

In this section, we introduce our data stream model and describe the basics for estimating *Probability Density Functions* (PDFs) using kernels. We further present the assumptions we made.

### 3.1 Data Stream Model

Like [13], we assume unbounded data streams of independent and identically distributed tuples $\boldsymbol{X}_1, \boldsymbol{X}_2, \ldots \in \mathbb{R}^d$ with $d$ real valued attributes. Timestamps are not part of this model. There can be dependencies between attributes of one tuple. Hence the attribute value distribution of a single stream is multidimensional.

### 3.2 Estimation of PDFs

There are different options to estimate the PDF of a data stream. If the underlying parametric model is known, the estimation of the unknown parameters based on a sample is sufficient to determine the density of the stream. Nonparametric estimation is an alternative approach with no need for information about the underlying model. One well-known example for nonparametric estimation is KDE [14, 15].

A *Kernel Density Estimator* (KDE) is constructed from a sample $\boldsymbol{X}_1, \boldsymbol{X}_2, \ldots, \boldsymbol{X}_k$ with $\boldsymbol{X}_i = (X_{i,1}, \ldots, X_{i,d})$, $X_{i,j} \in \mathbb{R}$ as follows:

$$\hat{f}^{(k)}(\boldsymbol{x}) = \frac{1}{k}\sum_{i=1}^{k}\prod_{j=1}^{d}\frac{1}{h_j^{(k)}}K\left(\frac{x_j - X_{i,j}}{h_j^{(k)}}\right), \boldsymbol{x} \in \mathbb{R}^d. \tag{1}$$

The kernel function $K$ is an arbitrary one-dimensional symmetric PDF with mean 0. This means that every tuple in the sample is represented by a "bump" (kernel) and the KDE is the normalized sum of these kernels.

$h_j^{(k)}$ is the bandwidth in dimension $j$ for a sample of $k$ tuples. The bandwidth determines the width of the kernels. Different values for the bandwidth lead to different resulting density estimates (Fig. 1).

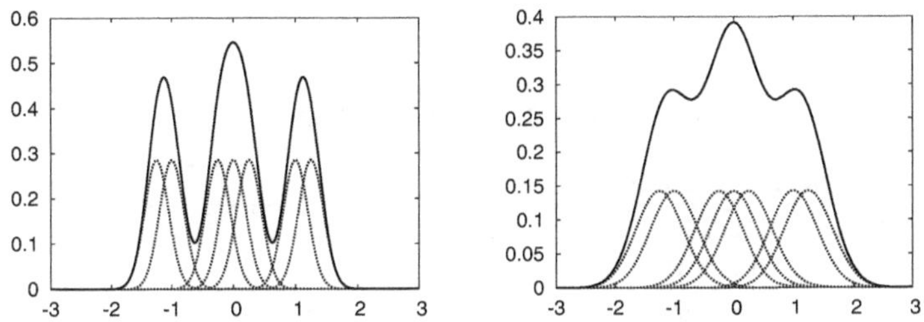


(a) $h^{(k)} = 0.2$ (b) $h^{(k)} = 0.4$

**Fig. 1.** The influence of the bandwidth on KDEs

One goal of density estimation is to minimize the difference between the estimated and the real density. Hence the choice of the right bandwidth is crucial. The following formula presented in [14] is one possible way to estimate the optimal bandwidth in dimension $j$ for a sample of $k$ $d$–dimensional tuples:

$$h_{j,\text{opt}}^{(k)} \approx \sigma_j \left(\frac{4}{d+2}\right)^{1/(d+4)} \cdot k^{-1/(d+4)}. \tag{2}$$

$\sigma_j$ is the standard deviation of the sample tuples in dimension $j$.

### 3.3 Assumptions

For every input stream, we assume constant rates and fixed densities. The number of tuples in a window is therefore known and fixed at runtime. Varying data rates could lead to varying densities, if e.g. an operator has a time-based window and if the data rate of the input stream and therefore the number of tuples in the window is varying. If rates or densities change in a relevant way during runtime, a recalculation might be necessary.

Our underlying model uses probability distributions over continuous values. With limited precision, it works well for discrete data streams, if there is a sufficiently high number of uniformly distributed distinct elements in the stream. We cannot support nominal attributes like strings. Specific values are approximated by defining an interval; e.g. equi-joins are simulated by overlapping ranges. As grouping relies on finding tuples with identical values in the grouping attributes, our approach does not support grouping. A definition of interval-based grouping is out of the scope of this paper.

# 4 Analytic Propagation

To propagate the densities of streams in a query graph, we need to estimate the output densities of all operators used in the graph. This can be achieved by modeling the operators' influence on their input densities. In this section, we describe the formulas we found for the operators described in [16], as it contains both adapted relational and stream operators. Table 2 describes all variables used in the formulas that are not explained in the text.

**Table 2.** List of identifiers

| **Identifier** | **Description** |
|---|---|
| $f$ | density of the output stream |
| $n$ | number of tuples in a window |
| $f_n$ | density of an aggregate with windowsize $n$ |
| $g, \tilde{g}$ | density of an input-stream |
| $p \in [0, 1]$ | filter predicate |
| $k$ | number of attributes to be projected out |
| $m$ | number of attributes not to be projected out |
| $\ell$ | number of input-streams |
| $g_j$ | density of the $j$-th input-stream |
| $\lambda_j$ | rate of the $j$-th input-stream |
| $o$ | number of attributes of the input-stream |
| $o_j$ | number of attributes of the $j$-th input-stream |
| $\boldsymbol{x}$ | $= (\boldsymbol{x}_1, \ldots, \boldsymbol{x}_\ell) = (x_{1,1}, \ldots, x_{1,o_1}, \ldots, x_{\ell,1}, \ldots, x_{\ell,o_\ell})$ |
| $\boldsymbol{t}$ | $= (\boldsymbol{t}_1, \ldots, \boldsymbol{t}_\ell) = (t_{1,1}, \ldots, t_{1,o_1}, \ldots, t_{\ell,1}, \ldots, t_{\ell,o_\ell})$ |
| $\boldsymbol{y}$ | $= (y_1, \ldots, y_o)$ |
| $\boldsymbol{s}$ | $= (s_1, \ldots, s_o)$ |
| $\boldsymbol{G}$ | mapping function |
| $\boldsymbol{G}^*$ | inverse mapping function |
| $J_{\boldsymbol{G}}$ | Jacobian determinant of $\boldsymbol{G}$ |

## 4.1 Union

The *Union* operator has $\ell$ input streams and one output stream. All input streams have the same schema, but they usually have different densities and input rates. Every tuple that arrives on one input stream is immediately forwarded to the output stream. Hence the output density is a weighted sum of the input streams' densities.

The weight for input stream $i$ is $\frac{\lambda_i}{\sum_{j=1}^{\ell} \lambda_j}$. The more tuples arrive on one input stream the higher its weight. The weights are normalized to guarantee that the result is a density. The output density is calculated as follows:

$$f(\boldsymbol{y}) = \frac{1}{\sum_{j=1}^{\ell} \lambda_j} \sum_{j=1}^{\ell} \lambda_j g_j(\boldsymbol{y}). \tag{3}$$

### 4.2 Filter

A *Filter* is an operator with a predicate $P$, one input stream, and one output stream. A tuple is only forwarded to the output stream if it satisfies the *Filter*'s predicate. The support of the output stream's density is therefore the support of the input stream's density minus the subset of $\mathbb{R}^n$ for which the predicate $P$ is not satisfied. The selectivity of the *Filter* $\int g(\boldsymbol{s})p(\boldsymbol{s})\,\mathrm{d}\boldsymbol{s}$ is needed to normalize the resulting density.

A function $p$ is defined as:

$$p(\boldsymbol{y}) = \begin{cases} 1 \text{ if } \boldsymbol{y} \text{ satisfies the predicate } P \\ 0 \text{ else} \end{cases}.$$

The resulting density can therefore be described as follows:

$$f(\boldsymbol{y}) = \frac{1}{\int g(\boldsymbol{s})p(\boldsymbol{s})\,\mathrm{d}\boldsymbol{s}} g(\boldsymbol{y})p(\boldsymbol{y}). \tag{4}$$

### 4.3 Join

The *Join* operator has $\ell$ input streams and one output stream. Each input stream may have a different schema and a different rate. A query defines a window for each input stream. *Join* tests each possible combination of tuples in these windows if it matches the join predicate $P$ and forwards it to the output stream, if it satisfies the predicate. The attribute value distribution of a tuple which is part of one of those combinations is independent of the window sizes and the input streams' rates. Hence the resulting density is basically a product density with a filter applied to it. The function $p$ is likewise defined as it was for the filter.

$$f(\boldsymbol{x}) = \frac{1}{\int p(\boldsymbol{t}) \prod_{j=1}^{\ell} g_j(\boldsymbol{t}_j)\,\mathrm{d}\boldsymbol{t}} p(\boldsymbol{x}) \prod_{j=1}^{\ell} g_j(\boldsymbol{x}_j) \tag{5}$$

If the predicate $P$ is always satisfied, the *Join* would basically be a Cartesian product between the windows over the input streams. Then the resulting density could simply be described as:

$$f(\boldsymbol{x}) = \prod_{j=1}^{\ell} g_j(\boldsymbol{x}_j). \tag{6}$$

### 4.4 Projection

A *Projection* operator removes certain attributes from each tuple that arrives on its single input stream. Therefore the resulting stream has a different schema. In the case of data stream processing, only duplicate preserving projection is considered. *Projection* could also rename the attributes in the schema, but this does not affect the output stream's density.

For the sake of simplicity we assume that the $m + k$ attributes are ordered in a way that the last $k$ attributes will be deleted by the *Projection*. If the input stream's attribute value distribution is $g : \mathbb{R}^{m+k} \to \mathbb{R}$, the output stream's distribution would be:

$$f(x_1, \dots, x_m) = \int g(x_1, \dots, x_m, \tau_1, \dots, \tau_k)\, \mathrm{d}\tau_1 \dots \mathrm{d}\tau_k. \tag{7}$$

### 4.5 Aggregate

The *Aggregate* operator applies an aggregate function to all tuples in a window over its single input stream. We assume that these tuples only have one attribute. All other attributes are projected out as follows:

$$g(x_j) = \int \cdots \int \tilde{g}(x_1, \dots, x_o)\, \mathrm{d}x_1 \dots\, \mathrm{d}x_{j-1}\, \mathrm{d}x_{j+1} \dots\, \mathrm{d}x_o.$$

Because we assume the rate to be constant, the number of tuples in a window is known, even for time based windows.

**Sum.** The output density of the sum of $n$ values is the convolution of the input densities.

$$f_n(x) = (\underbrace{g * \dots * g}_{n \text{ times}})(x) \tag{8}$$

**Average.** By means of the change of variables formula, the output density for the average of $n$ values can be derived from the formula for the sum of $n$ values.

$$f_n(x) = n \cdot (\underbrace{g * \dots * g}_{n \text{ times}})(nx) \tag{9}$$

**Maximum.** The distribution function of the maximum of $n$ values is:

$$F_n(x) = \left( \int_{-\infty}^{x} g(\tau)\, \mathrm{d}\tau \right)^n.$$

Hence the PDF of the output stream is:

$$f_n(x) = F_n'(x) = n g(x) \left( \int_{-\infty}^{x} g(\tau)\, \mathrm{d}\tau \right)^{n-1}. \tag{10}$$

**Minimum.** The density of the minimum of $n$ values is as follows:

$$f_n(x) = ng(x)\left(\int_x^{\infty} g(\tau)\,\mathrm{d}\tau\right)^{n-1}. \tag{11}$$

**Count.** Let $\delta$ be the Dirac delta function, with the property:

$$\int_{-\infty}^{\infty} \delta(x)\,\mathrm{d}x = 1.$$

The density of the count of $n$ values can be described as:

$$f_n(x) = \delta(x-n) = \begin{cases} +\infty,\ x = n \\ 0,\ x \neq n \end{cases}. \tag{12}$$

In reality, the rate is usually not constant but determined by the distribution of the inter-arrival times. Therefore the output density depends on the PDF of the inter-arrival times.

### 4.6 Map

The *Map* operator applies a function $\boldsymbol{G} : \mathbb{R}^m \rightarrow \mathbb{R}^m$ to every single input tuple $\boldsymbol{x} = (x_1, \ldots, x_m)$ producing output tuples $\boldsymbol{y} = (y_1, \ldots, y_m)$. If $\boldsymbol{G}$ fulfills the requirements of the change of variables formula, the output density is:

$$f(\boldsymbol{x}) = g(\boldsymbol{G}^*(\boldsymbol{x}))\frac{1}{|J_{\boldsymbol{G}}(\boldsymbol{G}^*(\boldsymbol{x}))|}. \tag{13}$$

If $\boldsymbol{G}$ is an affine transformation $\boldsymbol{G}(\boldsymbol{x}) = \boldsymbol{A}\boldsymbol{x} + \mathbf{c}$ then the output stream's density can be described as:

$$f(\boldsymbol{x}) = g(\boldsymbol{A}^{-1}(\boldsymbol{x} - \mathbf{c}))\frac{1}{|\det(\boldsymbol{A})|}. \tag{14}$$

### 4.7 BSort

The *BSort* operator approximately sorts its input stream by applying a certain number of bubble-sort passes. Because the output tuples are the same as the input tuples but possibly in a different order, the operator's output density is the same as its input density.

$$f(\boldsymbol{y}) = g(\boldsymbol{y}) \tag{15}$$

### 4.8 Resample

The *Resample* operator has two input streams and aligns tuples coming from the second input stream with tuples from the first input stream. To achieve this, the *Resample* operator interpolates tuples of the second input stream to match the time stamp of a tuple from the first input stream.

Under certain assumptions, a stream consisting of perfectly interpolated tuples has the same attribute value distribution as the original stream. These assumptions are manifold but out of the scope of this paper.

Let $g_1$ be the density of the first input stream and $g_2$ the density of the second input stream. Assuming a perfect interpolation, the resulting density is:

$$f(\boldsymbol{y}_1, \boldsymbol{y}_2) = g_1(\boldsymbol{y}_1) \cdot g_2(\boldsymbol{y}_2). \tag{16}$$

### 4.9 Summary

In this section, we have explained our formulas for the analytic estimation of probability distributions for several operators. These include the most important stream operators (*Filter*, *Join*, *Projection*, *Union*, and *Map*) as well as several aggregates, the *BSort*, and the *Resample* operator. For reference, the formulas are summarized in Table 3.

**Table 3.** Operators' output densities

| Operator | Output Density |
|---|---|
| Filter | $f(\boldsymbol{y}) = \frac{1}{\int g(\boldsymbol{s})p(\boldsymbol{s})\,\mathrm{d}\boldsymbol{s}} g(\boldsymbol{y})p(\boldsymbol{y})$ |
| Join | $f(\boldsymbol{x}) = \frac{1}{\int p(\boldsymbol{t})\prod_{j=1}^{\ell} g_j(\boldsymbol{t}_j)\,\mathrm{d}\boldsymbol{t}} p(\boldsymbol{x}) \prod_{j=1}^{\ell} g_j(\boldsymbol{x}_j)$ |
| Projection | $f(x_1,\ldots,x_m) = \int g(x_1,\ldots,x_m,\tau_1,\ldots,\tau_k)\,\mathrm{d}\tau_1\ldots\mathrm{d}\tau_k$ |
| Aggregate Sum | $f_n(x) = \underbrace{(g * \ldots * g)}_{n \text{ times}}(x)$ |
| Aggregate Avg | $f_n(x) = n \cdot \underbrace{(g * \ldots * g)}_{n \text{ times}}(nx)$ |
| Aggregate Max | $f_n(x) = ng(x)\left(\int_{-\infty}^{x} g(\tau)\,\mathrm{d}\tau\right)^{n-1}$ |
| Aggregate Min | $f_n(x) = ng(x)\left(\int_{x}^{\infty} g(\tau)\,\mathrm{d}\tau\right)^{n-1}$ |
| Aggregate Count | $f_n(x) = \delta(x-n)$ |
| Union | $f(\boldsymbol{y}) = \frac{1}{\sum_{j=1}^{\ell}\lambda_j}\sum_{j=1}^{\ell}\lambda_j g_j(\boldsymbol{y})$ |
| Map | $f(\boldsymbol{x}) = g(\boldsymbol{G}^*(\boldsymbol{x}))\frac{1}{\lvert J_G(\boldsymbol{G}^*(\boldsymbol{x}))\rvert}$ |
| Map (affine) | $f(\boldsymbol{x}) = g(\boldsymbol{A}^{-1}(\boldsymbol{x}-\mathbf{c}))\frac{1}{\lvert\det(\boldsymbol{A})\rvert}, \qquad \boldsymbol{G}(\boldsymbol{x}) = \boldsymbol{A}\boldsymbol{x}+\mathbf{c}$ |
| BSort | $f(\boldsymbol{y}) = g(\boldsymbol{y})$ |
| Resample | $f(\boldsymbol{y}_1, \boldsymbol{y}_2) = g_1(\boldsymbol{y}_1) \cdot g_2(\boldsymbol{y}_2)$ |

# 5 Numerical Propagation

In the previous section, we described an analytic method for estimating densities. This approach relies on finding formulas that describe each operator's output density. Thus, it is not applicable for operators for which no formulas are known (yet). This is a problem as there is currently no consensus about the basic set of data stream operators. Additionally, some *User-Defined Operator*s (UDOs) are hard or even impossible to model.

In order to overcome this problem, we developed a method for numerically estimating the output densities of operators.

This method consists of two steps: In the first step (configuration phase), we build a numerical model that describes an operator instance's behavior. As the model depends on the operator's configuration (e.g. filter predicate), it is computed when the operator is instantiated and its configuration is known. This model is independent of the actual input distributions which need not be known at this time.

The second step (application phase) is performed when the query graph is instantiated. It combines knowledge of the actual input distributions with the model of the operator in order to describe the output distributions.

The advantage of this two-step approach is that the computationally expensive model building needs to be performed only once for each operator instance. The second step has to be done every time an operator graph is instantiated. During optimization, several query graphs may be instantiated for a single query. It is the optimizer's duty to choose the best one. Fortunately, the second step can be computed relatively quickly.

After outlining some requirements and limitations of this approach, we will describe both steps in detail.

## 5.1 Requirements

In order to apply the numerical estimation, a number of requirements have to be fulfilled. These requirements are detailed below.

**Determinism.** Obviously, operators have to act deterministically. An indeterministic operator may behave differently between the test and the real execution, rendering the test results worthless. Additionally, an operator's output may only depend on its input but not on its state because it is not feasible to model all possible states. We model windows as additional input dimensions.

**Continuity.** As an operator cannot be tested with all possible input values, we must assume that small variations in the input values only lead to small variations in the output values. More formally, an operator has to be continuous on subsets of its domain.

**Known Domain.** In order to test an operator with an uniform input distribution, the domain of the input streams has to be known in advance as it is not possible to test with an uniform distribution on an infinite domain. This knowledge may be gained by testing and stored in the metadata catalog.

For operators that have intermediate streams as input, the domain of the intermediate streams has to be known as well. We solve this problem by topologically ordering the query graph and deriving the domain of the intermediate streams from the knowledge about input streams and intermediate operators. This requires the operator graph to be acyclic.

**Independence Of Rates.** As we do not model the influence of rates on an operator's behavior, we require that an operator is independent of the rates of its input streams. The most common rate-dependent operators are time-based windows. We sketch an idea for coping with time-based windows in Sect. 5.4.

### 5.2 Test with Uniform Distribution (Configuration Phase)

In order to describe the influence of an operator on its output streams, it is tested with synthetic inputs. This yields a model of an operator's behavior. The model is built when the operator is deployed, as it depends on the configuration of the operator as well as knowledge of its input domains.

The operator is tested with $k$ input values that are randomly and uniformly chosen from its input domains. The value of $k$ has to be carefully chosen to balance accuracy versus memory requirements. Each input value is stored together with its corresponding output value. If a given input value does not produce any output, it is stored nevertheless, together with a flag that denotes that no output was produced. This will be required for selectivity estimation. Together the input and output values form the operator model.

### 5.3 Estimating Densities (Application Phase)

When the operator graph is instantiated, we measure the actual densities of input streams and estimate the densities of intermediate streams. The input densities are then combined with the operator model in order to yield the actual output densities.

For each combination of input and output values in the model, we compute a weight which is based on the input densities. The estimated output density is a weighted sum of kernels based on the output values in the previously calculated operator model.

The weight of each kernel is given by the following equation:

$$g_i = u(\boldsymbol{G}^*(\boldsymbol{X}_i)).$$

Here, $u$ is the actual input density, $\boldsymbol{G}^*$ is the operator's inverse mapping function of the operator model. $\boldsymbol{X}_i$ is an output value in the operator model.

As the integral over a density has to be 1, the weights have to be normalized. This condition holds if the sum of all weights in (17) equals 1.

$$g_i^* = \frac{g_i}{\sum_{j=1}^{k} g_j}$$

Finally, we just have to apply a weighted version of (1) as suggested in [17]. The output of this equation is the estimated output density.

$$\hat{f}^{(k)}(\boldsymbol{x}) = \sum_{i=1}^{k} g_i^* \prod_{j=1}^{d} \frac{1}{h_j^{(k)}} K\left(\frac{x_j - X_{i,j}}{h_j^{(k)}}\right), \boldsymbol{x} \in \mathbb{R}^d \tag{17}$$

The optimal bandwidths $h_j^{(k)}$ can be estimated with (2) in Sect. 3.2.

**Selectivity Estimation.** The selectivity of an operator can be easily derived from the available information. Remember that input values which produce no output are not excluded from the operator model. Thus, after the weights of the kernels are known for the actual input, the selectivity is just the ratio of the sum of weights for kernels without output and the sum of weights for all kernels.

### 5.4 Further Work

The approach described in this section may still be improved in numerous ways. We sketch the two extensions which in our opinion promise the greatest benefits.

**Compression.** The models for operators with high dimensions or large domains require a large number of kernels for accurate results. This leads to high memory usage as well as increased computational costs at runtime. One solution to this problem might be cluster kernels [2].

The basic idea is to combine several kernels to a single one by means of clustering. For best results, the right choice of clusters is crucial. This choice largely depends on the function that computes the distance between two kernels. It turns out that neither the distance between input values $d_i$ nor the distance between output values $d_o$ is a good choice. The combination of these distances $d = \sqrt{d_i^2 + d_o^2}$ however gives adequate results. Some additional thought is required to determine which information has to be stored for each kernel. [2] discusses several possibilities.

**Time-based Windows.** As in Sect. 4, windows are modeled as additional dimensions. This is not directly feasible for time-based windows, as their size is unknown which leads to an unknown number of dimensions. It may however be possible to transform an operator in a way that the window size is set to a fixed maximum value. Then the actual window size depending on the rate is modeled as an additional parameter. For this approach, it is necessary to determine an upper bound for the window size.

### 5.5 Summary

The approach described in this section allows to estimate the value distributions for operators for which no analytic formula is known. If an analytic description of an operator is available, it is preferred to the numerical approach. The numerical approach is however more general and allows to model e.g. user defined operators. As both approaches have their merits, they should be combined.

## 6 Synthesis

The propagation of densities works by using the estimated output densities of an operator model as input densities of the successive operator models in the operator graph. If the analytic method is applicable for modeling an operator, it should be used, because it is more precise and less computationally intensive. The numerical approach can model unknown operators such as UDOs. This section gives an overview of the integration

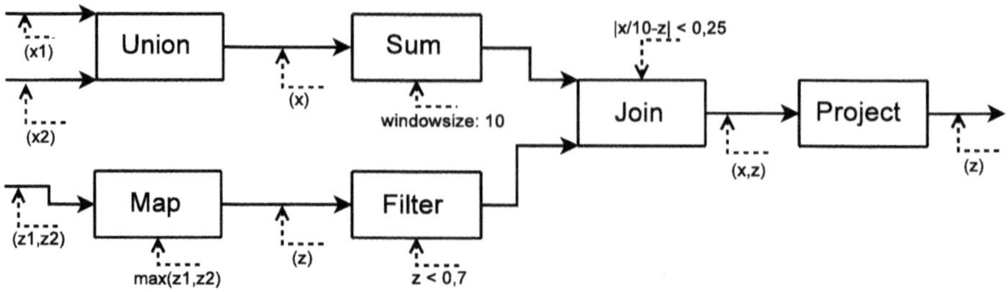


**Fig. 2.** The operator graph used in our experiments

of both methods in query graphs and has a complex example query for evaluation purposes. The evaluation uses our implementations of KDEs for the common data-stream operators and a generic implementation that realizes the numerical approach. Finally, we evaluate the results of our estimates and describe the impact of the number of kernels on the quality of our estimations.

### 6.1 Integration of Analytic and Numerical Propagation

As the numerical method uses KDEs, we decided to implement the analytic methods with KDEs, too. This ensures compatibility of both methods that supports direct combination of both kinds of operator models. As the estimation of the PDFs are implemented as KDEs, all operator models use KDEs and are derived from an abstract class `KernelEstimator`. It defines an interface that supports the determination of the density for any multidimensional point, the dimensionality, and the support of the density. For most of the operators having analytic formulas, we provided an implementation. We did not implement the formulas for *Resample*, *BSort*, and *Aggregate Count* because they are trivial. The *Map* operator would require an implementation of the change of variables formula, which is out of scope of this paper. However, our numerical approach is well suited to estimate the output densities of the *Map* operator.

The decision to use KDEs leads to some problems. A direct implementation of the analytic model for the *Join* operator may create too many kernels. We decided to reduce some kernels by dropping them randomly; a more precise method would be using cluster kernels [2]. The integrals with variable boundaries in the formulas for maximum (10) and minimum (11) prohibit a direct representation as KDEs. Hence our implementation constructs a new KDE, which represents the output density calculated using our exact method.

For the numerical method, we distinguish "configuration phase" and "application phase", as the generic implementation of the numerical method does not have intrinsic formulas for the manipulation of PDFs. In the configuration phase, it is crucial to create uniformly distributed input values. Input values that don't generate output values also have to be stored in order to determine the selectivity in the application phase later. In the application phase, i.e. using this instance in a query graph, the output density of the model operator can be determined by weighting the output values according to the input density.

```
stream S1(x1 float)
stream S2(x2 float)
stream S3(z1 float,z2 float)

UnionStream(x):
    S1 UNION S2

AggStream(x):
    SELECT SUM(x) FROM UnionStream[rows 10]

MapStream(z):
    SELECT MAX(z1,z2) FROM S3

FilterStream(z):
    SELECT z FROM MapStream WHERE z < 0.7

JoinStream(x,z):
    SELECT x,z FROM FilterStream[rows 10],
        AggStream[rows 10]
    WHERE x/10-z < 0.25
        AND x/10-z > -0.25

ProjectStream(z):
    SELECT z FROM JoinStream
```

**Listing 1.** The CQL query belonging to the operator graph (Fig. 2)

## 6.2 Evaluation

We tested the methods presented in Sects. 4 and 5 with several synthetic data streams. The densities of these streams consisted of sums of normal distributions $\mathcal{N}(\mu, \sigma^2)$ or multidimensional normal distributions $\mathcal{N}^k(\mu, \sigma^2)$. For this evaluation, we compared output densities estimated with our approach to the actual output densities. We either calculated the real output densities, if it was feasible, or, otherwise, we simulated the operators and measured the resulting output densities with KDEs.

To evaluate the estimation of densities, we utilized the *Mean Squared Error* (MSE). The actual density $f$ was compared to estimated densities $\hat{f}_j^{(n)}$, constructed from $n$ kernels, at 1000 random points $x_{i,j}$ equally distributed over the support of $f$. Because of this randomness, we took the mean of 5 comparisons to get significant results.

$$\mathrm{MSE} = \frac{1}{5} \sum_{j=1}^{5} \frac{1}{1000} \sum_{i=1}^{1000} \left( f(x_{i,j}) - \hat{f}_j^{(n)}(x_{i,j}) \right)^2 \tag{18}$$

We also evaluated the selectivity estimation using the *Mean Relative Error* (MRE). Estimated selectivities $\hat{s}_i^{(n)}$, calculated with $n$ kernels, were compared to the actual selectivity $s$.

$$\mathrm{MRE} = \frac{1}{20} \sum_{i=1}^{20} \frac{\left| s - \hat{s}_i^{(n)} \right|}{s} \tag{19}$$

We calculated the bandwidth for the KDEs using (2) from [14]. Our experiments showed that this estimate for the bandwidth might not be the optimal choice. Hence we carried out the tests for different bandwidths. In the following, $h$ always represents the

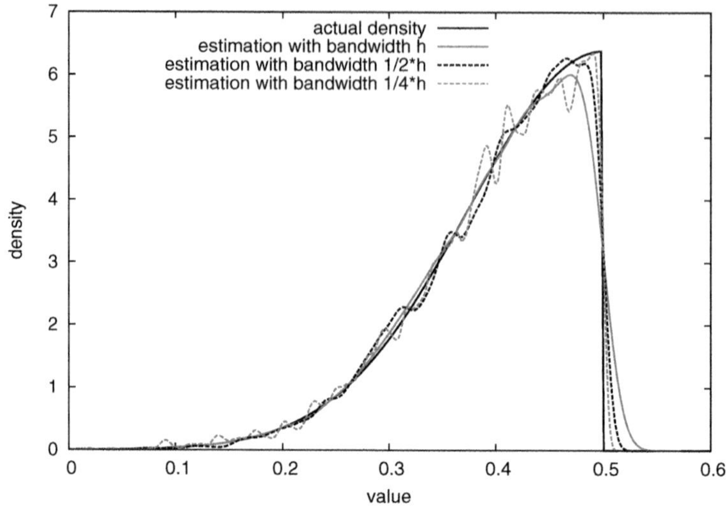


**Fig. 3.** Output density of a *Filter* operator with the predicate $x < 0.5$

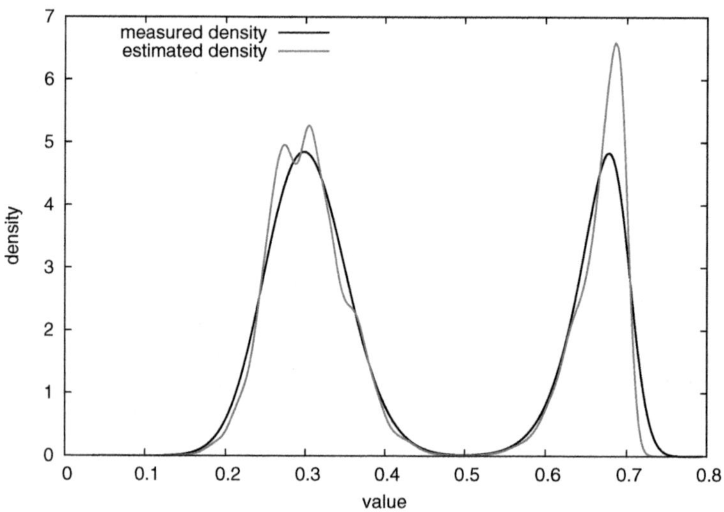


**Fig. 4.** Output density of the operator graph

bandwidth calculated with (2). Fig. 3 shows the output density of a *Filter* operator, estimated with our implementation of the analytic method using different bandwidths. The input density was $\mathcal{N}(1/2, (1/8)^2)$ and the *Filter*'s predicate was $x < 0.5$. $\frac{1}{2}h$ seemed to be the best choice for the bandwidth in our experiments (Fig. 3). Therefore more precise methods to estimate the optimal bandwidth should be implemented. Some possible methods are described in [15].

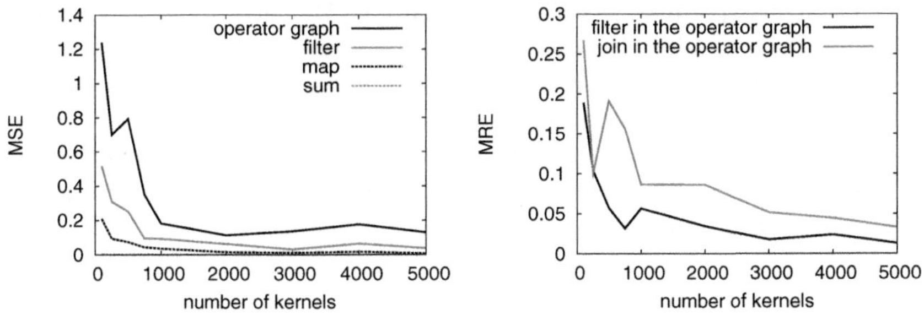


(a) MSE (b) MRE

**Fig. 5.** MSE and MRE of the operator graph

We also tested our methods with an operator graph, which is depicted in Fig. 2. The corresponding *Continuous Query Language* (CQL) query [18] is shown in Listing 1. The densities of the input streams of the *Union* operator were $g_{S_1} = \mathcal{N}(1/4, (1/16)^2) + \mathcal{N}(3/4, (1/16)^2)$ and $g_{S_2} = \mathcal{N}(1/2, (1/8)^2)$ with equal rates. The density of the input stream of the *Map* operator was $g_{S_3} = \mathcal{N}^2(1/4, (1/16)^2) + \mathcal{N}^2(3/4, (1/16)^2)$. Both the numerical and the analytic method were utilized to estimate the output density of this operator graph. The numerical method was used for the *Map* operator, and the output densities of the other operators were estimated by means of the analytic method. Fig. 4 shows the estimated output density compared to the output density measured using a KDE. Because of the *Filter* operator, the actual density should be zero for every value greater than $0.7$. This is neither true for the measured nor for the estimated density, because they were both constructed from KDEs known for blurring discontinuities. In Fig. 5, the MSE is depicted for some operators in the graph and different numbers of kernels and it also shows the MRE for the selectivity estimates for the *Filter* and *Join* operator in the graph.

Our evaluation shows that the prototypic implementation of our methods is able to produce suitable density and selectivity estimates for a complex query graph.

## 7 Conclusions and Future Work

In this paper, we showed a well working method for estimating densities within query graphs of DSSs. This work is especially important, if data rates of internal streams are relevant for cost models as it is in distributed data stream processing. With our approach, we can estimate densities of both inner and output streams within the query graph without executing the query. This estimation facilitates choosing a good physical plan.

We proposed formulas for calculating output densities for a core set of relevant stream operators and called this "analytic propagation". For other operators, we proposed a numerical method that works without specific formulas. This might be necessary for application-specific operators like UDOs.

By means of an experimental evaluation, we used KDEs in order to integrate numerical and analytic propagation. The estimation used a concrete query graph. We compared the calculated results of our estimations with the correct results of a simulation. This comparison shows the accuracy of our approach.

In our future work, we plan to use this density estimation as a basis for selectivity estimation in the cost estimator of DSAM. We hope to get better operator placement decisions by having a more precise basis of decision-making.

## References

1. Daum, M., Fischer, M., Kiefer, M., Meyer-Wegener, K.: Integration of Heterogeneous Sensor Nodes by Data Stream Management. In: Proceedings of the 10th International Conference on Mobile Data Management: Systems, Services and Middleware (MDM), pp. 525–530. IEEE Computer Society, Los Alamitos (2009)
2. Heinz, C., Seeger, B.: Towards Kernel Density Estimation over Streaming Data. In: Proceedings of the 13th International Conference on Management of Data (COMAD), Delhi, India (2006)
3. Heinz, C., Seeger, B.: Adaptive Wavelet Density Estimators over Data Streams. In: Proceedings of the 19th International Conference on Scientific and Statistical Database Management (SSDBM), p. 35. IEEE Computer Society, Washington (2007)
4. Merrett, T.H., Otoo, E.J.: Distribution Models of Relations. In: Proceedings of the 5th International Conference on Very Large Data Bases (VLDB), VLDB Endowment, pp. 418–425 (1979)
5. Muthuswamy, B., Kerschberg, L.: A Detailed Statistical Model for Relational Query Optimization. In: Proceedings of the 13th ACM Annual Conference, The range of computing: mid-80's perspective, pp. 439–448. ACM, New York (1985)
6. Mannino, M.V., Chu, P., Sager, T.: Statistical profile estimation in database systems. ACM Computing Surveys (CSUR) 20(3), 191–221 (1988)
7. Heinz, C., Kramer, J., Riemenschneider, T., Seeger, B.: Toward Simulation-Based Optimization in Data Stream Management Systems. In: Proceedings of the IEEE International Conference on Data Engineering, ICDE (2008)
8. Blohsfeld, B., Heinz, C., Seeger, B.: Maintaining nonparametric estimators over data streams. In: Proceedings of the GI-Fachtagung für Datenbanksysteme in Business, Technologie und Web, BTW (2005)
9. Gunopulos, D., Kollios, G., Tsotras, J., Domeniconi, C.: Selectivity estimators for multidimensional range queries over real attributes. The International Journal on Very Large Data Bases (VLDBJ) 14(2), 137–154 (2005)
10. Viglas, S.D., Naughton, J.F.: Rate-Based Query Optimization for Streaming Information Sources. In: Proceedings of the 2002 ACM SIGMOD International Conference on Management of Data (SIGMOD), pp. 37–48. ACM Press, New York (2002)
11. Meyerhöfer, M.: Messung und Verwaltung von Softwarekomponenten für die Performancevorhersage. PhD thesis, University of Erlangen-Nuremberg (2007)
12. Hamlet, D., Mason, D., Woit, D.: Properties of Software Systems Synthesized from Components. In: Component-Based Software Development: Case Studies, pp. 129–159. World Scientific Publishing Company, Singapore (2004)
13. Heinz, C.: Density Estimation over Data Streams. PhD thesis, University of Marburg (2007)
14. Silverman, B.: Density Estimation for Statistics and Data Analysis. Monographs on Statistics and Applied Probability. Chapman and Hall, London (1986)

15. Scott, D.W.: Multivariate Density Estimation. Wiley Interscience, Hoboken (1992)
16. Abadi, D.J., Carney, D., Cetintemel, U., Cherniack, M., Convey, C., Lee, S., Stonebraker, M., Tatbul, N., Zdonik, S.: Aurora: a new model and architecture for data stream management. The International Journal on Very Large Data Bases (VLDBJ) 12(2), 120–139 (2003)
17. Zhou, A., Cai, Z., Wei, L., Qian, W.: M-Kernel Merging: Towards Density Estimation over Data Streams. In: Proceedings of the 8th International Conference on Database Systems for Advanced Applications (DASFAA), pp. 285–292. IEEE Computer Society, Washington (2003)
18. Arasu, A., Babu, S., Widom, J.: The CQL continuous query language: semantic foundations and query execution. The International Journal on Very Large Data Bases (VLDBJ) 15(2), 121–142 (2006)

# Spatio-temporal Event Stream Processing in Multimedia Communication Systems

Mingyan Gao[1], Xiaoyan Yang[2], Ramesh Jain[1], and Beng Chin Ooi[2]

[1] University of California, Irvine
{gaom,jain}@ics.uci.edu
[2] National University of Singapore
{yangxia2,ooibc}@comp.nus.edu.sg

**Abstract.** Emerging multimedia communication environments, such as Environment-to-Environment (E2E) systems, require detecting complex events in environments using multimodal sensory data. Based on these spatio-temporal events, systems select and send data from appropriate sensors. Most existing stream processing systems consider temporal streams of alpha-numeric data and provide efficient approach to deal with queries in these environments. In cases where events are detected in different sensory data types, including audio and video collected at different locations, new approaches need to be developed to represent, combine, and process events to answer queries. In this paper, we present our approach in managing event stream processing to address the needs of a real time E2E system being developed in our laboratory. We introduce the modeling of our problem, and describe in detail the filtering and matching algorithms for querying spatio-temporal event stream. Experimental results demonstrate the efficacy and efficiency of our approach.

## 1 Introduction

Stream processing has been gaining attention in the database community in recent years [1,2,3,4,5]. Clearly, there are many applications of streams, ranging from network monitoring system and stock markets to emerging applications such as the RFID tracking system. Among these applications, processing of event stream has attracted particular interests lately. In these applications, event stream is usually modeled as a sequence of tuples [3,4], each of which consists of a primary timestamp and several attributes. One important task in these applications is to understand the current situation of the system, based on which proper decision can be automatically made. To realize such goal, it is important to develop query processing techniques that facilitate the definition and detection of events in the streams. Efforts have been made to define complex event processing (CEP) in information systems [6].

In many emerging applications, however, data streams may come from different live sensors, such as video cameras and microphones. Such data streams pose a greater challenge due to the more complex semantics of events in sensory data. Moreover, many applications may require events to be defined based on spatially distributed sensors where the semantics of events depends on both temporal and spatial relationships between events. In these applications, sensory data stream is first processed for the

M. Gertz and B. Ludäscher (Eds.): SSDBM 2010, LNCS 6187, pp. 602–620, 2010.

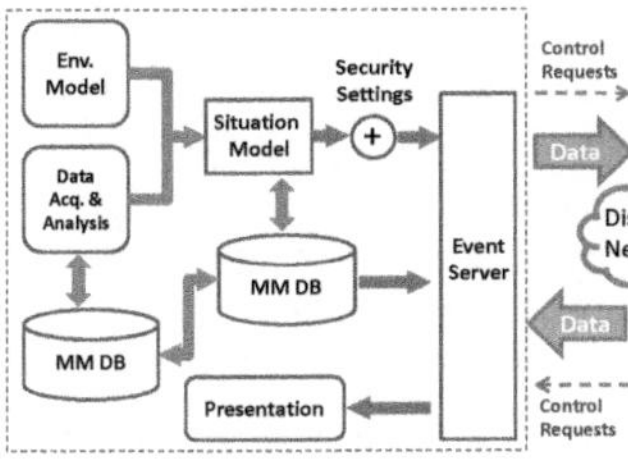


**Fig. 1.** E2E System

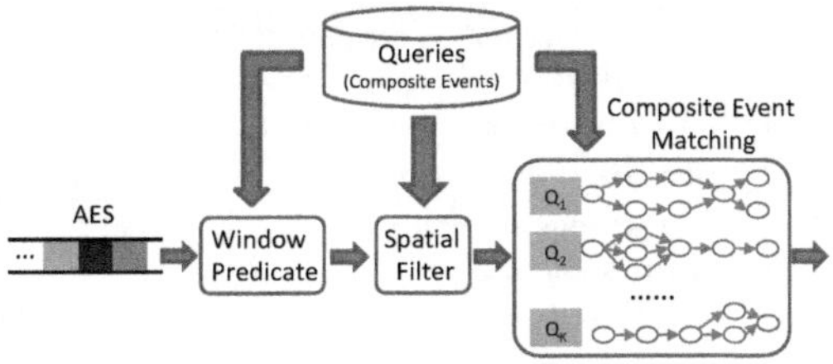


**Fig. 2.** System Architecture

appropriate features to be detected, and then transformed to stream of atomic events. Afterwards the spatio-temporal atomic event streams are examined for the detection of more complex events, which would aid the intelligence on situation level. Environment-to-Environment(E2E) is such a multimedia communication system. We give a brief introduction to E2E system before introducing our problem.

Environment-to-Environment (E2E) connection has been developed as a new form of communication that allows users to connect their natural physical environments for communications [7,8,9]. The goal is to design an architecture that pushes sensors and other devices into a supporting role in the background and to focus on natural human interaction. Figure 1 [9] shows the architecture for an E2E node. The 'Data acquisition and analysis' (DAA) component converts data from each sensor into data events. The translation of sensor based data events into application events uses a physical model of environment. This is handled via the Environment Model (EM) which creates indices between various sensors and overall physical environment. The actual semantic understanding of the event requires additional contextual information to be added by Situation Model (SM). The SM represents all the domain-dependent information required to support application functionality. As can be seen, in this application, heterogeneous data streams are collected at different locations and these streams are converted to atomic data event streams, which should then be combined into higher level application event streams. Many emerging applications in telepresence [10], surveillance [11], as well as ethnographic studies [12] have similar characteristics.

Let us consider one example to illustrate the problems involved in our event processing system. Suppose that we are dealing with a sensor rich environment where there are cameras,microphones, RFID detectors, and motion detectors at many different locations to cover all areas of a multi-storey hospital building. The system should detect events such as '*Dr. Miller went from Radiation Therapy area to meet a patient Mr. Jones in Oncology ward*'. This event can be considered to be composed of sub-events '*Dr. Miller leaving Radiation Therapy in the basement*', '*Dr. Miller catching an elevator*', '*Dr. Miller leaving elevator on the fifth floor*', '*Dr. Miller walking to room 518*' and '*Dr. Miller greeting Mr. Jones*'. The five sub-events are depicted in Figure 3, each of which consists of specific spatio-temporal information. For example, sub-event $AE_2$ is captured in the elevator stopping at the basement. Considering the event occurrence time, the five sub-events happened in sequential order.

In the rest of the paper, we call a *sub-event* in the previous example an atomic event. Events that are constructed from atomic events are called *composite events*. The

| Atomic Events of Dr. Miller | |
|---|---|
| ID | Event Description |
| $AE_1$ | Leaving Radiation Therapy in the basement |
| $AE_2$ | Catching an elevator |
| $AE_3$ | Leaving elevator on the fifth floor |
| $AE_4$ | Walking to room 518 |
| $AE_5$ | Greeting Mr. Jones |

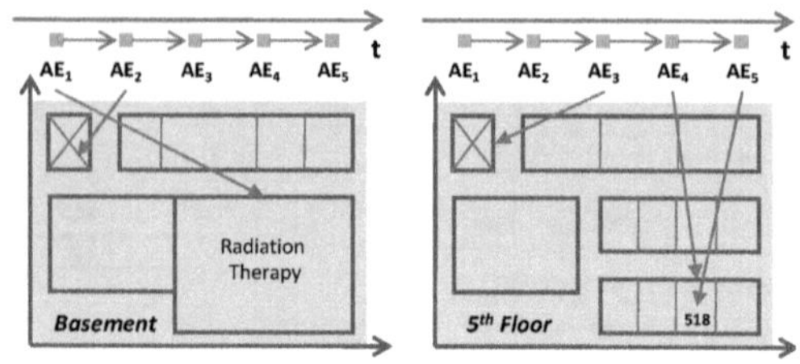


**Fig. 3.** Examples of Atomic Events

problem now becomes that given an atomic event stream with spatio-temporal information, how our system detects pre-defined composite events efficiently.

### 1.1 Challenges and Contributions

To solve the problem, the following challenges should be carefully considered. First, events in our problem carry spatial information. Suppose we are interested in events at different locations, how to efficiently filter incoming sequences of atomic events is a challenge. Second, real-life composite events usually involve concurrently as well as sequentially occurred atomic events, which makes the processing of complex temporal relationships between atomic events another challenge.

In this paper, we propose an event processing strategy to address the above challenges. To the best of our knowledge, there is no prior work on processing spatio-temporal data in event streams. Our main contributions are: 1) We provide precise semantics for the new class of spatio-temporal composite event queries in multimedia communication systems; 2) We implement an Event Processor for efficient detection of composite events, which includes a spatial filtering and a graph matching process; 3) We conducted a comprehensive experimental study, the results of which demonstrate the effectiveness and the efficiency of our system.

Rest of the paper is organized as follows. We introduce the problem formulation in Section 2, and discuss the related work in Section 3. In Section 4, we describe the general system architecture and the spatial filter component. Section 5 presents our graph model and matching algorithms. Experiments and results are demonstrated in Section 6. The paper is concluded in Section 7.

## 2 Problem Formulation

### 2.1 Atomic Event and Atomic Event Stream

Atomic event is the finest data and semantic unit in our system. It indicates the occurrence of a real life event, which captures one *type* of happening on one *person* at one *spatio-temporal* point. We represent an atomic event using a tuple, as defined below:

**Definition 1.** *An atomic event is a tuple e (Pid, $T_s$, $T_e$, LocRec$(x_1, y_1, x_2, y_2)$, $E_t$), where Pid is the person ID, $T_s$ and $T_e$ are the start and end time respectively, and LocRec is the location where the event happened, and $E_t$ is the event type.*

Different from [3,4,13,5], an atomic event in our system needs not to be instantaneous, and can last for a period of time. This is because each atomic event corresponds to a real life event, the span of which could be an interval. Instantaneous events are represented as $T_s = T_e$. Each time point in this paper is an integer in $\mathbb{N}$; while the spatial geometry considered is a 2D plane. ($x_1$, $y_1$) and ($x_2$, $y_2$) in *LocRec* define the coordinates of the bottom-left and top-right corner of a rectangular respectively. When the location of an event is a spatial point, we have $x_1 = x_2$ and $y_1 = y_2$. Event type $E_t$ could be 'walking', 'talking', 'entering room' and etc. The complete set of $E_t$ that can be recognized by the system is defined by the DAA component (Section 1.1).

The input to our system is a stream of atomic events.

**Definition 2.** *An atomic event stream is defined as:* $AES = e_1, e_2, ..., e_i, ...$, *where each* $e_i$ *is an atomic event, and atomic events are ordered by their end time* $T_e$.

Atomic events may have same start and end time ($T_s$ and $T_e$). In our model atomic events arrive in order of end time, and no out-of-order arrival is considered.

### 2.2 Temporal Relationships and Patterns

**Temporal Relationships.** Base temporal relationships between intervals were advanced in Allen's Interval Algebra [14], as shown in Table 1. Symmetric relations are omitted due to space limitations. We adopt this proposal to describe the relationships between events.

**Table 1.** Temporal Relationships and corresponding Temporal Patterns

| Base relationships | Equivalent to |
|---|---|
| $e_1$ takes place before $e_2$ | $SEQ(e_1.T_e, e_2.T_s)$ |
| $e_1$ meets $e_2$ | $EQ(e_1.T_e, e_2.T_s)$ |
| $e_1$ overlaps with $e_2$ | $SEQ(e_1.T_s, e_2.T_s, e_1.T_e, e_2.T_e)$ |
| $e_1$ starts $e_2$ | $SEQ(EQ(e_1.T_s, e_2.T_s), e_1.T_e, e_2.T_e)$ |
| $e_1$ during $e_2$ | $SEQ(e_2.T_s, e_1.T_s, e_1.T_e, e_2.T_e)$ |
| $e_1$ finishes $e_2$ | $SEQ(e_2.T_s, e_1.T_s, EQ(e_1.T_e, e_2.T_e))$ |
| $e_1$ is equal to $e_2$ | $SEQ(EQ(e_1.T_s, e_2.T_s), EQ(e_1.T_e, e_2.T_e))$ |

**Basic Temporal Patterns.** We now introduce five basic temporal patterns $SEQ, EQ, CONJ, DISJ, NEG$, which are designed to express the temporal relationships of atomic events. Each temporal pattern is specified by a *temporal requirement*, which defines the occurrence and order of atomic events. Also, every temporal pattern is associated with one *induced time bound* ($ITB = [T_s, T_e]$) indicating the time boundary of this pattern, which is computed from the time points of atomic events in the pattern.

First, $SEQ$ and $EQ$ are defined to express sequential and concurrent relationship respectively. In the following definition, $i \in [1, n]$, $e$ is an atomic event, $t_i \in \{s, e\}$.
1) Pattern $P_1 = SEQ(e_1.T_{t_1}, ..., e_i.T_{t_i}, ..., e_n.T_{t_n})$, requires that $e_1.T_{t_1} < ... < e_i.T_{t_i} < ... < e_n.T_{t_n}$. The *induced time bound* $ITB_{P_1}$ is $[e_1.T_{t_1}, e_n.T_{t_n}]$.
2) Pattern $P_2 = EQ(e_1.T_{t_1}, ..., e_i.T_{t_i}, ..., e_n.T_{t_n})$, requires that $e_1.T_{t_1} = ... = e_i.T_{t_i} = ... = e_n.T_{t_n}$. $ITB_{P_2} = [e_1.T_{t_1}, e_1.T_{t_1}]$.

Besides these two patterns, we also support three general ones: conjunction ($CONJ$), disjunction($DISJ$) and negation($NEG$). However, in most of the existing event stream processors [4,3], when considering temporal relationships of events, only sequential patterns ($SEQ$) are studied, while $CONJ$ and $DISJ$ are ignored.
3) Pattern $P_3 = CONJ(e_1, ..., e_i, ..., e_n)$, requires that each $e_i$ occurs, but no time order is required among these events. $ITB_{P_3} = [min(e_i.T_s), max(e_i.T_e)]$.
4) Pattern $P_4 = DISJ(e_1, ..., e_i, ..., e_n)$, requires that non-empty subset of these events occurs, but no time order requirement among these atomic events.
$ITB_{P_4} = [min(e_j.T_s), max(e_j.T_e)], j \in [1, n]$ and $e_j$ occurs.
5) Pattern $P_5 = NEG(e)$ ($e$ is an atomic event), requires that $e$ does not occur. Given the infinity of time, it is infeasible to negate an event without proper time constraints. Therefore in this paper, we consider a negation when it is bounded by two events. Pattern $P_5 = NEG(e, e_p.T_{t_p}, e_q.T_{t_q})$ ($e_p, e_q$ are atomic events, $t_p, t_q \in \{s, e\}$), requires no occurrence of $e$ between $e_p.T_{t_p}$ and $e_q.T_{t_q}$. $ITB_{P_5} = [e_p.T_{t_p}, e_q.T_{t_q}]$.

**Nested Temporal Patterns.** Up till now, only atomic events are considered in the basic temporal patterns. However, they could be easily extended to support nested temporal patterns by treating (basic) patterns as atomic events and their corresponding $ITB$ as their time points. The definitions are omitted due to space limitations.

For example, given pattern P, and its associated $ITB_P = [T_s, T_e]$, pattern $P' = SEQ(e_1.T_{t_1}, ..., P, ..., e_n.T_{t_n})$ requires that $e_1.T_{t_1} < ... < P.T_s < P.T_e < ... < e_n.T_{t_n}$.

The temporal patterns are defined to help formulate composite events which will be discussed in the following section.

### 2.3 Composite Events and Queries

Composite event is semantically more meaningful event. It is defined over a set of constituting events, which can be atomic events or composite events. Users describe their interests through the specification of composite event, which includes the temporal patterns of constituting events as well as predicates on other attributes of atomic events, i.e. $PID$, $LocRec$ and $E_t$. Predicates of $Pid$ and $E_t$ are equality comparison on values, e.g. $Pid = 123$, $E_t =' walking'$, while predicates of $LocRec$ can be comparison on either spatial points or area ranges, e.g. $4 <= x < 8, 7 <= y < 11$. Besides, predicates between sequential atomic events in pattern $SEQ$ are also allowed. For example, the specification can have the temporal pattern $SEQ(e_1.T_s, e_2.T_s)$ and predicate $e_2.T_s - e_1.T_s < 2sec$. At last, a window predicate is defined, which specifies the time limit that one composite event could maximally last, e.g. in 10 mins.

The specification of a composite event essentially forms a standing query $Q$, pre-registered in the system. When atomic event stream $AES$ flow by, queries in the system will be answered on the fly. In order to make it easier for users to specify composite events, we use a SQL-like declarative language introduced in [3,5] to express queries.

An example of composite event and corresponding query is given as follows.

**Example 1.** Here is a scenario when Tom and John at the office in US start the weekly meeting with Mohan in Singapore. Tom is in his office room 2059 equipped with 8 cameras and 4 microphones (and many other devices as part of E2E). The system determines that he is working on his desk ($e_1$). At this time, John enters the room ($e_2$).

Then John talks to Tom about calling Mohan in Singapore for the meeting ($e_3$). Tom connects with Mohan for discussions ($e_4$). For further discussions Tom and John will go to the Lab in the CalIT2 building. Connectivity should be maintained so that the discussion can continue from the Lab. To satisfy such requirement, our system should be able to recognize the occurrence of this composite event. There are four atomic events ($e_i, 1 \leq i \leq 4$ as indicated above) constituting the composite event. Specification of the composite event declaratively in SQL-like query language is the following:

SELECT SEQ(CONJ($e_1, e_2$), $e_3, e_4$)
WHERE $e_1.Pid =' Tom'$ AND $e_1.E_t =' working'$
AND $e_2.Pid =' John'$ AND $e_2.E_t =' entering\ room'$
AND $e_3.Pid =' John'$ AND $e_3.E_t =' talking'$
AND $e_4.Pid =' Tom'$ AND $e_4.E_t =' connecting'$
AND $e_1.LocRec = Rec(Rm2059)$ AND $e_2.LocRec = Rec(Rm2059)$
AND $e_3.LocRec = Rec(Rm2059)$ AND $e_4.LocRec = Rec(Rm2059)$

Note that 'Tom', 'John', 'walking' etc. actually refer to their *Pid/Et* values, while $Rec(Rm2059)$ refers to spatial coordinates of room 2059.

In the rest of the paper, 'composite event' and 'query' will be used interchangeably.

### 2.4 Problem

Our problem could now be formulated as: given composite events $QS = \{Q_1, ..., Q_i, ..., Q_n\}$ registered in system and the incoming atomic event stream $AES$, find subsequences of atomic events from $AES$ that match queries in $QS$. A formal definition of matching is defined as follows.

**Definition 3.** *Given a query $Q = (P, PS)$ specified by user, where P is a (nested) temporal pattern and $PS$ is a predicates set, a sequence of atomic events $S = e_{s1}, ..., e_{si}, ..., e_{sn}$ is a match of Q if S satisfies both temporal requirement of P and every predicate in $PS$.*

## 3 Related Work

Much work has been done in active database systems on composite event detection [13,15,16], and a comprehensive study of the semantics of composite events can be found in [17]. Among the work, basic methods such as tree-based approach [13], Petri Nets model [15] and finite automata [16] have been proposed. But, as noted in [5], arbitrary tree plans in Snoop [13] may suffer from poor performance; Petri Nets are too complicated to put into practice use; and concurrent relationships are not supported in Ode [16].

Pub/Sub event systems [18,19] offer an asynchronous communication paradigm between publishers and subscribers, on which a large amount of user subscriptions can be handled over event streams. However, the expressiveness of user interests is limited. Especially complex temporal patterns are not addressed in these systems.

Meanwhile, data stream processors such as Telegraph CQ [1], STREAM [2] and Borealis [20] have been proposed to handle continuous queries over stream data. Operations such as projections, selections, aggregations and joins over time windows can be efficiently evaluated. Although the expressiveness provided by stream processors is much more complex than that in Pub/Sub systems, stream data processors become clumsy when processing complex temporal patterns, where every temporal relationship in patterns have to be specified as an individual predicate and evaluated separately.

Recently, NFA-based event systems as Cayuga [4] and SASE [3] have been developed to support complex event detection over high-rate event streams. User queries are transformed to NFA models, by which pattern matching is supported. However, as we mentioned above, these systems only consider sequential pattern matching and do not support concurrent temporal relationships among events as in our work. ZStream [5] deploys tree-based query plans as in [16] and is able to process concurrent events and their adjust query plans according to their cost model. However, their method may suffer from the risk of generating large numbers of intermediate results, which is not ideal for high volume event processing. Besides, complex spatial constraints, which are essential in our applications, are not efficiently supported and utilized in existing systems.

Work [21,22] has also been done in the graphic area, utilizing hash functions for spatial information compression. Similarly in the AI area, much work [23,24] has been done on simple temporal problems. Algorithms have been presented to solve temporal constraint satisfaction problems. We have borrowed from [23] the idea of splitting an event into two nodes which represent start and end time respectively.

## 4 Event Processor

In this section, we introduce the main components of our event stream processor. We propose a spatial filter that efficiently removes irrelevant incoming events based on their spatial values. In Section 5, a matching algorithm is proposed that refines the filtering result and detects the composite event.

### 4.1 System Architecture

We first describe the system architecture, as shown in Figure 2. The input to our system is an atomic event stream $AES$ ordered by $T_e$. All composite events are pre-registered as queries. The query engine consists of three main components: window predicate processor, spatial filter and composite event matching processor. Window predicates of queries are pushed to the front. If a composite event does not have a window predicate, an appropriate timeout value (e.g. every 30 seconds, which is a tunable parameter in systems) will be set up to stop the buffering process and form a window of atomic events, which is then fed to the spatial filter. If the window of atomic events survives the filtering, it is sent to the composite event matching process, which will generate the final matching subsequences from the input stream.

### 4.2 Spatial Filter

We now introduce the design of spatial filter. When a window of incoming atomic events is matched to a composite event, *all* the spatial predicates specified in this composite event must be satisfied. It is desirable to have an approach that is able to check the satisfaction of all spatial predicates in one shot and avoid multiple examinations of individual spatial predicate. Based on this observation, we propose a spatial filter that utilizes fast spatial signature comparison to filter unrelated sequences of events.

We apply bloom filter as the data structure of spatial signature, for several reasons: 1) There is no false negative; 2) It is space-efficient; 3) By utilizing bloom filter, the problem of 2D comparison is reduced to 1D comparison.

The construction of signature has the following steps: 1) partition the plane into grids and assign an unique ID to each cell; 2) map the spatial areas covered by composite events or incoming window of atomic events to cells. 3) compute the signature from the cell IDs returned from Step 2. Given a set of atomic events $ES = \{e_1, ..., e_n\}$ and $w$ different hash functions $\{h_1, ..., h_w\}$, the spatial signature of $ES$ is a bloom filter (a bit vector) $b$ of size $m$, with all bits $b_i$ sets to 1, where $i = h_k(e_j.LocRec.to\_cell\_ids())\ mod\ m$, $i \in [1, m], j \in [1, n], k \in [1, w]$.

Spatial signature is built for both registered composite events as well as incoming windows of atomic events. For each $Q_i$ in $QS$, we generate its spatial signature $B_{Q_i}$. Similarly, when an incoming window of atomic events $ES$ arrives, we construct a spatial signature $b_{ES}$ for it by using the same hash functions. We then compare $b_{ES}$ with each $B_{Q_i}$, if $b_{ES}\ AND\ B_{Q_i} = 0$ holds, which means that $ES$ does not cover any spatial area of $Q_i$, $ES$ will be filtered out immediately. Otherwise, $ES$ is forwarded to the composite event matching component for further processing.

## 5 Composite Event Matching

In this section, we introduce the composite event matching processor, which is designed to find a subsequence from the incoming window of atomic events that satisfies a given query $Q$. When evaluating standing queries under streaming mode, it is inefficient to buffer a large number of events for post processing in terms of both space and time cost. We address this problem by first introducing a graph structure to effectively model temporal patterns in queries. Based on this model, we propose a matching algorithm, which is able to obtain query results by one-pass examination of incoming events.

### 5.1 Graph Representation

We model a composite event as a directed graph, which is an effective way to represent relationships between atomic events. Consider a composite event $Q$, which consists of a set of atomic events $\{e_1, ..., e_n\}$. We discuss the construction of $Q$'s graph representation $G(V, E)$ in this section.

First, we construct the node set $V$ of $G$. For each $e_i$ of $Q$, if $e_i$ is non-instantaneous, two nodes $n_{e_i.T_s}$ and $n_{e_i.T_e}$, tagged as "start" and "end" respectively, are added to $V$. If $e_i$ is instantaneous, one node $n_{e_i}$, tagged as "none", is added to $V$. Each node stores attributes *Pid*, *LocRec*, $E_t$, *start/end tag* and *edge_type*. *Edge_type* of node $n$ represents the temporal pattern between node $n$ and its parent nodes. It is assigned to each node at edge construction step. The set of *edge_type* is $\{root, subroot, seq, eq, conj, disj, seq + neg, eq + neg, conj + neg, disj + neg\}$, details of which are given below. Each node is also associated with one matching slot and a candidate list to store matching instance and candidates. During edge construction, we will expand $V$ by adding

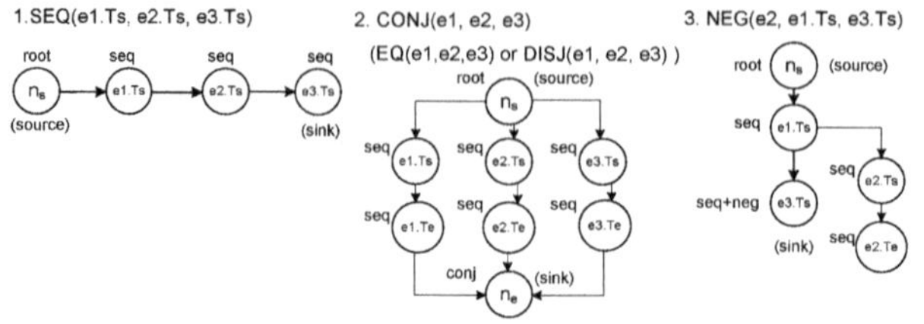


**Fig. 4.** Graph Elements

some function nodes, which are introduced to complete the graph and not intended to be matched by any events. Particularly, we designate the node whose in-degree is 0 as "source", and the node whose out-degree is 0 as "sink".

Next, we introduce the construction of edge set $E$ based on the temporal patterns of $Q$. We first explain the edge building for 5 basic temporal patterns, examples of which are illustrated in Figure 4. Let $e_i$ denote an atomic event, $t_i \in \{s, e\}$ and $i \in [1, n]$.
1) $SEQ(e_1.T_{t_1}, ..., e_i.T_{t_i}, ..., e_n.T_{t_n})$. One function node $n_s$ is added to $V$. For each $e_i.T_{t_i}$, we add one edge from $n_{e_i.T_{t_i}}$ to $n_{e_{i+1}.T_{t_{i+1}}}$ $(i \in [1, n-1])$. Also an edge is added from $n_s$ to $n_{e_1.T_{t_1}}$. In this graph, the source node is $n_s$ and the sink node is $n_{e_n.T_{t_n}}$. *Edge_type* is set as *root* for the source node $n_s$, and *seq* for all other nodes.
2) $EQ(e_1.T_{t_1}, ..., e_i.T_{t_i}, ..., e_n.T_{t_n})$. Two function nodes $n_s$ and $n_e$ are inserted into $V$. For each $e_i.T_{t_i}$, one edge is added from $n_s$ to $n_{e_i.T_{t_i}}$, and another from $n_{e_i.T_{t_i}}$ to $n_e$. The source is $n_s$ and the sink is $n_e$. *Edge_type* is set as *root* for $n_s$, *eq* for $n_e$, and *seq* for all other nodes.
3) $CONJ(e_1, ..., e_i, ..., e_n)$. Same as $EQ$, two function nodes $n_s$ and $n_e$ are added to $V$. For each $e_i$, we add one edge from $n_s$ to $n_{e_i.T_s}$, one from $n_{e_i.T_s}$ to $n_{e_i.T_e}$, and another from $n_{e_i.T_e}$ to $n_e$. The source is $n_s$ and the sink is $n_e$. *Edge_type* is set as *root* for $n_s$, *conj* for $n_e$, and *seq* for all other nodes.
4) $DISJ(e_1, ..., e_i, ..., e_n)$. Edges and function nodes are added in the same way as for pattern $CONJ$. However, *edge_type* is set as *root* for $n_s$, *disj* for $n_e$, and *seq* for all other nodes.
5) $NEG(e_i, e_p.T_{t_p}, e_q.T_{t_q})$ ($e_p, e_q$ are atomic events, $t_p, t_q \in \{s, e\}$). One function node $n_s$ is added to $V$. We add one edge from $n_s$ to $n_{e_p.T_{t_p}}$, one from $n_{e_p.T_{t_p}}$ to $n_{e_q.T_{t_q}}$, one from $n_{e_p.T_{t_p}}$ to $n_{e_i.T_s}$, and one from $n_{e_i.T_s}$ to $n_{e_i.T_e}$. The source is $n_s$, and the sink is $n_{e_q.T_{t_q}}$. *Edge_type* is set as *root* for $n_s$, *seq+neg* for $n_{e_q.T_{t_q}}$, and *seq* for all other nodes. Specifically, we call the subgraph including $n_{e_i.T_s}$ and $n_{e_i.T_e}$ a *negated* subgraph, with $n_{e_i.T_s}$ as the *negated* source and $n_{e_i.T_e}$ the *negated* sink. A *negated link* to the negated sink is stored at $n_{e_q.T_{t_q}}$. Note that this link is not an edge in graph $G$.

Based on the edge building of basic temporal patterns, we briefly introduce the construction of nested graph pattern. Suppose pattern $P_i$ is nested in $P_j$. For $P_j$, the graph of $P_i$ is treated as a blackbox, whose source and sink serve as interface. The construction is implemented in a hierarchical fashion. Graphs of inner nested patterns are built first, which are then connected to the outside nodes through its interface. For example, consider building the graph $G'$ for $NEG(P_1, P_2, P_3)$. We first created graphs for each $P_i$. Then one edge is added from $P_2.n_e$ to $P_3.n_s$, and one from $P_2.n_e$ to $P_1.n_s$. For $G'$, the source is $P_2.n_s$ and the sink is $P_3.n_e$. The negated source is $P_1.n_s$ and the negated

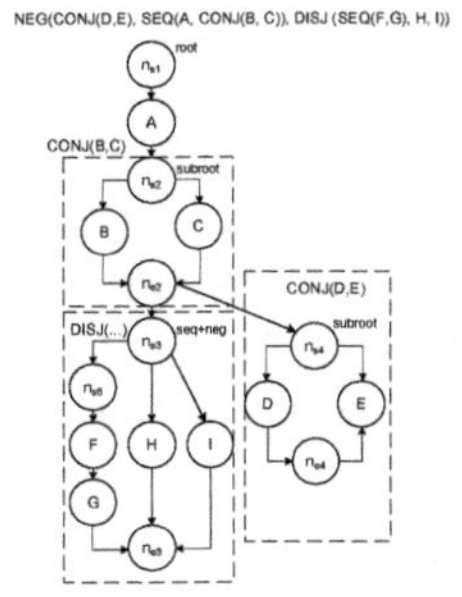


**Fig. 5.** A Temporal Graph Example

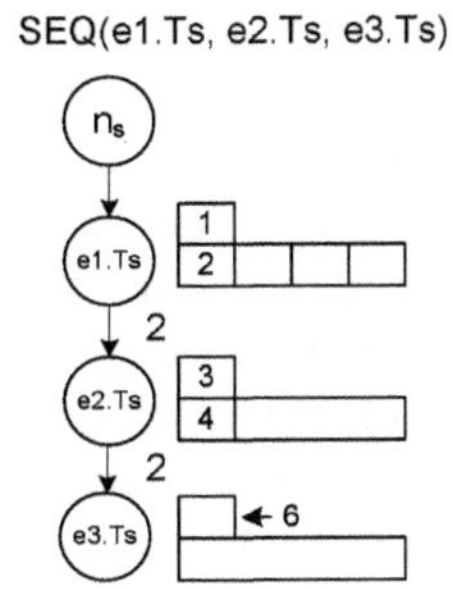


**Fig. 6.** Graph Example for Backtrack

sink is $P_1.n_e$. A *negated link* pointing to the negated sink is stored in $P_3.n_s$. Lastly, we modify the *edge_type* of $P_1.n_s$ to *subroot* and that of $P_3.n_s$ to *seq+neg*. Figure 5 shows example of a complex nested pattern. Each capital letter in the pattern represents an atomic event or a time point.

Edges can be weighted. For example, consider one edge $e = (n_1, n_2)$ with $e.weight = h$, and the *edge_type* of $n_2$ is *seq*. Then the requirement is $n_1.time < n_2.time <= n_1.time + h$. This representation is especially useful when the time of an event needs to be bounded in a range. If $e$ is unweighted, then $n_1.time < n_2.time$.

### 5.2 Graph Matching Algorithm

We propose a graph matching algorithm based on the graph $G$ of composite event $Q$. We call nodes in $G$ query nodes, and nodes created for input atomic events input nodes. If an input node $t$ satisfies temporal requirements and all other predicates of query node $n$, $t$ is *matched* to $n$. We call $t$ an *instance* of $n$, and store it in $n$'s matching slot. If more input nodes are mapped to $n$ after $t$, they are stored in the candidate list $L$ of $n$. $G$ is matched if all query nodes in $G$ have been matched by some input nodes.

The graph matching algorithm is shown in Algorithm 1. The input is a window of atomic events, and the output is a subsequence from the window that matches graph $G$. First, for each incoming atomic event $e_i$, method *SplitEventsAndSort* in line 2

**Algorithm 1.** Graph Matching $M$

```
1  begin
2      T ← SplitEventsAndSort(e1, e2, ..., en);
3      while T ≠ ∅ and !G.isMatched() do
4          t ← T.pop();
5          n ← G.getNodes(t);
6          if n is NULL then deleteInputNode(T, G, t); continue;
7          r ← G.checkMatches(n, t);
8          if r is TRUE then continue;
9          else deleteInputNode(T, G, t);
10     end
11     if G.isMatched() then return G.buildResult() ;
12     else return FAILED;
13 end
```

splits it and creates two input nodes $n_{s_i}$ and $n_{e_i}$, tagged as *start* and *end* respectively. $n_{s_i}$ and $n_{e_i}$ store the start and end time of $e_i$ as well as other attributes from atomic events. Besides, a pointer to each other is saved, in case when matching of one input node fails, the pair can be removed together. The method then sorts these input nodes in ascending order of time. Next, we pop up input nodes and match them to nodes in $G$. After one input node $t$ is popped up (line 4), method $getNodes(t)$ (line 5) finds query nodes in $G$ that have the same values on person id, event type and start/end tag as $t$. To improve performance, we build one hash table $H$, which maps triplet $< person\ id, event\ type, start/end\ tag >$ to a set of query nodes in $G$. $getNodes(t)$ looks up hash table $H$, and returns a set of query nodes. $t$ is then tested if it falls into the spatial rectangle covered by any query node in this set. Notice that when there are identical atomic events in composite event, i.e. the same person at the same location doing the same type of event but at different time, it is possible to match $t$ to multiple $n$. In this paper, we do not consider such case and leave it as future work. So $t$ can be mapped to at most one node. If $t$ is not mapped to any query node, $deleteInputNode(T, G, t)$ is invoked to properly remove $t$ and its associated pair node. The process goes back to line 3. Otherwise, if $t$ is mapped to $n$, $checkMatches(n, t)$ is invoked to examines whether $t$ satisfies the temporal requirement of $n$. If this is true, $t$ is stored in $n$; otherwise, call $deleteInputNode(T, G, t)$. The while loop (line 3-10) stops when input nodes are exhausted or $G$ is matched. If $G$ is matched, the sequences of atomic events from instances of query nodes in $G$ are returned (line 11); otherwise, algorithm returns FAILED (line 12).

Note that there are different selection criteria when returning matching instances. For example, we can return the first matching sequence, or return every possible matching sequences. In this paper, we return the first sequence for simplicity. Results of all possible sequences can be easily supported if necessary.

Method $checkMathces(n, t)$ examines the matching of incoming atomic events. Clearly, matching of an input node $t$ to a query node $n$ given $n$'s temporal requirements depends on several factors: 1) temporal relationships between node $n$ and its parent nodes; 2) whether $n$'s parents are matched, and the time of their instances; 3) edge weights; 4) the time of $t$.

Several observations from edge construction are helpful in designing the algorithm. 1) Input nodes can only be mapped to non-function query nodes, whose *edge_type* is either *seq* or $seq + neg$; 2) Each non-function query node has only one parent, whose *edge_type* can be *root*, *subroot*, and *seq*; 3) Nodes whose *edge_type* is *subroot* have only one parent, which can have any *edge_type*. Based on these observations, we design the matching process (Algorithm 2). Note that before matching starts, if $n$ has already had a matching instance, $t$ is directly inserted into candidate list and return.

As $n$'s *edge_type* is either *seq* or *seq+neg*, $n$ has one and only one incoming edge denoted as $e = (n_p, n)$. $checkParents(n_p)$ is invoked (line 2) to check whether $n_p$ has been matched. If $n_p$ has not been matched, $n$ cannot be matched either, given the sequential requirement between $n_p$ and $n$. Therefore, FALSE is returned (line 3). If $n_p$ has been matched by some instance $t_p$, the temporal requirement between $n_p$ and $n$ is $n.time > t_p.time$. If the edge is weighted by $h$, the temporal requirement is $t_p.time < n.time <= t_p.time + h$. If $t$ satisfies the requirement (line 5), and its *edge_type* is

**Algorithm 2.** *checkMatches(n, t)*

```
1  begin
2      r, time ← checkParents(n.n_p);
3      if r is FALSE then return FALSE;
4      else
5          if t satisfies TimeRequirement(time) then
6              if n's edge_type is seq then return TRUE;
7              else
8                  if n is negated by negated pattern then return FALSE;
9                  else return TRUE;
10             end
11         else if t.time > t_p.time + h and n's edge_type is seq then
           Backtrack(G, n); checkMatches(n, t);
12         else return FALSE;
13     end
14 end
```

$seq$, then $t$ is matched to $n$. We return TRUE (line 6). However, if the $edge\_type$ of $t$ is $seq + neg$, further check on the occurrence of the negated pattern is required. Followed the negated link of $n$ pointing to the negated sink $n_{neg}$, we call $checkParents(n_{neg})$ to test whether $n_{neg}$ is matched. If $n_{neg}$ is not matched, then $t$ matches $n$ (line 9). In case it is matched, we need to backtrack from $n$. The matching instance and candidates of $n_p$ with time before that of $n_{neg}$ are removed. If $n_p$ finds a new match among candidates, we call $checkMatches(n, t)$ to re-match $t$ to $n$. Otherwise, $n_p$ is left unmatched and $t$ cannot match $n$. If the edge $e$ is weighted by $h$, and $t$ and all future input nodes after $t$ cannot get matched as long as $t_p$ works as the instance of $n_p$, backtrack from $n$ is required (line 11). In all other cases, matching fails (line 12).

Method $checkParents(n_p)$ mainly examines whether $n_p$ has been matched and if so, return the time of $n_p$. If $n_p$ has been matched by an instance $t_p$, $t_p.time$ is returned. Otherwise, if $n_p$ has not been matched and $n_p$ is a non-function node, FALSE is returned; if $n_p$ is a function node, we need to analyze its relationship with its parents and calculate its time from the parents. This step involves examination of all possible $edge\_type$. Readers may refer to [25] for more details.

Method $Backtrack(G, n)$ checks the candidates of $n$'s parent node $n_p$, and verify whether $n_p$ can be matched by one of them. If it is matched, return TRUE; otherwise, return FALSE. Besides, negated subgraphs (if any) should be reset properly. Algorithm details can be found at [25].

### 5.3 Complexity Analysis

Now, we discuss the complexity of our matching algorithm. Assume the size of the incoming window of atomic events is $n$. We first discuss the complexity of $SplitEventsAndSort$. For each $e_i$ ($i \in [1, n]$), it is split into two input nodes, and inserted to a priority queue. The complexity of inserting and sorting in a priority queue is $O(n \log n)$, which is the complexity of $SplitEventsAndSort$. Complexity of matching an input node depends on the number of its parent nodes. When checking relationships of equality, conjunction and disjunction, more than one parent nodes are examined. Therefore, the complexity relies on the maximum number of parent nodes in these types of relationships. Assume the maximum in-degree in graph $G$ is $m_1$. Since each input node can be matched at most once, the complexity of matching an input node is $O(m_1 n)$. Similarly, when doing backtrack, the complexity of dropping a matched input node depends on the number of its child nodes, as all its children need to be reset. Assume the maximum out-degree of a node in $G$ is $m_2$. Since each input node can be dropped at most once, the complexity of dropping a match is $O(m_2 n)$. To sum up, the complexity of Algorithm 1 is $O(m_1 n + m_2 n + n \log n)$.

## 6 Performance Study

We have implemented our event detection processor in C++ using compiler G++ 4.3 on Ubuntu 9.04 in a machine equipped with a Core 2 Duo 2.4Hz CPU and a 2GB memory. In this section, we evaluate the performance of our prototype system. We first study the effectiveness of spatial filtering. We learn by experiments the appropriate size of bloom filter and number of hash functions under different data. We also examine the effect of grid partition over spatial filtering. Next we study how our graph matching algorithm performs given the complxity of graphs and occurrence of backtrack. Extensive experiments demonstrate the effectiveness and efficiency of our system.

### 6.1 Performance of Spatial Filtering

In order to test the performance of spatial filter, we generate queries and input atomic events with spatial information only, which consists of spatial areas and points. Consider a space of size $3000 \times 3000$. We first generate 10 queries, each consisting of 20 spatial areas as rectangles defined by bottom left node $(x_1, y_1)$ and top right node $(x_1 + r_x, y_1 + r_y)$. $x_1$ and $y_1$ are randomly generated within $[0, 3000)$ while $r_x$ and $r_y$ are within $[0, 60)$ such that point $(x_1 + r_x, y_1 + r_y)$ is within the $3000 \times 3000$ space. For each query, we then generate 10000 windows of atomic events, each consisting around 30 spatial points. We first generate spatial points that are varied around queries, as it would be very hard for purely random generated spatial points to match a query. Given a query spatial area $(x_1, y_1, r_x, r_y)$, we generate one or several points $(x, y)$ based on the parameters shown in Table 2. Besides, we insert 1 or 2 randomly generated points into each window at probability of 0.2 independently. Inserting extra randomly generated points is to add more variations to the input data.

**Signature Size and Number of Hash Functions.** In the first experiment, we examine the effect of signature size and number of hash functions on the FPR (false positive rate) of bloom filter. We fixed the cell size to 15 leading to a $200 \times 200$ grid over the space. Each spatial area in the query covers 1 to 25 grid cells. Notice that there are only points in the input data. If an input window covers at least one cell for each spatial area specified in the query, we consider it a cell-based match of the query. A true match of a query must be a cell-based match; while a cell-based match may not be a true match of the origin query, as points may belong to a cell which is partially covered by a query area. A false positive of bloom filter in our scenario is that when an input window is considered a match of the query, it is not a cell-based matched of the query. We vary the size of the bloom filter and number of hash functions and measure the corresponding false positive. Assume $n$ is the number of input windows that pass

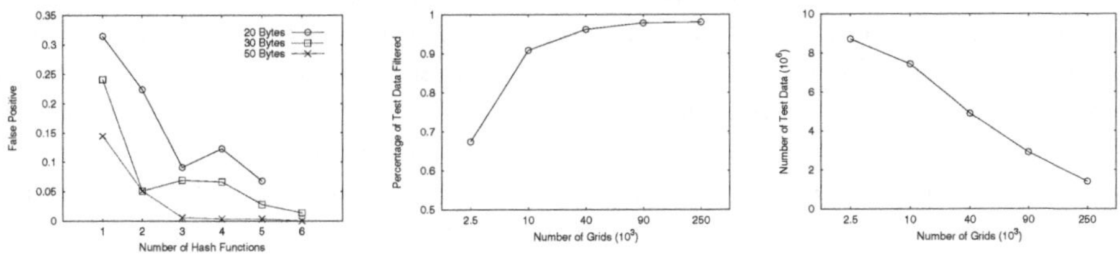


(a) False Positive Rate of Bloom Filter

(b) Savings of Spatial Filtering

(c) Throughput of Spatial Filtering

**Fig. 7.** Performance of Spatial Filtering

**Table 2.** Parameters of Data Generation

| Variations to spatial points | Probability |
|---|---|
| $x = x_1 + (1\|2\|3) \times 15$ | 0.2 |
| $y = y_1 + (1\|2\|3) \times 15$ | 0.2 |
| insert $(1\|2\|3)$ spatial points, $x = x_1 + d_x, d_x \in [0, 15)$, $y = y_1 + d_y, d_y \in [0, 15)$. | 0.1 |
| $x = x_1, y = y_1$ | 0.5 |

**Table 3.** Queries and Test Data

| Type | Number of Input |
|---|---|
| True match | 107.6 |
| Cell-based match | 380.4 |
| Spatial filter | 594.1 |

through spatial filter; $m$ is the number of test data that are cell-based match of the query. The FPR of bloom filter as $\frac{n-m}{n}$ is shown in Figure 7(a). For a query of 20 spatial areas and an input window with around 30 points, a bloom filter with size of 30 bytes and 3 hash functions could achieve FPR less than 0.07.If we increase the bloom filter size to 50 bytes, using 3 hash functions makes its FPR to be less than 0.006. Through this experiment we found that a bloom filter of modest size could achieve very low FPR and serves well for filtering purpose. Further, as we only need to maintain the spatial signature for each query in the main memory, the space cost is low. Next we show the savings of spatial filtering. We first measure the percentage of input data that could be filtered by spatial filter (shown in Table 3). On average 107.6 test data are true matches of the original query over the 10 sample queries and their corresponding 10000 input data. Consider the $200 \times 200$ grid over the space in the previous experiment. The worst case false positive ($> 0.3$) is obtained when using a bloom filter of size 20 bytes and only 1 hash function. Even in that situation, the spatial filter only returns on average 594.1 test data (shown in Table 3) and more than 9400 test data is filtered.

**Cell Size.** Next we examine the performance of spatial filter under different cell size. We fixed the bloom filter with size 50 bytes and apply 6 hash functions, under which the FPR is 0. We vary the cell size from 60 to 6. The results are shown in Figure 7(b). It is easy to understand that the smaller the cell size, the more we could filtered. The smaller the cell size is, the less probability that a non-match point is allocated with the same cell as the query area, leading to more accurate spatial signature. However, we could already achieve that over 96% input are filtered with cell size of 15 in the $200 \times 200$ grid.

Although decreasing the cell size increases the filtering performance of spatial filter, it is at the cost of throughput. In Figure 7(c) we plot the number of input data our spatial filter could process per second under different grid partition. We can see that the throughput of spatial filter decreases with smaller cell size. This is because when the cell size decreases, an area in the query would cover more cells and they are all hashed to the same value. In the implementation, we grouped all cells covered by an area together and map them to one cell. When a cell id of a test data comes, we look it up in these groups and find its corresponding cell and send that to the hash functions. A smaller cell size means larger groups, which increases the look up time.

**Number of Spatial Areas.** Lastly, we examine the effect of number of spatial areas in the query on the performance of spatial filter. We generate another 4 groups of queries consisting of 4, 8, 12 and 16 spatial areas. Each group consists of 10 queries. For each query, we generate 10000 input data. Queries and data are generated in the same way as that of previous experiments. The underlying grid is $200 \times 200$. Similar to previous experiments, we use a bloom of size 50 bytes and 6 hash functions. Assume $n_1$ is the number of input data returned by spatial filter after pruning, and $n_2$ is the number of test data that truly match the query. We measure $\frac{n_1 - n_2}{n_2}$. The results are shown in Figure 8. With increasing number of spatial areas in query, the pruning effect of spatial filter decreases as more test data are returned compared to true matches of query. This is because the errors brought by grid partition accumulate with increasing number of spatial areas involved in a query.

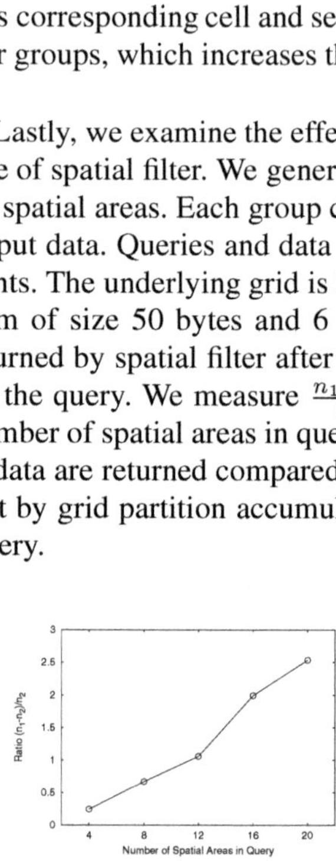


**Fig. 8.** Effect of Number of Spatial Areas in Query

## 6.2 Performance of Graph Matching

**Complexity of Query Graph.** In this experiment, we study how the complexity of a query graph affects the matching performance. Complexity of a query graph relies on three factors: 1) size of the graph, 2) density of the graph, and 3) weight on edges. The size of a graph is measured by the number of nodes, which is mostly decided by the number of atomic events in the query composite event. It is also partly influenced by temporal patterns, since different number of function nodes are introduced from different patterns. Non-sequential patterns, i.e. $EQ$, $CONJ$ and $DISJ$, bring in more function nodes in graph construction. The density is measured by the number of edges in the graph, which is mainly decided by the number of non-sequential patterns between atomic events as well as number of atomic events in each pattern. Weight on edges specifies whether there is a temporal predicate between events.

To test the effects resulted from these factors, we implement a query graph generator that randomly creates query graphs following the graph properties described in Section 5.3. Based on the analysis above, parameters and their associated values are set for generator, as shown in Table 4. $N$ expresses the total number of non-function nodes in graph. $P$ is the probabilities of non-sequential temporal pattern in graph. As said, this probabilities also decides the number of function nodes. When $P$ is 0, the graph consists only sequentially related nodes and negation nodes. $B$ captures the number of nodes in a non-sequential relationship. $P$ and $B$ jointly determine the graph density. $C$ represents whether edges in graph are weighted or not. Weights are added only on edges between nodes whose $edge\_type$ is $seq$.

**Table 4.** Parameters of Graph Generator

| Description | Values |
|---|---|
| $N$:Number of Nodes | 10,20,50,100 |
| $P$:Percent of Non-seq Patterns | 0,0.3,0.6 |
| $B$:Branch Num | [3-5] |
| $C$:Weight | with/without weights |

**Table 5.** Parameters of Test Streams

| Description | Values |
|---|---|
| $T$:Backtrack Times | [1...4] |
| $N_b$:Number of Nodes Backtracked | [2...8] |
| $W$:Percent of Data Backtracked | 0, 25%, 50%, 75%, 100% |

Given a setting of above parameters, we generate a query graph in the following way. We maintain a queue and a $cnt$ as number of created nodes. The queue is initially enqueued with a default root, and $cnt$ is set to 0. While the queue is not empty, we pop up a node $n$. Based on value of $P$, we randomly select a temporal pattern between $n$ and its children. We then pick a number $childCnt$ from $B$'s value range, and set $min(childCnt, N-cnt)$ as the $n$'s children number. We update the count, create child nodes, and enqueue them to the queue. Note that for $NEG$, in our experiments, only negation on one atomic event is tested. So the negated subgraph is made up of start and end node. The process stops when $N - cnt$ becomes 0. Then we stop expanding from children, and add enough function nodes to complete the graph.

Besides, we implement a test data generator which generates windows of test atomic events. Given a query graph, a test window of atomic events can be easily profiled to be either matched or not matched to the query. Queries and test data are stored as files in disk and preloaded into memory before running the experiments.

Experiments are carried out based on the value settings in Table 4. For each parameter setting $S$, 10 query graphs are randomly generated. For each of the 10 graphs, we randomly generate 10000 windows of test atomic events. In this experiment, we profile the test data to be backtrack free, and the number of nodes in the test data is set around $[0.9N, 1.1N]$. We run matching of each query, and compute the average time as the running time of $S$. For each setting $S$, throughput is calculated by dividing the total number of windows, 10000, by the running time. Experiment result is shown in Figure 9.

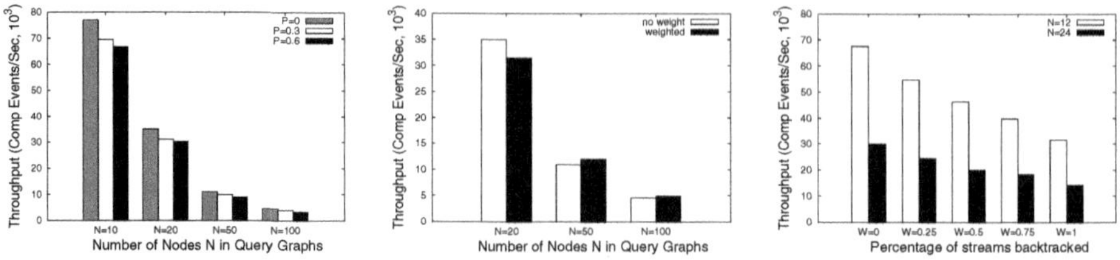


(a) Graphs with No Edge Weight

(b) Comparison on Edge Weight

(c) Test Data that Needs Backtrack

**Fig. 9.** Throughput of Graph Matching

Figure 9(a) shows the system throughput when there is no weight on edges in query graphs. We can see that the processing throughput is very large. When $N = 10, P = 0$, throughput reaches 76920 windows of events per second. It is easy to find that throughput drops as graph size grows, and the drop rate is roughly proportional to the number of nodes. Even in the case when $N = 100, P = 0.6$, our system still processes as many as 3000 windows of test data per second. In real applications, one query composite event usually has much fewer number of atomic events than 100. Besides, from the figure we also see that graphs that have the same $N$ but larger $P$ take longer time to process, and the matching of which yields less throughput. This is easy to understand since the matching of a non-function node requires only one or two (in case of negation) checkings of parent nodes, while the matching of a function node needs checking $B = [3-5]$ parent nodes. But the difference of throughput is indeed very little, which means the performance is still largely decided by the number of non-function nodes. Figure 9(b) compares the throughput between graphs with and without weight on edges. It can be seen that the performance of these two types of graphs are very close to each other. Processing of the two cases are identical for backtrack-free data, except the calculation of time requirement, whose influence on performance is almost neglectable.

**Backtrack.** In this section, we examine how backtrack affects the overall performance.

We know that backtrack happens at a node when: 1) matching instance of the node is too "old" and prevents its children from being matched by future input nodes, 2) the node is negated, and we check whether it has any candidate that can't be negated (Section 5.3). In order to make backtrack happen in test data, we profile the test data in three aspects, as shown in Table 5. First, we set the number of nodes that need to be backtracked, $N_b$. For example, suppose we have a graph as in Figure 6. Now $n_{e_1.T_s}$ and $n_{e_2.T_s}$ have been matched by instances at time 1 and 3. A node mapped to $n_{e_3.T_s}$ arrives at time 6. Given $e_3.T_s <= e_2.T_s + 2$, $n_{e_2.T_s}$ has to be backtracked. However, time of its first candidate instance is 4, which can not match $n_{e_2.T_s}$ as long as time of the instance at $n_{e_1.T_s}$ is 1. So backtrack from $n_{e_1.T_s}$ is recursively called. Second, we select number of times that backtrack happen in a test data, $T$. Thirdly, we can also tune the percentage of test data in need of backtrack, $W$. Assume $T$ and $N_b$ are uniformly distributed over their domains $D_T$, $D_{N_b}$, then the expected total number of non-function nodes checked for a given percentage $W$ in one matching process would be

$E(N_{total}) = N + W * \sum_{T_i \in D_T} T_i/|D_T| * \sum_{N_{b_i} \in D_{N_b}} N_{b_i}/|D_{N_b}|$

We set $N = 12, 24$, $P = 0.3$, and generate 2 queries for each $N$ and $P$ combination. Then for each query, and a value from $W$, we generate 10000 groups of test data. Throughput result is in Figure 9(c). When $W = 0$, no test data needs to be backtracked; when $W = 1$, all the test windows have to backtrack for $T = [1, 4]$ times. For example, when $N = 12$, the total expected number of nodes backtracked when $W = 1$ in a graph is $N_{total} = 24.5$, which is around twice of $N_{total} = 12$ for $W = 0$. We can see from the figure, the throughput of $W = 1$ is roughly around half of $W = 0$. This observation again demonstrates that the processing rate in our system is almost constant, and the throughput is mostly decided by the number of processed nodes in a graph.

## 7 Conclusion

In this paper, we presented a formal discussion on spatio-temporal events detection in multimedia communication systems. We analyzed the challenges, defined the model, and proposed techniques to solve the problem. A spatial filter scheme that can effectively prune unrelated events is designed. Also, we implemented the graph matching algorithm that is able to detect temporal relationship efficiently. Experiments prove that our work has large throughput ability as well as supporting complex semantic events. In future, we plan to incorporate complex spatial relationships into the semantic of complex events. Also, Kleene closure could be introduced to represent more complex temporal relationships. With such extension on semantics, careful improvement on processing techniques should also be designed. Besides, optimizations for multi-query processing is one of our future work as well.

## Acknowledgements

Xiaoyan Yang and Beng Chin Ooi were supported by Singapore NRF grant R-252-000-376-279.

## References

1. Chandrasekaran, S., Cooper, O., Deshpande, A., Franklin, M.J., Hellerstein, J.M., Hong, W., Krishnamurthy, S., Madden, S., Reiss, F., Shah, M.A.: Telegraphcq: Continuous dataflow processing. In: SIGMOD Conference, p. 668 (2003)
2. Arasu, A., Babcock, B., Babu, S., Datar, M., Ito, K., Nishizawa, I., Rosenstein, J., Widom, J.: Stream: The stanford stream data manager. In: SIGMOD Conference, p. 665 (2003)
3. Agrawal, J., Diao, Y., Gyllstrom, D., Immerman, N.: Efficient pareoattern matching over event streams. In: SIGMOD Conference, pp. 147–160 (2008)
4. Demers, A., Gehrke, J., Hong, M., Riedewald, M., White, W.: Towards expressive publish/subscribe systems. In: Ioannidis, Y., Scholl, M.H., Schmidt, J.W., Matthes, F., Hatzopoulos, M., Böhm, K., Kemper, A., Grust, T., Böhm, C. (eds.) EDBT 2006. LNCS, vol. 3896, pp. 627–644. Springer, Heidelberg (2006)

5. Mei, Y., Madden, S.: Zstream: a cost-based query processor for composite event detection. In: SIGMOD Conference (2009)
6. Luckham, D.: Complex event processing, http://complexevents.com
7. Singh, V.K., Pirsiavash, H., Rishabh, I., Jain, R.: Towards environment-to-environment (e2e) multimedia communication systems. Multimedia Tools Appl. 44(3), 361–388 (2009)
8. Rishabh, I., Singh, V., Pirsiavash, H., Jain, R.: Environment to environment (e2e) communication systems for collaborative work. In: Poster session: Computer Supported Cooperative Work (2008)
9. Singh, V.K., Pirsiavash, H., Rishabh, I., Jain, R.: Towards environment-to-environment (e2e) multimedia communication systems. In: SAME 2008: Proceeding of the 1st ACM international workshop on Semantic ambient media experiences (2008)
10. Cisco: Telepresence-cisco systems, http://www.cisco.com/en/US/netsol/ns669/networking_solutions_solution_segment_home.html
11. Sweden, I.C.: Skyview surveillance application, http://www.instrumentcontrol.se/index.php/products/skyviewsurveillance
12. Hellerstein, J.M., Condie, T., Garofalakis, M.N., Loo, B.T., Maniatis, P., Roscoe, T., Taft, N.: Public health for the internet (phi). In: CIDR, pp. 332–340 (2007)
13. Chakravarthy, S., Krishnaprasad, V., Anwar, E., Kim, S.K.: Composite events for active databases: Semantics, contexts and detection. In: VLDB 1994: Proceedings of the 20th International Conference on Very Large Data Bases, San Francisco, CA, USA, pp. 606–617 (1994)
14. Allen, J.F.: Maintaining knowledge about temporal intervals. Commun. ACM 26(11), 832–843 (1983)
15. Gatziu, S., Fritschi, H., Vaduva, A.: Samos an active object-oriented database system: Manual. Technical report (1996)
16. Gehani, N.H., Jagadish, H.V., Shmueli, O.: Event specification in an active object-oriented database. In: SIGMOD 1992: Proceedings of the 1992 ACM SIGMOD international conference on Management of data, pp. 81–90. ACM, New York (1992)
17. Zimmer, D.: On the semantics of complex events in active database management systems. In: ICDE 1999: Proceedings of the 15th International Conference on Data Engineering, p. 392. IEEE Computer Society, Washington (1999)
18. Aguilera, M.K., Strom, R.E., Sturman, D.C., Astley, M., Chandra, T.D.: Matching events in a content-based subscription system. In: PODC, pp. 53–61 (1999)
19. Fabret, F., Jacobsen, H.A., Llirbat, F., Pereira, J., Ross, K.A., Shasha, D.: Filtering algorithms and implementation for very fast publish/subscribe. In: SIGMOD Conference, pp. 115–126 (2001)
20. Cherniack, M., Balakrishnan, H., Balazinska, M., Carney, D., Çetintemel, U., Xing, Y., Zdonik, S.B.: Scalable distributed stream processing. In: CIDR (2003)
21. Lefebvre, S., Hoppe, H.: Perfect spatial hashing. In: SIGGRAPH 2006: ACM SIGGRAPH 2006 Papers, pp. 579–588. ACM, New York (2006)
22. Teschner, M., Heidelberger, B., Müller, M., Pomerantes, D., Gross, M.H.: Optimized spatial hashing for collision detection of deformable objects. In: VMV, pp. 47–54 (2003)
23. Dechter, R., Meiri, I., Pearl, J.: Temporal constraint networks. Artif. Intell. 49(1-3), 61–95 (1991)
24. Bliek, C., Sam-Haroud, D.: Path consistency on triangulated constraint graphs. In: IJCAI, pp. 456–461 (1999)
25. Spatio-Temporal Event Stream Processings in Multimedia Communication Systems. Technical Report, http://www.comp.nus.edu.sg/~yangxia2/ep-tr.pdf

# Stratified Reservoir Sampling over Heterogeneous Data Streams

Mohammed Al-Kateb and Byung Suk Lee

Department of Computer Science, The University of Vermont, Burlington VT, USA
{malkateb,bslee}@cs.uvm.edu

**Abstract.** *Reservoir sampling* is a well-known technique for random sampling over data streams. In many streaming applications, however, an input stream may be naturally *heterogeneous*, i.e., composed of sub-streams whose statistical properties may also vary considerably. For this class of applications, the conventional reservoir sampling technique does not guarantee a statistically sufficient number of tuples from each sub-stream to be included in the reservoir, and this can cause a damage on the statistical quality of the sample. In this paper, we deal with this heterogeneity problem by *stratifying* the reservoir sample among the underlying sub-streams. We particularly consider situations in which the stratified reservoir sample is needed to obtain reliable estimates at the level of either the entire data stream or individual sub-streams. The first challenge in this stratification is to achieve an optimal allocation of a fixed-size reservoir to individual sub-streams. The second challenge is to adaptively adjust the allocation as sub-streams appear in, or disappear from, the input stream and as their statistical properties change over time. We present a stratified reservoir sampling algorithm designed to meet these challenges, and demonstrate through experiments the superior sample quality and the adaptivity of the algorithm.

## 1 Introduction

Sampling is the process of selecting some members of a population for the purpose of deriving estimates of the population using only the selected members [10] [14]. The basic sampling scheme is *random sampling* in which each member of the population has an identical chance of being in the sample. Random sampling usually generates consistent and unbiased estimates of the original population, and it has been used in a wide range of application domains such as approximate query processing (e.g., [23]) and data stream processing (e.g., [20]).

For applications in which data are available in the form of an incoming *stream*, sampling has two major challenges. First, the size of the data stream is usually unknown a priori and, therefore, it is not possible to predetermine the sample fraction (or sampling rate) before the sampling starts. Second, in most cases the data arriving in a stream cannot be stored and, therefore, have to be processed sequentially in a single pass. A technique commonly used to overcome these challenges is the *reservoir sampling* [15] [22], which selects a random sample of a fixed size without replacement from a stream of an unknown size.

M. Gertz and B. Ludäscher (Eds.): SSDBM 2010, LNCS 6187, pp. 621–639, 2010.

**Table 1.** Mean and standard deviation of bidding amount of two FCC auctions [2]

| Auction Item | Mean | Std dev |
|---|---|---|
| FCC 700 MHz Guard Band | 73964.29 | 24591.07 |
| FCC Analog TV Stations | 263800.00 | 39115.21 |

For many streaming applications, however, we make two key observations. First, an input stream may be composed of *sub-streams* that correspond to different groups whose statistical properties, specifically *mean* and *variance*, may vary significantly. We refer to this class of data streams as *heterogeneous* data streams. Second, the application may naturally demand using a sample to derive estimates at the level of either the entire data stream or individual sub-streams.

Consider, for example, the application of the Federal Communications Commission (FCC) auction system [2] through which auctions for licenses of electromagnetic spectrum are conducted electronically over the Internet. In this application, an auction data stream is composed of *multiple sub-streams* each of which represents the biddings in a particular auction. Moreover, an auction data stream can be *heterogeneous*, as the mean and the variance of bidding amounts vary significantly from one auction to another depending on the type of an auction item (see Table 1). From the application standpoint, the scope of sampling differs in two ways. On one hand, a sample of *all* bidding amounts can be used to perform a set of analyses on the entire auction data stream, e.g., the median of bidding amounts across all auctions. On the other hand, a sample of the bidding amounts in *individual* auctions can be utilized to generate the estimate for each individual auction, e.g., the median of bidding amounts in each auction.

For such applications with heterogeneous data streams, the conventional reservoir sampling technique does not guarantee a statistically sufficient number of tuples to be included in the reservoir for *every* sub-stream. The inevitable consequence of this is a damage to the statistical quality of the sample. Furthermore, the technique is only used for the purpose of maintaining one random sample of a fixed size from all tuples seen so far in an input stream. Therefore, it is not suitable when multiple random sub-samples are needed to obtain the estimates of individual sub-streams. In other words, it is not appropriate for the purpose of producing a *sub-sample* stored in a *sub-reservoir* for each *sub-stream.*

The research literature addresses an analogous heterogeneity problem in the context of database systems through *stratified sampling* [9] [13]. In this sampling scheme [10], a population is initially clustered into homogenous disjoint strata. Then, a sample is taken randomly from each stratum. Stratified sampling is particularly preferred if the statistical properties of strata vary considerably [14]. Statistical properties are typically mean and variance or, equivalently, *coefficient of variation (CV)* which is the ratio of the standard deviation to the mean.

In no existing work, however, *data stream* has been the target of a stratified sampling algorithm. When applied to data streams, stratified sampling inherits the challenges of random sampling over a data stream and poses the following additional challenges. First, usually neither the number of sub-streams nor their statistical properties are known in advance. Thus, it is not possible to optimally allocate a stratified sample to sub-streams prior to sampling. Second, the membership of a data stream and the statistical properties of the member sub-streams may change over time. Hence, the allocation should have the ability to adapt to these changes.

In this paper, we address the problem of maintaining a stratified reservoir sample over heterogeneous data streams for applications that demand reliable estimates at the level of either the entire data stream or individual sub-streams. There are two specific problems to be solved. The first one is to allocate a given fixed-size reservoir optimally among sub-streams, and the second one is to adjust the allocation as new sub-streams appear or existing sub-streams disappear (e.g., due to punctuation) or their statistical properties change over time.

To solve the allocation problem, we adopt a statistical method known as the *power allocation* [6]. By controlling what is called the *power* parameter, this method allows to allocate a given sample size optimally [6] when the estimates are required from the data stream or from the individual sub-streams. To adapt to changes in data stream membership and sub-streams statistical properties, *uniformity* of the sample of each sub-stream should be maintained as the corresponding sample size changes over time. For this we use a simple variation of the *adaptive-size reservoir sampling* technique (from our prior work) [5], which maintains the uniformity of a reservoir sample with a required degree of confidence after the reservoir size is adjusted in the middle of sampling.

Two sets of experiments have been conducted using synthetic and real datasets. In the first set of experiments, we compare the stratified and the conventional reservoir sampling algorithms with respect to the sample quality – specifically, sample *accuracy* and sample *precision*[1] – for different number of input sub-streams and for varying degree of heterogeneity among the sub-streams. The results of this experiment show that the stratified algorithm outperforms the conventional algorithm by nearly an order of magnitude in both sample quality metrics. In the second set of experiments, we examine how adaptively the stratified reservoir sampling algorithm adjusts the allocation of the fixed reservoir sample size. The results of this experiment show the stratified reservoir sampling quickly adjusting the sub-sample sizes when the $CV$s of the member sub-streams change and when a new sub-stream appears or an exiting sub-stream expires.

Main contributions of this paper can be summarized as follows.

- It identifies and motivates the problem of stratified reservoir sampling over heterogeneous data streams.
- It presents an algorithm for maintaining a stratified reservoir sample over a heterogeneous data stream when the sample is used to obtain either one estimate from the whole stream or multiple estimates from the sub-streams.
- It empirically shows the superiority of the proposed algorithm (with respect to the precision and accuracy of the sample) and demonstrates its adaptivity.

---

[1] Sample accuracy is the degree of closeness of the estimate to its true value. Sample precision is the degree to which the estimates from different samples taken from the same data set vary from one another.

The rest of the paper is organized as follows. Section 2 gives an overview of the reservoir sampling and stratified sampling techniques. Section 3 formulates the research problem and presents the proposed stratified sampling algorithm. Section 4 presents and discusses the experiment results. Section 5 reviews related work. Section 6 concludes this paper and suggests future work.

# 2 Background

This section provides backgrounds on reservoir sampling and stratified sampling.

## 2.1 Reservoir Sampling

*Reservoir sampling* [15] [22] is a technique for selecting a uniform random sample of a fixed size without replacement from an input stream of an unknown size. Initially, the algorithm (see Algorithm 1) places all tuples in a reservoir $r$ until the reservoir (of the size of $|r|$ tuples) becomes full. After that, each $k^{th}$ tuple is accepted for inclusion in the reservoir with the probability of $\frac{|r|}{k}$ and an accepted tuple replaces a randomly selected tuple in the reservoir.

---

**Algorithm 1.** *Conventional Reservoir Sampling* (CRS)

**Require:** $|r|$ // *size of a reservoir r*
$k = 0$
**for** each tuple arriving from the input stream **do**
  $k = k + 1$
  **if** $k \leq |r|$ **then**
    add the tuple to the reservoir
  **else**
    decide with the probability $\frac{|r|}{k}$ whether to accept the tuple
    **if** the tuples is accepted **then**
      replace a randomly selected tuple in the reservoir with the accepted tuple
    **end if**
  **end if**
**end for**

---

Reservoir sampling guarantees that a reservoir always holds a *uniform* sample of the $k$ tuples seen so far [15]. After the $k^{th}$ tuple arrives, each of the $k$ tuples has the equal probability $\frac{|r|}{k}$ to be included in the reservoir. That is, each of the $\binom{k}{|r|}$ different possible samples has the same probability $\frac{1}{\binom{k}{|r|}}$ to represent $r$.

## 2.2 Stratified Sampling

Stratified sampling [10] [14] is a sampling scheme in which a heterogeneous population $R$ is initially clustered into $n$ disjoint homogeneous strata, $R_1$, $R_2$, ..., $R_i$, ..., $R_n$, and then a sample $r_i$ is taken randomly from each stratum $R_i$. Every member of $R$ should belong to one and only one stratum (i.e., $R_i \cap R_j = \phi$ $(i \neq j)$ and $R_1 \cup R_2 \cup ... \cup R_i \cup ... \cup R_n = R$). A stratified sample of a given size is expected to have higher statistical precision (i.e., lower sampling error) than a random sample of the same size taken from the same population when the statistical properties (i.e., mean and variance) of strata vary considerably.

Allocating a given sample size $|r|$ to different strata is a fundamental issue in stratified sampling. Obviously, the allocation is under the constraint on the the sum of the sub-sample sizes assigned to individual strata, $|r_1|, |r_2|, ..., |r_n|$:

$$\sum_{i=1}^{n} |r_i| \leq |r| \tag{1}$$

There are two allocation methods commonly used for a stratified sample, the *proportional* allocation [14] and the *Neyman* allocation [14]. Under the *proportional* allocation, the sample size of each stratum is determined in proportion to the size of the stratum:

$$|r_i| = |r| \times \frac{|R_i|}{|R|} \tag{2}$$

where $R$ denotes the whole population, $R_i$ denotes a stratum, and $|R|$ and $|R_i|$ denote the sizes of $R$ and $R_i$, respectively. Under the *Neyman* allocation, the sample size of each stratum is determined in proportion to the standard deviation as well as the size of the stratum:

$$|r_i| = |r| \times \frac{\sigma_i \times |R_i|}{\sum_{j=1}^{n} \sigma_j \times |R_j|} \tag{3}$$

where $\sigma_i$ denotes the standard deviation of $R_i$.

## 3 Stratified Reservoir Sampling

The proposed stratified reservoir sampling algorithm is described in this section. As mentioned in Section 1, there are two technical issues to resolve in the proposed algorithm: (1) determining the optimal sizes of sub-samples for each sub-stream, and (2) maintaining the uniformity of sub-samples as their sizes change. In this section, we first formulate the problem formally in Section 3.1 and discuss our approaches to the two technical issues in Sections 3.2 and 3.3 and then summarize them into one algorithm in Section 3.4.

### 3.1 Problem Formulation

The problem of allocating a fixed-size reservoir to sub-streams is an adaptive optimization problem formulated as follows. An input data stream $S$ consists of $n$ sub-streams $S_1$, $S_2$, ..., $S_n$. Each sub-stream $S_i$ $(i = 1, 2, ..., n)$ is a sequence of tuples $s_{i_1}, s_{i_2}, ...$ such that $S_i \cap S_j = \phi$ $(i \neq j)$ and $\cup_{S_i} = S$. Given a total available size of $|r|$ tuples in a reservoir $r$, the objective is to allocate $|r|$ *optimally* among the $n$ sub-streams subject to the following constraint at any point in time $t$:

$$\sum_{i=1}^{n} |r_i(t)| \leq |r| \tag{4}$$

where $r_i(t)$ denotes the sample allocated for $S_i$ at time point $t$ and $|r_i(t)|$ denotes its size. The optimality criterion is the sample quality, and there is some minor

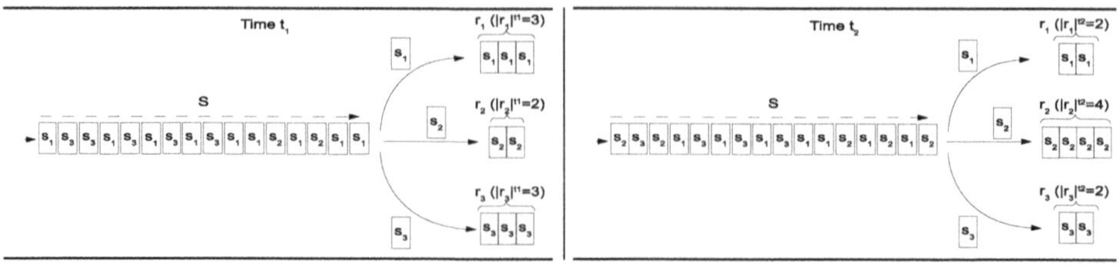


**Fig. 1.** An illustration of stratified reservoir sampling

difference in the specific criteria depending on which purpose (i.e., one whole sample or individual sub-samples) the sample is used for (details in Section 3.2).

Figure 1 illustrates the processing of stratified reservoir sampling. It shows that the sizes of sub-samples $r_1$, $r_2$, and $r_3$ have respectively decreased, increased, and decreased from $t_1$ to $t_2$ while the same total sample size remains the same.

### 3.2 Optimal Stratified-Reservoir Allocation

For the flexible aim of generating estimates from the whole sample or from separate sub-samples, the commonly used *Neyman allocation* is not adequate enough since it is geared for the former case only. To overcome this limit, we adopt another statistical method, known as *power allocation*, [6]. The power allocation method provides a way to allocate the sample to different strata whether the sample is used to generate a single estimate for the underlying population as a whole or multiple estimates separately for each of the underlying strata. This flexibility is enabled by a control parameter called the *power* of allocation.

Formally, the size of a sample, $|r_i|$, assigned to a stratum $R_i$ is computed as

$$|r_i| = |r| \times \frac{\sigma_i \times \left( \left( \sum_{j=1}^{|R_i|} y_{ij} \right)^q \right) / \left( \frac{\sum_{j=1}^{|R_i|} y_{ij}}{|R_i|} \right)}{\sum_{k=1}^{n} \sigma_k \times \left( \left( \sum_{j=1}^{|R_k|} y_{kj} \right)^q \right) / \left( \frac{\sum_{j=1}^{|R_k|} y_{kj}}{|R_k|} \right)} \tag{5}$$

where $y_{ij}$ denotes the sampling attribute value of the $j^{th}$ member in $R_i$, $\sigma_i$ denotes the standard deviation of the sampling attribute values in $R_i$, and $q$ denotes the power of allocation.

When the stratified sample is used of the *entire population*, power allocation aims to minimize the sampling variance of the estimator of the whole stratified sample, where the sampling variance is formulated as

$$\sum_{i=1}^{n} \sigma_i \times \frac{|R_i| \times (|R_i| - |r_i|)}{|r_i|} \tag{6}$$

In this case, it achieves an optimal allocation by setting the power value to 1. Note that this results in the exact Neyman allocation, that is

$$|r_i| = |r| \times \frac{\sigma_i \times \left( \left( \sum_{j=1}^{|R_i|} y_{ij} \right)^1 \right) / \left( \frac{\sum_{j=1}^{|R_i|} y_{ij}}{|R_i|} \right)}{\sum_{k=1}^{n} \sigma_k \times \left( \left( \sum_{j=1}^{|R_k|} y_{kj} \right)^1 \right) / \left( \frac{\sum_{j=1}^{|R_k|} y_{kj}}{|R_k|} \right)} = |r| \times \frac{\sigma_i \times |R_i|}{\sum_{k=1}^{n} \sigma_k \times |R_k|} \tag{7}$$

When the stratified sample is used at the level of *individual strata*, Neyman allocation may cause the sampling variances of some strata to be larger than those achievable by considering strata individually. Power allocation's remedy for this deficiency is to allocate sub-sample sizes in proportion to CV of each stratum, which is achieved by setting the power to 0. In this case,

$$|r_i| = |r| \times \frac{\sigma_i \times \left(\left(\sum_{j=1}^{|R_i|} y_{ij}\right)^0\right) / \left(\frac{\sum_{j=1}^{|R_i|} y_{ij}}{|R_i|}\right)}{\sum_{k=1}^{n} \sigma_k \times \left(\left(\sum_{j=1}^{|R_k|} y_{kj}\right)^0\right) / \left(\frac{\sum_{j=1}^{|R_k|} y_{kj}}{|R_k|}\right)} = |r| \times \frac{\sigma_i / \left(\frac{\sum_{j=1}^{|R_i|} y_{ij}}{|R_i|}\right)}{\sum_{k=1}^{n} \sigma_k / \left(\frac{\sum_{j=1}^{|R_k|} y_{kj}}{|R_k|}\right)} \tag{8}$$

Applying this power allocation to data stream gives the following formula for determining sub-sample sizes at any point in time $t$.

$$|r_i(t)| = |r| \times \frac{\sigma_i(t) \times \left(\left(\sum_{j=1}^{|S_i(t)|} y_{ij}\right)^q\right) / \left(\frac{\sum_{j=1}^{|S_i(t)|} y_{ij}}{|S_i(t)|}\right)}{\sum_{k=1}^{n} \sigma_k(t) \times \left(\left(\sum_{j=1}^{|S_k(t)|} y_{kj}\right)^q\right) / \left(\frac{\sum_{j=1}^{|S_k(t)|} y_{kj}}{|S_k(t)|}\right)} \tag{9}$$

where $|r_i(t)|$ denotes the size of a sub-sample allocated for a sub-stream $S_i$ at time point $t$, $\sigma_i(t)$ denotes the running standard deviation[2] of the sampling attribute values in $S_i$ up to $t$, and $|S_i(t)|$ denotes the number of tuples processed up to $t$ from $S_i$.

### 3.3 Maintaining Sample Uniformity

As mentioned in Section 1, we use the *adaptive-size reservoir sampling* algorithm (ARS) [5] (see Algorithm 2) to maintain the uniformity of each sub-sample as its size decreases or increases as a result of optimal allocation.

ARS is based on the concept of uniformity confidence ($UC$), which refers to the probability that a sampling algorithm generates a uniform random sample after the sample size changes in the middle of sampling. A theoretical study in [5] concludes that if the reservoir size decreases, the sample uniformity can be maintained in the *reduced* reservoir with 100% confidence by randomly evicting tuples from the original reservoir.

In contrast, if the reservoir size increases, it is not possible to attain 100% confidence in the *enlarged* reservoir. It is possible, however, to ensure the uniformity confidence above a given threshold. The steps are as follows. First, ARS finds the minimum number of incoming tuples that should be considered to refill the enlarged reservoir such that the resulting uniformity confidence exceeds the given threshold (Equation 10). Then, it decides probabilistically on the number of tuples to retain in the enlarged reservoir and randomly evicts the remaining

[2] Running standard deviation is required for the calculations in the power allocation method. For this, we use an efficient recurrence relation [21], known as the *updating* method, that is capable of calculating the standard deviation in a single scan of the data and providing precise calculation even when the data values are relatively large.

number of tuples (Equation 11). Eventually, it fills the room available in the enlarged reservoir from the incoming tuples.

$$UC(k, |r|, \delta, m) = \frac{\sum_{x=\max\{0,(|r|+\delta)-m\}}^{|r|} \binom{k}{x}\binom{m}{|r|+\delta-x}}{\binom{k+m}{|r|+\delta}} \times 100 \tag{10}$$

$$p(x) = \frac{\binom{k}{x}\binom{m}{|r|+\delta-x}}{\binom{k+m}{|r|+\delta}} \tag{11}$$

In this paper, we use a simple variation of ARS in which the number of incoming tuples required to refill an enlarged reservoir is computed as[3]

$$m = \frac{\delta \times k}{|r|} \tag{12}$$

**Algorithm 2.** *Adaptive-size Reservoir Sampling* (ARS)

```
Require: |r| // size of a reservoir r
         k // number of tuples seen so far
         ζ // uniformity confidence threshold
while true do
   while the reservoir size |r| does not change do
      continue sampling using CRS (Algorithm 1)
   end while
   if reservoir size is decreased by δ then
      randomly evicts δ tuples from the reservoir
   else
      // i.e., reservoir size is increased by δ
      find the minimum value of m (Equation 10) such that UC >= ζ
      flip a biased coin to decide on x, the number of tuples to retain in the reservoir (Equation 11)
      randomly evict |r| − x tuples from the reservoir
      select δ + |r| − x tuples from the incoming m tuples using CRS (Algorithm 1)
   end if
end while
```

### 3.4 Stratified Reservoir Sampling Algorithm

Based on the discussions above, our stratified reservoir sampling algorithm works as shown in Algorithm 3. In this algorithm, the input stream $S$ is treated as a *set* of sub-streams $S_1$, $S_2$, etc, and $ALG_i$ refers to the sampling algorithm currently in use for the sub-stream $S_i$.

In the initialization phase of the algorithm (Lines 1-15), the first $|r|$ tuples in a data stream $S$ are added to the reservoir while the running statistics of sub-streams are being updated (Lines 3-4). The sampling starts using CRS for all new sub-streams (Lines 5-8) and, once the reservoir becomes full, the size of a sub-reservoir is initialized in proportion to the number of tuple seen so far from the corresponding sub-stream (Lines 13-15).

In the sampling phase (Lines 16-41), each time a new tuple $s$ arrives from a sub-stream $S_i$, the algorithm decides to sample $s$ using CRS if $S_i$ is a new

[3] The rationale for computing the value of $m$ in this way is a simple heuristic that, since $r$ has been filled from $k$ tuples so far, the room for additional $\delta$ tuples should be filled in proportion to $\frac{k}{|r|}$, that is, $\delta \times \frac{k}{|r|}$ tuples. This heuristic facilitates the use of the ARS by eliminating the need to conduct an expensive search to find the optimum value of $m$ using Equation 10, which is an inverse-mapping problem.

**Algorithm 3.** Stratified Reservoir Sampling *(SRS)*

```
Require: |r| // size of a reservoir r
         q // power of allocation
         Δ // sample reallocation time interval
   // ***************INITIALIZATION PHASE***************
1: for each new tuple s arriving from a sub-stream S_i do
2:    if reservoir r is not full then
3:       add s to r
4:       update the running statistics of S_i
5:       if S_i ∉ S // i.e., S_i is a new sub-stream then
6:          S = S U {S_i}
7:          ALG_i = CRS // start sampling using CRS
8:       end if
9:    else
10:      break // go to line 13
11:   end if
12: end for
13: for each S_i ∈ S do
14:    |r_i| = size(S_i) // initialize sub-reservoir sizes
15: end for
   // ****************SAMPLING PHASE****************
16: while true do
17:    for each new tuple s arriving from a sub-stream S_i do
18:       if S_i ∉ S // i.e., S_i is a new sub-stream then
19:          S = S U {S_i}
20:          ALG_i = CRS // start sampling using CRS
21:       end if
22:       sample s into the sub-reservoir r_i using ALG_i // either CRS or ARS
23:       update the running statistics of S_i
24:       if the time interval Δ has passed then
25:          break // go to line 28 to calculate sub-reservoir sizes
26:       end if
27:    end for
28:    for each sample r_i allocated to sub-stream S_i do
29:       if S_i expires from S // e.g., due to a punctuation then
30:          S = S - {S_i}
31:          |r_i(t)| = 0
32:       else
33:          calculate |r_i(t)| for S_i using Equation 9 with the given value of q
34:          if |r_i(t)| has changed as a result then
35:             ALG_i = ARS (Algorithm 2)
36:          else
37:             ALG_i = CRS (Algorithm 1)
38:          end if
39:       end if
40:    end for
41: end while
```

sub-stream (Lines 18-21). Then, the algorithm samples $s$ into $r_i$ using the corresponding sampling algorithm (i.e., either CRS or ARS) while updating its running statistics (Lines 22-23 and 28-40). Periodically, the algorithm reallocates the reservoir size optimally among sub-streams (Lines 24-26). Specifically, if a sub-stream has expired from the input stream (e.g., due to the presence of a punctuation), the memory of the sub-reservoir of that sub-stream is released (Lines 29-31). Otherwise, the algorithm calculates the optimal sample size for the sub-stream (Line 33). If the size of $r_i$ changes as a result, then the algorithm switches over to ARS to continue sampling the incoming $S_i$ tuples (Lines 34-35). Note that ARS quickly resumes CRS once the size adjustment is handled. If the size of $r_i$ does not change, then the algorithm samples the incoming $S_i$ tuples using CRS (Line 37).

# 4 Performance Evaluation

We conduct two sets of experiments. The first set of experiments evaluates the performance of the *stratified reservoir sampling (SRS)* algorithm against the *conventional reservoir sampling (CRS)* algorithm with respect to the sample quality. The second set demonstrates the adaptivity of the SRS to the changes of data stream membership and the statistical characteristics of member sub-streams. In this section, the design and setup of the experiments are described in Section 4.1 and the results of the experiments are presented in Section 4.2.

## 4.1 Experiment Design and Setup

Intuitively, two factors affect the performances of algorithms over a data stream consisting of multiple heterogeneous sub-streams: the number of sub-streams and the degree of heterogeneity among the sub-streams. These two parameters are thus used in the comparisons between SRS and CRS.

**Performance Metrics.** The two kinds of sample quality mentioned in Section 1 are used to compare the performances of SRS and CRS: *accuracy* and *precision*. Specifically, we use the *error in estimated mean (EEM)*, the difference between the mean value estimated from the sample and the actual mean value, as the metric of sample accuracy. The estimated mean for a random sample is calculated as

$$\frac{1}{|r|} \times \sum_{i=1}^{|r|} y_i \tag{13}$$

where $y_i$ denotes the value of the sampling attribute of the $i^{th}$ tuple in a sample $r$ [10]. Extended from it, the estimated mean for a stratified sample is calculated as

$$\sum_{i=1}^{|n|} \left( \frac{|S_i|}{|S|} \times \left( \frac{1}{|r_i|} \sum_{j=1}^{|r_i|} y_{ij} \right) \right) \tag{14}$$

where $y_{ij}$ denotes the value of sampling attribute of the $j^{th}$ tuple in a sub-sample $r_i$ [10].

On the other hand, we use the *standard error (SE)*, a common statistical quantification of the sample precision, as the metric of sample precision. The SE is a measure of how precise the sample is; the larger the SE, the lower the statistical precision of the sample is, and vice versa. The SE for a random sample is computed as

$$\sqrt{\left( \left( 1 - \left( \frac{|r|}{|S|} \right) \right) \times \left( \frac{\sigma^2}{|S|} \right) \right)} \tag{15}$$

where $\sigma^2$ denotes the variance of the entire sample [10]. Extended from it, the SE for a stratified sample is computed as

$$\frac{1}{|S|} \times \sqrt{\sum_{i=1}^{n} |S_i|^2 \times \left( 1 - \frac{|r_i|}{|S_i|} \right) \times \left( \frac{{\sigma_i}^2}{|r_i|} \right)} \tag{16}$$

where ${\sigma_i}^2$ denotes the variance of the $i^{th}$ sub-sample [10].

**Datasets.** Experiments are conducted using both synthetic and real datasets. Synthetic datasets are used to examine the effect of the statistical characteristics of an input data stream on the quality of the sample. Now, we describe the process of synthetic dataset generation and outline the profile of the real datasets.

***Synthetic Datasets.*** A synthetic data stream is generated bottom up, that is, by first generating sub-streams and then combining them to form one stream. The sampling attribute value in each sub-stream $S_i$ has the *doubly-truncated normal distribution* [19], i.e., the normal distribution with bounded lower and upper ends. Formally, if a random variable $X \backsim N(\mu, \sigma)$ has the normal distribution such that $\infty \leq l \leq X \leq u \leq \infty$, then $X$ is considered to have a doubly-truncated normal distribution with the probability density function

$$pdf\,(x;\mu,\sigma,l,u) = \frac{\frac{1}{\sigma}\phi\left(\frac{x-\mu}{\sigma}\right)}{\Phi\left(\frac{u-\mu}{\sigma}\right) - \Phi\left(\frac{l-\mu}{\sigma}\right)} \tag{17}$$

where $\phi(x)$ is the probability density function of the standard normal distribution, and $\Phi(x)$ is its cumulative distribution function [19]. This distribution is used in many applications like inventory management and financial applications, in which the values are naturally constrained within a certain bound [16].

The datasets are synthesized from a different number of sub-streams ($n$) and with a varying degree of heterogeneity among the sub-streams (*DH*). *DH* is defined as the ratio of the *inter-sub-stream* variability to the *intra-sub-stream* variability. With the variability expressed in terms of *CV* [6], we define *DH* as the ratio of the *standard deviation* among the CVs of sub-streams ($\sigma_{[CV]}$) to the *average* of the CVs of sub-streams ($\mu_{[CV]}$). With the doubly-truncated normal distribution in place, we know that the standard deviation of the sampling attribute values of a sub-stream $S_i$ is bounded by half the range of these values. This means that each $CV_i$ is bounded within the range of 0 to 1. Consequently, *DH* is also bounded within the range of 0 to 1.

Given the values of $n$ and *DH*, the synthetic dataset generator works as follows. First, it sets the value of $\mu_{[CV]}$ to 0.5 (note $0 < \mu_{[CV]} \leq 1$) and calculates the value of $\sigma_{[CV]}$ accordingly. Second, it generates $n$ random numbers from a doubly-truncated normal distribution with $\mu_{[CV]}$, $\sigma_{[CV]}$, $l_{[CV]} = \mu_{[CV]} - \sigma_{[CV]}$, and $u_{[CV]} = \mu_{[CV]} + \sigma_{[CV]}$. The $n$ random numbers generated correspond to the *CV*s of the $n$ sub-streams. Third, for $S_i$, the synthetic dataset generator uses the value of $CV_i$ to assign the values of $\mu_{[S_i]}$ and $\sigma_{[S_i]}$ randomly such that $\frac{\sigma[S_i]}{\mu_{[S_i]}} = CV_i$. Finally, the generator produces the values of $S_i$ from a doubly-truncated normal distribution with $\mu_{[S_i]}$, $\sigma_{[S_i]}$, $l_i = \mu_{[S_i]} - \sigma_{[S_i]}$, and $u_i = \mu_{[S_i]} + \sigma_{[S_i]}$.

Figure 2 shows an example of different datasets with varying degree of heterogeneity. In this example, the number of sub-streams is 10 and the values of *DH* are set to 30%, 50%, and 70%. When *DH* is relatively low (e.g., 30% in Figure 2(a)), we see that most of the sub-streams have *wide* and *similar* spreads of sampling attribute values. The wide spread of each sub-stream indicates that the variability within each sub-stream is high, and the similar spreads among sub-streams indicates that the variability across sub-streams is low. These two combined indicate a low degree of heterogeneity in the entire stream. In

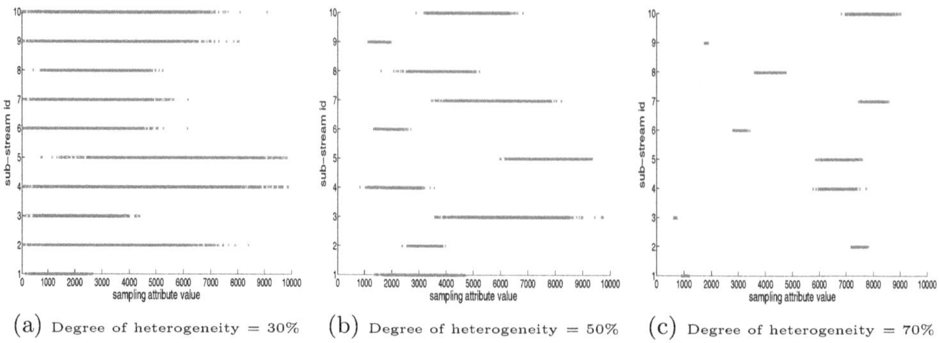


**Fig. 2.** Scatter plots of synthetic datasets with different degrees of heterogeneity

contrast, when the *DH* is relatively high (e.g., 70% in Figure 2(c)), we see that most sub-streams have narrow and dissimilar spreads of the sampling attribute values. This is the converse of the Figure 2(a) case above, and thus indicates a high degree of heterogeneity in the entire stream.

***Real Datasets.*** Two kinds of real datasets are used, one (SENS) in the wireless sensor networks application and one (AUCT) in the auction application.

- The SENS real dataset is weather measurements from sensors deployed through the Intel Berkeley Research lab to gather time-stamped topology information, along with humidity, temperature, light and voltage values [1]. SENS is a projection of this data on two attributes, *sensor mote id* and *temperature measurement* acquired from 55 motes. (Data from three motes have incomplete readings and thus have been discarded.). SENS is characterized with a *low* degree of heterogeneity. The low degree of heterogeneity among the temperature readings of different motes is due to the fact that temperatures of nearby regions are expected to be close to each other.
- The AUCT real dataset is for auctions conducted over the Internet through the Federal Communications Commission (FCC) [2]. The entire dataset consists of 55 auction sub-datasets. Each sub-dataset contains bidding information of one auction. We have merged the 55 auction sub-datasets into one single dataset. The order of tuples in the resulting dataset is shuffled and the resulting tuples are projected on two attributes, *auction ID* and *bidding amount.* AUCT is characterized with a *high* degree of heterogeneity. The high degree of heterogeneity of the bidding amounts is intuitive since the bidding amounts can vary to a large extent depending on the auction item.

### 4.2 Experiment Results

**Sample Quality.** In this set of experiments, we compare sample accuracy and precision between SRS and CRS. Given that SRS is meant to support both the case of using a sample to obtain the estimate of the entire data stream and the case of using a sample to obtain the estimates of individual sub-streams, experiments are done to report the results in both cases. We refer to the former case as the WHOLE-SAMPLE case and the latter case as the SUB-SAMPLE case[4]. In the SUB-SAMPLE case, the results are reported as the *average square* value of the sample quality metric used. The results of the experiments demonstrate that in both cases SRS outperforms CRS in sample accuracy as well as precision by nearly an order of magnitude.

***Whole-sample Case.*** Figures 3(a) and 3(b) show the SRS accuracy against the CRS accuracy using the synthetic datasets for different degree of heterogeneity and for different number of sub-streams, respectively. Figure 3(a) shows that the degree of heterogeneity has a major influence on the sample accuracy. For a low degree of heterogeneity, (e.g., 10%), we observe that there is only a minor improvement of SRS accuracy over CRS accuracy. The level of improvement, however, increases as the degree of heterogeneity increases. For a high degree of heterogeneity, (e.g., 70% or higher), we see that the SRS accuracy is higher than the CRS accuracy by more than an order of magnitude. The reason for this is that CRS does not consider any heterogeneity between sub-streams whereas SRS does. On the other hand, Figure 3(b) shows that the performance improvement of SRS over CRS is more or less constant regardless of the number of sub-streams. This makes sense because the accuracy of CRS is not affected by the number of sub-streams (Equation 13) and because the accuracy of SRS is primarily influenced by the size and the values of sub-streams (Equation 14).

Figures 4(a) and 4(b) show similar results for the sample precision by demonstrating that the degree of heterogeneity has dominant effect on the precision.

Figure 5 shows the results from using the real datasets AUCT and SENS. The results are consistent with the results from using the synthetic datasets. The figure shows that the improvement of SRS over CRS is higher for for the AUCT dataset than SENS with regard to both sample accuracy and sample precision. This is due to the higher degree of heterogeneity of the AUCT dataset.

***Sub-sample Case.*** Figures 6 and 7 show the results for sub-sample accuracy and sub-sample precision, respectively, using the synthetic dataset. These results report the average square value of EEM (for accuracy) and SE (for precision) per sub-sample. As we see in Figure 6(a), the sub-sample accuracy of SRS improves over the accuracy of CRS linearly with the degree of heterogeneity. Likewise, Figure 7(a) shows a similar trend for the sub-sample precision. From Figure 6(b) and Figure 7(b) we observe that the number of sub-streams is irrelevant to the performance of both SRS and CRS at the level of individual sub-samples.

The results from using the SENS and AUCT real datasets in Figure 8 are similar to those in Figures 6 and 7.

**SRS Adaptivity.** In this set of experiments, we demonstrate the adaptivity of the SRS by showing the change in the allocation of a stratified reservoir sample as

[4] In the experiments, $q$ is assigned the values of 1 and 0 for the WHOLE-SAMPLE case and the SUB-SAMPLE case, respectively. (Recall Section 3.2).

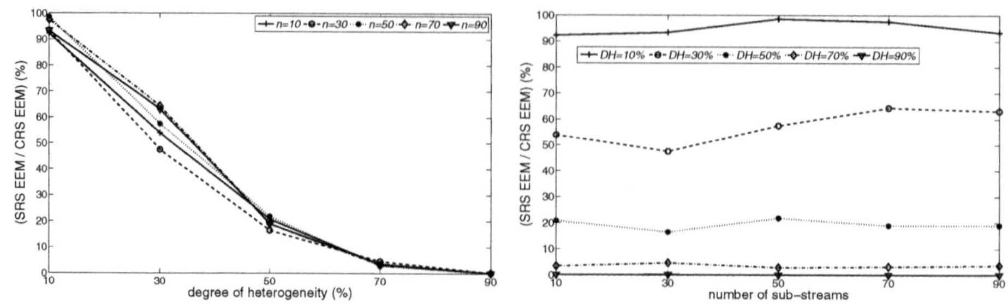


(a) Effect of the degree of heterogeneity (b) Effect of the number of sub-streams

**Fig. 3.** WHOLE-SAMPLE accuracy - synthetic datasets

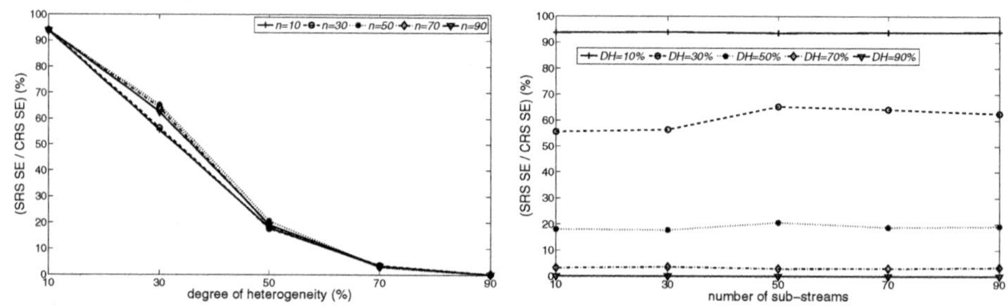


(a) Effect of the degree of heterogeneity (b) Effect of the number of sub-streams

**Fig. 4.** WHOLE-SAMPLE precision - synthetic datasets

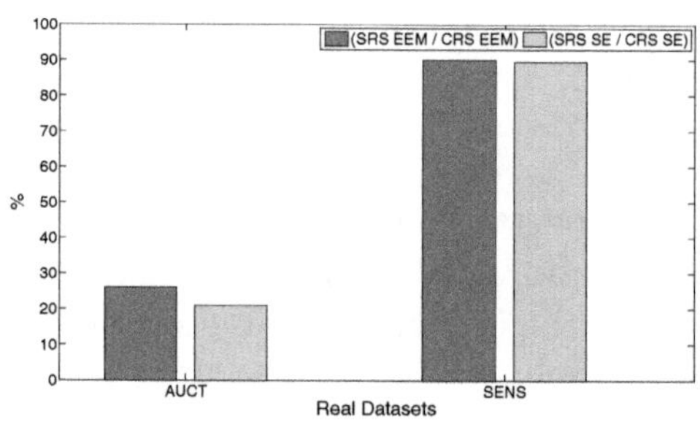


**Fig. 5.** WHOLE-SAMPLE accuracy and precision - real datasets

a new sub-stream appears in, or an exiting sub-stream expires from, the input stream (i.e., with respect to *data stream membership*) and as the statistical properties of individual sub-streams change over time (i.e., with respect to *sub-streams' stationariness*). Results presented in this section show the change in sub-reservoir sizes over time for five sub-streams synthetically generated and for five sub-streams selected from the AUCT and SENS real datasets. (Only five sub-streams are used for better visibility. Results for a larger number of sub-streams look similar.)

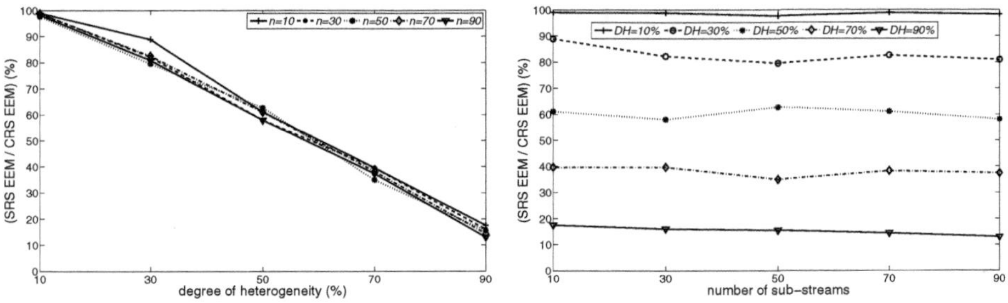


(a) Effect of the degree of heterogeneity (b) Effect of the number of sub-streams

**Fig. 6.** SUB-SAMPLE accuracy - synthetic datasets

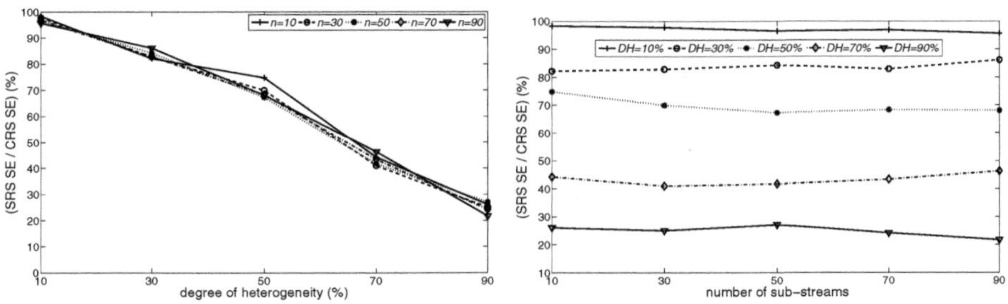


(a) Effect of the degree of heterogeneity (b) Effect of the number of sub-streams

**Fig. 7.** SUB-SAMPLE precision - synthetic datasets

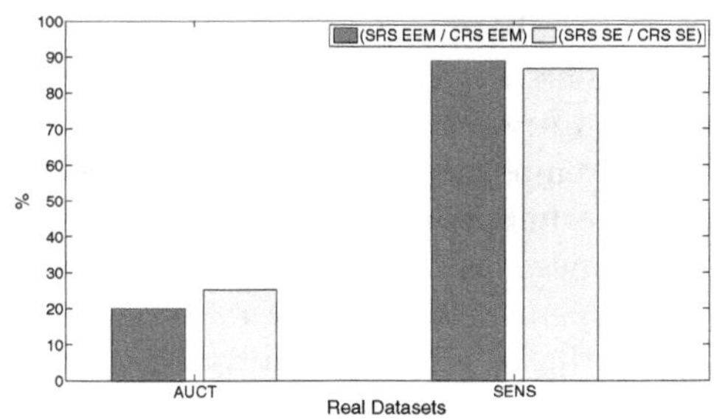


**Fig. 8.** SUB-SAMPLE accuracy and precision - real datasets

Figure 9 shows the adaptivity of SRS from using synthetic datasets. When *DH* is low (10%) (Figure 9(a)), the sub-reservoir sizes for the sub-streams are relatively close to one another compared with the case of a higher *DH* (90%) (Figure 9(b)). The observed influence of the *DH* on the closeness of the sub-reservoir sizes is reasonable since the allocation of sub-reservoir size is subject to the heterogeneity of the sub-streams.

Figures 9(a) and 9(b) also show that the sizes of sub-reservoirs change more frequently in the early stages of sampling and less frequently as the sampling

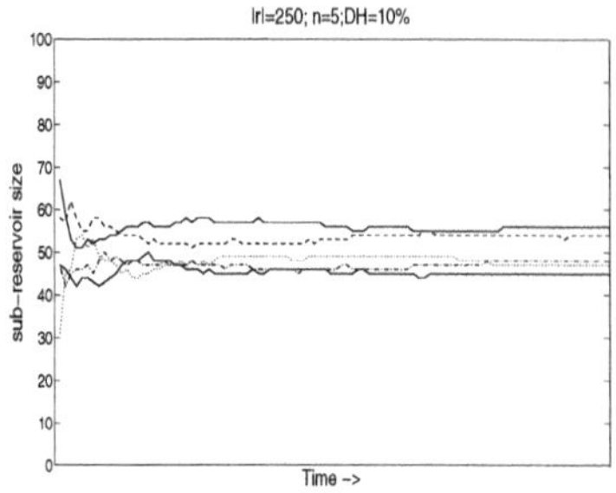


(a) Low degree of heterogeneity

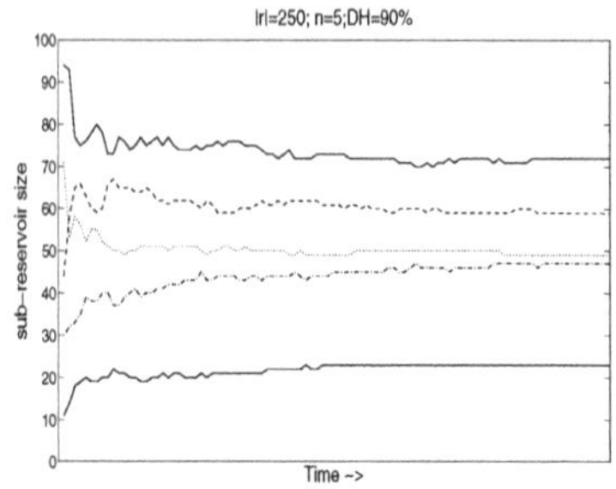


(b) High degree of heterogeneity

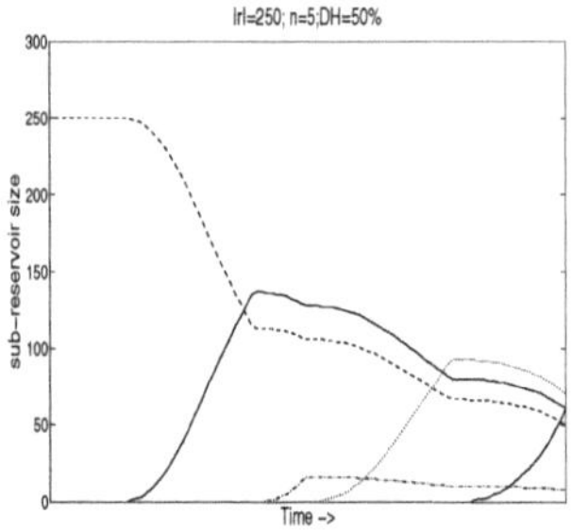


(c) Stream membership

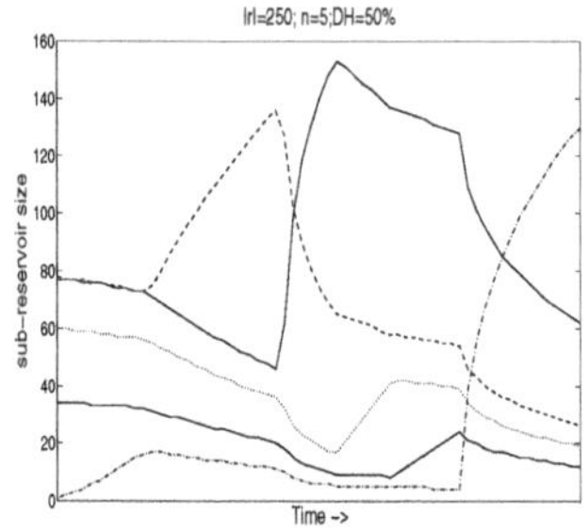


(d) Stream non-stationariness: Less frequent change in running statistics

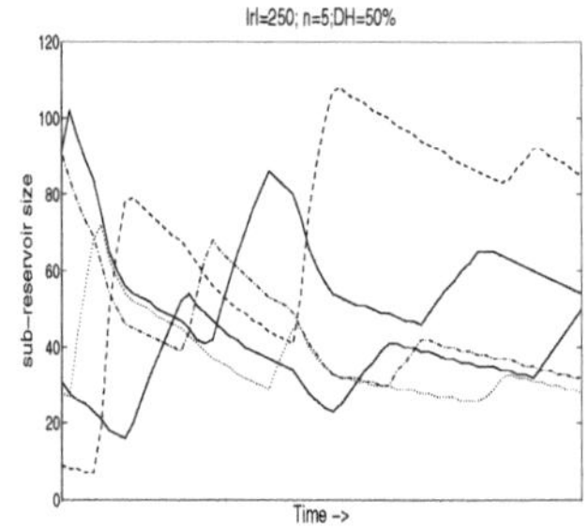


(e) Stream non-stationariness: more frequent change in running statistics

**Fig. 9.** SRS adaptivity - synthetic datasets

progresses. The frequent change in the early stages is attributed to the significance of the difference in the sub-streams running statistics. As the sampling progresses, the change in a sub-stream statistics relative to the changes in the statistics of other sub-streams becomes smaller and, therefore, does not cause so much frequent changes in sub-reservoir sizes. This trend is in part due to the fact that the underlying sub-streams are stationary in their statistical properties.

In order to conduct experiments to study the influence of data stream membership and non-stationariness, we modify the generation of synthetic datasets as follows. For data stream membership, we make the sub-streams appear in sequence. For non-stationariness, we periodically re-generate $n$ random numbers that correspond to the $CV$s of $n$ sub-streams such that the overall $DH$ among them is preserved (recall Section 4.1).

Figure 9(c) shows that when a new sub-stream appears in a data stream, the SRS adapts to this situation by releasing memory from the sub-reservoirs of existing sub-streams and allocating the released memory to the sub-reservoirs of the new sub-stream. Figure 9(d) shows that when the running statistics of some sub-streams change over time, SRS decreases (or increases) the sizes of some exiting sub-reservoirs and increases (or decreases) the sizes of other exiting sub-reservoirs. A reduced sub-reservoir size may increase afterwards, and vice versa. The frequency of the change in sub-reservoir sizes is relative to the frequency of the change in the running statistics of sub-streams. (Figure 9(e) shows the case of more frequent change in the running statistics compared to Figure 9(d)).

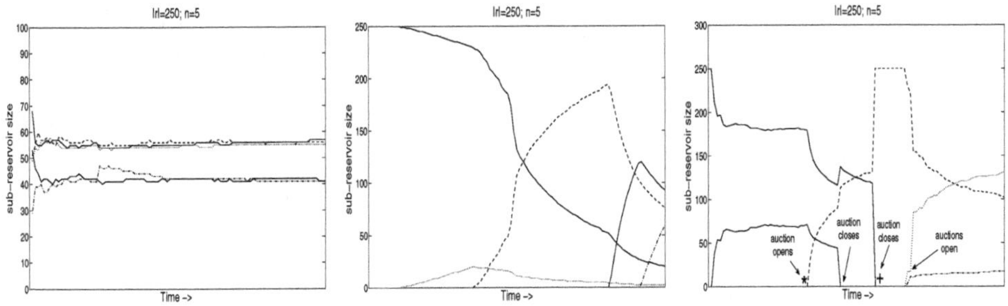


(a) SENS (b) AUCT (c) AUCT: auctions open and close

**Fig. 10.** SRS adaptivity - real datasets

Figure 10(a) shows the change of sub-reservoir sizes using SENS real dataset. This dataset represents the case in which sub-streams all exist from the beginning of the input stream and their statistics remain stationary over time. In other words, readings from different sensors scattered to collect temperature information in a certain area are likely to be generated *altogether* from the time the data collection begins. Besides, the change of temperature readings is expected to be similar at any time of the day. Consequently, all sub-reservoir sizes show little change over time.

Figure 10(b) shows the change of sub-reservoir sizes using AUCT real dataset. This dataset represents the case in which sub-streams are added one after another and their statistics change over time. Indeed, in auctions applications, it is unlikely that all auctions (represented by sub-streams) start simultaneously; they are expected to start one after another. Besides, the bidding amount of an auction item naturally increases over time, making the statistics of an auction sub-stream non-stationary. As a consequence, we see significant changes of sub-reservoir sizes over time.

Figure 10(c) further shows the adaptivity of SRS under the scenario of auctions going open and then closed while sampling progresses. When a new auction opens, memory has to be released from existing sub-reservoirs and allocated to the sub-reservoir of the newly opened auction sub-stream (see the point marked with $*$). When an auction closes from further bids (because the auction is forced to close, the auction expires, the auction item is sold, etc.), the sub-reservoir size of the closed auction sub-stream is released and allocated to the sub-reservoirs of the sub-streams of auctions still open (see the point marked with $+$).

## 5 Related Work

*Reservoir sampling* technique was proposed by McLeod [15]. Vitter [22] improved the algorithm's performance through more optimization studies. Reservoir sampling has been used in many database applications including clustering [12], data warehousing [7], spatial data management [17], and approximate query processing [23]. Besides the conventional reservoir algorithm, various reservoir-based sampling algorithms have been proposed in the research literature for various applications. Examples of such algorithms include reservoir sampling with replacement (i.e., with duplicates being allowed in the sample) [18], sampling from an evolving dataset (i.e., in the presence of insertions and deletions) [11], biased reservoir sampling (i.e., to bias the sample over time using a given bias function) [4], and adaptive-size reservoir sampling [5] (i.e., to allow the reservoir size to be adjusted in the middle of sampling). In contrast to the existing research on reservoir sampling, our work addresses the problem of *stratifying* a *reservoir sample* rather than maintaining a single reservoir sample.

*Stratified sampling* has been used for approximate query processing in database systems [3] [8] [9] [13]. *Congressional sampling* [3] proposes to use stratified sampling approach to solve the problem of providing accurate approximate answers of a set of grouped aggregation queries using pre-computed biased samples of the data. In [8], stratified sampling is used in the problem of identifying an appropriate sample selection for answering aggregation queries approximately with the goal of minimizing error in the query result under a given query workload. A comprehensive study of the work proposed in [8] is presented in [9]. The work in [13] solves the problem of using stratified sampling to calculate approximate results of low selectivity aggregation queries. All this work pertains to databases, which makes our work different in addressing *stratified sampling* for *data streams.*

## 6 Conclusion and Future Work

In this paper, we studied the problem of maintaining a stratified sample over data streams which consist of multiple sub-streams with large statistical variations. First, we discussed the motivation of this new research problem in real-world applications. Second, we discussed an optimal allocation method of a fixed-size reservoir, which can be used whether the sample is needed to generate estimates of the whole data stream or the sub-streams on an individual basis. Third, we presented a sampling algorithm which uses the proposed allocation method to adjust the allocation of a stratified reservoir sample among sub-streams adaptively as sub-streams appear in, or disappear from, the input stream and as their statistical properties change over time. Finally, through experiments, we demonstrated the adaptivity of the proposed algorithm and its superiority over the conventional reservoir sampling algorithm with regard to the sample quality.

Several issues are open for future work. One issue is to extend the proposed algorithm to handle *multi-variate* sampling situation in which an input stream has multiple sampling attributes and an estimate is needed from each sampling attribute. In this situation, it may be required to compromise the allocation of a stratified reservoir sample with respect to the target estimates. Another is to explore the utility of the proposed algorithm in more real-world applications.

## Acknowledgments

The authors would like to thank the members of Intel Berkeley Research lab for graciously granting the permission to use their sensor datasets in the experiments. The authors would also like to thank the Federal Communications Commission for making their auctions data available to use in the experiments.

This material is based upon work supported by the National Science Foundation under Grant No. IIS-0415023.

## References

1. Intel lab data, `http://berkeley.intel-research.net/labdata/`
2. FCC Auctions, `http://wireless.fcc.gov/auctions/default.htm`
3. Acharya, S., Gibbons, P.B., Poosala, V.: Congressional samples for approximate answering of group-by queries. In: SIGMOD 2000, pp. 487–498 (2000)
4. Aggarwal, C.C.: On biased reservoir sampling in the presence of stream evolution. In: VLDB 2006, pp. 607–618 (2006)
5. Al-Kateb, M., Lee, B.S., Wang, X.S.: Adaptive-size reservoir sampling over data streams. In: SSDBM 2007, pp. 22–33 (2007)
6. Bankier, M.D.: Power allocations: Determining sample sizes for subnational areas. The American Statistician, American Statistical Association 42, 174–177 (1988)
7. Brown, P.G., Haas, P.J.: Techniques for warehousing of sample data. In: ICDE 2006, pp. 6–17 (2006)
8. Chaudhuri, S., Das, G., Narasayya, V.: A robust, optimization-based approach for approximate answering of aggregate queries. In: SIGMOD 2001, pp. 295–306 (2001)
9. Chaudhuri, S., Das, G., Narasayya, V.: Optimized stratified sampling for approximate query processing. ACM Trans. Database Syst. 32(2), 9 (2007)
10. Cochran, W.G.: Sampling Techniques, 3rd edn. John Wiley, Chichester (1977)
11. Gemulla, R., Lehner, W., Hass, P.J.: Maintaining bounded-size sample synopses of evolving datasets. The VLDB Journal 17(2), 173–201 (2008)
12. Guha, S., Rastogi, R., Shim, K.: CURE: an efficient clustering algorithm for large databases. In: SIGMOD 1998, pp. 73–84 (1998)
13. Joshi, S., Jermaine, C.M.: Robust stratified sampling plans for low selectivity queries. In: ICDE, pp. 199–208 (2008)
14. Lohr, S.L. (ed.): Sampling: Design and Analysis. Duxbury Press (1999)
15. McLeod, A., Bellhouse, D.: A convenient algorithm for drawing a simple random sample. Applied Statistics 32, 182–184 (1983)
16. Norgaard, R., Killeen, T.: Expected utility and the truncated normal distribution. Management Science 26, 901–909 (1980)
17. Olken, F., Rotem, D.: Sampling from spatial databases. In: ICDE 2003, pp. 199–208 (2003)
18. Park, B.-H., Ostrouchov, G., Samatova, N.F., Geist, A.: Reservoir-based random sampling with replacement from data stream. In: SDM 2004 (2004)
19. Patel, J.K., Read, C.B.: Handbook of the Normal Distribution. CRC, Boca Raton (1996)
20. Srivastava, U., Widom, J.: Memory-limited execution of windowed stream joins. In: VLDB 2004, pp. 324–335 (2004)
21. LeVeque, R.J., Chan, T.F., Golub, G.H.: Algorithms for computing the sample variance: Analysis and recommendations. The American Statistician, American Statistical Association 37, 242–247 (1983)
22. Vitter, J.S.: Random sampling with a reservoir. ACM Trans. Math. Softw. 11(1), 37–57 (1985)
23. Wu, Y.-L., Agrawal, D., El Abbadi, A.: Query estimation by adaptive sampling. In: ICDE 2002, pp. 639–648 (2002)

# Tree Induction over Perennial Objects

Zaigham Faraz Siddiqui and Myra Spiliopoulou

Otto-von-Guericke-University of Magdeburg,
Magdeburg 39106, Germany
{siddiqui,myra}@iti.cs.uni-magdeburg.de

**Abstract.** We study the tree induction over a stream of *perennial* objects. The perennial objects are dynamic in nature and *cannot be forgotten.* The objects come from a multi-table stream, e.g., streams of `Customer` and `Transaction`. As the Transactions arrive, the perennial Customers' profiles *grow* and accumulate over time. To perform tree induction, we propose a tree induction algorithm that can handle perennial objects. The algorithm also encompasses a method that identifies and adapts to the concept drift in the stream. We have also incorporated a conventional classifier (kNN) at the leaves to further improve the classification accuracy of our algorithm. We have evaluated our method on a synthetic dataset and the PKDD Challenge 1999 dataset.

## 1 Introduction

Traditional mining algorithms designed for the analysis of stream data assume that objects enter the horizon of observation, are processed to the effect of learning and adapting the model (e.g., a decision tree or a set of clusters), and are then forgotten. This paradigm has been motivated by the obvious fact that it is pragmatically impossible and practically unnecessary to maintain each data point registered by a sensor or recorded in a server log for longer time than needed to update the underlying model. However, in many applications, the *ephemeral* data points constituting the data stream are part of complex *perennial* objects that (a) may not be forgotten and (b) constitute themselves a stream. Stream mining over perennial objects is a new problem for which conventional techniques for model learning and adaptation must be reconsidered. In this paper we propose a solution for the task of tree induction over a stream.

Perennial objects occur in more applications than one might think at first. Consider a hospital that maintains records for patients with a chronic disease, a company that keeps a customer warehouse, or a group of scientists that study a system of at least two stars, one of which are visible while the others are perceived only through the seemingly aperiodic effects they cause on the plasma, luminosity and trajectory of the visible one. The patients, the customers and the stars (of yet unknown number) are perennial objects, for which activities are recorded. The more activities are recorded, the more is captured in the model of the objects. At the same time, new objects are recorded: new patients with the same disease are registered at the hospital, new customers are recorded in the warehouse,

M. Gertz and B. Ludäscher (Eds.): SSDBM 2010, LNCS 6187, pp. 640–657, 2010.

while the observations on further star systems are recorded and can be exploited for model learning. Hence, the perennial objects constitute themselves a stream. Capacity limitations may force the deletion of old activities and even of old objects (e.g., customers that have attrited since long or patients that deceased long ago), but their properties must be remembered by the model for the case that similar objects might show up.

The implications of perennial objects on stream mining are manifold. First, perennial objects are relational by nature: they are composed of simpler objects (1-n relationship) or associated to further objects of different kind (m-n relationship). For example, patients are associated to test results, medical treatments and pharmaceutical products given to them. Model learning over a static set of such objects can be successfully accomplished with methods of multi-relational data mining [1], but learning over a stream is a new problem, as we explained in [2,3], where we have proposed first solutions. Second, perennial objects cause concept drift of a very particular kind: in conventional classification, an object has a given label, e.g., a customer is trustworthy or not, an Alzheimer patient either exhibits pacing or does not; the label of a perennial object may change though, i.e., the customer may stop being trustworthy, while the patient may start exhibiting pacing (by the nature of the Alzheimer illness). Such drifts must be captured by the model, while retaining the circumstances (data) before and after the drift for use upon further similar objects. This calls for a new kind of model adaptation. Finally, as mentioned before, even if some perennial objects must be moved out of storage, their contribution in the model should be retained, at least for some (application-specific) time period.

In this paper, we propose a new approach for classification over a stream of perennial objects, taking account of the above challenges. We build upon our earlier work on multi-relational stream mining to combine the stream of perennial objects and the streams of simpler objects (transactions, activities and similar) associated to them into a "multi-table stream" upon which a classifier can be applied. We then extend the incremental tree induction algorithm CVFDT proposed by Hulten et al. [4] for a conventional data stream into an adaptive learner for a stream of perennial objects. The extensions are twofold: the new algorithm can deal with the fact that the objects are perennial, hence their contribution to the model may not be forgotten, and with the concept drift incurring as some perennial objects change their label.

The paper is organized as follows. In the next section we discuss related work; since classification of perennial objects is a new problem, the publications of relevance are those dealing with stream classification for conventional data streams. In section 3, we present our new tree induction algorithm, including a method for the aging of the objects that contribute to the tree nodes, and a method for the adaptation of the nodes in the presence of the new art of concept drift. In section 4, we compare our approach to a baseline algorithm for synthetic datasets and for a real dataset to which we have imputed concept drift. The last section concludes our study with a summary and a list of open issues.

## 2 Related Work

One of the first works to address the issue of incremental tree induction was the work of Schlimmer and Granger [5]. Their proposed method ID4 is an extension to the ID3 method of Quinlan [6]. It processes each example (tuple/object with its label) as it arrives and learns the tree incrementally. All statistics needed to compute the entropy of each attribute and choose the one with lowest entropy, $X_a$, are stored at the nodes. At a later timepoint, if $X_a$ no longer has the lowest entropy, it is replaced by the one with lowest entropy. In doing so ID4 also discards all the sub-trees below node $X_a$. If the choice of decision attributes changes often during training, then sub-trees will be discarded repeatedly. this makes ID4 sensitive to the ordering of incoming examples, rendering certain concepts unlearnable by the algorithm.

Utgoff proposed two methods for incremental construction of decision trees; ID5 [7] and ID5R [8]. The basic idea of keeping the statistics at the nodes is similar to [5]. However, instead of keeping concise statistics, they store complete examples. The monitoring of entropy $E(X_a)$ for a candidate attribute $X_a$ is as in [5]. However, when another attribute $X_b$ exhibits the lowest entropy, ID5 restructures the tree only to ensure that $X_b$ becomes the root; unlike the algorithm in [5], it still keeps the original sub-trees without changing them. ID5R [8] also shifts $X_b$ at the root, but then proceeds recursively with re-structuring below it. Due to this, ID5 is unable to guarantee that the tree would be similar to that of an ID3 algorithm given the same examples, while ID5R does.

All of the above algorithms induce decision tree by a greedy search mechanism that requires restructuring the tree, if the selection for a specific split attribute $X_a$ (the "split decision") needs to be revised. The method of Gratch induces a decision that is significantly different from the greedy approaches [9]. Gratch notes that the optimal split decision cannot be achieved without a finite sample, so the proposed method " selects an attribute that is within $\epsilon$ of the best with probability $1-\delta$, taking as many examples as are sufficient to ensure a decision of this [given] quality."

More recently, Domingos and Hulten presented their incremental decision tree induction method VFDT [10]. They note (with Catlett [11]) that a small subset of training examples is sufficient to select the best split attribute for a given node. They use the so-called *Hoeffding bound* to determine the number of training examples that are required. More formally, consider a real-valued random variable $r$ whose range is $R$. Suppose we have made $n$ independent observations of this variable and computed their mean $\bar{r}$. The Hoeffding bound states that, with probability $1-\delta$, the true mean of $r$ is in $[\bar{r}-\epsilon, \bar{r}+\epsilon]$, where

$$\epsilon = \sqrt{\frac{R^2 ln(1/\delta)}{2n}} \tag{1}$$

At each timepoint, VFDT applies the Hoeffding bound upon the difference $\Delta G$ between the information gain of the best split attribute $G(X_a)$ and of the second best attribute $G(X_b)$. In particular, assume that the two attributes deliver (asymptotically) the same gain, i.e., they are interchangeable. The true mean of their difference would then be zero and $\Delta G$ would be less than $0 + \epsilon$, where $\epsilon$ is computed as in Eq.1 with $n$ being the number of examples seen thus far. Hence, if $\Delta G$ is found to be larger than $0 + \epsilon$, then the best split attribute $X_a$ is significantly better than the second one, and VFDT uses it as a new leaf node, growing the tree upon it. If $\Delta G$ is less than $\epsilon$, then VFDT postpones the split until a best split is found that is significantly better than the second best.

Hulten et al. extended the VFDT to deal with concept drift: the CVFDT updates the tree as soon as the learned concept starts to change [4]. They also introduce a notion of window that stores only the most recent objects and removes the old ones, i.e., those that fall out of the window.

Gama et al. makes use of The algorithm $\text{VFDT}_C$ of Gama et al. makes use of a minimal set of statistics (they call them "sufficient statistics") calculated at the leaves [12]. $\text{VFDT}_C$ is an extension of the original VFDT [10] that employs Naïve Bayes at each leaf node to assign the node's members to the classes with help of these statistics. They show that they achieve better performance and can also recognize concept drift by detecting performance degradation. Their proposed system can also handle numerical attributes.

All aforementioned algorithms operate on a single stream of data and under a fixed schema. As we explain in section 3.1, a multi-relational stream of perennial objects implies combining individual streams at each timepoint; this combination of streams incurs a change in the schema. Furthermore, stream classifiers assume that objects are seen only once, while perennial objects are seen more than once and experience changes - including changes in their label.

Partially relevant to our idea of stream classification upon multi-relational objects is the SRPT algorithm proposed by McGovern et al. [13]: the algorithm operates upon spatio-temporal data of numerical nature (e.g., timeseries of meteorological phenomena like wind updrafts), accompanied by nominal attributes that summarize the timeseries or check conditions upon them (e.g., whether the observed mean of a specific timeseries exceeds a specific threshold or whether some explicitly defined event has been observed in the most recent timepoints)[1]. The objective of SRPT is to *probabilistically* assign each object (e.g., a storm) composed of multiple timeseries to a set of predefined classes (e.g., the classes "positive", "negative" and "maybe" for storms). Since the timeseries are read incrementally, SRPT can be interpreted as a stream mining algorithm; since it operates on multiple streams, it is relational. Dissimilarly to our problem specification, though, SRPT does not deal with nominal attributes. Since the products purchased by a customer or the medical treatments of a patient cannot transfer to timeseries, and since SRPT assumes only a priori defined nominal *meta*-data, SRPT does not seem to transfer to the problem we want to solve.

---

[1] There is not much text in [13] on what art of summarization information should be used in the general case, how it is to be computed and updated efficiently, nor about the space it consumes. The authors mention possible examples of meta-information for an example application, though.

**Table 1.** Symbols and Parameters

| Notation | Description |
|---|---|
| $\mathcal{X}^{\mathcal{B}}$ | schema of the multi-table stream |
| $x$ | a propositionalized object |
| $t_i$ | the $i^{th}$ timepoint |
| $w$ | size of the sliding window as number of timepoints |
| $\mathcal{S}_i$ | set of non-propositionalized stream objects arrived in $(t_{i-1}, t_i]$ |
| $\mathcal{W}_i$ | set of propositionalized stream objects arrived in $(t_{i-1}, t_i]$ |
| $\mathcal{R}$ | root node of the tree induced by TrIP |
| $T$ | a node of the induction tree |
| $a_{T,i}$ | age of node $T$ at timepoint $t_i$ |
| $Q_{T,i}$ | accuracy of the subtree with root $T$ at timepoint $t_i$ |
| $var_{T,i}$ | variance in the accuracy of the children $T$ at timepoint $t_i$ |
| $s_{T,i}$ | support of node $T$ at timepoint $t_i$: number of objects in $T$ at $t_i$ |
| $\delta$ | confidence threshold for the computation of the Hoeffding Bound |
| $\tau$ | tie breaker – used to do a split when the Hoeffding Bound results in a tie |
| $n$ | minimum number of objects that must be in a leaf node before it is checked whether the node can be split; used to compute the Hoeffding Bound |
| $l$ | minimum number of objects that must be in a leaf node after a split |
| $f$ | minimum number of objects that must be in a node before a check for concept drift is performed |
| $s_t$ | minimum support threshold in $[0, 1]$ for a leaf before it starts to age |

## 3 Our Classification Method for Perennial Objects

Our ***Tr**ee **I**nduction algorithm for **P**erennial objects* (**TrIP**) has several components. The first is an *incremental propositionalization* algorithm that combines the stream of perennial objects with further streams (of perennial or ephemeral objects) transferring them into a single stream for mining. This component is coupled with a sliding window mechanism that replaces outdated perennial objects with their up to date version and forgets those that are not needed for the current version of the model. The tree induction and adaptation with help of alternate trees is based on CVFDT [4], but this component has been extended to cover the particularities of perennial objects, including a new form of concept drift. Object labeling at the leaf nodes is done with help of a conventional classifier, as does the VFDT$_c$ [12], but instead of Naïve Bayes we use the k-Nearest Neighbors classifier. We present each component in turn in the following subsections. The notation and parameters are presented in Table 1.

### 3.1 Combining Multiple Streams

As discussed earlier (c.f. Section 1), perennial objects are composed of multiple interrelated streams. We transform these streams into a single stream, a *multi-table stream*, using the method presented in [2].

In the following, we use the tables in Figure 1 as a running example: we see a multi-table stream composed of multiple tables arriving at different speeds.

**Original Schema**

**Transaction**

| TID | CID | PID | Time |
|---|---|---|---|
| 1 | 1 | 1 | 1 |
| 2 | 1 | 1 | 1 |
| 3 | 2 | 1 | 1 |
| 4 | 2 | 2 | 1 |
| 5 | 1 | 2 | 2 |
| 6 | 1 | 2 | 2 |
| 7 | 2 | 1 | 2 |
| 8 | 1 | 3 | 3 |
| 9 | 3 | 3 | 3 |

**Customer**

| CID | Name | Married | Income |
|---|---|---|---|
| 1 | David | S | 20000 |
| 2 | Tom | M | 65000 |
| 3 | Harris | M | 90000 |

**Product**

| PID | Price | Category |
|---|---|---|
| 1 | 100 | Book |
| 2 | 50 | DVD |
| 3 | 25 | CD |

**Natural Join**

| TID | CID | Name | Married | Income | PID | Price | Category | Time |
|---|---|---|---|---|---|---|---|---|
| 1 | 1 | David | S | 20000 | 1 | 100 | Book | 1 |
| 2 | 1 | David | S | 20000 | 1 | 100 | Book | 1 |
| 3 | 2 | Tom | M | 65000 | 1 | 100 | Book | 1 |
| 4 | 2 | Tom | M | 65000 | 2 | 50 | DVD | 1 |
| 5 | 1 | David | S | 20000 | 2 | 50 | DVD | 2 |
| 6 | 1 | David | S | 20000 | 2 | 50 | DVD | 2 |
| 7 | 2 | Tom | M | 65000 | 1 | 100 | Book | 2 |
| 8 | 1 | David | S | 20000 | 3 | 25 | CD | 3 |
| 9 | 3 | Harris | M | 90000 | 3 | 25 | CD | 3 |

**Propositionalised Table**

| CID | Name | Married | Income | Count | AVG_P | MIN_P | MAX_P | Count_Book | Count_DVD | Time |
|---|---|---|---|---|---|---|---|---|---|---|
| 1 | David | S | 20000 | 2 | 100 | 100 | 100 | 2 | 0 | 1 |
| 2 | Tom | M | 65000 | 2 | 75 | 50 | 100 | 1 | 1 | 1 |
| 1 | David | S | 20000 | 4 | 75 | 50 | 100 | 2 | 2 | 2 |
| 2 | Tom | M | 65000 | 3 | 83.333 | 50 | 100 | 2 | 1 | 2 |
| 1 | David | S | 20000 | 3 | 41.667 | 25 | 50 | 1 | 2 | 3 |
| 3 | Harris | M | 90000 | 1 | 25 | 25 | 25 | 1 | 0 | 3 |

**Fig. 1.** Objects of (a) a multi-table stream on customers, transactions and products, (b) n-way join of the `Customer` data with transaction and product information and (c) propositionalized version of the same target `Customer`

The stream of "Customer" data is associated with a stream of products and a stream of transactions. We observe the Customer stream as the *target stream*, in the sense that this is the stream on which we want to perform classification, exploiting also the information from the other streams. It is obvious that the number of products purchased by each customer changes over time and so is the information accumulated about each customer's product preferences and regularity of purchases. It is also obvious that a customer object must be joined with all transactions of this account, and be thus kept for as long as such transactions are expected; customer objects are perennial (and so are products). On the other hand, the transactions themselves may be discarded immediately after being read; they are ephemeral.

Using our method of [2] we assign a *cache* and secondary storage for long-term maintenance to each stream of perennial objects and a *sliding window* to each stream of ephemeral objects. In the example of Figure 1, a sliding window of two time units (depicted by dotted arrows) is specified for "Transaction" and caches are defined for "Customer" and for "Product"; each of those caches can accommodate two objects.

Propositionalization is performed incrementally at each timepoint $t_i$ on the contents of each cache and window. It starts with a semi-join between the contents of the cache for the target perennial stream $\mathcal{T}_0$ and the cache/window of each stream $\mathcal{T}_j$ associated to $\mathcal{T}_0$. Hence, for each stream $\mathcal{T}_j$ that is in 1-to-m or m-to-n relationship to $\mathcal{T}_0$, each object $x \in \mathcal{T}_0$ is associated with the set of matching objects $matches(x) \subset \mathcal{T}_j$.

Then, the propositionalization algorithm summarizes the objects in this set into a single *sub-object*. To summarize the values of each numerical attribute $A$ in $matches(x)$, we generate four attributes: the *min*, *max*, *count* and *average* of the

**Algorithm 1.** TrIP: Tree Induction for Perennial Objects

**Input** . $\mathcal{X}^{\mathcal{B}}, \mathcal{S}, n, f, w, k, l, \delta$

1 Create root node $\mathcal{R}$
2 Initialize counters
3 **for** $t_i = t_1$ **to** *STREAM_END* **do**
4     $\mathcal{W}_i \leftarrow$ `IncProp`$(\mathcal{X}^{\mathcal{B}}, \mathcal{S}_i)$
5     **foreach** $x \in \mathcal{W}_i$ **do**
6         **if** $x.id \in (\mathcal{W}_{i-w}, \mathcal{W}_{i-1}]$ **then**
7             `RecursivelyForget`$(\mathcal{R}, x)$
8         `ClassifyNPresent`$(\mathcal{R}, x, k)$
9         **foreach** *n objects* **do**
10             `GrowNAdaptSubtree`$(\mathcal{R}, f, l)$
11     **foreach** $x \in \mathcal{W}_j \mid j = i - w$ **do**
12         `RecursivelyForget`$(\mathcal{R}, x)$

**Function** `RecursivelyForget`$(T, x)$

**Input** . $T, x$

**if** $x.tp \geq T.tp \wedge x.ID \geq T.firstID$ **then**
    Decrease counters of the statistics w.r.t. $x$
    $T_c \leftarrow$ `ParseIntoChild`$(x)$
    `RecursivelyForget`$(T_c, x)$
**foreach** $T_{alt} \in$ `GetAltTrees`$(T)$ **do**
    `RecursivelyForget`$(T_{alt}, x)$

**Function** `ClassifyNPresent`$(T, x, k)$

**Input** . $T, x, k$

**if** $T$ *is leaf* **then**
    $cl$ = label of $x$     `/* kNN at leaf */`
Increase counters of statistics w.r.t. $x$
**if** $T$ *is not leaf* **then**
    $T_c \leftarrow$ `ParseIntoChild`$(x)$
    $cl$ = `ClassifyNPresent`$(T_c, x, k)$
**foreach** $T_{alt} \in$ `GetAltTrees`$(T)$ **do**
    `ClassifyNPresent`$(T_{alt}, x, k)$
return $cl$

**Function** `GrowNAdaptSubtree`$(T, f, l)$

**Input** . $T, f, l$

**if** $T$ *is leaf* **then**
    `SplitUsingTheBestAtt`$(T)$
    Select $l$ atts with best gain for kNN
**else**
    `AgeTree`$(T)$
    `ReplaceWithAltTree`$(T)$
    **for** *every f objects seen* **do**
        **do** `ValidateSplit`$(T)$
    **forall** $T_c \in$ `GetChildren`$(T)$ **do**
        `GrowNAdaptSubtree`$(T_c, f, l)$
    **forall** $T_{alt} \in$ `GetAltTrees`$(T)$ **do**
        `GrowNAdaptSubtree`$(T_{alt}, f, l)$

$A$ values seen in $matches(x)$. To summarize each nominal attribute $A$, we generate as many columns($r_A$) for $A$ as there are distinct values in $\bigcup_x matches(x)$ at $t_0$. The domain of $A$ may change after $t_0$, in the sense that previously unseen values emerge, while old values are no more referenced. If the domain grows larger than $r_A$, then values are grouped into $r_A$ clusters on similarity: two values of $A$ are similar, if they are referenced by similar objects. At the end of the propositionalization phase, each object of the (perennial) target stream is expanded by summarized attribute values from each stream associated with it.

### 3.2 Growing and Adapting a Decision Tree over Perennial Objects

TrIP grows a decision tree incrementally upon the propositionalized data. We depict the high-level process as Algorithm 1. TrIP first initializes the root of the tree (line 1). It takes as input the multiple interrelated streams $S_i$ at timepoint $t_i$ and summarizes them into a single propositionalized window $\mathcal{W}_i$ (line 4). Then, each object $x$ from $\mathcal{W}_i$ is recursively presented to the model (line 8), starting from $\mathcal{R}$. The object is incorporated in the tree and when at least $n$ objects have been presented, TrIP expands the tree by leaf node splitting (line 10). Periodically, TrIP updates and forgets outdated perennial objects (line 7 & 12).

**Dealing with Outdated Perennial Objects.** The stream of perennial objects cannot be propositionalized once and forever: as new perennial or ephemeral objects arrive, the target schema needs to be updated – adding, modifying and deleting columns, as explained in section 3.1, as well as the perennial objects seen thus far. Hence, TrIP employs a sliding window of length $w$ timepoints: at timepoint $t_i$ the newest block of objects $\mathcal{S}_i$ (cf. Table 1) is read in and propositionalized into $\mathcal{W}_i$. Then, outdated perennial objects must be forgotten. We distinguish two cases, as described below.

Perennial objects are kept up-to-date by the arriving ephemeral objects that reference them. If for a perennial object $x$, there is no ephemeral object seen for the last $w$ timepoints, then $x$ carries no new information and is unlikely to influence the current model. Hence, we remove such objects from the model. Obviously, the objects themselves are not eliminated from secondary storage.

The second case of outdated perennial objects concerns object replacement. In particular, let $x$ be a perennial object and $x_j$ its content at timepoint $t_j$, composed of the data in $\mathcal{T}_0$ and the propositionalized data on $x$ from the other streams. If a new instance $x_i$ arrives at $t_i > t_j$, then it replaces the old one.

The process of forgetting the impact of outdated perennial objects is undertaken by Function `RecursivelyForget()`. To do so, it maintains for each node $T$ the timepoint $tp$ at which it was created, as well as the identifier $firstID$ of the first object placed in this node. Then, at a timepoint $t > tp$, the function ignores all objects that have appeared before $tp$ for the last time and those that have identifiers less than $firstID$ and have not been seen within the last $w$ timepoints. The statistics on the contents of node $T$ and of its subtrees are updated accordingly.

**Growing a decision tree on a propositionalized stream.** TrIP starts building the decision tree from the root $\mathcal{R}$, which is originally the only node and a leaf. For each node, TrIP maintains the same statistics in it as CVFDT: for each encountered attribute $A$ and value $v$ of this attribute and for each class label $k$, it counts the number of objects having $A = v$ and label $k$. These counters are initialized and maintained separately for each node as it is created.

When an object $x$ arrives, it is recursively presented to the tree, starting from the root node. The process is undertaken by Function `ClassifyNPresent`. When $x$ is presented to a node $T$, $T$ first updates the relevant counter (c.f. `ClassifyNPresent`, line 3) and then passes it down to the relevant child node (lines 5 & 6). If the currently traversed node is a leaf, before an object is incorporated, it is assigned a label (line 2).

Once $n$ objects have been presented to a *leaf* node $T$, TrIP (like CVFDT) considers $T$ as a candidate for split and expands the tree. This process is undertaken by the Function `GrowNAdaptSubtree` and is invoked recursively from TrIP. First, it computes the gain $G(X_m)$ for every attribute $X_m$ Next, for the best and second best split attributes $X_a$ and $X_b$ it calculates $\Delta G = G(X_a) - G(X_b)$ and computes the Hoeffding bound $\epsilon$ on the true mean of $\Delta G$ with confidence $\delta$ (cf. Eq. 1). As explained in Section 2, if $\Delta G > \epsilon$, then $T$ is split on $X_a$, otherwise the split decision is postponed and further objects are read and processed.

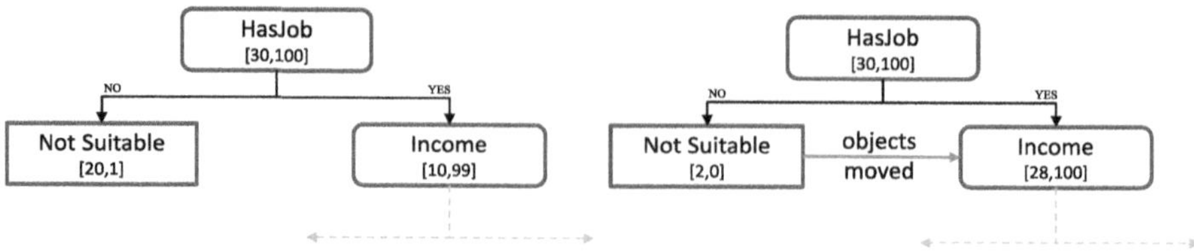


**Fig. 2.** Tree losing support as objects change their label

As a node sees more and more objects, $n$ increases and $\epsilon$ decreases (cf. Eq. 1). As long as $\Delta G$ remains less than $\epsilon$, no split can be performed. To avoid spending time on attributes with very close gain, TrIP, like CVFDT, uses a tie breaking mechanism: once the value of $\epsilon$ drops below a threshold $\tau$, the algorithm is forced to make a split on the current best attribute.

Next to the leaf node splitting (line 2), Function `GrowNAdaptSubtree` also selects the best attributes to be used in the classifier at the leaf nodes (line 3) and is also responsible for node adaptation to concept drift. Adaptation is attempted after the arrival of at least $f$ objects at the node (line 8). We elaborate on these steps hereafter.

**Tree ageing and generation of alternate trees.** Similarly to CVFDT, TrIP maintains alternate trees as means for fast adaptation to concept drift. However, concept drift upon a stream of perennial objects occurs in two ways: (1) some perennial objects change their label as time passes; (2) the number of objects associated with each label changes as time passes. The second type is the conventional concept drift. The first type occurs only upon perennial objects because of their very nature, and is independent of the second type. For both types of drift, we must take account of the fact that changes in the number of objects having a given label may be of temporary nature only. We explain this by means of an example.

*Example 1.* Assume a partner matching site, in which a set of persons are registered. The objective is to learn the concept "get a spouse". Assume that the tree $T$ shown in Figure 2 to be the one learned till timepoint $t_i$. The current best split attribute is "HasJob" with both left and right subtree accommodating a sufficient number of objects. At a later timepoint $t_j$, some objects currently in the left subtree get a job and then a partner. This means that the number of objects in the left subtree decreases and the gain for the attribute "HasJob" may drop as well. This renders the current split suboptimal and forces the algorithm to choose a new split attribute and start growing an alternate subtree under it.

However, the original concept may well re-appear and the number of objects in the left subtree may start growing again. When new objects that are consistent with the replaced sub-tree start arriving again, it would take some time before the algorithm re-learns the discarded concept. Hulten et al. also identified re-learning of a discarded periodical concept as a direction for future work [4].

TrIP checks for concept drift every $f$ objects seen during maintenance (Algo 4, line 8). TrIP inspects each node $T$ if the split attribute $X_s$ is still the best split decision or not. In case $X_s \neq X_a$, i.e., current split attribute $X_s$ is not the best split attribute any more, TrIP makes sure if an improved split can be installed at $T$ using $X_a$. If a new split can be made, it initializes an *alternate* sub-tree $T_{alt}$ (rooted at $parent(T)$) with $X_a$ as the new split attribute, separately. To avoid excessive alternate tree generation, tie breaking condition is made tighter, i.e., $\Delta G \leq \epsilon < \frac{\tau}{2}$. Hulten et al. points out that a simple approach would be to replace $T$ as soon as an alternate tree $T_{alt}$ with a split anchored at $X_a$ is generated [4] . This would ensure that the induced tree, rooted at $\mathcal{R}$, is always as accurate as possible. However, it would force $T_{alt}$ (with 2 leaves only) to do the job that was earlier done by a whole sub-tree. Similarly to the CVFDT, TrIP waits for the accuracy of alternate tree $T_{alt}$ to be greater than $T$ and then replaces $T$ with $T_{alt}$ (Algo 4, line 6). However, due to the dynamic nature of the perennial objects, TrIP employs a different method for the adaptation.

To deal with the pitfalls of accepting a short-lived concept, TrIP checks whether the accuracy of the tree deteriorates, whether each node of the tree still represents, i.e., "is supported by", an adequate number of perennial objects, *and* for how long the tree has (or has not) received support. Informally, we model for a (sub-)tree (a) the quality of the concept in it, (b) the support, i.e., the number of objects accommodated in it and (c) its age as the time elapsed since quality deterioration has started in it. By this, a tree of good quality is not aging, even if its support drops.

More formally, TrIP calculates for each node $T$ two coefficients, support and quality. For the internal decision nodes (not the leaf nodes), these two coefficients are further used for calculating the age $a_{T,i}$ of $T$ at timepoint $t_i$. The support coefficient calculates the penalty for the children of T with support less that the threshold $s_t$ (cf. Table 1). The formula for support penalty for child $c$ is shown in Equation 2, where, $s_{c,max}$ is maximum observed support for child node $c$ and $s_{c,i}$ is the current support.

$$supportCoeff(T, t_i) = \sum_{c \in child(T)} \begin{cases} \frac{s_{c,max} - s_{c,i}}{s_{c,max}} & if\ s_{c,i} < s_t \times s_{c,max} \\ 0 & if\ s_{c,i} \geq s_t \times s_{c,max} \end{cases} \quad (2)$$

The quality coefficient calculates the change in the classification accuracy of a node at timepoint $t_i$ from that in $t_{i-1}$.The formula for calculating the quality coefficient is shown in Equation 3

$$qualityCoeff(T, t_i) = \begin{cases} (1 - var_{T,i})\Delta Q_T & if\ \Delta Q_T > (1-\delta)^e \\ Q_{T,i} - 0.5 & otherwise \end{cases} \quad (3)$$

where $\Delta Q_T = Q_{T,i} - Q_{T,i-1}$ and $Q_{T,i}$ and $Q_{T,i-1}$ are the classification accuracy of tree $T$ at $t_i$ and $t_{i-1}$ respectively and $var_{T,i}$ is the variance in the classification accuracy of the children of $T$ (cf. Table 1). The variance among the children of $T$ is used to capture the case where one child/subtree $c$ has much lower quality than the other: then, the quality coefficient of $T$ itself is not affected, thus preventing a premature aging of the whole subtree under $T$. The quality coefficient of $c$ itself will be low, hence $c$ will age faster. Then, the age of an internal node at timepoint $t_i$ is computed upon the age of the node at the previous timepoint, and the node's support and quality coefficients:

$$a_{T,i} = a_{T,i-1} + supportCoeff(T, t_i) - qualityCoeff(T, t_i) \tag{4}$$

The maintenance procedure is recursively invoked at each tree node $T$ (cf. function specification and line 5). At node $T$, TrIP checks if the attribute $X_s$ originally used to split the node is still the best split decision. If not , i.e., another attribute $X_a$ provides a split of higher gain, then TrIP starts growing an alternate (sub-)tree $T_{alt}$ and split using $X_a$. Similarly to CVFDT, TrIP replaces $T$ with $T_{alt}$ only if (and after) the accuracy of $T$ has dropped below that of $T_{alt}$. Dissimilarly to CVFDT, TrIP retains $T$ even if its accuracy dropped, and then starts increasing its age. $T$ is discarded only if its age exceeds a certain threshold, which is expected to capture background knowledge about periodicity in the application. If the threshold is not exceeded, $T$ is available and its quality is checked at each timepoint: if its quality improves, it "rejuvenates", i.e., its age decreases, as can be seen in Eq.4.

**Using kNN classifier in the leaves of the decision tree.** In the application phase of conventional classification, an object moves down the tree and is accommodated in the leaf describing it best. Then, the label assigned to the object is usually the majority label of that leaf node. In the learning phase of stream classification, objects also travel the tree down to a leaf node and are assigned the majority label of that node, until there are enough objects collected to allow for tree refinement. Gama et al. observe that this approach may be inconvenient: the VFDT stream classifier [10] requires hundreds of objects before it can make a decision about splitting a leaf further to improve the accuracy. The problem is particularly acute if the classes are balanced at the leaf node: although there may be means for separating the objects and growing the tree further, the algorithm is prevented from doing so, until the node has grown very large. The VFDT$_C$ of Gama et al. is therefore using a Naïve Bayes classifier to assign labels to the objects of the leaf nodes [12].

In TrIP, we also invoke a classifier at each leaf node to decide about the labels of the objects in it. Instead of Naïve Bayes, we opt for a k-nearest-neighbors classifier (kNN). The overhead of kNN is higher than that of Naïve Bayes, but it allows us to capture the similarity among perennial objects of different sizes in a more seamless way. Moreover, to reduce the overhead, TrIP invokes kNN for only a fraction of the attributes: it consults the statistics at the current leaf and chooses $l$ attributes with the best gain.

## 4 Experiments

We use two datasets, a synthetic and a real dataset, for our evaluation. The real dataset, called "Financial" dataset, comes from the PKDD Challenge of 1999 and is multi-relational. Both datasets are labeled. Our objective is to study the performance of our methods over a stream of perennial objects. To this purpose, we designed a variety of experiments that deal with the effect of window size and tree aging on quality.

### 4.1 Experiments on Synthetic Data

**Dataset "Marriage".** The synthetic data is called "marriage dataset". It is a small dataset with 3 features and 200 data instances that are used to test specific aspects of TrIP. The objects in the dataset are dynamic. They are persons labeled on whether they are likely to find a match or not on the basis of their age, income and marital status. The underlying data generating process remains static. However, the objects can change property values and their class labels. This "movement" of objects gives impression.

**Trip Variants for the Synthetic Dataset.** For the marriage dataset, as there are no multiple streams, we use $w = 5, 7$ time units and vary $age_{MAX} = 0, 4, \infty$. When $age_{MAX} = 0$, a subtree rooted at $T$ that no longer has best split decision at its root can be immediately replaced once the accuracy of alternate tree $T_{alt}$ becomes better. When $age_{MAX} = 4$, $T$ can be replaced by $T_{alt}$ only if $a_{T,i} >= age_{MAX}$. When $age_{MAX} = \infty$, $T$ never gets replaced by $T_{alt}$ as it never really reaches $age_{MAX}$. We name the strategies as Quick (QR), Deferred (DR) and No Replacement (NR), respectively. The other tree parameters are: $n = 4$, $f = 8$, $\delta = 0.9$, $\tau = 0.1$, $s_t = 0.1$. As the dataset has only three attributes, simple majority voting is used for classification at the leaves rather than a kNN classifier.

**Experimental Results.** The objects are persons who have registered themselves and evolve over time. They grow old, their income changes from year to year and their marital status changes as well. The underlying data generating process remains unchanged until $t_{30}$, where we have imputed a concept drift for the last 5 timepoints.

In the left part of Figure 3 we show the accuracy of strategies QR, DR and NR for$w = 5$. From timepoint $t_1$ to $t_{10}$ all the strategies are in a learning

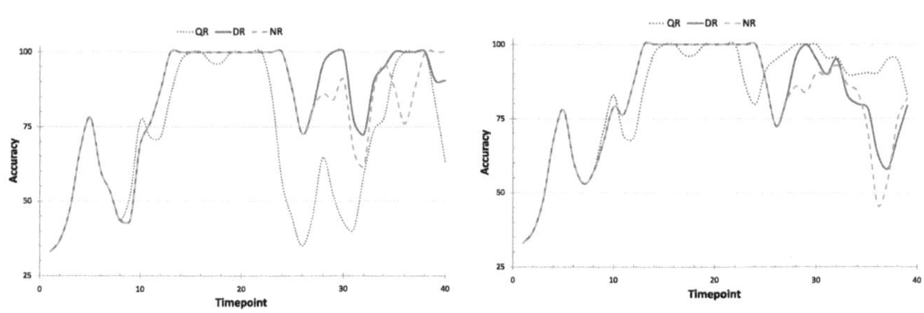


**Fig. 3.** The performance of strategies (left) $w = 5$, (right) $w = 7$ timepoints

phase: they perform similarly and have identical trees. Until $t_6$ the main split attribute at the root was *MaritalStatus* and anyone already married was deemed as unsuitable to find a match. By timepoint $t_6$ the arriving objects are singles, while most of the old ones have become single again. This renders the previous split decision invalid. Strategies QR and DR start growing alternate trees. It needs to be stressed here that conventional algorithm would try and forget the concept;however it is important to keep the concept for objects that would come in future and are consistent with it.

At timepoint $t_{10}$ strategy QR replaces the subtree with invalid split decision by the alternate tree with better accuracy. The alternate tree for strategy DR, although it has better accuracy, does not replace the original subtree as it has not yet reached $age_{MAX} = 4$. To adapt to the new data, strategy DR as well as NR are forced to expand their trees by further split decisions.

From $t_{10}$ to $t_{20}$ all trees stabilize because the objects that arrive are mostly consistent with them. Married individuals cause a fluctuation in the accuracy for strategy NR.

Around $t_{22}$ the new objects cause a drop in accuracy for all strategies. The strategies QR and DR replace their subtrees: it is quite obvious that QR would do a tree replacement; DR is forced to replace the tree because of aging for one of its decision nodes. The drop in accuracy has greater effect than the loss in support (c.f. Equation 3). As a result the tree with low accuracy ages faster. And by the time the original tree in DR is overtaken by its alternate tree in terms of accuracy, it reaches $age_{MAX}$ and thus, is replaced.

Around $t_{25}$ objects with *MaritalStatus=true* start arriving again. Strategies DR and NR that have maintained the trees from earlier timepoints show no drop in performance. However, these objects result in drop in accuracy for strategy QR as it had replaced its tree at $t_{10}$. It starts growing the alternate tree again but it takes time before the outdated information can be replaced.

As new objects with a different concept are introduced around $t_{30}$ , strategy NR's performance deteriorates. While strategies QR and NR recover by replacing their tree with the alternate ones. We expected strategy NR to show the worst performance during this period but even this one recovers. On closely inspecting the results, it became apparent, that the due to an already expanded tree, it is able to manage the incoming data in its leaves. Although the split decision w.r.t. to gain criteria are not valid any more, it still has competent accuracy but is more sensitive due to over fitting.

In the left of Fig 3, we show the performance for $w = 7$. The strategies behave similarly to $w = 5$, expect strategy QR whose performance does not deteriorate much during $t_{20}$ to $t_{30}$. This is probably due to the larger $w$ as it is able to make better informed split decision based on *MaritalStatus* than in $w = 5$.

### 4.2 Experiments on Real Data

**The Dataset "Financial" of the PKDD '99 Challenge.** Financial dataset is a multi-relational. The tables represent the activities (transaction and loans request etc.) of bank customers. These customers have been granted loans and

**Table 2.** Tables and their statistics

| **Tables** | C<br>`Accounts` | C<br>`Districts` | `Clients` | W<br>`Orders` | `Cards` | W<br>`Transactions` |
|---|---|---|---|---|---|---|
| **Objects** | 682<br>(A/C)606 (B/D)76 | 77 | 827 | 1513 | 170 | 191,556 |

**Table 3.** Strategies on Financial dataset

| *Acronym* | `Accounts` | `District` | `Transaction` | $r$ | $age_{MAX}$ | $\delta$ | $\tau$ | $n$ | $f$ | $k$ | $l$ |
|---|---|---|---|---|---|---|---|---|---|---|---|
| FIN1-DR | 100 | 20 | | | | | | 200 | 400 | | |
| FIN2-DR | 200 | 40 | $w = 30$ | 3 | 5 | 0.95 | 0.2 | 200 | 400 | 2 | 3 |
| FIN3-DR | 300 | 50 | | | | | | 300 | 600 | | |
| REF-DR | $\infty$ | $\infty$ | $w = 30$ | $\infty$ | 5 | 0.95 | 0.2 | 400 | 800 | 2 | 3 |

are paying it back over a period 01/93 to 12/98. In Table 2, we depict the tables of the Financial dataset; the target table is underlined. In the first column, $C$ stands for streams associated with a cache, $W$ stands for window, rest are used as static tables. A loan is associated with an account which in turn may belong to one or more clients. The type of credit cards and orders made through each account are recorded, however the main load comes from the transaction stream. Already during PKDD Challenge classes A, C and B, D were merged into *loan-trusted* and *loan-risk*, respectively. We do the same.

This dataset puts forwards a difficult learning problem. The class distributions are not only very skewed to begin with; they also reflect the state of accounts only when they have matured, i.e., class labels become applicable at a much later timepoint than when the objects were introduced.

**Trip Variants for Dataset "Financial".** For the Financial dataset, the amount of information that becomes available as the multi-table stream progresses has an impact upon the quality of the classification results. This remembered information is affected by the size of the cache and the sliding window over individual streams. We have thus varied these values for the streams Accounts, District and Transaction.

The strategies we use are depicted in Table 3. Strategy FIN2-DR uses a cache of size 200 for the stream Account and of size 40 for the districts, a sliding window of size *window* = 30 months for Transaction stream, 3 columns to store nominal values (c.f. Section 3.1), $age_{MAX} = 5$ to perform deferred replacement, update tree every $n = 200$ objects, check for concept drift every $f = 400$ objects etc. We test these strategies against our reference strategy that has unlimited storage and knows the future.

Due to large number of moving Account objects, the window size $w = 30$ used by TrIP to forget outdated objects (c.f. Section 3.2) has little impact. Most objects are frequently updated and never become obsolete. We conducted experiments with $age_{MAX} = 0, 5, 10$. However, we report results for $age_{MAX} = 5$ as only two strategies (i.e., FIN1-DR and FIN3-DR) experience change in performance after timepoint $t_{60}$.

**Evaluation Measure.** Our evaluation measure is the "Area under the ROC curve" (AUC), a measure derived from the *Receiver Operating Characteristic*, commonly known as the ROC curve. As the name implies, the ROC curve is a plot: it combines two curves that measure the performance of a binary classifier. In particular, let $C_p, C_n$ be the number of positive, resp. negative examples, let $T_p$ be the number of positive examples recognized as such by the classifier, and let $T_n$ be the number of negative examples recognized as such by the classifier.

Following Bradley [14], a classifier's *sensitivity* is defined as $P(T_p) = \frac{T_p}{C_p}$, while its *specificity* is $P(T_n) = \frac{T_n}{C_n}$ , i.e., the complement of the so-called "$\alpha$-error" $1-P(T_n)$. The ROC curve consists of the sensitivity curve and the $\alpha$-error curve, when the decision threshold is varied. The AUC is the area under those two meeting curves; Bradley provides a formula for the computation of this are (Eq. 7, page 2 of [14]). According to Wikipedia[2], the AUC is equal to the probability that a classifier will rank a randomly chosen positive instance higher than a randomly chosen negative one.

**Experimental Results.** In the Financial dataset, the stream Account contains perennial objects; a cache (c.f. Section 3.1) is used to accommodate the most active accounts and the ephemeral transactions on them. Initially, all accounts are empty. As transactions are recorded for an account, it becomes either "loan-risk" or "loan-trusted" class.

In [15], it is pointed out that object identifiers may be useful in some learning tasks. In a stream scenario, this may be more likely than in a static scenario: if identifiers are generated sequentially. For example during the KDD Cup 2008, in one of the tasks a leak was detected in Patient IDs [16]. This leak gave away the information about a patient having breast cancer or not. Such a leak might not be desirable in a real scenario. That said, some identifiers can convey demographic information about the objects. For example, individual cheques in a cheque books are sequentially numbered. If two accounts have similar cheque numbers it may be likely that they belong to the same region where the books were issued. This can implicitly convey demographic information that might not be present explicitly. Therefore, we report two experiments for the financial dataset. In one we exploit the identifiers of the ephemeral objects like transaction and card that reference the accounts, while ignore the identifiers from these objects in the other.

In Figure 4 we depict the performance of each strategy on the financial dataset with $w = 30$. In the left side of the figure, we show the AUC values for strategies with varying cache sizes, when the identifiers from the ephemeral objects not exploited. Initially, the AUC values are zero as TrIP only gathers sufficient statistics about the the incoming objects and does not grow the tree.

[2] Lemma: "ROC curve", accessed Jan. 19, 2010.

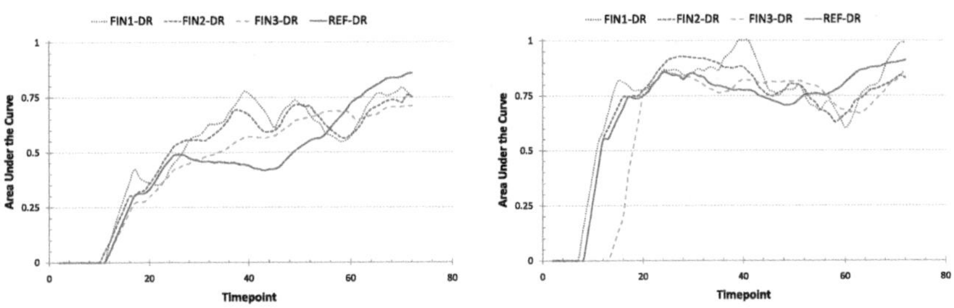


**Fig. 4.** Performance of different strategies over financial dataset (left) without IDs (right) with IDs

Around $t_{10}$, first splits are performed almost simultaneously for all strategies. It must be stressed here that accounts are perennial objects defined by their transactions. Initially there is only static information available about the accounts, e.g., the information about the owner(s) and types of card they hold etc. There is little or no information on transaction. Moreover, the class labels attributed to the accounts reflect their state after many transactions have accumulated on them, i.e., they indicate their final states, which is unknown at early timepoints. For this reason almost all the strategies perform poorly at the beginning.

At the beginning, the arrival of accounts is rather slow. As the stream progress and information accumulates, subsequent splits are performed faster. The first strategy to experience a rise in AUC is FIN1-DR around timepoint $t_{25}$. FIN1-DR is also the strategy with the smallest cache of 100 accounts. By this time more than 100 accounts have arrived. The propositionalization algorithm (c.f Section 3.1) keeps those objects inside the cache that are referenced most often, i.e., they have most ephemeral objects associated with them. For FIN1-DR with its small cache size, this means that accounts with fewer transactions and less information are not considered for propositionalization. It focuses on the informative accounts and shows large AUC. All other strategies have larger caches and store less informative accounts as well. These account cannot be easily classified and result in bad performance. At later timepoints, (i.e., around $t_{30}$) the strategies FIN2-DR and FIN3-DR also register improvements in their AUCs. They reach their cache size limits and start focusing on mature accounts.

Unlike other strategies, the performance of the Reference (with its infinite cache size), deteriorates between timepoints $t_{25}$ and $t_{50}$. During this time many accounts with very little information arrive, the Reference strategy remembers all of them.

Although, the strategies with smaller cache sizes (i.e., FIN1-DR and FIN2-DR) show good AUCs during the middle time period, they are also the most unstable ones. Strategies with larger caches (i.e., FIN3-DR and Reference) have a more stable performance. A possible reason is that due to their smaller sizes, even a single misclassification for FIN1-DR and FIN2-DR gets severely punished by the AUC measure as class distributions are fairly skewed.

After timepoint $t_{55}$, only very few new accounts arrive, the last one at $t_{60}$. For the next 12 timepoints, all accounts keep evolving as new transactions arrive for them. The AUC for the Reference strategy also registers a rise towards the end since there are no immature accounts to perturb it. It outperforms all strategies as there is very little information loss.

In the right-side of the Figure 4 we depict the performance of the strategies with the same parameter settings but with exploiting the identifiers. By contrasting the results to those at the left side of the Fig 4 we see that identifiers from the referring ephemeral objects carry valuable implicit information and all the strategies get a boost in their AUC values. The identifier attribute that conveys most information is the *Maximum Transaction ID* from among the set of transactions performed by an account while other identifiers are also utilized at some timepoint or the other. The relative performance of the strategies with and without identifier are quite similar. The strategies that benefit most are the ones with small caches, i.e., FIN1-DR and FIN2-DR, during $t_{35}$ to $t_{45}$ and $t_{20}$ to $t_{35}$, respectively. At late timepoints, the Reference strategy again has best performance.

## 5 Conclusion

We have presented TrIP, a tree induction algorithm for stream classification over a new type of data - a stream of *perennial* objects. Unlike the objects in a conventional stream, perennial objects, like patients or customers, may not be forgotten as the stream progresses, because new data on them may yet arrive and their properties may change - including their label.

Perennial objects are multi-relational by nature. We have built upon our earlier work on multi-table stream mining to propose the TrIP algorithm that processes a propositionalized stream of perennial objects and learns a decision tree for the objects seen thus far. When perennial objects are not referenced for a long time, TrIP moves them off the memory cache, so their impact on the model is reduced. When perennial objects change their label, the model must be adapted. For model adaptation, TrIP maintains alternate trees and chooses among them on the grounds of their accuracy, support and age: TrIP lets a tree grow in age as soon as its quality deteriorates, but rejuvenates it when its quality improves. We have experimented with TrIP upon synthetic and real data and studied the impact of the impact of tree ageing on model adaptation to concept drift and the role of re-appearing objects on model learning.

Our work begins the investigation of a new problem. In this study, we have focused on building a first classification algorithm for it, but many issues remain to be dealt with. One issue is the tradeoff between remembering re-occurring perennial objects and overfitting the model to them. Another, more technical issue is the adaptation of further conventional stream classification algorithms to streams of perennial objects, and the comparison of their performance.

## References


1. Džeroski, S.: Multi-relational data mining: An introduction. SIGKDD Explorations Newsletter 5(1) (2003)
2. Siddiqui, Z.F., Spiliopoulou, M.: Combining multiple interrelated streams for incremental clustering. In: Proc of 21st International Conference on Scientific and Statistical Database Management, SSDBM 2009, Springer, Heidelberg (2009)
3. Siddiqui, Z.F., Spiliopoulou, M.: Stream clustering of growing objects. In: Gama, J., Costa, V.S., Jorge, A.M., Brazdil, P.B. (eds.) DS 2009. LNCS, vol. 5808, pp. 433–440. Springer, Heidelberg (2009)
4. Hulten, G., Spencer, L., Domingos, P.: Mining time-changing data streams. In: The 7th ACM SIGKDD International Conference on Knowledge Discovery and Data Mining, KDD 2001, pp. 97–106. ACM, New York (2001)
5. Schlimmer, J.C., Granger, J.R.H.: Incremental learning from noisy data. Machine Learning 1(3), 317–354 (1986)
6. Quinlan, J.R.: Learning from noisy data. In: Proceedings of the Second International Machine Learning Workshop, Urbana-Champaign, IL, pp. 58–64 (1983)
7. Utgoff, P.E.: Id5: An incremental id3. In: Proceedings of the 5th International Conference on Machine Learning, ICML 1988, pp. 107–120. Morgan Kaufman, San Francisco (1988)
8. Utgoff, P.E.: Incremental induction of decision trees. Machine Learning 4 (1989)
9. Gratch, J.: Sequential inductive learning. In: Proceedings of the 13th National Conference on Artificial Intelligence, AAAI 1996, pp. 779–786 (1996)
10. Domingos, P., Hulten, G.: Mining high-speed data streams. In: The 6th ACM SIGKDD International Conference on Knowledge Discovery and Data Mining, KDD 2000, pp. 71–80. ACM Press, New York (2000)
11. Catlett, J.: Megainduction: Machine Learning on Very Large Databases. PhD thesis, University of Sydney, Sydney, Australia (1991)
12. Gama, J., Rocha, R., Medas, P.: Accurate decision trees for mining high-speed data streams. In: The 9th ACM SIGKDD International Conference on Knowledge Discovery and Data Mining, KDD 2003, pp. 523–528. ACM, New York (2003)
13. McGovern, A., Hiers, N., Collier, M., Gagne II, D.J., Brown, R.A.: Spatiotemporal relational probability trees. In: Proceedings of the 2008 IEEE International Conference on Data Mining, ICDM 2008, Pisa, Italy, pp. 935–940 (2008)
14. Bradley, A.P.: The use of the area under the ROC curve in the evaluation of machine learning algorithms. Pattern Recognition 30(7), 1145–1159 (1997)
15. Kroegel, M.A.: On Propositionalization for Knowledge Discovery in Relational Databases. PhD thesis, University of Magdeburg, Germany (2003)
16. Perlich, C., Melville, P., Liu, Y., Swirszcz, G., Lawrence, R.D., Rosset, S.: Breast cancer identification: Kdd cup winner's report. SIGKDD Explorations Newsletter 10(2), 39–42 (2008)

# Author Index

**Batch number: 10584007**

Printed by Printforce, the Netherlands